YEARBOOK OF AMERICAN & CANADIAN CHURCHES 2004

Previous Issues

Year of Publication/Title		*Editor*
1917	Federal Council Year Book	H. K. Carroll
1918	Yearbook of the Churches	C. F. Armitage
1919	Yearbook of the Churches	C. F. Armitage
1920	Yearbook of the Churches	S. R. Warburton
1922	Yearbook of the Churches	E. O. Watson
1923	Yearbook of the Churches	E. O. Watson
1925	Yearbook of the Churches	E. O. Watson
1927	The Handbook of the Churches	B. S. Winchester
1931	The New Handbook of the Churches	Charles Steizle
1933	Yearbook of American Churches	H. C. Weber
1935	Yearbook of American Churches	H. C. Weber
1937	Yearbook of American Churches	H. C. Weber
1939	Yearbook of American Churches	H. C. Weber
1941	Yearbook of American Churches	B. Y. Landis
1943	Yearbook of American Churches	B. Y. Landis
1945	Yearbook of American Churches	B. Y. Landis
1947	Yearbook of American Churches	B. Y. Landis, G. F. Ketcham
1949	Yearbook of American Churches	G. F. Ketcham
1951	Yearbook of American Churches	G. F. Ketcham
1952	Yearbook of American Churches	B. Y. Landis
1953	Yearbook of American Churches	B. Y. Landis
1954	Yearbook of American Churches	B. Y. Landis
1955	Yearbook of American Churches	B. Y. Landis
1956	Yearbook of American Churches	B. Y. Landis
1957	Yearbook of American Churches	B. Y. Landis
1958	Yearbook of American Churches	B. Y. Landis
1959	Yearbook of American Churches	B. Y. Landis
1960	Yearbook of American Churches	B. Y. Landis
1961	Yearbook of American Churches	B. Y. Landis
1962	Yearbook of American Churches	B. Y. Landis
1963	Yearbook of American Churches	B. Y. Landis
1964	Yearbook of American Churches	B. Y. Landis
1965	Yearbook of American Churches	B. Y. Landis
1966	Yearbook of American Churches	C. H. Jacquet
1967	Yearbook of American Churches	L. B. Whitman
1968	Yearbook of American Churches	L. B. Whitman
1969	Yearbook of American Churches	C. H. Jacquet
1970	Yearbook of American Churches	C. H. Jacquet
1971	Yearbook of American Churches	C. H. Jacquet
1972	Yearbook of American Churches	C. H. Jacquet
1973	Yearbook of American & Canadian Churches	C. H. Jacquet
1974	Yearbook of American & Canadian Churches	C. H. Jacquet
1975	Yearbook of American & Canadian Churches	C. H. Jacquet
1976	Yearbook of American & Canadian Churches	C. H. Jacquet
1977	Yearbook of American & Canadian Churches	C. H. Jacquet
1978	Yearbook of American & Canadian Churches	C. H. Jacquet
1979	Yearbook of American & Canadian Churches	C. H. Jacquet
1980	Yearbook of American & Canadian Churches	C. H. Jacquet
1981	Yearbook of American & Canadian Churches	C. H. Jacquet
1982	Yearbook of American & Canadian Churches	C. H. Jacquet
1983	Yearbook of American & Canadian Churches	C. H. Jacquet
1984	Yearbook of American & Canadian Churches	C. H. Jacquet
1985	Yearbook of American & Canadian Churches	C. H. Jacquet
1986	Yearbook of American & Canadian Churches	C. H. Jacquet
1987	Yearbook of American & Canadian Churches	C. H. Jacquet
1988	Yearbook of American & Canadian Churches	C. H. Jacquet
1989	Yearbook of American & Canadian Churches	C. H. Jacquet
1990	Yearbook of American & Canadian Churches	C. H. Jacquet
1991	Yearbook of American & Canadian Churches	C. H. Jacquet, Alice M. Jones
1992	Yearbook of American & Canadian Churches	Kenneth B. Bedell, Alice M. Jones
1993	Yearbook of American & Canadian Churches	Kenneth B. Bedell
1994	Yearbook of American & Canadian Churches	Kenneth B. Bedell
1995	Yearbook of American & Canadian Churches	Kenneth B. Bedell
1996	Yearbook of American & Canadian Churches	Kenneth B. Bedell
1997	Yearbook of American & Canadian Churches	Kenneth B. Bedell
1998	Yearbook of American & Canadian Churches	Eileen W. Lindner
1999	Yearbook of American & Canadian Churches	Eileen W. Lindner
2000	Yearbook of American & Canadian Churches	Eileen W. Lindner
2001	Yearbook of American & Canadian Churches	Eileen W. Lindner
2002	Yearbook of American & Canadian Churches	Eileen W. Lindner
2003	Yearbook of American & Canadian Churches	Eileen W. Lindner

Seventy-second Issue Annual

YEARBOOK OF AMERICAN & CANADIAN CHURCHES 2004

Edited by Eileen W. Lindner

Prepared and edited for the
National Council of the Churches of Christ in the U.S.A.
475 Riverside Drive, New York, NY 10115-0050

Published and Distributed
by Abingdon Press
Nashville

YEARBOOK OF AMERICAN & CANADIAN CHURCHES
2004

Telephone: (212) 870-2031

Fax: (212) 870-2817

E-mail: yearbook@ncccusa.org

Printed in the United States of America
ISBN 0-687-00666X
ISSN 0195-9034
Library of Congress catalog card number
16-5726

Preparation of this *Yearbook* is an annual project of the National Council of the Churches of Christ in the United States of America.

This is the seventy-second edition of a yearbook that was first published in 1916. Previous editions have been entitled: *Federal Council Yearbook* (1916-1917), *Yearbook of the Churches* (1918-1925), *The Handbook of the Churches* (1927), *The New Handbook of the Churches* (1928), *Yearbook of American Churches* (1933-1972), and *Yearbook of American & Canadian Churches* (1973-2003).

Eileen W. Lindner *Editor*
Marcel A. Welty *Associate Editor*
Elizabeth C. During *Assistant Editor*

Contents

Editor's Preface ... vii

I

PERSPECTIVES ON AMERICA'S RELIGIOUS LANDSCAPE

Trends & Developments, 2003 ... 9
Reception: Learning the Lessons of Research on Theological Education ... 16
—Eileen W. Lindner, Ph.D.

II

DIRECTORIES

1. United States Cooperative Organizations, National ... 21
2. Canadian Cooperative Organizations, National ... 49
3. Religious Bodies in the United States ... 58
   Religious Bodies in the United States Arranged by Family ... 170
4. Religious Bodies in Canada ... 173
   Religious Bodies in Canada Arranged by Family ... 203
5. The Electronic Church ... 205
6. Sources of Religion-Related Research ... 211
   I. Directory of Selected Research Organizations ... 211
   II. Directory of Selected Faith Traditions in America ... 219
7. United States Regional and Local Ecumenical Bodies ... 226
   Index of Select Programs for U.S. Regional and Local Ecumenical Bodies ... 263
8. Canadian Regional and Local Ecumenical Bodies ... 286
9. Theological Seminaries and Bible Colleges in the United States ... 289
10. Theological Seminaries and Bible Colleges in Canada ... 309
11. Religious Periodicals in the United States ... 315
12. Religious Periodicals in Canada ... 340
13. Church Archives and Historical Records Collections ... 348

III

STATISTICAL SECTION

Guide to Statistical Tables ... 357
1. Membership Statistics in Canada ... 358
2. Membership Statistics in the United States ... 365
3. Membership Statistics for the National Council of the Churches of Christ U.S.A. ... 378
4. Selected Statistics of Church Finances—Canadian Churches ... 380
5. Selected Statistics of Church Finances—United States Churches ... 382

Trends in Seminary Enrollment ... 388

IV

A CALENDAR FOR CHURCH USE

A Calendar for Church Use, 2004–2007 ... 391

V

INDEXES

Organizations ... 395
Individuals ... 404

Editor's Preface

Advent 2003 finds us preparing the seventy-second edition of the *Yearbook of American & Canadian Churches* and once again acknowledging the ever-changing religious context of our times. This 2004 edition is accessible in both hardcopy and in electronic format that can be accessed over the Internet using the unique pass code printed on the inside back cover of this volume. Updated information is reflected in the electronic edition three times during the year, June, September and December.

Recognizing the Contributions of Many

The field of church statistics is complex and, of necessity, filled with inconsistencies. In recent years, electronic reporting has enabled greater amounts of time at each data collection level to raise questions and to recalculate and refine reports. We at the *Yearbook* are pleased to take our place in this important task of annually capturing a snapshot of American religious life. Reflection upon such findings tells us much about ourselves as well as the institutional religious life in a country which has been referred to as a "nation with the soul of a church."

Our colleagues in the compilation of each edition of the *Yearbook* are the thousands, perhaps tens of thousands, of individuals who keep church records. We rely and build upon the efforts of church pastors, deacons, secretaries, and vestrymen and women who carefully review and report church membership statistics and financial giving. We acknowledge the contributions of those at congregational, regional, and especially denominational levels who respond with good cheer (most of the time!) and expeditiously (at least at our second request!) in furnishing us with the detailed data we require in the format that we request. We hope that being a part of the record and analysis offered by the *Yearbook* contributes to their sense of satisfaction for a job well done.

For various chapters of the *Yearbook* we are indebted to specific individuals for their assistance in gathering, analyzing, and corroborating the information we publish. As she has for the last several years, Nancy Merrill of the Association of Theological Schools in the United States and Canada has furnished us with the data and analysis concerning seminary enrollments. Likewise, Mark Duffy, Director of Archives of the Episcopal Church USA, has reviewed the chapter on church archives and historical records collections. Our colleague Ernest Rubenstein, Librarian of the Interchurch Center in New York, is a regular and reliable consultant to us. Likewise, Seth Kasten, Librarian at the Burke Library of Union Theological Seminary in New York, is ever ready to offer able assistance and counsel. Dale Dickerson of the Evangelical Lutheran Church in America helped us to confirm the dates for the calendar. Cathy Lavendar of the United States Census Bureau assured that the Statistical Abstract remains current with *Yearbook* data.

As we selected this year's theme of Theological Education we found wise counsel in Barbara G. Wheeler, President of Auburn Seminary; Daniel O. Aleshire, Executive Director of the Association of Theological Schools in the US and Canada; and Dale T. Irvin, Academic Dean at New York Theological Seminary. All directed us toward valuable resources that contributed much to our understanding of this complex field.

Annual production of the *Yearbook* requires a variety of skills and commitments within our own editorial offices. Associate Editor Marcel A. Welty gives leadership and prodigious effort to the logistics of researching, requesting, compiling, confirming, correcting, formatting, and preparing data for analysis. Elizabeth C. During contributes substantially to the administering and recording of the prodigious data, and negotiating the thousands of person-to-person contacts that work requires. Earl Davis is invaluable as the Editor's Assistant, aiding in confirming data and preparing the theme chapter text for publication. Almost as closely associated with us as those we see each day are our colleagues and friends of long standing, John and Sylvia Ronsvalle, of the empty tomb, inc. Nationally recognized for their steadfast attention to the patterns of church giving, the Ronsvalles are unfailingly gracious in providing expert assistance and in enabling our own analysis.

At Abingdon we rely upon Rebekah D. Sharp to convert our manuscript into a publication, and Paul Franklyn and Rebecca Burgoyne to be certain that the electronic edition, with the paper edition, is available to our readers.

On behalf of those readers, we extend our gratitude for the wisdom, skill, patience, and generosity of those we acknowledge here. No small group of individuals could hope to have the knowledge needed to compile a text as far ranging as the *Yearbook.* Our efforts strengthened by the contributions of all those named above have led to the 2004 edition of the *Yearbook of American & Canadian Churches*; we wish to express our deepest thanks to each of them.

The 2004 Edition Highlights

- Reports on a robust 215 U.S. church bodies with record high total membership exceeding 161 million. The U.S. retains a higher level of church affiliation than most western industrial societies.
- Signals the changes in church demography and membership affiliation with the movement of a Pentecostal church (Church of God [Cleveland, TN]) into the twenty-five largest churches. Seven of the largest twenty curches remain predominantly African American Churches.
- Reports receipt of more than $31 billion by 59 reporting churches. Analysis indicates stable income with 1.25% growth, uncorrected for inflation. Benevolent giving likewise remained stable at 15% of total giving.
- Provides an overview of a century's research in theological education and argues that a broader stakeholder group, including those concerned about faith based participation in the civil society debates might give greater attention to recent findings.
- While total giving to churches continued to rise, the proportion of church finances committed to benevolent purposes continued to trend downward, reaching a new low of 14% of total church giving.
- Despite a well-documented clergy shortage, notably in the Catholic Church and for small and/or rural parishes, the *total* number of students enrolled in theological education continues to grow and is now at a high of over 75,000 students nationwide in ATS member schools.
- The nearly thirty year trend in increasing numbers of women enrolled in theological education remains stable and can be considered a permanent feature of the demography of theological students.

Eileen W. Lindner
Editor
New York, Advent 2003

I

PERSPECTIVES ON AMERICA'S RELIGIOUS LANDSCAPE

Trends & Developments, 2004

Methodological Considerations

The *Yearbook of American & Canadian Churches* reports annually on data gathered from national religious bodies that reflect the religious affiliations and financial giving patterns of hundreds of millions of Americans. However, these data generally represent information gathered two calendar years prior to the year of publication. For instance, data reported in this 2004 edition of the *Yearbook* reflects information for 2002 that was collected by national church structures in 2003 and reported to the *Yearbook* for publication. This "lag time" often leads our readers to ask if such data is out of date by the time it is printed. In response, we would give a qualified "no." Massive national agencies, such as the churches reporting through the *Yearbook*, move in their institutional lives at nearly imperceptible rates of speed. Moreover, given the vast size and complexity of such organizations, partial data reported more frequently might well have the unintended effect of conveying a sense of "trend" to momentary or regionally isolated patterns of affiliation and/or financial giving. Now in the seventy-second year of publication, the *Yearbook* believes that an annual review of data continues to provide an appropriate interval for tracking the changes in institutional patterns.

No single standard for data collection exists to apply across the variety of ecclesiastical structures reported in the *Yearbook*. Moreover, the definitions of membership and related terms differ widely from one church structure to another. This lack of universal definition and collection methodology has frequently led to questions about the validity and reliability of self-reported data. Recognizing the limitations of the data reported herein, we continue to have confidence in the overall value of trends and other findings based on these figures and this methodology. While church data collection and analytical practices differ across various institutional and organizational margins, they tend to be remarkably consistent *within* specific organizations over time. This consistency within organizations brings a greater degree of confidence to the relative data of a given church over time. For the same reason, we believe the *relative* size of one church to another as reported here provides an accurate picture, even while lacking a degree of absolute precision of membership statistics, particularly over time. Thus we believe that the Southern Baptist Convention is roughly twice the size of the United Methodist Church, for example, and that changes relative to each other over several years are probably an accurate reflection of actual membership trends. Moreover, these data are the most exacting figures presently available, and thus serve as the national standard.

The seven decades of record keeping represented by the *Yearbook of*

Table 1
INCLUSIVE MEMBERSHIP 1890–2002

Year	Membership	Source	Year	Membership	Source
1890	41,699,342	CRB	1966	125,778,656	YBAC
1906	35,068,058	CRB	1967	126,445,110	YBAC
1916	41,926,852	CRB	1968	128,469,636	YBAC
1926	54,576,346	CRB	1969	128,505,084	YBAC
1931	59,268,764	CH	1970	131,045,053	YBAC
1932	60,157,392	CH	1971	131,389,642	YBAC
1933	60,812,624	CH	1972	131,424,564	YBAC
1934	62,007,376	CH	1973	131,245,139	YBAC
1935	62,678,177	CH	1974	131,871,743	YBACC
1936	55,807,366	CRB	1975	131,012,953	YBACC
1936	63,221,996	CH	1976	131,897,539	YBACC
1937	63,848,094	CH	1977	131,812,470	YBACC
1938	64,156,895	YBAC	1978	133,388,776	YBACC
1940	64,501,594	YBAC	1979	133,469,690	YBACC
1942	68,501,186	YBAC	1980	134,816,943	YBACC
1944	72,492,699	YBAC	1981	138,452,614	YBACC
1945	71,700,142	CH	1982	139,603,059	YBACC
1946	73,673,182	CH	1983	140,816,385	YBACC
1947	77,386,188	CH	1984	142,172,138	YBACC
1948	79,435,605	CH	1985	142,926,363	YBACC
1949	81,862,328	CH	1986	142,799,662	YBACC
1950	86,830,490	YBAC	1987	143,830,806	YBACC
1951	88,673,005	YBAC	1988	145,383,739	YBACC
1952	92,277,129	YBAC	1989	147,607,394	YBACC
1953	94,842,845	YBAC	1990	156,331,704	YBACC
1954	97,482,611	YBAC	1991	156,629,918	YBACC
1955	100,162,529	YBAC	1992	156,557,746	YBACC
1956	103,224,954	YBAC	1993	153,127,045	YBACC
1957	104,189,678	YBAC	1994	158,218,427	YBACC
1958	109,557,741	YBAC	1995	157,984,194	YBACC
1959	112,226,905	YBAC	1996	159,471,758	YBACC
1960	114,449,217	YBAC	1997	157,503,033	YBACC
1961	116,109,929	YBAC	1998*	150,105,525	YBACC
1962	117,946,002	YBAC	1999*	151,161,906	YBACC
1963	120,965,238	YBAC	2000*	152,134,407	YBACC
1964	123,307,449	YBAC	2001	158,952.292	YBACC
1965	124,682,422	YBAC	2002	161,145,004	YBACC

*Note: The 1998–2000 editions of the *Yearbook* excluded the membership of the National Baptist Convention, USA, Inc., as the church re-assessed its membership figures. The omission of these data explain what appears to be a drop in total membership from 1997 to 1998 and likewise the restoration of these figures explains the apparent increase in total membership from 2000 to 2001.

CRB—*Census of Religious Bodies*, Bureau of the Census, Washington
CH—*The Christian Herald*, New York
YBAC—*Yearbook of American Churches*, New York
YBACC—*Yearbook of American and Canadian Churches*, New York

American & Canadian Churches is contained on a comprehensive Historic Archive on CD-ROM (which contains membership and financial data from 1916-1999). This CD provides a longitudinal backdrop for the analysis that follows. Only through such a longitudinal study of growth and decline in membership are we able to capture and analyze the emerging patterns. Our annual trends analysis should be regarded as a snapshot taken at a discrete moment in history. The meaning of the figures within that snapshot will best be given definition by the larger and longer context of which they are a part.

The reader is invited to utilize both the current edition and the *Yearbook of American & Canadian Churches*' historic CD to test and amplify the analysis that follows. To obtain the Historic Archive on CD-ROM call (888)870-3325 or visit www.electronicchurch.org.

Table 2
US MEMBERSHIP CHURCH RANKING: Largest 25 Churches

Denomination Name	Current Ranking (2004 Edition)	Inclusive Membership	Increase Decrease
The Catholic Church	1(1)	66,407,105	1.74%
Southern Baptist Convention	2(2)	16,247,736	1.21%
The United Methodist Church	3(3)	8,251,042	-0.57%
The Church of God in Christ	4(4)	5,499,875	***0.00%***
The Church of Jesus Christ of Latter-day Saints	5(5)	5,410,544	1.88%
Evangelical Lutheran Church in America	6(6)	5,038,006	-1.21%
National Baptist Convention, USA, Inc.	7(7)	5,000,000	***0.00%***
National Baptist Convention of America, Inc.	8(8)	3,500,000	***0.00%***
Presbyterian Church (USA)	9(9)	3,407,329	-1.41%
Assemblies of God	10(10)	2,687,366	2.30%
The Lutheran Church—Missouri Synod (LCMS)	11(11)	2,512,714	-1.08%
African Methodist Episcopal Church	12(12)	2,500,000	***0.00%***
National Missionary Baptist Convention of America	12(12)	2,500,000	***0.00%***
Progressive National Baptist Convention, Inc.	12(12)	2,500,000	***0.00%***
Episcopal Church	15(15)	2,333,628	0.01%
Churches of Christ	16(16)	1,500,000	***0.00%***
Greek Orthodox Archdiocese of America	16(16)	1,500,000	***0.00%***
Pentecostal Assemblies of the World, Inc.	16(16)	1,500,000	***0.00%***
American Baptist Churches in the USA	19(20)	1,484,291	2.87%
African Methodist Episcopal Zion Church	20(19)	1,430,795	-1.18%
United Church of Christ	21(21)	1,330,985	-2.07%
Baptist Bible Fellowship International	22(22)	1,200,000	***0.00%***
Christian Churches and Churches of Christ	23(23)	1,071,616	***0.00%***
Jehovah's Witnesses	24(25)	1,022,397	3.33%
Church of God (Cleveland, Tenn.)	25(26)	944,857	1.38%

Percentages in ***Bold Italics*** *signify that no membership report was submitted for the 2004 Edition of the* Yearbook.

Last Year's Ranking

Denomination Name	Inclusive Membership Figures Reported in Last Year's Yearbook
The Catholic Church	65,270,444
Southern Baptist Convention	16,052,920
The United Methodist Church	8,298,460
The Church of God in Christ	5,499,875
The Church of Jesus Christ of Latter-day Saints	5,310,598
Evangelical Lutheran Church in America	5,099,877
National Baptist Convention USA, Inc.	5,000,000
National Baptist Convention of America, Inc.	3,500,000
Presbyterian Church (USA)	3,455,952
Assemblies of God	2,627,029
The Lutheran Church—Missouri Synod (LCMS)	2,540,045
African Methodist Episcopal Church	2,500,000
National Missionary Baptist Convention of America	2,500,000
Progressive National Baptist Convention, Inc.	2,500,000
Episcopal Church	2,333,327
Churches of Christ	1,500,000
Greek Orthodox Archdiocese of America	1,500,000
Pentecostal Assemblies of the World, Inc.	1,500,000
African Methodist Episcopal Zion Church	1,447,934
American Baptist Churches in the U.S.A.	1,442,824
United Church of Christ	1,359,105
Baptist Bible Fellowship International	1,200,000
Christian Churches and Churches of Christ	1,071,616
The Orthodox Church in America	1,000,000
Jehovah's Witnesses	998,403

Table 3
PATTERNS OF US MEMBERSHIP CHANGE OF SELECTED LARGE CHURCHES 1999–2002

Denomination	1999 Membership Change	Percentage Change	2000 Membership Change	Percentage Change	2001 Membership Change	Percentage Change	2002 Membership Change	Percentage Change
The Catholic Church	373,048	0.60	1,291,546	2.07	1,587,414	2.49	1,136,661	1.74
Southern Baptist Convention	122,400	0.77	108,552	0.68	92,612	0.58	194,816	1.21
The United Methodist Church	-33,841	-0.40	-36,708	-0.44	-42,494	-0.51	-47,418	-0.57
Evangelical Lutheran Church in America	-28,557	-0.55	-23,749	-0.46	-26,042	-0.51	-61,871	-1.21
The Church of Jesus Christ of Latter-day Saints	90,358	1.78	95,418	1.87	101,771	1.95	99,946	1.88
Presbyterian Church (USA)	-13,775	-0.39	-75,852	-2.13	-29,380	-0.84	-48,623	-1.41
The Lutheran Church—Missouri Synod	-11,964	-0.46	-28,352	-1.10	-14,043	-0.55	-27,331	-1.08
Assemblies of God	48,719	1.90	3,029	0.12	49,469	1.92	60,337	2.30
American Baptist Churches in the USA	-53,012	-3.64	-17,479	-1.20	5,915	0.41	41,467	2.87

Table 4
US FINANCIAL SUMMARIES 1995-2002

Year	Number Reporting	Full or Confirmed Members	Inclusive Members	Total Contributions	Per Capita Full or Confirmed Members	Per Capita Inclusive Members	Total Congregational Contributions
1995	55	43,104,555	48,115,704	$21,433,517,908	$497.24	$445.46	$17,743,597,668
1996	55	43,321,039	50,047,599	$24,970,133,464	$576.40	$498.93	$20,422,403,297
1997	58	44,804,383	49,936,836	$25,181,416,276	$562.03	$504.27	$21,212,711,615
1998	62	44,574,101	49,679,497	$26,242,626,313	$588.74	$528.24	$22,202,379,038
1999	62	44,288,906	49,196,965	$26,997,610,588	$609.58	$548.77	$22,801,548,715
2000	65	44,401,451	49,178,675	$29,464,889,024	$663.60	$599.14	$24,475,897,453
2001	62	45,359,589	49,828,003	$31,041,852,581	$684.35	$622.98	$26.587,142,109
2002	59	43,694,611	47,773,814	$31,465,090,286	$720.11	$658.63	$26,908,804,274

Year	Per Capita Full or Confirmed Members	Per Capita Inclusive Members	Total Benevolences	Per Capita Full or Confirmed Members	Per Capita Inclusive Members	Benevolences as a Percentage of Total Contributions
1995	$411.64	$368.77	$3,689,920,239	$85.60	$76.69	17%
1996	$471.42	$408.06	$3,739,584,874	$86.32	$74.72	15%
1997	$473.45	$424.79	$3,968,704,661	$88.58	$79.47	16%
1998	$498.10	$446.91	$4,040,247,275	$90.64	$81.33	15%
1999	$514.84	$463.47	$4,197,087,981	$94.77	$85.31	16%
2000	$551.24	$497.69	$4,988,352,266	$112.35	$101.43	17%
2001	$586.14	$533.58	$4,510,958,817	$99.45	$90.53	15%
2002	$615.84	$563.25	$4,555,191,495	$104.25	$95.35	14%

Table 1 Longitudinal Inclusive Membership

This table represents a longitudinal view of aggregated membership totals for all churches reporting to the *Yearbook*. These data do not reflect the entirety of national church membership since some churches either do not gather such data or do not report them to the *Yearbook*. As the 2003 *Yearbook* noted in its theme chapter on megachurches, these figures do not include membership of independent congregations of any size. Substantial numbers of church members, therefore, are not accounted for in nationally-gathered membership data. With well over 161 million adherents, the churches collectively continue to maintain a substantial organizational and institutional presence within the United States.

Table 2 U.S. Membership Church Ranking

This table allows comparison in size as determined by membership of the largest 25 churches in the nation. Dwarfing any single other church is the Catholic Church, reporting nearly 66 million adherents.

The remainder of the top 25 are Protestant Churches with two exceptions: the Greek Orthodox Archdiocese, which is ranked 16th, and the Jehovah's Witnesses, which is ranked 24th. In comparison with the findings from the 2003 *Yearbook,* the rankings of the top 25 largest churches remain stable as would be expected. In light of current data, the Amercian Baptist Churches in the USA rose from 20th to 19th, reporting a substantial 2.87% increase. This growth rate of nearly 3% exceeds that of any other protestant church reporting. The African Methodist Episcopal Zion Church declined in the rankings from 19th to 20th, reporting a decline in estimated membership of 1.18% in substantial contrast to its previous estimated gain of 11% reported in the 2003 *Yearbook*. Such a decline in membership following a year of rapid increase may be explained by a small portion of those new members failing to continue their membership a second year. The Orthodox Church in America, previously ranked 25th, reported a membership decline of 100,000 (10%), reflecting a multi year adjustment in its estimated membership data. The Church of God (Cleveland, TN), reporting a membership gain of 1.38%, moves into the ranking as the 25th largest church. The Jehovah's Witnesses, reporting an increase of 3.33%, moved from the 25th to the 24th place.

The patterns of affiliation reflected in this table offer a numerical view and summary of American church history. Protestantism has, since the founding of the democracy, enjoyed cultural hegemony accompanied throughout by a consistent substantial Catholic presence. Four of the largest 25 churches are Pentecostal in belief and practice, reflecting the continuing increase in numbers of adherents to Pentecostal traditions. The Pentecostal churches are: The Church of God in Christ; Assemblies of God; Pentecostal Assemblies of the World, Inc.; and the Church of God (Cleveland, Tenn.).

Likewise, the top 15 churches, those with membership exceeding two million members, reflect the constancy of the Historic Black Churches. Six of the fifteen largest churches (The Church of God in Christ; National Baptist Convention USA; National Baptist Church of America, Inc.; National Missionary Baptist Convention of America; Progressive National Baptist Convention; African Methodist Episcopal Church) are predominately African American churches. This, of course, is reflective of the historic strength of the church within the African American community.

The Church of Jesus Christ of Latter-day Saints, an American-born church, continues to grow remarkably, remaining the fifth largest church in the nation. Among the 15 largest churches the LDS also reports the highest rate of growth at 1.88% in the last year (which is virtually the same as the previous growth rate). Given the American legacy of religious freedom, new faith traditions and variations on inherited traditions alike have found a receptive climate for growth.

Table 3 Patterns of Membership Gains and Losses

Broadly held on-going interest in patterns of membership gain and loss has prompted the *Yearbook* to offer five-year longitudinal data on a selected group of large churches notable for their diversity regarding theology, governance, and social location. Table 3 reports these patterns for 1999-2002.

In recent years, the Church of Jesus Christ of Latter-day Saints, the Catholic Church, and the Assemblies of God have reported consistency in both *direction* and *rate* of change. This pattern continues with a modest increase in the rate of growth for the Assemblies of God. The Southern Baptist Convention, that had been reporting a slowing rate of membership gain, in the current data reports a significant increase in the rate of gain from 0.58% to 1.21%.

Perhaps the most notable change in these data is in the instance of the American Baptist Churches. After reporting a decline in membership in 1999 and 2000, a change of *direction* from loss to gain in membership was reported in 2001, albeit a very modest increase of .41%. Current data continues to reflect growth, but at an accelerated rate of 2.87%. This rate of increase in membership for the American Baptist Churches exceeds that of all other churches in this sample.

The 2003 *Yearbook* reported a similar *rate* of membership losses among the Evangelical Lutheran Church in America, United Methodist Church, Presbyterian Church (USA), and Lutheran Church–Missouri Synod between 0.5% and 1.5% for each church. These churches continue to reflect similar rates of membership decline but a slightly accelerated rate of loss of between (1.21%, 0.57%, 1.41%, 1.08% respectively.); only the United Methodist Church, the largest church in this sample, maintains a lower 0.57% rate of loss.

Table 4 Financial Trends

Second only to the interest in membership trends is the interest of media and the church world alike in the financial trends reported in the *Yearbook.* While not all churches report their financial information to the *Yearbook,* the 59 churches that have provided full data for the 2004 edition provide an important glimpse into United States church giving. More than $31 billion dollars are accounted for in the reports of these churches and this, of course, is but a portion of the whole of church giving. For instance, the Church of Jesus Christ of Latter-day Saints does not provide financial data but is a church in which financial giving is a prominent feature of membership; we would expect commitment to be quite high.

The financial reporting for this 2004 *Yearbook* is based on the financial income reports of the 59 churches reporting figures. The nearly 48 million inclusive members contributed a total of more than $31 billion, marking an increase in the total amount of income to the churches. It is particularly useful to view this increase in its per capita terms. The $659 contributed per person is an increase of $36.00 (5.7%) per person from the previous year. While the increase in per capita giving exceeds the official inflation figure for 2002, it must be remembered that some individuals will be contributing to parishes with a declining number of members. In such settings, it is doubtful that this increase will offset the financial loss associated with membership decline.

Benevolence giving for 2002 is reported at the level of 14%, marking a new low in such giving. Caution must be exercised generalizing from this new data since it is based upon the experience of 59 specific denominations. Even with this caveat a continued downward trend in benevolence giving will be a matter of deep concern to many. While admittedly reporting on a far smaller sample and reflecting a much lower level of giving, the percentage of benevolence giving for Canadian churches is consistently in the 19%-20% range compared to the current U.S. figure of 14%.

This year's 14% percent U.S. benevolence giving is a new low in *Yearbook* reporting over the period of the last decade, and warrants further comment. The overall increase in giving to the churches, at this reporting, is occurring simultaneously with a declining posture in benevolence as a percentage. The churches that seek generosity from their supporters have not, at least in this sample, matched that generosity, or even held constant, in their own patterns of giving. The practical consequences of such a decline translates in local settings to less support for church-sponsored day care, fewer soup kitchens meals, less emergency help to persons with medical problems, or reduced transportation for the elderly. Such a decline is occurring even as reports of requests for aid at shelters and soup kitchens are rising.

No one has given greater attention to church giving patterns than John and Sylvia Ronsvalle. For a fulsome discussion of the giving patterns of churches, see their *The State of Church Giving* series of publications, by writing: empty tomb, inc., P.O. Box 2404, Champaign, IL 61825, or through www.emptytomb.org.

Reception: Learning the Lessons of Research on Theological Education

Eileen W. Lindner, Ph.D.

In 1983, Edward Farley began his landmark *Theologia: The Fragmentation and Unity of Theological Education* with an assertion so stark as to demand attention. He said, "Complaints about theological education are as old as theological education itself." While no doubt true, there have been seasons of greater focus on theological education throughout the last century as well as relatively long periods of quiescence on the subject. The appearance of Farley's work served to invigorate contemporary inquiries into aspects of theological education which have been generative of fresh insight and which have identified emerging challenges.

In keeping with long established practice, the *Yearbook of American & Canadian Churches* annually draws attention to important areas of church related research. In focusing on theological education in this 2004 edition, the *Yearbook* once again surveys and reports on the status of research conducted relative to the annual theme rather than conducting primary research of its own. Our hope in taking such an approach is to gather in a single place an overview of important literature on a timely topic and to identify implications for churches and for society. Consistent with *Yearbook* practice, we have provided a bibliography as well a special reference to the studies from the Auburn Center for the Study of Theological Education. (See box on pg. 18.)

A variety of factors contributed to our selection of theological education for this year's theme. It has been a full century since the publication of Charles Briggs "A Plea for the Higher Study of Theology" in the *American Journal of Theology* (July 1904). It has been eighty years since Robert L. Kelly published his study of 161 theological schools in *Theological Education in America* and seventy years since the publication of the four volume study of *The Education of American Ministers,* by William Adams Brown, Mark A. May, and Frank K. Shuttleworth. These latter two studies applied social science methodologies to provide both qualitative and quantitative analysis of theological education. This foundational work did much to set an enduring standard in scope and methodology for subsequent studies. These studies established a scope of research to include analysis of students, faculty, governance, finances, content, and outcomes of theological education.

Moreover, the study of theological education has attracted some of the most influential theological minds of the last century. In 1956 H. Richard Niebuhr, Daniel Day Williams, and James M. Gustafson published *The Purpose of the Church and its Ministry,* and in 1957 published *The Advancement of Theological Education,* utilizing the framework and scope established by earlier studies. These works concluded with a number of recommendations addressed to both theological seminaries and churches. In the first half of the twentieth century the focus of these inquiries was almost exclusively upon mainline Protestant schools, with a single chapter devoted to African American seminaries. In more recent decades Robert W. Lynn has tirelessly researched the history of theological education and given counsel and leadership to many scholars and studies. In 1993 David Kelsey published *Between Athens and Berlin: The Theological Debate,* contributing especially to the discussion of content and purpose of theological education. That same year Barbara G. Wheeler and Linda-Marie Delloff published "Reaching Out" in conjunction with the launch of the Auburn Seminary Center for the Study of Theological Education.

Auburn Seminary President Barbara G. Wheeler has been particularly prolific, contributing nine studies and myriad articles, lectures, and book chapters on varied aspects of theological education (see inset for listing). These contemporary studies, while providing comparative analysis to earlier studies, also extend the scope of study to raise new questions probing further the context in which theological education takes place. Other contemporary studies, notably those of Katarina Schuth, have contributed to the literature about Roman Catholic theological education. R. Albert Mohler and D. G. Hart have examined *Theological Education in the Evangelical Tradition* (see bibliography). Throughout the last several decades the Association of Theological Schools has made an invaluable contribution, particularly in longitudinal quantitative data, excerpts of which are published annually in the *Yearbook of American & Canadian Churches* (see Section III). Thus, the various anniversaries of seminal studies and the burgeoning literature offered compelling reasons to devote our theme chapter to research in theological education in the 2004 edition of the *Yearbook.*

Writing in the mid-twentieth century, H. Richard Niebuhr wrote "...our schools, like our churches and our ministers have no clear conceptions of what they are doing but are carrying on traditional actions, making separate responses, various pressures exerted by churches and society, contriving uneasy compromises among many values, engaging in little quarrels symptomatic of undefined issues trying to improve their work by adjusting minor parts of the academic machine or by changing the specifications of the raw material to be treated." (*The Purpose of the Church and its Ministry,* pg. 101)

The dynamics and conundrums which confronted the task of theological education a half century ago have not yielded but, rather, have been joined by an ever-increasing clash of values. In addition to the internal disputes about theological education there are questions to be pondered about the relationship of the theological enterprise to the community as a whole. Elizabeth Lynn and Barbara G. Wheeler reported in "Missing Connections" (*Auburn Studies,* No. 6, September 1999) that, in the four communities they studied, seminaries were scarcely known and little understood beyond the confines of their own inner circles. While there is room to debate whether the educational goals of a seminary are best served through engagement with the surrounding community or not, the absence of such relationships is seldom helpful in areas such as recruitment and fundraising.

Thus, theological education—while beset within and without by foundational questions of meaning, purpose, and goals—nonetheless continues to prepare men and women for ministry and professions in which theological competence is desirable or required. The research findings of those cited here and those of many others offer a rich bounty of both quantitative and qualitative data on subjects such as the changing demography of students, the prospects for attracting high quality faculty in future years, trends in financial support for theological education, and myriad other foci. The whole theological enterprise is served by the availability of reliable data and thoughtful analysis, which can only play a constructive role as seminaries seek to meet these challenges.

This literature has been well received by those engaged in theological education where it has stimulated thinking, discussion, debate, and remedial action. The Auburn studies, in particular, have been noted for their clarity, careful analysis, thoughtful discussion, and intellectual accessibility.

Yet it is not only the academy that might benefit from this utilitarian research. While some national church agencies have made good use of the materials, by and large pastors, congregations, and those outside the church interested in the religiously motivated voice in society have not yet discovered it. As critical components of the civil society, churches exercise moral authority and influence, that is often derived from and expressed by the theologically trained within the various churches. The nature of the preparations of such persons ultimately has meaning for society as a whole.

While the primary audiences for such literature will remain the academy and denominational and university personnel concerned with theological education, a wider audience for these studies might be hoped for in the future. The findings of these studies, in the aggregate, are highly consequential for church leadership development but also for the degree to which local congregations might look to theological seminaries as resources for ministry, theological discernment, and lay leadership development. In recent years, the broader society's expressed enthusiasm for faith-based initiatives (especially in social service), whatever the motivation may be, might be better informed about capacity and competence of church institutions by engagement with this literature.

Auburn Center Studies		
Reaching Out Auburn Seminary Launches the Center for the Study of Theological Education.	**Lean Years, Fat Years** Changes in the Financial Support of Protestant Theological Education	**Manna From Heaven?** Theological and Rabbinical Student Debt
True and False The First in a Series of Reports from a Study of Theological School Faculty	**Tending Talents** The Second in a Series of Reports from a Study of Theological School Faculty	**Missing Connections** Public Perceptions of Theological Education and Religious Leadership
The Big Picture Strategic Choices for Theological Schools	**Is There A Problem?** Theological Students and Religious Leadership for the Future	**In Whose Hands?** A Study of Theological School Trustees

Studies available online at *auburnsem.org/studies/pubs.shtml*

In the field of ecumenical theological exchange the last quarter century has seen an emphasis placed upon the idea of 'reception.' Reception is that process by which the insights of ecumenical encounter are gradually and mutually appropriated by the churches. It is not only, nor even most centrally, a process of legitimization but more profoundly a process of appropriation and amendment of life and understanding. The high quality and volume of the body of research available on theological education today warrants such reception from several quarters within church and society. It is our hope that it receives such attention both for the betterment of the theological enterprise as well as for the common good.

A Selected Bibliography on Theological Education

Banks, Robert J. *Reenvisioning Theological Education: Exploring a Missional Alternative to Current Models*. Grand Rapids, Mich.: Eerdmans, 1999.

Browning, Don S., David Polk, and Ian S. Evison, eds. *The Education of the Practical Theologian: Responses to Joseph Hough and Jon Cobb's 'Christian Identity and Theological Education.'* Atlanta, Ga.: Scholars Press, 1989.

Cannon, Katie G. and Mud Flower Collective. *God's Fierce Whimsy: Christian Feminism and Theological Education*. New York, N.Y.: Pilgrim Press, 1985.

Carey, Patrick W. and Earl C. Muller, eds. *Theological Education in the Catholic Tradition*. New York, N.Y.: Crossroads, 1997.

Carroll, Jackson, Barbara G. Wheeler, Daniel O. Aleshire, and Penny Long Marler. *Being There: Culture and Formation in Two Theological Schools*. New York, N.Y.: Oxford University Press, 1997.

Cetuk, Virginia Samuel. *What to Expect in Seminary: Theological Education As Spiritual Formation*. Nashville, Tenn.: Abingdon Press, 1998.

Cherry, Conrad. *Hurrying Toward Zion: Universities, Divinity Schools, and American Protestantism*. Bloomington, Ind.: Indiana University Press, 1995.

Chopp, Rebecca S. *Saving Work: Feminist Practices of Theological Education*. 1st ed. Louisville, Ky.: Westminster John Knox Press, 1995.

Farley, Edward. *The Fragility of Knowledge: Theological Education in the church and the University*. Philadelphia, Pa.: Fortress Press, 1988.

Farley, Edward. *Theologia: The Fragmentation and Unity of Theological Education*. Philadelphia, Pa.: Fortress Press, 1983.

Gilpin, W. Clark. *A Preface to Theology*. Chicago, Ill.: The University of Chicago Press, 1996.

Hough, Joseph C. and John B. Cobb. *Christian Identity and Theological Education*. Chico, Calif.: Scholars Press, 1985.

Hough, Joseph C. and Barbara G. Wheeler. *Beyond Clericalism: the Congregation As a Focus for Theological Education*. Scholars Press Studies in Religious and Theological Scholarship. Atlanta, Ga.: Scholars Press, 1988.

Kelsey, David H. *To Understand God Truly: What's Theological About A Theological School*. Louisville, Ky.: Westminster/John Knox Press, 1992.

Kelsey, David H. *Between Athens and Berlin: The Theological Education Debate*. Grand Rapids, Mich.: Eerdmans, 1993.

Kelsey, David H. and Barbara G. Wheeler. *New Ground: The Foundations and Future of the Theological Education Debate*. Robert R. Williams ed. *Theology and the Interhumans*. Valley Forge, Pa.: Trinity Press International, 1995.

Kinast, Robert L. *Let Ministry Teach: A Guide to Theological Reflection.* Collegeville, Minn.: Liturgical Press, 1996.

Leith, John H. *Crisis in the Church: The Plight of Theological Education.* 1st ed. Louisville, Ky.: Westminster/John Knox Press, 1992.

Mohler, R. Albert and D. G. Hart. *Theological Education in the Evangelical Tradition.* Grand Rapids, Mich.: Baker Books, 1996.

Palmer, Parker. *The Courage to Teach: Exploring the Inner Landscape of a Teacher's Life.* San Francisco, Calif.: Jossey-Bass, 1998.

Palmer, Parker, Barbara Wheeler, and James Fowler. Eds. *Caring for the Commonweal: Education for Religious and Public Life.* Macon, Ga.: Mercer University Press, 1990.

Sarles, Harvey B. *Teaching as Dialogue: A Teacher's Study.* Lanham: University Press, 1993.

Schuth, Katarina. *Seminaries, Theologates, and the Future of Church Ministry: an Analysis of Trends and Transitions.* Collegeville, Minn.: Liturgical Press, 1999.

Thistlewaite, Susan B. and George F. Cairns, eds. *Beyond Theological Tourism: Mentoring as a Grassroots Approach to Theological Education.* Maryknoll: Orbis, 1994.

Wheeler, Barbara G. and Edward Farley, eds. *Shifting Boundaries: Contextual Approaches to the Structure of Theological Education.* Louisville, Ky.: Westminster/John Knox Press, 1991.

Wood, Charles. *Vision and Discernment: An Orientation in Theological Study.* Atlanta, Ga.: Scholars Press, 1985.

Youngblood, Robert L., World Evangelical Fellowship, and Study Unit on Theological Education. *A Reader in Theological Education.* Driebergen, Exeter: Study Unit on Theological Education, WEF Theological Commission. Paternoster Distributor, 1983.

Articles

Ferris, Robert W. and Billy Graham Center. *Renewal in Theological Education: Strategies for Change.* BGC Monograph. Wheaton, Ill.: Billy Graham Center, Wheaton College, 1990.

Fletcher, John C. *The Futures of Protestant Seminaries.* Washington, D.C.: Alban Institute, 1983.

Kelsey, David H. and Barbara G. Wheeler. "Thinking About Theological Education," *Theological Education* (autumn 1991).

Langford, Jeremy. "Working at a Distance: New Learning Technologies Bring the Classroom to the Learner," *In Trust* (spring 1998): 8-13.

Patterson, Elizabeth. "The Questions of Distance Education," *Theological Education* 13.1 (1996): 59-74.

Waits, James L. "An Educator Looks Ahead: Challenges Met Make for New Ones to Come," *In Trust* (summer 1998): 6-8.

Wheeler, Barbara G. "Argument and Allies: The Yale Consultations and Recent Writings about Theological Education," *Theological Education,* Vol. 21, No. 1 (autumn 1994).

Wheeler, Barbara G. with Jackson Carroll, Daniel O. Aleshire, and Penny Long Marler "Snapshots at Two Schools: How Seminary Culture Shapes the Student's Learning," *In Trust* (autumn 1998).

II

DIRECTORIES

1. United States Cooperative Organizations, National

The organizations listed in this section are cooperative religious organizations that are national in scope. Regional cooperative organizations in the United States are listed in Directory 7, "United States Regional and Local Ecumenical Bodies."

The Alban Institute, Inc.

Founded in 1974, the Alban Institute, Inc. (www.alban.org) is a nonprofit, nondenominational membership organization which provides resources for vital congregations. Through its book publishing, *Congregations* magazine, education programs, consulting, training services, and research, the Alban Institute provides resources and services—including www.congregationalresources.org, its online resource database—to congregations and judicatories of all denominations and their lay and ordained leaders.

The Institute has long been a pioneer in identifying, researching and publishing information about key issues in the religious world such as conflict management, clergy transition, leadership, worship and congregation size transitions. The Institute's resources include over 100 book titles, over 40 courses offered nationally each year, and a staff of senior and regional consultants located across the country ready to assist local congregations. Individuals, congregations, and institutions support Alban's work and maintain their cutting-edge skills for ministry through membership in the Institute and through donations of Alban's products and services.

Headquarters

7315 Wisconsin Ave., Ste. 1250 W, Bethesda, MD 20814-3211 Tel. (800)486-1318
Website: www.alban.org
Media Contact, Dir. of Research, Dr. Ian Evison

Officers

Pres., The Rev. James P. Wind, PhD

American Bible Society

In 1816, pastors and laymen representing a variety of Christian denominations gathered in New York City to establish an organization "to disseminate the Gospel of Christ throughout the habitable world." Since that time the American Bible Society (ABS) has continued to provide God's Word, without doctrinal note or comment, wherever it is needed and in the language and format the reader can most easily use and understand. The ABS is the servant of the denominations and local churches.

The American Bible Society is committed to promoting personal engagement with the Holy Scriptures. A new special emphasis is placed on reaching the souls of America's youth through literacy training and faith-based hip-hop music with the goal of changed lives.

Today the ABS serves more than 100 denominations and agencies, and its board of trustees is composed of distinguished laity and clergy drawn from these Christian groups.

Fifty-five years ago the American Bible Society played a leading role in the founding of the United Bible Societies, a federation of 135 national Bible Societies around the world that enables global cooperation in Scripture translation, publication and distribution in more than 200 countries and territories. The ABS contributes approximately 45 percent of the support provided by the UBS to those national Bible Societies which request support to meet the total Scripture needs of people in their countries.

The work of the ABS is supported through gifts from individuals, local churches, denominations, and cooperating agencies.

Headquarters

National Service Center, 1865 Broadway, New York, NY 10023 Tel. (212)408-1200
Media Contact, Senior Manager, Media Relations, Roy Lloyd Tel. (212)408-8731, Fax (212)408-1456, rlloyd@americanbible.org

Officers

Chpsn., Rev. R. Lamar Vest
Vice Chpsn., Harold Bennett
Pres., Dr. Eugene B. Habecker
Senior Vice Pres. for Organizational Marketing, Robert L. Briggs
Senior Vice Pres. for Publishing Unit, John Cruz
Senior Vice Pres. for Programs, Rev. Trevón Gross

Vice Pres. for People Resources, Angelo Agrafiotis
Vice Pres. and General Counsel, Peter Rathbun
Vice Pres. for Office of Latino Affairs, Emilio Reyes
Associate Vice Pres. and Dean, Nida Institute, Dr. Robert Hodgson
Associate Vice Pres. for Finance and Administration, Donald Cavanaugh
Associate Vice Pres. for Product Marketing, Thomas Durakis
Associate Vice Pres. for Operations, Publishing Unit, Gary Ruth

DEPARTMENT HEADS

Senior Dir. for ILLM, Stephen King
Dir. of Market Research, Cheryl Berlamino
Dir. of Administrative Services, John Colligan
Dir. of Technology, William Cook
Dir. of Research, Nida Institute, Dr. Joseph Crockett
Dir. of Product Development, ABSinteractive, Nicholas Garbidakis
Dir. of Fulfillment Services, Gary Golden
Dir. of Customer and Inventory Management, Dr. John Greco
Dir. of The Gallery and Art Initiatives, Dr. Ena Heller
Dir. of Editorial Services and Product Development, Charles Houser
Dir. of Publishing Services, Anne Hughes
Dir. of Creative Services, H. Lee Manis
Dir. of Financial Services, Dennis Morgan
Dir. of Investment and Special Projects, Nicholas Pagano
Dir. of People Resources, Sharon Roberts
Dir. of International Business Development, ABSi, Andrew Rugege
Dir. of Program Implementation, Rev. John Scott
Dir. of Direct Response Sales, Brian Sherry
Dir. of Trade and Ministry Sales, William Sinclair
Dir. of Major Gifts, Melinda Trine
Dir. of Program Development, Karmen Wynick

American Council of Christian Churches

The American Council of Christian Churches is a Fundamentalist multidenominational organization whose purposes are to provide information, encouragement, and assistance to Bible-believing churches, fellowships, and individuals; to preserve our Christian heritage through exposure of, opposition to, and separation from doctrinal impurity and compromise in current religious trends and movements; to protect churches from religious and political restrictions, subtle or obvious, that would hinder their ministries for Christ; and to promote obedience to the inerrant Word of God.

Founded in 1941, The American Council of Christian Churches (ACCC) is a multidenominational agency for fellowship and cooperation among Bible-believing churches in various denominations and fellowships—Bible Presbyterian Church, Evangelical Methodist Church, Fellowship of Fundamental Bible Churches (formerly Bible Protestant), Free Presbyterian Church of North America, Fundamental Methodist Church, Independent Baptist Fellowship of North America, Independent Churches Affiliated—along with hundreds of independent churches. The total membership nears 2,000,000. Each denomination retains its identity and full autonomy, but cannot be associated with the World Council of Churches, National Council of Churches, or National Association of Evangelicals.

Commissions: Chaplaincy, Education, Laymen, Literature, Missions, Radio and Audio Visual, Relief, Youth.

Headquarters

P.O. Box 5455, Bethlehem, PA 18015 Tel. (610)865-3009 Fax (610)865-3033
Media Contact, Exec. Dir., Dr. Ralph Colas

Officers

Pres., Dr. John McKnight
Vice Pres., Rev. Mark Franklin
Exec. Sec., Dr. Ralph Colas
Sec., Rev. Craig Griffith
Treas., Rev. Thomas Hamilton.

American Friends Service Committee

Founded: 1917. Regional offices: 9. Founded by and related to the Religious Society of Friends (Quakers) but supported and staffed by individuals sharing basic values regardless of religious affiliation. Attempts to relieve human suffering and find new approaches to world peace and social justice through nonviolence. Work in 22 countries includes development and refugee relief, peace education, and community organizing. Sponsors off-the-record seminars around the world to build better international understanding. Conducts programs with US communities on the problems of minority groups such as housing, employment, and denial of legal rights. Maintains Washington, D.C. office to present AFSC experience and perspectives to policymakers. Seeks to build informed public resistance to militarism. A co-recipient of the Noble Peace Prize. Programs are multiracial, nondenominational, and international.

Divisions: Community Relations Unit, International Programs, Peacebuilding Unit

Headquarters

1501 Cherry St., Philadelphia, PA 19102 Tel. (215)241-7000 Fax (215)241-7275

Officers

Presiding Clerk, Paul Lacey
Treas., James Fletcher
Gen. Sec., Mary Ellen McNish

The American Theological Library Association

The American Theological Library Association (ATLA) is a library association that works to improve theological and religious libraries and librarianship by providing continuing education, developing standards, promoting research and experimental projects, encouraging cooperative programs, and publishing and disseminating research tools and aids. Founded in 1946, ATLA currently has a membership of over 245 institutions and 550 individuals.

Headquarters

250 S. Wacker Dr., Suite 1600, Chicago, IL 60606-5889 Tel. (312)454-5100 Fax (312) 454-5505

Media Contact, Web Editor, Jonathan West

Officers

Pres., Paul Schrodt, Methodist Theological School in Ohio, 3081 Columbus Pike, P.O. Box 8004, Delaware, OH 43015-8004

Vice Pres., Paul F. Stuehrenberg, Yale University Divinity School Library, 409 Prospect St., New Haven, CT 06511

Sec., Anne Womack, Vanderbilt University Divinity Library, 419 21st Ave. S, Nashville, TN 37240-0007

Exec. Dir., Dennis A. Norlin, ATLA, 250 S. Wacker Dr., Suite 1600, Chicago, IL 60606-5889

American Tract Society

The American Tract Society is a nonprofit, interdenominational organization, instituted in 1825 through the merger of most of the then-existing tract societies. As one of the earliest religious publishing bodies in the United States, ATS has pioneered in the publishing of Christian books, booklets, and leaflets. The volume of distribution has risen to over 35 million pieces of literature annually. For free samples or a free catalog contact 1-800-54-TRACT.

Headquarters

P.O. Box 462008, Garland, TX 75046 Tel. (972)276-9408 Fax (972)272-9642

Media Contact, Dir. of Marketing, Mark A. Brown

Officers

Chpsn., John A. Mawhinney

The American Waldensian Society

The American Waldensian Society (AWS) promotes ministry linkages, broadly ecumenical, between U.S. churches and Waldensian (Reformed)-Methodist constituencies in Italy and Waldensian constituencies in Argentina-Uruguay. Founded in 1906, AWS aims to enlarge mission discovery and partnership among overseas Waldensian-Methodist forces and denominational forces in the U.S.

AWS is governed by a national ecumenical board, although it consults and collaborates closely with the three overseas Waldensian-Methodist boards.

The Waldensian experience is the earliest continuing Protestant experience

Headquarters

American Waldensian Society, VistaCorn, Ste. #1, 1902 Vultee St., Allentown, PA 18103-2958 Tel. (866)825-3373 Fax (610)797-9723

Email: info@waldensian.org

Website: www.waldensian.org

Media Contact, Exec. Dir., Rev. Frank G. Gibson Jr.

Officers

Pres., The Rev. Francis Rivers, '05 PC (USA)

Vice Pres., The Rev. Gabriella Lettini, '05 WC

Sec., Ms. June Rostan, '06

Treas., The Rev. Dick Sanner, '06 PC (USA)

Exec. Dir., Rev. Frank G. Gibson Jr.

Appalachian Ministries Educational Resource Center (AMERC)

The mission of AMERC is to promote contextual, cross-cultural education for theological students, faculties, ministers, and other Christian leaders. Working through an ecumenical consortium of theological schools and denominational judicatories, AMERC supports experiential learning about the theological, spiritual, social, economic, and environmental aspects of Appalachian culture, especially for rural and small town settings for ministry.

Since 1985, AMERC has provided quality educational programs and learning experiences for seminaries and other religious leaders interested in ministry in Appalachia and other rural areas. The centerpiece of these programs has been and continues to be in-depth, contextually based dialogue with local people engaged in creative ministries, exploring with them social, economic, political, ecological, cultural, and religious issues. Intense theological reflection is used to understand these issues through the eyes of faith, equipping students and other leaders for ministry in the Appalachian context.

In the new millennium AMERC's form of ministry has changed. AMERC is now supporting its consortium of members by providing program grants, technical and library support, and leadership consultation. The consortium seminaries and other groups, in turn, design and offer an even wider variety of experiential programs in rural and small town ministry in the context of Appalachia. Both seminary, for credit, and continuing education courses are offered. In 2000 AMERC launched its Grants Program for members of the consortium. Since that time AMERC has funded 20 winter and summer Travel Seminars, a spring course with an immersion component, a Seminary Faculty Immersion experience, a summer intern program, a consultation, and six continuing education events with grants of up to $15,000.

Headquarters

300 Harrison Rd., Berea, KY 40403 Tel. (859) 986-8789 Fax (859)986-2576

Email: bpoage@amerc.org

Website: www.amerc.org

Media Contact, Rev. Dr. Bennett; Exec. Dir., D. Poage; Exec. Assistant, Marsha Baker

Officers

Chpsn., Rev. Dr. Leon Carroll, Columbia Theological Seminary

Vice Chpsn., Rev. Dr. Bill J. Leonard, Wake Forest University Divinity School

Sec., Ms. Tena Willemsma, Commission on Religion in Appalachia

Treas., Mr. Jim Strand, Berea College

The Associated Church Press

The Associated Church Press was organized in 1916. Its members include periodicals and Websites of major Protestant, Catholic, Orthodox, and ecumenical groups in the U.S., Canada, and abroad; individual members who supply publishing services on a freelance or student basis; and affiliate members who supply the Christian press with news, information, and vendor services. It is a professional Christian journalistic association seeking to promote excellence among editors and writers, recognize achievements, and represent the interests of the religious press. It sponsors seminars, conventions, awards programs, and workshops for editors, staff people, and business managers. It is active in postal rates and regulations on behalf of the religious press.

Headquarters

1410 Vernon St. Stoughton , WI 53589-2248 Tel. (608)877-0011 Fax (608)877-0062

Website: www.theacp.org

Media Contact, Exec. Dir., Mary Lynn Hendrickson

Officers

Exec. Dir., Mary Lynn Hendrickson, 1410 Vernon St., Stoughton, WI 53589-2248 Tel. (608)877-0011, Fax (608)877-0062, acpoffice@earthlink.net

Pres., Victoria A. Rebeck, *The Minnesota Connect*, 122 W. Franklin, Ste. 400, Minneapolis, MN 55404-2472 Tel. (612)870-0058, ext. 232, Fax (612)870-1260, victoria.rebeck@mnumc.org

Vice Pres., Jerry Van Marter, Presbyterian News Service, 100 Witherspoon St., Louisville, KY 40202-1396 Tel. (502)569-5493, Fax (502) 569-8073, jerryv@ctr.pcusa.org

Past Pres., Bob Terry, *The Alabama Baptist*, 3310 Independence Dr., Birmingham, AL 35209-5602 Tel. (205)870-4720, Fax (205)870-8957, bterry@alabapnews.org

Treas., Tim Postuma, *The Banner*, 2850 Kalamazoo Ave. SE, Grand Rapids, MI 49560-0001 Tel. (616)224-0793, Fax (616)224-0834, postumat@crcpublications.org

The Associated Gospel Churches

Organized in 1939, The Associated Gospel Churches (AGC) endorses chaplains primarily for strong evangelical Independent Baptist and Bible Churches to the U.S. Armed Forces. The AGC has been recognized by the U.S. Department of Defense for 65 years as an Endorsing Agency, and it supports a strong national defense. The AGC also endorses VA chaplains, police, correctional system, and civil air patrol chaplains.

The AGC provides support for its constituent churches, seminaries, Bible colleges, and missionaries.

The AGC believes in the sovereignty of the local church, the historic doctrines of the Christian faith, and the infallibility of the Bible.

The AGC is a member of the National Conference on Ministry to the Armed Forces (NCMAF) and the Endorsers Conference for Veterans Affairs Chaplaincy (ECVAC).

Headquarters

National Hdqt., P.O. Box 733, Taylors, SC 29687 Tel. (864)268-9617 Fax (864)268-0166

Media Contact, Pres., Billy Baugham, D.D.

Officers

Commission on Chaplains, Pres. and Chpsn., Billy Baugham, D.D.

Vice Pres., Rev. Chuck Flesher

Sec.-Treas., Eva Baugham

Exec. Committee, Chaplain (Captain) James Poe, USN Member

Association of Catholic Diocesan Archivists

The Association of Catholic Diocesan Archivists, which began in 1979, has been committed to the active promotion of professionalism in the management of diocesan archives. The Association meets annually; in the even years it has its own summer conference, in the odd years it meets in conjunction with the Society of American Archivists. Publications include *Standards for Diocesan Archives*, *Access Policy for Diocesan Archives*, and the quarterly *Bulletin*.

Headquarters

Archives & Records Center, 711 W. Monroe, 60661, IL 60661 Tel. (312)831-0711 Fax (312) 736-0488

Media Contact, Ms. Nancy Sandlebac

Officers

Pres., Msgr. Francis J. Weber, 15151 San Fernando Mission Blvd., Mission Hills, CA 91345 Tel. (818)365-1501

Vice Pres., Dr. Charles Nolan, 1100 Chartres St., New Orleans, LA 70116 Tel. (504)529-2651 Fax (504)529-2001

Sec.-Treas., Sr. Catherine Louise LaCoste, C.S.J., 10291/2 Hayes Ave., San Diego, CA 92103 Tel. (619)298-6608

Bd. Members: Kinga Perzynska, P.O. Box 13124, Capital Station, Austin, TX 78711 Tel. (512)476-6296 Fax (512)476-3715; Timothy Cary, P.O. Box 07912, Milwaukee, WI 19807 Tel. (414)769-3407 Fax (414)769-3408; Lisa May, P.O. Box 907, 1700 San Jacinto, Houston, TX 77001 Tel. (713)659-5461 Fax (713)759-9151; John J. Treanor, 711 W. Monroe, Chicago, IL 60661 Tel. (312)736-5150 Fax (312)736-0488; Bernice Mooney, 27 C St., Salt Lake City, UT 84103-2397 Tel. (801)328-8641 Fax (801)328-9680

Newsletter Editor, Nancy Sandleback

ADRIS-Association for the Development of Religious Information Services

The Association for the Development of Religious Information Services was established in 1971 to facilitate coordination and cooperation among information services that pertain to religion. Its goal is a worldwide network that is interdisciplinary, interfaith, and interdenominational to serve both administrative and research applications. ADRIS publishes an e-zine and provides internet consulting services.

Headquarters

ADRIS Newsletter Office, P.O. Box 210735, Nashville, TN 37221-0735 Tel. (615)429-8744 Fax (508)632-0370

Media Contact, Ezine Ed., Edward W. Dodds, P.O. Box 210735, Nashville, TN 37221-0735 Tel. (615)429-8744Fax (508)632-0370

Association of Gospel Rescue Missions

The Association of Gospel Rescue Missions (AGRM), formerly the International Union of Gospel Missions, is an association of 300 rescue missions and other ministries that serve more than 7 million homeless and needy people in the inner cities of the US, Canada, and overseas each year. Since 1913, AGRM member ministries have offered emergency food and shelter, evangelical outreach, Christian counsel, youth and family services, prison and jail outreach, rehabilitation, and specialized programs for the mentally ill, the elderly, the urban poor, and street youth. The AGRM operates RESCUE College, an Internet-based distance education program to prepare and train rescue mission workers. The AGRM sponsors Alcoholics Victorious, a network of Christian support groups.

Headquarters

1045 Swift, Kansas City, MO 64116-4127 Tel. (816)471-8020 Fax (816)471-3718

Media Contact, Exec. Dir., Rev. Stephen E. Burger or Phil Rydman

Officers

Exec. Dir., Rev. Stephen E. Burger

Pres., Mr. Rick Alvis, P.O. Box 817, Indianapolis, IN 46206 Tel. (317)635-3575 Fax (317)687-3629

Vice Pres., Mr. Tom Zobel, P.O. Box 461, Salem, OR 97308 Tel. (503)362-3983 Fax (503)399-8673

Sec., Rev. James Harriger, 205 Commercial St., Springfield, MO 65803 Tel. (417)831-9980 Fax (417)831-9980

NATIONAL PROGRAM UNITS AND STAFF

Education, Rev. Michael Liimatta

Exec. Asst., Tammy Sharp

Newsletter and Magazine, Stephen E. Burger; Philip Rydman

Convention, Stephen E. Burger

Business Admn., Len Conner

Historian, Delores Burger

Communications, Phillip Rydman

Expansion, Gary Meek

Development, Ken Fast

Association of Statisticians of American Religious Bodies

This Association was organized in 1934 and grew out of personal consultations held by representatives from the *Yearbook of American Churches*, the National (now Official) Catholic Directory, the Jewish Statistical Bureau, and the Methodist (now The United Methodist), Lutheran, and Presbyterian churches.

ASARB has a variety of purposes: to bring together those officially and professionally responsible for gathering, compiling, and publishing denominational statistics; to provide a forum for the exchange of ideas and sharing of problems in statistical methods and procedure; and to seek such standardization as may be possible in religious statistical data.

Headquarters

c/o John P. Marcum, Presbyterian Church (USA), 100 Witherspoon St., Rm. 2623, Louisville, KY 40202-1396 Tel. (502)569-5161 Fax (502)569-5163

Media Contact, Sec.-Treas., John P. Marcum

Officers

Pres., Rich Houseal, Church of the Nazarene, 6401 The Paseo, Kansas City, MO 64131 Tel. (816)333-7000, ext. 2473, Fax (816)361-5202, rhouseal@nazarene.org

1st Vice Pres., Mary Gautier, Center for Applied Research in the Apostolate, Georgetown University, Washington, D.C. 20057 Tel. (202) 687-8086, Fax (202)687-8083, gautierm@georgetown.edu

2nd Vice Pres., Craig This, Office of Research, United Methodist Church, 601 W. Riverview Avenue, Dayton, OH 45406 Tel. (937)227-9415, Fax (937)227-9407, cthis@gcom-umc.org

Sec.-Treas., John P. Marcum, Presbyterian

Church (USA), 100 Witherspoon St., Louisville, KY 40202-1396 Tel.(502)569-5161, Fax(502) 333-7161, jmarcum@ctr.pcusa.org

MEMBERS-AT-LARGE

Larry Steinmetz, Year Book Office, Christian Church (Disciples of Christ), P.O. Box 1986, Indianapolis, IN 46206-1986 Tel. (317)635-3100, Fax (317)635-3700, 1steinmetz@ddi.disciples.org

Major Diana E. Smith, The Salvation Army, 440 West Nyack Road, Box C-635, West Nyack, NY 10994-1739 Tel. (845)620-7382, Fax (845) 620-7766, Diana_smith@use.salvationarmy.org

The Association of Theological Schools in the United States and Canada

The Association of Theological Schools is the accrediting and program agency for graduate theological education in North America. Its member schools offer graduate professional and academic degrees for church-related professions.

Headquarters

10 Summit Park Dr., Pittsburgh, PA 15275-1103 Tel. (412)788-6505 Fax (412)788-6510

Media Contact, Dir. Of Comm., Nancy Merrill, Tel. (412)788-6505

Officers

Pres., David L. Tiede, Luther Seminary, St. Paul, MN

Vice Pres., Cynthia Campbell, McCormick Theological Seminary, Chicago, IL

Sec., Clarence G. Newsome, Howard University School of Divinity, Washington, D.C.

Treas., Thomas R. Johnson, Kirkpatrick and Lockhart, Pittsburgh, PA

Staff

Exec. Dir., Daniel O. Aleshire

Blanton-Peale Institute

Blanton-Peale Institute is dedicated to helping people overcome emotional obstacles by joining mental health expertise with religious faith and values. The Blanton-Peale Graduate Institute provides advanced training in marriage and family therapy, psychotherapy, and pastoral care for ministers, rabbis, sisters, priests, and other counselors. The Blanton-Peale Counseling Centers provide counseling for individuals, couples, families, and groups. Blanton-Peale also offers a nationwide telephone support service for clergy, social service agencies, and other employers, and promotes interdisciplinary communication among theology, medicine, and the behavioral sciences. Blanton-Peale was founded in 1937 by Dr. Norman Vincent Peale and psychiatrist Smiley Blanton, M.D.

Headquarters

3 W. 29th St., New York, NY 10001 Tel. (212)725-7850 Fax (212)689-3212

Officers

Chpsn., John Allen
Vice Chpsn., Arthur Caliandro
Sec., Janet E. Hunt
Treas., Mary McNamara
Pres. & CEO, Dr. Holly Johnson

Bread For The World

Bread for the World is a nonprofit, nondenominational Christian citizen's movement of 45,000 members that advocates specific hunger policy changes and seeks justice for hungry people at home and abroad. Founded in 1974, Bread for the World is supported by more than 45 Protestant, Catholic, and Evangelical denominations and church agencies. Rooted in the gospel of God's love in Jesus Christ, its 45,000 members write, call, and visit their members of Congress to win specific legislative changes that help hungry people and place the issue of hunger on the nation's policy agenda.

Bread for the World works closely with Bread for the World Institute. The Institute seeks to inform, educate, nurture, and motivate concerned citizens for action on policies that affect hungry people.

Headquarters

50 F St. NW, Ste. 500, Washington, D.C. 20001 Tel. (202)639-9400 Fax (202)639-9401

Media Contact, Shawnda Eibl

Officers

Pres., Rev. David Beckmann
Bd. Chpsn., Matthew McHugh.
Bd. Vice Chpsn., Eleanor Butt Crook

Campus Crusade for Christ International

Campus Crusade for Christ International is an interdenominational, evangelistic, and discipleship ministry dedicated to helping fulfill the Great Commission through the multiplication strategy of "win-build-send." Founded in 1951 on the campus of UCLA, the organization now includes 60 plus separate ministries and special projects reaching out to almost every segment of society. There are more than 27,000 staff members and 226,000 trained volunteers in 190 countries.

Headquarters

100 Lake Hart Dr., Orlando, FL 32832 Tel. (407) 826-2000 Fax (407)826-2120

Media Contact, James Woelbern

Officers

Chairman & Pres., Stephen B. Douglass
Chief Operating Officer, J. Roger Bruehl
Chief Fin. Officer, Roger L. Craft

CARA–Center for Applied Research in the Apostolate

CARA–the Center for Applied Research in the Apostolate is a not-for-profit research organization of the Roman Catholic Church. It operates on the premise that not only theological principles but also findings of the social sciences must be the basis for pastoral care.

CARA's mission since its founding in 1964 has been "to discover, promote, and apply modern techniques and scientific informational resources for practical use in a coordinated and effective approach to the Church's social and religious mission in the modern world, at home and overseas."

CARA performs a wide range of research studies and consulting services. Since its roots are Roman Catholic, many of its studies are done for dioceses, religious orders, parishes, and the United States Conference of Catholic Bishops. Interdenominational studies are also performed. Publishes *The CARA Report*, a research newsletter on Catholic Church related topics, four times a year and *The Catholic Ministry Formation Directory*, a guide and statistical compilation of enrollments for Catholic seminaries, diaconate formation programs, and lay ministry formation programs.

Headquarters

Georgetown University, Washington, D.C. 20057-1203 Tel. (202)687-8080 Fax (202) 687-8083 Email: cara@georgetown.edu

Media Contact, Exec. Dir., Dr. Bryan Froehle

Officers

Bishop John J. Leibrecht, Chpsn., CARA Board of Directors

Periodical

The Catholic Ministry Formation Directory

Center on Conscience & War (NISBCO)

CCW (formerly NISBCO), formed in 1940, is a nonprofit service organization supported by individual contributions and related to more than thirty religious organizations. Its purpose is to defend and extend the rights of conscientious objectors to war. CCW provides information on how to register for the draft while documenting one's convictions as a conscientious objector, how to cope with penalties if one does not cooperate, and how to qualify as a conscientious objector while in the Armed Forces. It also provides information for counselors and the public about conscientious objection, military service, and the operation of the draft. It provides information to and support for conscientious objectors in other countries.

As a national resource center it assists research in its area of interest including the peace witness of religious bodies. Its staff provides referral to local counselors and attorneys and professional support for them. Through publications and speaking, CCW encourages people to decide for themselves what they believe about participation in war and to act on the basis of the dictates of their own informed consciences.

Headquarters

1830 Connecticut Ave. NW, Washington, D.C. 20009-5732 Tel. (202)483-2220 Fax (202) 483-1246

Media Contact, Exec. Dir., J. E. McNeil

Officers

Exec. Dir., J. E. McNeil
Chpsn., Jonathan Ogle
Sec., James Feldman
Treas., Mary Miller

Center for Parish Development

The Center for Parish Development is an ecumenical, nonprofit research and development agency whose mission is to help church bodies learn to become faithful expressions of God's mission in today's postmodern, post-Christendom world. Founded in 1968, the Center brings to its client-partners a strong theological orientation, a missional ecclesial paradigm with a focus on faithful Christian communities as the locus of mission, research-based theory and practice of major change, a systems approach, and years of experience working with national, regional, and local church bodies.

The Center staff provides research, consulting and training support for church organizations engaging in major change. The Center is governed by a 12-member Board of Directors.

Headquarters

1525 E. 55th St., Suite 201, Chicago, IL 60615 Tel. (773)752-1596 Fax (773)752-5093

Media Contact, Office Manager, Beatrice Vansen

Officers

Chpsn., Charles J. Cook, 606 Ratherview Pl., Austin, TX 78768
Vice Chpsn., Stephen B. Bevens, 5401 S. Cornell Avenue, Chicago, IL 60615
Sec., Delton Krueger, 10616 Penn Ave. S, Bloomington, MN 55431
Exec. Dir., Paul M. Dietterich

Chaplaincy of Full Gospel Churches

The Chaplaincy of Full Gospel Churches (CFGC) is a unique coalition of 239 nondenominational churches and networks of churches united for the purpose of being represented in military and civilian chaplaincies. Since its inception in 1984, CFGC has grown rapidly. Today CFGC represents over 8 million American Christians.

Churches, fellowships, and networks of churches which affirm the CFGC statement of faith that "Jesus is Savior, Lord and Baptizer in the Holy Spirit today, with signs, wonders and gifts following" may join the endorsing agency. CFGC represents its 239 member-networks of churches (consisting of over 60,000 churches nationwide) before the Pentagon's Armed Forces Chaplains Board, the National Conference of Ministry to the Armed Forces, Endorsers Conference for Veterans Affairs Chaplaincy, Federal Bureau of Prisons, Association of Professional Chaplains, and other groups requiring professional chaplaincy endorsement. The organization also ecclesiastically credentials professional counselors.

Headquarters

2715 Whitewood Dr., Dallas, TX 75233 Tel. (214)331-4373 Fax (214)333-4401
Media Contact, Rev. Dr. E. H. Jim Ammerman

Officers

Pres. & Dir., Rev. Dr. E. H. Jim Ammerman
Vice Pres., Lt. Col. Ed Leach, US Army (Retired)

Christian Council on Persons with Disabilities

Created in 1988, the Christian Council on Persons with Disabilities (CCPD) is a coalition of churches, nonprofit organizations, and individuals advocating an evangelical perspective concerning people with disabilities and their place in God's world. The coalition provides a national voice for Christians involved in disability ministry, framing the Christian community's response to issues relating to disability.

CCPD provides information and responses on issues specifically relating to the church such as accessibility, disability theology, and outreach, as well as disability-related issues of concern to the general public such as genetic research, end-of-life care, and cloning.

Advocacy, professional development, networking, and education are all part of the coalition's activities. Annual conferences (both national and regional), chapter groups, and mentoring programs are part of the coalition's strategy in strengthening the network of disability ministry.

Headquarters

1100 W. 42nd Street, Ste. 223, Indianapolis, IN 46208 Tel. (317)923-CCPD
Email: info@ccpd.org
Website: www.ccpd.org

Officers

Exec. Dir., LisaRose Hall
Vice Pres., Charlie Chivers of Waupaca, WI
Treas., Stan Higgins, of Rohnert Park, CA
Sec., Connie Hutchinson of Placetia, CA

Christian Endeavor International

Christian Endeavor International is a Christ-centered, youth-oriented ministry which assists local churches in reaching young people with the gospel of Jesus Christ, discipling them in the Christian faith, and equipping them for Christian ministry and service in their local church, community, and world. It trains youth leaders for effective ministry and provides opportunities for Christian inspiration, spiritual growth, fellowship, and service. Christian Endeavor International reaches across denominational, cultural, racial, and geographical boundaries. All materials are on the internet at www.teamce.com

Headquarters

309 South Main St., Mount Vernon, OH 43050 Tel. (800)260-3234 Fax (740)397-0198
Email: info@teamce.com
Website: www.teamce.com
Media Contact, Exec. Dir., Wesley Whatley

Officers

Pres., Jonathan Stewart
Exec. Dir., Wesley Whatley

Christian Management Association

Christian Management Association (CMA) provides leadership training, management resources, and strategic networking relationship for leaders and managers of Christian organizations and growing churches. Its membership represents senior leaders and departmental managers from more than 1,500 larger Christian organizations and mega-churches in the US. CMA publishes *Christian Management Report* magazine, *CMA Management* monthly e-newsletter, *CMA Compensation Handbook for Christian Ministries*, www.CMAonline.org website, CMA Management Tape Library, and other resources. CMA provides the latest leadership and management trends and tools through its annual leadership and management conference for Christian organizations and churches, CEO Dialogues one-day roundtables, CMA Executive Leadership Program, CMA Chapters, CMA Online Job Market, CMA Sponsored Programs, and CMA Money-Savers. It also sponsors the Best Christian Place to Work annual survey and the annual CMA Management Award. Annual membership is open to Christian organizations, ministries, and churches. Organizations that provide products or services for Christian organizations and churches may apply for business membership. For complete membership information, go to www.CMAonline.org.

Headquarters

P.O. Box 4090, San Clemente, CA 92674 Tel. (800)727-4CMA Fax (949)487-0927
Website: www.CMAonline.org
CEO, John Pearson, John@CMAonline.org; Dir. of Management Resources, DeWayne Herbrandson, DeWayne@CMAonline.org

Officers for 2003-2004

Chmn., Jerry E. White, Pres., The Navigators
Vice Chmn., Mark G. Holbrook, Pres./CEO, ECCU
Treas., Frederick J. Rudy, Consultant
Sec., Mark A. Bankord, Managing Partner, Cap Trust Asset Management

Officers

Chmn., James A. Gwinn (Pres., CRISTA Ministries)
Vice Chpsn., Molly Davis Scott (Pres., The Molly Davis Scott Company)
Sec.-Treas., James A. Canning (Chief Financial Officer, World Vision International)
CEO, John Pearson

A Christian Ministry in the National Parks

This ministry is recognized by over 40 Christian denominations and extends the ministry of Christ to the millions of people who live, work, and vacation in our National Parks. Ministry Staff Members conduct services of worship in the parks on Sundays. The staff are employed by park concessionaires and have full-time jobs in which their actions, attitudes, and commitment to Christ serve as witness. Room and board are provided at a minimal cost; minimum commitment of 90 days needed.

Officers

Dir., The Rev. Richard P. Camp Jr.
Deputy Dir., Gordon Compton

Church Growth Center—Home of Church Doctor Ministries

The Church Growth Center is an interfaith, nonprofit, professional organization which exists to bring transformational change of the Christian church toward the effective implementation of the Lord's Great Commission, to make disciples of all people. This effort is done through consultations, resources, and educational events.

Founded in 1978 by Kent R. Hunter, president and chairman of the board, the Church Growth Center offers several services including church consultations by experienced consultants, cutting edge resources through The Church Doctor™ Resource Center, and educational events at churches and organizations in the way of providing speakers and resources at seminars, workshops, and conferences. The quarterly newsletter is the *Church Doctor Report*.

Headquarters

P.O. Box 145, 1230 US Highway Six, Corunna, IN 46730 Tel. (800)626-8515 Fax (260)281-2167
Website: www.churchdoctor.org
Media Contact, Assistant to Pres., Cindy Warren

Officers

Pres., Dr. Kent R. Hunter, Dmin, PhD
Vice Pres., Jim Manthei
Treas., Wayne Register

Church Women United in the USA

Church Women United in the USA is a grassroots ecumenical movement of one-half million Protestant, Orthodox, Roman Catholic, and other Christian women organized into more than 1,200 local and state units throughout the United States and Puerto Rico. Founded in 1941, CWU works in coalition with religious and secular groups on issues of peace and justice. CWU hosts three ecumenical worhip services each year, with World Day of Prayer being the most widely celebrated. The priority for 2000-2004 is "Strengthening Families Worldwide in the 21st Century."

Headquarters

NATIONAL OFFICE
475 Riverside Dr., Ste. 500, New York, NY 10115 Tel. (800)CWU-5551 or (212)870-2347 Fax (212)870-2338
Media Contact, Roberto Vasquez Tel. (212)870-3339, allamoso@churchwomen.org
LEGISLATIVE OFFICE
CWU Washington Ofc., 100 Maryland Ave. NE, Rm. 100, Washington, D.C. 20002 Tel. (202) 544-8747 Fax (202)544-9133
Legislative Dir., Wash. Ofc., Roberto Vazquez, tlheath@churchwomen.org
UNITED NATIONS OFFICE
475 Riverside Dr., Ste. 500, New York, NY 10115 Tel. (212)661-3856
ADMINISTRATION
Controller/Operations Manager, Roberto Vazquez, rvazquez@churchwomen.org

Officers

Pres., Jerrye Champion, Scottsdale, AZ
Vice Pres., Dorothy Krieger, Bloomingfield, CO
Sec., Carol Kolsti, Austin, TX
Treas., Jane Gray, Columbus, OH
Regional Coordinators: Central, Helen Traudt, Lincoln, NE; East Central, Margaret Tweet, Rock Island, IL; Mid-Atlantic, Blanche Crim, Dover, DE; Northeast, Marilyn Lariviere, Hyannis, MA; Northwest, Edna Best, Billings, MT; South Central, Martha Moody Boone, Keithville, LA; Southeast, Mona Hayes, Nashville, TN; Southwest, Martha DeWarf, Tucson, AZ

Churches Uniting in Christ

Churches Uniting in Christ (CUIC) was inaugurated on January 20, 2002, in Memphis TN as a new relationship among nine communions which agreed to start living more fully into their unity in Christ. CUIC is the successor to the Consultation on Church Union (COCU) which was organized in 1962 to explore the formation of a uniting church. At the 1999 COCU Plenary the nine member communions affirmed eight "Marks" of Churches Uniting in Christ and agreed to move into the new relationship of covenanted communion to be called Churches Uniting in Christ. Following confirmation actions by each of the communions, all nine communions officially constituted Churches Uniting in Christ. The nine member communions are: The African Methodist Episcopal Church, the African Methodist Episcopal Zion Church, the Christian Church (Disciples of Christ), the Christian Methodist Episcopal Church, The Episcopal Church, the International Council of

Community Churches, the Presbyterian Church (USA), the United Church of Christ, and the United Methodist Church. Also participating at present is one Partner in Mission and Dialogue, the Evangelical Lutheran Church in America. Other communions are exploring various possibilities for relating to CUIC.

CUIC is a bold venture, expressed through the participating communions' covenant to seek to live a new relationship that bears witness to a church that is truly catholic, truly evangelical, and truly reformed. Among the goals for bearing witness to that unity are two very challenging endeavors: to heed the "emphatic call to 'erase racism' by challenging the system of white privilege that has so distorted life in this society and in the churches themselves" and to "provide a foundation for the mutual recognition and reconciliation of ordained ministry by the members of Churches Uniting in Christ by the year 2007." Notably, the commitment to address racism is named as a hallmark of the new relationship and, following the Inaugural ceremony,on Dr. Martin Luther King Jr. Day, January 21, 2002, the Heads of Communion signed an Appeal to the Churches to work together for the eradication of racism.

The Ecumenical Officers of each of the communions will carry major responsibility for the engagement of their congregations and members in the CUIC relationship. Neighboring congregations are encouraged to celebrate the Eucharist together; invite the participation of each in services of baptism, ordinations, and installation as well as other special events in the congregations' lives; and to discover ways in which they might witness together in combating social injustices, especially racism. In addition to the representational Coordinating Council, three task forces will work to enhance the collaborative endeavors of CUIC: Ministry, Racism, and Local and Regional Ecumenism.

US COOPERATIVE ORGANIZATIONS

Headquarters

700 Prospect Ave., Cleveland, OH 44115-1100 Tel. (216)736-3294 Fax (216)736-329

Email: cuic@ucc.org

Media Contact, The Rev. Dr. Bertrice Y. Wood

Officers

Dir., The Rev. Dr. Bertrice Y. Wood, 700 Prospect Ave., Cleveland, OH 44115-1100 Tel. (216)736-3294, cuicwood@ucc.org/cuic@ucc.org

Pres. of the Coordinating Council, Bishop Melvin G. Talbert (United Methodist Church), 108 Rausch Drive, Brentwood, TN 37027

Vice Pres., The Dr. Suzanne Webb (Christian Church/Disciples of Christ), P.O. Box 299, Elyria, OH 44036

Sec., The Rev. C. Dana Krutz (Episcopal Church/USA), Louisiana Interchurch Conference, 660 North Foster Dr., Ste. A-225, Baton Rouge, LA 70806

Treas., Elder James N. Tse (Presbyterian Church/USA), 87-17 85th St., Woodhaven, NY 11421

COORDINATING COUNCIL REPRESENTATIVES FROM MEMBER COMMUNIONS

African Methodist Episcopal Church, Bishop Vashti McKenzie and Bishop Gregory Ingram

African Methodist Episcopal Zion Church, The Rev. Dr. Harrison Bonner, 12 Eldridge St., Waterbury, CT 06704

Christian Church (Disciples of Christ), The Rev. Dr. Suzanne Webb

Christian Methodist Episcopal Church, Bishop Ronald Cunningham

The Episcopal Church (USA), The Rev. C. Dana Krutz

International Council of Community Churches, Mr. Abraham Wright, 1912-3 Rosemary Hills Drive, Silver Spring, MD 20910

Presbyterain Church (USA), Elder James N. Tse

United Church of Christ, The Rev. Lydia Veliko, 700 Prospect Avenue, Cleveland, OH 44115-1100

The United Methodist Church, Bishop Melvin G. Talbert

Evangelical Council for Financial Accountability

Founded in 1979, the Evangelical Council for Financial Accountability has the purpose of helping Christ-centered, evangelical, nonprofit organizations earn the public's trust through their ethical practices and financial accountability. ECFA assists its over 1,050 member organizations in making appropriate public disclosure of their financial practices and accomplishments, thus materially enhancing their credibility and support potential among present and prospective donors.

Headquarters

440 W. Jubal Early Drive Ste. 130, Winchester, VA 22601-6319 Tel. (540)535-0103 Fax (540) 535-0533

Media Contact, Pres., Paul D. Nelson

Officers

Pres., Paul D. Nelson

Vice Pres., Dan Busby

Evangelical Press Association

The Evangelical Press Association is an organization of editors and publishers of Christian periodicals which seeks to promote the cause of Evangelical Christianity and enhance the influence of Christian journalism.

Headquarters

314 Dover Rd., Charlottesville, VA 22901 Tel. (804)973-5941 Fax (804)973-2710

Media Contact, Exec. Dir., Ronald Wilson

Officers

Pres., David Neff, *Christianity Today*, 465 Gundersen Dr., Carol Stream, IL 60188

Pres.-Elect, Terry White, *Inside Journal*, P.O. Box 17429, Washington, D.C. 20041-0429
Treas., Lamar Keener, *Christian Times*, P.O. Box 2606, El Cajon, CA 92021
Sec., Jeanette Thomason, *Aspire*, 107 Kenner Ave., Nashville, TN 37205
Advisor, Dean Ridings, *Christian Camp & Conference Journal*, P.O. Box 62189, Colorado Springs, CO 80962-2189
Advisor, Brian Peterson, *New Man*, 600 Rinehart Rd., Lake Mary, FL 32746
Exec. Dir., Ronald Wilson

Faith & Values Media

(See also National Interfaith Cable Coalition, Inc.)

Faith & Values Media is a nation's largest coalition of Jewish and Christian faith groups dedicated to media production, distribution, and promotion. It is a service of the National Interfaith Cable Coalition, Inc., established in 1987.

Faith & Values Media member association includes more than 40 faith groups and religious organizations representing 200,000 congregations and 120 million congregants. Its mission is to use television and other media to promote the vitality of religious experience in everyday life.

Programming from Faith & Values Media is available on Hallmark Channel (available through local cable for satellite providers) and on www.faithandvalues.com

Headquarters

74 Trinity Place, Suite 1550, New York, NY 10006 Tel. (212)406-4121 Fax (212)406-4105
Email: www.faithandvalues.com
Media Contact, Nina Katzander

Officers

Chpsn., Dr. Daniel Paul Matthews
Vice Chpsn., Elder Ralph Hardy Jr.
Sec., Rabbi Paul J. Menitoff
Treas., Betty Elam

Staff

Pres. and CEO, Edward J. Murray
Vice Pres., Beverly Judge

Federation of Christian Ministries

The Federation of Christian Ministries is an ecumenical faith community founded in 1968 as the Society of Priests for a Free Ministry. FCM stresses inclusiveness, opening its membership to men and women of varying faith backgrounds who share its vision of an ecumenical, nondenominational community.

FCM's educational branch, Global Ministries University, offers online degree completion courses at both the undergraduate and graduate level for adult learners in the field of ministry (contact: info@federationofchristianministries.org).

FCM ministers serve in many ways. Some lead local house churches and parishes, or are chaplains in nursing homes, correctional facilities, or hospitals. Others serve as spiritual counselors, offer healing ministries, and promote groups dedicated to peace and justice.

Headquarters

1905 Bugbee Rd., Ionia, MI 48846-9663 Tel. (800)538-8923 or (616)527-0419 Fax (616) 527-0419
Email: info@federationofchristianministries.org or ejkalmanek@home.ionia.com
Media Contact, Pres. Bridget Mary Meehan Tel. (703)379-2487, Fax (703)379-2487, sofiabmm@aol.com

Officers

Chpsn., Jan & Paul Reithmaier, 7415 K Triwoods Dr., Shrewsbury, MO 63119-4456 Tel. (314) 962-6220, p.reithmaier@worldnet.att.net
Pres., Bridget Mary Meehan, 5856 Glen Forest Dr., Falls Church, VA 22041-2528 Tel. (703)379-2487, Fax (703)379-2487, sofiabmm@aol.com
Treas., Roger J. Fecher, 8330 Catamaran Dr., Indianapolis, IN 46236-9585 Tel. (317)826-8940, rjfecher@aol.com
Secs./Central Office, Edward & Judy Kalmanek, 1905 Bugbee Rd., Ionia, MI 48846-9663 Tel. (616)527-0419, ejkalmanek@home.ionia.com
Development Directors, Jean & Mike Conley, 355 Hillcrest St., El Segundo, CA 90245-2910 Tel. (310)322-7983, jeannx@aol.com
Members at Large: Gerald Grudzen, 6331 Mountford Dr., San Jose, CA 95123-5246 Tel. (408)629-6146, grudzen@yahoo.com; William Manseau, 12 Catherwood Rd., Tewksbury, MA 01876-2620 Tel. (978)851-5547, manseau@comcast.net

REGIONAL VICE PRESIDENTS

Pacific Region: Brad Krick & Valerie Morgan-Krick, P.O.Box 12099, Tacoma, WA 98412-0099 Tel. (253)473-8959, btkrick@qwest.net
Mountains & Plains Region: Bill Dix, 19060 Nelson Fork Rd., Deerwood, MN 56444-7911 Tel. (281)534-3110, dixie@emily.net
Great Lakes Region: Tom Leonhardt & Carolyn Horvath, 1709 W. 69th St., Cleveland, OH 44102-2957 Tel. (216)651-4362, cartomhl@earthlink.net
Southern Region: Marge & Tom Wilt, 1565 Gores Landing Rd. SW, Ocean Isle Beach, NC 28469-6343 Tel. (910)755-6730, wiltma@aol.com
Northeast Region: Michaelita & Thomas Quinn, 93 Post Rd., Danbury, CT 06810-8367 Tel. (203)792-6968, quinnems@aol.com

Foundation for a Conference on Faith and Order in North America

A Foundation for a Conference on Faith and Order is a not-for-profit organization dedicated to promoting the unity of the North America Churches by keeping before the Churches the gospel call to unity in Faith and Order. It engages in educational studies and programs that relate to issues affecting Faith and Order, and promotes, plans, and administers conferences on Faith and Order in North America. The purpose of these conferences is to encourage and promote the unity of the Churches in Faith and Order.

Headquarters

99 Park Ave., Suite 298-A, New York, NY 10016 Tel. (212)332-0031

MEMBERS OF THE BOARD

Bishop Vinton Anderson
Dr. Wallace M. Alston Jr.
The Rev. Canon Alyson Barnett-Cowan
Dr. Susan E. Davies
Archbishop Demetrios
Dr. Robert M. Franklin
Dr. Donna Geernaert, SC
Dr. Thomas W. Gillespie
The Right Rev. Richard F. Grein
Dr. Robert W. Jenson
Dr. Cheryl Bridges Johns
William Cardinal Keeler
Dr. Kevin W. Mannoia
Bishop Donald J. McCoid
Dr. Richard Mouw
Dr. Willam G. Rusch
Dr. George Vandervelde
Dr. Eldin Villafane
The Rev. Portia Turner Williamson

Friends World Committee for Consultation (Section of the Americas)

The Friends World Committee for Consultation (FWCC) was formed in 1937. There has been an American Section as well as a European Section from the early days and an African Section was organized in 1971. In 1974 the name Section of the Americas was adopted by that part of the FWCC with constituency in North, Central, and South America and in the Caribbean area. In 1985 the Asia-West Pacific Section was organized. The purposes of FWCC are summarized as follows: To facilitate loving understanding of diversities among Friends while discovering together, with God's help, a common spiritual ground, and to facilitate full expression of Friends' testimonies in the world.

Headquarters

Section of the Americas Headquarters
1506 Race St., Philadelphia, PA 19102 Tel. (215) 241-7250 Fax (215)241-7285
Email: americas@fwcc.quaker.org
Website: www.quaker.org/fwcc/americas/americas.html
Media Contact, Exec. Sec., Margaret Fraser
Latin American Office, Guerrero 223 Pte., Zona Centro, Cd. Mante, TAM 89800 Mexico

Officers

Exec. Sec., as well as 5 full-time employees

The Fund for Theological Education, Inc.

Begun in 1954 with the goal of supporting excellence in the profession of ministry, the Fund for Theological Education has enjoyed a long and rich history, providing gifted women and men with nearly 5,000 fellowships and generating innovative new programs for support of persons preparing for ministry and theological teaching. Supported by individuals and grants from a group of US Foundations, FTE envisions new and imaginative programs to encourage diversity and excellence in the churches and seminaries of North America.

Headquarters

825 Houston Mill Rd., Suite 250, Atlanta, GA 30329 Tel. (404)727-1450 Fax (404)727-1490
Email: fte@thefund.org
Website: www.thefund.org, www.exploreministry.org

Officers

Pres., Ann Svennungsen
Vice Pres. For Advancement, Jack Gilbert
Dir., Expanding Horizons Partnership, Dr. Sharon Watson Fluker
Dir., Partnership for Excellence, Melissa Wiginton

Glenmary Research Center

The Research Center is a department of the Glenmary Home Missioners, a Catholic society of priests and brothers. The Center was established in 1966 to serve the rural research needs of the Catholic Church in the United States. Its research has led it to serve ecumenically a wide variety of church bodies. Local case studies as well as quantitative research is done to understand better the diversity of contexts in the rural sections of the country. The Center's statistical profiles of the nation's counties cover both urban and rural counties.

Headquarters

1312 Fifth Ave. N., Nashville, TN 37208 Tel. (615)256-1905 Fax (615)251-1472

Officers

Pres., Rev. Daniel Dorsey, P.O. Box 465618, Cincinnati, OH 45246-5618
1st Vice Pres., Rev. Robert Poandl, P.O. Box 465618, Cincinnati, OH 45246-5618
2nd Vice Pres., Rev. Dominic Duggins, P.O. Box 465618, Cincinnati, OH 45246-5618
Treas., Ms. Teri Heckenmueller, P.O. Box 465618, Cincinnati, OH 45246-5618
Dir., Kenneth M. Sanchagrin, PhD, ksanchagrin@glenmary.org

Graymoor Ecumenical & Interreligious Institute (GEII)

Graymoor Ecumenical & Interreligious Institute has its roots in the Graymoor Ecumenical Institute which was founded in 1967 by the

Franciscan Friars of the Atonement to respond to the Friars' historical concern for Christian Unity in light of the theological and ecumenical developments arising from the Second Vatican Council.

In 1991, in response to developments in both the Institute and the wider ecumenical scene, the Graymoor Ecumenical Institute was expanded into an information and service organization with a mission of Christian Unity and interreligious dialogue. Today, the Graymoor Ecumenical & Interreligious Institute employs several means to acomplish this goal. Among these are specialization desks for African American Churches; Evangelical and Free Churches; Lutheran, Anglican, and Roman Catholic Affairs; Interreligious Dialogue; and Social Ecumenism. Another is the annual Week of Prayer of Christian Unity—a world-wide observance initiated in 1908 by the Rev. Paul Wattson, co-founder of the Society of the Atonement—the theme and text of which are now chosen and prepared by the Pontifical Council for Promoting Christian Unity and representatives of the World Council of Churches. The Institute publishes the monthly journal *Ecumenical Trends* to keep clergy and laity abrest of developments in the ecumenical and interreligious movements; provides membership in, and collaboration with, national and local ecumenical and interreligious organizations and agencies; and cooperates with individuals engaged in ecumenical and interreligious work.

Over the years, the Graymoor Ecumenical & Interreligious Institute has sponsored and co-sponsored meetings, colloquia, and workshops in areas of ecumenical and interreligious dialogue. These have been as diverse as colloquia between African-American and Hispanic Pentecostal scholars; Christians, Muslims, and Jews; state Councils of Churches; and interfaith training workshops for Christian leaders.

Headquarters

475 Riverside Dr., Rm. 1960, New York, NY 10115-1999 Tel. (212)870-2330 Fax (212) 870-2001

Staff

General Ecumenical and Interreligious Dialogue Desk, Dir., Rev. James Loughran, SA, Tel. (212)870-2330

Lutheran, Anglican, Roman Catholic Research Desk, Assoc. Dir., Lorelei F. Fuchs, SA, MA, STL, Tel. (212)870-2330, 100772.372@compuserve.com

Ecumenical Trends, Editor, Assoc. Dir., Kevin McMorrow, SA, Graymoor, Route 9, P.O. Box 300, Garrison, NY 10524-0300 Tel. (845)424-3671, ext. 3120, Kmcmorrow@ atonementfriars.org

Ecumenical Desk, Assoc. Ed., Rev. Wildfred Tyrrell, SA Tel. (212)870-2330

Business Office/Week of Prayer for Christian Unity, Graymoor, Rt. 9, P.O. Box 300, Garrison, NY 10524-0300 Tel. (845)424-3671, ext. 2109, Fax (845)424-2163, rsullivan@ atonementfriars.org

Inter-Varsity Christian Fellowship of the USA

Inter-Varsity Christian Fellowship is a non-profit, interdenominational student movement that ministers to college and university students and faculty in the United States. Inter-Varsity began in the United States when students at the University of Michigan invited C. Stacey Woods, then General Secretary of the Canadian movement, to help establish an Inter-Varsity chapter on their campus. Inter-Varsity Christian Fellowship–USA was incorporated two years later, in 1941.

Inter-Varsity's uniqueness as a campus ministry lies in the fact that it is student-initiated and student-led. Inter-Varsity strives to build collegiate fellowships that engage their campus with the gospel of Jesus Christ and develop disciples who live out biblical values. Inter-Varsity students and faculty are encouraged in evangelism, spiritual discipleship, serving the church, human relationships, righteousness, vocational stewardship, and world evangelization. A triennial missions conference held in Urbana, Illinois, jointly sponsored with Inter-Varsity–Canada, has long been a launching point for missionary service.

Headquarters

6400 Schroeder Rd., P.O. Box 7895, Madison, WI 53707 Tel. (608)274-9001 Fax (608)274-7882

Media Contact, Dir. of Development Services, Carole Sharkey

Officers

Pres. & CEO, Stephen A. Hayner

Vice Pres., C. Barney Ford; Robert A. Fryling; Samuel Barkat; Ralph Thomas; Jim Malliet

Bd. Chpsn., Virginia Viola

Bd. Vice Chpsn., E. Kenneth Nielson

Interfaith Impact for Justice and Peace

Interfaith Impact for Justice and Peace is the religious community's united voice in Washington. It helps Protestant, Jewish, Muslim, and Catholic national organizations have clout on Capitol Hill and brings grassroots groups and individual and congregational members to Washington and shows them how to turn their values into votes for justice and peace.

Interfaith Impact for Justice and Peace has established the following Advocacy Networks to advance the cause of justice and peace: Justice for Women, Health Care, Hunger and Poverty, International Justice and Peace, Civil and Human Rights. The Interfaith Impact Foundation provides an annual Legislative Briefing for their members.

Members receive the periodic Action alerts on initiatives, voting records, etc., and a free subscription to the Advocacy Networks of their choice.

Headquarters

100 Maryland Ave. NE, Ste. 200, Washington, D.C. 20002 Tel. (202)543-2800 Fax (202)547-8107

Media Contact, Jane Hull Harvey

Officers

Chpsn. of Bd., Jane Hull Harvey (United Methodist Church)

MEMBERS

African Methodist Episcopal Church
African Methodist Episcopal Zion Church
Alliance of Baptists
American Baptist Churches, USA: Washington Office; World Relief Office
American Ethical Union
American Muslim Council
Center of Concern
Christian Methodist Episcopal (CME) Church
Christian Church (Disciples of Christ)
Church of the Brethren
Church Women United
Commission on Religion in Appalachia
Episcopal Church
Episcopal Urban Caucus
Evangelical Lutheran Church in America
Federation of Southern Cooperatives–LAF
Federation for Rural Empowerment
Graymoor Ecumenical and Interreligious Institute
Jesuit Social Ministries
Maryknoll Fathers and Brothers
Moravian Church in America
National Council of Churches of Christ: Church World Service; Washington Office
National Council of Jewish Women

NETWORK

Peoria Citizens Committee
Presbyterian Church (USA)
Progressive National Baptist Convention
Presbyterian Hunger Fund
Reformed Church in America
Rural Advancement Fund
Society of African Missions
Southwest Organizing Project
Southwest Voter Registration-Education Project
Toledo Metropolitan Ministries
Union of American Hebrew Congregations
Unitarian Universalist Association
Unitarian Universalist Service Committee
United Church of Christ: Bd. for Homeland Ministries; Bd. for World Ministries; Hunger Action Ofc.; Ofc. of Church in Society
United Methodist Church: Gen. Bd. of Church & Society; Gen. Bd. of Global Ministries Natl. Div.; Gen. Bd. of Global Ministries Women's Div.; Gen. Bd. of Global Ministries World Div.
Virginia Council of Churches
Western Organization of Resource Councils

Interreligious Foundation for Community Organization (IFCO)

IFCO is a national ecumenical agency created in 1966 by several Protestant, Roman Catholic, and Jewish organizations to be an interreligious, interracial agency for support of community organization and education in pursuit of social justice. Through IFCO, national and regional religious bodies collaborate in development of social justice strategies and provide financial support and technical assistance to local, national, and international social-justice projects.

IFCO serves as a bridge between the churches and communities and acts as a resource for ministers and congregations wishing to better understand and do more to advance the struggles of the poor and oppressed. IFCO conducts workshops for community organizers and uses its national and international network of organizers, clergy, and other professionals to act in the interest of justice.

Churches, foundations, and individual donors use IFCO services as a fiscal agent to make donations to community organizing projects.

IFCO's global outreach includes humanitarian aid shipments through its Pastors for Peace program to Cuba, Haiti, Nicaragua, Honduras, and Chiapas, Mexico.

Headquarters

402 W. 145th St., New York, NY 10031 Tel. (212)926-5757 Fax (212)926-5842
Media Contact, Dir. of Communications, Gail Walker

Officers

Pres., Rev. Schuyler Rhodes
Vice Pres. & Treas., Marilyn Clement

The Kairos Institute, Inc.

The Kairos Institute provides quality support, consultation, and in-depth educational opportunities to the professional, medical, mental health, and religious communities and promotes assistance, consultation, education, and care to families of exceptional children. It's clergy consultation service provides care to many denominations and clergy. "Career Path" offers candidate assessment for ordination and consultation for clergy in transition.

Headquarters

107 Green Ave., Madison, NJ 07940 Tel. (973) 966-9099 Fax (973)377-8509

Officers

Exec. Dir., Rev. Robert Clark

The Liturgical Conference

Founded in 1940 by a group of Benedictines, the Liturgical Conference is an independent, ecumenical, international association of persons concerned about liturgical renewal and meaningful worship. The Liturgical Conference is known chiefly for its periodicals, books, and materials on worship-related concerns in cooperation with various church groups.

Headquarters

P.O. Box 31, Evanston, IL 60201

Officers

Pres., Frank C. Senn
Vice Pres., R. Byron Anderson
Sec., Robert Rimbo
Treas., Victor Cinson

Lombard Mennonite Peace Center

The Lombard Mennonite Peace Center (LMPC) is a nonprofit organization with the mission "to proclaim Christ's good news, the gospel of peace and justice—and to be active in the sacred ministry of reconciliation." With an emphasis on equipping clergy and churches to function in healthy ways, LMPC offers training in conflict transformation and in a family systems approach to church leaders' management of themselves and their congregations.

One- and two-day educational workshops and a five-day Mediation Skills Training Institute for Church Leaders are offered throughout the US. Ongoing clergy clinics provide church leaders with regular opportunities to reflect on their own functioning. LMPC also provides educational events, consultation, and mediation services for congregations and judicatories of all denominations, as well as consultation for individual clergy.

Founded in 1983 as a ministry of a local congregation, LMPC became an independent, 501(c)3 corporation in 1997.

Headquarters

1263 S. Highland Avenue, Suite 1N, Lombard, IL 60148 Tel. (630)627-0507 Fax (630)627-0519

Email: admin@LMPeaceCenter.org

Website: www.LMPeaceCenter.org

Officers

Exec. Dir., Richard G. Blackburn

The Lord's Day Alliance of the United States

The Lord's Day Alliance of the United States, founded in 1888 in Washington, D.C., is the only national organization whose sole purpose is the preservation and cultivation of Sunday, the Lord's Day, as a day of rest and worship. The Alliance also seeks to safeguard a Day of Common Rest for all people regardless of their faith. Its Board of Managers is composed of representatives from 25 denominations. It serves as an information bureau, publishes a magazine, *Sunday*, and furnishes speakers and a variety of materials such as pamphlets, videos, posters, radio spot announcements, cassettes, news releases, articles for magazines, and television programs.

Headquarters

2930 Flowers Rd. S, Atlanta, GA 30341-5532 Tel. (770)936-5376 or (800)746-4422, ext. 376 Fax (770)936-5385

Email: tnorton@1dausa.org

Website: www.sundayonline.org

Media Contact, Exec. Dir. & Ed., Rev. Timothy A. Norton

Officers

Pres., Dr. Roger A. Kvam

Pres. Emeritus, Paul J. Craven

Senior Vice Pres., Wendell J. Schaal

Vice Pres., Brian W. Hanse, David C. McNair, Eugene J. Nicodemus, W. David Sapp, William B. Shea

Sec., Donald R. Pepper

Asst. Sec., Betty Jo Craft

Treas., E. Larry Eidson

Lutheran World Relief

Lutheran World Relief (LWR) is an overseas development and relief agency based in Baltimore which responds quickly to natural and man-made disasters and supports more than 160 long-range development projects in countries throughout Africa, Asia, the Middle East, and Latin America.

Founded in 1945 to act on behalf of Lutherans in the United States, LWR has as its mission "to support the poor and oppressed overseas in their efforts to meet basic human needs and participate with dignity and equity in the life of their communities; and to alleviate human suffering resulting from natural disaster, war, social conflict, or poverty."

Headquarters

700 Light St., Baltimore, MD 21230-3850 Tel. (410)230-2700 Fax (410)230-2882

Media Contact, Jonathan C. Frerichs

Officers

Pres., Kathryn F. Wolford

The Mennonite Central Committee

The Mennonite Central Committee is the relief and service agency of North American Mennonite and Brethren in Christ Churches. Representatives from Mennonite and Brethren in Christ groups make up the MCC, which meets annually in June to review its program and to approve policies and budget. Founded in 1920, MCC administers and participates in programs of agricultural and economic development, education, health, self-help, relief, peace, and disaster service. MCC has about 900 workers serving in 60 countries in Africa, Asia, Europe, Middle East, and South, Central, and North America.

MCC has service programs in North America that focus both on urban and rural poverty areas. There are also North American programs focusing on such diverse matters as community conciliation, employment creation, and criminal justice issues. These programs are administered by two national bodies—MCC US and MCC Canada.

Contributions from North American Mennonite and Brethren in Christ churches provide the largest part of MCC's support. Other sources of financial support include the contributed earnings of volunteers, grants from private and government agencies and contributions from Mennonite churches abroad. The total income in FYE 2001, including material aid contributions, amounted to $63.2 million.

MCC tries to strengthen local communities by

working in cooperation with local churches or other community groups. Many personnel are placed with other agencies, including missions. Programs are planned with sensitivity to locally felt needs.

Headquarters

21 S. 12th St., P.O. Box 500, Akron, PA 17501-0500 Tel. (717)859-1151 Fax (717)859-2171

Canadian Office: 134 Plaza Dr., Winnipeg, MB R3T 5K9 Tel. (204)261-6381 Fax (204)269-9875

Media Contact, Exec. Dir., Ronald J.R. Mathies, P.O. Box 500, Akron, PA 17501 Tel. (717)859-1151 Fax (717)859-2171

Officers

Exec. Directors.: Intl., Ronald J.R. Mathies; Canada, Donald Peters; USA, Jose Ortiz

National Association of Ecumenical and Interreligious Staff

NAEIS is an association of professional staff in ecumenical and interreligious work. Founded as the Association of Council Secretaries in 1940, the Association was widened to include program staff in 1971, and renamed the National Association of Ecumenical Staff. It has included staff of any faith engaged in interreligious work since 1994.

NAEIS was established to provide creative relationships and to encourage mutual support and personal and professional growth. This is accomplished through training programs, through exchange and discussion of common concerns at conferences, and through the publication of the *Corletter*, in collaboration with NCCC Ecumenical Networks.

Headquarters

Best reached through Janet Leng, Membership Officer, P.O. Box 7093, Tacoma, WA 98406-0093 Tel. (253)759-0142, naeisjan@aol.com

Officers

Pres., 2003-2005: Barbara White, Social Services, Church of God in Christ, 3500 W. Mother Daniel's Way, Milwaukee, WI 53209 Tel. (44)466-1800, uniquebarbara@hotmail.com

Vice Pres., 2003-2005: The Rev. Samuel Muyskens, Interfaith Ministers, Wichita 829 North Market Street, Wichita, KS 67214-1157 Tel. (512)451-2062

Immediate Past. Pres.: Julia Sibley Juras, SC Christian Action Council P.O. Box 3248, Columbia SC 29230-3248 Tel. (803)786-7115

Sec., 2003-2005: Rev. Peggy Crawford, Church of Scientology, 1010 Hurley Way, Ste. 505, Sacramento, CA 95825 Tel. (916)925-2545

Trea., Ste.B, Portland, OR 97201-4297 Tel. (503) 221-1054

The National Association of Evangelicals

The National Association of Evangelicals (NAE) is a voluntary fellowship of evangelical denominations, churches, organizations, and individuals demonstrating unity in the body of Christ by standing for biblical truth, speaking with a representative voice, and serving the evangelical community through united action, cooperative ministry, and strategic planning.

The association is comprised of approximately 43,000 congregations nationwide from 50 member denominations and fellowships, as well as several hundred independent churches. The membership of the association includes over 250 parachurch ministries and educational institutions. Through the cooperative ministry of these members, NAE directly and indirectly benefits over 27 million people. These ministries represent a broad range of theological traditions, but all subscribe to the distinctly evangelical NAE Statement of Faith. The association is a nationally recognized entity by the public sector with a reputation for integrity and effective service.

The cooperative ministries of the National Association of Evangelicals demonstrate the association's intentional desire to promote cooperation without compromise.

Headquarters

NAE–Washington, 701 "G" Street SW, Washington, D.C. 20024 Tel. (202)789-1011 Fax (202)842-0392

Media Contact, Rev. Rich Cizik Tel. (202)789-1011

STAFF

Vice Pres. of Ministry Development, Rev. John N. Mendez

Vice Pres. of Governmental Affairs, Rev. Rich Cizik

MEMBER DENOMINATIONS

Advent Christian General Conference
Assemblies of God
Association of Vineyard Churches
Baptist General Conference
The Brethren Church
Brethren in Christ Church
Christian & Missionary Alliance
Christ Community Church
Christian Church of North America
Christian Reformed Church in Noth America
Christian Union
Church of God, Cleveland, TN
Church of God, Mountain Assembly
Church of the Nazarene
United Brethren in Christ Church
Churches of Christ in Christian Union
Congregational Holiness Church
Conservative Baptist Assoc. of America
Conservative Congregational Christian Conf.
Conservative Lutheran Association
Elim Fellowship

Evangelical Church of North America
Evangelical Congregational Church
Evangelical Free Church of America
Evangelical Friends Intl.–North America
Evangelical Mennonite Church
Evangelical Methodist Church
Evangelical Presbyterian Church
Evangelistic Missionary Fellowship
Fellowship of Evangelical Bible Churches
Fire-Baptized Holiness Church of God of the Americas
Free Methodist Church of North America
General Association of General Baptists
Intl. Church of the Foursquare Gospel
Intl. Pentecostal Church of Christ
Intl. Pentecostal Holiness Church
Mennonite Brethren Churches, USA
Missionary Church, Inc.
Open Bible Standard Churches
Pentecostal Church of God
Pentecostal Free Will Baptist Church
Presbyterian Church in America
Primitive Methodist Church, USA
Reformed Episcopal Church
Reformed Presbyterian Church of N.A.
Salvation Army
Regional Synod of Mid-America (Reformed Church in America)
Wesleyan Church
Worldwide Church of God

National Bible Association

The National Bible Association is an autonomous, interfaith organization of lay people who advocate regular Bible reading and sponsor National Bible Week (Thanksgiving week) each November. Program activities include public service advertising, distribution of nonsectarian literature, and thousands of local Bible Week observances by secular and religious organizations. The Association also urges constitutionally acceptable use of the Bible in public school classrooms (i.e., the study of the Bible in literature). All support comes from individuals, corporations, and foundations.

Founded in 1940 by a group of business and professional people, the Association offers daily Bible readings in several English and Spanish translations on its website and has the IRS nonprofit status of a 501(c)(3) educational association.

Headquarters

1865 Broadway, New York, NY 10023 Tel. (212) 408-1390 Fax (212)408-1448
Media Contact, Pres., Thomas R. May

Officers

Cpsn., Philip J. Clements
Vice Cpsns., Robert Cavalero, John W. Pugsley, John M. Templeton Jr., MD
Pres., Thomas R. May
Treas., Paul Werner
Sec., J. Marshall Gage

The National Conference for Community and Justice

The National Conference for Community and Justice, founded in 1927 as the National Conference of Christians and Jews, is a human relations organization dedicated to fighting bias, bigotry, and racism in America. The NCCJ promotes understanding and respect among all races, religions, and cultures through advocacy, conflict resolution, and education.

Programmatic strategies include interfaith and interracial dialogue, youth leadership workshops, workplace training, human relations research, and the building of community coalitions. NCCJ has 65 regional offices staffed by approximately 350 people. Nearly 200 members comprise the National Board of Advisors and members from that group form the 27-member National Board of Directors. Each regional office has its own Regional Board of Directors with a total of about 2,800. The National Board of Advisors meets once annually, the National Board of Directors at least three times annually.

Headquarters

475 Park Ave. S, New York, NY 10016 Tel. (212)545-1300 Fax (212)545-8053
Media Contact, Dir. of Communications, Diane Powers

Officers

Pres. & CEO, Sanford Cloud Jr.

National Conference on Ministry to the Armed Forces

The Conference is an incorporated civilian agency. Representation in the Conference with all privileges of the same is open to all endorsing or certifying agencies or groups authorized to provide chaplains for any branch of the Armed Forces.

The purpose of this organization is to provide a means of dialogue to discuss concerns and objectives and, when agreed upon, to take action with the appropriate authority to support the spiritual ministry to and the moral welfare of Armed Forces personnel.

Headquarters

4141 N. Henderson Rd., Ste. 13, Arlington, VA 22203 Tel. (703)276-7905 Fax (703)276-7906
Media Contact, Jack Williamson

Staff

Coord., Jack Williamson
Admn. Asst., Maureen Francis

Officers

Chpsn., David Peterson
Chpsn.-elect, Robert Jemerson
Sec., Lemuel Boyles
Treas., John Murdoch

National Council of the Churches of Christ in the USA

The National Council of the Churches of Christ in the USA is the preeminent expression in the United States of the movement toward Christian unity. The NCC's 36 member communions—including Protestant, Orthodox, and Anglican church bodies—work together on a wide range of activities that further Christian unity, that witness to the faith, that promote peace and justice, and that serve people throughout the world. Over 50 million US Christians belong to churches that hold Council membership. The Council was formed in 1950 in Cleveland, Ohio, by the action of representatives of the member churches and by the merger of 12 previously existing ecumenical agencies, each of which had a different program focus. The roots of some of these agencies go back to the 19th century.

Headquarters

475 Riverside Dr., New York, NY 10115. Tel. (212)870-2141

Media Contact, Dir. of News Services, Ms. Carol J. Fouke, Tel. (212)870-2252

GENERAL OFFICERS

Pres., Bishop Thomas L. Hoyt

Gen. Sec., Rev. Dr. Robert W. Edgar

Immediate Past Pres., Ms. Elenie K. Huszagh, Esq.

Sec., Bishop Vicken Aykazian

Treas., Ms. Clare Chapman

Vice Pres., Church World Service and Witness, Rev. Patrick Mauney

Vice Pres., National Ministries, Dr. Audrey Miller

Vice Pres.-at-Large, Bishop Jon S. Enslin, Rev. Dr. Bertrice Wood; Ms. Barbara Ricks Thompson

THE GENERAL SECRETARIAT

Gen. Sec., Rev. Dr. Robert W. Edgar Tel. (212)870-2141 Fax (212)870-2817

Special Assist. to the Gen. Sec. for the Poverty Mobilization, Rev. Dr. Paul Sherry Tel. (212)870-2361

DEVELOPMENT

Dir. of Development, Mr. John A. Briscoe

Special Assist. to the Gen. Sec. for Planned Giving Endowment, Mr. Jon Sherry Tel. (804) 928-6222

RESEARCH AND PLANNING

Deputy Gen. Sec. for Research and Planning, Rev. Dr. Eileen W. Lindner Tel. (212)870-2333

YEARBOOK OF AMERICAN & CANADIAN CHURCHES

Editor, Rev. Dr. Eileen W. Lindner Tel. (212)870-2031

Assoc. Ed, and Technical Coord., Rev. Marcel A. Welty Tel. (212)870-2379

Assistant Ed., Ms. Elizabeth C. During Tel. (212)870-2031 Fax (212)870-2817

Assistant to the Ed., Mr. Earl Davis Tel. (212) 870-2333

WASHINGTON OFFICE

110 Maryland Ave. NE Washington, D.C. 20002 Tel. (202)544-2350 Fax (202)543-1297

Assoc. Gen. Sec. for Public Witness and Dir. Wash. Office, Ms. Brenda Girton-Mitchell, Esq.

Washington Communication Officer, Ms. Leslie C. Tune Tel. (202)544-2350 ext.11

National Religious Partnership for the Environment, Mr. Doug Grace Tel. (202)544-5530 or (202)544-3110

COMMUNICATION COMMISSION

Tel. (212)870-2227 Fax (212)870-2030

Associate Gen. Sec. for Communication and Interpretation, Mr. Wesley M. Pattillo

Dir., News Services, Ms. Carol J. Fouke Tel. (212)870-2252

Dir., Interpretation Resources, Ms. Sarah Vilankulu Tel. (212)870-2228

Coord. of Television Programming, Ms. Shirley W. Struchen Tel. (212)870-2227

JUSTICE AND ADVOCACY

Justice for Women, Program Dir., Karen M. Hessel, M.Div. Tel. (212)870-2421

UNITY PROGRAMS

Assoc. Gen. Sec. for Faith and Order, Dr. Ann K. Riggs, 110 Maryland Ave. NE, Washington, D.C. 20002 Tel. (202)544-2350

Assoc. Gen. Sec. for Interfaith Relations, The Rev. Dr. Shanta D. Premawardhana Tel. (212)870-2560

Interim Assoc. Gen. Sec. for International Affairs, Dr. Tony Kireopoulos Tel. (212)870-3422

EDUCATION AND LEADERSHIP MINISTRIES

Assoc. Gen. Sec. for Education and Leadership Ministries., Rev. Patrice Rosner Tel. (212)870-2738

Assoc. Dir., Rev. Garland Pierce, Tel. (212)870-2267

RELATED ORGANIZATIONS

Agricultural Missions, Exec. Dir., Dr. Winston Carroo Tel. (212)870-2554

Interfaith Center for Corporate Responsibility, Exec. Dir., Sr. Patricia Wolf, RSM Tel. (212) 870-2295

Natl. Farm Worker Ministry, Exec. Dir., Ms. Virginia Nesmith, 438 N. Skinner Blvd., St. Louis, MO 63130 Tel. (314)726-6470

ADMINISTRATION AND FINANCE

Tel. (212)870-2361 Fax (212)870-3112

Assoc. Gen. Sec. for Administration and Finance, Ms. Leora E. Landmesser

Controller, Ms. Karen Wang Tel. (212)870-3351 Fax (212)870-3112

Dept. of Business Services Tel. (212)870-2181

CHURCH WORLD SERVICE AND WITNESS

Tel. (212)870-2061 Fax (212)870-3523

Exec. Dir., Rev. John L. McCullough Tel. (212) 870-2175

Deputy Dir., Operations and CFO, Ms. Joanne Rendall Tel. (219)264-3102 ext. 332

Deputy Dir., Programs, Ms. Kirsten M. Laursen Tel. (212)870-2798

Chief Development Officer, Peter D. Crouch Tel. (219)264-3102 ext. 454
Dir., Human Resources, Mr. Bernard Kirchhoff Tel. (219)264-3102 ext. 346
Dir., Mission Relationships & Witness Program, Mr. David Weaver Tel. (212)870-2818
Acting Dir., Education & Advocacy for International Justice & Human Rights, Ms. Kirsten M. Laursen Tel. (212)870-2377
Interim Dir., Social and Economic Development, Mr. Martin Coria Tel. (212)870-2074
Dir., Emergency Response, Mr. Rick Augsburger Tel. (212)870-3154
Dir., Immigration & Refugee Program, Rev. Joseph Roberson Tel. (212)870-2178

CONSTITUENT BODIES (with membership dates)

African Methodist Episcopal Church (1950)
African Methodist Episcopal Zion Church (1950)
The Alliance of Baptists in the USA (2000)
American Baptist Churches in the USA (1950)
The Antiochian Orthodox Christian Archdiocese of North America (1966)
Armenian Apostolic Church, Diocese of the (1957)
Christian Church (Disciples of Christ) (1950)
Christian Methodist Episcopal Church (1950)
Church of the Brethren (1950)
Coptic Orthodox Church (1978)
The Episcopal Church (1950)
Evangelical Lutheran Church in America (1950)
Friends United Meeting (1950)
Greek Orthodox Archdiocese of America (1952)
Hungarian Reformed Church in America (1957)
Intl. Council of Community Churches (1977)
Korean Presbyterian Church in America, Gen. Assembly of the (1986)
Malankara Orthodox Syrian Church, Diocese of America (1998)
Mar Thoma Church (1997)
Moravian Church in America, Northern Province, Southern Province (1950)
National Baptist Convention of America, Inc. (1950)
National Baptist Convention, USA, Inc. (1950)
National Missionary Baptist Convention of America (1995)
Orthodox Church in America (1950)
Philadelphia Yearly Meeting of the Religious Society of Friends (1950)
Polish Natl. Catholic Church of America (1957)
Presbyterian Church (USA) (1950)
Progressive Natl. Baptist Convention, Inc. (1966)
Reformed Church in America (1950)
Russian Orthodox Church in the USA, Patriarchal Parishes of the (1966)
Serbian Orthodox Church in the USA & Canada (1957)
The Swedenborgian Church (1966)
Syrian (Syriac) Orthodox Church of Antioch (Archdiocese of the US and Canada) (1960)
Ukrainian Orthodox Church of the USA(1950)
United Church of Christ (1950)
The United Methodist Church (1950)

National Institute of Business and Industrial Chaplains

NIBIC is the professional organization for workplace chaplains that includes members from a wide variety of denominations and work settings, including corporations, manufacturing plants, air and sea ports, labor unions, and pastoral counseling centers. NIBIC has six membership categories, including Clinical, Professional, Affiliates, and Organizational.

NIBIC works to establish professional standards for education and practice; promotes and conducts training programs; provides mentoring, networking, and chaplaincy information; encourages research and public information dissemination; and communicates with business leaders and conducts professional meetings. NIBIC publishes a quarterly newsletter and co-sponsors *The Journal of Pastoral Care*. A public membership meeting and training conference is held annually.

Headquarters

7100 Regency Square Blvd., Ste. 210, Houston, TX 77036-3202 Tel. (713)266-2456 Fax (713) 266-0845
Media Contact, Rev. Diana C. Dale, 7100 Regency Square Blvd., Ste. 210, Houston, TX 77036-3202 Tel. (713)266-2456 Fax (713) 266-0845

Officers

Executive Dir., Rev. Diana C. Dale, D.Min.
Pres., Rev. Timothy Bancroft, D.Min.
Vice Pres., Rev. Stephen Holden
Treas., Rev. Gregory Edwards
Board Member, Rev. Robert L. Lewis Jr., STM

National Interfaith Cable Coalition, Inc. (NICC)

The National Interfaith Cable Coalition, Inc. (NICC) was formed as a not-for-profit 501(c)3 corporation, in December, 1987, and is currently comprised of nearly 70 associated faith groups from the Jewish and Christian traditions.

In September 1988, NICC launched a religious cable network called VISN (Vision Interfaith Satellite Network), now known as Odyssey Network. Today, Odyssey is owned and operated by Crown Media Holdings, Inc., in which NICC is a strategic investor. Odyssey provides a mix of high-quality family entertainment and faith-based programming. NICC provides 30 hours a week of programming on the network.

In 2000, NICC adopted Faith & Values Media as its service mark and expanded its mission to include a significant Web presence (www.FaithandValues.com) and plans for a full-time digital channel.

Headquarters

74 Trinity Place, Ste. 1550, New York, NY 10006 Tel. (212)406-4121 Fax (212)406-4105
Website: www.FaithandValues.com
Media Contact, Melissa Gonzalez

Officers

Chpsn., Dr. Daniel Paul Matthews
Vice Chpsn., Elder Ralph Hardy Jr.
Sec., Rabbi Paul J. Menitoff
Treas., Betty Elam

Staff

Pres. and CEO, Edward J. Murray
Vice Pres., Beverly Judge

National Interfaith Coalition on Aging

The National Interfaith Coalition on Aging (NICA), a constituent unit of the National Council on Aging, is composed of Protestant, Roman Catholic, Jewish, and Orthodox national and regional organizations and individuals concerned about the needs of older people and the religious community's response to problems facing the aging population in the United States. NICA was organized in 1972 to address spiritual concerns of older adults through religious sector action.

Mission Statement: The National Interfaith Coalition on Aging (NICA), affiliated with the National Council on the Aging (NCOA), is a diverse network of religious and other related organizations and individual members which promotes the spiritual well being of older adults and the preparation of persons of all ages for the spiritual tasks of aging. NICA serves as a catalyst for new and effective research, networking opportunities, resource development, service provision, and dissemination of information.

Headquarters

c/o NCOA, 300 D St. SW, 801 Ste., Washington, D.C. 20024 Tel. (202)479-6655 Fax (202)479-0735
Media Contact, Rita Chow, Ed.D.

Officers

Chpsn., Jane Stenson
Chpsn.-Elect, Rev. Ron Field
Past Chpsn., Rev. Dr. Robert W. Carlson
Sec., Rev. Dr. James W. Ellor
Dir., Dr. Rita K. Chow

National Religious Broadcasters

National Religious Broadcasters is an association of Christian communicators, 1,500 organizations which produce religious programs for radio and television and other forms of electronic mass media or operate stations carrying predominately religious programs. NRB member organizations are responsible for more than 75 percent of all religious radio and television in the United States, reaching an average weekly audience of millions by radio, television, and other broadcast media.

Dedicated to the communication of the Gospel, NRB was founded in 1944 to safeguard free and complete access to the broadcast media. By encouraging the development of Christian programs and stations, NRB helps make it possible for millions to hear the good news of Jesus Christ through the electronic media.

Headquarters

9510 Technology Dr., Manassas, VA 20110 Tel. (703)330-7000 Fax (703)330-7100
Media Contact, Pres., -vacant-
Exec. Vice Pres., Michael Glenn

Officers

Chmn., Glenn R. Plummer, Christian Television Network, Detriot, MI
1st Vice Chmn., Michael D. Little, Christian Broadcasting Network, Virginia Beach, VA
2nd Vice Chmn., Bill A. Blount, Blount Communications, Warwick, RI
Sec., William Skelton, Love Worth Finding Ministries, Memphis, TN
Treas., James A. Gwinn, CRISTA Ministries, Seattle, WA

National Woman's Christian Temperance Union

The National WCTU is a not-for-profit, nonpartisan, interdenominational organization dedicated to the education of our nation's citizens, especially children and teens, on the harmful effects of alcoholic beverages, other drugs, and tobacco on the human body and the society in which we live. The WCTU believes in a strong family unit and, through legislation, education, and prayer, works to strengthen the home and family.

WCTU, which began in 1874 with the motto, "For God and Home and Every Land," is organized in 58 countries.

Headquarters

1730 Chicago Ave., Evanston, IL 60201 Tel. (708) 864-1396
Media Contact, Sarah F. Ward Tel. (765)345-7600

Officers

Pres., Sarah F. Ward, 33 N. Franklin, Knightstown, IN 46148, sarah@wctu.org
Vice Pres., Rita Wert, 2250 Creek Hill Rd., Lancaster, PA 17601
Promotion Dir., Nancy Zabel, 1730 Chicago Ave., Evanston, IL 60201-4585
Treas., Faye Pohl, P.O. Box 739, Meade, KS 67864
Rec. Sec., Dorothy Russell, 18900 Nestueca Dr., Cloverdale, OR 97112

MEMBER ORGANIZATIONS

Loyal Temperance Legion (LTL), for boys and girls ages 6-12
Youth Temperance Council (YTC), for teens through college age

North American Baptist Fellowship

Organized in 1964, the North American Baptist Fellowship is a voluntary organization of Baptist Conventions in Canada and the United States, functioning as a regional body within the Baptist World Alliance. Its objectives are (a) to promote fellowship and cooperation among Baptists in North America and (b) to further the aims and objectives of the Baptist World Alliance so far as these affect the life of the Baptist churches in North America. Its membership, however, is not identical with the North American membership of the Baptist World Alliance. Church membership of the Fellowship bodies is more than 28 million.

The NABF assembles representatives of the member bodies once a year for exchange of information and views in such fields as evangelism and education, missions, stewardship promotion, lay activities, and theological education. It conducts occasional consultations for denominational leaders on such subjects as church extension. It encourages cooperation at the city and county level where churches of more than one member group are located.

Headquarters

Baptist World Alliance Bldg., 405 N. Washington St., Falls Church VA 22046
Media Contact, Dr. Denton Lotz

Officers

Pres., Dr. Robert Ricker, 2002 S. Arlington Heights Rd., Arlington Heights, IL 60005, rricker@baptistgeneral.org
Vice Pres., Dr. David Emmanuel Goatley, 300 I St. NE, Suite 104, Washington, D.C. 20002, degoatley@aol.com
Vice Pres., Dr. Phillip Wise, 300 West Main St., Box 2025, Dothan, AL 36301, philip@fbc-dothan.org
Vice Pres., Dr. Gary Nelson, 7185 Millcreek Dr., Mississauga, ON l5N 5R4, Canada, nelsong @cbmin.org

MEMBER BODIES

American Baptist Churches in the USA
Baptist General Conference
Canadian Baptist Federation
General Association of General Baptists
National Baptist Convention of America
National Baptist Convention, USA, Inc.
Progressive National Baptist Convention, Inc.
Seventh Day Baptist General Conference
North American Baptist Conference
Southern Baptist Convention

Oikocredit–Ecumenical Development Cooperative Society

Based in the Netherlands, EDCS is often called "the churches' bank for the poor." EDCS borrows funds from churches, religious communities, and concerned individuals and re-lends the funds to enterprises operated by low-income communities. Launched in 1975 through an initiative of the World Council of Churches, EDCS is organized as a cooperative of religious institutions and is governed by annual membership meetings and an elected board of religious leaders and development and financial professionals.

An international network of 15 EDCS Regional Managers is responsible for lending funds to cooperative enterprises and microcredit institutions. At the present time over $220 million is at work in coffee shops, fishing enterprises, handicraft production, truck farming, and many other commercial ventures owned and operated by poor people.

EDCS is represented in the United States by the Ecumenical Development Corporation–USA (EDC–USA), a 501(c)3 non-profit corporation. American individuals and congregations can invest in EDCS by purchasing one, three, and five year notes paying 0-2% interest that are issued by EDC–USA.

US Headquarters

P.O. Box 11000, Washington, D.C. 20008 Tel.(202)265-0607 Fax (202)265-7029
Email: office.us@oikocredit.org
Website: www.oikocredit.org
Media Contact, Regional Manager for North America, The Rev. Louis L. Knowles

Officers, EDC–USA

Exec. Dir., Rev. Terry Province
Chpsn., Gary Cook
Vice Chpsn., Richard Gist
Treas., Mary Pat Brennan

Parish Resource Center, Inc.

Parish Resource Center, Inc. promotes, establishes, nurtures, and accredits local Affiliate Parish Resource Centers. Affiliate centers educate, equip, and strengthen subscribing congregations of all faiths by providing professional consultants, resource materials, and workshops. The Parish Resource Center was founded in 1976. In 2002, there were 5 free-standing affiliates located in Lancaster, Pa.; Long Island, N.Y.; Denver, Colo.; Dayton, Ohio; and New York City. These centers serve congregations from 49 faith traditions.

Headquarters

633 Community Way, Lancaster, PA 17603 Tel. (717)299-2223 Fax (717)299-7229
Media Contact, Pres., Dr. D. Douglas Whiting

Officers

Chpsn., Margaret M. Obrecht
Vice Chpsn., Sidney Lovett
Sec., Sally Bures
Treas., Stephen C. Eyre
Pres., Dr. D. Douglas Whiting

Pentecostal-Charismatic Churches of North America

The Pentecostal-Charismatic Churches of North America (PCCNA) was organized October 19, 1994, in Memphis, Tenn. This organizational meeting came the day after the Pentecostal Fellowship of North America (PFNA) voted itself out of existence in order to make way for the new fellowship.

The PFNA had been formed in October 1948

in Des Moines, Iowa. It was composed of white-led Pentecostal denominations. The move to develop a multiracial fellowship began when the PFNA Board of Administration initiated a series of discussions with African-American Pentecostal leaders. The first meeting was held July 10-11, 1992, in Dallas, Tex. A second meeting convened in Phoenix, Ariz., January 4-5, 1993. On January 10-11, 1994, 20 representatives from each of the two groups met in Memphis to make final plans for a Dialogue which was held in Memphis, October 1994.

This racial reconciliation meeting has been called "The Memphis Miracle." During this meeting the PFNA was disbanded, and the PCCNA was organized. The new organization quickly adopted the "Racial Reconciliation Manifesto." Subsequent meetings were held in Memphis, Tenn. (1996); Washington, D.C. (1997); Tulsa, Ok. (1998); and Hampton, Va. (1999).

In an effort to further increase the spirit of reconciliation, the PCCNA meeting of 2000 was held during the North American Renewal Service committee (NARSC) Conference in St. Louis, Mo. Furthermore, the PCCNA acted as host for the 19th Pentecostal World Conference held in Los Angeles, Calif., May 2001.

Headquarters

1910 W. Sunset Blvd., Ste. 200, Los Angeles, CA 90026-0176 Tel. (213)484-2400 ext. 309 Fax (213)413-3824

Media Contact, Dr. Ronald Williams

Officers

PCCNA EXECUTIVE BOARD

Co-Chpsn., Bishop James D. Leggett, International Pentecostal Holiness Church, P.O. Box 12609, Oklahoma City, OK 73157-2609 Tel. (405)787-7110 ext. 3302, Fax (405)787-3650, jdl@iphc.org

Co-Chpsn., Bishop George D. McKinney, St. Stephen's Church of God in Christ, 5825 Imperial Ave., San Diego, CA 92114 Tel. (619) 262-2671, Fax (619)262-8335, ststephens@pcsinter.net

First Vice Chpsn., Bishop Oswill Williams, Church of God of Prophecy, Cleveland, TN 37320-3000 Tel. (423)559-5444, Fax (423) 559-5219, ossie@wingnet.net

Second Vice Chpsn., Rev. Jeff Farmer, Open Bible Standard Churches, 2020 Bell Ave., Des Moines, IA 50315-1096 Tel. (515)288-6761 Fax (515)288-2510

Sec., Dr. Lamar Vest, Church of God, P.O. Box 2430, Cleveland, TN 37320-2430 Tel. (423)478-7137 Fax (423)478-7443

Treas., Dr. Ronald Williams, Intl. Church of the Foursquare Gospel, P.O. Box 26902, Los Angeles, CA 90026 Tel. (213)989-4221, Fax (213)989-4544, ron@foursquare.org

ADVISORS

Rev. Billy Joe Daugherty, Victory Christian Center, 7700 S. Lewis Ave., Tulsa, OK 74136-7700 Tel. (918)493-1700 Fax (918)491-7795

Rev. Thomas Trask, Assemblies of God, 1445 Boonville Ave., Springfield, MO 65802 Tel. (417)862-2781 ext. 3000 Fax (417)862-8558

Bishop Barbara Amos, Mt. Sinai Holy Church of America, 1010 E. 26th St. , Norfolk, VA 23504 Tel. (757)624-1950 Fax (757)625-6648

Project Equality, Inc.

Project Equality is a nonprofit national interfaith program for affirmative action and equal employment opportunity.

Project Equality serves as a central agency to receive and validate the equal employment commitment of suppliers of goods and services to sponsoring organizations and participating institutions, congregations, and individuals. Employers filing an accepted Annual Participation Report are included in the Project Equality "Buyer's Guide."

Workshops, training events and consultant services in affirmative action, diversity, and equal employment practices in recruitment, selection, placement, transfer, promotion, discipline, and discharge are also available to sponsors and participants. Project Equality is a leader in transforming the society to true inclusiveness.

Headquarters

Pres., 7132 Main St., Kansas City, MO 64114-1406 Tel. (816)361-9222 or (877)PE-IS-EEO Fax (816)361-8997

Media Contact, Pres., Rev. Kirk P. Perucca

Officers

Chpsn., Gloria Folds
Vice Chpsn., Salvador Mendoza
Sec., Barbara George
Treas., Carla Shaw
Pres., Rev. Kirk P. Perucca

SPONSORS-ENDORSING ORGANIZATIONS

American Baptist Churches in the USA
American Friends Service Committee
American Jewish Committee
Assoc. Of Junior Leagues, Intl.
Central Conference of American Rabbis
Church of the Brethren
The Episcopal Church
Evangelical Lutheran Church in America
National Council of Churches of Christ in the USA
National Education Association
Presbyterian Church (USA)
Reorganized Church of Jesus Christ of Latter-day Saints
The United Methodist Church
Unitarian Universalist Association
United Church of Christ
United Methodist Assoc. of Health & Welfare Ministries
YWCA of the USA

The Protestant Hour, Inc.

The Protestant Hourr, Inc. is an interdenominational organization dedicated to the purpose of producing ecumenical media resources. The Flagship productions are the weekly radio show "Day 1," formerly "The Protestant Hour," and the "Day 1" television program (produced in association with Faith & Values Media), airing Sunday mornings on Hallmark Channel. The Website www.day1.net provides additional text and audio resources. Participating denominations include the Episcopal Media Center, Evangelical Lutheran Church in America, Presbyterian Church (USA), United Church of Christ, and the United Methodist Church.

Headquarters

644 West Peachtree St, Suite 300, Atlanta, GA 30308-1925 Tel. (404)815-9110 Fax (404) 815-0258

Website: www.day1.net

Media Contact, Nan Ross

Officers

Bd. Chpsn., Ms. Harriet Tumlin Jobson

Vice Chpsn., Bishop L. Bevel Jones, III

Pres., Peter M. Wallace

Treas., Edward Stoners Jr.

Sec., Ann Gillies

Religion In American Life, Inc.

Religion In American Life (RIAL) is a unique cooperative program of some 50 major national religious groups (Catholic, Eastern Orthodox, Jewish, Protestant, Muslim, etc.). It provides services for denominationally-supported, congregation-based outreach and growth projects such as the current Invite a Friend program. These projects are promoted through national advertising campaigns reaching the American public by the use of all media. The ad campaigns are produced by a volunteer agency with production-distribution and administration costs funded by denominations and business groups, as well as by individuals.

Since 1949, RIAL ad campaign projects have been among the much coveted major campaigns of The Advertising Council. This results in as much as $35 million worth of time and space in a single year, contributed by media as a public service. Through RIAL, religious groups demonstrate respect for other traditions and the value of religious freedom. The RIAL program also includes seminars and symposia, research and leadership awards and produces a weekly syndicated radio broadcast, "SpiriTalk".

Headquarters

2001 W. Main St., Suite 120, Stamford, CT 06902 Tel. (203)355-1220 Fax (203)355-1221

Media Contact, Exec. Admin., Martha Mesiti Tel. (203)355-1220

Executive Committee

Natl. Chpsn., Thomas S. Johnson (Chmn. & CEO, Greenpoint Bank, NY)

Chpsn. of Bd., Rev. Dr. Gordon Sommers

Vice Chpsns., Bishop Khajag Barsamian, Primate (Armenian Church of America); Most Rev. William Cardinal Keeler, Archbishop of Baltimore; Rabbi Ronald B. Sobel (Cong. Emanu-El of the City of N.Y.)

Sec.,Timothy A. Hultquist (Morgan Stanley Dean Witter)

Treas., Robertson H. Bennett (Smith Barney)

Staff

Pres. & CEO, Robert B. Lennick, Rabbi, D.Min.

Exec. Admin., Martha Mesiti

The Religion Communicators Council, Inc.

RCC is an international, interfaith, interdisciplinary association of professional communicators who work for religious groups and causes. It was founded in 1929 and is the oldest nonprofit professional public relations organization in the world. RCC's more than 600 members include those who work in communications and related fields for church-related institutions, denominational agencies, non- and interdenominational organizations and communications firms who primarily serve religious organizations.

Members represent a wide range of faiths, including Presbyterian, Baptist, Methodist, Lutheran, Episcopalian, Mennonite, Roman Catholic, Seventh-day Adventist, Jewish, Salvation Army, Brethren, Bahá'í, Disciples, Latter-day Saints, and others.

On the national level, RCC sponsors an annual three-day convention and has published six editions of a *Religious Public Relations Handbook* for churches and church organizations, as well as a videostrip, The Church at Jackrabbit Junction. Members receive a quarterly newsletter (*Counselor*). There are 11 regional chapters.

RCC administers the annual Wilbur Awards competition to recognize high quality coverage of religious values and issues in the public media. Wilbur winners include producers, reporters, editors, and broadcasters nationwide. To recognize communications excellence within church communities, RCC also sponsors the annual DeRose-Hinkhouse Awards for its own members.

In 1970, 1980, 1990, and 2000 RCC initiated a global Religious Communications Congress bringing together thousands of persons from Western, Eastern, and Third-World nations who are involved in communicating religious faith.

Headquarters

475 Riverside Dr., Rm. 1948A, New York, NY 10115-1948 Tel. (212)870-2985 Fax (212) 870-3578

Exec. Dir., Shirley Whipple Struchen Tel. (212) 870-2402, SSTRUCHEN@RCN.COM

Officers

Pres., Michael A. Hickcox, Dir. Of Communications, New England Conference, UMC, P.O. Box 249, Lawrence, MA 01842-0449 Tel. (978)682-7676 ext. 2, Fax (978)682-7677, communicate@neumc.org

Vice Pres., Anuttama Dasa, Communications Dir.,

US COOPERATIVE ORGANIZATIONS

ISKCON, Hare Krishna, 10310 Oaklyn Drive, Potomac, MD 20854 Tel. (301)299-9707, Fax (301)299-5025, anuttama.acbsp@ pamho.net

Religion News Service

Religion News Service (RNS) has provided news and information to the media for almost 70 years. Owned by the Newhouse News Service, it is staffed by veteran jounalists who cover stories on all of the world religions as well as trends in ethics, morality, and spirituality.

RNS provides a daily news service, a weekly news service, and photo and graphic services. The daily service is available via the AP Data Features wire, or email. The weekly report is available by wire or email. RNS's Photos Service features stock images, news photography, and related graphics. RNS also offers Religion Press Release Services, which distributes press releases and advisories to religion editors. RNS is syndicated in the United States by Universal Press Syndicate and in Canada by Canadian Press.

Headquarters

1101 Connecticut Ave. NW, Ste. 350, Washington, D.C. 20036 Tel. (202)463-8777 Fax (202)463-0033

Email: info@religionnews.com

Website: www.religionnews.com

Officers

Editor, David Anderson

Religion Newswriters Association

Founded in 1949, the RNA is a professional association of religion news editors and reporters on secular daily and weekly newspapers, news services, news magazines, radio, and television stations. It sponsors seven annual contests for excellence in religion news coverage in the secular press. Annual meetings are held in the fall.

Headquarters

P.O. Box 2037, Westerville, OH 43086 Tel. (614)891-9001 Fax (614) 891-9774

Email: mason@religionwriters.com

Website: www. Religionwriters.com

Media Contact, Exec. Dir., Debra Mason

Religious Conference Management Association, Inc.

The Religious Conference Management Association, Inc. (RCMA) is an interfaith, nonprofit, professional organization of men and women who have responsibility for planning and/or managing meetings, seminars, conferences, conventions, assemblies, or other gatherings for religious organizations.

Founded in 1972, RCMA is dedicated to promoting the highest professional performance by its members and associate members through the mutual exchange of ideas, techniques, and methods.

Today RCMA has more than 3,200 members and associate members.

The association conducts an annual conference and exposition which provides a forum for its membership to gain increased knowledge in the arts and sciences of religious meeting planning and management.

Headquarters

One RCA Dome, Ste. 120, Indianapolis, IN 46225 Tel. (317)632-1888 Fax (317)632-7909

Website: www.RCMAWEB.ORG

Media Contact, Exec. Dir., Dr. DeWayne S. Woodring

Officers

Pres., Dr. Jack Stone, Church of the Nazarene, 6401 The Paseo, Kansas City, MO 64131-1213

Vice Pres., Ms. Linda M. de Leon, General Conference Seventh-Day Adventist Church, 12501 Old Columbia Pike, Silver Spring, MD 20904

Sec.-Treas., Dr. Melvin Worthington, Natl. Assoc. of Free Will Baptists, 4878 Ayden Golf Club Rd., Ayden, NC 28513

Exec. Dir., Dr. DeWayne S. Woodring

The Seminary Consortium for Urban Pastoral Education (SCUPE)

Founded in 1976, SCUPE is an interdenominational agency committed to the development of individuals, congregations, and organizations for leadership in urban ministry. For individuals, we offer three accredited graduate-level academic programs: the semester- and/or summer-term Graduate Theological Urban Studies program for seminary students; an MA in Community Development degree developed in partnership with North Park University; and Nurturing the Call, a year-long sequence of graduate courses in theology and ministry for urban pastors who have not previously attended seminary.

SCUPE also consults to other ministries and urban institutions, providing specially-designed training programs around issues including diversity, strategic planning, leadership development, and human resource mobilization. We operate an urban ministry resource center and publish the Resource Review, as well as other occasional materials, as a service to the urban church. Every two years, SCUPE also organizes the Congress on Urban Ministry as a training and networking event for those in urban ministry.

Headquarters

200 N. Michigan Ave., Suite 502, Chicago, IL 60601 Tel. (312)726-1200 Fax (312)726-0425

Media Contact, Pres., Dr. David Frenchak

Dir. of Development, Mark Walden

Officers

Chpsn., Rev. Donald Sharp

Vice Chpsn., Ms. Cheryl Hammock

Treas., Mr. Case Hoogendoorn

Sec., Dr. Bill VanWyngaarden

Lead Program Staff

Pres., Dr. David Frenchak

Co-Directors, MA in Community Development,

Rev. Carol Ann McGibbon & Dr. Arthur Lyons
Dir., Graduate Theological Urban Studies, Rev. Bill Wylie-Kellermann
Coordinator, Special Events, Ms. Angela Janssen
Dir., Nurturing the Call, Rev. Kazi Joshua

Transnational Association of Christian Colleges and Schools (TRACS)

TRACS was established in 1979 to promote the welfare, interests, and development of postsecondary institutions, whose mission is characterized by a distinctly Christian purpose, as defined in our Foundational Standards. TRACS is a voluntary, non-profit, self-governing organization that provides accreditation to Christian postsecondary institutions offering certificates, diplomas, and/or degrees. TRACS is recognized by both the United States Department of Education, and the Council for Higher Education Accreditation, as a national accrediting body for Christian institutions, colleges, universities, and seminaries. The geographic territory of TRACS currently consists of the United States and its territories.

Headquarters

P.O. Box 328, Forest, VA 24551 Tel. (434)525-9539 Fax (434)525-9538
Email: info@tracs.org
Website: www.tracs.org
Media Contact, Exec. Dir., Dr. Russell G. Fitzgerald

Officers

Accreditation Commission Chairman, Dr. Samuel R. Chand
Exec. Dir., Dr. Russell G. Fitzgerald
Assoc. Exec. Dir., Dr. Jeff McCann

United Ministries in Higher Education

United Ministries in Higher Education is a cooperative effort to provide religious programs and services to those engaged in higher education ministries.

Headquarters

7407 Steele Creek Rd., Charlotte, NC 28217 Tel. (704)588-2182 Fax (704)588-3652
Media Contact, Res. Sec., Linda Danby Freeman

Officers

Treas., Kathy Carson
Personnel Service, Kathy Carson, 11720 Borman Dr., Ste. 240, St.Louis, MO 63146 Tel. (314)991-3000 Fax (314)991-2957
Resource Center, Linda Danby Freeman

PARTICIPATING DENOMINATIONS

Christian Church (Disciples of Christ)
Presbyterian Church (USA)
United Church of Christ

United Religions Initiative

The purpose of the United Religions Initiative is to promote enduring, daily interfaith cooperation; to end religiously motivated violence; and to create cultures of peace, justice, and healing for the Earth and all living beings.

The United Religions initiative is a growing, global community of over 130 Cooperation Circles, involving thousands of people around the world. The URI is inspired by the leadership potential inherent in every individual, leadership that is discovered and deepened through dialogue with others when dreams are shared and cooperative destinies are realized. The individuals who make up the URI network are committed to interfaith peacebuilding, recognizing that, for peace to prevail on earth, "peace must begin with me." They believe that by talking with others who come from different faiths, cultures, or spiritual traditions, all involved can begin to better understand their own beliefs and recognize their common bonds.

The URI seeks to create safe spaces throughout the world where these interfaith partnerships can be seeded, and the ideas and initiatives that they spark can be practically applied. With the mandate in the URI Charter that each Cooperation Circle represents at least three different faith traditions, the very act of coming together builds peace by creating interfaith cooperation among neighbors and within communities where it may never before have been possible. The Charter "Guidelines for Action" affirms the "essentially self-organizing nature" of the Cooperation Circles and empowers CC participants to "choose what they want to do" while providing guidance for community building. The Guidelines assure that all URI activities and actions demonstrate the following heartfelt considerations: (a) sharing the wisdom and cultures of different faith traditions; (b) nurturing cultures of healing and peace; (c) upholding human rights; (d) supporting the health of the entire Earth; (e) integrating spirituality in issues of economic justice; and (f) providing grassroot support for all URI activities.

The initial vision for the United Religions Initiative began in 1993 with a dream by its founder, Bishop William Swing. He writes that it came with "a sudden realization that religions, together, have a vocation to be a force for good in the world." In just seven years, tens of thousands of people in more than sixty countries around the world have responded to this vision with a resounding "Yes!" Their affirmations have taken on a myriad of forms. For example, during the 72 Hours Project at the turn of the Millennium, over a million people in 40 countries participated in 200 projects for peace. Highlights included a 12-day interfaith pilgrimage across Pakistan and the celebration of 1 million signatures on a petition to ban handguns in Rio de Janeiro.

Headquarters

P.O. Box 29242, San Francisco, CA 94129-0242 Tel. (415)561-2300 Fax (415)562-2313
Media Contact, Kristin Swenson

Staff

Exec. Dir., Rev. Cn Charles P. Gibbs
Peacebuilding, Barbara H. Hartford & Sarah Talcott
Global Fundraising, Philanthropy, Jennifer Kirk & LaTonya Trotter
Membership and Organizational Development, Sally Mahe & Cory Robertson
Visions for Peace Among Religions Project, Nancy Nielsen
Annual Giving and Knowledge Management, Sarah Talcott
Financial Manager, Ray Signer

GLOBAL COUNCIL

President and Founding Trustee, Bishop William Swing
AFRICA
Malawi, Joyce N'goma
Uganda, Despina Namwembe
Mozambique, Sabapath Alagiah
ASIA
Pakistan, James Channan
Korea, Jinwol Lee
India, Mohinder Singh
EUROPE
Netherlands, Annie Imbens
United Kingdom, Deepak Naik
Germany, Karimah Stauch
LATIN AMERICA AND THE CARIBBEAN
Argentina, Rosalia Guiterrez
Mexico, Jonathan Rose
Chile, Gerado Gonzalez
MIDDLE EAST
Israel, George Khory
Israel, Yehuda Stolov
Egypt, Mohamed Mosaad
MULTI-REGIONAL/NON-GEOGRAPHIC
Yoland Trevino
Jack Lundin
Munirah Shahidi
NORTH AMERICA
United States of America, Don Frew
United States of America, Kay Lindhal
United States of America, Heng Sure
THE PACIFIC
New Zealand, George Armstrong
Philippines, Bonifacio Quirog
Philippines, Shakuntala Moorjani-Vaswani
TRANSITION ADVISORY COMMITTEE
Iftekhar Hai
Rita Semel
Bob Walter

The United States Conference of Religions for Peace (USCRP)

The United States Conference of Religions for Peace (USCRP) provides a forum for the nation's religious bodies based upon respect for religious differences. In today's world, cooperation among religions offers an important opportunity to mobilize and coordinate the great moral and sociological capacities for constructive action inherent in religious communities.

USCRP provides American religious bodies with opportunities for the following, to identify shared commitments to constructive social development, justice, and peace; to coordinate their efforts with other religious groups on behalf of widely-shared concerns; and to design, undertake, and evaluate joint action projects.

Headquarters

USCRP, 777 United Nations Plaza, New York, NY 10017 Tel. (212)338-9140 (212)983-0566

Officers

Sec. Gen./Exec. Dir., Rev. Bud Heckman, Bheckman@usrp.org
Moderator, V. Rev. Leonid Kishkovsky

Vellore Christian Medical College Board (USA), Inc.

The Vellore Christian Medical College Board (USA) has been linked since 1900 to the vision of a young American medical doctor, Dr. Ida S. Scudder, who founded Christian Medical College and Hospital in Vellore, India. Dr. Ida's vision was to train women in all the healing arts so that they could treat women and their families. Today, after 100 years of teaching and service, the College and Hospital is directed by an Indian woman, Dr. Joyce Ponnaiya. The Vellore Christian Medical College Board (USA) supports the work of Christian Medical College and Hospital in Vellore through exchange personnel programs including volunteers to Vellore and senior CMC staff receiving fellowships to study and work in the United States over 3 month periods. The Vellore Board also assists CMC&H with Capital Campaigns and high tech medical equipment.

Headquarters

475 Riverside Dr., Rm. 243, New York, NY 10115 Tel. (212)870-2640 Fax (212)870-2173
Media Contact, President, Dr. Louis L. Knowles louknowles@vellorecmc.org

Officers

Pres., Dr. Louis L. Knowles
Chpsn., Dr. Mani M. Mani, 5137 West 60th Terrace, Mission, KS 66205
Vice Chpsn., Miriam Ballert, 7104 Olde Oak Ct., Prospect, KY 40059
Sec., Mrs. Edwina Youth, 211 Blue Ridge Dr., Levittown, PA 19057
Treas., Michael Holt, 352 Pines Lake Dr. East, Wayne, NJ 07470

World Council of Churches, United States Office

The United States Conference of the World Council of Churches was formed in 1938 when the WCC itself was still in the "Process of Formation." Henry Smith Leiper, an American with many national and international connections, was given the title of "Associate General Secretary" of the WCC and asked to carry out WCC work in the US. After the World Council of Churches was officially born in 1948 in Amsterdam, Netherlands, Leiper raised millions of dollars for WCC programs.

Today the US Conference of the WCC is composed of representatives of US member churches of the worldwide body. The US Office of the WCC works to develop relationships among the churches, advance the work of WCC and interpret the council in the United States.

Headquarters

475 Riverside Dr., Rm. 915, New York, NY 10115 Tel. (212)870-2533 Fax (212)870-2528

Media Contact, Philip E. Jenks

Officers

WCC Pres. from North America and Moderator, Rev. Kathryn Bannister (United Methodist Church)

Vice Moderator, Bishop McKinley Young (African Methodist Episcopal Church)

Vice Moderator and Treas., The Very Rev. Leonid Kishkovsky (Orthodox Church in America)

Staff

Program Exec. for the U.S., Deborah DeWinter Tel. (212)870-2522

Office Admn., Gloria Feliciano (212)870-3260

World Day of Prayer

World Day of Prayer is an ecumenical movement initiated and carried out by Christian women in 170 countries who conduct a common day of prayer on the first Friday of March to which all people are welcome. There is an annual theme for the worship service that has been prepared by women in a different country each year. For 2004, the women of Panama have prepared a worship service on the theme, "In Faith, Women Shape the Future." The offering at the WDP Worship is gathered by each WDP National or Regional Committee and given to help people who are in need. For 2005 the WDP will be led by women from Poland and the theme will be, "Let Our Light Shine."

Headquarters

World Day of Prayer International Comm., 475 Riverside Dr., Rm. 560, New York, NY 10115 Tel. (212)870-3049 Fax (212)864-8648

Media Contact, Exec. Dir., Eileen King

Officers

Chpsn., Sylvia Lisk Vanhaverbeke

Treas., Karen Prudente

Africa, Suzie Bayiha II; Assah E. Mgonja

Asia, Junko Matsuura; Woranut Pantupong

Caribbean and North America, Waveney Benjamin; Annette Poitier

Europe, Inge Lise Lollike; Ewa Walter

Latin America, Elisabeth Delmonte; Ormara Nolla

Middle East, Laila Carmi; Nadia Menes

Pacific, Jannice Graham, Joanna S. Matigai-Vilitama

Member-at-Large for Orthodox Churches, Marija Ciceva-Aleksic

World Methodist Council–North American Section

The World Methodist Council, one of the 30 or so "Christian World Communions," shares a general tradition which is common to all Christians.

The world organization of Methodists and related United Churches is comprised of 74 churches with roots in the Methodist tradition. These churches, found in 130 countries, have a membership of more than 34 million.

The Council's North American Section, comprised of 10 Methodist and United Church denominations, provides a regional focus for the Council in Canada, the United States, and Mexico. The North American Section meets at the time of the quinquennial World Conference and Council, and separately as Section between world meetings. The Section met in Rio de Janeiro, Brazil in August, 1996 during the 17th World Methodist Conference to elect its officers for the 1997-2001 quinquennium. 2001-2006 officers were elected in Brighton, England, July 2001.

North American Churches related to the World Methodist Council have a membership of approximately 16 million and a church community of more than 30 million.

Headquarters

P.O. Box 518, Lake Junaluska, NC 28745 Tel. (828)456-9432 Fax (828)456-9433

Media Contact, Gen. Sec., Joe Hale

Officers

Section Pres., Bishop Neil L. Irons, 900 S. Arlington Ave., Rm. 214, Harrisburg, PA 17109-5097 Tel. (717)652-6705 Fax (717)652-5109

First Vice Pres., Bishop Thomas L. Hoyt, CME Church

Vice Pres., Bishop John R. Bryant, AME Church; Bishop Cecil Bishop, AMEZ Church; Bishop Richard D. Snyder, Free Methodist Church; Bishop Gracela Alverez, Methodist Church in Mexico; Bishop Keith Elford, Free Methodist Church of Canada; Rev. Carol Hancock, United Church of Canada; Dr. Jack Stone, Church of the Nazarene; Dr. Earle L. Wilson, The Wesleyan Church

Chmn., Finance Committee, Dr. Donald V. Fites

Treas., Dr. James W. Holsinger, Jr.

Asst. Treas., Edna Alsdurf

Gen. Sec., Dr. Joe Hale

World Officers from North America, Dr. Frances M. Alguire, Dr. Maxie D. Dunnam, Bishop Donald Ming

World Vision

World Vision is an international, Christian relief and development organization working to promote the well being of all people—especially that of children. Established in 1950 to care for Asian orphans, World Vision has grown to embrace the larger issues of community development and advocacy for the poor in its mission to help children and their families build sustainable futures. Working on six continents, World Vision is one of the largest Christian relief and development organizations in the world. World Vision US, one of the members of this international partnership also works in the US to alleviate poverty and its effects, focusing on key metro areas. Programs that are geared to the church include the 30 Hour Famine and Love Loaf. The Church Relations department faciliates partnerships between churches and local or international projects.

Headquarters

P.O. Box 9716, Federal Way, WA 98063-9716 Tel. (253)815-1000,

Media Contact, Dean Owen Tel. (253)815-2158

Officers

Pres., Richard Stearns

Vice Pres., Scott Jackson, Atul Tandon, Bruce Wilkinson, Julie Regnier

YMCA of the USA

The YMCA is one of the largest private voluntary organizations in the world, serving about 30 million people in more than 100 countries. In the United States, more than 2,000 local branches, units, camps, and centers annually serve more than 14 million people of all ages, races, and abilities. About half of those served are female. No one is turned away because of an inability to pay.

The Y teaches youngsters to swim, organizes youth basketball games, and offers adult aerobics. But the Y represents more than fitness—it works to strengthen families and help people develop values and behavior that are consistent with Christian principles.

The Y offers hundreds of programs including day camp for children, child care, exercise for people with disabilities, teen clubs, environmental programs, substance abuse prevention, family nights, job training, and many more programs from infant mortality prevention to overnight camping for seniors.

The kind of programs offered at a YMCA will vary; each is controlled by volunteer board members who make their own program, policy, and financial decisions based on the special needs of their community. In its own way, every Y works to build strong kids, strong families, and strong communities.

The YMCA was founded in London, England, in 1844 by George Williams and friends who lived and worked together as clerks. Their goal was to save other live-in clerks from the wicked life of the London streets. The first members were evangelical Protestants who prayed and studied the Bible as an alternative to vice. The Y has always been nonsectarian and today accepts those of all faiths at all levels of the organization.

Headquarters

101 N. Wacker Dr., Chicago, IL 60606 Tel. (312) 977-0031 Fax (312)977-9063

Media Contact, Media Relations Manager, Arnie Collins

Officers

Board Chpsn., Daniel E. Emerson

Exec. Dir., David R. Mercer

(Int.) Public Relations Assoc., Mary Pyke Gover

YWCA of the USA

The YWCA of the USA is comprised of 313 affiliates in communities and on college campuses across the United States. It serves one million members and program participants. It seeks to empower women and girls to enable them—coming together across lines of age, race, religious belief, economic and occupational status—to make a significant contribution to the elimination of racism and the achievement of peace, justice, freedom, and dignity for all people.

Headquarters

Empire State Building, 350 Fifth Ave., Ste. 301 New York, NY 10118 Tel. (212)273-7800 Fax (212)465-2281

Media Contact, Khristina Lew

Officers

National Pres., Leticia Paez

Sec., Carol O. Markus

Chief Exec. Officer, Margaret Tyndall

Youth for Christ–USA

Founded in 1944, as part of the body of Christ, our vision is to see every young person in every people group in every nation have the opportunity to make an informed decision to be a follower of Jesus Christ and become a part of a local church.

There are 220 locally controlled YFC programs serving in cities and metropolitan areas of the United States.

YFC's Campus Life Club program involves teens who attend approximately 58,236 high schools in the United States. YFC's staff now numbers approximately 1,000. In addition, nearly 10,000 part-time and volunteer staff supplement the full-time staff. Youth Guidance, a ministry for nonschool-oriented youth includes group homes, court referrals, institutional services, and neighborhood ministries. The year-round conference and camping program involves approximately 200,000 young people each year. Other ministries include D.C. Ministries, World Outreach, Project Serve, and Teen Moms. Independent, indigenous YFC organizations also work in 127 countries overseas.

Headquarters

US Headquarters, P.O. Box 228822, Denver, CO 80222 Tel. (303)843-9000 Fax (303)843-9002

Canadian Organization, 2540 5th Ave. NW, Calgary, AB T2N 0T

Media Contact, Pres., Roger Cross

Officers

United States, Pres., Roger Cross

Canada, Pres., -vacant-

Intl. Organization, Pres., Jean-Jacques Weiler

2. Canadian Cooperative Organizations, National

In most cases, the organizations listed here work on a national level and cooperate across denominational lines. Regional cooperative organizations in Canada are listed in Directory 8, "Canadian Regional and Local Ecumenical Bodies."

Aboriginal Rights Coalition (ARC)

ARC works towards the transformation of the relationship between Canadian society and Aboriginal peoples. Through education, research, advocacy, and action, this coalition of national churches, faith bodies, and regional groups works in solidarity with Aboriginal peoples. ARC seeks to embody true partnership by building authentic alliances in the global struggle for Aboriginal justice.

Headquarters

153 Laurier Ave. E, 2nd Floor, Ottawa, ON K1N 6N8 Tel. (613)235-9956 Fax (613)235-1302

E-mail: arc@istar.ca

Media Contact, Natl. Coord., Ed Bianchi

Officers

Co-Chairs., Richard Renshaw, Mildred Poplar

Natl. Coord., Ed Bianchi

MEMBER ORGANIZATIONS

Anglican Church of Canada
Canadian Conference of Catholic Bishops
Canadian Religious Conference
Council of Christian Reformed Churches in Canada
Evangelical Lutheran Church in Canada
Mennonite Central Committee
Oblate Conference in Canada
Presbyterian Church of Canada
Religious Society of Friends (Quakers)
Society of Jesus (Jesuits)
Canadian Unitarian Council
United Church of Canada

Association of Canadian Bible Colleges

The Association brings into cooperative association Bible colleges in Canada that are evangelical in doctrine and whose objectives are similar. Services are provided to improve the quality of Bible college education in Canada and to further the interests of the Association by means of conferences, seminars, cooperative undertakings, information services, research, publications, and other projects.

Headquarters

Box 4000, Three Hills, AB T0M 2N0 Tel. (403) 443-3051 Fax (403)443-5540

Media Contact, Sec.-Treas., Peter Doell, peter.doell@pbi.ab.ca

Officers

Pres., Larry J. McKinney, Tel. (204)433-7488 Fax (204)433-7158

Vice Pres., Dr. Arthur Maxwell, Tel. (506)432-4400 Fax (506)432-4425

Sec.-Treas., Peter Doell, Tel. (403)443-3051 Fax (403)443-5540

Members-at-Large: Nil Lavallee Tel. (705)748-9111 Fax (705)748-3931; Wendy Thomas Tel. (306)545-1515 Fax (306)545-0201; Earl Marshall Tel. (519)651-2869 Fax (519)651-2820

Canadian Bible Society

The Canadian Bible Society is a nondenominational and interconfessional organization that exists to translate, publish, distribute, and encourage the use of the Scriptures, without doctrinal note or comment. Bible Society work was begun in Canada in 1804 by the British and Foreign Bible Society. In 1906, the various auxiliaries of the British and Foreign Bible Society joined together to form the Canadian Bible Society. Today, the Canadian Bible Society has 16 district offices across Canada, a Scripture Translation Office in Kitchener, a French Services Office in Montreal, and a National Support Office in Toronto. Additionally, the Bermuda Bible Society is constituted as an Associate District of the Canadian Bible Society. The Society holds quarterly Board meetings involving one elected representative from each of the districts and from the francophone sector. About 90% of the Society's revenue comes through the generosity of Canadian supporters in the form of donations, bequests, and annuity income. Through the Canadian Bible Society's membership in the United States Societies' fellowship, over 81 million Bibles, Testaments, and Portions were distributed globally in 2002. The complete Bible has been published in over 400 languages, with at least one book of the Bible availabe in 2,303 languages.

Headquarters

C.B.S. National Support Office, 10 Carnforth Rd., Toronto, ON M4A 2S4 Tel. (416)757-4171 Fax (416)757-3376

Officers

National Director, Rev. Glen R. Pitts, 10 Carnforth Rd., Toronto, ON M4A 2S4 Tel. (416)757-4171, Fax (416)757-1292, gpitts@biblesociety.ca

Chief Operating Officer, Mr. Wally Sherwin, 10 Carnforth Rd., Toronto, ON M4A 2S4 Tel.

(416)757-4171, Fax (416)757-1292, wsherwin@biblesociety.ca

Dir. of Scripture Translation, Mr. Hart Wiens, Frederick Mall (2nd Floor), 385 Frederick Street, Kitchener, ON N2H 2P2 Tel. (519)741-8285, Fax (519)741-8357, hwiens@biblesociety.ca

Directeur du Secteur francophone, M. Serge Rhéaume, 4050 avenue du Parc-Lafontaine, Montreal, QC H2L 3M8 Tel. (514)524-7873, Fax (514)524-6116, srheaume@societebiblique.ca

Dir. of Ministry Funding, Mr. Erwin van Laar, 10 Carnforth Rd., Toronto, ON M4A 2S4 Tel. (416)757-4171, Fax (416)757-3376, evanlaar@biblesociety.ca

Distribution Manager, Mr. David Duncan, 10 Carnforth Rd., Toronto, ON M4A 2S4 Tel. (416) 757-4171, Fax (416)757-3376, dduncan@biblesociety.ca

Human Resources Manager/Volunteer Program Coordinator, Mrs. Linda Donohoe, 10 Carnforth Rd., Toronto, ON M4A 2S4 Tel. (416)757-4171, Fax (416)757-3376, ldonohoe@biblesociety.ca

Canadian Centre for Ecumenism

The Centre has facilitated understanding and cooperation among believers of various Christian traditions and world religions since 1963. An active interdenominational Board of Directors meets annually.

Outreach: *Ecumenism*, a quarterly publication, develops central themes such as Rites of Passage, Sacred Space, Interfaith Marriages, Care of the Earth, etc. through contributions from writers of various churches and religions in addition to its regular ecumenical news summaries, book reviews, and resources.

A specialized library is open to the public for consultation in the areas of religion, dialogue, evangelism, ethics, spirituality, etc.

Conferences and sessions are offered on themes such as Ecumenism and Pastoral Work, Pluralism, World Religions, Prayer and Unity.

Headquarters

2065 Sherbrooke St. W. Montreal, QC H3H 1G6 Tel. (514)937-9176 Fax (514)937-4986

Email: ccocce@total.net

Website: www.total.net/~ccocce

Officers

Media Contact, Bernice Baranowski

Associate Directors, Emmanuel Lapierre, O.P.

Dir., Gilles Bourdeau, O.F.M.

Assistant Dir., Angelika Piché

The Canadian Council of Churches

The Canadian Council of Churches was organized in 1944. Its basic purpose is to provide the churches with an agency for conference and consultation and for such common planning and common action as they desire to undertake. It encourages ecumenical understanding and action throughout Canada through local councils of churches. It also relates to the World Council of Churches and other agencies serving the worldwide ecumenical movement.

The Council has a Governing Board which meets semiannually and an Executive Committee. Program is administered through two commissions—Faith and Witness, Justice and Peace.

Headquarters

3250 Bloor St. W, 2nd Floor, Toronto, ON M8X 2Y4 Tel. (416)972-9494 ext. 22 Fax (416)l236-4532

Email: ccchurch@web.net

Website: www.web.net/~ccchurch

Media Contact, Rev. Dr. Karen Hamilton

Officers

Pres., Bishop Andre Vallee

Vice Presidents, Rev. Michael Winnowski, Fr. Shenork Sovin, Ms. Karen MacKay Llewellyn

Treas., Nancy Bell

Treas. Emeritus, Mr. Jack Hart

Gen. Secretary., Rev. Dr. Karen Hamilton

MEMBER CHURCHES

The Anglican Church of Canada

The Armenian Orthodox Church–Diocese of Canada

Baptist Convention of Ontario and Quebec

British Methodist Episcopal Church*

Canadian Conference of Catholic Bishops

Christian Church (Disciples of Christ)

Coptic Orthodox Church of Canada

Christian Reformed Church in North America–Canadian Ministries

Ethiopian Orthodox Church in Canada

Evangelical Lutheran Church in Canada

Greek Orthodox Metropolis of Toronto, Canada

Orthodox Church in America, Diocese of Canada

Polish National Catholic Church

Presbyterian Church in Canada

Reformed Church in Canada

Religious Society of Friends–Canada Yearly Meeting

Salvation Army–Canada and Bermuda

The Ukrainian Orthodox Church

The United Church of Canada

**Associate Member*

Canadian Evangelical Theological Association

In May 1990, about 60 scholars, pastors and other interested persons met together in Toronto to form a new theological society. Arising out of the Canadian chapter of the Evangelical Theological Society, the new association established itself as a distinctly Canadian group with a new name. It sponsored its first conference as CETA in Kingston, Ontario, in May 1991.

CETA provides a forum for scholarly contributions to the renewal of theology and church in Canada. CETA seeks to promote theological work which is loyal to Christ and his Gospel, faithful to the primacy and authority of Scripture, and responsive to the guiding force of the historic creeds and Protestant confessions of the Christian Church. In its newsletters and conferences, CETA seeks presentations that will speak to a general theologically-educated audience rather than to specialists.

CETA has special interest in evangelical points of view upon and contributions to the wider conversations regarding religious studies and church life. Members therefore include pastors, students, and other interested persons as well as professional academicians. CETA currently includes about 100 members, many of whom attend its annual conference in the early summer. It publishes the *Canadian Evangelical Review* and supports an active internet discussion group, which may be accessed by emailing ceta-l@egroups.com.

Headquarters

Dr. Hans Boersma, Trinity Western University, 7600 Glover Rd., Langley, BC V2Y 1Y1 Tel. (604)513-2121

Email: hansb@twu.ca

Media Contact, Dr. Hans Boersma

Officers

Pres., Dr. Hans Boersma

Sec.-Treas., Dr. David Guretzki

Editor, *Canadian Evengelical Review*, Dr. Archie Pell

Exec. Member, Mr. Stephen Martin

Canadian Tract Society

The Canadian Tract Society was organized in 1970 as an independent distributor of Gospel leaflets to provide Canadian churches and individual Christians with quality materials proclaiming the Gospel through the printed page. It is affiliated with the American Tract Society, which encouraged its formation and assisted in its founding, and for whom it serves as an exclusive Canadian distributor. The CTS is a nonprofit international service ministry.

Headquarters

P.O. Box 2156, LCD 1, Brampton, ON L6T 3S4 Tel. (905)457-4559 Fax (905)457-0529

Media Contact, Mgr., Donna Croft

Officers

Dir.-Sec., Robert J. Burns

Dir., John Neufeld

Dir., Patricia Burns

Canadian Society of Biblical Studies–Société Canadienne des Études Bibliques

The object of the Society shall be to stimulate the critical investigation of the classical biblical literatures, together with other related literature, by the exchange of scholarly research both in published form and in public forum.

Headquarters

Dept. of Religion and Culture, Wilfrid Laurier University, Waterloo, ON N2L 3C5 Tel. (519)884-0710 ext.3323 Fax (519)884-9387

Media Contact, Exec. Sec., Dr. Michel Desjardins

Officers

Pres., Gary Knoppers, Classics & Ancient Mediterranean Studies, Penn State University, 101 Weaver Building, University Park, PA 16802-5500, gxk7@psu.edu

Vice Pres., David J. Hawkin, Dept. of Religious Studies, Memorial University St. John's, NFLD A1C 5S7, dhawkin@mun.ca

Exec. Sec., Michele Murray, Dept. of Religion, Bishop's University, Lennoxville, PQ J1M 1Z7, mmurray@ubishops.ca

Treas., Dietmar Neufeld, Department of Classical, Near Eastern and Religious Studies, University of British Columbia, Vancouver, BC V6T 1Z1, Tel. (604)822-4065, dneufeld@interchange.ubc.ca

Communications Officer, John L. McLaughlin, Faculty of Theology, University of St. Michael's College, 81 St. Mary Street, Toronto, ON M5S 1J4, johnl.mclaughlin@utoronto.ca

Programme Coord., J. Glen Taylor, Wycliffe College, 5 Hoskin Ave., Toronto, ON M5S 1H7, glen.taylor@utoronto.ca

Student Liaison Officer, Mona Tokarek LaFosse, Centre for the Study of Religion University of Toronto, Unit 63 - 14 Williamsburg Rd., Kitchener, ON N2E 1W1, lafosse@golden.net

The Church Army in Canada

The Church Army in Canada has been involved in evangelism and Christian social service since 1929.

Headquarters

105 Mountain View Dr., Saint John, NB E2J 5B5 Tel. (888)316-8169 Fax (506)642-4005,

Media Contact, National Dir., Capt. R. Bruce Smith, bsmith@churcharmy.com

Officers

National Dir., Capt. R. Bruce Smith

Bd. Chmn., Mr. Peter Bloom

The Churches' Council on Theological Education in Canada, An Ecumenical Foundation

The Churches' Council (CCTE, EF) maintains an overview of theological education in Canada on behalf of its constituent churches and functions as a bridge between the schools of theology and the churches which they serve.

Founded in 1970 with a national and ecumenical mandate, the CCTE, EF provides resources for research into matters pertaining to theological education, opportunities for consultation and cooperation, and a limited amount of funding in the form of grants for the furtherance of ecumenical iniatives in theological education.

Headquarters

60 St. Clair Avenue E, Ste. 302, Toronto, ON M4T 1N5 Tel. (416)928-3223 Fax (416)928-3563

Email: ccte@web.ca

Website: www.web.net/~ccte

Media Contact, Exec. Dir., Dr. Stewart Gillan

Officers

Bd. of Dir., Chpsn., Dr. Richard C. Crossman, Waterloo Lutheran Seminary, 75 University Ave. W, Waterloo, ON N2L 3C5

Bd. of Dir., Vice Chpsn., Sr. Ellen Leonard, CSJ, Univ. of St. Michaels's College, 81 St. Mary St., Toronto, ON M5S 1J4

Treas., Mr. Ralph Kendall, 9 Sari Cres., Toronto, ON M1E 4W3, ralph.sheila@home.com

Exec. Dir., Dr. Stewart Gillan

MEMBER ORGANIZATIONS

The General Synod of the Anglican Church of Canada

Canadian Baptist Ministries

The Evangelical Lutheran Church in Canada

The Presbyterian Church in Canada

The Canadian Conference of Catholic Bishops

The United Church of Canada

Ecumenical Coalition for Economic Justice (ECEJ)

The Ecumenical Coalition for Economic Justice (ECEJ) enables member churches to have a more effective public voice in advocating for a just, moral, and sustainable economy. ECEJ undertakes research, education, and advocacy to promote economic policy alternatives that are grounded in a Christian perspective. Sponsoring denominations include: the Anglican Church of Canada, the Canadian Catholic Bishops Conference, the Evangelical Lutheran Church in Canada, the Presbyterian Church in Canada, and the United Church of Canada. ECEJ also acts as a link to social movements and coalitions to bring a collective church presence to them and to inform our own analysis.

The program focus of the next three years will be to advance alternative economic policies which support our vision of an "economy of hope." This includes proposing different ways to assess economic prosperity, challenging the growth model, envisioning a new model for social programs in global economy, and presenting alternative fiscal and monetary policies.

ECEJ publishes a quarterly briefing paper on current issues, *the Economic Justice Report*, as well as education and action resources.

An Administrative Committee oversees ECEJ and is made up of representatives from the sponsoring denominations as well as participating members which currently include the School Sisters of Notre Dame, the Scarboro Foreign Mission, and the Religious Society of Friends (Quaker).

Headquarters

77 Charles St. W, Ste. 402, Toronto, ON M5S 1K5 Tel. (416)921-4615 Fax (416)922-1419

Media Contact, Educ. & Communications, Jennifer Henry

Officers

Co-Chpsn., Doryne Kirby

Co-Chpsn., Jim Marshall

Staff

Research, John Dillon

Women & Economic Justice Programme, Kathryn Robertson

Education-Communication, Jennifer Henry

Administration-Finance, Diana Gibbs

Evangelical Fellowship of Canada

The Fellowship was formed in 1964. There are 31 denominations, 124 organizations, 1,200 local churches, and 11,000 individual members.

Its purposes are "fellowship in the gospel" (Phil. 1:5), "the defence and confirmation of the gospel" (Phil. 1:7), and "the furtherance of the gospel" (Phil. 1:12). The Fellowship believes the Holy Scriptures, as originally given, are infallible and that salvation through the Lord Jesus Christ is by faith apart from works.

In national and regional conventions the Fellowship urges Christians to live exemplary lives and to openly challenge the evils and injustices of society. It encourages cooperation with various agencies in Canada and overseas that are sensitive to social and spiritual needs.

Headquarters

Office, 600 Alden Rd. Ste. 300, Markham, ON L3R 0E7 Tel. (905)479-5885 Fax (905)479-4742

Mailing Address, M.I.P. Box 3745, Markham, ON L3R 0Y4

Media Contact, Pres., Dr. Gary Walsh, 600 Alden Rd., Ste. 300, Markham, ON L3R 0E7 Tel. (905)479-5885 Fax (905)479-4742

Officers

Pres., Dr. Gary Walsh

Chpsn., Dr. Paul Magnus

Vice Chpsn., Dr. Rick Penner

Treas., Lt. Col. David Luginbuhl

Past Pres., Dr. Brian Stiller

EXECUTIVE COMMITTEE

Rev. Scott Campbell, Rev. Carson Pue, Ms. Ruth Andrews, Rev. Stewart Hunter, Ms. Jacqueline Dugas, Dr. Rick Penner, Lt. Col. David Luginbuhl, Dr. Ralph Richardson, Rev. Abe Funk, Rev. Gillis Killam, Dr. Paul Magnus, Rev. Winston Thurton

Task Force on Evangelism (Vision Canada), Interim Chair, Gary Walsh

Social Action Commission, Chpsn., Dr. James Read

Education Commission, Chpsn., Dr. Glenn Smith

Women in Ministry Task Force, Chpsn., Rev. Eileen Stewart-Rhude

Aboriginal Task Force, Co-Chairs, Ray Aldred; Wendy Peterson

Religious Liberties Commission, Chpsn., Dr. Paul Marshall

Task Force on Global Mission, Chpsn., Dr. Geoff Tunnicliffe

Inter-Varsity Christian Fellowship of Canada

Inter-Varsity Christian Fellowship is a non-profit, interdenominational student movement centering on the witness to Jesus Christ in campus communities, universities, colleges, and high schools and through a Canada-wide Pioneer Camping program. It also ministers to professionals and teachers through Nurses and Teacher Christian Fellowship.

IVCF was officially formed in 1928-29 by the late Dr. Howard Guinness, whose arrival from Britain challenged students to follow the example of the British Inter-Varsity Fellowship by organizing themselves into prayer and Bible study fellowship groups. Inter-Varsity has always been a student-initiated movement emphasizing and developing leadership in the campus to call Christians to outreach, challenging other students to a personal faith in Jesus Christ, and studying the Bible as God's revealed truth within a fellowship of believers. A strong stress has been placed on missionary activity, and the triennial conference held at Urbana, Ill. (jointly sponsored by US and Canadian IVCF) has been a means of challenging many young people to service in Christian vocations. Inter-Varsity works closely with and is a strong believer in the work of local and national churches.

Headquarters

Unit 17, 40 Vogell Rd., Richmond Hill, ON L4B 3N6 Tel. (905)884-6880 Fax (905)884-6550

Media Contact, Gen. Dir., Rob Regier

Officers

Gen. Dir., Rob Regier

Interchurch Communications

Interchurch Communications is made up of the communication units of the Anglican Church of Canada, the Evangelical Lutheran Church in Canada, the Presbyterian Church in Canada, the Canadian Conference of Catholic Bishops (English Sector), and the United Church of Canada. ICC members collaborate on occasional video or print coproductions and on addressing public policy issues affecting religious communications.

Headquarters

3250 Bloor St. W, Etobicoke, ON M8X 2Y4

Media Contact, Chpsn., Douglas Tindal, Anglican Church of Canada, 600 Jarvis St., Toronto, ON M4Y 2J6 Tel. (416)924-9199 ext. 286, Fax (416)968-7983, doug.tindal@national.anglican.ca

MEMBERS

Mr. Douglas Tindal, Anglican Church of Canada, 600 Jarvis St., Toronto, ON M4Y 2J6 Tel. (416)924-9199 ext.286, Fax (416)968-7983, dtindal@national.anglican.ca

Mr. William Kokesch, Canadian Conference of Catholic Bishops, 90 Parent Ave., Ottawa, ON K1N 7B1 Tel. (613)241-9461, Fax (613)241-8117, kokesch@cccb.ca

Mr. Merv Campone, Evangelical Lutheran Church in Canada, 305-896 Cambie St., Vancouver, BC V6B 2P6 Tel. (604)888-4562, Fax (604)687-6593, mcampone@spiritscall. com

Rev. Keith Knight, Presbyterian Church in Canada, 50 Wynford Dr., Don Mills, ON M3C 1J7 Tel. (416)441-1111, Fax (416)441-2825, kknight@presbyterian.ca

Mr. Gordon How, United Church of Canada, 3250 Bloor St. W., Etobicoke, ON M8X 2Y4 Tel. (416)231-7680, Fax (416)231-3103, ghow@uccan.org

Religious Television Associates, 3250 Bloor St. W., Etobicoke, ON M8X 2Y4 Tel. (416)231-7680 Fax (416)232-6004

John Howard Society of Ontario

The John Howard Society of Ontario is a registered nonprofit charitable organization providing services to individuals, families, and groups at all stages in the youth and criminal justice system. The Society also provides community education on critical issues in the justice system and advocacy for reform of the justice system. The mandate of the Society is the prevention of crime through service, community education, advocacy and reform.

Founded in 1929, the Society has grown from a one-office service in Toronto to 17 local branches providing direct services in the major cities of Ontario and a provincial office providing justice policy analysis, advocacy for reform and support to branches.

Headquarters

6 Jackson Pl., Toronto, ON M6P 1T6 Tel. (416) 604-8412 Fax (416)604-8948

Media Contact, Exec. Dir., William Sparks

Officers

Pres., Susan Reid-MacNevin, Dept. of Sociology, Univ. Of Guelph, Guelph, ON N1G 2W1

Vice Pres., Richard Beaupe, 4165 Fernand St., Hamner, ON B3A 1X4

Treas., Jack Battler, Waterloo, ON

Sec., Peter Angeline, OISE, 252 Bloor St. W., Toronto, ON

Exec. Dir., William Sparks

LOCAL SOCIETIES

Collins Bay; Hamilton; Kingston; Lindsay; London; Niagara; Oshawa; Ottawa; Peel; Peterborough; Sarnia; Sault Ste. Marie; Sudbury; Thunder Bay; Toronto; Waterloo; Windsor

John Milton Society for the Blind in Canada

The John Milton Society for the Blind in Canada is an interdenominational Christian charity founded by Hellen Keller whose mandate is producing Christian publications for adults or young people who are blind, deafblind, or visually impaired. As such, it produces *Insight*, a large-print magazine; *Insound*, a cassette magazine; and *In Touch*, a braille magazine. The John Milton Society also features an audio cassette library called the Library in Sound, which contains Christian music, sermons, seasonal materials, and workshops. All services are available free upon request to blind persons.

Headquarters

40 St. Clair Ave. E, Ste. 202, Toronto, ON M4T 1M9 Tel. (416)960-3953 Fax (416)960-3570
Website: www.jmsblind.ca
Media Contact, Ex. Dir., The Rev. Barry R. Brown

Officers

Exec. Dir., The Rev. Barry R. Brown, bbrown@jmsblind.ca
Pres., The Rev. Gerald Hunt

Lutheran Council in Canada

The Lutheran Council in Canada was organized in 1967 and is a cooperative agency of the Evangelical Lutheran Church in Canada and Lutheran Church–Canada.

The Council's activities include communications, coordinative service and national liaison in social ministry, chaplaincy and scout activity.

Headquarters

302-393 Portage Ave., Winnipeg, MB R3B 3H6 Tel. (204)984-9150 Fax (204)984-9185
Media Contact, Pres., Rev. Ralph Mayan, 3074 Portage Ave., Winnipeg, MB R3K 0Y2 Tel. (204)895-3433 Fax (204)897-4319

Officers

Pres., Rev. Ralph Mayan
Treas., -vacant-
Sec., Rev. Leon C. Gilbertson
Vice Pres., Bishop Telmore Sartison

Mennonite Central Committee Canada (MCCC)

Mennonite Central Committee Canada was organized in 1964 to continue the work which several regional Canadian inter-Mennonite agencies had been doing in relief, service, immigration, and peace. All but a few of the smaller Mennonite groups in Canada belong to MCC Canada.

MCCC is part of the Mennonite Central Committee (MCC) International which has its headquarters in Akron, Pa. from where most of the overseas development and relief projects are administered. In 2000-2001 MCCC's income was $25 million, about 47 percent of the total MCC income. There were 408 Canadians out of a total of 867 MCC workers serving in North America and abroad during the same time period.

The MCC office in Winnipeg administers projects located in Canada. Domestic programs of Voluntary Service, Native Concerns, Peace and Social Concerns, Food Program, Employment Concerns, Ottawa Office, Victim-Offender Ministries, Mental Health, and Immigration are all part of MCC's Canadian ministry. Whenever it undertakes a project, MCCC attempts to relate to the church or churches in the area.

Headquarters

134 Plaza Dr., Winnipeg, MB R3T 5K9 Tel. (204)261-6381 Fax (204)269-9875
Communications, Rick Fast, 134 Plaza Dr., Winnipeg, MT R3T 5K9 Tel. (204)261-6381 Fax (204)269-9875

Officers

Exec. Dir., Donald Peters

Project Ploughshares

Founded in 1976, Project Ploughshares is a Canadian ecumenical nongovernmental organization that carries out policy research, analysis, dialogue, and public education programs in Canada and internationally to identify, develop, and advance approaches that build peace, prevent war, and promote the peaceful resolution of political conflict. Project Ploughshares is sponsored by the Canadian Council of Churches and is affiliated with the Institute of Peace and Conflict Studies, Conrad Grebel University College, University of Waterloo. Publications include the *Ploughshares Monitor* (quarterly), *The Armed Conflicts Report* (annually), and *Briefings and Working Papers* (occasional).

Headquarters

Project Ploughshares, 57 Erb St. West, Waterloo, ON, Canada N2L 6C2 Tel. (519) 888-6541 Fax (519)885-0188
Email: plough@ploughshares.ca
Website: www.ploughshares.ca
Media Contact, Dir., Ernie Regehr

Officers

Chpsn., Moira Hutchinson
Treas., Philip Creighton

SPONSORING ORGANIZATIONS

Anglican Church of Canada
Canadian Catholic Organization for Development & Peace
Canadian Unitarian Council
Canadian Voice of Women for Peace
Canadian Yearly Meeting, Religious Society of Friends
Evangelical Lutheran Church in Canada
Mennonite Central Committee Canada
Presbyterian Church in Canada
United Church of Canada

Religious Television Associates

Religious Television Associates was formed in the early 1960s for the production units of the Anglican, Baptist, Presbyterian, Roman Catholic Churches, and the United Church of Canada. In the intervening years, the Baptists have withdrawn and the Lutherans have joined. RTA provides an ecumenical umbrella for joint productions in broadcasting and development education. The directors are the heads of the Communications Departments participating in Interchurch Communications.

Headquarters

c/o The United Church of Canada, 3250 Bloor St. W., Etobicoke, ON M8X 2Y4 Tel. (416)231-7680 ext. 4076 Fax (416)231-3103

Media Contact, Shane Chadden

MEMBER ORGANIZATIONS

The Anglican Church of Canada
Canadian Conference of Catholic Bishops
The Canadian Council of Churches
The Evangelical Lutheran Church in Canada
The Presbyterian Church in Canada
The United Church of Canada

Scripture Union

Scripture Union is an international interdenominational missionary movement working in 130 countries. Scripture Union aims to work with the churches to make God's Good News known to children, young people, and families, and to encourage people of all ages to meet God daily through the Bible and prayer.

In Canada, a range of daily Bible guides are offered to individuals, churches, and bookstores for people from age four through adult. Sunday School curriculum and various evangelism and discipling materials are also offered for sale. A program of youth and family evangelism, including beach missions and community-based evangelistic holiday clubs, is also undertaken.

Headquarters

1885 Clements Rd., Unit 226, Pickering, ON L1W 3V4 Tel. (905)427-4947 Fax (905)427-0334,

Media Contact, Pres., John Irwin, jirwinc617@rogers.com

Officers

Chpsn. of the Board, Harold Murray, 216 McKinnon Pl. NE, Calgary, AB T2E 7B9 Tel. (403)276-4716, hjmurray@home.com

Pres., John W. Irwin, 1885 Clements Rd., Unit 226, Pickering, ON L1W 3V4, jirwinc617@rogers.com

Student Christian Movement of Canada

The Student Christian Movement of Canada was formed in 1921 from the student arm of the YMCA. It has its roots in the Social Gospel movements of the late 19th and early 20th centuries. Throughout its intellectual history, the SCM in Canada has sought to relate the Christian faith to the living realities of the social and political context of each student generation.

The present priorities are built around the need to form more and stronger critical Christian communities on Canadian campuses within which individuals may develop their social and political analyses, experience spiritual growth and fellowship, and bring Christian ecumenical witness to the university.

The Student Christian Movement of Canada is affiliated with the World Student Christian Federation.

Headquarters

310 Danforth Ave., Toronto, ON M4K 1N6 Tel. (416)463-4312 Fax (416)466-6854

Media Contact, Natl. Coord., Susannah Schmidt

Officers

Natl. Coord., Susannah Schmidt

Taskforce on the Churches and Corporate Responsibility

The Taskforce on the Churches and Corporate Responsibility is a national ecumenical coalition of the major churches in Canada. Official representatives from the General Synod of the Anglican Church of Canada, the Canadian Conference of Catholic Bishops, the Evangelical Lutheran Church in Canada, the Presbyterian Church in Canada, the Religious Society of Friends (Quakers), the United Church of Canada, CUSO, the YWCA, and a number of religious orders of women and men, serve as links between the Taskforce and the decision-making structures of the members. The Taskforce assists the members in implementing policies adopted by the churches in the areas of corporate responsibility. Among the policies and issues placed on the agenda of the Taskforce by the participating churches are: principles for global corporate responsibility and bench marks for measuring business performance, corporate operating practices and codes of operation conduct, environmental reporting, human rights and Aboriginal land rights in relation to corporate conduct, social and environmental issues relative to corporate global citizenship, corporate governance issues, responsible investing issues.

Headquarters

129 St. Clair Ave., W, Toronto, ON M4V 1N5 Tel. (416)923-1758 Fax (416)927-7554

Media Contact, Coord., Daniel Gennarelli Tel. (416)923-1758 Fax (416)927-7554

Officers

Coord., Daniel Gennarelli
Bd. Co-Chpsns., Tim Ryan; David Hallman
Treas., Doug Peter
Chpsn., Corp. Governance Comm., Richard Soo

Co-Chpsns. Inter-Church Comm. on Ecology, Joy Kennedy, Jim Profit

MEMBERS

Anglican Church of Canada
Basilian Fathers
Baptist Convention Ontario–Quebec
Canadian Conference of Catholic Bishops
Canadian Religious Conference
Christian Reformed Church in Canada
Conference religieuse canadiene–Quebec
Congregation of Notre Dame
Evangelical Lutheran Church in Canada
Grey Sisters of the Immaculate Conception
Jesuit Fathers of Upper Canada
Les Soeurs de Sainte-Anne
Oblate Conference of Canada
Presbyterian Church in Canada
Redemptorist Fathers
Religious Hospitallers of St. Joseph
Religious Society of Friends (Quakers)
School Sisters of Notre Dame
Scarboro Foreign Mission Society
Sisterhood of St. John the Divine
Sisters of Charity–Mount St. Vincent
Sisters of Charity of the Immaculate Conception
Sisters of Mercy Generalate
Sisters of St. Ann, Victoria
Sisters of St. Joseph of Hamilton
Sisters of St. Joseph–Diocese of London
Sisters of Service of Canada
Sisters of St. Joseph–Sault Ste. Marie
Sisters of St. Joseph–Toronto
Sisters of the Holy Names of Jesus & Mary Windsor, ON
Sisters of Holy Names of Jesus and Mary, Longueil, P.Q.
Sisters of Providence of St. Vincent dePaul
Sisters of St. Martha
Toronto United Church Council
United Church of Canada
Ursulines of Chatham Union
Young Women's Christian Association

Ten Days for Global Justice

Supported by five of Canada's major Christian denominations, Ten Days is dedicated to helping people discover, examine, and reflect on the ways global and domestic structures and policies promote and perpetuate poverty and injustice for the majority of the world's people. Ten Days is an education and action program that attempts to influence the policies and practice of Canadian churches, government, business, labour, education, and the media.

Headquarters

KAIROS: Canadian Ecumenical Justice Initiatives/ Initiatives oecuméniques canadiennes pour la justice
129 St. Clair Ave. W, Toronto, ON, Canada M4V 1N5 Tel. (416)463-5312 ext. 237 or (877)403-8933 Fax (416)463-5569
Websites: www.kairoscanada.org and www.web.ca/~ tendays
Media Contact, Natl. Coord., Team Leader, Canadian Justice Cluster, Dennis Howlett, dhowlett@kairoscanada.org

Staff

Natl. Coord., Dennis Howlett
Coord. for Leadership Dev. & Regional Communication, David Reid
Resource Coord., Julie Graham
Admn. Asst., Ramya Hemachandra

MEMBER ORGANIZATIONS

Anglican Church of Canada
Canadian Cath. Orgn. for Dev. & Peace
Evangelical Lutheran Church in Canada
Presbyterian Church in Canada
United Church of Canada

Women's Inter-Church Council of Canada

Women's Inter-Church Council of Canada is a national Christian women's council that encourages women to grow in ecumenism, to strengthen ecumenical community, to share their spirituality and prayer, to engage in dialogue about women's concerns, and to stand in solidarity with one another. The Council calls women to respond to national and international issues affecting women and to take action together for justice. WICC sponsors the World Day of Prayer and Fellowship of the Least Coin in Canada. Human rights projects for women are supported and a quarterly magazine, *Making Waves*, distributed.

Headquarters

Suite 201, 394 Bloor St. W, Toronto, ON M5S 1X4 Tel. (416)929-5184 Fax (416)929-4064
Media Contact, Communications Coord., Gillian Barfoot

Officers

Pres., Joyce Christie
Exec. Dir., Rev. Karen Hincke

CHURCH MEMBER BODIES

African Methodist Episcopal, Anglican Church of Canada, Canadian Baptist Ministries, Christian Church (Disciples of Christ), Evangelical Lutheran Church in Canada, Mennonite Central Committee, Presbyterian Church in Canada, Religious Society of Friends, Roman Catholic Church, The Salvation Army in Canada, United Church of Canada

World Vision Canada

World Vision Canada is a Christian humanitarian relief and development organization. Although its main international commitment is to translate child sponsorship into holistic, sustainable community development, World Vision also allocates resources to help Canada's poor and complement the mission of the church.

World Vision's Reception Centre assists government-sponsored refugees entering Canada. The NeighbourLink program mobilizes church volunteers to respond locally to people's needs. A quarterly publication, *Context*, provides data on the Canadian family to help churches effectively reach their communities. The development education program provides resources on development issues. During the annual 30-Hour Famine, people fast for 30 hours while discussing poverty and raising funds to support aid programs.

Headquarters

6630 Turner Valley Rd., Mississauga, ON L5N 2S4 Tel. (905)821-3030 Fax (905)821-1356
Media Contact, Philip Maher Tel. (905)567-2726

Officers

Pres., Dave Toycen
Vice Pres.: Intl. & Govt. Relations, Linda Tripp; Natl. Programs, Don Posterski; Fin. & Admin., Charlie Fluit; Donor Development Group, Brian Tizzard

Young Men's Christian Association in Canada

The YMCA began as a Christian association to help young men find healthy recreation and meditation, as well as opportunities for education, in the industrial slums of 19th century England. It came to Canada in 1851 with the same mission in mind for young men working in camps and on the railways.

Today, the YMCA maintains its original mission, helping individuals to grow and develop in spirit, mind and body, but attends to those needs for men and women of all ages and religious beliefs. The YMCA registers 1.5 million participants in 250 communities that are served by 64 autonomous associations across Canada.

The program of each association differs according to the needs of the community, but most offer one or more programs in each of the following categories: health and fitness, child care, employment councelling and training, recreation, camping, community support and outreach, international development, and short-term accommodation.

The YMCA encourages people of all ages, races, abilities, income, and beliefs to come together in an environment which promotes balance in life, breaking down barriers, and helping to create healthier communities.

Headquarters

42 Charles St. E, 6th Floor., Toronto, ON M4Y 1T4 Tel. (416)967-9622 Fax (416)967-9618
Media Contact, Sol Kasimer

Officers

Chpsn., Ray Mantha
CEO, Sol Kasimer

Young Women's Christian Association of/du Canada

The YWCA of/du Canada is a national voluntary organization serving 44 YWCAs and YM/YWCAs across Canada. Dedicated to the development and improved status of women and their families, the YWCA is committed to service delivery and to being a source of public education on women's issues and an advocate of social change. Services provided by YWCAs and YM/YWCAs include adult education programs, residences and shelters, child care, fitness activities, wellness programs, and international development education. As a member of the World YWCA, the YWCA of/du Canada is part of the largest women's organization in the world.

Headquarters

80 Gerrard St. E, Toronto, ON M5B 1G6 Tel. (416)593-9886 Fax (416)971-8084
Media Contact, Int. CEO, Margaret MacKenzie

Officers

Pres., Ann Mowatt

Youth for Christ–Canada

Youth For Christ is an interdenominational organization founded in 1944 by Torrey Johnson. Under the leadership of YFC's 11 national board of directors, Youth For Christ–Canada cooperates with churches and serves as a mission agency reaching out to young people and their families through a variety of ministries.

YFC seeks to have maximum influence in a world of youth through high-interest activities and personal involvement. Individual attention is given to each teenager through small group involvement and counselling. These activities and relationships become vehicles for communicating the message of the Gospel.

Headquarters

822-167 Lombard Ave., Winnipeg, MB R3B 0V3 Tel. (204)989-0056 Fax (204)989-0067

Officers

Natl. Dir., Randy L. Steinwand

3. Religious Bodies in the United States

The United States, with its staunch constitutional stance on religious freedom and successive waves of immigrants over the last three centuries, has proved to be a fertile soil for the development of varied Christian traditions. In the directory that follows, some 216 distinct church traditions are represented. Many of these groups represent the processes of dividing and re-uniting that are a hallmark of American religious life. Many churches listed here represent those with a long tradition in Europe, Africa, or Asia predating their American tenure. Others are American-born churches. The researcher may be helped by consulting the churches grouped by tradition at the end of this directory in the section entitled, "Religious Bodies in the United States Arranged by Families." In this section, all the Baptists bodies are listed together, all the Lutheran bodies, Methodists, etc.

The following directory information is supplied by the national headquarters of each church. Each listing contains a brief description of the church, followed by the national headquarters contact information, which includes a mailing address, telephone and fax numbers, email and website addresses (when available), and the name of the media contact. After the headquarters, there are data regarding the church officers or leaders, including names, titles, and contact information (when contact information differs from the headquarters). There is a staggering array of churches, each with its own form of organization; not all of them refer to their leaders as "officers." In some places, the reader will find the term "Bishops," "Board Members," or "Executives" in place of "Officers." Finally, when applicable, each entry contains a list of the names of church publications.

The churches are printed in alphabetical order by the official name of the organization. There are a few instances in which certain churches are more commonly known by another name. In such cases, the reader is referred incidentally within the text to the appropriate official name. Churches that are member communions of the National Council of the Churches of Christ in the USA are marked with an asterisk (*).

Other useful information about the churches listed here can be found in other chapters or directories within the book: Statistical information for these churches can be found in the tables toward the end of this book in Chapter III. Further, more extensive information about the publications listed in this directory can be found in Directory 11, "Religious Periodicals in the United States." For a list of church websites, see Directory 5, "The Emerging Electronic Church."

The organizations listed here represent the denominations to which the vast majority of church members in the United States belong. It does not include all religious bodies functioning in the United States. *The Encyclopedia of American Religions* (Gale Research Inc., P.O. Box 33477, Detroit Mich. 48232-5477) contains names and addresses of additional religious bodies.

Advent Christian Church

The Advent Christian Church is a conservative, evangelical denomination which grew out of the Millerite movement of the 1830s and 1840s. The members stress the authority of Scripture; justification by faith in Jesus Christ alone; the importance of evangelism, disciple-making, and world missions; and the soon visible return of Jesus Christ.

Organized in 1860, the Advent Christian Church maintains headquarters in Charlotte, NC, with regional offices in Rochester, N.H.; Princeton, N.C.; Ellisville, Mo.; Sumas, Wash.; and Lenoir, N.C. Missions are maintained in India, Nigeria, Ghana, Japan, Liberia, Croatia, New Zealand, Malaysia, the Philippines, Mexico, South Africa, Namibia, Honduras, China, Kenya, Malawi, Mozambique, Congo, Romania, and Memphis, Tenn.

The Advent Christian Church maintains doctrinal distinctives in three areas—conditional immortality, the sleep of the dead until the return of Christ, and belief that the kingdom of God will be established on earth made new by Jesus Christ.

Headquarters

P.O. Box 23152, Charlotte, NC 28227 Tel. (704) 545-6161 ext. 202 Fax (704)573-0712
Email: acpub@adventchristian.org
Website: www.adventchristian.org
Media Contact, Exec. Dir., David E. Ross

Officers

Pres., Rev. Ronald P. Thomas, 10210 229th Ln., Live Oak, FL 32064
Exec. Dir., David E. Ross
Sec., Rev. Thomas S. Warren II, 8912 Snow Hill Ln., Jacksonville, FL 32221
Appalachian Vice Pres., Rev. R. Franklin Hall, 148 Wildwood Rd. NE, Lenoir, NC 28645
Central Vice Pres., Mr. Homer Easley, 1529 Southlawn Pl., Aurora, IL 60506
Eastern Vice Pres., Rev. Glenn Rice, 130 Leighton St., Bangor, ME 04401
Southern Vice Pres., Rev. Brent Ross, 3635 Andrea Lee Ct., Snellville, GA 30278-4941
Western Vice Pres., Brad Neil, 4035 S. 275th Pl., Auburn, WA 98001
The Woman's Home & Foreign Mission Soc., Pres., Randee Davis, 2201 Old Farm Rd., Hudson, NC 28638

Periodicals

Advent Christian News, The Advent Christian Witness, Insight, Maranatha, Henceforth..., Coast to Coast on Campus, Leadership Letter, Prayer and Praise

African Methodist Episcopal Church*

This church began in 1787 in Philadelphia when persons in St. George's Methodist Episcopal Church withdrew as a protest against color segregation. In 1816 the denomination was started, led by Rev. Richard Allen who had been ordained deacon by Bishop Francis Asbury and was subsequently ordained elder and elected and consecrated bishop.

Headquarters

3801 Market St., Suite 300, Philadelphia, PA 29204 Tel. (215)662-0506

Email: Administrator@amecnet.org

Website: www.amecnet.org

Officers

Senior Bishop, Bishop John Hurst Adams, Presiding Bishop, Eleventh Episcopal District, African Methodist Episcopal Church, 101 E. Union St., Ste. 301, Jacksonville, FL 32202 Tel. (904)355-4310 Fax (904)356-1617

Chief Ecumenical & Urban Affairs Officer, Bishop Theodore Larry Kirkland, African Methodist Episcopal Church, 4519 Admiralty Way, Marina delRey, CA 90292 Tel. (310)577-8530, Fax (310)577-8540, bishopkirkland@aol.com

Pres., Gen. Bd., Bishop John Richard Bryant, Presiding Bishop, Fifth Episcopal District, African Methodist Episcopal Church, 1900 W. 48th St., Los Angeles, CA 90062 Tel. (323) 296-1487

Pres. Council of Bishops 2003-2004, Bishop Richard Allen Norris, Presiding Bishop, Fourteenth Episcopal District, African Methodist Episcopal Church, 1626 N. 72nd St., Philadelphia, 19151 Tel. (215)477-9467 Fax (215)477-0233

GENERAL OFFICERS

Dr. Clement W. Fugh; Dr. Richard Allen Norris; Dr. Kenneth H. Hill; Dr. Johnny Barbour Jr.; Dr. George F. Flowers; Dr. Dennis C. Dickerson; Dr. Jerome V. Harris; Dr. George L. Champion Sr.; Dr. Ricky Spain

Bishop Zedekiah LaZett Grady (First Episcopal Dist.); Bishop Vinton Randolph Anderson (Second Episcopal Dist.); Bishop Robert Vaughn Webster (Third Episcopal Dist.); Bishop Philip Robert Cousin Sr. (Fourth Episcopal Dist.); Bishop John Richard Bryant (Fifth Episcopal Dist.); Bishop Frank Curtis Cummings (Sixth Episcopal Dist.); Bishop Henry Allen Belin Jr. (Seventh Episcopal Dist.); Bishop Cornal Garnett Henning Sr. (Eighth Episcopal Dist.); Bishop Theodore Larry Kirkland (Ninth Episcopal Dist.); Bishop McKinley Young (Tenth Episcopal Dist.); Bishop John Hurst Adams (Eleventh Episcopal Dist.); Bishop Richard Allen Chappelle Sr. (Twelfth Episcopal Dist.); Bishop Frederick Hilborn Talbot (Thirteenth Episcopal Dist.); Bishop Richard Franklin Norris (Fourteenth Episcopal Dist.); Bishop Gregory Gerald McKinley Ingram (Fifteenth Episcopal Dist.); Bishop William Phillips DeVeaux (Sixteenth Episcopal Dist.); Bishop Preston Warren Williams (Seventeenth Episcopal Dist.); Bishop Vashti Murphy McKenzie (Eighteenth Episcopal Dist.); Bishop Adam Jefferson Richardson (Nineteenth Episcopal Dist.); Bishop Theodore Larry Kirkland (Ecumenical Officer)

Periodicals

The Christian Recorder, A.M.E. Review, Journal of Christian Education, Secret Chamber, Women's Missionary Magazine, Voice of Mission, YPD Newsletter

African Methodist Episcopal Zion Church*

The A.M.E. Zion Church is an independent body, having withdrawn from the John Street Methodist Church of New York City in 1796. The first bishop was James Varick.

Headquarters

Dept. of Records & Research, 3225 W. Sugar Creek Rd., Charlotte, NC 28269 Tel.(704)599-4630 Fax (704)688-2549

Email: jlgsa@aol.com

Media Contact, Gen. Sec-Aud., Dr. W. Robert Johnson, IIIF

BOARD OF BISHOPS
Officers

*Pres., Richard Keith Thompson, 2159 Vaughn Ln., Montgomery, AL 36106; Office: 808 S. Lawrence St., Montgomery, AL 36104-5055 Tel. (334)269-6365, Fax (334)269-6369, alflamez@Bellsouth.net; Washington address: P.O. Box 55458, Washington, D.C. 20040 Tel. (202)723-8993 Fax (202)722-1840

Sec., I. Strickland, Marshall Haywood, 2000 Cedar Circle Dr., Baltimore, MD 21228 Tel. (410)744-7330 Fax (410)788-5510

Assistant Sec., Clarence Carr, 2600 Normandy Dr., Greendale, MO 63121 Tel. (314)727-2931 Fax (314)727-0663; Office: 2645 Hord Ave., St. Louis, MO 63136 Tel. (314)867-8067

Treas., George Washington Carver Walker Sr., 137 Talcott Notch Rd., Farmington, CT 06032 Tel. (860)676-8414 Fax (860)676-8424; Mailing Address: P. O. Box 483, Farmington, CT 06034

*Note: Presidency rotates every six months according to seniority.

MEMBERS

ACTIVE

George Edward Battle Jr., 18403 Dembridge Ln., Davidson, NC 28036 Tel. (704)895-2236, gebenced@bellsouth.net; Office: Two Wachovia Center, 301 S. Tryon St., Suite 1755, Charlotte, NC 28202 Tel. (704)332-7600 Fax (704)343-3745

Cecil Bishop, 2663 Oakmeade Dr., Charlotte, NC 28270 Tel. (704) 846-9370, Fax (704)846-9371, PiedBishop@aol.com

Warren Matthew Brown, 22 Crowley Dr., Randolph, MA 02368 Tel. (781)961-2434 Fax (781)961-2939

Clarence Carr, 2600 Normandy Dr., Greendale, MO 63121 Tel. (314)727-2931 Fax (314)727-0663; Office: 2645 Hord Ave., St. Louis, MO 63136 Tel. (314)867-8067

Samuel Chuka Ekemam Sr., Office: 98 Okigwe Road, P. O. Box 1149, Owerri, Nigeria, West Africa; Home Tel. from US: (011)234-82-441-700 (1pm-5pm est) or (011)234-83-231-303 Alt. Quick Tel.: (011)234-90-500-436; Office/Fax from US: (011)234-83-232-271 amezion@infoweb.abs.net

Nathaniel Jarrett Jr., 18031 S. Pheasant Lake Dr., Tinley Park, IL 60477 Tel. (708)802-9873 Fax (708)429-3911

Joseph Johnson, 1408 Jack White Dr., Rock Hill, SC 29732 Tel. (803)328-1068, BishopJJ85@RHTC.net; Mailing Address: P.O. Box 608, Matthews, NC 28106 Fax (803)980-0793

Enoch Benjamin Rochester, Home and Office: 129 Sagebush Dr., Belleville, Il 62221 Tel. (618)257-8481 Fax (618)257-9520

I. Strickland , Marshall Hayward, 2000 Cedar Circle Dr., Baltimore, MD 21228 Tel. (410) 744-7330 Fax (410)788-5510

Richard Keith Thompson,1259 Vaughn Ln., Montgomery, AL 36106 Office: 808 S. Lawrence Street, Montgomery, AL 36104-5055 Tel. (334)269-6365, Fax (334)269-6369, alflamez@Bellsouth.net; Washington address: P.O. Box 55458, Washington, D.C. 20040, Tel. (202)723-8993 Fax (202)722-1840

George Washington Carver Walker Sr., 137 Talcott Notch Rd., Farmington, CT 06032 Tel. (860)676-8414 Fax (860)676-8424; Mailing Address: P. O. Box 483, Farmington, CT 06034

Milton Alexander Williams, 12904 Canoe Ct., Fort Washington, MD 20744 Tel. (301)292-0002 Fax (301)292-6655; Office: 8700 Central Ave., Suite 307, Landover, MD 20785 Tel. (301)499-6890 Fax (301)499-6893

RETIRED

William Alexander Hilliard, 690 Chicago Blvd., Detroit, MI 48202

John Henry Miller Sr., Springdale Estates, 8605 Caswell Court, Raleigh, NC 27612 Tel. (919) 848-6915

EPISCOPAL ASSIGNMENTS

Piedmont Episcopal District: Blue Ridge, West Central North Carolina, Western North Carolina, and Jamaica Conferences: Cecil Bishop

North Eastern Episcopal District: New England, New York, Western New York, and Bahamas Islands Conferences: George Washington Carver Walker Sr.

Mid-Atlantic II Episcopal District: East Tennessee-Virginia, India, London-Birmingham, Manchester- Midland, Philadelphia-Baltimore, Virginia and Angola Conferences: Milton A. Williams

Eastern West Africa Episcopal District: Central Nigeria, Lagos-West Nigeria, Nigeria, Northern Nigeria, Rivers, Mainland, Cross River, South Eastern, and Southern Conferences: Samuel Chuka Ekemam Sr.

Eastern North Carolina Episcopal District: Albemarle, Cape Fear, Central North Carolina, North Carolina, and Virgin Islands Conferences: George Edward Battle Jr.

South Atlantic Episcopal District: Georgia, Palmetto, Pee Dee, and South Carolina Conferences: Joseph Johnson

Alabama/Florida Episcopal District: Alabama, Cahaba, Central Alabama, North Alabama, South Alabama, West Alabama, Florida, and South Florida Conferences: Richard Keith Thompson

Mid-West Episcopal District: Indiana, Kentucky, Michigan, Missouri, Tennessee, Central Africa (Malawi and Mozambique) and South Africa Conferences: Enoch Benjamin Rochester

Mid-Atlantic I Episcopal District: Allegheny, New Jersey, Ohio, Guyana, Trinidad-Tobago, and Barbados Conferences: I. Strickland, Marshall Haywood

Western Episcopal District: Alaska, Arizona, California, Oregon-Washington, Southwest Rocky Mountain, and Colorado Conferences: Clarence Carr

Southwestern Delta: Arkansas, Louisiana, Oklahoma, South Mississippi, West Tennessee-Mississippi, and Texas Conferences: Nathaniel Jarrett Jr.

Western West Africa: Cote D'Ivore, East Ghana, Liberia, Mid-Ghana, North Ghana, Togo, and West Ghana Conferences: Warren Matthew Brown

General Officers nd Departments

Address and telephone number for all Departments (except where indicated) is 3225 W. Sugar Creek Rd., Charlotte, NC 28269 Tel. (704) 599-4630 and Mailing Address for all Departments (except where indicated) is P.O. Box 26670, Charlotte, NC 28221.

Dept. of Records and Research: Robert W. Johnson III, General Secretary-Auditor Fax (704)688-2549, j1gas@aol.com or wajohnson @amezhqtr.org

Dept. of Finance: Shirley Welch, Chief Financial Officer, Fax (704)688-2553, shwelch@amezhqtr.org

Star of Zion: Micahel Lisby, Editor, Fax (704) 688-2546, editor@thestarofzion.org.

A.M.E. Zion Quarterly Review and Historical Society: James D. Armstrong, Secretary-Editor, P.O. Box 33247, Charlotte, NC 28233 Fax (704)688-2544, jaarmstrong@amezhqtr.org

Heritage Hall, Livingstone College, Dr. Phyllis Galloway, Dir., 701 W. Monroe St., Salisbury, NC 28144 Tel. (704)216-6094

Dept. of Overseas Missions and Missionary Seer: Kermit DeGraffenreidt, Sec.-Editor, 475 Riverside Dr., Room 1935, New York, NY 10115 Tel. (212)870-2952 Fax (212)870-2808

Dept. of Brotherhood Pensions and Ministerial Relief: David Miller, Sec.-Treas., Fax (704) 599-4580, damiller@amezhqtr.org; Mailing Address: P. O. Box 217114, Charlotte, NC 28221.

Christian Education Dept.: Raymon Hunt, Gen. Sec., Fax (704)688-2550, rehunt@amezhqtr. org

Dept. of Church School Literature: Mary A. Love, Editor, Fax (704)688-2548, malove@amezhqtr.org

Dept. of Church Extension and Home Missions: Terrence J. Jones, Sec.-Treas., Fax (704)688-2552, tejones@amezhqtr.org

Bureau of Evangelism: Darryl B. Starnes, Dir., P.O. Box 217258, Charlotte, NC 28221-7258 Fax (704)688-2547, dastarnes@amezhqtr.org

Public Affairs and Convention Manager: George E.McKain II, Dir., 943 W. 1st North St., Summerville, SC 29483 Tel. (843)873-2475, Fax (843) 873-6673, Zionpagem2@aol.com, Info Line (888)496-2100

Dept. of Health and Social Concerns: Bernard Sullivan, Dir., 201 W. Franklin Blvd., Gastonia, NC 28052 Tel. (704)861-2004 Fax (704)864-7641, ststep@bellsouth.net

A.M.E. Zion Publishing House: David Miller, (Interim) Gen. Manager, Fax (704)688-2541, damiller@amezhqtr.org

JUDICIAL COUNCIL

OFFICERS

Pres., Honorable Adele M. Riley, 625 Ellsworth Dr., Dayton, Ohio 45426

George L. Blackwell, 220 N. Elm St., Williamston, NC 27892

Charlotte D. Brown, Esq. P.O. Box 4104, Salisbury, NC 28144

MEMBERS

William Clinton King Jr., Esq., 401 Wood Street, Ste. 1310, Pittsburgh, PA 15222; Home: 963 Wellesley Rd., Pittsburgh, PA 15206

Kennedy Bedford, Esq., 135 B Burton Rd., West Didsbury, Manchester M208JP, England; Home: 16 Colshaw Rd., Manchester, M23 2 QN, Manchester, England

Jewett L. Walker, 910 Bridle Path Ln., Charlotte, NC 21221

Reid R. White Jr., 6608 Cartwright Dr., Columbia, SC 29223

Neville Tucker, Esq., 865 S. Figueroa, Suite 2640, Los Angeles, CA 90017

CONNECTIONAL LAY COUNCIL

Pres., David A. Aiken Sr., 115-21 142nd St., South Ozone Park, NY 11436 Tel. (718)322-1893, Fax (718)529-6045, laypresident@worldnet.att.net

First Vice Pres., Raymond Richmond Jr., 456 Stillwood Dr., Jackson, MS 39206-5142 Tel. (601)979-2353 or (601)982-7401, raymondrichmond@ccaixjsums.edu

Second Vice Pres., Regina W. Rivera, 10828 Kilpatrick Ln., Glen Allen, VA 23059 Tel. (804)264-2689, Cell (804)306-8102, Fax (804) 264-9777, regrivera@aol.com

Sec., Mary J. Matthews, P.O. Box 3155, Sanford, NC 27331 Tel. (191)775-2058 Fax (919)499-1187

Treas., Connie Bell Beverly, 822 Polk St., Charlotte, NC 28206-2930 Tel. (704)331-9818 Fax (704)688-2552

Financial Sec., Jerry L. McCombs, P.O. Box 2718, Newton, NC 28658 Tel. (828)464-9609 Page (828)325-1910, Fax (828)466-1496, jlm-cableman@charter.net

Chaplain, Annie M. Williams, 2416 Heyward Brockington Rd., Columbia, SC 29203-9081 Tel. (803)754-8561 or (803)647-3570

Editor, *"The laity Speaks,"* Rhandi M. Stith, Carrington Arms, Apt 10L, 33 Lincoln Ave., New Rochelle, NY 10801 Tel. (914)235-3596, Fax (914)637-2518, RANDHIM@AOL.COM

Pres. Emeritus, Betty V. Stith, Carrington Arms, Apt 10L, 33 Lincoln Ave., New Rochelle, NY 10801 Tel. (914)235-3596 Fax (914)637-2518

GENERAL OFFICERS OF THE WOMAN'S HOME AND OVERSEAS MISSIONARY SOCIETY

General Pres., Dr. Adlise Ivey Porter, 14500 Abington Rd., Detroit, MI 48227 Tel. (313) 270-3280 Fax (313)270-4988

First Vice Pres., Mrs. Margie J. Bonner, 12 Eldridge St., Waterbury, CT 06704 Tel. (203) 756-1829

Second Vice Pres., Dr. Sandra L. Gaston, 1808 Heather Hill Ct., Flossmoor, Il 60422 Tel. (708)957-0114 Fax (708)957-4629

Exec. Sec., Mrs. Alice Steele Robinson, P.O. Box 26846, Charlotte, NC 28221 Tel. (704)599-4630 Fax (704)688-2554;

Recording Sec., Mrs. Vivian W. Brown, 3130 Greenvale Way, Decatur, GA 30034 Tel. (770) 593-1566

General Treas., Mrs. Elease W. Johnson, P.O. Box 25582, Charlotte, NC 28229 Tel. (704) 573-3262, Office (704)599-4630, eljohnson@amezhqtr.org

General Coordinator of YAMS, Mrs. Sandra B.

Crowder, 960 Autumn Harvest Dr., Virginia Beach, VA 23464 Tel. (757)495-8728

Sec. of Young Women, Mrs. Millicent D. Thomas, 12904 Canoe Ct., Fort Washington, MD 20744 Tel. (301)292-0002 Fax (301)292-6655

Superintendent of Buds of Promise, Mrs. Vicki L. Lewis, 110 S. Bayou Street, Mobile, AL 36602 Tel. (251)438-4945

Secretary, Bureau of Supplies, Mrs. Annette E. Whitted, P.O. Box 994, Salisbury, NC 28145 Tel. (704)633-0278 Fax (704)639-1433

Chmn., Life Members Council, Mrs. Juletha N. French, 500 State St., Mobile, AL 36603 Tel. (251)438-4096

Editor, Woman's Section, *Missionary Seer*, Mrs. Ruth J. Stevens, 1080 Lincoln Pl., Brooklyn, NY 11213 Tel. (718)604-3681 Fax (718) 604-2094

Periodicals

Star of Zion, Quarterly Review, Church School Herald, Missionary Seer, Vision Focus, Evangel

Albanian Orthodox Archdiocese in America

The Albanian Orthodox Church in America traces its origins to the groups of Albanian immigrants which first arrived in the United States in 1886, seeking religious, cultural, and economic freedoms denied them in the homeland.

In 1908 in Boston, the Rev. Fan Stylian Noli (later Archbishop) served the first liturgy in the Albanian language in 500 years, to which Orthodox Albanians rallied, forming their own diocese in 1919. Parishes began to spring up throughout New England and the Mid-Atlantic and Great Lakes states. In 1922, clergy from the United States traveled to Albania to proclaim the self-governance of the Orthodox Church in the homeland at the Congress of Berat.

In 1971 the Albanian Archdiocese sought and gained union with the Orthodox Church in America, expressing the desire to expand the Orthodox witness to America at large, giving it an indigenous character. The Albanian Archdiocese remains vigilant for its brothers and sisters in the homeland and serves as an important resource for human rights issues and Albanian affairs, in addition to its programs for youth, theological education, vocational interest programs, and retreats for young adults and women.

Headquarters

523 E. Broadway, S. Boston, MA 02127

Website: www.oca.org

Media Contact, Sec., Dorothy Adams Tel. (617) 268-1275 Fax (617)268-3184

Officers

Metropolitan Herman Tel. (617)268-1275

Chancellor, V. Rev. Arthur E. Liolin, 60 Antwerp St., East Milton, MA 02186 Tel. (617)698-3366

Lay Chpsn., William Poist, 40 Forge Village Rd., Westford, MA 01885 Tel. (978)392-0759

Treas., Cynthia Vasil Brown, 471 Capt. Eames Circle, Ashland, MA 01721 (508)881-0072

Albanian Orthodox Diocese of America

This Diocese was organized in 1950 as a canonical body administering to the Albanian faithful. It is under the ecclesiastical jurisdiction of the Ecumenical Patriarchate of Constantinople (Istanbul).

Headquarters

6455 Silver Dawn Ln., Las Vegas, NV 89118 Tel. (702)365-1989 Fax (702)365-1989

Media Contact, Rt. Rev. Bishop Ilia

Officers

Rt. Rev. Bishop Ilia, 6455 Silver Dawn Ln., Las Vegas, NV 89118 Tel. (702)365-1989 Fax (702)365-1989

The Allegheny Wesleyan Methodist Connection (Original Allegheny Conference)

This body was formed in 1968 by members of the Allegheny Conference (located in Eastern Ohio and Western Pennsylvania) of the Wesleyan Methodist Church, which merged in 1966 with the Pilgrim Holiness Church to form The Wesleyan Church.

The Allegheny Wesleyan Methodist Connection is composed of persons "having the form and seeking the power of godliness, united in order to pray together, to receive the word of exhortation, and to watch over one another in love, that they may help each other to work out their salvation." There is a strong commitment to congregational government and to holiness of heart and life. There is a strong thrust in church extension within the United States and in missions worldwide.

Headquarters

P.O. Box 357, Salem, OH 44460 Tel. (330)337-9376

Email: awmc@juno.com

Website: c1web.com/local_info/churches/aw.html

Media Contact, Pres., Rev. William Cope

Officers

Pres., Rev. William Cope, P.O. Box 357, Salem, OH 44460

Vice Pres., Rev. David Blowers, 1231 Conser Dr., Salem, OH 44460

Sec., Rev. Ray Satterfield, Rt. 4, Box 300, Salem, WV 26426

Treas., James Kunselman, 1022 Newgarden Ave., Salem, OH 44460

Periodicals

The Allegheny Wesleyan Methodist

The Alliance of Baptists*

The Alliance of Baptists is an association of individuals and churches dedicated to the preservation of historic Baptist principles, freedoms, and traditions, and to the expression of our ministry and mission through cooperative relationships with other Baptist bodies and the larger Christian community.

From its inception in early 1987, the Alliance has stood for those values that have distinguished the Baptist movement from its beginnings nearly four centuries ago—the freedom and accountability of every individual in matters of faith, the freedom of each congregation under the authority of Jesus Christ to determine its own ministry and mission, and religious freedom for all in relationship to the state.

Headquarters

1328 16th St. NW, Washington, D.C. 20036 Tel. (202)745-7609 Fax (202)745-0023

Website: www.allianceofbaptists.org

Media Contact, Exec. Dir., Rev. Dr. Stan Hastey

Officers

Exec. Dir., Rev. Dr. Stan Hastey

Assoc. Dir., Jeanette Holt

Pres., Craig Henry, Monroe, LA Tel. (318)388-4400

Vice Pres., The Rev. Shanta Premawardhana, New York, NY Tel. (212)870-2560

Sec., Mary Sue Brookshire, Atlanta, GA Tel. (404)727-3064

Periodicals

Connections

The American Association of Lutheran Churches

This church body was constituted on November 7, 1987. The AALC was formed by laity and pastors of the former American Lutheran Church in America who held to a high view of Scripture (inerrancy and infallibility). This church body also emphasizes the primacy of evangelism and world missions and the authority and autonomy of the local congregation.

Congregations of the AALC are distributed throughout the continental United States from Long Island, N.Y., to Los Angeles. The primary decision-making body is the General Convention, to which each congregation has proportionate representation.

Headquarters

The AALC National Office, 801 W. 106th Street, Ste. 203, Minneapolis, MN 55420-5630 Tel. (952)884-7784 Fax (952)884-7894

Email: aa2taalc@aol.com

Website: www.taalc.com

Media Contact, Admn. Asst. to the AALC, Rev Charles D. Eidum, 801 W. 106th Street, Ste. 203, Minneapolis, MN 55420-5630 Tel. (952)884-7784, Fax (952)884-7894, aa2taalc@ aol.com

Officers

Presiding Pastor, Rev. Thomas V. Addland, 801 W. 106th St., Ste. 203, Minneapolis, MN 55420-5630 Tel. (952)884-7784, Fax (952) 884-7894, aa2taalc@aol.com

Asst. Presiding Pastor, Rev. John A. Anderson, 310 Seventh St., Ames, IA 50010 Tel. (515) 232-3815, jjamiela@aol.com

Sec. to The AALC, Rev. Harold C. Johnson, 7001 San Antonio NE, Ste. S, Albuquerque, NM 87109 Tel. (505)828-0172, christrayof hope@juno.com

Treas., Rev. Dale Zastrow, 700 Second Ave. NE, Minot, ND 58703 Tel. (701)839-7474

Periodicals

The Evangel

The American Baptist Association

The American Baptist Association (ABA) is an international fellowship of independent Baptist churches voluntarily cooperating in missionary, evangelistic, benevolent, and Christian education activities throughout the world. Its beginnings can be traced to the landmark movement of the 1850s. Led by James R. Graves and J.M. Pendleton, a significant number of Baptist churches in the South, claiming a New Testament heritage, rejected as extrascriptural the policies of the newly formed Southern Baptist Convention (SBC). Because they strongly advocated church equality, many of these churches continued doing mission and benevolent work apart from the SBC, electing to work through local associations. Meeting in Texarkana, Tex., in 1924, messengers from the various churches effectively merged two of these major associations, the Baptist Missionary Association of Texas and the General Association, forming the American Baptist Association.

Since 1924, mission efforts have been supported in Australia, Africa, Asia, Canada, Central America, Europe, India, Israel, Japan, Korea, Mexico, New Zealand, South America, and the South Pacific. An even more successful domestic mission effort has changed the ABA from a predominantly rural southern organization to one with churches in 48 states.

Through its publishing arm in Texarkana, the ABA publishes literature and books numbering into the thousands. Major seminaries include the Missionary Baptist Seminary, founded by Dr. Ben M. Bogard in Little Rock, Ark.; Texas Baptist Seminary, Henderson, Tex.; Oxford Baptist Institute, Oxford, Miss.; and Florida Baptist Schools in Lakeland, Fla.

While no person may speak for the churches of the ABA, all accept the Bible as the inerrant Word of God. They believe Christ was the virgin-born Son of God, that God is a triune God, that the only church is the local congregation of scripturally baptized believers, and that the work of the church is to spread the gospel.

Headquarters

4605 N. State Line Ave., Texarkana, TX 75503 Tel. (903)792-2783

Email: bssc@abaptist.org

Website: www.abaptist.org

Media Contact, Steve Reeves, Public Relations Director

Officers

Pres., David Butimore, Sr., 197 W. Railto Ave., Clovis, CA 93612

Vice Pres., Neal Clark, Rt. 1, Box 48A, Daingerfield, TX 75638; John Owen, P.O. Box 142, Bryant, AR 72089; Donald R. Price, 210 West Mill St., Malvern, 72104

Recording Clerks, Larry Clements, 270 Tracy Dr., Monticello, AR 71655; Lonnie Wiggins, 1114 Occidental St., Redlands, CA 92374

Publications: Editor in Chief, Bill Johnson; Bus. Mgr., Wayne Sewell, 4605 N. State Line Ave., Texarkana, TX 75503

Meeting Arrangements Director, Edgar N. Sutton, P.O. Box 240, Alexander, AR 72002

Sec.-Treas. of Missions, Randy Cloud, P.O. Box 1050, Texarkana, TX 75504

American Baptist Churches in the USA*

Originally known as the Northern Baptist Convention, this body of Baptist churches changed the name to American Baptist Convention in 1950 with a commitment to "hold the name in trust for all Christians of like faith and mind who desire to bear witness to the historical Baptist convictions in a framework of cooperative Protestantism."

In 1972 American Baptist Churches in the USA was adopted as the new name. Although national missionary organizational developments began in 1814 with the establishment of the American Baptist Foreign Mission Society, and continued with the organization of the American Baptist Publication Society in 1824 and the American Baptist Home Mission Society in 1832, the general denominational body was not formed until 1907. American Baptist work at the local level dates back to the organization by Roger Williams of the First Baptist Church in Providence, R.I. in 1638.

Headquarters

American Baptist Churches Mission Center

P.O. Box 851, Valley Forge, PA 19482-0851 Tel. (610)768-2000 Fax (610)768-2320

Website: www.abc-usa.org

Media Contact, Dir., Office of Comm., Richard W. Schramm, Tel. (610)768-2077 Fax (610) 768-2320, richard.schramm@abc-usa.org

Officers

Pres., Margaret Johnson

Vice Pres., Arlee Griffin

Budget Review Officer, Melva Gray

Gen. Sec., A. Roy Medley, Tel. (610)768-2273, roy.medley@abc-usa.org

Assoc. Gen. Sec.-Treas., Cheryl H. Wade, Tel. (610) 768-2280, cheryl.wade@abc-usa.org

REGIONAL ORGANIZATIONS

Central Region, ABC of, Fred A. Ansell, 5833 SW 29th St., Topeka, KS 66614-2499

Chicago, ABC of Metro, Leonard Thompson, Sr., 28 E. 8765 W. Higgins Road., Ste. 240, Chicago, IL 60631

Cleveland Baptist Assoc., Dennis E. Norris, 6060 Rockside Woods Blvd., Ste. 317, Cleveland, OH 44131

Connecticut, ABC of, Lowell H. Fewster, 100 Bloomfield Ave., Hartford, CT 06105-1097

Dakotas, ABC of, Riley H. Walker, 1101 W. 22nd St., Sioux Falls, SD 57105-1699

District of Columbia Bapt. Conv., Jeffrey Haggray, 1628 16th St., NW, Washington, D.C. 20009-3099

Evergreen Baptist Association, Marcia Patton, Transitional Minister, 409 Third Ave., South Ste. A, Kent, WA 98032

Great Rivers Region, ABC of, J. Dwight Stinnett, P.O. Box 3786, Springfield, IL 62708-3786

Indiana, ABC of, Larry D. Mason, 1350 N. Delaware St., Indianapolis, IN 46202-2493

Indianapolis, ABC of Greater, Larry D. Sayre, 1350 N. Delaware St., Indianapolis, IN 46202-2493

Los Angeles, ABC of, Samuel S. Chetti, 605 W. Olympic Blvd., Ste. 700, Los Angeles, CA 90015-1426

Maine, ABC of, Alfred Fletcher, 107 Winthrop St., P.O. Box 617, Augusta, ME 04332-0667

Massachusetts, ABC of, Robert Wallace, Interim, 20 Milton St., Dedham, MA 02026-2967

Metropolitan New York, ABC of, James O. Stallings, 475 Riverside Dr., Rm. 432, New York, NY 10115-0432

Michigan, ABC of, Michael A. Williams, 4578 S. Hagadorn Rd., East Lansing, MI 48823-5396

Mid-American Baptist Churches, Marshall Peters, Ste. 15, 2400 86th St., Des Moines, IA 50322-4380

Nebraska, ABC of, Susan E. Gillies, 6404 Maple St., Omaha, NE 68104-4079

New Jersey, ABC of, Lee Spitzer, 3752 Nottingham Way, Ste. 101, Trenton, NJ 08690-3802

New York State, ABC of, William A. Carlsen, 5842 Heritage Landing Dr., East Syracuse, NY 13057-9359

Northwest, ABC of, Charles Revis, 601 S. Ross Point Road, Post Falls, ID 83854-7726

Ohio, ABC of, Robert H. Roberts, Interim, 136 N. Galway Dr., P.O. Box 376, Granville, OH 43023-0376

Oregon, ABC of, W. Wayne Brown, 0245 SW Bancroft St., Ste. G, Portland, OR 97201-4270
Pacific Southwest, ABC of the, Dale V. Salico, 970 Village Oaks Dr., Ste. 101, Covina, CA 91724-3679
Pennsylvania & Delaware, ABC of, Clayton R. Woodbury, 106 Revere Ln., Coatesville, PA 19320
Philadelphia Baptist Assoc., James E. McJankin Jr., 100 N. 17th St., Philadelphia, PA 19103-2736
Pittsburgh Baptist Assoc., Lawrence O. Swain, 429 Forbes Ave., #1620, Pittsburgh, PA 15219-1604
Puerto Rico, Baptist Churches of, Cristino Diaz-Montanez, Calle Mayaguez #21, San Juan, PR 00917
Rhode Island, ABC of, Donald R. Rasmussen, P.O. Box 330, Exeter, RI 02822
Rochester-Genesee Region, ABC of, Alan Newton, 151 Brooks Ave., Rochester, NY 14619-2454
Rocky Mountains, ABC of, Louise B. Barger, 3900 Wadsworth Blvd. Suite 365, Lakewood, CO 80235-2220
South, ABC of the, Walter L. Parrish, II, 5124 Greenwich Ave., Baltimore, MD 21229-2393
Vermont-New Hampshire, ABC of, Z. Allen Abbott, Wheeler Professional Park, One Oak Ridge Rd., Bldg. 3, Suite 4A, West Lebanon, NH 03784-3121
West, ABC of the, Paul D. Borden, 2420 Camino Ramon, Ste. 140, San Ramon, CA 94583-4207
West Virginia Baptist Convention, Lloyd D. Hamblin Jr., P.O. Box 1019, Parkersburg, WV 26102-1019
Wisconsin, ABC of, Arlo R. Reichter, 15330 W. Watertown Plank Rd., Elm Grove, WI 53122-2391

BOARDS

Bd. of Educational Ministries: Interim Exec. Dir., Arthur Munson; Pres., H. Jay Flu-allen
American Baptist Assembly: Green Lake, WI 54941; Pres., Kenneth P. Giacoletto
American Baptist Historical Society: 1106 S. Goodman St., Rochester, NY 14620 or P.O. Box 851, Valley Forge, PA 19482-0851; Admn. Archivist, Deborah B. VanBroekhoven; Pres., Esther Irish
American Baptist Men: Pres., Cody Pollington
American Baptist Women's Ministries: Exec. Dir., Virginia Holmstrom; Pres., Lois Chiles
Ministerial Leadership Commission: Exec. Dir., Ivan George
Bd. of Intl. Ministries: Exec. Dir., Hector Cortez; Pres., Kirkpatrick Cohall
Bd. of Natl. Ministries: Exec. Dir., Aidsand F. Wright-Riggins; Pres., Susan Maybeck
Ministers & Missionaries Benefit Bd.: Exec. Dir., Sumner M. Grant; Pres., George Tooze, 475 Riverside Dr., New York, NY 10115
Minister Council: Dir., Carole (Kate) H. Harvey; Pres., Joseph Kutter

Periodicals

Tomorrow Magazine, The Secret Place, American Baptist Quarterly, American Baptists In Mission

The American Carpatho-Russian Orthodox Greek Catholic Church

The American Carpatho-Russian Orthodox Greek Catholic Church is a self-governing diocese that is in communion with the Ecumenical Patriarchate of Constantinople. The late Patriarch Benjamin I, in an official Patriarchal Document dated Sept. 19, 1938, canonized the Diocese in the name of the Orthodox Church of Christ.

Headquarters

312 Garfield St., Johnstown, PA 15906 Tel. (814) 539-4207 Fax (814)536-4699
Email: archdiocese@goarch.org
Website: www.goarch.org
Media Contact, Chancellor, V. Rev. Protopresbyter Frank P. Miloro Tel. (814)539-8086 Fax (814) 536-4699

Officers

Bishop, Metropolitan Nicholas Smisko, 312 Garfield St., Johnstown, PA 15906 Tel. (814)539-4207 Fax (814)536-4699
Chancellor, V. Rev. Protopresbyter Frank P. Miloro, 127 Chandler Ave., Johnstown, PA 15906 Tel. (814)539-9143, Fax (814)536-4699, acrod@helicon.net
Treas., V. Rev. Protopresbyter Ronald A. Hazuda, 115 East Ave., Erie, PA 16503 Tel. (814)453-4902

Periodicals

The Church Messenger

American Evangelical Christian Churches

Founded in 1944, the AECC is composed of individual ministers and churches who are united in accepting "Seven Articles of Faith." These seven articles are—the Bible as the written word of God, the Virgin birth, the deity of Jesus Christ, Salvation through the atonement, guidance of our life through prayer, the return of the Saviour, and the establishment of the Millennial Kingdom.

The American Evangelical Christian Churches offers the following credentials—Certified Christian Worker, Commission to Preach, Licensed Minister, and Ordained Minister—to those who accept the Seven Articles of Faith, who put unity in Christ first, and are approved by AECC. AECC seeks to promote the gospel through its ministers, churches, and missionary activities.

Churches operate independently with all decisions concerning local government left to the individual churches. The organization also has ministers in Canada, England, Bolivia, Philippines Thailand, Brazil, and South America.

Headquarters

P.O. Box 47312, Indianapolis, IN 46227 Tel. (863)314-9370 Fax (863)314-9570
Email: alpha@strato.net
Website: www.aeccministries.com
Media Contact, International Mod., Dr. Otis O. Osborne, 51 Wells Rd., Barton, NY 13734-1818

Officers

INTERNATIONAL OFFICERS

Mod., Dr. Charles Wasielewski, Box 51, Wells Rd., Barton, NY 13734 Tel. (607)565-4074
Sec., Dr. Gene McClain, 520 Blooming Pike, Morgantown, IN 46160 Tel. (812)597-5021
Treas., Dr. Michael Ward Sr., 4802 Chervil Ct., Indianapolis, IN 46237 Tel. (317)888-2095
Bd. Member, Dr. Allen Kent, 550 E. Shoeline Drive, Long Beach, CA 90802 Tel. (562)590-7294
Bd. Member, Dr. David Burgess, 5420 Caribbean Pl., Jonesboro, AR 72404 Tel. (870)802-1010

REGIONAL MODERATORS

Northwest Region, Rev. Alvin House, P.O. Box 393, Darby MT 59829 Tel. (406)821-3141
Central-West Region, Rev. Charles Clark, Box 314, Rockport, IL 62370 Tel. (217)437-2507
Far West Region, Pastor Richard Cuthbert, 1195 Via Serville, Cathedral City, CA 92234 Tel. (706)321-6682
Lowell Ford, 397 Shamrock Ln., Newark, OH, 43055 Tel. (614)309-3419
Northeast Region, Rev. John Merrill, P.O. Box 183, East Smithfield, PA 18817 Tel. (717)596-4598
East Region, James R. Brown, 17404 W. Washington, Hagerstown, MD 21740 Tel. (301)797812f1
Southeast Region, Rev. James Fullwood, 207 5th Avenue NE, Lutz, FL 33549

STATE MODERATORS

Rev. James Brown, Maryland
Rev. John W. Coats, Delaware
Brenda Osborne, New York
Dr. Berton G. Heleine, Illinois
Rev. R. Eugene Hill, New Jersey
Rev. Kenneth Pope, Washington
Rev. Art Mirek, Michigan
Rev. Charles Jennings, Pennsylvania
Rev. Jerry Myers, Indiana

FOREIGN OUTREACH MINISTRIES

American Evangelical Christian Churches–Canada:
Regional Moderator, Dr. Stephen K. Massey, 730 Ontario St., Suite 709, Toronto, Ontario M4X 1N3, Canada Tel. (416)323-9076
Philippine Evangelical Christian Churches:
Dir., Rev. Alan A. Olubalang, P.O. Box 540, Cotabato City, Philippines 9600
American Evangelical Christian Churches–Philippines:
Regional Moderator, Rev. Oseas Andres, P.O. Box 2695, Central Post Office, 1166 Q.C. Metro Manila, Philippines 430-6549

Periodicals

The American Evangelical Christian Churches Newsletter (Monthly)

American Rescue Workers

Major Thomas E. Moore was National Commander of Booth's Salvation Army when a dispute flared between Booth and Moore. Moore resigned from Booth's Army and, due to the fact that Booth's Army was not incorporated at the time, Moore was able to incorporate under said name. The name was changed in 1890 to American Salvation Army. In 1913 the current name, American Rescue Workers, was adopted.

It is a national religious social service agency which operates on a quasimilitary basis. Membership includes officers (clergy), soldiers/adherents (laity), members of various activity groups, and volunteers who serve as advisors, associates and committed participants in ARW service functions.

The motivation of the organization is the love of God. Its message is based on the Bible. This is expressed by its spiritual Ministry, the purposes of which are to preach the gospel of Jesus Christ and to meet human needs in his name without discrimination. It is a branch of the Christian Church... A Church with a Mission.

Headquarters

Operational Headquarters, 25 Ross St., Williamsport, PA 17701 Tel. (570)323-8693 Fax (570) 323-8694
National Field Office, 1209 Hamilton Blvd., Hagerstown, MD 21742 Tel. (301)797-0061
Email: amerscwk@pcspower.net
Website: www.arwus.com
Media Contact, Natl. Communication Sec./Natl Special Services Dir., Col. Robert N. Coles, Rev., Natl. Field Ofc. Fax (301)797-1480

Officers

Commander-In-Chief & Pres. Of Corp., General Claude S. Astin Jr., Rev
Chief of Staff, Col. Larry D. Martin
Natl. Bd. Pres., Col. George B. Gossett, Rev.
Ordination Committee, Chpsn., Gen. Paul E. Martin, (Emeritus) Rev.
Natl. Chief Sec., Major Dawn R. Astin, NQ-643 Elmira St., Williamsport, PA 17701

Periodicals

The Rescue Herald (Editor-in-Chief, Col. Robert N. Cole, Rev).

The Antiochian Orthodox Christian Archdiocese of North America*

The spiritual needs of Antiochian faithful in North America were first served through the Syro-Arabian Mission of the Russian Orthodox

Church in 1895. In 1895, the Syrian Orthodox Benevolent Society was organized by Antiochian immigrants in New York City. Raphael Hawaweeny, a young Damascene clergyman serving as professor of Arabic language at the Orthodox theological academy in Kazan, Russia, came to New York to organize the first Arabic-language parish in North America in 1895, after being canonically received under the omophorion of the head of the Russian Church in North America. Saint Nicholas Cathedral, now located at 355 State St. in Brooklyn, is considered the "mother parish" of the Archdiocese.

On March 12, 1904, Hawaweeny became the first Orthodox bishop to be consecrated in North America. He traveled throughout the continent and established new parishes. The unity of Orthodoxy in the New World, including the Syrian Greek Orthodox community, was ruptured after the death of Bishop Raphael in 1915 and by the Bolshevik revolution in Russia and the First World War. Unity returned in 1975 when Metropolitan Philip Saliba of the Antiochian Archdiocese of New York and Metropolitan Michael Shaheen of the Antiochian Archdiocese of Toledo, Ohio, signed the Articles of Reunification, ratified by the Holy Synod of the Patriarchate. Saliba was recognized as the Metropolitan Primate and Shaheen as Auxiliary Archbishop. A second auxiliary to the Metropolitan, Bishop Antoun Khouri, was consecrated at Brooklyn's Saint Nicholas Cathedral, in 1983. A third auxiliary, Bishop Basil Essey was consecrated at Wichita's St. George Cathedral in 1992. Two additional bishops were added in 1994, Bishop Joseph Zehlaoui and Bishop Demetri Khoury.

The Archdiocesan Board of Trustees (consisting of 60 elected and appointed clergy and lay members) and the Metropolitan's Advisory Council (consisting of clergy and lay representatives from each parish and mission) meet regularly to assist the Primate in the administration of the Archdiocese. Currently, there are 240 parishes and missions in the Archdiocese.

Headquarters

358 Mountain Rd., Englewood, NJ 07631 Tel. (201)871-1355 Fax (201)871-7954

Email: FrJoseph@antiochian.org

Website: www.antiochian.org

Media Contact, Father Thomas Zain, 52 78th St., Brooklyn, NY 11209 Tel. (718)748-7940 Fax (718)855-3608

Officers

Primate, Metropolitan Philip Saliba, 358 Mountain Rd., Englewood, NJ 07631

Auxiliary, Bishop Antoun Khouri, 358 Mountain Rd., Englewood, NJ 07631

Auxiliary, Bishop Joseph Zehlaoui, 454 S. Lorraine Blvd., Los Angeles, CA 90020

Auxiliary, Bishop Basil Essey, 1559 N. Woodlawn, Wichita, KS 67208

Auxiliary, Bishop Demetri Khoury, 2656 Pemberton Dr., Toledo, OH 43606

Periodicals

The Word, Again Magazine

Apostolic Catholic Assyrian Church of the East, North American Dioceses

The Holy Apostolic Catholic Assyrian Church of the East is the ancient Christian church that developed within the Persian Empire from the day of Pentecost. The Apostolic traditions testify that the Church of the East was established by Sts. Peter, Thomas, Thaddaeus, and Bartholomew from among the Twelve and by the labors of Mar Mari and Aggai of the Seventy. The Church grew and developed carrying the Christian gospel into the whole of Asia and islands of the Pacific. Prior to the Great Persecution at the hands of Tamer'leng the Mongol, it is said to have been the largest Christian church in the world.

The doctrinal identity of the church is that of the Apostles. The church stresses two natures and two Qnume in the One person; Perfect God/Perfect man. The church gives witness to the original Nicene Creed, the Ecumenical Councils of Nicea and Constantinople, and the church fathers of that era. Since God is revealed as Trinity, the appellation "Mother of God" is rejected for the "Ever Virgin Blessed Mary Mother of Christ." We declare that she is Mother of Emmanuel, God with us!

The church has maintained a line of Catholicos Patriarchs from the time of the Holy Apostles until this present time. Today, the present occupant of the Apostolic Throne is His Holiness Mar Dinkha IV, 120th successor to the See of Selucia Ctestiphon.

Headquarters

Catholicos Patriarch, His Holiness Mar Dinkha, IV, Metropolitanate Residence, The Assyrian Church of the East, Baghdad, Iraq

Email: ABSoro@aol.com

Website: www.cired.org/ace.html

Media Contact, Rev. Chancellor C. H. Klutz, 7201 N. Ashland, Chicago, IL 60626 Tel. (773)465-4777 Fax (773)465-0776

BISHOPS–NORTH AMERICA

Diocese Eastern USA, His Grace Bishop Mar Aprim Khamis, 8908 Birch Ave., Morton Grove, IL 60053 Tel. (847)966-0617 Fax (847)966-0012; Chancellor to the Bishop, Rev. Chancellor C. H. Klutz, 7201 N. Ashland, Chicago, IL 60626 Tel. (773)465-4777 Fax (773)465-0776

Diocese Western USA, -vacant-, St. Joseph Cathedral, 680 Minnesota Ave., San Jose, CA 95125 Tel. (408)286-7377 Fax (408)286-1236

Diocese of Canada, His Grace Bishop Mar Emmanuel Joseph, St. Mary Cathedral, 57 Apted Ave., Weston, ON M9L 2P2 Tel. (416)744-9311

Comm. on Inter-Church & Religious Ed., His Grace Bishop Mar Bawai, Diocese of Seattle in WA, 165 NW 65th, Seattle, WA 98117 Tel. (206)789-1843

Periodicals

Qala min M'Dinkha (Voice from the East)

Apostolic Catholic Orthodox Church

The Apostolic Catholic Orthodox Church (ACOC) is a communion of persons gathered for worship and public ministry outreach within the Christian Apostolic tradition. The ACOC is creedal, renewal-oriented, and is a part of the autocephalous (self-ruling) Old Catholic Movement, which has its origins in the ancient Catholic Church of the Netherlands. The immediate history of the Old Catholic churches comes out of the reform movement that took place after the First Vatican Council (1869-70). The ACOC maintains a friendly relationship with the Old Catholic Church in the Netherlands.

The bishops of the newly forming churches received episcopal consecration in valid Apostolic lines from the church of the Netherlands, based in Utrecht, which had been a fully autonomous Catholic church. These churches became known as "Old Catholic" in reference to their insistence upon return to the basic tenets of Apostolic Christianity, and as defined by the seven Ecumenical Councils of the undivided Eastern and Western Christian churches.

The Old Catholic independent church movement came to the United States as early as the 1880's. Bishop DeLandes Berghes, an Austrian nobleman, ordained and consecrated a bishop with valid Old Catholic Apostolic lines, was sent to North America in 1914. The ACOC derives its lines of Apostolic Succession from two of the bishops he consecrated in 1916, Carmel Henry Carfora and William Francis Brothers.

The Apostolic Catholic Orthodox Church finds matters of discipline, administration, and procedure to be important, but not as essential as matters of faith. For example, clerical celibacy (which is a matter of discipline) is optional among Old Catholics. In the ACOC, Holy Orders are open to both women and men, single or married.

Matters of faith in the Apostolic Catholic Orthodox Church are the same as in most other liturgical churches. For example, the Offices of bishop, priest, and deacon exist for the service of spiritual leadership in facilitating expressions of life with God—in the celebration of the sacraments, counseling and pastoral care, teaching, and public advocacy of Gospel values. The sacraments are never denied to any person on grounds of gender, race, or marital status. The Holy Eucharist is the center of worship for the ACOC and all who are baptized are welcomed at the Lord's Table.

The Apostolic Catholic Orthodox Church emphasizes the importance of the life of the church as community, that all may be one in Christ (John 17), through mutual helpfulness, ministering to one another and all creation in love, through the diversity of personal giftedness and sensitivity to the particular needs of those being served. The church values and promotes spiritually based, courageous, and compassionate ministry to both personal and global needs. Ongoing spiritual growth is to be nourished through sacred study and contemplative prayer. The ACOC values ecumenical dialogue as an expression of the life of the church.

Headquarters

7100 Regency Sq., Suite 210, Houston, TX 77036-3202 Tel (713)266-2456 or (713)977-2855 Fax(713)266-0855

Officers

Presiding Bishop, Most Rev. Diana C. Dale, 7100 Regency Sq., Suite 210, Houston, TX 77036 Tel (713)266-2456

Treas., Elizabeth F. Burleigh, J.D., 7100 Regency Sq., Suite 212, Houston, TX 77036 Tel (713) 334-0499

Ecumenical Officer, Very Rev. Robert L. Lewis Jr., P.O. Box 6482, Plymouth, MA 02362 Tel. (508)667-1729

Register Agent, Most Rev. Lance Beizer, J.D., P.O. Box 1121, Campbell, CA 9009-1121

BOARD REGIONAL REPRESENTATIVES

West: Rev. H. Rogers Thomson, 203 E. Shoreacres Blvd., Shoreacres TX, 77571

Mid-Continent: Rev. Robert M. Palmer, 871 Stone Blvd., Nolensville, TN 37135

Atlantic: Very Rev. Robert L. Lewis Jr., P.O.Box 6482, Plymouth, MA 02362

Other Organizations: Institute of Worklife Ministry, 7100 Regency Sq., Suite 210, Houston, TX 77036-3202 Tel (713)266-2456 Fax (713)266-0855

Periodicals

ACOC Quarterly Bulletin, Worklife Quarterly Newsletter

Apostolic Christian Church (Nazarene)

This body was formed in America by an immigration from various European nations from a movement begun by Rev. S. H. Froehlich, a Swiss pastor, whose followers are still found in Switzerland and Central Europe.

Headquarters

Apostolic Christian Church Foundation, 1135 Sholey Rd., Richmond, VA 23231 Tel. (804) 222-1943 Fax (804)236-0642

Media Contact, Exec. Dir., James Hodges

Officers

Exec. Dir., James Hodges

Apostolic Christian Churches of America

The Apostolic Christian Churches of America has its roots in the early 1830s in Switzerland and Samuel Froehlich, a young divinity student who had experienced a religious conversion based on the pattern found in the New Testament. The church he founded, known then as Evangelical Baptist, spread to surrounding countries. A Froehlich associate, Elder Benedict Weyeneth, established the church's first American congregation in 1847 in upstate New York. In America, where the highest concentration today is in the Midwest farm belt, the church became known as Apostolic Christian.

Church doctrine is based on a literal interpretation of the Bible, the infallible Word of God. The church believes that a true faith in Christ's redemptive work at Calvary is manifested by a sincere repentance and conversion. Members strive for sanctification and separation from worldliness as a consequence of salvation, not as a means to obtain it. Security in Christ is believed to be conditional based on faithfulness. Uniform observance of scriptural standards of holiness are stressed. Holy Communion is confined to members of the church. Male members are willing to serve in the military, but do not bear arms. The holy kiss is practiced and women wear head coverings during prayer and worship.

Doctrinal authority rests with a council of elders, each of whom serves as a local elder (bishop). Both elders and ministers are chosen from local congregations, do not attend seminary and serve without compensation. Sermons are delivered extemporaneously as led by the Holy Spirit, using the Bible as a text.

Headquarters

3420 N. Sheridan Rd., Peoria, IL 61604

Email: Questions@ApostolicChristian.org

Website: www.apostolicchristian.org/

Media Contact, Sec., William R. Schlatter, 14834 Campbell Rd., Defiance, OH 43512 Tel. (419) 393-2621, Fax (419)393-2144, wrschlatter@juno.com

Officers

Sec., Elder (Bishop) William R. Schlatter, 14834 Campbell Rd., Defiance, OH 43512 Tel. (419)393-2621 Fax (419)393-2144

Periodicals

The Silver Lining

Apostolic Episcopal Church

On Sept. 23-24, 2000 in New York City, The Apostolic Episcopal Church signed Concordats of Intercommunion with the following Christian Churches—The Anglican Independent Communion, The Ethiopian Orthodox Coptic Archdiocese of North and South America, The Uniate Western Orthodox Catholic Church, and the Byelorussian Orthodox National Church in Exile under the administration of His Beatitude Yury I.

In effect, the Apostolic Episcopal Church thus became a Uniate Western Rite of the Orthodox Church of the East, using the 1928 Book of Common Prayer. In 1905, under the guidance of Archbishop Tikhon Bellavin (later Patriarch of Moscow), the Holy Synod in St. Petersburg approved the use of the Anglican Liturgy for Western Rite Orthodox Christians. Today this usage is called the Rite of St. Tikhon and is in use among many Orthodox Western Rite Jurisdictions.

This Pilgrimage to Orthodoxy among Anglicans began in 1712 with the Non-Jurors Anglican Hierarchy and faithful. These Non-Jurors were Anglican Clergy who in 1689 refused allegiance to King William III and Queen Mary, the usurpers who had overthrown King James II. In 1712 Metropolitan-Bishop Arsenios of the Alexandrine Patriarchate visited England and received many of these "British Katholicks" into the Orthodox Church.

Headquarters

World Mission HQS and the Editorial Office of the Tover of St. Cassian: 80-46 234 St. Jamaica, NY 11427-2116, Attn. Editor: the Rt. Rev. Francis C. Spataro DD Tel. (718)740-4134

The Province of Guyana and the Caribbean, c/o The Rev. Lloyd U. Samuel OCR, P.O. Box 10844, Georgetown, Guyana, South America 630875.

Ohio OCR Vicariate: the V. Rev. Michael B. Reed, St. Peter the Aleut Mission, 3423 Hunter Dr., N. Olmstead, OH 44070 Tel. (216)779-0272

Queens, NY, OCR Vicariate: the Rev. Pedro Bravo-Guzman, AIELC, POB 2465, Astoria, NY 11102

Belgium Mission: St. Michael's, Domein Fort 3, Frans Beirenlaan 2A, 2150 Borsbeek, Belgium

Email: osbm_ny@yahoo.com

Website: www.cinemaparallel.com/AECSynod.html and http://netministries.org/see/churches/ch04671

Media Contact, The Rt. Rev. Paget E.J. Mack OSBM, P.O. Box 170234, Brooklyn, NY 11217-0234 Tel. (718)622-0072

Officers

Pres., The Rt. Rev. Francis C. Spataro, DD, OCR

Diocesan Bishop, The Rt. Rev. Paget E.J.Mack, OSBM, OCR

AIELC Visitor, The Rt. Rev. Peter P. Brennan, OCR

Vicar for Guyana & the Caribbean, Rev Lloyd U. Samuel, OCR

Vicar for Ohio, The V. Rev. Michael B. Reed, OCR

Vicar for Queens, NY, The Rev. Pedro Bravo-Guzman, OCR

International Primate for the OCR, The M. Rev. Bertil Persson, THD, OCR

Belgium Mission, The Rt. Rev. Walter M. C. Walgraeve, OCR

The Order of Corporate Reunion; The Vilatte Guild/Society of St. Cassian

Periodicals

The Tover of St. Cassian

Apostolic Faith Mission Church of God

The Apostolic Faith Mission Church of God was founded and organized July 10, 1906, by Bishop F. W. Williams in Mobile, Ala.

Bishop Williams was saved and filled with the Holy Ghost at a revival in Los Angeles under Elder W. J. Seymour of The Divine Apostolic Faith Movement. After being called into the ministry, Bishop Williams went out to preach the gospel in Mississippi, then moved on to Mobile.

On Oct. 9, 1915, the Apostolic Faith Mission Church of God was incorporated in Mobile under Bishop Williams, who was also the general overseer of this church.

Headquarters

Ward's Temple, 806 Muscogee Rd., Cantonment, FL 32533

Media Contact, Natl. Sunday School Supt., Bishop Thomas Brooks, 3298 Toney Dr., Decatur, GA 30032 Tel. (404)284-7596

BOARD OF BISHOPS

Presiding Bishop, Donice Brown, 2265 Welcome Cir., Cantonement, FL 32535 Tel. (904)968-5225

Bishop T.C. Tolbert Sr., 226 Elston Ave., Anniston, AL, 36201; Bishop John Crum, 4236 Jackson St., Birmingham, AL 35217; Bishop Samuel Darden, 25 Taunton Ave., Hyde Park, MA 02136; Bishop James Truss, P.O. Box 495, Lincoln, AL 35096; Bishop T.C. Tolbert Jr., 768 Grayton Rd., Ohatchee, AL 36271; Bishop Thomas Brooks, 3298 Toney Drive, Decatur, GA 30032 Tel. (404)284-7596 Fax (404)284-7173; Bishop Jonny Cunningham, P.O. Box 472, Century, FL 32535 Tel. (850) 256-2443

NATIONAL DEPARTMENTS

Missionary Dept., Pres., Rosa Tolbert, Anniston, AL

Youth Dept., Pres., Johnny Kennedy, Birmingham, AL

Sunday School Dept., Supt., Thomas Brooks, Decatur, GA

Mother Dept., Pres., Mother Bessie Davis, 1003 Northeast St., Pensacola, FL 32501

INTERNATIONAL DEPARTMENTS

Monrovia, Liberia: Bishop Beter T. Nelson, Box 3646, Bush Rhode Islane, Monrovia, Liberia

Periodicals

The Three-Fold Vision (quarterly)

Apostolic Faith Mission of Portland, Oregon

The Apostolic Faith Mission of Portland, Oreg., was founded in 1907. It had its beginning in the Latter Rain outpouring on Azusa Street in Los Angeles in 1906.

Some of the main doctrines are: justification by faith which is a spiritual new birth, as Jesus told Nicodemus and as Martin Luther proclaimed in the Great Reformation; sanctification, a second definite work of grace; the Wesleyan teaching of holiness; and the baptism of the Holy Ghost as experienced on the Day of Pentecost and again poured out at the beginning of the Latter Rain revival in Los Angeles.

Mrs. Florence L. Crawford, who had received the baptism of the Holy Ghost in Los Angeles, brought this Latter Rain message to Portland on Christmas Day 1906. It has spread to the world by means of literature which is still published and mailed everywhere without a subscription price. Collections are never taken in the meetings and the public is not asked for money.

Camp meetings have been held annually in Portland, Oreg. since 1907, with delegations coming from around the world.

Missionaries from the Portland headquarters have established churches in Korea, Japan, the Philippines and many countries in Africa.

Headquarters

6615 SE 52nd Ave., Portland, OR 97206 Tel. (503)777-1741 Fax (503)777-1743

Media Contact, Superintendent, Darrel D. Lee

Website: www.apostolicfaith.org

Officers

President, Rev. Darrel D. Lee

Periodicals

Higher Way

Apostolic Lutheran Church of America

Organized in 1872 as the Solomon Korteniemi Lutheran Society, this Finnish body was incorporated in 1929 as the Finnish Apostolic Lutheran Church in America and changed its name to Apostolic Lutheran Church of America in 1962.

This body stresses preaching the Word of God. There is an absence of liturgy and formalism in worship. A seminary education is not required of pastors. Being called by God to preach the Word is the chief requirement for clergy and laity. The church stresses personal absolution and forgiveness of sins, as practiced by Martin Luther, and the importance of bringing converts into God's kingdom.

Headquarters

P.O. Box 2948, Battle Ground, WA 98604-2948

Website: www.apostolic-lutheran.org

Media Contact, Secretary, Ivan M. Seppala

Officers

Chmn., Richard C. Juuti, RRI, Bentley, AB T0C 0J0, Canada

Treas., Ben Johnson, 98920 Keller Rd., Astoria, OR 97103

Sec., Ivan M. Seppala, 332 Mt. Washington Way, Clayton, CA 94517

Periodicals

Christian Monthly

Apostolic Orthodox Catholic Church of North America

Also, legally known as the American Orthodox Catholic Church. The Christian Church was established by the Lord Jesus Christ and His Holy Apostles in Jerusalem in 33 A.D. From Jerusalem, the Church spread to other centers of the known world, including Constantinople (founded in 37 A.D.) and Kiev (45 A.D.), founded by St. Andrew the First-Called Holy Apostle. In 864, missionaries of the Church of Constantinople further extended the Orthodox Christian Faith in present-day Russia. In 988, Russia's Prince Vladimir converted and declared Orthodoxy the State religion, while hundreds of thousands were baptized in the Dnieper River at Kiev. The resulting Russian Orthodox Church became the greatest safe-guard and body of Orthodox Christians in the world.

The history of American Orthodox Catholic Christianity began in 1794 when Russian Orthodox Church missionaries established the first Orthodox mission on North American soil at present-day Kodiak, Alaska. Their missionary efforts continued down the Pacific coast in 1824, then across the whole continent. Being the canonical founder of Orthodox Christianity in North America, the Russian Orthodox Church maintained and presided over all Orthodox missions, churches, and Christians throughout North America without question or challenge for over 100 years. However, the 1917 Bolshevik Revolution, which resulted in severe persecution and imprisonment of the Russian Orthodox Mother Church, also resulted in the unrestrained rise of old-country nationalism and great ethnic turbulence between Orthodox Catholic Christians and their churches in North America. They seperated and divided, often violently, along ethnic and nationalist lines, with each creating their own old-world ethnic administrations. The once long-held unity and single Orthodox Church canonical administration in North America was destroyed.

The Apostolic Orthodox Catholic Church (AOCC) is canonically independent and indigenous to North America and comprised of bishops, clergy, and faithful, possessing unbroken Apostolic Succession since the time of Jesus Christ's appointment of His Twelve Holy Apostles to the present day through American Orthodoxy's Luminary and Defender, Russian Orthodox Prelate-Archbishop Aftimios Ofiesh of Blessed Memory.

The AOCC maintains unquestionable, canonical Apostolic Succession passed on to its bishops through its Russian Orthodox Mother Church by Archbishop Aftimios Ofiesh, his succeeding Bishops Sophronios Beshara and Christopher Contogeorge, their legal successors and through consecrating support of such memorable Orthodox leaders as Russian Patriarchal Exarch of North America Metropolitan Benjamin Fedchenkov and Albanian Orthodox Church Metropolitan Theophan Noli. In 1945, the Apostolic Succession and Canonicity of these bishops "and their successors" were declared in binding agreement to be unquestionable, valid, authentic, and independent by the Orthodox Church Ecumenical Patriarchate of Constantinople, and recognition was furthermore attested to in 1951. English-speaking and non-ethnic restrictive, the AOCC's further validity is evidenced by its life, mind, discourse, and teaching all being governed and directed in accordance with the Sacred Canons of the Most Ancient Holy Orthodox Catholic Church. The AOCC embraces the ideals and theology of Orthodoxy and freedom which Archbishop Aftimios Ofiesh stood for, taught, and passed on by selfless devotion and love for Christ and His Church, and by his personal example.

Headquarters

AOCC Chancery, P.O. Box 1834, Glendora, CA 91740-1834 Tel. (626)335-7369

Email: aoccna.relations@usa.com

Website: www.ForMinistry.com/91740AOCCA

Media Contact, Rt. Rev. Fr. Bartimaeus, Archpriest, Ecumenical Relations Officer, 2324 9th St., South, Great Falls, MT 59405 Tel./Fax (406)452-0674

Officers

Presiding Bishop, Most Rev. Gorazd

Second-Presiding Bishop, Most Rev. Aftimios II

Bishop Sec., Most Rev. Angelo Ricci

Synod of Bishops & Dioceses

Most Rev. Gorazd (C. W. Imgram), Bishop of the Diocese of Los Angeles & Greater Pacific, P.O. Box 1834, Glendora, CA 91740-1834 Tel. (626)335-7369, cwingram@webtv.net

Most Rev. Aftimios II (L. Sinclair), Bishop of the Diocese of the Rocky Mountains & Midwest, 4696 SE Horseshoe Ct., Salem, OR 97301 Tel. (503)375-6175, BaftimII@aol.com,

Most Rev. Richard (Ingram), Bishop of the Diocese of Indiana, 2741 Edgewood Street, Portage, IN 46368-2774

Most Rev. John (Kelly), Bishop of the Diocese of New York; Federal Endorser: Military, Federal Prisons& Veteran Administration Chaplains, NC/MAF-EC/VAC National Board; 4-20 Green Way Ave., Manorville, NY 11949 Tel. (516)878-4172, Bishop-NY@webtv.net

Most Rev. Angelo (Ricci), Bishop of the Diocese of the Eastern States, 37 Shippee School House Rd., Foster, RI 02825 Tel. (401)647-2867

ADDITIONAL CHURCH

American Othordox Catholic Church (Refer to: Apostolic Orthodox Catholic Church)

SEMINARY

Holy Trinity Apostolic Orthodox Catholic Seminary, P.O. Box 1834, Glendora, CA 91740-1834

Periodicals

Carpenter's Workshop

Apostolic Overcoming Holy Church of God, Inc.

The Right Reverend William Thomas Phillips (1893-1973) was thoroughly convinced in 1912 that Holiness was a system through which God wanted him to serve. In 1916 he was led to Mobile, Ala., where he organized the Ethiopian Overcoming Holy Church of God. In April 1941 the church was incorporated in Alabama under its present title.

Each congregation manages its own affairs, united under districts governed by overseers and diocesan bishops and assisted by an executive board comprised of bishops, ministers, laymen, and the National Secretary. The General Assembly convenes annually.

The church's chief objective is to enlighten people of God's holy Word and to be a blessing to every nation. The main purpose of this church is to ordain elders, appoint pastors, and send out divinely called missionaries and teachers. This church enforces all ordinances enacted by Jesus Christ. The church believes in water baptism (Acts 2:38; 8:12; and 10:47), administers the Lord's Supper, observes the washing of feet (John 13:4-7), believes that Jesus Christ shed his blood to sanctify the people and cleanse them from all sin, and believes in the resurrection of the dead and the second coming of Christ.

Headquarters

1120 N. 24th St., Birmingham, AL 35234

Email: traydoc@mindspring.com

Media Contact, Dr. Juanita R. Arrington, Business Manager, A.O.H. Church of God Public Relations Department

Officers

Presiding Senior Bishop & Exec. Head, Rt. Rev. Jasper Roby

Periodicals

The People's Mouthpiece

Armenian Apostolic Church of America

Widespread movement of the Armenian people over the centuries caused the development of two seats of religious jurisdiction of the Armenian Apostolic Church in the World—the See of Etchmiadzin, in Armenia, and the See of Cilicia, in Lebanon.

In America, the Armenian Church functioned under the jurisdiction of the Etchmiadzin See from 1887 to 1933, when a division occurred within the American diocese over the condition of the church in Soviet Armenia. One group chose to remain independent until 1957, when the Holy See of Cilicia agreed to accept them under its jurisdiction.

Despite the existence of two dioceses in North America, the Armenian Church has always functioned as one church in dogma and liturgy.

Headquarters

Eastern Prelacy, 138 E. 39th St., New York, NY 10016 Tel. (212)689-7810 Fax (212)689-7168

Western Prelacy, 6252 Honolulu Ave., La Crecsenta, CA 91214 Tel. (818)248-7737 Fax (818)248-7745

Email: prelacy@gis.net

Website: www.armprelacy.org

Media Contact, Vazken Ghougassian

Officers

Eastern Prelacy, Prelate, Archbishop Oshagan Choloyan

Eastern Prelacy, Chpsn., Richard Sarajian, Esq.

Western Prelacy, Prelate, Archbishop Moushegh Mardirossian

Western Prelacy, Chpsn., Avo Donoyan

DEPARTMENTS

Eastern Prelacy Offices, Exec. Dir., Vazken Ghougassian

AREC, Armenian Religious Educ. Council, Exec. Coord., Deacon Shant Kazanjian

ANEC, Armenian Natl. Educ. Council, Exec. Coord., Gilda Kupelian

Periodicals

Outreach

Armenian Apostolic Church, Diocese of America*

The Armenian Apostolic Church was founded at the foot of the biblical mountain of Ararat in the ancient land of Armenia, where two of Christ's Holy Apostles, Saints Thaddeus and Bartholomew, preached Christianity. In 303 A.D. the historic Mother Church of Etchmiadzin was founded by Saint Gregory the Illuminator, the first Catholicos of All Armenians. This cathedral still stands and serves as the center of the Armenian Church. A branch of this Church was established in North America in 1889. The first church building was consecrated in 1891 in Worcester, Mass. The first Armenian Diocese was set up in 1898 by the then-Catholicos of All Armenians, Mgrditch Khrimian. Armenian immigrants built the first Armenian church in the new world in Worcester, Mass., under the jurisdiction of Holy Etchmiadzin.

In 1927, the churches and the parishes in California were formed into a Western Diocese and the parishes in Canada formed their own diocese in 1984. Other centers of major significance of the Armenian Apostolic Church are the Catholicate of Cilicia, now located in Lebanon, the Armenian Patriarchate of Jerusalem, and the Armenian Patriarchate of Constantinople.

Headquarters

Eastern Diocese, 630 Second Ave., New York, NY 10016-4885 Tel. (212)686-0710 Fax (212) 779-3558

Western Diocese, 3325 North Glenoaks Blvd., Burbank, CA 91504 Tel. (818)558-7474 Fax (818)558-6333

Canadian Diocese, 615 Stuart Ave., Outremont, QC H2V 3H2 Tel. (514)276-9479 Fax (514) 276-9960

Media Contact, Dir., Public Relations, Chris Zakian, Eastern Diocese

Officers

EASTERN DIOCESE

Primate, Archbishop Khajag Barsamian, Eastern Diocese Ofc.

Diocesan Council, Chpsn., Haig Dadourian, 415 Madison Ave., 7th Fl., New York, NY 10017

WESTERN DIOCESE

Primate, His Em. Archbishop Vatche Hovsepian, Western Diocese Ofc.

Diocesan Council, Chpsn., Dn. Dr. Varouj Altebarmakian, 7290 North San Pedro, Fresno, CA 93011

Diocesan Council, Sec., Mr. John Yaldezian, 23221 Aetna St., Woodland Hills, CA 91367 Tel. (B) (818)346-6163

CANADIAN DIOCESE

Primate, His Em. Archbishop Hovnan Derderian

Diocesan Council, Chpsn., Mr. Takvor Hopyan, 20 Pineway,Blvd., Willowdale, ON M2H 1A1, Canada Tel (B) (416)222-2639

Diocesan Council Secretary, Mr. Vahe Ketli, 750 Montpellier, # 909, St. Laurens, QC H4L 5A7, Canada Tel (R) (514)747-1347

Periodicals

The Armenian Church, The Mother Church

Assemblies of God

From a few hundred delegates at its founding convention in 1914 at Hot Springs, Ark., the Assemblies of God has become one of the largest church groups in the modern Pentecostal movement with over 40 million adherents worldwide. Throughout its existence it has emphasized the power of the Holy Spirit to change lives and the participation of all members in the work of the church.

The revival that led to the formation of the Assemblies of God and numerous other church groups early in the 20th century began during times of intense prayer and Bible study. Believers in the United States and around the world received spiritual experiences like those described in the Book of Acts. Accompanied by baptism in the Holy Spirit and its initial physical evidence of "speaking in tongues," or a language unknown to the person, their experiences were associated with the coming of the Holy Spirit at Pentecost (Acts 2), so participants were called Pentecostals.

The church also believes that the Bible is God's inspired infallible Word to man, that salvation is available only through Jesus Christ, that divine healing is made possible through Christ's suffering, and that Christ will return again for those who love him. In recent years, this Pentecostal revival has spilled over into almost every denomination in a wave of revival sometimes called the charismatic renewal.

Assemblies of God leaders credit their church's rapid and continuing growth to its acceptance of the New Testament as a model for the present-day church. Aggressive evangelism and missionary zeal at home and abroad characterize the denomination.

Assemblies of God believers observe two ordinances—water baptism by immersion and the Lord's Supper, or Holy Communion. The church is trinitarian, holding that God exists in three persons—Father, Son and Holy Spirit.

Headquarters

1445 Boonville Ave., Springfield, MO 65802 Tel. (417)862-2781 Fax (417)862-8558

Email: info@ag.org

Website: www.ag.org/top/

Media Contact, Dir. of Public Relations, Juleen Turnage Fax (417)862-5554

EXECUTIVE PRESBYTERY

Gen. Supt., Thomas E. Trask

Asst. Supt., Charles T. Crabtree

Gen. Sec., George O. Wood

Gen. Treas., James E. Bridges

World Missions, Exec. Dir., John Bueno

Home Missions, Exec. Dir., Charles Hackett

Great Lakes, Charles Crank, 8750 Purdue Rd., Indianapolis, IN 46268 Tel. (317)872-9812

Gulf, L. Alton Garrison, P.O. Box 191670, Little Rock, AR 72219 Tel. (501)568-2194

North Central, David Argue, 1111 Old Cheney Rd., Lincoln, NE 68512 Tel. (402)421-1111

Northeast, H. Robert Rhoden, P.O. Box 1045, FairFax, VA 22030 Tel. (703)273-7805

Northwest, Warren Bullock, Suite Y150, 9930 Evergreen Way, Everett, WA 98204 Tel. (425)423-0222

South Central, J. Don George, 3000 W. Airport Freeway, Irving, TX 75062

Southeast, Dan Betzer, 4701 Summerlin Rd., Ft. Myers, FL 33919 Tel. (941)936-6277

Southwest, Richard Dresselhaus, 8404 Phyllis Pl., San Diego, CA 92123 Tel. (858)560-1870

Language Area, Spanish, Jesse Miranda, 3257 Thaxton, Hacienda Heights, CA 91745 Tel.

(714)668-6196
Language Area, Other, Nam Soo Kim, 130-30 31st Ave., 4th Fl, Flushing, NY 11354 Tel. (718)321-7800
Ethnic Fellowship, Zollie Smith, P.O. Box 70, Somerset, NJ 08875

INTERNATIONAL HEADQUARTERS

Division of the Treasury, Gen. Treas., James E. Bridges
Division of Christian Education, Natl. Dir., Debrorah Gill
Division of Church Ministries, Exec. Liaison, Charles Crabtree
Division of World Missions, Exec. Dir., John Bueno
Division of Home Missions, Exec. Dir., Charles Hackett
Div. of Publication, Gospel Publishing House, Natl. Dir., Arlyn Pember

Periodicals

Enrichment–A Journal for Pentecostal Ministry, At Ease, Caring, High Adventure, Club Connection, Pentecostal Evangel, Woman's Touch, Heritage, On Course

Assemblies of God International Fellowship (Independent/ Not affiliated)

April 9, 1906 is the date commonly accepted by Pentecostals as the 20th-century outpouring of God's spirit in America, which began in a humble gospel mission at 312 Azusa St. in Los Angeles. This spirit movement spread across the United States and gave birth to the Independent Assemblies of God (Scandinavian). Early pioneers instrumental in guiding and shaping the fellowship of ministers and churches into a nucleus of independent churches included Pastor B.M. Johnson, founder of Lakeview Gospel Church in 1911; Rev. A. A. Holmgren, a Baptist minister who received his baptism of the Holy Spirit in the early Chicago outpourings, was publisher of Sanningens Vittne, a voice of the Scandinavian Independent Assemblies of God, and also served as secretary of the fellowship for many years; Gunnar Wingren, missionary pioneer in Brazil; and Arthur F. Johnson, who served for many years as chairman of the Scandinavian Assemblies.

In 1935, the Scandinavian group dissolved its incorporation and united with the Independent Assemblies of God of the US and Canada which by majority vote of members formed a new corporation in 1986, Assemblies of God International Fellowship (Independent/Not Affiliated).

Headquarters

6325 Marindustry Dr., San Diego, CA 92121 Tel. (858)677-9701 Fax (858)677-0038
Email: admin@agifellowship.org
Website: www.agifellowship.org
Media Contact, Exec. Dir. & Ed., Rev. T. A. Lanes

Officers

Exec. Dir., Rev. T. A. Lanes
Sec., Rev. George E. Ekeroth
Treas., M. J. Ekeroth
Canada, Sec., Harry Nunn, Sr., 15 White Crest Ct., St. Catherines, ON 62N 6Y1

Periodicals

The Fellowship Magazine

Associate Reformed Presbyterian Church (General Synod)

The origin of the Associate Reformed Presbyterian Church began in Scotland with the Covenanters of the 17th century and Seceder movement of the 18th. The Covenanters broke from the established Church of Scotland to eventually form separate "praying societies," which led to the Reformed Presbyterian Church of Scotland. The Seceders, about a hundred years later, became the Associate Church of Scotland.

The Associate Reformed Presbyterian Church stems form the 1782 merger of these two groups in America. In 1822 the "Synod of the South" was granted independent status from the national body. It continued to hold to the 1799 Constitution of the church with no changes, and probably consisted of around 2,000 members. The present Associate Reformed Presbyterian Church (General Synod) is the ongoing denomination resulting from that actions, the original "General Synod" of the denomination having become a part of the United Presbyterian Church.

The government is by a three-layered court system—the local "Session", the regional "Presbytery," and the national "General Synod"—each of which is composed of both ruling and teaching elders. The Standards of the denomination include the Westminster Confession of Faith, the Catechisms, and the Forms of Government, Worship, and Discipline.

Headquarters

Associate Reformed Presbyterian Center, One Cleveland St., Greenville, SC 29601-3696 Tel. (864)232-8297 Fax (864)271-3729
Email: dragondraw@aol.com
Website: www.arpsynod.org
Media Contact, Principal Clk., Rev. C. Ronald Beard, DD, 3132 Grace Hill Rd., Columbia, SC 29204 Tel. (803)787-6370.
Moderator, Mr. David Sides, One Cleveland St. Greenville, SC 29601

AGENCIES AND INSTITUTIONS
In the A.R. Presbyterian Center in Greenville:

Admn. Ser. Dir., Ed Hogan
Christian Education, Dir., Dr. David Vickery
Church Extension, Dir., Rev. James T. Corbitt, DD
Publications, Editor, E. Benton Johnston
Treas., Guy H. Smith, III

World Witness, Bd. of Foreign Missions, Exec. Sec., John E. Mariner

OTHER INSTITUTIONS

Bonclarken Assembly, Dir., James T. Brice, 500 Pine St., Flat Rock, NC 28731 Tel. (704)692-2223

Erskine College, Pres., Rev. John L. Carson, PhD, Due West, SC 29639 Tel. (864)379-8759

Erskine Theological Seminary, Dean, Ralph J. Gore Jr., PhD, Due West, SC 26939 Tel. (864) 379-8885

Periodicals

The Associate Reformed Presbyterian, The Adult Quarterly

The Association of Free Lutheran Congregations

The Association of Free Lutheran Congregations, rooted in the Scandinavian revival movements, was organized in 1962 by a Lutheran Free Church remnant which rejected merger with The American Lutheran Church. The original 42 congregations were joined by other like-minded conservative Lutherans, and there has been a sixfold increase in the number of congregations. Members subscribe to the Apostles', Nicene, and Athanasian creeds; Luther's Small Catechism; and the Unaltered Augsburg Confession. The Fundamental Principles and Rules for Work (1897) declare that the local congregation is the right form of the kingdom of God on earth, subject to no authority but the Word and the Spirit of God.

Distinctive emphases are: (1) the infallibility and inerrancy of Holy Scriptures as the Word of God; (2) congregational polity; (3) the spiritual unity of all believers, resulting in fellowship and cooperation transcending denominational lines; (4) evangelical outreach, calling all to enter a personal relationship with Jesus Christ; (5) a wholesome Lutheran pietism that proclaims the Lordship of Jesus Christ in all areas of life and results in believers becoming the salt and light in their communities; (6) a conservative stance on current social issues.

A two-year Bible school and a theological seminary are in suburban Minneapolis. The AFLC is in fellowship with sister churches in Brazil, Mexico, and India.

Headquarters

3110 E. Medicine Lake Blvd., Minneapolis, MN 55441 Tel. (763)545-5631 Fax (763)545-0079

Email: webmaster@aflc.org

Website: www.aflc.org

Media Contact, Pres., Rev. Robert L. Lee

Officers

Pres., Rev. Robert L. Lee, 3110 E. Medicine Lake Blvd. Minneapolis, MN 55441 Tel. (763)545-5631, Fax (763)545-0079, president@aflc.org

Vice Pres., Rev. Elden K. Nelson, 932 S. Candy Circle, Kandiyohi, MN 56251 Tel. (320)382-6550, efnelson@charter.net or vpres@aflc.org

Sec., Rev. Brian Davidson, 3110 E. Medicine Lake Blvd., Minneapolis, MN 55441 Tel. (763)545-5631, Fax (763)545-0079, briand@aflc.org

Periodicals

The Lutheran Ambassador

Baptist Bible Fellowship International

Organized on May 24, 1950 in Fort Worth, Tex., the Baptist Bible Fellowship was founded by about 100 pastors and lay people who had grown disenchanted with the policies and leadership of the World Fundamental Baptist Missionary Fellowship, an outgrowth of the Baptist Bible Union formed in Kansas City in 1923 by fundamentalist leaders from the Southern Baptist, Northern Baptist, and Canadian Baptist Conventions. The BBF elected W. E. Dowell as its first president and established offices and a three-year (now four-year with a graduate school) Baptist Bible College.

The BBF statement of faith was essentially that of the Baptist Bible Union, adopted in 1923, a variation of the New Hampshire Confession of Faith. It presents an infallible Bible, belief in the substitutionary death of Christ, his physical resurrection, and his premillennial return to earth. It advocates local church autonomy and strong pastoral leadership and maintains that the fundamental basis of fellowship is a missionary outreach. The BBF vigorously stresses evangelism and the international missions office reports 901 adult missionaries working on 110 fields throughout the world.

There are BBF-related churches in every state of the United States, with special strength in the upper South, the Great Lakes region, southern states west of the Mississippi, Kansas, and California. There are seven related colleges and one graduate school or seminary.

A Committee of Forty-Five, elected by pastors and churches within the states, sits as a representative body, meeting in three subcommittees, each chaired by one of the principal officers—an administration committee chaired by the president, a missions committee chaired by a vice president, and an education committee chaired by a vice president.

World Mission Service Center

Baptist Bible Fellowship Missions Bldg., 720 E. Kearney St., Springfield, MO 65803 Tel. (417)862-5001 Fax (417)865-0794; Mailing Address: P.O. Box 191, Springfield, MO 65801

Email: csbc@cherrystreet.org

Website: www.bbfi.org

Media Contact, Mission Dir., Dr. Bob Baird, P.O. Box 191, Springfield, MO 65801

Officers

Pres., Rev. Bill Monroe, P.O. Box 12809, Florence, SC 29504 Tel. (843)662-0453 Work Tel. (417)862-5001

First Vice Pres., Rev. Mike Peper, 4150 Market St., Aston, PA 19014 Tel. (610)497-0700 Work Tel. (417)862-5001

Second Vice Pres., Keith Gillming, 3025 N. Lindbergh Blvd., St. Louis, MO 63074 Tel. (314)291-6919

Sec., Rev. Don Elmore, P.O.Box 7150, Springdale, AR 72766 Tel. (479)751-4255

Treas., Rev. Ken Armstrong, 2200 Prairin St., Emporia, KS Tel. (316)342-4142

Periodicals

The Baptist Bible Tribune, The Preacher, Global Partners

Baptist General Conference

The Baptist General Conference, rooted in the pietistic movement of Sweden during the 19th century, traces its history to Aug. 13, 1852. On that day a small group of believers at Rock Island, Ill., under the leadership of Gustaf Palmquist, organized the first Swedish Baptist Church in America. Swedish Baptist churches flourished in the upper Midwest and Northeast, and by 1879, when the first annual meeting was held in Village Creek, Iowa, 65 churches had been organized, stretching from Maine to the Dakotas and south to Kansas and Missouri.

By 1871, John Alexis Edgren, an immigrant sea captain and pastor in Chicago, had begun the first publication and a theological seminary. The Conference grew to 324 churches and nearly 26,000 members by 1902. There were 40,000 members in 1945 and 135,000 in 1993.

Many churches began as Sunday schools. The seminary evolved into Bethel, a four-year liberal arts college with 1,800 students, and theological seminaries in Arden Hills, Minn. and San Diego, Calif. Missions and the planting of churches have been main objectives both in America and overseas. Today churches have been established in the United States, Canada, and Mexico, as well as twenty countries overseas. In 1985 the churches of Canada founded an autonomous denomination, The Baptist General Conference of Canada.

The Baptist General Conference is a member of the Baptist World Alliance, the Baptist Joint Committee on Public Affairs, and the National Association of Evangelicals. It is characterized by the balancing of a conservative doctrine with an irenic and cooperative spirit. Its basic objective is to seek the fulfillment of the Great Commission and the Great Commandment.

Headquarters

2002 S. Arlington Heights Rd., Arlington Heights, IL 60005 Tel. (847)228-0200 Fax (847)228-5376

Email: gmarsh@baptistgeneral.org

Website: www.bgcworld.org

Officers

Pres. & Chief Exec. Officer, Dr. Gerald Sheveland, 2002 S. Arlington Hts. Rd., Arlington Heights, IL 60005 Tel. (847)228-0200, Fax (847)228-5376, jsheveland@baptistgeneral.org

Exec, Vice-Pres., Ray Swatkowski 2002 S. Arlington Hts. Rd., Arlington Heights, IL 60005 Tel. (847)228-0200, Fax (847)228-5376, rswatkowski@baptistgeneral.org

Director of Mission Advance, Dr. Lou Petrie, 2002 S. Arlington Hts. Rd., Arlington Heights, IL 60005 Tel. (847)228-0200, Fax (847)228-5376, lpetrie@baptistgeneral.org

Director of Finance, Stephen R. Schultz, 2002 S. Arlington Hts. Rd., Arlington Heights, IL 60005 Tel. (847)228-0200, Fax (847)228-5376, sschultz@baptistgeneral.org

Director of National Ministries, Rev. Paul Johnson, 2002 S. Arlington Hts. Rd., Arlington Heights, IL 60005 Tel. (847)228-0200, Fax (847)228-5376, pauljchp@aol.com

Director of International Ministries, Dr. Ronald Larson, 2002 S. Arlington Hts. Rd., Arlington Heights, IL 60005 Tel. (847)228-0200, Fax (847)228-5376, rlarson@aol.com

OTHER ORGANIZATIONS

Bd. of Trustees, Bethel College & Seminary, Pres., Dr. George K. Brushaber, 3900 Bethel Dr., St. Paul, MN 55112

Periodicals

BGC World

Baptist Missionary Association of America

A group of regular Baptist churches organized in associational capacity in May, 1950, in Little Rock, Ark., as the North American Baptist Association. The name changed in 1969 to Baptist Missionary Association of America. There are several state and numerous local associations of cooperating churches. In theology, these churches are evangelical, missionary, fundamental, and, for the most part, premillennial.

Headquarters

9219 Sibly Hole Rd., Little Rock, AR Tel. (501) 455-4977 Fax (501)455-3636

Mailing Address: P.O. Box 193920, Little Rock, AR 72219-3920

Email: bmaam@bmaam.com

Website: www.bmaam.com

Media Contact, Dir. of Baptist News Service, Kenneth W. Vanderslice, P.O. Box 97, Jacksonville, TX 75766 Tel. (903)586-2501 Fax (903)586-0378

Officers

Pres., Ronald Morgan, 208 N. Arkansas St., Springhill, LA 71075-2704

Vice Pres., Leon J. Carmical, 85 Midway Church Rd., Sumrall, MS 39428; David T. Watkins, 1 Pineridge St., Magnolia, AR 71753

Rec. Sec., Rev. Ralph Cottrell, P.O. Box 1203, Van, TX 75790; Don J. Brown, P.O. Box 8181, Laruel, MS 39441; James Ray Raines, 5609 N. Locust, N. Little Rock, AR 72116

DEPARTMENTS

Missions, Gen. Sec., Rev. F. Donald Collins, P.O. Box 193920, Little Rock, AR 72219-3920

Publications, Ed.-in-Chief, Rev. James L. Silvey, 311 Main St., P.O. Box 7270, Texarkana, TX 75505

Christian Education, Bapt. Missionary Assoc. Theological Sem., Pres., Dr. Charley Holmes, Seminary Heights, 1530 E. Pine St., Jacksonville, TX 75766

Baptist News Service, Dir., Rev. Kenneth W. Vanderslice, P.O. Box 97, Jacksonville, TX 75766

Life Word Broadcast Ministries, Dir., Rev. George Reddin, P.O. Box 6, Conway, AR 72032

Armed Forces Chaplaincy, Exec. Dir., Bobby C. Thornton, P.O. Box 240, Flint, TX 75762

BMAA Dept. of Church Ministries, Donny Parish, P.O. Box 10356, Conway, AR 72033

Daniel Springs Encampment, James Speer, P.O. Box 310, Gary, TX 75643

Ministers Resource Services, Craig Branham, 4001 Jefferson St., Texarkana, TX 75501

OTHER ORGANIZATIONS

Baptist Missionary Assoc. Brotherhood, Pres., Bill Looney, 107 Bearskin Dr., Sherwood, AR 72120

National Women's Missionary Auxiliary, Pres., Mrs. Bill Skinner, RR1 Box 213 B, Mineola, TX 75773-9742 Tel. (903)365-2465

Periodicals

The Gleaner

Beachy Amish Mennonite Churches

The Beachy Amish Mennonite Church was established in 1927 in Somerset County, Penn. following a division in the Amish Mennonite Church in that area. As congregations in other locations joined the movement, they were identified by the same name. There are currently 97 churches in the United States, 9 in Canada and 34 in other countries. Membership in the United States is 7,059, according to the 1996 Mennonite Yearbook.

Beachy Churches believe in one God eternally existent in three persons (Father, Son, and Holy Spirit); that Jesus Christ is the one and only way to salvation; that the Bible is God's infallible Word to us, by which all will be judged; that heaven is the eternal abode of the redeemed in Christ; and that the wicked and unbelieving will endure hell eternally.

Evangelical mission boards sponsor missions in Central and South America, Belgium, Ireland, and in Kenya, Africa.

The Mission Interests Committee, founded in 1953 for evangelism and other Christian services, sponsors homes for handicapped youth and elderly people, mission outreaches among the North American Indians in Canada, and a mission outreach in Europe.

Headquarters

Media Contact, Paul L. Miller, 7809 S. Herren Rd. Partridge, KS 67566 Tel. (620)567-2286

Officers

Amish Mennonite Aid, Sec.-Treas., Vernon Miller, 2675 US 42 NE, London, OH 43140 Tel. (614)879-8616

Mission Interests Committee, Sec.-Treas., Melvin Gingerich, 42555 900W, Topeka, IN 46571 Tel. (219)593-9090

Choice Books of Northern Virginia, Supervisor, Simon Schrock, 4614 Holly Ave., FairFax, VA 22030 Tel. (703)830-2800

Calvary Bible School, HC 61, Box 202, Calico Rock, AR 72519 Tel. (501)297-8658; Sec.-Treas., Elmer Gingerich, HC 74, Box 282, Mountain View, AR 72560 Tel. (501)296-8764

Penn Valley Christian Retreat, Bd. Chmn., Wayne Schrock, RR 2, Box 165, McVeytown, PA 17015 Tel. (717)529-2935

Periodicals

The Calvary Messenger

Berean Fundamental Church Fellowship

Founded 1932 in North Platte, Nebr., this body emphasizes conservative Protestant doctrines.

Headquarters

Box 1264 Kearney, NE 68848 Tel (308)234-5374 Fax (308)234-5373

Email: office@bereanfellowship.org

Website: www.bereanfellowship.org

Media Contact, Pres., Pastor Doug Shada

Officers

Pres., Doug Shada

Vice Pres., Richard Crocker, 419 Lafayette Blvd., Cheyenne, WY 82009 Tel. (307)635-5914

Sec., Roger Daum, 1510 O Street, Cozad, NE 69130 Tel. (308)784-3675

Treas., Virgil Wiebe, P.O. Box 6103, Lincoln, NE 68506

Exec. Advisor, Curt Lehman Tel. (402)483-4840

The Bible Church of Christ, Inc.

The Bible Church of Christ was founded on March 1, 1961 by Bishop Roy Bryant Sr. Since that time, the Church has grown to include congregations in the United States, Africa, and India. The church is trinitarian and accepts the Bible as the divinely inspired Word of God. Its doctrine includes miracles of healing, deliverance, and the baptism of the Holy Ghost.

Headquarters

1358 Morris Ave., Bronx, NY 10456 Tel. (718) 588-2284 Fax (718) 992-5597
Email: bccbookstore@earthlink.net
Website: www.thebiblechurchofchrist.org
Media Contact, Pres., Bishop Roy Bryant Sr.

Officers

Pres., Bishop Roy Bryant Sr.
Sec., Mother Sissieretta Bryant
Treas., Elder Artie Burney

EXECUTIVE TRUSTEE BOARD

Chpsn., Bishop Eddie Citronnelli, 100 W. 2nd St., Mount Vernon, NY 10550 Tel. (914)664-4602
Exec. Admn., Sr. Hermenia Benjamin

OTHER ORGANIZATIONS

Bookstore, Mgr., Evangelist Beryl C. Foster Tel. (718)293-1928
Foreign Missions, Pres., Sr. Autholene Smith
Home Missions, Pres., Evangelist Mary Jackson
Min. of Education, Minister Abraham Jones
Min. of Music, Ray Crenshaw
Prison Ministry Team, Pres., Evangelist Marvin Lowe
Public Relations, Deacon Abraham Jones
Publications, Dir., Deaconess Betty Hamilton
Sunday Schools, Gen. Supt., Elder A. M. Jones
Theological Institute, Pres., Dr. Roy Bryant Sr.; Dean, Elder A. M. Jones
Vessels Unto Honor Deliverance Ministries, Pres., Evangelist Antoinette Cannaday
Women's Committee, Natl. Chpsn., Sissieretta Bryant
Youth, Pres., Deacon Tommy Robinson

Presiding Elders,
Delaware, Elder Edward Cannon, RR Box 70-B5, Daimond Acre, Dagsboro, DE 19939 Tel. (302)732-3351
Virginia, Elder jesse Alton, 221 Keith Rd., Newport News, VA 23606 Tel. (804)930-2445
Mount Vernon, Elder Artie Burney, 100 W. 2nd St., Mount Vernon, NY 10550 Tel. (914)664-4602
Bronx, Elder Anita Robinson, 1358 Morris Ave., Bronx, NY 10456 Tel. (718)588-2284
Annex, Elder Reginald Gullette, 1069 Morris Ave., Bronx, NY 10456 Tel. (718)992-4653
Schenectady, New York, Elder Monica Hope, 1132 Congress St., Schenectady, New York 12303 Tel. (518)382-5625
North Carolina, Elder Raymond Shepard, 512 W. Vernon Ave. Kinston, NC 28502 Tel. (252)527-7739
India, Dr. B. Veeraswamy, 46-7-34, Danavaya Peta, Rajahmunry, India, 533103
Haiti, Antoine Polycarpe, P.O. Box 197, Port-au-Prince, Haiti
St. Croix, Elder Floyd Thomas, 1-J Diamond Ruby, P.O. Box 5183, Sunny Isles, Christiansted, St. Croix Tel. (809)778-1002

Periodicals

The Voice, The Gospel Light, The Challenge

Bible Fellowship Church

The Bible Fellowship Church grew out of divisions in the Mennonite community in Pennsylvania in the 1850s. Traditional church leadership resisted the freedom of expression and prayer meetings initiated by several preachers and church leaders. These evangelical Mennonites formed the Evangelical Mennonite Society. Over the next two decades, various like-minded groups in Canada, Ohio, and Pennsylvania joined the Society.

In 1959 the Conference became the Bible Fellowship Church and new articles of faith were ratified. They now hold a unique combination of Reformed doctrines with insistence on "Believer Baptism" and Premillennialism.

Headquarters

Bible Fellowship Church, 3000 Fellowship Dr., Whitehall, PA 18052
Email: bfc@bfc.org
Website: www.bfc.org/
Media Contact, David J. Watkins, 2270 Little Rd., Perkiomenville, PA 18074 Tel. (610)754-7463

Officers

Chmn., William G. Schlonecker
Vice Chmn., Randall A. Grossman
Sec., David A. Thomann
Asst. Sec., Robert W. Smock

BOARDS AND COMMITTEES

Bd. of Dir., Bible Fellowship Church
Bd. of Christian Education
Bd. of Extension
Bible Fellowship Church Homes, Inc.
Bd. of Pensions
Bd. of Pinebrook Bible Conference
Bd. of Missions
Bd. of Publication and Printing
Bd. of Victory Valley Camp
Bd. of Higher Education

Periodicals

Fellowship News

Bible Holiness Church

This church came into being about 1890 as the result of definite preaching on the doctrine of holiness in some Methodist churches in southeastern Kansas. It became known as The Southeast Kansas Fire Baptized Holiness Association. The name was changed in 1945 to The Fire Baptized Holiness Church and in 1995 to Bible Holiness Church. It is entirely Wesleyan in doctrine, episcopal in church organization, and intensive in evangelistic zeal.

Headquarters

304 Camp Dr., Independence, KS 67301 Tel. (316)331-3049
Media Contact, Gen. Supt., Leroy Newport

Officers

Gen. Supt., Leroy Newport

Gen. Sec., Wayne Knipmeyer, Box 457, South Pekin, IL 61564
Gen. Treas., Robert Davolt, 523 2nd St., Oswego, KS 67356

Periodicals

The Flaming Sword, John Three Sixteen

Bible Way Church of Our Lord Jesus Christ World Wide, Inc.

This body was organized in 1957 in the Pentecostal tradition for the purpose of accelerating evangelistic and foreign missionary commitment and to effect a greater degree of collective leadership than leaders found in the body in which they had previously participated.

The doctrine is the same as that of the Church of Our Lord Jesus Christ of the Apostolic Faith, Inc., of which some of the churches and clergy were formerly members.

This organization has churches and missions in Africa, England, Guyana, Trinidad, and Jamaica, and churches in 25 states in America. The Bible Way Church is involved in humanitarian as well as evangelical outreach with concerns for urban housing, education, and economic development.

Headquarters

4949 Two-Notch Rd., Columbia, SC 29204 Tel. (800)432-5612 Fax (803)691-0583
Email: mr.ed5strings@worldnet.att.net
Website: www.biblewaychurch.org
Media Contact, Chief Apostle, Presiding Bishop Huie Rogers

Officers

Presiding Bishop, Bishop Huie Rogers, 4949 Two Notch Rd., Columbia, SC 29204 Tel. (800)432-5612 Fax (803)691-0583
Gen. Sec., Bishop Edward Williams, 5118 Clarendon Rd., Brooklyn, NY 11226 Tel. (718)451-1238

Brethren in Christ Church

The Brethren in Christ Church was founded in Lancaster County, Penn. in about the year 1778 and was an outgrowth of the religious awakening which occurred in that area during the latter part of the 18th century. This group became known as "River Brethren" because of their original location near the Susquehanna River. The name "Brethren in Christ" was officially adopted in 1863. In theology they have accents of the Pietist, Anabaptist, Wesleyan, and Evangelical movements.

Headquarters

General Church Office, P.O. Box A, Grantham, PA 17027 Tel. (717)697-2634 Fax (717)697-7714
Email: RRoss@BIC-church.org
Website: www.bic-church.org/index.htm
Media Contact, Dr. Warren L. Hoffman, Mod., Tel. (717)697-2634 Fax (717)697-7714

Officers

Dr. Warren L. Hoffman, Mod., P.O. Box A, Grantham, PA 17027 Tel. (717)697-2634 Fax (717)697-7714
Dr. Kenneth O. Hoke, Gen. Sec., P.O. Box A, Grantham, PA 17027 Tel. (717)697-2634 Fax (717)697-7714
Elizabeth Brown, Treas., P.O. Box A, Grantham, PA 17027 Tel. (717)697-2634 Fax (717)697-7714.

OTHER ORGANIZATIONS

General Conference Board: Chpsn., Dr. Mark Garis, 504 Swartley Rd., Hatfield, PA 19440
Bd. for World Missions: Chair, Dr. Grace Holland, 21A Junction Rd., Dillsburg, PA 17019-9469; Exec. Dir., Rev. John Brubaker, P.O. Box 390, Grantham, PA 17027-0390
Bd. for Stewardship Services: Chair, Terry Hoke; Exec. Dir., Rev. Phil Keefer, Box A, Grantham, PA 17027; Pension Fund Trustees, Eric Mann, Chair
Bd. for Media Ministries: Chair, Mark Witman, 590 Meadowview Circle, Greencastle, PA 17225-1032; Publishing House, Exec. Dir., Roger Williams, Evangel Press, P.O. Box 189, Nappanee, IN 46550
Brethren in Christ Foundation: Chair, Donald Winters; CEO, Elvin H. Peifer, P.O. Box 290, Grantham, PA, 17027-0290

Periodicals

The Visitor, Yes!, Shalom

Brethren Church (Ashland, Ohio)

The Brethren Church (Ashland, Ohio) was organized by progressive-minded German Baptist Brethren in 1883. They reaffirmed the teaching of the original founder of the Brethren movement, Alexander Mack, and returned to limited congregational government.

Headquarters

524 College Ave., Ashland, OH 44805 Tel. (419) 289-1708 Fax (419)281-0450
Email: brethren@brethrenchurch.org
Website: www.brethrenchurch.org
Media Contact, Editor of Publications

Officers

Executive Dir., Rev. Ken Hunn
Dir. Of Pastoral Ministries, Rev. David Cooksey
Dir. Of Administrative Services, Mr. Stanley Gentle

Periodicals

The Brethren Evangelist

The Catholic Church

The largest single body of Christians in the United States, The Catholic Church is under the spiritual leadership of His Holiness the Pope. Its establishment in America dates back to the priests who accompanied Columbus on his second voyage to the New World. A settlement, later discontinued, was made in 1565 at St. Augustine, Fla. The continuous history of this Church in the Colonies began at St. Mary's in Maryland, in 1634.

INTERNATIONAL ORGANIZATION

His Holiness the Pope, Bishop of Rome, Vicar of Jesus Christ, Supreme Pontiff of the Catholic Church.

Pope John Paul II, Karol Wojtyla (born May 18, 1920; installed Oct. 22, 1978)

APOSTOLIC NUNCIO TO THE UNITED STATES

Archbishop Gabriel Montalvo, 3339 Massachusetts Ave. NW, Washington, D.C. 20008 Tel. (202) 333-7121 Fax (202)337-4036

U.S. ORGANIZATION

United States Conference of Catholic Bishops, 3211 Fourth St. NE, Washington, D.C. 20017-1194 Tel. (202)541-3000

The United States Conference of Catholic Bishops (USCCB) is an assembly of the hierarchy of the United States and the US Virgin Islands who jointly exercise certain pastoral functions on behalf of the Christian faithful of the United States. The purpose of the Conference is to promote the greater good which the Church offers humankind, especially through forms and programs of the apostolate fittingly adapted to the circumstances of time and place. This purpose is drawn from the universal law of the Church and applies to the episcopal conferences which are established all over the world for the same purpose.

The bishops themselves constitute the membership of the Conference and are served by a staff of over 350 people, priests, and religious located at the Conference headquarters in Washington, D.C. There is also a small Office of Film and Broadcasting in New York City and a branch office of Migration and Refugee Services in Miami.

The Conference is organized as a corporation in the District of Columbia. Its purposes under civil law are: "To unify, coordiante, encourage, promote and carry on Catholic activities in the United States; to organize and conduct religious, charitable and social welfare work at home and abroad; to aid in education; to care for immigrants; and generally to enter into and promote by education, publication and direction the objects of its being."

On July 1, 2001 the NCCB and the USCC were combined to form the United states Conference of Catholic Bishops (USCCB). The USCCB continues all of the work formerly done by the NCCB and the USCC with the same staff. The bishops themselves form approximately 50 committees, each with its own particular responsibility.

Website: www.usccb.org

UNITED STATES CONFERENCE OF CATHOLIC BISHOPS (USCCB)

GENERAL SECRETARIAT

General Sec., Msgr. William P. Fay

Assoc. Gen. Sec., Mr. Bruce E. Egnew, Msgr. David Malloy, Sr. Lourdes Sheehan, RSM

Officers

Pres., Bishop Wilton D. Gregory

Vice Pres., Bishop William S. Skylstad

Treas., Bishop Henry J. Mansell

Sec., Bishop William B. Friend

USCCB STANDING COMMITTEES

Administrative Committee, Chmn., Bishop Wilton D. Gregory

Executive Committee, Chmn., Bishop Wilton D. Gregory

Committee on Budget and Finance, Chmn., Bishop Henry J. Mansell

Committee on Personnel, Bishop Wilton D. Gregory

Committee on Priorities and Plans, Chmn., Bishop Wilton D. Gregory

African American Catholics, Chmn., Bishop J. Terry Steib, SVD

American Bishops' Overseas Appeal, Chmn., Bishop Wilton D. Gregory

American College Louvain, Chmn., Bishop Edward K. Braxton

Boundaries of Dioceses and Provinces, Chmn., Bishop Wilton D. Gregory

Canonical Affairs, Chmn., Bishop A. James Quinn

Church in Latin America, Chmn., Bishop Edmond Carmody

Consecrated Life, Chmn., Bishop Sean P. O'Malley, OFM

Diaconate, Chmn., Bishop Robert C. Morlino

Doctrine, Chmn., Bishop Donald W. Trautman

Ecumenical and Interreligious Affairs, Chmn., Bishop Tod D. Brown

Subcommittee on Interreligious Dialogue, Chmn., Bishop Joseph J. Gerry, OSB

Evangelization, Chmn., Bishop Michael W. Warfel

Hispanic Affairs, Chmn., Bishop Arthur N. Tafoya

Home Missions, Chmn., Bishop Paul A. Zipfel

Laity, Chmn., Bishop John J. McRaith

Subcommittee on Lay Ministry, Chmn., Bishop Joseph P. Delaney

Subcommittee on Youth and Young Adults, Chmn., Bishop Kevin M. Britt

Liturgy, Chmn., Archbishop Oscar H. Lipscomb

Marriage and Family Life, Chmn., Bishop J. Kevin Boland

Migration, Chmn., Bishop Thomas G. Wenski

North American College Rome, Chmn., Edwin F. O'Brien

Pastoral Practices, Chmn., Bishop James R. Hoffman

Priestly Formation, Chmn., Bishop George H. Niederauer

Priestly Life and Ministry, Chmn., Bishop John R. Gaydos
Pro-Life Activities, Chmn., Anthony Cardinal Bevilacqua
Relationship Between Eastern and Latin Catholic Churches, Chmn., Bishop Basil H. Losten
Science and Human Values, Chmn., Bishop John S. Cummins
Selection of Bishops, Chmn., Bishop Wilton D. Gregory
Vocations, Chmn., Bishop Kevin M. Britt
Woman in Society and in the Church, Chmn., Bishop Edward P. Cullen
World Mission, Chmn., Bishop Gregory M. Aymond

USCCB AD HOC COMMITTEES

Agricultural Issues, Chmn., Bishop William S. Skylstad
Aid to the Catholic Church in Central and Eastern Europe, Chmn., Adam Cardinal Maida
Bishops' Life and Ministry, Chmn., Bishop Robert H. Brom
Catholic Charismatic Renewal, Chmn., Bishop Sam G. Jacobs
Catholic Health Care Issues and the Church, Chm., Bishop Robert C. Morlino
Committee for the Special Assembly 2004, Chmn., Bishop Dennis M. Shnurr
Economic Concerns of the Holy See, Chmn., Archbishop James P. Keleher
National Review Board, Chmn., the Honorable Frank Keating, Governor of Oklahoma
Native American Catholics, Chmn., Bishop Donald E. Pelotte, SSS
Nomination of Conference Officers, Chmn., Archbishop Daniel E. Pilarezyk
Oversee the Use of the Catechism, Chmn., Archbishop Daniel M. Buechlein, OSB
Review of Scripture Translations, Chmn., Bishop Arthur J. Serratelli
Sexual Abuse, Chmn., Bishop Harry J. Flynn
Shrines, Chmn., Archbishop James P. Keleher
Stewardship, Chmn., Bishop Sylvester D. Ryan

USCCB EXECUTIVE COMMITTEES

Administrative Board, Chmn., Bishop Wilton D. Gregory
Executive Committee, Chmn., Bishop Wilton D. Gregory
Committee on Budget and Finance, Chmn., Bishop Henry J. Mansell
Committee on Personnel, Chmn., Bishop Wilton D. Gregory
Committee on Priorities and Plans, Chmn., Bishop Wilton D. Gregory

USCCB DEPARTMENTAL COMMITTEES

Catholic Campaign for Human Development, Chmn., Bishop George V. Murray
Communications, Chmn., Bishop Joseph A. Galante
Domestic Policy, Chmn., Theodore Cardinal McCarrick
International Policy, Chmn., Bernard Cardinal Law
Education, Chmn., Bishop Donald W. Wuerl
Advisory Committee on Public Policy and Catholic Schools, Chmn., Bishop Donald W. Wuerl
Bishops and Catholic College and University Presidents, Chmn., Bishop Donald W. Wuerl
Catechesis, Chmn., Bishop Donald W. Wuerl
Sapientia Christiana, Chmn., Bishop John P. Boles

For information on related organizations and individual dioceses, consult the *Official Catholic Directory* (published annually by P.J. Kenedy and Sons) and the USCCB website (www.usccb.org).

Periodicals

Catholic News Service, L'Osservatore Romano, The Living Light, Origins, Lay Ministry Update, Bishops Committee on the Liturgy Newsletter, life Insight, SEIA Newsletter on the Eastern Churches and Ecumenism, Law Briefs, Catholic Trends

Christ Catholic Church

The church is a catholic communion established in 1968 to minister to the growing number of people who seek an experiential relationship with God and who desire to make a total commitment of their lives to God. The church is catholic in faith and tradition. Participating cathedrals, churches, and missions are located in several states.

Headquarters

405 Kentling Rd., Highlandville, MO 65669 Tel. (417)443-3951
Website: christcatholicchurch.freeyellow.com/
Media Contact, Archbishop, Most Rev. Karl Pruter, bishopkarl@juno.com

Officers

Archbishop, Most Rev. Karl Pruter, P.O. Box 98, Highlandville, MO 65669 Tel. (417)443-3951
Order of St. John of the Cross, Abbot Fr. Frank Bracelin, 1002 16th Pl., Kelso, WA 98626

Periodicals

St. Willibrord Journal

Christ Community Church (Evangelical-Protestant)

This church was founded by the Rev. John Alexander Dowie on Feb. 22, 1896 at Chicago, Ill. In 1901 the church founded the city of Zion, Ill. and moved their headquarters there. Theologically, the church is rooted in evangelical orthodoxy. The Scriptures are accepted as the rule of faith and practice. Other doctrines call for belief in the necessity of repentance for sin and personal trust in Christ for salvation.

The Christ Community Church is a denominational member of The National Association of Evangelicals. It has work in six other nations in addition to the United States. Branch ministries are found in Tonalea, Ariz.; Lindenhurst, Ill.; and Toronto, Canada.

Headquarters

2500 Dowie Memorial Dr., Zion, IL 60099 Tel. (847)746-1411 Fax (847)746-1452

Officers

Senior Pastor, Ken Langley

Christadelphians

The Christadelphians are a body of people who believe the Bible to be the divinely inspired word of God, written by "Holy men who spoke as they were moved by the Holy Spirit" (2 Peter 1:21). They believe that the Old Testament presents God's plan to establish His Kingdom on earth in accord with the promises He made to Abraham and David and that the New Testament declares how that plan works out in Jesus Christ, who died a sacrificial death to redeem sinners. They believe in the personal return of Jesus Christ as King, to establish "all that God spoke by the mouth of his holy prophets from of old" (Acts 3:21). They believe that at Christ's return many of the dead will be raised by the power of God to be judged. Those whom God deems worthy will be welcomed into eternal life in the Kingdom on earth. Christadelphians believe in the mortality of man; in spiritual rebirth requiring belief and immersion in the name of Jesus; and in a godly walk in this life. They have no ordained clergy, and are organized in a loose confederation of 2,500 autonomous congregations (ecclesias) in approximately 150 countries. They are conscientiously opposed to participation in war. They endeavor to be enthusiastic in work, loyal in marriage, generous in giving, dedicated in preaching, and cheerful in living.

The denomination was organized in 1844 by a medical doctor, John Thomas, who came to the United States from England in 132, having survived a near shipwreck in a violent storm. This experience effected him profoundly, and he vowed to devote his life to a search for the truth of God and a future hope from the Bible.

Headquarters

Media Contact, Trustee, Norman D. Zilmer, Christadelphian Action Society, 1000 Mohawk Dr., Elgin, IL 60120-3148 Tel. (847) 741-5253, Fax (847)888-3334, Nzilmer@aol.com

Website: www.christadelphia.org, www.Tidings.org, www.wcfoundation.org

Leaders

Co-Ministers: Norman Fadelle, 815 Chippewa Dr., Elgin, IL 60120, Nfadelle@juno.com; Norman D. Zilmer, 1000 Mohawk Dr., Elgin, IL 60120, Nzilmer@aol.com

Periodicals

Christadelphian Tidings, Christadelphian Advocate

Christian Brethren (also known as Plymouth Brethren)

Christian Brethren churches are bound together by common beliefs and practices but not by central organization. They are committed to the inerrancy of Scripture, to Trinitarian doctrine, and to the evangelical message of salvation by faith apart from works or sacrament. Their most recognizable feature is the weekly observance of the Lord's Supper as the focus of a full length service of worship, not prearranged and not clergy-led.

Originating in England and Ireland in the late 1820s, the Brethren were influenced by the counsel of Anthony Norris Groves, an English dentist, and the teaching of John Nelson Darby, an Irish clergyman. They recovered aspects of church practice and simplicity that had been obscured in the course of the centuries, such as an unwillingness to establish denominational govering structures and a reluctance to accept sectarian names. The nickname Plymouth has replaced Plymouth Brethren for the open branch of the movement in Canada and the British Commonwealth and, to some extent, in the United States. Neither name has legal status, except where required by national governments. There are no central offices and no corporate property in the USA or Canada.

In the late 1840s the movement divided. The open assemblies, led initially by George Mueller of orphanage fame, stressed evangelism and foreign missions. It has grown to be the larger of the two branches. The autonomy of local congregations permits variations in practice and generally avoids wide-ranging division.

The other branch focused more on doctrinal and ecclesiastical issues. From it came notable Bible teachers like Darby, William Kelly, C.H. Mackintosh (CHM), and F.W. Grant. Their books have had a wide influence, especially among premillennialists. These assemblies stress the interdependency of congregations. Local church decisions on doctrine and discipline are generally held to be binding on all assemblies. At times, when actions were debatable, division spread throughout the group. By 1900, there were seven or eight main groups. Since 1925, some divisions have been healed, reducing that number to three or four.

Correspondent

James A. Stahr, 327 W. Prairie Ave., Wheaton, IL 60187-3408 Tel. (630)665-3757

RELATED ORGANIZATIONS

Interest Ministries, 2060 Stonington Ave., Suite 101, Hoffman Estates, IL 60195

Christian Missions in Many Lands, P.O. Box 13, Spring Lake, NJ 07762-0013

Stewards Foundation, 14285 Midway Rd., Ste. 330, Addison, TX 75001-3622

International Teams, 411 W. River Rd., Elgin, IL 60123

Emmaus Bible College, 2570 Asbury Rd., Dubuque, IA 52001-3044

Stewards Ministries, 18-3 E. Dundee Rd., Ste. 100, Barrington, IL 60010

Believers Bookshelf, P.O. Box 261 Sunbury, PA 17801

Christian Church (Disciples of Christ) in the United States and Canada*

Born on the American frontier in the early 1800s as a movement to unify Christians, this body drew its major inspiration from Thomas and Alexander Campbell in western Pennsylvania and Barton W. Stone in Kentucky. Developing separately, the "Disciples," under Alexander Campbell, and the "Christians," led by Stone, united in 1832 in Lexington, Ky.

The Christian Church (Disciples of Christ) is marked by informality, openness, individualism, and diversity. The Disciples claim no official doctrine or dogma. Membership is granted after a simple statement of belief in Jesus Christ and baptism by immersion—although most congregations accept transfers baptized by other forms in other denominations. The Lord's Supper—generally called Communion—is open to Christians of all persuasions. The practice is weekly Communion, although no church law insists upon it.

Thoroughly ecumenical, the Disciples helped organize the National and World Councils of Churches. The church is a member of the Churches Uniting in Christ. The Disciples and the United Church of Christ have declared themselves to be in "full communion" through the General Assembly and General Synod of the two churches. Official theological conversations have been going on since 1967 directly with the Roman Catholic Church.

Disciples have vigorously supported world and national programs of education, agricultural assistance, urban reconciliation, care of persons with retardation, family planning, and aid to victims of war and calamity. Operating ecumenically, Disciples' personnel or funds work in more than 100 countries outside North America.

Three manifestations or expressions of the church (general, regional, and congregational) operate as equals, with strong but voluntary covenantal ties to one another. Entities in each manifestation manage their own finances, own their own property, and conduct their own programs. A General Assembly meets every two years and has voting representation from each congregation.

Headquarters

Disciples Center, 130 E. Washington St., P.O. Box 1986, Indianapolis, IN 46206-1986 Tel. (317)635-3100 Fax (317)635-3700

Email: cmiller@cm.disciples.org

Website: www.disciples.org

Media Contact, Communication Ministries, Exec. Dir., -vacant-

Officers

Gen. Minister & Pres., William Chris Hobgood Tel. (317)713-2401, chobgood@ogmp.disciples.org

Mod., Charisse Gillett, 3292 Hunters Point, Lexington, KY 40515 Tel. (859)281-3569, Fax (859)281-3547, cgillett@transy.edu

1st Vice Mod., Douglas Skinner, Northway Christian Church, 7202 Northway Hwy., Dallas, TX 75225 Tel. (214)361-6641, Fax (214) 361-3941

2nd Vice Mod., Manny Collaxo, EDS Federal Government, 12000 Research Parkway, Suite 100, Orlando, FL 21826 Tel (407)207-8990, Fax (407)207-8993, manny.collazo@eds.com

GENERAL OFFICERS

Gen. Min. & Pres., William Chris Hobgood, chobgood@ogmp.disciples.org

Assoc. Gen. Min. & Vice Pres., William H. Edwards, bedwards@ogmp.disciples.org

Assoc. Gen. Min. & Admin. Sec. of the National Convocation, Timothy M. James, tjames@ogmp.disciples.org

ADMINISTRATIVE UNITS

Board of Church Extension, dba Church Extension, Pres., James L. Powell, 130 E. Washington St., P.O. Box 7030, Indianapolis, IN 46207-7030 Tel. (317)635-6500, Fax (317)635-6534, bce@churchextension.org

Christian Board of Publication (Chalice Press), Pres., Cyrus N. White, 1221 Locust St., Suite 1200, P.O. Box 179, St. Louis, MO 63166-0179 Tel. (314)231-8500 or (800)366-3383, Fax (314)231-8524, customerservice@cbp21.com

Christian Church Foundation, Inc., Pres., Gary W. Kidwell Tel. (317)635-3100 or (800)366-8016, Fax (317)635-1991, jcullumb@ccf.disciples.org

Church Finance Council, Inc., Pres., Lois Artis, jedmundson@cfc.disciples.org

Council on Christian Unity, Inc., Pres., Robert K. Welsh, Tel (317)713-2586, Fax (317)713-2588, rozanne@ccu.disciples.org

Disciples of Christ Historical Society, Pres., Peter M. Morgan, 1101 19th Ave. S., Nashville, TN 37212-2196 Tel. (615)327-1444, Fax (615)327-1445, mail@dishistsoc.org

Division of Higher Education, Pres., Dennis L. Landon, 11477 Olde Cabin Rd., Ste. 310, St. Louis, MO 63141-7130 Tel. (314)991-3000, Fax (314)991-2957, dhe@dhedisciples.org

Division of Homeland Ministries, Disciples Home Missions, Pres., Arnold C. Nelson Jr. Tel. (317)635-3100 or (888)346-2631, Fax (317) 635-4426 homelandministries@dhm.disciples.org

Division of Overseas Ministries, Pres., David A. Vargas Fax (317)635-4323, dom@disciples.org

National Benevolent Association, Pres., Cindy Dougherty, 11780 Borman Dr., St. Louis, MO 63146-4157 Tel. (314)993-9000, Fax (314) 993-9018, nba@nbacares.org

Pension Fund, Pres., James P. Hamlett, 130 E. Washington St., Indianapolis, IN 46204-3645 Tel. (317)634-4504, Fax (317)634-4071, pfccl@pension.disciples.org

REGIONAL UNITS OF THE CHURCH

Alabama/Northwest Florida, Regional Minister, John P. Mobley, 861 Highway 52, Helena, AL 35080 Tel. (205)425-5246, Fax (205)423-0963, alnwfl@aol.com

Arizona, Regional Minister, Dennis L. Williams, 4423 N. 24th St., Ste 700, Phoenix, AZ 85016-5544 Tel. (602)468-3815 Fax (602)468-3816, azregion@worldnet.att.net

California, Northern-Nevada, Regional Minister, Pres., Charles R. Blaisdell, 9260 Alcosta Blvd., C-18, San Ramon, CA 94583-4143 Tel. (925)556-9900, Fax (925)556-9904, info@ccncn.org

Canada, Regional Minister, F. Thomas Rutherford, P.O. Box 23030, 417 Wellington St., St. Thomas, ON N5R 6A3 Tel. (519)633-9083, Fax (519)637-6407, ccic@netrover.com

Capital Area, Regional Minister, Lari R. Grubbs, 11501 Georgia Ave., Ste. 400, Wheaton, MD 20902-1955 Tel (301)942-8266, Fax (301) 942-8366, lgrubbs@cccadisciples.org

Central Rocky Mountain Region, Exec. Regional Min., Ronald L. Parker, 2950 Tennyson #300, Denver, CO 80212-3091 Tel. (303)561-1790, Fax (303)561-1795, info@crmrdoc.org

Florida, Regional Minister, William C. Morrison, Jr., 924 N. Magnolia Ave., Ste. 200, Orlando, FL 32803-3845 Tel. (407)843-4652, Fax (407) 843-0272, RegionalOffice@floridadisciples.org

Georgia, Interim Regional Minister, Zena S. McAdams, 2370 Vineville Ave., Macon, GA 31204-3163 Tel. (478)743-8649 or (800)755-0485, Fax (478)741-1508, ccinga@bellsouth.net

Great River Region, Co-Executive Regional Ministers, Barbara E. Jones and William E. McKnight, 9302 Geyer Springs Rd, P.O.Box 192058, Little Rock, AR 72219-2058 Tel. (501)562-6053 or (800)241-5531, Fax (501) 562-7089

Idaho, South, Regional Minister, Larry Crist, 6465 Sunrise Ave., Nampa, ID 83686-9461 Tel. (208)468-8976, Fax (208)468-8973, ccsi1@mindspring.com

Illinois and Wisconsin, Regional Minister, Pres., Herbert L. Knudsen, 1011 N. Main St., Bloomington, IL 61701-1753 Tel. (309)828-6293, Fax (309)829-4612, herb@cciwdisciples.org

Indiana, Regional Minister, Richard L. Spleth, 1100 W. 42nd St., Indianapolis, IN 46208-3375 Tel. (317)926-6051, Fax (317)931-2034, cci@ccindiana.org

Kansas, Regional Minister, Pres., Patsie Sweeden, 2914 SW MacVicar Ave., Topeka, KS 66611-1787 Tel. (785)266-2914, Fax (785)266-0174, ccks@ksmessenger.org

Kansas City, Greater, Regional Min., Pres., Paul J. Diehl, Jr., 5700 Broadmoor, Ste. 702, Mission, KS 66202-2405 Tel. (913)432-1414, Fax (913)432-3598, ksdisciple@aol.com

Kentucky, General Minister, Janet M. Ehrmantraut, 1125 Red Mile Rd., Lexington, KY 40504-2660 Tel. (859)233-1391, Fax (859)233-2079, cck@ccinky.net

Michigan, Regional Minister, Morris Finch Jr., 2820 Covington Ct., Lansing, MI 48912-4830 Tel. (517)372-3220, Fax (517)372-2705, ccmr@michigandisciples.org

Mid-America Region, Regional Minister, Danny Stewart, 3000 Jack Stocker Rd. P.O. Box 104298, Jefferson City, MO 65110-4298 Tel. (573)636-8149, Fax (573)636-2889, ccma@socket.net

Montana, Regional Minister, Ruth A, Fletcher, 1019 Central Ave., Great Falls, MT 59401-3784 Tel. (406)452-7404, Fax (406)452-7404, ccm@imt.net

Nebraska, Regional Ministers, Kenneth W. Moore, 1268 S. 20th St., Lincoln, NE 68502-1612 Tel. (402)476-0359 or (800)580-8851, Fax (402)476-0350, ccnebraska@alltel

North Carolina, Regional Minister, John M. Richardson, 509 NE Lee St., P.O. Box 1568, Wilson, NC 27894-1568 Tel. (252)291-4047, Fax (252)291-3338, ccnc@ncdisciples.org

Northeastern Region, Co-Regional Ministers, Lonnie F. Oates & Wesley R. Bourdette, 475 Riverside Dr., Rm. 1950, New York, NY 10115-1999 Tel. (212)870-2734, Fax (870) 2735, n.christian.church@worldnet.att.net

Northwest Region, Regional Minister, Pres., Jack Sullivan Jr., 6558-35th Ave. SW, Seattle, WA 98126-2899 Tel. (206)938-1008, Fax (206) 933-1163, nwrcc@disciplesnw.org

Ohio, Interim Regional Pastor, Pres., Suzanne J. Webb, 38007 Butternut Ridge Rd., P.O. Box 299, Elyria, OH 44036-0299 Tel. (440)458-5112, Fax (440)458-5114, ccio@christianchurchinohio.org

Oklahoma, Regional Pastor, Thomas R. Jewell, 301 N.W. 36th St., Oklahoma City, OK 73118-8661 Tel. (405)528-3577, Fax (405)528-3584, tjewell@okdisciples.org

Oregon, Co-Regional Ministers, Douglas Wirt & Cathy Myers-Wirt, 0245 SW Bancroft St., Ste. F, Portland, OR 97239-4267 Tel. (503)226-7648, Fax (503)226-0598, odmail@oregondisciples.org

Pacific Southwest Region, Regional Minister, Pres., Don W. Shelton, 2401 N. Lake Ave., Altadena, CA 91001-2418 Tel. (626)296-0385, Fax (626)296-1280, pswr@discipleswr

Pennsylvania, Regional Minister, W. Darwin Collins, 670 Rodi Rd., Pittsburgh, PA 15235-4524 Tel. (412)731-7000, Fax (412)731-4515, wdar@padisciples.org

South Carolina, Regional Minister, Sotello V. Long, 5103 Rhett Ave., P.O. Box 5135, North Charleston, SC 29405-5135 Tel. (843)744-5786, Fax (843)744-5787, rcccsc@aol.com

Southwest Region, Interim Regional Minister, Donald B. Manworren, 3209 S. University Dr., Fort Worth, TX 76109-2239 Tel. (817) 926-4687, Fax (817) 926-5121, ccsw@ csw.org

Tennessee, Regional Minister, Pres., Glen J. Stewart, 50 Vantage Way, Ste. 251, Nashville, TN 37228-1523 Tel. (615)251-3400, Fax (615)251-3415, ccdctn@yahoo.com

Upper Midwest Region, Regional Minister, Pres., Richard L. Guentert, 3300 University Ave., P.O. Box 41217, Des Moines, IA 50311-0504 Tel. (515)255-3168, Fax (515)255-2625, rg@uppermidwestcc.org

Virginia, Regional Minister, George Lee Parker, 518 Brevard St., Lynchburg, VA 24501-3547 Tel. (434)846-3400, Fax (434)528-4919, linda@ccwv.org

West Virginia, Regional Minister, William B. Allen, 1400 Washington Ave., P.O. Box 264, Parkersburg, WV 26102-0264 Tel. (304)428-1681, Fax (304)428-1684, ccwv@prodigy.com

Periodicals

DiscipleWorld, Call To Unity

Christian Church of North America, General Council

Originally known as the Italian Christian Church, its first General Council was held in 1927 at Niagara Falls, N.Y. This body was incorporated in 1948 at Pittsburgh, Penn., and is described as Pentecostal but does not engage in the "the excesses tolerated or practiced among some churches using the same name."

The movement recognizes two ordinances—baptism and the Lord's Supper. Its moral code is conservative and its teaching is orthodox. Members are exhorted to pursue a life of personal holiness, setting an example to others. A conservative position is held in regard to marriage and divorce. The governmental form is, by and large, congregational. District and National officiaries, however, are referred to as Presbyteries led by Overseers.

The group functions in cooperative fellowship with the Italian Pentecostal Church of Canada and the Evangelical Christian Churches–Assemblies of God in Italy. It is an affiliate member of the Pentecostal Fellowship of North America and of the National Association of Evangelicals.

Headquarters

1294 Rutledge Rd., Transfer, PA 16154-2299 Tel. (724)962-3501 Fax (724)962-1766

Email: cnna@nauticom.net

Website: www.ccna.org

Exec. Sec., Terri Metcalfe; Admin. Asst., Chris Marini

Officers

Executive Bd., Gen. Overseer, Rev. John DelTurco, 1294 Rutledge Rd., Transfer, PA 16154

Exec. Vice Pres., Rev. Charles Gay, 26 Delafield Dr., Albany, NY 12205

Asst. Gen. Overseers, Rev. Joseph Shipley 44-19 Francis Lewis Blvd., Bayside, NY 11361; Rev. Vincent Prestigiacomo, 21 Tyler Hill Rd., Jaffrey, NH 03452; Rev. Michael Trotta, 224 W. Winter Ave., New Castle, PA 16101; Rev. Douglas Bedgood Sr., 442 Trinidad Ln., Teadkwood Village, Largo, FL 33770

DEPARTMENTS

Benevolence, Rev. John Del Turco, P.O. Box 1198, Hermitage, PA 16148

Home Missions, Rev. Richard George

Faith, Order & Credentials, Rev. Rev. Joseph Shipley, 44-19 Francis Lewis Blvd., Bayside, NY 11361

Missions, Rev. Mark Charles, 1067 Stevens Blvd. Eastlake, OH 44095

Publications Relations, Rev. John Tedesco, 1188 Heron Rd., Cherry Hill, NJ 08003

Lay Ministries, Rev. Carmine Zottoli, 27D Shear Hill Rd., Mahopac, NY 10541

Education, Rev. Lucian Gandolfo, 3141 Highland Dr., Easton, PA. 18045

Periodicals

Vista

Christian Churches and Churches of Christ

The fellowship, whose churches were always strictly congregational in polity, has its origin in the American movement to "restore the New Testament church in doctrine, ordinances, and life" initiated by Thomas and Alexander Campbell, Walter Scott, and Barton W. Stone in the early 19th century.

Headquarters

Media Contact, N. American Christian Convention Dir., Rod Huron, 4210 Bridgetown Rd., Box 11326, Cincinnati, OH 45211 Tel. (513) 598-6222 Fax (513)598-6471

Email: Jowston@cwv.edu

Website: www.cwv.net/christ'n/

Conventions

North American Christian Convention, Dir., Rod Huron, 4210 Bridgetown Rd., Box 11326, Cincinnati, OH 45211 Tel. (513)598-6222; NACC Mailing Address, Box 39456, Cincinnati, OH 45239

National Missionary Convention, Coord., Walter Birney, Box 11, Copeland, KS 67837 Tel. (316)668-5250

Eastern Christian Convention, Kenneth Meade, 5300 Norbeck Rd., Rockville, MD 20853 Tel. (301)460-3550

Periodicals

Christian Standard, Restoration Herald, Horizons, The Lookout

The Christian Congregation, Inc.

The Christian Congregation is a denominational evangelistic association that originated in 1787 and was active on the frontier in areas adjacent to the Ohio River. The church was an unincorporated organization until 1887. At that time, a group of ministers who desired closer cooperation formally constituted the church. The charter was revised in 1898 and again in 1970.

Governmental polity basically is congregational. Local units are semi-autonomous. Doctrinal positions, strongly biblical, are essentially universalist in the sense that ethical principles, which motivate us to creative activism, transcend national boundaries and racial barriers. A central tenet, John 13:34-35, translates to such respect for sanctity of life that abortions on demand, capital punishment, and all warfare are vigorously opposed. All wars are considered unjust and obsolete as a means of resolving disputes.

Early leaders were John Chapman, John L. Puckett, and Isaac V. Smith. Bishop O. J. Read was chief administrative and ecclesiastic officer for 40 years until 1961. Rev. Dr. Ora Wilbert Eads has been general Superintendent since 1961. Ministerial affiliation for independent clergymen is provided.

Headquarters

812 W. Hemlock St., LaFollette, TN 37766

Email: Revalnas@aol.com

Website: netministries.org/see/churches.exe/ch 10619

Media Contact, Gen. Supt., Rev. Ora W. Eads, DD Tel. (423)562-6330

Officers

Gen. Supt., Rev. Ora W. Eads, DD

Christian Methodist Episcopal Church*

The Christian Methodist Episcopal Church (CME) is a historically African-American denomination that was established in Jackson, Tennessee in 1870 when a group of former slaves, representing eight annual conferences of the Methodist Episcopal Church South organized the Colored Methodist Episcopal Church in America. In 1954 at its General Conference in Memphis, Tenn. it was overwhelmingly voted to change the term "Colored" to "Christian". On January 3, 1956 the official name became Christian Methodist Episcopal Church. Its boundaries reach from the continental United States, Alaska, Haiti, Jamaica, and the West African countries of Nigeria, Ghana, and Liberia. One of its most significant witnessing arenas has been the education of African Americans. Today the CME Church supports Paine College, August, Ga.; Lane College, Jackson, Tenn.; Miles College, Birmingham, Ala.; Texas College, Tyler, Tex.; and the Phillips School of Theology in Atlanta, Ga.

Headquarters

First Memphis Plaza, 4466 Elvis Presley Blvd., Memphis, TN 38116

Media Contact, Exec. Sec., Attorney Juanita Bryant, 3675 Runnymede Blvd., Cleveland Hts., OH 44121 Tel. (216)382-3559, Fax (216) 382-3516, juanbr4law@aol.com

Officers

Exec. Sec., Attorney Juanita Bryant, 3675 Runnymede Blvd., Cleveland Hts., OH 44121 Tel. (216)382-3559, Fax (216)382-3516, juanbr4law@aol.com

Sec. Gen. Conf., Rev. John Gilmore, 111 S. Highland, Suite 334, Memphis, TN 38111 Tel. (901)323-3514

OTHER ORGANIZATIONS

Christian Education: Gen. Sec., Dr. Carmichael Crutchfield, 4466 Elvis Presley Blvd., Ste. 214, Box 193, Memphis, TN 38116-7100 Tel. (901)345-0580 Fax (901)345-4118

Lay Ministry: Gen. Sec., Dr. Victor Taylor, 9560 Drake Ave., Evenston, IL 60203 Tel. (800) 782-4335 ext. 6029, Fax (312)345-6056, victav @idt.net

Evangelism & Missions: Gen. Sec., Dr. Willie C. Champion, 102 Pearly Top Dr., Glen Heights, TX 75154 Tel. (214)372-9505

Finance: Sec., Dr. Joseph C. Neal Jr., P.O. Box 75085, Los Angeles, CA 90075 Tel. (323)233-5050

Editor: *The Christian Index,* Dr. Kenneth E. Jones, P.O. Box 431, Fairfield, AL 35064 Tel. (205)929-1640, Fax (205)791-1910, Goodoc@ aol.com

Publication Services: Gen. Sec., Rev. William George, 4466 Elvis Presley Blvd., Memphis, TN 38116 Tel. (901)345-0580 Fax (901)767-8514

Personnel Services: Gen. Sec., Rev. Tyrone T. Davis, P.O. Box 74, Memphis, TN 38101-0074 Tel. (901)345-4100

Women's Missionary Council: Pres., Mrs. Elnora Hamb, 4466 Elvis Presley Blvd., Memphis, TN 38116 Tel. (901)345-0580

BISHOPS

First District: Bishop William H. Graves, Sr., 4466 Elvis Presley Blvd., Ste. 222, Memphis, TN 38116 Tel. (901)345-0580

Second District: Bishop E. Lynn Brown, 5115 Rollman Estate Dr., Cincinnati, OH 45236 Tel. (513)772-8622

Third District: Bishop Paul A. G. Stewart Sr., 5925 W. Florissant Ave., St. Louis, MO 63136 Tel. (314)381-3111

Fourth District, Bishop Thomas L. Hoyt, Jr., 109 Holcomb Dr., Shreveport, LA 71103 Tel. (318) 222-6284

Fifth District, Bishop Lawerence L. Reddick III, 310 18th St., N, Ste. 400D, Birmingham, AL 35203 Tel. (205)655-0346

Sixth District, Bishop Othal H. Lakey, 2001 M.L. King, Jr. Dr. SW, Ste. 423, Atlanta, GA 30310 Tel. (404)752-7800

Seventh District, Bishop Charles L. Helton 6524 16th St. NW, Washington, D.C. 20012 and 5337 Ruth Dr., Charlotte, NC 28215 Tel. (704)536-8067

Eighth District, Bishop Marshall Gilmore, Sr., 1616 E. Illinois, Dallas, TX 75216 Tel. (214)372-9073

Ninth District, Bishop Henry M. Williamson, 3844 W. Slauson Ave., Ste. 1, Los Angeles, CA 90043 Tel. (213)294-3830

Tenth District, Bishop Ronald M. Cunningham, P.O. Box 27147, Memphis, TN 38167 Tel. (901)274-1070

Retired, Bishop Caesar D. Coleman, 1000 Longmeadow Ln., DeSoto, TX 75115; Bishop Richard O. Bass Sr., 1556 Delton Pl., Midfield, AL 35228; Bishop Oree Broomfield Sr., 3505 Springrun Dr., Decatur, GA 30032; Bishop Nathaniel L. Linsey, Canterbury Subdivision, 190 Squire Ln., Fayettsville, GA 30214 Tel. (770)460-6897; Bishop Dotcy I. Isom, 4326 Richwood Place, Memphis, TN 36125 Tel. (901)753-8123

Periodicals

The Christian Index, The Missionary Messenger

The Christian and Missionary Alliance

The Christian and Missionary Alliance was formed in 1897 by the merger of two organizations begun in 1887 by Dr. Albert B. Simpson: The Christian Alliance and the Evangelical Missionary Alliance. The Christian and Missionary Alliance is an evangelical church which stresses the sufficiency of Jesus as Savior, Sanctifier, Healer, and Coming King and has earned a worldwide reputation for its missionary accomplishments. The Canadian districts became autonomous in 1981 and formed The Christian and Missionary Alliance in Canada.

NATIONAL OFFICES

P.O. Box 35000, Colorado Springs, CO 80935-3500 Tel. (719)599-5999 Fax (719)593-8234

Email: info@cmalliance.org

Website: www.cmalliance.org

Media Contact, Peter Burgo, Asst. Vice Pres. for Advancement

Officers

Pres., Rev. Peter N. Nanfelt, DD

Corp. Vice Pres., Rev. Abraham H. Poon, DMin

Corp. Sec., Rev. David L. Goodin

Vice Pres., for Advancement, Rev. David F. Presher, DMin.

Vice Pres. for International Ministries, Rev. Robert L. Fetherlin, DMin.

Vice Pres. for National Church Ministries, Rev. Donald A. Wiggins, DMin.

Vice Pres. for Operations/Finance, Mr. Duane A. Wheeland, LLD/CPA

BOARD OF DIRECTORS

Chpsn., Rev. Rockwell L. Dillaman, DD

Vice Chpsn., Rev. Robert L. Thune

DISTRICTS

Cambodian, Rev. Nareth May, 1616 S. Palmetto Ave., Ontario, CA 91762 Tel. (909)988-9434

Central, Rev. Gordon F. Meier, DMin, 1218 High St., Wadsworth, OH 44281 Tel. (330)336-2911

Central Pacific, Rev. R. Douglas Swinburne, Jr., 715 Lincoln Ave., Woodland, CA 95695 Tel. (530)662-2500

E. Pennsylvania, Rev. J. Wayne Springgs, 1200 Spring Garden Dr., Middletown, PA 17057 Tel. (717)985-9240

Great Lakes, Rev. Jeffrey P. Brown, 2250 Huron Pkwy, Ann Arbor, MI 48104 Tel. (734)677-8555

Haitian South, Rev. Joe Kong (Interim Director), P.O. Box 35000, Colorado Springs, CO 80935 Tel. (719)265-2052

Hmong, Rev. Timothy T. Vang, 12287 Pennsylvania St., Thornton, CO 80241 Tel. (303)252-1793

Korean, Rev. Paul H. Lee, 713 W. Commonwealth Ave., Ste. C, Fullerton, CA 92832 Tel. (714)879-5201

Metropolitan, Rev. John F. Soper, P.O. Box 7060, 275 Sussex Ave., Ste. B, Newark, NJ 07107 Tel. (973)412-7025

Mid-America, Rev. Randall S. Burg, 1301 S. 119th St., Omaha, NE 68144 Tel. (402)330-1888

Mid-Atlantic, Rev. Randall B. Corbin, D.Min., Jr., 292 Montevue Lane, Frederick, MD 21702 Tel. (301)620-9934

Midwest, Rev. M. Fred Polding, D.Miss., 260 Glen Ellyn Road, Bloomingdale, IL 60108 Tel. (630)893-1355

Native American, Rev. Craig S. Smith, 19019 N. 74th Dr., Glendale, AZ 85308 Tel. (623)561-8134

New England, Rev. Richard E. Bush, D.Min., P.O. Box 288, South Easton, MA 02375 Tel. (508)238-3820

Northeastern, Rev. David J. Phillips, 6275 Pillmore Dr., Rome, NY 13440 Tel. (315)336-4720

Northwestern, Rev. Craig L. Strawser, 6425 CTYRD 30 #740, St., Bonifacius, MN 55375 Tel. (952)446-9318

Ohio Valley, Rev. P. David Klinsing, D.Min., 4050 Executive Park Dr., Ste.402, Cincinnati, OH 45241 Tel. (513)733-4833

Pacific NW, Rev. Kelvin J. Gardiner, P.O. Box 1030, Canby, OR 97013 Tel. (503)266-2238

Puerto Rico, Rev. Rosilio Roman III-Cruz, P.O. Box 191794, San Juan, PR 00919 Tel. (787) 281-0101

Rocky Mountain, Rev. Timothy P. Owen, DMin, 2545 St. Johns Ave., Billings, MT 59102 Tel. (406)656-4233

South Atlantic, Rev. L. Ferrell Towns, 10801 Johnston Rd., Ste. 125, Charlotte, NC 28226 Tel. (704)543-0470

South Pacific, Rev. Donald M. Brust, 4130 Adams St., Ste. A, Riverside, CA 92504 Tel. (909) 351-0111

Southeastern, Rev. Mark T. O' Farrell, D.D., P.O. Box 720430, Orlando, FL 32872-0430 Tel. (407)823-9662

Southern, Rev. Fred G. King, 5998 Deerfoot Parkway, Trussville, AL 35173 Tel. (205)661-9585

Southwestern, Rev. Daniel R. Wetzel, 5600 E. Loop 820 South, Ste. 100, Fort Worth, TX 76119 Tel. (817)561-0879

Spanish Central, Rev. José Bruno, P.O. Box 5477, McAllen, TX 78504 Tel. (956)565-1600

Spanish Eastern, Rev. Marcelo Realpe, P.O.Box 865, Union City, NJ 07087 Tel. (201)866-7202

Vietnamese, Dr. Tai Anh Nguyen, Th.D., 2275 W. Lincoln Ave., Anaheim, CA 92801 Tel. (714)491-8007

W. Great Lakes, Rev. Gary E. Russell, W. 6107 Aerotech Dr., Appleton, WI 54914 Tel. (920) 734-1123

W. Pennsylvania, Rev. Palmer L. Zerbe, P.O.Box 600, Punxsutawney, PA 15767 Tel. (814)938-6920

NATIONAL ETHNIC ASSOCIATIONS

African-American, Pres., Rev. Terrence L. Nichols, 120 Lancaster Way, Vallejo, CA 94591 Tel. (707)310-3926; Exec. Sec., Rev. Gus H. Brown, 688 Diagonal Rd., Akron, OH 44320 Tel. (330)376-4653

Chinese, Pres., Rev. Abraham K. Poon, D.Min., 2360 McLauglin Ave., San Jose, CA 95122-3560 Tel. (408)280-1021

Dega, Pres., Rev. Ha Giao Cilpam, 3119 Westerwood Dr., Charlotte, NC 28214 Tel. (704)393-7159

Filipino, Pres., Exec. Dir., Rev. Abednego Ferrer, 20143 Royal Ave., Hayward, CA 94541 Tel. (510)887-6261

Haitian, Pres., Rev. Emmanuel Seide, 14 Glen Rd., West Hempstead, NY 11552 Tel. (516) 594-1046

ETHNIC/CULTURAL MINISTRIES

Arab & South Asian, Rev. Joseph S. Kong, P.O. Box 35000, Colorado Springs, CO 80935 Tel. (719)599-5999 ext. 2052

Alliance Jewish Ministry, Rev. Abraham Sandler, 9820 Woodfern Rd., Philadelphia, PA 19115 Tel. (215)676-5122

Periodicals

Alliance Life

Christian Reformed Church in North America

The Christian Reformed Church represents the historic faith of Protestantism. Founded in the United States in 1857 and active in Canada since 1908, it asserts its belief in the Bible as the inspired Word of God, and is creedally united in the Belgic Confession (1561), the Heidelberg Catechism (1563), and the Canons of Dort (1618-19).

Headquarters

2850 Kalamazoo Ave. SE, Grand Rapids, MI 49560 Tel. (616)224-0744 Fax (616)224-5895

Email: btgh@crcna.org

Website: www.crcna.org

Media Contact, Gen. Sec., Dr. David H. Engelhard

Officers

Gen. Sec., Dr. David H. Engelhard

Exec. Dir. of Ministries, Dr. Peter Borgdorff

Canadian Ministries Dir., Rev. William Veenstra, 3475 Mainway, P.O. Box 5070 STN LCR 1, Burlington, ON L7R 3Y8

Director of Finance and Administration, Mr. John Bolt

OTHER ORGANIZATIONS

The Back to God Hour, Dir. of Ministries, Dr. Calvin L. Bremer, International Headquarters, 6555 W. College Dr., Palos Heights, IL 60463

Christian Reformed Home Missions, Dir., Rev. John A. Rozeboom

Christian Reformed World Missions, US, Dir., Dr. Gary Bekker

Christian Ref. World Missions, Canada, Dir., Albert Karsten, 3475 Mainway, P.O. Box 5070 STN LCR 1, Burlington, ON L7R 3Y8

Christian Reformed World Relief, US, Dir., Andrew Ryskamp

Christian Reformed World Relief, Canada, Dir., H. Wayne deJong, 3475 Mainway, P.O. Box 5070 STN LCR 1, Burlington, ON L7R 3Y8

CRC Publications, Dir., Gary Mulder

Ministers' Pension Fund, Admn., Kenneth Horjus

Periodicals

The Banner

Christian Union

Organized in 1864 in Columbus, Ohio, the Christian Union stresses the oneness of the Church with Christ as its only head. The Bible is the only rule of faith and practice and good fruits the only condition of fellowship. Each local church governs itself.

Headquarters

316 Rexford Dr., Fort Wayne, IN 46816-1085 Tel. (260)456-7882 Fax (260)456-7802 (on request)

Website: www.christianunion.com

Media Contact, Pres., Rev. Phil Harris

Officers

Pres., Rev. Phil Harris, 316 Rexford Dr., Fort Wayne, IN 46816-1085 Tel. (260)456-7802

Vice Pres., Rev. Marion Hunerdosse, 1844 W. Kansas, Liberty, MD 64068-1919 Tel. (816) 781-5044

Sec., Joseph Cunningham, 1005 N. 5th St., Greenfield, OH 45123 Tel. (937)981-3476

Asst. Sec., Jim Eschenbrenner, 30055 130th Ave., Hedrick, IA 52563-8539 Tel. (641)653-4945

Treas., Rev. Neil Skiles, 80 Licking View Dr., Heath, OH 43056-1530 Tel. (740)522-4845, Fax 740-522-6076, skiles@adelphia.net

Periodicals

The Christian Union Witness (Monthly Magazine), P.O.Box 361, Greenfiled, OH 45123 Tel. (937)981-2760, Joseph Cunningham, Editor/Manager/Publisher

Church of the Brethren*

Eight German Pietists/Anabaptists, including their leader, Alexander Mack, founded the Brethren movement in 1708 in Schwarzenau, Germany. Begun in reaction to spiritual stagnation in state churches, the Brethren formed their own movement, modeled on the first-century church. They practice church discipline, believer baptism, anointing, and the love feast. They have no other creed than the New Testament, hold to principles of nonviolence, no force in religion, Christian service, and simplicity. They migrated to the colonies beginning in 1710 and settled at Germantown, Penn., moving westward and southward over the next 200 years. Emphasis on religion in daily life led to the formation of Brethren Volunteer Service in 1948, which continues today.

Headquarters

Church of the Brethren General Offices, 1451 Dundee Ave., Elgin, IL 60120-1694 Tel. (847) 742-5100 Fax (847)753-6103

Washington Office Email:

Email: generalboard@brethren.org

Brethren Service Center, 500 Main Street, P.O. Box 188, New Windsor, MD 21776-0188 Tel. (410)635-8710 Fax (410)635-8789

Email: bsc_gb@brethren.org

Washington Office, 337 North Carolina Ave. SE, Washington, D.C. 20003-2004 Tel. (202)546-3202 Fax (202)544-5852

Email: washington_office_gb@brethren.org

Media Contact, Walt Wiltschek, Dir. of Brethren Identity, Elgin Office.

Email: cobweb@brethren.org

Website: www.brethren.org

Officers

Moderator, Christopher D. Bowman, 210 N. Wall St., Martinsburg, PA 16662-1252 Tel. (814) 793-2422, Fax (814)793-3755, mburgcob@nb.net

Moderator, Jim Hardenbrook, 11030 Orchard Ave., Nampa, ID 83651-8258 Tel. (208)466-3321, jobrook@msn.com

Sec., Fred W. Swartz, 10047 Nokesville Rd., Manassas, VA 20110-4131 Tel. (703)369-3947, Swartz@emountain.net

GENERAL BOARD STAFF

Gen. Sec., Stanley J. Noffsinger, 1451 Dundee Ave., Elgin, IL 60120-1694 Tel. (847)742-5100 ext. 201, Fax (847)742-8212, snoffsinger_gb@brethren.org

Manager of Office Operations, Jon Kobel, 1451 Dundee Ave., Elgin, IL 60120-1694 Tel. (847)742-5100 ext. 202, Fax (847)742-8212, jkobel_gb@brethren.org

Dir., Human Resources, Mary Lou Garrison, 1451 Dundee Ave., Elgin, IL 60120-1694 Tel. (847)742-5100 ext. 258, Fax (847)742-8212, mgarrison-gb@brethren.org

LEADERSHIP TEAM

Gen. Sec., Stanley J. Noffsinger, 1451 Dundee Ave., Elgin, IL 60120-1694 Tel. (847)742-5100 ext. 201, Fax (847)742-8212, snoffsinger_gb@brethren.org

Exec. Dir., Centralized Resources and Chief Financial Officer/Treasurer, Judy E. Keyser, 1451 Dundee Ave., Elgin, IL 60120-1694 Tel. (847)742-5100 ext. 270, Fax (847)742-6103, jkeyser_gb@brethren.org

Exec. Dir. and Publisher, Brethren Press, Wendy McFadden, 1451 Dundee Ave., Elgin, IL 60120-1694 Tel. (847)742-5100 ext. 278, Fax (847)742-1407, wmcfadden_gb@brethren.org

Exec. Dir. of Congregational Life Ministries, Glenn F. Timmons, 1451 Dundee Ave., Elgin, IL 60120-1694 Tel. (847)742-5100 ext. 282, Fax (847)742-6103, gtimmons_gb@brethren.org

Exec. Dir. of Global Mission Partnerships, Mervin B. Keeney, 1451 Dundee Ave., Elgin, IL 60120-1694 Tel. (847)742-5100 ext. 226, Fax (847)742-6103, mission_gb@brethren.org

Exec. Dir., Brethren Service Center, Roy Winter, P.O. Box 188, New Windsor, MD 21776-0188 Tel. (410)635-8748, Fax (410)635-8739, rwinter_ gb@brethren.org

Periodicals

Messenger

Church of Christ

Joseph Smith and five others organized the Church of Christ on April 6, 1830 at Fayette, N.Y. In 1864 this body was directed by revelation through Granville Hedrick to return in 1867 to Independence, Mo. to the "consecrated land" dedicated by Joseph Smith. They did so and purchased the temple lot, dedicated in 1831.

Headquarters

Temple Lot, 200 S. River St., P.O. Box 472, Independence, MO 64051 Tel. (816)833-3995

Website: http://church-of-christ.com

Media Contact, Gen. Church Rep., William A. Sheldon, P.O. Box 472, Independence, MO 64051 Tel. (816)833-3995

Officers

Council of Apostles, Sec., Apostle Smith N. Brickhouse, P.O. Box 472, Independence, MO 64051

Gen. Bus. Mgr., Bishop Alvin Harris, P.O. Box 472, Independence, MO 64051

Periodicals

Zion's Advocate

The Church of Christ (Holiness) USA

The Church of Christ (Holiness) USA has a Divine commission to propagate the gospel throughout the world, to seek the conversion of sinners, to reclaim backsliders, to encourage the sanctification of believers, to support divine healing, and to advance the truth for the return of our Lord and Savior Jesus Christ. This must be done through proper organization.

The fundamental principles of Christ's Church have remained the same. The laws founded upon these principles are to remain unchanged. The Church of Christ (Holiness) USA is representative in form of government; therefore, the final authority in defining the organizational responsibilities rests with the national convention. The bishops of the church are delegated special powers to act in behalf of or speak for the church. The pastors are ordained ministers, who, under the call of God and His people, have divine oversight of local churches. However, the representative form of government gives ministry and laity equal authority in all deliberate bodies. With the leadership of the Holy Spirit, Respect, Loyalty, and Love will greatly increase.

Headquarters

329 East Monument Street, P.O. Box 3622, Jackson, MS 39207 Tel. (601)353-0222 Fax (601)353-4002

Email: Everything@cochusa.com

Website: www.cochusa.com/main.htm

Media Contact, Maurice D. Bingham, EdD, Senior Bishop

BOARD OF BISHOPS

Senior Bishop, Maurice D. Bingham, EdD
Eastern Diocese, Bishop Lindsay E. Jones
North Central Diocese, Bishop Bennett Wolfe
Northern Diocese, Bishop Emery Lindsay
Pacific Northwest Diocese, Bishop Robert Winn
South Central Diocese, Bishop Joseph Campbell
Southeastern Diocese, Bishop Victor P. Smith
Southwestern Diocese, Bishop Vernon Kennebrew
Western Diocese, Bishop Robert Winn
Board Member, Bishop James K. Mitchell

Church of Christ, Scientist

The Church of Christ, Scientist, was founded in 1879 by Mary Baker Eddy "to commemorate the word and works of our Master [Christ Jesus], which should reinstate primitive Christianity and its lost element of healing" (Church Manual, p. 17). Central to the Church's mission is making available worldwide Mrs. Eddy's definitive work on health and Bible-based Christian healing, *Science and Health With Key to the Scriptures*, as well as its publications, Internet sites, and broadcast programs, all of which respond to humanity's search for spiritual answers to today's pressing needs.

The Church also maintains an international speakers' bureau to introduce the public to Christian Science and Mrs. Eddy. Christian Science practitioners, living in hundreds of communities worldwide are available full-time to pray with anyone seeking comfort and healing. And Christian Science teachers hold yearly classes for those interested in a more specific understanding of how to practice the Christian Science system of healing.

The worldwide activities and business of the Church are transacted by a five-member Board of Directors in Boston. About 2,000 congregations, each democratically organized and governed, are located in approximately 75 countries. The church has no clergy. Worship services are conducted by lay persons elected to serve as Readers. Each church maintains a Reading Room —a bookstore open to the community for spiritual inquiry and research—as well as a Sunday School where young people discuss the contemporary relevance of ideas from the Bible and Science and Health.

Headquarters

The First Church of Christ, Scientist, 175 Huntington Ave., Boston, MA 02115

Website: www.spirituality.com

Media Contact, Mgr., Comm. on Publication, Gary A. Jones Tel. (617)450-3300 Fax (617) 450-7397

Officers

Board of Directors, Virginia S. Harris, Walter D. Jones, M. Victor Westberg, Mary Ridgway, Mary Metzner Trammell

Pres., Hans-Joachim Trapp
Treas., Walter D. Jones
Clk., Mary Ridgway
First Reader, Candace duMars
Second Reader, William E. Moody

Periodicals

The Christian Science Monitor (www. csmonitor.com), *The Christian Science Journal, Christian Science Sentinel, The Herald of Christian Science* (13 languages), Christian Science Quarterly Bible Lessons in 16 languages and English Braille

Church of God (Anderson, Indiana)

The Church of God (Anderson, Indiana) began in 1881 when Daniel S. Warner and several associates felt constrained to forsake all denominational hierarchies as formal creeds, trusting solely in the Holy Spirit as their overseer and the Bible as their statement of belief. These people saw themselves at the forefront of a movement to restore unity and holiness to the church; not to establish another denomination, but to promote primary allegiance to Jesus Christ so as to transcend denominational loyalties.

Deeply influenced by Wesleyan theology and Pietism, the Church of God has emphasized conversion, holiness, and attention to the Bible. Worship services tend to be informal, accentuating expository preaching and robust singing.

There is no formal membership. Persons are assumed to be members on the basis of witness to a conversion experience and evidence that supports such witness. The absence of formal membership is also consistent with the church's understanding of how Christian unity is to be achieved—that is, by preferring the label Christian before all others.

The Church of God is congregational in its government. Each local congregation is autonomous and may call any recognized Church of God minister to be its pastor and may retain him or her as long as is mutually pleasing. Ministers are ordained and disciplined by state or provincial assemblies made up predominantly of ministers. National program agencies serve the church through coordinated ministries and resource materials.

There are Church of God congregations in 89 foreign countries, most of which are resourced by one or more missionaries. There are slightly more Church of God adherents overseas than in North America.

GENERAL OFFICES

CHURCH OF GOD MINISTRIES, INC.:

Gen. Dir., Pres., Ronald V. Duncan P.O. Box 2420, Anderson, IN 46018-2420 Tel. (765) 642-0256 Fax (765)642-5652

Includes Congregational Ministries, Outreach Ministries, and Resource & Linking Ministries

Email: JMartin@chog.org

Website: www.chog.org

Media Contact, Sam Collins, Communications Coordinator, scollins@chog.org

OTHER CHURCH OF GOD ORGANIZATIONS

Board of Pensions, Pres., Exec. Sec.-Treas., Jeffery A. Jenness, Box 2299, Anderson, IN 46018

Warner Press, Inc., Pres., Eric King, Box 2499, Anderson, IN 46018

Anderson University, Pres., James L. Edwards, 1100 E. 5th St., Anderson, IN 46012

Mid-America Christian University, Pres., John Fozard, 3500 SW 119th St., Oklahoma City, OK 73170

Warner Pacific College, Pres., Jay A. Barber, Jr., 2219 SE 68th Ave, Portland, OR 97215

Warner Southern College, Pres., Gregory V. Hall, 13895 Hwy 27, Lake Wales, FL 33859

Women of the Church of God, Exec. Dir., Linda J. Mason, Box 2328, Anderson, IN 46018

Bd. of Church Extension, Pres., J. Perry Grubbs, Box 2069, Anderson, IN 46018

Periodicals

Missions Magazine, Pathways to God, Communion, People to People, YMI Update

The Church of God in Christ

The Church of God in Christ was founded in 1907 in Memphis, Tenn., and was organized by Bishop Charles Harrison Mason, a former Baptist minister who pioneered the embryonic stages of the Holiness movement beginning in 1895 in Mississippi.

Its founder organized four major departments between 1910-1916: the Women's Department, the Sunday School, Young Peoples Willing Workers, and Home and Foreign Mission.

The Church is trinitarian and teaches the infallibility of scripture, the need for regeneration, and subsequent baptism of the Holy Ghost. It emphasizes holiness as God's standard for Christian conduct. It recognizes as ordinances Holy Communion, Water Baptism, and Feet Washing. Its governmental structure is basically episcopal with the General Assembly being the Legislative body.

Headquarters

Mason Temple, 938 Mason St., Memphis, TN 38126 Tel. (901)947-9300; Mailing Address: P.O. Box 320, Memphis, TN 38101

Temple Church Of God In Christ, 672 S. Lauderdale St., Memphis, TN 38126 Tel. (901) 527-9202

Email: EJOHNCOGIC@aol.com

Website: netministries.org/see/churches/ch00833

GENERAL OFFICES

Office of the Presiding Bishop, Presiding Bishop, Bishop Chandler D. Owens Tel. (901) 947-9338

Office of the General Sec., Gen. Sec., Bishop W. W. Hamilton Tel. (901)947-9358

Office of the Financial Sec., Sec., Bishop Frank O. White Tel. (901)947-9310

Office of the Treasurer, Treas., Bishop Samuel L. Lowe Tel. (901)947-9381

Office of the Bd. of Trustees, Chmn., Elder Dwight Green Tel. (901)947-9326

Office of the Chief Operating Officer at World Headquarters, Elder A.Z. Hall Jr., 930 Mason Street, Memphis, TN Tel. (901)947-9358

Office of the Clergy Bureau, Dir., Bishop W. W. Hamilton Tel. (901)974-9358

Office of Supt. of National Properties, Supt., Elder Marles Flowers Tel. (901)947-9330

Office of Accounting, Chief Financial Officer, Ms. Sylvia H. Law Tel. (901)947-9361

Department of Evangelism, Pres., Elder Richard White, Atlanta, GA Tel. (404)361-7020

Department of Missions, Pres., Bishop Carlis L. Moody, Tel. (901)947-9316; Vice Pres., Elder Jesse W. Denny

Dept. of Music, Pres., Ms. LuVoinia Whittley, 20205 Augusta Dr., Olympia Fields, IL 60461 Tel. (312)626-1970

Dept. of Sunday Schools, Gen. Supt., Bishop Jerry Macklin, 1027 W. Tennyson Rd., Hayward, CA 94544 Tel. (510)783-9377

Dept. of Women, Pres./Gen. Supervisor, Mother Willie Mae Rivers, P.O. Box 1052, Memphis, TN 38101 Tel. (901)775-0600

Dept. of Youth (Youth Congress), Pres., Elder J. Drew Sheard, 7045 Curtis Dr., Detroit, MI 48235 Tel. (313)864-7170

Church of God in Christ Book Store, Mgr., Geraldine Miller, 285 S. Main St., Memphis, TN 38103 Tel. (901)947-9304

Church of God in Christ Publishing House, CEO, Dr. David A. Hall Sr., Tel. (901)947-9342

Board of Publications, Chmn., Bishop R.L.H. Winbush Tel. (901)947-9342

Periodicals

The Whole Truth, The Voice of Missions

Church of God in Christ, International

The Church of God in Christ, International was organized in 1969 in Kansas City, Mo., by 14 bishops of the Church of God in Christ of Memphis, Tenn. The doctrine is the same, but the separation came because of disagreement over polity and governmental authority. The Church is Wesleyan in theology (two works of grace) but stresses the experience of full baptism of the Holy Ghost with the initial evidence of speaking with other tongues as the Spirit gives utterance.

Headquarters

170 Adelphi St., Brooklyn, NY 11205 Tel. (718) 625-9175

Email: laity@cogic.org

Website: www.cogic.org/main.htm

Media Contact, Natl. Sec., Rev. Sis. Sharon R. Dunn

Officers

Presiding Bishop, Most Rev. Carl E. Williams Sr.

Vice Presiding Bishop, Rt. Rev. J. P. Lucas, 90 Holland St., Newark, NJ 07103

Sec.-Gen., Deacon Dennis Duke, 360 Colorado Ave., Bridgeport, CT 06605

Exec. Admn., Horace K. Williams, Word of God Center, Newark, NJ

Women's Dept., Natl. Supervisor, Evangelist Elvonia Williams

Youth Dept., Pres., Dr. Joyce Taylor, 137-17 135th Ave. S, Ozone Park, NY 11420

Music Dept., Pres., Isaiah Heyward

Bd. of Bishops, Chpsn., Bishop J. C. White, 360 Colorado Ave., Bridgeport, CT 06605

Church of God in Christ, Mennonite

The Church of God in Christ, Mennonite was organized by the evangelist/reformer John Holdeman in Ohio. The church unites with the faith of the Waldenses, Anabaptists, and other such groups throughout history. Emphasis is placed on obedience to the teachings of the Bible, including the doctrine of the new birth and spiritual life, noninvolvement in government or the military, head-coverings for the women, beards for the men, and separation from the world shown by simplicity in clothing, homes, possessions, and lifestyle. The church has a worldwide membership of about 19,630, largely concentrated in the United States and Canada.

Headquarters

P.O. Box 313, 420 N. Wedel Ave., Moundridge, KS 67107 Tel. (620)345-2532 Fax (620)345-2582

Media Contact, Dale Koehn, P.O. Box 230, Moundridge, KS 67107 Tel. (620)345-2532 Fax (620)345-2582

Periodicals

Messenger of Truth

Church of God (Cleveland, Tennessee)

It is one of America's oldest Pentecostal churches founded in 1886 as an outgrowth of the holiness revival under the name Christian Union. In 1907 the church adopted the organizational name Church of God. It has its foundation upon the principles of Christ as revealed in the Bible. The Church of God is Christian, Protestant, foundational in its doctrine, evangelical in practice, and distinctively Pentecostal. It maintains a centralized form of government and a commitment to world evangelization. The first church of Canada was established in 1919 in Scotland Farm, Manitoba. Paul H. Walker became the first overseer of Canada in 1931.

Headquarters

Intl. Offices, 2490 Keith St. NW, Cleveland, TN 37320 Tel. (423)472-3361 Fax (423)478-7066

Website: www.churchofgod.cc/default_nav40.asp

Media Contact, Dir. of Communications, Michael L. Baker, P.O.Box 2430, Cleveland, TN 37320-2430 Tel. (423)478-7112 Fax (423)478-7066

EXECUTIVES

Gen. Overseer, R. Lamar Vest

Asst. Gen. Overseers, T. L. Lowery, Bill F. Sheeks, Orville Hagan

Sec.-Gen., Gene D. Rice

Canada–Eastern, Rev. Andrew Binda, P.O.Box 2036, Brampton, ON L6T 3TO Tel. (905)793-2213 Fax (905) 793-9173

Canada–Western, Rev. Raymond W. Wall, Box 54055, 2640 52 St. NE, Calgary, AB T1Y 6S6 Tel. (403)293-8817 Fax (403)293-8832

Canada–Quebec–Maritimes, Rev. Jaques Houle, 19 Orly, Granby, QC J2H 1Y4 Tel. (514)378-4442 Fax (514) 378-8646

Canada–National, Rev. Ralph R. Glagau, P.O.Box 333, Stn B, Etobicoke, ON M9W 5L3 Tel. (416)741-9222 Fax (416)741-3717

DEPARTMENTS

Benefits Board, CEO, Arthur Rhodes
Business & Records, Dir., Julian B. Robinson
Care Ministries, Dir., John D. Nichols
Chaplains Commission, Dir., Robert D. Crick
Communications, Media Ministries, Dir., Michael L. Baker
Education–European Bible Seminary, Dir., John Sims
Education–Hispanic Institute of Ministry, Dir., Jose D. Montanez
Education–International Bible College, Pres., Cheryl Busse
Education–Lee University, Pres., C. Paul Conn
Education–Patten College, Pres., Gary Moncher
Education–Puerto Rico Bible School, Pres., Ildefonso Caraballo
Education–School of Ministry, Chancellor, Paul L. Walker
Education–Theological Seminary, Pres., Steven J. Land
Evangelism & Home Missions, Dir., Larry J. Timmerman
Evangelism–Black Ministries, Dir., Asbury R. Sellers
Evangelism–Cross-Cultural Min., Dir., Wallace J. Sibley
Evangelism–Hispanic Ministry, Dir., Esdras Betancourt
Evangelism–Native American Ministries, Dir., Douglas M. Cline
Lay Ministries, Dir., Leonard Albert
Legal Services, Dir., Dennis W. Watkins
Men/Women of Action, Dir., Hugh Carver
Ministerial Development, Dir., Larry G. Hess
Ministry to Israel, Dir., J. Michael Utterback
Ministry to the Military, Dir., Robert A. Moore
Music Ministries, Dir., Delton Alford
Pentecostal Resource Center, Dir., Don Smeeton
Pentecostal Research Center, David G. Roebuck
Publications, Dir., Daniel F. Boling
Stewardship, Dir., Al Taylor
Women's Ministries, Coordinator, Oleda Adkinson
World Missions, Dir., Lovell R. Cary
Youth & Christian Education, Dir., John D. Childers

Periodicals

Church of God Evangel, Church of God Evangelica, Save Our World, Ministry Now Profiles

Church of God by Faith, Inc.

Founded 1914, in Jacksonville Heights, Fla., by Elder John Bright, this church believes the word of God as interpreted by Jesus Christ to be the only hope of salvation and Jesus Christ the only mediator for people.

Headquarters

1315 Lane Ave. S, Suite 6, Jacksonville, FL 32205 Tel. (904)783-8500 Fax (904)783-9911
Email: natl-hq@cogbf.org
Website: www.cogbf.org
Media Contact, Ofc. Mgr., Sarah E. Lundy

Officers

Presiding Bishop, James E. McKnight, P.O. Box 121, Gainesville, FL 32601
Treas., Elder Theodore Brown, 93 Girard Pl., Newark, NJ 07108
Ruling Elders, Elder John Robinson, 300 Essex Dr., Ft. Pierce, FL 33450; Elder D. C. Rourk, 207 Chestnut Hill Dr., Rochester, NY 14617
Exec. Sec., David C. Rourk, 207 Chestnut Hill Dr., Rochester, NY 14617

Church of God General Conference (Oregon, IL and Morrow, GA)

This church is the outgrowth of several independent local groups of similar faith. Some were in existence as early as 1800, and others date their beginnings to the arrival of British immigrants around 1847. Many local churches carried the name Church of God of the Abrahamic Faith.

State and district conferences of these groups were formed as an expression of mutual cooperation. A national organization was instituted at Philadelphia in 1888. Because of strong convictions on the questions of congregational rights and authority, however, it ceased to function until 1921, when the present General Conference was formed at Waterloo, Iowa.

The Bible is accepted as the supreme standard of faith. Adventist in viewpoint, the second (premillenial) coming of Christ is strongly emphasized. The church teaches that the kingdom of God will be literal, beginning in Jerusalem at the time of the return of Christ and extending to all nations. Emphasis is placed on the oneness of God and the Sonship of Christ, that Jesus did not pre-exist prior to his birth in Bethlehem, and that the Holy Spirit is the power and influence of God. Membership is dependent on faith, repentance, and baptism by immersion.

The work of the General Conference is carried on under the direction of the board of directors. With a congregational church government, the General Conference exists primarily as a means of mutual cooperation and for the development of yearly projects and enterprises.

The headquarters and Bible College were moved to Morrow, Ga. in 1991.

Headquarters

P.O. Box 100,000, Morrow, GA 30260 Tel. (404) 362-0052 Fax (404)362-9307
Email: info@abc-coggc.org
Website: www.abc-coggc.org
Media Contact, David Krogh

Officers

Pres., Mr. Tim Jones, Box 100,000, Morrow , GA 30260 Tel. (404)362-9307, tjones@abc-coggc.org
Chpsn., Charles Bottolfs, 43137 Happywoods Rd., Hammond, LA 70403 Tel. (985)542-1555, bottdlcg@I055.com

Vice Chpsn., Pastor Greg Demmitt, 825 E. Drake Dr., Tempe, AZ 85283 Tel. (480)820-9885, demitt@amug.org

Sec., Keith Williams, 3250 Vermont Ave SW, Grandville, MI 49418 Tel. (616)538-9181, kdkwilliams@earthlink.net

Treas., Paul Duncan, 1044 Cottrell Hill, Lenoir, NC 28645 Tel. (616)878-7118, 1mpen@juno.com

OTHER ORGANIZATIONS

Bus. Admn., Operations Manager, Mr. Gary Burnham, Box 100,000, Morrow, GA 30260 Tel. (404)362-0052, Fax (404)362-9307, gburnham@abc-coggc.org

Atlanta Bible College, Pres., Dr. Brian Atra, Box 100,000, Morrow, GA 30260 Tel. (404)362-0052, Fax (404)362-9307, drbia@yahoo.com

Periodicals

The Restitution Herald, A Journal From the Radical Reformation, Church of God Progress Journal

Church of God, Mountain Assembly, Inc.

The church was formed in 1895 and organized in 1906 by J. H. Parks, S. N. Bryant, Tom Moses and William Douglas.

Headquarters

164 N. Florence Ave., P.O. Box 157, Jellico, TN 37762 Tel. (423)784-8260 Fax (423)784-3258

Email: cgmahdq@jellico.com

Website: www.cgmahdq.org

Media Contact, Gen. Sec.-Treas., Rev. Alfred Newton Jr.

Officers

Gen. Overseer, Rev. Cecil Johnson

Asst. Gen. Overseer, World Missions Dir., Rev. Lonnie Lyke

Gen. Sec.-Treas., Rev. Alfred Newton Jr.

Youth Ministries & Camp Dir., Rev. Ken Ellis

Periodicals

The Gospel Herald

Church of God of Prophecy

The Church of God of Prophecy is one of the churches that grew out of the work of A.J. Tomlinson in the first half of the 20th century. Historically, it shares a common heritage with the Church of God (Cleveland, Tenn.) and is in the mainstream of the classical Pentecostal-holiness tradition.

At the death of A.J. Tomlinson in 1943, M.A. Tomlinson was named General Overseer and served until his retirement in 1990. He emphasized unity and fellowship unlimited by racial, social, or political differences. The next General Overseer, Billy D. Murray Sr., who served from 1990 until his retirement in 2000, emphasized a commitment to the promotion of Christian unity and world evangelization. In July 2000, Fred S. Fisher Sr. was duly selected to serve as the fourth General Overseer of the Church of God of Prophecy.

From its beginnings, the Church has based its beliefs on "the whole Bible, rightly divided," and has accepted the Bible as God's Holy Word, inspired, inerrant, and infallible. The church is firm in its commitment to orthodox Christian belief. The Church affirms that there is one God, eternally existing in three persons—Father, Son, and Holy Spirit. It believes in the deity of Christ, His virgin birth, His sinless life, the physical miracles He performed, His atoning death on the cross, His bodily resurrection, His ascension to the right hand of the Father, and His Second coming. The church professes that salvation results from grace alone through faith in Christ, that regeneration by the Holy Spirit is essential for the salvation of sinful men, and that sanctification by the blood of Christ makes possible personal holiness. It affirms the present ministry of the Holy Spirit by Whose indwelling believers are able to live godly lives and have power for service. The church believes in, and promotes, the ultimate unity of believers as prayed for by Christ in John 17. The church stresses the sanctity of human life and is committed to the sanctity of the marriage bond and the importance of strong, loving Christian families. Other official teachings include Holy Spirit baptism with tongues as initial evidence; manifestation of the spiritual gifts; divine healing; premillenial second-coming of Christ; total abstinence from the use of tobacco, alcohol, and narcotics; water baptism by immersion; the Lord's supper and washing of the saints' feet; and a concern for moderation and holiness in all dimensions of lifestyle.

The Church is racially integrated on all levels, including top leadership. Women play a prominent role in church affairs, serving in pastoral roles and other leadership positions. The church presbytery has recently adopted plurality of leadership in the selection of a General Oversight Group. This group consists of eight bishops located around the world who, along with the General Overseer, are responsible for inspirational leadership and vision casting for the church body.

The Church has local congregations in all 50 states and more than 100 nations worldwide. Organizationally there is a strong emphasis on international missions, evangelism, youth and children's ministries, women's and men's ministries, stewardship, communications, publishing, leadership development, and discipleship.

INTERNATIONAL OFFICES

P.O. Box 2910, Cleveland, TN 37320-2910

Email: betty@cogop.org

Website: www.cogop.org

Media Contact, Natl. Overseer, Levy Clarke, 5145 Tomken Rd., Mississauga, ON L4 W1P1 Tel. (905)625-1278 Fax (905)625-1316.

Officers

Gen. Overseer, Bishop Fred S. Fisher Sr.

General Presbyters: Sherman Allen, Sam Clements, Daniel Corbett, Clayton Endecott, Miguel Mojica, José Reyes Sr., Felix Santiago, Brice Thompson

International Offices Ministries: Dirs.; Finance, Communications, and Publishing, Oswill Williams; Global Outreach and Administrative Asst. to the General Presbyters, Randy Howard; Leadership Development and Discipleship Ministries, Larry Duncan.

Periodicals

White Wing Messenger (ENG), *Victory* (Youth Magazine/Sunday School Curriculum), *The Happy Harvester, White Wing Messenger* (Spanish).

The Church of God (Seventh Day), Denver, Colorado

The Church of God (Seventh Day) began in southwestern Michigan in 1858, when a group of Sabbath-keepers led by Gilbert Cranmer refused to give endorsement to the visions and writings of Ellen G. White, a principal in the formation of the Seventh-Day Adventist Church. Another branch of Sabbath-keepers, which developed near Cedar Rapids, Iowa, in 1860, joined the Michigan church in 1863 to publish a paper called *The Hope of Israel*, the predecessor to the *Bible Advocate*, the church's present publication. As membership grew and spread into Missouri and Nebraska, it organized the General Conference of the Church of God in 1884. The words "Seventh Day" were added to its name in 1923. The headquarters of the church was in Stanberry, MO, from 1888 until 1950, when it moved to Denver.

The Church teaches salvation is a gift of God's grace, and is available solely by faith in Jesus Christ, the Savior; that saving faith is more than mental assent, it involves active trust and repentance from sin. Out of gratitude, Christians will give evidence of saving faith by a lifestyle that conforms to God's commandments, including the seventh-day Sabbath, which members observe as a tangible expression of their faith and rest in God as their Creator and Redeemer. The church believes in the imminent, personal, and visible return of Christ; that the dead are in an unconscious state awaiting to be resurrected, the wicked to be destroyed, and the righteous to be rewarded to eternal life in the presence of God on a restored earth. The church observes two ordinances, baptism by immersion and an annual Communion service accompanied by foot washing.

Headquarters

330 W. 152nd Ave., P.O. Box 33677, Denver, CO 80233 Tel. (303)452-7973 Fax (303)452-0657

Email: offices@cog7.org

Website: www.cog7.org

Media Contact, Pres., Whaid Rose

MINISTRIES

Missions Ministries: Dir., William Hicks; Church Planting Dir., Mike Vlad; Home Missions Dir., Ralph Diaz; Missions Abroad, Dir., William Hicks

Publications/Bible of Advocate Press: Dir., John Crisp

Ministerial Training System: Chmn., Harvey Fischer

Young Adult Ministry: Dir., Tony & Becky Riggs

Youth Ministry: Dirs., Kurt & Kristi Lang

Women's Ministry: Dir., Mary Ling

Periodicals

The Bible Advocate (English & Spanish), *Pulse* (English & Spanish)

The Church of Illumination

The Church of Illumination was organized in 1908 for the express purpose of establishing congregations-at-large; offering a spiritual, esoteric, philosophic interpretation of the vital biblical teachings, thereby satisfying the inner spiritual needs of those seeking spiritual truth, yet permitting them to remain in, or return to, their former church membership.

Headquarters

Beverly Hall, 5966 Clymer Rd., Quakertown, PA 18951 Tel. (800)779-3796

Email: bevhall@comcat.com

Website: www.soul.org

Media Contact, Dir. General, Gerald E. Poesnecker, P.O. Box 220, Quakertown, PA 18951 Tel. (215)536-7048 Fax (215)536-7058

Officers

Dir.-General, Gerald E. Poesnecker, P.O. Box 220, Quakertown, PA 18951

The Church of Jesus Christ (Bickertonites)

This church was organized in 1862 at Green Oak, PA, by William Bickerton, who obeyed the Restored Gospel under Sidney Rigdon's following in 1845.

Headquarters

Sixth & Lincoln Sts., Monongahela, PA 15063 Tel. (412)258-3066

Media Contact, Exec. Sec., John Manes, 2007 Cutter Dr., McKees Rocks, PA 15136 Tel. (412)771-4513

Officers

Pres., Dominic Thomas, 6010 Barrie, Dearborn, MI 48126

First Counselor, Paul Palmieri, 319 Pine Dr., Aliquippa, PA 15001 Tel. (412)378-4264

Second Counselor, Robert Watson, Star Rt. 5, Box 36, Gallup, NM 87301

Exec. Sec., John Manes, 2007 Cutter Dr., McKees Rocks, PA 15136 Tel. (412)771-4513

Periodicals

The Gospel News

The Church of Jesus Christ of Latter-day Saints

This church was organized April 6, 1830, at Fayette, NY by Joseph Smith. Members believe Joseph Smith was divinely directed to restore the gospel to the earth, and that through him the keys to the Aaronic and Melchizedek priesthoods and temple work also were restored. Members believe that both the Bible and the Book of Mormon (a record of the Lord's dealings with His people on the American continent 600 B.C.–421 A.D.) are scripture. Membership is over eleven million.

In addition to the First Presidency, the governing bodies of the church include the Quorum of the Twelve Apostles, the Presidency of the Seventy, the Quorums of the Seventy, and the Presiding Bishopric.

Headquarters

47 E. South Temple St., Salt Lake City, UT 84150 Tel. (801)240-1000 Fax (801)240-1167

Website: www.lds.org

Media Contact, Dir., Media Relations, Michael Otterson Tel. (801)240-1111 Fax (801)240-1167

Officers

Pres., Gordon B. Hinckley

1st Counselor, Thomas S. Monson

2nd Counselor, James E. Faust

Quorum of the Twelve Apostles: Pres., Boyd K. Packer, L. Tom Perry, David B. Haight, Neal A. Maxwell, Russell M. Nelson, Dallin H. Oaks, M. Russell Ballard, Joseph B. Wirthlin, Richard G. Scott, Robert D. Hales, Jeffrey R. Holland, Henry B. Eyring

AUXILIARY ORGANIZATIONS

Sunday Schools: Gen. Pres., Cecil O. Samuelson Jr.

Relief Society: Gen. Pres., Bonnie D. Parkin

Young Women: Gen. Pres., Margaret Nadauld

Young Men: Gen. Pres., F. Melvin Hammond

Primary: Gen. Pres., Coleen K. Menlove

Periodicals

The Ensign, Liahona, The New Era, Friend Magazine

Church of the Living God (Motto, Christian Workers for Fellowship)

The Church of the Living God was founded by William Christian in April 1889 at Caine Creek, Ark. It was the first black church in America without Anglo-Saxon roots and not founded by white missionaries.

Chief Christian, as he is now referred, was born a slave in Mississippi on Nov. 10, 1856, and grew up uneducated. In 1875, he united with the Missionary Baptist Church and began to preach. In 1888, he left the Baptist Church and began what was known as Christian Friendship Work. Believing himself to have been inspired by the Spirit of God through divine revelation and close study of the Scriptures, he was led to the truth that the Bible refers to the church as The Church of the Living God (I Timothy 3:15). In 1889, he established the Church of the Living God organization.

The organization is nondenominational, nonsectarian, and Trinitarian and believes in the infallibility of the Scriptures. It emphasizes believer's baptism by immersion, the use of water and unleavened bread element in the Lord's Supper, and the washing of feet that is required only when one unites with the church.

The local organizations are know as "Temples" rather than as "Churches" and are subject to the authority of the general assembly. The presiding officer is styled as "Chief Bishop." The ministry includes bishops, overseers, evangelists, pastors, missionaries, and local preachers. The Executive Board is in charge of the operation of the entire organization, at, the absence of the Annual Assembly, Synod, Annual, General Assembly meets quadrennial.

The Church of the Living God, now headquartered in Cincinnati, Ohio, has been in existence for more than 114 years. It is represented by approximately 10,000 members throughout 25 states within the US. The presiding officer, Chief Bishop W.E. Crumes, has led the organization for more than 30 years.

Headquarters

430 Forest Ave., Cincinnati, OH 45229 Tel. (513)569-5660 Fax (513)569-5661

Media Contact, Chief Bishop, W. E. Crumes

Executive Board

Chief Bishop, W. E. Crumes, 430 Forest Ave., Cincinnati, OH 45229

Vice Chief Bishop, Robert D. Tyler, 3802 Bedford, Omaha, NE 68110

Exec. Sec., Bishop C. A. Lewis, 1360 N. Boston, Tulsa, OK 73111

Gen. Sec., Elder Raymond Powell Sr., 2159 E. 95th St., Chicago, IL 60617

Gen. Treas., Elder Harry Hendricks, 11935 Cimarron Ave., Hawthorne, CA 90250

Bishop E.L. Bowie, 2037 NE 18th St., Oklahoma City, OK 73111

Bishop Leroy Smith Jr., 1418 Faraday, Peoria, IL 61605

Bishop Jeff Ruffin, 302 E. Monte Way, Phoenix, AZ 85040

Bishop S.E. Shannon, 1034 S. King Hwy., St. Louis, MO 63110

Bishop Elbert Jones, 4522 Melwood, Memphis, TN 38109

Bishop Harold Edwards, P.O.Box 411489, Dallas, TX 75249

NATIONAL DEPARTMENTS

Convention Planning Committee

Young People's Progressive Union

Christian Education Dept.

Sunday School Dept.
Natl. Evangelist Bd.
Natl. Nurses Guild
Natl. Women's Work Dept.
Natl. Music Dept.
Natl. Usher Board
Natl. Sec. Office

Periodicals

The Gospel Truth

Church of the Lutheran Brethren of America

The Church of the Lutheran Brethren of America was organized in December 1900. Five independent Lutheran congregations met together in Milwaukee, Wisc., and adopted a constitution patterned very closely on that of the Lutheran Free Church of Norway.

The spiritual awakening in the Midwest during the 1890s crystallized into convictions that led to the formation of a new church body. Chief among the concerns were church membership practices, observance of Holy Communion, confirmation practices, and local church government.

The Church of the Lutheran Brethren practices a simple order of worship with the sermon as the primary part of the worship service. It believes that personal profession of faith is the primary criterion for membership in the congregation. The Communion service is reserved for those who profess faith in Christ as savior. Each congregation is autonomous and the synod serves the congregations in advisory and cooperative capacities.

The synod supports a world mission program in Cameroon, Chad, Japan, and Taiwan. Approximately 40 percent of the synodical budget is earmarked for world missions. A growing home mission ministry is planting new congregations in the United States and Canada. Affiliate organizations operate several retirement, nursing homes, conference, and retreat centers.

Headquarters

1020 Alcott Ave. W, Box 655, Fergus Falls, MN 56538 Tel. (218)739-3336 Fax (218)739-5514
Email: clba@clba.org
Website: www.clba.org
Media Contact, Pres., Rev. Joel Egge

Officers

Pres., Rev. Joel Egge
Vice Pres., Rev. David Rinden
Sec., Rev. Richard Vettrus, 707 Crestview Dr., West Union, IA 52175
Exec. Dir. of Finance, Bradley Martinson
Lutheran Brethren Schools Representative, Dr. Eugene Boe
World Missions, Exec. Dir., Rev. Matthew Rogness
Home Missions, Exec. Dir., Rev. Armin Jahr
Church Services, Exec. Dir., Rev. Brent Juliot
Youth Ministries, Exec. Dir., Nathan Lee

Periodicals

Faith & Fellowship

Church of the Lutheran Confession

The Church of the Lutheran Confession held its constituting convention in Watertown, S.D., in August of 1960. The Church of the Lutheran Confession was begun by people and congregations who withdrew from church bodies that made up what was then known as the Synodical Conference over the issue of unionism. Following such passages as I Corinthians 1:10 and Romans 16:17-18, the Church of the Lutheran Confession holds the conviction that mutual agreement with the doctrines of Scripture is essential and necessary before exercise of church fellowship is appropriate.

Members of the Church of the Lutheran Confession uncompromisingly believe the Holy Scriptures to be divinely inspired and therefore inerrant. They subscribe to the historic Lutheran Confessions as found in the Book of Concord of 1580 because they are a correct exposition of Scripture.

The Church of the Lutheran Confession exists to proclaim, preserve, and spread the saving truth of the gospel of Jesus Christ, so that the redeemed of God may learn to know Jesus Christ as their Lord and Savior and follow him through this life to the life to come.

Headquarters

501 Grover Rd., Eau Claire, WI 54701 Tel. (715) 836-6622
Email: JohnHLau@juno.com
Website: www.clclutheran.org
Media Contact, Pres., Daniel Fleischer Tel. (361) 241-5147

Officers

Pres., Rev. John Schierenbeck, 3015 Ave. K NW, Winter Haven, FL 33881
Mod., Prof. Ronald Roehl, 515 Ingram Dr. W., Eau Claire, WI 54701
Vice Pres., Rev. Mark Bernthal, 3232 West Point Rd., Middleton, WI 53562 Tel. (608)233-2244
Sec., Rev. James Albrecht, 102 Market St., P.O. Box 98 Okebena, MN 55432-2408
Treas., Dr. James Sydow, 500 Grover Rd., Eau Claire, WI 54701
Archivist, Prof. David Lau, 507 Ingram Dr., Eau Claire, WI 54701
Statistician, Dr. James Sydow, 500 Grover Rd., Eau Claire, WI 54701

Periodicals

The Lutheran Spokesman, Journal of Theology

Church of the Nazarene

The Church of the Nazarene resulted from the merger of three independent holiness groups. The Association of Pentecostal Churches in America, located principally in New York and

New England, joined at Chicago in 1907 with a largely West Coast body called the Church of the Nazarene and formed the Pentecostal Church of the Nazarene. A southern group, the Holiness Church of Christ, united with the Pentecostal Church of the Nazarene at Pilot Point, Tex., in 1908. In 1919 the word "Pentecostal" was dropped from the name. Principal leaders in the organization were Phineas Bresee, William Howard Hoople, H.F. Reynolds, and C.B. Jernigan. The first congregation in Canada was organized in November 1902 by Dr. H.F. Reynolds in Oxford, Nova Scotia.

The Church of the Nazarene emphasizes the doctrine of entire sanctification, or Christian Holiness. It stresses the importance of a devout and holy life and a positive witness before the world by the power of the Holy Spirit. Nazarenes express their faith through evangelism, compassionate ministries, and education.

Nazarene government is representative, a studied compromise between episcopacy and congregationalism. Quadrennially, the various districts elect delegates to a general assembly at which six general superintendents are elected.

The international denomination has 9 liberal arts colleges, two graduate seminaries, 43 Bible colleges, two schools of nursing, and a junior college. The church maintains over 600 missionaries in 119 world areas. World services include medical, educational, and religious ministries. Books, periodicals, and other Christian literature are published at the Nazarene Publishing House.

The church is a member of the Christian Holiness Partnership and the National Association of Evangelicals.

Headquarters

6401 The Paseo, Kansas City, MO 64131 Tel. (816)333-7000 Fax (816)822-9071

Email: ssm@nazarene.org

Website: www.nazarene.org

Media Contact, Gen. Sec./Headquarters Operations Officer (HOO), Dr. Jack Stone Tel. (816)333-7000 ext. 2517

Officers

Gen. Supts., James H. Diehl, Paul G. Cunningham, Jerry D. Porter, Jim L. Bond, W. Talmadge Johnson, Jesse C. Middendorf

Gen. Sec./Headquarters Operation Officer (HOO), Jack Stone

Gen. Treas./Headquarters Financial Officer (HFO), Marilyn McCool

OTHER ORGANIZATIONS

General Bd., Sec., Jack Stone; Treas., Robert Foster

USA–Canada Mission, Evangelism, Dir., Tom Nees

Clergy Services, Dir., Ron Blake

Communications, Dir., Michael Estep

NCN Productions, Dir., David Anderson

World Literature Ministries, Dir., Ray Hendrix

Int. Bd. of Educ., Ed. Commissioner, Jerry Lambert

Pensions & Benefits Services USA & Intl., Don Walter

Adult Min., Dir., David Felter

Children's Min., Dir., Lynda Boardman

Curriculum, Dir., Randy Cloud

NYI Min., Dir., Gary Hartke

World Mission Div., Dir., Louie Bustle

Nazarene Mission International, Dir., Nina Gunter

Mission Strategy, Dir., Tom Nees

Information Technology and Research, Dir., Dale Jones

Periodicals

Holiness Today, Preacher's Magazine, Cross Walk, Grow Magazine

Church of Our Lord Jesus Christ of the Apostolic Faith, Inc.

This church body was founded by Bishop R.C. Lawson in Columbus, Ohio, and moved to New York City in 1919. It is founded upon the teachings of the apostles and prophets, Jesus Christ being its chief cornerstone.

Headquarters

2081 Adam Clayton Powell Jr. Blvd., New York, NY 10027 Tel. (212)866-1700

Website: www.apostolic-faith.org

Media Contact, Exec. Sec., Bishop T.E. Woolfolk, P.O. Box 119, Oxford, NC 27565 Tel. (919)693-9449, Fax (919)693-6115, tewmsw @gloryroad.net

Officers

Board of Apostles, Chief Apostle, Bishop William L. Bonner

Presiding Apostle, Bishop James I. Clark Jr., Bishop Frank S. Solomon

Vice Pres., Bishop J. P. Steadman, Bishop Mathew A. Norwood, Bishop Gentle L. Groover, Bishop Wilbur L. Jones, Bishop Robert L. Sanders

Bd. of Bishops, Chmn., Bishop Henry A. Moultrie II

Bd. of Presbyters, Pres., Elder Michael A. Dixon

Exec. Sec., Bishop Thomas E. Woolfolk

Natl. Rec. Sec., Bishop Fred Rubin Sr.

Natl. Fin. Sec., Bishop Clarence Groover

Natl. Corr. Sec., Bishop Raymond J. Keith Jr.

Natl Treas., Elder Richard D. Williams

Periodicals

Contender For The Faith, Minute Book

Church of the United Brethren in Christ

The Church of the United Brethren in Christ had its beginning with Philip William Otterbein and Martin Boehm, who were leaders in the revival movement in Pennsylvania and Maryland from the late 1760s into the early 1800s.

On Sept. 25, 1800, they and others associated

with them formed a society under the name of United Brethren in Christ. Subsequent conferences adopted a Confession of Faith in 1815 and a constitution in 1841. The Church of the United Brethren in Christ adheres to the original constitution as amended in 1957, 1961, and 1977.

Headquarters

302 Lake St., Huntington, IN 46750 Tel. (260) 356-2312 Fax (260)356-4730 ext. 210

Website: www.ub.org

Media Contact, Communications Dir., Steve Dennie, sdennie@ub.org

Officers

Bishop, Rev. Paul Hirschy
Finance Dir., Janet Bilyew
Dept. of Education,Dir., Dr. G. Blair Dowden
Global Ministries, Dir., Rev. Gary Dilley
Communications, Dir., Mr. Steve Dennie

Churches of Christ

Churches of Christ are autonomous congregations whose members appeal to the Bible alone to determine matters of faith and practice. There are no central offices or officers. Publications and institutions related to the churches are either under local congregational control or are independent of any congregation. Churches of Christ shared a common fellowship in the 19th century with the Christian Churches/Churches of Christ and the Christian Church (Disciples of Christ). This fellowship ended in the decadeds following the American Civil War due to erosion of confidence in Scripture among many of those who would go on to form these other groups. This shift in belief embraced theistic evolution, doubted the complete truth of Scripture, and permitted unscriptual practices into the work and worship of the church. Chief among the changes in practice were the use of instrumental music in worship, permitting women to officiate in worship services, and conducting the work of the church through centralized agencies. Churches of Christ, following this division, remained strongly united in their belief in the inerrancy and sufficiency of Scripture. From this standpoint they affirm faith in one God who subsists in three persons: Father, Son, and Holy Spirit. They teach that salvation is through the sacrificial death of Christ and is available to all who come to God through repentance and faith, initially expressed through confession of faith and baptism by immersion. Churches of Christ follow the New Testament pattern to direct every facet of the teaching and work of the church.

Headquarters

Media Contact, Ed., *Gospel Advocate,* Mr. Neil Anderson, P.O. Box 150, Nashville, TN 37202 Tel. (800)251-8446 Fax (615)254-7411

Periodicals

Action; Christian Woman, Christian Bible Teacher, The Christian Chronicle, Firm Foundation, Gospel Advocate, Guardian of Truth, Restoration Quarterly, 21st Century Christian, Rocky Mountain Christian, The Spiritual Sword, Word and Work

Churches of Christ in Christian Union

Organized in 1909 at Washington Court House, Ohio, as the Churches of Christ in Christian Union, this body believes in the new birth and the baptism of the Holy Spirit for believers. It is Wesleyan, with an evangelistic and missionary emphasis.

The Reformed Methodist Church merged with the Churches of Christ in Christian Union in 1952.

Headquarters

1426 Lancaster Pike, Box 30, Circleville, OH 43113 Tel. (740)474-8856 Fax (740)477-7766

Media Contact, Dir. of Comm., Rev. Ralph Hux

Officers

Gen. Supt., Dr. Daniel Tipton
Asst. Gen. Supt., Rev. Ron Reese
Gen. Treas., Mr. Mark Taylor
Gen. Bd. of Trustees, Chpsn., Dr. Daniel Tipton; Vice Chpsn., Rev. Ron Reese
District Superintendents, West Central District, Rev. Ron Reese; South Central District, Rev. Don Spurgeon; Northeast District, Rev. Brad Dixon; West Indies District, Rev. Michael Aubrey

Periodicals

The Evangelical Advocate

Churches of God, General Conference

The Churches of God, General Conference (CGGC) had its beginnings in Harrisburg, Penn., in 1825.

John Winebrenner, recognized founder of the Church of God movement, was an ordained minister of the German Reformed Church. His experience-centered form of Christianity—particularly the "new measures" he used to promote it, his close connection with the local Methodists, his "experience and conference meetings" in the church, and his "social prayer meetings" in parishioners' homes—resulted in differences of opinion and the establishment of new congregations. Extensive revivals, camp meetings, and mission endeavors led to the organization of additional congregations across central Pennsylvania and westward through Ohio, Indiana, Illinois, and Iowa.

In 1830 the first system of cooperation between local churches was initiated as an "eldership" in eastern Pennsylvania. The organization of other elderships followed. General Eldership was organized in 1845, and in 1974 the official name of the denomination was changed from General Eldership of the Churches of God in North America to its present name.

The Churches of God, General Conference, is composed of 8 conferences in the United States and 1 conference in Haiti. The polity of the church is presbyterial in form. The church has mission ministries in the southwest among native Americans and is extensively involved in church planting and whole life ministries in Bangladesh, Brazil, Haiti, and India.

The General Conference convenes in business session triennially. An Administrative Council composed of 16 regional representatives is responsible for the administration and ministries of the church between sessions of the General Conference.

Headquarters

Legal Headquarters, United Church Center, Rm. 213, 900 S. Arlington Ave., Harrisburg, PA 17109 Tel. (717)652-0255

Administrative Offices, General Conf. Exec. Dir., Pastor Wayne W. Boyer, 700 E. Melrose Ave., P.O. Box 926, Findlay, OH 45839 Tel. (419)424-1961 Fax (419)424-3343

Email: director@cggc.org

Website: www.cggc.org

Media Contact, Editor, Rachel L. Foreman, P.O. Box 926, Findlay, OH 45839 Tel. (419) 424-1961, Fax (419)424-3343, communications@ cggc org

Officers

Pres., Pastor Robert L. Eatherton, P.O.Box 366, Columbia City, IN 46725-0366 Tel. (260)244-4042, Fax (260)244-9663, director@midwest-cggc.org

Sec., Pastor E. David Green, 700 E. Melrose Ave., P.O. Box 1132, Findlay, OH 45839 Tel. (419)423-7694, Fax (419)423-9092, GLCdirector@cggc.org

Treas., Robert E. Stephenson, 700 E. Melrose Ave., P.O. Box 926, Findlay, OH 45839 Tel. (419)424-1961, Fax (419)424-3433, treasurer@ cggc.org

DEPARTMENTS

Cross-Cultural Ministries: Pastor Don Dennison

Pensions: Mr. James P. Thomas

Denominational Communications: Rachel L. Foreman

Church Renewal: Pastor Mark A. Hosler

Church Planting: Pastor Charles A. Hirschy

Youth & Family Ministries: Susan L. Callaway

CGWM–Churches of God Women's Ministries

Periodicals

The Church Advocate, The Gem, The Missionary Signal

Community of Christ

Community of Christ's mission is to proclaim Jesus Christ and promote communities of joy, hope, love, and peace. Founded on April 6, 1830, this Christian denomination is present in nearly 50 nations with approximately 250,000 members worldwide. The church's Temple, located in the international headquarters complex, is dedicated to peace, reconciliation, and healing of the Spirit. Priesthood includes both men and women.

Headquarters

International Headquarters, 1001 W. Walnut, Independence, MO 54050-3562 Tel. (816) 833-1000 Fax (816)521-3096

Email: snaylor@CofChrist.org

Website: www.CofChrist.org

Media Contacts: Kendra Friend, kfriend@ cofchrist.org, or Jennifer Killpack, jkillpack@ cofchrist.org

Officers

FIRST PRESIDENCY

Pres., W. Grant McMurray, gmcmurray@cofchrist. org

Counselor, Kenneth N. Robinson, krobinson@ cofchrist.org

Counselor, Peter A. Judd, pjudd@cofchrist.org

Council of Twelve Apostles: Pres., Stephen M. Veazey, sveazey@cofchrist. org

PRESIDING BISHOPRIC

Presiding Bishop, Larry R. Norris, lnorris@ cofchrist.org

Counselor, Stassi D. Cramm, scramm@cofchrist. org

Counselor, Stephen M. Jones, sjones@cofchrist. org

Presiding Evangelist: Danny A. Belrose, dbelrose@ cofchrist.org

World Church Sec., A. Bruce Lindgren, blindgren@ cofchrist.org

Public Relations Fax (816)521-3043

Kendra Friend, kfriend@cofchrist.org

Jennifer Killpack, jkillpack@cofchrist.org

Periodicals

Herald; Restoration Witness, Face to Face

Congregational Holiness Church

This body was organized in 1921 and embraces the doctrine of Holiness and Pentecost. It carries on mission work in Mexico, Honduras, Costa Rica, Cuba, Brazil, Guatemala, India, Nicaragua, El Salvador, Venezula, Panama, Chile, Argentina, Belize, Zimbabwe, Haiti, and Peru.

Headquarters

3888 Fayetteville Hwy., Griffin, GA 30223 Tel. (404)228-4833 Fax (404)228-1177

Email: chchurch@bellsouth.net

Website: www.chchurch.com

Media Contact, Gen. Supt., Bishop Ronald Wilson

EXECUTIVE BOARD

Gen. Supt., Bishop Ronald Smith

1st Asst. Gen. Supt., Rev. William L. Lewis

2nd Asst. Gen. Supt., Rev. Wayne Hicks

Gen. Sec., Rev. Leslee Bailey

Gen. Treas., Rev. Stephen Phillips

World Missions Supt., Rev. Billy Anderson

Periodicals

The Gospel Messenger

Conservative Baptist Association of America (CBAmerica)

The Conservative Baptist Association of America (now known as CBAmerica) was organized May 17, 1947 at Atlantic City, N.J. The Old and New Testaments are regarded as the divinely inspired Word of God and are therefore infallible and of supreme authority. Each local church is independent, autonomous, and free from ecclesiastical or political authority.

CBAmerica provides wide-ranging support to its affiliate churches and individuals through nine regional associations. CBA offers personnel to assist churches in areas such as growth and health, conflict resolution, and financial analysis. The association supports its clergy with retirement planning, referrals for new places of ministry, and spiritual counseling. The Conservative Baptist Women's Ministries assists women in the church to be effective in their personal growth and leadership.

Each June or July there is a National Conference giving members an opportunity for fellowship, inspiration, and motivation.

Headquarters

1501 W. Mineral Ave., Suite B, Littleton, CO 80120-5612 Tel. (888)627-1995 or (720)283-3030 Fax (720)283-3333

Email: cba@cbamerica.org

Website: www.cbamerica.org

Media Contact, Exec. Dir., Dr. Dennis L. Gorton

OTHER ORGANIZATIONS

CBInternational, Exec. Dir., Dr. Hans Finzel, 1501 W. Mineral Ave., Littleton, CO 80120-5612

Mission to the Americas, Exec. Dir., Rev. Rick Miller, Box 828, Wheaton, IL 60189

Conservative Baptist Higher Ed. Council, Dr. Bert Downs, Western Seminary, 5511 S. E. Hawthorne Blvd., Portland, OR 97215

Periodicals

Front Line Turnings

Conservative Congregational Christian Conference

In the 1930s, evangelicals within the Congregational Christian Churches felt a definite need for fellowship and service. By 1945, this loose association crystallized into the Conservative Congregational Christian Fellowship, committed to maintaining a faithful, biblical witness.

In 1948 in Chicago, the Conservative Congregational Christian Conference was established to provide a continuing fellowship for evangelical churches and ministers on the national level. In recent years, many churches have joined the Conference from backgrounds other than Congregational. These churches include Community or Bible Churches and churches from the Evangelical and Reformed background that are truly congregational in polity and thoroughly evangelical in conviction. The CCCC welcomes all evangelical churches that are, in fact, congregational. The CCCC believes in the necessity of a regenerate membership, the authority of the Holy Scriptures, the Lordship of Jesus Christ, the autonomy of the local church, and the universal fellowship of all Christians.

The Conservative Congregational Christian Conference is a member of the World Evangelical Congregational Fellowship (formed in 1986 in London, England) and the National Association of Evangelicals.

Headquarters

7582 Currell Blvd., Ste. #108, St. Paul, MN 55125 Tel. (651)739-1474 Fax (651)739-0750

Email: CCCC4@juno.com

Website: www.ccccusa.org/

Media Contact, Conf. Min., Mrs. Diane Johnson

Officers

Pres., Rev. Larry Scovil, 317 W. 40th Street, Scottsbluff, NE 69361

Vice Pres., Rev. Nicholas Granitsas, 68 Enstis St., Revere, MA 02151

Conf. Min., Rev. Clifford R. Christensen, 944 Stratford Law, Burnsville, MN 55337

Controller, Mr. Orrin Bailey, 4260 East Lake Rd., Muskegon, MI 49444

Treas., Rev. Tay Kersey, 8450 Eastwood Rd., Moundsview, MN 55112

Sec., Rev. Peter Murdy, 4 Plympton St., Middleboro, MA 02346

Editor, Mrs. Carol Wells, 2789 Wimbledon Ridge, Woodbury, MN 55125

Historian, Rev. Milton Reimer, 507 Central Ave., New Rockford, ND 58356

Periodicals

Foresee

Conservative Lutheran Association

The Conservative Lutheran Association (CLA) was originally named Lutheran's Alert National (LAN) when it was founded in 1965 by 10 conservative Lutheran pastors and layman meeting in Cedar Rapids, Iowa. Its purpose was to help preserve from erosion the basic doctrines of Christian theology, including the inerrancy of Holy Scripture. The group grew to a worldwide constituency, similarly concerned with maintaining the doctrinal integrity of the Bible and the Lutheran Confessions.

Headquarters

Trinity Lutheran Church, 4101 E. Nohl Ranch Rd., Anaheim, CA 92807 Tel. (714)637-8370

Website: www.tlcanaheim.com/CLA/

Media Contact, Pres., Rev. P. J. Moore, PastorPJ@ix.netcom.com

Officers

Pres., Rev. P. J. Moore, 4101 E. Nohl Ranch Rd., Anaheim, CA 92807 Tel. (714)637-8370

Vice Pres., Rev. Dr. R. H. Redal, 409 Tacoma Ave. N, Tacoma, WA 98403 Tel. (206)383-5528

Faith Seminary, Dean, Rev. Dr. Michael J. Adams, 3504 N. Pearl St., P.O. Box 7186, Tacoma, WA 98407 Tel. (888)777-7675 Fax (206)759-1790

Coptic Orthodox Church*

This body is part of the ancient Coptic Orthodox Church of Alexandria, Egypt which is currently headed by His Holiness Pope Shenouda III, 116th Successor to St. Mark the Apostle. Egyptian immigrants have organized many parishes in the United States. Copts exist outside Egypt in Africa, Europe, Asia, Australia, Canada, and the United States. The total world Coptic community is estimated at 27 million. The church is in full communion with the other members of the Oriental Orthodox Church Family: the Syrian Orthodox Church, Armenian Orthodox Church, Ethiopian Orthodox Church, the Syrian Orthodox Church in India, and the Eritrean Orthodox Church.

Headquarters

5 Woodstone Dr., Cedar Grove, NJ 07009

3803 W. Mission Blvd., Pomona, CA 91766 Tel. (909)865-8378 Fax (909)865-8348

Email: Webmaster@coptic.org

Website: www.coptic.org

Media Contact, Fr. Isaac Boulos Azmy, P.O. Box 4960, Diamond Bar, CA 91765

Officers

Bishop of Los Angeles, Bishop Serapion, 3803 3803 W. Mission Blvd., Pomona, CA 91766 Tel. (909)865-8378, Fax (909)865-8348, bishopserapion@lacopts.org

Periodicals

Agape Magazine, El Keraza

Cumberland Presbyterian Church

The Cumberland Presbyterian Church was organized in Dickson County, Tenn., on Feb. 4, 1810. It was an outgrowth of the Great Revival of 1800 on the Kentucky and Tennessee frontier. The founders were Finis Ewing, Samuel King, and Samuel McAdow, ministers in the Presbyterian Church who rejected the doctrine of election and reprobation as taught in the Westminster Confession of Faith.

By 1813, the Cumberland Presbytery had grown to encompass three presbyteries, which constituted a synod. This synod met at the Beech Church in Sumner County, Tenn., and formulated a "Brief Statement" which set forth the points in which Cumberland Presbyterians dissented from the Westminster Confession. These points are:

1. That there are no eternal reprobates;
2. That Christ died, not for some, but for all people;
3. That all those dying in infancy are saved through Christ and the sanctification of the Spirit;
4. That the Spirit of God operates on the world, or as coextensively as Christ has made atonement, in such a manner as to leave everyone inexcusable.

From its birth in 1810, the Cumberland Presbyterian Church grew to a membership of 200,000 at the turn of the century. In 1906 the church voted to merge with the then-Presbyterian Church. Those who dissented from the merger became the nucleus of the continuing Cumberland Presbyterian Church.

Headquarters

1978 Union Ave., Memphis, TN 38104 Tel. (901)276-4572 Fax (901)272-3913

Email: assembly@cumberland.org

Website: www.cumberland.org

Media Contact, Stated Clk., Rev. Robert D. Rush Fax (901)276-4578

Officers

Mod., Rev. Dr. Charles McCaskey, 679 Canter Ln., Cookeville, TN 38501 Tel. (931)526-6585, charles_mccaskey @presbyteriancumberlan.com

Stated Clk., Rev. Robert D. Rush Tel. (901)276-4572 ext. 3325, Fax (901)276-4578, rdr@cumberland.org

General Assembly Council, Exec. Dir., Davis Gray Tel. (901)276-4572 ext. 3316, Fax (901) 272-3913, dg@cumberland.org

INSTITUTIONS

Cumberland Presbyterian Children's Home, Exec. Dir., Dr. Judith B. Keith, Drawer G, Denton, TX 76202 Tel. (940)382-5112, Fax (940)387-0821, cpch@cpch.org

Cumberland Presbyterian Center, Tel.(901)276-4572 Fax (901)272-3913 or (901)276-4578

Memphis Theological Seminary, Pres., Dr. Timothy Weber, tweber@mts.edu, 168 E. Parkway S, Memphis, TN 38104 Tel. (901) 458-8232 Fax (901)452-4051;

Bethel College, Pres., Dr. Robert Prosser, 325 Cherry St., McKenzie, TN 38201 Tel. (901)352-4004, Fax (901)352-4069, rprosser@bethel-college.edu

Historical Foundation, Archivist, Susan K. Gore, 1978 Union Avenue, Memphis, TN 38104 Tel. (901)276-8602, Fax (901)272-3913, skg@cumberland.org

BOARDS

Bd. of Christian Education, Exec. Dir., Claudette Pickle, 1978 Union Ave., Memphis, TN 38104 Tel. (901)276-4572 ext. 3323, Fax (901)272-3913, chp@cumberland.org

Bd. of Missions, Exec. Dir., Rev. Michael Sharpe, 1978 Union Ave., Memphis, TN

38104 Tel. (901)276-9988, Fax (901)272-3913, mgs@cumberland.org

Bd. of Stewardship, Exec. Sec., Rev. Richard Magrill, 1978 Union Ave., Memphis, TN 38104 Tel (901)276-4572 ext. 3307, jrm@cumberland.org

Bd. of The *Cumberland Presbyterian*, Editor, Mrs. Patricia White, P.O. Box 935, Antioch, TN 37011 Tel. (615)731-5556, cpmag@comcast.net

Commission on the Ministry, 1978 Union Ave., Memphis, TN 38104 Tel (901)276-4572 ext. 3335, Fax (901)272-3913; Rev. Chris Joiner, Dir. of Ministry, caj@cumberland.org

Periodicals

The Cumberland Presbyterian, The Missionary Messenger

Cumberland Presbyterian Church in America

This church, originally known as the Colored Cumberland Presbyterian Church, was formed in May 1874. In May 1869, at the General Assembly meeting in Murfreesboro, Tenn., Moses Weir of the Black delegation sucessfully appealed for help in organizing a separate African church so that: Blacks could learn self-reliance and independence; they could have more financial assistance; they could minister more effectively among Blacks; and they could worship close to the altar, not in the balconies. He requested that the Cumberland Presbyterian Church organize Blacks into presbyteries and synods; develop schools to train black clergy; grant loans to assist Blacks to secure hymnbooks, Bibles, and church buildings; and establish a separate General Assembly.

In 1874 the first General Assembly of the Colored Cumberland Presbyterian Church met in Nashville. The moderator was Rev. P. Price and the stated clerk was Elder John Humphrey.

The denomination's General Assembly, the national governing body, is organized around its three program boards and agencies: Finance, Publication and Christian Education, and Missions and Evangelism. Other agencies of the General Assembly are under these three program boards.

The church has four synods (Alabama, Kentucky, Tennessee, and Texas), 15 presbyteries and 153 congregations. The CPC extends as far north as Cleveland, Ohio, and Chicago, Ill., as far west as Marshalltown, Ia., and Dallas, Tex., and as far south as Selma, Ala.

Headquarters

Media Contact, Stated Clk., Rev. Dr. Robert Stanley Wood, 226 Church St., Huntsville, AL 35801 Tel. (205)536-7481 Fax (205)536-7482

Email: mleslie598@aol.com

Website: www.cumberland.org/cpca/

Officers

Mod., Rev. Endia Scruggs, 1627 Carroll Rd., Harvest, AL 35749

Stated Clk., Rev. Dr. Rorbert Stanley Wood, 226 Church St., Huntsville, AL 35801 Tel. (205)536-7481

SYNODS

Alabama, Stated Clk., Arthur Hinton, 511 10th Ave. NW, Aliceville, AL 35442

Kentucky, Stated Clk., Mary Martha Daniels, 8548 Rhodes Ave., Chicago, IL 60619

Tennessee, Stated Clk., Elder Clarence Norman, 145 Jones St., Huntington, TN 38334

Texas, Stated Clk., Arthur King, 2435 Kristen, Dallas, TX 75216

Periodicals

The Cumberland Flag

Elim Fellowship

The Elim Fellowship, a Pentecostal Body established in 1947, is an outgrowth of the Elim Missionary Assemblies formed in 1933.

It is an association of churches, ministers, and missionaries seeking to serve the whole Body of Christ. It is of Pentecostal conviction and charismatic orientation, providing ministerial credentials and counsel and encouraging fellowship among local churches. Elim Fellowship sponsors leadership seminars at home and abroad and serves as a transdenominational agency sending long-term, short-term, and tent-making missionaries to work with national movements.

Headquarters

1703 Dalton Rd., Lima, NY 14485 Tel. (585)582-2790 Fax (585)624-1229

Email: 75551.743@compuserve.com

Website: www.ElimFellowship.org

Media Contact, Gen. Sec., Paul Anderson

Officers

Pres., Bernard J. Evans

Vice Pres., Ron Burgio

Gen. Treas., Stephanie Zeller

Periodicals

Elim Herald

Episcopal Church*

The Episcopal Church entered the colonies with the earliest settlers at Jamestown, Va., in 1607 as the Church of England. After the American Revolution, it became autonomous in 1789 as The Protestant Episcopal Church in the United States of America. (The Episcopal Church became the official alternate name in 1967.) Samuel Seabury of Connecticut was elected the first bishop and consecrated in Aberdeen by bishops of the Scottish Episcopal Church in 1784.

In organizing as an independent body, the Episcopal Church created a bicameral legislature, the General Convention, modeled after the new US Congress. It comprises a House of Bishops and a House of Deputies and meets every three years. A 38-member Executive

Council, which meets three times a year, is the interim governing body. An elected presiding bishop serves as Primate and Chief Pastor.

After severe setbacks in the years immediately following the Revolution because of its association with the British Crown and the fact that a number of its clergy and members were Loyalists, the church soon established its own identity and sense of mission. It sent missionaries into the newly settled territories of the United States, establishing dioceses from coast to coast, and also undertook substantial missionary work in Africa, Latin America, and the Far East. Today, the overseas dioceses are developing into independent provinces of the Anglican Communion, the worldwide fellowship of 36 churches in communion with the Church of England and the Archbishop of Canterbury.

The beliefs and practices of The Episcopal Church, like those of other Anglican churches, are both Catholic and Reformed, with bishops in the apostolic succession and the historic creeds of Christendom regarded as essential elements of faith and order, along with the primary authority of Holy Scripture and the two chief sacraments of Baptism and Eucharist.

EPISCOPAL CHURCH CENTER

815 Second Ave., New York, NY 10017 Tel. (212)716-6240 or (800)334-7626 Fax (212) 867-0395 or (212)490-3298

Email: jrollins@ecusa.anglican.org

Website: www.ecusa.anglican.org

Media Contact, Dir. of News & Info., James Solheim Tel. (212)922-5385

Officers

Presiding Bishop & Primate, Most Rev. Frank Tracy Griswold

Vice Pres. & Assist. to the Presiding Bishop for Administration, Patricia C. Mordecai

Assistant to the Presiding Bishop for Communication, Barbara L. Braver

Treas., -vacant-

Canon to the Primate and Presiding Bishop, The Rev. Canon Carlson Gerdau

House of Deputies, Pres., The Very Rev. George L. Werner

Exec. Officer of the General Convention, Sec. Of the House of Deputies, Sec. Of the Domestic and Foreign Missionary Society, and Sec. Of the Executive Council, The Rev. Rosemari Sullivan

OFFICE OF THE PRESIDING BISHOP

Presiding Bishop, Most Rev. Frank Tracy Griswold Tel. (212)922-5322

Vice Pres. Assistant to the Presiding Bishop for Administration, Patricia Mordecai Tel. (212)922-5313

Canon to the Presiding Bishop, Rev. Canon Carl Gerdau Tel. (212)922-5282

Exec. Dir., Church Deployment Office, The Rev. James G. Wilson Tel. (212)922-5251

Coordinator for Ministry Development, The Rev. Dr. Melford E. Holland Jr. Tel. (212)922-5246

Exec. Dir., Office of Pastoral Dev., Rt. Rev. F. Clayton Mathews Tel. (212)716-6163

Exec. Sec., General Board of Examining Chaplains, The Rev. Locke E. Bowman Jr. Tel. (919)489-1422

Chaplaincy, Suffragan Bishop for the Armed Services, Healthcare and Prison Ministries, Rt. Rev. George Packard Tel. (212)922-5240

Chaplaincy, Suffragan Bishop for American Churches in Europe, Rt. Rev. Pierre W. Whalon Tel. (011)33-1-472-01792

Dir., Ecumenical and Interfaith Relations, The Rt. Rev. Canon C. Christopher Epting Tel. (212)716-6220

ADMINISTRATION AND FINANCE

Treasurer of the Domestic and Foreign Missionary Society and of the General Convention, -vacant-, Tel. (212)922-5296

Controller, Thomas Hershkowitz Tel. (212)922-5366

Archivist, Mark Duffy Tel. (800)525-9329

Human Resources, John Colon Tel. (212)922-5158

SERVICE, EDUCATION, AND WITNESS

Asst. to the Presiding Bishop for Program, -vacant-

Dir., Anglican and Global Relations, The Rev. Canon Patrick Mauney Tel. (212)716-6223

Editor, *Episcopal Life,* Jerry Hames Tel. (212) 716-6009

Interim Dir., Media Services, -vacant- Tel. (212) 922-5386

Dir., News & Information, James Solheim Tel. (212)922-5385

Dir., Migration Ministries, Richard Parkins Tel. (212)716-6252

Dir., Peace & Justice Ministries, The Rev. Brian Grieves Tel. (212)922-5207

Dir., Ministries to the Young & Young Adult Ministries Staff Officer, Thomas Chu Tel. (212)922-5267

Exec Dir., Episcopal Relief and Development, Sandra Swan Tel. (212)716-6020

BISHOPS IN THE USA

(C)= Coadjutor; (S)= Suffragan; (A)= Assistant

Address, Right Reverend

Presiding Bishop & Primate: Most Rev. Frank Tracy Griswold; Pastoral Dev., The Rt. Rev. F. Clayton Matthews

Alabama: Henry N. Parsley Jr., 521 N. 20th St., Birmingham, AL 35203 Tel. (205)715-2066

Alaska: Mark MacDonald, David Elsensohn, 1205 Denali Way, Fairbanks, AK 99701-4137 Tel. (907)452-3040

Albany: Daniel W. Herzog, 68 S. Swan St., Albany, NY 12210-2301 Tel. (518)465-4737

Arizona: Robert Shahan, 114 W.Roosevelt, Phoenix, AZ 85003-1406 Tel. (602)254-0976

Arkansas: Larry E. Maze, P.O. Box 162668, Little Rock, AR 72216-4668 Tel. (501)372-2168

Atlanta: John Neil Alexander, 2744 Peachtree Rd. NW, Atlanta, GA 30363 Tel. (404)365-1010

Bethlehem: Paul Marshall, 333 Wyandotte St., Bethlehem, PA 18015 Tel. (610)691-5655

California: William E. Swing, 1055 Taylor St., San Francisco, CA 94115 Tel. (415)288-9712

Central Florida: John H. Howe, 1017 E. Robinson St., Orlando, FL 32801 Tel. (407)423-3567

Central Gulf Coast: Philip M. Duncan II, P.O. Box 13330, Pensacola, FL 32591-3330 Tel. (904)434-7337

Central New York: Gladstone B. Adams III, 310 Montgomery St., Ste. 200, Syracuse, NY 13202 Tel. (315)474-6596

Central Pennsylvania: Michael Creighton, P.O. Box 11937, Harrisburg, PA 17108 Tel. (717)236-5959

Chicago: William D. Persell, 65 E. Huron St., Chicago, IL 60611 Tel. (312)751-4200

Colorado: William J. Winterrowd, 1300 Washington St., Denver, CO 80203 Tel. (303) 837-1173

Connecticut: Andrew D. Smith, 1335 Asylum Ave., Hartford, CT 06105 Tel. (203)233-4481

Dallas: James M. Stanton, 1630 Garrett St., Dallas, TX 75206 Tel. (214)826-8310

Delaware: Wayne P. Wright, 2020 Tatnall St., Wilmington, DE 19802 Tel. (302)656-5441

East Carolina: Clifton Daniel III, P.O. Box 1336, Kinston, NC 28501 Tel. (919)522-0885

East Tennessee: Charles Von Rosenberg, 401 Cumberland Ave., Knoxville, TN 37902-2302 Tel. (615)521-2900

Eastern Michigan: Edward Leidel, 4611 Swede Ave., Midland, MI 48642 Tel. (517)752-6020

Eastern Oregon: William O. Gregg, P.O. Box 620, The Dalles, OR 97058 Tel. (541)298-4477; Easton Lacaut, P.O. Box 1027, Easton, MD 21601 Tel. (410)822-1919

Eau Claire: Keith B. Whitmore, 510 S. Farwell St., Eau Claire, WI 54701 Tel. (715)835-3331

El Camino Real: Richard Shimpfky, P.O. Box 1903, Monterey, CA 93940 Tel. (408)394-4465

Florida: Stephen H. Jecko, 325 Market St., Jacksonville, FL 32202 Tel. (904)356-1328

Fond du Lac: Russell E. Jacobus, P.O. Box 149, Fond du Lac, WI 54936 Tel. (414)921-8866

Fort Worth: Jack Iker, 6300 Ridgelea Pl., Ste. 1100, Fort Worth, TX 76116 Tel. (817)738-9952

Georgia: Henry Louttit, Jr., 611 E. Bay St., Savannah, GA 31401 Tel. (912)236-4279

Hawaii: Richard Chang, 229 Queen Emma Sq., Honolulu, HI 96813 Tel. (808)536-7776

Idaho: Harry B. Bainbridge, P.O. Box 936, Boise, ID 83701 Tel. (208)345-4440

Indianapolis: Catherine M. Waynick,1100 W. 42nd St., Indianapolis, IN 46208 Tel. (317)926-5454

Iowa: Alan Scarfe, 225 37th St., Des Moines, IA 50312 Tel. (515)277-6165

Kansas: William E. Smalley, 833-35 Polk St., Topeka, KS 66612 Tel. (913)235-9255

Kentucky: Edwin F. Gulick, 600 E. Maine, Louisville, KY 40202 Tel. (502)584-7148

Lexington: Stacy F. Sauls, P.O. Box 610, Lexington, KY 40586 Tel. (606)252-6527

Long Island: Orris G. Walker, 36 Cathedral Ave., Garden City, NY 11530 Tel. (516)248-4800

Los Angeles: J. Jon Bruno; Chester Talton (S), P.O. Box 2164, Los Angeles, CA 90051 Tel. (213)482-2040

Louisiana: Charles E. Jenkins, 1623 7th St., New Orleans, LA 70115-4411 Tel. (504)895-6634

Maine: Chilton Knudsen, 143 State St., Portland, ME 04101 Tel. (207)772-1953

Maryland: Bob Ihloff, 4 E. University Pkwy., Baltimore, MD 21218-2437 Tel. (410)467-1399

Massachusetts: M. Thomas Shaw, SSJE; Barbara Harris (S), 138 Tremont St., Boston, MA 02111 Tel. (617)482-5800

Michigan: Wendell N. Gibbs, 4800 Woodward Ave., Detroit, MI 48201 Tel. (313)832-4400

Milwaukee: Roger J. White, 804 E. Juneau Ave., Milwaukee, WI 53202 Tel. (414)272-3028

Minnesota: James L. Jelinek, 430 Oak Grove St., #306, Minneapolis, MN 55403 Tel. (612)871-5311

Mississippi: Alfred C. Marble, P.O. Box 23107, Jackson, MS 39225-3107 Tel. (601)948-5954

Missouri: G. Wayne Smith, 1210 Locust St., St. Louis, MO 63103 Tel. (314)231-1220

Montana: -vacant-, 515 North Park Ave., Helena, MT 59601 Tel. (406)442-2230

Nebraska: James E. Krotz, 200 N. 62nd St., Omaha, NE 68132 Tel. (402)341-5373

Nevada: Katharin Jefferts Schori, P.O. Box 6357, Reno, NV 89513 Tel. (702)737-9190

New Hampshire: V. Gene Robinson, 63 Green St., Concord, NH 03301 Tel. (603)224-1914

New Jersey: -vacant-, 808 W. State St., Trenton, NJ 08618

New York: Mark Sisk, 1047 Amsterdam Ave., New York, NY 10025 Tel. (212)316-7413

Newark: Jack Croneberger; Jack McKelvey (S), 24 Rector St., Newark, NJ 07102 Tel. (201)622-4306

North Carolina: Michael B. Curry, 201 St. Albans Dr., Raleigh, NC 27619 Tel. (919)787-6313

North Dakota: Andrew H. Fairfield, P.O. Box 10337, Fargo, ND 58106-0337 Tel. (701)235-6688

Northern California: Jerry A. Lamb, P.O. Box 161268, Sacramento, CA 95816 Tel. (916) 442-6918

Northern Indiana: Eduard S. Little, 117 N. Lafayette Blvd., South Bend, IN 46601 Tel. (219)233-6489

Northern Michigan: James Kelsey, 131 E. Ridge St., Marquette, MI 49855 Tel. (906)228-7160

Northwest Texas: C. Wallis Ohl Jr., P.O. Box 1067, Lubbock, TX 79408 Tel. (806)763-1370

Northwestern Pennsylvania: Robert D. Rowley, 145 W. 6th St., Erie, PA 16501 Tel. (814)456-4203

Ohio: J. Clark Grew; Arthur B. Williams, (S), 2230 Euclid Ave., Cleveland, OH 44115 Tel. (216)771-4815

Oklahoma: Robert M. Moody; William J. Cox, (A), 924 N. Robinson, Oklahoma City, OK 73102 Tel. (405)232-4820

Olympia: Vincent W. Warner, P.O. Box 12126, Seattle, WA 98102 Tel. (206)325-4200

Oregon: Robert Louis Ladehoff, P.O. Box 467, Portland, OR 97034 Tel. (503)636-5613

Pennsylvania: Charles Bennison, 240 S. 4th St., Philadelphia, PA 19106 Tel. (215)627-6434

Pittsburgh: Robert W. Duncan, Jr., 325 Oliver Ave., Pittsburgh, PA 15222 Tel. (412)281-6131

Quincy: Keith L. Ackerman, 3601 N. North St., Peoria, IL 61604 Tel. (309)688-8221

Rhode Island: Geralyn Wolf, 275 N. Main St., Providence, RI 02903 Tel. (401)274-4500

Rio Grande: Terence Kelshaw, 4304 Carlisle St. NE, Albuquerque, NM 87107 Tel. (505)881-0636

Rochester: William G. Burrill, 935 East Ave., Rochester, NY 14607 Tel. (716)473-2977

San Diego: Gethin B. Hughes, St. Paul's Church, 2728 6th Ave., San Diego, CA 92103 Tel. (619)291-5947

San Joaquin: John-David Schofield, 4159 E. Dakota Ave., Fresno, CA 93726 Tel. (209)244-4828

South Carolina: Edward L. Salmon, P.O. Box 20127, Charleston, SC 29413-0127 Tel. (843) 722-4075

South Dakota: Creighton Robertson, 500 S. Main St., Sioux Falls, SD 57102-0914 Tel. (605) 338-9751

Southeast Florida: Leopold Frade, 525 NE 15th St., Miami, FL 33132 Tel. (305)373-0881

Southern Ohio: Herbert Thompson, Jr.; Kenneth Price, (S), 412 Sycamore St., Cincinnati, OH 45202 Tel. (513)421-0311

Southern Virginia: David C. Bane Jr., 600 Talbot Hall Rd., Norfolk, VA 23505 Tel. (804)423-8287

Southwest Florida: Rogers S. Harris, P.O. Box 491, St. Petersburg, FL 33731 Tel. (941)776-1018

Southwestern Virginia: John B. Lipscomb, P.O. Box 2279, Roanoke, VA 24009 Tel. (703)342-6797

Spokane: James E. Waggoner, 245 E. 13th Ave., Spokane, WA 99202 Tel. (509)624-3191

Springfield: Peter H. Beckwith, 821 S. 2nd St., Springfield, IL 62704 Tel. (217)525-1876

Tennessee: Bertram M. Herlong, One LaFleur Bldg., Ste. 100, 50 Vantage Way, Nashville, TN 37228 Tel. (615)251-3322

Texas: Claude E. Payne, 3203 W. Alabama St., Houston, TX 77098 Tel. (713)520-6444

Upper South Carolina: Dorsey F. Henderson Jr., P.O. Box 1789, Columbia, SC 29202 Tel. (803)771-7800

Utah: Carolyn Irish, 231 E. First St. S., Salt Lake City, UT 84111 Tel. (801)322-4131

Vermont: Thomas C. Ely, Rock Point, Burlington, VT 05401 Tel. (802)863-3431

Virginia: Peter J. Lee (S), 110 W. Franklin St., Richmond, VA 23220 Tel. (804)643-8451

Washington: John B. Chane, Episc. Church House, Mt. St. Alban, Washington, D.C. 20016 Tel. (202)537-6555

West Missouri: John Buchanan, P.O. Box 413216, Kansas City, MO 64141 Tel. (816)471-6161

West Tennessee: James M. Coleman, 692 Poplar Ave., Memphis, TN 38105 Tel. (901)526-0023

West Texas: James E. Folts; Earl N. MacArthur (S), P.O. Box 6885, San Antonio, TX 78209 Tel. (210)824-5387

West Virginia: William M. Klusmeyer, P.O. Box 5400, Charleston, WV 25361-0400 Tel. (304)344-3597

Western Kansas: Vernon Strickland, P.O. Box 2507, Salina, KS 67402 Tel. (913)825-1626

Western Louisiana: D. Bruce MacPherson Jr., P.O. Box 2031, Alexandria, LA 71309-2031 Tel. (318)442-1304

Western Massachusetts: Gordon P. Scruton, 37 Chestnut St., Springfield, MA 01103 Tel. (413)737-4786

Western Michigan: Edward L. Lee, 2600 Vincent Ave., Kalamazoo, MI 49008 Tel. (616)381-2710

Western New York: J. Michael Garrison, 1114 Delaware Ave., Buffalo, NY 14209 Tel. (716)881-0660

Western North Carolina: Robert H. Johnson, P.O. Box 369, Black Mountain, NC 28711 Tel. (704)669-2921

Wyoming: Bruce Caldwell, 104 S. 4th St., Laramie, WY 82070 Tel. (307)742-6606

Am. Churches in Europe–Jurisdiction: Pierre W. Whalon, The American Cathedral, 23 Avenue Georges V, 75008, Paris, France

Navajoland Area Mission: Steven Plummer, P.O. Box 40, Bluff, UT 84512 Tel. (505)327-7549

Periodicals

Episcopal Life

The Episcopal Orthodox Church

This body was incorporated in 1964 as a self-governing Anglican church. The Church upholds orthodox theology and traditional liturgical practice, using the 1928 Book of Common Prayer and the Authorized Version of the Bible for public worship. The Chuch is committed to the three ancient Creeds of the Christian faith, the genuine spiritual power of the Sacraments, and the sufficiency and inspiraton of the Scriptures, as expressed in the Thirty-Nine Articles of Religion and the Book of Common Prayer. The Church is the United States member of the Orthodox Anglican Communion, the creation of which it authorized in 1967. The Orthodox Anglican

Communion is a fellowship of churches around the world that use the traditional editions of the Book of Common Prayer and adhere to conservative theology. In 1971 the Church opened its own theological educational institution; clergy in the United States are trained at the denomination's school, St. Andrew's Theological college and Seminary.

Headquarters

464 County Home Road, Lexington, NC 27292 Tel. (336)236-9565 Fax (336)236-4822
Email: eoc@orthodoxanglican.net
Website: www.orthodoxanglican.net

Officers

Presiding Bishop, The Most Rev. Dr. Scott E. McLaughlin, The Chancery of the Archdiocese, 464 County Home Road, Lexington, NC 27292 Tel. (336)236-9565, Fax (336)236-4822, abpmclaughlin@orthodoxanglican.net

Periodicals

The Episcopal Orthodox Encounter

The Estonian Evangelical Lutheran Church

For information on the Estonian Evangelical Lutheran Church (EELC), please see the listing in Chapter 4, "Religious Bodies in Canada."

Headquarters

383 Jarvis St., Toronto, ON M5B 2C7
Email: konsistoorium@eelk.ee
Website: www.eelk.ee/

The Evangelical Church

The Evangelical Church was born June 4, 1968 in Portland, Oreg., when 46 congregations and about 80 ministers, under the leadership of V. A. Ballantyne and George Millen, met in an organizing session. Within two weeks, a group of about 20 churches and 30 ministers from the Evangelical United Brethren and Methodist churches in Montana and North Dakota became a part of the new church. Richard Kienitz and Robert Strutz were the superintendents.

Under the leadership of Superintendent Robert Trosen, the former Holiness Methodist Church became a part of the Evangelical Church in 1969, bringing its membership and a flourishing mission field in Bolivia. The Wesleyan Covenant Church joined in 1977, with its missionary work in Mexico, in Brownsville, Tex. and among the Navajos in New Mexico.

The Evangelical Church in Canada, where T. J. Jesske was superintendent, became an autonomous organization on June 5, 1970. In 1982, after years of discussions with the Evangelical Church of North America, a founding General Convention was held at Billings, Mont., where the two churches united. In 1993 the Canadian conference merged with the Canadian portion of the Missionary Church to form the Evangelical Missionary Church. The new group maintains close ties with their American counterparts. Currently there are nearly 150 US congregations of the Evangelical Church. The headquarters is located in Minneapolis, Minn..

The following guide the life, program, and devotion of this church: faithful, biblical, and sensible preaching and teaching of those truths proclaimed by scholars of the Wesleyan-Arminian viewpoint; an itinerant system which reckons with the rights of individuals and the desires of the congregation; and local ownership of all church properties and assets.

The church is officially affiliated with the Christian Holiness Partnership, the National Association of Evangelicals, Wycliffe Bible Translators, World Gospel Mission, and OMS International. The denomination has nearly 150 missionaries.

Headquarters

Denominational Office, 9421 W. River Rd., Minneapolis, MN 55444 Tel. (763)421-2589 Fax (763)424-9230
Email: jsditzel@juno.com
Website: www.quakertownecna.com/conferences.html or www.ecm@usfamily.net
Media Contact, Gen. Supt., Dr. William Vermillion

Officers

Gen. Supt., Dr. William Vermillion, 9421 W. River Rd., Minneapolis, MN 55444
Denominational Sec., Dr. Bruce Moyer, P.O. Box 29, University Park, IA 52595 Tel. (641)673-8391
Exec. Dir., Evangelical Church Mission, Rev. Duane Erickson, 9421 W. River Rd., Minneapolis, MN 55444

Periodicals

HeatBeat, The Evangelical Challenge

The Evangelical Church Alliance

What is known today as the Evangelical Church Alliance began in 1887 under the name "World's Faith Missionary Association." Years later, on March 28, 1928, a nonprofit organization was incorporated in the state of Missouri under the same name. In October 1931, the name "Fundamental Ministerial Association" was chosen to reflect the organization's basis of unity.

On July 21, 1958, during the annual convention at Trinity Seminary and Bible College in Chicago, Ill., a more comprehensive constitution was created and the name was changed to "The Evangelical Church Alliance."

The ECA licenses and ordains ministers who are qualified, providing them with credentials from a recognized ecclesiastical body; provides training courses through the Bible Extension Institute for those who have not had the opportunity to attend Seminary or Bible School; provides Associate Membership for churches and Christian organizations giving opportunity for fellowship and networking with other evangelical ministers and organizations who share the same goals and mission, while remaining autonomous; provides endorsement for military, prison, hospital, and other institutional chaplains; provides Regional Conferences and an Annual International Conference where members can find fellowship, encouragement and training; and cooperates with churches in finding new pastors when they have openings.

ECA is an international, nonsectarian, Evangelical organization.

Headquarters

205 W. Broadway St., P.O. Box 9, Bradley, IL 60915 Tel. (815)937-0720 Fax (815)937-0001
Email: info@ecainternational.org
Website: www.ecainternational.org/
Media Contact, Pres./CEO, Dr. George L. Miller

Officers

Pres./CEO, Dr. George L. Miller

Periodicals

The Evangel

The Evangelical Congregational Church

This denomination had its beginning in the movement known as the Evangelical Association, organized by Jacob Albright in 1796. A division which occurred in 1891 in the Evangelical Association resulted in the organization of the United Evangelical Church in 1894. An attempt to heal this division was made in 1922, but a portion of the United Evangelical Church was not satisfied with the plan of merger and remained apart, taking the above name in 1928. This denomination is Wesleyan-Arminian in doctrine, evangelistic in spirit, and Methodist in church government, with congregational ownership of local church property.

Congregations are located from New Jersey to Illinois. A denominational center, two retirement villages, and a seminary are located in Myerstown, Penn.. Three summer youth camps and four camp meetings continue evangelistic outreach. A worldwide missions movement includes conferences in North East India, Liberia, Mexico, Costa Rica, and Japan. The denomination is a member of National Association of Evangelicals.

Headquarters

Evangelical Congregational Church Center, 100 W. Park Ave., Myerstown, PA 17067 Tel. (800) 866-7581 Fax (717)866-7383
Email: eccenter@eccenter.com
Website: www.eccenter.com/church/
Media Contact, Bishop, Rev. Michael W. Sigman Tel. (717)866-7581

Officers

Presiding Bishop, Rev. Michael W. Sigman
1st Vice Chpsn., Rev. Gary Brown
Sec., Rev. Kirk Marks
Asst. Sec., Rev. Robert Stahl, Lancaster, PA; Rev. Dirk Pogue, Chicago, IL; Rev. Sterling Trimmer, Red Lion, PA; Rev. Gregory Dimick, Hartfield, PA
Treas., Patricia Hartman, Annville, PA
E.C.C. Retirement Village, Exec. Dir., Rev. Bruce Hill Fax (717)866-6448
Evangelical School of Theology, Pres., Dr. Kirby N. Keller Fax (717)866-4667

OTHER ORGANIZATIONS

Evangelism & Discipleship Commission, Chpsn., Bishop Michael Sigman
Leadership Commission, Chpsn., Bishop Michael Sigman
Church Health Commission, Chpsn., Rev. Fred Moury
Church Planting Commission, Chpsn,, Rev. Keith Miller
Church Services Commission, Chpsn., Rev. Keith Miller
Global Ministries Commission, Chpsn., Rev. John Ragsdale
Bd. of Pensions, Pres., William Kautz, New Cumberland, PA; Business Mgr., Rev. Keith R. Miller, Myerstown, PA 17067

Periodicals

Window on the World (Global Ministries Commission)

The Evangelical Covenant Church

The Evangelical Covenant Church has its roots in historic Christianity as it emerged during the Protestant Reformation, in the biblical instruction of the Lutheran State Church of Sweden and in the great spiritual awakenings of the 19th century.

The Covenant Church adheres to the affirmations of the Protestant Reformation regarding the Holy Scriptures, believing that the Old and the New Testament are the Word of God and the only perfect rule for faith, doctrine, and conduct. It has traditionally valued the historic confessions of the Christian church, particularly the Apostles' Creed, while at the same time emphasizing the sovereignty of the Word over all creedal interpretations. It has especially cherished the pietistic restatement of the doctrine of justification by faith as basic to its dual task of evangelism and Christian nurture. It recognizes the New Testament emphasis upon personal faith in Jesus Christ as Savior and Lord, the reality of a fellowship of believers which acknowledges but transcends theological differences, and the belief in baptism and the Lord's Supper as divinely ordained sacraments of the church.

While the denomination has traditionally practiced the baptism of infants, in conformity with its principle of freedom it has also recognized the practice of believer baptism. The principle of personal freedom, so highly esteemed by the Covenant, is to be distinguished from the individualism that disregards the centrality of the Word of God and the mutual responsibilities and disciplines of the spiritual community.

Headquarters

5101 N. Francisco Ave., Chicago, IL 60625 Tel. (773)784-3000 Fax (773)784-4366
Email: president@covoffice.org
Website: www.covchurch.org/
Media Contact, Sally A. Johnson, sally.johnson@covchurch.org

Officers

Pres., Dr. Glenn R. Palmberg
Vice Pres., Rev. Donn Engebretson
Administrative V.P., Dr. Mary C. Miller
Financial V.P., Dr. Dean A. Lundgren

ADMINISTRATIVE BOARDS

Bd. of Church Growth & Evangelism, Exec. Dir., Rev. Gary B. Walter
Executive Board, Chpsn., Rev. Curt Peterson,
Bd. of Covenant Women Ministries, Exec. Minister, Rev. Ruth Y. Hill
Bd. Of Nominations, Advisory Member, Rev. Dr. Mary C. Miller
Bd. of the Ordered Ministry, Exec. Minister, Rev. Dr. David Kersten
Bd. of Pensions & Benefits, Dir. of Pensions, Rev. Dr. Mary C. Miller
Bd. of Benevolence, Pres. of Covenant Ministries of Benevolence, David A. Dwight, 5145 N. California Ave., Chicago, IL 60625
North Park University, Pres., Dr. David G. Horner, 3225 W. Foster Ave., Chicago, IL 60625
North Park Theological Seminary, Pres. and Dean, Dr. John E. Phelan Jr.

SERVICE ORGANIZATIONS

National Covenant Properties, Pres., David W. Johnson, 5101 N. Francisco, Chicago, IL 60625 Tel. (773)784-3000
Covenant Trust Company, Pres., Charles A. Walles, 5101 N. Francisco, Chicago, IL 60625 Tel. (773)784-9911

REGIONAL CONFERENCES OF THE ECC

Central Conference, Supt., Rev. Herbert M. Freedholm, 3319 W. Foster Ave., Chicago, IL 60625 Tel. (773)267-3060
East Coast Conference, Supt., Rev. Robert C. Dvorak, 52 Missionary Rd., Cromwell, CT 06416 Tel. (860)635-2691
Great Lakes Conference, Supt., Rev. Richard Lucco, 70 W. Streetsboro St., P.O. Box 728, Hudson, OH 44236 Tel. (330)655-9345
Midwest Conference, Supt., Rev. Kenneth P. Carlson, 13304 W. Center Rd. #229, Omaha, NE 68144 Tel. (402)334-3060
North Pacific Conference, Supt., Rev. Mark A. Novak, 9311 SE 36th St., Ste 120, Mercer Island, WA 98040 Tel. (206)275-3903
Northwest Conference, Supt., Rev. Paul Erickson, 4721 E. 31st St., Minneapolis, MN 55406 Tel. (612)721-4893
Pacific Southwest Conference, Supt., Rev. Evelyn M. R. Johnson, 1333 Willow Pass Rd., Ste 212, Concord, CA 94502 Tel. (925)677-2140
Southeast Conference, Supt., Rev. Kurt A. Miericke, 1759 W. Broadway St., #7, Oviedo, FL 32765 Tel. (407)977-8009
ECC of Canada, Supt., Rev.Jeffrey Anderson, 2791 Pembina Hwy., Winnipeg, MN R3T 2H5 Tel. (204)269-3437
Midsouth Conference, Conference Supt., Rev. Garth T Bolinder, 8411 Greenwood Cir., Lenexa, KS 66215 Tel. (785)888-1825
ECC of Alaska, Field Dir., P.O. Box 770749, Eagle River, AK 99577 Tel. (907)694-6348

Periodicals

Covenant Companion, Covenant Quarterly, Covenant Home Altar

The Evangelical Free Church of America

In October 1884, 27 representatives from Swedish churches met in Boone, Iowa, to establish the Swedish Evangelical Free Church. In the fall of that same year, two Norwegian-Danish groups began worship and fellowship (in Boston and in Tacoma) and by 1912 had established the Norwegian-Danish Evangelical Free Church Association. These two denominations, representing 275 congregations, came together at a merger conference in 1950.

The Evangelical Free Church of America is an association of local, autonomous churches across the United States and Canada, blended together by common principles, policies, and practices. A 12-point statement addresses the major doctrines but also provides for differences of understanding on minor issues of faith and practice.

Overseas outreach includes 500 missionaries serving in 31 countries.

Headquarters

901 E. 78th St., Minneapolis, MN 55420-1300 Tel. (612)854-1300 Fax (612)853-8488
Email: president@efca.org
Website: www.efca.org/
Media Contact, Exec. Dir. of Ministry Advancement, Timothy Addington

Officers

Acting Pres./Exec. Vice Pres., Rev. William Hamel
Moderator, Ronald Aucutt, 3417 Silver Maple Pl., Falls Church, VA 22042
Vice Moderator, Rev. Mark J. Wold, 41827 Higgins Way, Fremont, CA 94539
Sec., Dr. Roland Peterson, 235 Craigbrook Way NE, Fridley, MN 55432
Vice Sec., Rev. William S. Wick, 92 S. Main, Northfield, VT 05663
Chief Fin. Ofc., Robert Peterson
Exec. Dir., Evangelical Free Church Mission, Dr. Ben Swatsky
Assoc. Dir. of Mission USA, Rev. Steve Hudson

Periodicals

Evangelical Beacon, Pursuit

Evangelical Friends International–North American Region

The organization restructured from Evangelical Friends Alliance in 1990 to become internationalized for the benefit of its world-wide contacts. The North America Region continues to function within the United States as EFA formerly did. The organization represents one corporate step of denominational unity, brought about as a result of several movements of spiritual renewal within the Society of Friends. These movements are: (1) the general evangelical renewal within Christianity, (2) the new scholarly recognition of the evangelical nature of 17th-century Quakerism, and (3) EFA, which was formed in 1965.

The EFA is conservative in theology and makes use of local pastors. Sunday morning worship includes singing, Scripture reading, a period of open worship, and a sermon by the pastor.

Headquarters

5350 Broadmoor Cir. NW, Canton, OH 44709 Tel. (330)493-1660 Fax (330)493-0852

Email: efcer@aol.com

Website: www.evangelical-friends.org

Media Contact, Gen. Supt., Dr. John P. Williams Jr.

YEARLY MEETINGS

Evangelical Friends Church, Eastern Region, Wayne Ickes, 5350 Broadmoor Cir. NW, Canton, OH 44709 Tel. (330)493-1660 Fax (330)493-0852

Rocky Mountain YM, John Brawner, 3350 Reed St., Wheat Ridge, CO 80033 Tel. (303)238-5200 Fax (303)238-5200

Mid-America YM, Duane Hansen, 2018 Maple, Wichita, KS 67213 Tel. (316)267-0391 Fax (316)267-0681

Northwest YM, Mark Ankeny, 200 N. Meridian St., Newberg, OR 97132 Tel. (503)538-9419 Fax (503)538-9410

Alaska YM, Sam Williams, P.O. Box 687, Kotzebue, AK 99752 Tel. (907)442-3906

Friends Church Southwest, YM, Linda Coop, P.O. Box 1607, Whittier, CA 90609-1607 Tel. (562)947-2883 Fax (562)947-9385

Periodicals

The Friends Voice

Evangelical Lutheran Church in America*

The Evangelical Lutheran Church in America (ELCA) was organized April 30–May 3, 1987, in Columbus, Ohio, bringing together the 2.25 million-member American Lutheran Church, the 2.85 million-member Lutheran Church in America, and the 100,000-member Association of Evangelical Lutheran Churches.

The ELCA is, through its predecessors, the oldest of the major US Lutheran churches. In the mid-17th century, a Dutch Lutheran congregation was formed in New Amsterdam (now New York). Other early congregations were begun by German and Scandinavian immigrants to Delaware, Pennsylvania, New York, and the Carolinas.

The first Lutheran association of congregations, the Pennsylvania Ministerium, was organized in 1748 under Henry Melchior Muhlenberg. Numerous Lutheran organizations were formed as immigration continued and the United States grew.

In 1960, the American Lutheran Church (ALC) was created through a merger of an earlier American Lutheran Church (formed in 1930), the Evangelical Lutheran Church (begun in 1917), and the United Evangelical Lutheran Church in America (started in 1896). In 1963 the Lutheran Free Church, formed in 1897, merged with the ALC.

In 1962, the Lutheran Church in America (LCA) was formed by a merger of the United Lutheran Church (formed in 1918) with the Augustana Lutheran Church (begun in 1860), the American Evangelical Lutheran Church (founded in 1872), and the Finnish Lutheran Church or Suomi Synod (founded in 1891).

The Association of Evangelical Lutheran Churches arose in 1976 from a doctrinal split with the Lutheran Church–Missouri Synod.

The ELCA, through its predecessor church bodies, was a founding member of the Lutheran World Federation, the World Council of Churches, and the National Council of the Churches of Christ in the USA.

The church is divided into 65 geographical areas or synods. These 65 synods are grouped into nine regions for mission, joint programs, and service.

Headquarters

8765 W. Higgins Rd., Chicago, IL 60631 Tel. (773)380-2700 Fax (773)380-1465

Email: info@elca.org

Website: www.elca.org

Media Contact, Dir. for News, John Brooks Tel. (773)380-2958 Fax (773)380-2406

Officers

Presiding Bishop, Rev. Mark S. Hanson

Sec., Rev. Dr. Lowell G. Almen

Treas., Ms. Christina L. Jackson-Skelton

Vice Pres., -vacant-

Exec. for Admn., Rev. Charles S. Miller

Office of the Bishop, Exec. Assts. for Federal Chaplaincies, Exec. Asst., Ms. Myrna J. Sheie

DIVISIONS

Div. for Congregational Min., Co-Exec. Dir., Rev. Mark R. Moller-Gunderson; Co-Exec. Dir., Rev. M. Wyvetta Bullock; Bd. Chpsn., Ms. Karen Walhof; Lutheran Youth Organization, Pres., Leota Thomas-Breitfeld

Div. for Higher Educ. and Schools, Exec. Dir.,

Rev. Dr. Leonard G. Schulze; Bd. Chpsn., Mr. Raymond E. Bailey

Div. for Global Mission, Exec. Dir., Rev. Rafael Malpica Padilla; Bd. Chpsn., Ms. Christine S. Mummert

Div. for Ministry, Exec. Dir., Rev. Stanley N. Olson; Bd. Chpsn., Mr. Kevin J. Boatright

Div. for Outreach, Exec. Dir., Rev. Dr. Richard A. Magnus Jr.; Bd. Chpsn., Ms. Dorothy Baumgartner

Div. for Church in Society, Exec. Dir., Rev. Rebecca S. Larson; Chpsn., Rev. Denver W. Bitner

COMMISSIONS

Comm. for Multicultural Ministries, Exec. Dir., Rev. Frederick E.N. Rajan; Chpsn., Rev. Grace G. El-Yateem

Comm. for Women, Exec. Dir., Joanne Chadwick; Chpsn., Ms. Agnes S. McClain

CHURCHWIDE UNITS

Conference of Bishops, Asst. to the Bishop, Rev. Kathie Bender Schwich; Chpsn., Rev. Donald J. McCoid

ELCA Foundation, Exec. Dir., The Rev. Donald M. Hallberg; Chpsn., Mr. David D. Swartling

ELCA Publishing House, Exec. Dir., Ms. Beth A. Lewis; Bd. Chpsn., Mr. Timothy I. Maudlin

ELCA Bd. of Pensions, Exec. Dir., John G. Kapanke; Bd. Chpsn, Mr. Kenneth G. Bash

Women of the ELCA, Exec. Dir., Ms. Linda Post Bushkofsky; Bd. Chpsn., Ms. Mary Ellen Kiesner

DEPARTMENTS

Dept. for Communication, Dir., Rev. Eric C. Shafer

Dept. for Ecumenical Affairs, Dir., Rev. Randall R. Lee; Committee Chpsn., Rev. John K. Stendahl

Dept. for Human Resources, Dir., Ms. Else Thompson

Dept. for Research & Evaluation, Dir., Dr. Kenneth W. Inskeep

Dept. for Synodical Relations, Dir., Rev. Kathie Bender Schwich

SYNODICAL BISHOPS

REGION 1

Alaska, Rev. Ronald D. Martinson, 1847 W. Northern Lights Blvd., #2, Anchorage, AK 99517-3343 Tel. (907)272-8899 Fax (907) 274-3141

Northwest Washington, Rev. Wm Chris Boerger, 5519 Pinney Ave. N, Seattle, WA 98103-5899 Tel. (206)783-9292 Fax (206)783-9833

Southwestern Washington, Rev. Robert D. Hofstad, 420 121st St. S, Tacoma, WA 98444-5218 Tel. (253)535-8300 Fax (253)535-8315

Eastern Washington/Idaho, Rev. Martin D. Wells, 314 South Spruce St., Ste. A, Spokane, WA 99204-1098 Tel. (509)838-9871 Fax (509)838-0941

Oregon, Rev. Paul R. Swanson, 2800 N. Vancouver Ave., Ste. 101, Portland, OR 97227-1643 Tel. (503)413-4191 Fax (503) 413-2407

Montana, Rev. Dr. Richard R. Omland, 2415 13th Ave. S, Great Falls, MT 59405-5199 Tel. (406)453-1461 Fax (406)761-4632

Regional Coord., Mr. Steven H. Lansing, Region 1, 766-B John St., Seattle, WA 98109-5186 Tel. (206)624-0093 Fax (206)626-0987

REGION 2

Sierra Pacific, Rev. David G. Mullen, 401 Roland Way, #215, Oakland, CA 94621-2011 Tel. (510)430-0500 Fax (510)430-8730

South West California, Bishop, Rev. Dean W. Nelson, 1300 E. Colorado St., Glendale, CA 91205-1406 Tel. (818)507-9591 Fax (818)507-9627

Pacifica, Rev. Murray D. Finck, 23655 Via Del Rio, Ste. B, Yorba Linda, CA 92887-2738 Tel. (714)692-2791 Fax (714)692-9317

Grand Canyon, Rev. Michael J. Neils, Interchurch Center 4423 N. 24th St., Ste. 400, Phoenix, AZ 85016-5544 Tel. (602)957-3223 Fax (602)956-8104

Rocky Mountain, Rev. Allan C. Bjornberg, 455 Sherman St., Ste. 160, Denver, CO 80203 Tel. (303)777-6700 Fax (303)733-0750

Regional Coord., Ms. Margaret Schmitt Ajer, Region 2, 3755 Avocado Blvd., PMB 411, La Mesa, CA 91941 Tel (619)460-9312 Fax (619)460-9314

REGION 3

Western North Dakota, Rev. Duane C. Danielson, 1614 Capitol Way, P.O. Box 370, Bismarck, ND 58502-0370 Tel. (701)223-5312 Fax (701)223-1435

Eastern North Dakota, Rev. Richard J. Foss, 1703 32nd Ave. S, Fargo, ND 58103-5936 Tel. (701)232-3381 Fax (701)232-3180

South Dakota, Rev. Andrea F. DeGroot-Nesdahl, Augustana College, 29th & S. Summit, Sioux Falls, SD 57197-0001 Tel. (605)247-4011 Fax (605)274-4028

Northwestern Minnesota, Rev. Rolf P. Wangberg, Concordia College, 901 8th St. S, Moorhead, MN 56562-0001 Tel. (218)299-3019 Fax (218)299-3363

Northeastern Minnesota, Rev. E. Peter Strommen, 1105 E. Superior St., Upper Suite, Duluth, MN 55802-2085 Tel. (218)724-4424 Fax (218) 724-4393

Southwestern Minnesota, Rev. Jon V. Anderson 175 E. Bridge St., P.O. Box 499, Redwood Falls, MN 56283-0499 Tel. (507)637-3904 Fax (507)637-2809

Minneapolis Area, Rev. Craig E. Johnson, 122 W. Franklin Ave., Ste. 600, Minneapolis, MN 55404-2474 Tel. (612)870-3610 Fax (612) 870-0170

Saint Paul Area, Rev. Peter Rogness, 105 W. University Ave., St. Paul, MN 55103-2094 Tel. (651)224-4313 Fax (651)224-5646

Southeastern Minnesota, Rev. Harold L. Usgaard, Assisi Heights, 1001 14th St. NW, Ste. 300, Rochester, MN 55901-2511 Tel. (507)280-9457 Fax (507)280-8824

Regional Coord., Rev. Craig A. Boehlke, Region 3, Luther Seminary, 2481 Como Ave., St. Paul, MN 55108-1445 Tel. (651)649-0454 ext. 232 Fax (651)649-0468

REGION 4

Nebraska, Rev. David L.deFreese, 4980 S. 118th St., Ste. D, Omaha, NE 68137-2220 Tel. (402)896-5311 Fax (402)896-5354

Central States, Rev. Dr. Gerald L. Mansholt, 3210 Michigan Ave., 4th Fl., Kansas City, MO 64109 Tel. (816)861-6584 Fax (816)861-4753

Arkansas/Oklahoma, Rev. Floyd M. Schoenhals, 693 S. 66th E. Ave., Ste. 310, Tulsa, OK 74133-1760 Tel. (918)492-4288 Fax (918) 491-6275

Northern Texas/Northern Louisiana, Rev. Kevin S. Kanouse, 1230 Riverbend Dr., Ste. 105, P.O. Box 560587, Dallas, TX 75356-0587 Tel. (214)637-6865 Fax (214)637-4805

Southwestern Texas, Rev. Ray Tiemann, 1090 Oestreich Dr., Seguin, TX 78155 Tel. (830)379-9900 Fax (830)379-9990

Texas/Louisiana Gulf Coast, Rev. Paul J. Blom, 12707 North Fwy., #580, Houston, TX 77060-1239 Tel. (281)873-5665 Fax (281)875-4716

Acting Regional Coord., Rev. Donald R. Just, Region 4, 7016 Ameranth Ln., Austin, TX, 78723 Tel. (512)272-9677 Fax (512)272-9699

REGION 5

Metropolitan Chicago, Rev. Paul R. Landahl, 1420 W. Dickens Ave., Chicago, IL 60614-3004 Tel. (773)248-0021 Fax (773)248-8455

Northern Illinois, Rev. Gary M. Wollersheim, 103 W. State St., Rockford, IL 61101-1105 Tel. (815) 964-9934 Fax (815)964-2295

Central/Southern Illinois, Rev. Warren D. Freiheit, 524 S. Fifth St., Springfield, IL 62701-1822 Tel. (217)753-7915 Fax (217) 753-7976

Southeastern Iowa, Rev. Philip L. Hougen, 2635 Northgate Dr., P.O. Box 3167, Iowa City, IA 52244-3167 Tel. (319)338-1273 Fax (319) 351-8677

Western Iowa, Rev. Michael A. Last, 318 E. Fifth St., P.O. Box 577, Storm Lake, IA 50588-0577 Tel. (712)732-4968 Fax (712)732-6540

Northeastern Iowa, Rev. Steven L. Ullestad, 201-20th St. SW, P.O. Box 804, Waverly, IA 50677-0804 Tel. (319)352-1414 Fax (319) 352-1416

Northern Great Lakes, Rev. Thomas A. Shrenes, 1029 N. Third St., Marquette, MI 49855-3588 Tel. (906)228-2300 Fax (906)228-2527

Northwest Synod of Wisconsin, Rev. Robert D. Berg, 12 W. Marshall St., P.O. Box 730, Rice Lake, WI 54868-0730 Tel. (715)234-3373 Fax (715)234-4183

East/Central Synod of Wisconsin, Rev. James A. Justman, 16 Tri-Park Way, Appleton, WI 54914-1658 Tel. (920)734-5381 Fax (920) 734-5074

Greater Milwaukee, Rev. Paul W. Stumme-Diers, 1212 S. Layton Blvd., Milwaukee, WI 53215-1653 Tel. (414)671-1212 Fax (414) 671-1756

South/Central Synod of Wisconsin, Rev. George G. Carlson, 2909 Landmark Pl., Ste. 202, Madison, WI 53713-4237 Tel. (608)270-0201 Fax (608)270-0202

La Crosse Area, Rev. April Ulring Larson, 3462 Losey Blvd. S., La Crosse, WI 54601-7217 Tel. (608)788-5000 Fax (608)788-4916

Regional Coord., Rev. Carl R. Evenson, Region 5, 675 Deerwood Dr., Ste. 4., Neenah, WI 54956-1629 Tel. (920)720-9880 Fax (920) 720-9881

REGION 6

Southeast Michigan, Rev. Robert A. Rimbo, 218 Fisher Bldg., 3011 W. Grand Ave., Detroit, MI 48202-3011 Tel. (313)875-1881 Fax (313) 875-1889

Northwest Lower Michigan, Rev. Gary L. Hansen, 801 S. Waverly Rd., Ste. 201, Lansing, MI 48917-4254 Tel. (517)321-5066 Fax (517)321-2612

Indiana/Kentucky, Rev. James R. Stuck, 911 E. 86th St., Ste. 200, Indianapolis, IN 46240-1840 Tel. (317)253-3522 Fax (317)254-5666

Northwestern Ohio, Rev. Marcus C. Lohrmann, 621 Bright Rd., Findlay, OH 45840-6987 Tel. (419)423-3664 Fax (419)423-8801

Northeastern Ohio, Rev. Marcus J. Miller, 1890 Bailey Rd., Cuyahoga Falls, OH 44221-5259 Tel. (330)929-9022 Fax (330)929-9018

Southern Ohio, Rev. Dr. Callon W. Holloway Jr., 300 S. 2nd St., Columbus, OH 43215-5001 Tel. (614)464-3532 Fax (614)464-3422

Regional Coord., Marilyn McCann Smith, Region 6, P.O. Box 91, 119 1/2 N. Main St. Bluffton, OH 45817 Tel. (419)369-4006 Fax (419)369-4007

REGION 7

New Jersey, Rev. E. Roy Riley Jr., 1930 State Highway. 33, Hamilton Square, Trenton, NJ 08690-1799 Tel. (609)586-6800 Fax (609) 586-1597

New England, Rev. Margaret G. Payne, 20 Upland St., Worcester, MA 01607-1624 Tel. (508)791-1530 Fax (508)797-9295

Metropolitan New York, Rev. Stephen P. Bouman, Interchurch Center, 475 Riverside Dr., Ste.1620, New York, NY 10115 Tel. (212) 665-0732 Fax (212)665-8640

Upstate New York, Rev. Marie C. Jerge, 890 E. Brighton Ave., Syracuse, NY 13205 Tel. (315)446-2502 Fax (315)446-4642

Northeastern Pennsylvania, Rev. Dr. David R. Strobel, 4865 Hamilton Blvd., Wescosville,

PA 18106-9705 Tel. (610)395-6891 Fax (610)398-7083

Southeastern Pennsylvania, Rev. Roy G. Almquist, 506 Haws Ave., Norristown, PA 19401-4543 Tel. (610)278-7342 Fax (610) 696-2782

Slovak Zion, Rev. Wilma S. Kucharek, 124 Barbero Dr., Torrington, CT 06790, P.O. Box 1003 06790-1003 Tel. (860)482-6100 Fax (860)482-7463

Regional Coord., Judith A. Spindt, Region 7, Lutheran Theol. Seminary at Philadelphia, Hagan Hall, 7301 Germantown Ave., Philadelphia, PA 19119-1794 Tel. (215)248-6319 Fax (215)248-7377

REGION 8

Northwestern Pennsylvania, Rev. Ralph E. Jones, 308 Seneca St., 5th Fl., Oil City, PA 16301 Tel. (814)677-5706 Fax (814)676-8591

Southwestern Pennsylvania, Rev. Donald J. McCoid, 9625 Perry Hwy., Pittsburgh, PA 15237-5590 Tel. (412)367-8222 Fax (412) 369-8840

Allegheny, Rev. Gregory R. Pile, 701 Quail Ave., Altoona, PA 16602-3010 Tel. (814)942-1042 Fax (814)941-9259

Lower Susquehanna, Rev. Carol S. Hendrix, 900 S. Arlington Ave., Ste. 208, Harrisburg, PA 17109-5031 Tel. (717)652-1852 Fax (717) 652-2504

Upper Susquehanna, Rev. Dr. A. Donald Main, Rt. 192 & Reitz Blvd., P.O. Box 36, Lewisburg, PA 17837-0036 Tel. (570)524-9778 Fax (570)524-9757

Delaware/Maryland, Rev. Dr. H. Gerard Knoche, 700 Light St., Baltimore, MD 21230-3850 Tel. (410)230-2860 Fax (410)230-2871

Metropolitan Washington, D.C., Rev. Theodore F. Schneider, 1030-15th St. NW, Ste 1010, Washington, D.C. 20005-1503 Tel. (202)408-8110 Fax (202)408-8114

West Virginia/Western Maryland, Rev. Ralph W. Dunkin, The Atrium, 503 Morgantown Avenue, Ste. 100, Fairmont, WV 26554-4374 Tel. (304)363-4030 Fax (304)366-9846

Regional Coord., Rev. James E. Miley, Region 8, Lutheran Theological Sem. at Gettysburg, 61 Seminary Ridge, Gettysburg, PA 17325-1795 Tel. (717)334-6286 ext. 2133 Fax (717)334-0323

REGION 9

Virginia, Rev. James F. Mauney, Roanoke College, 221 College Ln., Bittle Hall, P.O. Drawer 70, Salem, VA 24153-0070 Tel. (540)389-1000 Fax (540)389-5962

North Carolina, Rev. Leonard H. Bolick, 1988 Lutheran Synod Dr., Salisbury, NC 28144-4480 Tel. (704)633-4861 Fax (704)638-0508

South Carolina, Rev. David A. Donges, 1003 Richland St., P.O. Box 43, Columbia, SC 29202-0043 Tel. (803)765-0590 Fax (803)252-5558

Southeastern,, Rev. Ronald B. Warren, 100 Edgewood Ave. NE, Ste. 1600, Atlanta, GA 30303 Tel. (404)589-1977 Fax (404)521-1980

Florida/Bahamas, Rev. Edward R. Benoway, 3838 W. Cypress St., Tampa, FL 33607-4897 Tel. (813)876-7660 Fax (813)870-0826

Caribbean, Rev. Margarita Martinez, PMB Num 359 Ste. 1, 425 CARR 693, Ste. 1, Dorado, PR 00646-4802 Tel. (787)273-8311 Fax (787) 796-3365

Regional Coord., Rev. Harvey Huntley, Region 9, Lutheran Theological Southern Seminary, 4201 N. Main St., Columbia, SC 29203 Tel. (803)461-3263 Fax (803)461-3380

Periodicals

The Lutheran, Lutheran Partners, Lutheran Woman Today, Seeds for the Parish

Evangelical Lutheran Synod

The Evangelical Lutheran Synod had its beginning among the Norwegian settlers who brought with them their Lutheran heritage. The Synod was organized in 1853. It was reorganized in 1918 by those who desired to adhere to the synod's principles not only in word but also in deed.

The Synod owns and operates Bethany Lutheran College and Bethany Lutheran Theological Seminary. It has congregations in 20 states and maintains foreign missions in Peru, Chile, the Czech Republic, and Ukraine. It operates a seminary in Lima, Peru and in Ternopil, Ukraine.

Headquarters

6 Browns Ct., Mankato, MN 56001 Tel. (507) 344-7356 Fax (507)344-7426

Email: gorvick@blc.edu

Website: www.EvLuthSyn.org

Media Contact, Pres., John A. Moldstad

Officers

Pres., Rev. John A. Moldstad, 6 Browns Ct., Mankato, MN 56082

Sec., Rev. Craig Ferkenstad, Rt. 3, Box 40, St. Peter, MN 56082

Treas., Keith Wiederhoeft, 6 Browns Ct., Mankato, MN 56001

Vice Pres., Rev. Glenn Obengerger, 12309 Pacific Ave., Tacoma, WA 98444

OTHER ORGANIZATIONS

Lutheran Synod Book Co., Bethany Lutheran College, 700 Luther Dr., Mankato, MN 56001

Bethany Lutheran Theological Seminary, 6 Browns Ct., Mankato, MN 56001

Periodicals

Lutheran Sentinel, Lutheran Synod Quarterly, Young Branches, Oak Leaves, Mission News

Evangelical Mennonite Church—now listed as Fellowship of Evangelical Churches

Evangelical Methodist Church

The Evangelical Methodist Church was organized in 1946 at Memphis, Tenn., largely as a movement of people who opposed modern liberalism and wished for a return to the historic Wesleyan position. In 1960, it merged with the Evangel Church (formerly Evangelistic Tabernacles) and with the People's Methodist Church in 1962.

Headquarters

P.O. Box 17070, Indianapolis, IN 46217 Tel. (317)780-8017 Fax (317)780-8078

Email: headquarters@emchurch.org

Website: www.emchurch.org/

Media Contact, Gen. Conf. Sec.-Treas., Rev. James A. Coulston

Officers

Gen. Supt., Dr. Edward W. Williamson

Gen. Conf. Sec.-Treas., Rev. James A. Coulston

Evangelical Presbyterian Church

The Evangelical Presbyterian Church (EPC), established in March 1981, is a conservative denomination of 9 geographic presbyteries, 8 in the United States and one in Argentina. From its inception with 12 churches, the EPC has grown to 190 churches with a membership of over 69,610.

Planted firmly within the historic Reformed tradition and evangelical in spirit, the EPC places high priority on church planting and development along with world missions. Eighty missionaries serve the church's mission.

Based on the truth of Scripture and adhering to the Westminster Confession of Faith plus its Book of Order, the denomination is committed to the "essentials of the faith." The historic motto "In essentials, unity; in nonessentials, liberty; in all things, charity" catches the irenic spirit of the EPC, along with the Ephesians theme, "truth in love."

The Evangelical Presbyterian Church is a member of the World Alliance of Reformed Churches, National Association of Evangelicals, World Evangelical Fellowship, and the Evangelical Council for Financial Accountability.

Headquarters

Office of the General Assembly, 29140 Buckingham Ave., Ste. 5, Livonia, MI 48154 Tel. (734)261-2001 Fax (734)261-3282

Email: EPCHURCH@epc.org

Website: www.epc.org

Media Contact, Stated Clk., Rev. Michael Glodo, 29140 Buckingham Ave., Ste. 5, Livonia, MI 48154 Tel. (734)261-2001 Fax (734)261-3282

Officers

Administration Committee, Chmn., Mr. Knox Sherer, 921-F Mathews Mint Hill Rd., Mathews, NC 28105

Board of Pension & Benefits, Chmn., Mr. John Baird, c/o EPC, 29140 Bucklingham Ave., #5, Livonia, MI 48154

Committee on Fraternal Relations, Chmn., Rev. Craig Vanbiber, Calvary Presbyterian, 6100 Richfield Rd., Flint, MI 48506

Committee on National Outreach, Chmn., Rev. Eli Morris, Hope Presbyterian, 8500 Walnut Grove Rd., Cordova, TN 38018

Committee on Presbytery Review, Chmn., Mr. Jay Curtis, 3018 Forest Club Dr., Plant City, FL 33566

Committee on World Outreach, Chmn., Rev. Ed Randal, Northwest EPC, 17820 NE 101st Court, Redmond, WA 98052

Committee on Ministerial Vocation, Chmn., Mr. Ron DeHaas, Box 397, Owosso, MI 48867

Committee on Christian Educ. & Publ. , Chmn., Rev. Waring Porter, Knox Presbyterian, 25700 Crocker Blvd., Harrison Township, MI 48045

Committee on Women's Ministries, Chmn., Mrs. Vicki Oliver, 18414 Glastonbury Dr., Livonia, MI 48152

Committee on Theology, Chmn., Rev. Don Sweeting, Cherry Creek Presbyterian, 10150 E. Belleview Ave., Englewood, CO 80111

Committee on Student and Young Adult Ministries, Chmn., Mr. Freddie Albaugh, Knox Presbyterian, 25700 Crocker Blvd., Harrison Township, MI 48045

PRESBYTERIES

Central South, Stated Clk., Rev. Dennis Flach, New Covenant Evangelical Presbyterian Church, P.O. Box 842, Natchez, MS 39121

East, Stated Clk., Dr. Frank Johnson, 36 Slape Ave., Salem, NJ 08079

Florida, Stated Clk., Rev. Robert Garment, Trinity EPC, 5150 Oleander, Ft. Pierce, FL 34982

Mid-America, Stated Clk., Mr. Dexter Kuhlman, 1926 Prospector Ridge, Ballwin, MO 63011

Mid-Atlantic, Stated Clk., Dr. Howard Shockley, 58 Bear Trail, Fairview, NC 28730

Midwest, Stated Clk., Mr. John C. Manon, P.O. Box 6047, Auburn, IN 46706-6047

Southeast, Stated Clk., Rev. Bill Sharp, 1222 Village Green Dr., Chattanooga, TN 39343

West, Stated Clk., Mr. Cecil Matthews, 4677 Springmeadow Lane, Castle Rock, CO 80104

St. Andrews, Stated Clk., Rev. Jorge Lumsden, Temperley Church, Gral Paz 191, (1834) Temperley PCIA Buenos Aires, Argentina

Fellowship of Evangelical Bible Churches

Formerly known as Evangelical Mennonite Brethren, this body emanates from the Russian immigration of Mennonites into the United States (1873-74). Established with the emphasis on true repentance, conversion, and a committed life to Jesus as Savior and Lord, the conference was founded in 1889 under the leadership of Isaac Peters and Aaron Wall. The founding churches were located in Mountain Lake, Minn., and in Henderson and Jansen, Nebr. The conference has since grown to a fellowship of 43 churches with approximately 4,500 members in Argentina, Canada, Paraguay, and the United States.

Foreign missions have been a vital ingredient of the total ministry. Today, one missionary is serving for every 35 members in the home churches. The fellowship does not develop and administer foreign mission fields of its own, but actively participates with existing evangelical "faith" mission agencies. The fellowship has missionaries serving under approximately 40 different agencies around the world.

The church holds fast to the inerrancy of Scripture, the deity of Christ, and the need for spiritual regeneration of man from his sinful natural state by faith in the death, burial, and resurrection of Jesus Christ as payment for sin. Members look forward to the imminent return of Jesus Christ and retain a sense of urgency to share the gospel with those who have never heard of God's redeeming love.

Headquarters

3339 N. 109th Plz., Omaha, NE 68164 Tel. (402) 965-3860 Fax (402)965-3871

Email: info@febcministries.org or febcoma@aol.com

Website: members.aol.com/febcoma/index.html

Admn., Paul Boeker, 3339 N. 109th Plz., Omaha, NE 68164 Tel. (402)965-3860 Fax (402)965-3871

Officers

Pres., Mr. Gerald Epp, P.O. Box 86, Waldheim, SK S0K 4R0 Tel. (306)945-2023, ggepp@sk.sympatico.ca

Vice Pres., Rev. Charles Tschetter, 9001 Q St., Omaha, NE 68127-3548, cbcomaha@aol.com

Rec. Sec., Stan Seifert, 1002-3190 Gladwin Road, Abbotsford, BC V2T 5T2 Tel. (604) 852-3253 Fax (604)852-7887

Admn., Paul Boeker, 3339 N. 109th Plz., Omaha, NE 68164 Tel. (402)965-3860 Fax (402)965-3871, febcoma@aol.com

Ministries Coord., Harvey Schultz, 3011 3rd Ave. East, P.O. Box 8, Waldheim, SK S0K 4R0 Tel. (306)945-2220, Fax (306)945-2088, hesals@aol.com

Comm. on Churches, Chpsn., Rev. Paul Carpenter, 401 Nebraska St., Box 141, Jansen, NE 68377-0141 Tel. (402)424-2645, jb95208@alltel.net

Comm. on Education, Chpsn., Ray Reimer, 5005 Adams, Lincon, NE 68504 Tel. (402)466-6409, rayreimer@juno.com

Comm. on Missions, Chpsn., Dennis Wiens, 11260 N. Summit, Kansas City, MO 64155 Tel. (816)734-3798, dwiens@gmu.org

Comm. of Trustees, Chpsn., William Ginter, Box 326 Morris MB ROG 1KO, Canada Tel. (204) 746-2612, wginter@escape.ca

Comm. on Church Planting, Chpsn., Jim Ingle, 806 Leprechaun LN, Papillion, NE 68046-2111 Tel. (402)339-1221, jandpingle@cox.net

Comm. on Women's Ministries, Chpsn., Ruth Epp, Box 86, Waldheim, SK S0K 4R0 Tel. (306)945-2023, ggepp@sk.sympatico.ca

Periodicals

Fellowship Focus

Fellowship of Fundamental Bible Churches

The churches in this body represent the 1939 separation from the Methodist Protestant Church, when some 50 delegates and pastors (approximately one-third of the Eastern Conference) withdrew to protest the union of the Methodist Protestant Church with the Methodist Episcopal Church and the Methodist Episcopal Church South, and what they considered the liberal tendencies of those churches. These churches subsequently changed their name to the Bible Protestant Church. In 1985, this group again changed its name to the Fellowship of Fundamental Bible Churches to more accurately define their position.

As fundamentalists, this group strongly adheres to the historic fundamentals of the faith, including the doctrine of separation. This group accepts a literal view of the Bible and, consequently, accepts premillennial theology and a pretribulational rapture.

The churches are currently located in New Jersey, New York, Pennsylvania, Virginia, Michigan, and California. It is a fellowship of independent Bible and Baptist churches. Baptism by immersion and the Lord's Supper, as a memorial, are recognized as ordinances. There are currently 21 churches representing 1,500 members. This constituent body is a member of the American Council of Christian Churches.

The Fellowship of Fundamental Bible Churches owns and operates Tri-State Bible Camp and Conference Center in Montague, N.J., oversees a mission board called Fundamental Bible Missions, and conducts a Bible Institute called Fundamental Bible Institute.

Headquarters

P.O. Box 206, Penns Grove, NJ 08069

Email: FFBC-USA@juno.com

Website: www.churches-ffbc.org/

Media Contact, Sec., Rev. Edmund G. Cotton, 80 Hudson St., Port Jervis, NY 12771 Tel. (914) 856-7695

Officers

Pres., Rev. Mark Franklin, 284 Whig Ln., Monroeville, NJ 08343 Tel. (609)881-0057

Vice Pres., Rev. Gary Myers, P.O. Box 191, Meshoppen, PA 18630 Tel. (717)833-4898

Sec., Rev. Edmund G. Cotton, 80 Hudson St., Port Jervis, NY 12771 Tel. (914)856-7695

Treas., Ken Thompson, 501 N. Main St., Elmer, NJ 08318 (865)358-0515

Fellowship of Grace Brethren Churches

A division occurred in the Church of the Brethren in 1882 on the question of the legislative authority of the annual meeting. It resulted in the establishment of the Brethren Church under a legal charter requiring congregational government. This body divided in 1939 with the Grace Brethren establishing headquarters at Winona Lake, Ind., and the Brethren Church at Ashland, Ohio.

Headquarters

Media Contact, Fellowship Coord., Rev. Thomas Avey, P.O. Box 386, Winona Lake, IN 46590 Tel. (219)269-1269 Fax (219)269-4066

Email: fgbc@fgbc.org

Website: www.fgbc.org

Officers

Mod., Dr. Galen Wiley, 22713 Ellsworth Ave., Minerva, OH 44657

1st Mod.-Elect, Dr. James Custer, 2515 Carriage Rd., Powell, OH 43065

2nd Mod.-Elect, Dr. Ron Manahan, 2316 E. Kemo Ave., Warsaw, IN 46580

Fellowship Coord., Rev. Thomas Avey, P.O. Box 386, Winona Lake, IN 46590 Tel. (219)269-1269 Fax (219)269-4066

Sec., Fellowship Coord., Rev. Thomas Avey, P.O. Box 386, Winona Lake, IN 46590

Treas., Thomas Staller, 2311 S. Cost-a-Plenty Dr., Warsaw, IN 46580

OTHER BOARDS

Grace Brethren International Missions, Exec. Dir., Rev. Tom Julien, P.O. Box 588, Winona Lake, IN 46590

Grace Brethren Home Missions, Exec. Dir., Larry Chamberlain, P.O. Box 587, Winona Lake, IN 46590

Grace College and Seminary, Pres., Ronald E. Manahan, 200 Seminary Dr., Winona Lake, IN 46590 Tel. (210)372-5100

Brethren Missionary Herald Co., Pub. & Gen. Mgr., James Bustram, P.O. Box 544, Winona Lake, IN 46590

CE National, Exec. Dir., Rev. Ed Lewis, P.O. Box 365, Winona Lake, IN 46590

Grace Brethren Navajo Ministries, Dir., Steve Galegor, Counselor, NM 87018

Grace Village Retirement Community, Admn., Jeff Carroll, P.O. Box 337, Winona Lake, IN 46590

Natl. Fellowship of Grace Brethren Ministries, Pres., Dr. Steve Taylor, 132 Summerall Ct., Aiken, SC 29801

Women's Missionary Council, Pres., Janet Minnix, 3314 Kenwick Tr. SW, Roanoke, VA, 24015

Grace Brethren Men International, Pres., Morgan Burgess, 163 N. Franklin St., Delaware, OH 43015

Fellowship of Evangelical Churches

The Evangelical Mennonite Church is an American denomination in the European free church tradition, tracing its heritage to the Reformation period of the 16th century. The Swiss Brethren of that time believed that salvation could come only by repentance for sins and faith in Jesus Christ, that baptism was only for believers, and that the church should be separate from controls of the state. Their enemies called them Anabaptists, since they insisted on rebaptizing believers who had been baptized as infants. As the Anabaptist movement spread to other countries, Menno Simons became its principal leader. In time his followers were called Mennonites.

In 1693 a Mennonite minister, Jacob Amman, insisted that the church should adopt a more conservative position on dress and style of living and should more rigidly enforce the "ban"—the church's method of disciplining disobedient members. Amman's insistence finally resulted in a division within the South German Mennonite groups; his followers became known as the Amish.

Migrations to America, involving both Mennonites and Amish, took place in the 1700s and 1800s, for both religious and economic reasons.

The Evangelical Mennonite Church was formed in 1866 out of a spiritual awakening among the Amish in Indiana. It was first known as the Egly Amish, after its founder Bishop Henry Egly. Bishop Egly emphasized regeneration, separation, and nonconformity to the world. His willingness to rebaptize anyone who had been baptized without repentance created a split in his church, prompting him to gather a new congregation in 1866. The conference, which has met annually since 1895, united a number of other congregations of like mind. This group became The Defenseless Mennonite Church in 1898 and has been known as the Evangelical Mennonite Church since 1948. At the 2003 convention, the delegates voted to change the name to Fellowship of Evangelical Churches.

Headquarters

1420 Kerrway Ct., Fort Wayne, IN 46805 Tel. (260)423-3649 Fax (260)420-1905

Email: emcintlmin@aol.com

Media Contact, Admn. Asst., Lynette Augsburger

Officers

Pres., Mr. Ronald J. Habegger

Chpsn., Rev. Roger Andrews, 12509 Chapel Cove, Fort Wayne, IN 46845

Vice Chpsn., Rev. Bryce Winteregg, 11331 Coldwater Rd., Ft. Wayne, IN 46845

Sec., Gene Rupp, c/o Taylor University, 236 W. Reade Ave., Upland, IN 46989

Treas., Alan Rupp, 5724 Spring Oat Ct., Fort Wayne, IN 46845

Free Christian Zion Church of Christ

This church was organized in 1905 at Redemption, Ark., by a company of African-American ministers associated with various denominations. Its polity is in general accord with that of Methodist bodies.

Headquarters

1315 S. Hutchinson St., Nashville, AR 71852 Tel. (501)845-4933

Media Contact, Gen. Sec., Shirlie Cheatham

Officers

Chief Pastor, Willie Benson, Jr.

Free Methodist Church of North America

The Free Methodist Church was organized in 1860 in Western New York by ministers and laymen who had called the Methodist Episcopal Church to return to what they considered the original doctrines and lifestyle of Methodism. The issues included human freedom (anti-slavery), freedom and simplicity in worship, free seats so that the poor would not be discriminated against, and freedom from secret oaths (societies) so the truth might be spoken freely at all times. The founders emphasized the teaching of the entire sanctification of life by means of grace through faith.

The denomination continues to be true to its founding principles. It communicates the gospel and its power to all people without discrimination through strong missionary, evangelistic, and educational programs. Six colleges, a Bible college, and numerous overseas schools train the youth of the church to serve in lay and ministerial roles.

Its members covenant to maintain simplicity in life; worship; daily devotion to Christ; and responsible stewardship of time, talent, and finance.

Headquarters

World Ministries Center, 770 N. High School Rd., Indianapolis, IN 46214 Tel. (317)244-3660 Fax (317)244-1247; Mailing Address: P.O. Box 535002, Indianapolis, IN 46253 Tel. (800)342-5531

Email: info@fmcna.org

Website: www.freemethodistchurch.org

Media Contact, Yearbook Ed., P.O. Box 535002, Indianapolis, IN 46253

Officers

Bishops: Bishop Roger W. Haskins Jr., Bishop Joseph F. James, Bishop Leslie L. Krober, Bishop Richard D. Snyder, Bishop Jim Tuan, Bishop Abner Chauke

General Conference Sec., Miss Carol Bartlett

Dir. of Administraion and Finance, Mr. Gary Kilgore

Free Methodist Communications, Rev. Douglas Newton

Free Methodist World Missions, Dr. Arthur Brown

Men's Ministries Inl.,, Dir., Rev. Jeffrey Johnson

Women's Ministries Intl.,, Pres., Mrs. Beth Webb

Periodicals

Light and Life Magazine, Free Methodist World Mission People

Friends General Conference

Friends General Conference (FGC) is an association of fourteen yearly meetings open to all Friends meetings which wish to be actively associated with FGC's programs and services. Friends General Conference includes Baltimore, Canadian, Illinois, Lake Erie, New England, New York, Northern, Ohio Valley, Philadelphia, South Central, and Southeastern Yearly Meetings; Alaska Friends Conference, Southern Appalachian Yearly Meeting and Association, and Piedmont Friends Fellowship; plus seven independently affiliated monthly meetings. Friends General Conference is primarily a service organization with the stated purpose of nurturing the spiritual life within its constituency of predominantly unprogrammed Friends. FGC offers services to all Friends, but has no authority over constituent meetings. A Central Com-mittee, to which constituent Yearly Meetings name appointees (in proportion to membership), and its Executive Committee are responsible for the direction of FGC's programs and services which include a bookstore, conferences, and traveling ministries program. The 1995 Central Committee approved the following Minute of Purpose:

Friends General Conference is a Quaker organization in the unprogrammed tradition of the Religious Society of Friends which primarily serves affiliated yearly and monthly meetings. It is our experience that:

—Faith is based on direct experience of God.

—Our lives witness this experience individually and corporately.

—By answering that of God in everyone, we build and sustain inclusive community.

Friends General Conference provides resources and opportunities that educate and invite members and attenders to experience, individually and corporately, God's living presence, and to discern and follow God's leadings. Friends General Conference reaches out to seekers and to other religious bodies inside and outside the Religious Society of Friends.

Headquarters

1216 Arch St., 2B, Philadelphia, PA 19107 Tel. (215)561-1700 Fax (215)561-0759

Email: friends@fgcquaker.org

Website: www.fgcquaker.org

Media Contact, Gen. Sec., Bruce Birchard

Officers

Gen. Sec., Bruce Birchard

Presiding Clerk, Janice Domanik

Treas., Mike Hubbart

YEARLY MEETINGS

Alaska Friends Conference: Clerk, Bill Schoder-Ehri, 480 Grubstake Ave., Homer, AK Tel. (907)479-5257, lovenest@ptialaska.net

*Baltimore: Clerk, Lamar Matthew, 17100 Quaker Ln., Sandy Spring, MD 20860 Tel. (301)774-7663, bymrsf@igc.org

*Canadian: Clerk, John Calder, 91A Fourth Ave., Ottawa, ON K1S 2L1 Tel. (613)235-8553, cym-office@quaker.ca

Illinois: Clerk, Margaret Katranides, 620 Fairview Ave., St. Louis, MO 63119-1809 Tel. (217) 384-9591, shaworth@prairienet.org or katrani@juno.org

Lake Erie: Clerk, Don Nagler, 1360 Tomah Dr., Mt. Pleasant, MI 48858 Tel. (419)874-6738, dfn@journey.com

*New England: Clerk, Deana Chase, 901 Pleasant St., Worcester, MA 01602-1908 Tel. (508)754-6760, neym@ultranet.com

*New York: Clerk, Linda Chidsey, 15 Rutherford Pl., New York, NY 10003 Tel. (212)673-5750, nyym@compuserve.com

Northern: Clerk, Christopher Sammond, 1718 10th St., Menomonie, WI 54751 Tel. (612) 529-9652, clsammond@aol.com (numeral 1)

Ohio Valley: Clerk, Cindi Goslee, P.O. Box 20066, Cincinnati, OH 45220 Tel. (513)281-8831, cemg@earthlink.net

Philadelphia: Clerk, Arlene Kelly, 1515 Cherry St., Philadelphia, PA 19102 Tel. (215)241-7210, joanb@pym.org; Staff, Thomas Jeavons, thomj@pym.org

Piedmont Friends Fellowship: Clerk, David Bailey, 1712 Lakemont Dr., Greensboro, NC 27410 Tel. (336)854-1225, DLLOYDBAI@aol.com

South Central: Clerk, Jan Michael, 1422 S. Western Stillwater, OK 74074-6832 Tel. (405) 624-0778, jdmichael@aol.com

*Southeastern: Clerk, Lyn Cope-Robinson, P.O. Box 510975, Melbourne Beach, FL 3295 Tel. (321)724-1162, admin@seym.org

Southern Appalachian: Clerk, Sharon Annis, P.O. Box 2191, Abington, VA 24212-2191 Tel. (276)628-5852

**also affiliated with Friends United Meeting*

Periodicals

Friends Journal

Friends United Meeting*

Friends United Meeting was organized in 1902 (the name was changed in 1963 from the Five Years Meeting of Friends) as a confederation of North American yearly meetings to facilitate a united Quaker witness in missions, peace work Christian education and outreach.

Today Friends United Meeting is comprised of 26 full-member and 3 association member yearly meetings representing about half the Friends in the world. FUM's current work includes programs of mission and service, leadership development, and outreach. FUM publishes Christian education curriculum, books of Quaker history and religious thought, and a magazine, *Quaker Life*.

Headquarters

101 Quaker Hill Dr., Richmond, IN 47374-1980 Tel. (765)962-7573 Fax (765)966-1293

Email: info@fum.org

Website: www.fum.org

Media Contact, Gen. Sec., Retha McCutchen

Officers

Presiding Clk., Brent McKinney

Treas., Don Garner

Gen. Sec., Retha McCutchen

DEPARTMENTS

World Missions: Dir., Colin Senth

North American Ministries: Dir., Ben Richmond

Quaker Hill Bookstore: Mgr., (interim)

Quaker Life: Ed., Trish Edwards-Konic

Friends United Press: Ed., Barbara Mays

YEARLY MEETINGS

Baltimore Yearly Meeting: 17100 Quaker Ln., Sandy Spring, MD 20860-1296 Tel. (301)774-7663 or (800)962-4766, Fax (301)774-7087, www.bymrsf@igc.org; Clerk, Lamar Matthew; Gen. Sec., Frank Massey

Bware Yearly Meeting: P.O. Box 179, Suna, Kenya; Gen. Sect., Samuel Kaguni; Gen Supt., Epainitus Adego; Presiding Clerk, Jonathan M. Sande

Canadian Yearly Meeting: 91-A Fourth Ave., Ottawa ON K1S 2L1, Canada Tel. & Fax (613)235-8553 Fax (613)235-1753; Clerk, George McClure; Website: www.cym@web.net

Central Yearly Meeting: P.O. Box 1510, Kakamega, Kenya, E. Africa; Gen. Supt., Evans Nyenzo

Chavakali Yearly Meeting: P.O. Box 102, Chavakali, Kenya, East Africa; Gen. Sec., Andrew Mukulu; Clerk, Wilson Andenya

Calle 20 #118 Esquina Paz, Reparto Vista, Alegre 80300, Hoguin, Cuba

Cuba Yearly Meeting: Calle 20 #118 Esquina Paz, Reparto Vista Alegre, 80300 Holguin, Cuba; Pres., Maria Renya Yi,

East Africa Yearly Meeting of Friends: (Kaimosi) P.O. Box 35, Tiriki, Kenya, East Africa; Presiding Clerk, Matthew Tsimbaki; Gen. Sec., Ephraim Konsolo; Gen. Supt., Erastus Kesohole

East Africa Yearly Meeting of Friends (North) : P.O. Box 544, Kitale, Kenya, East Africa; Gen. Sec., Geoffrey M. Wukwanja; Gen. Supt., Titus Adira; Presiding Clerk, H. M Mukwanja

VIHIGA Yearly Meeting of Friends: P.O. Box 160, Vihiga, Kenya, East Africa; Presiding Clerk, Joseph Kisia; Gen. Sec., Lam Kisanya Osodo; Gen. Supt., Gilbert Akenga Oyando

Elgon East Yearly Meeting: P.O. Box 2322, Kitale, Kenya, East Africa; Gen. Supt., Maurice Simiyu; Gen. Sec., Philip Musungu; Presiding Clerk, John Kitui

Elgon Religious Society of Friends (West): P.O. Box 4, Lugulu Via Webuye, Kenya, East Africa; General Sec., Tom Isiye; Gen. Supt., John Ngoya; Presiding Clerk, Charles Mbachi

Evangelical Friends Church Uganda: P.O. Box 129, Mbale, Uganda, East Africa; Gen. Supt., Simon Tsapwe; Gen. Sec., Peter Kutosi

Great Plains Yearly Meeting: 1262 Richland Rd., Lacon, IL 61540 Tel. (309)246-8397, mesnerret@cconline.net; Clerk, Neil Mesner

Indiana Yearly Meeting: 4715 N. Wheeling Ave., Muncie, IN 47304-1222 Tel. (765)284-6900, Fax (765)284-8925, iyminfo@iym.org; Clerk, Susan Kirkpatrick; Gen. Supt., Alan Weinacht

Iowa Yearly Meeting: Box 657, Oskaloosa, IA 52577-0657 Tel. (641)673-9717, Fax (641) 673-9718, wpdc9717@wmpenn.edu; Clerk, Margaret Stoltzfus; Gen. Supt., Ron Bryan

Jamaica Yearly Meeting: 4 Worthington Ave., Kingston 5, Jamaica WI Tel. (876)926-7371

Kakamega Yearly Meeting: P.O. Box 465, Kakamega, Kenya, East Africa; Gen. Sec., Jonathan Shisanya; Presiding Clerk, Blastus Wawire; Gen. Supt., Meschack Musindi

Lugari Yearly Meeting: P.O. Box 483, Turbo, Kenya, East Africa; Gen. Sec., David A. Mulama; Presiding Clerk, Joshuah Lilande; Gen. Supt., Japheth Vidolo

Malava Yearly Meeting: P.O. Box 26, Malava, Kenya, East Africa; Gen. Sec., Andrew Namasaka Mulongo; Presiding Clerk, Samson Marani; Gen. Supt., Enoch Shinachi

Nairobi Yearly Meeting: P.O. Box 8321, Nairobi, Kenya, East Africa; Gen. Supt., Benson Simiyu; Gen. Sec., Zablon Isaac Malenge; Vice Pres., Nilson Shivachi

New England Yearly Meeting: 901 Pleasant St., Worcester, MA 01602-1908 Tel. (508)754-6760, neym@neym.org; Clerk, Deana Chase; Field Sec., Jonathan Vogel-Borne

New York Yearly Meeting: 15 Rutherford Pl., New York, NY 10003 Tel. (212)673-5750, office@nyym.org; Clerk, Linda Chidsey; Admin. Sec., Helen Garay Toppins

North Carolina Yearly Meeting: 5506 W. Friendly Ave., Greensboro, NC 27410 Tel. (336)292-6957, ncfriends@juno.com; Clerk, Brent McKinney; Gen. Supt., John Porter

Southeastern Yearly Meeting: P.O. Box 510795, Melbourne Beach, FL 32951-0795 Tel. (321)724-1162; Adm. Sec., Lyn Cope-Robinson, seym@bv.net

Tanzania Yearly Meeting: P.O. Box 151, Mugumu, Serengeti, Tanzania; Gen. Supt. & Clerk, Joseph Lavuna Oguma

Tuloi Yearly Meeting: P.O. Box 102, Kapsabet, Kenya, East Africa; Presiding Clerk, Joseph Anyonge Mulama; Gen. Supt., Solomon Mwanzi; Gen. Sec., Frederick Inyangu

Uganda Yearly Meeting: P.O. Box 2384, Mbale, Uganda, East Africa; Gen. Supt., Francis Wamala; Gen. Sec., Andrew H.S. Kurima; Clerk, Sylvester Khasufa

Vokoli Yearly Meetings: P.O. Box 266, Wodanga, Kenya, East Africa; Gen. Sec., Javan Chondo; Presiding Clerk, Hannington Mbato; Gen Supt., Thomas Kivuya

Western Yearly Meeting: P.O. Box 70, Plainfield, IN 46168 Tel (317)839-2789 and (317)839-2849 Fax (317)839-2616; Gen. Supt., Curt Shaw; Clerk, Mary Lee Cimer

Wilmington Yearly Meeting: Pyle Center Box 1194, Wilmington, OH 45177 Tel (937)382-2491, Fax (937)382-7077, phackney@wilmington.edu; Clerk, Gary Farlow; Exec. Sec., Marvin Hall

Periodicals

Quaker Life, Trish Edwards-Konic

Full Gospel Assemblies International

The Full Gospel Assemblies International was founded in 1962 under the leadership of Dr. Charles Elwood Strauser. The roots of Full Gospel Assemblies may be traced to 1947 with the beginning of the Full Gospel Church of Coatesville, Penn. As an Assemblies of God Pentecostal church, the Full Gospel Church of Coatesville was active in evangelization and educational ministries to the community. In service to the ministers and students of the Full Gospel Church ministries, the Full Gospel Trinity Ministerial Fellowship was formed in 1962, later changing its name to Full Gospel Assemblies International.

Retaining its original doctrine and faith, Full Gospel Assemblies is Trinitarian, believing that the Bible is God's infallible Word to mankind, baptism in the Holy Spirit according to Acts 2, divine healing is made possible by the sufferings of our Lord Jesus Christ, and in the imminent return of Christ for those who love him.

The body of Full Gospel Assemblies is an evangelical missionary fellowship sponsoring ministry at home and abroad, composed of self-governing ministries and churches. Congregations, affiliate ministries and clerical body are located throughout the United States and over 15 countries of the world.

Headquarters

3170 Lincoln Hwy, Parkesburg, PA

Mailing Address, P.O. Box 1230, Coatesville, PA 19320 Tel. (610)857-2357 Fax (610)857-3109

Media Contact, Simeon Strauser

Officers

Gen. Supt., Dr. AnnaMae Strauser

Exec. Dir. of Ministry, J. Victor Fisk

Exec. Dir of Admn., Simeon Strauser

Exec. Dir. of Communications, Archie Neale

Exec. Sec., Betty Stewart

Exec. Trustee, Edward Popovich

Periodicals

Full Gospel Ministries Outreach Report

Full Gospel Fellowship of Churches and Ministers International

In the early 1960s a conviction grew in the hearts of many ministers that there should be closer fellowship between the people of God who believed in the apostolic ministry. At the same time, many independent churches were experiencing serious difficulties in receiving authority from the IRS to give governmentally accepted tax-exempt receipts for donations.

In September 1962 a group of ministers met in Dallas, Tex., to form a Fellowship to give expression to the essential unity of the Body of Christ under the leadership of the Holy Spirit— a unity that goes beyond individuals, churches, or organizations. This was not a movement to build another denomination, but rather an effort to join ministers, churches, and ministry organizations of like mind across denominational lines.

To provide opportunities for fellowship and to support the objectives and goals of local and national ministries, regional conventions and an annual international convention are held.

Headquarters

1000 N. Belt Line Rd., Irving, TX 75061 Tel. (214)492-1254

Email: FGFCMI@aol.com

Website: www.fgfcmi.org/

Media Contact, Sec., Dr. Harry Schmidt

Officers

Pres., Dr. Don Arnold, P.O. Box 324, Gadsden, AL 35901

1st Vice Pres., Dr. Ray Chamberlain

Sec., Dr. Harry Schmidt

Treas., Rev. Gene Evans, P.O. Box 813 Douglasville, GA 30133

CFO, Dr. S.K. Biffle, 1000 N. Belt Line Rd., Irving, TX 75061

Ofc. Sec., Mrs. Anita Sullivan

Receptionist, Mrs. Nita Biffle

Vice Pres.-at-Large, Rev. Maurice Hart, P.O. Box 4316, Omaha, NE 68104; Rev. Don Westbrook, 3518 Rose of Sharon Rd., Durham, NC 27705

Chmn. of Evangelism, David Ellis

Chmn. of Mission, Dr. Ray Chamberlain

Chmn. of Youth, Rev. Steven K. Biffle, 3833 Westervill Rd., Columbus, OH 43224

Past Pres., Dr. James Helton

REGIONAL VICE PRESIDENTS

Southeast: Rev. Gene Evans, P.O. Box 813, Douglasville, GA 30133

South Central: Rev. Robert J. Miller, P.O. Box 10621, Killeen, TX 76547

Southwest: Rev. Arlie Branson, 12504 4th St., Yucaipa, CA 92399

Northeast: Rev. David Ellis, 3636 Winchester Rd., Allertown, PA 18104

North Central: Rev. Raymond Rothwell, P.O. Box 367, Eaton, OH 45320

Northwest: Rev. Ralph Trask, 3212 Hyacinth NE, Salem, OR 97303

Periodicals

Fellowship Tidings

Fundamental Methodist Church, Inc.

This group traces its origin through the Methodist Protestant Church. It withdrew from The Methodist Church and organized on August 27, 1942.

Headquarters

1034 N. Broadway, Springfield, MO 65802

Media Contact, Dist. Supt., Rev. Ronnie Howerton, 1952 Highway H, Monett, MO 65708 Tel. (417)235-3849

Officers

Treas., Wayne Blades, Rt. 1, Crane, MO 65633 Tel. (417)723-8123

Sec., Betty Nicholson, Rt. 2, Box 397, Ash Grove, MO 65604 Tel. (417)672-2268

Dist. Supt., Rev. Ronnie Howerton, 1952 Highway H, Monett, MO 65708 Tel. (417) 235-3849

General Association of General Baptists

Similar in doctrine to those General Baptists organized in England in the 17th century, the first General Baptist churches were organized on the Midwest frontier following the Second Great Awakening. The first church was established by the Rev. Benoni Stinson in 1823 at Evansville, Ind.

Stinson's major theological emphasis was general atonement—"Christ tasted death for every man." The group also allows for the possibility of apostasy. It practices open Communion and believer's baptism by immersion.

Called "liberal" Baptists because of their emphasis on the freedom of man, General Baptists organized a General Association in 1870 and invited other "liberal" Baptists (e.g., "Free Will" and Separate Baptists) to participate.

The policy-setting body is composed of delegates from local General Baptist churches and associations. Each local church is autonomous but belongs to an association. The group currently consists of more than 60 associations in 16 states, as well as associations in the Philippines, Guam, Saipan, Jamaica , Honduras, and India. Ministers and deacons are ordained by a presbytery.

The denomination operates Oakland City University in Oakland City, Ind., and Nursing Homes in Illinois and Missouri. General Baptists belong to the Baptist World Alliance, the North American Baptist Fellowship, and the National Association of Evangelicals.

Headquarters

100 Stinson Dr., Poplar Bluff, MO 63901 Tel. (573)785-7746 Fax (573)785-0564

Media Contact, Exec. Dir., Dr. Ron Black

Officers

Mod., Rev. Bill McMillen

Clk., Mr. Tommy Roberts

Exec. Dir., Dr. Ron Black

OTHER ORGANIZATIONS

International Missions, Dir., Rev. Jack Eberhardt

National Missions, Dir., Rev. Ron Byrd

Women's Ministries, Dir., Barbara Wigger

Oakland City University, Chancellor/Pres., Dr. James Murray, 143 North Lucretia St., Oakland City, IN 47660

Congregational Ministries, Dir., Rev. Mike Warren, 100 Stinson Dr., Poplar Bluff, MO 63901

Pastoral Ministries, Dir., Rev. Fred Brittain, 100 Stinson Dr., Poplar Bluff, MO 63901

Admin., Financial Services, Financial Officer, Linda McDonough, 100 Stinson Dr., Poplar Bluff, MO 63901

Stinson Press, Inc., Pres., Rev. Dale Bates, 400 Stinson Dr., Poplar Bluff, MO 63901

Nursing Home Board, CEO Rev. Jack Cole, Rt. #2, Box 650, Campbell, MO 63933

Compassionate Care Adoption Agency, Dir., Dr. John Clanton, Rt. 3, Box 12B, Oakland City, IN 47660

Periodicals

The General Baptist Messenger, Capsule, Voice, Church Talk, Pastor Talk

General Association of Regular Baptist Churches

This association was founded in May, 1932, in Chicago by a group of churches which had withdrawn from the Northern Baptist Convention (now the American Baptist Churches in the USA) because of doctrinal differences. Its Confession of Faith, which it requires all churches to subscribe to, is essentially the old, historic New Hampshire Confession of Faith with a premillennial ending applied to the last article.

The churches of the General Association of Regular Baptist Churches voluntarily join together to accomplish four goals: (1) Champion Biblical truth—committed to communicating the whole counsel of God in its timeless relevance; (2) Impact the world for Christ—obeying the Lord's Great Commission to take the life-changing gospel to the entire world; (3) Perpetuate its Baptist heritage—faithfully promoting its Scriptural legacy and identity; (4) Advancing GARBC churches—strengthening existing churches and planting new churches for the purposes of evangelism and edification.

Headquarters

1300 N. Meacham Rd., Schaumburg, IL 60173 Tel. (847)843-1600 Fax (847)843-3757

Email: garbc@garbc.org

Website: www.garbc.org

Media Contact, Natl. Rep., Dr. John Greening

Officers

Chpsn., Rev. Bryce Augsburger

Vice Chpsn., David Warren

Treas.,Dr. David Gower

Sec., Rev. David Strope

Natl. Rep., Dr. John Greening

Periodicals

Baptist Bulletin, Energy Newsletter

General Church of the New Jerusalem

The General Church of the New Jerusalem, also called the New Church, was founded in 1897. It is based on the teachings of the 18th Century scientist Emanuel Swedenborg, and stresses the oneness of God, who is the Lord Jesus Christ; a life of faith and love in service to others; in true married love; and in life after death.

Headquarters

P.O. Box 743, Bryn Athyn, PA 19009 Tel. (215)938-2682

Email: svsimpso@newchurch.edu

Website: www.newchurch.org

Media Contact, Ed., Church Journal, Donald L. Rose, Box 277, Bryn Athyn, PA 19009 Tel. (215)947-6225 Fax (215)947-3078

Officers

Presiding Bishop, Rt. Rev. P. M. Buss

Sec., Susan V. Simpson

Treas., William W. Buick

Periodicals

New Church Life

General Conference of Mennonite Brethren Churches

A small group, requesting that closer attention be given to prayer, Bible study, and a consistent lifestyle, withdrew from the larger Mennonite Church in the Ukraine in 1860. Anabaptist in origin, the group was influenced by Lutheran pietists and Baptist teachings and adopted a quasi-congregational form of church government. In 1874 and years following, small groups of these German-speaking Mennonites left Russia, settled in Kansas and then spread to the Midwest west of the Mississippi and into Canada. Some years later, the movement spread to California and the West Coast. In 1960, the Krimmer Mennonite Brethren Conference merged with this body.

Today the General Conference of Mennonite Brethren Churches conducts services in many European languages as well as in Vietnamese, Mandarin, and Hindi. It works with other denominations in missionary and development projects in 25 countries outside North America.

Headquarters

4812 E. Butler Ave., Fresno, CA 93727 Tel. (209) 452-1713 Fax (209)452-1752

Media Contact, Exec. Sec., Marvin Hein

Officers

Mod., Ed Boschman, 12630 N. 103rd Ave., Suite 215, Sun City, AZ 85351

Asst. Mod., Herb Kopp, 200 McIvor Ave., Winnipeg, NB R20 028

Sec., Valerie Rempel

Exec. Sec., Marvin Hein

Periodicals

Christian Leader, Mennotite Bretheren Herald

Grace Gospel Fellowship

The Grace Gospel Fellowship was organized in 1944 by a group of pastors who held to a dispensational interpretation of Scripture. Most had ministries in the Midwest. Two prominent leaders were J.C. O'Hair of Chicago and Charles Baker of Milwaukee. Subsequent to 1945, a Bible Institute was founded (now Grace Bible College of Grand Rapids, Mich.), and a previously organized foreign mission (now Grace Ministries International of Grand Rapids) was affiliated with the group. Churches have now been established in most sections of the country.

The body has remained a fellowship, each church being autonomous in polity. All support for its college, mission, and headquarters is on a contributory basis.

The binding force of the Fellowship has been the members' doctrinal position. They believe in the Deity and Saviorship of Jesus Christ and subscribe to the inerrant authority of Scripture. Their method of biblical interpretation is dispensational, with emphasis on the distinctive revelation to and the ministry of the apostle Paul.

Headquarters

Media Contact, Pres., Ken Parker, 2125 Martindale SW, P.O. Box 9432, Grand Rapids, MI 49509 Tel. (616)245-0100 Fax (616)241-2542

Email: ggfinc@aol.com

Website: www.ggfusa.org/

Officers

Pres., Roger G. Anderson

OTHER ORGANIZATIONS

Grace Bible College, Pres., Rev. Bruce Kemper, 1011 Aldon St. SW, Grand Rapids, MI 49509

Grace Ministries Intl., Exec. Dir., Dr. Samuel Vinton, 2125 Martindale Ave. SW, Grand Rapids, MI 49509

Prison Mission Association, Gen. Dir., Nathan Whitham, P.O. Box 1587, Port Orchard, WA 98366-0140

Grace Publications Inc. , Exec. Dir., Roger G. Anderson, 2125 Martindale Ave. SW, Grand Rapids, MI 49509

Bible Doctrines to Live By, Exec. Dir., Lee Homoki, P.O. Box 2351, Grand Rapids, MI 49501

Periodicals

Truth

Greek Orthodox Archdiocese of America*

THE ORTHODOX CHURCH

The Orthodox Church today, numbering over 250 million worldwide, is a communion of self-governing Churches, each administratively independent of the other, but united by a common faith and spirituality. Their underlying unity is based on identity of doctrines, sacramental life, and worship, which distinguishes Orthodox Christianity. All recognize the spiritual preeminence of the Ecumenical Patriarch of Constantinople who is acknowledged as primus inter pares, first among equals. All share full communion with one another. The living tradition of the Church and the principles of concord and harmony are expressed through the common mind of the universal episcopate as the need arises. In all other matters, the internal life of each independent Church is administered by the bishops of that particular Church. Following the ancient priciple of the one people of God in each place and the universal priesthood of all believers, the laity share equally in the responsibility for the preservation and propagation of the Christian faith and Church.

THE GREEK ORTHODOX ARCHIODESE OF AMERICA

Before the establishment of an Archdiocese in the Western Hemisphere there were numerous communities of Greek Orthodox Christians. The first Greek Orthodox community in the Americas was founded in New Orleans, La. by a small colony of Greek merchants. History also records that on June 26, 1768 the first Greek colonists landed at St. Augustine, Fla., the oldest city in America. The first permanent community was founded in New York City in 1892, today's Archdiocesan Cathedral of the Holy Trinity and the See of the Archbishop of America. The Greek Orthodox Archdiocese of North and South America was incorporated in 1921 and officially recognized by the State of New York in 1922.

The Greek Orthodox Archdiocese of America is under the jurisdiction of the Ecumenical Patriarchate of Constantinople and is composed of an Archdiocesan District—New York and eight dioceses: New Jersey, Chicago, Atlanta, Detroit, San Francisco, Pittsburgh, Boston, and Denver. It is governed by the Archbishop and the Synod of Bishops. The Synod of Bishops is headed by the Archbishop and comprised of the Bishops who are in charge of a diocese. It has all the authority and responsibility which the Church canons provide for a provincial synod.

Headquarters

8-10 E. 79th St., New York, NY 10021 Tel. (212) 570-3500 Fax (212)570-3569

Email: archdiocese@goarch.org

Website: www.goarch.org

Media Contact, Nikki Stephanopoulos, Dir., News and Information/Public Affairs Tel. (212) 570-3530, Fax (212)774-0215, nikki@goarch.org

HOLY EPARCHIAL SYNOD OF BISHOPS

His Eminence Archbishop Demetrios, Primate of the Greek Orthodox Archdiocese of America, Exarch of the Atlantic and Pacific Oceans, Chairman of the Holy Synod of Bishops, Greek Orthodox Church in America, 8-10 E. 79th St., New York, NY 10021 Tel. (212)570-3500 Fax (212)570-3592

DIOCESES

His Eminence Metropolitan Iakovos of Chicago, Metropolis of Chicago,40 E. Burton Pl., Chicago, IL 60610 Tel. (312)337-4130 Fax (312)337-9391

His Eminence Metropolitan Anthony of San Francisco, Metropolis of San Francisco, 372 Santa Clara Ave., San Francisco, CA 94127 Tel. (415)753-3075 Fax (415)753-1165

His Eminence Metropolitan Maximos of Pittsburgh, Metropolis of Pittsburgh, 5201 Ellsworth Ave., Pittsburgh, PA 15232 Tel. (412)621-5529 Fax (412)621-1522

His Eminence Metropolitan Methodios of Boston, Metropolis of Boston, 162 Goddard Ave., Brookline, MA 02146 Tel. (617)277-4742 Fax (617)739-9229

His Eminence Metropolitan Isaiah of Denver, Metropolis of Denver, 4610 E. Alameda Ave., Suite D1, Denver, CO 80222 Tel. (303)333-7794 Fax (303)333-7796

His Eminence Metropolitan Alexios of Atlanta, Metropolis of Atlanta, 2480 Clairmont Rd. NE, Atlanta, GA 30329 Tel. (404)634-9345 Fax (404)634-2471

His Eminence Metroplitan Nicholas of Detroit, Metropolis of Detroit, 19405 Renfrew Rd., Detroit, MI 48221 Tel. (313)664-5433 Fax. (313)864-5543

Hs Eminence Metropolitan Evangelos of New Jersey, Metropolis of New Jersey, 629 Springfield Rd., Kenilworth, NJ 07033 Tel. (908)686-0003 Fax (908)686-0046

His Grace Bishop Gerasimos of Krateia, Chief Sec.

Auxiliary Bishops: His Grace Bishop Dimitrios of Xanthos, His Grace Bisop Savas of Troas, His Grace Bishop Gerasimos of Krateia, His Grace Bishop Andonios of Phasiane

CLERGY/LAITY CONGRESS

The Clergy/Laity Congress, the highest legislative body of the Archdiocese, is convened biennially and presided over by the Archbishop. It is concerned with all matters, other than doctrinal or canonical, affecting the life, growth, and unity of the Church; the institutions, finances, administration, educational, and philanthropic concerns; and its increasing growing role in the life of the nations of the Western Hemisphere. The delegates are the pastors and elected lay representatives.

There are 540 parishes, 800 priests, and approximately 1.5 million faithful in the Greek Orthodox Archdiocese of America

THE ARCHDIOCESAN COUNCIL

The Archdiocesan Council is the deliberative body of the Greek Orthodox Archdiocese which meets in the interim period between Clergy/Laity Congresses, held every two years.

Executive Committee, Chmn., His Eminence Archbishop Demetrios

THE HOLY SYNOD OF BISHOPS

Vice Chmn., Michael Jaharis; Treas., Peter Dion; Sec., Nicholas Bouras; George Behrakis; Dr. John Collis; John Pappajohn; John Payiavlas; Georgia Skeadas; Anthony Stefanis; Legal Counselor to the Archdiocese, Emanuel G. Demos

INSTITUTIONS

Archdiocesan Cathedral of the Holy Trinity: Dean, The Rev. Dr. Robert G. Stephanopoulos, 319-337 E. 74th St., New York, NY 10021 Tel. (212)288-3215 Fax (212)288-5876

Website: www.thecathedral.goarch.org

Hellenic College/Holy Cross School of Theology: Pres., The Rev. Nicholas Triantafilou, 50 Goddard Ave., Brookline, MA 02445 Tel. (617) 731-3500, Fax (617)850-1460, admission@hchc.edu

Saint Basil Academy: Dir., The Rev. Constantine L. Sitaras, 79 Saint Basil Rd., Garrison, NY 10524 Tel. (845)424-3500, Fax (845)424-4172, stbasil@bestweb.net, Website: www.stbasil.goarch.org

St. Michael's Home: Dir., His Grace Bishop Andonios of Phasiane, 3 Lehman Terr., Yonkers, NY 10705 Tel. (914)476-3374, Fax (914)476-1744, Stmichaelshome@msn.com, Website: stmichael.goarch.org

ARCHDIOCESE OF NEW YORK

Office of the Archbishop: Dir., Alice Keurian

Office of the Chancellor: Chancellor, His Grace Bishop Savas of Troas

Office of Administration: Exec. Dir., Jerry Dimitriou,

ARCHDIOCESAN DEPARTMENTS

Registry, Finance, Stewardship & LOGOS, Religious Education, Greek Education, Communications, Internet Ministries, Information Technologies, Youth and Young Adults, Camping Ministry, Ionian Village Ecumenical, Interfaith/Interchurch Marriages, Archives, Benefits

Related Organizations, auxiliaries

Ladies Philoptochos Society, Presbyters Council, Sisterhood of Presvyteres, Retired Clergy of America, National Forum of Greek Orthodox Musicians, Hellenic Cultural Center, Archons of the Ecumenical Patriarchate, Archbishop Iakovos

Leadership 100 Endowment Fund, St. Photios National Shrine, International Orthodox Christian Charities(IOCC), Orthodox Christian Mission Center, Trinity Children & Family Services.

OTHER JURISDICTIONS OF THE ECUMENICAL PATRIARCHATE IN THE USA

Albanian Orthodox Diocese in America; Belarusian Council of Orthodox Churches in North America; American Carpatho-Russian Orthodox Greek Catholic Diocese of the USA; Ukrainian Orthodox Church of the USA

Periodicals

The Orthodox Observer, observer@goarch.org

Television Ministry: Greek Orthodox Telecommunications (GOTelecom)

The Holy Eastern Orthodox Catholic and Apostolic Church in North America, Inc.

Canonically established by the Russian Orthodox Synod of Bishops in North America on Feb. 2, 1927, this church was incorporated on Feb. 1, 1928 by Archbishop Aftimios Ofiesh, the first Archbishop-president. Archbishop Aftimios continued as head of this church until he reposed in July 1966. The name and logo are registered service marks of this church. We are a western rite Church but some of our clergy do celebrate the Eastern Liturgy.

The first Synod included Archbishop Aftimios and Bishops Sophronios and Zuk. Over the years, many have claimed to be this Church, its successor, this Church under a different name, or having our lines. These are members of the independent movement who claim to have lines of apostolic succession that are traced back to us but not recognized by this or any canonical Church since they were not administered in accordance to the Rudder (Canons) of the Orthodox Church.

Headquarters

Monastery: St. Pachomius Monastery, P.O.Box 8122, Columbus, OH 43201 Tel. (614)297-8055

Primate, Metropolitan Victor

Email: tmetropolitan@theocacna.org

Website: www.theocacna.org

Officers

Archbishop Peter Mar Kepa, Archdiocese of the East

Metropolitan Victor, Archdiocese of the West

Bishop Christopher, Diocese of Houston, TX

Bishop Cassian, Diocese of Columbus, OH

Bishop Arthur, Diocese of Michigan

SYNOD ADVISORS

Archbishop James

Bishop Donald

Society: The Society of Clerks Secular of St. Basil, est. 1931

Periodicals

Orthicon and *Orthodox Catholic Review*

Holy Ukrainian Autocephalic Orthodox Church in Exile

This church was organized in a parish in New York in 1951 by Ukrainian laymen and clergy who settled in the Western Hemisphere after World War II. In 1954 two bishops, immigrants from Europe, met with clergy and laymen and formally organized the religious body.

Headquarters

103 Evergreen St., W. Babylon, NY 11704

Officers

Admn., Rt. Rev. Serhij K. Pastukhiv Tel. (516) 669-7402

House of God, Which is the Church of the Living God, the Pillar and Ground of the Truth, Inc.

This body, founded by Mary L. Tate in 1919, is episcopally organized.

Headquarters

1301 N. 58th St., Philadelphia, PA 19131

Media Contact, Sec., Rose Canon, 515 S. 57th St., Philadelphia, PA 19143 Tel. (215)474-8913

Officers

Bishop, Raymond W. White, 6107 Cobbs Creek Pkwy., Philadelphia, PA 19143 Tel. (215)748-6338

Hungarian Reformed Church in America*

A Hungarian Reformed Church was organized in New York in 1904 in connection with the Reformed Church of Hungary. In 1922, the Church in Hungary transferred most of its congregations in the United States to the Reformed Church in the US. Some, however, preferred to continue as an autonomous, self-supporting American denomination, and these formed the Free Magyar Reformed Church in America. This group changed its name in 1958 to Hungarian Reformed Church in America.

This church is a member of the World Alliance of Reformed Churches, Presbyterian and Congregational, the World Council of Churches, and the National Council of Churches of Christ.

Headquarters

Bishop's Office, 13 Grove St., Poughkeepsie, NY 12601 Tel. (914)454-5735

Officers

Bishop, Rt. Rev. Alexander Forro

Chief Lay-Curator, Prof. Stephen Szabo, 464 Forest Ave., Paramus, NJ 07652

Gen. Sec. (Clergy), Rt. Rev. Stefan M. Torok, 331 Kirkland Pl., Perth Amboy, NJ 08861 Tel. (908)442-7799

Gen Sec. (Lay), Zoltan Ambrus, 3358 Maple Dr., Melvindale, MI 48122

Eastern Classes: Dean (Senior of the Deans, Chair in Bishop's absence), Very Rev. Imre Bertalan, 10401 Grosvenor Pl., #1521, Rockville, MD 20852 Tel. (301)493-5036 Fax (301)571-5111; Lay-Curator, Balint Balogh, 519 N. Muhlenberg St., Allentown, PA 18104

New York Classes: Supervisor, Rt. Rev. Alexander Forro; Lay-Curator, Laszlo B. Vanyi, 229 E. 82nd St., New York, NY 10028

Western Classes: Dean, V. Rev. Andor Demeter, 3921 W. Christy Dr., Phoenix, AZ 85029; Lay-Curator, Zolton Kun, 2604 Saybrook Dr., Pittsburgh, PA 15235

Periodicals

Magyar Egyhaz

Hutterian Brethren

Small groups of Hutterites derive their names from Jacob Hutter, a 16th-century Anabaptist who taught true discipleship after accepting Jesus as Saviour, advocated communal ownership of property, and was burned as a heretic in Austria in 1536.

Many believers are of German descent and still use their native tongue at home and in church. Much of the denominational literature is produced in German and English. "Colonies" share property, practice non-resistance, dress plainly, do not participate in politics, and operate their own schools. There are 428 colonies with 42,000 members in North America. Each congregation conducts its own youth work through Sunday school. Until age 15, children attend German and English school which is operated by each colony. All youth ages 15 to 20 attend Sunday school. They are baptized as adults upon confession of faith, around age 20.

Headquarters

Media Contact, Philip J. Gross, 3610 N. Wood Rd., Reardon, WA 99029 Tel. (509)299-5400, Fax (509)299-3099, philsjg@juno.com

Officers

Smiedleut Chmn., No. 1, Jacob Waldner, Blumengard Colony, Box 13 Plum Coulee, MB R0G 1R0 Tel. (204)829-3527

Smiedleut Chmn., No. 2, Jacob Wipf, Spring Creek Colony, 36562 102 Street, Forbes, ND 58439 Tel. (701)358-8621

Dariusleut, Chmn., No. 1, Martin Walter, Springpoint Colony, Box 249, Pincher Creek, AB T0K 1W0 Tel. (403)553-4368

Lehrerleut, Chmn., Rev. John Wipf, Rosetown Colony, Box 1509, Rosetown, SK S0L 2V0 Tel. (306)882-3344

IFCA International, Inc.

This group of churches was organized in 1930 at Cicero, Ill., by representatives of the American Council of Undenominational Churches and representatives of various independent churches. The founding churches and members had separated themselves from various denominational affiliations. Founders included J. Oliver Buswell of Wheaton College, Billy McCarrell of Cicero Bible Church and Moody Bible Institute, and M.R. DeHaan of Grand Rapids, Mich. and Radio Bible Class. Members have included J. Vernon McGee, Charles Ryrie, John Walvoord, and John MacArthur.

The IFCA provides a way for independent churches and ministers to unite in close fellowship and cooperation, in defense of the fundamental teachings of Scripture and in the proclamation of the gospel of God's grace.

Today it consists of 1,000 associated churches and 1,200 individual members (pastors, professors, missionaries, chaplains, and other Christian workers).

Headquarters

3520 Fairlanes, Grandville, MI 49418 Tel. (616)531-1840 Fax (616)531-1814; Mailing Address, P.O. Box 810, Grandville, MI 49468-0810

Email: office@ifca.org

Website: www.ifca.org

Media Contact, Exec. Dir., Rev. Les Lofquist

Officers

Exec. Dir., Rev. Les Lofquist

Pres., Dr. Roy Sprague, Lakewood, WA

Periodicals

The Voice

International Church of the Foursquare Gospel

Founded by Aimee Semple McPherson in 1927, the International Church of the Foursquare Gospel proclaims the message of Jesus Christ the Savior, Healer, Baptizer with the Holy Spirit, and Soon-coming King. Headquartered in Los Angeles, this evangelistic missionary body of believers consists of nearly 1,907 churches in the United States and Canada.

The International Church of the Foursquare Gospel is incorporated in the state of California and governed by a Board of Directors who direct its corporate affairs. A Foursquare Cabinet—consisting of the Corporate Officers, Board of Directors, and District Supervisors of the various districts of the Foursquare Church in the United States and other elected or appointed members—serves in an advisory capacity to the President and the Board of Directors.

Each local Foursquare Church is a subordinate unit of the International Church of the Foursquare Gospel. The pastor of the church is appointed by the Board of Directors and is responsible for the spiritual and physical welfare of the church. To assist and advise the pastor, a church council is elected by the local church members.

Foursquare Churches seek to build strong

believers through Christian education, Christian day schools, youth camping and ministry, Foursquare Women International who support and encourage Foursquare missionaries abroad, radio and television ministries, the *Foursquare World Advance* Magazine, and 554 Bible Colleges worldwide.

Worldwide missions remains the focus of the Foursquare Gospel Church with 35,223 churches and meeting places, 48,451 national Foursquare pastors, leaders, and 3,865,827 members with a combined constituency nearing 5 million in 170 countries around the globe. The Church is affiliated with the Pentecostal/Charismatic Churches of North America, National Association of Evangelicals, and the World Pentecostal Fellowship.

Headquarters

1910 W. Sunset Blvd., Ste. 200, P.O. Box 26902, Los Angeles, CA 90026-0176 Tel. (213)989-4234 Fax (213)989-4590

Email: comm@foursquare.org

Website: www.foursquare.org

Media Contact, Editor, Dr. Ron Williams

CORPORATE OFFICERS

Pres., Dr. Paul C. Risser

Vice Pres., Dr. Jared D. Roth

Gen. Supvr., Rev. Glenn C. Burris, Jr.

Dir. of Missions Intl., Rev. Michael Larkin

Corporate Sec., Rev. Arthur J. Gray, II

Treas., Mr. Brent R. Morgan

BOARD OF DIRECTORS

Corporate Officers (listed above), Mark Simon, Rev. James Cecil, George Cline, Rick J. Danna, Daniel Hicks, Kenneth R. Johnson, Farrell G. Lemings, Steve H. Overman, Ron S. Pinkston, Michael E. Posey, Ivy Stanton, Devorah N. Titus, Ronald D. Williams (observer), Cheryl L. Vincent (recording secretary).

DISTRICT SUPERVISORS

Fred Parker, Ralph E. Moore, Larry R. Spousta, James C. Scott, F. Stan Simmons, Tom S. Ferguson, Jeffrey A. Kolodziej, Wayne Cordeiro, Dennis Easter, Daniel K. Ussery, Donald D. Long, Robert M. Booth

FOURSQUARE CABINET

Corp. Officers (listed above), Board of Directors (listed above), District Supervisors (listed above), Cosette M. Conaway, James P. Freund, Mark T. Harris, Louis J. Locke, Mary L. Phillips, David W. Wing, Enrique Zone, Richard E. Scott, James Walz, Kenneth J. Authier, Scott G. Bauer, J. Richard Casteel, Gary A. Clouse, Frederick T. Donaldson, Dale R. Evrist, Jesus De Paz, Santiago Gallegos, Kenneth W. Hart, Robert E. Hasty, Robb J. Hattem, Jack W. Hayford, James W. Hayford, John F. Honold, L. Don Jackson, C. Marty Jenkins, Gregory L. Massanari, Tony W. Maupin, Ronald D. Mehl, Teri L. Orewiler, Alex J. Pacheco, Mark G. Pickerill, Randy A. Remington, Terry D. Risser, B. Ted Roberts, Dwight L. Saunders, C. Steven Schell, Burton E. Smith, Sharon C. Snow, Dan R. Stewart, Ronald E. Swor, James A. Tolle, Richard J. Trees, Roger A. Whitlow, Stanley M. Wilson, Joe K. Wittwer

SUPPORT MINISTRIES

Natl. Dept. of Youth: Natl. Youth Minister, Walter R. Hoefflin

Natl. Dept. of Chr. Educ.: Dir., Rev. Rick Wulfestieg

Natl. Dept. of Foursquare Women Intl.: Kimberly Dirmann

All of the above can be reached through the corporate address: International Church of the Foursquare Gospel, P.O. Box 26902, Los Angeles, CA 90026 Tel. (888)635-04234, Fax (213) 989-4590, comm@foursquare.org, Website: www.foursquare.org

Periodicals

Foursquare World Advance

International Council of Community Churches*

This body is a fellowship of locally autonomous, ecumenically minded, congregationally governed, non-creedal Churches. The Council came into being in 1950 as the union of two former councils of community churches, one formed of black churches known as the Biennial Council of Community Churches in the United States and elsewhere and the other of white churches known as the National Council of Community Churches.

Headquarters

21116 Washington Pky., Frankfort, IL 60423-3112 Tel. (815)464-5690 Fax (815)464-5692

Media Contact, Exec. Dir., Rev. Michael E. Livingston

Officers

Pres., Grace O'Neal

Vice Pres., Rev. Herbert Freitag

Vice Pres., Rev.Leroy McCrewy

Sec., Rev. Gary Batey

Treas., Rev. Martin Singley III

OTHER ORGANIZATIONS

Commission on Laity and Church Relations: Fran Langille

Commission on Ecumenical Relations: Rev. Herman Harmelink III

Commission on Clergy Relations: Rev. Carol Parrish

Commission on Faith, Justice & Mission: Rev. Dr. Jeffrey Newhall

Women's Christian Fellowship: Pres., Catherine Luckett

Samaritans (Men's Fellowship) : Pres., Nicholas Brame

Young Adult Fellowship: Pres., Susan Frazier
Youth Fellowship: Pres., Britney Gardner

Periodicals

The Christian Community, The Inclusive Pulpit, Key Lay Notes, Clergy comminique

The International Pentecostal Church of Christ

At a General Conference held at London, Ohio, Aug. 10, 1976, the International Pentecostal Assemblies and the Pentecostal Church of Christ consolidated into one body, taking the name International Pentecostal Church of Christ.

The International Pentecostal Assemblies is the successor of the Association of Pentecostal Assemblies and the International Pentecostal Missionary Union. The Pentecostal Church of Christ was founded by John Stroup of Flatwoods, Ky., on May 10, 1917 and was incorporated at Portsmouth, Ohio, in 1927. The International Pentecostal Church of Christ is an active member of the Pentecostal/Charismatic Churches of North America, as well as a member of the National Association of Evangelicals.

The priorities of the International Pentecostal Church of Christ are to be an agency of God for evangelizing the world, to be a corporate body in which people may worship God, and to be a channel of God's purpose to build a body of saints being perfected in the image of His Son.

The Annual Conference is held each year during the first full week of August in London, Ohio.

Headquarters

2245 St. Rt. 42 SW, P.O. Box 439, London, OH 43140 Tel. (740)852-4722 Fax (740)852-0348
Email: hqipcc@aol.com
Website: members.aol.com/hqipcc/
Media Contact, Gen. Overseer, Clyde M. Hughes

EXECUTIVE COMMITTEE

Gen. Overseer, Clyde M. Hughes, P.O. Box 439, London, OH 43140 Tel. (740)852-4722 Fax (740)852-0348
Asst. Gen. Overseer, B.G. Turner, RR5, Box 1286, Harpers Ferry, WV 25425 Tel. (304)535-221 Fax (304)535-1357
Gen. Sec., Asa Lowe, 513 Johnstown Rd., Chesapeake, VA 23322 Tel. (757)547-4329
Gen. Treas., Ervin Hargrave, P.O. Box 439, London, OH 43140 Tel. (740)852-4722 Fax (740)852-0348
Dir. of Global Missions, Dr. James B. Keiller, P.O. Box 18145, Atlanta, GA 30316 Tel. (404) 627-2681 Fax (404)627-0702

DISTRICT OVERSEERS

Central District: Lindsey Hayes, 609 Lansing Rd., Akron, OH 44312 Tel. (330)784-3453
Mid-Eastern District: H. Gene Boyce, 705 W. Grubb St., Hertford, NC 27944 Tel. (252)426-5403
Mountain District: Terry Lykins, P.O. Box 131, Staffordsville, KY 41256 Tel. (606)297-3282
New River District: Calvin Weikel, RR #2, Box 300, Ronceverte, WV 24970 Tel. (304)647-4301
North Central District: Edgar Kent, P.O. Box 275, Hartford, MI 49057 Tel. (616)621-3326
North Eastern District: Wayne Taylor, 806 8th St., Shenandoah, VA 22849 Tel. (540) 652-8090
South Eastern District: Frank Angie, 2507 Old Peachtree Rd., Duluth, GA 30097 Tel. (770) 476-5196
Tri-State District: Cline McCallister, 5210 Wilson St., Portsmouth, OH 45662 Tel. and Fax (740)776-6357
Portugese District: Pedro Messias, 34 Woodside Ave., Danbury, CT 06810 Tel. (203)790-9628

OTHER ORGANIZATIONS

Beulah Heights Bible College: Pres., Samuel R. Chand, P.O. Box 18145, Atlanta, GA 30316 Tel. (404)627-2681 Fax (404)627-0702
Women's Ministries: Gen. Pres., Janice Boyce, 121 W. Hunters Tr., Elizabeth City, NC 27909 Tel. and Fax (252)338-3003
Pentecostal Ambassadors: Dustin Hughes, National Youth Dir., P.O. Box 439, London, OH 43140 Tel. (740)852-0448 Fax (740)852-0348
National Christian Education Dept.: Dir., Dustin Hughes, P.O. Box 439, London, OH 43140 Tel. (740)852-0448 Fax (740)852-0348

Periodicals

The Bridegroom's Messenger, The Pentecostal Leader

International Pentecostal Holiness Church

This body grew out of the National Holiness Association movement of the last century, with roots in Methodism. Beginning in the South and Midwest, the church represents the merger of the Fire-Baptized Holiness Church (founded by B. H. Irwin in Iowa in 1895), the Pentecostal Holiness Church (founded by A.B. Crumpler in Goldsboro, N.C., in 1898), and the Tabernacle Pentecostal Church (founded by N.J. Holmes in 1898).

All three bodies joined the ranks of the pentecostal movement as a result of the Azusa Street revival in Los Angeles in 1906 and a 1907 pentecostal revival in Dunn, N.C., conducted by G. B. Cashwell, who had visited Azusa Street. In 1911 the Fire-Baptized and Pentecostal Holiness bodies merged in Falcon, N.C., to form the present church; the Tabernacle Pentecostal Church was added in 1915 in Canon, Ga.

The church stresses the new birth, the Wesleyan experience of sanctification; the pentecostal baptism in the Holy Spirit, evidenced by speaking in tongues; divine healing; and the premillennial second coming of Christ.

Headquarters

P.O. Box 12609, Oklahoma City, OK 73157-2609 Tel. (405)787-7110 Fax (405)789-3957
Email: jdl@iphc.org (for Bishop Leggett)
Website: www.iphc.org
Media Contact, Admn. Asst.

Officers

Gen. Supt., Bishop James D. Leggett, jdl@iphc.org
Vice Chpsn., Exec. Dir. Of World Missions Ministries, Rev. M. Donald Duncan
Exec. Dir. of Evangelism USA, Dr. Ronald Carpenter Sr.
Exec. Dir. of Church Education Ministries, Dr. A.D. Beacham Jr.
Exec. Dir. of Stewardship Ministries/Gen. Sec.-Treas., Rev. Edward W. Wood

OTHER ORGANIZATIONS

The Publishing House (LifeSprings): CEO, Greg Hearn, Franklin Springs, GA 30639
Women's Ministries: Exec. Dir., Mrs. Jewelle Stewart
Men's Ministries: Exec. Dir., Col. Jack Kelley, P.O. Box 53307, Fayetteville, NC 28305-3307

Periodicals

IssacharFile; Women's Ministries Today, Evangelism USA, Worldorama, Discipleship Matters

Jehovah's Witnesses

Modern-day Jehovah's Witnesses began in the early 1870s when Charles Taze Russell was the leader of a Bible study group in Allegheny City, Penn. In July 1879, the first issue of *Zion's Watch Tower and Herald of Christ's Presence* (now called *The Watchtower,* which is published in more than 140 languages with a circulation of upwards of 25 million) appeared. In 1884 Zion's Watch Tower Tract Society was incorporated, later changed to Watch Tower Bible and Tract Society. Congregations spread into other states and countries, and followers witnessed from house to house.

By 1913, printed sermons were in four languages in 3,000 newspapers in the United States, Canada and Europe. Hundreds of millions of books, booklets, and tracts were distributed. Publication of the magazine now known as *Awake!* began in 1919. Today, it is published in more than 80 languages and has a circulation of upwards of 22,000,000. In 1931, the name Jehovah's Witnesses, based on Isaiah 43:10-12, was adopted.

During the 1930s and 1940s Jehovah's Witnesses fought many court cases in the interest of preserving freedom of speech, press, assembly, and worship. They have won a total of 43 cases before the United States Supreme Court. A missionary training school was established in 1943, and has been a major factor in the international expansion of the Witnesses. There are now 6.3 million Witnesses in 234 lands.

Jehovah's Witnesses believe in one almighty God, Jehovah, who is the Creator of all things. They believe in Jesus Christ as God's Son, the first of His creations. While Jesus is now an immortal spirit in heaven, ruling as King of God's Kingdom, he is still subject to his heavenly Father, Jehovah God. Christ's human life was sacrificed as a ransom to open up for obedient mankind the opportunity of eternal life. With Christ in heaven, 144,000 individuals chosen from among mankind will rule in righteousness over an unnumbered great crowd who will survive the destruction of wickedness and receive salvation into an earth cleansed of evil. (Rev. 7:9, 10; 14:1-5). These, along with the resurrected dead, will transform the earth into a global earthly paradise and will have the prospect of living forever on it.

Headquarters

25 Columbia Heights, Brooklyn, NY 11201-2483 Tel. (718)560-5000
Website: www.watchtower.org
Media Contact, Office of Public Information, J. R. Brown
Editorial Contact, Writing Department, James N. Pellechia

Officers

Watch Tower Bible and Tract Society of Pennsylvania, Pres., Don Adams

Periodicals

Awake!, The Watchtower

Korean Presbyterian Church in America, General Assembly of the*

This body came into official existence in the United States in 1976 and is currently an ethnic church, using both the Korean and English languages.

Headquarters

General Assembly of the Korean Presbyterian Church in America, 17200 Clark Ave., Bellflower, CA 90706 Tel. (714)816-1100 Fax (714)816-1120

Officers

Gen. Sec., Rev. Seung Koo Choi, 3146 W. Ball Rd., #31, Anaheim, CA 92804 Tel. (714)816-1100
Moderator, Rev. Dr Se Won Han, Youn Nak Church of NY Tel. (718)335-3194 Fax (718) 335-3607

The Latvian Evangelical Lutheran Church in America

This body was organized into a denomination on Aug. 22, 1975 after having existed as the Federation of Latvian Evangelical Lutheran Churches in America since 1955. This church is a regional constituent part of the Lutheran Church of Latvia Abroad, a member of the Lutheran World Federation, and the World Council of Churches.

The Latvian Evangelical Lutheran Church in America works to foster religious life, traditions, and customs in its congregations in harmony with the Holy Scriptures; the Apostles', Nicean, and Athanasian Creeds; the unaltered Augsburg Confession; Martin Luther's Small and Large Catechisms; and other documents of the Book of Concord.

The LELCA is ordered by its Synod (General Assembly), executive board, auditing committee, and district conferences.

Headquarters

2140 Orkla Dr., Golden Valley, MN 55427 Tel. (612)722-0174

Email: ucepure@aol.com

Media Contact, Juris Pulins, 9531 Knoll Top Rd., Union, IL 60180 Tel. (815)923-5919, pulins@flash.net

Officers

Pres., Rev. Uldis Cepure Tel. (612)546-3712

Vice Pres., Rev. Anita Varsbergs, 9908 Shelburne Terr., 312, Gathersburg, MD 20878 Tel. (301) 251-4151

Sec., Girts Kugars, 5209 Douglas Ave., Kalamazoo, MI 49004 Tel. (616)381-3798

Treas., Vilmars Beinikis, 17 John Dr., Old Bethpage, NY 11804 Tel. (516)293-8432

Periodicals

Cela Biedrs, Lelba Zinas

Liberal Catholic Church (International)

Founded as a reorganization of the Dutch Old Catholic Church in 1915-16. In 1941 a controversy broke out in the Church regarding whether or not certain teachings of Theosophy (reincarnation, etc.) were to become official teachings of the Church. This was resolved by a court decision holding we (the non-Theosophist party) were the legal Liberal Catholic Church.

Headquarters

741 Cerro Gordo Ave., San Diego, CA 92102 Tel. & Fax (619)239-0637

Email: liberalcatholic@aol.com

Website: www.liberalcatholic.org

Officers

Pres. and Regionary Bishop, The Most Rev. James P. Roberts, Jr., 39 Claire Ave., New Rochelle, NY 10804 Tel. (914)636-7917, Bppal32@aol.com

Vice Pres. and Presiding Bishop, The Most Rev. Charles W. Finn, 741 Cerro Gordo Ave., San Diego, CA 92102 Tel. and Fax (619)239-0637, abpchas@msn.com

Sec.-Treas., The Most Rev. Dean Bekken, P.O.Box 26044, San Diego, CA 92196-0044 Tel. and Fax (858)689-8610, mrbekken@abac.com

Other Organizations

St. Alban Theological Seminary: P.O. Box 2507, Frisco, TX 75034-2507 Tel. (214)636-6719, liberalcatholic@aol.com

St. Alban Press: 741 Cerro Gordo Avenue, San Diego, CA 92102 Tel. and Fax (858)689-8610, info@liberalcatholic.org

Periodicals

Community, P.O.Box 2507, Frisco, TX 75034-2507 Tel. (214)636-6719

The Liberal Catholic Church–Province of the United States of America

The Liberal Catholic Church was founded Feb. 13, 1916 as a reorganization of the Old Catholic Church in Great Britain with the Rt. Rev. James I. Wedgwood as the first Presiding Bishop. The first ordination of a priest in the United States was Fr. Charles Hampton, later a Bishop. The first Regionary Bishop for the American Province was the Rt. Rev. Irving S. Cooper (1919-1935).

Headquarters

Pres., The Rt. Rev. William S.H. Downey, 1206 Ayers Ave., Ojai, CA 93023 Tel. (805)646-2573 Fax (805)646-2575

Email: bshp052497@aol.com

Website: www.thelcc.org

Media Contact, Regionary Bishop, The Rt. Rev. William S.H. Downey

Officers

Pres. and Regionary Bishop, The Rt. Rev. William S.H. Downey

Vice Pres., Rev. L. Marshall Heminway, P.O. Box 19957 Hampden Sta., Baltimore, MD 21211-0957

Sec. (Provincial), Rev. Lloyd Worley, 1232 24th Avenue Ct., Greeley, CO 80631 Tel. (303)356-3002

Provost, Rev. Lloyd Worley

Treas., Rev. Milton Shaw

BISHOPS

Regionary Bishop for the American Province, The Rt. Rev. William S.H. Downey

Aux. Bishops of the American Province: Rt. Rev. Dr. Robert S. McGinnis Jr., 3612 N. Labarre Rd., Metaire, LA 70002; Rt. Rev. Joseph L. Tisch, P.O. Box 1117, Melbourne, FL 32901; Rt. Rev. Dr. Hein VanBeusekom, 12 Krotona Hill, Ojai, CA 93023; Rt. Rev. Ruben Cabigting, P.O. Box 270, Wheaton, IL 60189; The Rt. Rev. Lawrence Smith 9740 S. Avers Ave., Evergreen Park, IL

Periodicals

Ubique

The Lutheran Church–Missouri Synod (LCMS)

The Lutheran Church–Missouri Synod, which was founded in 1847, has more than 6,000 congregations in the United States and works in 74 other countries. It has 2.6 million members and is the second-largest Lutheran denomination in North America.

Christian education is offered for all ages. The North American congregations operate the largest elementary and secondary school systems of any Protestant denomination in the nation, and 17,042 students are enrolled in 12 LCMS institutions of higher learning.

Traditional beliefs concerning the authority and interpretation of Scripture are important. The synod is known for mass-media outreach through "The Lutheran Hour" on radio; "This Is The Life" dramas on television; and the products of Concordia Publishing House, the third-largest Protestant publisher, whose Arch Books children's series has sold more than 60 million copies.

An extensive network of more than 1,000 volunteers in 58 work centers produces Braille, large-type, and audiocassette materials for the blind and visually impaired. Sixty-three of the Eighty-five deaf congregations affiliated with US. Also, there are 16 centers in the US sponsored by LCMS Blind Missions where Blind people are trained for Christian outreach. Lutheran denominations are LCMS, and many denominations use the Bible lessons prepared for developmentally disabled persons.

The involvement of women is high, although they do not occupy clergy positions. Serving as teachers, deaconesses, and social workers, women comprise approximately half of total professional workers.

The members' responsibility for congregational leadership is a distinctive characteristic of the synod. Power is vested in voters' assemblies, generally comprised of adults of voting age. Synod decision making is given to the delegates at triennial national and district conventions, where the franchise is equally divided between lay and pastoral representatives.

Headquarters

The Lutheran Church–Missouri Synod, Intl. Center, 1333 S. Kirkwood Rd., St. Louis, MO 63122-7295

Email: infocenter@lcms.org

Website: www.lcms.org

Media Contact, Dir., News & Information, Rev. David Mahsman Tel. (314)996-1227

Dir., Public Affairs, Mr. David Strand Tel. (314) 996-1229

Manager, News Bureau, Mr. Joe Isenhower Tel. (314)996-1231 Fax (314)996-1126

Officers

Pres., Dr. Gerald B. Kieschnick

1st Vice Pres., Rev. Daniel Preus

2nd Vice Pres., Dr. Wallace R. Schulz

3rd Vice Pres., Dr. Robert H. King

4th Vice Pres., Dr. Paul L. Maier

5th Vice Pres., Dr. William C. Weinrich

Sec., Dr. Raymond L. Hartwig

Treas., Mr. Thomas Kuchta

Admn. Officer of Bd. of Dir., Dr. Bradford L. Hewitt

Exec. Dir., Human Resources, Barb Ryan

Bd. of Directors: Dr. Karl L. Barth, Milwaukee, WI; Dr. Betty Duda, Oviedo, FL; Ernest E. Garbe, Dieterich, IL; Dr. Jean Garton, Benton, AR; Oscar H. Hanson, Lafayette, CA; Ted Kober, Billings, MT; Christian Preus, Plymouth, MN; Rev. James E. Fandrey, Omaha, NE; Dave Hook, Fort Wayne, IN; Elizabeth A. Fluegel, Alexandria, VA; Dr. Robert T. Kuhn, Oviedo, FL; Dr. Edwin Trapp Jr., Dallas, TX

BOARDS AND COMMISSIONS

Communication Services: Exec. Dir., Rev. J. Thomas Lapacka

Mission Services: Exec. Dir., Rev. Robert Roegner

Higher Education Services: Exec. Dir., Dr. William F. Meyer

Human Care Ministries: Exec. Dir., Rev. Matthew Harrison

Worker Benefit Plans: Pres., Paul W. Uiddeke

Lutheran Church–Missouri Synod Foundation: Pres., -vacant-

Lutheran Church Ext. Fund–Missouri Synod: Pres., Merle Freitag

District and Congregational Services: Exec. Dir., Dr. Le Roy Wilke

Black Ministries Services: Exec. Dir., -vacant-

ORGANIZATIONS

Concordia Publishing House: Interim Pres., Rev. Paul McCain, 3558 S. Jefferson Ave., St. Louis, MO 63118-3968

Concordia Historical Institute: Interim Dir., Dr. Martin Noland, Concordia Seminary, 801 De Mun Ave., St. Louis, MO 63105

Intl. Lutheran Laymen's League: Exec. Dir., Rodger W. Hebermehl, 2185 Hampton Ave., St. Louis, MO 63139-2983

KFUO Radio: Dir., Rev. Dennis Stortz

Intl. Lutheran Women's Missionary League: Pres., Virginia Linda Reiser, 3558 S. Jefferson Ave., St. Louis, MO 63118-3910

Periodicals

The Lutheran Witness, Reporter

Malankara Orthodox Syrian Church, Diocese of America*

The American Diocese of the Malankara Orthodox Syrian Church is in full accord with the Mother Church—Malankara Orthodox Syrian Church, also known as the Indian Orthodox Church. The diocese is a national or missionary entity of the Indian Orthodox Church. The Malankara Orthodox Syrian Church established an American diocese in 1978 to serve her immigrant members in America. This diocese is a new phenomenon with great challenges and potentials, composed of immigrant Indian Orthodox members and their American-born children. Now that some years have passed, the immigrant church is entering into an indigenous era with the second generation Indian Orthodox members. Currently there are 60 parishes, 68 clergy, and about 12,000 members of this church in the United States. The diocese is still growing with immigrants and native-born members.

The Malankara Orthodox Syrian Church has claimed its roots in the Apostolic ministry of Apostle St. Thomas, who was martyred in India, since 52 A.D. Although there is not much available about the early history of the Indian Church, it is known that later it was influenced by Roman Catholicism, and then Protestant missionaries of the post Reformation period. During the sixteenth century, there arose an increased relationship with the Oriental churches with the arrival of Syrian Bishops. Although different segments of Christianity have been flourishing in India, the Church maintained a close faith in the Non-Chalcedonian councils.

The Malankara Orthodox Syrian Church has got its name "Malankara" from Maliankara, a nearby town of Dodungalloor where St. Thomas is believed to have arrived in 52 A.D.; "Orthodox" comes from the faith of the fathers (non-Chalcedonian faith); "Syrian" comes from its connection with the Syrian Orthodox Church's traditions, practices, liturgy, language, and liturgical calendar.

Headquarters

80-34 Commonwealth Blvd., Bellerose, NY 11426 Tel. (718)470-9844 Fax (718)470-9219
Email: Malankara@malankara.org
Website: www.malankara.org/american.htm
Media Contact, His Grace Mathews Mar Barnabas, Diocesan Metropolitan

Officers

Diocesan Metropolitan, His Grace Mathews Mar Barnabas
Diocesan Sec., Rev. Fr. M. Johnson, Secretary to the Metropolitan and Diocesan Office

Periodicals

*Diocesan Voice (*A quarterly publication of the Diocese, Family, and Youth Conference); *Souvenir* (An annual publication of the F & Y Conference of the Diocese); *Directory of the Diocese*

Mar Thoma Syrian Church of India*

According to tradition, the Mar Thoma Church was established as a result of the apostolic mission of St. Thomas, the apostle in 52 A.D. Church history attests to the continuity of the community of faithful, throughout the long centuries in India. The liturgy and faith practices of the Church were based on the relationship between the Church in Kerala, India (which St. Thomas founded) with the East-Syrian and Persian Churches. This started in the 3rd century and continued up to the 16th century. In the 17th century, the Malabar Church of St. Thomas (as the Church in Kerala was known) renewed her relationship with the Orthodox Patriarchate of Antioch as part of the resistance to forced Latinization by the Portuguese. This process also led to the development of the Kerala Episcopacy, whereby the first Indian Bishop Mar Thoma I was consecrated in Kerala.

The Mar Thoma Church retains her Eastern Orthodoxy. She follows an Orthodox (true) worship form and liturgy, believes in the catholicity of grace, and is missionary and evangelistic in approach. She derives Episcopal succession from the Syrian Orthodox Church of Antioch and follows Eastern Reformed Theology. She is independent, autonomous, and indigenous, constitutionally combining democratic values and Episcopal authority. She has been in full communion with the Anglican Church since 1954.

The Diocese of North America was organized in 1988 in order to serve the needs of the immigrant community. It has a membership of around 6,000 families in 68 parishes.

Headquarters

Sinai Mar Thoma Center, 2320 S. Merrick Avenue, Merrick, New York 11566 Tel. (516) 377-3311 Fax (516)377-3322
Email: webmaster@marthomachurch.org
Website: www.marthomachurch.org/

Officers

Diocesan Bishop, The Rt. Rev. Dr. Euyakim Mar Coorilos
Diocesan Bishop's Sec., Rev. Dr. John Joseph
Diocesan Treas., Dr. P. John Lincoln

Periodicals

Mar Thoma Messenger

Mennonite Church USA

Mennonite Church USA, with 113,000 members, is one of several denominations that traces their beginnings to the Protestant Reformation in the early 1500s. Mennonites hold common core beliefs with other Christian denominations, but they live out God's call is some ways that make them distinct. Mennonites believe in giving ultimate loyalty to God rather than to the nations in which they live. They believe that Jesus revealed a way for people to live peacefully and nonviolently, and they seek to be peacemakers in everyday life.

Mennonite Church USA is committed to sharing its faith and passion for Jesus with others and is open to anyone who confesses Jesus Christ as Lord and Savior and wants to live as Jesus taught.

The vision statement of Mennonite Church USA reads, "God calls us to be follower of Jesus Christ and, by the power of the Holy Spirit, to grow as communities of grace, joy, and peace, so that God's healing and hope flow through us to the world."

Mennonite Church USA—its congregations, area conferences, Executive Board, ministry offices, and churchwide agencies—focus on three priorities:

1. Becoming a missional church, by discerning God's will and joining in God's mission.

2. Developing leaders, young and old, for a missional church.

3. Strengthening relationships with Mennonites and other Christians around the globe to extend the reign of God on earth.

Mennonite Church USA lists as its strengths a high level of integrity recognized in both society and the religious community, high church attendance (90% of members attend church regularly), expanded global awareness through exposure to other world cultures, strong commitment to nonviolence and use of conflict resolution skills, above average giving to the work of the church, a natural communitarian impulse demonstrated by an emphasis on congregational relationships and mutual accountabilities, strong support of volunteer efforts, relief and service activities, and a holistic theology that holds word and deed together.

Headquarters

Great Plains Office: 722 Main St., P.O. Box 347, Newton, KS 67114 Tel. (316)283-5100 Fax (316)283-0454

Great Lakes Office: 500 S. Main St., P.O. Box 1245, Elkhart, IN 46515-1245 Tel. (574)294-7523 Fax (574)293-1892

Email: info@MennoniteUSA.org

Website: www.MennoniteChurchUSA.org

Toll free phone number for churchwide agencies: (866)866-2872

Media contact, Director of Communication, Cindy Snider Tel. (316)283-5100, cindyS@mennoniteusa.org

Officers

Moderator, Duane Oswald, 1111 E. Herndon Ave., Suite 308, Fresno, CA 93720-3100 Tel. (559)261-9070, doswald@avantehealth.com

Moderator-Elect, Roy Williams, 22642 Newfield Ct., Land O'Lakes FL 34639 Tel. (813)966-4244, rrrsjw@aol.com

Exec. Dir., James M. Schrag, 722 Main St., P.O. Box 347, Newton, KS 67114 Tel. (316)283-5100, jims@mennoniteusa.org

Associate Exec. Dir., J. Ron Byler, 500 S. Main St., P.O. Box 1245, Elkhart, IN 46515 Tel. (574)294-7523, ronb@mennoniteusa.org

Other Organizations

Mennonite Education Agency: Exec. Dir., Carlos Romero, 63846 County Road, 35 Ste. 1, Goshen, IN 46528-9621 Tel. (574)642-3164, Fax (574) 642-4863, carlosr@mennoniteeducation.org

Mennonite Mission Network: Exec. Dir., Stanley Green, 500 S. Main Box 370, Elkhart, IN 46515-0370 Tel. (574)294-7523, stanleyg@mennonitemission.net

Mennonite Mutual Aid: Pres., Howard Brenneman, P.O. Box 486, Goshen, IN 46527 Tel. (219)533-9511, howard.brenneman@mma-online.org

Mennonite Publishing Network: Exec. Dir., Ron Rempel, 616 Walnut Ave., Scottdale, PA 15683 Tel. (724)887-8500, rrempel@mph.org

Periodicals

The Mennonite, Leader, Rejoice!, Mennonite Historical Bulletin, Mennonite Quarterly Review, On the Line, Purpose, Story Friends, WITH

The Missionary Church

The Missionary Church was formed in 1969 through a merger of the United Missionary Church (organized in 1883) and the Missionary Church Association (founded in 1898). It is evangelical and conservative with a strong emphasis on missionary work and church planting.

There are three levels of church government with local, district, and general conferences. There are 11 church districts in the United States. The general conference meets every two years. The denomination operates one college in the United States.

Headquarters

3811 Vanguard Dr., P.O. Box 9127, Ft. Wayne, IN 46899-9127 Tel. (260)747-2027 Fax (260) 747-5331

Email: mcdenomusa@aol.com

Website: www.mcusa.org

Media Contact, Pres., Rev. William Hossler

Officers

Pres., Rev. William Hossler

Vice Pres., Rev. Joel DeSelm

Sec., Rev. Dave Engbrecht

Treas., Darrel Schlabach

Dir. of US Ministries, Rev. Robert Ransom

Dir. of World PartnersUSA, Rev. David Mann

Healthy Church Initiatives Coordinator, Dr. Dan Riemenschneider

Servant Leadership Coordinator, Rev. Greg Getz

Support Ministries Coordinator, Rev. Ron Phipps

Pastoral Leadership Institute Dir., Rev. Greg Getz

Dir. of Development/Communications, Dr. Tom Murphy

Dir. of Ad. Services, David Von Gunten

Dir. of Financial Services, Neil Rinehart

Youth Dir., Eric Liechty

Children's Dir., Mrs. Pam Merillat

Senior Adult Ministry Dir., Dr. Charles Cureton

Missionary Men Liaison, Rev. Ron Phipps

Missionary Women Intl. Pres., Charlotte Beals

Missionary Church Investment Foundation, Mr. Eric Smith

Periodicals

Missionary Church Today

Moravian Church in America (Unitas Fratrum)*

In 1735 German Moravian missionaries of the pre-Reformation faith of Jan Hus came to Georgia, in 1740 to Pennsylvania, and in 1753 to North Carolina. They established the American Moravian Church, which is broadly evangelical, ecumenical, liturgical, "conferential" in form of government, and has an episcopacy as a spiritual office. The Northern and Southern Provinces of the church operate on a semi-autonomous basis.

Headquarters

Denominational offices or headquarters are called the Provincial Elders' Conference.

See addresses for Northern and Southern Provinces

NORTHERN PROVINCE HEADQUARTERS

1021 Center St., P.O. Box 1245, Bethlehem, PA 18016-1245 Tel. (610)867-7566 Fax (610) 866-9223

Media Contact, Ms. Deanna Hollenbach

PROVINCIAL ELDERS' CONFERENCE

Northern Province: Pres., Rev. David L. Wickmann, P.O. Box 1245, Bethlehem, PA 18016-1245, gray@mcnp.org

Western District: Pres., Rev. Lawrence Christianson, P.O. Box 386, Sun Prairie, WI 53590, christlr@aol.com

Canadian District: Pres., Mr. Graham Kerslake, 10910 Harvest Lake Way NE, Calgary, AB T3K 4L1, gkerslake@thealtusgroup.com

Other Members: Nancy Baldwin, Paul DeTilla, Glenn Hertzog, Graham Kerslake, Carol Messina

Comptroller, Theresa E. Kunda, 1021 Center St., P.O. Box 1245, Bethlehem, PA 18016-1245, theresa@mcnp.org

SOUTHERN PROVINCE HEADQUARTERS

459 S. Church St., Winston-Salem, NC 27101; Mailing address: Drawer O, Winston-Salem, NC 27108 Tel. (336)725-5811 Fax (336)723-1029

Email: rsawyer@mcsp.org

Website: www.moravian.org (for Moravian Church, Northern and Southern Province)

PROVINCIAL ELDERS' CONFERENCE

Pres., Rev. Dr. Robert E. Sawyer

Vice Pres., Mrs. Betsy Bombick

Sec. –vacant-

Treas., Mr. Richard Cartner, Drawer M, Salem Station, Winston-Salem, NC 27108

Other Members: Ms. Donna Hurt, Rev. Tom Shelton, Rev. Richard Sides

Asst. to Pres., Robert Hunter, rhunter@mcsp.org

ALASKA PROVINCE

P.O. Box 545, 361 3rd Ave., Bethel, AK 99559

Email: gary@mcnp.org

Website: www.moravian.org

PROVINCIAL ELDERS' CONFERENCE

Pres., Rev. Isaac Amik

Vice Pres., Rev. William H. Nicholson

Sec., Rev. Peter Green

Treas., Steven M. Alaexie

Dir. of Theological Education, Rev. Will Updegrove

Periodicals

The Moravian

National Association of Congregational Christian Churches

This association was organized in 1955 in Detroit, Mich., by delegates from Congregational Christian Churches committed to continuing the Congregational way of faith and order in church life. Participation by member churches is voluntary.

Headquarters

P.O. Box 288, Oak Creek, WI 53154 Tel. (414)764-1620 Fax (414)764-0319

Email: naccc@naccc.org

Website: www.naccc.org

Media Contact, Assoc. Exec. Sec., Rev. Dr. Donald P. Olsen, 8473 S. Howell Ave., Oak Creek, WI 53154 Tel. (414)764-1620 Fax (414)764-0319

Officers

Exec. Sec., Rev. Dr. Thomas M. Richard, 8473 South Howell Ave., Oak Creek, WI 53154

Assoc. Exec. Secs., Rev. Phil Jackson and Rev. Dr. Donald P. Olsen

Periodicals

The Congregationalist

National Association of Free Will Baptists

This evangelical group of Arminian Baptists was organized by Paul Palmer in 1727 at Chowan, N.C. Another movement (teaching the same doctrines of free grace, free salvation, and free will) was organized June 30, 1780, in New Durham, N.H., but there was no connection with the Southern organization except for a fraternal relationship.

The Northern line expanded more rapidly and extended into the West and Southwest. This body merged with the Northern Baptist Convention Oct. 5, 1911, but a remnant of churches reorganized into the Cooperative General Association of Free Will Baptists Dec. 28, 1916, at Pattonsburg, Mo.

Churches in the Southern line were organized into various conferences from the beginning and finally united in one General Conference in 1921.

Representatives of the Cooperative General Association and the General Conference joined Nov. 5, 1935, to form the National Association of Free Will Baptists.

Headquarters

5233 Mt. View Rd., Antioch, TN 37013-2306 Tel. (615)731-6812 Fax (615)731-0771; Mailing Address: P.O. Box 5002, Antioch, TN 37011-5002

Email: webmaster@nafwb.org
Website: www.nafwb.org/
Media Contact, Exec. Sec., Keith Burden

Officers

Exec. Sec., Keith Burden
Mod., Rev. Carl Cheshier, P.O. Box 7208, Moore, OK 73153

DENOMINATIONAL AGENCIES

Free Will Baptist Foundation: Exec. Dir., William Evans
Free Will Baptist Bible College: Pres., Mathew Pinson
Foreign Missions Dept.: Dir., Rev. James Forlines
Home Missions Dept.: Dir., Rev. Larry Powell
Bd. of Retirement: Dir., Rev. William Evans
Historical Commission: Chpsn., Dr. Darrell Holley, 3606 West End Ave., Nashville, TN 37205
Comm. for Theological Integrity: Chpsn., Rev. Leroy Forlines, 3606 West End Ave., Nashville, TN 37205
Music Comm.: Chpsn., Rev. Randy Sawyer, 2316 Union Rd., Gastonia, NC 28054
Media Comm.: Chpsn., Rev. Steve Faison, 719 N. Cleveland St., Arlington, VA. 22201
Sunday School & Church Training Dept.: Dir., Rev. Ron Hunter
Women Nationally Active for Christ: Exec. Sec., Majorie Workman
Master's Men Dept.: Dir., Rev. Kenneth Akers

Periodicals

Attack, A Magazine for Christian Men, Contact, Free Will Bible College Bulletin, Co-Laborer, Free Will Baptist Gem, Heartbeat, AIM

National Baptist Convention of America, Inc.*

The National Baptist Convention of America, Inc., was organized in 1880. Its mission is articulated through its history, constitution, articles of incorporation, and by-laws. The Convention (corporate churches) has a mission statement with 14 objectives including fostering unity throughout its membership and the world Christian community by proclaiming the gospel of Jesus Christ, validating and propagating the Baptist doctrine of faith and practice and its distinctive principles throughout the world, and harnessing and encouraging the scholarly and Christian creative skills of its membership for Christian writing and publications.

Headquarters

Liaison Officer, Dr. Richard A. Rollins, 777 S. R.L. Thornton Fwy., Ste. 205, Dallas, TX 75203 Tel. (214)946-8913 Fax (214)946-9619

Officers

Pres., Dr. E. Edward Jones, 1327 Pierre Ave., Shreveport, LA 71103 Tel. (318)221-3701 Fax (318)222-7512
Gen. Rec. Sec., Dr. Clarence C. Pennywell, 2016 Russell Rd., Shreveport, LA 71107
Corres. Sec., Rev. E.E. Stafford, 6614 S. Western Ave., Los Angeles, CA 90047
Liaison Officer, Dr. Richard A. Rollins, 777 S. R.L. Thornton Frwy., Ste. 205, Dallas, TX 75203 Tel. (214)946-8913 Fax (214)946-9619

Periodicals

The Lantern

National Baptist Convention, USA, Inc.*

The National Baptist Convention, one of the oldest African American organization in the nation, traces it history back to 1895. It was formed as a cosolidation of the Baptist Foreign Mission Convention (1880), Consolidated American Baptist Convention (1896), and the National Baptist Educational Convention (1882). Rev. W.H. Alpine of Alabama was the first president of the Baptist Foreign Mission Board which later became the Baptist Foreign Mission Convention, USA.

The constitution of the convention 1895 states: "Whereas, It is the sense of the Colored Baptists of the United States of America, convened in the city of Atlanta, Georgia, September 28, 1895 in the several organizations as 'The Baptist Foreign Mission Convention of the United States of America,' hithero engaged in Mission work on the West Coast of Africa: and the 'National Baptist Convention' which has been engaged in mission work in the United States of America, and the 'National Baptist Educational Convention,' which has sought to look after the educational interest that the interest of the way of the Kingdom of God requires that the several bodies above named should, and do now, unite in one body. Therefore, we do now agree to and adopt the following constitution:

This body shall become known and styled, The National Baptist Convention of the United States of America.

The object of this convention shall be 'to do mission work in the United States of America, in Africa, and elsewhere and to foster the cause of education.' Dr. L.M. Luke was elected the first Corresponding S ecretary of the Foreign Board. In October, 1896 Rev. L.G. Jordan, pastor of the Union Baptist Church of Philadelphia was selected successor of Luke"

(*The Epoch of Negro Baptists and The Foreign Mission Board, NBC, USA, Inc.*, Dr. Edward A. Freeman, The Central Seminary Press 1953.)

In September 1915 at the annual meeting of the convention the constitution was revised with the following changes:

"The particular business and object of this Convention shall be to promote a growth and propagamation of religion, morality, and intelligence among the races of mankind, by engaging in missionary work in the United States of

America, and elsewhere, by fostering the cause of education and publishing and circulating literature, and in providing the necessary ways and means for carrying on such work."

Headquarters

1700 Baptist World Center Dr., Nashville, TN 37207 Tel. (615)228-6292 Fax (615)226-5935

Officers

Pres., Dr. William J. Shaw, 1700 Baptist World Center Dr., Nashville, TN 37207 Tel. (615)228-6292 Fax (615)226-5935

Gen. Sec., Dr. Harry Blake, Mt. Canaan Baptist Church, 1666 Alston St., Shreveport, LA 71101, Tel. (318)227-9993

Periodicals

Mission Herald

National Missionary Baptist Convention of America*

The National Missionary Baptist Convention of America was organized in 1988 as a separate entity from the National Baptist Convention of America, Inc., after a dispute over control of the convention's publishing efforts. The new organization intended to remain committed to the National Baptist Sunday Church School and Baptist Training Union Congress and the National Baptist Publishing Board.

The purpose of the National Missionary Baptist Convention of America is to serve as an agency of Christian education, church extension and missionary efforts. It seeks to maintain and safeguard full religious liberty and engage in social and economic development.

Headquarters

1404 E. Firestone, Los Angeles, CA 90001 Tel. (323)582-0090 Fax (323)582-1226

Website: www.nmbca.com

Media Contact, Dr. W. T. Snead Sr.

Officers

Pres., Dr. W. T. Snead Sr.

Vice Pres., At-large, Dr. Harvey E. Leggett, 866 Monroe St., Ypsilanti, MI 48197

Vice Pres., Ecumenical Affairs, Dr. F. Benjamin Davis, 1535 Dr. A.J. Brown Blvd. N., Indianapolis, IN 46202

Vice Pres., Auxiliaries, T.J. Prince, 2219 Sea Island Dr., Dallas, TX 75232

Vice Pres., Boards, Dr. O. E. Piper, 4220 W. 18th St., Chicago, IL 60623

Vice Pres., Financial Affairs, J.A. Boles, 2001 South J St., Tacoma, WA 98405

Pres., National Baptist Publishing Bd., Dr. T.B. Boyd, III, 6717 Centennial Blvd., Nashville, TN 37209

Gen. Sec., Dr. Melvin V. Wade, 4269 S. Figueroa, Los Angeles, CA 90037

Corres. Sec., Dr. H.J. Johnson, 2429 South Blvd., Dallas, TX 75215

Treas., Dr. W.N. Daniel, 415 W. Englewood Ave., Chicago, IL 60612

Rec. Sec., Dr. Lonnie Franks, Crocker, TX

National Organization of the New Apostolic Church of North America

This body is a variant of the Catholic Apostolic Church which began in England in 1830. The New Apostolic Church distinguished itself from the parent body in 1863 by recognizing a succession of Apostles.

Headquarters

3753 N. Troy St., Chicago, IL 60618

Email: info@nak.org

Website: www.nak.org

Media Contact, Sec. & Treas., Ellen E. Eckhardt Tel. (773)539-3652 Fax (773)478-6691

Officers

Pres., Rev. Rev. Richard C. Freund, 1 Mikel Ln., Glen Head, NY 11545-1591

Vice Pres., Rev. John W. Fendt, Jr., 2 Willets Ln., Plandome, NY 11030-1023

Vice Pres., Rev. Leonard R Kolb, 5250 Robinhood Ln., Erie, PA 16509-2563

Vice Pres. Rev. Karl H. Hoffman, 35 Tradewinds Cir., Tequesta, FL 33469-2041

Treas. and Sec., Ellen E. Eckhardt, 6380 N. Indian Rd., Chicago, IL 60646

Asst. Sec., Rev. John E. Doderer, 171 Shore Rd., Glen Cove, NY 11542

Treas. and Sec., Ellen E. Eckhardt, 6380 N. Indian Rd., Chicago, IL 60646

Asst. Treas. and Asst. Sec., Rev. John E. Doderer, 171 Shore Rd., Glen Cove, NY 11542

National Primitive Baptist Convention, Inc.

Throughout the years of slavery and the Civil War, the Negro population of the South worshipped with the white population in their various churches. At the time of emancipation, their white brethren helped them establish their own churches, granting them letters of fellowship, ordaining their deacons and ministers, and helping them in other ways.

The doctrine and polity of this body are quite similar to that of white Primitive Baptists, yet there are local associations and a national convention, organized in 1907.

Each church is independent and receives and controls its own membership. This body was formerly known as Colored Primitive Baptists.

Headquarters

6433 Hidden Forest Dr., Charlotte, NC 28213 Tel. (704)596-1508

Media Contact, Elder T. W. Samuels

Officers

Natl. Convention, Pres., Elder T.W. Samuels Tel. (704)596-3153

Natl. Convention, Vice Pres., Elder Ernest Ferrell, Tallahassee, FL

Natl. Convention, Chmn. Bd. of Dirs., Elder Ernest Ferrell, Tallahassee, FL

Natl. Church School Training Union, Pres., Jonathan Yates, Mobile, AL

Natl. Ushers Congress, Pres., Bro. Carl Batts, 21213 Garden View Dr., Maple Heights, OH 44137

Publishing Bd., Chpsn., Elder E. W. Wallace, Creamridge, NJ

Women's Congress, Pres., Betty Brown, Cocoa Beach, FL

Natl. Laymen's Council, Pres., Densimore Robinson, Huntsville, AL

Natl. Youth Congress, Pres., Robert White, Trenton, NJ

National Spiritualist Association of Churches

This organization is made up of believers that Spiritualism is a science, philosophy, and religion based upon the demonstrated facts of communication between this world and the next.

Headquarters

NSAC General Offices, Rev. Sharon L. Snowman, Secretary, P.O. Box 217, Lily Dale, NY 14752-0217

Email: nsac@nsac.org

Website: www.nsac.org

Media Contact, Mr. Robert Egby, 720 Almonesson, Westville, NJ 08093

Officers

Pres., Rev. Barbara Thurman, 200 Marina Vista Rd., Larkspur, CA 94939-2144

Vice Pres., Rev. Pamla Ashlay, 11811 Watertown Plank Rd., Milwaukee, WI 53226

Sec., Rev. Sharon L. Snowman, P.O. Box 217, Lily Dale, NY 14752 Tel. (716)595-2000 Fax (716)595-2020

Treas., Rev. Lelia Cutler, 7310 Medfield St. #1, Norfolk, VA 23505

OTHER ORGANIZATIONS

Department of Education, Dir., Rev. Barbara Starr, 4245 Woodmont Rd., Great Cacapon, WV 25422

Department of Lyceums, Dir., Rev. Arsenia Williams, 10913 S. Parnell, Chicago, IL 60628

Department of Missionaries, Dir., Rev. E. Ann Otzelberger, 4332 Woodlynne Ln., Orlando, FL 32812-7562

Department of Phenomenal Evidence, Dirs., Revs. Lisa and Thomas Butler, 3415 Socrates Dr., Reno, NV 89512

Department of Public Relations, Dir., Mary Montgomery Clifford, 2426 North Kimball St., Chicago, IL 60647

Department of Publications, Dir., John Rothamel, Jr., 7851 Foxfarm Ln., Glen Burnie, MD 21061-6324

NSAC Healing Center, Pres., Rev. Gene Pfortmiller, 3521 W. Topeka Drive, Glendale, AZ 85308-2325

NSAC Minsterial Association, Pres., Rev. Barbara Star, NST, 4245 Woodmont Rd., Great Cacapon, WV 25422

National Spiritualist Teachers Club, Pres., Rev. E. Ann Otzelberger, NST, 4332 Woodlynne Ln., Orlando, FL 32812

Spiritualist Healers League, Pres., Rev. Gene Pfortmiller, NST, 3521 W. Topeka Dr., Glendale, AZ 85308-2325

Licentiate Ministers & Certified Mediums Society, Pres., Rev. Janet Tisdale, NST, 1616 N. Alta Mesa Dr., #51, Mesa, AZ 85205

The Stow Memorial Foundation, Sec., Rev. Sharon L. Snowman, P.O. Box 217, Lily Dale, NY 14752 Tel. (716)595-2000 Fax (716)595-2020

Spiritualist Benevolent Society, Inc., P.O. Box 217, Lily Dale, NY 14752

Netherlands Reformed Congregations

The Netherlands Reformed Congregations organized denominationally in 1907. In the Netherlands, the so-called Churches Under the Cross (established in 1839, after breaking away from the 1834 Secession congregations) and the so-called Ledeboerian churches (established in 1841 under the leadership of the Rev. Ledeboer, who seceded from the Reformed State Church), united in 1907 under the leadership of the then 25-year-old Rev. G.H. Kersten, to form the Netherlands Reformed Congregations. Many of the North American congregations left the Christian Reformed Church to join the Netherlands Reformed Congregations after the Kuyperian presupposed regeneration doctrine began making inroads.

All Netherlands Reformed Congregations, office-bearers, and members subscribe to three Reformed Forms of Unity: The Belgic Confession of Faith (by DeBres), the Heidelberg Catechism (by Ursinus and Olevianus), and the Canons of Dort. The Heidelberg Catechism is preached weekly, except on church feast days.

Headquarters

Media Contact, Rev. C. Vogelaar, 2339 Deer Trail Dr. NE, Grand Rapids, MI 49505 Tel. (616)364-9889 Fax (616)364-9979

OTHER ORGANIZATIONS

Netherlands Reformed Book and Publishing: 1233 Leffingwell NE, Grand Rapids, MI 49505

Periodicals

The Banner of Truth, Paul (mission magazine), *Insight Into* (for young people), *Learning and Living* (for school and home)

The New Church—See General Church of the New Jerusalem

North American Baptist Conference

The North American Baptist Conference was begun by immigrants from Germany. The first church was organized by the Rev. Konrad Fleischmann in Philadelphia in 1843. In 1865, delegates of the churches met in Wilmot, Ontario, and organized the North American Baptist Conference. Today, only a few churches still use the German language, mostly in a bilingual setting.

The Conference meets in general session once every three years for fellowship, inspiration, and to conduct the business of the Conference through elected delegates from the local churches. The General Council, composed of representatives of the various Associations and Conference organizations and departments, meets annually to determine the annual budget and programs for the Conference and its departments and agencies. The General Council also makes recommendations to the Triennial Conference on policies, long-range plans, and election of certain personnel, boards, and committees.

Approximately 60 missionaries serve in Brazil, Cameroon, Japan, Mexico, Nigeria, Philippines, and Russia. Eight homes for the aged are affiliated with the Conference and 11 camps are operated on the association level.

Headquarters

1 S. 210 Summit Ave., Oakbrook Terrace, IL 60181 Tel. (630)495-2000 Fax (630)495-3301

Media Contact, Marilyn Schaer

Officers

Exec. Dir., Rev. Ron Berg, 1 S. 210 Summit Ave., Oakbrook Terrace, IL 60181 Tel. (630) 495-2000, Fax (630)475-3301, Pyntema@nabconf.org

OTHER ORGANIZATIONS

Intl. Missions Dept.: Dir., Ron Salzman

Home Missions Dept.: Dir., Rev. Bob Walther

Church Extension Investors Fund: Dir., Les D. Collins

Periodicals

NABtoday

North American Old Roman Catholic Church (Archdiocese of New York)

This body is identical with the Roman Catholic Church in faith but differs from it in discipline and worship. The Mass is offered with the appropriate rite either in Latin or in the vernacular. All other sacraments are taken from the Roman Pontifical. This jurisdiction allows for married clergy.

Primatial Headquarters

60 St. Felix St., Brooklyn, NY 11217-1206 Tel. (718)855-0600 Fax (718)522-1231

Media Contact, Chancellor, Most Rev. Albert J. Berube

Officers

Primate, The Most Rev. Herve L. Quessy

Chancellor, Most Rev. Albert J. Berube

Diocese of New York, Ordinary, Most Rev. Albert J. Berube

Diocese of Montreal & French Canada, Ordinary, Most Rev. Herve L. Quessy

Old German Baptist Brethren Church

This group separated from the Church of the Brethren (formerly German Baptist Brethren) in 1881 in order to preserve and maintain historic Brethren Doctrine.

Headquarters

Vindicator Ofc. Ed., Steven L. Bayer, 6952 N. Montgomery County Line Rd., Englewood, OH 45322-9748 Tel. (937)884-7531

Periodicals

The Vindicator

Old Order Amish Church

The congregations of this Old Order Amish group have no annual conference. They worship in private homes. They adhere to the older forms of worship and attire. This body has bishops, ministers, and deacons.

Headquarters

LeRoy Beachy, Beachy Amish Mennonite Church, 4324 SR 39, Millersburg, OH 44654 Tel. (216)893-2883

Old Order (Wisler) Mennonite Church

This body arose from a separation of Mennonites dated 1872, under Jacob Wisler, in opposition to what were thought to be innovations.

The group is in the Eastern United States and Canada. Each state, or district, has its own organization and holds semi-annual conferences.

Headquarters

Media Contact, Amos B. Hoover, 376 N. Muddy Creek Rd., Denver, PA 17517 Tel. (717)484-4849 Fax (717)484-104

Open Bible Standard Churches

Open Bible Standard Churches originated from two revival movements: Bible Standard Conference (founded in Eugene, Oreg., under the leadership of Fred L. Hornshuh in 1919) and Open Bible Evangelistic Association (founded in Des Moines, IA, under the leadership of John R. Richey in 1932).

Similar in doctrine and government, the two groups amalgamated on July 26, 1935 as "Open Bible Standard Churches, Inc." with headquarters in Des Moines, Iowa.

The original group of 210 ministers has enlarged to incorporate over 2,479 ministers and 1,397 churches in 36 countries. The first missionary left for India in 1926. The church now ministers in Asia, Africa, South America, Europe, Canada, Mexico, Central America, and the Caribbean Islands.

Historical roots of the parent groups reach back to the outpouring of the Holy Spirit in 1906 at Azusa Street Mission in Los Angeles and to the full gospel movement in the Midwest. Both groups were organized under the impetus of pentecostal revival. Simple faith, freedom from fanaticism, emphasis on evangelism and missions, and free fellowship with other groups were characteristics of the growing organizations.

The highest governing body of Open Bible Standard Churches meets biennially and is composed of all ministers and one voting delegate per 100 members from each church. A National Board of Directors, elected by the national and regional conferences, conducts the business of the organization. Official Bible College is Eugene Bible College in Oregon.

Open Bible Standard Churches is a charter member of the National Association of Evangelicals and of the Pentecostal/Charismatic Churches of North America. It is a member of the Pentecostal World Conference.

National Office

2020 Bell Ave., Des Moines, IA 50315 Tel. (515)288-6761 Fax (515)288-2510

Email: info@openbible.org

Website: www.openbible.org

Media Contact, Exec. Dir., Communications & Resources, Jeff Farmer Tel. (515)288-6761 Fax (515)288-2510

Officers

Pres., Jeffrey E. Farmer, 2020 Bell Ave., Des Moines, Iowa 50315 Tel. (515)288-6761, Fax (515)288-2510, jeff@openbible.org

Esq., Sec.-Treas., Teresa A. Beyer, 2020 Bell Ave., Des Moines, Iowa 50315 Tel (515)288-6761, Fax (515)288-2510, tbeyer@openbible.org

Dir., of Intl. Min., Paul V. Canfield, 2020 Bell Ave., Des Moines, Iowa 50315 Tel. (515)288-6761, Fax (515)288-2510, missions@openbible.org

Periodicals

Message of the Open Bible

The (Original) Church of God, Inc.

This body was organized in 1886 as the first church in the United States to take the name "The Church of God." In 1917 a difference of opinion led this particular group to include the word "Original" in its name. It is a holiness body and believes in the whole Bible, rightly divided, using the New Testament as its rule and government.

Headquarters

P.O. Box 592, Wytheville, VA 24382

Media Contact, Gen. Overseer, Rev. William Dale Tel. (800)827-9234

Officers

Gen. Overseer, Rev. William Dale

Asst. Gen. Overseer, Rev. Alton Evans

Periodicals

The Messenger

The Orthodox Church in America*

The Orthodox Church of America entered Alaska in 1794 before its purchase by the United States in 1867. Its canonical status of independence (autocephaly) was granted by its Mother Church, the Russian Orthodox Church, on April 10, 1970, and it is now known as The Orthodox Church in America.

Headquarters

P.O. Box 675, Syosset, NY 11791-0675 Tel. (516)922-0550 Fax (516)922-0954

Website: www.oca.org

Media Contact, Dir. of Communications, V. Rev. John Matusiak, 1 Wheaton Center, # 912, IL 60187 Tel. (630)668-3071, Fax (708)923-1706, jjm@oca.org

Officers

Primate, Archbishop of Washington, Metropolitan of All America & Canada, Most Blessed Herman

Chancellor, V. Rev. Robert S. Kondratick, P.O. Box 675, Syosset, NY 11791 Tel. (516)922-0550 Fax (516)922-0954

SYNOD

Chpsn., His Beatitude Herman, P.O. Box 675, Syosset, NY 11791

Archbishop of New York, Most Rev. Peter, 33 Hewitt Ave., Bronxville, NY 10708

Archbishop of Pittsburgh & Western PA, Most Rev. Kyrill, P.O. Box R, Wexford, PA 15090

Archbishop of Dallas, Archbishop Dmitri, 4112 Throckmorton, Dallas, TX 75219

Bishop of Sitka, Anchorage, and Alaska, Rt. Rev. Nikolai, 513 E. 24 Ave., Ste. #3, Anchorage, AK 99503

Archbishop of Detroit, Rt. Rev. Nathaniel, P.O. Box 309, Grass Lake, MI 49240-0309

Bishop of Chicago, Rt. Rev. Job, 927 N. LaSalle, Chicago, IL 60610

Bishop of San Francisco, Rt. Rev. Tikhon, 649 North Robinson St., Los Angeles, CA 90026

Bishop of Ottawa and Canada, Rt. Rev. Seraphim, P.O. Box 179, Spencerville, ON K0E 1X0 Tel. (613)925-5226

Retired Bishop, Rt. Rev. Mark, 9511 Sun Pointe Dr., Boynton Beach, FL 33437

Auxiliary Bishop of Baltimore, Rt. Rev. Nikon, P.O. Box 149, Southbridge, MA 01550 Tel. (508)764-3222

Auxiliary Bishop of Dearborn Heights, Rt. Rev.

Irinev, 23300, Davison Ave. W, Detriot, MI 48223 Tel. (313)533-3413
Retired Metropolitan, the Most Blessed Theodosius, P.O. Box 70, Hamlin, PA 18477
Retired Archbishop, the Most Rev. Gregory, P.O. Box 94, Jackson, NJ 08527-0094

Periodicals

The Orthodox Church, Annual Sourcebook, Church Directory

The Orthodox Presbyterian Church

On June 11, 1936, certain ministers, elders, and lay members of the Presbyterian Church in the USA withdrew from that body to form a new denomination. Under the leadership of the late Rev. J. Gresham Machen, noted conservative New Testament scholar, the new church determined to continue to uphold the Westminster Confession of Faith as traditionally understood by Presbyterians and to engage in proclamation of the gospel at home and abroad.

The church has grown modestly over the years and suffered early defections, most notably one in 1937 that resulted in the formation of the Bible Presbyterian Church under the leadership of Dr. Carl McIntire. It now has congregations throughout the states of the continental United States.

The denomination is a member of the North American Presbyterian and Reformed Council and the International Council of Reformed Churches.

Headquarters

607 N. Easton Rd., Bldg. E, Box P, Willlow Grove, PA 19090-0920 Tel. (215)830-0900 Fax (215)830-0350
Website: www.opc.org
Media Contact, Stated Clerk, Rev. Donald J. Duff, duff.1@opc.org

Officers

Moderator of General Assembly, The Rev. Douglas B. Clawson, Box P, Willow Grove, PA 19090
Stated Clk., Rev. Donald J. Duff

Periodicals

New Horizons in the Orthodox Presbyterian Church

Patriarchal Parishes of the Russian Orthodox Church in the USA*

This group of parishes is under the direct jurisdiction of the Patriarch of Moscow and All Russia, His Holiness Aleksy II, in the person of a Vicar Bishop, His Grace Mercurius, Bishop of Zaraisk.

Headquarters

St. Nicholas Cathedral, 15 E. 97th St., New York, NY 10029 Tel. (212)831-6294 Fax (212)427-5003
Email: bmercurius@ruscon.com
Website: www.orthodox.net
Media Contact, Sec. to the Bishop, Hierodeacon Joseph Tel. (212)996-6638

Officers

Secretary to the Bishop, Hierodeacon Joseph

Pentecostal Assemblies of the World, Inc.

This organization is an interracial Pentecostal holiness of the Apostolic Faith, believing in repentance; baptism in Jesus's name; and being filled with the Holy Ghost, with the evidence of speaking in tongues. It originated in the early part of the century in the Middle West and has spread throughout the country.

Headquarters

3939 Meadows Dr., Indianapolis, IN 46205 Tel. (317)547-9541
Media Contact, Admin., John E. Hampton Fax (317)543-0512

Officers

Presiding Bishop, Norman L. Wagner
Asst. Presiding Bishop, James E. Tyson
Bishops: Arthus Brazier, George Brooks, Ramsey Butler, Morris Golder, Francis L. Smith, Francis L., Brooker T. Jones, C. R. Lee, Robert McMurray, Philip L. Scott, William L. Smith, Samuel A. Layne, Freeman M. Thomas, James E. Tyson, Charles Davis, Willie Burrell, Harry Herman, Jeremiah Reed, Jeron Johnson, Clifton Jones, Robert Wauls, Ronald L. Young, Henry L. Johnson, Leodis Warren, Thomas J. Weeks, Eugene Redd, Thomas W. Weeks, Sr., Willard Saunders, Davis L. Ellis, Earl Parchia, Vanuel C. Little, Norman Wagner, George Austin, Benjamin A. Pitt, Markose Thopil, John K. Cole, Peter Warkie, Norman Walters, Alphonso Scott, David Dawkins
Gen. Sec, Dr. Aletha Cushinberry
Assist. Gen Sec., Suffragan Bishop Noel Jones
Gen. Treas., Elder James Loving
Asst. Treas., Dist. Eld. Charles Ellis III

Periodicals

Christian Outlook

Pentecostal Church of God

Growing out of the pentecostal revival at the turn of the century, the Pentecostal Church of God was organized in Chicago on Dec. 30, 1919, as the Pentecostal Assemblies of the USA. The name was changed to Pentecostal Church of God in 1922, in 1934 it was changed again to The Pentecostal Church of God of America, Inc., and finally the name became the Pentecostal Church of God (Incorporated) in 1979.

The International Headquarters was moved from Chicago, Ill. to Ottumwa, Iowa, in 1927; then to Kansas City, Mo., in 1933; and finally to Joplin, Mo., in 1951.

The denomination is evangelical and pentecostal in doctrine and practice. Active membership in the National Association of Evangelicals and the Pentecostal/Charismatic Churches North America is maintained.

The church is Trinitarian in doctrine and teaches the absolute inerrancy of the Scripture from Genesis to Revelation. Among its cardinal beliefs are the doctrines of salvation, which includes regeneration; divine healing, as provided for in the atonement; the baptism in the Holy Ghost, with the initial physical evidence of speaking in tongues; and the premillennial second coming of Christ.

Headquarters

4901 Pennsylvania, P.O. Box 850, Joplin, MO 64802 Tel. (417)624-7050 Fax (417)624-7102
Email: pcg@pcg.org
Website: www.pcg.org
Media Contact, Gen. Sec., Dr. Ronald R. Minor

Officers

Gen. Supt/Bishop., Dr. Phil L. Redding
Gen. Sec., Dr. Ronald R. Minor

OTHER GENERAL EXECUTIVES

Dir. of World Missions, Rev. Loyd L. Naten
Dir. of Indian Missions, Dr. C. Don Burke
Dir. of Youth Ministries, Rev. Reggie O. Powers
Dir. of Home Missions/Evangelism, Rev. Stephen E. Oates

ASSISTANT GENERAL SUPERINTENDENTS/BISHOPS

Northwestern Division: Rev. Jamie J. Joiner
Southwestern Division: Rev. Michael W. Jacobsen
North Central Division: Rev. Donald R. Dennis
South Central Division: Rev. Leon A. McDowell
Northeastern Division: Rev. Charles R. Mosier
Southeastern Division: Rev. C.W. Goforth

OTHER DEPARTMENTAL OFFICERS

Bus. Mgr., Rev. R. Alan Greagrey
Director of Women's Ministry, Mrs. Sharon K. Redding
Christian Educ., Dir., Mrs. Billie L. Palumbo

Periodicals

The Pentecostal Messenger

Pentecostal Fire-Baptized Holiness Church

Organized in 1918, this group consolidated with the Pentecostal Free Will Baptists in 1919. It maintains rigid discipline over members.

Headquarters

P.O. Box 261, La Grange, GA 30241-0261 Tel. (706)884-7742
Media Contact, Gen. Mod., Wallace B. Pittman, Jr.

Officers

Gen. Treas., Alan Sparkman, 1961 Norjon circle, Clio, SC 29525, Tel. 843-586-9095
Gen. Sec., Joel Powell, 16841 Springs Mill Rd., Lauringbury, NC 28352, Tel. (901)462-3379
Gen. Mod., Wallace B. Pittman Jr.
Gen. Supt. Mission Bd., Jerry Powell, Rt. 1, Box 384, Chadourn, NC 28431

Periodicals

Faith and Truth

The Pentecostal Free Will Baptist Church, Inc.

The Cape Fear Conference of Free Will Baptists, organized in 1855, merged in 1959 with The Wilmington Conference and The New River Conference of Free Will Baptists and was renamed the Pentecostal Free Will Baptist Church, Inc. The doctrines include regeneration, sanctification, the Pentecostal baptism of the Holy Ghost, the Second Coming of Christ, and divine healing.

Headquarters

P.O. Box 1568, Dunn, NC 28335 Tel. (910)892-4161 Fax (910)892-6876
Website: www.pfwb.org/
Media Contact, Gen. Supt., Preston Heath, pheath@intrstar.net

Officers

Gen. Supt., Rev. Preston Heath
Asst. Gen. Supt., Jim Wall
Gen. Sec., Mr. Stephen Garriss
Gen. Treas., Mr. Dewayne Weeks
Christian Ed. Dir., Rev. Randy Barker
World Witness Dir., Rev. Hobbs
Gen. Services Dir., Ms. Cathy Muzingo
Ministerial Council Dir., Rev. Ed Taturn
Ladies' Auxiliary Dir., Dollie Davis
Heritage Bible College, Pres., Dr. Dwarka Ramphal
Crusader Youth Camp, Dir., Rev. Randy Barker

OTHER ORGANIZATIONS

Heritage Bible College
Crusader Youth Camp
Blessings Bookstore: 1006 W. Cumberland St., Dunn, NC 28334 Tel. (910)892-2401

Periodicals

The Messenger

Philadelphia Yearly Meeting of the Religious Society of Friends*

PYM traces its roots to the yearly meeting of 1681 in Burlington, N.J. For more than three centuries, PYM has served Monthly Meetings and Quarterly Meetings throughout eastern Pennsylvania, southern New Jersey, northern Maryland, and Delaware. In general, the activities of PYM are organized under five Standing Committees—Standing Committee on Worship and Care, Standing Committee on Education, Standing Committee on Peace and Concerns, Standing Committee on Support and Outreach, and Standing Committee on General Services.

Headquarters

Philadelphia Yearly Meeting, 1515 Cherry St., Philadelphia, PA 19102-1479 Tel. (215)241-7211 Fax (215)567-2096

Website: www.pym.org

Officers

Presiding Clerk, Gretchen Castle

Clerk of Interim Meeting, Chris Mahon

Gen. Sec., Thomas Jeavons

Clerk, Standing Committee on Worship and Care, Edward Breadfires, James Morrissey

Clerk, Standing Committee on Education, Deborah Lyons

Clerk, Standing Committee on Peace and Concerns, Howard Cell

Clerk, Standing Committee on Support and Outreach, Frances Dreisback, Pamela Carter

Clerk, Standing Committee on General Services, Anne Moore

Pillar of Fire

The Pillar of Fire was founded by Alma Bridwell White in Denver on Dec. 29, 1901 as the Pentecostal Union. In 1917, the name was changed to Pillar of Fire. Alma White was born in Kentucky in 1862 and taught school in Montana where she met her husband, Kent White, a Methodist minister who was a University student in Denver.

Because of Alma White's evangelistic endeavors, she was frowned upon by her superiors, which eventually necessitated her withdrawing from Methodist Church supervision. She was ordained as Bishop and her work spread to many states; to England; and, since her death, to Liberia, West Africa, Malawi, East Africa, Yugoslavia, Spain, India, and the Philippines.

The Pillar of Fire organization has a college and two seminaries stressing Biblical studies. It operates eight separate schools for young people. The church continues to keep in mind the founder's goals and purposes.

Headquarters

P.O. Box 9159, Zarephath, NJ 08890 Tel. (732) 356-0102

Western Headquarters: 1302 Sherman St., Denver, CO 80203 Tel. (303)427-5462

Email: info@zarephath.edu

Website: www.gospelcom.net/pof/

Media Contact, 1st Vice Pres., Robert B. Dallenbach, 3455 W. 83 Ave., Westminster, CO 80031 Tel. (303)427-5462 Fax (303)429-0910

Officers

Pres. and Gen. Supt., Dr. Robert B. Dallenbach

1st Vice Pres. and Asst. Supt., Rev. Joseph Gross

2nd Vice Pres./Sec.-Treas., Lois R. Stewart

Trustees: Kenneth Cope, S. Rea Crawford, Lois Stewart, Dr. Donald J. Wolfram, Robert B. Dallenbach, Rob W. Cruver, Joseph Gross

Periodicals

The Pillar Monthly

Polish National Catholic Church of America*

After a number of attempts to resolve differences regarding the role of the laity in parish administration in the Roman Catholic Church in Scranton, Penn., this Church was organized in 1897. With the consecration to the episcopacy of the Most Rev. F. Hodur, this Church became a member of the Old Catholic Union of Utrecht in 1907.

Headquarters

Office of the Prime Bishop, 1006 Pittston Ave., Scranton, PA 18505 Tel. (570)346-9131

Email: ads22244@aol.com

Website: www.PNCC.org/

Media Contact, Prime Bishop, Most Rev. Robert M. Nemkovich, 1006 Pittston Ave., Scranton, PA 18505 Tel. (570)346-9131 Fax (570)346-2188

Officers

Prime Bishop, Most Rev. Robert M. Nemkovich, 115 Lake Scranton Rd., Scranton, PA 18505

Central Diocese: Bishop, Rt. Rev. Casimir Grotnik, 529 E. Locust St., Scranton, PA 18505

Eastern Diocese: Bishop, Rt. Rev. Thomas J. Gnat, 166 Pearl St., Manchester, NH 03104

Buffalo-Pittsburgh Diocese: Bishop, Rt. Rev. Thaddeus S. Peplowski, 5776 Broadway, Lancaster, NY 14086

Western Diocese: Rt. Rev. Robert M. Dawidziuk, 920 N. Northwest Hwy., Park Ridge, IL 60068; Rt. Rev. Jan Dawidziuk (Auxilliery Bp.) 1901 Wexford Ave., Parma, OH 44134

Canadian Diocese: Bishop, Sede Vacante, 186 Cowan Ave., Toronto, ON M6K 2N6

Ecumenical Officer, V. Rev. Anthony Mikovsky

Periodicals

God's Field, Polka

Presbyterian Church in America

The Presbyterian Church in America is an Evangelical, Reformed covenant community of churches in the United States and Canada committed to a common doctrinal standard (The Westminster Standards), mutual accountability (representative church government), and cooperative ministry. The PCA traces its historical roots to the First General Assembly of the Church of Scotland of 1560; the establishment of the Presbytery of Philadelphia, 1789; and the General Assembly of the Southern Presbyterian Church, Augusta in 1861. Organized in 1973 by conservative churches formerly associated with the Presbyterian Church in the United States, the Church was first known as the National Presbyterian Church but changed its name in 1974 to the Presbyterian Church in America. The

PCA seeks to be "Faithful to the Scriptures, True to the Reformed Faith, and Obedient to the Great Commission." In 1982 the Reformed Presbyterian Church, Evangelical Synod joined the PCA bringing with it a rich tradition that had antecedents in colonial America.

The PCA holds to the ancient creeds of the Church such as the Apostles' Creed and the Nicene Creed and has a firm commitment to its doctrinal standards—The Westminster Confession of Faith, Larger and Shorter Catechisms—that have been significant in Presbyterianism since 1645. These doctrinal standards reflect the distinctives of the Reformed tradition, Calvinism, and Covenant Theology. Ministers, ruling elders, and deacons are required to subscribe to the Westminster Standards in good faith. Individuals are received by a Session as communing members of the Church upon their profession of faith in Jesus Christ as Lord and Saviour, their promise to live a Christian lifestyle, and their commitment to worship and service in the Church.

The PCA is a connectional Church, led by ruling elders (lay leaders) and teaching elders (ministers). The Session governs a local congregation, the Diaconate carries out mercy ministries. The Presbytery is responsible for regional matters and the General Assembly is responsible for national matters in the USA and Canada. Cooperative ministry is carried out through over sixty Presbyteries and ten General Assembly Ministries.

The educational institutions of the Church are Covenant College of Lookout Mountain,GA and Covenant Theological Seminary of St. Louis, Mo. The PCA and the Orthodox Presbyterian Church participate in a joint publication venture, Great Commission Publications, for the publication of Christian Education materials.

In its ecumenical relations the PCA is a member of the North American Presbyterian and Reformed Council, the National Association of Evangelicals, and the World Reformed Fellowship.

The General Assembly approved a statement of purpose: "It is the purpose of the PCA to bring glory to God as a worshipping and serving community until the nations in which we live are filled with churches that make Jesus Christ and His word their chief joy, and the nations of the world, hearing the Word, are discipled in obedience to the Great Commission."

The Church has grown beyond its origin in the southeastern states to have congregations in forty-nine states in the USA and in several provinces of Canada. Growth is due to the PCA's ministry in evangelism, discipleship, church planting, church renewal, and campus ministry. Indicative of her concern for cross-cultural ministry, the PCA has the largest international missionary force in Presbyterian Church history.

Headquarters

1700 N. Brown Rd., Lawrenceville, GA 30043-8122, Tel. (678)825-1000

Email: ac@pcanet.org

Website: www.pcanet.org

Officers

Moderator, Dr. Skip Ryan, Park Cities PC, 4124 Oak Lawn Ave., Dallas, TX 75219 Tel. (214)224-2500, webmaster@pcpc.org

Stated Clerk/Coordinator of Administration, Dr. L. Roy Taylor, 1700 N. Brown Rd., Suite 105, Lawrenceville, GA 30043-8122 Tel. (678)825-1100, ac@pcanet.org

Christian Education & Publications Coordinator, Dr. Charles Dunahoo, 1700 N. Brown Rd., Suite 102, Lawrenceville, GA 30043-8122 Tel. (678)825-1100, cep@pacnet.org

Mission to the World Coordinator, Dr. Paul D. Kooistra, 1600 N. Brown Rd., Lawrenceville, GA 30043-8141 Tel. (678)823-0004, mtw@mtw.org

Mission to North America Coordinator, Dr. James C. Bland, 1700 N. Brown Rd., Suite 101, Lawrenceville, GA 30043-8122 Tel. (678)825-1200, mna@pcanet.org

Reformed University Ministries Coordinator, Dr. Rod Mays, 1700 N. Brown Rd., Suite 104, Lawrenceville, GA 30043-8122 Tel. (678)825-1070, rum@pcanet.org

PCA Foundation Pres., Mr. Randy Stair, 1700 N. Brown Rd., Suite 103, Lawrenceville, GA 30043-8122 Tel. (678)825-1040, pcaf@pcanet.org

Insurance-Annuities Pres., Mr. James L. Hughes, 1700 N. Brown Rd., Suite 106, Lawrenceville, GA 30043-8122 Tel. (678)825-1260, iar@pcanet.org

Ridge Haven Conference Dir., Rev. Morse Up De Graff, P.O. Box 969, Rosman, NC 28772 Tel. (828)862-3916, Fax (828)884-6988, ridgehaven@citcom.net

Covenant College Pres., Mr. Niel Nielson, 14049 Scenic Hwy, Lookout Mountain, GA 30750 Tel. (706)820-1560, Fax (706)820-2165, webmaster@covenant.edu

Covenant Theological Seminary Pres., Dr. Bryan Chapell, 12330 Conway Rd., St. Louis, MO 63141-8697 Tel. (314)434-4044, Fax (314) 434-4819, webmaster@covenantseminary.edu

Periodicals

Equip; Covenant, Multiply, The View, Network, PCANews.com

Presbyterian Church (USA)*

The Presbyterian Church (USA) was organized June 10, 1983, when the Presbyterian Church in the United States and the United Presbyterian Church in the United States of America united in Atlanta. The union healed a major division which began with the Civil War when Presbyterians in the South withdrew from the Presbyterian Church in the United States of America to form the Presbyterian Church in the Confederate States.

The United Presbyterian Church in the United

States of America had been created by the 1958 union of the Presbyterian Church in the United States of America and the United Presbyterian Church of North America. Of those two uniting bodies, the Presbyterian Church in the USA dated from the first Presbytery organized in Philadelphia, about 1706. The United Presbyterian Church of North America was formed in 1858, when the Associate Reformed Presbyterian Church and the Associate Presbyterian Church united.

Strongly ecumenical in outlook, the Presbyterian Church (USA) is the result of at least 10 different denominational mergers over the last 250 years. A restructure, adopted by the General Assembly meeting in June 1993, has been implemented. The Presbyterian Church (USA) dedicated its new national offices in Louisville, Ky. in 1988.

Headquarters

100 Witherspoon St., Louisville, KY 40202 Tel. (888)728-7228 Fax (502)569-5018

Email: presytel@pcusa.org

Website: www.pcusa.org

Media Contact, Assoc. Dir. for Communications, Ann Giles Tel. (502)569-5515 Fax (502)569-8073

Officers

Mod., Susan Andrews, 100 Witherspoon St., Louisville KY 40202 Tel. (888)728-7228

Vice Mod., Charles Easley, 100 Witherspoon St., Louisville KY 40202 Tel. (888)728-7228

Stated Clk., Clifton Kirkpatrick,100 Witherspoon St., Louisville KY 40202 Tel. (888)728-7228

THE OFFICE OF THE GENERAL ASSEMBLY

100 Witherspoon St., Louisville KY 40202-1396 Tel. (888)728-7228 ext. 5424 Fax (502)569-8005

Stated Clk., Rev. Clifton Kirkpatrick

Strategic Operations: Dir., Rev. Gradye Parsons

Middle Governing Body Relations: Coord., Rev. Gary Torrens

Dept. of the Stated Clerk: Dir., Loyda Aja

Dept. of Constitutional Services: Dir., Rev. Mark Tammen

Ecumenical & Agency Relations: Dir., Rev. Robina Winbush

Dept. of Communication & Technology: Dir., Rev. Kerry Clements

Dept. of Hist.: Philadelphia, 425 Lombard St., Philadelphia, PA 19147 Tel. (215)627-1852 Fax (215)627-0509; Dir., Frederick J. Heuser Jr.; Deputy Dir., Margery Sly

GENERAL ASSEMBLY COUNCIL

Exec. Dir., John J. Detterick

Deputy Exec. Dir., Kathy Luekert

Worldwide Ministries Division: Dir., Rev. Marian McClure

Congregational Ministries Division: Dir., Donald G. Campbell

National Ministries Division: Dir., Rev. Curtis A. Kearns Jr.

Mission Support Services: Dir., Joey Bailey

BOARD OF PENSIONS

200 Market St., Philadelphia, PA 19103-3298 Tel. (800)773-7752 Fax (215)587-6215

Chpsn. of the Bd., Earldean V. S. Robbins

Pres. & CEO, Robert W. Maggs Jr.

PRESBYTERIAN CHURCH (USA) FOUNDATION

200 E. Twelfth St., Jeffersonville, IN 47130 Tel. (812)288-8841 Fax (502)569-5980

Chpsn. of the Bd., James Henderson

Pres. & CEO, Robert E. Leech

PRESBYTERIAN CHURCH (USA) INVESTMENT & LOAN PROGRAM, INC.

Tel. (800)903-7457 Fax (502)569-8868

Chpsn. of the Board, Ben McAnally

Pres. & CEO, -vacant-

PRESBYTERIAN PUBLISHING CORPORATION

Chpsn. of the Bd., Robert Bohl

Pres. & CEO, Davis Perkins

SYNOD EXECUTIVES

Alaska/Northwest: Rev. Doug Kelly, 217 6th Ave. N., Seattle, WA 98109 Tel. (206)448-6403

Boriquen in Puerto Rico: Rev. Harry Fred Del Valle, Ave. Hostos Edificio 740, Cond. Medical Center Plaza, Ste. 216, Mayaguez, PR 00680 Tel. (787)832-8375

Covenant: Rev. Larry Edwards, 1911 Indian Wood Cir #B Tel. (419)754-4050

Lakes & Prairies: Rev. Grant Lowe, 8012 Cedar Ave. S., Bloomington, MN 55425-1210 Tel. (612)854-0144

Lincoln Trails: Rev. Jay Hudson, 1100 W. 42nd St., Indianapolis, IN 46208-3381 Tel. (317)923-3681

Living Waters: Rev. P. David Snellgrove, 318 Seaboard Ln, Ste. 205, Franklin, TN 37067 Tel. (615)261-4008

Mid-America: Rev. John L. Williams, 6400 Glenwood, Ste. 111, Overland Park, KS 66202-4072 Tel. (913)384-3020

Mid-Atlantic: Rev. Davis Yeuell, P.O. Box 27026, Richmond, VA 23261-7026 Tel. (804)342-0016

Northeast: Rev. Robert Howell White Jr., 5811 Heritage Landing Dr., East Syracuse, NY 13057-9360 Tel. (315)446-5990

Pacific: Rev. Robert Brinks, 8 Fourth St., Petaluma, CA 94952-3004 Tel. (707)765-1772

Rocky Mountains: Rev. Zane Buxton,3025 West 37th Ave., Ste.206, Denver, CO 80211-2799 Tel. (303)477-9070

South Atlantic: Rev. Reginald Parsons, 118 E. Monroe St., Ste. 3, Jacksonville, FL 32202 Tel. (904)356-6070

Southern California & Hawaii: Rev. John N.

Langfitt, 1501 Wilshire Blvd., Los Angeles, CA 90017-2293 Tel. (213)483-3840

Southwest: Rev. Janet DeVries, 4423 N. 24th St., Ste. 800, Phoenix, AZ 85016 Tel. (602)468-3800

The Sun: Rev. Judy R. Fletcher, 920 S. I 35 E, Denton, TX 76205-7898 Tel. (940)382-9656

The Trinity: Rev. Jim Cushman, 3040 Market St., Camp Hill, PA 17011-4599 Tel. (717)737-0421

Periodicals

American Presbyterians, Journal of Presbyterian History, Presbyterian News Service "News Briefs", Church & Society Magazine, Horizons, Presbyterians Today, Interpretation, Presbyterian Outlook

Primitive Advent Christian Church

This body split from the Advent Christian Church. All its churches are in West Virginia. The Primitive Advent Christian Church believes that the Bible is the only rule of faith and practice and that Christian character is the only test of fellowship and communion. The church agrees with Christian fidelity and meekness; exercises mutual watch and care; counsels, admonishes, or reproves as duty may require; and receives the same from each other as becomes the household of faith. Primitive Advent Christians do not believe in taking up arms.

The church believes that three ordinances are set forth by the Bible to be observed by the Christian church: (1) baptism by immersion; (2) the Lord's Supper, by partaking of unleavened bread and wine; (3) feet washing, to be observed by the saints' washing of one another's feet.

Headquarters

Media Contact, Sec.-Treas., Roger Wines, 1971 Grapevine Rd., Sissonville, WV 25320 Tel. (304)988-2668

Officers

Pres., Herbert Newhouse, 7632 Hughart Dr., Sissonville, WV 25320 Tel. (304)984-9277

Vice Pres., Roger Hammons, 273 Frame Rd., Elkview, WV 25071 Tel. (304)965-6247

Sec. & Treas., Roger Wines, 1971 Grapevine Rd., Sissonville, WV 25320 Tel. (304)988-2668

Primitive Baptists

This large group of Baptists, located throughout the United States, opposes all centralization and modern missionary societies. They preach salvation by grace alone.

Headquarters

P.O. Box 38, Thornton, AR 71766 Tel. (501)352-3694

Media Contact, Elder W. Hartsel Cayce

Officers

Elder W. Hartsel Cayce

Elder Lasserre Bradley Jr., Box 17037, Cincinnati, OH 45217 Tel. (513)821-7289

Elder S. T. Tolley, P.O. Box 68, Atwood, TN 38220 Tel. (901)662-7417

Periodicals

Baptist Witness, The Christian Baptist, The Primitive Baptist, For the Poor

Primitive Methodist Church in the USA

Hugh Bourne and William Clowes, local preachers in the Wesleyan Church in England, organized a daylong meeting at Mow Cop in Staffordshire on May 31, 1807, after Lorenzo Dow, an evangelist from America, told them of American camp meetings. Thousands attended and many were converted but the Methodist church, founded by the open-air preacher John Wesley, refused to accept the converts and reprimanded the preachers.

After waiting for two years for a favorable action by the Wesleyan Society, Bourne and Clowes established The Society of the Primitive Methodists. This was not a schism, Bourne said, for "we did not take one from them... it now appeared to be the will of God that we... should form classes and take upon us the care of churches in the fear of God." Primitive Methodist missionaries were sent to New York in 1829. An American conference was established in 1840.

Missionary efforts reach into Guatemala, Spain, and other countries. The denomination joins in federation with the Evangelical Congregational Church, the United Brethren in Christ Church, and the Southern Methodist Church, and is a member of the National Association of Evangelicals.

The church believes the Bible is the only true rule of faith and practice, the inspired Word of God. It believes in one Triune God, the Deity of Jesus Christ, the Deity and personality of the Holy Spirit, the innocence of Adam and Eve, the Fall of the human race, the necessity of repentance, justification by faith of all who believe, regeneration witnessed by the Holy Spirit, sanctification by the Holy Spirit, the second coming of the Lord Jesus Christ, the resurrection of the dead and conscious future existence of all people, and future judgments with eternal rewards and punishments.

Headquarters

Media Contact, Pres., Rev. Kerry Ritts, 723 Preston Ln., Hatboro, PA 19040 Tel. (215)675-2639 or (215)672-1576

Email: pmconf@juno.com

Website: www.primitivemethodistchurch.org

Officers

Pres., Rev. Kerry R. Ritts, 723 Preston Ln., Hatboro, PA 19040-2321 Tel. (215)672-1576

Vice Pres., Rev. Reginald H. Thomas, 110 Pittston Blvd., Wilkes-Barre, PA 18702-9620 Tel. (570)823-3425

Recording Sec., Rev. Allan Rupert, 207 Whitmore Ave., Mayfield, PA 18433-1738 Tel. (570)876-2234

General. Sec., Rev. David Allen Jr., 1199 Lawrence St., Lowell, MA 01852-5526 Tel. (978)453-2052, pahson@earthlink.net

Treas., Mr. Raymond C. Baldwin, 18409 Mill Run Ct., Leesburg, VA 20176-4583, Rbaldwin32 @aol.com

Progressive National Baptist Convention, Inc.*

This body held its organizational meeting in Cincinnati in November, 1961. Subsequent regional sessions were followed by the first annual session in Philadelphia in 1962.

Headquarters

601 50th Street NE, Washington, D.C. 20019 Tel. (202)396-0558 Fax (202)398-4998

Media Contact, Gen. Sec., Dr. Tyrone S. Pitts

Officers

Pres., Dr. Bennett W. Smith, Sr., St. John Baptist Church, 184 Goodell St., Buffalo, NY 14204

Gen. Sec., Dr. Tyrone S. Pitts

OTHER ORGANIZATIONS

Dept. of Christian Education: Exec. Dir., Dr. C. B. Lucas, Emmanuel Baptist Church, 3815 W. Broadway, Louisville, KY 40211

Women's Dept.: Mildred Wormley, 218 Spring St., Trenton, NJ 08618

Home Mission Bd.: Exec. Dir., Rev. Archie LeMone Jr.

Congress of Christian Education: Pres., Rev. Harold S. Diggs, Mayfield Memorial Baptist Church, 700 Sugar Creek Rd. W, Charlotte, NC 28213

Baptist Global Mission Bureau: Dr. Ronald K. Hill, 161-163 60th St., Philadelphia, PA 19139

Nannie Helen Burroughs School Tel. (202)398-5266

Periodicals

Baptist Progress

Protestant Reformed Churches in America

The Protestant Reformed Churches (PRC) have their roots in the sixteenth century Reformation of Martin Luther and John Calvin, as it developed in the Dutch Reformed churches. The denomination originated as a result of a controversy in the Christian Reformed Church in 1924 involving the adoption of the "Three Points of Common Grace." Three ministers in the Christian Reformed Church—the Reverends Herman Hoeksema, George Ophoff, and Henry Danhof—and their consistories (Eastern Avenue, Hope, and Kalamazoo, respectively) rejected the doctrine. Eventually these men were deposed, and their consistories were either deposed or set outside the Christian Reformed Church. The denomination was formed in 1926 with three congregations. Today the denomination is comprised of some twenty-seven churches (more than 6,000 members) in the USA and Canada.

The presbyterian form of church government as determined by the Church Order of Dordt is followed by the PRC. The doctrinal standards of the PRC are the Reformed confessions—the Heidelberg Catechism, Belgic Confession of Faith, and Canons of Dordrecht. The doctrine of the covenant is a cornerstone of their teaching. They maintain an unconditional, particular covenant of grace that God establishes with His elect.

Headquarters

16511 South Park Ave., South Holland, IL 60473 Tel. (708)333-1314

Website: www.prca.org

Media Contact, Stat. Clk., Don Doezema, 4949 Ivanrest Ave., Grandville, MI 49418 Tel. (616)531-1490, doezema@prca.org

Officers

Stat. Clk., Don Doezema, 4949 Ivanrest Ave., Grandville, MI 49418 Tel. (616)531-1490, Fax (616)531-3033, doezema@prca.org

Periodicals

The Standard Bearer

Quakers—See Friends

Reformed Catholic Church

The Reformed Catholic Church was founded in 1988 and incorporated in 1989 as an alternative to the structures and strictures of the Roman Catholic Church, without denying basic catholic beliefs of faith and love, spirituality and community, prayer and sacramentality. The Reformed Catholic Church is a federation of independent churches offering a progressive alternative in the Catholic tradition. It is a newly formed rite, as in the tradition of the Orthodox churches of the Catholic tradition and the Old Catholic Church of Utrecht. It remains a Catholic Church, and its priets are considered Catholic priests.

Headquarters

Good Shepherd Rectory, P.O. Box 725, Hampton Bays, NY 11946 Tel. (516)723-2012

Email: berzol@apollo3.com

Website: www.geocities.com/WestHollywood/4136/

Media Contact, Archbishop, Most Rev. Robert J. Allmen, DD

Officers

Archbishop, Most Rev. Robert J. Allmen, DD

Reformed Church in America*

The Reformed Church in America was established in 1628 by the earliest settlers of New York. It is the oldest Protestant denomination with a continuous ministry in North America.

Until 1867 it was known as the Reformed Protestant Dutch Church.

The first ordained minister, Domine Jonas Michaelius, arrived in New Amsterdam from The Netherlands in 1628. Throughout the colonial period, the Reformed Church lived under the authority of the Classis of Amsterdam. Its churches were clustered in New York and New Jersey. Under the leadership of Rev. John Livingston, it became a denomination independent of the authority of the Classis of Amsterdam in 1776. Its geographical base was broadened in the 19th century by the immigration of Reformed Dutch and German settlers in the midwestern United States. The Reformed Church now spans the United States and Canada.

The Reformed Church in America accepts as its standards of faith the Heidelberg Catechism, Belgic Confession, and Canons of Dort. It has a rich heritage of world mission activity. It claims to be loyal to reformed tradition which emphasizes obedience to God in all aspects of life.

Although the Reformed Church in America has worked in close cooperation with other churches, it has never entered into merger with any other denomination. It is a member of the World Alliance of Reformed Churches, the World Council of Churches, and the National Council of the Churches of Christ in the United States of America. In 1998 it also entered into a relationship of full communion with the Evangelical Lutheran Church in America, Presbyterian Church (USA), and the United Church of Christ by way of the Formula of Agreement.

Headquarters

475 Riverside Dr., New York, NY 10115 Tel. (212)870-2841 Fax (212)870-2499

Email: kbaker@rca.org

Website: www.rca.org

Media Contact, Communication Officer, Phil Tanis, 4500 60th St. SE, Grand Rapids, MI 49512 Tel. (616)698-7071 Fax (616)698-6606

OFFICERS AND STAFF OF GENERAL SYNOD

Pres., The Rev. David Schutt, 475 Riverside Dr., 18th Floor, New York, NY 10115

Gen. Synod Council, Moderator, The Rev. Steven Brooks, 475 Riverside Dr., 18th Floor, New York, NY 10115

Gen. Sec., The Rev. Wesley Granberg-Michaelson, 475 Riverside Dr., 18th Floor, New York, NY 10115

Policy, Planning & Administrative Services, Dir. & Assistant Sec., The Rev. Kenneth Bradsell

Office of Ministry Services, Dir., The Rev. Dr. Gregg Mast

Congregational Services/Evangelism & Church Development Services, Dir., The Rev. Richard Welscott

Finance Services, Treas., Ms. Susan Converse

Mission Services, Dir., The Rev. Bruce Menning

African-American Council, Exec. Dir., The Rev. Dr. Glen Missick

Council for Hispanic Ministries, Exec. Sec., The Rev. Brigido Cabrera

Native American Indian Ministries Council, -vacant-

Council for Pacific/Asian-American Ministries, Exec. Sec., Ms. Ella Campbell

OTHER ORGANIZATIONS

Board of Benefits Services, Dir., Mr. Jack Dalenberg, 7 Salt Creek Ln., Suite 107, Hinsdale, IL 60521; Pres., The Rev. Robert White; Sec., The Rev. Kenneth Bradsell

RCA Foundation, Dir., Mr. Larryl Humme, 7 Salt Creek Ln., Suite 107, Hinsdale, IL 60521

RCA Building and Extension Fund, Fund Exec., Mr. Paul Karssen, 612 8th St. SE, Orange City, IA 51014

Periodicals

Perspectives, The Church Herald

Reformed Church in the United States

Lacking pastors, early German Reformed immigrants to the American colonies were led in worship by "readers." One reader, schoolmaster John Philip Boehm, organized the first congregations near Philadelphia in 1725. A Swiss pastor, Michael Schlatter, was sent by the Dutch Reformed Church in 1746. Strong ties with the Netherlands existed until the formation of the Synod of the German Reformed Church in 1793.

The Eureka Classis—organized in North and South Dakota in 1910 and strongly influenced by the writings of H. Kohlbruegge, P. Geyser, and J. Stark—refused to become part of the 1934 merger of the Reformed Church with the Evangelical Synod of North America, holding that it sacrificed the Reformed heritage. (The merged Evangelical and Reformed Church became part of the United Church of Christ in 1957.) Under the leadership of pastors W. Grossmann and W. J. Krieger, the Eureka Classis in 1942 incorporated as the continuing Reformed Church in the United States.

The growing Eureka Classis dissolved in 1986 to form a Synod with four regional classes. An heir to the Reformation theology of Zwingli and Calvin, the Heidelberg Catechism, the Belgic Confession, and the Canons of Dort are used as the confessional standards of the church. The Bible is strictly held to be the inerrant, infallible Word of God.

The RCUS supports Dordt College, Mid-America Reformed Seminary, New Geneva Theological Seminary, West Minster Theological Seminary in California, and Hope Haven. The RCUS is the official sponsor to the Reformed Confessing Church of Zaire.

Headquarters

Media Contact, Rev. Frank Walker Th.M., 6121

Pine Vista Way, Elk Grove City, CA 95758-4205 Tel. (661)827-9885
Email: TriWheeler@aol.com
Website: www.rcus.org

Officers

Pres., Rev. Vernon Pollema, 235 James Street, Shafter, CA 93263 Tel. (661)746-6907

Vice Pres., Rev. Robert Grossmann, Th.M., 1905 200th St., Garner, IA 50438 Tel. (515)923-3060

Stated Clk., Rev. Frank Walker Th.M., 5601 Spring Blossom St., Bakersfield, CA 93313-6025 Tel. (661)827-9885

Treas., Clayton Greiman, 2115 Hwy. 69, Garner, IA 50438 Tel. (515)923-2950

Periodicals

Reformed Herald

Reformed Episcopal Church

The Reformed Episcopal Church was founded December 2, 1873 in New York City by Bishop George D. Cummins, an assistant bishop in the Protestant Episcopal Church from 1866 until 1873. Cummins and other evangelical Episcopalians were concerned about the exclusiveness propagated by what they perceived to be an excessive ritualism then sweeping the church. Throughout the late 1860s, evangelicals and ritualists clashed over ceremonies, vestments, open or closed communion, the Articles of Religion, interpretation of the meaning of the sacraments, and the understanding of Apostolic Succession.

In October, 1873, other bishops of the Episcopal Church publicly attacked Cummins in major newspapers for participating in an ecumenical communion service sponsored by the Evangelical Alliance. Cummins resigned from the Episcopal Church and drafted a call to organize a new Episcopal Church for the "purpose of restoring the old paths of their fathers." On December 2, 1873, a Declaration of Principles which expressed the evangelical understanding of the Articles of Religion was adopted. Dr. Charles Edward Cheney of Chicago was elected as bishop to serve with Bishop Cummins. The Second General Council, meeting in May 1874 in New York City, approved a Constitution and Canons and adopted the 1785 Proposed Book of Common Prayer for use in the new Church.

In recent years the Reformed Episcopal Church has revised the Prayer Book to conform to the 1662 and 1928 Books of Common Prayer. The Church still embraces the Thirty Nine Articles of Religion, and has approved the Chicago-Lambeth Quadrilateral of 1886-1888.

There are presently five geographic diocese in the United States and Canada, as well as various missionary jurisdictions including India, Liberia, the West Indies, and others.

The Reformed Episcopal Church is a member of the National Association of Evangelicals.

Headquarters

826 2nd Ave, Blue Bell, PA 19422-1257 Tel. (215)483-1196 Fax (215)483-5235
Email: wycliffe@jps.net
Website: recus.org
Media Contact, Rt. Rev. Leonard Riches
Media Contact, Rt. Rev. Royal U. Grote Jr., Church Growth Office, 211 Byrne Ave., Houston, TX 77009 Tel. (713)862-4929

Officers

Pres. & Presiding Bishop, Rt. Rev. Leonard W. Riches

Vice Pres., Rt. Rev. Royal U. Grote Jr.

Sec., Rev. Walter Banek

Treas., Rev. Jon W. Abboud

OTHER ORGANIZATIONS

Bd. of Foreign Missions: Pres., Dr. Barbara J. West, 316 Hunters Rd., Swedesboro, NJ 08085 Tel. (609)467-1641

Bd. of Natl. Church Extension: Pres., Rt. Rev. Royal U. Grote Jr., 211 Byrne Ave., Houston, TX 77009 Tel. (713)862-4929

Publication Society: Pres., Rt. Rev. Royal U. Grote; Orders, Rev. Jonathan S. Riches, 7372 Henry Ave., Philadelphia, PA 19128 Tel. (215)956-0655

The Reapers: Pres., Susan Higham, 472 Leedom St., Jenkintown, PA 19046

Committee on Women's Work: Pres., Joan Workowski, 1162 Beverly Rd., Rydal, PA 19046

BISHOPS

Leonard W. Riches Sr., 85 Smithtown Rd., Pipersville, PA 18947 Tel. (215)483-1196 Fax (215)294-8009

Royal U. Grote Jr., 211 Byrne Ave., Houston, TX 77009

James C. West Sr., 408 Red Fox Run, Summerville, SC 29485

Robert H. Booth, 1611 Park Ave., #212, Quakertown, PA 18951

Gregory K. Hotchkiss, 318 E. Main St., Somerville, NJ 08876

George B. Fincke, 155 Woodstock Circle, Vacaville, CA 95687-3381

Daniel R. Morse, 11259 Wexford Dr., Eads, TN 38025

Michael Fedechko, Box 2532, New Liskeard, ON P0J 1P0

Charles W. Dorrington, 626 Blanshard St., Victoria, BC V8W 3G6

Ray R. Sutton, 3421 Madison Park Blvd., Shreveport, LA 71104

Periodicals

Reformed Episcopalians

Reformed Mennonite Church

This is a small group of believers in Pennsylvania, Ohio, Michigan, Illinois, and Ontario, Canada who believe in nonresistance of evil, nonconformity to the world, and who practice separation from unfaithful worship. They believe that Christian unity is the effect of brotherly love and are of one mind and spirit. Their church was established in 1812 by John Herr who agreed with the teachings of Menno Simon as well as those of Jesus Christ.

Headquarters

Lancaster County only: Reformed Mennonite Church, 602 Strasburg Pike, Lancaster, PA 17602

Media Contact, Bishop, Glenn M. Gross Tel. (717)697-4623

Officers

Bishop Glenn M. Gross, 906 Grantham Rd., Mechanicsburg, PA 17055

Reformed Methodist Union Episcopal Church

The Reformed Methodist Union Episcopal church was formed after a group of ministers withdrew from the African Methodist Episcopal Church following a dispute over the election of ministerial delegates to the General Conference.

These ministers organized the Reformed Methodist Union church during a four-day meeting beginning on January 22, 1885 at Hills Chapel (now known as Mt. Hermon RMUE church), in Charleston, S.C. The Rev. William E. Johnson was elected president of the new church. Following the death of Rev. Johnson in 1896, it was decided that the church would conform to regular American Methodism (the Episcopacy). The first Bishop, Edward Russell Middleton, was elected, and "Episcopal" was added to the name of the church. Bishop Middleton was consecrated on Dec. 5, 1896, by Bishop P. F. Stephens of the Reformed Episcopal Church.

Headquarters

1136 Brody Ave., Charleston, SC 29407

Media Contact, Gen. Secretary, Brother Willie B. Oliver, P.O. Box 1995, Orangeburg, SC 29116 Tel. (803)536-3293

Officers

Bishop, Rt. Rev. Leroy Gethers Tel. (803)766-3534

Asst. Bishop, Rt. Rev. Jerry M. DeVoe Jr.

Gen. Sec., Brother Willie B. Oliver

Treas., Rev. Daniel Green

Sec. of Education, Rev. William Polite

Sec. of Books Concerns, Sister Ann Blanding

Sec. of Pension Fund, Rev. Joseph Powell

Sec. of Church Extension, Brother William Parker

Sec. of Sunday School Union, Sister Wine

Sec. of Mission, Rev. Warren Hatcher

Reformed Presbyterian Church of North America

Also known as the Church of the Covenanters, this church's origin dates back to the Reformation days of Scotland when the Covenanters signed their "Covenants" in resistance to the king and the Roman Church in the enforcement of state church practices. The Church in America has signed two "Covenants" in particular, those of 1871 and 1954.

Headquarters

Media Contact, Stated Clk., Louis D. Hutmire, 7408 Penn Ave., Pittsburgh, PA 15208 Tel. (412)731-1177 Fax (412)731-8861

Email: RPTrustees@aol.com

Website: www.reformedpresbyterian.org/

Officers

Mod., Rev. William J. Edgar, 25 Lawrence Rd., Broomall, PA 19008 Tel. (610)353-1371

Clk., J. Bruce Martin, 310 Main St., Ridgefield Park, NJ 07660 Tel. (201)440-5993

Asst. Clk., Raymond E. Morton, 411 N. Vine St., Sparta, IL 62286 Tel. (618)443-3419

Stated Clk., Louis D. Hutmire, 7408 Penn Ave., Pittsburgh, PA 15208 Tel. (412)731-1177

Periodicals

The Covenanter Witness

Reformed Zion Union Apostolic Church

This group was organized in 1869 at Boydton, Va., by Elder James R. Howell of New York, a minister of the AME Zion Church, with doctrines of the Methodist Episcopal Church.

Headquarters

Rt. 1, Box 64 D, Dundas, VA 23938 Tel. (804) 676-8509

Media Contact, Bishop G. W. Studivant

Officers

Exec. Brd., Chair, Rev. Hilman Wright Tel. (804)447-3988

Sec., Joseph Russell Tel. (804)634-4520

Religious Society of Friends (Conservative)

These Friends mark their present identity from separations occurring by regions at different times from 1845 to 1904. They hold to a minimum of organizational structure. Their meetings for worship—which are unprogrammed and based on silent, expectant waiting upon the Lord—demonstrate the belief that all individuals may commune directly with God and may share equally in vocal ministry.

They continue to stress the importance of the Living Christ and the experience of the Holy Spirit working with power in the lives of individuals who obey it.

YEARLY MEETINGS

North Carolina YM: Robert Gosner, P.O. Box 489, Woodland, NC 27897 Tel. (252)587-2571

Iowa YM: Deborah Frisch, Clerk, 916 41st St., Des Moines, Iowa 50312-2612

Ohio YM: S. S. Smith, Clerk, 61830 Sandy Ridge Rd., Barnesville, OH 43713

Religious Society of Friends (Unaffiliated Meetings)

Though all groups of Friends acknowledge the same historical roots, 19th-century divisions in theology and experience led to some of the current organizational groupings. Many newer yearly meetings, often marked by spontaneity, variety, and experimentation and hoping for renewed Quaker unity, have chosen not to identify with past divisions by affiliating in traditional ways with the larger organizations within the Society. Some of these unaffiliated groups have begun within the past 25 years.

YEARLY MEETINGS

Central Yearly Meeting (I): Supt., Jonathan Edwards, 5597 West County Rd., 700 N, Ridgeville, IN 47380 Tel. (765)857-2347 Fax (765)857-2347

Intermountain Yearly Meeting (I): Clerk, Ted Church, 10801 Lagrima de Oro N.E.- Apt 86,1 Albuquerque, NM 87111 Tel. (505)898-5306, Fax (505)899-0936, tchurch@comcast.net

North Pacific Yearly Meeting (I): Contact,, Helen Dart, 3311 NW Polk, Corvallis, OR 97330 Tel. (541)485-6589, Fax (541)345-7664, npym@teleport.com

Pacific Yearly Meeting (I): Clerk, Shan Cretin, 402 15th St., Santa Monica, CA 90402-2232 Tel. (301)393-7660, pacificym@juno.com

Membership

Central Yearly Meeting: 287 Members

Intermountain Yearly Meeting: 997 Members

North Pacific Yearly Meeting: 865 Members

Pacific Yearly Meeting: 1,480 Members

Periodicals

Friends Bulletin

The Romanian Orthodox Church in America

The Romanian Orthodox Church in America is an autonomous Archdiocese chartered under the name of "Romanian Orthodox Archdiocese in America." The diocese was founded in 1929 and approved by the Holy Synod of the Romanian Orthodox Church in Romania in 1934. The Holy Synod of the Romanian Orthodox Church granted ecclesiastical autonomy in American Diocese on July 12, 1950. The Diocese continues to hold dogmatic and canonical ties with the Holy Synod and the Romanian Orthodox Patriarchate of Romania.

In 1951, approximately 40 parishes with their clergy from the United States and Canada separated from this church. In 1960, they joined the Russian Orthodox Greek Catholic Metropolia, now called the Orthodox Church in America, which reordained for these parishes a bishop with the title "Bishop of Detroit and Michigan."

On June 11, 1973 the Holy Synod of the Romanian Orthodox church elevated the Bishop of Romanian Orthodox Missionary Episcopate in America to the rank of Archbishop.

Headquarters

P.O. Box 27, Skokie, IL 60076-0027 Tel. (847)674-3900, Fax (847)674-4110

Email: ArchNicolae@aol.com

Website: www.romarch.org

Media Contact, Archdiocesan Secretary, V. Rev. Fr. Nicholas Apostola, 44 Midland St., Worcester, MA 01602-4217 Tel. (508)845-0088, Fax (508)845-8850, Nicholas.Apostola@verizon.net

Officers

Archbishop, His Eminence Dr. Nicolae Condrea, P.O. Box 27, Skokie, IL 60076-0027 Tel. (847) 674-3900, Fax (847)674-4110, ArchNicolae@aol.com

Vicar, V. Rev. Fr. Ioan Ionita, 17601 Wentworth Ave., Lansing, IL 60438-2074 Tel./Fax (708) 474-0340, Tintari@aol.com

Inter-Church Relations, Dir., V. Rev. Fr. Nicholas Apostola, 44 Midland St., Worcester, MA 01602-4217 Tel. (508)845-0088 Fax (508) 845-8850, Nicholas.Apostola@verizon.net

Periodicals

Credinta-The Faith

The Romanian Orthodox Episcopate of America

This body of Eastern Orthodox Christians of Romanian descent is part of the Autocephalous Orthodox Church in America; for complete description and listing of officers, please see its entry in Directory 3, "Religious Bodies in the United States."

Headquarters

2525 Grey Tower Rd., Jackson, MI 49201 Tel. (517)522-4800; Mailing Address: P.O. Box 309, Grass Lake, MI 49240-0309

Email: roeasolia@aol.com

Website: www.roea.org

Media Contact, Ed.-Sec., Rev. Protodeacon David Oancea, P.O. Box 185, Grass Lake, MI 49240-0185 Tel. (517)522-3656

Officers

Ruling Hierarch, Most Rev. Archbishop Nathaniel Popp

Dean for All Canada and the Western Provinces, Very Rev. Daniel Nelson , 2855 Helmsing St., Regina, SK S4V OW7 Tel. (306)761-2379

Periodicals

Solia–The Herald, Good News–Buna Vestire (in Canada only)

The Russian Orthodox Church Outside of Russia

This group was organized in 1920 to unite in one body of dioceses the missions and parishes of the Russian Orthodox Church outside of Russia. The governing body, set up in Constantinople, was sponsored by the Ecumenical Patriarchate. In November 1950, it came to the United States. The Russian Orthodox Church Outside of Russia emphasizes being true to the old traditions of the Russian Church. It is not in communion with the Moscow Patriarchate.

Headquarters

75 E. 93rd St., New York, NY 10128 Tel. (212) 534-1601 Fax (212)426-1086

Media Contact, Dep. Sec., Bishop Gabriel

Synod of Bishops

Pres., His Eminence Metropolitan Vitaly

Sec., Archbishop of Syracuse and Trinity, Laurus

Dep. Sec., Bishop of Manhattan, Gabriel Tel. (212)722-6577

Periodicals

Living Orthodoxy, Orthodox Family, Orthodox Russia (Russian), *Orthodox Voices, Pravoslavnaya Rus, Pravoslavnaya Zhisn, Orthodox America*

The Salvation Army

The Salvation Army—founded in 1865 by William Booth (1829-1912) in London, England, and introduced into America in 1880—is an international religious and charitable movement organized and operated on a paramilitary pattern and is a branch of the Christian church. To carry out its purposes, The Salvation Army has established a widely diversified program of religious and social welfare services which are designed to meet the needs of children, youth, and adults in all age groups.

Headquarters

615 Slaters Ln., Alexandria, VA 22313 Tel. (703) 684-5500 Fax (703)684-5538

Media Contact, Community Relations & Devel., Major George Hood Tel. (703)684-5526 Fax . . .

Officers

Natl. Commander, Commissioner W. Todd Bassett

Natl. Chief Sec., Lt. Colonel Larry Bosh

Media Contact, Community Relations & Devel., Major George Hood

TERRITORIAL ORGANIZATIONS

Central Territory: 10 W. Algonquin Rd., Des Plaines, IL 60016 Tel. (847)294-2000 Fax (847)294-2299, Territorial Commander, Commissioner Kenneth Baillie

Eastern Territory: 440 W. Nyack Rd., P.O. Box C-635, West Nyack, NY 10994 Tel. (914)620-7200 Fax (914)620-7766, Territorial Commander, Commissioner Lawrence Moretz

Southern Territory: 1424 Northeast Expressway, Atlanta, GA 30329 Tel. (404)728-1300 Fax (404)728-1331, Territorial Commander, Commissioner Philip Needham

Western Territory: 180 E. Ocean Blvd., Long Beach, CA Tel. (562)436-7000 Fax (562)491-8792, Territorial Commander, Commissioner Linda Bond

Periodicals

The War Cry

The Schwenkfelder Church

The Schwenkfelders are the spiritual descendants of the Silesian nobleman Caspar Schwenkfeld von Ossig (1489-1561), a scholar, reformer, preacher, and prolific writer who endeavored to aid in the cause of the Protestant Reformation. A contemporary of Martin Luther, John Calvin, Ulrich Zwingli, and Phillip Melanchthon, Schwenkfeld sought no following, formulated no creed, and did not attempt to organize a church based on his beliefs. He labored for liberty of religious belief, for a fellowship of all believers and for one united Christian church.

He and his cobelievers supported a movement known as the Reformation by the Middle Way. Persecuted by state churches, ultimately 180 Schwenkfelders exiled from Silesia emigrated to Pennsylvania. They landed at Philadelphia on Sept. 22, 1734. In 1782, the Society of Schwenkfelders, the forerunner of the present Schwenkfelder Church, was formed. The church was incorporated in 1909.

The General Conference of the Schwenkfelder Church is a voluntary association for the Schwenkfelder Churches at Palm, Worcester, Lansdale, Norristown, and Philadelphia, Penn.

They practice adult baptism and dedication of children, and observe the Lord's Supper regularly with open Communion. In theology, they are Christo-centric; in polity, congregational; in missions, world-minded; in ecclesiastical organization, ecumenical.

The ministry is recruited from graduates of colleges, universities, and accredited theological seminaries. The churches take leadership in ecumenical concerns through ministerial associations, community service and action groups, councils of Christian education, and other agencies.

Headquarters

105 Seminary St., Pennsburg, PA 18073 Tel. (215)679-3103

Media Contact, Dennis Moyer

Officers

Mod., John Graham, Collegeville, PA 19426

Sec., Frances Witte, Central Schwenkfelder Church, Worcester, PA 19490

Treas., Syl Rittenhouse, 1614 Kriebel Rd., Lansdale, PA 19446

Periodicals

The Schwenkfeldian

Separate Baptists in Christ

The Separate Baptists in Christ are a group of Baptists found in Indiana, Ohio, Kentucky, Tennessee, Virginia, West Virginia, Florida, and North Carolina dating back to an association formed in 1758 in North Carolina and Virginia.

Today this group consists of approximately 100 churches. They believe in the infallibility of the Bible, the divine ordinances of the Lord's Supper, feetwashing, baptism, and that those who endureth to the end shall be saved.

The Separate Baptists are Arminian in doctrine, rejecting both the doctrines of predestination and eternal security of the believer.

At the 1991 General Association, an additional article of doctrine was adopted. "We believe that at Christ's return in the clouds of heaven all Christians will meet the Lord in the air, and time shall be no more," thus leaving no time for a literal one thousand year reign. Seven associations comprise the General Association of Separate Baptists.

Headquarters

Media Contact, Clk., Greg Erdman, 10102 N. Hickory Ln., Columbus, IN 47203 Tel. (812)526-2540

Email: mail@separatebaptist.org

Website: www.separatebaptist.org

Officers

Mod., Rev. Jim Goff, 1020 Gagel Ave., Louisville, KY 40216

Asst. Mod., Rev. Jimmy Polston, 785 Kitchen Rd., Mooresville, IN 46158 Tel. (317)831-6745

Clk., Greg Erdman, 10102 N. Hickory Ln., Columbus, IN 47203 Tel. (812)526-2540

Asst. Clk., Rev. Mattew Cowan, 174 Oak Hill School Rd., Lot 30, Smiths Grove, KY 42171 Tel. (270)678-5599

Serbian Orthodox Church in the USA and Canada*

The Serbian Orthodox Church is an organic part of the Eastern Orthodox Church. As a local church it received its autocephaly from Constantinople in 1219 A.D.

In 1921, a Serbian Orthodox Diocese in the United States of America and Canada was organized; in 1963, it was reorganized into three dioceses; and in 1983 a fourth diocese was created for the Canadian part of the church. The Serbian Orthodox Church in the USA and Canada received its administrative autonomy in 1928. However, it remains canonically an integral part of the Serbian Orthodox Patriarchate with its See in Belgrade. The Serbian Orthodox Church is in absolute doctrinal unity with all other local Orthodox Churches.

Headquarters

St. Sava Monastery, P.O. Box 519, Libertyville, IL 60048 Tel. (847)367-0698

Email: oea@oea.serbian-church.net

Website: oea.serbian-church.net/

Bishops

Metropolitan of Midwestern America, Most Rev. Metropolitan Christopher

Bishop of Canada, Georgije, 5A Stockbridge Ave., Toronto, ON M8Z 4M6 Tel. (416)231-4009

Bishop of Eastern America, Rt. Rev. Bishop Mitrophan, P.O. Box 368, Sewickley, PA 15143 Tel. (412)741-5686

Diocese of Western America, Bishop Jovan, 2541 Crestline Terr., Alhambra, CA 91803 Tel. (818)264-6825

OTHER ORGANIZATIONS

Brotherhood of Serbian Orth. Clergy in USA & Canada: Pres., V. Rev. Nedeljko Lunich, Joliet, IL, Merrilville, IN

Federation of Circles of Serbian Sisters

Serbian Singing Federation

Periodicals

The Path of Orthodoxy

Seventh-day Adventist Church

The Seventh-day Adventist Church grew out of a worldwide religious revival in the mid-19th century. People of many religious persuasions believed Bible prophecies indicated that the second coming or advent of Christ was imminent.

When Christ did not come in the 1840s, a group of these disappointed Adventists in the United States continued their Bible studies and concluded they had misinterpreted prophetic events and that the second coming of Christ was still in the future. This same group of Adventists later accepted the teaching of the seventh-day Sabbath and became known as Seventh-day Adventists. The denomination organized formally in 1863.

The church was largely confined to North America until 1874, when its first missionary was sent to Europe. Today, over 53,502 congregations meet in 203 countries. Membership exceeds 12 million and increases between four and a half to five percent each year.

In addition to a mission program, the church has the largest worldwide Protestant parochial school system with approximately 5,650 schools with more than 1,056,000 students on elementary through college and university levels.

The Adventist Development and Relief Agency (ADRA) helps victims of war and natural disasters, and many local congregations have community service facilities to help those in need close to home.

The church also has a worldwide publishing ministry with 56 printing facilities producing magazines and other publications in over 343 languages and dialects. In the United States and Canada, the church sponsors a variety of radio and television programs, including *Christian Lifestyle* Magazine, It Is Written, Breath of Life, Ayer, Hoy, y Mañana, Voice of Prophecy, and La Voz de la Esperanza.

The North American Division of Seventh-day Adventist includes 58 Conferences which are grouped together into nine organized Union Conferences. The various Conferences work under the general direction of these Union Conferences.

Headquarters

12501 Old Columbia Pike, Silver Spring, MD 20904-6600 Tel. (301)680-6000
Email: kjones@gc.adventist.org
Website: www.adventist.org
Media Contact, Dir., Archives & Statistics, Bert Haloviak

WORLDWIDE OFFICERS

Pres., Jan Paulsen
Sec., Matthew A. Bediako
Treas., Robert E. Lemon

WORLDWIDE DEPARTMENTS

Adventist Chaplaincy Ministries: Dir., Richard O. Stenbakken
Children's Ministries: Dir., Linda Koh
Education: Dir., C. Garland Dulan
Communication: Dir., Rajmund Dabrowski
Family Ministries: Dir., Ronald M. Flowers
Health Ministries: Dir., Allan R. Handysides
Ministerial Assoc.: Dir., James A. Cress
Public Affairs & Religious Liberty: Dir., John Graz
Publishing: Dir., Jose Luis Campos
Sabbath School & Personal Ministries: James W. Zackrison
Stewardship: Dir., Benjamin C. Maxson
Trust Services: Jeffrey K. Wilson
Women's Ministries: Ardis D. Stenbakken
Youth: Baraka G. Muganda

NORTH AMERICAN OFFICERS

Pres., Don C. Schneider
Vice Pres., Debra Brill, Clarence E. Hodges, James W. Gilley, Gerald Kovalski, Alvin M. Kibble, Manuel Vasquez
Sec., Roscoe J. Howard III
Assoc. Sec., Rosa T. Banks
Treas., Juan R. Prestol
Assoc. Treas., Michael Park, Del L. Johnson, Kenneth W. Osborn

NORTH AMERICAN ORGANIZATIONS

Atlantic Union Conf.: Pres., Donald G. King, P.O. Box 1189, South Lancaster, MA 01561-1189
Canada: Seventh-day Adventist Church in Canada (see Directory 4, "Religious Bodies in Canada")
Columbia Union Conf.: Pres., Harold L. Lee, 5427 Twin Knolls Rd., Columbia, MD 21045
Lake Union Conf.: Pres., Walter L. Wright, P.O. Box C, Berrien Springs, MI 49103
Mid-America Union Conf.: Pres., Dennis N. Carlson, P.O. Box 6128, Lincoln, NE 68506
North Pacific Union Conf.: Pres., Jere D. Patzer, P.O. Box 871150, Vancouver, WA 98687
Pacific Union Conf.: Pres., Thomas J. Mostert Jr., P.O. Box 5005, Westlake Village, CA 91359
Southern Union Conf.: Pres., Gordon L. Retzr, P.O. Box 849, Decatur, GA 30031
Southwestern Union Conf.: Pres., Max A. Trevino, P.O. Box 4000, Burleson, TX 76097

Periodicals

ADRA Works; Advent View; The Adventist Chaplain; Adventist Review; ASI Magazine; ASI Update; Audit Trails; AWR Transmissions; AWR Current; AWRecorder; AWResource; Children's Friend; Christian Record; Client Connection; College and University Dialogue; Collegiate Quarterly; Cornerstone Youth Resource Magazine; Cornerstone Connections; Elder's Digest; Encounter; For God and Country; Geoscience Reports; Guide, Insight; It is Written Channels; The Journal of Adventist Education; Kid's Ministry Ideas; Liberty; Lifeglow; Listen; Literature Evangelist; Message; Ministry, Mission—children, youth, adult; Origins; Our Little Friend; Primary Treasure; Publishing Mirror; Sabbath School Teaching Aids; Sabbath School Program Helps; Sabbath School Leadership; Shabbat Shalom; Shepherdess International Journal; Signs of the Times; The Student; Telenotes; Vibrant Life; Voice of Prophecy News; The Window; Winner; Women of Spirit; Young and Alive; Youth Ministry ACCENT

Seventh Day Baptist General Conference, USA and Canada

Seventh Day Baptists emerged during the English Reformation, organizing their first churches in the mid-1600s. The first Seventh Day Baptists of record in America were Stephen and Ann Mumford, who emigrated from England in 1664. Beginning in 1665 several members of the First Baptist Church at Newport, R.I. began observing the seventh day Sabbath, or Saturday. In 1671, five members, together with the Mumfords, formed the first Seventh Day Baptist Church in America at Newport.

Beginning about 1700, other Seventh Day Baptist churches were established in New Jersey and Pennsylvania. From these three centers, the denomination grew and expanded westward. They founded the Seventh Day Baptist General Conference in 1802.

The organization of the denomination reflects an interest in home and foreign missions, publications, and education. Women have been encouraged to participate. From the earliest years, religious freedom has been championed for all and the separation of church and state advocated.

Seventh Day Baptists are members of the Baptist World Alliance and Baptist Joint Committee. The Seventh Day Baptist World Federation has 17 member conferences on six continents.

Headquarters

Seventh Day Baptist Center, 3120 Kennedy Rd., P.O. Box 1678, Janesville, WI 53547-1678 Tel. (608)752-5055 Fax (608)752-7711
Email: sdbgen@inwave.com

Website: www.seventhdaybaptist.org
Media Contact, Ex. Sec., Calvin Babcock

OTHER ORGANIZATIONS

Seventh Day Baptist Missionary Society: Exec. Dir., Kirk Looper, 119 Main St., Westerly, RI 02891

Seventh Day Bapt. Bd. of Christian Ed.: Exec. Dir., Dr. Ernest K. Bee Jr., Box 115, Alfred Station, NY 14803

Women's Soc. of the Gen. Conference: Pres., Mrs. Ruth Probasco, 858 Barrett Run Rd., Bridgeton, NJ 08302

American Sabbath Tract & Comm. Council: Dir. of Communications, Rev. Kevin J. Butler, 3120 Kennedy Rd., P.O. Box 1678, Janesville, WI 53547

Seventh Day Baptist Historical Society: Historian, Don A. Sanford, 3120 Kennedy Rd., P.O. Box 1678, Janesville, WI 53547

Seventh Day Baptist Center on Ministry: Dir. of Pastoral Services, Rev. Rodney Henry, 3120 Kennedy Rd., P.O. Box 1678, Janesville, WI 53547

Periodicals

Sabbath Recorder

Southern Baptist Convention

The Southern Baptist Convention was organized on May 10, 1845 in Augusta, Ga.. Cooperating Baptist churches are located in all 50 states, the District of Columbia, Puerto Rico, American Samoa, and the Virgin Islands. The members of the churches work together through 1,198 district associations and 41 state conventions or fellowships. The Southern Baptist Convention has an Executive Committee and 12 national agencies—four boards, six seminaries, one commission, and one auxiliary organization.

The purpose of the Southern Baptist Convention is "to provide a general organization for Baptists in the United States and its territories for the promotion of Christian missions at home and abroad and any other objects such as Christian education, benevolent enterprises, and social services which it may deem proper and advisable for the furtherance of the Kingdom of God". (Constitution, Article II)

The Convention exists in order to help the churches lead people to God through Jesus Christ.

From the beginning, there has been a mission desire to share the Gospel with the peoples of the world. The Cooperative Program is the basic channel of mission support. In addition, the Lottie Moon Christmas Offering for Foreign Missions and the Annie Armstrong Easter Offering for Home Missions support Southern Baptists' world mission programs.

In 2002, there were more than 5,300 foreign missionaries serving in foreign countries and more than 5,200 home missionaries serving in North America.

Headquarters

901 Commerce St., Nashville, TN 37203 Tel. (615)244-2355

Website: www.sbc.net

Media Contact, Vice Pres. for Convention Relations, A. William Merrell Tel. (615)244-2355, Fax (615)782-8684, bmerrell@sbc.net

Officers

Pres., Jack Graham, 6801 W. Park Blvd., Plano, TX 75093

Recording Sec., John Yeats, P.O. Box 12130, Oklahoma City, OK 73112

Executive Committee: Pres., Morris H. Chapman; Vice Pres., Business & Finance, Jack Wilkerson; Vice Pres., Convention News, Will Hall; Vice Pres., Convention Relations, A. William Merrell; Vice Pres., Convention Policy, Augie Boto; Vice Pres., Cooperative Program, David E. Hankins

GENERAL BOARDS AND COMMISSION

International Mission Board: Pres., Jerry A. Rankin, 3806 Monument Ave, Richmond, VA 23230 Tel. (804)353-0151 ext. 1207

North American Mission Board: Pres., Robert E. Reccord, 4200 No. Point Pkwy, Alpharetta, GA 30022-4176 Tel. (770) 410-6000

Annuity Board: Pres., O. S. Hawkins, 2401 Cedar Springs Rd, Dallas, TX 75201 Tel. (214)720-0511

LifeWay Christian Resources: Pres., James T. Draper Jr., One Lifeway Plaza, Nashville, TN 37234 Tel. (615)251-2000

Ethics and Religious Liberty Commission: Pres., Richard D. Land, 901 Commerce St., Suite 550, Nashville, TN 37203 Tel. (615)244-2495

STATE CONVENTIONS

Alabama: Rick Lance, 2001 E. South Blvd., Montgomery, AL 36116 Tel. (334)288-2460

Alaska: David N. Baldwin, 1750 O'Malley Rd., Anchorage, AK 99507 Tel. (907)344-9627

Arizona: Steve Bass, 2240 N. Hayden Rd., Ste. 100 Scottsdale, AZ 85257 Tel. (480)945-0880

Arkansas: Emil Turner, 525 W. Capitol, Little Rock, AR 72201 Tel. (501)376-4791

California: Fermin A. Whittaker, 678 E. Shaw Ave., Fresno, CA 93710 Tel. (559)229-9533 ext. 230

Colorado: Mark Edlund, 7393 S. Alton Way, Centennial, CO 80112 Tel. (303)771-2480 ext. 222

District of Columbia: Rev. Jeffrey Haggray, 1628 16th St. NW, Washington, D.C. 20009 Tel. (202)265-1526

Florida: John Sullivan, 1230 Hendricks Ave., Jacksonville, FL 32207 Tel. (904)396-2351

Georgia: Dr. J. Robert White, 2930 Flowers Rd., S, Atlanta, GA 30341 Tel. (770)455-0404

Hawaii: Veryl F. Henderson, 2042 Vancouver Dr., Honolulu, HI 96822 Tel. (808)946-9581 ext. 229

Illinois: Exec. Dir, Wendell Lung, 3085 Stevenson Dr, Springfield, IL 62703 Tel. (217)786-2600

Indiana: Stephen P. Davis, 900 N. High School Rd., Indianapolis, IN 46214 Tel. (317)241-9317

Iowa: Jimmy L. Barrentine, Suite #27, 2400 86th St., Des Moines, IA 50322 Tel. (515)278-1566 ext. 1200

Kansas-Nebraska: R. Rex Lindsay, 5410 SW Seventh St., Topeka, KS 66606 Tel. (785)228-6800

Kentucky: Bill F. Mackey, 10701 Shelbyville Rd., Louisville, KY 40253-0433 Tel. (502) 245-4101

Louisiana: Dean Doster, 1250 MacArthur Dr., Alexandria, LA 71303 Tel. (318)448-3402

Maryland/Delaware: David H. Lee, 10255 Old Columbia Rd., Columbia, MD 21046 Tel. (410)290-5290

Michigan: Michael R. Collins, 64 W. Columbia Ave, Bldg. 2, Pontiac, MI 48340 Tel. (248)332-6426

Minnesota/Wisconsin: Leo Endel, Exec. Dir., 519 16th St. SE, Rochester, MN 55904 Tel. (507)282-3636

Mississippi: James R. Futral, 515 Mississippi St., Jackson, MS 39201 Tel. (601)968-3800

Missouri: Exec. Dir., David Clippard, 400 E. High Street, Jefferson City, MO 65101 Tel. (573)635-7931

Nevada: Thane Barnes, Exec. Dir., 406 California Ave., Reno, NV 89509 Tel. (775)786-0406

New England: James Wideman, 87 Lincoln St., Northboro, MA 01532 Tel. (508)393-6013 ext. 224

New Mexico: Claude W. Cone, 5325 Wyoming NE, Albuquerque, NM 87109 Tel. (505)924-2300

New York: J. B. Graham, 6538 Baptist Way, East Syracuse, NY 13057 Tel. (315)433-1001

North Carolina: James H. Royston, 205 Convention Dr., Cary, NC 27511 Tel. (919) 467-5100, ext. 102

Northwest, Jeff Iorg, 3200 NE 109th Ave., Vancouver, WA 98682 Tel. (360)882-2100 ext. 121

Ohio: Exec. Dir., Jack P. Kwok, 1680 E. Broad St., Columbus, OH 43203 Tel. (614)258-8491

Oklahoma: Anthony L. Jordan, 3800 N. May Ave., Oklahoma City, OK 73112 Tel. (405)942-3800

Pennsylvania/South Jersey: David C. Waltz, 4620 Fritchey St., Harrisburg, PA 17109 Tel. (717) 652-5856

South Carolina: B. Carlisle Driggers, 190 Stoneridge Dr., Columbia, SC 29210 Tel. (803)765-0030

Tennessee: James M. Porch, 5001 Maryland Way, Brentwood, TN 37027 Tel. (615)371-2090

Texas: (BGCT) Baptist General Convention of Texas, Charles R. Wade, 333 N. Washington, Dallas, TX 75246 Tel. (214)828-5100

Texas: (SBTC) Southern Baptists of Texas, James W. Richards, 1304 W. Walnut Hill Ln., Suite 220, Irving, TX 75038 Tel. (972)953-0878

Utah-Idaho: Tim Clark, P.O. Box 1347, Draper, UT 84020 Tel. (801)572-5350

Virginia: (BGAV) Baptist General Association of Virginia, John V. Upton Jr., 2828 Emerywood Pkwy, Richmond, VA 23226 Tel. (804)915-2430

Virginia: (SBCV) Southern Baptist Conservatives of Virginia, H. Doyle Chauncey, 4101 Cox Rd., Suite 100, Glen Allen, VA 23060 Tel. (804)270-1848

West Virginia: Terry L. Harper, Number One Missions Way, Scott Depot, WV 25560 Tel. (304)757-0944

Wyoming: Randy Sprinkle, 3925 Casper Mountain Rd., Casper, WY 82601 Tel. (307) 472-4087

FELLOWSHIPS

Dakota Southern Baptist Fellowship: W.D. "Doc" Lindsey, P.O. Box 6028, Bismarck, ND 58506 Tel. (701)255-3765

Montana Southern Baptist Fellowship: Jeffery A. Clark, 1130 Cerise Rd., Billings, MT 59101 Tel. (406)252-7537

Canadian Convention of Southern Baptists: Gerry Taillon, 100 Convention Way, Cochrane, Alberta T4C 2G2 Tel. (403)932-5688

Periodicals

The Commission, SBC Life, On Mission

Southern Methodist Church

Organized in 1939, this body is composed of congregations desirous of continuing in true Biblical Methodism and preserving the fundamental doctrines and beliefs of the Methodist Episcopal Church, South. These congregations declined to be a party to the merger of the Methodist Episcopal Church; The Methodist Episcopal Church, South; and the Methodist Protestant Church into The Methodist Church.

Headquarters

P.O. Box 39, Orangeburg, SC 29116-0039 Tel. (803)536-1378 Fax (803)535-3881

Email: smchq@juno.com

Media Contact, Pres., Rev. Bedford F. Landers

Officers

Pres., Rev. Bedford F. Landers

Dir. of Admin. & Fin., Rev. Dan Shapley

Dir. of Foreign Missions, Rev. Paul Zellmer, P.O. Box 39, Orangeburg, SC 29116-0039

Southern Methodist College: Pres., position vacant, P.O. Box 1027, Orangeburg, SC 29116-1027

The Eastern Conf.: Vice Pres., Rev. John T. Hucks Jr., 221 Pinewood Dr., Rowesville, SC 29133

Alabama/Florida/Georgia Conf.: Vice Pres., Rev. Bob Waites, 220 South Trace Lane, Hooves, AL 35244

Mid-South Conf.: Vice Pres.,

South-Western Conf.: Vice Pres., Rev. Ira Schilling, 106 Albert Dr., Haughton, LA 71037

Gen. Conf., Treas., Rev. Dan Shapley, P.O. Drawer A, Orangeburg, SC 29116-0039

Periodicals

The Southern Methodist

Sovereign Grace Believers

The Sovereign Grace Believers are a contemporary movement which began its stirrings in the mid-1950s when some pastors in traditional Baptist churches returned to a Calvinist theological perspective.

The first "Sovereign Grace" conference was held in Ashland, Ky., in 1954 and since then conferences of this sort have been sponsored by various local churches on the West Coast, Southern and Northern states, and Canada. This movement is a spontaneous phenomenon concerning reformation at the local church level. Consequently, there is no interest in establishing a Sovereign Grace Baptist "Convention" or "Denomination." Each local church is to administer the keys to the kingdom.

Most Sovereign Grace Believers formally or informally relate to the "First London" (1646), "Second London" (1689), or "Philadelphia" (1742) Confessions.

There is a wide variety of local church government in this movement. Many Calvinist Baptists have a plurality of elders in each assembly. Other Sovereign Grace Believers, however, prefer to function with one pastor and several deacons.

Membership procedures vary from church to church but all require a credible profession of faith in Christ, and proper baptism as a basis for membership.

Calvinistic Baptists financially support gospel efforts (missionaries, pastors of small churches at home and abroad, literature publication and distribution, radio programs, etc.) in various parts of the world.

Headquarters

Media Contact, Corres., Jon Zens, P.O. Box 548, St. Croix Falls, WI 54024 Tel. (651)465-6516 Fax (651)465-5101

Email: jon@searchingtogether.org

Website: www.searchingtogether.org

Periodicals

Searching Together, Sound of Grace

The Swedenborgian Church*

Founded in North America in 1792 as the Church of the New Jerusalem, the Swedenborgian Church was organized as a national body in 1817 and incorporated in Illinois in 1861. Its biblically-based theology is derived from the spiritual, or mystical, experiences and exhaustive biblical studies of the Swedish scientist and philosopher Emanuel Swedenborg (1688-1772).

The church centers its worship and teachings on the historical life and the risen and glorified present reality of the Lord Jesus Christ. It looks with an ecumenical vision toward the establishment of the kingdom of God in the form of a universal Church, active in the lives of all people of good will who desire and strive for freedom, peace, and justice for all. It is a member of the NCCC and active in many local councils of churches.

With churches and groups throughout the United States and Canada, the denomination's central administrative offices and its seminary, "Swedenborg House of Studies," are located in Newton, MA and Berkeley, Calif. Affiliated churches are found in Africa, Asia, Australia, Canada, Europe, the United Kingdom, Japan, South Korea, and South America. Many philosophers and writers have acknowledged their appreciation of Swedenborg's teachings.

Headquarters

11 Highland Ave., Newtonville, MA 02460 Tel. (617)969-4240 Fax (617)964-3258

Email: manager@swedenborg.org

Website: www.swedenborg.org

Media Contact, Central Ofc. Mgr., Martha Bauer

Officers

Pres., Rev. Ronald P. Brugler, 489 Franklin St. N, Kitchener, ON, Canada N2A 1Z2

Vice Pres., Christine Laitner, 10 Hannah Court, Midland, MI 48642

Rec. Sec., Gloria Toot, 10280 Gentlewind Dr., Montgomery, OH 45242

Treas., Lawrence Conant, 290 Berlin St., Apt. 89, Clinton, MA 01510 Tel. (978)368-6269

Ofc. Mgr., Martha Bauer

Periodicals

The Messenger, Our Daily Bread

Syrian (Syriac) Orthodox Church of Antioch*

The Syrian Orthodox Church of Antioch traces its origin to the Patriarchate established in Antioch by St. Peter the Apostle. It is under the supreme ecclesiastical jurisdiction of His Holiness the Syrian Orthodox Patriarch of Antioch and All the East, now residing in Damascus, Syria. The Syrian Orthodox Church—composed of several archdioceses, numerous parishes, schools, and seminaries—professes the faith of the first three Ecumenical Councils of Nicaea, Constantinople, and Ephesus, and numbers faithful in the Middle East, India, the Americas, Europe, and Australia.

The first Syrian Orthodox faithful came to North America during the late 1800s, and by 1907 the first Syrian Orthodox priest was ordained to tend to the community's spiritual needs. In 1949, His Eminence Archbishop Mor Athanasius Y. Samuel came to America and was soon appointed Patriarchal Vicar. The Archdiocese was officially established in 1957. In 1995, the Archdiocese of North America was divided into three separate Patriarchal Vicariates (Eastern United States, Western United States, and Canada), each under a hierarch of the Church.

There are 15 official archdiocesan parishes and three mission congregations in the United States, located in Arizona, California, District of Columbia, Florida, Indiana, Illinois, Massachusetts, Michigan, New Jersey, New York, Oregon, Rhode Island, and Texas. In Canada, there are seven official parishes, four in the Province of Ontario, two in the Province of Quebec, and one in the Province of Alberta.

Headquarters

Archdiocese for the Eastern US, 260 Elm Ave., Teaneck, NJ 07666 Tel. (201)801-0660 Fax (201)801-0603

Archdiocese of Los Angeles and Environs, 417 E. Fairmount Rd., Burbank, CA 91501 Tel. (818)845-5089 Fax (818)845-5436

Email: syrianoc@syrianorthodoxchurch.org

Website: www.syrianorthodoxchurch.org

Media Contact, Archdiocesan Gen. Sec., V. Rev. Chorepiscopus John Meno, 260 Elm Ave., Teaneck, NJ 07666 Tel. (201)907-0122 Fax (201)907-0551

Officers

Archdiocese for Eastern US, Archbishop, Mor Cyril Aphrem Karim

Archdiocese of Los Angeles and Environs, Archbishop, Mor Clemis Eugene Kaplan

The Syro-Russian Orthodox Catholic Church

The Syro-Russian Orthodox Catholic Church was originally established in May of 1892 as the American Orthodox Catholic Archdiocese of America; this was canonized by His Holiness Ignatius Peter III, Patriarch of Antioch. It was this same Patriarch that issued the Bull for the consecration of its first Archbishop Metropolitan, Timotheos Vilathi, as named by Patriarch Ignatius. Because the jurisdiction also has some Western Rite parishes, the Synod has been named "Romano Byzantine Synod of Bishops." First parishes of this jurisdiction were established in Wisconsin among Belgians, Italians, Slavs, and other ethnic groups. After Archbishop Timotheos' consecration, parishes were later formed in Ohio, Illinois, and New York, and some missionary work begun in Canada.

After much disagreement with the Patriarchate concerning administration and the Council of Chalcedon (which the Patriarchate did not accept concerning the two natures of Christ), on January 1, 1910, a Consistory was held concerning the future of the Archdiocese of America. The Bishops agreed upon and decided that, "Our reality as a branch, a part of the true Catholic and Orthodox Church of God, is not dependent upon the recognition of any ecclesiastical authority outside the Councils of our own American Ecclesiastical Consistory and National Synod of Bishops and Clergy." Archbishop Timotheos believed strongly in the truths of the Council of Chalcedon, and the rights of the American Church to name its own bishops, and from here the Church was known as Autocephalous and severed form the Patriarchate of Antioch. However, after this time several schisms occurred that gave way to some heretical newly established "churches" that caused the Church to eventually be renamed "Syro-Russian Orthodox Catholic." In the 1970s, after the retirement for health reasons of Archbishop John, Archbishop Joseph of Blessed Memory became the newly enthroned Metropolitan Hierarch of the Church. He possessed Apostolic Succession from both the Syrian and Russian Orthodox Churches later giving the Synod the name of Syro-Russian Orthodox Catholic Church. In 1987, before his death, a meeting was held at St. Paul's Monastery in LaPorte, Ind. and Very Right Reverend Archimandrite Stephen (Thomas) was duly elected metropolitan Hierarch. He was consecrated Bishop on October 18, 1987, by Archbishop Joseph assisted by Archbishop George and Bishop Norman at St. Mary's Chapel, LaPorte, Ind.; and the following year enthroned as Metropolitan Archbishop Hierarch. Archbishop Stephen has caused the Church to grow throughout the world. In 1994-1996, he endured many sufferings as the result of some clergy who went astray and since deposed of their faculties and offices. Since that time, the Church has experienced peace, growth, and new viability. The official liturgy of the Church is the Divine Liturgy of Saint James, the oldest liturgy of the Christian Church authored by St. James the Brother of our Lord. In addition, as with all other Orthodox Churches, the Liturgy of Saint Basil is used ten times a year, and the Presanctified Liturgy as prescribed. The Traditions of Holy Orthodoxy are observed in the administration of the Holy Mysteries (Sacraments) and, as is practice in the Russian Orthodox Church, Holy Myron (Chrism) is consecrated by the Metropolitan Hierarch on Holy Thursday and distributed to the clergy of the Church.

Some western customs exist within the Church. Hyperveneration is given to icons that memorialize the saints and events in the life of Jesus Christ and the Holy Theotokos Mary. It follows the Gregorian Calendar and the Orthodox date of Pascha (Easter). The Romano Byzantine Synod of Bishops, and the Syro-Russian Orthodox Catholic Church, strongly believes in the separation of Church and State, and in the administration of healing by licensed practitioners, and by the clergy in the Mystery of Holy Unction. The Synodal Metropolinate has received official recognition from the Hellenic (Greek) Orthodox Church of Athens, and has been involved in ecumenical dialogue with the Orthodox Patriarchate of Jerusalem, the Russian Orthodox Patriarchate, and more recently has opened dialogue with the Ukrainian Autocephalous Orthodox Church. There is one monastic order, The Monastic

Community of Saint Basil, open to men and women that is headquartered in England. The canonical diocese of the Church and their Bishops are Archbishop Stephen (United States), Bishop Andreas (Guatemala), Bishop Benjamin (Bangladesh), Bishop Cristobal (Spain), Bishop John (India), Bishop Joseph (Africa), Bishop Pedro (Cuba), and retired Chorbishop John (United States). The Diocese of Pakistan currently is served by a Vicar General as the result of an episcopal vacancy there. Vicars serve the mission territories of Belgium, Kenya, Tanzania, and soon a Bishop (George) will be consecrated for the United Kingdom. The Church of Bangladesh recently united with the Syro-Russian Orthodox Catholic Church, and the independent Diocese of Bogota is now in dialogue with Metropolitan Stephen concerning union. Clergy are trained for the Church through Holy Family Collegiate Seminary of Tacoma, Wash., St. Basil's Seminary of Havana, Cuba, or St. Efrem's Seminary of Cordoba, Spain. A distance education program for mature candidates is offered through Romano Byzantine College (Virginia). The national headquarters at this time is at St. Mary the Theotokos Pro-Cathedral in Duluth, Minnesota.

Headquarters

St. Mary the Theotokos Pro-Cathedral, 5907 Grand Ave, Duluth, MN 55087 Tel. (218)624-0202

Email: rbsocc@juno.com

Periodicals

Orthodox Christian Herald

Triumph the Church and Kingdom of God in Christ Inc. (International)

This church was given through the wisdom and knowledge of God to the Late Apostle Elias Dempsey Smith on Oct. 20, 1897, in Issaquena County, Miss., while he was pastor of a Methodist church.

The Triumph Church, as this body is more commonly known, was founded in 1902. Its doors opened in 1904 and it was confirmed in Birmingham, Ala., with 225 members in 1915. It was incorporated in Washington, D.C. in 1918 and currently operates in 31 states and overseas. The General Church is divided into 13 districts, including the Africa District.

Triumphant doctrine and philosophy are based on the principles of life, truth, and knowledge; the understanding that God is in man and expressed through man; the belief in manifested wisdom; and the hope for constant new revelations. Its concepts and methods of teaching the second coming of Christ are based on these and all other attributes of goodness.

Triumphians emphasize that God is the God of the living, not the God of the dead.

Headquarters

213 Farrington Ave. SE, Atlanta, GA 30315

Media Contact, Bishop C. W. Drummond, 7114 Idlewild, Pittsburg, PA 15208 Tel. (412)731-2286

Officers

Chief Bishop, Bishop C. W. Drummond, 7114 Idlewild, Pittsburgh, PA 15208 Tel. (412)731-2286

Gen. Bd of Trustees, Chmn., Bishop Leon Simon, 1028 59th St., Oakland, CA 94608 Tel. (415)652-9576

Gen. Treas., Bishop Hosea Lewis, 1713 Needlewood Ln., Orlando, FL 32818 Tel. (407)295-5488

Gen. Rec. Sec., Bishop Zephaniah Swindle, Box 1927, Shelbyville, TX 75973 Tel. (409)598-3082

True Orthodox Church of Greece (Synod of Metropolitan Cyprian), American Exarchate

The American Exarchate of the True (Old Calendar) Orthodox Church of Greece adheres to the tenets of the Eastern Orthodox Church, which considers itself the legitimate heir of the historical Apostolic Church.

When the Orthodox Church of Greece adopted the New (or Gregorian) Calendar in 1924, many felt that this breach with tradition compromised the Church's festal calendar, based on the Old (or Julian) Calendar, and its unity with world Orthodoxy. In 1935, three State Church Bishops returned to the Old Calendar and established a Synod in Resistance, the True Orthodox Church of Greece. When the last of these Bishops died, the Russian Orthodox Church Abroad consecrated a new Hierarchy for the Greek Old Calendarists and, in 1969, declared them a Sister Church.

In the face of persecution by the State Church, some Old Calendarists denied the validity of the Mother Church of Greece and formed two synods, now under the direction of Archbishop Chrysostomos of Athens and Archbishop Andreas of Athens. A moderate faction under Metropolitan Cyprian of Oropos and Fili does not maintain communion with the Mother Church of Greece, but recognizes its validity and seeks a restoration of unity by a return to the Julian Calendar and traditional ecclesiastical polity by the State Church. About 1.5 million Orthodox Greeks belong to the Old Calendar Church.

The first Old Calendarist communities in the United States were formed in the 1930s. The Exarchate under Metropolitan Cyprian was established in 1986. Placing emphasis on clergy education, youth programs, and recognition of the Old Calendarist minority in American Orthodoxy, the Exarchate has encouraged the establishment of monastic communities and missions. Cordial contacts with the New Calendarist and other Orthodox communities are encouraged. A center for theological training and Patristic studies has been established at the Exarchate headquarters in Etna, Calif.

In July 1994, the True Orthodox Church of

Greece (Synod of Metropolitan Cyprian), the True Orthodox Church of Romania, the True Orthodox Church of Bulgaria, and the Russian Orthodox Church Abroad entered into liturgical union, forming a coalition of traditionalist Orthodox bodies several million strong.

Headquarters

St. Gregory Palamas Monastery, P.O. Box 398, Etna, CA 96027-0398 Tel. (530)467-3228 Fax (530)467-5828

Media Contact, Exarch in America, His Eminence, Archbishop Chrysostomos

Officers

Acting Synodal Exarch in America, His Grace Bishop Auxentios

Chancellor of the Exarchate, The Very Rev. Raphael Abraham, 3635 Cottage Grove Ave. SE, Cedar Rapids, IA 52403-1612

Periodicals

Orthodox Tradition (quarterly theological journal)

Ukrainian Orthodox Church of the USA*

The Ukrainian Orthodox Church of the USA has its origin in the ancient lands of Rus-Ukraine (present day Ukraine). It was to the inhabitants of these lands that the Apostle Andrew first preached the Gospel. Christianization began early in the history of Rus-Ukraine by missionaries from the Orthodox Christian See of Constantinople. In 988 A.D., the Saintly Prince Volodymyr, crowned a process of Christian Evangelization begun in the 4th century, by personally accepting Orthodox Christianity and inspiring his subjects to do the same. The baptism of Volodymyr, his household, and the inhabitants of Kyiv, altered the face of Kyivan Rus-Ukraine and Slavic history for all time. Kyiv became the spiritual heart of Orthodox Christians in Rus-Ukraine. It was from this See that missionaries were sent into every corner of St. Volodymyr's realm. Through their efforts, the Gospel was preached and new communities were established. The Mother Church of Kyiv and its See of Saint Sophia, modeled after Constantinople's See of the same name, gave birth to many Orthodox Christian centers and communities in the west, east, and north of the Dnipro river, among them the Orthodox Christian See of Moscow, Russia (Rosia).

The Ukrainian Orthodox Church of USA ministers to the needs of the faithful whose ancestral roots are in Ukraine. The Church found haven in America in the early 1920s. Its first bishop, Metropolitan Ioan (John) Teodorovych, arrived from Ukraine in 1924 and shepherded the Church as Metropolitan until his death in 1971. His successor, Archbishop Mstyslav, arrived in the USA in 1950, and shepherded the Church as Metropolitan from 1971 until his death in 1993. It was Metropolitan Mstyslav who, as a consequence of Ukraine's independence, was named Patriarch of Kyiv and All Ukraine in 1990. Previous to 1996 there were two Ukrainian Orthodox jurisdictions in the USA. Formal unification of the Ukrainian Orthodox Church of the USA, shepherded by His Beatitude Metropolitan Constantine, and the Ukrainian Orthodox Church of America, shepherded by His Grace Bishop Vsevolod, was concluded in November 1996.

Headquarters

Saint Andrew the Firstcalled Apostle Ukrainian Orthodox Church Center, P.O. Box 495, South Bound Brook, NJ 08880 Tel. (732)356-0090 Fax (732)356-5556

Email: uocofusa@aol.com

Website: www.uocofusa.org

Media Contact, His Eminence Antony, Archbishop of New York, Consistory President

Officers

Metropolitan, His Beatitude Constantine, 1803 Sidney Street, Pittsburgh, PA 15203

CENTRAL EPARCHY

Eparchial Bishop: Metropolitan Constantine

Eparchial See: St. Volodymyr Cathedral, 5913 State Rd., Parma, OH 44134 Tel. (440)885-1509

Eparchial Territory: Florida, Georgia, Ohio, Western Pennsylvania

EASTERN EPARCHY

Eparchial Bishop: Archbishop Antony.

Eparchial Seat: St. Volodymyr Cathedral, 160 West 82nd St. New York, NY 10024 Tel. (212)873-8550

Eparchial Territory: Connecticut, Delaware, Massachusetts, Maryland, New Jersey, New York, Pennsylvania, and Rhode Island

WESTERN EPARCHY

Eparchial Bishop: Archbishop Vsevolod

Eparchial Seat: St. Volodymyr Cathedral, 2230-50 West Cortez St. Chicago, IL 60622 Tel. (312)278 2827

Eparchial Territory: Arizona, California, Colorado, Illinois, Indiana, Michigan, Minnesota, North Dakota, Nebraska, Oregon, Washington, Wisconsin, Ontario Province

COUNCIL OF BISHOPS OF THE UKRAINIAN ORTHODOX CHURCH OF THE USA

Metropolitan Constantine - Chair

Achbishop Antony - Secretary

Achbishop Vsevolod - Member

METROPOLITAN COUNCIL MEMBERS

Archimandrite Andriy, Vice Chmn

Protopresbyter William Diakiw

Protopresbyter Frank Estocin, JCB

Protopriest John Nakonachny

Protopriest Michael Kochis

Protopriest Eugene Meschisen

Protopriest Bazyl Zawierucha

Dr. Gayle Woloschak, English Language Sec.

Mr. Emil Skocypec
Dr. Paul Micevych
Dr. George Krywolap, Ukrainian Language Sec.
Dr. Anatol Lysyj
Mrs. Helen Greenleaf
Mr. Michael Kapeluck
Daria Pishko, Ukrainian Orthodox League Pres.
Mrs. Nadia Mirchuk, United Ukrainian Orthodox Sisterhoods Pres.
Mr. Michael Heretz, Saint Andrew Society, Pres.
CONSISTORY
Consistory Pres., His Eminence Antony, Archbishop of New York, P.O. Box 495, South Bound Brook, NJ 08880 Tel. (732)356-0090, Fax (732)356-5556, uocofusa@aol.com
Vice Pres., Protopresbyter Willam Diakiw
Sec., Protopriest Frank Estocin
Treas., Mr. Emil Skocypec
Member, Protopriest John Nakonachny
Member, Protopriest Bazyl Zawierucha
Member, Dr. George Krywolap

Periodicals

Ukrainian Orthodox Word, Vira

Unitarian Universalist Association of Congregations

HISTORY: The Unitarian Universalist Association (UUA), created in 1961 through a consolidation of the Universalist Church of America with the American Unitarian Association, combines two liberal religious traditions. The religion traces its roots back to Europe where, in 1569, the Transylvanian king, John Sigismund (1540-1571), issued an edict of religious freedom. The religious philosophy led to the organization of the Universalists in this country in 1793, and the Unitarians (organized here in 1825).

BELIEFS: Founders of Universalism believed in universal salvation of all humans by God, while founders of Unitrarianism believed in the unity of God (as opposed to the Trinity). Unitarian Universalism is a liberal, creedless religion with Judeo-Christian roots. It draws also from Eastern, humanist, and other religious traditions, and encourages its members to seek religious truth out of their own reflection and experience. The denomination teaches tolerance and respect for other religious viewpoints, and affirms the worth and dignity of every person.

ORGANIZATION AND GOVERNMENT: The Unitarian Universalist Association consists of over 1,010 congregations in the United States and Canada, with over 220,000 members, and is served by more than 1,100 ministers. The Association is the fastest-growing liberal religion in North America, and this year completed its twenty-first consecutive year of growth, at an average annual rate of nearly 2 percent. Each member congregation within the UUA is governed independently. In North America, the Association is made up of 20 Districts (served by a District Executive who is a member of the UUA staff), with each congregation having district affiliation. The Association is governed by an elected Board of Trustees, chaired by an elected Moderator. An elected President, three vice presidents, and directors of five departments form the Executive Staff that administers the daily activities of the Association.

The General Assembly, held each June in a different UUA District, serves as the Association's annual business meeting. The UUA includes Departments of Ministry and Professional Leadership, Lifespan Faith Development, Congregational Services, Identity Based Ministries, District Services, Advocacy and Witness, Financial Development, and Communications. The *World*, published bimonthly, is the denominational journal. Beacon Press, an internationally honored publishing house, is wholly owned by the Unitarian Universalist Association.

Headquarters

25 Beacon St., Boston, MA 02108 Tel. (617) 742-2100 Fax (617) 367-3237
Website: www.uua.org
Media Contact, John Hurley, Dir. of Information, Tel. (617)742-2100 ext. 131, jhurley@uua.org

Officers

Pres., The Rev. William Sinkford
Moderator, Diane Olson
Exec. Vice Pres., Kathleen C. Montgomery

Periodicals

UU World, InterConnections

United Christian Church

The United Christian Church originated about 1864. There were some ministers and laymen in the United Brethren in Christ Church who disagreed with the position and practice of the church on infant baptism, voluntary bearing of arms, and belonging to oath-bound secret combinations. This group developed into United Christian Church, organized at a conference held in Campbelltown, Penn., on May 9, 1877. The principal founders of the denomination were George Hoffman, John Stamn, and Thomas Lesher. Before they were organized, they were called Hoffmanites.

The United Christian Church has district conferences, a yearly general conference, a general board of trustees, a mission board, a board of directors of the United Christian Church Home, a camp meeting board, a young peoples' board, and local organized congregations.

It believes in the Holy Trinity and the inspired Holy Scriptures with the doctrines they teach. The church practices the ordinances of Baptism, Holy Communion, and Foot Washing.

It welcomes all into its fold who are born again, believe in Jesus Christ as Savior and Lord, and have received the Holy Spirit.

Headquarters

c/o John P. Ludwig Jr., 523 W. Walnut St., Cleona, PA 17042 Tel. (717)273-9629

Media Contact, Presiding Elder, John P. Ludwig Jr.

Officers

Presiding Elder, Elder John P. Ludwig Jr.

Conf. Sec., Mr. Lee Wenger, 1625 Thompson Ave., Annville, PA 17003

Conf. Moderator, Elder Gerald Brinser, 2360 Horseshoe Pike, Annville, PA 17003

OTHER ORGANIZATIONS

Mission Board: Pres., Elder John P. Ludwig Jr.; Sec., Elder David Heagy, 4129 Oak St., Lebanon, PA 17042; Treas., LeRoy Bomgardner, 1252 Royal Rd., Annville, PA 17003

United Church of Christ*

The United Church of Christ was constituted on June 25, 1957 by representatives of the Congregational Christian Churches and of the Evangelical and Reformed Church, in Cleveland, OH.

The Preamble to the Constitution states: "The United Church of Christ acknowledges as its sole head, Jesus Christ ... It acknowledges as kindred in Christ all who share in this confession. It looks to the Word of God in the Scriptures, and to the presence and power of the Holy Spirit... It claims... the faith of the historic Church expressed in the ancient creeds and reclaimed in the basic insights of the Protestant Reformers. It affirms the responsibility of the Church in each generation to make this faith its own in... worship, in honesty of thought and expression, and in purity of heart before God.... it recognizes two sacraments, Baptism and the Lord's Supper."

The creation of the United Church of Christ brought together four unique traditions:

(1) Groundwork for the Congregational Way was laid by Calvinist Puritans and Separatists during the late 16th–early 17th centuries, then achieved prominence among English Protestants during the civil war of the 1640s. Opposition to state control prompted followers to emigrate to the United States, where they helped colonize New England in the 17th century. Congregationalists have been self-consciously a denomination from the mid-19th century.

(2) The Christian Churches, an 18th-century American restorationist movement, emphasized Christ as the only head of the church, the New Testament as their only rule of faith, and "Christian" as their sole name. This loosely organized denomination found in the Congregational Churches a like disposition. In 1931, the two bodies formally united as the Congregational Christian Churches.

(3) The German Reformed Church comprised an irenic aspect of the Protestant Reformation, as a second generation of Reformers drew on the insights of Zwingli, Luther, and Calvin to formulate the Heidelberg Catechism of 1563. People of the German Reformed Church began immigrating to the New World early in the 18th century, the heaviest concentration in Pennsylvania. Formal organization of the American denomination was completed in 1793. The church spread across the country. In the Mercersburg Movement, a strong emphasis on evangelical catholicity and Christian unity was developed.

(4) In 19th-century Germany, Enlightenment criticism and Pietist inwardness decreased longstanding conflicts between religious groups. In Prussia, a royal proclamation merged Lutheran and Reformed people into one United Evangelical Church (1817). Members of this new church way migrated to America. The Evangelicals settled in large numbers in Missouri and Illinois, emphasizing pietistic devotion and unionism; in 1840 they formed the German Evangelical Church Society in the West. After union with other Evangelical church associations, in 1877 it took the name of the German Evangelical Synod of North America.

On June 25, 1934, this Synod and the Reformed Church in the US (formerly the German Reformed Church) united to form the Evangelical and Reformed Church. They blended the Reformed tradition's passion for the unity of the church and the Evangelical tradition's commitment to the liberty of conscience inherent in the gospel.

Headquarters

700 Prospect Avenue, Cleveland, OH 44115 Tel. (216)736-2100 Fax (216)736-2103 Toll-free (866)822-8224

Email: kellys@ucc.org

Website: www.ucc.org

Media Contact, Rev. Robert Chase, 700 Prospect Ave., Cleveland, OH 44115 Tel. (216)736-2173 Fax (216)736-2223

Officers

Gen. Minister and Pres., Rev. John H. Thomas

Assoc. Gen. Minister, Ms. Edith A. Guffey

Exec. Minister, Wider Church Ministries, Ms. Olivia Masih White

Exec. Minister, Justice and Witness Ministries , Ms. Bernice Powell Jackson

Exec. Minister, Local Church Ministries, Rev. José A. Malayang

Chair, Executive Council, Rev. M. Winston Baldwin, Jr.

Vice Chair, Executive Council, Ms. Reba Walker

Mod., General Synod , Rev. Norman W. Jackson

Asst. Mod., General Synod, Ms. Annie Wynn Neal

Asst. Mod., General Synod, Mr. Chris Smith

ORGANIZATIONS

Office of General Ministries: National Office, 700 Prospect Ave., Cleveland, OH 44115 Tel. (216)736-2100 Fax (216)736-2103, General Minister and Pres., Rev. John H. Thomas; Associate General Minister, Ms. Edith A. Guffey

Justice and Witness Ministries: National Office, 700 Prospect Ave., Cleveland, OH 44115 Tel.

(216)736-3700 Fax (216)736-3703; Franklinton Center at Bricks, P.O. Box 220, Whitakers, NC Tel. (252)437-1723 Fax (252)437-1278; Washington Office, 110 Maryland Ave. NE, Room 207, Washington, D.C. Tel. (202)543-1517 Fax (202)543-5994; Exec. Minister, Ms. Bernice Powell Jackson; Exec. Associate, Rev. Carl P. Wallace

Local Church Ministries: Tel. (216)736-3800 Fax (216)736-3803, Exec. Minister, Rev. José A. Malayang

Wider Church Ministries: National Offices, 700 Prospect Ave., Cleveland, OH 44115 Tel. (216)736-3200 Fax (216)736-3203; 475 Riverside Dr., New York, NY 10115; Disciples of Christ Division of Overseas Ministries, P.O. Box 1986, Indianapolis, IN 46206 Tel. (317) 635-3100 Fax (317)635-4323; Exec. Minister, Ms. Olivia Masih White; Exec. Associate to the Exec. Minister, Rev. William R. Johnson

Pension Boards: Main Office, 475 Riverside Dr., New York, NY 10115 Tel. (212)870-2777 Fax (212)870-2877; National Office, 700 Prospect Ave., Cleveland, OH 44115 Tel. (216)736-2271 Fax (216)736-2274; Exec. Vice Pres., Mr. Michael A. Downs

United Church Foundation, Inc.: 475 Riverside Dr., New York, NY 10115 Tel. (212)870-2582 Fax (212)870-2366; Exec.Vice Pres., Mr. Donald G. Hart

Council for American Indian Ministry: 471 3rd St., Box 412, Excelsior, MN 55331 Tel. (952) 474-3532; Executive Director, Rev. Kim Mammedaty

Council for Health and Human Services Ministries: National Office, 700 Prospect Ave., Cleveland, OH 44115 Tel. (216)736-2250 Fax (216)736-2251; Exec. Dir., Rev. Bryan W. Sickbert

CONFERENCES

Western Region

California, Nevada, Northern: Rev. Mary Susan Gast, 21425 Birch St., Hayward, CA 94541-2131

California, Southern: Rev. Daniel F. Romero and Rev. Jane E. Heckles, 2401 N. Lake Ave., Altadena, CA 91001

Hawaii: -vacant- 15 Craigside Pl., Honolulu, HI 96817

Montana/Northern Wyoming: Rev. John M. Schaeffer, 2016 Alderson Ave., Billings, MT 59102

Central Pacific: Rev. Hector Lopez and Rev. Eugene Ross, 0245 SW Bancroft St., Ste. E, Portland, OR 97201

Rocky Mountain: Vacant, 12560 W. Cedar Drive, Lakewood, CO 80228

Southwest: Rev. Ann C. Rogers-Witte, 4423 N. 24th St., Ste. 600, Phoenix, AZ 85016

Pacific Northwest: Rev. Stephanie Boughton Haines, 6218 Beacon Ave. S, Seattle, WA 98108; Rev. Randall Hyvonen, 411 S. Washington St., Spokane, WA 99204

West Central Region

Iowa: Rev. Susan J. Ingham, 600 42nd St., Des Moines, IA 50312

Kansas/Oklahoma: Vacant, 1248 Fabrique, Wichita, KS 67218

Minnesota: Rev. Clyde Steckel, 122 W. Franklin Ave., Rm. 323, Minneapolis, MN 55404

Missouri, Mid South: Rev. A. Gayle Engel, 461 E. Lockwood Ave., St. Louis, MO 63119

Nebraska: Vacant, 825 M St., Lincoln, NE 68508

Northern Plains: Rev. Wade Schemmel Jr., 227 W. Broadway, Bismarck, ND 58501

South Dakota: Rev. Gene E. Miller, 3500 S. Phillips Ave., #121, Sioux Falls, SD 57105-6864

Great Lakes Region

Illinois: Rev. Jane Fishler Hoffman, 1840 Westchester Blvd., Westchester, IL 60154

Illinois South: Vacant, Box 325, 1312 Broadway, Highland, IL 62249

Indiana/Kentucky: Rev. Stephen C. Gray, 1100 W. 42nd St., Indianapolis, IN 46208

Michigan: Rev. Kent J. Ulery, P.O. Box 1006, East Lansing, MI 48826

Ohio: Rev. David V. Schwab, 6161 Busch Blvd.,#95, Columbus, OH 43229

Wisconsin: Rev. David Moyer, 4459 Gray Rd., Box 435, De Forest, WI 53532-0495

Southern Region

Florida: Rev. M. Douglas Borko, 924 Magnolia Ave., Orlando, FL 32803

South Central: Rev. Mark H. Miller, 6633 E. Hwy. 290, #200, Austin, TX 78723-1157

Southeast: Rev. Timothy C. Downs, 756 W. Peachtree St., NW, Atlanta, GA 30308

Southern: Rev. Steve Camp, 217 N. Main St., Box 658, Graham, NC 27253

Middle Atlantic Region

Central Atlantic: Rev. John R. Deckenback, 916 S. Rolling Rd., Baltimore, MD 21228

New York: Rev. Geoffrey A. Black, 5800 Heritage Landing Dr., Suite 2D, East Syracuse, NY 13057

Penn. Central:Vacant, The United Church Center, Rm. 126, 900 S. Arlington Ave., Harrisburg, PA 17109

Penn. Northeast: Rev. Alan C. Miller, 431 Delaware Ave., P.O. Box 177, Palmerton, PA 18071

Penn. Southeast: Rev. F. Russell Mittman, Jr., 505 Second Ave., P.O. Box 400, Collegeville, PA 19426

Penn West: Rev. Alan McLarty, 320 South Maple Ave., Greensburg, PA 15601

Puerto Rico: Rev. Luis Rosario, Box 8609, Caguas, PR 00762

New England Region

Connecticut: Rev. Davida Foy Crabtree, 125 Sherman St., Hartford, CT 06105

Maine: Rev. Jean M. Alexander, Rev. David R. Gaewski, 68 Main St., P.O. Box 966, Yarmouth, ME 04096

Massachusetts: Rev. Nancy Taylor, P.O. Box 2246, 1 Badger Rd., Framingham, MA 01701

New Hampshire: Vacant, 140 Sheep Davis Rd., Pembroke, NH 03275

Rhode Island: Vacant, 56 Walcott St., Pawtucket, RI 02860

Vermont: Rev. Arnold I. Thomas, 285 Maple St., Burlington, VT 05401

Nongeographic

Calvin Synod: Rev. Louis Medgyesi, 607 Plum St., Fairport Harbor, OH 44077

Periodicals

United Church News, Common Lot, Courage in the Struggle for Justice and Peace

United Holy Church of America, Inc.

The United Holy Church of America, Inc. is an outgrowth of the great revival that began with the outpouring of the Holy Ghost on the Day of Pentecost. The church is built upon the foundation of the Apostles and Prophets, Jesus Christ being the cornerstone.

During a revival of repentence, regeneration, and holiness of heart and life that swept through the South and West, the United Holy Church was born. The founding fathers had no desire to establish a denomination but were pushed out of organized churches because of this experience of holiness and testimony of the Spirit-filled life.

On the first Sunday in May 1886, in Method, N.C., what is today known as the United Holy Church of America, Inc. was born. The church was incorporated on Sept. 25, 1918.

Baptism by immersion, the Lord's Supper, and feet washing are observed. The premillennial teaching of the Second Coming of Christ, Divine healing, justification by faith, sanctification as a second work of grace, and Spirit baptism are accepted.

Headquarters

5104 Dunstan Rd., Greensboro, NC 27405 Tel. (336)621-0669

Email: books@mohistory.org

Media Contact, Gen. Statistician, Ms. Jacquelyn B. McCain, 1210 N. Euclid Ave., Apt. A, St. Louis, MO 63113-2012 Tel. (314)367-8351 Fax (314)367-1835

GENERAL ADMINISTRATION

Gen. Pres., The Rt. Rev. Odell McCollum, 707 Woodmark Run, Gahanna, OH 43230 Tel. (614)475-4713 Fax (614)475-4713

Gen. Vice Pres., Bishop Elijah Williams, 901 Briarwood St., Reidsville, NC 27320 Tel. (919)349-7275

Gen. 2nd Vice Pres., The Rt. Rev. Kenneth O. Robinson Sr., 33 Springbrook Rd., Nanuet, NY 10954-4423 Tel. (914)425-8311 Fax (914) 352-2686

Gen. Rec. Sec., Rev. Mrs. Elsie Harris, 2304 Eighth St., Portsmouth, VA 23704 Tel (757) 399-0926

Asst. Rec. Sec., Mrs. Cassandra Jones, 3869 JoAnn Dr., Cleveland, OH 44122 Tel. (216)921-0097

Gen. Fin. Sec., Vera Perkins-Hughes, P.O. Box 6194, Cleveland, OH Tel. (216)851-7448

Asst. Fin. Sec., Bertha Williams, 4749 Shaw Dr., Wilmington, NC 28405 Tel. (919)395-4462

Gen. Corres. Sec., Ms. Gwendolyn Lane, 3069 Hudson St., Columbus, OH 43219

Gen. Treas., Louis Bagley, 8779 Wales Dr., Cincinnati, OH 45249 Tel. (513)247-0588

GENERAL OFFICERS

Gen Pres. Missionary Dept.: Rev. Ardelia M. Corbett, 519 Madera Dr., Youngstown, OH 44504 Tel. (216)744-3284

Gen. Evangelism & Extension Dept.: Pres., Elder Clifford R. Pitts, 3563 North 14th St., Milwaukee, WI 53206 Tel. (414)244-1319

Gen. Bible Church School Dept.: Superintendent, Robert L. Rollins, 1628 Avondale Ave., Toledo, OH 43607 Tel. (419) 246-4046

Gen. Y.P.H.A.: Pres., Elder James W. Brooks, Rt. 3 Box 105, Pittsboro, NC 27312 Tel. (919)542-5357

Gen. Ushers Department: Pres., Ms. Sherly M. Hughes, 1491 East 191st St., #H-604, Euclid, OH 44117 Tel. (216)383-0038

Gen. Educ. Dept.: Elder Roosevelt Alston, 168 Willow Creek Run, Henderson, NC 27636 Tel. (919)438-5854

Gen. Music Dept.: Chpsn., Rosie Johnson, 2009 Forest Dale Dr., Silver Spring, MD 20932

Gen. Historian: Dr. Chester Gregory Sr., 1302 Lincoln Woods Dr., Baltimore, MD 21228 Tel. (410)788-5144

Gen. Counsel: Mr. Joe L. Webster, Esq., Attorney-At-Law, P.O. Box 2301, Chapel Hill, NC 27515-2301 Tel. (919)542-5150

UHCA Academy: Dir., Ms. Stephanie Davis, The United Holy Church of America, Inc., 5104 Dunstan Road, Greensboro, NC 27405 Tel. (336)621-0069

Gen. Statistician: Ms. Jacquelyn B. McCain, 1210 N. Euclid Ave., Apt. A, St. Louis, MO 63113-2012 Tel. (314)367-8351 Fax (314) 367-1835

PRESIDENTS OF CONVOCATIONAL DISTRICTS

Barbados Dist.: The Rt. Rev. Jestina Gentles, 5 West Ridge St., Britton's Hill, St. Michael, BH2 Barbados, West Indies Tel. (246)427-7185

Bermuda Dist.: The Rt. Rev. Calvin Armstrong, P.O. Box 234, Paget, Bermuda Tel. (441)296-0828 or (441)292-8383

Central Western Dist.: Bishop Bose Bradford, 6279 Natural Bridge, Pine Lawn, MO 63121 Tel. (314)355-1598

Ghana, West Africa Dist.: The Rt. Rev. Robert Blount, 231 Arlington Ave., Jersey City, NJ 07035 Tel. (201)433-5672

New England Dist.: The Rt. Rev. Lowell Edney, 85 Woodhaven St., Mattapan, MA 02126 Tel. (617)296-5366

Northern Dist.: The Rt. Rev. Kenneth O. Robinson, Sr., 33 Springbrook Rd., Nanuet, NY 10954 Tel. (914)425-8311

Northwestern Dist.: The Rt. Rev. M. Daniel Borden, 8655 North Melody Lane, Macedonia, OH 44056 Tel. (330)468-0270

Pacific Coast Dist.: The Rt. Rev. Irvin Evans, 235 Harvard Rd., Linden, NJ 07036 Tel. (908)925-6138

Southeastern Dist.: The Rt. Rev. James C. Bellamy, 1825 Rockland Dr. SE, Atlanta, GA 30316 Tel. (404)241-1821

Southern Dist.–Goldsboro: The Rt. Rev. Ralph E. Love Sr., 200 Barrington Rd., Greenville, NC 27834 Tel. (252)353-0495

Southern Dist.–Henderson: The Rt. Rev. Jesse Jones, 608 Cecil Street, Durham, NC 27707 Tel. (919)682-8249

St. Lucia Dist.: The Rt. Rev. Carlisle Collymore, P.O. Box 51, Castries, St. Lucia, West Indies Tel. (758)452-5835

Virginia Dist.: The Rt. Rev. Albert Augson, 1406 Melton Ave., Richmond, VA 23223 Tel. (804) 222-0463

West Virginia Dist.: The Rt. Rev. Alvester McConnell, Route 3, Box 263, Bluefield, WV 24701 Tel. (304)248-8046

Western North Carolina Dist.: The Rt. Rev. Elijah Williams, 901 Briarwood St., Reidsville, NC 27320-7020 Tel. (336)349-7275

Periodicals

The Holiness Union, The United Holy Church General Church Organ

United House of Prayer

The United House of Prayer was founded and organized as a hierarchical church in the 1920s by the late Bishop C. M. Grace, who had built the first House of Prayer in 1919 in West Wareham, Mass., with his own hands. The purpose of the organization is to establish, maintain, and perpetuate the doctrine of Christianity and the Apostolic Faith throughout the world among all people; to erect and maintain houses of prayer and worship where all people may gather for prayer and to worship the almighty God in spirit and in truth, irrespective of denomination or creed; and to maintain the Apostolic faith of the Lord and Savior, Jesus Christ.

Headquarters

1117 7th St. NW, Washington, D.C. 20001 Tel. (202)289-0238 Fax (202)289-8058

Media Contact, Apostle S. Green

Officers

CEO, Bishop S. C. Madison, 1665 N. Portal Dr. NW, Washington, D.C. 20012 Tel. (202)882-3956 Fax (202)829-4717

NATIONAL PROGRAM STAFF

The Gen. Assembly: Presiding Officer, Bishop S. C. Madison, 1665 N. Portal Dr. NW, Washington, D.C. 20012 Tel. (202)882-3956 Fax (202)829-4717

Gen. Council Ecclesiastical Court: Clerk, Apostle R. Price, 1665 N. Portal Dr. NW, Washington, D.C. 20012 Tel. (202)882-3956 Fax (202)829-4717

Nationwide Building Program: General Builder, Bishop S. C. Madison, 1665 N. Portal Dr. NW, Washington, D.C. 20012 Tel. (202)882-3956 Fax (202)829-4717

Special Projects: Dir., Apostle S. Green

Annual Truth & Facts Publication: Exec. Editor, Bishop S. C. Madison, 1665 N. Portal Dr. NW, Washington, D.C. 20012 Tel. (202)882-3956 Fax (202)829-4717

The United Methodist Church*

The United Methodist Church was formed April 23, 1968, in Dallas by the union of The Methodist Church and The Evangelical United Brethren Church. The two churches shared a common historical and spiritual heritage. The Methodist Church resulted in 1939 from the unification of three branches of Methodism—the Methodist Episcopal Church; the Methodist Episcopal Church, South; and the Methodist Protestant Church.

The Methodist movement began in 18th-century England under the preaching of John Wesley, but the Christmas Conference of 1784 in Baltimore is regarded as the date on which the organized Methodist Church was founded as an ecclesiastical organization. It was there that Francis Asbury was elected the first bishop in this country.

The Evangelical United Brethren Church was formed in 1946 with the merger of the Evangelical Church and the Church of the United Brethren in Christ, both of which had their beginnings in Pennsylvania in the evangelistic movement of the 18th and early 19th centuries. Philip William Otterbein and Jacob Albright were early leaders of this movement among the German-speaking settlers of the Middle Colonies.

Headquarters

Information, InfoServ, United Methodist Information Service: Dir., Mary Lynn Holly Tel. (800)251-8140 Fax (615)742-5423

Email: infoserv@umcom.umc.org

Website: www.umc.org

Media Contact, Dir., United Methodist News Service Tel. (615)742-5470, Fax (615)742-5469, newsdesk@umcom.umc.org

Officers

General Conference, Sec., Carolyn M. Marshall, 204 N. Newlin St., Veedersburg, IN 47987

Council of Bishops: Pres., Bishop Sharon Brown Christopher, 400 Chatham Rd. Ste. 100, Springfield, IL 62704-1495 Tel. (217)726-8071, Fax (217)726-8074, ILAREAUMC@ aol.com; Sec., Bishop Sharon Zimmerman Rader, 750 Windsor St. Ste. 303, Sun Prairie, WI 53590-2149 Tel. (608)837-8526, Fax (608) 837-0281, EpiscopalOffice@WisconsinUMC. org

JURISDICTIONAL BISHOPS:

North Central Jurisdiction

Chicago Episcopal Area: Bishop C. Joseph Sprague, 77 W. Washington St. Ste. 1820, Chicago, IL 60602-2904 Tel. (312)346-9766 ext. 101, Fax (312)214-9031, JSPRAGUE@umcnic.org

Dakotas Episcopal Area: Bishop Michael J. Coyner, 3910 25th St. S, Fargo, ND 58104-6880 Tel. (701)232-2241, Fax (701)232-2615, BISHOPCOYNER@juno.com

Illinois Episcopal Area: Bishop Sharon Brown Christopher, 400 Chatham Rd. Ste. 100, Springfield, IL 62704-1495 Tel. (217)726-8071, Fax (217)726-8074, ILAREAUMC@aol.com

Indiana Episcopal Area: Bishop Woodie W. White, 1100 W. 42nd St., Ste. 210, Indianapolis, IN 46208-3382 Tel. (317)924-1321, Fax (317)924-1380, BishopWhite@inareaumc.org

Iowa Episcopal Area: Bishop Gregory V. Palmer, 500 E. Court Ave., Ste. C, Des Moines, IA 50309-2019 Tel. (515)283-1996 ext. 102, Fax (515)283-8672, bishop.palmer@iaumc.org

Michigan Episcopal Area: Bishop Linda Lee (2164 University Park Dr., Ste. 250, Okemos, MI 48864), P.O. Box 25068, Lansing, MI 48909-5068 Tel. (517)347-4030, Fax (517)347-4003, MAREAUMC@tir.com

Minnesota Episcopal Area: Bishop John L. Hopkins, 122 W. Franklin Ave. Rm. 200, Minneapolis, MN 55404-2472 Tel. (612)870-4007, Fax (612)870-3587, jhopkins@msn.com

Ohio East Episcopal Area: Bishop Jonathan D. Keaton (8800 Cleveland Ave. NW), P.O. Box 2800, North Canton, OH 44720-0800 Tel. (330)499-3972 ext. 112, Fax (330)497-4911, jonathan@eocumc.com

Ohio West Episcopal Area: Bishop Bruce R. Ough, 32 Wesley Blvd., Worthington, OH 43085-3585 Tel. (614)844-6200 ext. 215, Fax (614)781-2625, Bishop@wocumc.org

Wisconsin Episcopal Area: Bishop Sharon Zimmerman Rader, 750 Windsor St. Ste. 303, Sun Prairie, WI 53590-2149 Tel. (608)837-8526, Fax (608)837-0281, EpiscopalOffice@WisconsinUMC.org

Northeastern Jurisdiction

Albany Episcopal Area: Bishop Susan M. Morrison, 215 Lancaster St., Albany, NY 12210-1131 Tel. (518)426-0386, Fax (518)426-0347, AlbEpisArea@Worldnet.att.net

Boston Episcopal Area: Bishop Susan W. Hassinger (276 Essex St. 5th Fl. 01840), P.O. Box 249, Lawrence, MA 01842-0449 Tel. (978)682-7555 ext. 30, Fax (978)682-9555, bishopsoffice@neumc.org

Harrisburg Episcopal Area:, Bishop Neil L. Irons, 303 Mulberry Dr. Ste. 100, Mechanicsburg, PA 17050-3141 Tel. (717) 766-7871 ext. 3100, Fax (717)766-3210, bishop@ cpcumc.org

New Jersey Episcopal Area: Bishop Alfred Johnson, 1001 Wickapecko Dr., Ocean, NJ 07712-4733 Tel. (732)359-1010, Fax (732)359-1019, Bishop@gnjumc.org

New York Episcopal Area: Bishop Ernest Shaw Lyght, 20 Soundview Ave., White Plains, NY 10606-3302 Tel. (914)615-2221, Fax (914)615-2246, Bishop@NYAC.com

New York West Episcopal Area: Bishop Violet L. Fisher, 1010 East Ave, Rochester, NY 14607-2220 Tel. (585)271-3400, Fax (585)271-3404, nywaumc@frontiernet.net

Philadelphia Episcopal Area: Bishop Peter D. Weaver (Madison & Monroe Blvd.), P.O. Box 820, Valley Forge, PA 19482-0820 Tel. (610)666-9090 ext. 233, Fax (610)666-9181, bishop@epaumc.org

Pittsburgh Episcopal Area: Bishop Hae-Jong Kim (1204 Freedom Rd.), P.O. Box 5002, Cranberry Township, PA 16066-1902 Tel. (724)776-1499/1599, Fax (724)776-1683, HAEJONGKIM@aol.com

Washington Episcopal Area (D.C.) : Bishop Felton Edwin May, 100 Maryland Ave. NE, Ste. 510, Washington, D.C. 20002-5611 Tel. (202)546-3110, Fax (202)546-3186, bishop-may@bwcumc.org

West Virginia Episcopal Area: Bishop S. Clifton Ives, United Methodist Center, 900 Washington St. E. Ste. 300, Charleston, WV 25301-1710 Tel. (304)344-8330, Fax (304)344-8330, WVareaumc@aol.com

South Central Jurisdiction

Arkansas Episcopal Area: Bishop Janice Riggle Huie, 723 Center St., Little Rock, AR 72201-4399 Tel. (501)324-8019, Fax (501)324-8018, bishophuie@arumc.org

Dallas Episcopal Area: Bishop William B. Oden (3300 Mockingbird Ln. Rm. 358, 75205), P.O. Box 600127, Dallas, TX 75360-0127 Tel. (214)522-6741, Fax (214)528-4435, DallasBishop@hpumc.org

Fort Worth Episcopal Area: Bishop Ben R. Chamness, 464 Bailey Ave., Fort Worth, TX 76107-2153 Tel. (817)877-5222, Fax (817)332-4609, bishop@ctcumc.org

Houston Episcopal Area: Bishop Alfred L. Norris, 5215 Main St., Houston, TX 77002-9792 Tel. (713)528-6881, Fax (713)529-7736, ijarratt@methodists.net

Kansas Episcopal Area: Bishop Albert Frederick Mutti (4201 SW 15th St.), P.O. Box 4187, Topeka, KS 66604-0187 Tel. (785)272-0587, Fax (785)272-9135, kansasbishop@kansaseast.org

Louisiana Episcopal Area: Bishop William W. Hutchinson, 527 North Blvd., Baton Rouge, LA 70802-5700 Tel. (225)346-1646 ext. 212, Fax (225)387-3662, laumc@premier.net

Missouri Episcopal Area: Bishop Ann Brookshire Sherer, 4800 Santana Cir., Ste. 100, Columbia, MO 65203-7138 Tel. (573)441-1770, Fax (573)441-0765, sherer@ cunet.org

Nebraska Episcopal Area: Bishop Rhymes H. Moncure Jr. (2641 N. 49th St.), P.O. Box 4553, Lincoln, NE 68504-0553 Tel. (402)466-4955, Fax (402)466-7931, bishop@umcneb.org

Northwest Texas/New Mexico Episcopal Area: Bishop D. Max Whitfield, 7920 Mountain Rd. NE, Albuquerque, NM 87110-7805 Tel. (505) 255-8786, Fax (505)255-8738, whitmax@nmconfum.com

Oklahoma Episcopal Area: Bishop Bruce P. Blake (2420 N. Blackwelder Ave.), P.O. Box 60467, Oklahoma City, OK 73106-0467 Tel. (405)530-2025, Fax (405)530-2040, cnoble@okumc.org

San Antonio Episcopal Area: Bishop Joel N. Martinez (16400 Huebner Rd., 78248), P.O. Box 781688, San Antonio, TX 78278-1688 Tel. (210)408-4500, Fax (210)408-4501, bishop@umcswtx.org

Southeastern Jurisdiction

Alabama/West Florida Episcopal Area: Bishop Larry M. Goodpaster, 312 Interstate Park Dr., Montgomery, AL 36109-5408 Tel. (334)277-1787, Fax (334)277-0109, bishop.awf@knology.net

Birmingham Episcopal Area: Bishop Robert E. Fannin, 898 Arkadelphia Rd., Birmingham, AL 35204-5011 Tel. (205)322-8665, Fax (205)322-8938, Rfannin@umcna.bsc.edu

Charlotte Episcopal Area: Bishop Charlene P. Kammerer (3400 Shamrock Dr., 28215), P.O. Box 18750, Charlotte, NC 28218-0750 Tel. (704)535-2260, Fax (704)535-9160, jclark@wnccumc.org

Columbia Episcopal Area: Bishop J. Lawrence McCleskey, 4908 Colonial Dr., Ste. 108, Columbia, SC 29203-6000 Tel. (803)786-9486, Fax (803)754-9327, bishop@umcsc.org

Florida Episcopal Area: Bishop Timothy Wayne Whitaker (1122 E. McDonald St., 33801), P.O. Box 1747, Lakeland, FL 33802-1747 Tel. (863)688-4427, Fax (863)687-0568, bishop@flumc.org

Holston Episcopal Area: Bishop Ray W. Chamberlain Jr. (9915 Kingston Pike Ste. C, 37922), P.O. Box 32939, Knoxville, TN 37930-2939 Tel. (865)690-4080, Fax (865) 690-7112, bishop@holston.org

Louisville Episcopal Area: Bishop James R. King, Jr., 7400 Floydsburg Rd., Crestwood, KY 40014-8202 Tel. (502)425-4240, Fax (502) 425-9232, jking@kyumc.org

Mississippi Episcopal Area, Bishop Kenneth L. Carder (321 Mississippi St., 39201), P.O. Box 931, Jackson, MS 39205-0931 Tel. (601)948-4561, Fax (601)948-5981, bishop@mississippi-umc.org

Nashville Episcopal Area: Bishop William W. Morris, 520 Commerce St., Ste. 201, Nashville, TN 37203-3714 Tel. (615)742-8834, Fax (615)742-3726, umcoffice@aol.com

North Georgia Episcopal Area: Bishop G. Lindsey Davis (4511 Jones Bridge Cir. NW, 30092), P.O. Box 922997 Norcross, GA 30010-2997 Tel. (678)533-1360, Fax (678) 533-1361, bishop@ngumc.org

Raleigh Episcopal Area: Bishop Marion M. Edwards (1307 Glenwood Ave., Rm. 203), P.O. Box 10955, Raleigh, NC 27605-0955 Tel. (919)832-9560 ext. 243, Fax (919)832-4721, bishopmme@nccumc.org

Richmond Episcopal Area: Bishop Joe E. Pennel, Jr. (10330 Staples Mill Rd.), P.O. Box 1719, Glen Allen, VA 23060-0659 Tel. (804)521-1100, Fax (804)521-1171, bod@vaumc.org

South Georgia Episcopal Area: Bishop B. Michael Watson (3370 Vineville Ave. Ste. 101, 31204), P.O. Box 13616, Macon, GA 31208-3616 Tel. (478)475-9286, Fax (478)475-9248, bishopsga@aol.com

Western Jurisdiction

Denver Episcopal Area: Bishop Warner H. Brown Jr., 2200 S. University Blvd., Denver, CO 80210-4797 Tel. (303)733-3736 ext. 601, Fax (303)733-5047, bishop@bishopbrown.org

Los Angeles Episcopal Area: Bishop Mary Ann Swenson (110 S. Euclid Ave., 91101), P.O. Box 6006, Pasadena, CA 91102-6006 Tel. (626)568-7312, Fax (626)568-7377, calpacbishop@earthlink.net

Phoenix Episcopal Area: Bishop William W. Dew Jr., 1550 E. Meadowbrook Ave., Phoenix, AZ 85014-4040 Tel. (602)266-6956 ext. 209, Fax (602)279-1355, Bishop@desertsw.org

Portland Episcopal Area: Bishop Edward W. Paup, 1505 SW 18th Ave., Portland, OR 97201-2599 Tel. (503)226-1530, Fax (503) 228-3189, bishop@umoi.net

San Francisco Episcopal Area: Bishop Beverly J. Shamana (1276 Halyard Dr., 95691), P.O. Box 980250, West Sacramento, CA 95798-0250 Tel. (916)374-1510, Fax (916)372-9062, bishop@calnevumc.org

Seattle Episcopal Area: Bishop Elias G. Galvan, 2112 3rd Ave., Ste. 301, Seattle, WA 98121-2333 Tel. (206)728-7674, Fax (206)728-8442, bishop@pnwumc.org

Periodicals

Mature Years, El Intérprete, New World Outlook, Newscope, Interpreter, Methodist History, Christian Social Action, Pockets, Response, Social Questions Bulletin, United Methodist Reporter, United Methodist Review, Quarterly Review, Alive Now, Circuit Rider, El Aposento Alto, Weavings–A Journal of the Christian Spiritual Life, The Upper Room

United Pentecostal Church International

The United Pentecostal Church International came into being through the merger of two oneness Pentecostal organizations—the Pentecostal Church, Inc., and the Pentecostal Assemblies of

Jesus Christ. The first of these was known as the Pentecostal Ministerial Alliance from its inception in 1925 until 1932. The second was formed in 1931 by a merger of the Apostolic Church of Jesus Christ with the Pentecostal Assemblies of the World.

The church contends that the Bible teaches that there is one God who manifested himself as the Father in creation, in the Son in redemption, and as the Holy Spirit in regeneration; that Jesus is the name of this absolute deity; and that water baptism should be administered in his name, not in the titles Father, Son and Holy Ghost (Acts 2:38; 8:16; and 19:6).

The Fundamental Doctrine of the United Pentecostal Church International, as stated in its Articles of Faith, is "the Bible standard of full salvation, which is repentance, baptism in water by immersion in the name of the Lord Jesus Christ for the remission of sins, and the baptism of the Holy Ghost with the initial sign of speaking with other tongues as the Spirit gives utterance."

Further doctrinal teachings concern a life of holiness and separation, the operation of the gifts of the Spirit within the church, the second coming of the Lord, and the church's obligation to take the gospel to the whole world.

Headquarters

8855 Dunn Rd., Hazelwood, MO 63042 Tel. (314)837-7300 Fax (314)837-4503

Media Contact, Gen. Sec.-Treas., Rev. Jerry Jones

Officers

Gen. Supt., Rev. Kenneth F. Haney

Asst. Gen. Supts., Rev. Jesse F. Williams and Rev. Randy Keyes

Gen. Sec.-Treas., Rev. Jerry Jones

Dir. of Foreign Missions, Rev. Bruce Howell

Gen. Dir. of Home Missions, Rev. Jack Cunningham

Editor-in-Chief, Rev. J. L. Hall

Gen. Sunday School Dir., Rev. Gary Erickson

Youth Pres., Rev. Todd Gaddy

OTHER ORGANIZATIONS

Pentecostal Publishing House: Mgr., Rev. Marvin Curry

Ladies Ministries: Pres., Gwyn Oakes

Harvestime Radio Broadcast: Dir., Rev. N. A. Ursham and Coordinator, Rev. J. Hugh Rose

Stewardship Dept.: Dir., Rev., Stephen Drur

Division of Education: Supt., Rev. Arless Glass

Word Aflame Publications: Editor, Rev. Richard Davis

Public Relations: Contact Church Administration

Historical Society & Archives

Urshan Graduate School of Theology

Periodicals

The Pentecostal Herald, World Harvest Today, The North American Challenge, Preserving Christian Homes, Conqueror, Reflections, Forward, Apostolic Man

The United Pentecostal Churches of Christ

In a time when the Church of Jesus Christ is challenged to send the "Evening Light Message" to the uppermost part of the Earth, a group of men and women came together on May 29, 1992 at the Pentecostal Church of Christ in Cleveland, Ohio to form what is now called The United Pentecostal Churches of Christ.

Organized and established by Bishop Jesse Delano Ellis II, the United Pentecostal Churches of Christ is about the business of preparing people to see the Lord of Glory. The traditional barriers of yesteryear must not keep saints or like faith apart ever again and this fellowship of Pentecostal, Apostolic Independent Churches have discovered the truth of Our Lord's Prayer in the seventeenth chapter of Saint John, "that they may all be One."

The United Pentecostal Churches of Christ is a fellowship of holiness assemblies which has membership in the universal Body of Christ. As such, we preserve the message of Christ's redeeming love through His atonement and declare holiness of life to be His requirement for all men who would enter into the Kingdom of God. We preach repentence from sin, baptism in the Name of Jesus Christ, a personal indwelling of the Holy Spirit, a daily walk with the Lord and life after death. Coupled with the cardinal truths of the Church are the age old customs of ceremony and celebration.

Headquarters

10515 Chester Ave. (at University Circle), Cleveland, OH 44106 Tel. (216)721-5935 Fax (216)721-6938

Media Contact, Public Relations., Rev. W. Michelle James Williams

REGIONAL OFFICE

493-5 Monroe St., Brooklyn, New York 11221 Tel. (718)574-4100 Fax (718)574-8504

Media Contact, Secretary General., Rev. Rodney McNeil Johnson

Officers

Presiding Bishop and Gen. Overseer, Bishop J. Delano Ellis II, Cleveland, OH

Asst. Presiding Bishop, Bishop Carl Halloway Montgomery II, Baltimore, MD

Sec. Gen., Bishop James R. Chambers, Brookyn, NY

Pres. Of Pentacostal Youth Congress, Overseer Darryl D. Woodson, Memphis, TN

Periodicals

The Pentecostal Flame

United Zion Church

A branch of the Brethren in Christ which settled in Lancaster County, Penn., the United Zion Church was organized under the leadership of Matthias Brinser in 1855.

Headquarters

United Zion Retirement Community, 722 Furnace Hills Pk., Lititz, PA 17543

Media Contact, Bishop, Carl Eberly, 270 Clay School Rd., Ephrata, PA 17522 Tel. (717)733-3932

Officers

Gen. Conf. Mod., Bishop Carl Eberly, 270 Clay School Rd., Ephrata, PA 17522 Tel. (717)733-3932

Asst. Mod., Rev. John Leisey

Gen. Conf. Sec., Rev. Clyde Martin

Gen. Conf. Treas., Kenneth Kleinfelter, 919 Sycamore Lane, Lebanon, PA 17042

Periodicals

Zion's Herald

Unity of the Brethren

Czech and Moravian immigrants in Texas (beginning about 1855) established congregations which grew into an Evangelical Union in 1903 and, with the accession of other Brethren in Texas, into the Evangelical Unity of the Czech-Moravian Brethren in North America. In 1959, it shortened the name to the original name used in 1457, the Unity of the Brethren (Unitas Fratrum, or Jednota Bratrska).

Headquarters

4009 Hunter Creek, College Station, TX 77845

Media Contact, Sec. of Exec. Committee, Ginger McKay, 148 N. Burnett, Baytown, TX 77520

Officers

Pres., Kent Laza, 4009 Hunter Creek, College Station, TX 77845

1st Vice Pres., Rev. Michael Groseclose, 902 Church St., Belleville, TX 77418 Tel. (512)365-6890

Sec. of Exec. Committee, Ginger McKay, 148 N. Burnett, Baytown, TX 77520

Fin. Sec., Rev. Joseph Polasek, 4241 Blue Heron, Bryan, TX 77807

Treas., Arranna Jakubik, P.O. Box 408, Snook, TX 77878

OTHER ORGANIZATIONS

Bd. of Christian Educ.: Dir., Donald Ketcham, 900 N. Harrison, West, TX 76691

Brethren Youth Fellowship: Pres., Jamie Brooke Bryan, 1231 Four Corners, West, TX 76691

Friends of the Hus Encampment: Jim Baletka, 727 San Benito, College Station, TX 77845

Christian Sisters Union: Pres., Janet Pomykal, P.O. Box 560, Brenham, TX 77834

Sunday School Union: Pres., Dorothy Kocian, 107 S. Barbara Dr., Waco, TX 76705

Youth Director: Kimberly Stewart, 1500 Lawnmont Dr., Apt. 208, Round Rock, TX 78664

Periodicals

Brethren Journal: Editor, Rev.Milton Maly, 6703 FM 2502, Brenham, TX 77833; Bus Mngr., Jean Maly, 6703 FM 2502, Brenham, TX 77833

Universal Fellowship of Metropolitan Community Churches

The Universal Fellowship of Metropolitan Community Churches was founded Oct. 6, 1968 by the Rev. Troy D. Perry in Los Angeles, with a particular but not exclusive outreach to the gay community. Since that time, the Fellowship has grown to include congregations throughout the world.

The group is Trinitarian and accepts the Bible as the divinely inspired Word of God. The Fellowship has two sacraments, baptism and holy communion, as well as a number of traditionally recognized rites such as ordination.

This Fellowship acknowledges "the Holy Scriptures interpreted by the Holy Spirit in conscience and faith, as its guide in faith, discipline, and government." The government of this Fellowship is vested in its General Council (consisting of Elders and District Coordinators), clergy, and church delegates, who exert the right of control in all of its affairs, subject to the provisions of its Articles of Incorporation and By-Laws.

Headquarters

8704 Santa Monica Blvd., 2nd Floor, West Hollywood, CA 90069-4548 Tel. (310)360-8640 ext. 226 Fax (310)360-8680

Email: communications@ufmcchq.com

Website: www.ufmcchq.com

Media Contact, Dir. of Communications, Jim Birkett

Officers

Mod., Rev. Elder Troy D. Perry

Vice Mod., Rev. Elder Nancy L. Wilson

Treas., Rev. Elder Donald Eastman

Clk., Rev. Elder Darlene Garner

Elder Mel Johnson, PMB #63, 2261 Market St., San Francisco, CA 94114-1600

Rev. Elder Nori Rost, 214 S. Prospect St., Colorado Springs, CO 80903

Rev. Elder Hong Kia Tan, 72 Fleet Rd., Hampstead, London, NW3 2QT England

Deputy Chief Executive Officer, Jane Wagner, 8704 Santa Monica Blvd., 2nd Floor, W. Holywood, CA 90069-4548

Dir., Communications, Jim Birkett, 8704 Santa Monica Blvd., 2nd Floor, W. Hollywood, CA 90069-4548

OTHER COMMISSIONS & COMMITTEES

Min. of Global Outreach: Field Dir., Rev. Judy Dahl

Commission on the Laity: Chpsn., Stan Kimer

Clergy Credentials & Concerns: Admn., Rev. Justin Tanis

UFMCC AIDS Ministry: AIDS Liaison., Rev. Robert Griffin

Chief Financial Officer: Margaret Mahlman, 8704 Santa Monica Blvd., 2nd Floor, West Hollywood, CA 90069-4548

Periodicals

Keeping in Touch, UFMCC E-Mail News Service (FREE)

Volunteers of America

Volunteers of America is a national, nonprofit, spiritually-based organization providing local human service programs and opportunities for individual and community involovement. Founded in 1896 by Christian social reformers Ballington and Maud Booth, Volunteers of America provides about 100 different types of programs and services in more than 400 communities nationwide for abused and neglected children, youth at risk, the elderly, people with disabilities, homeless individuals and families, and many others.

Headquarters

1660 Duke St., Alexandria, VA 22314-3427 Tel. (800)899-0089
Email: voa@voa.org
Website: www.voa.org

Officers

Chpsn., Frances Hesselbein
Pres., Charles W. Gould, 1660 Duke St., Alexandria, VA. 22314 Tel. (703)341-5000
Dir., of Ecclesiastical Services, Harry V. Quiett,1660 Duke St., Alexandria, VA 22314 Tel. (703)341-5054, Hquiett@voa.org

Periodicals

Spirit

The Wesleyan Church

The Wesleyan Church was formed on June 26, 1968, through the union of the Wesleyan Methodist Church of America (1843) and the Pilgrim Holiness Church (1897). The headquarters was established at Marion, Ind., and relocated to Indianapolis in 1987.

The Wesleyan movement centers around the beliefs, based on Scripture, that the atonement in Christ provides for the regeneration of sinners and the entire sanctification of believers. John Wesley led a revival of these beliefs in the 18th century.

When a group of New England Methodist ministers led by Orange Scott began to crusade for the abolition of slavery, the bishops and others sought to silence them. This led to a series of withdrawals from the Methodist Episcopal Church. In 1843, the Wesleyan Methodist Connection of America was organized and led by Scott, Jotham Horton, LaRoy Sunderland, Luther Lee, and Lucius C. Matlack.

During the holiness revival in the last half of the 19th century, holiness replaced social reform as the major tenet of the Connection. In 1947 the name was changed from Connection to Church and a central supervisory authority was set up.

The Pilgrim Holiness Church was one of many independent holiness churches which came into existence as a result of the holiness revival. Led by Martin Wells Knapp and Seth C. Rees, the International Holiness Union and Prayer League was inaugurated in 1897 in Cincinnati. Its purpose was to promote worldwide holiness evangelism and the Union had a strong missionary emphasis from the beginning. It developed into a church by 1913.

The Wesleyan Church is now spread across most of the United States and Canada and in over 70 other countries. The Wesleyan World Fellowship was organized in 1972 to unite Wesleyan mission bodies developing into mature churches. The Wesleyan Church is a member of the Christian Holiness Partnership, the National Association of Evangelicals, and the World Methodist Council.

Headquarters

P.O. Box 50434, Indianapolis, IN 46250 Tel. (317)570-5100
Email: gensupts@wesleyan.org
Website: www.wesleyan.org
Media Contact, Gen. Sec., Dr. Ronald D. Kelly Tel. (317)570-5154, Fax (317)570-5280, kellyr@wesleyan.org

Officers

General Superintendents
Dr. Earle L. Wilson Tel. (317)570-5146, Fax (317)570-5255, wilsone@wesleyan.org
Dr. Thomas E. Armiger Tel. (317)570-5147, Fax (317)570-5255, armigert@wesleyan.org
Dr. David W. Holdren Tel. (317)570-5148, Fax (317)570-5255, holdrend@wesleyan.org
General Officers
Gen. Sec., Dr. Ronald D. Kelly Tel. (317)570-5154, Fax (317)570-5280, kellyr@wesleyan.org
Gen. Treas., Donald M. Frase Tel. (317)570-5150, Fax (317)570-5285, frased@wesleyan.org
Gen. Publisher, Mr. Donald D. Cady Tel. (317)570-5317, Fax (317)570-5370, cadyd@wesleyan.org
Gen. Director of Communications, Dr. Norman G. Wilson Tel. (317)570-5156, Fax (317)570-5260, wilsonn@wesleyan.org
Gen. Dir. of Sunday School & Discipleship, Dr. Ray E. Barnwell Sr. Tel. (317)570-5180, Fax (317)570-5290, barnwelr@wesleyan.org
Gen. Dir. of Evangelism & Church Growth, Dr. Jerry Pence Tel. (317)570-5125, Fax (317) 570-5265, pencej@wesleyan.org
Gen. Dir. of Education & the Ministry, Rev. Kerry D. Kind Tel. (317)570-5130, Fax (317) 570-5270, kindk@wesleyan.org
Gen. Dir. of World Missions, Dr. Donald L. Bray Tel. (317)570-5160, Fax (317)570-5256, brayd@wesleyan.org
Gen. Dir. of Youth, Rev. Ross A. DeMerchant Tel. (317)570-5140, Fax (317)570-5257, demerchr@wesleyan.org
Auxiliaries/Subsidiary Agencies
Estate Planning: Gen. Dir., Rev. Larry J. Moore Tel. (317)570-5162, Fax (317)570-5273, castleh@wesleyan.org
Wesleyan Investment Foundation: Gen. Dir., Dr.

Craig A. Dunn Tel. (317)570-5136, Fax (317)570-6190, wif@wesleyan.org
Wesleyan Pension Fund: Gen. Dir., Mr. Robert L. (Bobby) Temple Tel. (317)570-5131, Fax (317)570-5253, templer@wesleyan.org
Wesleyan Women: Mrs. Nancy Heer Tel. (317)570-5164, heern@wesleyan.org
Wesleyan Kids for Mission: Mrs. Peggy Camp Tel. (317)570-5164, Fax (317)570-5254, heern@wesleyan.org or wwi@wesleyan.org
Wesleyan Men: Dr. Jerry Pence Tel. (317)570-5125, Fax (317)570-5265, pencej@wesleyan.org
Address Service: Tel. (317)570-5200
Archives & Historical Library: Tel. (317)570-5145
Computer Information Services: Tel. (317)570-5121
Wesleyan Publishing House: Tel. (317)570-5300

Periodicals

Wesleyan Woman; The Wesleyan Advocate, Wesleyan World

Wesleyan Holiness Association of Churches

This body was founded Aug. 4, 1959 near Muncie, Ind. by a group of ministers and laymen who were drawn together for the purpose of spreading and conserving sweet, radical, scriptural holiness. These men came from various church bodies. This group is Wesleyan in doctrine and standards.

Headquarters

1141 N. US Hwy 27, Fountain City, IN 47341-9757 Tel. (765)584-3199
Media Contact, Gen. Sec.-Treas., Rev. Robert W. Wilson, RR3 Box 218, Selinsgrove, PA 17870

Officers

Gen. Supt., Rev. John Brewer
Asst. Gen. Supt., Rev. Armen O. Rhoads, 7812 Portland Ave., Tacoma, WA 98404
Gen. Sec.-Treas., Rev. Robert W. Wilson, RR3 Box 218, Selinsgrove, PA 17870 Tel. (570) 539-9821
Gen. Youth Pres., Rev. Nathan Shockley, 504 W. Tyrell St., St. Louis, MI 48880 Tel. (517)681-2591

Periodicals

Eleventh Hour Messenger

Wisconsin Evangelical Lutheran Synod

Organized in 1850 at Milwaukee, Wisc., by three pastors sent to America by a German mission society, the Wisconsin Evangelical Lutheran Synod still reflects its origins, although it now has congregations in 50 states and three Canadian provinces. It supports missions in 26 countries.

The Wisconsin Synod federated with the Michigan and Minnesota Synods in 1892 in order to more effectively carry on education and mission enterprises. A merger of these three Synods followed in 1917 to give the Wisconsin Evangelical Lutheran Synod its present form.

Although at its organization in 1850 WELS turned away from conservative Lutheran theology, today it is ranked as one of the most conservative Lutheran bodies in the United States. WELS confesses that the Bible is the verbally inspired, infallible Word of God and subscribes without reservation to the confessional writings of the Lutheran Church. Its interchurch relations are determined by a firm commitment to the principle that unity of doctrine and practice are the prerequisites of pulpit and altar fellowship and ecclesiastical cooperation. It does not hold membership in ecumenical organizations.

Headquarters

2929 N. Mayfair Rd., Milwaukee, WI 53222 Tel. (414)256-3888 Fax (414)256-3899
Email: webbin@sab.wels.net
Website: www.wels.net
Dir. of Communications, Rev. Gary Baumler

Officers

Pres., Rev. Karl R. Gurgel, 2929 N. Mayfair Rd., Milwaukee, WI 53222
1st Vice Pres., Rev. Wayne D. Mueller, 2929 N. Mayfair Rd., Milwaukee, WI 53222 Tel (414)256-3888 Fax (414)256-3899
2nd Vice Pres., Rev. Thomas Zarling, 6 Wiltshire Ct. E, Sterling, VA 20165
Sec., Teacher Steven Lemke, 1108 Ontario Ave., Sheboygan, WI, 53081

OTHER ORGANIZATIONS

Bd. for Ministerial Education: Admn., Rev. Peter Kruschel
Bd. for Parish Services: Admn., Rev. Bruce Becker
Bd. for Home Missions: Admn., Rev. Harold J. Hagedorn
Bd. for World Missions: Admn., Rev. Daniel Koelpin

Periodicals

Wisconsin Lutheran Quarterly, Forward in Christ, Lutheran Leader, The Lutheran Educator, Mission Connection

Religious Bodies in the United States Arranged by Families

The following list of religious bodies appearing in the Directory Section of the *Yearbook* shows the "families," or related clusters, into which American religious bodies can be grouped. For example, there are many communions that can be grouped under the heading "Baptist" for historical and theological reasons. It should not be assumed, however, that all denominations under one family heading are necessarily consistent in belief or practice. The family clusters tend to represent historical factors more often than theological or practical ones. These family categories provide one of the major pitfalls when compiling church statistics because there is often a tendency to combine the statistics by "families" for analytical and comparative purposes. Such combined totals are deeply flawed, even though they are often used as variables for sociological analysis. The arrangement by families offered here is intended only as a general guide for conceptual organization when viewing the broad sweep of American religious culture.

Religious bodies that can not be categorized under family headings appear alphabetically and are not indented in the following list.

Adventist Bodies

Advent Christian Church
Church of God General Conference (Oregon, IL and Morrow, GA)
Primitive Advent Christian Church
Seventh-day Adventist Church

American Evangelical Christian Churches
American Rescue Workers

Anglican Bodies

Episcopal Church
The Episcopal Orthodox Church
Reformed Episcopal Church

Apostolic Christian Church (Nazarene)
Apostolic Christian Churches of America
Apostolic Episcopal Church

Baptist Bodies

The Alliance of Baptists in the USA
The American Baptist Association
American Baptist Churches in the USA
Baptist Bible Fellowship International
Baptist General Conference
Baptist Missionary Association of America
Conservative Baptist Association of America
General Association of General Baptists
General Association of Regular Baptist Churches
National Association of Free Will Baptists
National Baptist Convention of America, Inc.
National Baptist Convention, USA, Inc.
National Missionary Baptist Convention of America
National Primitive Baptist Convention, Inc.
North American Baptist Conference
Primitive Baptists
Progressive National Baptist Convention, Inc.
Separate Baptists in Christ
Seventh Day Baptist General Conference, USA and Canada
Southern Baptist Convention
Sovereign Grace Believers

Berean Fundamental Church

Brethren (German Baptists)

Brethren Church (Ashland, Ohio)
Church of the Brethren
Fellowship of Grace Brethren Churches
Old German Baptist Brethren

Brethren, River

Brethren in Christ Church
United Zion Church

The Catholic Church
Christ Community Church (Evangelical-Protestant)
Christadelphians
Christian Brethren (also known as Plymouth Brethren)
The Christian Congregation, Inc.
The Christian and Missionary Alliance
Christian Union
The Church of Christ (Holiness) USA
Church of Christ, Scientist
The Church of Illumination
Church of the Living God
Church of the Nazarene

Churches of Christ—Christian Churches

Christian Church (Disciples of Christ)
Christian Churches and Churches of Christ
Churches of Christ
Churches of Christ in Christian Union

Churches of God

Church of God (Anderson, Indiana)
The Church of God (Seventh Day), Denver, Colorado

Church of God by Faith, Inc.
Churches of God, General Conference

Churches of the New Jerusalem

General Church of the New Jerusalem
The Swedenborgian Church

Conservative Congregational Christian Conference

Eastern Orthodox Churches

Albanian Orthodox Archdiocese in America
Albanian Orthodox Diocese of America
The American Carpatho-Russian Orthodox Greek Catholic Church
The Antiochian Orthodox Christian Archdiocese of North America
Apostolic Catholic Assyrian Church of the East, North American Dioceses
Apostolic Orthodox Catholic Church
Greek Orthodox Archdiocese of America
The Holy Eastern Orthodox Catholic and Apostolic Church in North America, Inc.
Holy Ukrainian Autocephalic Orthodox Church in Exile
The Orthodox Church in America
Patriarchal Parishes of the Russian Orthodox Church in the USA
The Romanian Orthodox Church in America
The Romanian Orthodox Episcopate of America
The Russian Orthodox Church Outside of Russia
Serbian Orthodox Church in the U.S.A. and Canada
The Syro-Russian Orthodox Catholic Church, Romano-Byzantine Synod
True Orthodox Church of Greece (Synod of Metropolitan Cyprian), American Exarchate
Ukrainian Orthodox Church of the USA

The Evangelical Church
The Evangelical Church Alliance
The Evangelical Congregational Church
The Evangelical Covenant Church
The Evangelical Free Church of America
Fellowship of Fundamental Bible Churches
Free Christian Zion Church of Christ

Friends

Evangelical Friends International–North American Region
Friends General Conference
Friends United Meeting
Philadelphia Yearly Meeting of the Religious Society of Friends
Religious Society of Friends (Conservative)
Religious Society of Friends (Unaffiliated Meetings)

Grace Gospel Fellowship

House of God, Which is the Church of the Living God, the Pillar and Ground of the Truth, Inc.
Independent Fundamental Churches of America/ IFCA International, Inc.
International Council of Community Churches
Jehovah's Witnesses

Latter Day Saints (Mormons)

Church of Christ
The Church of Jesus Christ of Latter-day Saints
The Church of Jesus Christ (Bickertonites)
Community of Christ

The Liberal Catholic Church— Province of the United States of America

Lutheran Bodies

The American Association of Lutheran Churches
Apostolic Lutheran Church of America
The Association of Free Lutheran Congregations
Church of the Lutheran Brethren of America
Church of the Lutheran Confession
Conservative Lutheran Association
The Estonian Evangelical Lutheran Church
Evangelical Lutheran Church in America
Evangelical Lutheran Synod
The Latvian Evangelical Lutheran Church in America
The Lutheran Church–Missouri Synod
Wisconsin Evangelical Lutheran Synod

Mennonite Bodies

Beachy Amish Mennonite Churches
Bible Fellowship Church
Church of God in Christ, Mennonite
Fellowship of Evangelical Bible Churches
Fellowship of Evangelical Churches
General Conference of Mennonite Brethren Churches
Hutterian Brethren
Mennonite Church, USA
Old Order Amish Church
Old Order (Wisler) Mennonite Church
Reformed Mennonite Church

Methodist Bodies

African Methodist Episcopal Church
African Methodist Episcopal Zion Church
Allegheny Wesleyan Methodist Connection (Original Allegheny Conference)
Bible Holiness Church
Christian Methodist Episcopal Church
Evangelical Methodist Church
Free Methodist Church of North America
Fundamental Methodist Church, Inc.
Primitive Methodist Church in the U.S.A.
Reformed Methodist Union Episcopal Church
Reformed Zion Union Apostolic Church

Southern Methodist Church
The United Methodist Church
The Wesleyan Church

The Metropolitan Church Association, Inc.
The Missionary Church

Moravian Bodies

Moravian Church in America (Unitas Fratrum)
Unity of the Brethren

National Association of Congregational Christian Churches
National Organization of the New Apostolic Church of North America
National Spiritualist Association of Churches
North American Old Roman Catholic Church (Archdiocese of New York)

Old Catholic Churches

Apostolic Catholic Orthodox Church
Christ Catholic Church
Liberal Catholic Church (International)

Oriental Orthodox Churches

Armenian Apostolic Church of America
Armenian Apostolic Church, Diocese of America
Coptic Orthodox Church
Syrian (Syriac) Orthodox Church of Antioch

Pentecostal Bodies

Apostolic Faith Mission of Portland, Oregon
Apostolic Faith Mission Church of God
Apostolic Overcoming Holy Church of God, Inc.
Assemblies of God
Assemblies of God International Fellowship (Independent/Not affiliated)
The Bible Church of Christ, Inc.
Bible Way Church of Our Lord Jesus Christ World Wide, Inc.
Christian Church of North America, General Council
Church of God of Prophecy
Church of God (Cleveland, Tennessee)
Church of God in Christ, International
The Church of God In Christ
Church of God, Mountain Assembly, Inc.
Church of Our Lord Jesus Christ of the Apostolic Faith, Inc.
Congregational Holiness Church
Elim Fellowship
Full Gospel Assemblies International
Full Gospel Fellowship of Churches and Ministers International
International Church of the Foursquare Gospel
The International Pentecostal Church of Christ
International Pentecostal Holiness Church
Open Bible Standard Churches
The (Original) Church of God, Inc.
Pentecostal Assemblies of the World, Inc.
Pentecostal Church of God
Pentecostal Fire-Baptized Holiness Church
The Pentecostal Free Will Baptist Church, Inc.
Pillar of Fire
United Holy Church of America, Inc.
United Pentecostal Church International
The United Pentecostal Churches of Christ

Polish National Catholic Church of America

Reformed Bodies

Associate Reformed Presbyterian Church (General Synod)
Christian Reformed Church in North America
Cumberland Presbyterian Church
Cumberland Presbyterian Church in America
Evangelical Presbyterian Church
Hungarian Reformed Church in America
Korean Presbyterian Church in America, General Assembly of the Netherlands Reformed Congregations
The Orthodox Presbyterian Church
Presbyterian Church in America
Presbyterian Church (USA)
Protestant Reformed Churches in America
Reformed Church in America
Reformed Church in the United States
Reformed Presbyterian Church of North America
United Church of Christ

Reformed Catholic Church
The Salvation Army
The Schwenkfelder Church

Thomist Churches

Malankara Orthodox Syrian Church, Diocese of America
Mar Thoma Syrian Church of India

Triumph the Church and Kingdom of God in Christ Inc. (International)
Unitarian Universalist Association of Congregations

United Brethren Bodies

Church of the United Brethren in Christ
United Christian Church

United House of Prayer
Universal Fellowship of Metropolitan Community Churches
Volunteers of America
Wesleyan Holiness Association of Churches

4. Religious Bodies in Canada

A large number of Canadian religious bodies were organized by immigrants from Europe and elsewhere, and a smaller number sprang up originally on Canadian soil. In the case of Canada, moreover, many denominations that transcend the US–Canada border have headquarters in the United States.

A final section in this directory lists churches according to denominational families. This can be a helpful tool in finding a particular church if you don't know the official name. Complete statistics for Canadian churches are found in the statistical section in Chapter 3: Table 1 contains membership figures, and Table 4 contains giving figures. Addresses for periodicals are found in the directory entitled, "Religious Periodicals in Canada."

The Pentecostal Assemblies of Canada

This body is incorporated under the Dominion Charter of 1919 and is also recognized in the Province of Quebec as an ecclesiastical corporation. Its beginnings are to be found in the revivals at the turn of the century, and most of the first Canadian Pentecostal leaders came from a religious background rooted in the Holiness movements.

The original incorporation of 1919 was implemented among churches of eastern Canada only. In the same year, a conference was called in Moose Jaw, Saskatchewan, to which the late Rev. J. M. Welch, general superintendent of the then-organized Assemblies of God in the US, was invited. The churches of Manitoba and Saskatchewan were organized as the Western District Council of the Assemblies of God. They were joined later by Alberta and British Columbia. In 1921, a conference was held in Montreal, to which the general chairman of the Assemblies of God was invited. Eastern Canada also became a district of the Assemblies of God, joining Eastern and Western Canada as two districts in a single organizational union.

In 1920, at Kitchener, Ontario, eastern and western churches agreed to dissolve the Canadian District of the Assemblies of God and unite under the name "The Pentecostal Assemblies of Canada."

Today the Pentecostal Assemblies of Canada operates throughout the nation and in about 30 countries around the world. Religious services are conducted in more than 25 different languages in the 1,100 local churches in Canada. Members and adherents number about 230,000. The number of local churches includes approximately 100 Native congregations.

Headquarters

2450 Milltower Court, Mississauga, ON L5N 5Z6 Tel. (905)542-7400 Fax (905)542-7313

Officers

Gen. Supt., Rev. William D. Morrow

Asst. Supt., for Ministerial Services, Rev. David E. Hazzard

Asst. Supt. for Financial Resources, Rev. David Ball

DISTRICT SUPERINTENDENTS

British Columbia: Rev. D. R. Wells, 20411 Douglas Crescent, Langley, BC V3S 4B6 Tel. (604)533-2232 Fax (604)533-5405

Alberta: Rev. Lorne D. McAlister, 10585-111 St., #101, Edmonton, AB T5H 3E8 Tel. (403)426-0084 Fax (403)420-1318

Saskatchewan: Rev. J. I. Guskjolen, 3488 Fairlight Dr., Saskatoon, SK S7M 3Z4 Tel. (306)683-4646 Fax (306)683-3699

Manitoba: Rev. R.W. Pierce, 187 Henlow Bay, Winnipeg, MB R3Y 1G4 Tel. (204)940-1000 Fax (204)940-1009

Western Ontario: Rev. D.A Shepherd, 3214 S. Service Rd., Burlington, ON L7N 3J2 Tel. (905) 637-5566 Fax (905)637-7558

Eastern Ontario and Quebec: Rev. R. T. Hilsden, Box 337, Cobury, ON K9A 4K8 Tel. (905) 373-7374 Fax (905)373-1911

Quebec: Rev. G.C. Connors, 911, boul Roland-Therrien, Longueuil, QC JAJ 4L3 Tel (4005) 442-2732 Fax (405) 442-3818

Maritime Provinces: Rev. Douglas Moore, Box 1184, Truro, NS B2N 5H1 Tel. (902)895-4212 Fax (902)897-0705

BRANCH CONFERENCES

Slavic Conferences: Eastern District, Rev. A. Muravski, 445 Stevenson Rd., Oshawa, ON L1J 5N8 Tel (905)576-3584; Western District, Rev. Michael Brandebura, 4108-134 Ave., Edmonton, AB T5A 3M2 Tel (780)743-2410 Fax (780)473-2410

Finnish Conference: Rev. E. Ahonen, 1920 Argyle Dr., Vancouver, BC V5P 2A8 Tel (604)321-0555 Fax (604)321-0555

Periodicals

Testimony (The official magazine of The Pentecostal Assemblies of Canada), *Enrich* (National Leadership Magazine), *Contact* (Magazine for those 50 years +), *HonorBound* (Magazine for Men)

The Anglican Church of Canada

Anglicanism came to Canada with the early explorers such as Martin Frobisher and Henry Hudson. Continuous services began in Newfoundland about 1700 and in Nova Scotia in 1710. The first Bishop, Charles Inglis, was appointed to Nova Scotia in 1787. The numerical

CANADIAN RELIGIOUS BODIES

strength of Anglicanism was increased by the coming of American Loyalists and by massive immigration both after the Napoleonic wars and in the later 19th and early 20th centuries.

The Anglican Church of Canada has enjoyed self-government for over a century since 1893 and is an autonomous member of the worldwide Anglican Communion. The General Synod, which normally meets triennially, consists of the Archbishops, Bishops, and elected clerical and lay representatives of the 30 dioceses. Each of the Ecclesiastical Provinces—Canada, Ontario, Rupert's Land, and British Columbia—is organized under a Metropolitan and has its own Provincial Synod and Executive Council. Each diocese has its own Diocesan Synod.

Headquarters

Church House, 80 Hayden St., Toronto, ON M4Y 3G2 Tel. [Switchboard] (416)924-9192 [Voice mail] (416)924-9199 Fax (416)968-7983,

E-mail: info@national.anglican.ca

Website: www.anglican.ca

Media Contact, Mr. Sam Galati Vianney (Sam) Carriere

GENERAL SYNOD OFFICERS

Primate of the Anglican Church of Canada, -vacant- (election May 2004)

Prolocutor, Ms. Dorothy Davies-Flindall

Gen. Sec., Ven. James B. Boyles

Treas., Gen. Synod, Mr. James Cullen

DEPARTMENTS AND DIVISIONS

Faith, Worship & Ministry: Dir., Rev. Canon Alyson Barnett-Cowan

Financial Management and Dev.: Dir., Mr. James Cullen

Inform. Resources: Dir., Mr. Vianney (Sam) Carriere

Partnerships: Dir., Dr. Eleanor Johnson

Pensions: Dir., Ms. Judith Robinson

Primate's World Relief and Dev. Fund: Dir., Mr. Andrew Ignatieff

METROPOLITANS (ARCHBISHOPS)

British Columbia: The Most Rev. David P. Crawley, 1876 Richter St., Kelowna, BC V1Y 2M9 Tel. (250)762-3306 Fax (250)762-4150

Ecclesiastical Province of, Canada: The Most Rev. Andrew S. Hutchison, 1444 Union Ave., Montreal, QC H3A 2B8 Tel. (514)843-6577, Fax (514)843-32221, bishops.office@ montreal.anglican.ca

Ontario: The Most Rev. Terence E. Finlay, 135 Adelaide St. East, Toronto, ON M5C 1L8 Tel. (416)363-6021, Fax (416)363-3683, tfinlay@ toronto.anglican.ca

Rupert's Land: The Most Rev. John R. Clarke, Box 6868, Peace River, AB T8S 1S6 Tel. (780)624-2767, Fax (780)624-2365, bpath@ telusplanet.net

DIOCESAN BISHOPS

Algoma: The Rt. Rev. Ronald Ferris, Box 1168, Sault Ste. Marie, ON P6A 5N7 Tel. (705)256-5061, Fax (705)946-1860, dioceseofalgoma@on.aibn.com

Arctic: The Rt. Rev. Andrew P. Atagotaalnuk, 4910 51st St., Box 190, Yellowknife, NT X1A 2N2 Tel. (867)873-5432, Fax (867)873-8478, diocese@theedge.ca

Athabasca: The Most Rev. John R. Clarke, Box 6868, Peace River, AB T8S 1S6 Tel. (780)624-2767, Fax (780)624-2365, bpath@telusplanet.net

Brandon: Rt. Rev. James D. Njegovan, Box 21009 WEPO, Brandon, MB R7B 3W8 Tel. (204)727-7550, Fax (204)727-4135, bishopbdn @mts.net

British Columbia: -vacant-, 900 Vancouver St., Victoria, BC V8V 3V7 Tel. (250)386-7781, Fax (250)386-4013, bishop@acts.bc.ca

Caledonia: The Rt. Rev. William J. Anderson, Box 278, Prince Rupert, BC V8J 3P6 Tel. (250)624-6013, Fax (250)624-4299, synod-ofc@citytel.net

Calgary: Bishop, The Rt. Rev. Barry C.B. Hollowell, #560, 1207 11th Ave., SW, Salgary, AB T3C 0M5 Tel. (403)243-3673, Fax (403) 243-2182, synod@calgary.anglican.ca

Cariboo: for matters pertaining to clergy and Anglican parishes of the Central Interior: The Rev. Canon Gordon Light, 608 Sutherland Ave., Kelowna, BC V1Y 5X1 Tel (250)763-0099, Fax (250)762-9173, apci@silk.net

Central Newfoundland: The Rt. Rev. Donald A. Young, 34 Fraser Rd., Gander, NF A1V 2E8 Tel. (709)256-2372, Fax (709)256-2396, bishopcentral@nfld.net

Eastern Newfoundland and Labrador: The Rt. Rev. Donald F. Harvey, 19 King's Bridge Rd., St. John's, NF A1C 3K4 Tel. (709)576-6697, Fax (709)576-7122, dharvey@anglicanenl.nf.net

Edmonton: The Rt. Rev. Victoria Matthews, 10035-103 St., Edmonton, AB T5J 0X5 Tel. (780)439-7344, Fax (780)439-6549, bishopv@telusplanet.net

Fredericton: The Rt. Rev. Claude E.W. Miller, 115 Church St., Fredericton, NB E3B 4C8 Tel. (506)459-1801, Fax (506)459-8475, bishfton@ nbnet.nb.ca

Huron: The Rt. Rev. Bruce H. W. Howe, 190 Queens Ave., London, ON N6A 6H7 Tel. (519) 434-6893, Fax (519)673-4151, bishops@ huron.anglican.ca

Keewatin: Rt. David N. Ashdown, 915 Ottawa St., Keewatin, ON P0X 1C0 Tel. (807)547-3353, Fax (807)547-3356, diocese ofkeewatin @gokenora.com

Kootenay: Archbishop, The Most Rev. David P. Crawley, 1876 Richter St., Kelowna, BC V1Y 2M9 Tel. (250)762-3306, Fax (250)762-4150, diocese_of_kootenay@telus.net

Montreal: The Most Rev. Andrew S. Hutchison, 1444 Union Ave., Montreal, QC H3A 2B8 Tel. (514)843-6577, Fax (514)843-3221, bishops.office@montreal.anglican.ca

Moosonee: The Rt. Rev. Caleb J. Lawrence, Box 841, Schumacher, ON P0N 1G0 Tel. (705) 360-1129, Fax (705)360-1120, dmoose@domaa.ca

New Westminster: The Rt. Rev. Michael C. Ingham, 580-401 W. Georgia St., Vancouver, BC V6B 5A1 Tel. (604)684-6306, Fax (604) 684-7017, bishop@vancouver.anglican.ca

Niagara: The Rt. Rev. Ralph Spence, 252 James St. N, Hamilton, ON L8R 2L3 Tel. (905)527-1278, Fax (905)527-1281, bishop@niagara.anglican.ca

Nova Scotia and Prince Edward Is.: The Rt. Rev. Frederick J. Hiltz, 5732 College St., Halifax, NS B3H 1X3 Tel. (902)420-0717, Fax (902)425-0717, office@nspeidiocese.ca

Ontario: The Rt. Rev. George L. R. Bruce, 90 Johnson St., Kingston, ON K7L 1X7 Tel. (613)544-4774, Fax (613)547-3745, synod@ontario.anglican.ca

Ottawa: The Rt. Rev. Peter R. Coffin, 71 Bronson Ave., Ottawa, ON K1R 6G6 Tel. (613)232-7124, Fax (613)232-7088, dayadmin@ottawa.anglican.ca

Qu'Appelle: The Rt. Rev. Duncan D. Wallace, 1501 College Ave., Regina, SK S4P 1B8 Tel. (306)522-1608, Fax (306)352-6808, quappelle@ca sasktel.net

Quebec: The Rt. Rev. Bruce Stavert, 31 rue des Jardins, Quebec, QC G1R 4L6 Tel. (418)692-3858, Fax (418)692-3876, synodoffice@quebec.anglican.ca

Rupert's Land: The Rt. Rev. Donald D. Phillips, 935 Nesbitt Bay, Winnipeg, MB R3T 1W6 Tel. (204)922-4200, Fax (204)922-4219, general@rupertsland.ca

Saskatchewan: The Rt. Rev. Anthony Burton, 1308 5th Ave. East, Prince Albert, SK S6V 2H7 Tel. (306)763-2455, Fax (306)764-5172, synod@sasktel.net

Saskatoon: The Archbishop, -vacant-, Box 1965, Saskatoon, SK S7K 3S5 Tel. (306)244-5651, Fax (306)933-4606, anglicanbishop@sasktel.net

Toronto: The Most Rev. Terence E. Finlay, 135 Adelaide St. E, Toronto, ON M5C 1L8 Tel. (416)363-6021, Fax (416)363-3683, tfinlay@toronto.anglican.ca

Western Newfoundland: The Rt. Rev. Percy D. Coffin, 25 Main St., Corner Brook, NF A2H 1C2 Tel. (709)639-8712, Fax (709)639-1636, dsownc@nf.aibn.com

Yukon: The Rt. Rev. Terry Buckle, Box 4247, Whitehorse, YT Y1A 3T3 Tel. (867)667-7746, Fax (867)667-6125, synof@dioyukon.org

Periodicals

Anglican Journal (National Newspaper), *Ministry Matters*

The Antiochian Orthodox Christian Archdiocese of North America

The approximately 100,000 members of the Antiochian Orthodox community in Canada are under the jurisdiction of the Antiochian Orthodox Christian Archdiocese of North America with headquarters in Englewood, NJ. There are churches in Edmonton, Winnipeg, Halifax, London, Ottawa, Toronto, Windsor, Montreal, Saskatoon, Hamilton, Vancouver, Charlottestown, PEI, Calgary, and Mississauga.

Headquarters

Metropolitan Philip Saliba, 358 Mountain Rd., Englewood, NJ 07631 Tel. (201)871-1355 Fax (201)871-7954

Email: abouna@aol.com

Website: www.antiochian.org

Media Contact, Rev. Fr. Thomas Zain, 355 State Street, Brooklyn, NY 11217 Tel. (718)855-6225 Fax (718)855-3608

Periodicals

The Word, Again, Handmaiden

Apostolic Christian Church (Nazarene)

This church was formed in Canada as a result of immigration from various European countries. The body began as a movement originated by the Rev. S. H. Froehlich, a Swiss pastor, whose followers are still found in Switzerland and Central Europe.

Headquarters

Apostolic Christian Church Foundation, 1135 Sholey Rd., Richmond, VA 23231 Tel. (804) 222-1943

Media Contact, James Hodges

Officers

Exec. Dir., James Hodges

The Apostolic Church in Canada

The Apostolic Church in Canada is affiliated with the worldwide organization of the Apostolic Church with headquarters in Great Britain (www.apostolicworld.net). A product of the Welsh Revival (1904-1908), its Canadian beginnings originated in Nova Scotia in 1927. Today its main centers are in Nova Scotia, Ontario, and Quebec. This church is evangelical, fundamental, and Pentecostal, with special emphasis on the ministry gifts listed in Ephesians 4:11-12.

Headquarters

27 Castlefield Ave., Toronto, ON M4R 1G3

Website: www.apostolic.ca

Media Contact, Pres., Rev. John Kristensen, 685 Park St. S, Peterborough, ON K9J 3S9 Tel. (705)742-1618, Fax (705)742-2948, jkristensen@sympatico.ca

Officers

Pres., Rev.John Kristensen, 685 Park St. S, Peterborough, ON K9J 3S9 Tel. (705)742-1618, Fax (705)742-2948, jkristensen@sympatico.ca

Natl. Sec., Rev. D. Karl Thomas, 220 Adelaide St., London, ON N6B 344 Tel. (519)438-7036

Periodicals

Canadian News Up-Date; The News Magazine of the Apostolic Church in Canada

Apostolic Church of Pentecost of Canada Inc.

This body was founded in 1921 at Winnipeg, Manitoba, by Pastor Frank Small. Doctrines include belief in eternal salvation by the grace of God, baptism of the Holy Spirit with the evidence of speaking in tongues, and water baptism by immersion in the name of the Lord Jesus Christ.

Headquarters

#119-2340 Pegasus Way NE, Calgary, AB T2E 8M5
E-mail:acop@acop
Website: www.acop.ca
Media Contact, Admn., Rev. Wes Mills Tel. (403)273-5777 Fax (403)273-8102

Officers

Mod., Rev. G. Killam
Admin., Rev. Wes Mills
Mission Director, Rev. Brian Cooper

Periodicals

Fellowship Focus, Apostolic Women's Ministry (AWM) Newsletter, Apostolic Children's Ministry Newsletter

Armenian Evangelical Church

Founded in 1960 by immigrant Armenian evangelical families from the Middle East, this body is conservative doctrinally, with an evangelical, biblical emphasis. The polity of churches within the group differ, with congregationalism being dominant, but there are presbyterian Armenian Evangelical churches as well. Most of the local churches have joined main-line denominations. All of the remaining Armenian Evangelical (congregational or presbyterian) local churches in the United States and Canada have joined with the Armenian Evangelical Union of North America.

Headquarters

Armenian Evangelical Church of Toronto, 2851 John St., P.O. Box 42015, Markham, ON L3R 5R0 Tel. (905)305-8144
Media Contact, Chief Editor, Rev. Yessayi Sarmazian

A.E.U.N.A. OFFICERS

Min. to the Union, Rev. Karl Avakian, 1789 E. Frederick Ave., Fresno, CA 93720
Mod., Rev. Bernard Geulsgeugian
Min., Rev. Yessayi Sarmazian

Periodicals

Armenian Evangelical Church

Armenian Holy Apostolic Church–Canadian Diocese

The Canadian branch of the ancient Church of Armenia founded in A.D. 301 by St. Gregory the Illuminator was established in Canada at St. Catharines, Ontario, in 1930. The diocesan organization is under the jurisdiction of the Holy See of Etchmiadzin, Armenia. The Diocese has churches in St. Catharines, Hamilton, Toronto, Ottawa, Vancouver, Mississauga, Montreal, Laval, Windsor, Halifax, Winnipeg, Edmonton, and Calgary.

Headquarters

Diocesan Offices, Primate, Canadian Diocese, Archbishop Hovnan Derderian, 615 Stuart Ave., Outremont, QC H2V 3H2 Tel. (514)276-9479 Fax (514)276-9960
Email: adiocese@aol.com
Website: www.canarmdiocese.org
Media Contact, Exec. Dir., Deacon Hagop Arslanian

Officers

Sec., Silva Mangassarian
Webmaster, Albert Yeglikian

Associated Gospel Churches

The Associated Gospel Churches (AGC) traces its historical roots to the 1890s. To counteract the growth of liberal theology evident in many established denominations at this time, individuals and whole congregations seeking to uphold the final authority of the Scriptures in all matters of faith and conduct withdrew from those denominations and established churches with an evangelical ministry. These churches defended the belief that "all Scripture is given by inspiration of God" and also declared that the Holy Spirit gave the identical word of sacred writings of holy men of old, chosen by Him to be the channel of His revelation to man.

At first, this growing group of independent churches was known as the Christian Workers' Churches of Canada, and by 1922 there was desire for forming an association for fellowship, counsel, and cooperation. Several churches in southern Ontario banded together under the leadership of Dr. P. W. Philpott of Hamilton and Rev. H. E. Irwin, K. C. of Toronto.

When a new Dominion Charter was obtained on March 18, 1925, the name was changed to Associated Gospel Churches. Since that time the AGC has steadily grown, spreading across Canada by invitation to other independent churches of like faith and by actively beginning new churches.

Headquarters

3228 S. Service Rd., Burlington, ON L7N 3H8 Tel. (905)634-8184 Fax (905)634-6283
Email: admin@agcofcanada.com
Website: www.agcofcanada.com
Administrative Assistant, Donna Leung, c-o 3228 S. Service Rd., Burlington, ON L7N 3H8 Tel. (905)634-8184, Fax (905)634-6283, donna @agcofcanada.com

Officers

Pres., Rev. A.F. (Bud) Penner, 3228 South Service Rd., Burlington, ON L7N 3H8 Tel. (905)634-8184 Fax (905)634-6283

Mod., Mrs. Debra Teakle, 2589 Noella Cres., Niagara Falls, ON L2J 3H7 Tel./Fax (905)356-4767

Sec.-Treas., Mr. Charles Lyle, 54 Silverbirch Blvd. RR#1, Mount Hope, ON LOR 1WO Tel. (905)679-5495 Fax (905)679-5511

Periodicals

Insidedge

Association of Regular Baptist Churches (Canada)

The Association of Regular Baptist Churches was organized in 1957 by a group of churches for the purpose of mutual cooperation in missionary activities. The Association believes the Bible to be God's word, stands for historic Baptist principles, and opposes modern ecumenism.

Headquarters

17 Laverock St., Tottenham, ON L0G 1W0 Tel. (905)936-3786

Officers

Chmn., Rev. S. Kring, 67 Sovereen St., Delhi, ON N4B 1L7

Baptist Convention of Ontario and Quebec

The Baptist Convention of Ontario and Quebec is a family of 386 churches in Ontario and Quebec, united for mutual support and encouragement and united in missions in Canada and the world.

The Convention was formally organized in 1888. Its one educational institution, McMaster Divinty College, was founded in 1887. The Convention works through the all-Canada missionary agency, Canadian Baptist Ministries. The churches also support the Sharing Way, the relief and development arm of Canadian Baptist Ministries.

Headquarters

195 The West Mall, Ste. 414, Etobicoke, ON M9C 5K1 Tel. (416)622-8600 Fax (416)622-2308

Media Contact, Exec. Min., Dr. Ken Bellous

Officers

Past Pres., Rev. Ian Dixon
President, Mrs. Brenda Mann
1st Vice Pres., Mr. Roger Harris
2nd Vice Pres., Rev. John Torrance
Treas.-Bus. Admn., Nancy Bell
Exec. Min., Dr. Ken Bellous

Periodicals

The Canadian Baptist

Baptist General Conference of Canada

The Baptist General Conference was founded in Canada by missionaries from the United States. Originally a Swedish body, BGC Canada now includes people of many nationalities and is conservative and evangelical in doctrine and practice.

Headquarters

4306-97 St. NW, Edmonton, AB T6E 5R9 Tel. (780)438-9127 Fax (780)435-2478

Media Contact, Exec. Dir., Rev. Abe Funk

Officers

Exec. Dir., Rev. Abe Funk, 4306-97 St. NW, Edmonton, AB T6E 5R9 Tel. (780)438-9127 Fax (780)435-2478

Exec. Dir., Gordon Sorensen, BGC Stewardship Foundation

DISTRICTS

Baptist Gen. Conf.– Central Canada

Baptist General Conference in Alberta: Exec. Min., Dr. Cal Netterfield, 5011 122nd A St., Edmonton, AB T6H 3S8 Tel. (780)438-9126 Fax (780)438-5258

British Columbia Baptist Conference: Exec. Min., Rev. Walter W. Wieser, 7600 Glover Rd., Langley, BC V2Y 1Y1 Tel. (604)888-2246 Fax (604)888-0046

Baptist General Conf. in Saskatchewan

Periodicals

BGC Conference Corner

Baptist Union of Western Canada

Headquarters

302, 902-11 Ave. SW, Calgary, AB T2R 0E7

Media Contact, Exec. Min., Dr. Gerald Fisher

Officers

Pres., Mr. Bill Mains, 4576 Rainer Crescent, Prince George, BC V2K 1X4

Exec. Minister, Dr. Gerald Fisher, 302, 902-11 Ave. SW, Calgary, AB T2R 0E7

Alberta Area Minister: Rev. Ed Dyck, 302, 902-11 Ave. SW, Calgary, AB T2R 0E7

BC Area Minister: Dr. Paul Pearce, 201, 20349-88th Ave., Langely, BC V1M 2K5

SK-MB Area Minister: Dr. Robert Krahn, 414 Cowley Pl., Saskatoon, SK S7N 3X2

Carey Theological College: Principal, Dr. Brian Stelck, 5920 Iona Dr., Vancouver, BC V6T 1J6

Baptist Resources Centre: 302, 902-11 Ave. SW, Calgary, AB T2R 0E7

The Bible Holiness Movement

The Bible Holiness Movement, organized in 1949 as an outgrowth of the city mission work of the late Pastor William James Elijah Wakefield, an early-day Salvation Army officer, has been headed since its inception by his son, Evangelist Wesley H. Wakefield, its Bishop-General.

It derives its emphasis on the original Methodist faith of salvation and scriptural holiness from the late Bishop R. C. Horner. It adheres to the common evangelical faith in the Bible, the Deity, and the atonement of Christ. It stresses a personal experience of salvation for the repentant sinner, of being wholly sanctified for the believer, and of the fullness of the Holy Spirit for effective witness.

Membership involves a life of Christian love and evangelistic and social activism. Members are required to totally abstain from liquor and tobacco. They may not attend popular amusements or join secret societies. Divorce and remarriage are forbidden. Similar to Wesley's Methodism, members are, under some circumstances, allowed to retain membership in other evangelical church fellowships. Interchurch affiliations are maintained with a number of Wesleyan-Arminian Holiness denominations.

Year-round evangelistic outreach is maintained through open-air meetings, visitation, literature, and other media. Noninstitutional welfare work, including addiction counseling, is conducted among minorities. There is direct overseas famine relief, civil rights action, environment protection, and antinuclearism. The movement sponsors a permanent committee on religious freedom and an active promotion of Christian racial equality.

The movement has a world outreach with branches in the United States, India, Nigeria, Philippines, Ghana, Liberia, Cameroon, Kenya, Zambia, South Korea, Mulawi, and Tanzania. It also ministers to 89 countries in 42 languages through literature, radio, and audiocassettes.

Headquarters

Box 223, Postal Stn. A, Vancouver, BC V6C 2M3 Tel. (250)492-3376

Media Contact, Bishop-General, Evangelist Wesley H. Wakefield, P.O. Box 223, Postal Stn. A, Vancouver, BC V6C 2M3 Tel. (250)492-3376

DIRECTORS

Bishop-General, Evangelist Wesley H. Wakefield (Intl. Leader)

Evangelist M. J. Wakefield, Penticton, BC

Pastor Vincente & Mirasal Hernando, Phillipines

Pastor & Mrs. Daniel Stinnett, 1425 Mountain View W., Phoenix, AZ 85021

Evangelist I. S. Udoh, Abak, Akwalbom, Nigeria, West Africa

Pastor Richard & Laura Wesley, Protem, Monrovia, Liberia

Pastor Choe Chong Dee, Cha Pa Puk, S. Korea

Pastor S. A. Samuel, Andra, India

Pastor and Mrs. Daniel Vandee, Ghana, W. Africa

Periodicals

Hallelujah!

Brethren in Christ Church, Canadian Conference

The Brethren in Christ, formerly known as Tunkers in Canada, arose out of a religious awakening in Lancaster County, PA late in the 18th century. Representatives of the new denomination reached Ontario in 1788 and established the church in the southern part of the present province. Presently the conference has congregations in Ontario, Alberta, Quebec, and Saskatchewan. In theology they have accents of the Pietist, Anabaptist, Wesleyan, and Evangelical movements.

Headquarters

Brethren in Christ Church, Gen. Ofc., P.O. Box A, Grantham, PA 17027-0901 Tel. (717)697-2634 Fax (717)697-7714

Canadian Headquarters, Bishop's Ofc., 2619 Niagara Pkwy., Ft. Erie, ON L2A 5M4 Tel. (905)871-9991

Media Contact, Mod., Dr. Warren L. Hoffman, Brethren in Christ Church Gen. Ofc.

Officers

Mod., Bishop Darrell S. Winger, 416 North Service Road, Suite 1, Oakville, ON L6H 5R2 Tel. (905)339-2335 Fax (905)337-2120

Sec., Betty Albrecht, RR 2, Petersburg, ON N0B 2H0

Periodicals

Evangelical Visitor, "Yes", Shalom

British Methodist Episcopal Church of Canada

The British Methodist Episcopal Church was organized in 1856 in Chatham, ON and incorporated in 1913. It has congregations across the Province of Ontario.

Headquarters

430 Grey Street, London, ON N6B 1H3 Tel.

Media Contact, Gen. Sec., Rev. Jacqueline Collins, 47 Connolly St., Toronto, ON M6N 4Y5 Tel. (416)653-6339

Officers

Gen. Supt., Rt. Rev. Dr. Douglas Birse, R.R. #5, Thamesville, ON N0P 2K0 Tel. (519)692-3628

Asst. Gen. Supt., Maurice M. Hicks, 3 Boxdene Ave., Scarborough, ON M1V 3C9 Tel. (416) 298-5715

Gen. Sec., Rev. Jacqueline Collins, 47 Connolly St., Toronto, ON M6N 4Y5 Tel. (416)653-6339

Gen. Treas., Ms. Hazel Small, 7 Wood Fernway, North York, ON M2J 4P6 Tel. (416)491-0313

Periodicals

B.M.E. Church Newsletter

Canadian and American Reformed Churches

The Canadian and American Reformed Churches accept the Bible as the infallible Word of God, as summarized in The Belgic Confession of Faith (1561), The Heidelberg Cathechism (1563), and The Canons of Dort (1618-1619). The federation was founded in Canada in 1950 and in the United States in 1955.

Headquarters

Synod, 607 Dynes Rd., Burlington, ON L7N 2V4

Canadian Reformed Churches: Ebenezer Canadian Reformed Church, 607 Dynes Rd., Burlington, ON L7N 2V4

Theological College: Dr. N. H. Gootjes, 110 W. 27th St., Hamilton, ON L9C 5A1 Tel. (905) 575-3688 Fax (905)575-0799

Media Contact, Rev. G. Nederveen, 3089 Woodward Ave., Burlington, ON L7N 2M3 Tel. (905)681-7055 Fax (905)681-7055

Periodicals

Reformed Perspective, A Magazine for the Christian Family; Evangel, The Good News of Jesus Christ; Clarion, The Canadian Reformed Magazine; Diakonia-A Magazine of Office-Bearers; Book of Praise; Koinonia, A periodical of the Ministers of the CARC; Horizon, A quarterly magazine published by the League of CARC Women Societies; A Gift from Heaven, A Reformed Bible course.

Canadian Baptist Ministries

The Canadian Baptist Ministries has four federated member bodies: (1) Baptist Convention of Ontario and Quebec, (2) Baptist Union of Western Canada, (3) the United Baptist Convention of the Atlantic Provinces, and (4) Union d'Églises Baptistes Françaises au Canada (French Baptist Union). Its main purpose is to act as a coordinating agency for the four groups for mission in all five continents.

Headquarters

7185 Millcreek Dr., Mississauga, ON L5N 5R4 Tel. (905)821-3533 Fax (905)826-3441

Website: www.cbmin.org

Media Contact, Communications, David Rogelstad, daver@cbmin.org

Officers

Pres., Doug Coomas

Gen. Sec., Rev. Gart Nelson, NelsonG@cbmin.org

Canadian Conference of Mennonite Brethren Churches

The conference was incorporated November 22, 1945.

Headquarters

3-169 Riverton Ave., Winnipeg, MB R2L 2E5 Tel. (204)669-6575 Fax (204)654-1865

Media Contact, Exec. Dir., Dave Wiebe

Officers

Mod., Jascha Boge, 261 Bonner Ave., Winnipeg, MB R2G 1B3 Tel. (204)663-1414

Asst. Mod., Ralph Gliege, Box 67, Hepburn, SK S0K 1Z0 Tel. (306)947-2030

Sec., Gerald Janzen, 32145 Austin Ave., Abbotsford, BC V2T 4P4

Periodicals

Mennonite Brethren Herald, Mennonitische Rundschau, IdeaBank, Le Lien, Expression, Chinese Herald

Canadian Convention of Southern Baptists

The Canadian Convention of Southern Baptists was formed at the Annual Meeting, May 7-9, 1985, in Kelowna, British Columbia. It was formerly known as the Canadian Baptist Conference, founded in Kamloops, British Columbia, in 1959 by pastors of existing churches.

Headquarters

100 Convention Way, Cochrane, AB T4C 2G2 Tel. (403)932-5688 Fax (403)932-4937

E-mail: office@ccsb.ca

Media Contact, Exec. Dir.-Treas., Rev.Gerald Taillon

Officers

Exec. Dir.-Treas., Gerald Taillon, 17 Riverview Close, Cochrane, AB T4C 1K7

Pres., Alan Braun, 334 Norton St., Penticton, BC V2A 4H7

Periodicals

The Baptist Horizon

Canadian District of the Moravian Church in America, Northern Province

The work in Canada is under the general oversight and rules of the Moravian Church, Northern Province, general offices for which are located in Bethlehem, Penn.. For complete information, see "Religious Bodies in the United States" section of the Yearbook.

Headquarters

1021 Center St., P.O. Box 1245, Bethlehem, PA 18016-1245

Media Contact, Rev. David Wickmann

Officers

Pres., Mr. Graham Kerslake, 10910 Harvest Lake Way NE, Calgary, AB T3K 4L1 Tel (403)508-7765 Fax (403)226-2467

Periodicals

The Moravian

Canadian Evangelical Christian Churches

The Canadian Evangelical Christian Church is an international, full-gospel new apostolic denomination, emphasizing the New Testament apostolic paradigm pattern which recognizes the ministry gifts beyond the apostle, prophet, evangelist, pastor, and teacher to spread the Gospel, according to Ephesians 4:11,12. The congregations are associated through full-gospel doctrine that is in combination with Calvinistic and Arminian beliefs. Each and every congregation is connected with CECC as congregational and ordination is supervised by National Office.

Headquarters

General Superintendent, Rev. David P. Lavigne, 410-125 Lincoln Rd., Waterloo, ON N2J 2N9 Tel. (519)880-9110 or (888)981-8881 Fax (519)725-5578

E-mail: cecc@rogers.com

Website: www.cecconline.org or www.cetsonline.com

Officers

Gen. Supt., Rev. David P. Lavigne, 410-125 Lincoln Rd., Waterloo, ON N2J 2N9 Tel. (519)725-5578 or (888)981-8881, Fax 519-725-5578, cecc@rogers.com

Exec. Dir., Rev. Otto Ferber, 139 Ste. Ann Ave., Box 237, St. Agatha, ON N0B 2L0 Tel. (519) 886-8809

Gen. Sec., Rev. Bill St. Pierre, Box 7, Oro, ON N3P 1B9 Tel. (888)297-5551

Canadian Yearly Meeting of the Religious Society of Friends

Canadian Yearly Meeting of the Religious Society of Friends was founded in Canada as an offshoot of the Quaker movement in Great Britain and colonial America. Genesee Yearly Meeting (founded 1834), Canada Yearly Meeting (Orthodox) (founded in 1867), and Canada Yearly Meeting (founded in 1881), united in 1955 to form the Canadian Yearly Meeting. Canadian Yearly Meeting is affiliated with Friends United Meeting and Friends General Conference. It is also a member of Friends World Committee for Consultation.

Headquarters

91A Fourth Ave., Ottawa, ON K1S 2L1 Tel. (613)235-8553 or (888)296-3222 Fax (613) 235-1753

E-mail: cym-office@quaker.ca

Media Contact, Gen. Sec.-Treas., —

Officers

Gen. Sec.-Treas., —

Clerk, John Calder

Archivist, Jane Zavitz Bond

Archives, Arthur G. Dorland, Pickering College, 389 Bayview St., Newmarket, ON L3Y 4X2 Tel. (416)895-1700

Periodicals

The Canadian Friend, Quaker Concern

Christ Catholic Church International

Christ Catholic Church International now has churches and/or missions in 17 countries spread over four continents. They are located in the United States, Canada, Norway, Sweden, Bolivia, Poland, England, Portugal, Bahamas, Belgium, Trinidad-Tobago, Germany, Viet Nam, Colombia, Paraguay, Australia, and Croatia. Some countries have active churches and missions, some just missions and/or prayer groups.

CCCI is an Orthodox-Catholic Communion tracing Apostolic Succession through the Old Catholic and Orthodox Catholic Churches.

The church ministers to a growing number of people seeking an experiential relationship with their Lord and Savior Jesus Christ in a Sacramental and Scripture-based church. As one of the three founding members of FOCUS—Federation of Orthodox Catholic Churches United Sacramentally—CCCI is working to bring together Old and Orthodox Catholicism into one united church under the headship of Jesus Christ.

Headquarters

5165 Palmer Ave., P.O. Box 73, Niagara Falls, ON L2E 6S8 Tel. (905)354-2329 Fax (905) 354-9934

E-mail: dwmullan@sympatico.ca

Website: www3.sympatico.ca/dwmullan

Media Contact, The Rt. Rev. John W. Brown, 1504-75 Queen St., Hamilton, ON L8R 3J3 Tel. (905)527-9089, Fax (905)354-9934, bishopjohn@primus.ca

Officers

PRESIDING ARCHBISHOP

The Most Rev. Donald Wm. Mullan, 6190 Barker St., Niagara Falls, ON L2G 1Y4 Tel. (905)354-2329, Fax (905)357-9934, dmullan1@home.com

ARCHBISHOPS

The Most Rev. Kyrillos Markskog, Skoldgatan 3 C, S-212 29 Malmo, Sweden Tel. +(040) 930088, cyril@mbox301.swipnet.se

The Most Rev. Jose Ruben Garcia Matiz, Calle 52, Sur #24A-35-Bq. #1, Ap. 301, Santa Fe de Bogota, D.C., Colombia, South America Tel. (57)71447 87, jorugama@col1.telecom.com. co

BISHOPS

The Rt. Rev. Richard Blalack, 220 Cold Indian Springs Rd., Wayside, NJ 07712 Tel. (732) 542-1370, Fax (732)922-6430, rblalack@monmouth.com

The Rt. Rev. Curtis Bradley, 5567 E. 97th Pl., Thornton, CO 80209 Tel. (303)451-0683, cbrad99@aol.com

The Rt. Rev. John Wm. Brown, 1504-75 Queen St., N. Hamilton, ON L8R 3J3 Tel. (905)522-6240, bishopjohn@primus.ca

The Rt. Rev. James Judd, 1624 Luella St. N., St. Paul, MN 55119-3017 Tel. (651)776-3172, jrjudd@aol.com

The Rt. Rev. Trond Hans Farner Kverno, Jarhaug, N-2750 Gran, Norway Tel. (47)61-32-75-37, tkverno@online.no

The Rt. Rev. Gerard La Plante, 715 E. 51st Ave., Vancouver, BC V5X 1E2 Tel. (604)327-1066, Fax (604)327-1066, oldcatholic@telus.ca

The Rt. Rev. Luis Fernando Hoyos Maldonado,

A.A. 24378 Santa Fe de Bogota, D.C., Colombia, South America Tel. (57)276-68-16, jourgama@col1.telecom.com.co

The Rt. Rev. L.M. (Mac) McFerran, #206-6020 E. Boulevard, Vancouver, BC Tel. (604)261-2494

The Rt. Rev. Jose Moises Moncada Quevedo, A.A. 24378 Santa Fe de Bogota, D.C., Colombia, South America Tel. (57)276-68-16, jourgama@col1.telecom.com.co

The Rt. Rev. Jerome Robben, P.O. Box 566, Chesterfield, MO 63006-0566 Tel. (314)205-8422, abbajn17@aol.com

The Rt. Rev. Andrzej J. Sarwa, ul. Krucza 16 27-600 Sandomierz, Poland Tel./Fax 084-(015) 833-21-41, andrzej-san@poczta.wp.pl

The Rt. Rev. Robert Smith, 824 Royal Oak Dr., Orlando, FL 32809 Tel (407)240-7833, yshwa@webtv.net

SEMINARY

St. Mary's Seminary: The Very Rev. Del Baier, 8287 Lamont, Niagara Falls, ON L2G 7L4 (offering on-site and correspondence programs)

The New Order of St. Francis (Priests, Brothers and Sisters): Sec. General, Rev. Bro. Sean Ross, 5768 Summer St., Niagara Falls, ON L2G 1M2

Periodicals

St. Luke Magazine, The Franciscan

Christian Brethren (also known as Plymouth Brethren)

The Christian Brethren are a loose grouping of autonomous local churches, often called "assemblies." They are firmly committed to the inerrancy of Scripture and to the evangelical doctrine of salvation by faith alone apart from works or sacrament. Characteristics are a weekly Breaking of Bread and freedom of ministry without a requirement of ordination. For their history, see "Religious Bodies in the United States" in the Directories section of this Yearbook.

CORRESPONDENT

James A. Stahr, 327 W. Praire Ave., Wheaton, IL 60187 USA Tel. (630)665-3757

RELATED ORGANIZATIONS

Christian Brethren Church in the Province of Quebec: Exec. Sec., Marj Robbins, P.O. Box 1054, Sherbrooke, QC J1H 5L3 Tel. (819)820-1693 Fax (819)821-9287

MSC Canada, Administrator: William Yuille, 509-3950 14th Ave., Markham, ON L3R 0A9 Tel. (905)947-0468 Fax (905)947-0352

Vision Ministries Canada: Dir., Gord Martin, P.O. Box 28032, Waterloo, ON N2L 6J8 Tel. (519)725-1212 Fax (519)725-9421

Periodicals

News of Quebec

Christian Church (Disciples of Christ) in Canada

Disciples have been in Canada since 1810, and were organized nationally in 1922. This church served the Canadian context as a region of the whole Christian Church (Disciples of Christ) in the United States and Canada.

Headquarters

Christian Church in Canada, P.O. Box 23030, 417 Wellington St., St. Thomas, ON N5R 6A3 Tel. (519)633-9083 Fax (519)637-6407

Email: ccic@netrover.com

Media Contact, Reg. Min., F. Thomas Rutherford

Officers

Mod., Peter Fountain, P.O. Box 344, Milton, NS B0T 1P0 Tel. (902)354-5988, pjfountain@auracom.com

Reg. Min., F. Thomas Rutherford, P.O. Box 23030, 417 Wellington St., St. Thomas, ON N5R 6A3 Tel. (519)633-9083, Fax (519)637-6407, ccic@netrover.com

Periodicals

Canadian Disciple

Christian Churches/Churches of Christ

Congregations who later identified with the American Restoration or Stone-Campbell Movement were organized by Scotch Baptists and former Presbyterians, many of whom were influenced by the Haldanes of Edinburgh, Scotland. The first congregation was organized at Cross Roads, Prince Edward Island in 1812 with more organized across the Maritime colonies (later, Canadian provinces) and in the colony of "Canada West" (now, Ontario) by the 1820s. By the 1820s, these congregations began contact with the Thomas and Alexander Campbell and their publications were widely distributed or reprinted. By the late 19th century in Ontario, these congregations began to drift apart over the use of musical instruments in worship—an issue surfaced by differing approaches to the interpretation and authority of Scripture. In the Maritimes, however, this split did not occur. By 1948, however, the Maritime congregations split apart over "open membership" and support or non-support of institutions which came to later form the Disciples of Christ in Canada. A similar schism occurred over the same issues among Disciples of Christ in Ontario.

In western Canada, a number of Disciples of Christ who immigrated to Canada beginning about 1880 until 1930 organized congregations in Manitoba, Saskatchewan, Alberta, and British Columbia. Not until late 1950s did the controversy over super-congregational institutions affect these congregations. By 1970, most congregations identified with the North American Christian Convention, an annual, non-delegated, preaching and teaching convention of Christian Churches and Churches of Christ in the US, but they continued to cooperate at various levels with Disciples of Christ, and, later, with a capella Churches of Christ, as well as several evangelical Protestant traditions. The first congregation organized was Cross Roads Christian Church, Cross Roads, Prince Edward Island, Canada, 1812. These congregations identify with the 19th-century "Restoration Movement" (also known as the "Stone-Campbell Movement") which came to be known as "Disciples of Christ." From about 1948 and 1970, when the Disciples of Christ in Canada first moved toward and, then, declared a formal denominational structure, 65-70 congregations did not identify with this structure preferring to remain free, congregationally-governed fellowships. While especially in western Canada these congregations cooperate and fellowship with congregations identified with the Disciples of Christ in Canada, a capella Churches of Christ, and people and congregations of several other traditions, they generally tend to identify with the interpretation of the Restoration or Stone-Campbell Movement as exemplified by US Christian Churches and Churches of Christ in affinity with the North American Christian Convention, an annual, non-delegated, preaching and teaching convention.

Headquarters

Media Contact: Russell Edson Kuykendall, 25 Grenville St., 1507, Toronto ON M4Y 2X5 Tel (416)895-1098, kuykendall@canada.com

Christian and Missionary Alliance in Canada

A Canadian movement—dedicated to the teaching of Jesus Christ the Saviour, Sanctifier, Healer, and Coming King—commenced in Toronto in 1887 under the leadership of the Rev. John Salmon. Two years later, the movement united with The Christian Alliance of New York, founded by Rev. A. B. Simpson, becoming the Dominion Auxiliary of the Christian Alliance, Toronto, under the presidency of the Hon. William H. Howland. Its four founding branches were Toronto, Hamilton, Montreal, and Quebec. The movement focused on the deeper life and missions. In 1980, the Christian and Missionary Alliance in Canada became autonomous. Its General Assembly is held every two years.

Headquarters

30 Carrier Dr., Suite 100, Toronto, ON M9W 5T7 Tel. (416)674-7878 Fax (416)674-0808

Email: info@cmacan.org

Media Contact, Dir. of Communications, Barrie Doyle

Officers

Pres., Dr. Franklin Pyles, pylesf@cmacan.org

Vice Pres., Global Ministries, Dr. Ray Downey, downeyr@cmacan.org

Vice Pres., Fin., Paul D. Lorimer, lorimerp @cmacan.org

Vice Pres., Canadian Ministries, Rev. C. Stuart Lightbody, lightbodys@cmacan.org

Vice Pres., Advancement, Rev. David Freeman, freemand@cmacan.org

Chairman of the Board, Dr. T. V. Thomas

Secretary of the Board, Connie Driedger

Periodicals

Alliance Life

Christian Reformed Church in North America

Canadian congregations of the Christian Reformed Church in North America have been formed since 1908. For detailed information about this denomination, please refer to the listing for the Christian Reformed Church in North America in Directory 3, "Religious Bodies in the United States."

Headquarters

United States Office, 2850 Kalamazoo Ave. SE, Grand Rapids, MI 49560 Tel. (616)224-0744 Fax (616)224-5895

Canadian Office, 3475 Mainway, P.O. Box 5070 STN LCR 1, Burlington, ON L7R 3Y8 Tel. (905)336-2920 Fax (905)336-8344

Website: www.crcna.org

Media Contact, Gen. Sec., Dr. David H. Engelhard, US Office, Director of Communication, Mr. Henry Hess, Canadian Office

Officers

Gen. Sec., Dr. David H. Engelhard, US Office

Exec. Dir.-Ministries, Dr. Peter Borgdorff, US Office

Dir. of Fin.& Administration, Mr. John Bolt, US Office

Periodicals

The Banner

Church of God (Anderson, Ind.)

This body is one of the largest of the groups which have taken the name "Church of God." Its headquarters are at Anderson, Indiana. It originated about 1880 and emphasizes Christian unity.

Headquarters

Western Canada Assembly, Chpsn., Horst Depner, 4717-56th St., Camrose, AB T4V 2C4

Tel. (780)672-0772 Fax (780)672-6888

Eastern Canada Assembly, Chpsn., Jim Wiebe, 38 James St., Dundas, ON L9H 2J6

Email: admincoo@cable-lynx.net, baughman@ cable-lynx.net

Website: www.chog.ca

Media Contact for Western Canada, Exec. Dir. Of Ministry Services, John D. Campbell, 4717 56th St., Camrose, AB T4V 2C4 Tel. (780) 672-0772 Fax (780)672-6888

Periodicals

College News & Updates, The Gospel Contact, The Messenger

Church of God in Christ (Mennonite)

The Church of God in Christ (Mennonite) was organized by the evangelist-reformer John Holdeman in Ohio. The church unites with the faith of the Waldenses, Anabaptists, and other such groups throughout history. Emphasis is placed on obedience to the teachings of the Bible, including the doctrine of the new birth and spiritual life; noninvolvement in government or the military; a head-covering for women; beards for men; and separation from the world shown by simplicity in clothing, homes, possessions, and lifestyle. The church has a worldwide membership of about 19,300, largely concentrated in the United States and Canada.

Headquarters

P.O. Box 313, 420 N. Wedel Ave., Moundridge, KS 67107 Tel. (620)345-2532 Fax (620)345-2582

Media Contact, Dale Koehn, P.O. Box 230, Moundridge, KS 67107 Tel. (620)345-2532 Fax (620)345-2582

Periodicals

Messenger of Truth

Church of God (Cleveland, Tenn.)

It is one of America's oldest Pentecostal churches founded in 1886 as an outgrowth of the holiness revival under the name Christian Union. In 1907 the church adopted the organizational name Church of God. It has its foundation upon the principles of Christ as revealed in the Bible. The Church of God is Christian, Protestant, foundational in its doctrine, evangelical in practice and distinctively Pentecostal. It maintains a centralized form of government and a commitment to world evangelization.

The first church in Canada was extablished in 1919 in Scotland Farm, Manitoba. Paul H. Walker became the first overseer of Canada in 1931.

Headquarters

Intl. Offices, 2490 Keith St. NW, Cleveland, TN 37320 Tel. (423)472-3361 Fax (423)478-7066

Media Contact, Dir. of Communications, Michael L. Baker, P.O. Box 2430, Cleveland, TN 37320-2430 Tel. (423)478-7112 Fax (423)478-7066

EXECUTIVES

Gen. Overseer, R. Lamar Vest

Assistant Gen. Overseers, T.L. Lowery, Bill F. Sheeks, Orville Hagan

Gen. Sec.-Treas., Gene D. Rice

DEPARTMENTS

Benefits Board: CEO, Arthur Rhodes

Business & Records: Dir., Julian B. Robinson

Care Ministries: Dir., John D. Nichols

Chaplains Commission: Dir., Robert D. Crick

Communications, Media Ministries: Dir., Michael L. Baker

Education–European Bible Seminary: Dir., John Sims

Education–Hispanic Institute of Ministry: Dir., Jose D. Montanez

Education–International Bible College: Pres., Cheryl Busse

Education–Lee University: Pres., C. Paul Conn

Education–Patten College: Chancellor, Bebe Patten

Education–Puerto Rico Bible School: Pres., Iledfonso Caraballo

Education–School of Ministry: Chancellor, Paul L. Walker

Education–Theology Seminary: Pres., Stephen J. Land

Evangelism & Home Missions

Canada–Eastern: Rev. Canute Blake, P.O. Box 2036, Brampton, ON L6T 3TO Tel. (905)793-2213 Fax (905)793-9173

Canada–Western: Rev. Raymond W. Wall, Box 54055, 2640 52 St. NE, Calgary, AB T1Y 6S6 Tel. (403)293-8817 Fax (403)293-8832

Canada–Quebec/Maritimes: Rev. Jacques Houle, 19 Orly, Granby, QC J2H 1Y4 Tel. (514)378-4442 Fax (514)378-8646

Periodicals

Church of God Evangel, Editorial Evangelica

The Church of God of Prophecy in Canada

The Church of God of Prophecy is one of the churches that grew out of the work of A. J. Tomlinson in the first half of the twentieth century. Historically it shares a common heritage with the Church of God (Cleveland, Tenn.) and is in the mainstream of the classical Pentecostal-holiness tradition.

At the death of A.J. Tomlinson in 1943, M. A. Tomlinson was named General Overseer and served until his retirement in 1990. He emphasized unity and fellowship unlimited by racial, social, or political differences. The next General Overseer, Billy D. Murray Sr., who served from 1990 until his retirement in 2000, emphasized a commitment to the promotion of Christian unity and world evangelization. In July 2000, Fred S. Fisher Sr. was duly selected to serve as the fourth General Overseer of the Church of God of Prophecy.

From its beginnings, the Church has based its beliefs on "the whole Bible, rightly divided," and has accepted the Bible as God's Holy Word, inspired, inerrant, and infallible. The church is firm in its commitment to orthodox Christian belief. The Church affirms that there is one God, eternally existing in three persons—Father, Son, and Holy Spirit. It believes in the deity of Christ,

His virgin birth, His sinless life, the physical miracles He performed, His atoning death on the cross, His bodily resurrection, His ascension to the right hand of the Father, and His Second coming. The church professes that salvation results from grace alone through faith in Christ, that regeneration by the Holy Spirit is essential for the salvation of sinful men, and that sanctification by the blood of Christ makes possible personal holiness. It affirms the present ministry of the Holy Spirit by Whose indwelling believers are able to live godly lives and have power for service. The church believes in, and promotes, the ultimate unity of believers as prayed for by Christ in John 17. The church stresses the sanctity of human life and is committed to the sanctity of the marriage bond and the importance of strong, loving Christian families. Other official teachings include Holy Spirit baptism, with tongues as initial evidence; manifestation of the spiritual gifts; divine healing; premillenial second-coming of Christ; total abstinence from the use of tobacco, alcohol, and narcotics; water baptism by immersion; the Lord's supper and washing of the saints' feet; and a concern for moderation and holiness in all dimensions of lifestyle.

The Church is racially integrated on all levels, including top leadership. Women play a prominent role in church affairs, serving in pastoral roles and other leadership positions. The church presbytery has recently adopted plurality of leadership in the selection of a General Oversight Group. This group consists of eight bishops located around the world who, along with the General Overseer, are responsible for inspirational leadership and vision casting for the church body.

The Church has local congregations in all 50 states and more than 100 nations worldwide. Organizationally there is a strong emphasis on international missions, evangelism, youth and children's ministries, women's and men's ministries, stewardship, communications, publishing, leadership development, and discipleship.

Headquarters

CHURCH OF GOD OF PROPHECY INTERNATIONAL OFFICES

P.O. Box 2910, Cleveland, TN 37320-2910

Media Contact, National Overseer, Levy Clarke, 5145 Tomken Rd, Mississauga, ON L4 W1P1 Tel. (905) 625-1278, Fax (905)-625-1316.

Officers

Gen. Overseer, Bishop Fred S. Fisher Sr.

General Presbyters: Sherman Allen, Sam Clements, Daniel Corbett, Clayton Endecott, Miguel Mojica, José Reyes Sr., Felix Santiago, Brice Thompson

International Offices Ministries Dirs.: Finance, Communications, and Publishing, Oswill Williams; Global Outreach and Administrative Asst. to the General Presbyters, Randy Howard; Leadership Development and Discipleship Ministries, Larry Duncan.

Periodicals

White Wing Messenger (ENG), *Victory* (Youth Magazine/Sunday School Curriculum), *The Happy Harvester, White Wing Messenger* (Spanish)

The Church of Jesus Christ of Latter-day Saints in Canada

The Church has had a presence in Canada since the early 1830's. Joseph Smith and Brigham Young both came to Eastern Canada as missionaries. There are now 157,000 members in Canada in more than 400 congregations.

Leading the Church in Canada are the presidents of over 40 stakes (equivalent to a diocese). World headquarters is in Salt Lake City, UT (See "US Religious Bodies" chapter of the Directories section of this Yearbook).

Headquarters

50 E. North Temple St., Salt Lake City, UT 84150

Media Contact, Public Affairs Dir., Bruce Smith, 1185 Eglinton Ave., Box 116, North York, ON M3C 3C6 Tel. (416)431-7891 Fax (416)438-2723

Church of the Lutheran Brethren

The Church of the Lutheran Brethren of America was organized in December 1900. Five independent Lutheran congregations met together in Milwaukee, Wisc., and adopted a constitution patterned very closely to that of the Lutheran Free Church of Norway.

The spiritual awakening in the Midwest during the 1890s crystallized into convictions that led to the formation of a new church body. Chief among the concerns were church membership practices, observance of Holy Communion, confirmation practices, and local church government.

The Church of the Lutheran Brethren practices a simple order of worship with the sermon as the primary part of the worship service. It believes that personal profession of faith is the primary criterion for membership in the congregation. The Communion service is reserved for those who profess faith in Christ as savior. Each congregation is autonomous and the synod serves the congregations in advisory and cooperative capacities.

The synod supports a world mission program in Cameroon, Chad, Japan, and Taiwan. Approximately 40 percent of the synodical budget is earmarked for world missions. A growing home mission ministry is planting new congregations in the United States and Canada. Affiliate organizations operate several retirement-nursing homes, conference, and retreat centers.

Headquarters

1020 Alcott Ave. W, P.O. Box 655, Fergus Falls, MN 56538 Tel. (218)739-3336 Fax (218)739-5514

Email: rmo@clba.org
Website: www.clba.org
Media Contact, Rev. Brent Juliot

Officers

Pres., Rev. Arthur Berge, 72 Midridge Close SE, Calgary, AB T2X 1G1

Vice Pres., Rev. Luther Stenberg, P.O. Box 75, Hagen, SK S0J 1B0

Sec., Mr. Alvin Herman, 3105 Taylor St. E., Saskatoon, SK S7H 1H5

Treas., Edwin Rundbraaten, Box 739, Birch Hills, SK S0J 0G0

Youth Coord., Rev. Harold Rust, 2617 Preston Ave. S, Saskatoon, SK S7J 2G3

Periodicals

Faith and Fellowship

Church of the Nazarene in Canada

The first Church of the Nazarene in Canada was organized in November, 1902, by Dr. H. F. Reynolds. It was in Oxford, Nova Scotia. The Church of the Nazarene is Wesleyan Arminian in theology, representative in church government, and warmly evangelistic.

Headquarters

20 Regan Rd., Unit 9, Brampton, ON L7A 1C3 Tel. (905)846-4220 Fax (905)846-1775

Email: national@nazarene.ca

Website: www.nazarene.ca

Media Contact, Gen. Sec., Dr. Jack Stone, 6401 The Paseo, Kansas City, MO 64131 Tel. (816)333-7000 Fax (816)822-9071

Officers

Natl. Dir., Dr. William E. Stewart, 20 Regan Rd. Unit 9, Brampton, ON L7A 1C3 Tel. (905) 846-4220 Fax (905)846-1775

Exec. Asst., John T. Martin, 20 Regan Rd. Unit 9, Brampton, ON L7A 1C3 Tel. (905)846-4220 Fax (905)846-1775

Churches of Christ in Canada

Churches of Christ are autonomous congregations, whose members appeal to the Bible alone to determine matters of faith and practice. There are no central offices or officers. Publications and institutions related to the churches are either under local congregational control or independent of any one congregation.

Churches of Christ shared a common fellowship in the 19th century with the Christian Churches–Churches of Christ and the Christian Church (Disciples of Christ). Fellowship was broken after the introduction of instrumental music in worship and centralization of church-wide activities through a missionary society. Churches of Christ began in Canada soon after 1800, largely in the middle provinces. The few pioneer congregations were greatly strengthened in the mid-1800s, growing in size and number.

Members of Churches of Christ believe in the inspiration of the Scriptures, the divinity of Jesus Christ, and immersion into Christ for the remission of sins. The New Testament pattern is followed in worship and church organization.

Headquarters

Media Contact, Man. Ed., Gospel Herald, Max Craddock, 5 Lankin Blvd., ON M4J 4W7 Tel. (416)461-7406, Fax (416)424-1850, maxc@strathmorecofc.ca

Periodicals

Gospel Herald

Community of Christ

Founded April 6, 1830, by Joseph Smith Jr., the church was reorganized under the leadership of the founder's son, Joseph Smith III, in 1860. The Church is established in 38 countries including the United States and Canada, with nearly a quarter of a million members. A biennial world conference is held in Independence, Mo. The current president is W. Grant McMurray.

Headquarters

World Headquarters Complex, P.O. Box 1059, Independence, MO 64051 Tel. (816)833-1000 Fax (816)521-3095

Ontario Regional Ofc., 390 Speedvale Ave. E., Guelph, ON N1E 1N5

Media Contact, Public Relations Coordinator, Susan Naylor

CANADIAN REGIONS AND DISTRICTS

North Plains & Prairie Provinces Region: Regional Admn., Kenneth Barrows, 84 Hidden Park NW, Calgary, AB T3A 5K5; Alberta District, R.A. (Ryan) Levitt, #325, 51369 Range Rd., Sherwood Park, AB T8C 1H3; Saskatchewan District, Robert G. Klombies, 202 Saskatchewan Crescent W, Saskatoon, SK S7M 0A4

Pacific Northwest Region: Regional Admn., Raymond Peter, P.O. Box 18469, 4820 Morgan, Seattle, WA 98118; British Columbia District, E. Carl Bolger, 410-1005 McKenzie Ave., Victoria, BC V8X 4A9

Ontario Region: Regional Admn., Larry D. Windland, 390 Speedvale Ave. E., Guelph, ON N1E 1N5; Chatham District, David R. Wood, 127 Mount Pleasant Crescent, Wallaceburg, ON N8A 5A3; Grand River District, C. Allen Taylor, R R 2, Orangeville, ON L9W 2Y9; London District, William T. Leney Jr., 18 Glendon Road, Stratford, ON N5A 5B3; Niagara District, Willis L. Hopkin, 765 Rymal Rd. E, Hamilton, ON L8W 1B6; Northern Ontario District, Douglas G. Bolger, 482 Timmins St., North Bay, ON P1B 4K7; Ottawa District, Marion Smith, 70 Mayburry St., Hull, QC J9A 2E9; Owen Sound District, Robin M. Duff, P.O. Box 52, Owen Sound, ON N1K 5P1; Toronto Metropole, Kerry J. Richards, 74 Parkside Dr., Brampton, ON L6Y 2G9

Periodicals

Saints Herald

Congregational Christian Churches in Canada

This body originated in the early 18th century when devout Christians within several denominations in the northern and eastern United States, dissatisfied with sectarian controversy, broke away from their own denominations and took the simple title "Christians." First organized in 1821 at Keswick, Ontario, the Congregational Christian Churches in Canada was incorporated on Dec. 4, 1989 as a national organization. In doctrine, the body is evangelical, being governed by the Bible as the final authority in faith and practice. It believes that Christian character must be expressed in daily living; it aims at the unity of all true believers in Christ that others may believe in Him and be saved. In church polity, the body is democratic and autonomous. It is also a member of The World Evangelical Congrega--tional Fellowship.

Headquarters

241 Dunsdon St. Ste. 405, Brantford, ON N3R 7C3 Tel. (519)751-0606 Fax (519)751-0852

Media Contact, Past Pres., Jim Potter, 8 Church St., Waldemar, ON L0N 1G0 Tel. (519)928-5561

Officers

Pres., Rev. Michael Shute

Exec. Dir., Rev.David Schrader

Sec., Rev. Ron Holden

Convention of Atlantic Baptist Churches

The United Baptist Convention of the Atlantic Provinces is the largest Baptist Convention in Canada. Through the Canadian Baptist Ministries, it is a member of the Baptist World Alliance.

In 1763 two Baptist churches were organized in Atlantic Canada; one in Sackville, New Brunswick and the other in Wolfville, Nova Scotia. Although both these churches experienced crises and lost continuity, they recovered and stand today as the beginning of organized Baptist work in Canada.

Nine Baptist churches met in Lower Granville, Nova Scotia in 1800 and formed the first Baptist Association in Canada. By 1846 the Maritime Baptist Convention was organized, consisting of 169 churches. Two streams of Baptist life merged in 1905 to form the United Baptist Convention. This is how the term "United Baptist" was derived. Today there are 554 churches within 21 associations across the Convention.

The Convention has two educational institutions: Atlantic Baptist University in Moncton, New Brunswick, a Christian Liberal Arts University; and Acadia Divinity College in Wolfville, Nova Scotia, a Graduate School of Theology. The Convention engages in world mission through Canadian Baptist Ministries, the all-Canada mission agency. In addition to an active program of home mission, evangelism, training, social action, and stewardship, the Convention operates ten senior citizen complexes and a Christian bookstore.

Headquarters

1655 Manawagonish Rd., Saint John, NB E2M 3Y2 Tel. (506)635-1922 Fax (506)635-0366

Email: cabc@baptist.atlantic.ca

Website: www.baptist.atlantic.ca

Media Contact, Exec. Minister, Dr. Harry G. Gardner

Officers

Pres. (2002-2003), Dr. Malcom Card, 125 Beatty St., Woodstock, NB E7M 6A4 Tel. (506)324-8021 Fax (506)328-2460

Pres. (2003-2004), Dr. Lionel Moriah, 107 Ashgrove Ave., Dartmouth, NS B2V 1G2 Tel. (902)429-0690 Fax (902)429-0886

Vice Pres. (2002-2003), Dr. Lionel Moriah, 107 Ashgrove Ave., Dartmouth, NS B2V 1G2 Tel. (902)429-0690 Fax (902)429-0886

Exec. Min., Dr. Harry G. Gardner, 1655 Manawagonish Rd., Saint John, NB E2M 3Y2 Tel. (506)635-1922, Fax (506)635-0366, harry.gardner@baptistt-atlantic.ca

Dir. of Operations., Daryl MacKenzie, 1655 Manawagonish Rd., Saint John, NB E2M 3Y2 Tel. (506)635-1922, Fax (506)635-0366, darryl.mackenzie@baptistt-atlantic.ca

Dir. of Atlantic Baptist Mission, Dr. Malcolm Beckett, 1655 Manawagonish Rd., Saint John, NB E2M 3Y2 Tel. (506)635-1922, Fax (506) 635-0366, malcolm.beckett@baptistt-atlantic.ca

Dir. of Youth and Family, Rev. Bruce Fawcett, 1655 Manawagonish Rd., Saint John, NB E2M 3Y2 Tel. (506)635-1922, Fax (506)635-0366, bruce.fawcett@baptistt-atlantic.ca

Dir. Of Development, Rev. Greg Jones, 1655 Manawagonish Rd., Saint John, NB E2M 3Y2 Tel. (506)635-1922, Fax (506)635-0366, greg.jones@baptistt-atlantic.ca

Part-time Dir. Of Public Witness and Social Concern, Dr. Lois P. Mitchell c/o 1655 Manawagonish Rd., Saint John, NB E2M 3Y2 Tel. (506)635-1922, Fax (506)635-0366, lois.mitchell@baptistt-atlantic.ca

The Coptic Orthodox Church in Canada

The Coptic Orthodox Church in North America was begun in Canada in 1964 and was registered in the province of Ontario in 1965. The Coptic Orthodox Church has spread rapidly since then. The total number of local churches in both Canada and the USA exceeded one hundred. Two dioceses; a monastery with a bishop, monks, and novices; and two theological seminaries were established in the USA.

The Coptic Orthodox Church is the church of Alexandria founded in Egypt by St. Mark the Apostle in the first century A.D. She is a hierarchical church and the administrative governing body of each local church is an elected Board of Deacons approved by the Bishop. The current patriarch of the church is H. H. Pope Shenouda III, Pope of Alexandria and Patriach of the see of St. Mark. The Coptic Orthodox Church is a member of the Canadian Council of Churches.

Headquarters

St. Mark's Coptic Orthodox Church, 41 Glendinning Ave., Scarborough, ON M1W 3E2 Tel. (416)494-4449 Fax (416)494-2631

Email: mail@coptorthodox.ca

Website: www.stmark.toronto.on.coptorthodox.ca

Media Contact, Fr. Ammonius Guirguis Tel. (416) 494-4449, Fax (416)494-2631, frammonius@coptorthodox.ca

Elim Fellowship of Evangelical Churches and Ministers

The Elim Fellowship of Evangelical Churches and Ministers, a Pentecostal body, was established in 1984 as a sister organization of Elim Fellowship in the United States.

This is an association of churches, ministers, and missionaries seeking to serve the whole body of Christ. It is Pentecostal and has a charismatic orientation.

Headquarters

379 Golf Road, R.R. #6, Brantford, ON N3T 5L8 Tel. (519)753-7266 Fax (519)753-5887

Email: elim@bfree.on.ca

Website: Bfree.ON.ca/comdir/churchs/elim

Ofc. Mgr., Larry Jones

Officers

Pres., Howard Ellis, 102 Ripley Crescent., Kitchener, ON N2N 1V4

Vice Pres., Rev. Errol Alchin, 1694 Autumn Crescent, Pickering, ON L1V 6X5

Sec.-Treas., Larry Jones, 107 Hillside Ave., Paris ON K2G 4N1

COUNCIL OF ELDERS

Rev. Bud Crawford, Brampton, ON

Rev. Howard Ellis, Kitchener, ON

Rev. Bernard Evans, Lima, NY

Rev. Claude Favreau, Drummondville, Quebec

Rev. Aubrey Phillips, Blairsville, GA

The Estonian Evangelical Lutheran Church Abroad

The Estonian Evangelical Lutheran Church (EELC) was founded in 1917 in Estonia and reorganized in Sweden in 1944. The teachings of the EELC are based on the Old and New Testaments, explained through the Apostolic, Nicean, and Athanasian confessions; the unaltered Confession of Augsburg; and other teachings found in the Book of Concord.

Headquarters

383 Jarvis St., Toronto, ON M5B 2C7 Tel. (416) 925-5465 Fax (416)925-5688

Website: www.eelk.ee/~e.e.l.k./

Media Contact, Archbishop, Rev. Udo Petersoo, udo.petersoo@eelk.ee

Officers

Archbishop, The Rev. Udo Petersoo

Gen. Sec., Mr. Ivar Nippak

Sec./Clerk, Mrs. Evi Jaaguste

Periodicals

Eesti Kirik

The Evangelical Covenant Church of Canada

A Canadian denomination organized in Canada at Winnipeg in 1904 which is affiliated with the Evangelical Covenant Church of America and with the International Federation of Free Evangelical Churches, which includes 31 federations in 26 countries.

This body believes in the one triune God as confessed in the Apostles' Creed, that salvation is received through faith in Christ as Saviour, and that the Bible is the authoritative guide in all matters of faith and practice. Christian Baptism and the Lord's Supper are accepted as divinely ordained sacraments of the church. As descendants of the 19th-century northern European pietistic awakening, the group believes in the need of a personal experience of commitment to Christ, the development of a virtuous life, and the urgency of spreading the gospel to the "ends of the world."

Four Core Values: To be a Missional Church, To be a Biblical Church, To be a Devotional Church, and to be a Connnectional Church.

Four Ministry Priorities: Leadership Development, Church Planting & Mission, Church Renewal/Transition, and Christian Services.

Headquarters

P.O. Box 34025, RPO Fort Richmond, Winnipeg, MB R3T 5T5

Media Contact, Supt., Jeff Anderson

Officers

Pres./Supt., Rev. Jeff Anderson, P.O. 34025, RPO Fort Richmond, Winnipeg, MB R3T 5T5

Chpsn., Rod Johnson, Box 217, Norquay, SK S0A 2V0

Sec., Judy Nelson, Box 194, Norquay, SK S0A 2V0

Treas., Ingrid Wildman, Box 93, Norquay, SK S0A 2V0

Periodicals

The Covenant Messenger

Evangelical Free Church of Canada

The Evangelical Free Church of Canada traces its beginning back to 1917 when the church in

Enchant, Alberta opened its doors. Today the denomination has 139 churches from the West Coast to Quebec. Approximately 80 missionaries are sponsored by the EFCC in 17 countries. The Evangelical Free Church is the founding denomination of Trinity Western University in Langley, British Columbia. Church membership is 7,920; average attendance is 18,496

Headquarters

Mailing Address, P.O. Box 850 LCD1, Langley, BC V3A 8S6 Tel. (604)888-8668 Fax (604) 888-3108; Location, 7600 Glover Rd., Langley, BC

Email: efcc@twu.ca

Website: www.efcc.ca

Media Contact, Exec. Sec., Carol Jones, P.O. Box 850 LCD1, Langley, BC V3A 8S6 Tel. (604)888-8668 Fax (604)888-3108

Officers

President, Dr. Ron Unruh, P.O. Box 850 LCD 1, Langley, BC, Canada V3A 8S6 Tel (604)888-8668, Fax (604)888-3108, efcc@twu.ca

Periodicals

The Pulse

Evangelical Lutheran Church in Canada

The Evangelical Lutheran Church in Canada was organized in 1985 through a merger of The Evangelical Lutheran Church of Canada (ELCC) and the Lutheran Church in America–Canada Section.

The merger is a result of an invitation issued in 1972 by the ELCC to the Lutheran Church in America–Canada Section and the Lutheran Church–Canada. Three-way merger discussions took place until 1978 when it was decided that only a two-way merger was possible. The ELCC was the Canada District of the ALC until autonomy in 1967.

The Lutheran Church in Canada traces its history back more than 200 years. Congregations were organized by German Lutherans in Halifax and Lunenburg County in Nova Scotia in 1749. German Lutherans, including many United Empire Loyalists, also settled in large numbers along the St. Lawrence and in Upper Canada. In the late 19th century, immigrants arrived from Scandinavia, Germany, and central European countries, many via the United States. The Lutheran synods in the United States have provided the pastoral support and help for the Canadian church.

Headquarters

302-393 Portage Ave., Winnipeg, MB R3B 3H6 Tel. (204)984-9150 Fax (204)984-9185

Media Contact, Bishop, Rev. Raymond L. Schultz

Periodicals

Canada Lutheran, Esprit

The Evangelical Mennonite Conference

The Evangelical Mennonite Conference is a modern church of historic Christian convictions, tracing its indebtedness to the Radical Reformation, which, in turn, is rooted in the Protestant Reformation of the 16th century. The Centre of faith, and of Scripture, is found in Jesus Christ as Saviour and Lord.

The church's name was chosen in 1959. It's original name, Kleine Gemeinde (which means "small church"), reflected its origins as a renewal movement among Mennonites in southern Russia. Klaas Reimer, a minister, was concerned about a decline of spiritual life and discipline in the church and inappropriate involvement in the Napoleanic War. About 1812, Reimer and others began separate worship services and two years later were organized as a small group.

Facing increasing government pressure, particularly about military service, the group migrated to North America in 1874 to 1875. Fifty families settled in Manitoba and 36 in Nebraska. Ties between the groups weakened and eventually the US group gave up its KG identity. The KG survived several schisms and migrations, dating from its years in Russia through the 1940s.

As an evangelical church, The Evangelical Mennonite Conference holds that Scripture has final authority in faith and practice, a belief in Christ's finished work, and that assurance of salvation is possible. As Mennonite, the denomination has a commitment to discipleship, baptism upon confession of faith, community, social concern, nonviolence, and the Great Commission. As a conference, it seeks to encourage local churches, to work together on evangelism and matters of social concern, and relates increasingly well to other denominations.

In the year 2000 its membership surpassed 7,000, with many more people as treasured adherents and a wider circle of ministry influence. Membership is for people baptized on confession of faith (usually in adolescence or older). Children are considered safe in Christ until they reach an age where they are accountable for their own spiritual decision and opt out; they are considered part of the church, while full inclusion occurs upon personal choice.

The Conference has 50 churches from British Columbia to Ontario (33 in Manitoba) and roughly 147 mission workers in 25 countries. The cultural make-up of the Conference is increasingly diverse, though its Dutch/German background remains dominant nationally. Ten churches have pastors or leaders who are of non-Dutch/German background.

Some churches have a multiple leadership pattern (ministers and deacons can be selected from within the congregation), others have new patterns. Most churches support their leading minister full time. Its church governance moved from a bishop system to greater local congregational autonomy. It currently functions as a conference of churches with national boards, a conference council, and a moderator.

Woman can serve on most national boards, as conference council delegates, as missionaries, and within a wide range of local church activities, while they can be selected locally, they cannot currently serve as nationally recognized or commissioned ministers.

It is a supporting member of Mennonite Central Committee and the Evangelical Fellowship of Canada. About 80 percent of its national budget goes toward mission work in Canada and other countries.

Headquarters

Box 1268, 440 Main St., Steinbach, MB R0A 2A0 Tel. (204)326-6401 Fax (204)326-1613

Email: emconf@mts.net

Media Contact, Conf. Pastor, David Thiessen

Officers

Conf. Mod., Harvey Plett
General Sec., Len Barkman
Conference Pastor, David Thiessen
Bd. of Missions: Exec. Sec., Len Barkman
Bd. of Missions: Foreign Sec., Lester Olfert
Bd. of Church Ministries: Exec. Sec.-Editor, Terry M. Smith
Canadian Sec., Conf. Pastor, David Thiessen
Conference Youth Minister, Gerald Reimer

Periodicals

The Messenger

Evangelical Mennonite Mission Conference

This group was founded in 1936 as the Rudnerweider Mennonite Church in Southern Manitoba and organized as the Evangelical Mennonite Mission Conference in 1959. It was incorporated in 1962. The Annual Conference meeting is held in July.

Headquarters

Box 52059, Niakwa P.O., Winnipeg, MB R2M 5P9 Tel. (204)253-7929 Fax (204)256-7384

Email: emmc@mb.sympatico.ca

Media Contact, John Bergman, Box 206, Niverville, MB R0A 1E0 Tel. (204)388-4775, Fax (204)388-4775, jbergman@mb.sympatico.ca

Officers

Mod., David Penner, 906-300 Sherk St., Leamington, ON N8H 4N7
Vice Mod., Carl Zacharias, R.R. #1, Box 205, Winkler, MB R6W 4A1
Sec., Darrell Dyck, R.R. #1, Box 186, Winkler, MB R6W 4A1
Dir. of Conference Ministries, Jack Heppner
Dir. of Missions, Rev. Leonard Sawatzky
Business Admin., Henry Thiessen

OTHER ORGANIZATIONS

The Gospel Message: Box 1622, Saskatoon, SK S7K 3R8 Tel. (306)242-5001 Fax (306)242-6115; 210-401-33rd St. W, Saskatoon, SK S7L 0V5 Tel. (306)242-5001;
Radio Pastor, Rev. Ed Martens

Periodicals

EMMC Recorder

The Evangelical Missionary Church of Canada

This denomination was formed in 1993 with the merger of The Evangelical Church of Canada and The Missionary Church of Canada. The Evangelical Missionary Church of Canada maintains fraternal relations with the worldwide body of the Missionary Church, Inc. and with the Evangelical Church of North America.The Evangelical Church of Canada was among those North American Evangelical United Brethern Conferences which did not join the EUB in merging with the Methodist Church in 1968. The Missionary Church of Canada is Anabaptist in heritage. Its practices and theology were shaped by the Holiness Revivals of the late 1800s. The Evangelical Missionary Church consists of 135 churches in two conferences in Canada.

Headquarters

4031 Brentwood Rd., NW, Calgary, AB T2L 1L1 Tel. (403)250-2759 Fax (403)291-4720

Media Contact, Exec. Dir., Missions and Administration, G. Keith Elliott

Email: info@emcc.ca

Officers

Pres., Rev. David Crouse, 4031Brentwood Rd. NW, Calgary, AB Tel (403)250-2759 Fax (403)291-4720
Canada East District, Dist. Supt., Rev. Phil Delsaut, 130 Fergus Ave., Kitchener, ON N2A 2H2 Tel. (519)894-9800
Canada West District, Acting Dist. Supt., Rev. Don Adolf, 4031 Brentwood Rd. NW, Calgary, AB T2L 1L1 Tel. (403)250-2759 Fax (403) 291-4720

The Fellowship of Evangelical Baptist Churches in Canada

This organization was founded in 1953 by the merging of the Union of Regular Baptist Churches of Ontario and Quebec with the Fellowship of Independent Baptist Churches of Canada.

Headquarters

679 Southgate Dr., Guelph, ON N1G 4S2 Tel. (519)821-4830 Fax (519)821-9829

Media Contact, Pres., Rev. Terry D. Cuthbert, president@fellowship.ca

Officers

Pres., Rev. Terry D. Cuthbert
Chmn., Rev. Dan Shurr

Periodicals

B.C. Fellowship Baptist, The Evangelical Baptist, Intercom

Foursquare Gospel Church of Canada

The Western Canada District was formed in 1964 with the Rev. Roy Hicks as supervisor. Prior to 1964 it had been a part of the Northwest District of the International Church of the Foursquare Gospel with headquarters in Los Angeles, Calif.

A Provincial Society, the Church of the Foursquare Gospel of Western Canada, was formed in 1976; a Federal corporation, the Foursquare Gospel Church of Canada, was incorporated in 1981 and a national church formed. The provincial society was closed in 1994.

Headquarters

#100 8459 160th St., Surrey, BC V3S 3T9
Email: fgcc@canada.com
Media Contact, Pres. & Gen. Supervisor, Timothy J. Peterson, #100-8459 160th St., Surrey, BC V4N 1B4 Tel. (604)543-8414 Fax (604)543-8417

Officers

Pres. & Gen. Supervisor, Timothy J. Peterson

Periodicals

VIP Communique

Free Methodist Church in Canada

The Free Methodist Church was founded in New York in 1860 and expanded in 1880. It is Methodist in doctrine, evangelical in ministry, and emphasizes the teaching of holiness of life through faith in Jesus Christ.

The Free Methodist Church in Canada was incorporated in 1927 after the establishment of a Canadian Executive Board. In 1959 the Holiness Movement Church merged with the Free Methodist Church. Full autonomy for the Canadian church was realized in 1990 with the formation of a Canadian General Conference. Mississauga, Ontario, continues to be the location of the Canadian Headquarters.

The Free Methodist Church ministers in 50 countries through its World Ministries Center in Indianapolis, Ind.

Headquarters

4315 Village Centre Ct., Mississauga, ON L4Z 1S2 Tel. (905)848-2600 Fax (905)848-2603
Email: ministrycentre@fmc-canada.org
Website: www.fmc-canada.org
Media Contact, Dan Sheffield

Officers

Bishop, Rev. Keith Elford
Dir. of Admn. Ser., Norman Bull
Dir. Of Global and Intercultural Ministries, Rev. Dan Sheffield
Supt., Personnel, Rev. Alan Retzman
Supt., Growth Ministries, in transition

Periodicals

The Free Methodist Herald

Free Will Baptists

As revival fires burned throughout New England in the mid- and late 1700s, Benjamin Randall proclaimed his doctrine of Free Will to large crowds of seekers. In due time, a number of Randall's converts moved to Nova Scotia. One such believer was Asa McGray, who was to become instrumental in the establishment of several Free Baptist churches. Local congregations were organized in New Brunswick. After several years of numerical and geographic gains, disagreements surfaced over the question of music, Sunday school, church offerings, salaried clergy, and other issues. Adherents of the more progressive element decided to form their own fellowship. Led by George Orser, they became known as Free Christian Baptists.

The new group faithfully adhered to the truths and doctrines which embodied the theological basis of Free Will Baptists. Largely through Archibald Hatfield, contact was made with Free Will Baptists in the United States in the 1960s. The association was officially welcomed into the Free Will Baptist family in July 1981, by the National Association.

Headquarters

5233 Mt. View Rd., Antioch, TN 37013-2306 Tel. (615)731-6812 Fax (615)731-0771
Media Contact, Mod., Dwayne Broad, RR 3, Bath, NB E0J 1E0 Tel. (506)278-3771

Officers

Mod., Dwayne Broad
Promotional Officer, Dwayne Broad

General Church of the New Jerusalem

The Church of the New Jerusalem, also called The New Church, is a Christian Church founded on the Bible and the Writings of Emanuel Swedenborg (1688-1772). These Writings were first brought to Ontario in 1835 by Christian Enslin.

Headquarters

c/o Olivet Church, 279 Burnhamthorpe Rd., Etobicoke, ON M9B 1Z6 Tel. (416)239-3054 Fax (416)239-4935
Website: www.newchurch.org
Media Contact, Exec. Vice-Pres., Rev. Michael D. Gladish, Mgladish@interlog.com

Officers

Pres., Rt. Rev. P. M. Buss, Bryn Athyn, PA 19009
Exec. Vice-Pres., Rev. Michael D. Gladish
Sec., Carolyn Bellinger, 110 Chapel Hill Dr., Kitchener, ON N2G 3W5
Treas., James Bellinger, 2 Shaver Court, Etobicoke, ON M9B 4P5

Periodicals

New Church Canadian

Greek Orthodox Metropolis of Toronto (Canada)

Greek Orthodox Christians in Canada are under the jurisdiction of the Ecumenical Patriarchate of Constantinople (Istanbul).

Headquarters

86 Overlea Blvd., Toronto, ON M4H 1C6 Tel. (416)429-5757 Fax (416)429-4588

E-mail: gocanada@total.net

Media Contact, Orthodox Way Committee

Officers

Metropolitan Archbishop of the Metropolis of Toronto (Canada), His Eminence Metropolitan Archbishop Sotirios

Periodicals

Orthodox Way

Independent Assemblies of God International (Canada)

This fellowship of churches has been operating in Canada for over 58 years. It is a branch of the Pentecostal Church in Sweden. Each church within the fellowship is completely independent.

Headquarters

1211 Lancaster St., London, ON N5V 2L4 Tel. (519)451-1751 Fax (519)453-3258

Media Contact, Gen. Sec., Rev. Harry Wuerch, jwuerch@odyssey.on.ca

Officers

Gen. Sec., Rev. Harry Wuerch, 1211 Lancaster St., London, ON N5V 2L4

Treas., Rev. David Ellyatt, 1795 Parkhurst Ave., London, ON N5V 2C4, david.ellyatt@odyssey.on.ca

Periodicals

The Mantle (published in March, July & October)

Independent Holiness Church

The former Holiness Movement of Canada merged with the Free Methodist Church in 1958. Some churches remained independent of this merger and they formed the Independent Holiness Church in 1960, in Kingston, Ontario. The doctrines are Methodist and Wesleyan. The General Conference is every three years, with the next meeting in 2004.

Headquarters

Rev. R. E. Votary, 1564 John Quinn Rd., R.R.1, Greely, ON K4P 1J9 Tel. (613)821-2237

Media Contact, Gen. Sec., Dwayne Reaney, 5025 River Rd. RR #1, Manotick, ON K4M 1B2 Tel. (613)692-3237

Officers

Gen. Supt., Rev. R. E. Votary, 1564 John Quinn Rd., Greeley, ON K4P 1J9

Gen. Sec., Dwayne Reaney

Additional Officers: E. Brown, 104-610 Pesehudoff Cresc., Saskatoon, SK S7N 4H5; D. Wallace, 1456 John Quinn Rd., R#1, Greely, ON K4P 1J9

Periodicals

Gospel Tidings

The Italian Pentecostal Church of Canada

This body had its beginnings in Hamilton, Ontario, in 1912 when a few people of an Italian Presbyterian Church banded themselves together for prayer and received a Pentecostal experience of the baptism in the Holy Spirit. Since 1912, there has been a close association with the teachings and practices of the Pentecostal Assemblies of Canada.

The work spread to Toronto, then to Montreal, where it also flourished. In 1959, the church was incorporated in the province of Quebec. The early leaders of this body were the Rev. Luigi Ippolito and the Rev. Ferdinand Zaffuto. The churches carry on their ministry in both the English and Italian languages.

Headquarters

6724 Fabre St., Montreal, QC J2G 2Z6 Tel. (514)279-1100 Fax (514)279-1131

Media Contact, Gen. Sec., Rev. John Della-Foresta, 12216 Pierre Baillargeon, Montreal, QC H1E 6R7 Tel. (514)494-6969

Officers

Gen. Supt., Rev. Daniel Mortelliti, 6724 Fabre St., Montreal, QC J2G 2Z6 Tel. (514)279-1100 Fax (514)279-1131

Gen. Sec., Rev. John DellaForesta, 12216 Pierre Baillargeon, Montreal, QC H1E 6R7 Tel. (514)494-6969

Gen. Treas., Rev. David Quackenbush, 6724 Fabre St., Montreal, QC H2G 2Z6 Tel. (514) 593-1944 Fax (514)593-1835

Overseer, Rev. David DiStaulo, 5811 Maurice Duplessis, Montreal QC H1G 1Y2, Tel. (514) 328-3131

Overseer, Rev. Joseph Manafo, 22 Sparrow Ave., Toronto ON M6A 1L4, Tel. (416) 787-0341

Periodicals

Voce Evangelica–Evangel Voice

Jehovah's Witnesses

For a description of Jehovah's Witnesses see "Religious Bodies in the United States" in this edition of the Yearbook.

Headquarters

25 Columbia Heights, Brooklyn, NY 11201-2483 Tel. (718)560-5600 Fax (718)560-5619

Canadian Branch Office, Box 4100, Halton Hills, ON L7G 4Y4

Media Contact, Director, Public Affairs Office, James N. Pellechia

Media Contact, Public Affairs Office in Canada, Dennis Charland

Lutheran Church–Canada

Lutheran Church–Canada was established in 1959 at Edmonton, Alberta, as a federation of Canadian districts of the Lutheran Church–Missouri Synod; it was constituted in 1988 at Winnipeg, Manitoba, as an autonomous church.

The church confesses the Bible as both inspired and infallible, the only source and norm of doctrine and life and subscribes without reservation to the Lutheran Confessions as contained in the Book of Concord of 1580.

Headquarters

3074 Portage Ave., Winnipeg, MB R3K 0Y2 Tel. (204)895-3433 Fax (204)897-4319

Email: info@lutheranchurch.ca

Media Contact, Dir. of Comm., Ian Adnams, communications@lutheranchurch.ca

Officers

Pres., Rev. Ralph Mayan, 3074 Portage Ave., Winnipeg, MB R3K 0Y2 Tel. (204)895-3433, Fax (204)897-4319, president@lutheranchurch.ca

Pres. Emeritus, Rev. Dr. Edwin Lehman, 686 Lee Ridge Rd., Edmonton AB T6K 0P2 Tel. (780) 462-9608, Fax (780)468-2172, edwinlehman@shaw.ca

Honorary Pres., Rev. Dr. Elroy Treit, 74-3180 East 58 Avenue, Vancouver BC V5S 3S8 Tel. (604)434-9700

1st Vice Pres., Rev. Daniel Rinderknecht, Box 1, Site 1 RR4, Stony Plain, AB T7Z 1X4 (2008) Tel./Fax (780)963-773, sjohnlcc@telusplanet.net,

2nd Vice Pres., Rev. James Fritsche, 1541 St. Mary's Rd., Winnipeg, MB R2M 3V8 (2008) Tel. (204)256-5548, Fax (519)745-7165, rekrestick@sympatico.ca

Sec., Rev. William Ney, 5021-52 Ave., Stony Plain, AB T7Z 1C1 (2002) Tel. (780)963-4144, Fax (780)963-3800, revney@telusplanet.net

Treas., Mr. Dwayne Cleave, 3074 Portage Avenue, Winnipeg, MB R3K 0Y2 Tel. (204) 895-3433, Fax (204)897-4319, treasurer@lutheranchurch.ca

DISTRICT OFFICES

Alberta-British Columbia: Pres., Rev. D. Schiemann, 7100 Ada Blvd., Edmonton, AB T5B 4E4 Tel. (403)474-0063, Fax (403)477-9829, info@lccabc.ca

Central: Pres., Rev. T. Prachar, 1927 Grant Dr., Regina, SK S4S 4V6 Tel. (306)586-4434, Fax (306)586-0656, tprachar@accesscomm.ca

East: Pres., Rev. A. Maleske, 275 Lawrence Ave., Kitchener, ON N2M 1Y3 Tel. (519)578-6500, Fax (519)578-3369, lcced@aol.com

Periodicals

The Canadian Lutheran

Mennonite Church Canada

Mennonite Church Canada began (formerly Conference of Mennonites in Canada) was founded in 1903 by 15 praire congregations. In the late 1990s it merged with the Mennonite Church to become Mennonite Church Canada. The first Mennonites came to Canada in 1786, moving from Pennsylvania in Conestoga wagons. Over the next 150 years, more arrived by ship from Europe in at least four successive waves. Its members hold to traditional Christian beliefs, believer's baptism, and congregational polity. They emphazes practical Christianity, opposition to war, service to others, and personal ethics.

Some people who have joined the Mennonite body in recent years have arrived from Asia, from Africa, or from Latin and South America. Native brothers and sisters, whose people were here long before the first conastoga wagons arrived, have added their voices to the mix. Further immigration from Russia in the 1920s and 1940s increased the group which is now located in all provinces from New Brunswick to British Columbia. In recent years a variety of other ethnic groups, including native Canadians, have joined the conference. Meanwhile, French-speaking and English-speaking Canadians from the wider community have enriched the Mennonite people. Together we are Christian believers moving into the future under the umbrella of the Mennonite Church Canada.

Mennonite Church Canada is affiliated with Mennonite Church USA whose offices are at Newton, Kans. and Elkhart, Ind. (See, Mennonite Church USA description in the section "Religious Bodies in the United States")

Headquarters

600 Shaftesbury Blvd., Winnipeg, MB R3P 0M4 Tel. (204)888-6781 Fax (204)831-5675

Website: www.mennonitechurch.ca

Media Contact, Dan Dyck, ddyck@mennonitechurch.ca

Officers

Chpsn., Henry Krause

Gen. Sec., Dan Nighswander

Periodicals

Canadian Mennonite

North American Baptist Conference

Churches belonging to this conference emanated from German Baptist immigrants of more than a century ago. Although scattered across Canada and the US, they are bound together by a common heritage, a strong spiritual unity, a Bible-centered faith, and a deep interest in missions.

Note: The details of general organization, officers, and periodicals of this body will be found in the North American Baptist Conference directory in the "Religious Bodies in the United States" section of this Yearbook.

Headquarters

1 S. 210 Summit Ave., Oakbrook Terr., IL 60181 Tel. (630)495-2000 Fax (630)495-3301

Media Contact, Marilyn Schaer

Officers

Exec. Dir., Dr. Philip Yntema

Periodicals

N.A.B. Today

The Old Catholic Church of Canada

The church was founded in 1948 in Hamilton, Ontario. The first bishop was the Rt. Rev. George Davis. The Old Catholic Church of Canada accepts all the doctrines of the Eastern Orthodox Churches and, therefore, not Papal Infallibility or the Immaculate Conception. The ritual is Western (Latin Rite) and is in the vernacular language. Celibacy is optional.

Headquarters

2185 Sheridan Park Dr., Apt. 105, Mississauga, ON L5K 1C7 Tel. (905)855-3643

Media Contact, Bishop, The Right Rev. Pat Davies, Vicar General

Officers

Vicar General and Auxiliary Bishop, The Rt. Rev. A.C. Keating, PhD, 5066 Forest Grove Crest, Burlington, ON L7L GG6 Tel. (905) 681-9983

Old Order Amish Church

This is the most conservative branch of the Mennonite Church and direct descendants of Swiss Brethren (Anabaptists) who emerged from the Reformation in Switzerland in 1525. The Amish, followers of Bishop Jacob Ammann, became a distinct group in 1693. They began migrating to North America about 1736; all of them still reside in the United States or Canada. They first migrated to Ontario in 1823 directly from Bavaria, Germany and later from Pennsylvania and Alsace-Lorraine. Since 1953 more Amish have migrated to Ontario from Ohio, Indiana, and Iowa.

In 2003 there were 26 congregations in Ontario, each being autonomous. No membership figures are kept by this group, and there is no central headquarters. Each congregation is served by a bishop, two ministers, and a deacon, all of whom are chosen from among the male members by lot for life.

Officers

Correspondent, Pathway Publishers, David Luthy, Rt. 4, Aylmer, ON N5H 2R3

Periodicals

Blackboard Bulletin, Herold der Wahreit, The Budget, The Diary, Die Botschaft, Family Life, Young Companion

Open Bible Faith Fellowship of Canada

This is an Evangelical, Full Gospel Fellowship of Churches and Ministries emphasizing evangelism, missions, and the local church for success in the present harvest of souls. OBFF was chartered January 7, 1982.

Headquarters

Niagara Celebration Church, P.O. Box 968, St. Catharines, ON L2R 6Z4 Tel. (905)646-0970

Media Contact, Exec. Dir., Randy Neilson

Officers

Pres., Peter Youngren
Vice Pres., Peter Morgan
Exec. Dir., Randy Neilson
Sec.-Treas., George Woodward
Dir., Jim Buslon
Dir., Greg Newman

Orthodox Church in America (Canada Section)

The Archdiocese of Canada of the Orthodox Church in America was established in 1916. First organized by St. Tikhon—martyr Patriarch of Moscow, previously Archbishop of North America—it is part of the Russian Metropolia and its successor, the autocephalous Orthodox Church in America.

The Archdiocesan Council meets twice yearly, the General Assembly of the Archdiocese takes place every three years. The Archdiocese is also known as "Orthodox Church in Canada."

Headquarters

P.O. Box 179, Spencerville, ON K0E 1X0 Office Tel. (613)925-5226 Home Tel. (613)925-3004 Fax (613)925-1521

E-mail: zoe@ripnet.com

Officers

Bishop of Ottawa & Canada, The Rt. Rev. Seraphim, Chancellor, V. Rev. Dennis Pinach, 17319

Treas., Nikita Lopoukhine, 55 Clarey Ave., Ottawa, ON K1S 2R6

Eastern Sec., Olga Jurgens, P.O. Box 179, Spencerville, ON K0E 1X0

ARCHDIOCESAN COUNCIL

Clergy Members: Rev. Lawrence Farley, Rev. R.S. Kennaugh, Rev. Larry Reinheimer, Igumen Irenee Rochon, Rev. James Griggs, Rev. Rodion Luciuk

Lay Members: David Grier, John Hadjinicolaou, Denis Lessard, Mother Sophia (Zion), David Rystephanuk, Rod Tkachuk, Geoff Korz

Ex Officio: Chancellor, Treas., Eastern Sec., Western Sec.

Periodicals

Canadian Orthodox Messenger

Patriarchal Parishes of the Russian Orthodox Church in Canada

This is the diocese of Canada of the former Exarchate of North and South America of the Russian Orthodox Church. It was originally founded in 1897 by the Russian Orthodox Archdiocese in North America.

Headquarters

St. Barbara's Russian Orthodox Cathedral, 10105 96th St., Edmonton, AB T5H 2G3

Media Contact, Sec.-Treas., Victor Lopushinsky, #303 9566-101 Ave., Edmonton, AB T5H 0B4 Tel. (780)455-9071

Officers

Admn., Archbishop of Kashira, Most Rev. Mark, 10812-108 St., Edmonton, AB T5H 3A6 Tel. (780)420-9945

The Pentecostal Assemblies of Newfoundland

This body began in 1911 and held its first meetings at Bethesda Mission at St. John's. It was incorporated in 1925 as The Bethesda Pentecostal Assemblies of Newfoundland and changed its name in 1930 to The Pentecostal Assemblies of Newfoundland.

Headquarters

57 Thorburn Rd., Box 8895, Stn. "A", St. John's, NF A1B 3T2 Tel. (709)753-6314 Fax (709) 753-4945

Email: paon@paon.nf.ca

Media Contact, Gen. Supt., A. Earl Batstone, 57 Thorburn Rd., Box 8895, Stn. "A", St. John's, NF A1B 3T2

GENERAL EXECUTIVE OFFICERS

Gen. Supt., A. Earl Batstone, 57 Thorburn Rd., Box 8895, Stn. "A", St. John's, NF A1B 3T2

Gen. Sec.-Treas., Clarence Buckle, 57 Thorburn Rd., Box 8895, Stn. "A", St. John's, NF A1B 3T2

Ex. Dir. of Home Missions, Barry Q. Grimes, 57 Thorburn Rd., Box 8895, Stn. "A", St. John's, NF A1B 3T2

Ex. Dir. of Ch. Ministries, Robert H. Dewling, 57 Thorburn Rd., Box 8895, Stn. "A", St. John's, NF A1B 3T2

PROVINCIAL DIRECTORS

Sunday School Ministries: Alvin F. Peddle, Box 40, Baytona, NF A0G 2J0

Children's Ministries: Lorinda R. Moulton, Box 56, New Harbour, NF A0B 2P0

Women's Ministries: Nancy L. Hunter, 12 Harp Pl., Paradise, NF A1L 1G9

Men's Ministries: Norman C. Joy, 2 Firgreen Ave., Mount Pearl, NF A1N 1T7

Youth Ministries: B. Dean Brenton, Box 21100, St. John's, NF A1B 3L5

Mature Adult Ministries: Clayton Rice, 29 Diana Rd., St. John's, NF A1B 1H7

Family Ministries: Eva M. Winsor, 26 Ireland Dr., Grand Falls-Windsor, NF A2A 2S6

AUXILIARY SERVICES

Chaplain for Institutions, Roy A. Burden, 293 Frecker Dr., St. John's, NF A1E 5T8

Pentecostal Senior Citizens Home: Administrator, Beverley Bellefleur, Box 130, Clarke's Beach, NF A0A 1W0

Evergreen Manor: Summerford, NF A0G 4E0

Pastoral Enrichment Ministries: Gary D. & Eva M. Winsor, 26 Ireland Dr., Grand Falls-Windsor, NF A2A 2S6

Memorial University of Newfoundland: Chaplain, Gregory R. Dewling, Memorial University of Newfoundland, Box 102, St. John's, NF A1C 5S7

Emmanuel Convention Centre: Administrator, Ronald M. Dicks, Box 1558, Lewisporte, NF A0G 3A0

World Missions Promotions: A. Scott Hunter, 12 Harp Place, Paradise, NF A1L 1G9

Good Tidings: Managing Editor, Burton K. Janes, 57 Thornburn Rd., Box 8895, Stn. "A", St. John's, NF A1B 3T2

Periodicals

Good Tidings

Presbyterian Church in America (Canadian Section)

Canadian congregations of the Reformed Presbyterian Church, Evangelical Synod, became a part of the Presbyterian Church in America when the RPCES joined PCA in June 1982. Some of the churches were in predecessor bodies of the RPCES, which was the product of a 1965 merger of the Reformed Presbyterian Church in North America, General Synod and the Evangelical Presbyterian Church. Others came into existence later as a part of the home missions work of RPCES. Congregations are located in seven provinces, and the PCA is continuing church extension work in Canada. The denomination is committed to world evangelization and to a continuation of historic Presbyterianism. Its officers are required to subscribe to the Reformed faith as set forth in the Westminster Confession of Faith and Catechisms.

Headquarters

Media Contact, Dr. Dominic Aquila, Editor PCANet.org, New Geneva Seminary, 3622 E. Galley Rd,, Colorado Springs, CO, 80909 Tel. (719)573-5395 Fax, (719)573-5398, daquila6@aol.com

Website: www.PCANet.org

Periodicals

Equip for Ministry, Multiply, Network

Presbyterian Church in Canada

This is the nonconcurring portion of the Presbyterian Church in Canada that did not become a part of The United Church of Canada in 1925.

Headquarters

50 Wynford Dr., Toronto, ON M3C 1J7 Tel. (416)441-1111 Fax (416)441-2825

Website: www.presbyterian.ca

Media Contact, Principal Clk., Rev. Stephen Kendall or

Associate Sec. for Resource Production & Communication, Mr. Keith Knight

Officers

Principal Clk., Rev. Stephen Kendall

Periodicals

Channels, The Presbyterian Message, Presbyterian Record, Glad Tidings, La Vie Chrétienne

Reformed Church in Canada

The Canadian region of the Reformed Church in America was organized under the General Synod of the Reformed Church in America. The RCA in Canada has 41 churches which includes three classes (lower assemblies). The reformed churches in Canada are member congregations of the Reformed Church in America and the Regional Synod of Canada (one of eight RCA regional synods established by the General Synod) and three classes: Ontario, Canadian Prairies, and British Columbia.

The first ordained minister, Domine Jonas Micahelius, arrive in New Amsterdam from The Netherlands in 1628. Throughout the colonial period, the Reformed Church lived under the authority of the Classis of Amsterdam. Its churches were clustered in New York and New Jersey. Under the leadership of Rev. John Livingston, it became a denomination independent of the authority of the Classis of Amsterdam in 1776. Its geographical base was broadened in the 19th century by the immigration of Reformed Dutch and German settlers in the midwestern United States. The Reformed Church now spans the United States and Canada. The Reformed Church in America accepts as its standards of faith the Heidelberg Catechism, Belgic Confession, and Canons of Dort. It has a rich heritage of world mission activity. It claims to be loyal to reformed tradition which emphasizes obedience to god in all aspects of life.

Although the Reformed Church in America has worked in close cooperation with other churches, it has never entered into merger with any other denomination. It is a member of the World Alliance of Reformed Churches, the World Council of Churches, and the National Council of the Churches of Christ in the United States of America. In 1998 it also entered into a relationship of full communion with the Evangelical Lutheran Church in America, Presbyterian Church (USA), and the United Church of Christ by way of the Formula of Agreement.

Headquarters

475 Riverside Dr., Rm. 1812, New York, NY 10115 Tel. (212)870-2841 Fax (212)870-2499

Website: www.rca.org

Media Contact, Dir., Communication and Production Services, Kim Nathan Baker, 4500 60th St. SE, Grand Rapids, MI 49512 Tel. (616)698-7071 Fax (616)698-6606

OFFICERS AND STAFF OF GENERAL SYNOD

Regional Synod of Canada: Exec. Sec., -vacant-

Pres., The Rev. Steven Brooks, 475 Riverside Dr., 18th Floor, New York, NY 10115

General Synod Council: Moderator, Ms. Carol Mutch, 475 Riverside Dr., 18th Floor, New York, NY 10115

Gen. Sec., The Rev. Wesley Granberg-Michaelson, 475 Riverside Dr., 18th Floor, New York, NY 10115

Policy, Planning & Administrative Services: Dir. & Assistant Sec., The Rev. Kenneth Bradsell

Ministry & Personnel Services: Dir., The Rev. Dr. Vernon Hoffs

Congregational Servcies-Evangelism & Church Development Services: Dir., The Rev. Richard Welscott

Finance Services: Treas., Ms. Susan Converse

The Reformed Episcopal Church of Canada

The Reformed Episcopal Church is a separate entity. It was established in Canada by an act of incorporation given royal assent on June 2, 1886. It maintains the founding principles of episcopacy (in historic succession from the apostles), Anglican liturgy and Reformed doctrine, and evangelical zeal. In practice it continues to recognize the validity of certain nonepiscopal orders of evangelical ministry. The Church has reunited with the Reformed Episcopal Church and is now composed of two Dioceses in this body—the Diocese of Central and Eastern Canada and the Diocese of Western Canada and Alaska.

Headquarters

Box 2532, New Liskeard, ON P0J 1P0 Tel. (705) 647-4565 Fax (705)647-4565

Email: fed@nt.net

Website: www.reformedepiscopal.com

Media Contact, Pres., Rt. Rev. Michael Fedechko, MDiv, DD

Officers

Pres., Rt. Rev. Michael Fedechko, 320 Armstrong St., New Liskeard, ON P0J 1P0

Sec., Janet Dividson, 224 Haliburton,New Liskeard, ON P0J 1P0

BISHOPS

Diocese of Central & Eastern Canada: Rt. Rev. Michael Fedechko, 320 Armstrong St., New Liskeard, ON P0J 1P0 Tel. (705)647-4565 Fax (705)647-4565

Diocese of Western Canada & Alaska: Rt. Rev. Charles W. Dorrington, 54 Blanchard St., Victoria, BC V8X 4R1 Tel. (604)744-5014 Fax (604)388-5891

Periodicals

The Messenger

Reinland Mennonite Church

This group was founded in 1958 when 10 ministers and approximately 600 members separated from the Sommerfelder Mennonite Church. In 1968, four ministers and about 200 members migrated to Bolivia. The church has work in five communities in Manitoba and one in Ontario.

Headquarters

Bishop William H. Friesen, P.O. Box 96, Rosenfeld, MB R0G 1X0 Tel. (204)324-6339

Media Contact, Deacon, Henry Wiebe, Box 2587, Winkler, MB R6W 4C3 Tel. (204)325-8487

The Roman Catholic Church in Canada

The largest single body of Christians in Canada, the Roman Catholic Church is under the spiritual leadership of His Holiness the Pope. Catholicism in Canada dates back to 1534, when the first Mass was celebrated on the Gaspé Peninsula on July 7, by a priest accompanying Jacques Cartier. Catholicism had been implanted earlier by fishermen and sailors from Europe. Priests came to Acadia as early as 1604. Traces of a regular colony go back to 1608 when Champlain settled in Quebec City. The Recollets (1615), followed by the Jesuits (1625) and the Sulpicians (1657), began the missions among the native population. The first official Roman document relative to the Canadian missions dates from March 20, 1618. Bishop François de Montmorency-Laval, the first bishop, arrived in Quebec in 1659. The church developed in the East, but not until 1818 did systematic missionary work begin in western Canada.

In the latter 1700s, English-speaking Roman Catholics, mainly from Ireland and Scotland, began to arrive in Canada's Atlantic provinces. After 1815 Irish Catholics settled in large numbers in what is now Ontario. The Irish potato famine of 1847 greatly increased that population in all parts of eastern Canada.

By the 1850s the Catholic Church in both English- and French-speaking Canada had begun to erect new dioceses and found many religious communities. These communities did educational, medical, and charitable work among their own people as well as among Canada's native peoples. By the 1890s large numbers of non-English and non-French-speaking Catholics had settled in Canada, especially in the Western provinces. In the 20th century the pastoral horizons have continued to expand to meet the needs of what has now become a very multicultural church.

The Canadian Conference of Catholic Bishops is the national association of the Latin and Eastern Catholic Bishops of Canada. Its main offices are in Ottawa, Ontario.

Headquarters

CANADIAN ORGANIZATION

Conférence des évêques catholiques du Canada - Canadian Conference of Catholic Bishops, 2500 Don Reid Dr., Ottawa, ON k1H 2J2 Tel. (613)241-9461 Fax (613)241-9048

Email: cecc@cccb.ca

Website: www.cccb.ca

Media Contact, M. Sylvain Salvas, salvas@cccb.ca (French Sector); Deacon William Kokesch, Kokesch@cccb.ca (English Sector); Tel. (613)241-7538 or (800)769-1147, publi@cccb.ca

Officers

Gen. Secretariat of the Canadian Conference of Catholic Bishops

Gen; Sec., Msgr. Peter Schonenbach, P. H.

Associate Gen. Secs.: M. Benoît Bariteau (French Sector), Mr. Bede Hubbard (English Sector)

EXECUTIVE COMMITTEE

Pres., Most Rev. Jacques Barthelet, C.S.V.

Vice Pres., Most Rev. Brendan O'Brien

Co-Treas., Most Rev. André Gaumond and Most Rev. Anthony F. Tonnos

EPISCOPAL COMMISSIONS–NATIONAL LEVEL

Social Affairs: Most Rev. Jean Gagnon

Canon Law: Most Rev. Jean-Guy Couture

Relations with Assoc. of Clergy, Consecrated Life & Laity: Most Rev. Brendan O'Brien

Evangelization of Peoples: Most Rev. Peter A. Sutton, O.M.I.

Christian Unity, Religious Relations with the Jews, and Interfaith Dialogue: Most Rev. Thomas Collins

Theology: Most Rev. Paul-André Durocher

EPISCOPAL COMMISSIONS–SECTOR LEVEL

Communications sociales: Most Rev. Martin Veillette

Social Communication: Most Rev. J. Faber MacDonald

Éducation chrétienne: Most Rev. Arthé Guimond

Christian Education, Most Richard Grecco

Liturgie: Most Rev. Bertrand Blanchet

Liturgy: Most Rev. Douglas Crosby, O.M.I.

OFFICES

Affaires sociales/Social Affairs: Dir., Mr. Joe Gunn

Communications: Dir. (French Sector), M. Sylvain Salvas; Dir. (English Sector), Deacon William Kokesch

Droit canonique-inter-rites/Canon Law-Inter-rite: Sec., Msgr. Peter Schonenbach, P.H.

Éditions-Publications: Dir., Mme Johanne Gnassi

Éducation chrétienne: Sec., Mme Adele Bolduc

Évangelisation des peuples-Evangelization of Peoples: Dir., Mme Adèle Bolduc

Liturgie/Liturgy: Dir. (French Sector), M. Gaëtan Baillargeon; Dir. (English Sector), Sr. Donna Kelly

National Office of Religious Education: Dir., Ms. Joanne Chafe

Christian Unity, Religious Relations with the Jews, and Interfaith Dialogue: Dir., Sr.

Mary Jean Goulet, C.S.C.

Relations avec les associations du clergé, de la vie conseacrée et du laïcat/Relations with Association of Clergy, Consecrated Life, and Laity: Sec., Ms. Jennifer Leddy

Théologie/Theology: Dir., P. Richard Côté, O.M.I.

Tribunal d'appel du Canada/The Canadian Appeal Tribunal: Vicaire judiciaire-Judicial Vicar, P. Pierre Allard, S.M.

REGIONAL EPISCOPAL ASSEMBLIES

Atlantic Episcopal Assembly/Assemblée des évêques de l'Atlantique: Pres., Most Rev. Raymond Lahey; Vice Pres., Most Rev. Terrence Prendergast, S.J. and Most Francois

Thibodeau, C.J.M.; Sec.-Treas.,Léo Grégoire, I.V. Dei Tel. (506)735-5578 Fax (506)735-4271

Assemblée des évêques du Québec: Pres., Most Rev. Raymond St-Gelais C.S.C.; Vice Prés., Most Rev. Gilles Cazabon, O.M.I.; Secrétaire général, M. Pierre Gaudette Tel. (514)274-4323 Fax (514)274-4383

Ontario Conference of Catholic Bishops/ Conférence des évêques catholiques de l'Ontario: Pres., Most Rev. Jean-Louis Plouffe; Vice Pres., Most Rev. Matthew F.Ustrzycki; Sec.-Treas., Mr. Thomas J. Reilly Tel. (306)682-1788 Fax (306)682-1766

MILITARY ORDINARIATE/ORDINARIAT MILITAIRE

Bishop, Most Rev. Donald J. Theriault, Military Ordinariate of Canada, Canadian Forces Support Unit (Ottawa), Uplands Site Building 469, Ottawa, ON K1A 0K2 Tel. (613)998-8747 Fax (613)991-1056

Canadian Religious Conference: Sec. Gen., Sr. Jocelyne Fallu, FDLS, 4135 rue de Rouen, Montréal, Québec H1V 1G5 Tel. (514)259-0856 Fax (514)259-0857

Catholic Organization for Life and Family/ Organisme catholizque pour la vie et la famille: Co-Dirs., Ms. Diane Dupras (French Sector), Ms. Jennifer Leddy (English Sector) Tel. (613) 241-9461, Fax (613)241-9048, indigen@cccb.ca

Periodicals

National Bulletin on Liturgy, Foi et Culture (Bulletin natl. de liturgie)

Romanian Orthodox Church in America (Canadian Parishes)

The first Romanian Orthodox immigrants in Canada called for Orthodox priests from their native country of Romania. Between 1902 and 1914, they organized the first Romanian parish communities and built Orthodox churches in different cities and farming regions of western Canada (Alberta, Saskatchewan, Manitoba) as well as in the eastern part (Ontario and Quebec).

In 1929, the Romanian Orthodox parishes from Canada joined with those of the United States in a Congress held in Detroit, Mich., and asked the Holy Synod of the Romanian Orthodox Church of Romania to establish a Romanian Orthodox Missionary Episcopate in America. The first Bishop, Policarp (Morushca), was elected and consecrated by the Holy Synod of the Romanian Orthodox Church and came to the United States in 1935. He established his headquarters in Detroit with jurisdiction over all the Romanian Orthodox parishes in the United States and Canada.

In 1950, the Romanian Orthodox Church in America (i.e., the Romanian Orthodox Missionary Episcopate in America) was granted administrative autonomy by the Holy Synod of the Romanian Orthodox Church of Romania; only doctrinal and canonical ties remain with this latter body.

In 1974 the Holy Synod of the Romanian Orthodox Church of Romania recognized and approved the elevation of the Episcopate to the rank of the Romanian Orthodox Archdiocese in America and Canada and completed the administrative autonomy.

Headquarters

Romanian Orthodox Archdiocese in America and Canada, P.O. Box 27 Skokie, IL 60076

Officers

Archbishop, Most Rev. Nicolae Condrea, P.O. Box 27 Skokie, IL 60076 Tel. (847)674-3900, Fax (847)674-4110, archnicolee@aol.com

Vicar, V. Rev. Fr. Ioan Ionita, 17527 Wenthworth Ave., Lansing, IL 60438 Tel. (708)889-9768

Sec., V. Rev. Fr. Nicholas Apostola, 44 Midland St. Worchester, MA 01602-4217 Tel. (508) 845-0088 Fax (508)752-8180

Periodicals

Credinte–The Faith

The Romanian Orthodox Episcopate of America (Jackson, MI)

This body of Eastern Orthodox Christians of Romanian descent is part of the Autocephalous Orthodox Church in America. For complete description and listing of officers, please see Directory 3, "Religious Bodies in the United States."

Headquarters

2535 Grey Tower Rd., Jackson, MI 49201; Mailing Address: P.O. Box 309, Grass Lake, MI 49240-0309 Tel. (517)522-4800 Fax (517) 522-5907

Email: roeasolia@aol.com

Website: www.roea.org

Media Contact, Ed.-Sec., Rev. Protodeacon David Oancea, P.O. Box 185, Grass Lake, MI 49240-0185 Tel. (517)522-3656 Fax (517) 522-5907

Officers

Ruling Hierarch, Most. Rev. Archbishop Nathaniel Popp

Dean for All Canada and the Western Provinces, Very Rev. Daniel Nenson, 2855 Helmsing St., Regina, SK S4V 0W7 Tel. (306)761-2379

Periodicals

Solia–The Herald, Good News–Buna Vestire (in Canada only)

The Salvation Army in Canada

The Salvation Army, an evangelical branch of the Christian Church, is an international movement founded in 1865 in London, England. The ministry of Salvationists, consisting of clergy (officers) and laity, comes from a commitment to Jesus Christ and is revealed in practical service, regardless of race, color, creed, sex, or age.

The goals of The Salvation Army are to preach the gospel, disseminate Christian truths, instill Christian values, enrich family life, and improve the quality of all life.

To attain these goals, The Salvation Army operates local congregations, provides counseling, supplies basic human needs, and undertakes spiritual and moral rehabilitation of any needy people who come within its influence.

A quasi-military system of government was set up in 1878, by founder General William Booth (1829-1912). Converts from England started Salvation Army work in London, Ontario, in 1882. Two years later, Canada was recognized as a Territorial Command, and since 1933 it has included Bermuda. An act to incorporate the Governing Council of The Salvation Army in Canada received royal assent on May 19, 1909.

Headquarters

2 Overlea Blvd., Toronto, ON M4H 1P4 Tel. (416)425-2111

Website: www.salvationarmy.ca

Media Contact, Major Len Miller, Tel. (416)425-6153 Fax (416)425-6157, len-miller@can.salvationarmy.org

Officers

Territorial Commander, Commissioner Bill Luttrell

Territorial Pres., Women's Organizations, Commissioner Gwen Lutterell

Chief Sec., Col. Bob Redhead

Sec. for Personnel, Lt. Col. Wayne Pritchett

Bus. Adm. Sec., Lt. Col. Susan McMillan

Fin. Sec., Major Paul Goodyear

Program Sec., Lt. Col. David Luginbuhl

Public Rel., Major Len Millar

Property Sec., Major Neil Watt

Periodicals

The War Cry, Faith & Friends, En Avant!, The Young Soldier, The Edge, Catherine, Horizons

Serbian Orthodox Church in the USA and Canada, Diocese of Canada

The Serbian Orthodox Church is an organic part of the Eastern Orthodox Church. As a local church it received its autocephaly from Constantinople in A.D. 1219. The Patriarchal seat of the church today is in Belgrade, Yugoslavia. In 1921, a Serbian Orthodox Diocese in the United States of America and Canada was organized. In 1963, it was reorganized into three dioceses, and in 1983 a fourth diocese was created for the Canadian part of the church. The Serbian Orthodox Church is in absolute doctrinal unity with all other local Orthodox Churches.

Headquarters

7470 McNiven Rd., R.R. #3, Campbellville, ON L0P 1B0 Tel. (905)878-0043 Fax (905)878-1909

Email: vladika@istocnik.com

Website: www. istocnik.com

Media Contact, Rt. Rev. Georgije

Officers

Serbian Orthodox Bishop of Canada, Rt. Rev. Georgije

Dean of Western Deanery, V. Rev. Mirko Malinovic, 924 12th Ave., Regina, SK S4N 0K7 Tel. (306)352-2917

Dean of Eastern Deanery, V. Rev. Zivorad Subotic, 351 Mellville Ave., Westmount, QC H3Z 2Y7 Tel./Fax (514)931-6664

Periodicals

Istocnik, Herald of the Serbian Orthodox Church–Canadian Diocese

Seventh-day Adventist Church in Canada

The Seventh-day Adventist Church in Canada is part of the worldwide Seventh-day Adventist Church with headquarters in Silver Spring, Md. (See "Religious Bodies in the United States" section of this Yearbook for a fuller description.) The Seventh-day Adventist Church in Canada was organized in 1901 and reorganized in 1932.

Headquarters

1148 King St. E, Oshawa, ON L1H 1H8 Tel. (905)433-0011 Fax (905)433-0982

Media Contact, Nilton D. Amorim

Officers

Pres., Daniel R. Jackson

Sec., Nilton D. Amorim

Treas., Gerald M. Northam

DEPARTMENTS

Under Treas., Brent Burdick

Asst. Treas., Joyce Jones

Computer Services, Brian Ford

Education, Mike Lekic

Family Ministries, Celest Corkum, Ken Corkum

Health Ministries, Dave Higgins

Sabbath School and Personal Ministries, Gary Hodder

Trust Services, Brent Burdick

Youth, Frankie Lazarus

ADRA Canada, Oliver Lofton-Brook

Periodicals

Canadian Adventist Messenger

Syriac Orthodox Church of Antioch

The Syriac Orthodox Church professes the faith of the first three ecumenical councils of Nicaea, Constantinople, and Ephesus and numbers faithful in the Middle East, India, the Americas, Europe, and Australia. It traces its origin to the Patriarchate established in Antioch by St. Peter the Apostle and is under the supreme ecclesiastical jurisdiction of His Holiness the Syrian Orthodox Patriarch of Antioch and All the East, now residing in Damascus, Syria.

The Archdiocese of the Syrian Orthodox Church in the US and Canada was formally established in 1957. In 1995, the Archdiocese of North America was divided into three separate Patriarchal Vicariates, including one for Canada. The first Syrian Orthodox faithful came to Canada in the 1890s and formed the first Canadian parish in Sherbrooke, Quebec. Today five official parishes of the Archdiocese exist in Canada—two in Quebec and three in Ontario. There is also an official mission congregation in Calgary, Alberta and Ottawa, Ontario.

Headquarters

Archdiocese of Canada, The New Archdiocesan Centre, 4375 Henri-Bourassa Ouest, St.-Laurent, Quebec H4L 1A5, Canada Tel. (514) 334-6993 Fax (514)334-8233

Officers

Archbishop Mor Timotheos Aphrem Aboodi

Ukrainian Orthodox Church of Canada

Toward the end of the 19th century, many Ukrainian immigrants settled in Canada. In 1918, a group of these pioneers established the Ukrainian Orthodox Church of Canada (UOCC), today the largest Ukrainian Orthodox Church beyond the borders of Ukraine. In 1990, the UOCC entered into a eucharistic union with the Ecumenical Patriarchate at Constantinople (Istanbul).

Headquarters

Ukrainian Orthodox Church of Canada, Office of the Consistory, 9 St. Johns Ave., Winnipeg, MB R2W 1G8 Tel. (204)586-3093 Fax (204)582-5241

Email: consistory@uocc.ca

Website: www. uocc.ca

Media Contacts, Rev. Fr. Andrew Jarmus, 9st. John's Ave., Winnipeg, MB R2W 1G8 Tel. (204)586-3093 Fax (204)582-5241; Ms. M. Zurek, 9 St. Johns Ave., Winnipeg, MB R2W 1G8 Tel. (204)586-3093 Fax (204)582-5241

Officers

Primate, Most Rev. Metropolitan Wasyly Fedak, 9 St. Johns Ave., Winnipeg, MB R2W 1G8 Tel. (204)586-3093 Fax (204)582-5241

Chancellor, Rt. Rev. Dr. Oleg Krawchenko

Periodicals

Visnyk-The Herald-Le Messager (newspaper), *Ridna Nyva* (almanac/annual)

Union d'Eglises Baptistes Françaises au Canada

Baptist churches in French Canada first came into being through the labors of two missionaries from Switzerland, Rev. Louis Roussy and Mme. Henriette Feller, who arrived in Canada in 1835. The earliest church was organized in Grande Ligne (now St. Blaise), Quebec in 1838.

By 1900 there were 7 churches in the province of Quebec and 13 French-language Baptist churches in the New England states. The leadership was totally French Canadian.

By 1960, the process of Americanization had caused the disappearance of the French Baptist churches. During the 1960s, Quebec as a society began rapidly changing in all its facets: education, politics, social values, and structures. Mission, evangelism, and church growth once again flourished. In 1969, in response to the new conditions, the Grande Ligne Mission passed control of its work to the newly formed Union of French Baptist Churches in Canada, which then included 8 churches. By 2003 the French Canadian Baptist movement had grown to include 32 congregations present in three provinces: Quebec, New Brunswick, and Ontario.

The Union d'Églises Baptistes Françaises au Canada is a member body of the Canadian Baptist Ministries and thus is affiliated with the Baptist World Alliance.

Headquarters

2285 Avenue Papineau, Montreal, QC H2K 4J5 Tel. (514)526-6643 Fax (514)526-9269

Website: www.UnionBaptiste.com

Media Contact, Gen. Sec., Rev. Roland Grimard

Officers

Sec. Gen., Rev. Roland Grimard

Periodicals

Entre Novs

Union of Spiritual Communities of Christ (Orthodox Doukhobors in Canada)

The Doukhobors are Canadians of Russian origin living primarily in the western provinces of Canada, but their beginnings in Russia are unknown. The name "Doukhobors," or "Spirit Wrestlers," was given them in derision by the Russian Orthodox clergy in Russia as far back as 1785. The Doukhobors were persecuted by the church for rejecting Orthodoxy and, following the counsel of their leader, Peter V. Verigin, earned the wrath of the Tsarist government by destroying all of their weapons and adopting pacifism in 1895. In 1899 the Tsarist government allowed 8,000 Doukhobors to leave Russia in response to an international uproar over their persecution by the church and state. They made their way to Canada with the assistance of Count Leo Tolstoy, who saw in these people the living embodiment of his philosophy, the Religious Society of Friends (commonly known as Quakers) and other people of good will. They originally settled in Saskatchewan, but by 1911 the majority followed Verigin to Bristish Columbia because of government efforts to assismilate them.

The teaching of the Doukhobors is penetrated with the Gospel spirit of love. Worshiping God in the spirit, they affirm that the outward church and all that is performed in it and concerns it has no importance for them; the church is where two or three are gathered together, united in the name of Christ. They do not believe in icon worship or in intermediaries between themselves and God. Their spiritual teachings are founded on ancient tradition, which they call the "Book of Life," because it lives in their memory and hearts. In this book are psalms composed by their elders and leaders, partly formed out of the contents of the Bible, partly out of their historical experience. These are committed to memory by each succeeding generation. Doukhobors observe complete pacifism and nonviolence, are lacto-vegetarians, and attempt to maintain a communal lifestyle.

The majority of Canadian Doukhobors were reorganized in 1938 by Peter P. Verigin (son of P.V. Verigin) shortly before his death into the Union of Spiritual Communities of Christ to distinguish themselves from a radical offshoot who call themselves Sons of Freedom, and whose embrace of nudity and depravations has been sensationalized by the media and has stigmatized all Doukhobors. Today the USCC is governed by Trustees elected from member communities and administered by an elected Executive Committee headed by Honourary Chairman, John J. Verigin, CM OBC. The USCC executes the will and protects the interests of its member communities and its members living beyond south central British Columbia where the USCC is headquartered. The USCC is the largest organization of Doukhobors and maintains relations with other Doukhobor groups across Canada, in the USA, the Russian Federation, the Ukraine, and Georgia. The USCC also cooperates with other nongovernmental organizations working non violently to promote peace, justice, and respect for human didgnity and ecological integrity.

Headquarters

USCC Central Office, Box 760, Grand Forks, BC V0H 1H0 Tel. (250)442-8252 Fax (250) 442-3433

Media Contact, John J. Verigin, Sr.

Officers

Hon. Chmn. of the Exec. Comm., John J. Verigin, Sr.

Chpsn., Fred Bojey

Periodicals

ISKRA

United Brethren Church in Canada

Founded in 1767 in Lancaster County, Penn.; missionaries came to Canada about 1850. The first class was held in Kitchener in 1855, and the first building was erected in Port Elgin in 1867.

The Church of the United Brethren in Christ had its beginning with Philip William Otterbein and Martin Boehm, who were leaders in the revivalistic movement in Pennsylvania and Maryland during the late 1760s.

Headquarters

302 Lake St., Huntington, IN 46750 Tel. (219) 356-2312 Fax (219)356-4730

Officers

Pres., Rev. Brian Magnus, 120 Fife Rd., Guelph, ON N1H 6Y2 Tel. (519)836-0180

Treas., Brian Winger, 2233 Hurontario St., Apt. 916, Mississauga, ON L5A 2E9 Tel. (905)275-8140

The United Church of Canada

The United Church of Canada was formed on June 10, 1925, through the union of the Methodist Church, Canada; the Congregational Union of Canada; the Council of Local Union Churches; and 70 percent of the Presbyterian Church in Canada. The union culminated years of negotiation between the churches, all of which had integral associations with the development and history of the nation.

In fulfillment of its mandate to be a uniting as well as a United Church, the denomination has been enriched by other unions during its history. The Wesleyan Methodist Church of Bermuda joined in 1930. On January 1, 1968, the Canada Conference of the Evangelical United Brethren became part of The United Church of Canada. At various times, congregations of other Christian communions have also become congregations of the United Church.

The United Church of Canada is a full member of the World Methodist Council, the World Alliance of Reformed Churches (Presbyterian and Congregational), and the Canadian and World Councils of Churches.

The United Church is the largest Protestant denomination in Canada.

NATIONAL OFFICES

The United Church House, 3250 Bloor St. W, Ste. 300, Etobicoke, ON M8X 2Y4 Tel. (416) 231-5931 Fax (416)231-3103

Email: info@uccan.org

Website: www.uccan.org

Media Contact, Manager Public Relations & Info. Unit, Mary-Frances Denis

GENERAL COUNCIL

Mod., Marion Pardy

Gen. Sec., K. Virginia Coleman

Archivist, Sharon Larade, 73 Queen's Park Cr. E, Toronto, ON M5C 1K7 Tel. (416)585-4563, Fax (416)585-4584, uccvu.archives@utoronto.ca

Website: www. vicu.utoronto.ca/archives/archives.htm

ADMINISTRATIVE DIVISIONS

Communication: Gen. Sec., Gordon How

Finance: Gen. Sec., Steven Adams

Ministry Personnel & Education: Gen. Sec., Rev. Steven Chambers

Mission in Canada: Gen. Sec., Rev. David Iverson

World Outreach: Gen. Sec., Rev. Christopher Ferguson

CONFERENCE EXECUTIVE SECRETARIES

Alberta and Northwest: Rev. George H. Rodgers, 9911-48 Ave., NW, Edmonton, AB T6E 5V6 Tel. (780)435-3995, Fax (780)438-3317, coffice @anwconf.com

All Native Circle: Speaker, Dianne Cooper (interim), 367 Selkirk Ave., Winnipeg, MB R2W 2N3 Tel. (204)582-5518, Fax (204)582-6649, allnat@mb.aibn.com

Bay of Quinte: Rev. Wendy Bulloch, P.O. Box 700, 67 Mill St., Frankford, ON K0K 2C0 Tel. (613)398-1051, Fax (613)398-8894, bayq.conference@sympatico.ca

British Columbia: Rev. Debra A. Bowman, 4383 Rumble St., Burnaby, BC V5J 2A2 Tel. (604)431-0434, Fax (604)431-0439, bcconf@infoserve.net

Hamilton: Rev. Roslyn A. Campbell, Box 100, Carlisle, ON L0R 1H0 Tel. (905)659-3343, Fax (905)659-7766, office@hamconf.org

London: W. Peter Scott, 359 Windermere Rd., London, ON N6G 2K3 Tel. (519)672-1930, Fax (519)439-2800, lonconf@execulink.com

Manitoba and Northwestern Ontario: Rev. Roger A. Coll, 170 Saint Mary's Rd., Winnipeg, MB R2H 1H9 Tel. (204)233-8911, Fax (204)233-3289, office@confmnwo.mb.ca

Manitou: Rev. Rev. Jim Sinclair, 319 McKenzie Ave., North Bay, ON P1B 7E3 Tel. (705)474-3350, Fax (705)497-3597, manitou@efni.com

Maritime: Rev. Catherine H. Gaw, 32 York St., Sackville, NB E4L 4R4 Tel. (506)536-1334, Fax (506)536-2900, marconf@nbnet.nb,ca

Montreal and Ottawa: Rev. Rev. David C. Estey, 225-50 Ave., Lachine, QC H8T 2T7 Tel. (514)634-7015, Fax (514)634-2489, lachine@istar.ca

Newfoundland and Labrador: Rev. Clarence R. Sellers, 320 Elizabeth Ave., St. John's, NF A1B 1T9 Tel. (709)754-0386, Fax (709)754-8336, newlab@seascape.com

Saskatchewan: Rev. Bruce G. Faurschou (interim), 418 A. McDonald St., Regina, SK S4N 6E1 Tel. (306)721-3311, Fax (306) 721-3171, ucskco@sk.sympatico.ca

Toronto: Rev. David W. Allen, 65 Mayall Ave., Downsview, ON M3L 1E7 Tel. (416)241-2677, Fax (416)241-2689, torconf@web.net

Periodicals

Fellowship Magazine, United Church Observer, Mandate, Aujourd'hui Credo

United Pentecostal Church in Canada

This body, which is affiliated with the United Pentecostal Church, International (with headquarters in Hazelwood, Mo.) accepts the Bible standard of full salvation, which is repentance; baptism by immersion in the name of the Lord Jesus Christ for the remission of sins; and the baptism of the Holy Ghost, with the initial signs of speaking in tongues as the Spirit gives utterance. Other tenets of faith include the Oneness of God in Christ, holiness, divine healing, and the second coming of Jesus Christ.

Headquarters

United Pentecostal Church Intl., 8855 Dunn Rd., Hazelwood, MO 63042 Tel. (314)837-7300 Fax (314)837-4503

Media Contact, Gen. Sec.-Treas., Rev. C. M. Becton

DISTRICT SUPERINTENDENTS

Atlantic: Rev. Harry Lewis, P.O. Box 1046, Perth Andover, NB E0J 1V0

British Columbia: Rev. Paul V. Reynolds, 13447-112th Ave., Surrey, BC V3R 2E7

Canadian Plains: Rev. Johnny King, 615 Northmount Dr. NW, Calgary, AB T2K 3J6

Central Canadian: Rev. Clifford Heaslip, 4215 Roblin Blvd., Winnipeg, MB R3R 0E8

Newfoundland: Jack Cunningham

Nova Scotia: Superintendent, Rev. John D. Mean, P.O. Box 2183, D.E.P.S., Dartmouth, NS B2W 3Y2

Ontario: Rev. Carl H. Stephenson, 63 Castlegrove Blvd., Don Mills, ON M3A 1L3

Universal Fellowship of Metropolitan Community Churches

The Universal Fellowship of Metropolitan Community Churches is a Christian church which directs a special ministry within, and on behalf of, the gay and lesbian community. Involvement, however, is not exclusively limited to gays and lesbians, UFMCC tries to stress its openness to all people and does not call itself a "gay church."

Founded in 1968 in Los Angeles by the Rev. Troy Perry, the UFMCC has over 300 member congregations worldwide. Congregations are in Vancouver, Edmonton, Windsor, London, Toronto, Ottawa (2), Guelph, Fredericton, Winnipeg, Halifax, Barrie, and Belleville.

Theologically, the Metropolitan Community Churches stand within the mainstream of

Christian doctrine, being "ecumenical" or "interdenominational" in stance (albeit a "denomination" in their own right).

The Metropolitan Community Churches are characterized by their belief that the love of God is a gift, freely offered to all people, regardless of sexual orientation, and that no incompatibility exists between human sexuality and the Christian faith.

The Metropolitan Community Churches in Canada were founded in Toronto in 1973 by the Rev. Robert Wolfe.

Headquarters

Media Contact, Marcie Wexler, 33 Holly St., #1117, Toronto, ON M4S 2G8 Tel. (416)487-8429 Fax (416)932-1836

Officers

Eastern Canadian District, Rev. Marcie Wexler, 33 Holly St., #1117, Toronto, ON M4S 2G8 Tel. (416)487-8429

The Wesleyan Church of Canada

This group is the Canadian portion of The Wesleyan Church which consists of the Atlantic and Central Canada districts. The Central Canada District of the former Wesleyan Methodist Church of America was organized at Winchester, Ontario, in 1889 and the Atlantic District was founded in 1888 as the Alliance of the Reformed Baptist Church, which merged with the Wesleyan Methodist Church in July, 1966.

The Wesleyan Methodist Church and the Pilgrim Holiness Church merged in June, 1968, to become The Wesleyan Church. The doctrine is evangelical and Wesleyan Arminian and stresses holiness beliefs. For more details, consult the US listing under The Wesleyan Church.

Headquarters

The Wesleyan Church Intl. Center, P.O. Box 50434, Indianapolis, IN 46250-0434

Media Contact, Dist. Supt., Central Canada, Rev. Donald E. Hodgins, 17 Saint paul St., Belleview, ON K8N 1A4 Tel. (613)966-7527 Fax (613)968-6190

DISTRICT SUPERINTENDENTS

Central Canada: Rev. Donald E. Hodgins, 17 Saint paul St., Belleview, ON K8N 1A4, ccd@on.aibn.com

Atlantic: Rev. Dr. H. C. Wilson, 1600 Main st., Ste. 216, Moncton, NB E1E 1G5, ncwilson@nbnet.nb.ca

Periodicals

Central Canada, The Clarion

Religious Bodies in Canada Arranged by Families

The following list of religious bodies appearing in the Directory Section of the *Yearbook* shows the "families," or related clusters into which Canadian religious bodies can be grouped. For example, there are many communions that can be grouped under the heading "Baptist" for historical and theological reasons. It should not be assumed, however, that all denominations under one family heading are necessarily consistent in belief or practice. The family clusters tend to represent historical factors more often than theological or practical ones. These family categories provide one of the major pitfalls when compiling church statistics because there is often a tendency to combine the statistics by "families" for analytical and comparative purposes. Such combined totals are deeply flawed, even though they are often used as variables for sociological analysis. The arrangement by families offered here is intended only as a general guide for conceptual organization when viewing the broad sweep of Canadian religious culture.

Religious bodies that can not be categorized under family headings appear alphabetically and are not indented in the following list.

The Anglican Church of Canada
Apostolic Christian Church (Nazarene)
Armenian Evangelical Church
Associated Gospel Churches

Baptist Bodies

Association of Regular Baptist Churches (Canada)
Baptist Convention of Ontario and Quebec
Baptist General Conference of Canada
Baptist Union of Western Canada
Canadian Baptist Ministries
Canadian Convention of Southern Baptists
Convention of Atlantic Baptist Churches
The Fellowship of Evangelical Baptist Churches in Canada
Free Will Baptists
North American Baptist Conference
Union d'Eglises Baptistes Françaises au Canada

Brethren in Christ Church, Canadian Conference
Canadian District of the Moravian Church in America, Northern Province
Canadian Evangelical Christian Churches
Canadian Yearly Meeting of the Religious Society of Friends
Christ Catholic Church International
Christian Brethren (also known as Plymouth Brethren)
Christian and Missionary Alliance in Canada
Church of God (Anderson, Ind.)
Church of the Nazarene in Canada

Churches of Christ-Christian Churches

Christian Church (Disciples of Christ) in Canada
Churches of Christ in Canada

Congregational Christian Churches in Canada

Eastern Orthodox Churches

The Antiochian Orthodox Christian Archdiocese of North America
Greek Orthodox Metropolis of Toronto (Canada)
Orthodox Church in America (Canada Section)
Patriarchal Parishes of the Russian Orthodox Church in Canada
Romanian Orthodox Church in America (Canadian Parishes)
The Romanian Orthodox Episcopate of America (Jackson, MI)
Serbian Orthodox Church in the USA and Canada, Diocese of Canada
Ukrainian Orthodox Church of Canada

The Evangelical Covenant Church of Canada
Evangelical Free Church of Canada
The Evangelical Missionary Church of Canada
General Church of the New Jerusalem
Jehovah's Witnesses
Latter-Day Saints (Mormons)

The Church of Jesus Christ of Latter-day Saints in Canada

Community of Christ

Lutheran Bodies

Church of the Lutheran Brethren
The Estonian Evangelical Lutheran Church Abroad
Evangelical Lutheran Church in Canada
Lutheran Church–Canada

Mennonite Bodies

Canadian Conference of Mennonite Brethren Churches
Church of God in Christ (Mennonite)

The Evangelical Mennonite Conference
Evangelical Mennonite Mission Conference
Mennonite Church Canada
Old Order Amish Church
Reinland Mennonite Church

Methodist Bodies

British Methodist Episcopal Church of Canada
Free Methodist Church in Canada
Independent Holiness Church
The Wesleyan Church of Canada

The Old Catholic Church of Canada
Open Bible Faith Fellowship of Canada

Oriental Orthodox Churches

Armenian Holy Apostolic Church - Canadian Diocese
The Coptic Orthodox Church in Canada
Syriac Orthodox Church of Antioch

Pentecostal Bodies

The Apostolic Church in Canada
Apostolic Church of Pentecost of Canada Inc.
The Bible Holiness Movement
Church of God (Cleveland, Tenn.)
The Church of God of Prophecy in Canada
Elim Fellowship of Evangelical Churches and Ministers
Foursquare Gospel Church of Canada
Independent Assemblies of God International (Canada)
The Italian Pentecostal Church of Canada
The Pentecostal Assemblies of Canada
Pentecostal Assemblies of Newfoundland
United Pentecostal Church in Canada

Reformed Bodies

Canadian and American Reformed Churches
Christian Reformed Church in North America
Presbyterian Church in America (Canadian Section)
Presbyterian Church in Canada
Reformed Church in Canada

The Reformed Episcopal Church of Canada
The Roman Catholic Church in Canada
The Salvation Army in Canada
Seventh-day Adventist Church in Canada
Union of Spiritual Communities of Christ (Orthodox Doukhobors in Canada)
United Brethren Church in Canada
The United Church of Canada
Universal Fellowship of Metropolitan Community Churches

5. The Electronic Church

Church-related organizations use electronic media in highly creative and useful ways. Efficiencies inherent on the Internet, increasing access speeds, and inexpensive data management tools provide increasing opportunities for outreach and accessibility to vast data and information. Sites provided by religious organizations such as those listed in the Yearbook continue to innovate and improve dramatically in usability, quality and sophistication.

The World Wide Web (www) addresses listed below are merely suggested beginning points for exploring the vast interlinked web of church-related material.

Expanded and updated email and website information pertaining to US and Canadian religious organizations, and an expanded church body Internet listings are provided for Yearbook readers at: www.ElectronicChurch.org.

Included with purchase of this book is access to the Internet edition of the Yearbook. Updated directory and statistical resources are available online at: www.Cokesbury.com/Subscriptions/. Consult the inside back cover of this volume for instructions on accessing the Yearbook online.

Helpful Databases and Search Engines for Local Churches and Denominations

About.com—christianity.about.com

Academic Info—www.academicinfo.net/Christian.html

Adherents—www.adherents.com

All-in-one Christian Index—allinone.crossdaily.com

American Religion Data Archive—www.thearda.com

BeliefNet—www.beliefnet.org

Crosssearch.com—www.crosssearch.com

Open Directory Project—dmoz.org/Society/Religion_and_Spirituality/Christianity

Ecunet—www.ecunet.org

Hartford Institute for Religion Research—hirr.hartsem.edu

National Center for Charitable Statistics—www.nccs.urban.org

Religion Online—www.religion-online.org

Religious Movements—religiousmovements.lib.virginia.edu

Resources for American Christianity—www.resourcingchristianity.org

Virtual Religion Index—www.rci.rutgers.edu/~religion/vri

Yahoo Society and Culture Directory –
http://dir.yahoo.com/Society_and_Culture/Religion_and_Spirituality/Faiths_and_Practices/Christianity

Index of Electronic Addresses of Denominations listed in the US Religious Bodies Chapter of this Yearbook

Advent Christian Church—Email: acpub@adventchristian.org
Website: www.adventchristian.org

African Methodist Episcopal Church—Email: Administrator@amecnet.org
Website: www.amecnet.org

Albanian Orthodox Archdiocese in America—Web: www.oca.org

The Allegheny Wesleyan Methodist Connection (Original Allegheny Conference)—
Email: awmc@juno.com
Website: c1web.com/local_info/churches/aw.html

The Alliance of Baptists in the USA—Website: www.allianceofbaptists.org

The American Association of Lutheran Churches—Email: aa2taalc@aol.com
Website: www.taalc.com

The American Baptist Association—Email: bssc@abaptist.org
Website: www.abaptist.org

American Baptist Churches in the USA—Email: richard.schramm@abc-usa.org
Website: www.abc-usa.org

The American Carpatho-Russian Orthodox Greek Catholic Church—
Email: archdiocese@goarch.org
Website: www.goarch.org

THE ELECTRONIC CHURCH

American Evangelical Christian Churches—Email: alpha@strato.net
Website: www.aeccministries.com

American Rescue Workers—Email: amerscwk@pcspower.net
Website: www.arwus.com

The Antiochian Orthodox Christian Archdiocese of North America—
Email: FrJoseph@antiochian.org
Website: www.antiochian.org

Apostolic Catholic Assyrian Church of the East, North American Dioceses—Email: ABSoro@aol.com
Website: www.cired.org/ace.html

Apostolic Christian Churches of America—Email: Questions@ApostolicChristian.org
Website: www.apostolicchristian.org

Apostolic Episcopal Church—Email: osbm_ny@yahoo.com
Website: www.cinemaparallel.com/AECSynod.html

Apostolic Faith Mission of Portland, Oregon—Website: www.apostolicfaith.org

Apostolic Lutheran Church of America—Website: www.apostolic-lutheran.org

Apostolic Orthodox Catholic Church of North America—Email: aoccna.relations@usa.com

Apostolic Overcoming Holy Church of God, Inc.—Email: traydoc@mindspring.com

Armenian Apostolic Church of America—Email: prelacy@gis.net
Website: www.armprelacy.org

Assemblies of God—Email: info@ag.org
Website: www.ag.org/top/

Assemblies of God International Fellowship (Independent/Not affiliated)—
Email: admin@agifellowship.org
Website: www.agifellowship.org

Associate Reformed Presbyterian Church (General Synod)—Email: dragondraw@aol.com
Website: www.arpsynod.org

The Association of Free Lutheran Congregations—Email: webmaster@aflc.org
Website: www.aflc.org

Baptist Bible Fellowship International—Email: csbc@cherrystreet.org
Website: www.bbfi.org

Baptist General Conference—Email: gmarsh@baptistgeneral.org
Website: www.bgcworld.org

Baptist Missionary Association of America—Email: bmaam@bmaam.com
Website: www.bmaam.com

Berean Fundamental Church Fellowship—Email: office@bereanfellowship.org
Website: www.bereanfellowship.org

The Bible Church of Christ, Inc.—Email: bccbookstore@earthlink.net
Website: www.thebiblechurchofchrist.org

Bible Fellowship Church—Email: bfc@bfc.org
Website: www.bfc.org

Bible Way Church of Our Lord Jesus Christ World Wide, Inc.—
Email: mr.ed5strings@worldnet.att.net
Website: www.biblewaychurch.org

Brethren in Christ Church—Email: RRoss@BIC-church.org
Website: www.bic-church.org/index.htm

Brethren Church (Ashland, Ohio)—Email: brethren@brethrenchurch.org
Website: www.brethrenchurch.org

The Catholic Church—Website: www.usccb.org

Christ Catholic Church—Email: bishopkarl@juno.com
Website: christcatholicchurch.freeyellow.com

Christadelphians—Email: Nzilmer@aol.com Website: www.christadelphia.org

Christian Church (Disciples of Christ) in the United States and Canada—
Email: cmiller@cm.disciples.org

Christian Church of North America, General Council—Email: cnna@nauticom.net
Website: www.ccna.org

Christian Churches and Churches of Christ—Email: Jowston@cwv.edu
Website: www.cwv.net/christ'n/

The Christian Congregation, Inc.—Email: Revalnas@aol.com
Website: netministries.org/see/churches.exe/ch10619

Christian Methodist Episcopal Church—Email: juanbr4law@aol.com

The Christian and Missionary Alliance—Email: info@cmalliance.org
Website: www.cmalliance.org

Christian Reformed Church in North America—Email: btgh@crcna.org
Website: www.crcna.org

Christian Union—Website: www.christianunion.com

Church of the Brethren—Email: cobweb@brethren.org
Website: www.brethren.org

Church of Christ—Website: http://church-of-christ.com

The Church of Christ (Holiness) USA—Email: Everything@cochusa.com
Website: www.cochusa.com/main.htm

Church of Christ, Scientist—Website: www.spirituality.com

Church of God (Anderson, Indiana)—Email: JMartin@chog.org
Website: www.chog.org

The Church of God in Christ—Email: EJOHNCOGIC@aol.com
Website: netministries.org/see/churches/ch00833

Church of God in Christ, International—Email: laity@cogic.org
Website: www.cogic.org/main.htm

Church of God (Cleveland, Tennessee)—Website: www.churchofgod.cc/default_nav40.asp

Church of God by Faith, Inc.—Email: natl-hq@cogbf.org
Website: www.cogbf.org

Church of God General Conference (Oregon, IL and Morrow, GA)—Email: info@abc-coggc.org
Website: www.abc-coggc.org

Church of God, Mountain Assembly, Inc.—Email: cgmahdq@jellico.com
Website: www.cgmahdq.org

Church of God of Prophecy—Email: betty@cogop.org
Website: www.cogop.org

The Church of God (Seventh Day), Denver, Colorado—Email: offices@cog7.org
Website: www.cog7.org

The Church of Illumination—Email: bevhall@comcat.com
Website: www.soul.org

The Church of Jesus Christ of Latter-day Saints—Website: www.lds.org

Church of the Lutheran Brethren of America—Email: clba@clba.org
Website: www.clba.org

Church of the Lutheran Confession—Email: JohnHLau@juno.com
Website: www.clclutheran.org

Church of the Nazarene—Email: ssm@nazarene.org
Website: www.nazarene.org

Church of Our Lord Jesus Christ of the Apostolic Faith, Inc.—Email: tewmsw@gloryroad.net
Website: www.apostolic-faith.org

Church of the United Brethren in Christ—Email: sdennie@ub.org
Website: www.ub.org

Churches of God, General Conference—Email: director@cggc.org
Website: www.cggc.org

Community of Christ—Email: snaylor@CofChrist.org
Website: www.CofChrist.org

Congregational Holiness Church—Email: chchurch@bellsouth.net
Website: www.chchurch.com

Conservative Baptist Association of America (CBAmerica)—Email: cba@cbamerica.org
Website: www.cbamerica.org

Conservative Congregational Christian Conference—Email: CCCC4@juno.com
Website: www.ccccusa.org

Conservative Lutheran Association—Email: PastorPJ@ix.netcom.com
Website: www.tlcanaheim.com/CLA/

Coptic Orthodox Church—Email: Webmaster@coptic.org
Website: www.coptic.org

Cumberland Presbyterian Church—Email: assembly@cumberland.org
Website: www.cumberland.org

Cumberland Presbyterian Church in America—Email: mleslie598@aol.com
Website: www.cumberland.org/cpca/

Elim Fellowship—Email: 75551.743@compuserve.com
Website: www.ElimFellowship.org

Episcopal Church—Email: jrollins@ecusa.anglican.org
Website: www.ecusa.anglican.org

The Episcopal Orthodox Church—Email: eoc@orthodoxanglican.net
Website: orthodoxanglican.net

The Estonian Evangelical Lutheran Church—Email: konsistoorium@eelk.ee
Website: www.eelk.ee

The Evangelical Church—Email: jsditzel@juno.com
Website: quakertownecna.com/conferences.html

The Evangelical Church Alliance—Email: info@ecainternational.org
Website: www.ecainternational.org

The Evangelical Congregational Church—Email: eccenter@eccenter.com
Website: www.eccenter.com/church/

The Evangelical Covenant Church—Email: Elliott.johnson@covchurch.org
Website: www.covchurch.org

The Evangelical Free Church of America—Email: president@efca.org
Website: www.efca.org

Evangelical Friends International–North American Region—Email: efcer@aol.com
Website: www.evangelical-friends.org

Evangelical Lutheran Church in America—Email: info@elca.org
Website: www.elca.org

Evangelical Lutheran Synod—Email: gorvick@blc.edu
Website: www.EvLuthSyn.org

Evangelical Methodist Church—Email: headquarters@emchurch.org
Website: www.emchurch.org

Evangelical Presbyterian Church—Email: EPCHURCH@epc.org
Website: www.epc.org

Fellowship of Evangelical Bible Churches—Email: febcoma@aol.com
Website: members.aol.com/febcoma/index.html

Fellowship of Fundamental Bible Churches—Email: FFBC-USA@juno.com
Website: www.churches-ffbc.org

Fellowship of Grace Brethren Churches—Email: fgbc@fgbc.org
Website: www.fgbc.org

Fellowship of Evangelical Churches—Email: emcintlmin@aol.com

Free Methodist Church of North America—Email: info@fmcna.org
Website: www.freemethodistchurch.org

Friends General Conference—Email: friends@fgcquaker.org
Website: www.fgcquaker.org

Friends United Meeting—Email: info@fum.org
Website: www.fum.org

Full Gospel Fellowship of Churches and Ministers International—Email: FGFCMI@aol.com
Website: www.fgfcmi.org

General Association of Regular Baptist Churches—Email: garbc@garbc.org
Website: www.garbc.org

General Church of the New Jerusalem—Email: svsimpso@newchurch.edu
Website: www.newchurch.org

Grace Gospel Fellowship—Email: ggfinc@aol.com
Website: www.ggfusa.org

Greek Orthodox Archdiocese of America—Email: archdiocese@goarch.org
Website: www.goarch.org

The Holy Eastern Orthodox Catholic and Apostolic Church in North America, Inc.—
Email: tmetropolitan@theocacna.org
Website: www.theocacna.org

Hutterian Brethren—Email: philsjg@juno.com

IFCA International, Inc.—Email: office@ifca.org
Website: www.ifca.org

International Church of the Foursquare Gospel—Email: comm@foursquare.org
Website: www.foursquare.org

The International Pentecostal Church of Christ—Email: hqipcc@aol.com
Website: members.aol.com/hqipcc/

Jehovah's Witnesses—Website: www.watchtower.org

The Latvian Evangelical Lutheran Church in America—Email: pulins@flash.net

Liberal Catholic Church (International)—Website: Website: www.liberalcatholic.org

The Liberal Catholic Church—Province of the United States of America—
Email: bshp052497@aol.com
Website: www.thelcc.org

The Lutheran Church–Missouri Synod (LCMS)—Email: infocenter@lcms.org
Website: www.lcms.org

Malankara Orthodox Syrian Church, Diocese of America—Email: Malankara@malankara.org
Website: www.malankara.org/american.htm

Mar Thoma Syrian Church of India—Email: webmaster@marthomachurch.org
Website: www.marthomachurch.org

Mennonite Church USA—Email: info@MennoniteUSA.org
Website: www.MennoniteChurchUSA.org

The Missionary Church—Email: mcdenomusa@aol.com
Website: www.mcusa.org

Moravian Church in America (Unitas Fratrum)—Email: gary@mcnp.org
Website: www.moravian.org

National Association of Congregational Christian Churches—Email: naccc@naccc.org
Website: www.naccc.org

National Association of Free Will Baptists—Email: webmaster@nafwb.org
Website: www.nafwb.org

National Missionary Baptist Convention of America—Website: www.nmbca.com

National Organization of the New Apostolic Church of North America—Email: info@nak.org
Website: www.nak.org

National Spiritualist Association of Churches—Email: nsac@nsac.org
Website: www.nsac.org

Open Bible Standard Churches—Email: info@openbible.org
Website: www.openbible.org

The Orthodox Church in America—Email: jjm@oca.org
Website: www.oca.org

Patriarchal Parishes of the Russian Orthodox Church in the USA—Email: bmercurius@ruscon.com
Website: www.orthodox.net

Pentecostal Church of God—Email: pcg@pcg.org
Website: www.pcg.org

The Pentecostal Free Will Baptist Church, Inc.—Email: pheath@intrstar.net
Website: www.pfwb.org

Philadelphia Yearly Meeting of the Religious Society of Friends—Website: www.pym.org

Pillar of Fire—Email: info@zarephath.edu
Website: www.gospelcom.net/pof/

Polish National Catholic Church of America—Email: ads22244@aol.com
Website: www.PNCC.org

Presbyterian Church in America—Email: ac@pcanet.org
Website: www.pcanet.org

Presbyterian Church (USA)—Email: presytel@pcusa.org
Website: www.pcusa.org

Primitive Methodist Church in the USA—Email: pmconf@juno.com
Website: www.primitivemethodistchurch.org

Protestant Reformed Churches in America—Email: doezema@prca.org
Website: www.prca.org

Reformed Catholic Church—Email: berzol@apollo3.com
Website: www.geocities.com/WestHollywood/4136/

Reformed Church in America—Email: kbaker@rca.org
Website: www.rca.org

Reformed Church in the United States—Email: TriWheeler@aol.com
Website: www.rcus.org

Reformed Episcopal Church—Email: wycliffe@jps.net
Website: recus.org

Reformed Presbyterian Church of North America—Email: RPTrustees@aol.com
Website: www.reformedpresbyterian.org

The Romanian Orthodox Church in America—Email: ArchNicolae@aol.com
Website: www.romarch.org

The Romanian Orthodox Episcopate of America—Email: roeasolia@aol.com
Website: www.roea.org

Separate Baptists in Christ—Email: mail@separatebaptist.org
Website: www.separatebaptist.org

Serbian Orthodox Church in the USA and Canada—Email: oea@oea.serbian-church.net
Website: oea.serbian-church.net

Seventh-day Adventist Church—Email: kjones@gc.adventist.org
Website: www.adventist.org

Seventh Day Baptist General Conference, USA and Canada—Email: sdbgen@inwave.com
Website: www.seventhdaybaptist.org

Southern Baptist Convention—Email: bmerrell@sbc.net
Website: www.sbc.net

Southern Methodist Church—Email: smchq@juno.com

Sovereign Grace Believers—Email: jon@searchingtogether.org
Website: www.searchingtogether.org

The Swedenborgian Church—Email: manager@swedenborg.org
Website: www.swedenborg.org

Syrian (Syriac) Orthodox Church of Antioch—Email: syrianoc@syrianorthodoxchurch.org
Website: www.syrianorthodoxchurch.org

The Syro-Russian Orthodox Catholic Church—Email: rbsocc@juno.com

Ukrainian Orthodox Church of the USA—Email: uocofusa@aol.com
Website: www.uocofusa.org

Unitarian Universalist Association of Congregations—Email: jhurley@uua.org
Website: www.uua.org

United Church of Christ—Email: kellys@ucc.org
Website: www.ucc.org

United Holy Church of America, Inc.—Email: books@mohistory.org

The United Methodist Church—Email: infoserv@umcom.umc.org
Website: www.umc.org

Universal Fellowship of Metropolitan Community Churches—Email: communications@ufmcchq.com
Website: www.ufmcchq.com

Volunteers of America—Email: voa@voa.org
Website: www.voa.org

The Wesleyan Church—Email: gensupts@wesleyan.org
Website: www.wesleyan.org

Wisconsin Evangelical Lutheran Synod—Email: webbin@sab.wels.net
Website: www.wels.net

6. Sources of Religion-Related Research

I. Directory of Selected Research Organizations

The editorial office of the Yearbook of American & Canadian Churches receives innumerable requests for data about churches, religious organizations, attendance patterns, and comparative religion concerns. Sometimes we are able to furnish the requested data, but more often we refer the inquirer to other research colleagues in the field.

In response to such inquiries, the "Sources in Religion-Related Research" directory was initiated. In addition to asking each research organization to provide an overall description, each was also asked to indicate research foci (i.e. denominational, congregational, interfaith, gender, etc.). We also request a list of recurrent publications. Below, the organizations' responses to these questions are reported as clearly and completely as is possible. Contact information appears just beneath the title of each organization. In most cases, the organization's website provides further detailed information about current research projects.

Numerous other research centers in the area of American religious life, each with specific areas of concern, conduct timely and significant research. We hope that readers will find utility in this directory and we invite them to identify additional sources by email—yearbook@ncccusa.org—or by Fax (212) 870-2817.

American Academy of Religion (AAR)

AAR Executive Office
825 Houston Mill Rd., Ste. 300
Atlanta, GA 30329
Tel. (404)727-7920
Fax (404)727-7959
Email: aar@aarweb.org
Website: www.aarweb.org
Pres. 2003, Dr. Robert A. Orsi
Pres. 2004, Dr. Jane Damman McAuliffe
Exec. Dir., Dr. Barbara DeConcini

The AAR is the major learned society and professional association for scholars whose object of study is religion. Its mission—in a world where religion plays so central a role in social, political and economic events, as well as in the lives of communities and individuals—is to meet a critical need for ongoing reflection upon and understanding of religious traditions, issues, questions, and values. As a learned society and professional association of teachers and research scholars, the American Academy of Religion has over 8,500 members who teach in some 1,500 colleges, universities, seminaries, and schools in North America and abroad. The Academy is dedicated to furthering knowledge of religion and religious institutions in all their forms and manifestations. This is accomplished through Academy-wide and regional conferences and meetings, publications, programs, and membership services. Within a context of free inquiry and critical examination, the Academy welcomes all disciplined reflection on religion, both from within and outside of communities of belief and practice, and seeks to enhance its broad public understanding.

At the AAR's annual meeting, over 8,000 scholars gather to share research and collaborate on scholarly projects. The annual meeting sessions are grouped into over 70 program units, each representing an ongoing community of scholars who are collectively engaged in pursuing knowledge about a specific religious tradition or a specific aspect of religion. In addition, the AAR's ten regional organizations sponsor smaller annual meetings that are similar in structure to the Academy-wide meeting. All of the world's major religious traditions, as well as indigenous and historical religions, are explored in the work of AAR members.

Current or Recent Research

Currently, for example, the AAR offers Teaching Workshops for both junior and senior scholars. It is organizing efforts to gather data on the field to facilitate departmental planning and funding. A full explanation of the many current research projects is available on the AAR website, which is listed above.

Periodicals

The Journal of the American Academy of Religion is the scholarly periodical of the AAR. In addition, the AAR publishes a quarterly newsletter, *Religious Studies News, AAR Edition.*

American Religion Data Archive (ARDA)

Department of Sociology
The Pennsylvania State University
211 Oswald Tower
University Park, PA 16802-6207
Tel. (814)865-6258
Fax (814)863-7216
Email: arda@pop.psu.edu
Website: www.TheARDA.com
Dir., Dr. Roger Finke
Dir., Dr. Roger Finke

The American Religion Data Archive (ARDA) is an Internet-based archive that stores and distributes information from over 250 major data collections on American religion. Online features include interactive maps of state and county church membership rates; denominational profiles for counties, states, metropolitan areas, and the nation; basic statistics for all survey questions; and many other features. With the exception of the 2000 Religious Congregations and Membership Study, all data files can be downloaded. The ARDA (www.TheARDA.com) is supported by the Lilly Endowment and is housed in the Social Science Research Institute at the Penn State University.

Association of Theological Schools (ATS)

10 Summit Park Dr.
Pittsburgh, PA 15275-1103
Tel. (412)788-6505
Fax (412)788-6510
Email: ats@ats.edu
Website: www.ats.edu
Exec. Dir., Daniel O. Aleshire
Dir. of Communications and Membership Services, Nancy Merrill

The mission of The Association of Theological Schools in the United States and Canada (ATS) is to promote the improvement and enhancement of theological schools to the benefit of communities of faith and the broader public. The Association seeks to fulfill this mission by engaging in four core areas of work: (1) accreditation; (2) leadership education for administrative officers and faculty; (3) development of theological education, which involves the study of critical issues in theological education; and (4) data and communications.

The Association is a membership organization of approximately 250 graduate schools of theology—including Protestant, Roman Catholic, and Orthodox schools—both freestanding seminaries and university-related divinity schools. A full list of members is available on the above website.

Targeted areas of the Association's work currently include: Theological Schools and the Church, the Public Character of Theological Schools, the Character and Assessment of Learning for Religious Vocation, Race and Ethnicity in Theological Education, Education for Administrative Leaders and Development for Faculty, Women in Leadership in Theological Education, and Technology and Educational Practices.

Current or Recent Research

Current research is addressing the effective formation of seminary students for religious vocation and ministerial leadership. The project encompasses several goals: (1) increased understanding of the character of theological learning that includes intellectual content, professional skill, personal formation, and spiritual maturity; (2) effective assessment of theological learning in the context of the Master of Divinity degree program, in particular, and in the context of ministerial practice; (3) information about the relationship between the goals of theological learning and selected characteristics of current theological students; and (4) development of models of assessment of student learning for use by ATS member schools. Over the course of this four-year project, the Association will commission five research studies that will focus on: (1) current practices of educational assessment being employed in ATS schools; (2) best practices of educational assessment in graduate, professional education for human services professions; (3) a review of the literature on higher education outcomes assessment; (4) characteristics of students currently enrolled in theological education programs of study; and (5) church-denominational perspectives of the strengths and weaknesses of recent graduates of ATS schools.

Periodicals

Fact Book on Theological Education is published annually and provides statistical data on the member institutions. The Association publishes a journal, *Theological Education*, bi-annually, a bi-monthly newsletter entitled *Colloquy*, and the formal institutional documents of the Association entitled *Bulletin*, part 2 of which is the ATS membership list.

Auburn Theological Seminary

3041 Broadway
New York, NY 10027
Tel. (212)662-4315
Fax (212)663-5214
Email: krh@auburnsem.org
Website: www.auburnsem.org
Dir., Dr. Barbara G. Wheeler
Exec. Vice Pres., Rev. Katharine R. Henderson

Auburn Theological Seminary's mission is to strengthen religious leadership. It carries out its mission through programs of non-degree theological education for clergy and laity; through programs for Presbyterian students enrolled at its partner institution, Union Seminary in New York City; and by conducting research on theological education at its Center for the Study of Theological Education. Auburn was founded in 1818 in Auburn, N.Y.; it is currently located on Union Seminary's campus.

Auburn Seminary is related by covenant agreement with Presbyterian Church (USA), but most of its programs are ecumenical, and many have a multi-faith focus. The Center for the Study of Theological Education includes rabbinical schools and Protestant and Roman Catholic seminaries and divinity schools in its studies.

Research is conducted using a variety of methods, including survey and ethnographic research, structured interview and documentary research, research reports on surveys, and case studies. Reports of findings are frequently published with accompanying information on the history of the issue being studied and with theological commentaries written from a variety of perspectives.

Current or Recent Research

The Center is undertaking a systematic study of U.S. and Canadian M.Div. graduates from across the religious spectrum in order to find out how graduates have used their theological training, how many are in ministry five and ten years after graduation, and how they look back and assess their seminary experience. A second study underway is on seminary institutional advancement. Through analysis of available data, site visits and interviews, the researchers will examine the techniques, costs, best practices and barriers to effective fundraising in theological schools.

Periodicals

Auburn Studies, an occasional bulletin in which the Center publishes its research results. Research reports are also available on Auburn's website (listed above).

Barna Research Group, Ltd.

5528 Everglades Street
Ventura, CA 93003
Tel. (805)658-8885
Fax (805)658-7298
Website: www.barna.org
Pres., George Barna
Vice Pres., David Kinnaman

Barna Research Group works with Christian churches and parachurch ministries throughout the nation by providing primary research data related to cultural change and people's lifestyles, values, attitudes, beliefs, and religious practices. Its vision is to provide current accurate and reliable information, in bite-sized pieces and at reasonable costs, to ministries who will use the information to make better strategic decisions. They conduct primary research for ministries that commission such research, studying their community, their church, or special population. Barna also produces many research-based books, reports, and ministry tools to help churches understand the national context of ministry. Barna Research conducts seminars in many markets across the nation to inform church leaders of its findings, and to train church leaders in the application of that information. The organization works with churches from all Christian denominations.

Barna Research has no special research focus. It conducts projects based upon existing needs in the Church-at-large, or for its clients specifically, and analyzes all of its findings in relation to a minimum of three dozen population subgroups involved in the survey interviews. Methodologically, Barna Research uses both qualitative approaches (focus groups, depth interviews) and quantitative approaches (cross-sectional surveys, longitudinal studies, panel research). Data collection methods include telephone surveys, mail surveys, in-person interviews, on-line surveys, self-administered surveys, and focus groups.

Current or Recent Research

Barna Research conducts more than 50 studies each year, covering a broad range of topics. Some of the recent non-proprietary studies completed are focused on understanding the state of the Church, the habits of highly effective churches, worship efficacy, the unchurched, strategies and techniques for developing lay leaders, understanding effective discipleship processes, pastoral profiles, beliefs and core attitudes of religious donors, Biblical knowledge, and many others.

Periodicals

Barna Research offers a bi-weekly update on current information related to faith matters from its national non-proprietary research. This information is free to those who register for it at the website (listed above).

Center for the Study of Religion and American Culture

Indiana University
Purdue University at Indianapolis
425 University Blvd, Room 341
Indianapolis, IN 46202-5140
Tel. (317)274-8409
Fax (317)278-3354
Email: pgoff@iupui.edu
Website: www.iupui.edu/it/raac
Dir., Dr. Conrad Cherry

The Center for the Study of Religion and American Culture is a research and public outreach institute devoted to the promotion of the understanding of the relation between religion and other features of American culture. Research methods are both interdisciplinary and multidisciplinary. Established in 1989, the Center is based in the School of Liberal Arts and Indiana University/Purdue University at Indianapolis. Center activities include national conferences and symposia; commissioned books, essays, bibliographies, and research projects; fellowships for younger scholars; data based communication about developments in the field of American religion; a newsletter devoted to the promotion of Center activities; and the semi-annual scholarly periodical, *Religion and American Culture, A Journal of Interpretation.*

Current or Recent Research

The Center is presently overseeing two initiatives. The "Young Scholars in American Religion Program" is a multi-year project to assist early-career scholars in developing their teaching skills and research agendas. The "Centers and Institutes Project," meanwhile, brings together those organizations dedicated to the academic study of religion in the US in order to discuss common problems and solutions, as well as to identify areas for cooperative efforts. The work of these various centers and institutes will be highlighted in future issues of the "Newsletter from the Center for the Study of Religion and American Culture" and the Center's reception at the annual meeting of the American Academy of Religion.

We continue to explore other areas of potential research in the relation between religion and other aspects of American culture. As these projects materialize, they will be announced on this website and in the "Newsletter."

Periodicals

Religion and American Culture, A Journal of Interpretation. Center books include the series, "The Public Expressions of Religion in America."

empty tomb, inc.

301 North Fourth Street
P.O. Box 2404
Champaign, IL 61825-2404
Tel. (217)356-9519
Fax (217)356-2344
Email: research@emptytomb.org
Website: www.emptytomb.org
CEO, John L. Ronsvalle
Exec.Vice Pres., Sylvia Ronsvalle

empty tomb, inc. is a Christian research and service organization. On a local level, it coordinates direct services to people in need in cooperation with area congregations. On a national level, it studies church member giving patterns of historically Christian churches, including Roman Catholic, mainline and evangelical Protestant, Anabaptist, Pentecostal, Orthodox, and fundamentalist communions. empty tomb publishes the annual State of Church Giving series. Staff also work with a select number of congregations, discovering ways to reverse the negative giving trends indicated by national data, through its project, The National Money for Mission Program.

Current or Recent Research

Current research monitors and analyzes church member giving patters, and is published in "The State of Church Giving" series produced by empty tomb, inc. The description of dynamics affecting current giving patterns is presented in *Behind The Stained Glass Windows, Money Dynamics in The Church* (Grand Rapids, MI, Baker Books, 1996).

Periodicals

"The State of Church Giving" series is an annual publication. It considers denominational giving data, analysis of giving and membership trends, and other estimates of charitable giving. Each edition has featured a special focus chapter, which discusses giving issues. Past state of church giving special focus chapters are posted on the emptytomb website.

The Hartford Institute for Religion Research of Hartford Seminary

Hartford Seminary
77 Sherman Street
Hartford, CT 06105
Tel. (860)509-9543
Fax (860)509-9551
Email: hirr@hartsem.edu
Website: www.hirr.hartsem.edu
Dir. for Research, Dr. David A. Roozen:
Adm. Assistant, Mary Jane Ross

The Hartford Institute for Religion Research of Hartford Seminary was established in 1981, formalizing a research program initiated by the Seminary in 1974. Until recently, it was known as The Center for Social and Religious Research. The Institute's work is guided by a disciplined understanding of the interrelationship between (a) the inner life and resources of American religious institutions and (b) the possibilities and limits placed on those institutions by the social and cultural context into which God has called them.

Its twenty-one year record of rigorous, policy-relevant research, anticipation of emerging issues, commitment to the creative dissemination of learning, and strong connections to both theological education and the church has earned the Institute an international reputation as an important bridge between the scholarly community and the practice of ministry.

Current or Recent Research

Some of the titles of current projects at the Institute are: "Organizing Religious Work for the 21st Century: Exploring 'Denominationalism,'" "Cooperative Congregational Studies Project," "Congregational Consulting Services," "New England Religion Discussion Society (NERDS)," and "Congregational Studies Team." Descriptions of these programs are available on the Institute's website, listed above.

Periodicals

Praxis is Hartford Seminary's magazine, which focuses on the activities and faculty of the Seminary.

Institute for Ecumenical and Cultural Research

P.O. Box 6188
Collegeville, MN 56321-6188
Tel. (320)363-3366
Fax (320)363-3313
Email: iecr@iecr.org
Website: www.iecr.org
Exec. Dir., Dr. Patrick Henry (Dr. Don B. Ottenhoff, June 1)
Adm. Assistant, Stephanie Hart

The Institute for Ecumenical and Cultural Research brings together well-trained, creative, articulate men and women for careful thought and dialogue in a place of inquiry and prayer. The Resident Scholars Program welcomes researchers and their families for either individual semesters or an entire academic year. Resident scholars work on their own projects but meet once a week for seminars, and have other occasions for conversation. Each scholar presents a public lecture. Ecumenism happens at the Institute as people come to know one another in community. The Institute is an independent corporation, but shares in the Benedictine and academic life of Saint John's Abbey and University, and of the nearby Saint Benedict's Monastery and College of Saint Benedict. In the summer, the Institute uses its facilities for invitational consultations on subjects considered by the Board of Directors to be of special ecumenical interest.

In the Resident Scholars Program, the subjects of research are determined by the interests of the applicants who are invited to come by the Admissions Committee. While most of the work tends to be in traditional theological areas, we encourage people in all fields to consider applying, both because ecumenism is of concern across the spectrum of disciplines, and because the term "cultural" in our title extends our reach beyond theology and religious studies. In particular cases, work done here may have a denominational, congregational, or interfaith focus, but the Institute does not prescribe or delimit, in any narrow way, what is appropriate.

Current or Recent Research

Recent summer consultations have had the following titles: "Ecumenical Formation: The Heart of the Matter" and "Igniting Biblical Imagination." Among subjects dealt with in earlier years are "Prayer in the Ecumenical Movement," "Virtues for an Ecumenical Heart," "The Price of Disunity," "Living Faithfully in North America Today," "Orthodoxy at Home in North America," "Transmitting Tradition to Children and Young People," "The Nature of Christian Hope," "Women and the Church," "Jewish and Christian Relatedness to Scripture," and "Confessing Christian Faith in a Pluralistic Society."

Periodicals

Ecumenical People, Programs, Papers is a bi-annual newsletter containing brief sketches of resident scholars, reports on Institute programs, and, in nearly every issue, "An Occasional Paper" on a subject of ecumenical interest. The newsletter is free.

Institute for the Study of American Evangelicals (ISAE)

Wheaton College
Wheaton, IL 60187
Tel. (630)752-5437
Fax (630)752-5516
Email: isae@wheaton.edu
Website: www.wheaton.edu/isae
Dir., Dr. Edith Blumhofer
Reserch and Resource Assistant, Katria Delac

Founded in 1982, the Institute for the Study of American Evangelicals is a center for research and functions as a program of Wheaton College. The purpose of the ISAE is to encourage and support research on evangelical Christianity in the United States and Canada. The institute seeks to help evangelicals develop a mature understanding of their own heritage and to inform others about evangelicals' historical significance and contemporary role. For the most part, the ISAE focuses on historical research, with occasional sociological or economic researchers participating in the projects.

Current or Recent Research

One recent project entitled "Hymnody in American Protestantism" is a research project focusing on the history of hymnology in American religious life.

Periodicals

Evangelical Studies Bulletin (*ESB*) is designed to aid both the scholar and the layman in his or her education and research of evangelicalism. Issued quarterly, the bulletin contains articles, book reviews, notices, a calendar of events, and bibliographic information on the latest dissertations, articles, and books related to the study of evangelicals.

Institute for the Study of American Religion

P.O. Box 90709
Santa Barbara, CA 93190-0709
Tel. (805)967-7721
Fax (805)683-4876
Email: jgordon@linkline.com
Website: www.americanreligion.org
Dir., Dr. J. Gordon Melton
Associate Dir., Dr. James Beverley

The Institute for the Study of American Religion was founded in 1968 in Evanston, Ill. as a religious studies research facility with a particular focus upon the smaller religions of the United States. Those groups that it has concentrated upon have been known under a variety of labels including sect, cult, minority religion, alternative religion, non-conventional religion, spiritual movement, and new religious movement.

In the 1970s the Institute extended its attention to Canada and in the 1990s developed an even more global focus. In 1985, the institute moved to its present location in Santa Barbara, Calif. Over the years, the institute built a large collection of both primary and secondary materials on the religious groups and movements it studied. In 1985 this collection of more than 40,000 volumes and thousands of periodicals and archival materials was deposited with the Davidson Library at the University of California in Santa Barbara. The reference material exists today as the American Religions Collection and is open to scholars and the interested public. The institute continues to support the collection with donations of additional materials.

Current or Recent Research

Today the institute has two main foci. It monitors all of the religious denominations, organizations, and movements functioning in North America and regularly publishes reports drawing from that activity in a series of reference books. The most important of these reference books is the *Encyclopedia of American Religions* (Detroit, Gale Group, 7th ed., 2002). Among the most called for information is factual data on the many new and more controversial religious movements, which are popularly labeled as "cults." The institute's second focus developed out of its more recent refocusing on the international scene, provoked by the international life of most of the religious groups which it has studied in previous decades.

J.M. Dawson Institute of Church-State Studies at Baylor University

P.O. Box 97308
Waco, TX 76798-7308
Tel. (254)710-1510
Fax (254)710-1571
Email: derek_davis@baylor.edu
Website: www.baylor.edu/~Church_State
Dir., Dr. Derek Davis
Adm. Assistant, Wanda Gilbert

Baylor University established the J. M. Dawson Institute of Church-State Studies in 1957, so named in honor of an outstanding alumnus, an ardent advocate of religious liberty, and a distinguished author of publications on church and state. The Institute is the oldest and most well-established facility of its kind located in a university setting. It is exclusively devoted to research in the broad field of church and state and the advancement of religious liberty around the world.

From its inception in 1957, the stated purpose of the Institute has been to stimulate academic interest and encourage research and publication in the broad area of church-state relations. In carrying out its statement of purpose, the Institute has sought to honor a threefold commitment, to be interfaith, interdisciplinary, and international.

Current or Recent Research

Some current research includes: Government persecution of minority religions in Europe, original intent of Founding Fathers regarding religion and public life, Christian Right views on political activism, conservative versus moderate Baptist views on church-state relations, role of civil religion in America, and international treaties and religious liberty.

Periodicals

Journal of Church and State is the only scholarly journal expressly devoted to church-state relations.

The Louisville Institute

1044 Alta Vista Road
Louisville, KY 40205-1798
Tel. (502)895-3411
Fax (502)894-2286
Email: info@louisville-institute.org
Website: www.louisville-institute.org
Exec. Dir., Dr. James W. Lewis
Admn. Sect., Suzanne Case

The Louisville Institute is a Lilly Endowment program for the study of American religion based at the Louisville Presbyterian Seminary. As a program of Lilly Endowment, the Louisville Institute builds upon the Endowment's long-standing support of both leadership education and scholarly research on American religion, focusing on American Protestantism, American Catholicism, the historic African-American churches, and the Hispanic religious experience. The distinctive mission of the Louisville Institute is to enrich the religious life of American Christians and to encourage the revitalization of their institutions by bringing together those who lead religious institutions with those who study them, so that the work of each might stimulate and inform the other. The Louisville Institute seeks to fulfill its mission through a program of grant-making and conferences.

The work of the Louisville Institute focuses on religion in North America, with particular attention to three issues. The first, Christian faith and life, concerns the character and role of the theology and spirituality that are effectively at work in the lives of American Christians. The second, religious institutions, asks how America's religious institutions might respond most constructively in the midst of the bewildering institutional reconfiguration occurring in American society. The third, pastoral leadership, explores various strategies for improving the quality of religious leadership in North America. The various research projects employ a variety of disciplinary perspectives, including but not limited to, theology, history, ethics, and the social sciences. They may also be interdisciplinary in nature.

Current or Recent Research

Please see the Louisville Institute website (listed above) for lists of recent grants made by the Louisville Institute.

Periodicals

Intersection is a newsletter reporting on Institute activities.

The Pluralism Project

Harvard University
201 Vanserg Hall
25 Francis Avenue
Cambridge, MA 02138
Tel. (617)496-2481
Fax (617)496-2428
Email: staff@pluralism.org
Website: www.pluralsm.org
Dir., Dr. Diana L. Eck
Project Manager, Ellie J. Pierce

The Pluralism Project was developed by Dr. Diana L. Eck at Harvard University to study and document the growing religions diversity of the United States, with a special view to its new immigrant religious communities. The religious landscape of the US has radically changed in the past 30 years; in light of these changes, how Americans of all faiths begin to engage with one another in shaping a positive pluralism is one of the most important questions American society faces in the years ahead. In addressing these phenomena, the Project has three goals: 1) To document some further changes taking place in America's cities and towns by beginning to map their new religious demography with old and new mosques and Islamic centers, Sikh gurdwaras, Hindu and Jain temples, Buddhist temples and meditation centers, Zoroastrian and Taoist religious centers. 2) To begin to study how these religious traditions are changing as they take root in American soil and develop in a new context. How are they beginning to recreate their community life, religious institutions, rites and rituals, and forms of transmission in the cultural environment of the United States? 3) To explore how the United States is changing as we begin to appropriate this new religious diversity in our public life and institutions, and in emerging forms of interfaith relationships.

The Pluralism Project has the most comprehensive archive anywhere of the print materials of America's new immigrant religious communities: newsletters, serial publications, anniversary programs, handbooks, prayer books, calendars, and educational materials. The Project files also include research papers as well as a variety of materials donated directly by centers.

The Pluralism Project On-Line Directory maintains an extensive directory of religious centers in the United States. At present, this directory exists in a sortable database, with listings of nearly 3,000 centers across the US.

Current or Recent Research

The Pluralism Project produced a CD-ROM, *On Common Ground–World Religions in America*, to present some of the wide range of work that had emerged from three years of research. A further grant from the Ford Foundation has enabled the Project to extend its research on the American religious landscape.

Directory of Selected Faith Traditions in America

Compiling a directory of faith groups is an arduous but rewarding task in religiously plural America, in part because the very self-understanding and definition of community varies so greatly from faith group to faith group. In order to present a reasonably parallel and well-balanced listing of organizations for each faith, care must be taken not to impose categories or terms from one's own universe of understanding upon other contexts. The very terms, "church," "membership," "denomination, " "hierarchy"—which are essential constructs of certain Christian universes of understanding—are rendered meaningless when applied to other faith groups.

Further, it is important to remember that many religious traditions lack a centralized organization that speaks for the whole of the community. Often, this lack of centralization reflects the existence of several distinct forms or branches of the religion. In some instances, different ethnic groups immigrating to the US bring with them a distinctive form of their religion, which is particular to their culture of origin. In other cases, plural forms of a faith exist resulting from theological, political, or economic differences. Still other faith groups may be more tightly organized, but the religious center that provides guidance in matters of faith and, perhaps, even organizational discipline may not be in the United States. Hence, the organizations before us are not necessarily religious hierarchical organizations, but are often groups assembled for other purposes that are associated with a particular faith group, or subdivision of that faith group. Caution is advised in regarding these entries as one might regard a "church headquarters."

The compilation of any directory relies upon the existence of some common organizational structure within all the entities listed. Yet, when compiling a directory of faith groups, it cannot be assumed such organizational parallels exist. Oblique ways must be found to adequately represent individual faith groups. The many religious communities in the United States are associated with myriad organizations of all different types. Some of these are primarily places of worship, others are organizations seeking to represent either the religious community as a whole or some particular constituency within it. Others are community centers, some are educational groups, some are organizations particularly for women or youths, and some are political action groups. Still others are peace organizations or relief organizations. That said, a directory of this sort can not include an exhaustive list of organizations for each faith group nationwide. The omission of any particular organization or branch of any of the major faith groups listed does not reflect a deliberate attempt to homogenize the rich pluralities that exist within faith groups. Instead, the listings that follow are intended to provide the interested reader with a few initial contacts within each religious community.

Despite the above cautions, this directory provides a rich resource for readers and researchers who wish to learn more about other faith groups. The agencies listed here consist of organizations of importance within the communities they represent, and serve as excellent introductory points of contact with those communities.

In some cases, these religious communities are in a state of flux; the Internet is an excellent way to keep contact with changing religious organizations. There is a plethora of information available about nearly all religious traditions online, but sites vary widely in their accuracy and reliability. While nearly all Internet search engines will provide extensive links to information about specific religious traditions, the listing of suggested sites in Directory 5, "The Electronic Church," is a good starting point. For directory information about national interfaith organizations in the United States, please see Directory 1, "US Cooperative Organizations." For directory information on local interfaith organizations, please see Directory 7, "US Regional and Local Ecumenical Bodies."

BAHA'ISM

Baha'ism was founded in Persia during the late 19th century by Mirza Hussein Ali Nuri, also known as Baha'ullah, which means "Glory of God" in Arabic. Baha'i is an outgrowth of an earlier Persian religious movement called Babism, which was initiated by Mirza Ali Muhammad, who was referred to as the "Bab". In 1844, the Bab prophesied that in nineteen years a divine manifestation of God would appear. Shortly afterward, the Babis endured a massive period of persecution in which the Bab was martyred. In 1863, Baha'ullah, a close follower of the Bab, claimed that he, himself was this divine manifestation of God. Further, he claimed that he was the last in a line of such divine figures, which included Zoroaster, the Buddha, Christ, and Muhammad. Along these lines, Baha'ullah's teachings called for a religious universalism in which moral truths could be gleaned from all faiths. His son, Abd al-Baha, spread his father's teachings to the Western world, insisting on certain social principles such as universal equality of the sexes or races, and of religious adherence.

The Baha'i National Center of the USA
536 Sheridan Rd.
Wilmette, IL 60091
Website: www.bahai.org

This center can provide information about the Baha'i faith and provide contacts with Baha'i organizations throughout the country and the world. There are over 1,400 Baha'i local spiritual assemblies in the United States. The community is very concerned about issues involving peace, justice, racial unity, economic development, and education (among others) and has available resources on a number of these issues as well as on Baha'i scriptures and theology. The website listed above is the official Baha'i website on the Internet.

BUDDHISM

Buddhism began in northern India between the 6th-5th centuries B.C.E. with the teachings of Siddhartha Gautama, who is called the Buddha, which means "The One Who is Enlightened." Buddhism grew out of the Hindu tradition of the time, but it rejected certain fundamental philosophical, cosmological, social, hierarchical, and scriptural aspects of that tradition, which set the two deeply apart from each other. Most Buddhists believe that suffering is the central predicament of life, and that desires are the source of this suffering. One need only remove desires and it follows that suffering disappears as well. Buddhism has grown in different directions over the centuries among many different cultures, and its traditions have varied widely. All are usually characterized by an emphasis on meditation and compassion. Buddhism is divided into three major branches: *Theravada*, "the Way of the Elders;" *Mahayana* "the Great Vehicle;" and *Vajrayana*, "the Indestructible Vehicle" or path of devotion. Buddhism spread through parts of South Asia, the Himalayan region, all over China, Japan, and Korea, and deeply into South East Asia. Although its origins are Indian, Buddhism is almost entirely absent from that country. In the past hundred and fifty years, Buddhism has spread to the Western world. In this religious tradition, with few national bodies and great variation among particular branches and cultural expressions, organization is more localized than in some other faith groups.

American Buddhist Congress
4267 West Third St.
Los Angeles, CA 20020
Tel. (213)386-8139

An association of leaders from a variety of Buddhist traditions in the US.

Buddhist Churches of America
1710 Octavia Street
San Francisco, CA 94109
Tel. (415)776-5600
Fax (415)771-6293
Bishop, Ven. Hakubun Watanabe

The national body of Japanese Shin tradition was founded in 1899. It provides programmatic resources for local temples around the US.

Buddhist Council of the Midwest
2400 Prairie
Evanston, IL 60201
Tel. (847)869-4975
Website: www.members.ymc.net/jfred

A regional organization active in coordinating activities among the Buddhist communities in the mid-west.

Buddhist Sangha Council of Southern California
933 South New Hampshire Ave.
Los Angeles, CA 90006
Tel. (213)739-1270
Fax (213)386-6643

The umbrella organization of Buddhist communities in Southern California.

Texas Buddhist Council
8727 Radio Rd.
Houston, TX 77075

The regional coordinating body for Buddhists in Texas.

The Buddhist Peace Fellowship
P. O. Box 4650
Berkeley, CA 94704
Tel. (510)655-6169

Fax (510)655-1369
Email: bpf@bpf.org
Website: www.bpf.org

A national organization through which Buddhists of many traditions work for peace and justice.

HINDUISM

Hinduism has been evolving since roughly 1500 B.C.E. and has its origins in India. Most of the inhabitants of India are still Hindus, but many have emigrated to Europe, North America, East Africa, and South and South East Asia. The beliefs and practices of Hinduism vary so deeply and widely throughout India, and are so diffused throughout every aspect of life, that one may describe Hinduism not so much as a tradition, but more accurately as the collection of many traditions, encompassed by the great history and geography of India. Throughout its history, Hinduism has had an enormous propensity for the absorption of new elements into its practices and its understanding of deity. There is no central authority or priestly hierarchy that regulates the evolution of Hinduism; very few traditions are shared by all Hindus. Adaptations and evolutions can and do occur, but usually at the regional level. Simultaneously, ancient practices and beliefs persist in some places, where elsewhere, they have been long since replaced or never occurred. Nevertheless, all Hindus believe in the authority of the *Vedas*, the ancient scriptural tradition of India. All accept the *dharma*, or "way," of the four *varnas*, or social classes, which constitute the complex caste system, which is interwoven in the practice of the religion. Further, most Hindus worship Shiva or Vishnu or Devi, in addition to individual devotions to other deities or divine manifestations. Most Hindus are vegetarians.

The International Society for Krishna Consciousness
North American Communications
10310 Oaklyn Dr.
Potomac, MD 20854
Tel. (301)299-9707
Fax (301)299-5025
Email: anuttama.acbsp@com.bbt.se
Communications Dir., Anuttama Dasa

Council of Hindu Temples of North America
45-57 Bowne St.
Flushing, NY 11355
Tel. (800)99HINDU

One of a number of Hindu organizations, which connect Hindus in certain regions of the US.

American Hindus Against Defamation
8914 Rotherdam Ave.
San Diego, CA 92129
Tel. (619)484-4564
Email: ajay@hindunet.org
Dir., Mr. Ajay Shah

A new organization devoted to defending Hindus from stereotyping and discriminatory or defamatory acts/speech.

ISLAM

Islam began in 7th-century Arabia under the leadership of the Prophet Muhammad, to whom God (*Allah* in Arabic) revealed a collection of verses known as the *Holy Qur'an*. The word *islam* means "making peace through submission" and, in the context of religion, it means "submission to the will of God." A person who practices Islam is a Muslim, meaning, "one who is submitting to the will of God." A Muslim follows the teachings of the *Holy Qur'an*, which was presented to human kind by Muhammad, but which is the very word of the one and only God, and is therefore perfect and complete. Integral to the Muslim Tradition are the "Five Pillars of Islam," which are the five obligations each Muslim must uphold. The first of these is the *shahadah*, or profession of faith, which states, "There is no God but God, and Muhammad is his prophet." The second obligation is that a Muslim prays five times each day at prescribed times. Thirdly, a Muslim must pay the *zakat*, which is a form of mandatory almsgiving. Fourth, a Muslim is required to fast from dawn until sunset during the month of *Ramadan*, the ninth month of the Muslim year. And finally, if able, once in his/her lifetime, every Muslim is required to make a pilgrimage called the *Hajj* to the holy city of Mekkah, where the *ka'bah* is housed, a stone structure built by Abraham and Ishmael. Early in the history of the Islam, the religion split into two distinct branches, known as the Sunni and the Shiah, both of which contain sub-branches. Muslims worldwide constitute an enormous community that is rapidly spreading throughout North America as a result of recent immigration as well as conversion.

The Islamic Society of North America (ISNA)
P.O. Box 38
Plainfield, IN 46168
Tel. (317)839-8157
Website: www.isna.net
Gen. Sec., Dr. Sayyid M. Syeed

The Islamic Society of North America grew out of the Muslim Students Association and is one of the oldest national Muslim organizations in the United States. It has a varied program primarily serving the Muslim community, but also seeks to promote friendly relations between Muslims and non-Muslims. It has a speakers' bureau, film loans, library assistance program, and several other services. It has also has a number of publications. Since ISNA is well represented throughout much of the United States, it is a good initial contact. It has been very active in the area of interfaith relations.

The Islamic Circle of North America (ICNA)
166-26 89th Ave.
Jamaica, NY 11432
Tel. (718)658-1199
Website: www.icna.org

The Islamic Circle of North America is a smaller national organization than ISNA, but is involved in many of the same activities. They also have a presence in many different parts of the country and provide a number of resources both to Muslims and non-Muslims. ICNA also has been very active in the world of interfaith relations.

The Muslim American Society
The Ministry of W. Deen Mohammed
P.O. Box 1944
Calumet City, IL 60409

This is the community of Imam W. Deen Mohammed and represents the largest single grouping of orthodox African-American Muslims in the United States. It is important to distinguish this group from the Nation of Islam (Black Muslims). African Americans constitute probably the largest single group of Muslims in the United States. Given the loose structure of the organization, it is often both possible and helpful to make contact with a local mosque in your area.

The American Muslim Council
1212 New York Ave. NW
Washington, D.C. 20005
Tel. (202)789-2262
Website: www.amermuslim.org
Exec. Dir., Dr. Aly R. Abuzaakouk,

This organization exists, in part, to represent the political and social interests of American Muslims and to defend their rights. It often has information about Muslim reaction to national and international events and also publishes informative booklets and brochures that include basic information on Islam and a journalistic style sheet.

JAINISM

Jainism was founded in the 6th century B.C.E. in India by Vardhamana Jnatiputra (also known as Nataputta Mahavira, whom the Jains call *Jina*, which means "Spiritual Conqueror"). Mahavira was a contemporary of the Buddha and, to some extent, Buddhism was an important rival to Jainism at the time. Both grew out of the Hindu tradition but rejected certain of its aspects. Jains honor a number of saints, or prophets from remote history called *tirthankaras,* who had liberated themselves from the bondage of *karma,* and hence from the cycle of reincarnation. Mahavira is the 24th of these *tirthankaras*. Emulating these saints, one may free the soul from the shackles of *karma* and rebirth, by observing the "three jewels" of "right faith," "right knowledge," and "right conduct." There is a strong emphasis in Jainism on peacefulness, moderation, and the refusal to injure animals in any way. There are religious orders, called *yatis,* which observe strict vows. The laity hold a pious respect for the *yatis*. There are two main branches of Jainism, the *Digambara* ("sky-clad" or "naked") and the *Svetambara* ("white-clad"). Despite the fact that the Jains constitute a relatively small proportion of the Indian population, they have a great influence on the Hindu community. The essential philosophy of nonviolence had a great effect on the teachings of Gandhi in this century.

Federation of Jain Associations in North America
66 Viscount
Williamsville, NY 14221
Tel. (716)688-3030

Siddhachalam/International Mahavira Jain Mission
65 Mud Pond Rd.
Blairstown, NJ 07285
Tel. (908)362-9793
Website: www.imjn.org
A residential center for the teaching of the Jain way of life in the United States.

JUDAISM

Judaism is one of the world's oldest religions, encompassing a rich and complex tradition that has evolved over centuries and has given rise to, or influenced, other major world traditions. Numerous expressions of Judaism have always coexisted with one another, as they do today. The central concern shared by all is to live in relation to God and to follow God's will. Jews understand themselves to be in covenant with God, who is the one transcendent God, Creator of the Universe. God revealed the Torah to the people of Israel as his way of life. History brought the Jewish people into contact with many cultures and civilizations, contacts that continuously transformed the nature of their worship, the understanding of God's law, and even their conceptualization of peoplehood. At the time of the second Diaspora—or great migration of Jews throughout the Middle East, North Africa, and Europe at the beginning of the common era—was the rise of the Rabbinical Tradition, with its emphasis on the study of scripture. Today's Judaism has grown out of these roots. In the 19th century, Reform Judaism arose in Europe and the United States as one Jewish response to modernity. Conservative Judaism and Reconstructionism are branches of Jewish practice that first developed in America. Orthodox Judaism also has a number of modern forms.

American Jewish Committee
165 East 56th St.
New York, NY 10022
Tel. (212)751-4000
Fax (212)750-0326
Website: www.ajc.org
Exec. Dir., David A. Harris

Founded in 1906, The AJC protects the rights and freedoms of Jews worldwide, combats bigotry and anti-Semitism and promotes democracy and human rights for all. It is an independent community-relations organization, with strong interest in interreligious relations and public-policy advocacy. The AJC publishes the *American Jewish Yearbook*, and *Commentary* magazine.

The Anti-Defamation League of B'nai B'rith
823 United Nations Plaza
New York, NY 10017
Tel. (212)885-7707
Fax (212)867-0779
Website: www.adl.org
National Dir., Abraham H. Foxman

Since 1913, the Anti-Defamation League has been involved in combating and documenting anti-Semitism. It also works to secure fair treatment for all citizens through law, education, and community relations.

Jewish Council for Public Affairs
443 Park Avenue S, 11th Floor
New York, NY 10016
Tel. (212)684-6950
Fax (212)686-1353
Website: www.JewishPublicAffairs.org
Exec. Dir., Hannah Rosenthal

This national coordinating body for the field of Jewish community relations comprises 13 national and 122 local Jewish communal agencies. Through the Council's work, and in its collaboration with other religious groups, its constituent agencies work on public policy issues, both international and domestic.

Jewish Reconstructionist Federation
7804 Montgomery Ave., Suite 9
Elkins Park, PA 19027
Tel. (212)782-8500
Email: jfrnatl@aol.com
Exec. Dir., Rabbi Mordechai Liebling

Fosters the establishment and ongoing life of Reconstructionist congregations and fellowship groups. Publishes *The Reconstructionist* and other materials. Rabbis who relate to this branch of Judaism are often members of the Reconstructionist Rabbinical Association.

Union of American Hebrew Congregations
633 Third Avenue
New York, NY 10017
Tel. (212)650-4000
Fax (212)650-4169
Website: www.uahc.org
Pres., Rabbi Eric H. Yoffie

The central congregational body of Reform Judaism, founded in 1873. It serves approx. 875 affiliated temples and its members through religious, educational, cultural, and administrative programs and Women's, Men's, and Youth organizations. *Reform Judaism* is one of its publications. The Central Conference of American Rabbis is the affiliated rabbinical body.

The Union of Orthodox Jewish Congregations of America
11 Broadway
New York, NY 10004-1003
Tel. (212)563-4000
Fax (212)564-9058
Website: www.ou.org
Exec.Vice Pres., Rabbi Tzvi Hersh Weinreb

The national central body of Orthodox synagogues since 1898, providing kashrut supervision; women's and youth organizations; and a variety of educational, religious, and public policy programs and activities. Publishers of *Jewish Action* magazine and other materials. The Rabbinical Council of America is the related organization for Orthodox Rabbis.

The United Synagogue of Conservative Judaism
155 Fifth Ave.
New York, NY 10010-6802
Tel. (212)533-7800
Fax (212)353-9439
Website: www.uscj.org
Exec. Vice Pres., Rabbi Jerome M. Epstein

The International organization of 800 congregations, founded in 1913. Provides religious, educational, youth, community, and administrative programming. Publishes *United Synagogue Review* and other materials. The Rabbinical Assembly is the association of Conservative Rabbis.

NATIVE AMERICAN TRADITIONAL SPIRITUALITY

Native American spirituality is difficult to define or categorize because it varies so greatly across the continent. Further, it is deeply entwined with elements of nature which are associated with different geographical regions. For example, while Plains Indians possess a spiritual relationship with the buffalo, Indigenous Peoples from the Northwest share a similar relationship with salmon. Hence, the character of Native American spirituality is dependent, to some extent, on the surrounding geography and its incumbent ecosystems. Despite this great variety, there are some similarities which allow us to consider the many Native American forms of spirituality together. Contrary to popular belief, Native American peoples are monotheistic; they do not worship the sun or buffalo or salmon, but rather understand that these elements of nature are gifts from the "Great Mystery," and are parts of it. Today, while still working toward religious freedom in the United States, Native Americans are also struggling to protect sacred sites, which they consider to be comparable to "churches." But since these sites are actually part of the land, not man-made structures, many are constantly under attack for the natural resources they contain. Such exploitation of these resources is an offense to the Native American sense of spirituality, which views resources like timber, oil, and gold, as gifts from the Great Mystery. The struggle to protect and respect these sacred sites is a universal and essential part of Native American spirituality.

National Congress of American Indians (NCAI)
1301 Connecticut Ave. NW
Suite 200
Washington, D.C. 20036
Tel. (202)466-7767
Fax (202)466-7797
Email: jdossett@ncia.org
Website: www.ncai.org
Exec. Dir., Jacqueline Johnson

The National Congress of American Indians (NCAI), founded in 1944, is the oldest, largest and most representative national Indian organization serving the needs of a broad membership of American Indian and Alaska Native governments. NCAI stresses the need for unity and cooperation among tribal governments and people for the security and protection of treaty and sovereign rights. As the preeminent national Indian organization, NCAI is organized as a representative congress aiming for consensus on national priority issues.

The NCAI website contains links for a directory of Indian nations in the continental US and Alaska as well as a directory of tribal governments. There are also links to other Native American websites.

Native American Rights Fund (NARF)
1506 Broadway
Boulder, CO 80302
Tel. (303)447-8760
Fax (303)433-7776
Email: pereira@narf.org
Website: www.narf.org
Exec. Dir., John Echohawk

The Native American Rights Fund is the nonprofit legal organization devoted to defending and promoting the legal rights of the Indian people. NARF attorneys, most of whom are Native Americans, defend tribes who otherwise cannot bear the financial burden of obtaining justice in the courts of the United States. The NARF mission statement outlines five areas of concentration: 1) Preservation of tribal existence, 2) Protection of tribal natural resources, 3) Promotion of human rights, 4) Accountability of government, 5) Development of Indian law.

SIKHISM

Sikhism was founded by Guru Nanak during the 15th and 16th centuries C.E. in the state of Punjab in northwestern India. Nanak was greatly influenced by the teachings of Kabir, a Muslim who became deeply inspired by Hindu philosophies. Kabir's poems called for a synthesis between Islam and Hinduism. In the footsteps of Kabir's wisdom, Nanak drew upon elements of Bhakti Hinduism and Sufi Islam. He stressed the existence of a universal, single God, who transcends religious distinctions. Union with God is accomplished through meditation and surrender to the divine will. Nanak also called for the belief in reincarnation, karma, and also the cyclical destruction and recreation of the universe. However, he rejected the caste system, the devotion to divine incarnations, priesthood, and idol worship, all of which were elements of the Hindu tradition. Nanak was the first of ten *gurus*, or teachers. The fourth guru built the Golden Temple in Amritsar, the Sikh religious center. The fifth guru compiled the *Adi Granth*, a sort of hymn-book of spiritual authority. All male sikhs are initiated into the religious brotherhood called the *Khalsa*. Members of this order vow never to cut their beard or hair, to wear special pants, to wear an iron bangle as an amulet against evil, to carry a steel dagger, and a comb.

The Sikh Center of Orange County
2514 W. Warner Ave.
Santa Ana, CA 92704
Tel. (714)979-9328
Website: www.sikhcenter.org

The Sikh Center of Orange County describes itself as follows: "Our mission, in following the tradition and teaching of our honorable Guru Nanak, is to provide accurate, reliable and complete religious, social and cultural teachings and understanding of Sikhism and the people who practice it."

7. United States Regional and Local Ecumenical Bodies

One of the many ways Christians and Christian churches relate to one another locally and regionally is through ecumenical bodies. The membership in these ecumenical organizations is diverse. Historically, councils of churches were formed primarily by Protestants, but many local and regional organizations now include Orthodox and Roman Catholics. Many are made up of congregations or judicatory units of churches. Some have a membership base of individuals. Others foster cooperation between ministerial groups, community ministries, coalitions, or church agencies. While "council of churches" is a term still commonly used to describe this form of cooperation, other terms such as "conference of churches," "ecumenical councils," "churches united," "metropolitan ministries," are coming into use. Ecumenical organizations that are national in scope are listed in Directory 1, "United States Cooperative Organizations."

An increasing number of ecumenical bodies have been exploring ways to strengthen the interreligious aspect of life in the context of religious pluralism in the US today. Some organizations in this listing are fully interfaith agencies primarily through the inclusion of Jewish congregations in their membership. Other organizations nurture partnerships with a broader base of religious groups in their communities, especially in the areas of public policy and interreligious dialogue.

This list does not include all local and regional ecumenical and interfaith organizations in existence today. The terms regional and local are relative, making identification somewhat ambiguous. Regional councils may cover sections of large states or cross-state borders. Local councils may be made up of several counties, towns, or clusters of congregations. State councils or state-level ecumenical contacts exist in 45 of the 50 states. These state-level or multi-state organizations are marked with a "*". The organizations are listed alphabetically by state.

ALABAMA

Greater Birmingham Ministries

2304 12th Ave. N, Birmingham, AL 35234-3111 Tel. (205)326-6821 Fax (205)252-8458
Email: robert@gbm.org
Website: www.gbm.org
Media Contact, Robert Montgomery
Exec. Dir., Scott Douglas
Economic Justice: Co-Chpsn., Helen Holdefer, Betty Likis
Direct Services: Chpsn., Patty Warren
Faith in Community: Chpsn., Patricia Ross
Finance & Fund-Raising: Chpsn., Richard Ambrose
Pres., Tom Forsee
Treas., Helen Tibbs Wilson
Major Activities: Direct Service Ministries (Food, Utilities, Rent, and Nutrition Education, Shelter), Alabama Arise (Statewide legislative network focusing on low income issues), Economic Justice Issues (Low Income Housing and Advocacy, Health Care, Community Development, Jobs Creation, Public Transportation), Faith in Community Ministries (Interchurch Forum, Interpreting and Organizing, Bible Study)

Interfaith Mission Service

411-B Holmes Ave. NE, Huntsville, AL 35801 Tel. (256)536-2401 Fax (256)536-2284
Email: ims@hiwaay.net
Exec. Dir., Susan J. Smith
Pres., Richard C. Titus
Major Activities: Foodline and Food Pantry, Local FEMA Committee, Ministry Development, Clergy Luncheon, Workshops, Response to Community Needs, Information and Referral, Interfaith Understanding, Christian Unity, Homeless Needs, School Readiness Screenings

ALASKA

Alaska Christian Conference

Episcopal Diocese of Alaska, 1205 Denali Way, Fairbanks, AK 99701-4178 Tel. (907)452-3040
Email: mmcdonald@gci.net
Media Contact, Rt. Rev. Mark MacDonald
Pres., Rt. Rev. Mark MacDonald
Vice Pres., Rev. David I. Blanchett, 1100 Pullman Dr., Wasilla, AK 99654 Tel. (907)352-2517
Treas., Carolyn M. Winters, 2133 Bridgewater Dr., Fairbanks, AK 99709-4101 Tel. (907)456-8555
Major Activities: Legislative and Social Concerns, Resources and Continuing Education, New Ecumenical Ministries, Communication, Alcoholism (Education and Prevention), Family Violence (Education and Prevention), Native Issues, Ecumenical/Theological Dialogue, HIV-AIDS Education and Ministry, Criminal Justice

ARIZONA

Arizona Ecumenical Council*

4423 N. 24th St., Ste. 750, Phoenix, AZ 85016 Tel. (602)468-3818 Fax (602)468-3839
Media Contact, Exec. Dir. Dr. Paul Eppinger, Tel. (602)967-6040 Fax (602)468-3839
Exec. Dir., Dr. Paul Eppinger
Pres., Rev. Gail Davis, 4423 N. 24th St. Ste. 700, Phoenix, AZ 85016
Major Activities: Donohoe Ecumenical Forum Series, Political Action Team, Legislative Workshop, Arizona Ecumenical Indian Concerns Committee, Mexican-American Border Issues, ISN-TV, Disaster Relief, Break Violence-Build Community, Truckin' for Kids, "Souper Bowl," Gun Information and Safety Program

ARKANSAS

Arkansas Interfaith Conference*

P.O. Box 151, Scott, AR 72142 Tel. (501)961-2626
Email: aicark@aol.com
Media Contact, Conf. Exec., Mimi Dortch
Conf. Exec., Mimi Dortch
Pres., Rev. Steve Copley, P.O. Box 88 Gielett, AR 72055 (Methodist)
Sec., Imam John Hasan. P.O.Box 1607, Little Rock, AR 72203 (Muslim)
Treas., Jim Davis, Box 7239, Little Rock, AR 72217 (Catholic)
Major Activities: Institutional Ministry, Interfaith Executives' Advisory Council, Interfaith Relations, Church Women United, Our House–Shelter, Legislative Liaison, Ecumenical Choir Camp, Tornado Disaster Relief, Camp for Jonesboro School Children Massacre, Welfare Reform Work, Med Center Chaplaincy, Peace Service

CALIFORNIA

California Council of Churches-California Church Impact*

2715 "K" St., Ste. D, Sacramento, CA 95816 Tel. (916)442-5447 Fax (916)442-3036
Email: cccinfo@calchurches.org
Website: www.calchurches.org
Media Contact, Exec. Dir., The Rev. Rick Schlosser
Exec. Dir., The Rev. Rick Schlosser
Major Activities: Monitoring State Legislation, California IMPACT Network, Legislative Principles, Food Policy Advocacy, Family Welfare Issues, Health, Church-State Issues, Violence Prevention, Child Care Program–Capacity Coordinator to Increase Quality Child Care within California for the Working Poor, Building Bridges of Understanding: An Interfaith Response to Septerber 11

The Council of Churches of Santa Clara County

1710 Moorpark Ave., San Jose, CA 95128 Tel. (408)297-2660 Fax (408)297-2661
Email: councilchurches@aol.com
Media Contact, Interim Ex. Dir., Rev. R. Richard Roe
Interim Exec. Dir., Rev. R. Richard Roe
Pres., Rev. Dr. Kristin Sundquist
Major Activities: Social Education/Action, Ecumenical and Interfaith Witness, Affordable Housing, Environmental Ministry, Family/Children, Convalescent Hospital Ministries, Gay Ministry

The Ecumenical Council of Pasadena Area Churches

P.O. Box 41125, 444 E. Washington Blvd., Pasadena, CA 91114-8125 Tel. (626)797-2402 Fax (626)797-7353
Email: ecpac@prodigy.net
Exec. Dir., Rev. Frank B. Clark
Major Activities: Christian Education, Community Worship, Community Concerns, Christian Unity, Ethnic Ministries, Hunger, Peace, Food, Clothing Assistance for the Poor, Emergency Shelter

Fresno Metro Ministry

1055 N. Van Ness, Ste. H, Fresno, CA 93728 Tel. (559)485-1416 Fax (559)485-9109
Email: metromin@fresnometmin.org
Website: www.fresnometmin.org
Media Contact, Exec. Dir., Rev. Walter P. Parry
Exec. Dir., Rev. Walter P. Parry
Pres., Vida Samilian
Major Activities: Hunger Relief and Nutrition Advocacy, Cultural Diversity and Anti-Racism, Health Care Advocacy, Environmental Health, Public Education Concerns, Children's Needs, Biblical and Theological Education For Laity, Ecumenical and Interfaith Celebrations and Cooperation, Youth Needs, Community Network Building, Human Services Facilitation, Anti-Poverty Efforts, Hate Crime Prevention and Response

Interfaith Council of Contra Costa County

1543 Sunnyvale Ave., Walnut Creek, CA 94596 Tel. (925)933-6030 Fax (925)952-4554
Chaplains: Rev. Charles Tinsley, Rev. Duane Woida, Rev. Harold Wright, Laurie Maxwell
Pres., Rev. Steve Harms
Treas., Robert Bender
Major Activities: Institutional Chaplaincies, Community Education, Interfaith Cooperation, Social Justice

Interfaith Service Bureau

2212 K. St., Sacramento, CA 95816-4923 Tel. (916)456-3815 Fax (916)456-3816

Email: isbdexter@aol.com
Media Contact, Executive Dir., Dexter McNamara
Executive Dir., Dexter McNamara
Pres., Richard Montgomery
Vice Pres., Lloyd Hanson
Major Activities: Religious and Racial Cooperation and Understanding, Welfare Reform Concerns, Refugee Resettlement and Support, Religious Cable Television, Violence Prevention, Graffiti Abatement

Marin Interfaith Council

845 Olive Ave., Suite 110, Novato, CA 94945 Tel. (415)209-6278 Fax (415)209-6527
Email: administration@marininterfaithcouncil.org
Website: marininterfaithcouncil.org
Media Contact, Exec. Dir., Rev. Kevin F. Tripp
Exec. Dir., Rev. Kevin F. Tripp
Major Activities: Interfaith Dialogue, Education, Advocacy, Convening, Interfaith Worship Services and Commemorations

Northern California Interreligious Conference

534 22nd St., Oakland, CA 94612 Tel. (510)433-0822 Fax (510)433-0813
Email: NCIC@igc.org
Website: ncic.home.igc.org
Media Contact, Pres., Rev. Phil Lawson
Exec. Dir., Catherine Coleman
Pres., Rev. Phil Lawson
Vice Pres., Esther Ho
Sec., Robert Forsberg
Major Activities: Peace with Justice Commission; Interreligious Relationships Commission; Public Policy Advocacy; Welfare Reform; Founding member of California Council of Churches and of California Interfaith Power and Light; Soul of Justice, a spiritual and leadership concepts interactive performance troupe of teens and young adults; death penalty moratorium; video produced for sale for congregations/organizations to study legal, theological, and social implications of marriage and same gender marriage; widening our circle of religious groups participating; a cooperating circle of URL

Pacific and Asian American Center for Theology and Strategies (PACTS)

Graduate Theological Union, 2400 Ridge Rd., Berkeley, CA 94709 Tel. (510)849-0653
Email: pacts@igc.org
Media Contact, Dir., Kyle Minura
Dir., Kyle Minura
Pres., Ronald Nakasone
Major Activities: Collect and Disseminate Resource Materials; Training Conferences; Public Seminars; Women in Ministry; Racial and Ethnic Minority Concerns; Journal and Newsletter; Hawaii and Greater Pacific Programme; Sale of Sadao Watanabe Calendars; Informational Forums on Peace and Social Justice in Asian Pacific American Community and Asia-Pacific Internationally; Forums and Conferences for Seminarians Asian Pacific Heritage; holistic health and healing ministries; affirming support groups for gay, lesbian, transgender; and questioning Asian and Pacific Islanders.

Pomona Inland Valley Council of Churches

1753 N. Park Ave., Pomona, CA 91768 Tel. (909)622-3806 Fax (909)622-0484
Media Contact, Dir. of Development, Mary Kashmar
Pres., The Rev. Henry Rush
Acting Exec. Dir., The Rev. La Quetta Bush-Simmons
Sec., Ken Coates
Treas., Anne Ashford
Major Activities: Advocacy and Education for Social Justice, Ecumenical Celebrations, Hunger Advocacy, Emergency Food and Shelter Assistance, Farmer's Market, Affordable Housing, Transitional Housing

Ecumenical Council of San Diego County

1880 Third Ave. #13, San Diego, CA 92101
Email: johnston@ecsd.org
Website: www.ecsd.org
Exec. Dir., Rosemary Johnston
Deputy Dir., Rev. Glenn Allison
Pres., Art C. Cribbs
Treas., Rev. Robert Ard
Major Activities: Interfaith Shelter Network–Rational Shelter and El Nido Transitional Living Program, Emerging Issues, Faith Order and Witness, Worship and Celebration, Ecumenical Tribute Dinner, Advent Prayer Breakfast, AIDS Chaplaincy Program, Third World Opportunities, Seminars and Workshops, Called to Dance Assn., S.D. Names Project Quilt, Children's Sabbath Workshops and events, Edgemoor Chaplaincy, Stand for Children events, Continuing Education for clergy and laypersons, Inter-Religious Council

San Fernando Valley Interfaith Council

10824 Topanga Canyon Blvd., No. 7, Chatsworth, CA 91311 Tel. (818)718-6460 Fax (818)718-0734
Email: sfvic@earthlink.net
Website: www.sfvic.org
Media Contact, Communications Coord., Eileen Killoren, ext. 3002
Exec. Dir., Barry Smedberg, ext. 3011

Pres., Ms. Katherine Rousseau
Major Activities: Seniors Multi-Purpose Centers, Nutrition and Services, Meals to Homebound, Meals on Wheels, Interfaith Reporter, Interfaith Relations, Social Adult Day Care, Hunger/Homelessness, Volunteer Care-Givers, Clergy Gatherings, Food Pantries and Outreach, Social Concerns, Aging, Hunger, Human Relations, Child Abuse Program, Medical Service, Homeless Program, Disaster Response Preparedness, Immigration Services, Self-Sufficiency Program for Section 8 Families

South Coast Ecumenical Council

759 Linden Ave., Long Beach, CA 90813 Tel. (562)595-0268 Fax (562)490-9920
Email: SCEC2@earthlink.net
Website: www.southcoastecumenical.org
Media Contact, Exec. Dir., Rev. Ginny Wagener
Exec. Dir., Rev. Ginny Wagener
Farmers' Markets, Rev. Dale Whitney
Pres., Dottie Wine
Centro Shalom, Amelia Nieto
Major Activities: Homeless Support Services, Farmers' Markets, CROP Hunger Walks, Church Athletic Leagues, Community Action, Easter Sunrise Worships, Interreligious Dialogue, Justice Advocacy, Martin Luther King Jr. Celebration, Violence Prevention, Long Beach Interfaith Clergy, Publishing Area Religious Directories

Southern California Ecumenical Council

54 N. Oakland Ave., Pasadena, CA 91101-2086 Tel. (626)578-6371 Fax (626)578-6358
Email: scec1@earthlink.net
Website: scec.faithweb.com
Media Contact, Exec. Dir., Rev. Albert G. Cohen
Exec. Dir., Rev. Albert G. Cohen
Pres., Fr. Ashag Khatchadourian
Treas., Rev. Paul Lance
Sec., Ms. Lucy Guernsey
V.P. Special Events, Dr. Gwynne Guibord
Members at Large: Rev. Dr. Efstathios Mylonas, Ms. Laura Ramirez, Fr. Alexei Smith
Faith and Order Chair, Rev. Dr. Rod Parrott
Past Pres., Rev. Donald Smith
Major Activities: Consultation with the regional religious sector concerning the well being and spiritual vitality of this most diverse and challenging area

Westside Interfaith Council

P.O. Box 1402, Santa Monica, CA 90406 Tel. (310)394-1518 Fax (310)576-1895
Media Contact, Rev. Janet A. Bregar
Exec. Dir., Rev. Janet A. Bregar
Major Activities: Meals on Wheels, Community Religious Services, Convalescent Hospital Chaplaincy, Homeless Partnership, Hunger and Shelter Coalition

COLORADO

Colorado Council of Churches*

3690 Cherry Creek S. Dr., Denver, CO 80209 Tel. (303)825-4910 Fax (303)744-8605
Email: jryan@americanisp.net
Website: www.coloradocouncilofchurches.org
Media Contact, Council Executive, Rev. Dr. James R. Ryan
Pres., Rev. Sarah Leatherman-Young
Staff Assoc, Dori Wilson
Major Activities: Addressing issues of Christian Unity, Justice, and Environment

Interfaith Council of Boulder

3700 Baseline Rd., Boulder, CO 80303 Tel. (303)494-8094
Media Contact, Pres., Stan Grotegut, 810 Kalma Ave., Boulder, CO 80304 Tel. (303)443-2291
Pres., Stan Grotegut
Major Activities: Interfaith Dialogue and Programs, Thanksgiving Worship Services, Food for the Hungry, Share-A-Gift, Monthly Newsletter

CONNECTICUT

Association of Religious Communities

325 Main St., Danbury, CT 06810 Tel. (203)792-9450 Fax (203)792-9452
Email: arc325@aol.com
Media Contact, Exec. Dir., Rev. Phyllis J. Leopold
Exec. Dir., Rev. Phyllis J. Leopold
Pres., The Rev. Mark Lingle
Major Activities: Refugee Resettlement, Family Counseling, Family Violence Prevention, Affordable Housing, Interfaith Dialogue, Racial Justice

The Capitol Region Conference of Churches

60 Lorrain St., Hartford, CT 06105 Tel. (860)236-1295 Fax (860)236-8071
Email: crcc@conferenceofchurches.org
Website: www.conferenceofchurches.org
Media Contact, Exec. Dir., Rev. Shelley Copeland
Exec. Dir., Rev. Shelley Copeland
Pastoral Care & Training: Dir., Rev. Kathleen Davis
Aging Project: Dir., Barbara Malcolm
Community Organizer, Joseph Wasserman
Broadcast Ministry Consultant, Ivor T. Hugh
Pres., Mr. David O. White
Major Activities: Organizing for Peace and Justice, Aging, Legislative Action, Cooperative Broadcast Ministry, Ecumenical Cooperation, Interfaith Reconciliation, Chaplaincies, Low-Income Senior Empowerment, Anti-Racism Education

Center City Churches

40 Pratt Street, Ste. 210, Hartford, CT 06103-1601 Tel. (860)728-3201 Fax (860)549-8550

Email: info@ccchartford.org
Media Contact, Exec. Dir., Paul C. Christie
Exec. Dir., Paul C. Christie
Pres., Terry Davis
Treas., Frank Lord
Major Activities: Senior Services, Family Resource Center, Energy Bank, Food Pantry, Assistance and Advocacy, After-School Tutoring and Arts Enrichment, Summer Day Camp, Housing for persons with AIDS, Community Soup Kitchen

Christian Community Action

168 Davenport Ave., New Haven, CT 06519 Tel. (203)777-7848 Fax (203)777-7923
Email: cca@ccahelping.org
Website: www.ccahelping.org
Media Contact, Exec. Dir., The Rev. Bonita Grubbs
Exec. Dir., The Rev. Bonita Grubbs
Major Activities: Emergency Food Program, Used Furniture and Clothing, Security and Fuel, Emergency Housing for Families, Advocacy, Transitional Housing for Families

Christian Conference of Connecticut*

60 Lorraine St., Hartford, CT 06105 Tel. (860) 236-4281 Fax (860)236-9977
Email: ssidorak@aol.com
Website: www.christconn.org
Media Contact, Exec. Dir., Rev. Dr. Stephen J. Sidorak Jr.
Exec. Dir., The Rev. Dr. Stephen J. Sidorak Jr.
Pres., The Rev. Dr. Robert C. Dvorak
Vice Pres., The Most Rev. Daniel A. Cronin
Sec., The Rev. Samuel N. Slie
Treas., Mr. Minot B. Nettleton
Major Activities: Communications, Institutional Ministries, Connecticut Ecumenical Council on Addiction, Ecumenical Forum, Faith and Order, Social Concerns, Public Policy, Peace and Justice Convocation, Restorative Justice & Death Penalty, Interreligious Dialogue and Interreligious Action on Economic Justice, Housing and Human Services Ministry, Anti-Nuclear Activities, Problem Gambling

Council of Churches of Greater Bridgeport, Inc.

180 Fairfield Ave., Bridgeport, CT 06604 Tel. (203)334-1121 Fax (203)367-8113
Email: ccgb@ccgb.org
Website: www.ccgb.org
Media Contact, Exec. Dir., Rev. John S. Kidd
Exec. Dir., Rev. John S. Kidd
Pres., Ms. Collin Vice
Vice Pres., Rev. Dr. Brian Schofield-Bodt
Sec., Sharon Dobbins Alberson
Treas., Roger Perry
Major Activities: Youth in Crisis, Safe Places, Youth Shelter, Criminal Justice, Nursing Home and Jail Ministries, Local Hunger, Ecumenical Inter-Religious Relations, Prayer and Celebration, Covenantal Ministries, Homework Help, Summer Programs, Race Relations/Bridge Building,

Council of Churches and Synagogues of Southwestern Connecticut

461 Glenbrook Rd, Stamford, CT 06901 Tel. (203)348-2800 Fax (203)358-0627
Email: council@flvax.ferg.lib.ct.us
Website: www.interfaithcouncil.org
Media Contact, Communications Ofc., Lois Alcosser
Exec. Dir., Jack Penfield, Interim Director
Major Activities: Partnership Against Hunger, The Food Bank of Lower Fairfield County, Friendly Visitors and Friendly Shoppers, Senior Neighborhood Support Services, Christmas in April, Interfaith Programming, Prison Visitation, Friendship House, Help a Neighbor, Operation Fuel, Teaching Place

Greater Waterbury Interfaith Ministries, Inc.

84 Crown St., Waterbury, CT 06704 Tel. (203) 756-7831 Fax (203)419-0024
Media Contact, Exec. Dir., Carroll E. Brown
Exec. Dir., Carroll E. Brown
Pres., The Rev. Dr. James G. Bradley
Major Activities: Emergency Food Program, Emergency Fuel Program, Soup Kitchen, Ecumenical Worship, Christmas Toy Sale, Annual Hunger Walk

Manchester Area Conference of Churches

P.O. Box 3804, Manchester, CT 06045-3804 Tel. (860)647-8003
Media Contact, Exec. Dir., Denise Cabana
Exec. Dir., Denise Cabana
Dir. of Community Ministries: Joseph Piescik
Dept.of Ministry Development: Dir., Karen Bergin
Pres., Rev. Charles Ericson
Vice Pres., Theresa Ghabrial
Sec., Jean Richert
Treas., Clive Perrin
Major Activities: Provision of Basic Needs (Food, Fuel, Clothing, Furniture), Emergency Aid Assistance, Emergency Shelter, Soup Kitchen, Reentry Assistance to Sex-Offenders, Pastoral Care in Local Institutions, Interfaith Day Camp, Advocacy for the Poor, Ecumenical Education and Worship

New Britain Area Conference of Churches (NEWBRACC)

830 Corbin Ave., New Britain, CT 06052 Tel. (860)229-3751 Fax (860)223-3445
Media Contact, Exec. Dir., Michael Gorzoch
Exec. Dir., Michael Gorzoch
Pastoral Care-Chaplaincy: Rev. Ron Smith, Rev. Will Baumgartner, Rev. Rod Rinnel

Pres., Rev. Anne Marie Meyerhoffer
Treas., Joyce Chmura
Major Activities: Worship, Social Concerns, Emergency Food Bank Support, Communications-Mass Media, Hospital, Elderly Programming, Homelessness and Hunger Programs, Telephone Ministry

DELAWARE

The Christian Council of Delaware and Maryland's Eastern Shore*

2020 N. Tatnall Street, Wilmington, DE 19802 Tel. (302)-656-5441
Website: www.DeMdSynod.org
Media Contact, Pres., Bishop Wayne P. Wright, Diocese of Delaware, 2020 N. Tatnall Street, Wilmington, DE 19802
Pres., Bishop Wayne P. Wright, Diocese of Delaware, 2020 N. Tatnall Street, Wilmington, DE 19802
Moderator, The Rev. Patricia McClurg, Presbyterian Church (USA), E-62 Omega Drive, Newark, DE 19713
Major Activities: Exploring Common Theological, Ecclesiastical and Community Concerns, Racism, Prisons

DISTRICT OF COLUMBIA

The Council of Churches of Greater Washington

5 Thomas Circle NW, Washington, D.C. 20005 Tel. (202)722-9240 Fax (202)722-9241
Media Contact, Exec. Dir., The Rev. Rodger Hall Reed, Sr.
Pres., The Rev. Lewis Anthony
Exec. Dir., The Rev. Rodger Hall Reed, Sr.
Program Officer, Daniel M. Thompson
Major Activities: Promotion of Christian Unity/Ecumenical Prayer and Worship, Coordination of Community Ministries, Summer Youth Employment, Summer Camping–Inner City Youth, Supports wide variety of social justice concerns

InterFaith Conference of Metropolitan Washington

1426 Ninth St. NW, Washington, D.C. 20001-3344 Tel. (202)234-6300 Fax (202)234-6303
Email: ifc@interfaith-metrodc.org
Website: www.interfaith-metrodc.org
Media Contact, Exec. Dir., Rev. Dr. Clark Lobenstine
Exec. Dir., Rev. Dr. Clark Lobenstine
Admn. Sec., Najla Robinson
Pres., Rev. Elizabeth Orens
1st Vice Pres., Ms. Amrit Kaur
Chpsn., Mr. Jack Serber
Sec., Janice Sadeghian, PhD
Treas., Ms. Frances B. Albers
Major Activities: Interfaith Dialogue, Interfaith Concert, Racial and Ethnic Polarization, Youth Leadership Training, Hunger, Homelessness, Church-State Zoning Issues

FLORIDA

Christian Service Center for Central Florida, Inc.

808 W. Central Blvd., Orlando, FL 32805-1809 Tel. (407)425-2523 Fax (407)425-9513
Media Contact, Exec. Dir., Robert F. Stuart
Exec. Dir., Robert F. Stuart
Family Emergency Services: Dir., LaVerne Sainten
Alzheimers Respite: Dir., Mary Ellen Ort-Marvin
Fresh Start: Dir., Rev. Haggeo Gautier
Dir. of Mktg., Margaret Ruffier-Farris
Pres., Dr. Charles Horton
Treas., Rick Crandall
Sec., Annie Harris
Major Activities: Provision of Basic Needs (food, clothing, shelter), Emergency Assistance, Noon-time Meals, Sunday Church Services at Walt Disney World, Collection and Distribution of Used Clothing, Shelter and Training for Homeless, Respite for Caregivers of Alzheimers

Florida Council of Churches*

924 N. Magnolia Ave., Ste. 304, Orlando, FL 32803 Tel. (407)839-3454 Fax (407)246-0019
Email: fced@aol.com
Website: www.floridachurches.org
Media Contact, Exec. Dir., Rev. Fred Morris
Exec. Dir., Rev. Fred Morris
Associate Dir., H. Basil Nichols,
Project Director, Cherishing the Creation, Russell Gebet
Major Activities: Justice and Peace, Disaster Response, Legislation and Public Policy, Local Ecumenism, Farmworker Ministry, Cherishing the Creation (Environmental Stewardship)

GEORGIA

Christian Council of Metropolitan Atlanta

465 Boulevard SE, Atlanta, GA 30312 Tel. (404)622-2235 Fax (404)627-6626
Email: dojccma@aol.com
Media Contact, Dir. of Development & Communication, Jane Hopson Enniss
Exec. Dir., Rev. Dr. David O. Jenkins
Assoc. Dir., -vacant-
Pres., Rev. Elizabeth Rechter
Major Activities: Refugee Services, Commission on Children and Youth, Supervised Ministry, Homeless, Ecumenical and Interreligious Events, Persons with Handicapping Conditions, Women's Concerns, Task Force on Prison Ministry, Quarterly Forums on Ecumenical Issues, Faith and Order Concerns, Interracial and Intercultural Emphasis

Georgia Christian Council*

P.O. Box 7193, Macon, GA 31209-7193 Tel. (478)743-2085 Fax (478)743-2085
Email: lccollins@juno.com
Website: georgiachurches.org
Media Contact, Exec. Dir., Rev. Leland C. Collins
Exec. Dir., Rev. Leland C. Collins
Pres., Rev. Dr. Tom Neal, 2370 Vineville Ave., Macon, GA 31204
Sec., Rev. Scudder Edwards, 6865 Turner Ct., Cumming, GA 30131
Major Activities: Local Ecumenical Support and Resourcing, Legislation, Rural Development, Racial Justice, Networking for Migrant Coalition, Aging Coalition, GA To GA With Love, Medical Care, Prison Chaplaincy, Training for Church Development, Souper Bowl, Disaster Relief, Clustering, Development of Local Ecumenism

IDAHO

The Regional Council for Christian Ministry, Inc.

237 N. Water, Idaho Falls, ID 83403 Tel. (208) 524-9935
Exec. Sec., Wendy Schoonmaker
Major Activities: Island Park Ministry, Community Food Bank, Community Observances, Community Information and Referral Service, F.I.S.H.

ILLINOIS

Churches United of the Quad City Area

630 9th St., Rock Island, IL 61201 Tel. (309)786-6494 Fax (309)786-5916
Email: mjones@churchesunited.net
Website: www.churchesunited.net
Media Contact, Exec. Dir., Rev. Ronald Quay
Exec. Dir., Ronald Quay
Program Manager, Anne E. Wachal
Pres., Ms. Betty Yohnka
Pres.-Elect, Mr. Joseph Lindsay
Treas., Mr. Bill Schmidt
Major Activities: Jail Ministry, Hunger Projects, Minority Enablement, Criminal Justice, Radio/TV, Peace, Local Church Development, Living Wage

Community Renewal Society

332 South Michigan Ave. Suite 500, Chicago, IL 60604 Tel. (312)427-4830 Fax (312)427-6130
Email: csmorris@crs-ucc.org
Website: www.crs-ucc.org
Media Contact, Exec. Dir., Dr. Calvin S. Morris
To Be Faxed on 11-3-02
Major Activities:

Contact Ministries of Springfield

1100 E. Adams, Springfield, IL 62703 Tel. (217)753-3939 Fax (217)753-8643
Email: rtarrcm@springnetl.com
Media Contact, Exec. Dir., Rita Tarr
Exec. Dir., Rita Tarr
Major Activities: Information, Referral and Advocacy, Ecumenical Coordination, Low Income Housing Referral, Food Pantry Coordination, Prescription and Travel Emergency, Low Income Budget Counseling, 24 hours on call, Emergency Shelter On-site, Women with Children

Evanston Ecumenical Action Council

P.O. Box 1414, Evanston, IL 60204 Tel. (847)475-1150 Fax (847)475-2526
Website: members.aol.com/eeachome/eeac.html
Media Contact, Comm. Chpsn., Ken Wylie
Dir. Hospitality Cntr. for the Homeless, Sue Murphy
Co-Pres., Rev. Ted Miller, Rev. Hardist Lane
Treas., Caroline Frowe
Major Activities: Interchurch Communication and Education, Peace and Justice Ministries, Coordinated Social Action, Soup Kitchens, Multi-Purpose Hospitality Center for the Homeless, Worship and Renewal, Racial Reconciliation, Youthwork

Greater Chicago Broadcast Ministries

112 E. Chestnut St., Chicago, IL 60611-2014 Tel. (312)988-9001 Fax (312)988-9004
Email: gcbm@ameritech.net
Media Contact, Exec. Dir., Lydia Talbot
Pres., Bd. of Dir., Eugene H. Winkler
Exec. Dir., Lydia Talbot
Admn. Asst., Margaret Early
Major Activities: Television, Cable, Interfaith/Ecumenical Development, Social-Justice Concerns

The Hyde Park & Kenwood Interfaith Council

5745 S. Blackstone Ave., Chicago, IL 60637 Tel. (773)752-1911 Fax (773)752-2676
Media Contact, Exec. Dir., Lesley M. Radius
Exec. Dir., Lesley M. Radius
Pres., Rev. David Grainger
Sec., Barbara Krell
Major Activities: Interfaith Work, Hunger Projects, Community Development

Illinois Conference of Churches*

522 East Monroe, Ste. 208, Springfield, IL 62701 Tel. (217)522-7105 Fax (217)522-7100
Email: adminstaff@ilconfchurches.org
Website: ilconfchurches.org
Media Contact, Exec. Dir., Rev. David A. Anderson, davidanderson@ilconfchurhces.org
Exec. Dir., Rev. David A. Anderson
Assoc. Dir., -vacant-
Pres., Rev. Donald E. Mason

Major Activities: Unity and Relationships Commission, Council of Judicatory Executives, Ecumenical Forums and Retreats, Triennial Ecumenical Assembly, Church and Society Commission, Public Policy Ecumenical Network, Global Ecumenism on Cuba, Racism, Economic Justice, Universal Health Care

Oak Park-River Forest Community of Congregations

P.O. Box 3365, Oak Park, IL 60303-3365 Tel. (708)386-8802 Fax (708)386-1399
Website: www.mcs.net/~grossman/comcong.htm
Media Contact, Patricia C. Koko
Admn. Sec., Patricia C. Koko
Pres., Mr. Leonard Grossman
Treas., Rev. Mark Reshan
Major Activities: Community Affairs, Ecumenical/Interfaith Affairs, Youth Education, Food Pantry, Senior Citizens Worship Services, Interfaith Thanksgiving Services, Good Friday Services, UNICEF Children's Fund Drive, Blood Drive, Literacy Training, CROP-CWS Hunger Walkathon, Work with Homeless Through PADS (Public Action to Deliver Shelter), Diversity Education

Peoria Friendship House of Christian Service

800 NE Madison Ave., Peoria, IL 61603 Tel. (309)671-5200 Fax (309)671-5206
Media Contact, Exec. Dir., Beverly Isom
Pres. of Bd., David Dadds
Major Activities: Children's After-School, Teen Programs, Recreational Leagues, Senior Citizens Activities, Emergency Food/Clothing Distribution, Emergency Payments for Prescriptions, Rent, Utilities, Community Outreach, Economic Development, Neighborhood Empowerment, GED Classes, Family Literacy, Mother's Group, Welfare to Work Programs

INDIANA

The Associated Churches of Fort Wayne & Allen County, Inc.

602 E. Wayne St., Fort Wayne, IN 46802 Tel. (219)422-3528 Fax (219)422-6721
Email: Vernchurch@aol.com
Website: www.associatedchurches.org
Media Contact, Exec. Dir., Rev. Vernon R. Graham
Exec. Dir., Rev. Vernon R. Graham
Administrative Assistant, Elaine Williamson
Foodbank: Ellen Graham, John Kaiser, John Lassen, Jenny Varecha
Dir. Of Prog. Development & Mission Outreach, Ellen Graham
Dir. Of Weekday Religious Education, Kathy Rolf
Pres., Ruth Jansen, 15535 Lost Valley Dr., Ft. Wayne, IN 46845
Treas., Rev. Alycia Smith, 3223 Hobson Rd., Ft. Wayne, IN 46805
Major Activities: Weekday Religious Ed., Church Clusters, Church and Society Commission, Overcoming Racism, A Baby's Closet, CROP, Campus Ministry, Feeding the Babies, Food Bank System, Peace and Justice Commission, Welfare Reform, Endowment Development, Child Care Advocacy, Advocates Inc., Ecumenical Dialogue, Feeding Children, Vincent House (Homeless), A Learning Journey (Literacy), Reaching Out in Love, The Jail Ministry, The Smaritan Counseling Center.

Christian Ministries of Delaware County

401 E. Main St., Muncie, IN 47305 Tel. (317)288-0601 Fax (317)282-4522
Email: christianministries@netzero.net
Website: www.christianministries.ws
Media Contact, Exec. Dir., Marie Evans
Exec. Dir., Marie Evans
Pres., Dr. J. B. Black Jr.
Treas., Joan McKee
Major Activities: Baby Care Program, Youth Ministry at Detention Center, Community Church Festivals, Food Pantry, Emergency Assistance, CROP Walk, Social Justice, Family Life Education, Homeless Shelter (sleeping room only), Clothing and Household Items Available Free, Workshops for Low Income Clients, Homeless Apartments (short stays only at no cost), Programs and Workshops for Pastors and Churches in Community, Work with Schools Sponsoring Programs.

Church Community Services

629 S. 3rd Street, Elkhart, IN 46516-3241 Tel. (574)295-3673 Fax (574)295-5593
Email: ccs6293rd@aol.com
Website: www.soupofsuccess.com
Media Contact, Rev. Jeni Hiett Umble
Exec. Dir., Rev. Jeni Hiett Umble
Major Activities: Financial Assistance for Emergencies, Food Pantry, Information and Referral, Clothing Referral, Laundry Vouchers, Medication Vouchers, Transporta-tion Vouchers, Job and Life Skills Training Program for Women

The Church Federation of Greater Indianapolis, Inc.

1100 W. 42nd St., Ste. 345, Indianapolis, IN 46208 Tel. (317)926-5371 Fax (317)926-5373
Email: churches@churchfederationindy.org
Website: www.churchfederationindy.org
Media Contact, Comm. Consultant, Julie Foster
Exec. Dir., Rev. Dr. Angelique Walker-Smith
Pres., Rev. Dr. Joh Wantz
Treas., Hugh Moore
Major Activities: "Preserving Christian Diversity

& Impacting Our Society Through Unity in Christ": Organizing, Energizing, Mobilizing Since 1912 (John 17: 20-23), Benevolence Ministry–C.R.O.P. (Church World Service, Celebration of Hope Partnership; Racial Reconciliation), Clergy ID Badge Program, Faith and Fathers, FaithFest!, Family Congregation and Mentoring Program (FCMP), Greater Indianapolis Urban Forum, Hispanic/Latino Forum, Indiana Faith-Based Climate Change Campaign, Indianapolis Interfaith Airport Chaplaincy, Loving Our Children/Children's Sabbath, Greater Indianapolis Prayer Network to Stop the Violence-Ecumenical Project for Reconciliation and Healing, TV Broadcasts

Evansville Area Community of Churches, Inc.

713 N. 2nd Ave., Evansville, IN 47710 Tel. (812)425-3524 Fax (812)425-3525
Email: eacc@evansville.net
Media Contact, EACC Administrator and Weekday Director, Janet Battram
Weekday Dir., Janet Battram
Pres., Rev. G. Philip Hoy
Vice Pres., Evelyn Cave
Sec., Rev. C. E. Erickson
Treas., Rev. Will Jewsbury
Major Activities: Food Pantry System, Jail Ministry, Weekday Christian Ed., Ecumenical and Community Service and Activities

Indiana Partners for Christian Unity and Mission

P.O. Box 88790, Indianapolis, IN 46208-0790 Tel. (815)377-8228 Fax 815-377-8228
Email: indunity@aol.com
Website: www.IPCUM.org
Media Contact, James Dougans
Pres., Ms. Andrea Thomas
Treas., Mrs. Marilyn Moffett
Major Activities: Initiating dialogue on issues of social concern by organizing conferences on the death penalty, racism, welfare reform and violence; facilitating communication through an electronic newsletter and web site; promoting the National Day of Prayer and the Week of Prayer for Christian Unity; and advancing Churches Uniting in Christ.

Interfaith Community Council, Inc.

702 E. Market St., New Albany, IN 47150 Tel. (812)948-9248 Fax (812)948-9249
Email: icc@digicove.com
Media Contact, Exec. Dir., Houston Thompson
Exec. Dir., Houston Thompson
Programs–Emergency Assistance, Kathy Anderson
RSVP, Dir., Ceil Sperzel
Major Activities: Emergency Assistance, Retired Senior Volunteer Program, New Clothing and Toy Drives, Emergency Food Distribution, Homeless Prevention, Kids' Café, Youth Development Services

Lafayette Urban Ministry

525 N. 4th St., Lafayette, IN 47901 Tel. (317)423-2691 Fax (317)423-2693
Media Contact, Exec. Dir., Joseph Micon
Exec. Dir., Joseph Micon
Advocate Coord., Rebecca Smith
Public Policy Coord., Harry Brown
Pres., John Wilson
Major Activities: Social Justice Ministries with and among the Poor

United Religious Community of St. Joseph County

2015 Western Ave., Suite 336, South Bend, IN 46629 Tel. (574)282-2397 Fax (574)282-8014
Email: Cmayernick@urcsjc.org
Website: www.urcsjc.org
Media Contact, Exec. Dir., Rev. Carol L. Mayernick
Exec. Dir., Rev. Carol L. Mayernick
Pres., Dave Berkenes
Refugee Program: Dir., Carol McDonnell
Victim Impact Panel: Dir., Martha Sallows
Advocacy Centers: Dir., Linda Jung-Zimmerman
Major Activities: Religious Understanding, Interfaith/Ecumenical Education, Interfaith Newsletter *Torch*, CROP Walk, UDare2Care Interfaith Youth Event, On-site Prayer Ministry, Peacemaker Awards, Hunger Education, Housing and Homelessness Issues, Clergy Education and Support, Refugee Resettlement, Victim Assistance, Advocacy for the Needy

West Central Neighborhood Ministry, Inc.

1316 Broadway, Fort Wayne, IN 46802-3304 Tel. (219)422-6618 Fax (219)422-9319
Media Contact, Exec. Dir., Andrea S. Thomas
Exec. Dir., Andrea S. Thomas
Ofc. Mgr., J. R. Stopperich
Neighborhood Services: Dir., Carol Salge
Senior Citizens: Dir., Gayle Mann
Youth Dir., Laura Watt
Major Activities: After-School Programs, Teen Drop-In Center, Summer Day Camp, Summer Overnight Camp, Information and Referral Services, Food Pantry, Nutrition Program for Senior Citizens, Senior Citizens Activities, Tutoring, Developmental Services for Families and Senior Citizens, Parent Club

IOWA

Churches United, Inc.

1035 3rd Ave., Suite 202, Cedar Rapids, IA 52403-2463 Tel. (319)366-7163
Media Contact, Exec. Dir., Karla Twedt-Ball
Exec. Dir., Karla Twedt-Ball
Pres., Rev. David Loy

Treas., Rachel Bartol, 450 19th St. NW, Cedar Rapids, IA 52405
Major Activities: Communication-Resource Center for Member Churches, Community Information and Referral, Ecumenical City-wide Celebrations

Des Moines Area Religious Council

3816-36th St. Ste. 204, Des Moines, IA 50310 Tel. (515)277-6969 Fax (515)274-8389
Email: info@dmreligious.org
Website: dmreligious.org
Media Contact, Exec. Dir., Forrest Harms
Exec. Dir., Forrest Harms
Pres., Ginny Hancock
Pres.-Elect, Fr. Jim Kierman
Treas., Jim Houser
Major Activities: Outreach and Nurture, Education, Social Initiatives Advocacy, Mission, Emergency Food Pantry, Ministry to Widowed, Child Care Assistance, Compassion in Action.

Ecumenical Ministries of Iowa (EMI)*

3816-36th St., Ste. 202, Des Moines, IA 50310-4722 Tel. (515)255-5905 Fax (515)255-1421
Email: emofiowa@aol.com
Website: www.iowa.churches.org
Media Contact, Communications Coord., Mary Swalla Holme
Exec. Dir., Rev. Sarai Schnucker Beck
Major Activities: Facilitating the denomination-s'cooperative agenda of resourcing local expression of the church, Assess needs & develop responses through Justice and Unity Commissions

Iowa Religious Media Services*

3816 36th St., Des Moines, IA 50310 Tel. (515)277-2920 Fax (515)277-0842
Email: questions@irms.org
Website: www.irms.org
Media Contact, Director
Exec. Dir., Sharon E. Strohmaier
Educ. Consultant, -vacant-
Major Activities: Media Library for Churches in 7 Denominations in the Midwest; Provide Video Production Services for Churches, Nonprofit, and Educational organizations; will rent media to churches in the continental US (details on the website)

KANSAS

Cross-Lines Cooperative Council

736 Shawnee Ave., Kansas City, KS 66105 Tel. (913)281-3388 Fax (913)281-2344
Email: rhea@cross-lines.org
Website: www.cross-lines.org
Media Contact, Dir. of Dev., Bill Scholl
Exec. Dir., Marilynn Rudell
Dir. of Programs, Rev. Robert L. Moore
Major Activities: Emergency Assistance, Family Support Advocacy, Crisis Heating/Plumbing Repair, Thrift Store, Workcamp Experiences, Adult Education (GED and Basic English Literacy Skills), School Supplies, Christmas Store, Institute for Poverty and Empowerment Studies (Education on poverty for the non-poor)

Inter-Faith Ministries-Wichita

829 N. Market, Wichita, KS 67214-3519 Tel. (316)264-9303 Fax (316)264-2233
Email: smuyskens@juno.com
Media Contact, Exec. Dir., Sam Muyskens
Exec. Dir., Rev. Sam Muyskens
Adm. Asst., Kathy Freed
Inter-Faith Inn (Homeless Shelter): Dir., Sandy Swank
Operation Holiday: Dir., Ashley Davis
Dev.-Communications: Dir., -vacant-
Campaign to End Childhood Hunger: Connie Pace
Community Ministry: Cammie Funston
Racial Justice: Coord., Cammie Funston
Major Activities: Communications, Urban Education, Interreligious Understanding, Community Needs and Issues, Theology and Worship, Hunger, Family Life, Multi-Cultural Concerns

Kansas Ecumenical Ministries*

5833 SW 29th St., Topeka, KS 66614-2499 Tel. (785)272-9533 Fax (785)272-9533
Email: kemstaff@ecunet.org
Website: kemontheweb.org
Media Contact, Exec. Dir., Dr. Joe M. Hendrixson, joe.hendrixson@ecunet.org
Exec. Dir., Dr. Joe M. Hendrixson
Pres.,Winnie Crapson
Vice Pres., Marvin Zehr
Sec., Rev. Art Jaggard
Major Activities: State Council of Churches, Legislative Activities, Program Facilitation and Coordination, Education, Mother-to-Mother Program, Rural Concerns, Hate group Monitoring, Children and Families, Faith and Order

KENTUCKY

Eastern Area Community Ministries

P.O. Box 43049, Louisville, KY 40253-0049 Tel. (502)244-6141 Fax (502)254-5141
Email: easternacm@cs.com
Media Contact, Acting Exec. Dir., Sharon Eckler
Acting Exec. Dir., Sharon Eckler
Board Pres., Rev. Elwood Sturtevant
Board Sec., Mary Stephens
Board Treas., Homer Lacy Jr.
Youth and Family Services: Rachael Elrod
Older Adult Services: Associate Program Dir., Joni Snyder
Neighborhood Visitor Program: Acting Prog. Dir., Jane Parker

Major Activities: Emergency Assistance, Clothes Closet, Meals on Wheels, Community Worship Services, Good Start for Kids, Juvenile Court Diversion, Community Development, Transient Fund, Ministerial Association, Juvenile Court Diversion

Fern Creek-Highview United Ministries

7502 Tangelo Dr., Louisvlle, KY 40228 Tel. (502)239-7407 Fax (502)239-7454

Email: FernCreek.Ministries@crnky.org

Media Contact, Exec. Dir., Kay Sanders, 7502 Tangelo Dr., Louisville, KY 40228 Tel. (502)239-7407

Exec. Dir., Kay Sanders

Pres., David Pooler

Major Activities: Ecumenically supported social service agency providing services to the community, including Emergency Financial Assistance, Food/Clothing, Health Aid Equipment Loans, Information-Referral, Advocacy, Checks, Holiday Programs, Life Skills Training, Mentoring, Case Management, Adult Day-Care Program

Hazard-Perry County Community Ministries, Inc.

P.O. Box 1506, Hazard, KY 41702-1506 Tel. (606)436-0051 Fax (606)436-0071

Media Contact, Gerry Feamster-Roll

Exec. Dir., Gerry Feamster-Roll

Chpsn., Sarah Hughes

Vice Chpsn., Susan Duff

Sec., Virginia Campbell

Treas., Margaret Adams

Major Activities: Food Pantry/Crisis Aid Program, Day Care, Summer Day Camp, After-School Program, Christmas Tree, Family Support Center, Adult Day Care, Transitional Housing

Highlands Community Ministries

1140 Cherokee Rd., Louisville, KY 40204 Tel. (502)451-3695 Fax (502)451-3609

Email: hcmexecu@hotmail.com

Media Contact, Exec. Dir., Stan Esterle

Exec. Dir., Stan Esterle

Major Activities: Welfare Assistance, Children Day Care, Adult DayHealth Care, Social Services for Elderly, Housing for Elderly and Handicapped, Ecumenical Programs, Interfaith Programs, Community Classes, Activities for Children, Neighborhood and Business Organization

Kentuckiana Interfaith Community

1113 South 4th St., Suite 200, Louisville, KY 40203 Tel. (502)587-6265 Fax (502)540-5017

Email: interfaith@bellsouth.net

Website: www.neighborhoodlink.com/org/kic

Media Contact, Executive Director, Dr. Roy Fuller

Pres., Steven Johns-Boehme

Vice Pres., Ron Gaddie

Treas., Fr. Bill Hammer

Major Activities: Christian/Jewish, Islamic, Bahai Ministries in KY, Southern IN; Consensus Advocacy; Interfaith Dialogue; Community Hunger Walk; Racial Justice Forums; Network for Neighborhood-based Ministries; Hunger & Racial Justice Com-mission; Faith Channel/ Cable TV Station; Horizon News Paper; Police-Comm. Relations Task Force; Ecumenical Strategic Planning; Networking with Seminaries and Religious-Affiliated Institutions

Kentucky Council of Churches*

2549 Richmond Rd., Suite 302, Lexington, KY 40509 Tel. (859)269-7715 Fax (859)269-1240

Email: kcc@kycouncilofchurches.org

Website: www.kycouncilofchurches.org

Media Contact, Exec. Dir., Nancy Jo Kemper

Exec. Dir., Rev. Dr. Nancy Jo Kemper

Pres., The Rev. Ron Gaddie

Kentucky Interchurch Disaster Recovery Program: Coordinator., Rev. Dr. John Kays

Program Associate for Local Ecumenism, Rev. W. Chris Benham Skidmore

Major Activities: Christian Unity, Public Policy, Justice, Disaster Response, Peace Issues, Anti-Racism, Health Care Issues, Local Ecumenism, Rural Land/Farm Issues, Gambling, Capital Punishment

Ministries United South Central Louisville (M.U.S.C.L., Inc.)

1207 Hart Avenue, Louisville, KY 42013 Tel. (502)363-9087 Fax (502)363-9087

Media Contact, Ex. Dir., Rev. Antonio (Tony) Aja, MDiv Tel. (502)363-2383, Tony_Aja@pcusa.org

Ex. Dir., Rev. Antonio (Tony) Aja, MDiv

Airport Relocation Ombudsman, Rev. Phillip Garrett, MDiv Tel. (502)361-2706, philombud@aol.com

Senior Adults Programs: Dir., Mrs. Jeannine Blakeman, BSSW

Emergency Assistance: Dir., Mr. Michael Hundley

Low-Income Coord., Ms. Wanda Irvio

Youth Services: Dir., Rev. Bill Sanders, M.Div.

Volunteers Coord., Mrs. Carol Stemmle

Northern Kentucky Interfaith Commission, Inc.

901 York St., P.O. Box 72296, Newport, KY 41072 Tel. (859)581-2237 Fax (859)261-6041

Email: wneuroth@hotmail.com

Media Contact, Exec. Dir., Rev. William C. Neuroth

Pres., Ms. Wanda Trinkle

Sec., Ms. Cordelia Koplow

Treas., Ms. Peggy McEntee

Admin. Asst., Pat McDermott

Major Activities: Understanding Faiths, Meeting Spiritual and Human Needs, Enabling Churches to Greater Ministry

Paducah Cooperative Ministry

1359 S. 6th St., Paducah, KY 42003 Tel. (270) 442-6795 Fax (270)442-6812
Email: pcministry@hotmail.com
Media Contact, Dir., Heidi Suhrheinrich
Dir., Heidi Suhrheinrich
Chpsn., Rev. Larry mcBride
Vice Chpsn., Tommy Tucker
Major Activities: Programs for Hungry, Elderly, Poor, Homeless, Handicapped, Undereducated

St. Matthews Area Ministries

201 Biltmore Rd., Louisville, KY 40207 Tel. (502)893-0205 Fax (502)893-0206
Media Contact, Exec. Dir., Dan G. Lane
Exec. Dir., Dan G. Lane
Child Care, Dir., Janet Hennessey
Dir. Assoc., Eileen Bartlett
Major Activities: Child Care, Emergency Assistance, Youth Services, Interchurch Worship and Education, Housing Development, Counseling, Information and Referral, Mentor Program, Developmentally Disabled

South East Associated Ministries (SEAM)

6500 Six Mile Ln., Ste. A, Louisville, KY 40218 Tel. (502)499-9350
Media Contact, Mary Beth Helton
Exec. Dir., Mary Beth Helton
Life Skills Center: Dir., Robert Davis
Youth Services: Dir., Bill Jewel
Pres., David Ehresman
Treas., Bill Trusty
Major Activities: Emergency Food, Clothing, and Financial Assistance; Life Skills Center (Programs of Prevention and Case Management and Self-Sufficiency Through Education, Empowerment, Support Groups, etc.); Bloodmobile; Ecumenical Education and Worship; Juvenile Court Diversion; TEEN Court; Teen Crime and the Community

South Louisville Community Ministries

Peterson Social Services Center, 204 Seneca Trail, Louisville, KY 40214 Tel. (502)367-6445 Fax (502)361-4668
Email: slcm@crnky.org
Website: www.slcm.org
Media Contact, Exec. Dir., J. Michael Jupin
Bd. Chair., Greg Greenwood
Bd. Vice Chair., Jim Woodward
Bd. Treas., Greg Greenwood
Exec. Dir., Rev. J. Michael Jupin
Major Activities: Food, Clothing, and Financial Assistance; Home Delivered Meals; Transportation; Ecumenical Worship; Juvenile Ct. Diversion Program; Affordable Housing; Adult Day Care; Truancy Prevention; Senior Center

LOUISIANA

Greater Baton Rouge Federation of Churches and Synagogues

P.O. Box 626, Baton Rouge, LA 70821 Tel. (225) 925-3414 Fax (225)925-3065
Media Contact, Exec. Dir., Rev. Jeff Day
Exec. Dir., Rev. Jeff Day
Admn. Asst., Marion Zachary
Pres., Bette Lavine
Pres.-Elect, Tom Sylvest
Treas., Randy Trahan
Major Activities: Combating Hunger, Housing (Helpers for Housing), Interfaith Relations, Interfaith Concert, Race Relations

Greater New Orleans Federation of Churches

4640 S. Carrollton Ave, Suite 2B, New Orleans, LA 70119-6077 Tel. (504)488-8788 Fax (504) 488-8823
Exec. Dir., Rev. J. Richard Randels
Major Activities: Information and Referral, Food Distribution (FEMA), Forward Together TV Program, Seminars for pastors (e.g. church growth, clergy taxes, etc.), Police Chaplaincy, Fire Chaplaincy

Louisiana Interchurch Conference*

660 N. Foster Dr., Ste. A-225, Baton Rouge, LA 70806 Tel. (225)924-0213 Fax (225)927-7860
Email: lainterchurch@aol.com
Media Contact, Exec. Dir., Rev. C. Dana Krutz
Exec. Dir., Rev. C. Dana Krutz
Pres., The Rt. Rev. Charles E. Jenkins
Major Activities: Ministries to Aging, Prison Reform, Liaison with State Agencies, Ecumenical Dialogue, Institutional Chaplains, Racism, Environmental

MAINE

Maine Council of Churches*

15 Pleasant Ave., Portland, ME 04103 Tel. (207)772-1918 Fax (207)772-2947
Email: info@mainecouncilofchurches.org
Website: www.mainecouncilofchurches.org
Media Contact, Communications Director, Karen Caouette
Exec. Dir., Thomas C. Ewell
Assoc. Dir., Douglas Cruger
Admin. Asst., Sandra Buzzell
Pres., Br. Francis Blouin
Treas., Rev. Richard Swan
Major Activities: Criminal Justice Reform/Restorative Justice, Economic Justice, Environmental Justice, Peace Issues, Civil Rights

MARYLAND

Central Maryland Ecumenical Council*

Cathedral House, 4 E. University Pkwy., Baltimore, MD 21218 Tel. (410)467-6194 Fax (410)554-6387
Email: cmec@bcpl.net
Media Contact, Exec. Dir., Martha Young
Pres., Rev. Iris Farabee-Lewis
Major Activities: Interchurch Communications and Collaboration, Information Systems, Ecumenical Relations, Urban Mission and Advocacy, Staff for Judicatory Leadership Council, Commission on Dialogue, Commission on Church & Society, Commission on Admin. and Dev., Ecumenical Choral Concerts, Ecumenical Worship Services

Community Ministries of Rockville

114 West Montgomery Ave., Rockville, MD 20850 Tel. (301)762-8682 Fax (301)762-2939
Email: cmr114cmr@aol.com
Media Contact, Managing Dir., Agnes Saenz
Exec. Dir. & Comm. Min., Mansfield M. Kaseman
Managing Dir., Agnes Aaenz
Major Activities: Shelter Care, Emergency Assistance, Elderly Home Care, Affordable Housing, Political Advocacy, Community Education, Education to Recent Immigrants

Community Ministry of Montgomery County

114 West Montgomery Ave., Rockville, MD 20850 Tel. (301)762-8682 Fax (301)762-2939
Media Contact, Exec. Dir., Rebecca Wagner
Exec. Dir., Rebecca Wagner
Major Activities: Interfaith Clothing Center, Emergency Assistance Coalition, The Advocacy Function, Information and Referral Services, Friends in Action, The Thanksgiving Hunger Drive, Thanksgiving in February, Community Based Shelter

MASSACHUSETTS

Attleboro Area Council of Churches, Inc.

7 North Main St., Ste. 200, Attleboro, MA 02703 Tel. (508)222-2933 Fax (508)222-2008
Email: aacc@naisp.net
Media Contact, Pres., Bd. Of Directors, Rev. Ruth Shaver
Exec. Adm., Kathleen Trowbridge
Staff Asst., Food 'n Friends Program: Dir., Dorothy Embree
Hosp. Chplns., Rev. Dr. William B. Udall, Rev. Lynn MacLagan
Pres., Rev. Ruth Shaver, Minister of Christian Ed. And Family Life, Second Congregational Ch., 50 Pk. St., Attleboro, MA 02703
Treas., Mr. Richard Shaw, 70 Stanson Dr., N. Attleboro, MA 02760
Major Activities: Hospital Chaplaincy, Personal Growth-Skill Workshops, Ecumenical Worship, Interfaith Worship, Media Resource Center, Referral Center, Communications/ Publications, Community Social Action, Food 'n Friends Kitchens, Nursing Home Volunteer Visitation Program, Clergy Fellowship/ Learning Events

The Cape Cod Council of Churches, Inc.

320 Main St., P.O. Box 758, Hyannis, MA 02601 Tel. (508)775-5073
Media Contact, Exec. Dir., Diane Casey-Lee
Exec. Dir., Rev. Susan Royce Scribner
Pres., Mr. Barry Jones-Henry, Sr.
Chaplain, Cape Cod Hospital: Rev. William Wilcox
Chaplain, Falmouth Hospital: Rev. Allen Page
Chaplain, House of Correction & Jail: Rev. Thomas Shepherd
Chaplain, Rehabilitation Hospital of the Cape and Islands: Mrs. Elizabeth Stommel
Service Center & Thrift Shop, P.O. Box 125, Dennisport, MA 02639 Tel. (508)394-6361
Major Activities: Pastoral Care, Social Concerns, Religious Education, Emergency Distribution of Food, Clothing, Furniture, Referral and Information, Church World Service, Interfaith Relations, Media Presence, Hospital and Jail Chaplaincy, Arts and Religion

Cooperative Metropolitan Ministries

474 Centre St., Newton, MA 02158 Tel. (617)244-3650 Fax (617)630-9172
Email: coopmet@aol.com
Website: www.coopment.org
Media Contact, Exec. Dir., Claire Kashuck
Exec. Dir., Robert Stephens
Bd. Pres., Ricado Neal
Treas., Rev. John Odams
Clk., Anna Lee Court
Major Activities: Low Income, Suburban/Urban Bridges, Racial and Economic Justice

Council of Churches of Greater Springfield

39 Oakland St., Springfield, MA 01108 Tel. (413)733-2149 Fax (413)733-9817
Media Contact, Asst. to Dir., Edith Kaye
Exec. Dir., Rev. Karen L. Rucks
Community Min., Dir. Don A. Washington
Pres., The Rev. Dr. David Hunter
Treas., John Pearson, Esq
Major Activities: Advocacy, Emergency Fuel Fund, Peace and Justice Division, Community Ministry, Task Force on Racism, Hospital and Jail Chaplaincies, Pastoral Service, Crisis Counseling, Christian Social Relations, Relief

Collections, Ecumenical and Interfaith Relations, Ecumenical Dialogue with Roman Catholic Diocese, Mass Media, Church-Community Projects and Community Dialogues, Publication, "Knowing My Neighbor–Religious Beliefs and Traditions at Times of Death"

Greater Lawrence Council of Churches

117A S. Broadway, Lawrence, MA 01843 Tel. (978)686-4012
Email: pointer53a@aol.com
Media Contact, Exec. Dir., David Edwards
Exec. Dir., David Edwards
Pres., Carol Rabs
Vice Pres., Rev. Michael Graham
Admn. Asst., Linda Sullivan
Major Activities: Ecumenical Worship, Radio Ministry, Hospital and Nursing Home Chaplaincy, Church Women United, Afterschool Children's Program, Vacation Bible School

Inter-Church Council of Greater New Bedford

412 County St., New Bedford, MA 02740-5096 Tel. (508)993-6242 Fax (508)991-3158
Email: administration@inter-churchcouncil.org
Website: www.inter-churchcouncil.org
Media Contact, Min., Rev. Edward R. Dufresne, PhD
Exec. Min., Rev. Edward R. Dufresne, PhD
Pres., The Rev. David Lima
Treas., George Mock
Major Activities: Counseling, Spiritual Direction, Chaplaincy, Housing for Elderly and Disabled, Urban Affairs, Community Spiritual Leadership, Parish Nurse Ministry, Accounting and Spiritual Care for the Developmentally Challenged, Ecumenical and Interfaith Ministries, Advocacy for the Homeless, Support for Urban Schhol District, Opposition to Expanded Gambling

Massachusetts Commission on Christian Unity

82 Luce St, Lowell, MA 01852 Tel. (978)453-5423 Fax (978)453-5423
Email: kgordonwhite@msn.com
Media Contact, Exec. Dir., Rev. K. Gordon White
Exec. Sec., Rev. K. Gordon White
Pres., Rev. Fr. Edward O'Flaherty, Ecumenical Officer, Roman Catholic Archdiocese of Boston
Major Activities: Faith and Order Dialogue with Church Judicatories, Guidelines and Pastoral Directives for Inter-Church Marriages, Guidelines for Celebrating Baptism in an Ecumenical Context

Massachusetts Council of Churches*

14 Beacon St., Suite 416, Boston, MA 02108 Tel. (617)523-2771 Fax (617)523-1483
Email: www.council@masscouncilofchurches.org
Website: www.masscouncilofchurches.org
Media Contact, Dir., Rev. Dr. Diane C. Kessler
Exec. Dir., Rev. Dr. Diane C. Kessler
Assoc. Dir., Rev. Jill Wiley
Adjunct Assoc., Rev. Betsy Sowers
Pres., Rev. Canon Edward Rodman
Vice Pres., Rev. John Stendahl
Sec., Ms. Anne Nickerson
Treas., Mr. Robert Sarly
Major Activities: Christian Unity, Education and Evangelism, Social Justice and Individual Rights, Ecumenical Worship, Services and Resources for Individuals and Churches

Worcester County Ecumenical Council

4 Caroline St., Worcester, MA 01604 Tel. (508)757-8385 Fax (508)795-7704
Email: worcecumen@aol.com
Media Contact, Exec. Dir., Rev. Allyson D. Platt
The Rev. Allyson D. Platt, worcecumen@aol.com
Pres., Mrs. Fran Langille
Major Activities: Ecumenical Worship and Dialogue Networking Congregations Together in Partnerships of Mission, Education, and Spiritual Renewal; Clusters of Churches; Ecumenical Worship and Dialogue; Interfaith Activities; Resource Connection for Churches; Group Purchasing Consortium

MICHIGAN

Bay Area Ecumenical Forum

103 E. Midland St., Bay City, MI 48706 Tel. (517)686-1360
Media Contact, Rev. Karen Banaszak
Major Activities: Ecumenical Worship, Community Issues, Christian Unity, Education, CROP Walk

Berrien County Association of Churches

275 Pipestone, P.O. Box 1042, Benton Harbor, MI 49023-1042 Tel. (616)926-0030
Media Contact, Sec., Mary Ann Hinz
Pres., Osceola Skinner
Dir., Street Ministry, Rev. Yvonne Hester
Major Activities: Street Ministry, CROP Walk, Community Issues, Fellowship, Christian Unity, Hospital Chaplaincy Program, Publish Annual County Church Directory and Monthly Newsletter, Resource Guide for Helping Needy, Distribution of Worship Opportunity– Brochure for Tourists

Grand Rapids Area Center for Ecumenism (GRACE)

207 East Fulton, Grand Rapids, MI 49503-3210 Tel. (616)774-2042 Fax (616)774-2042

Email: dbaak@graceoffice.org

Website: www.graceoffice.org

Media Contact, Exec. Dir., Rev. David P. Baak

Leadership Team: Rev. David P. Baak, Lisa H. Mitchell, Rev. David G. May

Major Activities: AIDS Care Network (Client Services Education-Volunteer Services), Hunger Walk , Education-Relationships, Ecumenical Lecture, Christian Unity Worship/ Events, Interfaith Dialogue Conference, Affiliates, ACCESS–All County Churches Emergency Support System, FISH for My People-transportation, Publications (*Religious Community Directory*, *Grace Notes*), Racial Justice Institute, Mentoring Partners (Welfare Reform Response), West Michigan Call to Renewal (Response to Poverty Advocacy)

Greater Flint Council of Churches

310 E. Third St., Suite 600, Flint, MI 48502 Tel. (810)238-3691 Fax (810)238-4463

Email: gfcc1929@aol.com

Media Contact, Coord., Mrs. Constance D. Neely

Publicity Chpsn., Barbara Spaulding Westcott

President, Rev. Zoltan S. Sutto

Major Activities: Christian Education, Christian Unity, Christian Missions, Nursing Home Visitor, Church in Society, American Bible Society Materials, Interfaith Dialogue, Church Teacher Exchange Sunday, Directory of Area Faiths and Clergy, Thanksgiving and Easter Sunrise Services, CROP Walks

In One Accord

157 Capital Ave. NE, Battle Creek, MI 49017-3928 Tel. (269)966-2500 Fax (269)660-6665

Email: inoneaccordmi@aol.com

Website: www.skywebsite.com/In-One-Accord

Media Contact, Executive Director, Rev. Ron L. Keller

Pres., Rev. Craig Tatum

Vice Pres., Joy Rogers

Exec. Dir., Rev. Ron L. Keller

Treas., Paula McDaniel

Secretary, Mrs. Carla Dearing

Major Activities: CROP Walk, Week of Prayer for Christian Unity, Ecumenical Worship, Faith Health Network, Martin Luther King Jr. Community Service, Church Softball and Volleyball Leagues, Clergy Support Groups, Burmese Refugee Resettlement, Neighborhood Improvement Program, Racism Action Group, Building Spirituality In the Schools, Coordinated Lisiting of Area Churches and Partners, Clergy Forums.

The Jackson County Interfaith Council

425 Oakwood, P.O. Box 156, Clarklake, MI 49234-0156 Tel. (517)529-9721

Media Contact, Exec. Dir., Rev. Loyal H. Wiemer

Exec. Dir., Rev. Loyal H. Wiemer

Major Activities: Chaplaincy at Institutions and Senior Citizens Residences, Martin L. King Jr. Day Celebrations, Ecumenical Council Representation, Radio and TV Programs, Food Pantry, Interreligious Events, Clergy Directory

The Metropolitan Christian Council: Detroit-Windsor

1300 Sutie, 28 W. Adams, Detroit, MI 48226 Tel. (313)962-0340 Fax (313)962-9044

Email: councilweb@aol.com

Website: users.aol.com/councilweb/index.htm

Media Contact, Rev. Richard Singleton

Exec. Dir., Rev. Richard Singleton

Meals for Shut-ins: Prog. Dir., John Simpson, Add. Asst., Mrs. Elaine Kisner

Web Calendar: Supervisor, Mr. Gerald Morgan

Major Activities: Theological and Social Concerns, Ecumenical Worship, Educational Services, Electronic Media, Print Media, Meals for Shut-Ins, Summer Feeding Program

Michigan Ecumenical Forum*

809 Center St., Ste. 5, Lansing, MI 48906 Tel. (517)485-4395 Fax (517)482-8751

Email: ecumenicalforum@aol.com

Major Activities: Communication and Coordination, Support and Development of Regional Ecumenical Fora, Ecumenical Studies, Fellowship and Celebration, Church and Society Issues, Continuing Education

Muskegon County Cooperating Churches

1095 Third St., Suite 10, Muskegon, MI 49441-1976 Tel. (231)727-6000 Fax (231)727-6004

Media Contact, Program Coordinator, Delphine Hogston

Pres., Rev. Dr. Fred Halde

Major Activities: Local Faith Community Information Source, Racial Reconciliation, Dialogue, and Healing, Multiracial Family Support, Responsible Fathers Empowerment, Ecumenical Worship, Faith News TV Ministry, CROP Walk Against Hunger, Jewish-Christian Dialogue, Environmental Issues, Social Justice Issues.

SUBSIDIARY ORGANIZATIONS

Institute for Healing Racism–Muskegon

1095 Third St., Suite 10, Muskegon, MI 49441-1976 Tel. (231)727-6005 Fax (231)727-6004

Media Contact, Dir., Gordon Rinard

Major Activities: Racial Reconciliation, Dialogue and Healing, Multiracial Family Support

Muskegon Responsible Fathers' Initiative

1095 Third St., Suite 10, Muskegon, MI 49441-1976 Tel. (231)725-7268 Fax (231)728-4558

Media Contact, Christopher Sandford, Program Coordinator

Major Activities: Responsible Fathers Empowerment; Providing Education, Job Skills, and Support for Fathers to Connect and Support Their Children Financially, Emotionally, and Spiritually; Fatherhood Skills for Incarcerated Fathers; Teen Pregnancy Prevention

Community Uniting for Peace

1095 Third St., Suite 10, Muskegon, MI 49441-1976 Tel. (231)727-6000 Fax (231)727-6004

Media Contact, Sec., Delphine Hogston

Major Activities: Advocacy to Remove the Effects of Racism, Community Civil Rights Health Assessment Survey, Responsible Consumer Spending Initiative, Monthly Community Dialogue on Racial Issues

MINNESOTTA

Arrowhead Interfaith Council*

230 E. Skyline Pkwy, Duluth, MN 55811 Tel. (218)727-5020 Fax (218)727-5022

Media Contact, Pres., Alan Cutter

Pres., Alan Cutter

Vice Pres., Amy Berstein

Sec., John H. Kemp

Major Activities: Interfaith Dialogue, Joint Religious Legislative Coalition, Corrections Chaplaincy, Human Justice and Community Concerns, Community Seminars, Children's Concerns

Community Emergency Assistance Program (CEAP)

6840 78th Ave N, Brooklyn Park, MN 55445 Tel. (763)566-9600 Fax (763)566-9604

Email: smklein@isd.net

Website: www.ceap.homestead.com

Media Contact, Exec. Dir., Stephen Klein

Exec. Dir., Stephen Klein

Major Activities: Provision of Basic Needs (Food, Clothing), Emergency Financial Assistance for Shelter, Home Delivered Meals, Chore Services and Homemaking Assistance, Family Loan Program, Volunteer Services

Greater Minneapolis Council of Churches

1001 E. Lake St., P.O. Box 7509, Minneapolis, MN 55407-0509 Tel. (612)721-8687 Fax (612)722-8669

Email: info@gmcc.org

Website: www.gmcc.org

Media Contact, Dir. of Communications, Darcy Hanzlik

President and CEO, Rev. Dr. Gary B. Reierson, reierson@gmcc.org

Chair, Dorothy Bridges

Treas., Lester Swenson

Division Indian Work: Vice Pres. & Exec. Dir., Noya Woodrich, Dir. Of Programs, Denise Estey

Russ Ewald Center for Urban Service: Dir., Bruce Bjork

Minnesota FoodShare: Dir., Barbara Thell

Handyworks: Dir., Katherine Panasuk

Correctional Chaplains: Rev. Susan Allers Hatlie, Rev. Thomas Van Leer, Rev. Paula Nordhem, Rev. James Njoroge

Discover Learning Centers: Coord., LaDonna White

Div. of Indian Work: Dir., Youth Program, Louise Matson; Adult Services, Denise Estey; Teen Indian Parents, Leslie Walking Elk

Finance & Admin.: Vice Pres. and CFO., Dennis Anderson

Advancement: Sr. Vice Pres., Don R. Riggs

Urban Immersion Service Retreats: Assoc. Dir., Mike Manhard

Metro Paint-A-Thon: Coord., Julie Kinkaid

Discover Support Groups: Coord., Briana Franzmeier

Minnesota Churches Anti-Racism Initiative: Dir., James Addington

Church and Community Initiatives: Coord., Bruce Bjork

Major Activities: Indian Work (Emergency Assistance, Youth Leadership, Self-Sufficiency, Jobs Program, Teen Indian Parents Program, and Family Violence Program), Minnesota FoodShare, Metro Paint-A-Thon, Correctional Chaplaincy Program, HandyWorks, Anti-Racism Initiative, Child Advocacy, Social Justice Advocacy, Home Renovation, Affordable Housing, Urban Immersion Service Retreats, Welfare Reform, Economic Self-Sufficiency, Discover Support Groups, Job Readiness, Discover Learning Centers, Church and Community Initiatives

The Joint Religious Legislative Coalition

122 W. Franklin Ave., Rm. 315, Minneapolis, MN 55404 Tel. (612)870-3670 Fax (612)870-3671

Email: info@jrlc.org

Website: www.jrlc.org

Media Contact, Exec. Dir., Brian A. Rusche

Exec. Dir., Brian A. Rusche

Research Dir., Dr. James Casebolt

Network Organizer, Jody McCardle

Major Activities: Lobbying at State Legislature, Researching Social Justice Issues and Preparing Position Statements, Organizing Grassroots Citizen's Lobby

Metropolitan Interfaith Council on Affordable Housing (MICAH)

122 W. Franklin Ave., #310, Minneapolis, MN 55404 Tel. (612)871-8980 Fax (612)813-4501

Email: info@micah.org
Website: www.micah.org
Media Contact, Ex. Dir., Joy Sorensen Navarre
Ex. Dir., Joy Sorensen Navarre
Assoc. Dir., José Trejo
Congregational Organizers: Jodi Nelson, Jean Pearson, Rev. John Buzza, Rev. John Buzza
Sec., Sue Watlov Phillips
Pres., Rev. Paul Robinson
Vice Pres., Nancy L. Anderson
Treas., Joseph Holmberg
Past Pres., Kristine Reynolds
Major Activities: The Metropolitan Interfaith Council on Affordable Housing, MICAH, seeks to live out the prophetic vision that calls us "to do justice, to love mercy and to walk humbly with God." (Micah 6:8). We envision a metropolitan area where everyone without exception has a safe, decent and affordable home. MICAH will realize this vision through organizing congregations of faith and community partners to change the political climate and public policies so that all communities preserve and build affordable housing. MICAH's faith-based organizing creates power that produces results. During the past five years MICAH:
Mobilized congregations to build community support for 1,348 affordable homes for families with very low incomes
Prevented the demolition and gentrification of 1,919 structurally sound apartments. Half of the tenants were people of color or people with disabilities
Earned HUD's 1999 National Best Practices Award and the Headwaters Fund Social Justice Award in 2001

Minnesota Council of Churches*

122 W. Franklin Ave., Rm. 100, Minneapolis, MN 55404 Tel. (612)870-3600 Fax (612)870-3622
Email: mcc@mnchurches.org
Website: www.mnchurches.org
Media Contact, Exec. Dir., Rev. Peg Chemberlin, pegchemberlin@mnchurches.org
Exec. Dir., Rev. Peg Chemberlin, pegchemberlin@mn.churches.org
Dir. of Program Commissions, Rev. Deborah Manning, manningd@mnchurches.org
Refugee Services: Dir., Joel Luedtke, luedtkej@mnchurches.org
Indian Ministry: Field Organizer, Sandi Berlin, sandra.berlin@mnchurches.org
Communications: Dir., Christopher Dart, dartcel@mnchurches.org
Finance & Facilities: Dir., Douglas Swanson, swansond@mnchurches.org
Tri-Council Coordinating Commission: Co-Dirs., James Addington, Carmen Valenzuela
Joint Religious Legislative Coalition: Research Dir. & Admn. Asst., James Casebolt; Exec., Brian A. Rusche
Pres., Bishop John Hopkins
Major Activities: Minnesota Church Center, Life & Work, Rural Life-Ag Crisis, Racial Reconciliation, Indian Ministry, Legislative Advocacy, Refugee Services, Service to Newly Legalized/Undocumented persons, Unity and Relationships, Sexual Exploitation Within the Religious Community, Clergy Support, Jewish-Christian Relations, Muslim-Christian Relations, Tri-Council Coordinating Commission (Minnesota Churches Anti-Racism Initiative), Hindu-Christian Relations, Ecojustice, Peace Works, Minnesota Foodshare

St. Paul Area Council of Churches

1671 Summit Ave, St. Paul, MN 55105 Tel. (651) 646-8805 Fax (651)646-6866
Email: spacc@spacc.com
Website: www.spacc.com
Media Contact, Mary Kane
Exec. Dir., Rev. Grant Abbott
Dir. of Development, Kristi Anderson
Congregations in Community: Bob Walz
Congregations Concerned for Children: Peg Wangensteen
Project Spirit: Darcel Hill & Lucy Zanders
Project Home: Sara Liegl
Dept. of Indian Work: Sheila WhiteEagle
Pres. of the Board, Tara Mattessich
Treas., James Verlautz
Sec., Art Sidner
Major Activities: Education and Advocacy Regarding Children and Poverty, Assistance to Churches Developing Children's Parenting Care Services, Ecumenical Encounters and Activities, Indian Ministries, Leadership in Forming Cooperative Ministries for Children and Youth, After School Tutoring, Assistance to Congregations, Training Programs in Anti-Racism, Shelters for Homeless

Tri-Council Coordinating Commission

122 W. Franklin, Rm. 100, Minneapolis, MN 55404 Tel. (612)871-0229 Fax (612)870-3622
Email: naja@gmcc.org
Website: www.gmcc.org/tcc.html
Media Contact, Co-Dir., R. James Addington,
Assoc., Co-Dir., Rev. Carmen Valenzuela,
Exec. Committee: Rev. Peg Chemberlin, Rev. Gary Reierson, and Rev. Thomas Duke
Major Activities: Anti-Racism Training and Organizational Consultation, Institutional Anti-Racism Team Development and Coaching, Training and Coaching of Anti-Racism Trainers and Organizers (in cooperation with Cross Roads Ministry)

MISSISSIPI

Mississippi Religious Leadership Conference*

P.O. Box 68123, Jackson, MS 39286-8123 Tel. (601)924-7430 Fax (601)924-7430
Email: mrlc@netdoor.com

Media Contact, Exec. Dir., Rev. Paul Griffin Jones II, ThD, PhD
Exec. Dir.,Rev. Paul Griffin Jones II, ThD, PhD
Chair, Rev. Sue Cherney
Treas., Rev. Jim White
Major Activities: Cooperation among Religious Leaders, Lay-Clergy Retreats, Social Concerns Seminars, Disaster Task Force, Advocacy for Disadvantaged

MISSOURI

Council of Churches of the Ozarks

P.O. Box 3947, Springfield, MO 65808-3947 Tel. (417)862-3586 Fax (417)862-2129
Email: ccozarks@ccozarks.org
Website: www.ccozarks.org
Media Contact, Comm. Dir., Susan Jackson
Exec. Dir., Dr. David W. Hockensmith Jr.
Chief Operating Officer, Julie Guillebeau
Major Activities: Ministerial Alliance, Child Care Food Program–FDA Food Program, Child Care Resource and Referral, Connections Handyman Service, Crosslines– Food and Clothing Pantry, Daybreak Adult Day Care Center, Long-Term Care Ombuds-man Programs, Ozarks Food Harvest, Retired and Senior Volunteer Program, Sigma House–Treatment Center for Alcohol and Drug Abuse, Therapeutic Riding of the Ozarks

Ecumenical Ministries

#2 St. Louis Ave., Fulton, MO 65251 Tel. (573) 642-6065
Email: em_fulton@ecunet.org
Website: www.coin.missouri.edu/region/callaway/em.html
Media Contact, Exec., Dir., Rev. Bruce Edwards
Chair, Bd. Of Dir., William Jessop
Major Activities: Kingdom Hospice, CROP Hunger Walk, Little Brother and Sister, Unity Service, Senior Center Bible Study, County Jail Ministry, Fulton High School Baccalaureate Service, HAVEN House, Missouri Youth Treatment Center Ministry, Parish Nurses of Callaway

Interfaith Community Services

200 Cherokee St., P.O. Box 4038, St. Joseph, MO 64504-0038 Tel. (816)238-4511 Fax (816)238-3274
Email: DaveB@PonyExpress.net
Website: www.inter-serv.org
Media Contact, Exec. Dir., David G. Berger
Major Activities: Child Development, Neighborhood Family Services, Group Home for Girls, Retired Senior Volunteer Program, Nutrition Program, Mobile Meals, Southside Youth Program, Church and Community, Housing Development, Homemaker Services to Elderly, Emergency Food, Rent, Utilities, AIDS Assistance, Family Respite, Family and Individual Casework

Interfaith Partnership of Metropolitan St. Louis

418 E. Adams Ave., Kirkwood, MO 63122 Tel. (314)821-3808 Fax (314)821-6361
Email: ipstlouis@mindspring.com
Website: http//home.mindspring.com/~ipstlouis/
Media Contact, Barbara Russell
Dir., Barbara Russell
Pres., The Rev. Dr. Warren Crews
Cabinet Chpsn., Riley Leag
Major Activities: Speaking Out With a Concerted Faith Voice on Public Issues; Celebrating Our Diversity; Encouraging Respect for Our Faith Traditions Through Interfaith Dialogue, Music Events, Dinner Programs, and Public Forums; Projects That Promote Bridge-Building Across Racial, Religious, and Cultural Divides; Health Promotion Through Congregational Health Initiatives; Projects Responding to Hunger, Natural Disasters; Environmental Restoration; Improving Impoverished Neighborhoods

MONTANA

Montana Association of Churches*

180 24th St. W, Ste. G, Billings, MT 59102 Tel. (406)656-9779 Fax (406)656-2156
Email: montanachurches@earthlink.net
Website: www.montana-churches.org
Media Contact, Exec. Dir., Margaret MacDonald
Exec. Dir., Margaret E. MacDonald
Admn. Asst., Hung Vu
Pres., Rev. Jessica Crist, 401 4th Ave. N, Great Falls, MT 59401-2310
Pres.-Elect, Fr. Jay Peterson, Box 1399, Great Falls, MT 59403
Treas., Rev. Barbara Archer, 2210 Pryor Ln., Billings, MT 59102
Sec., Sharon Hoff-Brodowy, 665 Stadlev Rd., Helena, MT 59602
Major Activities: Montana Christian Advocates Network, Christian Unity, Junior Citizen Camp, Public Information, Ministries Development, Social Ministry, Faith Responses to Extremism and Racism, Renewing the Public Church, Montana Faith-Health Cooperative

NEBRASKA

Interchurch Ministries of Nebraska*

215 Centennial Mall S., Rm. 411, Lincoln, NE 68508-1888 Tel. (402)476-3391 Fax (402) 476-9310
Email: im50427@alltel.net
Website: www.interchurchministries.org
Media Contact, Exec., Mrs. Marilyn P. Mecham
Pres., Rev. Dr. Kenneth W. Moore
Treas., Rev. Dr. Peter Frazier-Koontz
Exec., Mrs. Marilyn Mecham
Adm. Asst., Sharon K. Kalcik
Health Ministry Coordinator, Ronnette L. Sailors
Domestic Violence Program Coordinator, Patricia L. Brown
Staff Support, Patricia L. Brown

Major Activities: Interchurch Planning and Development, Indian Ministry, Rural Church Strategy, United Ministries in Higher Education, Disaster Response, Rural Response Hotline, Health Ministry, Community Organizing Initiative Planning, Peace with Justice, Angel Connection, Domestic Violence Program, Faith Based Initiative

Lincoln Interfaith Council

140 S. 27th St., Ste. B, Lincoln, NE 68510-1301 Tel. (402)474-3017 Fax (402)475-3262
Email: mail@lincolninterfaith.org
Website: www.lincolninterfaith.org
Media Contact, Doug Boyd
Exec. Dir., Rev. Dr. Norman E. Leach
Pres., Mr. Larry Williams
Vice Pres., The Rev. Jay A. Vetter
Sec., Ms. Stephanie Dohner
Treas., Mrs. Prem Bansal
Past Pres., Mrs. Amrita Mahapatra
Media Specialist, Mr. Douglas Boyd
Urban Ministries: Rev. Dr. Norman E. Leach
Fiscal Mgr., Mrs. Jean Scali
Youth Activities: Coord., Todd Burnham
Hispanic Migrant Education Worker, Mrs. Marina Wray
Sudanese Migrant Education Worker, Mr. Samuel Chuol
Vietnamese Migrant Education Worker, Ms. Holly Ha Le
Scoutmaster Boy Scout Troop #911, Mr. Keak Chol
Alcohol/Tobacco/Drug Prevention Youth: Coord., Mr. Tam Vo
Soccer Coach, Mr. Izzaldin Badi
Faces of the Middle East: Coord., Mr. Nodri Al-Awady
Faces of the Middle East: Case Mgr., Mr. Omar Younis
Families First & Foremost Irqai Care: Coord., Mrs. Zainab Al-Batat
Faces of the Middle East Taekwon Do: Instructor, Mr. Ali Zabaidi
African Multicultural Community Center: Coordinator, Mr. David Tan
African Behavioral Healthcare Specialist, Mrs. Nyalam Gatrek
Building & Grounds, Mrs. Doc Le
Major Activities: Emergency Food Pantries System, MLK Jr. Observance, Healing Community Project, Interfaith Passover Seder, Week of Prayer Christian Unity, Festival of Faith and Culture, Holocaust Memorial Observance, Citizens Against Racism & Discrimination, HIV-AIDS, Community organization, Anti-Drug and Anti-Alcohol Abuse Projects, Youth Gang and Violence Prevention, Domestic Abuse Prevention, Migrant Child Education, Connecting Neighborhood Partnerships, American Citizenship Classes, Survival English for Pre-literate AmerAsians and Elderly Refugees, Ecumenical Deaf Ministry, Multi-Faith and Multi-Cultural Training, Faces of the Middle East Project, Crop Walk for Hunger, Unicef Drive, New Clergy Orientation, Directory of Clergy, Congregations & Religious Resources, Multi-Faith Planning Calendar Publication, "Faith Report," "Lincoln Faith & Culture" on Cable TV-13 and Kzum-FM Radio, African Multicultural Community Center

NEW HAMPSHIRE

New Hampshire Council of Churches*

140 Sheep Davis Road, Ste. 1, Pembroke, NH 03275 Tel. (603)224-1352 Fax (603)224-9161
Email: churches@nhchurches.org
Website: www.nhchurches.org
Media Contact, Exec. Dir., David Lamarre-Vincent, david@nhchurches.org
Exec. Dir., David Lamarre-Vincent
Pres., Rev. Robert Biron, St Thomas More, P.O.Box 620, Durham, NH 03824-0620
Treas., Mr. Alvah Chisholm
Major Activities: Statewide Ecumenical Work For Christian Unity, Interfaith Under-standing, and Social Justice

NEW JERSEY

Bergen County Council of Churches

58 James Street, Bergenfield, NJ 07621 Tel. (201)384-7505 Fax (201)384-2585
Email: bergenccc@hotmail.com
Media Contact, Pres., Rev. Dr. Stephen T. Giordano, Clinton Avenue Reformed Church, Clinton Ave. & James St., Bergenfield, NJ 07621 Tel. (201)384-2454 Fax (201)384-2585
Exec. Sec., Anne Annunziato
Major Activities: Ecumenical and Religious Institute, Brotherhood-Sisterhood Breakfast, Center for Food Action, Homeless Aid, Operation Santa Claus, Aging Services, Boy & Girl Scouts, Easter Dawn Services, Music, Youth, Ecumenical Representation, Support of Chaplains in Jails and Hospitals, Faith and Values Online project (www.njfaithandvalues.org), Welfare into Workplace

Ecclesia

700 West State St., Trenton, NJ 08618 Tel. (609) 394-9229
Media Contact, Secretary, Mrs. Tina Swan
Pres., Rev. Joseph P. Ravenell
Campus Chaplains: Rev. Nancy Schulter, Rev. Robert Wittin, Rev. Richard Kocses
Major Activities: Racial Justice, Children and Youth Ministries, Advocacy, CROP Walk, Ecumenical Worship, Hospital Chaplaincy, Church Women United, Campus Chaplaincy, Congregational Empowerment, Prison Chaplaincy, Substance Abuse Ministry Training

Metropolitan Ecumenical Ministry

525 Orange St., Newark, NJ 07107 Tel. 973-485-8100 Fax 973-485-1165

Media Contact, Consultant, Rev. M. L. Emory

Exec. Dir., C. Stephen Jones

Major Activities: Community Advocacy (education, housing, environment), Church Mission Assistance, Community and Clergy Leadership Development, Economic Development, Affordable Housing

Metropolitan Ecumenical Ministry Community Development Corp.

525 Orange St., Newark, NJ 07107 Tel. (973) 481-3100 Fax (201)481-7883

Email: memcdc@juno.com

Exec. Dir., Jacqueline Jones

Major Activities: Housing Development, Neighborhood Revitalization, Commercial/Small Business Development, Economic Development, Community Development, Credit Union, Home Ownership Counseling, Credit Repair, Mortgage Approval, Technical Assitance To Congregations

New Jersey Council of Churches*

176 W. State St., Trenton, NJ 08608 Tel. (609) 396-9546 Fax (609)396-7646

Media Contact, Public Policy Dir., Joan Diefenbach, Esq.

Pres., Rev. Jack Johnson

Sec., Beverly McNally

Treas., Marge Christie

Major Activities: Racial Justice, Children's Issues, Theological Unity, Ethics Public Forums, Advocacy, Economic Justice

NEW MEXICO

Faith Community Assistance Center

P.O. Box 15517, Santa Fe, NM 87592 Tel. (505)438-4782 Fax (505)473-5637

Media Contact, Barbara A. Robinson

Major Activities: Faith Community Assistance Center, Providing emergency assistance to the poor, Interfaith Dialogues/Celebrations/Visitations, Peace Projects, Understanding Hispanic Heritage, Newsletter

New Mexico Conference of Churches*

720 Vassar Dr. NE, Albuquerque, NM 87106-2724 Tel. (505)255-1509 Fax (505)256-0071

Email: nmcc@nmchurches.org

Website: www.nmchurches.org

Media Contact, Exec. Dir.., Rev. Barbara E Dua

Pres., Rev. Harold T. Nilsson

Treas., George Chynoweth

Exec. Dir., Rev. Barbara E. Dua

Major Activities: Affordable Housing, Social Justice Coalitions, Spiritual Life and Ministries

NEW YORK

Brooklyn Council of Churches

125 Ft. Greene Pl., Brooklyn, NY 11217 Tel. (718)625-5851 Fax (718)522-1231

Media Contact, Dir., Charles Henze

Program Dir., Charles Henze

Pres., Rev. John L. Pratt. Sr.

Treas., Rev. Charles H. Straut Jr.

Major Activities: Education Workshops, Food Pantries, Welfare Advocacy, Hospital and Nursing Home Chaplaincy, Church Women United, Legislative Concerns

Broome County Council of Churches, Inc.

William H. Stanton Center, 3 Otseningo St., Binghamton, NY 13903 Tel. (607)724-9130 Fax (607)724-9148

Email: mfrick@broomecouncil.ort

Website: www.broomecouncil.net

Media Contact, Rev. Dr. Murray Frick

Exec. Dir., Rev. Dr. Murray Frick

Exec. Asst., Brigitte Stella

Hospital Chaplains: Betty Pomeroy, Rev. David Rockwell

Jail Chaplain, Rev. Cris Mogenson

Aging Ministry: Coord., Linda McColgin

CHOW Prog.: Coord., Wendy Primavera

Pres., Dr. Thomas Kelly

Treas., Rey Hull

Caregiver Program: Coord., Joanne Kays

Community and Donor Relations: Dir., Dr. Murray Frick

Major Activities: Hospital and Jail Chaplains, Youth and Aging Ministries, Broome Bounty (Food Rescue Program), Emergency Hunger and Advocacy Program, Faith and Family Values, Ecumenical Worship and Fellowship, Media, Community Affairs, Peace with Justice, Day by Day Marriage Prep Program, Interfaith Coalition, Interfaith Volunteer Caregiver Program

Capital Area Council of Churches, Inc.

646 State St., Albany, NY 12203-3815 Tel. (518) 462-5450 Fax (518)462-5450

Email: capareacc@aol.com

Media Contact, Admn. Asst.,Kitt Jackson

Exec. Dir., Rev. John U. Miller

Admn. Asst.,Kitt Jackson

Pres., Rev. William Cotant

Treas., David Wood

Major Activities: Hospital Chaplaincy, Food Pantries, CROP Walk, Jail and Nursing Home Ministries, Martin Luther King Memorial Service and Scholarship Fund, Emergency Shelter for the Homeless, Campus Ministry, Ecumenical Dialogue, Forums on Social Concerns, Peace and Justice Education, Interfaith Programs, Legislative Concerns, Comm. Thanksgiving Day and Good Friday

Services, Annual Ecumenical Musical Celebration

Capital Region Ecumenical Organization (CREO)

812 N. Church St., Schenectady, NY 12305 Tel. (518)382-7505 Fax (518)382-7505
Email: mishamarvel@juno.com
Media Contact, Coord., Misha Marvel
Pres., Rev. Donna Elia, (PCUSA)
Vice Pres., Rev. John U. Miller (UCC)
Treas., Rev. Dr. Charles Lindhdm (ELCA)
Sec., Ms. Kitt Jackson (RCA)
Coord., Misha Marvel
Major Activities: Promote Cooperation/ Coordination Among Member Judicatories and Ecumenical Organizations in the Capital Region in Urban Ministries, Social Action

Chautaugua County Rural Ministry

127 Central Ave., P.O. Box 362, Dunkirk, NY 14048 Tel. (716)366-1787 Fax (716)366-1787
Email: ccrm@netsync.net
Website: www.ccrm.netsync.net
Exec. Dir., Kathleen Peterson
Major Activities: Chautaugua County Food Bank; Collection/Distribution of Furniture, Clothing, and Appliances; Homeless Services; Advocacy for the Poor; Soup Kitchen; Emergency Food Pantry; Thrift Store

Concerned Ecumenical Ministry to the Upper West Side

286 LaFayette Ave., Buffalo, NY 14213 Tel. (716) 882-2442 Fax (716)882-2477
Email: crieleygod@cembuffalo.org
Media Contact, Exec. Dir., The Rev. Catherine Rieley-Goddard
Pres., Ms. Priscilla Marsh
Major Activities: Community Center Serving Youth, Refugee Families, Seniors and the Hungry

Cortland County Council of Churches, Inc.

7 Calvert St., Cortland, NY 13045 Tel. (607)753-1002
Media Contact, Office Mgr., Joy Niswender
Exec. Dir., Rev. Donald M. Wilcox
Major Activities: College Campus Ministry, Hospital Chaplaincy, Nursing Home Ministry, Newspaper Column, Interfaith Relationships, Hunger Relief, CWS, CROP Walk, Leadership Education, Community Issues, Mental Health Chaplaincy, Grief Support, Jail Ministry

Council of Churches of Chemung County, Inc.

330 W. Church St., Elmira, NY 14901 Tel. (607)734-2294
Email: ecumenic2000@yahoo.com
Media Contact, Exec. Dir., Joan Geldmacher, Tel. (607)734-7622
Exec. Dir., Joan Geldmacher
Pres., Rev. Cathy S. Black, Westminster Presbyterian, 1009 Maple Ave., Elmira 14904, (609) 773-4374
Major Activities: CWS Collection, CROP Walk, UNICEF, Institutional Chaplaincies, Radio, Easter Dawn Service, Communications Network, Produce and Distribute Complete Church Directories, Representation on Community Boards and Agencies, Ecumenical Services, Interfaith Coalition, Taskforce on Children and Families, Compeer, Interfaith Hospitality Center

Council of Churches of the City of New York

475 Riverside Dr., Rm. 727, New York, NY 10115 Tel. (212)870-1020 Fax (212)870-1025
Email: JEHiemstra@aol.com
Media Contact, Exec. Dir., Dr. John E. Hiemstra
Exec. Dir., Dr. John E. Hiemstra
Pres., Rev. Calvin O. Butts
1st Vice Pres., Friend Carol Holmes
2nd Vice Pres., Rev. Carolyn Holloway
3rd Vice Pres., Ven. Michael Kendall
4th Vice Pres., Morris Gurley
Sec., Rev. N.J. L'Heureux, Jr.
Treas., Dr. John Cole
Major Activities: Radio and TV, Pastoral Care, Christ for the World Chapel, Kennedy International Airport, Coordination and Strategic Planning, Interfaith Coordinator, Religious Conferences, Referral and Advocacy, Youth Development, Directory of Churches and Database Available

Dutchess Interfaith Council, Inc.

9 Vassar St., Poughkeepsie, NY 12601 Tel. (914) 471-7333 Fax (914)471-7333
Email: dic@bestweb.net
Media Contact, Exec. Dir., Rev. Gail A. Burger
Exec. Dir., Rev. Gail A. Burger
Pres.,Rev. Gilbert E, McKenzie
Treas., Edward Koziol
Major Activities: CROP Hunger Walk, Interfaith Music Festival, Public Worship Events, Interfaith Dialogue, Christian Unity, Interfaith Youth Evening, Oil Purchase Group, HIV-AIDS Work, Weekly Radio Program, Racial Unity Work, Poverty Forums

Genesee County Churches United, Inc.

P.O. Box 547, Batavia, NY 14021 Tel. (716)343-6763
Media Contact, Pres., Captain Leonard Boynton, Salvation Army, 529 East Main St., Batavia, NY 14020 Tel. (716)343-6284
Pres., James Woodruff
Exec. Sec., Cheryl Talone
Chaplain, Rev. Peter Miller
Major Activities: Jail Ministry, Food Pantries, Serve Needy Families, Radio Ministry, Pulpit

Exchange, Community Thanksgiving, Ecumenical Services at County Fair

Genesee-Orleans Ministry of Concern

Arnold Gregory Memorial Complex, Suite 271
243 South Main St., Albion, NY 14411 Tel. (585) 589-9210 Fax (585)589-9617
Email: gomoc@rochester.rr.com
Media Contact, Exec. Dir., Marian M. Adrian, GNSH
Exec. Dir., Suzanne R. Noonan
Advocates: JoAnn McCowan, Cheryl Johnson
Pres., John W. Cebula, Esq.
Chaplain, Albion Correctional Facility: Sr. Dolores O'Dowd, GNSH
Major Activities: Advocacy Services for the Disadvantaged, Homeless, Ill, Incarcerated and Victims of Family Violence; Emergency Food, Shelter, Utilities, Medicines; just Friends (a mentoring program for children); Parenting Program; Furniture Program.

Greater Rochester Community of Churches

2 Riverside St., Rochester, NY 14613-1222 Tel. (585)254-2570 Fax (585)254-6551
Email: grcc@juno.com
Media Contact, Administrator., Elder Marie E. Gibson
Pres., Elizabeth A. LeValley, SSJ,
Vice Pres. for Program and Discipleship, Gloria Ulterino,
Justice Ministers and Outreach, Rev. Richard Myers,
Sec., Deacon Tom Driscoll,
Treas., Gary Hoyle
Major Activities: Ecumenical Worship, Christian Unity, Interfaith Health Care Coalition, Interfaith Dialogue, Annual Faith in Action Celebration, Rochester's Religious Community Directory, Religious Information/Resources, Justice Issues, Children's Emergency Fund, Commission on Christian-Jewish Relations, Commissions on Christian-Muslim Relations, Commissions on Jewish-Muslim Relations

InterReligious Council of Central New York

3049 E. Genesee St., Syracuse, NY 13224 Tel. (315)449-3552 Fax (315)449-3103
Email: mbowles@irccny.org
Website: www.irccny.org
Media Contact, Dir. Of Development, Renée Roeder
Executive Dir., Dr. James B. Wiggins
Pres., The Rev. William C. Redfield
Bus. Mgr., Laura J. Haley
Director for Resource Development, Renée Roeder
Pastoral Care Prog.: Dir., The Rev. Terry Culbertson
Refugee Resettlement Prog.: Dir. Hope Wallis
Senior Companion Prog.: Dir., Alethea Connolly
Long Term Ombudsman Prog.: Dir., Linda Kashdin
Covenant Housing Prog.: Dir., Kimberlee Dupcak
Southeast Asia Center: Dir., Mai Lan Putnam
Community Wide Dialogue on Racism, Race Relations and Racial Healing: Beth Broadway
InterReligious Council News: Ed., Renée Roeder
Major Activities: Pastoral Ministries, Community Ministries, Interreligious and Ecumenical Relations, Diversity Education, Worship, Community Advocacy and Planning

The Long Island Council of Churches

1644 Denton Green, Hempstead, NY 11550 Tel. (516)565-0290 Fax (516)565-0291
Email: licchemp@aol.com
Website: www.ncccusa.org/ecmin/licc
Media Contact, Exec. Dir., Thomas W. Goodhue
Exec. Dir., Rev. Thomas W. Goodhue
Pastoral Care: Dir., Rev. Richard Lehman
Social Services: Dir., Anne Vaughan, Tel. (516) 565-0390
Nassau County Ofc.: Social Services Sec., LaToya Walker
Suffolk County Ofc.: Food Program & Family Support, Carolyn Gumbs
Major Activities: Pastoral Care in Jails, Emergency Food, Family Support and Advocacy, Advocacy for Peace and Justice, Church World Service, Multifaith Education, Clergy-Laity Training, Newsletter, Church Directory, AIDS Interfaith of Long Island

Network of Religious Communities

1272 Delaware Ave., Buffalo, NY 14209-2496 Tel. (716)882-4793 Fax (716)882-3797
Email: ReligiousNet@aol.com
Website: ReligiousNet.org
Media Contact, Co-Exec. Dir., Rev. Dr. G. Stanford Bratton
Co-Exec. Dir. & COO, Rev. Dr. G. Stanford Bratton
Co-Exec. Dir., Rev. Francis X. Mazur
Pres., Rev. Jeff Carter (Church of God in Christ)
Vice Pres. For Program, The Rev. Dr. David McKee (General Presbyter, Presbytery of WNY)
Vice Pres. For Administration, Ms. Marlene Glickman (Dir., American Jewish Committee)
Sec., Ms. Sheila Nickson (Episcopal Church)
Treas., The Rev. Amos Acree (Disciples of Christ)
Chpsn., Interreligious Concerns, Rabbi Michael Feshbach, President Board of Rabbis
Chpsn., Personnel, The Rev. James Croglio (Diocese of Buffalo- Roman Catholic)
Chpsn., Membership, The Rev. Robert Grimm (United Church of Christ)
Chpsn., Riefler Enablement Fund, Mrs. Thelma Lanier (African Methodist Episcopal Church)

Chpsn., Public Issues, Rev. Merle Showers (United Methodist Church)
Chpsn., Religious Leaders Forum, Rev. Paul Litwin (Diocese of Buffalo -Roman Catholic)
Chpsn., Church Women United, Ms. Alma Arnold (United Church of Christ)
Program Coord., Ms. Maureen Gensler
Office Coord., Ms. Sally Giordano
Food For All: Dir., Patricia Griffin
Nutrition Outreach and Education: Coord., Ms. Carolyn Williams
Staff Assistant, Mr. Lamont Gist
Major Activities: Regionwide Interreligious Conversation, Hunger Advocacy, Food Distribution, Roll Call Against Racism, Buffalo Coalition for Common Ground, Ecumenical and Interreligious Relations and Celebrations, Radio/TV Broadcast and Production, Church Women United, Lay-Religious Leaders Education, Community Development, Chaplaincy, Yom Hashoah Commemoration Service, Aids Memorial Service, Police-Community Relations, CROP Walks

New York State Community of Churches, Inc.*

362 State St, Albany, NY 12210-1202 Tel. (518)436-9319 Fax (518)427-6705
Email: nyscoc@aol.com
Website: www.nyscommunityofchurches.org
Media Contact, Ms. Mary Lu Bowen
Executive Dir., Ms. Mary Lu Bowen
Pres., Bishop Susan M. Morrison
Corp. Sec., The Rev. Dr. Jon Norton
Treas., Bishop Marie C. Jerge
Convener, The Rev. Geoffrey A. Black
Coordinator of Chaplaincy Services, Ms. Damaris McGuire
Public Policy Advocate, The Rev. Daniel Hahn
Communications Coord, The Rev. Daniel Hahn
Admin. Asst., Sylvenia F. Cochran
Major Activities: Faith and Order, Interfaith Dialogue; State Chaplaincy and Public Policy Advocacy in the following areas: Anti-Racism, Campaign Reform, Criminal Justice System Reform, Disability, Ecomomic/Social Justice, Environmental, Health care, Homelessness/ Shelter, Hunger-Food Programs, Immigrant Issues, Public Education, Rural Issues, Substance Abuse, Violence, Women's Issues

The Niagara Council of Churches Inc.

St. Paul UMC, 723 Seventh St., Niagara Falls, NY 14301 Tel. (716)285-7505
Media Contact, Pres., Nessie S. Bloomquist, 7120 Laur Rd., Niagara Falls, NY 14304 Tel. (716)297-0698 Fax (716)298-1193
Exec. Dir., Ruby Babb
Pres., Nessie S. Bloomquist
Treas., Shirley Bathurst
Trustees Chpsn., Rev. Vincent Mattoni, 834 19th St., Niagara Falls, NY 14304
Major Activities: Ecumenical Worship, Bible Study, Christian Ed. and Social Concerns, Church Women United, Evangelism and Mission, Institutional Min. Youth Activities, Hymn Festival, Week of Prayer for Christian Unity, CWS Projects, Audio-Visual Library, UNICEF, Food Pantries and Kitchens, Community Missions Inc., Political Refugees, Eco-Justice Task Force, Migrant/Rural Ministries, Interfaith Coalition on Energy

Queens Federation of Churches

86-17 105th St., Richmond Hill, NY 11418-1597 Tel. (718)847-6764 Fax (718)847-7392
Email: qfc@queenschurches.org
Website: www.queenschurches.org
Media Contact, Rev. N. J. L'Heureux, Jr.
Exec. Dir., Rev. N. J. L'Heureux Jr.
York College Chaplain: Rev. Dr. Hortense Merritt
Pres., Rev. J. Karel Boersma
Treas., Annie Lee Phillips
Major Activities: Emergency Food Service, York College Campus Ministry, Blood Bank, Scouting, Christian Education Workshops, Planning and Strategy, Church Women United, Community Consultations, Seminars for Church Leaders, Online Directory of Churches and Synagogues, Christian Relations (Prot-RC), Chaplaincies, Public Policy Issues, N.Y.S. Interfaith Commission on Landmarking of Religious Property, Queens Interfaith Hunger Network, "The Nexus of Queens" (online weekly newspaper)

Rural Migrant Ministry

P.O. Box 4757, Poughkeepsie, NY 12602 Tel. (845)485-8627 Fax (845)485-1963
Email: rmmhope3@aol.com
Website: ruralmigrantministry.org
Media Contact, Exec. Dir., Rev. Richard Witt
Exec. Dir., Rev. Richard Witt
Pres., Melinda Trotti
Major Activities: Serving the Rural Poor and Migrants Through a Ministry of Advocacy and Empowerment, Youth Program, Latino Committee, Organization and Advocacy with and for Rural Poor and Migrant Farm Workers

Schenectady Inner City Ministry

930 Albany St., Schenectady, NY 12307-1514 Tel. (518)374-2683 Fax (518)382-1871
Email: sicm@knick.net
Website: www. Timesunion.com/community/sicm
Media Contact, Marianne Comfort
Urban Agent, Rev. Phillip N. Grigsby
Off. Mgr., Vjuana Anderson
Business Manager, Barbara Bieniek
Emergency Food: Patricia Obrecht
Pres., Crystal Hamelink
Food System: Marianne Comfort

Damien Center: Glenn Read
Youth/Cocoa House: Rachel Graham
Jobs, Etc: David Coplon
Summer Food: Rachel Graham
Housing Task Force: Rev. Phil Grigsby
Major Activities: Food Security, Advocacy, Housing, Neighborhood and Economic Issues, Ecumenical Worship and Fellowship, Community Research, Education in Congregations on Faith Responses to Social Concerns, Legislative Advocacy, CROP Walk, HIV-AIDS Ministry,Job Training and Placement Center, Summer Lunch for Youth, Study Circles Initiative on Embracing Diversity, EPRUS-Americorps, Community Crisis Nework, Housing Services and Advocacy, Youth Initiative, After-School Program, Committee for Social Justice, Theological Center, Emmett Street Initiative

Southeast Ecumenical Ministry

25 Westminster Rd., Rochester, NY 14607 Tel. (585)271-5350 Fax (585)271-8526
Email: sem@frontiernet.net
Media Contact, Laurie Jenkins
Dir., Laurie Jenkins
Pres., Ronald K. Fox
Major Activities: Transportation of Elderly and Disabled, Emergency Food Cupboard for Case Managers to Access for Their Clients, Supplemental Nutrition Program for Seniors, Community Health and Pharmacy Partnership (CHAPP).

Staten Island Council of Churches

2187 Victory Blvd., Staten Island, NY 10314 Tel. (718)761-6782
Media Contact, Exec. Sec., Mildred J. Saderholm, 94 Russell St., Staten Island, NY 10308 Tel. (718)761-6782
Pres., Rev. Gard Rowe
Exec. Sec., Mildred J. Saderholm
Major Activities: Support, Christian Education, Pastoral Care, Congregational Concerns, Urban Affairs

Troy Area United Ministries

17 First St., #2, Troy, NY 12180 Tel. (518)274-5920 Fax (518)271-1909
Email: info@TAUM.org
Website: www.taum.org
Media Contact, Exec. Dir., Rev. Donna Elia
Pres., Laura M. Rogers
Chaplain, R.P.I. And Russel Sage, Rev. Beth Illingworth
Damien Center: Dir., Glenn Read
Furniture Program: Dir., Michael Barrett
Major Activities: College Ministry, Nursing Home Ministry, CROP Walk, Homeless and Housing Concerns, Weekend Meals Program at Homeless Shelter, Community Worship Celebrations, Racial Relations, Furniture Program, Damien Center of Troy Hospitality for persons with HIV-AIDS, Computer Ministries, Youth Ministry

Wainwright House

260 Stuyvesant Ave., Rye, NY 10580 Tel. (914) 967-6080 Fax (914)967-6114
Media Contact, Exec. Dir., Judith W. Milinowski
Exec. Dir., Judith W. Milinowski
Pres., Dr. Robert A. Rothman
Exec. Vice Pres., Beth Adams Smith
Major Activities: Educational Program and Conference Center; Intellectual, Psychological, Physical and Spiritual Growth; Healing and Health

NORTH CAROLINA

Asheville-Buncombe Community Christian Ministry (ABCCM)

30 Cumberland Ave., Asheville, NC 28801 Tel. (704)259-5300 Fax (704)259-5923
Media Contact, Exec. Dir., Rev. Scott Rogers, Fax (704)259-5323
Exec. Dir., Rev. Scott Rogers
Pres., Stephen Williamson
Major Activities: Crisis Ministry, Jail/Prison Ministry, Shelter Ministry, Medical Ministry

Greensboro Urban Ministry

305 West Lee St., Greensboro, NC 27406 Tel. (910)271-5959 Fax (910)271-5920
Email: Guministry@aol.com
Website: www.greensboro.com/gum
Media Contact, Exec. Dir., Rev. Mike Aiken
Exec. Dir., Rev. Mike Aiken
Major Activities: Emergency Financial Assistance, Emergency Housing, Hunger Relief, Interfaith and Interracial Understanding, Justice Ministry, Chaplaincy with the Poor

North Carolina Council of Churches*

Methodist Bldg., 1307 Glenwood Ave., Ste. 162, Raleigh, NC 27605-3258 Tel. (919)828-6501 Fax (919)828-9697
Email: nccofc@nccouncilofchurches.org
Website: www.nccouncilofchurches.org
Media Contact, Communications Associate, Aleta Payne
Exec. Dir., Rev. J. George Reed
Program Associate, Sr. Evelyn Mattern
Communications Associate, Aleta Payne
Pres., Rev. Joseph C. Brown Jr., 709 Church St., Wilmington, NC 28409
Treas., Dr. James W. Ferree, 5108 Huntcliff Tr., Winston-Salem, NC 27104
Major Activities: Children and Families, Health Care Justice, Christian Unity, Women's Issues, Legislative Program, Criminal Justice, Farmworker Ministry, Rural Crisis, Racial Justice, Death Penalty, Poverty and Response to Welfare Changes, Climate Change, Public Education

NORTH DAKOTA

North Dakota Conference of Churches*

9195 70th Avenue SE, Ashley, ND 58413-9600 Tel. (701)647-2041 Fax (701)223-6075
Email: ndconchu@drtel.net
Media Contact, Executive Sec., Renee Gopal
Pres., Bishop Andrew Fairfield
Vice Pres., Bishop Michael Coyner
Treas., Christopher Dodson
Secretary, Rev. Arabella Meadows-Rogers
Executive Sec., Renee Gopal
Major Activities: Prison Chaplaincy, Rural Life Ministry, Faith and Order, North Dakota 101, Current Ecumenical Proposals

OHIO

Akron Area Association of Churches

350 S. Portage Path, Akron, OH 44320 Tel. (330)535-3112 Fax (330)374-5041
Email: aaac1@juno.com
Website: www.triple-ac.org
Media Contact, Exec. Dir., Chloe Ann Kriska
Bd. of Trustees, Pres., Rev. Dr. J. Wayman Butts
Vice Pres., Rev. Mark Frey
Sec., Dale Kline
Treas., Ms. Sherrie Petrochuk
Major Activities: Messiah Sing, Interfaith Council, Newsletters, Resource Center, Community Worship, Training of Local Church Leadership, Radio Programs, Clergy and Lay Fellowship Luncheons, Neighbor-hood Development, Community Outreach, Church Interracial Partnerships, Pastor Peer Group Program

Alliance of Churches

470 E. Broadway, Alliance, OH 44601 Tel. (330) 821-6648
Media Contact, Dir., Lisa A. Oyster
Dir., Lisa A. Oyster
Pres., Rev. Bud Hoffman
Treas., Betty Rush
Major Activities: Christian Education, Community Relations and Service, Ecumenical Worship, Community Ministry, Peacemaking, Medical Transportation for Anyone Needing It, Emergency Financial Assistance

Churchpeople for Change and Reconciliation

Box 488, Lima, OH 45802-0488 Tel. 419-224-2086 Fax 419-224-2086
Media Contact, Exec. Dir., Sharron Thirkill
Exec. Dir., Sharron Thirkill
Major Activities: Developing Agencies for Minorities, Poor, Alienated, and Despairing; Our Daily Bread Soup Kitchen

Council of Christian Communions of Greater Cincinnati

42 Calhoun St., Cincinnati, OH 45219-1525 Tel. (513)559-3151
Media Contact, Exec. Dir., Joellen W. Grady
Exec. Dir., Joellen W. Grady
Justice Chaplaincy: Assoc. Dir., Rev. Jack Marsh
Educ.: Assoc., Lillie D. Bibb
Pres., Rev. Damon Lynch III
Major Activities: Christian Unity and Interfaith Cooperation, Justice Chaplaincies, Police-Clergy Team, Adult and Juvenile Jail Chaplains, Religious Education

Greater Dayton Christian Connections

601 W. Riverview Ave., Dayton, OH 45406 Tel. (937)227-9485 Fax (937)227-9407
Email: gdcc@donet.com
Website: www.christianconnections.org
Media Contact, Exec. Dir., Rev. Darryl Fairchild
Exec. Dir., Darryl Fairchild
Pres., Rev. Burton Wolf
Major Activities: Information, Ecumenical and Interfaith Dialogue, Peace Making, Environmental Justice, Racial Reconciliation, Pastor Resources, Ministry Recruitment and Placement

Mahoning Valley Association of Churches

30 W. Front St., Youngstown, OH 44503 Tel. (330)744-8946 Fax (330)774-0018
Email: mvac@onecom.com
Media Contact, Exec. Dir., Elsie L. Dursi
Exec. Dir., Elsie L. Dursi
Pres., Jack Ritter
Treas., Ray Hurd
Major Activities: Communications, Christian Education, Ecumenism, Social Action, Advocacy

Metropolitan Area Church Council

760 E. Broad St., Columbus, OH 43205 Tel. (614)461-7103 Fax (614) 280-0352
Email: church_council@yahoo.com
Media Contact, Exec. Dir., Alvin Hadley
Pres., The Rev. Melvin Richardson
Vice Pres., The Rev. Frank Ball
Sec., Ms. Ariene Reynolds
Treas., Ms. Marilyn Shreffler
Exec. Dir., Alvin Hadley
Major Activities: Newspaper (published nine times annually), Annual Living Faiths Awards, Quarterly Racial Unity Services, Clergy Hospital Indentification Badges, Community Computer Center, Social Concerns Relating to Human Needs in Our Community, Older Adult Ministries, Collaborations to Facilitate Unity Among Religious Denominations

Metropolitan Area Religious Coalition of Cincinnati

Ste. 1035, 617 Vine St., Cincinnati, OH 45202-2423 Tel. (513)721-4843 Fax (513)721-4891
Email: marcc@fuse.net
Media Contact, Dir., Rev. Duane Holm
Pres., Sr. Joan Krimm, SNDdN

Dir., Rev. Duane Holm
Major Activities: Local Social Policy Decisions Chosen Annually
2003—Community-Police Relations, Public Education.

Ohio Council of Churches*

6877 N. High St., Ste. 206, Columbus, OH 43085-2516 Tel. (614)885-9590 Fax (614)885-6097
Email: mail@ohcouncilchs.org
Website: www.ohcouncilchs.org
Exec. Dir., Rev. Rebecca J. Tollefson
Public Policy: Dir., Tom Smith
Pres., Rev. Joseph W. Witmer
Vice Pres., Ms. Rhea Ballas
Treas., Rev. Dr. LaTaunya M. Bynum
Major Activities: Economic and Social Justice, Ecumenical Relations, Health Care Reform, Public Policy Issues, Theological Dialogue, Racial Relations, Education/Funding, Childcare/ Children Issues, Poverty/Welfare, Environment, Casino Gambling, Global Warming

Pike County Outreach Council

122 E. North St., Waverly, OH 45690-1146 Tel. (740)947-7151
Dir., Judy Dixon
Major Activities: Emergency Service Program, Self Help Groups, Homeless Shelter

Toledo Ecumenical Area Ministries

444 Floyd St., Toledo, OH 43620 Tel. (419)242-7401 Fax (419)242-7404
Media Contact, Admn., Nancy Lee Atkins
Metro-Toledo Churches United: Admn., Nancy Lee Atkins
Toledo Metropolitan Mission: Exec. Dir., Nancy Lee Atkins
Major Activities: Ecumenical Relations, Interfaith Relations, Food Program, Housing Program, Social Action, Public Education, Health Care, Urban Ministry, Employment, Welfare Rights, Housing, Mental Retardation, Voter Registration/Education, Substance Abuse Treatment, Youth Leadership, Children At-Risk, Elimination of Discrimination

Tuscarawas County Council for Church and Community

107 West High , Ste. B, New Philadelphia, OH 44663 Tel. (330)343-6012 Fax (330)343-9845
Media Contact, Barbara E. Lauer
Exec. Dir., Barbara E. Lauer
Pres., Zoe Ann Kelley, 201 E. 12th St., Dover, OH 44622
Treas., James Barnhouse, 120 N. Broadway, New Philadelphia, OH 44663
Major Activities: Human Services, Health, Family Life, Child Abuse, Housing, Educational Programs, Emergency Assistance, Legislative Concerns, Juvenile Prevention Program, Character Formation, Prevention Program for High Risk Children, Bimonthly newsletter–*The Pilot*

West Side Ecumenical Ministry

5209 Detroit Ave, Cleveland, OH 44102 Tel. (216)651-2037 Fax (216)651-4145
Email: Eotero@wsem.org
Website: www.wsem.org
Media Contact, Dir. of Marketing and Pub. Relations, Kami L. Marquardt
Pres. & CEO, Judith Peters
Chief Operation Officer, Adam Roth
Major Activities: WSEM is dedicated to serving urban low-income families by providing programs that encourage self-sufficiency. Three food pantries and outreach centers, a job-training program, early childhood, preschool, and schol-age child care, crisis intervention, counseling, youth services, a theatre education program and a senior nutrition program are among the services available. WSEM serves more than 56,000 children, families, and individuals annually with a staffing of more than 300 employees and 3,200 volunteers.

OKLAHOMA

Oklahoma Conference of Churches*

301 Northwest 36th St., Oklahoma City, OK 73118 Tel. (405)525-2928 Fax (405)525-2636
Email: okchurches@okchurches.org
Website: www.okchurches.org
Media Contact, Deborah Canary-Marshall
Exec. Dir., The Rev. Dr. Rita K. Newton
Pres., Rev. Mark Gibbens-Rickman
Major Activities: Christian Unity Issues, Community Building Among Members, Rural Community Care, Children's Advocacy, Day at the Legislature, Impact, Criminal Justice, Hunger and Poverty, Legislative Advocacy, Aging, Women's Issues

Tulsa Metropolitan Ministry

221 S. Nogales, Tulsa, OK 74127 Tel. (918)582-3147 Fax (918)582-3159
Email: tummtulsa@aol.com
Website: www.TUMM.org
Media Contact, Exec. Dir., Stephen Cranford
Exec. Dir., The Rev. Dr. Stephen V. Cranford
Pres., Rev. Sara Jo Waggoner
Vice Pres., Martin Belsky
Treas., Earl Tuers
Major Activities: Religious Understanding, Legislative Issues, Christian Unity Issues, Justice Issues, Against Racism, Disability Awareness, Directory of Metro. Religious Community,Airport Interfaith Chapel, Caring Companions, Native American Issues.

OREGON

Ecumenical Ministries of Oregon*

0245 S.W. Bancroft St., Ste. B, Portland, OR 97239 Tel. (503)221-1054 Fax (503)223-7007

Email: emo@emoregon.org
Website: www.emoregon.org
Media Contact, Dir. Of Development & Communications, Stephanie Howell,
Exec. Dir., David A. Leslie
Finance and Administrative Services: Dir., Gary B. Logsdon
Development & Communications: Dir., Stephanie Howell
Sponsors Organized to Assist Refugees: Vesna Vila
Russian Oregon Social Services: Yelena Sergeva
Portland International Community School: Skip Adams
Public Policy: Dir., Phillip Kennedy-Wong
Interfaith Network for Earth Concerns: Jenny Holmes
Parent Mentor Program: Patti Clothier
HIV Day Center: Lowen Berman
Shared Housing: Verlin Byers
Oregon Recovery Homes: Mike Morgester
Northeast Emergency Food Program: Millyellen Strayer
Pres., The Rev. Eugene Ross
Major Activities: Ecumenical Ministries of Oregon is a statewide association of seventeen christian denominations including Protestant, Roman Catholic, and Orthodox bodies working together to improve the lives of Oregonians through theological education and dialogue, public policy advocacy, environmental ministry, and community ministry programs.

PENNSYLVANIA

Allegheny Valley Association of Churches

1333 Freeport Rd., P.O. Box 236, Natrona Heights, PA 15065 Tel. (724)226-0606 Fax (724)226-3197
Email: avac@salsgiver.com
Website: www.avaoc.org
Media Contact, Exec. Dir., Karen Snair
Exec. Dir., Karen Snair
Pres., Rev. Dr. W. James Legge, 232 Tarentum-Culmerville Rd., Tarentum, PA 15084
Treas., Libby Grimm, 312 Butternut Ln., Tarentum, PA 15084
Major Activities: Ecumenical Services, Dial-a-Devotion, Walk for Hunger, Food Bank, Emergency Aid, Cross-on-the-Hill, AVAC Hospitality Network for Homeless Families, AVAC Volunteer Caregivers, Senior Citizen Housing/Pine Ridge Heights Senior Complex, AVAC Chaplaincy Program, Summer Camp for Children

Christian Associates of Southwest Pennsylvania

204 37th St., Suite 201, Pittsburgh, PA 15201 Tel. (412)688-9070 Fax (412)688-9091
Email: casp1817@aol.com
Website: www.casp.org
Media Contact, Dir. of Communications, Bruce J. Randolph
Exec., Dir., Rev. Dr. Donald B. Green
Chair of Council, Rev. Dr. Wayne Yost
Pres., Board of Delegates, Fr. Roger Statnick
Director of Communications, Bruce J. Randolph
Exec. Adm. Assistant, Tracie Ritchie
Dir. of Jail Chaplaincy Services, Rev. Ulli Klemm
Television Studio: Dir., Earl C. Hartman, Jr.
Protestant Chaplain–Shuman Youth Detention Center, Rev. Floyd Palmer
Protestant Chaplain, Rev. Dallas Brown
Jail Adm. Assistant, Karen Mack
Major Activities: Jail Chaplaincy, Youth-Incarceration Chaplaincies, Theological Dialogue/Religious Education, Racism/Interracial Understanding, Religious Leadership Forum, Christian Associates Television (CATV), *The Call*...Newsletter, Media Ministries, Internet Ministry, Indigent Burial Program

Christian Churches United of the Tri-County Area

413 South 19th St., Harrisburg, PA 17106-0750 Tel. (717)230-9550 Fax (717)230-9554
Email: ccuhbg@aol.com
Website: christianchurchesunited.com
Media Contact, Exec. Dir., Jaqueline P. Rucker
Exec. Dir., Jaqueline P. Rucker
Pres., Peter Pennington
Treas., James Smeltzer
Vice Pres., Patricia Bucek
Sec., Patricia Greenawald
HELP & LaCasa Ministries, -vacant-, P.O. Box 60750, Harrisburg, PA 17106-0750 Tel. (717)238-2851 Fax (717)238-1916
Major Activities: Volunteer Ministries to Prisons, HELP (Housing, Rent, Food, Medication, Transportation, Home Heating, Clothing), La Casa de Amistad (The House of Friendship) Social Services, AIDS Outreach, Prison Chaplaincy, Lend-A-Hand (Disaster Rebuilding)

Christians United in Beaver County

1098 Third St., Beaver, PA 15009 Tel. (724)774-1446 Fax (724)774-1446
Media Contact, Exec. Sec., Lois L. Smith
Exec. Sec., Lois L. Smith
Chaplains: Rev. Dennis Ugoletti, Rev. Anthony Massey, Rev. Kathleen Schoeneck, John Pusateri, Rev. Art Peters
Pres., Mrs. Delores Tisdale, 1021-5th Street, New Brighton, PA 15066
Treas., Mr. Richard Puryear, 2 McCabe Street, Sewickley, PA 15143
Major Activities: Christian Education, Evangelism, Social Action, Church Women United, United Church Men, Ecumenism,

Hospital, Detention Home and Jail Ministry, Behavioral Health Clinic.

East End Cooperative Ministry

250 N. Highland Ave., Pittsburgh, PA 15206 Tel. (412)361-5549 Fax (412)361-0151
Email: eecm@usaor.net
Media Contact, Michele Griffiths, Community Development Director
Exec. Dir., Myrna Zelenitz
Ass. Dir., Rev. Darnell Leonard
Major Activities: Food Pantry, Soup Kitchen, Men's Emergency Shelter, Drop-In Shelter for Homeless, Meals on Wheels, Casework and Supportive Services for Elderly, Information and Referral, Programs for Children and Youth, Bridge Housing Program for Men and PennFree for Women in Recovery and Their Children

Ecumenical Conference of Greater Altoona

PO Box 771, Altoona, PA 16693 Tel. (814)942-0512
Email: ecumenaltoona@charter.net
Media Contact, Exec. Dir., Susanna M. Tomlinson
Exec. Dir., Susanna M. Tomlinson
Major Activities: Religious Education, Workshops, Ecumenical Activities, Religious Christmas Parade, Campus Ministry, Community Concerns, Peace Forum, Religious Education for Mentally Challenged, and Interfaith Committee

Greater Bethlehem Area Council of Churches

1021 Center St., P.O. Box 1245, Bethlehem, PA 18016-1245 Tel. (610)867-8671 Fax (610) 866-9223
Email: gbacc@enter.net
Exec. Dir., Rev. Dr. Helen Baily Cochrane
Pres., William L. Cauller
Treas., Mr. David G. Boltz, 1831 Levering Place, Bethlem, PA. 18017
Major Activities: World-local hunger projects, Ecumenical Worship-Cooperation, Prison Ministry Programs, Support for Homeless and Welfare to Work Programs, Emergency Food Pantry, Support for Hospice and Share Care Programs, Regional Grave Bank, Support Summer Youth Camps and Church Sports League

Hanover Area Council of Churches

136 Carlisle St., Hanover, PA 17331-2406 Tel. (717)633-6353 Fax (717)633-1992
Email: cathy@sun-link.com
Website: www. netrax.net/~bouchard/hacc.htm
Exec. Dir., Cathy Ferree
Major Activities: Meals on Wheels, Provide a Lunch Program, Fresh Air Program, Clothing Bank, Hospital Chaplaincy Services, Congregational and Interfaith Relations, Public Ecumenical Programs and Services, State Park Chaplaincy Services & Children's Program, Compeer, Faith at Work, CROP Walk, Stolte Scholarship Fund, Community Needs

Inter-Church Ministries of Erie County

2216 Peach St., Erie, PA 16502 Tel. (814)454-2411
Voucher Program: Jeremy Stewart
Pres., Msgr. William E. Biebel, 230 10th St., Erie, PA 16501
Treas., Ms. Margaret Lorei
Major Activities: Local Ecumenism, Ministry with Aging, Social Ministry, Continuing Education, North West Pennsylvania Conference of Bishops and Judicatory Execs., Theological Dialogue, Coats for Kids, Voucher Program for Emergency Assistance

Lancaster County Council of Churches

134 E. King St., Lancaster, PA 17602 Tel. (717)291-2261 Fax (717)291-6403
Email: office@lccouncilofchurches.org
Media Contact, Executive Dir., Kim Y. Wittel
Pres., John Dieterly
Prescott House: Dir., John Stoudt
Encounter: Dir., Catherine Moon
CONTACT: Dir., Tina Schadewald
Service Ministry: Dir., Jaclyn Messersmith
Major Activities: Social Ministry, Residential Ministry to Youthful Offenders, CONTACT, Advocacy, Child Abuse Prevention

Lebanon County Christian Ministries

250 S. 7th St., P.O. Box 654, Lebanon, PA 17042 Tel. (717)274-2601
Email: lccm@lmf
Media Contact, Exec. Dir., Lillian Morales
Exec. Dir., Lillian Morales
Noon Meals Coord., Wenda Dinatale
Major Activities: H.O.P.E. (Helping Our People in Emergencies), Food & Clothing Bank, Free Meal Program, Commodity Distribution Program, Ecumenical Events

Lehigh County Conference of Churches

534 Chew St., Allentown, PA 18102 Tel. (610)433-6421 Fax (610)439-8039
Email: lccc@lccconfchurch.org
Website: www.lcconfchurch.org
Media Contact, Dir. of Development, Ira Faro
Exec. Dir., The Rev. Dr. Christine L. Nelson
Assoc. Dir., Marlene Merz
Pres., Mr. Charles Ehninger
1st Vice Pres., Rev. William Metzger
Sec., The Rev. Dr. David Charles Smith
Treas., Mr. Nelson Rabenold

Major Activities: Prison Chaplaincy Program, Social Concerns and Action, Clergy Dialogues, Daybreak Drop-In-Center for Mental Health–Adults, Soup Kitchen, Housing Advocacy Program, Pathways (Referral to Social Services), Street Contact, Linkage, Guardianship, Community Exchange, Homelessness Prevention, Pharmaceutical Assistance, Campbell Ecumenism-Unity lecture, Clothing Distribution, Aspires Mentoring Program, Ecumenical and Interfaith Services

Lewisburg Council of Churches

5. S. Asper Place, Lewisburg, PA 17837 Tel. (570)524-4834

Media Contact, Guy Temple, 139 Iron Cave Lane, Lewisburg, PA 17837 Tel (570)524-4877

Pres., Mrs. Janet Betzer, 1103 Market St., Lewisburg, PA 17837 Tel. (570) 524-2834

Treas., Mrs. Jan Temple, 139 Iron Cave Ln., Lewisburg, PA 17837 Tel. (570)524-4877

Major Activities: Supplementary and Emergency Food Pantries, Clothing Bank, CROP Walk, Week of Prayer for Christian Unity, Soup and Scripture Lenten Series, 3-hour Good Friday Service, Human Services Directory, Transient/Homeless Aid

Metropolitan Christian Council of Philadelphia

1501 Cherry St., Philadelphia, PA 19102-1429 Tel. (215)563-7854 Fax (215)563-6849

Email: geiger@mccp.org

Website: www.mccp.org

Media Contact, Assoc. Communications, Nancy L. Nolde

Exec. Dir., Rev. C. Edward Geiger

Assoc. Communications, Nancy L. Nolde

Office Mgr., Joan G. Shipman

Pres., Rev. Steven B. Laurence

First Vice Pres., Rev. G. Daniel Jones

Treas., A. Louis Denton, Esq.

Major Activities: Congregational Clusters, Public Policy Advocacy, Communication, Theological Dialogue (Christian and Interfaith), Women's Issues

North Hills Youth Ministry Counseling Center

802 McKnight Park Dr., Pittsburgh, PA 15237 Tel. (412)366-1300

Email: NHYM@SGI.NET

Media Contact, Exec. Dir., Rev. Ronald B. Barnes

Exec. Dir., Ronald B. Barnes

Major Activities: Elementary, Junior and Senior High School Individual and Family Counseling, Elementary Age Youth Early Intervention Counseling, Educational Programming for Churches and Schools, Youth Advocacy, Parent Education, Marital Counseling

Northside Common Ministries

P.O. Box 99861, Pittsburgh, PA 15233 Tel. (412)323-1163 Fax (412)323-1749

Email: NCM@city-net.com

Media Contact, Exec. Dir., Janet E. Holtz

Exec. Dir., Janet E. Holtz

Major Activities: Pleasant Valley Shelter for Homeless Men; Advocacy Around Hunger, Housing, Poverty, and Racial Issues; Community Food Pantry and Service Center; Supportive Housing

Northwest Interfaith Movement

6757 Greene St., Philadelphia, PA 19119 Tel. (215)843-5600 Fax (215)843-2755

Email: jejohnson@nim-phila.org

Website: www.nim-phila.org

Media Contact, Exec. Dir., Rabbi George M. Stern

Exec. Dir., Rabbi George M. Stern

Chpsn., Judy Weinstein

Long Term Care Program: Dir., Donald Carlin

Neighborhood Child Care Resource Prog.: Dir., Leslie S. Eslinger

Major Activities: Resources amd Technical Assistance for Child Care Programs, Conflict Mediation and Support for Nursing and Boarding Home Residents, Development of After-School Programs

Pennsylvania Conference on Interchurch Cooperation*

P.O. Box 2835, 223 North St., Harrisburg, PA 17105 Tel. (717)238-9613 Fax (717)238-1473

Email: staff@pacatholic.org

Website: www.pacatholic.org/ecumenism/index.htm

Media Contact, Carolyn Astfalk

Co-Staff: Dr. Robert J. O'Hara Jr., Rev. Gary Harke

Co-Chpsns.: Bishop Joseph Martino, Bishop Donald Main.

Major Activities: Theological Consultation, Social Concerns, Public Policy, Conferences and Seminars

The Pennsylvania Council of Churches*

900 S. Arlington Ave., Ste. 100, Harrisburg, PA 17109-5089 Tel. (717)545-4761 Fax (717) 545-4765

Email: pcc@pachurches.org

Website: www.pachurches.org

Media Contact, Exec. Dir., Rev. Gary L. Harke

Exec. Dir., Rev. Gary L. Harke

Public Policy, Dir., Kay S. Dowhower

Coord. for Contract Chaplaincy, Rev. Douglas Hodges

Coord. for Leisure Ministries, Dr. Paul L. Herring

Coord. For Direct Ministries, Rev. Douglas Hodges

Pres., Rev. Bishop A. Donald Main

Vice Pres., Rev. Clarice L. Chambers

Sec., Ms. Barbara Adams-Smetter

Treas., David B. Hoffman, CPA
Dir. Of Finance & Facilities, Janet A. Gulick
Major Activities: Racial/Ethnic Empowerment, Inter-church Dialogue, Trade Association Activities, Faith and Order, Seasonal Farmworker Ministry, Trucker/Traveler Ministry, Institutional Chaplaincy, Public Policy Advocacy and Education, Leisure Ministry, Conferences and Continuing Education Events, Disaster Response, Church Education, Global Warming Project, Public Education Initiative

Project of Easton, Inc.

330 Ferry St., Easton, PA 18042 Tel. (215)258-4361
Pres., Dr. John H. Updegrove
Vice Pres. Public Relations, Rev. Charles E. Staples
Vice Pres. Operations, Don Follett
Sec., Rosemary Reese
Treas., Steve Barsony
Exec. Dir., Maryellen Shuman
Major Activities: Food Bank, Adult Literacy Program, English as a Second Language, Children's Programs, Parents as Student Support, CROP Walk, Interfaith Council, Family Literacy, Emergency Assistance, Even Start Family Literacy

Reading Berks Conference of Churches

519 Elm St., P.O.Box 957, Reading, PA 19603 Tel. (610)375-6108 Fax (610)375-6205
Email: rdgbrkscc@comcast.net
Website: www.readingberksconferenceofchurches.com
Media Contact, Exec. Dir., Rev. Calvin Kurtz
Admin Asst., Donna Boyajcan
Exec. Dir., Rev. Calvin Kurtz
Pres., Fr. Thomas Pappalas
Treas., William Maslo
Major Activities: Institutional Ministry, Social Action, Migrant Ministry, CWS, CROP Walk for Hunger, Emergency Assistance, Prison Chaplaincy, Hospital Chaplaincy, Inter-church/Intercultural Services, Children and Youth Ministry, Healthy Family and Marriage Initiatives, Lazarus Project

Reading Urban Ministry

150 North 11th St, Reading, PA 19601 Tel. (610)374-6917 Fax (610)371-9791
Media Contact, Susan Sentz
Exec. Dir., Susan Sentz
Pres., David Hunsberger
Vice Pres., Darrin Love
Sec., Eleanor Hay
Treas., Sally Waters
Major Activities: Youth Ministry Program, Family Action Support Team (Parent Education and Child Abuse Prevention), Heal Thyself (offers a love-based reality)

South Hills Interfaith Ministries

1900 Sleepy Hollow Rd., South Park, PA 15129 Tel. (412)854-9120 Fax (412)854-9123
Website: www.shimcenters.org
Media Contact, Exec. Dir., Jerry Ellis
Prog. Dir., Director of Youth Programs, Sarah Henkel
Psychological Services, Don Zandier
Family Assistance Coord., Harry Dietz
Business Mgr., Amy Puglisi
Volunteer Coord., Barbara Houston
Major Activities: Basic Human Needs, Community Organization and Development, Inter-Faith Cooperation, Personal Growth, At-Risk Youth Development, Women in Transition, Elderly Support, After School Homework Club, Early Childhood Program (Preschool), Interfaith Educational Programs and Observances

United Churches of Lycoming County

202 E. Third St., Williamsport, PA 17701 Tel. (570)322-1110 Fax (570)326-4572
Email: uclc@sunlink.net
Website: www.uclc.org
Media Contact, Exec. Dir., Gwen Nelson Bernstine
Exec. Dir., Gwen Nelson Bernstine
Ofc. Sec., Linda Winter
Pres., Mrs. Mikey Kamienski, 515 Vallamont Dr., Williamsport, PA 17701
Treas., Mr. A. Blair Phillips, 1511 Fairview Dr., Montoursville, PA 17754
Shepherd of the Streets: Rev. J. Morris Smith, 669 Center St., Williamsport, PA 17701
Ecumenism: Dir., Rev. Louis Gatti, 3200 Lycoming Creek Rd., Williamsport, PA 17701
Educ. Ministries: Dir., Mrs. Deb Best, 522 N. Grier St., Williamsport, PA. 17701
Institutional Ministry: Dir., Rev. Darlene Little, 266 Wagner Rd., Williamsport, PA 17701
Radio/TV: Dir., Nan Porter, 953 South Market St., South Williamsport, PA 17702
Prison Ministry: Dir., Rev. Jerry and Mrs. Evadna Cline, 3336 W. Fourth St., Williamsport, PA 17701
Christian Social Concerns: Dir., Rev. Joyce Gensib, 1315 Cherry St., Williamsport, PA 17701
Major Activities: Ecumenism, Educational Ministries, Church Women United, Church World Service and CROP, Prison Ministry, Radio/TV, Nursing Homes, Fuel Bank, Food Pantry, Family Life, Shepherd of the Streets Urban Ministry, Peace Concerns, Housing Initiative, Interfaith Dialogue, Youth Ministry.

Wilkinsburg Community Ministry

710 Mulberry St., Pittsburgh, PA 15221 Tel. (412)241-8072 Fax (412)241-8315
Email: wcm15221@juno.com
Website: trfn.clpgh.org/wcm
Media Contact, Dir., Rev. Vivian Lovingood

Acting Dir., Elizabeth Mulvaney, MSW, LSW
Pres. Of Bd., Glenna Wilson, MSW, LSW
Major Activities: Hunger Ministry,Summer Reading Camp, Teen-Moms Infant Care, Meals on Wheels, Church Camp Scholarships, Utility Assistance, Clothing/Furniture Assistance, Case Management for Elderly Homebound Persons and Families, Soup Kitchen

Wyoming Valley Council of Churches

70 Lockhart St., Wilkes-Barre, PA 18702 Tel. (570)825-8543
Media Contact, Exec. Dir., Susan Grine Harper
Exec. Dir., Susan Grine Harper
Ofc. Sec., Sandra Karrott
Pres., Dn. Sergei Kapral
Treas., H. Merritt Hughes
Major Activities: Nursing Home Chaplaincy, Martin Luther King Jr. Fuel Drive in Association with Local Agencies, Hospital Referral Service, Choral Festival of Faith, Migrant Ministry, Ecumenical Pulpit Exchange Int., CROP Hunger Walk, Pastoral Care Ministries, Clergy Retreats and Seminars

York County Council of Churches

P.O. Box 1865, York, PA 17405-1865 Tel. (717) 854-9504 Fax (717)843-5295
Email: yccc@nfdc.net
Media Contact, Exec. Dir., Rev. David D. Danneberger
Pres., Mrs. Christina J. Iosue
Vice Pres., Rev. Donald Zobler
Exec. Dir., Rev. David D. Danneberger
Major Activities: Educational Development, Spiritual Growth and Renewal, Worship and Witness, Congregational Resourcing, Outreach and Mission

RHODE ISLAND

The Rhode Island State Council of Churches*

734 Hope St., Providence, RI 02906 Tel. (401) 861-1700 Fax (401)331-3080
Email: ricouncil@aol.com
Website: www.ricouncilof churches
Media Contact, Exec. Min., The Rev. John E. Holt
Exec. Min., The Rev. John E. Holt
Admn. Asst., Peggy MacNie
Pres., Mr. Frank Cook
Treas., George Weavill
Major Activities: Urban Ministries, TV, Institutional Chaplaincy, Advocacy/Justice and Service, Legislative Liaison, Faith and Order, Leadership Development, Campus Ministries

South Carolina Christian Action Council, Inc.*

P.O. Drawer 3248, Columbia, SC 29230 Tel. (803)786-7115 Fax (803)786-7116
Email: sccouncil@sccouncil.net
Website: www.sccouncil.net
Media Contact, Exec. Minister, Rev. Brenda Kneece
Exec. Minister, Rev. Brenda Kneece
Pres., The Rt. Rev. William "Bill" Skitton
Major Activities: Advocacy and Ecumenism, Continuing Education, Interfaith Dialogue, Citizenship and Public Affairs, Publications, Race Relations, Child Advocacy, Faith and Health, Environmental Stewardship

United Ministries

606 Pendleton St., Greenville, SC 29601 Tel. (864)232-6463 Fax (864)370-3518
Email: info@united-ministries.org
Website: www.united-ministries.org
Media Contact, Exec. Dir., Rev. Beth Templeton
Exec. Dir., Rev. Beth Templeton
Pres., Dr. Lynne Shackelford
Vice Pres., Marvin Quattlebaum Jr.
Sec., Rufus E. Perry
Treas., Gordon Gibson, Bill Hummers
Major Activities: Survival Programs (Emergency Assistance, Place of Hope–a Day Shelter for Homeless, Travelers Aid), Stabilization Program (Faith in Action, Follow), Barrier Removal Programs (Employment Readiness, Adult Education)

SOUTH DAKOTA

Association of Christian Churches of South Dakota*

100 S. Spring Ave., Suite 106, Sioux Falls, SD 57104-3626 Tel. (605)334-1980
Email: office@accsd.org
Website: www.accsd.org
Media Contact, Rev. Christian Franklin, First Christian Church, 524 W. 13th St., Sioux Falls, SD 57104-4309 Tel. (605)338-9474
Pres., Bd. Of Directors, Rev. Christian Franklin
Ofc. Mgr., Pat Willard
Major Activities: Ecumenical Forums, Continuing Education for Clergy, Legislative Information, Resourcing Local Ecumenism, Native American Issues, Ecumenical Fields Ministries, Rural Economic Development, Children at Risk

TENNESSEE

Metropolitan Inter Faith Association (MIFA)

P.O. Box 3130, Memphis, TN 38173-0130 Tel. (901)527-0208 Fax (901)527-3202
Media Contact, Dir., Media Relations, Caroline Vonicessler
Exec. Dir., Margaret Craddock
Major Activities: Emergency Services (Rent, Utility, Food, Clothing Assistance), Home-Delivered Meals and Senior Support Services, Youth Services, Homeless Programs

Tennessee Association of Churches*

103 Oak St., Ashland City, TN 37015 Tel. (615)792-4631

Pres., Rev. Steve Mosley

Treas., Paul Milliken

Major Activities: Faith and Order, Christian Unity, Social Concern Ministries, Governmental Concerns, Governor's Prayer Breakfast

Volunteer Ministry Center

103 South Gay St., Knoxville, TN 37902 Tel. (423)524-3926 Fax (423)524-7065

Media Contact, Exec. Dir., Angelia Moon

Exec. Dir., Angelia Moon

Pres., David Leech

Vice Pres., John Moxham

Treas., Doug Thompson

Major Activities: Homeless Program, Food Line, Crisis Referral Program, Subsidized Apartment Program, Counselling Program, Parenting Education for Single Parents

TEXAS

Austin Area Interreligious Ministries

701 Tillery St., Ste. 8, Austin, TX 78705 Tel. (512)386-9145 Fax (512)385-1430

Email: aaim@ammaustin.org

Website: www.ammaustin.org

Media Contact, Exec. Dir., Susan Wills, LPC

Exec. Dir., Susan Wills

Pres., Rev. Mel Waxler

Treas., Anita Maxwell

Major Activities: Youth at Risk Mentoring, Housing Rehabilitation, Broadcast Ministry, Interfaith Dialogues, Family Issues, Homeless Issues, Hunger Issues, Racial Reconciliation, ESL

Border Association for Refugees from Central America (BARCA), Inc.

P.O. Box 1725, Edinburg, TX 78540 Tel. (956)631-7447 Fax (956)687-9266

Email: barcainc@aol.com

Media Contact, Exec. Dir., Ninfa Ochoa-Krueger

Exec. Dir, Ninfa Ochoa-Krueger

Outreach Services: Dir., Juanita Ledesma

Major Activities: Food, Shelter, Clothing to Newly Arrived Indigent Immigrants and Refugees; Medical and Other Emergency Aid; Special Services to Children; Speakers on Refugee and Immigrant Concerns for Church Groups; Orientation, Advocacy, and Legal Services for Immigrants and Refugees

Corpus Christi Metro Ministries

1919 Leopard St., P.O. Box 4899, Corpus Christi, TX 78469-4899 Tel. (361)887-0151 Fax (361)887-7900

Email: edseeger@ccmetrominstries.com

Website: www.ccmetroministries.com

Media Contact, Exec. Dir., Rev. Edward B. Seeger

Exec. Dir., Rev. Edward B. Seeger

Admn. Dir., Ginger Flewelling-Leeds

Volunteer Dir., Ann Cox

Fin. Coord., Sue McCown

Loaves & Fishes: Dir., Ray Gomez

Emergency Services: Mgr., Elsa Haecker

Employment: Dir., Larry Curtis

Health and Human Services: Dir., Ann Cox

Major Activities: Free Cafeteria,Transitional Shelters, Job Readiness, Job Placement, Primary Health Care, Community Service Restitution, Emergency Clothing, Information and Referral, Case Management

East Dallas Cooperative Parish

P.O. Box 720305, Dallas, TX 75372-0305 Tel. (214)823-9149 Fax (214)823-2015

Email: edcp@swbell.net

Media Contact, Nancy Jellinek, Exec. Dir.

Pres., Debbie Thorpe

Major Activities: Emergency Food, Clothing, Job Bank, Medical Clinic, Legal Clinic, Tutorial Education, Home Companion Service, Pre-School Education, Hispanic Ministry, Activity Center for Low Income Older Adults, Pastoral Counseling, English Language Ministry, Pre-GED program

Greater Dallas Community of Churches

624 N. Good-Latimer #100, Dallas, TX 75204-5818 Tel. (214)824-8680 Fax (214)824-8726

Email: gdcc@churchcommunity.org

Media Contact, Exec. Dir., Ray Flachmeier

Exec. Dir., Ray Flachmeier

Assoc. Dirs., The Rev. Holsey Hickman, John Stoesz

AmeriCorps-Building Blocks: Dir., Wendy Hodges-Kent

Development Dir., Mary Sue Foster

Pres., Rev. George Mason, Ph.D.

Treas., Jerry McNabb

Major Activities: Interdenominational, Interfaith and Interracial Understanding and Joint Work, AmeriCorps-Building Blocks (Direct Service to Develop Inner City Children, Youth and Families), Summer Food and Reading, Hunger, Peacemaking, Public Policy, Social Justice, Faith and Life, Children's Health Outreach, Child Advocacy, Dismantaling Racism

Interfaith Ministries for Greater Houston

3217 Montrose Blvd., Houston, TX 77006 Tel. (713)522-3955 Fax (713)520-4663

Media Contact, Exec. Dir., Betty P. Taylor

Exec. Dir., Betty P. Taylor

Pres., Charles R. Erickson

Development: Dir., Sharon Ervine
Assoc. Exec. Dir., Larry Norton
Treas., Fort D. Flowers, Jr.
Sec., Darlene Alexander
Major Activities: Community Concerns, Hunger, Older Adults, Families, Youth, Child Abuse, Refugee Services, Congregational Relations and Development, Social Service Programs, Refugee Services, Hunger Coalition, Youth Victim Witness, Family Connection, Meals on Wheels, Senior Health, RSVP, Foster Grandparents

North Dallas Shared Ministries

2530 Glenda Ln., #500, Dallas, TX 75229 Tel. (214)620-8696 Fax (214)620-0433
Media Contact, Exec. Dir., J. Dwayne Martin
Exec. Dir., J. Dwayne Martin
Major Activities: Emergency Assistance, Job Counseling, ESL

Northside Inter-Church Agency (NICA)

1600 Circle Park Blvd., Fort Worth, TX 76106-8943 Tel. (817)626-1102 Fax (817)626-9043
Email: nicaagency@sbcglobal.net
Media Contact, Exec. Dir., Connie Nohoolewa
Exec. Dir., Connie Nohoolewa
Major Activities: Food, Clothing, Counseling, Information and Referral, Furniture and Household Items, Nutrition Education and Teen Program, Employment Services, Thanksgiving Basket Program, "Last Resort" Christmas Program, Community Networking, Ecumenical Worship Services, Volunteer Training, Newsletter, Senior Home Repairs, School Clothing Program, Advocacy

San Antonio Community of Churches

1101 W. Woodlawn, San Antonio, TX 78201 Tel. (210)733-9159 Fax (210)733-5780
Email: SACC@juno.com
Media Contact, Exec. Dir., Dr. Kenneth Thompson
Exec. Dir., Dr. Kenneth Thompson
Pres., Rev. Thomas Robinson
Major Activities: Christian Education, Missions, Infant Formula and Medical Prescriptions for Children of Indigent Families, Continuing Education For Clergy and Laity, Media Resource Center, Social Issues, Aging Concerns, Youth Concerns, Family Concerns, Sponsor Annual CROP Walk for Hunger, Peace and Anti-Violence Initiatives

San Antonio Urban Ministries

535 Bandera Rd., San Antonio, TX 78228
Media Contact, Sue Kelly
Exec. Dir., Sue Kelly
Pres., Rev. Leslie Ellison
Major Activities: Homes for Discharged Mental Patients, After School Care for Latch Key Children, Christian Based Community Ministry

Southeast Area Churches (SEARCH)

P.O. Box 51256, Fort Worth, TX 76105 Tel. (817)531-2211
Exec. Dir., Dorothy Anderson-Develrow
Major Activities: Emergency Assistance, Advocacy, Information and Referral, Community Worship, School Supplies, Direct Aid to Low Income and Elderly

Tarrant Area Community of Churches

P.O. Box 11471, Fort Worth, TX 76110-0471 Tel. (817)534-1790 Fax (817)534-1995
Email: revkm@flash.net
Pres., Regina Taylor
Treas., Don Hoak
Exec. Dir., Dr. Kenneth W. McIntosh
Major Activities: Eldercare Program, Children's Sabbath Sponsorship, Week of Prayer for Christian Unity, CROP Walk for Hunger Relief, Community Issues Forums, Family Pathfinders

Texas Conference of Churches*

1033 La Posada, Ste. 125, Austin, TX 78752 Tel. (512)451-0991 Fax (512)451-5348
Email: tcc@txconfchurches.org
Website: www.txconfchurches.org
Media Contact, Communications and Web Services, Liz Yeats
Exec. Dir., Dr. Carol M. Worthing
Office Manager, Caryn Wontor
Pres., The Most Rev. Michael Pfeifer, OMI
Major Activities: Faith and Order, Related Ecumenism, Christian-Jewish Relations, Church and Society Issues

United Board of Missions

1701 Bluebonnet Ave., P.O. Box 3856, Port Arthur, TX 77643-3856 Tel. (409)982-9412 Fax (409)985-3668
Media Contact, Admn. Asst., Carolyn Schwarr
Exec. Dir., Clark Moore
Pres., Glenda McCoy
Major Activities: Emergency Assistance (Food and Clothing, Rent and Utility, Medical, Dental, Transportation), Share a Toy at Christmas, Counseling, Back to School Clothing Assistance, Information and Referral, Hearing Aid Bank, Meals on Wheels, Super Pantry, Energy Conservation Programs, Job Bank Assistance to Local Residents Only

VERMONT

Vermont Ecumenical Council and Bible Society*

285 Maple St., Burlington, VT 05477 Tel. (802)864-7723

Email: info@vecbs.org
Website: www.vecbs.org
Media Contact, Admn. Asst., Betsy Wackernagel
Exec. Officer, Rev. Dr. Leonard Rowelll
Pres., Rev. Frederick Neu
Vice Pres., Bishop Thomas Ely
Treas., Mr. Joseph Cioffi
Major Activities: Christian Unity, Bible Distribution, Social Justice, Committee on Faith and Order, Committee on Peace, Justice and the Integrity of Creation

VIRGINIA

Virginia Council of Churches, Inc.*

1214 W. Graham Rd., Richmond, VA 23220-1409 Tel. (804)321-3300 Fax (804)329-5066
Email: Barton@vcc-net.org
Website: www.vcc-net.org
Media Contact, Gen. Min., Rev. Jonathan Barton
Gen. Min., Rev. Jonathan Barton
Migrant Head Start: Dir., Richard D. Cagan
Refugee Resettlement: Dir., Rev. Richard D. Cline
Weekday Rel. Educ.: Coord., Faye Drewry, 2699 Lanier Lane, McGaheysville, VA 22840
Campus Ministry Forum: Coord., Rev. Steve Darr, c-o Community College Ministries, 305 Washington St. NW, Blacksburg, VA 24060-4745
Major Activities: Faith and Order, Network Building and Coordination, Ecumenical Communications, Justice and Legislative Concerns, Educational Development, Rural Concerns, Refugee Resettlement, Migrant Ministries and Migrant Head Start, Disaster Coordination, Infant Mortality Prevention

WASHINGTON

Associated Ministries of Tacoma-Pierce County

1224 South I St., Tacoma, WA 98405-5021 Tel. (253)383-3056 Fax (253)383-2672
Email: info@associatedministries.org
Website: www. associatedministries.org
Media Contact, Exec. Dir., Rev. David T. Alger
Dir. Of Communications, Judy Jones
Pres., Rev. John Williams
Vice Pres., Rev. David Wold
Sec., Karen Davey
Treas., Jeff Cunningham
Exec. Dir., Rev. David T. Alger
Deputy Dir., Maureen Fife
Mental Health Chaplaincy: Dir., Julie Bradley
Project Interdependence: Dir., Valorie Crout
Paint Tacoma-Pierce Beautiful: Dir., Sallie Shawl
Development: Dir., S. Marion Sharp
Hilltop Action Coalition: Dir., Jeanie Peterson
Communication and Education: Dir., Judy Jones
Community Connections for Military Families: Dir., Sherrill Hendrick
Major Activities: County-wide Hunger Walk, Hunger Awareness, Economic Justice, Religious Education, Social Service Program Advocacy, Communication and Networking of Churches, Housing, Paint Tacoma-Pierce Beautiful, Mental Health Chaplaincy, Theological Dialogue, Welfare to Work Mentoring, Hilltop Action Coalition, Compeer, Homelessness, Youth Ministry, Ecumenical Formation, Community Connection for Military Families, Interfaith Roundtable

Associated Ministries of Thurston County

P.O. Box 1221, Olympia, WA 98507 Tel. (360)357-7224
Email: theamtc@aol.com
Website: www.amtcoly.org
Media Contact, Exec. Dir., Kathy Erlandson
Exec. Dir., Cheri Gonyaw
Pres., George Hinkel
Treas., Bob McCoy
Major Activities: Church Information and Referral, Interfaith Relations, Social and Health Concerns, Community Action, Social Justice

Center for the Prevention of Sexual and Domestic Violence

2400 N. 45th St, Suite 10, Seattle, WA 98103 Tel. (206)634-1903 Fax (206)634-0115
Email: cpsdv@cpsdv.org
Website: www.cpsdv.org
Media Contact, Rev. Dr. Marie M. Fortune
Executive Director, Rev. Kathryn J. Johnson, kjohnson@cpsdv.org
Founder & Senior Analyst, Rev. Dr. Marie M. Fortune, mfortune@cpsdv.org
Training & Education: Dir., Rev. Thelma Burgonio-Watson, burgonio@cpsdv.org
Jewish Program: Dir., Rabbi Cindy Enger, cenger@cpsdv.org
Clearinghouse: Coord., Dinah Hall, dhall@cpsdv.org
Finance Dir., Marion J. Ward
Major Activities: Prevention and Response Education, Clergy and Lay Training, Video and Print Resources, Bi-national Educational Ministry

Church Council of Greater Seattle

4759 15th Ave. NE, Seattle, WA 98105-4404 Tel. (206)525-1213 Fax (206)525-1218
Email: info@churchcouncilseattle.org
Website: www.churchcouncilseattle.org
Media Contact, Acting Executive Dir., Alice Woldt
Acting Executive Dir., Alice Woldt
Emergency Feeding Prog.: Dir., Arthur Lee
Friend to Friend: Dir., Marilyn Soderquist
Youth Chaplaincy Program: Dir. Chaplain, Rev. Benny Wright

The Sharehouse: Dir., Michal Nortness
The Homelessness Project: Dir., Nancy Dorman
Mission for Music & Healing: Dir., Susan Gallaher and Esther "Little Dove" John
Sound Youth-AmeriCorps: Dir., Cat Koehn
Academy of Religious Broadcasting: Dir., Rev. J. Graley Taylor
Board Chair, The Rev. David Meekhof
Board Treas., The Rev. Jeb Parr
The Source, Editor, Cynthia Adcock
Seattle Youth Garden Works: Dir., -vacant-
SW King County Mental Health Ministry: Dir., Natasha White
JOY Initiative: Prog. Dir., Rick Jump
St. Petersburg-Seattle Sister Churches Program: Chpsn., Nigel Taber-Hamilton
Asia Pacific Task Force: Contact Person, Akio Yanagihara
Commission on Racial Justice: Chpsn., -vacant-
Commission on Public Witness: Staff, Alice Woldt
Sel-Managed Housing Programs: Dir., Misti Uptain
Cuba Friendshipment Committee: Chpsn., Monica Zapeda
Palestinain Concerns Task Force: Chpsn., The Rev. Dr. William Cate and Dr. Farhat Ziadeh
Interfaith Network of Concern for the People of Iraq: Chpsn., The Rev. Rich Gamble and Andrew Fung
Major Activities: Children, Youth and Families, Hunger Relief, Global Peace and Justice, Housing and Homelessness, Pastoral Care, Services for the Aging, Public Witness, Interfaith and Ecumenical Relations, Publisher of the *The Source* (monthly ecumenical newspaper)

The Interfaith Association of Snohomish County

2301 Hoyt, P.O. Box 12824, Everett, WA 98206 Tel. (206)252-6672
Email: admin@.tiasccom
Website: www.tiasc.com
Media Contact, Exec. Dir., Janet Pope
Exec. Dir., Janet Pope
Pres., William Comfort
Major Activities: Housing and Shelter, Economic Justice, Hunger, Interfaith Worship and Collaboration

Northwest Harvest–E.M.M.

P.O. Box 12272, Seattle, WA 98102 Tel. (206) 625-0755 Fax (206)625-7518
Email: nharvest@blarg.net
Website: www. northwestharvest.org
Media Contact, Comm. Affairs Dir., Ellen Hansen
Exec. Dir., Ruth M. Velozo
Chpsn., Patricia Barcott
Major Activities: Northwest Harvest (Statewide Hunger Response), Cherry Street Food Bank (Community Hunger Response), Northwest Infants Corner (Special Nutritional Products for Infants and Babies)

Spokane Council of Ecumenical Ministries

1620 N. Monroe, Spokane, WA 99205 Tel. (509)329-1410 Fax (509)329-1409
Email: scem1620@aol.com
Media Contact, Admin. Asst., Marylin Ferguson
Dir., Kateri Caron
Chair, Fr. William Pugliese
Treas., Rev. Mark Randall
Sec., Linda Schearing
Major Activities: Camp PEACE, Multi-Cultural Human Relations, High School Youth Camp, Eastern Washington Legislative Conference, Churches Against Racism, Living Wage Movement, CROP Walk, Interfaith Thanksgiving Worship, Easter Sunrise Service, Ecumenical Sunday, Friend to Friend Visitation, Family Friend Project, Night Walk Ministry, Dir. of Churches and Community Agencies

Washington Association of Churches*

419 Occidental Ave. S, Ste. 201, Seattle, WA 98104-2886 Tel. (206)625-9790 Fax (206)625-9791
Email: wac@thewac.org
Website: www.thewac.org
Media Contact, Exec. Min., Rev. John C. Boonstra, boonstra@thewac.org
Director for Operations, Bette Schneider, schneider @thewac.org
Major Activities: Faith and Order, Ecumencial Dialogue, Justice Advocacy, Confronting Poverty, Hunger Action, Legislation, Denominational Ecumenical Coordination, Theological Formation, Leadership Development, Immigrant Rights Advocacy, Racial Justice Advocacy, International Solidarity, Environmental Justice Advocacy

WEST VIRGINIA

Greater Fairmont Council of Churches

P.O. Box 108, Fairmont, WV 26554 Tel. (304) 367-0962
Media Contact, President, Rev. Jeremiah Jasper
Pres., Rev. Jeremiah Jasper
Major Activities: Community Ecumenical Services, Youth and Adult Sports Leagues, CROP Walk Sponsor, Weekly Radio Broadcasts

The Greater Wheeling Council of Churches

1060 Chapline St., 110 Methodist Building, Wheeling, WV 26003 Tel. (304)232-5315

Media Contact, Exec. Dir., Kathy J. Burley
Exec. Dir., Kathy J. Burley
Hospital Notification Sec., Anna Lou Lenz
Pres., Martha J. Morris
Finance Chpn., Rev. Robert P. Johnson- Doug Clatterbuck
Major Activities: Christian Education, Evangelism, Christian Heritage Week Celebration, Institutional Ministry, Regional Jail Chaplaincy, Church Women United, Volunteer Chaplaincy Care at OVMC Hospital, School of Religion, Hospital Notification, Hymn Sing in the Park, Anti-Gambling Crusade, Pentecost Celebration, Clergy Council, Easter Sunrise Service, Community Seder, Church Secretaries Fellowship, National Day of Prayer Service, Videotape Library-Audiotape Library, Flood Relief Network of the Upper Ohio Valley

West Virginia Council of Churches*

2207 Washington St. E., Charleston, WV 25311-2218 Tel. (304)344-3141 Fax (304)342-1506
Email: wvcc@wvcc.org
Website: www.wvcc.org
Media Contact, Office Manager, Bob Rosier, bob@wvcc.org
Pres., Most Rev. Bernard W. Schmitt, D.D. (RC)
1st Vice Pres.,Rev. Dr. Randall F. Flanagan (UMC)
2nd Vice Pres., Ms. Patricia Harris, CC (DOC)
Sec., Rev. Dr. William B. Allen (DOC)
Treas., Very Rev. Frederick P. Annie (RC)
Major Activities: Disaster Response, Faith and Order, Family Concerns, Interfaith Relations, Peace and Justice, Government Concerns, Support Services Network

WISCONSIN

Center for Community Concerns

1501 Villa St., Racine, WI 53403 Tel. (414)637-9176 Fax (414)637-9265
Email: ccc1501@rootcom.net
Media Contact, Exec. Dir., Douglas G. Farrell
Exec. Dir., Sr. Douglas G. Farrell
Skillbank Coord., Eleanor Sorenson
Major Activities: Advocacy, Direct Services, Research, Community Consultant, Senior Citizen Service, Referral

Christian Youth Council

1715-52nd St., Kenosha, WI 53140 Tel. (262) 654-6200 x120 Fax (414)652-4461
Media Contact, Exec. Dir., Steven L. Nelson
Exec. Dir., Steven L. Nelson
Sports Dir., Jerry Tappen
Outreach Dir., Linda Osborne
Accountant, Debbie Cutts
Class Director, Jill Cox
Pres. & Chmn. of Board, Lon Knoedler
Gang Prevention: Dir., Sam Sauceda
Major Activities: Leisure Time Ministry, Institutional Ministries, Ecumenical Committee, Social Concerns, Outreach Sports (with a Christian Philosophy)

Interfaith Conference of Greater Milwaukee

1442 N. Farwell Ave., Ste. 200, Milwaukee, WI 53202 Tel. (414)276-9050 Fax (414)276-8442
Email: IFCGM@aol.com
Media Contact, Exec. Dir., Marcus White
Chpsn., Rev. Velma Smith
First Vice Chpsn., Archbishop Rembert G. Weakland
Second Vice Chpsn., Rev. Charles Graves
Sec., Paula Simon
Treas., Rev. Mary Ann Neevel
Exec. Dir., Marcus White
Consultant in Communications, Rev. Robert P. Seater
Major Activities: Economic Issues, Racism, CROP Walk, Public Policy, Suburban and Urban Partnerships, TV Programming, Peace and International Issues Committee, Annual Membership Luncheon, Religion Diversity, Restorative Justice

Madison Area Urban Ministry

2300 S. Park St., Madison, WI 53713 Tel. (608)256-0906 Fax (608)256-4387
Email: mum@emum.org
Website: www.emun.org
Media Contact, Office Manager, Jackie Austin
Exec. Dir., Mary K. Baum
Program Mgr., -vacant-
Major Activities: Community Projects, Dialogue/Forums, Social and Economic Justice

Wisconsin Council of Churches*

750 Windsor St. Ste. 301, Sun Prairie, WI 53590-2149 Tel. (608)837-3108 Fax (608)837-3038
Email: sanderson@wichurches.org
Website: www.wichurches.org
Media Contact, Comm. Coord., Jeanette Johnson
Exec. Dir., Exec. Dir., Scott D. Anderson
Assoc. Dir., -vacant-
Ofc. Mgr., Jeanette Johnson
Coord. for Local Ecumenism, Rev. Kenneth Pennings
Pres., Rev. Hal Murray
Treas., Dr. Robert Book
Accountant, Rick Fluechtling
Coord. for Program Support Services, Mr. Christopher Marceil
Major Activities: Social Witness, Migrant Ministry, Institutional Chaplaincy, Peace and Justice, Faith and Order, Rural Concerns, American Indian Ministries Council, Park Ministry, Wisconsin Housing Partnership, Nonviolence, Economic Justice, Corporate Responsibility

WYOMING

Wyoming Church Coalition*

P.O. Box 20812, Cheyenne, WY 82003-7017 Tel. (307)635-4251 Fax (307)637-4737

Email: wychco@aol.com

Media Contact, Mary Richey, Wyoming Church Coalition, PO Box 20812, Cheyenne, WY 82003

Chpsn., Joe Keys

Chaplain, Rev. Kenneth Martin

Bookkeeper, Mary Richey

Office Manager, Peg Edwards

Major Activities: Alternatives to Violence, Prison Ministry, Beyond Tolerance, Malicious Harrasment, Domestic Violence, Empowering the Poor and Oppressed, Peace and Justice, Public Health Issues, Welfare Reform, Death Penalty

Index of Select Programs for U.S. Regional and Local Ecumenical Bodies

For many years the *Yearbook of American & Canadian Churches* has published the previous chapter, "The Directory of US Regional and Local Ecumenical Bodies." Each entry of that directory contains a brief description of the diverse programs offered by each agency. However, researchers, pastors, service organizations, and theological seminaries often inquire about specific programs and which agencies carry out such programs. In response, we have created this chapter, which indexes the various regional and local ecumenical agencies by 25 different program areas. These program areas are the 25 that have been the most frequent subjects of inquiry in our office. We have collected this program information directly from these organizations by means of a simple response form. There is an enormous diversity of ministries and missions conducted by these diverse organizations. Most organizations pursue several kinds of programs at once. However, some of these may focus their efforts most especially on only one of their programs, their other programs may be less well developed than their specialty. Consequently, the extent to which any of these ministries is a priority for any particular organization cannot be inferred from this list. For detailed information about the nature and extent of any particular ministry, the reader is urged to contact the organization directly using the directory of "US Regional and Local Ecumenical Bodies," which is found in the pages just prior to this index.

AIDS/HIV Programs

Associated Ministries of Tacoma-Pierce County—Tacoma, WA
Bergen County Council of Churches—Bergenfield, NJ
Center City Churches—Hartford, CT
Christian Churches United of the Tri-County Area—Harrisburg, PA
Christian Conference of Connecticut—Hartford, CT
Council of Churches of Greater Bridgeport, Inc.—Bridgeport, CT
East Dallas Cooperative Parish—Dallas, TX
East End Cooperative Ministry—Pittsburgh, PA
Ecumenical Ministries of Oregon—Portland, OR
Grand Rapids Area Center for Ecumenism (GRACE)—Grand Rapids, MI
Greater Chicago Broadcast Ministries—Chicago, IL
Interfaith Community Services—St. Joseph, MO
Metropolitan Ecumenical Ministry—Newark, NJ
Mississippi Religious Leadership Conference—Jackson, MS
New Britain Area Conference of Churches (NEWBRACC)—New Britain, CT
New Mexico Conference of Churches—Albuquerque, NM
Reading Berks Conference of Churches—Reading, PA
The Rhode Island State Council of Churches—Providence, RI
Schenectady Inner City Ministry—Schenectady, NY
South Carolina Christian Action Council, Inc.—Columbia, SC
Southeast Ecumenical Ministry—Rochester, NY
Southern California Ecumenical Council—Pasadena, CA
Troy Area United Ministries—Troy, NY
United Churches of Lycoming County—Williamsport, PA
Wisconsin Council of Churches—Sun Prairie, WI
York County Council of Churches—York, PA

Anti-Racism Programs

Akron Area Association of Churches—Akron, OH
Arkansas Interfaith Conference—Scott, AR
Asheville-Buncombe Community Christian Ministry (ABCCM)—Asheville, NC
The Associated Churches of Fort Wayne & Allen County, Inc.—Fort Wayne, IN
Associated Ministries of Tacoma-Pierce County— Tacoma, WA
Association of Christian Churches of South Dakota—Sioux Falls, SD
Association of Religious Communities—Danbury, CT
Austin Area Interreligious Ministries—Austin, TX
Bergen County Council of Churches—Bergenfield, NJ
Berrien County Association of Churches—Benton Harbor, MI
Brooklyn Council of Churches—Brooklyn, NY
Broome County Council of Churches, Inc.—Binghamton, NY
Capital Region Ecumenical Organization (CREO)—Schenectady, NY
The Capitol Region Conference of Churches—Hartford, CT
Christian Associates of Southwest Pennsylvania—Pittsburgh, PA
Christian Council of Metropolitan Atlanta—Atlanta, GA

Christian Ministries of Delaware County—Muncie, IN
Church Council of Greater Seattle—Seattle, WA
The Church Federation of Greater Indianapolis, Inc.—Indianapolis, IN
Churchpeople for Change and Reconciliation—Lima, OH
Colorado Council of Churches—Denver, CO
Community Emergency Assistance Program (CEAP)—Brooklyn Park, MN
Community Renewal Society—Chicago, IL
Cooperative Metropolitan Ministries—Newton, MA
Council of Churches of the City of New York—New York, NY
Council of Churches of Greater Springfield—Springfield, MA
The Council of Churches of Santa Clara County—San Jose, CA
Council of Churches and Synagogues of Southwestern Connecticut—Stamford, CT
Dutchess Interfaith Council, Inc.—Poughkeepsie, NY
East Dallas Cooperative Parish—Dallas, TX
East End Cooperative Ministry—Pittsburgh, PA
Ecclesia—Trenton, NJ
Ecumenical Conference of Greater Altoona—Altoona, PA
The Ecumenical Council of Pasadena Area Churches—Pasadena, CA
Ecumenical Ministries of Oregon—Portland, OR
Evanston Ecumenical Action Council—Evanston, IL
Faith Community Assistance Center—Santa Fe, NM
Florida Council of Churches—Orlando, FL
Fresno Metro Ministry—Fresno, CA
Georgia Christian Council—Macon, GA
Grand Rapids Area Center for Ecumenism (GRACE)—Grand Rapids, MI
Greater Birmingham Ministries—Birmingham, AL
Greater Chicago Broadcast Ministries—Chicago, IL
Greater Dallas Community of Churches—Dallas, TX
Greater Dayton Christian Connections—Dayton, OH
Greater Minneapolis Council of Churches—Minneapolis, MN
Greater Rochester Community of Churches—Rochester, NY
The Greater Wheeling Council of Churches—Wheeling, WV
Greensboro Urban Ministry—Greensboro, NC
Illinois Conference of Churches—Springfield, IL
In One Accord—Battle Creek, MI
Indiana Partners for Christian Unity and Mission—Indianapolis, IN
Inter-Church Council of Greater New Bedford—New Bedford, MA
Interchurch Ministries of Nebraska—Lincoln, NE
Interfaith Conference of Greater Milwaukee—Milwaukee, WI
Interfaith Council of Contra Costa County—Walnut Creek, CA
Inter-Faith Ministries–Wichita—Wichita, KS
Interfaith Mission Service—Huntsville, AL
Interfaith Service Bureau—Sacramento, CA
InterReligious Council of Central New York—Syracuse, NY
Kansas Ecumenical Ministries—Topeka, KS
Kentuckiana Interfaith Community—Louisville, KY
Lincoln Interfaith Council—Lincoln, NE
The Long Island Council of Churches—Hempstead, NY
Madison Area Urban Ministry—Madison, WI
Mahoning Valley Association of Churches—Youngstown, OH
Massachusetts Council of Churches—Boston, MA
Metropolitan Christian Council of Philadelphia—Philadelphia, PA
The Metropolitan Christian Council: Detroit–Windsor—Detroit, MI
Metropolitan Ecumenical Ministry—Newark, NJ
Metropolitan Interfaith Council on Affordable Housing (MICAH)—Minneapolis, MN
Michigan Ecumenical Forum—Lansing, MI
Minnesota Council of Churches—Minneapolis, MN
Mississippi Religious Leadership Conference—Jackson, MS
Montana Association of Churches—Billings, MT
Muskegon County Cooperating Churches—Muskegon, MI
Network of Religious Communities—Buffalo, NY
New Britain Area Conference of Churches (NEWBRACC)—New Britain, CT
New Hampshire Council of Churches—Pembroke, NH
New Mexico Conference of Churches—Albuquerque, NM
North Carolina Council of Churches—Raleigh, NC
Northern California Interreligious Conference—Oakland, CA
Northside Common Ministries—Pittsburgh, PA
Northwest Interfaith Movement—Philadelphia, PA
Ohio Council of Churches—Columbus, OH
Oklahoma Conference of Churches—Oklahoma City, OK
Reading Berks Conference of Churches—Reading, PA
The Rhode Island State Council of Churches—Providence, RI

St. Paul Area Council of Churches—St. Paul, MN
San Fernando Valley Interfaith Council—Chatsworth, CA
Schenectady Inner City Ministry—Schenectady, NY
South Carolina Christian Action Council, Inc.—Columbia, SC
South Coast Ecumenical Council—Long Beach, CA
South Hills Interfaith Ministries—South Park, PA
Spokane Council of Ecumenical Ministries—Spokane, WA
Staten Island Council of Churches—Staten Island, NY
Tarrant Area Community of Churches—Fort Worth, TX
Texas Conference of Churches—Austin, TX
Tri-Council Coordinating Commission—Minneapolis, MN
Troy Area United Ministries—Troy, NY
Tulsa Metropolitan Ministry—Tulsa, OK
United Religious Community of St. Joseph County—South Bend, IN
Virginia Council of Churches, Inc.—Richmond, VA
Washington Association of Churches—Seattle, WA
West Virginia Council of Churches—Charleston, WV
Wyoming Church Coalition—Cheyenne, WY
York County Council of Churches—York, PA

Christian Education Programs

Akron Area Association of Churches—Akron, OH
The Associated Churches of Fort Wayne & Allen County, Inc.—Fort Wayne, IN
Associated Ministries of Tacoma-Pierce County— Tacoma, WA
Association of Christian Churches of South Dakota—Sioux Falls, SD
Attleboro Area Council of Churches, Inc.—Attleboro, MA
Bergen County Council of Churches—Bergenfield, NJ
Berrien County Association of Churches—Benton Harbor, MI
Brooklyn Council of Churches—Brooklyn, NY
Center for the Prevention of Sexual and Domestic Violence—Seattle, WA
Christian Associates of Southwest Pennsylvania—Pittsburgh, PA
Christian Ministries of Delaware County—Muncie, IN
Christians United in Beaver County—Beaver, PA
Churchpeople for Change and Reconciliation—Lima, OH
Colorado Council of Churches—Denver, CO
Council of Christian Communions of Greater Cincinnati—Cincinnati, OH
Council of Churches and Synagogues of Southwestern Connecticut—Stamford, CT
East Dallas Cooperative Parish—Dallas, TX
East End Cooperative Ministry—Pittsburgh, PA
Ecclesia—Trenton, NJ
Ecumenical Conference of Greater Altoona—Altoona, PA
Ecumenical Ministries of Oregon—Portland, OR
Evansville Area Community of Churches, Inc.—Evansville, IN
Florida Council of Churches—Orlando, FL
Georgia Christian Council—Macon, GA
Greater Bethlehem Area Council of Churches—Bethlehem, PA
Greater Chicago Broadcast Ministries—Chicago, IL
Greater Dayton Christian Connections—Dayton, OH
Greater Fairmont Council of Churches—Fairmont, WV
Greater Flint Council of Churches—Flint, MI
Greater New Orleans Federation of Churches—New Orleans, LA
The Greater Wheeling Council of Churches—Wheeling, WV
Greensboro Urban Ministry—Greensboro, NC
Highlands Community Ministries—Louisville, KY
Inter-Church Council of Greater New Bedford—New Bedford, MA
Iowa Religious Media Services—Des Moines, IA
Kentuckiana Interfaith Community—Louisville, KY
Kentucky Council of Churches—Lexington, KY
Lehigh County Conference of Churches—Allentown, PA
Mahoning Valley Association of Churches—Youngstown, OH
Metropolitan Christian Council of Philadelphia—Philadelphia, PA
The Metropolitan Christian Council: Detroit-Windsor—Detroit, MI
Metropolitan Ecumenical Ministry—Newark, NJ
Network of Religious Communities—Buffalo, NY
Northern Kentucky Interfaith Commission, Inc.—Newport, KY
Oklahoma Conference of Churches—Oklahoma City, OK
Peoria Friendship House of Christian Service—Peoria, IL
Queens Federation of Churches—Richmond Hill, NY
Reading Berks Conference of Churches—Reading, PA
The Rhode Island State Council of Churches—Providence, RI

San Antonio Community of Churches—San Antonio, TX
South Coast Ecumenical Council—Long Beach, CA
Staten Island Council of Churches—Staten Island, NY
Tarrant Area Community of Churches—Fort Worth, TX
Troy Area United Ministries—Troy, NY
United Churches of Lycoming County—Williamsport, PA
Wyoming Church Coalition—Cheyenne, WY
York County Council of Churches—York, PA

Clothing Distribution Programs

Arkansas Interfaith Conference—Scott, AR
Asheville-Buncombe Community Christian Ministry (ABCCM)—Asheville, NC
Associated Ministries of Tacoma-Pierce County—Tacoma, WA
Attleboro Area Council of Churches, Inc.—Attleboro, MA
Bergen County Council of Churches—Bergenfield, NJ
Border Association for Refugees from Central America (BARCA), Inc.—Edinburg, TX
Chautaugua County Rural Ministry—Dunkirk, NY
Christian Ministries of Delaware County—Muncie, IN
Churchpeople for Change and Reconciliation—Lima, OH
Community Emergency Assistance Program (CEAP)—Brooklyn Park, MN
Community Ministry of Montgomery County—Rockville, MD
Concerned Ecumenical Ministry to the Upper West Side—Buffalo, NY
Contact Ministries of Springfield—Springfield, IL
Cooperative Metropolitan Ministries—Newton, MA
Corpus Christi Metro Ministries—Corpus Christi, TX
Council of Churches of the Ozarks—Springfield, MO
East Dallas Cooperative Parish—Dallas, TX
East End Cooperative Ministry—Pittsburgh, PA
Eastern Area Community Ministries—Louisville, KY
The Ecumenical Council of Pasadena Area Churches—Pasadena, CA
Evanston Ecumenical Action Council—Evanston, IL
Fern Creek–Highview United Ministries—Louisvlle, KY
Greater Birmingham Ministries—Birmingham, AL
Greater Fairmont Council of Churches—Fairmont, WV
Greater Minneapolis Council of Churches—Minneapolis, MN
Greensboro Urban Ministry—Greensboro, NC
Inter-Church Ministries of Erie County—Erie, PA
Interfaith Community Council, Inc.—New Albany, IN
Interfaith Community Services—St. Joseph, MO
Inter-Faith Ministries–Wichita—Wichita, KS
Lancaster County Council of Churches—Lancaster, PA
Lebanon County Christian Ministries—Lebanon, PA
Lehigh County Conference of Churches—Allentown, PA
Lewisburg Council of Churches—Lewisburg, PA
Lincoln Interfaith Council—Lincoln, NE
The Long Island Council of Churches—Hempstead, NY
Metropolitan Ecumenical Ministry—Newark, NJ
Northside Inter-Church Agency (NICA)—Fort Worth, TX
Peoria Friendship House of Christian Service—Peoria, IL
Reading Berks Conference of Churches—Reading, PA
The Rhode Island State Council of Churches—Providence, RI
St. Paul Area Council of Churches—St. Paul, MN
South East Associated Ministries (SEAM)—Louisville, KY
South Hills Interfaith Ministries—South Park, PA
Staten Island Council of Churches—Staten Island, NY
West Side Ecumenical Ministry—Cleveland, OH
Wilkinsburg Community Ministry—Pittsburgh, PA

CROP Walks

Akron Area Association of Churches—Akron, OH
Asheville-Buncombe Community Christian Ministry (ABCCM)—Asheville, NC
The Associated Churches of Fort Wayne & Allen County, Inc.—Fort Wayne, IN
Associated Ministries of Thurston County—Olympia, WA
Association of Christian Churches of South Dakota—Sioux Falls, SD
Attleboro Area Council of Churches, Inc.—Attleboro, MA
Austin Area Interreligious Ministries—Austin, TX
Bergen County Council of Churches—Bergenfield, NJ
Berrien County Association of Churches—Benton Harbor, MI
Broome County Council of Churches, Inc.—Binghamton, NY

Capital Area Council of Churches, Inc.—Albany, NY
Chautaugua County Rural Ministry—Dunkirk, NY
Christian Associates of Southwest Pennsylvania—Pittsburgh, PA
Christian Ministries of Delaware County—Muncie, IN
Church Community Services—Elkhart, IN
The Church Federation of Greater Indianapolis, Inc.—Indianapolis, IN
Churches United of the Quad City Area—Rock Island, IL
Churchpeople for Change and Reconciliation—Lima, OH
Community Emergency Assistance Program (CEAP)—Brooklyn Park, MN
Council of Churches of Chemung County, Inc.—Elmira, NY
Council of Churches of the City of New York—New York, NY
Council of Churches of Greater Bridgeport, Inc.—Bridgeport, CT
The Council of Churches of Santa Clara County—San Jose, CA
Dutchess Interfaith Council, Inc.—Poughkeepsie, NY
East Dallas Cooperative Parish—Dallas, TX
East End Cooperative Ministry—Pittsburgh, PA
Ecclesia—Trenton, NJ
The Ecumenical Council of Pasadena Area Churches—Pasadena, CA
Ecumenical Ministries—Fulton, MO
Evanston Ecumenical Action Council—Evanston, IL
Evansville Area Community of Churches, Inc.—Evansville, IN
Florida Council of Churches—Orlando, FL
Greater Bethlehem Area Council of Churches—Bethlehem, PA
Greater Dallas Community of Churches—Dallas, TX
Greater Dayton Christian Connections—Dayton, OH
Greater Fairmont Council of Churches—Fairmont, WV
Greater Flint Council of Churches—Flint, MI
Greater Waterbury Interfaith Ministries, Inc.—Waterbury, CT
Greensboro Urban Ministry—Greensboro, NC
Hanover Area Council of Churches—Hanover, PA
In One Accord—Battle Creek, MI
Inter-Church Ministries of Erie County—Erie, PA
Interfaith Community Services—St. Joseph, MO
Interfaith Conference of Greater Milwaukee—Milwaukee, WI
Inter-Faith Ministries–Wichita—Wichita, KS
Lancaster County Council of Churches—Lancaster, PA
Lebanon County Christian Ministries—Lebanon, PA
Lehigh County Conference of Churches—Allentown, PA
Lewisburg Council of Churches—Lewisburg, PA
Lincoln Interfaith Council—Lincoln, NE
The Long Island Council of Churches—Hempstead, NY
Mahoning Valley Association of Churches—Youngstown, OH
The Metropolitan Christian Council: Detroit-Windsor—Detroit, MI
Metropolitan Ecumenical Ministry—Newark, NJ
Muskegon County Cooperating Churches—Muskegon, MI
Network of Religious Communities—Buffalo, NY
New Britain Area Conference of Churches (NEWBRACC)—New Britain, CT
Northside Inter-Church Agency (NICA)—Fort Worth, TX
Oak Park–River Forest Community of Congregations—Oak Park, IL
Peoria Friendship House of Christian Service—Peoria, IL
Pike County Outreach Council—Waverly, OH
Reading Berks Conference of Churches—Reading, PA
The Rhode Island State Council of Churches—Providence, RI
St. Paul Area Council of Churches—St. Paul, MN
San Antonio Community of Churches—San Antonio, TX
San Fernando Valley Interfaith Council—Chatsworth, CA
Schenectady Inner City Ministry—Schenectady, NY
South Coast Ecumenical Council—Long Beach, CA
Spokane Council of Ecumenical Ministries—Spokane, WA
Staten Island Council of Churches—Staten Island, NY
Tarrant Area Community of Churches—Fort Worth, TX
Troy Area United Ministries—Troy, NY
United Churches of Lycoming County—Williamsport, PA
United Religious Community of St. Joseph County—South Bend, IN
Wilkinsburg Community Ministry—Pittsburgh, PA
Wisconsin Council of Churches—Sun Prairie, WI
Worcester County Ecumenical Council—Worcester, MA
York County Council of Churches—York, PA

Programs with/for Persons with Disabilities

The Associated Churches of Fort Wayne & Allen County, Inc.—Fort Wayne, IN

Bergen County Council of Churches—Bergenfield, NJ
Christian Council of Metropolitan Atlanta—Atlanta, GA
Christian Ministries of Delaware County—Muncie, IN
Des Moines Area Religious Council—Des Moines, IA
Greater Chicago Broadcast Ministries—Chicago, IL
Greater Minneapolis Council of Churches—Minneapolis, MN
Inter-Church Council of Greater New Bedford—New Bedford, MA
InterReligious Council of Central New York—Syracuse, NY
Lincoln Interfaith Council—Lincoln, NE
Massachusetts Council of Churches—Boston, MA
Metropolitan Ecumenical Ministry—Newark, NJ
New Mexico Conference of Churches—Albuquerque, NM
Northside Inter-Church Agency (NICA)—Fort Worth, TX
Reading Berks Conference of Churches—Reading, PA
The Rhode Island State Council of Churches—Providence, RI
Southeast Ecumenical Ministry—Rochester, NY
Tulsa Metropolitan Ministry—Tulsa, OK
United Religious Community of St. Joseph County—South Bend, IN

Domestic Violence Programs

Associated Ministries of Tacoma–Pierce County—Tacoma, WA
Association of Christian Churches of South Dakota—Sioux Falls, SD
Association of Religious Communities—Danbury, CT
Bergen County Council of Churches—Bergenfield, NJ
Berrien County Association of Churches—Benton Harbor, MI
Center for the Prevention of Sexual and Domestic Violence—Seattle, WA
Chautaugua County Rural Ministry—Dunkirk, NY
Church Council of Greater Seattle—Seattle, WA
Council of Churches of Greater Bridgeport, Inc.—Bridgeport, CT
Dutchess Interfaith Council, Inc.—Poughkeepsie, NY
Ecumenical Ministries of Oregon—Portland, OR
Florida Council of Churches—Orlando, FL
Greater Chicago Broadcast Ministries—Chicago, IL
Greater Minneapolis Council of Churches—Minneapolis, MN
Indiana Partners for Christian Unity and Mission—Indianapolis, IN
Inter-Church Council of Greater New Bedford—New Bedford, MA
Interchurch Ministries of Nebraska—Lincoln, NE
Interfaith Service Bureau—Sacramento, CA
Lincoln Interfaith Council—Lincoln, NE
Madison Area Urban Ministry—Madison, WI
The Metropolitan Christian Council: Detroit–Windsor—Detroit, MI
Metropolitan Ecumenical Ministry—Newark, NJ
Mississippi Religious Leadership Conference—Jackson, MS
New Mexico Conference of Churches—Albuquerque, NM
Oklahoma Conference of Churches—Oklahoma City, OK
Peoria Friendship House of Christian Service—Peoria, IL
The Rhode Island State Council of Churches—Providence, RI
Ecumenical Council of San Diego County—San Diego, CA
St. Paul Area Council of Churches—St. Paul, MN
San Antonio Community of Churches—San Antonio, TX
Southeast Ecumenical Ministry—Rochester, NY
Spokane Council of Ecumenical Ministries—Spokane, WA
Staten Island Council of Churches—Staten Island, NY
Troy Area United Ministries—Troy, NY
West Side Ecumenical Ministry—Cleveland, OH
Wyoming Church Coalition—Cheyenne, WY

Economic/Social Justice Programs

Akron Area Association of Churches—Akron, OH
Arkansas Interfaith Conference—Scott, AR
The Associated Churches of Fort Wayne & Allen County, Inc.—Fort Wayne, IN
Associated Ministries of Tacoma–Pierce County—Tacoma, WA
Associated Ministries of Thurston County—Olympia, WA
Association of Christian Churches of South Dakota—Sioux Falls, SD
Austin Area Interreligious Ministries—Austin, TX
Bergen County Council of Churches—Bergenfield, NJ
Berrien County Association of Churches—Benton Harbor, MI
Brooklyn Council of Churches—Brooklyn, NY
Broome County Council of Churches, Inc.—Binghamton, NY
California Council of Churches–California Church Impact—Sacramento, CA

Capital Area Council of Churches, Inc.—Albany, NY
Capital Region Ecumenical Organization (CREO)—Schenectady, NY
The Capitol Region Conference of Churches—Hartford, CT
Chautaugua County Rural Ministry—Dunkirk, NY
Christian Associates of Southwest Pennsylvania—Pittsburgh, PA
Christian Community Action—New Haven, CT
Christian Council of Metropolitan Atlanta—Atlanta, GA
Christian Ministries of Delaware County—Muncie, IN
The Church Federation of Greater Indianapolis, Inc.—Indianapolis, IN
Churches United of the Quad City Area—Rock Island, IL
Churches United, Inc.—Cedar Rapids, IA
Colorado Council of Churches—Denver, CO
Community Emergency Assistance Program (CEAP)—Brooklyn Park, MN
Community Ministry of Montgomery County—Rockville, MD
Community Renewal Society—Chicago, IL
Cooperative Metropolitan Ministries—Newton, MA
Council of Churches of Chemung County, Inc.—Elmira, NY
Council of Churches of the City of New York—New York, NY
Council of Churches of Greater Bridgeport, Inc.—Bridgeport, CT
Council of Churches of Greater Springfield—Springfield, MA
The Council of Churches of Santa Clara County—San Jose, CA
Dutchess Interfaith Council, Inc.—Poughkeepsie, NY
Eastern Area Community Ministries—Louisville, KY
Ecclesia—Trenton, NJ
Ecumenical Conference of Greater Altoona—Altoona, PA
The Ecumenical Council of Pasadena Area Churches—Pasadena, CA
Ecumenical Ministries of Iowa (EMI)—Des Moines, IA
Ecumenical Ministries of Oregon—Portland, OR
Evanston Ecumenical Action Council—Evanston, IL
Faith Community Assistance Center—Santa Fe, NM
Florida Council of Churches—Orlando, FL
Fresno Metro Ministry—Fresno, CA
Georgia Christian Council—Macon, GA
Grand Rapids Area Center for Ecumenism (GRACE)—Grand Rapids, MI
Greater Birmingham Ministries—Birmingham, AL
Greater Chicago Broadcast Ministries—Chicago, IL
Greater Dallas Community of Churches—Dallas, TX
Greater Dayton Christian Connections—Dayton, OH
Greater Minneapolis Council of Churches—Minneapolis, MN
Greater Rochester Community of Churches—Rochester, NY
Illinois Conference of Churches—Springfield, IL
In One Accord—Battle Creek, MI
Inter-Church Council of Greater New Bedford—New Bedford, MA
Interchurch Ministries of Nebraska—Lincoln, NE
Interfaith Community Council, Inc.—New Albany, IN
Interfaith Community Services—St. Joseph, MO
Interfaith Conference of Greater Milwaukee—Milwaukee, WI
Interfaith Council of Contra Costa County—Walnut Creek, CA
Inter-Faith Ministries–Wichita—Wichita, KS
Interfaith Mission Service—Huntsville, AL
Interfaith Service Bureau—Sacramento, CA
InterReligious Council of Central New York—Syracuse, NY
Kansas Ecumenical Ministries—Topeka, KS
Kentuckiana Interfaith Community—Louisville, KY
Kentucky Council of Churches—Lexington, KY
Lancaster County Council of Churches—Lancaster, PA
Lehigh County Conference of Churches—Allentown, PA
Lincoln Interfaith Council—Lincoln, NE
The Long Island Council of Churches—Hempstead, NY
Madison Area Urban Ministry—Madison, WI
Maine Council of Churches—Portland, ME
Marin Interfaith Council—Novato, CA
Massachusetts Council of Churches—Boston, MA
Metropolitan Area Religious Coalition of Cincinnati—Cincinnati, OH
Metropolitan Christian Council of Philadelphia—Philadelphia, PA
The Metropolitan Christian Council: Detroit-Windsor—Detroit, MI
Metropolitan Ecumenical Ministry—Newark, NJ
Metropolitan Inter Faith Association (MIFA)—Memphis, TN
Metropolitan Interfaith Council on Affordable Housing (MICAH)—Minneapolis, MN
Michigan Ecumenical Forum—Lansing, MI
Minnesota Council of Churches—Minneapolis, MN
Mississippi Religious Leadership Conference—Jackson, MS

Montana Association of Churches—Billings, MT
Muskegon County Cooperating Churches—Muskegon, MI
Network of Religious Communities—Buffalo, NY
New Britain Area Conference of Churches (NEWBRACC)—New Britain, CT
New Hampshire Council of Churches—Pembroke, NH
New Mexico Conference of Churches—Albuquerque, NM
North Carolina Council of Churches—Raleigh, NC
North Dakota Conference of Churches—Ashley, ND
Northern California Interreligious Conference—Oakland, CA
Northside Inter-Church Agency (NICA)—Fort Worth, TX
Northwest Interfaith Movement—Philadelphia, PA
Oklahoma Conference of Churches—Oklahoma City, OK
Pennsylvania Conference on Interchurch Cooperation—Harrisburg, PA
The Pennsylvania Council of Churches—Harrisburg, PA
Peoria Friendship House of Christian Service—Peoria, IL
Queens Federation of Churches—Richmond Hill, NY
Reading Berks Conference of Churches—Reading, PA
The Rhode Island State Council of Churches—Providence, RI
Rural Migrant Ministry—Poughkeepsie, NY
St. Paul Area Council of Churches—St. Paul, MN
San Antonio Community of Churches—San Antonio, TX
San Fernando Valley Interfaith Council—Chatsworth, CA
Schenectady Inner City Ministry—Schenectady, NY
South Carolina Christian Action Council, Inc.—Columbia, SC
South Coast Ecumenical Council—Long Beach, CA
South East Associated Ministries (SEAM)—Louisville, KY
South Louisville Community Ministries—Louisville, KY
Southern California Ecumenical Council—Pasadena, CA
Spokane Council of Ecumenical Ministries—Spokane, WA
Staten Island Council of Churches—Staten Island, NY
Tarrant Area Community of Churches—Fort Worth, TX
Texas Conference of Churches—Austin, TX
Troy Area United Ministries—Troy, NY
Tulsa Metropolitan Ministry—Tulsa, OK
United Churches of Lycoming County—Williamsport, PA
United Religious Community of St. Joseph County—South Bend, IN
Vermont Ecumenical Council and Bible Society—Burlington, VT
Virginia Council of Churches, Inc.—Richmond, VA
Washington Association of Churches—Seattle, WA
West Virginia Council of Churches—Charleston, WV
Wilkinsburg Community Ministry—Pittsburgh, PA
Wisconsin Council of Churches—Sun Prairie, WI
Worcester County Ecumenical Council—Worcester, MA
Wyoming Church Coalition—Cheyenne, WY

Employment Assistance Programs

Bergen County Council of Churches—Bergenfield, NJ
Berrien County Association of Churches—Benton Harbor, MI
Chautaugua County Rural Ministry—Dunkirk, NY
Church Community Services—Elkhart, IN
Churchpeople for Change and Reconciliation—Lima, OH
Community Emergency Assistance Program (CEAP)—Brooklyn Park, MN
Contact Ministries of Springfield—Springfield, IL
Corpus Christi Metro Ministries—Corpus Christi, TX
Council of Churches of Greater Bridgeport, Inc.—Bridgeport, CT
East Dallas Cooperative Parish—Dallas, TX
East End Cooperative Ministry—Pittsburgh, PA
Eastern Area Community Ministries—Louisville, KY
Evanston Ecumenical Action Council—Evanston, IL
Fern Creek–Highview United Ministries—Louisvlle, KY
Genesee–Orleans Ministry of Concern—Albion, NY
Greater Minneapolis Council of Churches—Minneapolis, MN
Greensboro Urban Ministry—Greensboro, NC
Interfaith Community Council, Inc.—New Albany, IN
Lehigh County Conference of Churches—Allentown, PA
Lincoln Interfaith Council—Lincoln, NE
The Long Island Council of Churches—Hempstead, NY
Metropolitan Ecumenical Ministry—Newark, NJ

Network of Religious Communities—Buffalo, NY
Northside Inter-Church Agency (NICA)—Fort Worth, TX
Peoria Friendship House of Christian Service—Peoria, IL
The Rhode Island State Council of Churches—Providence, RI
Schenectady Inner City Ministry—Schenectady, NY
South East Associated Ministries (SEAM)—Louisville, KY
Southeast Ecumenical Ministry—Rochester, NY
United Ministries—Greenville, SC
Virginia Council of Churches, Inc.—Richmond, VA
West Side Ecumenical Ministry—Cleveland, OH

Environmental Programs

Associated Ministries of Tacoma–Pierce County—Tacoma, WA
Bergen County Council of Churches—Bergenfield, NJ
California Council of Churches–California Church Impact—Sacramento, CA
The Capitol Region Conference of Churches—Hartford, CT
Christian Conference of Connecticut—Hartford, CT
The Church Federation of Greater Indianapolis, Inc.—Indianapolis, IN
Colorado Council of Churches—Denver, CO
The Council of Churches of Santa Clara County—San Jose, CA
Ecumenical Ministries of Iowa (EMI)—Des Moines, IA
Ecumenical Ministries of Oregon—Portland, OR
Florida Council of Churches—Orlando, FL
Fresno Metro Ministry—Fresno, CA
Georgia Christian Council—Macon, GA
Greater Chicago Broadcast Ministries—Chicago, IL
Greater Dayton Christian Connections—Dayton, OH
The Greater Wheeling Council of Churches—Wheeling, WV
Inter-Church Council of Greater New Bedford—New Bedford, MA
Interfaith Conference of Greater Milwaukee—Milwaukee, WI
Interfaith Mission Service—Huntsville, AL
Kentucky Council of Churches—Lexington, KY
Lincoln Interfaith Council—Lincoln, NE
Louisiana Interchurch Conference—Baton Rouge, LA
Mahoning Valley Association of Churches—Youngstown, OH
Maine Council of Churches—Portland, ME
Marin Interfaith Council—Novato, CA
Metropolitan Christian Council of Philadelphia—Philadelphia, PA
The Metropolitan Christian Council: Detroit–Windsor—Detroit, MI
Metropolitan Ecumenical Ministry—Newark, NJ
Michigan Ecumenical Forum—Lansing, MI
Minnesota Council of Churches—Minneapolis, MN
Mississippi Religious Leadership Conference—Jackson, MS
Montana Association of Churches—Billings, MT
Muskegon County Cooperating Churches—Muskegon, MI
Network of Religious Communities—Buffalo, NY
New Hampshire Council of Churches—Pembroke, NH
New Mexico Conference of Churches—Albuquerque, NM
North Carolina Council of Churches—Raleigh, NC
Northern California Interreligious Conference—Oakland, CA
Northwest Interfaith Movement—Philadelphia, PA
Oklahoma Conference of Churches—Oklahoma City, OK
The Pennsylvania Council of Churches—Harrisburg, PA
The Rhode Island State Council of Churches—Providence, RI
Ecumenical Council of San Diego County—San Diego, CA
South Carolina Christian Action Council, Inc.—Columbia, SC
South Coast Ecumenical Council—Long Beach, CA
Southern California Ecumenical Council—Pasadena, CA
Texas Conference of Churches—Austin, TX
United Churches of Lycoming County—Williamsport, PA
Washington Association of Churches—Seattle, WA
West Virginia Council of Churches—Charleston, WV

Faith and Order Programs

Akron Area Association of Churches—Akron, OH
Allegheny Valley Association of Churches—Natrona Heights, PA
The Associated Churches of Fort Wayne & Allen County, Inc.—Fort Wayne, IN
Associated Ministries of Tacoma–Pierce County—Tacoma, WA
Association of Christian Churches of South Dakota—Sioux Falls, SD
Bergen County Council of Churches—Bergenfield, NJ

Berrien County Association of Churches—Benton Harbor, MI
Capital Area Council of Churches, Inc.—Albany, NY
Capital Region Ecumenical Organization (CREO)—Schenectady, NY
Christian Associates of Southwest Pennsylvania—Pittsburgh, PA
Christian Conference of Connecticut—Hartford, CT
The Christian Council of Delaware and Maryland's Eastern Shore—Wilmington, DE
Christian Council of Metropolitan Atlanta—Atlanta, GA
The Church Federation of Greater Indianapolis, Inc.—Indianapolis, IN
Churches United of the Quad City Area—Rock Island, IL
Colorado Council of Churches—Denver, CO
Council of Churches of the City of New York—New York, NY
Council of Churches of Greater Springfield—Springfield, MA
Council of Churches and Synagogues of Southwestern Connecticut—Stamford, CT
East Dallas Cooperative Parish—Dallas, TX
East End Cooperative Ministry—Pittsburgh, PA
Ecclesia—Trenton, NJ
Ecumenical Conference of Greater Altoona—Altoona, PA
The Ecumenical Council of Pasadena Area Churches—Pasadena, CA
Ecumenical Ministries of Iowa (EMI)—Des Moines, IA
Florida Council of Churches—Orlando, FL
Fresno Metro Ministry—Fresno, CA
Georgia Christian Council—Macon, GA
Greater Dayton Christian Connections—Dayton, OH
Greater New Orleans Federation of Churches—New Orleans, LA
Greater Waterbury Interfaith Ministries, Inc.—Waterbury, CT
The Greater Wheeling Council of Churches—Wheeling, WV
Highlands Community Ministries—Louisville, KY
Illinois Conference of Churches—Springfield, IL
In One Accord—Battle Creek, MI
Indiana Partners for Christian Unity and Mission—Indianapolis, IN
Inter-Church Council of Greater New Bedford—New Bedford, MA
Interchurch Ministries of Nebraska—Lincoln, NE
Interfaith Community Council, Inc.—New Albany, IN
Interfaith Community Services—St. Joseph, MO
Interfaith Council of Contra Costa County—Walnut Creek, CA
Inter-Faith Ministries–Wichita—Wichita, KS
InterReligious Council of Central New York—Syracuse, NY
Kansas Ecumenical Ministries—Topeka, KS
Kentuckiana Interfaith Community—Louisville, KY
Lancaster County Council of Churches—Lancaster, PA
Lehigh County Conference of Churches—Allentown, PA
Lincoln Interfaith Council—Lincoln, NE
Louisiana Interchurch Conference—Baton Rouge, LA
Massachusetts Commission on Christian Unity—Lowell, MA
Metropolitan Christian Council of Philadelphia—Philadelphia, PA
The Metropolitan Christian Council: Detroit–Windsor—Detroit, MI
Metropolitan Ecumenical Ministry—Newark, NJ
Michigan Ecumenical Forum—Lansing, MI
Minnesota Council of Churches—Minneapolis, MN
Mississippi Religious Leadership Conference—Jackson, MS
Montana Association of Churches—Billings, MT
Network of Religious Communities—Buffalo, NY
New Hampshire Council of Churches—Pembroke, NH
New Mexico Conference of Churches—Albuquerque, NM
North Carolina Council of Churches—Raleigh, NC
North Dakota Conference of Churches—Ashley, ND
Northern California Interreligious Conference—Oakland, CA
Northern Kentucky Interfaith Commission, Inc.—Newport, KY
Northside Inter-Church Agency (NICA)—Fort Worth, TX
Northwest Interfaith Movement—Philadelphia, PA
Oklahoma Conference of Churches—Oklahoma City, OK
The Pennsylvania Council of Churches—Harrisburg, PA
Queens Federation of Churches—Richmond Hill, NY
Reading Berks Conference of Churches—Reading, PA
Reading Urban Ministry—Reading, PA
The Rhode Island State Council of Churches—Providence, RI
Ecumenical Council of San Diego County—San Diego, CA
Schenectady Inner City Ministry—Schenectady, NY
South Coast Ecumenical Council—Long Beach, CA

Southern California Ecumenical Council—Pasadena, CA
Texas Conference of Churches—Austin, TX
Troy Area United Ministries—Troy, NY
Tulsa Metropolitan Ministry—Tulsa, OK
United Churches of Lycoming County—Williamsport, PA
United Religious Community of St. Joseph County—South Bend, IN
Vermont Ecumenical Council and Bible Society—Burlington, VT
Virginia Council of Churches, Inc.—Richmond, VA
Washington Association of Churches—Seattle, WA
West Virginia Council of Churches—Charleston, WV
Wisconsin Council of Churches—Sun Prairie, WI
Worcester County Ecumenical Council—Worcester, MA

Healthcare Issues

Arkansas Interfaith Conference—Scott, AR
Asheville–Buncombe Community Christian Ministry (ABCCM)—Asheville, NC
Bergen County Council of Churches—Bergenfield, NJ
Berrien County Association of Churches—Benton Harbor, MI
California Council of Churches–California Church Impact—Sacramento, CA
Christian Associates of Southwest Pennsylvania—Pittsburgh, PA
Christian Conference of Connecticut—Hartford, CT
Churchpeople for Change and Reconciliation—Lima, OH
Community Ministries of Rockville—Rockville, MD
Community Renewal Society—Chicago, IL
Corpus Christi Metro Ministries—Corpus Christi, TX
Council of Churches of the City of New York—New York, NY
Council of Churches of Greater Springfield—Springfield, MA
East Dallas Cooperative Parish—Dallas, TX
Eastern Area Community Ministries—Louisville, KY
Ecumenical Ministries—Fulton, MO
Ecumenical Ministries of Iowa (EMI)—Des Moines, IA
Ecumenical Ministries of Oregon—Portland, OR
Florida Council of Churches—Orlando, FL
Fresno Metro Ministry—Fresno, CA
Greater Chicago Broadcast Ministries—Chicago, IL
Greater Minneapolis Council of Churches—Minneapolis, MN
Greater Rochester Community of Churches—Rochester, NY
Greensboro Urban Ministry—Greensboro, NC
Illinois Conference of Churches—Springfield, IL
Inter-Church Council of Greater New Bedford—New Bedford, MA
Interchurch Ministries of Nebraska—Lincoln, NE
Interfaith Conference of Greater Milwaukee—Milwaukee, WI
Lincoln Interfaith Council—Lincoln, NE
The Long Island Council of Churches—Hempstead, NY
Louisiana Interchurch Conference—Baton Rouge, LA
Marin Interfaith Council—Novato, CA
The Metropolitan Christian Council: Detroit–Windsor—Detroit, MI
Metropolitan Ecumenical Ministry—Newark, NJ
Metropolitan Ecumenical Ministry Community Development Corp.—Newark, NJ
Michigan Ecumenical Forum—Lansing, MI
Mississippi Religious Leadership Conference—Jackson, MS
Montana Association of Churches—Billings, MT
Network of Religious Communities—Buffalo, NY
New Hampshire Council of Churches—Pembroke, NH
New Mexico Conference of Churches—Albuquerque, NM
Northwest Interfaith Movement—Philadelphia, PA
Peoria Friendship House of Christian Service—Peoria, IL
Pike County Outreach Council—Waverly, OH
The Rhode Island State Council of Churches—Providence, RI
Schenectady Inner City Ministry—Schenectady, NY
Southeast Ecumenical Ministry—Rochester, NY
Tarrant Area Community of Churches—Fort Worth, TX
Texas Conference of Churches—Austin, TX
Washington Association of Churches—Seattle, WA
West Virginia Council of Churches—Charleston, WV
Worcester County Ecumenical Council—Worcester, MA

Homelessness/Shelter Programs

Akron Area Association of Churches—Akron, OH
Allegheny Valley Association of Churches—Natrona Heights, PA
Arkansas Interfaith Conference—Scott, AR
Asheville–Buncombe Community Christian Ministry (ABCCM)—Asheville, NC
The Associated Churches of Fort Wayne & Allen County, Inc.—Fort Wayne, IN

Associated Ministries of Tacoma–Pierce County—Tacoma, WA
Associated Ministries of Thurston County—Olympia, WA
Attleboro Area Council of Churches, Inc.—Attleboro, MA
Austin Area Interreligious Ministries—Austin, TX
Bergen County Council of Churches—Bergenfield, NJ
Berrien County Association of Churches—Benton Harbor, MI
Capital Area Council of Churches, Inc.—Albany, NY
The Capitol Region Conference of Churches—Hartford, CT
Center City Churches—Hartford, CT
Chautaugua County Rural Ministry—Dunkirk, NY
Christian Churches United of the Tri-County Area—Harrisburg, PA
Christian Community Action—New Haven, CT
Christian Community Action—New Haven, CT
Christian Council of Metropolitan Atlanta—Atlanta, GA
Christian Ministries of Delaware County—Muncie, IN
Church Council of Greater Seattle—Seattle, WA
Churches United of the Quad City Area—Rock Island, IL
Churchpeople for Change and Reconciliation—Lima, OH
Colorado Council of Churches—Denver, CO
Community Emergency Assistance Program (CEAP)—Brooklyn Park, MN
Community Ministries of Rockville—Rockville, MD
Community Ministry of Montgomery County—Rockville, MD
Community Renewal Society—Chicago, IL
Contact Ministries of Springfield—Springfield, IL
Corpus Christi Metro Ministries—Corpus Christi, TX
Council of Churches of Greater Bridgeport, Inc.—Bridgeport, CT
The Council of Churches of Santa Clara County—San Jose, CA
East End Cooperative Ministry—Pittsburgh, PA
The Ecumenical Council of Pasadena Area Churches—Pasadena, CA
Ecumenical Ministries—Fulton, MO
Ecumenical Ministries of Oregon—Portland, OR
Evanston Ecumenical Action Council—Evanston, IL
Faith Community Assistance Center—Santa Fe, NM
Florida Council of Churches—Orlando, FL
Genesee–Orleans Ministry of Concern—Albion, NY
Greater Bethlehem Area Council of Churches—Bethlehem, PA
Greater Chicago Broadcast Ministries—Chicago, IL
Greensboro Urban Ministry—Greensboro, NC
Illinois Conference of Churches—Springfield, IL
Inter-Church Ministries of Erie County—Erie, PA
Interfaith Community Council, Inc.—New Albany, IN
Interfaith Community Services—St. Joseph, MO
Interfaith Conference of Greater Milwaukee—Milwaukee, WI
InterFaith Conference of Metropolitan Washington—Washington, D.C.
Inter-Faith Ministries-Wichita—Wichita, KS
Interfaith Mission Service—Huntsville, AL
InterReligious Council of Central New York—Syracuse, NY
Lehigh County Conference of Churches—Allentown, PA
Lewisburg Council of Churches—Lewisburg, PA
The Long Island Council of Churches—Hempstead, NY
Maine Council of Churches—Portland, ME
Marin Interfaith Council—Novato, CA
Metropolitan Area Religious Coalition of Cincinnati—Cincinnati, OH
Metropolitan Ecumenical Ministry—Newark, NJ
Metropolitan Inter Faith Association (MIFA)—Memphis, TN
Metropolitan Interfaith Council on Affordable Housing (MICAH)—Minneapolis, MN
Michigan Ecumenical Forum—Lansing, MI
Mississippi Religious Leadership Conference—Jackson, MS
Network of Religious Communities—Buffalo, NY
New Britain Area Conference of Churches (NEWBRACC)—New Britain, CT
New Mexico Conference of Churches—Albuquerque, NM
Northside Common Ministries—Pittsburgh, PA
Northside Inter-Church Agency (NICA)—Fort Worth, TX
Oak Park–River Forest Community of Congregations—Oak Park, IL
Paducah Cooperative Ministry—Paducah, KY
Peoria Friendship House of Christian Service—Peoria, IL
Pike County Outreach Council—Waverly, OH
Reading Berks Conference of Churches—Reading, PA
The Rhode Island State Council of Churches—Providence, RI
Ecumenical Council of San Diego County—San Diego, CA

St. Paul Area Council of Churches—St. Paul, MN
San Antonio Community of Churches—San Antonio, TX
Staten Island Council of Churches—Staten Island, NY
Tarrant Area Community of Churches—Fort Worth, TX
Troy Area United Ministries—Troy, NY
United Ministries—Greenville, SC
United Religious Community of St. Joseph County—South Bend, IN

Hunger/Food Programs

Allegheny Valley Association of Churches—Natrona Heights, PA
Arkansas Interfaith Conference—Scott, AR
Asheville-Buncombe Community Christian Ministry (ABCCM)—Asheville, NC
The Associated Churches of Fort Wayne & Allen County, Inc.—Fort Wayne, IN
Associated Ministries of Tacoma-Pierce County—Tacoma, WA
Associated Ministries of Thurston County—Olympia, WA
Association of Christian Churches of South Dakota—Sioux Falls, SD
Attleboro Area Council of Churches, Inc.—Attleboro, MA
Austin Area Interreligious Ministries—Austin, TX
Bergen County Council of Churches—Bergenfield, NJ
Berrien County Association of Churches—Benton Harbor, MI
Border Association for Refugees from Central America (BARCA), Inc.—Edinburg, TX
Brooklyn Council of Churches—Brooklyn, NY
Broome County Council of Churches, Inc.—Binghamton, NY
California Council of Churches-California Church Impact—Sacramento, CA
Capital Area Council of Churches, Inc.—Albany, NY
Center City Churches—Hartford, CT
Chautaugua County Rural Ministry—Dunkirk, NY
Christian Community Action—New Haven, CT
Christian Community Action—New Haven, CT
Christian Ministries of Delaware County—Muncie, IN
Church Community Services—Elkhart, IN
Church Council of Greater Seattle—Seattle, WA
The Church Federation of Greater Indianapolis, Inc.—Indianapolis, IN
Churches United of the Quad City Area—Rock Island, IL
Churches United, Inc.—Cedar Rapids, IA
Churchpeople for Change and Reconciliation—Lima, OH
Community Emergency Assistance Program (CEAP)—Brooklyn Park, MN
Community Ministry of Montgomery County—Rockville, MD
Concerned Ecumenical Ministry to the Upper West Side—Buffalo, NY
Contact Ministries of Springfield—Springfield, IL
Corpus Christi Metro Ministries—Corpus Christi, TX
Council of Churches of Greater Bridgeport, Inc.—Bridgeport, CT
Council of Churches of the Ozarks—Springfield, MO
Council of Churches and Synagogues of Southwestern Connecticut—Stamford, CT
Des Moines Area Religious Council—Des Moines, IA
East Dallas Cooperative Parish—Dallas, TX
East End Cooperative Ministry—Pittsburgh, PA
Eastern Area Community Ministries—Louisville, KY
Ecclesia—Trenton, NJ
The Ecumenical Council of Pasadena Area Churches—Pasadena, CA
Ecumenical Ministries of Oregon—Portland, OR
Evanston Ecumenical Action Council—Evanston, IL
Evansville Area Community of Churches, Inc.—Evansville, IN
Faith Community Assistance Center—Santa Fe, NM
Fern Creek-Highview United Ministries—Louisvlle, KY
Florida Council of Churches—Orlando, FL
Fresno Metro Ministry—Fresno, CA
Genesee County Churches United, Inc.—Batavia, NY
Genesee-Orleans Ministry of Concern—Albion, NY
Grand Rapids Area Center for Ecumenism (GRACE)—Grand Rapids, MI
Greater Bethlehem Area Council of Churches—Bethlehem, PA
Greater Birmingham Ministries—Birmingham, AL
Greater Chicago Broadcast Ministries—Chicago, IL
Greater Dallas Community of Churches—Dallas, TX
Greater Minneapolis Council of Churches—Minneapolis, MN
Greater New Orleans Federation of Churches—New Orleans, LA
Greater Waterbury Interfaith Ministries, Inc.—Waterbury, CT
Greensboro Urban Ministry—Greensboro, NC
Hanover Area Council of Churches—Hanover, PA

Highlands Community Ministries—Louisville, KY
In One Accord—Battle Creek, MI
Inter-Church Ministries of Erie County—Erie, PA
Interchurch Ministries of Nebraska—Lincoln, NE
Interfaith Community Council, Inc.—New Albany, IN
Interfaith Community Services—St. Joseph, MO
Inter-Faith Ministries–Wichita—Wichita, KS
Interfaith Mission Service—Huntsville, AL
InterReligious Council of Central New York—Syracuse, NY
Kentuckiana Interfaith Community—Louisville, KY
Lancaster County Council of Churches—Lancaster, PA
Lebanon County Christian Ministries—Lebanon, PA
Lehigh County Conference of Churches—Allentown, PA
Lewisburg Council of Churches—Lewisburg, PA
Lincoln Interfaith Council—Lincoln, NE
The Long Island Council of Churches—Hempstead, NY
Madison Area Urban Ministry—Madison, WI
The Metropolitan Christian Council: Detroit–Windsor—Detroit, MI
Metropolitan Ecumenical Ministry—Newark, NJ
Minnesota Council of Churches—Minneapolis, MN
Mississippi Religious Leadership Conference—Jackson, MS
Network of Religious Communities—Buffalo, NY
New Britain Area Conference of Churches (NEWBRACC)—New Britain, CT
Northside Common Ministries—Pittsburgh, PA
Northside Inter-Church Agency (NICA)—Fort Worth, TX
Northwest Harvest–E. M. M.—Seattle, WA
Oak Park–River Forest Community of Congregations—Oak Park, IL
Ohio Council of Churches—Columbus, OH
Paducah Cooperative Ministry—Paducah, KY
Peoria Friendship House of Christian Service—Peoria, IL
Pike County Outreach Council—Waverly, OH
Queens Federation of Churches—Richmond Hill, NY
The Rhode Island State Council of Churches—Providence, RI
St. Paul Area Council of Churches—St. Paul, MN
San Antonio Community of Churches—San Antonio, TX
San Fernando Valley Interfaith Council—Chatsworth, CA
Schenectady Inner City Ministry—Schenectady, NY
South Coast Ecumenical Council—Long Beach, CA
South East Associated Ministries (SEAM)—Louisville, KY
South Hills Interfaith Ministries—South Park, PA
South Louisville Community Ministries—Louisville, KY
Southeast Ecumenical Ministry—Rochester, NY
Staten Island Council of Churches—Staten Island, NY
United Churches of Lycoming County—Williamsport, PA
United Ministries—Greenville, SC
United Religious Community of St. Joseph County—South Bend, IN
Vermont Ecumenical Council and Bible Society—Burlington, VT
Washington Association of Churches—Seattle, WA
West Central Neighborhood Ministry, Inc.—Fort Wayne, IN
West Side Ecumenical Ministry—Cleveland, OH
Wilkinsburg Community Ministry—Pittsburgh, PA
Wisconsin Council of Churches—Sun Prairie, WI

Immigration Issues

Association of Religious Communities—Danbury, CT
Austin Area Interreligious Ministries—Austin, TX
Bergen County Council of Churches—Bergenfield, NJ
Border Association for Refugees from Central America (BARCA), Inc.—Edinburg, TX
Chautaugua County Rural Ministry—Dunkirk, NY
Christian Council of Metropolitan Atlanta—Atlanta, GA
Community Emergency Assistance Program (CEAP)—Brooklyn Park, MN
Community Ministries of Rockville—Rockville, MD
East Dallas Cooperative Parish—Dallas, TX
Eastern Area Community Ministries—Louisville, KY
Ecumenical Ministries of Iowa (EMI)—Des Moines, IA
Ecumenical Ministries of Oregon—Portland, OR
Fresno Metro Ministry—Fresno, CA
Greater Minneapolis Council of Churches—Minneapolis, MN
InterReligious Council of Central New York—Syracuse, NY
Lehigh County Conference of Churches—Allentown, PA

Lincoln Interfaith Council—Lincoln, NE
Marin Interfaith Council—Novato, CA
Minnesota Council of Churches—Minneapolis, MN
Network of Religious Communities—Buffalo, NY
Peoria Friendship House of Christian Service—Peoria, IL
The Rhode Island State Council of Churches—Providence, RI
San Antonio Community of Churches—San Antonio, TX
San Fernando Valley Interfaith Council—Chatsworth, CA
South Coast Ecumenical Council—Long Beach, CA
Staten Island Council of Churches—Staten Island, NY
United Religious Community of St. Joseph County—South Bend, IN
Virginia Council of Churches, Inc.—Richmond, VA
Washington Association of Churches—Seattle, WA

Interfaith Dialogue/Relationships

Akron Area Association of Churches—Akron, OH
Arkansas Interfaith Conference—Scott, AR
The Associated Churches of Fort Wayne & Allen County, Inc.—Fort Wayne, IN
Associated Ministries of Tacoma–Pierce County—Tacoma, WA
Associated Ministries of Thurston County—Olympia, WA
Association of Christian Churches of South Dakota—Sioux Falls, SD
Association of Religious Communities—Danbury, CT
Attleboro Area Council of Churches, Inc.—Attleboro, MA
Austin Area Interreligious Ministries—Austin, TX
Bergen County Council of Churches—Bergenfield, NJ
Berrien County Association of Churches—Benton Harbor, MI
Brooklyn Council of Churches—Brooklyn, NY
Broome County Council of Churches, Inc.—Binghamton, NY
California Council of Churches–California Church Impact—Sacramento, CA
Capital Area Council of Churches, Inc.—Albany, NY
The Capitol Region Conference of Churches—Hartford, CT
Center for the Prevention of Sexual and Domestic Violence—Seattle, WA
Christian Conference of Connecticut—Hartford, CT
The Christian Council of Delaware and Maryland's Eastern Shore—Wilmington, DE
Christian Council of Metropolitan Atlanta—Atlanta, GA
Christian Ministries of Delaware County—Muncie, IN
Church Council of Greater Seattle—Seattle, WA
The Church Federation of Greater Indianapolis, Inc.—Indianapolis, IN
Churches United of the Quad City Area—Rock Island, IL
Churches United, Inc.—Cedar Rapids, IA
Churchpeople for Change and Reconciliation—Lima, OH
Colorado Council of Churches—Denver, CO
Community Emergency Assistance Program (CEAP)—Brooklyn Park, MN
Community Ministries of Rockville—Rockville, MD
Community Ministry of Montgomery County—Rockville, MD
Community Renewal Society—Chicago, IL
Cooperative Metropolitan Ministries—Newton, MA
Council of Churches of Chemung County, Inc.—Elmira, NY
Council of Churches of the City of New York—New York, NY
Council of Churches of Greater Bridgeport, Inc.—Bridgeport, CT
Council of Churches of Greater Springfield—Springfield, MA
The Council of Churches of Santa Clara County—San Jose, CA
Council of Churches and Synagogues of Southwestern Connecticut—Stamford, CT
Des Moines Area Religious Council—Des Moines, IA
Dutchess Interfaith Council, Inc.—Poughkeepsie, NY
East Dallas Cooperative Parish—Dallas, TX
East End Cooperative Ministry—Pittsburgh, PA
Eastern Area Community Ministries—Louisville, KY
Ecclesia—Trenton, NJ
Ecumenical Conference of Greater Altoona—Altoona, PA
The Ecumenical Council of Pasadena Area Churches—Pasadena, CA
Ecumenical Ministries of Oregon—Portland, OR
Evanston Ecumenical Action Council—Evanston, IL
Faith Community Assistance Center—Santa Fe, NM
Florida Council of Churches—Orlando, FL
Fresno Metro Ministry—Fresno, CA
Georgia Christian Council—Macon, GA
Grand Rapids Area Center for Ecumenism (GRACE)—Grand Rapids, MI
Greater Bethlehem Area Council of Churches—Bethlehem, PA
Greater Birmingham Ministries—Birmingham, AL

Greater Chicago Broadcast Ministries—Chicago, IL
Greater Dayton Christian Connections—Dayton, OH
Greater Flint Council of Churches—Flint, MI
Greater New Orleans Federation of Churches—New Orleans, LA
Greater Rochester Community of Churches—Rochester, NY
Greater Waterbury Interfaith Ministries, Inc.—Waterbury, CT
Greensboro Urban Ministry—Greensboro, NC
Highlands Community Ministries—Louisville, KY
Indiana Partners for Christian Unity and Mission—Indianapolis, IN
Inter-Church Council of Greater New Bedford—New Bedford, MA
Interchurch Ministries of Nebraska—Lincoln, NE
Interfaith Community Council, Inc.—New Albany, IN
Interfaith Community Services—St. Joseph, MO
Interfaith Conference of Greater Milwaukee—Milwaukee, WI
InterFaith Conference of Metropolitan Washington—Washington, D.C.
Interfaith Council of Contra Costa County—Walnut Creek, CA
Inter-Faith Ministries–Wichita—Wichita, KS
Interfaith Mission Service—Huntsville, AL
Interfaith Service Bureau—Sacramento, CA
InterReligious Council of Central New York—Syracuse, NY
Iowa Religious Media Services—Des Moines, IA
Kentuckiana Interfaith Community—Louisville, KY
Kentucky Council of Churches—Lexington, KY
Lancaster County Council of Churches—Lancaster, PA
Lehigh County Conference of Churches—Allentown, PA
Lewisburg Council of Churches—Lewisburg, PA
Lincoln Interfaith Council—Lincoln, NE
The Long Island Council of Churches—Hempstead, NY
Mahoning Valley Association of Churches—Youngstown, OH
Maine Council of Churches—Portland, ME
Marin Interfaith Council—Novato, CA
Massachusetts Council of Churches—Boston, MA
Metropolitan Christian Council of Philadelphia—Philadelphia, PA
The Metropolitan Christian Council: Detroit–Windsor—Detroit, MI
Metropolitan Ecumenical Ministry—Newark, NJ
Metropolitan Interfaith Council on Affordable Housing (MICAH)—Minneapolis, MN
Michigan Ecumenical Forum—Lansing, MI
Minnesota Council of Churches—Minneapolis, MN
Mississippi Religious Leadership Conference—Jackson, MS
Montana Association of Churches—Billings, MT
Muskegon County Cooperating Churches—Muskegon, MI
Network of Religious Communities—Buffalo, NY
New Britain Area Conference of Churches (NEWBRACC)—New Britain, CT
New Hampshire Council of Churches—Pembroke, NH
New Mexico Conference of Churches—Albuquerque, NM
Northern California Interreligious Conference—Oakland, CA
Northern Kentucky Interfaith Commission, Inc.—Newport, KY
Northwest Interfaith Movement—Philadelphia, PA
Oklahoma Conference of Churches—Oklahoma City, OK
Paducah Cooperative Ministry—Paducah, KY
Pennsylvania Conference on Interchurch Cooperation—Harrisburg, PA
The Pennsylvania Council of Churches—Harrisburg, PA
Peoria Friendship House of Christian Service—Peoria, IL
Reading Berks Conference of Churches—Reading, PA
The Rhode Island State Council of Churches—Providence, RI
Ecumenical Council of San Diego County—San Diego, CA
San Antonio Community of Churches—San Antonio, TX
San Fernando Valley Interfaith Council—Chatsworth, CA
South Carolina Christian Action Council, Inc.—Columbia, SC
South Coast Ecumenical Council—Long Beach, CA
South Hills Interfaith Ministries—South Park, PA
Southern California Ecumenical Council—Pasadena, CA
Spokane Council of Ecumenical Ministries—Spokane, WA
Staten Island Council of Churches—Staten Island, NY
Texas Conference of Churches—Austin, TX
Troy Area United Ministries—Troy, NY
Tulsa Metropolitan Ministry—Tulsa, OK
United Churches of Lycoming County—Williamsport, PA
United Religious Community of St. Joseph County—South Bend, IN
Vermont Ecumenical Council and Bible Society—Burlington, VT

Virginia Council of Churches, Inc.—Richmond, VA
Washington Association of Churches—Seattle, WA
West Side Ecumenical Ministry—Cleveland, OH
West Virginia Council of Churches—Charleston, WV
Wisconsin Council of Churches—Sun Prairie, WI
Worcester County Ecumenical Council—Worcester, MA
Wyoming Church Coalition—Cheyenne, WY
York County Council of Churches—York, PA

Prison Chaplaincy

Arkansas Interfaith Conference—Scott, AR
Asheville-Buncombe Community Christian Ministry (ABCCM)—Asheville, NC
Association of Christian Churches of South Dakota—Sioux Falls, SD
Bergen County Council of Churches—Bergenfield, NJ
Broome County Council of Churches, Inc.—Binghamton, NY
Capital Area Council of Churches, Inc.—Albany, NY
Christian Associates of Southwest Pennsylvania—Pittsburgh, PA
Christian Churches United of the Tri-County Area—Harrisburg, PA
Christian Conference of Connecticut—Hartford, CT
Christians United in Beaver County—Beaver, PA
Church Council of Greater Seattle—Seattle, WA
The Church Federation of Greater Indianapolis, Inc.—Indianapolis, IN
Churches United of the Quad City Area—Rock Island, IL
Churches United, Inc.—Cedar Rapids, IA
Churchpeople for Change and Reconciliation—Lima, OH
Council of Christian Communions of Greater Cincinnati—Cincinnati, OH
Council of Churches of Greater Bridgeport, Inc.—Bridgeport, CT
The Council of Churches of Santa Clara County—San Jose, CA
Dutchess Interfaith Council, Inc.—Poughkeepsie, NY
Ecclesia—Trenton, NJ
Evansville Area Community of Churches, Inc.—Evansville, IN
Florida Council of Churches—Orlando, FL
Genesee County Churches United, Inc.—Batavia, NY
Greater Bethlehem Area Council of Churches—Bethlehem, PA
Greater Chicago Broadcast Ministries—Chicago, IL
Greater Minneapolis Council of Churches—Minneapolis, MN
The Greater Wheeling Council of Churches—Wheeling, WV
Inter-Church Ministries of Erie County—Erie, PA
Interfaith Council of Contra Costa County—Walnut Creek, CA
InterReligious Council of Central New York—Syracuse, NY
Lehigh County Conference of Churches—Allentown, PA
The Long Island Council of Churches—Hempstead, NY
Madison Area Urban Ministry—Madison, WI
Maine Council of Churches—Portland, ME
Mississippi Religious Leadership Conference—Jackson, MS
Network of Religious Communities—Buffalo, NY
New Hampshire Council of Churches—Pembroke, NH
North Dakota Conference of Churches—Ashley, ND
Reading Berks Conference of Churches—Reading, PA
The Rhode Island State Council of Churches—Providence, RI
St. Paul Area Council of Churches—St. Paul, MN
San Antonio Community of Churches—San Antonio, TX
Staten Island Council of Churches—Staten Island, NY
United Churches of Lycoming County—Williamsport, PA
United Religious Community of St. Joseph County—South Bend, IN
Wisconsin Council of Churches—Sun Prairie, WI
Wyoming Church Coalition—Cheyenne, WY
York County Council of Churches—York, PA

Public Education Advocacy

Akron Area Association of Churches—Akron, OH
Arkansas Interfaith Conference—Scott, AR
The Associated Churches of Fort Wayne & Allen County, Inc.—Fort Wayne, IN
Associated Ministries of Tacoma–Pierce County—Tacoma, WA
Austin Area Interreligious Ministries—Austin, TX
Bergen County Council of Churches—Bergenfield, NJ
California Council of Churches–California Church Impact—Sacramento, CA
Christian Ministries of Delaware County—Muncie, IN
Church Council of Greater Seattle—Seattle, WA
The Church Federation of Greater Indianapolis, Inc.—Indianapolis, IN

Churchpeople for Change and Reconciliation—Lima, OH
Colorado Council of Churches—Denver, CO
Community Emergency Assistance Program (CEAP)—Brooklyn Park, MN
Community Ministries of Rockville—Rockville, MD
Community Ministry of Montgomery County—Rockville, MD
Community Renewal Society—Chicago, IL
Council of Churches of the City of New York—New York, NY
East End Cooperative Ministry—Pittsburgh, PA
Ecumenical Conference of Greater Altoona—Altoona, PA
Ecumenical Ministries of Iowa (EMI)—Des Moines, IA
Ecumenical Ministries of Oregon—Portland, OR
Evanston Ecumenical Action Council—Evanston, IL
Florida Council of Churches—Orlando, FL
Greater Bethlehem Area Council of Churches—Bethlehem, PA
Greater Birmingham Ministries—Birmingham, AL
Greater Chicago Broadcast Ministries—Chicago, IL
Greater Fairmont Council of Churches—Fairmont, WV
Greater Waterbury Interfaith Ministries, Inc.—Waterbury, CT
The Greater Wheeling Council of Churches—Wheeling, WV
In One Accord—Battle Creek, MI
Inter-Church Council of Greater New Bedford—New Bedford, MA
Interchurch Ministries of Nebraska—Lincoln, NE
Interfaith Conference of Greater Milwaukee—Milwaukee, WI
Lehigh County Conference of Churches—Allentown, PA
Lincoln Interfaith Council—Lincoln, NE
The Long Island Council of Churches—Hempstead, NY
Madison Area Urban Ministry—Madison, WI
Maine Council of Churches—Portland, ME
Metropolitan Christian Council of Philadelphia—Philadelphia, PA
Metropolitan Ecumenical Ministry—Newark, NJ
Metropolitan Inter Faith Association (MIFA)—Memphis, TN
Metropolitan Interfaith Council on Affordable Housing (MICAH)—Minneapolis, MN
Mississippi Religious Leadership Conference—Jackson, MS
Network of Religious Communities—Buffalo, NY
New Hampshire Council of Churches—Pembroke, NH
North Carolina Council of Churches—Raleigh, NC
Northwest Interfaith Movement—Philadelphia, PA
Ohio Council of Churches—Columbus, OH
Peoria Friendship House of Christian Service—Peoria, IL
The Rhode Island State Council of Churches—Providence, RI
Ecumenical Council of San Diego County—San Diego, CA
San Antonio Community of Churches—San Antonio, TX
South Carolina Christian Action Council, Inc.—Columbia, SC
Spokane Council of Ecumenical Ministries—Spokane, WA
Tarrant Area Community of Churches—Fort Worth, TX
Tulsa Metropolitan Ministry—Tulsa, OK
Washington Association of Churches—Seattle, WA
Wisconsin Council of Churches—Sun Prairie, WI

Refugee Assistance Programs

Association of Religious Communities—Danbury, CT
Austin Area Interreligious Ministries—Austin, TX
Bergen County Council of Churches—Bergenfield, NJ
Border Association for Refugees from Central America (BARCA), Inc.—Edinburg, TX
The Capitol Region Conference of Churches—Hartford, CT
Christian Council of Metropolitan Atlanta—Atlanta, GA
Community Emergency Assistance Program (CEAP)—Brooklyn Park, MN
Ecumenical Ministries of Oregon—Portland, OR
Greater Minneapolis Council of Churches—Minneapolis, MN
Interfaith Service Bureau—Sacramento, CA
InterReligious Council of Central New York—Syracuse, NY
Lincoln Interfaith Council—Lincoln, NE
Metropolitan Ecumenical Ministry—Newark, NJ
Minnesota Council of Churches—Minneapolis, MN
Network of Religious Communities—Buffalo, NY
The Rhode Island State Council of Churches—Providence, RI
Staten Island Council of Churches—Staten Island, NY
United Religious Community of St. Joseph County—South Bend, IN
Virginia Council of Churches, Inc.—Richmond, VA

Rural Issues

Alaska Christian Conference—Fairbanks, AK
Association of Christian Churches of South Dakota—Sioux Falls, SD
Bergen County Council of Churches—Bergenfield, NJ
Border Association for Refugees from Central America (BARCA), Inc.—Edinburg, TX
Chautaugua County Rural Ministry—Dunkirk, NY
Ecumenical Ministries of Iowa (EMI)—Des Moines, IA
Ecumenical Ministries of Oregon—Portland, OR
Fresno Metro Ministry—Fresno, CA
Georgia Christian Council—Macon, GA
Interchurch Ministries of Nebraska—Lincoln, NE
Interfaith Conference of Greater Milwaukee—Milwaukee, WI
Kansas Ecumenical Ministries—Topeka, KS
Kentucky Council of Churches—Lexington, KY
Louisiana Interchurch Conference—Baton Rouge, LA
Madison Area Urban Ministry—Madison, WI
Minnesota Council of Churches—Minneapolis, MN
Montana Association of Churches—Billings, MT
North Carolina Council of Churches—Raleigh, NC
North Dakota Conference of Churches—Ashley, ND
Oklahoma Conference of Churches—Oklahoma City, OK
Pike County Outreach Council—Waverly, OH
Reading Berks Conference of Churches—Reading, PA
The Rhode Island State Council of Churches—Providence, RI
United Churches of Lycoming County—Williamsport, PA
Virginia Council of Churches, Inc.—Richmond, VA
West Virginia Council of Churches—Charleston, WV
Wisconsin Council of Churches—Sun Prairie, WI

Senior Citizen Programs

Allegheny Valley Association of Churches—Natrona Heights, PA
Associated Ministries of Tacoma–Pierce County—Tacoma, WA
Attleboro Area Council of Churches, Inc.—Attleboro, MA
Bergen County Council of Churches—Bergenfield, NJ
Capital Area Council of Churches, Inc.—Albany, NY
The Capitol Region Conference of Churches—Hartford, CT
Center City Churches—Hartford, CT
Christian Ministries of Delaware County—Muncie, IN
Christians United in Beaver County—Beaver, PA
Church Council of Greater Seattle—Seattle, WA
Churchpeople for Change and Reconciliation—Lima, OH
Community Emergency Assistance Program (CEAP)—Brooklyn Park, MN
Community Ministries of Rockville—Rockville, MD
Community Renewal Society—Chicago, IL
Concerned Ecumenical Ministry to the Upper West Side—Buffalo, NY
Council of Churches of Greater Springfield—Springfield, MA
Council of Churches of the Ozarks—Springfield, MO
Council of Churches and Synagogues of Southwestern Connecticut—Stamford, CT
East Dallas Cooperative Parish—Dallas, TX
Eastern Area Community Ministries—Louisville, KY
Ecumenical Ministries—Fulton, MO
Fern Creek-Highview United Ministries—Louisvlle, KY
Fresno Metro Ministry—Fresno, CA
Georgia Christian Council—Macon, GA
Greater Chicago Broadcast Ministries—Chicago, IL
Greater Minneapolis Council of Churches—Minneapolis, MN
Highlands Community Ministries—Louisville, KY
Inter-Church Council of Greater New Bedford—New Bedford, MA
Inter-Church Ministries of Erie County—Erie, PA
Interfaith Community Council, Inc.—New Albany, IN
Interfaith Community Services—St. Joseph, MO
Interfaith Council of Contra Costa County—Walnut Creek, CA
InterReligious Council of Central New York—Syracuse, NY
Lincoln Interfaith Council—Lincoln, NE
Metropolitan Ecumenical Ministry—Newark, NJ
Metropolitan Inter Faith Association (MIFA)—Memphis, TN
Mississippi Religious Leadership Conference—Jackson, MS
Northside Inter-Church Agency (NICA)—Fort Worth, TX
Northwest Interfaith Movement—Philadelphia, PA
Ohio Council of Churches—Columbus, OH
Oklahoma Conference of Churches—Oklahoma City, OK
Paducah Cooperative Ministry—Paducah, KY

Peoria Friendship House of Christian Service—Peoria, IL
The Rhode Island State Council of Churches—Providence, RI
San Antonio Community of Churches—San Antonio, TX
San Fernando Valley Interfaith Council—Chatsworth, CA
South Hills Interfaith Ministries—South Park, PA
South Louisville Community Ministries—Louisville, KY
Southeast Ecumenical Ministry—Rochester, NY
Staten Island Council of Churches—Staten Island, NY
Tarrant Area Community of Churches—Fort Worth, TX
Troy Area United Ministries—Troy, NY
Tulsa Metropolitan Ministry—Tulsa, OK
United Churches of Lycoming County—Williamsport, PA
West Central Neighborhood Ministry, Inc.—Fort Wayne, IN
West Side Ecumenical Ministry—Cleveland, OH
Wilkinsburg Community Ministry—Pittsburgh, PA

Substance Abuse Programs

Asheville-Buncombe Community Christian Ministry (ABCCM)—Asheville, NC
Bergen County Council of Churches—Bergenfield, NJ
Berrien County Association of Churches—Benton Harbor, MI
Christian Conference of Connecticut—Hartford, CT
Community Ministries of Rockville—Rockville, MD
Corpus Christi Metro Ministries—Corpus Christi, TX
Council of Churches of Greater Bridgeport, Inc.—Bridgeport, CT
Council of Churches of the Ozarks—Springfield, MO
East End Cooperative Ministry—Pittsburgh, PA
Ecumenical Ministries of Iowa (EMI)—Des Moines, IA
Ecumenical Ministries of Oregon—Portland, OR
Evanston Ecumenical Action Council—Evanston, IL
Greater Chicago Broadcast Ministries—Chicago, IL
Greensboro Urban Ministry—Greensboro, NC
Lehigh County Conference of Churches—Allentown, PA
Lincoln Interfaith Council—Lincoln, NE
The Metropolitan Christian Council: Detroit–Windsor—Detroit, MI
Metropolitan Ecumenical Ministry—Newark, NJ
Metropolitan Ecumenical Ministry Community Development Corp.—Newark, NJ
Mississippi Religious Leadership Conference—Jackson, MS
New Hampshire Council of Churches—Pembroke, NH
Pike County Outreach Council—Waverly, OH
The Rhode Island State Council of Churches—Providence, RI
San Antonio Community of Churches—San Antonio, TX
Southeast Ecumenical Ministry—Rochester, NY
West Side Ecumenical Ministry—Cleveland, OH

Theology and Worship Programs

Allegheny Valley Association of Churches—Natrona Heights, PA
Associated Ministries of Tacoma–Pierce County—Tacoma, WA
Attleboro Area Council of Churches, Inc.—Attleboro, MA
Bergen County Council of Churches—Bergenfield, NJ
Berrien County Association of Churches—Benton Harbor, MI
Broome County Council of Churches, Inc.—Binghamton, NY
Capital Area Council of Churches, Inc.—Albany, NY
Christian Associates of Southwest Pennsylvania—Pittsburgh, PA
Christian Conference of Connecticut—Hartford, CT
Christian Council of Metropolitan Atlanta—Atlanta, GA
Church Council of Greater Seattle—Seattle, WA
The Church Federation of Greater Indianapolis, Inc.—Indianapolis, IN
Churches United of the Quad City Area—Rock Island, IL
Colorado Council of Churches—Denver, CO
Council of Churches of the City of New York—New York, NY
Council of Churches of Greater Springfield—Springfield, MA
The Council of Churches of Santa Clara County—San Jose, CA
Council of Churches and Synagogues of Southwestern Connecticut—Stamford, CT
Dutchess Interfaith Council, Inc.—Poughkeepsie, NY
East Dallas Cooperative Parish—Dallas, TX
Ecumenical Conference of Greater Altoona—Altoona, PA
The Ecumenical Council of Pasadena Area Churches—Pasadena, CA
Ecumenical Ministries—Fulton, MO

Ecumenical Ministries of Iowa (EMI)—Des Moines, IA
Ecumenical Ministries of Oregon—Portland, OR
Florida Council of Churches—Orlando, FL
Georgia Christian Council—Macon, GA
Grand Rapids Area Center for Ecumenism (GRACE)—Grand Rapids, MI
Greater Bethlehem Area Council of Churches—Bethlehem, PA
Greater Chicago Broadcast Ministries—Chicago, IL
Greater Dayton Christian Connections—Dayton, OH
Greater Fairmont Council of Churches—Fairmont, WV
Greater New Orleans Federation of Churches—New Orleans, LA
Greater Rochester Community of Churches—Rochester, NY
The Greater Wheeling Council of Churches—Wheeling, WV
Greensboro Urban Ministry—Greensboro, NC
In One Accord—Battle Creek, MI
Indiana Partners for Christian Unity and Mission—Indianapolis, IN
Inter-Church Council of Greater New Bedford—New Bedford, MA
Inter-Church Ministries of Erie County—Erie, PA
Interchurch Ministries of Nebraska—Lincoln, NE
Interfaith Mission Service—Huntsville, AL
InterReligious Council of Central New York—Syracuse, NY
Kentuckiana Interfaith Community—Louisville, KY
Lehigh County Conference of Churches—Allentown, PA
Lincoln Interfaith Council—Lincoln, NE
The Long Island Council of Churches—Hempstead, NY
Louisiana Interchurch Conference—Baton Rouge, LA
Marin Interfaith Council—Novato, CA
Massachusetts Council of Churches—Boston, MA
Metropolitan Christian Council of Philadelphia—Philadelphia, PA
The Metropolitan Christian Council: Detroit–Windsor—Detroit, MI
Metropolitan Ecumenical Ministry—Newark, NJ
Michigan Ecumenical Forum—Lansing, MI
Muskegon County Cooperating Churches—Muskegon, MI
Network of Religious Communities—Buffalo, NY
New Britain Area Conference of Churches (NEWBRACC)—New Britain, CT
New Mexico Conference of Churches—Albuquerque, NM
Northern Kentucky Interfaith Commission, Inc.—Newport, KY
Northwest Interfaith Movement—Philadelphia, PA
Oak Park–River Forest Community of Congregations—Oak Park, IL
Ohio Council of Churches—Columbus, OH
Oklahoma Conference of Churches—Oklahoma City, OK
The Pennsylvania Council of Churches—Harrisburg, PA
The Rhode Island State Council of Churches—Providence, RI
San Antonio Community of Churches—San Antonio, TX
Schenectady Inner City Ministry—Schenectady, NY
South Carolina Christian Action Council, Inc.—Columbia, SC
South Coast Ecumenical Council—Long Beach, CA
South East Associated Ministries (SEAM)—Louisville, KY
South Louisville Community Ministries—Louisville, KY
Southern California Ecumenical Council—Pasadena, CA
Spokane Council of Ecumenical Ministries—Spokane, WA
Tarrant Area Community of Churches—Fort Worth, TX
Texas Conference of Churches—Austin, TX
Troy Area United Ministries—Troy, NY
United Religious Community of St. Joseph County—South Bend, IN
Vermont Ecumenical Council and Bible Society—Burlington, VT
Virginia Council of Churches, Inc.—Richmond, VA
Washington Association of Churches—Seattle, WA
Worcester County Ecumenical Council—Worcester, MA
Wyoming Church Coalition—Cheyenne, WY

Women's Issues

Associated Ministries of Tacoma–Pierce County—Tacoma, WA
Bergen County Council of Churches—Bergenfield, NJ
Berrien County Association of Churches—Benton Harbor, MI
Border Association for Refugees from Central America (BARCA), Inc.—Edinburg, TX
California Council of Churches–California Church Impact—Sacramento, CA
Center for the Prevention of Sexual and Domestic Violence—Seattle, WA
Chautaugua County Rural Ministry—Dunkirk, NY
Christian Council of Metropolitan Atlanta—Atlanta, GA
Christian Ministries of Delaware County—Muncie, IN

Church Community Services—Elkhart, IN
Church Council of Greater Seattle—Seattle, WA
Community Ministries of Rockville—Rockville, MD
Council of Churches of Greater Bridgeport, Inc.—Bridgeport, CT
The Council of Churches of Santa Clara County—San Jose, CA
East Dallas Cooperative Parish—Dallas, TX
East End Cooperative Ministry—Pittsburgh, PA
The Ecumenical Council of Pasadena Area Churches—Pasadena, CA
Ecumenical Ministries of Oregon—Portland, OR
Florida Council of Churches—Orlando, FL
Fresno Metro Ministry—Fresno, CA
Genesee–Orleans Ministry of Concern—Albion, NY
Georgia Christian Council—Macon, GA
Greater Birmingham Ministries—Birmingham, AL
Greater Chicago Broadcast Ministries—Chicago, IL
Inter-Church Council of Greater New Bedford—New Bedford, MA
Lincoln Interfaith Council—Lincoln, NE
Metropolitan Christian Council of Philadelphia—Philadelphia, PA
The Metropolitan Christian Council: Detroit–Windsor—Detroit, MI
Metropolitan Ecumenical Ministry—Newark, NJ
Mississippi Religious Leadership Conference—Jackson, MS
Network of Religious Communities—Buffalo, NY
New Mexico Conference of Churches—Albuquerque, NM
North Carolina Council of Churches—Raleigh, NC
Oklahoma Conference of Churches—Oklahoma City, OK
Peoria Friendship House of Christian Service—Peoria, IL
The Rhode Island State Council of Churches—Providence, RI
San Antonio Community of Churches—San Antonio, TX
South Hills Interfaith Ministries—South Park, PA
Spokane Council of Ecumenical Ministries—Spokane, WA
Staten Island Council of Churches—Staten Island, NY
United Religious Community of St. Joseph County—South Bend, IN
West Central Neighborhood Ministry, Inc.—Fort Wayne, IN
West Side Ecumenical Ministry—Cleveland, OH

Youth Activities

Arkansas Interfaith Conference—Scott, AR
Associated Ministries of Tacoma–Pierce County—Tacoma, WA
Association of Christian Churches of South Dakota—Sioux Falls, SD
Austin Area Interreligious Ministries—Austin, TX
Bergen County Council of Churches—Bergenfield, NJ
Berrien County Association of Churches—Benton Harbor, MI
Brooklyn Council of Churches—Brooklyn, NY
Center for the Prevention of Sexual and Domestic Violence—Seattle, WA
Christian Council of Metropolitan Atlanta—Atlanta, GA
Christian Ministries of Delaware County—Muncie, IN
Church Council of Greater Seattle—Seattle, WA
The Church Federation of Greater Indianapolis, Inc.—Indianapolis, IN
Colorado Council of Churches—Denver, CO
Community Renewal Society—Chicago, IL
Concerned Ecumenical Ministry to the Upper West Side—Buffalo, NY
Council of Churches of Greater Bridgeport, Inc.—Bridgeport, CT
Council of Churches of Greater Springfield—Springfield, MA
The Council of Churches of Santa Clara County—San Jose, CA
Dutchess Interfaith Council, Inc.—Poughkeepsie, NY
East Dallas Cooperative Parish—Dallas, TX
East End Cooperative Ministry—Pittsburgh, PA
Eastern Area Community Ministries—Louisville, KY
Ecclesia—Trenton, NJ
Ecumenical Ministries—Fulton, MO
Ecumenical Ministries of Oregon—Portland, OR
Evanston Ecumenical Action Council—Evanston, IL
Fresno Metro Ministry—Fresno, CA
Genesee-Orleans Ministry of Concern—Albion, NY
Greater Bethlehem Area Council of Churches—Bethlehem, PA
Greater Chicago Broadcast Ministries—Chicago, IL
Greater Fairmont Council of Churches—Fairmont, WV
Greater Minneapolis Council of Churches—Minneapolis, MN
Highlands Community Ministries—Louisville, KY
Inter-Church Council of Greater New Bedford—New Bedford, MA

Interfaith Community Council, Inc.—New Albany, IN
Interfaith Community Services—St. Joseph, MO
Interfaith Conference of Greater Milwaukee—Milwaukee, WI
Kentucky Council of Churches—Lexington, KY
Lehigh County Conference of Churches—Allentown, PA
Lincoln Interfaith Council—Lincoln, NE
Marin Interfaith Council—Novato, CA
The Metropolitan Christian Council: Detroit–Windsor—Detroit, MI
Metropolitan Ecumenical Ministry—Newark, NJ
Metropolitan Ecumenical Ministry Community Development Corp.—Newark, NJ
Metropolitan Inter Faith Association (MIFA)—Memphis, TN
Network of Religious Communities—Buffalo, NY
New Britain Area Conference of Churches (NEWBRACC)—New Britain, CT
New Mexico Conference of Churches—Albuquerque, NM
Northern California Interreligious Conference—Oakland, CA
Northside Inter-Church Agency (NICA)—Fort Worth, TX
Northwest Interfaith Movement—Philadelphia, PA
Peoria Friendship House of Christian Service—Peoria, IL
Reading Berks Conference of Churches—Reading, PA
Reading Urban Ministry—Reading, PA
The Rhode Island State Council of Churches—Providence, RI
Rural Migrant Ministry—Poughkeepsie, NY
St. Paul Area Council of Churches—St. Paul, MN
San Antonio Community of Churches—San Antonio, TX
Schenectady Inner City Ministry—Schenectady, NY
South East Associated Ministries (SEAM)—Louisville, KY
South Hills Interfaith Ministries—South Park, PA
South Louisville Community Ministries—Louisville, KY
Southeast Ecumenical Ministry—Rochester, NY
Spokane Council of Ecumenical Ministries—Spokane, WA
Staten Island Council of Churches—Staten Island, NY
Troy Area United Ministries—Troy, NY
United Churches of Lycoming County—Williamsport, PA
United Religious Community of St. Joseph County—South Bend, IN
West Central Neighborhood Ministry, Inc.—Fort Wayne, IN
West Side Ecumenical Ministry—Cleveland, OH
Worcester County Ecumenical Council—Worcester, MA

8. Canadian Regional and Local Ecumenical Bodies

Most of the organizations listed below are councils of churches in which churches participate officially, whether at the parish or judicatory level. They operate at the city, metropolitan area, or county level. Parish clusters within urban areas are not included.

Canadian local ecumenical bodies operate without paid staff, with the exception of a few which have part-time staff. In most cases, the name and address of the president or chairperson is listed. As these offices change from year to year, some of this information may be out of date by the time the *Yearbook of American & Canadian Churches* is published.

ALBERTA

Calgary Council of Churches

c/o Anna Tremblay, Ecumenical & Inter-religious Affairs, 120 17th Ave., Calgary, AB T2S 2T2 Tel. (403)218-5521

Calgary Inter-Faith Community Association

P.O. Box 93, Stn. M, Calgary, AB T2P 2G9 Tel. (403)262-5111

BRITISH COLUMBIA

Canadian Ecumenical Action

Coord., 1410 W. 12th Ave., Vancouver, BC V6H 1M8

Greater Victoria Council of Churches

c/o Rev. Edwin Taylor, St. Alban's Church, 1468 Ryan St. at Balmont, Victoria, BC V8R 2X1

Vancouver Council of Churches

Murray Moerman, 700 Kingsway, Vancouver, BC V5V 3C1 Tel. (604)420-0761

MANITOBA

Association of Christian Churches in Manitoba

The Rev. Ted Chell, President, 484 Maryland St., Winnipeg, Manitoba R3G 1M5 Tel. (204)774-3143 or (204)775-3536

NEW BRUNSWICK

Atlantic Ecumenical Council of Churches

Rev. Rufus Onyewuchi, 170 Daniel Ave., Saint John, NB E2K 4S7 Tel. (506)538-2491

First Miramichi Inter-Church Council

Pres., Ellen Robinson, Doaktown, NB E0C 1G0

Moncton Area Council of Churches

Rev. Yvon Berrieau, Visitation Ministry, Grand Digue, NB, E0A 1S0

United Church Maritime Conference— Inter-church Inter-faith Committee

Rev. Leslie Robinson, PO Box 174, Chipman, NB E0E 1C0 Tel. (506) 339-6626, maronf@nbnet.nb.ca

NEWFOUNDLAND

Atlantic Ecumenical Council of Churches

Pres., Rev. John E. Boyd, Box 637, 90 Victoria St., Amherst, NS B4H 4B4

St. John's Area Council of Churches

Rev. Canon Ralph Billard, 31 Hazelwood Cres., St. John's, NF, A1E 6B3 Tel. (709)579-0536

NOVA SCOTIA

Amherst and Area Council of Churches

Jean Miller, RR#3 1065 Hwy 204, Amherst, NS, B4H 3Y1 Tel. (902) 667-8107

Bridgewater Inter-Church Council

Pres., Wilson Jones, 30 Parkdale Ave., Bridgewater, NS B4V 1L8

Cornwallis District Inter-Church Council

Pres., Mr. Tom Regan, Centreville, RR 2, Kings County, NS BOT 1JO

Halifax-Dartmouth Council of Churches

Mrs. Betty Short, 3 Virginia Ave., Dartmouth, NS B2W 2Z4

Industrial Cape Breton Council of Churches
Rev. Karen Ralph, 24 Huron Ave., Sydney Mines, NS B1S 1V2

Kentville Council of Churches
Rev. Canon S.J.P. Davies, 325-325 Main St., Kentville, NS B4N 1C5

Lunenburg Queens BA Association
Mrs. Nilda Chute, 56 Hillside Dr., RR 4, Bridgewater, NS B4V 2W3

Mahone Bay Interchurch Council
Patricia Joudrey, R.R. #1, Blockhouse, NS B0J 1E0

Pictou Council of Churches
Sec., Rev. D. J. Murphy, P.O. Box 70, Pictou, NS B0K 1H0

Queens County Association of Churches
Mr. Donald Burns, Box 537, Liverpool, NS B0T 1K6

ONTARIO

Burlington Inter-Church Council
Mr. Fred Townsend, 425 Breckenwood, Burlington, ON L7L 2J6

Christian Leadership Council of Downtown Toronto
Chpsn., Ken Bhagan, 40 Homewood Ave., #509, Toronto, ON M4Y 2K2

Ecumenical Committee (Sault Ste. Marie)
Rev. William B. Kidd, 76 Eastern Ave., Sault Ste. Marie, ON P6A 4R2

Glengarry-Prescott-Russell Christian Council
Pres., Rev. G. Labrosse, St. Eugene's, Prescott, ON K0B 1P0

The Greater Toronto Council of Christian Churches
Sec., Father Damian MacPherson, 1155 Yonge St., Toronto M4T 1W2 Tel. (416)934-3400 ext.344

Hamilton & District Christian Churches Association
The Rev. Dr. John Johnston, 183 Chedoke Avenue, Hamilton, ON L8P 4P2 Tel. (905) 529-6896 or (905)528-2730 Fax (905) 521-2539

Ignace Council of Churches
Box 5, 205 Pine St., St. Ignace, ON P0T 1H0

Inter Church Council of Burlington
Michael Bittle, Box 62120 Burlington Mall R.P.O., Burlington, ON L7R 4K2 Tel. (905) 526-1523 Fax (509)526-9056
Email: mbittle@istar.ca
Website: http://home.istar.cal/mbittle/eo_schl.htm

Kitchener-Waterloo Council of Churches
Rev. Clarence Hauser, CR, 53 Allen St. E, Waterloo, ON N2J 1J3

London Inter-City Faith Team
Chpsn., David Carouthers, c/o United Church, 711 Colbourne St., London, ON N6A 3Z4

Massey Inter-Church Council
The Rev. Hope Jackson, Box 238, Massey, ON P0P 1P0 Tel. (705)865-2202

Ottawa Christian Council of the Capital Area
1247 Kilborn Ave., Ottawa, ON K1H 6K9

St. Catharines & Dist. Clergy Fellowship
Rev. Victor Munro, 663 Vince St., St. Catharines, ON L2M 3V8

Spadina-Bloor Interchurch Council
Chpsn., Rev. Frances Combes, c/o Bathurst St. United Church, 427 Bloor St. W, Toronto, ON M5S 1X7

Stratford & District Council of Churches
Chpsn., Rev. Ted Heinze, 202 Erie St., Stratford, ON N5A 2M8

Thorold Inter-Faith Council
1 Dunn St., St. Catharines, ON L2T 1P3

Thunder Bay Council of Churches
Rev. Richard Darling, 1800 Moodie St. E, Thunder Bay, ON P7E 4Z2

PRINCE EDWARD ISLAND

Atlantic Ecumenical Council
Sec., The Rev. Arthur J. Pendergast, Immaculate Conception Church, St. Louis, PEI C0B 1Z0 Tel. (902)963-2202 or (902)882-2610

Summerside Christian Council
Ms. A. Kathleen Miller, P.O. Box 1551, Summerside, PEI C1N 4K4

QUEBEC

AGAPÉ Deux-Montagnes
c/o Donald Tremblay, prêtre, cure de Saint-Agapit et president de AGAPÉ deux-Montagnes, 1002

chemin d'Oka, Deux-Montagnes, QC J7® 1L7 Tel. (450)473-9877

ACAT

Action des chrétiens pour l'abolition de la torture, 4839 rue de Bordeaux, Montréal, QC H2H 2A2 Tel. (514)890-6169.

Canadian Centre for Ecumenism/Centre d'oecuménisme

Rev. Gilles Bourdeau, 2065 Sherbrooke St. W, Montreal, QC H3H 1G6 Tel. (514)937-9176 Fax (514)937-2684

Centre Emmaüs

Centre de spiritualité des Églises d'Orient, 3774 chemin Queen-Mary, Montréal, QC, H3V 1A6 Tel. (514)276-2144 Fax (514)905-0223
Website: www.centre-emmaus.qc.ca

Direction Chrétienne

The Rev. Glen Smith, 1450 City Councillors, Suite 720, Montréal, QC H3A 2E6 Tel. (514) 878-3035 Fax (514) 878-8048
Email: info@direction.ca
Website: www.direction.ca

Conseil des Églises de Côte-des Neiges <<Sept Égliese—un seul Esprit>>

Notre-Dame-des-Neiges (Roman Catholic), Tel. (514)738-1987; Dominion Douglas (United Church of Canada), Tel. (514)486-1165, St. Kevin's (Roman Catholic), Tel. (514)733-5600; St. Paul's (Anglican), Tel. (514)733-2908, Mount Royal United (United Church of Canada), Tel. (514)739-7741; St. Peter's (Anglican), Tel. (514)739-4776; St. Pascal-Baylon (Roman Catholic), Tel. (514)738-1214.

Conseil interreligieux de Montréal

2065 rue Sherbrooke ouest, Montréal, QC, H3H 1G6 Tel. (514)937-9176 Fax (514)937-4986, Website: www.total.net/~ccocce.

The Ecumenical Group

c/o Mrs. C. Haten, 1185 Ste. Foy, St. Bruno, QC J3V 3C3

Hemmingford Ecumenical Committee

c/o Catherine Priest, Box 300, Hemmingford, QC J0L 1H0

Jewish-Christian Dialogue of Montreal

The Rabbi Leigh Lerner, Temple Emmanu-El-Beth Sholom, 4100 Sherbrooke St. W, Westmount, QC H3Z 1A5 Office Tel. (514) 937-3575 ext.207, Home Tel. (514)937-3708

Montréal Council of Churches

The Rev. Ralph Watson, 4995 Coronation Ave., Montréal, QC H4V 2E1 Tel. (514)482-3210

Montreal Association for the Blind Foundation

The Rev. Dr. John A. Simms, 7000 Sherbrooke St. W., Montreal, QC H4B 1R3 Tel. (514)489-8201

Muslim Christian Dialogue

Dr. Sheila McDonnough, Department of Religion, Concordia University, 1455 de Maisonneuve Blvd., Montreal, QC, H3G 1M8 Tel. (514)488-6308
Email: donou@vax2.concordia.ca

Radio Ville-Marie

Radio religieuse, 505 avenue de Mont-Cassin, Montréal, QC, H3L 1W7 Tel (514)382-3913 or (877)668-6601 Fax (514)858-0965
Email: cira@radiovm.com
Website: www.radiovm.com

ROQ

Réseau oecuménique du Québec (Quebec Ecumenical Network), le Centre canadien d'oecuménisme en assure le secretariat, 2065 rue Sherbrooke ouest, Montréal, QC. Tel. (514) 937-9176 Fax (514)937-4986
Email: ccocce@total.net

Réseau oecuménique justice et paix

C.P. 114, Succ. D. Montréal, QC H3K 3B9 Tel./Fax (514)937-2683
Email: info@justiceoaix.org

Unitas

Centre oecuménique de meditation chrétienne et de spiritualité, 3289 St-Jacques, Montréal, QC, H4C 1G8 Tel. (514)485-0009

SASKATCHEWAN

Humboldt Clergy Council

Fr. Leo Hinz, OSB, Box 1989, Humboldt, SK S0K 2A0

Melville Association of Churches

Attn., Catherine Gaw, Box 878, Melville, SK S0A 2P0

Regina Council of Churches

The Rev. Bud Harper, 5 Robinson Crescent, Regina, SK S4R 3R1 Tel. (306)545-3375

Prairie Centre for Ecumenism

Sister Anne Keffer, 250-B Second Ave. So, Saskatoon, SK S7K 1K9 Tel. (306)653-1633 Fax (306)653-1821
Email: pce@ecumenism.net

Saskatoon Council of Churches

Dr. Colin Clay, 250-B Second Ave. S, Saskatoon, SK S7K 1K9

9. Theological Seminaries and Bible Colleges in the United States

The following list includes theological seminaries, Bible colleges, and departments in colleges and universities in which ministerial training is given. Many denominations have additional programs.

Inclusion in or exclusion from this list implies no judgment about the quality or accreditation of any institution. Those schools that are members of the Association of Theological Schools are marked with an asterisk (*). Those schools that are accredited by the Transnational Association of Christian Colleges and Schools are marked with (†). Additional information about enrollment in ATS member schools can be found in the "Trends in Seminary Enrollment" section of Section III. Information about TRACS and ATS can be found in the United States Cooperative Organizations section of Section II.

Each of the listings include, when available: the institution name, denominational sponsor, location, the president or dean of the institution, telephone, fax numbers, email and website addresses.

Abilene Christian University Graduate School of Theology* (Churches of Christ), Jack R. Reese, Dean, College of Biblical Studies, ACU Box 29422 1850 N. Judge Ely Blvd., CBS Room 297, Abilene, TX 79699-9422 Tel. (915)674-3700 Fax (915)674-6180
Email: thompson@bible.acu.edu
Website: www.bible.acu.edu/GST

Alaska Bible College (Nondenominational), Steven J. Hostetter, Pres., P.O. Box 289, Glennallen, AK 99588 Tel. (907)822-3201 Fax (907)822-5027
Email: info@akbible.edu
Website: www.akbible.edu

Alliance Theological Seminary* (The Christian and Missionary Alliance), David E. Schroeder, Pres., 350 N. Highland Ave., Nyack, NY 10960-1416 Tel. (845)353-2020 Fax (845) 727-3002
Website: www.alliance.edu

American Baptist College (National Baptist Convention USA, Inc.), Dr. Forrest E. Harris, Pres., 1800 Baptist World Center Dr., Nashville, TN 37207 Tel. (615)228-7877 Fax (615)226-7855
Email: harrisfe@abcnash.edu

American Baptist Seminary of the West* (American Baptist Churches in the USA), Keith A. Russell, President, 2606 Dwight Way, Berkeley, CA 94704-3029 Tel. (510)841-1905 Fax (510)841-2446
Email: krussell@absw.edu
Website: www.absw.edu

American Christian College and Seminary† Dr. Fred Hambrick, Pres., 4300 Highline Boulevard, Suite #202, Oklahoma, OK 73108 Tel. (405)945-0100 Fax (405)945-0311
Email: info@accs.edu
Website: www.accs.edu

Anderson University School of Theology* (Church of God [Anderson, Ind.]), James L. Edwards, Pres., 1100 E. Fifth Street, Anderson, IN 46012-3495 Tel. (765)641-4032 Fax (765)641-3851
Website: www.anderson.edu/academics/sot

Andover Newton Theological School* (American Baptist Churches in the USA; United Church of Christ), Benjamin Griffin, Pres., 210 Herrick Rd., Newton Centre, MA 02459 Tel. (617)964-1100 Fax (617)558-9785
Email: admissions@ants.edu
Website: www.ants.edu

Appalachian Bible College (Nondenominational), Daniel L. Anderson, Pres., P.O. Box ABC, Bradley, WV 25818 Tel. (304)877-6428 or (800)6789 Fax (304)877-5082
Email: abc@abc.edu
Website: www.abc.edu

Aquinas Institute of Theology* (Catholic), Charles E. Bouchard, Pres., 3642 Lindell Blvd., St. Louis, MO 63108-3396 Tel. (314) 977-3882 Fax (314)977-7225
Email: aquinas@slu.edu
Website: www.ai.edu

Arizona College of the Bible (Interdenominational), Douglas K. Winn, Pres., 2045 W. Northern Ave., Phoenix, AZ 85021-5197 Tel. (602)995-2670 Fax (602)864-8183

Arlington Baptist College (Baptist), David Bryant, Pres., 3001 W. Division, Arlington, TX 76012-3425 Tel. (817)461-8741 Fax (817)274-1138

Asbury Theological Seminary* (Inter/ Multidenominational), Maxie D. Dunnam, Pres., 204 N. Lexington Ave., Wilmore, KY 40390-1199 Tel. (859)858-3581
Website: www.asburyseminary.edu

Ashland Theological Seminary* (Brethren Church [Ashland, Ohio]), Frederick J. Finks, Pres., 910 Center St., Ashland, OH 44805 Tel. (419)289-5161 Fax (419)289-5969
Email: ffinks@ashland.edu
Website: www.ashland.edu/seminary/seminary.html

Assemblies of God Theological Seminary* (Assemblies of God), Byron D. Klaus, Pres., 1435 N. Glenstone Ave., Springfield, MO 65802-2131 Tel. (417)268-1000 Fax (417) 268-1001
Email: agts@agseminary.edu
Website: www.agts.edu

Associated Mennonite Biblical Seminary* (Mennonite Church; General Conference Mennonite Church), J. Nelson Kraybill, Pres., 3003 Benham Ave., Elkhart, IN 46517-1999 Tel. (574)295-3726 Fax (574)295-0092
Email: nkraybill@ambs.edu
Website: www.ambs.edu

Athenaeum of Ohio* (Catholic), Gerald R. Haemmerle, Pres. and Rector, 6616 Beechmont Ave., Cincinnati, OH 45230-2091 Tel. (513) 231-2223 Fax (513)231-3254
Email: atheathenaeum.edu
Website: www.athenaeum.edu

Atlanta Christian College (Christian Churches and Churches of Christ), R. Edwin Groover, Pres., 2605 Ben Hill Rd., East Point, GA 30344 Tel. (404)761-8861 Fax (404)669-2024
Email: admissions@acc.edu
Website: www.acc.edu

Austin Presbyterian Theological Seminary* (Presbyterian Church [USA]), Theodore J. Wardlaw, Pres., 100 E. 27th St., Austin, TX 78705-5797 Tel. (512)472-6736 Fax (512) 479-0738
Website: www.austinseminary.edu

Azusa Pacific University* (Interdenominational), Jon R. Wallace, Pres., 901 E. Alosta, P.O. Box 7000, Azusa, CA 91702 Tel. (845)969-3434 Fax (845)969-7180
Website: www.apu.edu

Bangor Theological Seminary* (United Church of Christ), William C. Imes, Pres., 300 Union St., Bangor, ME 04401 Tel. (207)942-6781 Fax (207)942-4914
Email: jwiebe@bts.edu
Website: www.bts.edu

Baptist Bible College (Baptist Bible Fellowship International), Leland Kennedy, Pres., 628 E. Kearney, Springfield, MO 65803 Tel. (417)268-6060 Fax (417)268-6694

Baptist Bible College and Seminary (Baptist), Jim Jeffery, Pres., 538 Venard Rd., Clarks Summit, PA 18411 Tel. (570)586-2400 Fax (570)586-1753
Email: bbc@bbc.edu
Website: www.bbc.edu

Baptist Missionary Association Theological Seminary (Baptist Missionary Association of America), Charley Holmes, Pres., 1530 E. Pine St., Jacksonville, TX 75766- Tel. (903)586-2501 Fax (903)586-0378
Email: bmaisem@flash.net
Website: www.geocities.com/Athens/Acropolis/3386

Baptist Theological Seminary at Richmond* (Cooperative Baptist Fellowship), Thomas H. Graves, Pres., 3400 Brook Rd., Richmond, VA 23227 Tel. (804)355-8135 Fax (804)355-8182
Email: btsr@btsr.edu
Website: www.btsr.edu

Barclay College (Interdenominational), Maurice G. Chandler, Pres., 607 N Kingman, Haviland, KS 67059 Tel. (620)862-5252 Fax (620)862-5403
Email: barclaycollege@havilandtalco.com

Barry University Department of Theology and Philosophy* Mark E. Wedig, Chpsn. of the Department of Theology and Philosophy, 11300 Northeast Second Ave., Miami Shores, FL 33161-6695 Tel. (305)899-3469 Fax (305) 899-3385
Email: theology@mail.barry.edu
Website: www.barry.edu/artssciences/default.htm

Bay Ridge Christian College (Church of God [Anderson, Ind.]), Dr. Verda Beach, Pres., P.O. Box 726, Kendleton, TX 77451 Tel. (979)532-3982 Fax (979)532-4352
Email: brcccampus@wcnet.net
Website: brcconline.org

Beacon College & Graduate School (Non-denominational), Dr. Ian Bond, Vice Pres., 6003 Veterans Pkwy, Columbus, GA 31909 Tel. (706)323-5364 Fax (706)323-3236
Email: beacon.beacon.edu/webmaster@beacon.edu
Website: www.beacon.edu

Beeson Divinity School of Samford University* (Inter/Multidenominational), Timothy George, Dean, 800 Lakeshore Dr., Birmingham, AL 35229-2252 Tel. (205)726-2991 Fax (205) 726-2260
Email: jtprince@samford.edu
Website: www.Samford.Edu/schools/divinity.html

Berkeley Divinity School* (Episcopal Church), Joseph H. Britton, Interim Dean, 409 Prospect St., New Haven, CT 06511 Tel. (203)432-9285 Fax (203)432-9353
Website: www.yale.edu/divinity/bds

Bethany College of the Assemblies of God (Assemblies of God), Eugene F. Roop, Pres., 800 Bethany Dr., Richmond, VA 47374 Tel. (765)983-1800 Fax (765)983-1840
Email: info@fc.bethany.edu
Website: www.bethanyseminary.educ

Bethany Lutheran Theological Seminary (Evangelical Lutheran Synod), G. R. Schmeling, Pres., 6 Browns Ct., Mankato, MN 56001 Tel. (507)344-7354 Fax (507)344-7426
Email: gschmeli@blc.edu
Website: www.blts.edu

Bethany Theological Seminary* (Church of the Brethren), Eugene F. Roop, Pres., 615 National Rd. W., Richmond, IN 47374 Tel. (765)983-1800 Fax (765)983-1840
Email: roopge@bethanyseminary.edu
Website: www.bethanyseminary.edu

Bethel Seminary of the East* (Conservative Baptist Association of America; Baptist General Conference), Douglas W. Fombelle, Dean and Exec. Officer, 1605 N. Limekiln Pike, Dresher, PA 19025 Tel. (215)641-4801 Fax (215)641-4804
Website: www.bethel.edu

Bethel Seminary San Diego* (General Bapist Conference), John Lillis, Dean, 6116 Arosa St., San Diego, CA 92115-3902 Tel. (619)582-8188 Fax (619)583-9114
Website: www.bethel.edu

Bethel Theological Seminary* (Baptist General Conference), George K. Brushaber, Pres., 3949 Bethel Dr., St. Paul, MN 55112 Tel. (651)638-6180 Fax (651)638-6002
Email: webmaster@bethel.edu
Website: www.bethel.edu

Beulah Heights Bible College*† (The International Pentecostal Church of Christ), Samuel R. Chand, Pres., 892 Berne St. SE, Atlanta, GA 30316 Tel. (404)627-2681 Fax (404)627-0702
Email: bhbc@beulah.org
Website: www.beulah.org

Bexley Hall* (Episcopal Church), John R. Kevern, Pres. and Dean, 1100 S. Goodman St., Rochester, NY 14620-2589 Tel. (585)340-9550 Fax (585)340-9636
Email: bexleyhall@crds.edu
Website: www.bexley.edu

Bible Church of Christ Theological Institute (Nondenominational), Roy Bryant Sr., Pres., 1358 Morris Ave., Bronx, NY 10456-1402 Tel. (718)588-2284 Fax (718)992-5597
Website: www.thebiblechurchofchrist.org

Biblical Theological Seminary* (Inter/ Multidenominational), David G. Dunbar, Pres., 200 N. Main St., Hatfield, PA 19440 Tel. (215)368-5000 Fax (215)368-7002
Email: president@biblical.edu
Website: www.biblical.edu

Blessed John XXIII National Seminary* (Catholic), Francis D. Kelly, Rector, 558 South Ave., Weston, MA 02493-2699 Tel. (781)899-5500 Fax (781)899-9057
Website: www.ziplink.net~popejohn/index.html

Boise Bible College (Christian Churches and Churches of Christ), Dr. Charles A. Crane, Pres., 8695 Marigold St., Boise, ID 83714-Tel. (208)376-7731 Fax (208)376-7743
Email: boisebible@boisebible.edu
Website: www.boisebible.edu

Boston Baptist College† 950 Metropolitan Ave., Boston, MA 02136 Tel. (617)364-3510 Fax (617)364-0723
Email: admin@boston.edu
Website: www.boston.edu

Boston University (School of Theology)* (The United Methodist Church), Dr. Robert C. Neville, Dean, 745 Commonwealth Ave., Boston, MA 02215 Tel. (617)353-3050 Fax (617)353-3061
Website: www.bu.edu/STH/

Brite Divinity School, Texas Christian University* (Christian Church [Disciples of Christ]), Newell Williams, Pres., TCU Box 298130, Ft. Worth, TX 76129-0002 Tel. (817) 257-7575 Fax (817)257-7305
Email: t.palmer@tcu.edu
Website: www.brite.tcu.edu/brite/

California Christian College† (Association of Free Will Baptists), Wendell Walley, Pres., 4881 E. University Ave., Fresno, CA 93703 Tel. (559) 251-4215 Fax (559) 251-4231
Email: cccfresno@aol.com
Website: www.calchristiancollege.org

Calvary Bible College and Theological Seminary (Independent Fundamental Churches of America), James L. Anderson, Pres., 15800 Calvary Rd., Kansas City, MO 64147-1341 Tel. (800)326-3960 Fax (816)331-4474

Calvin Theological Seminary* (Christian Reformed Church in North America), Cornelius Plantinga Jr., Pres., 3233 Burton St.

SE, Grand Rapids, MI 49546-4387 Tel. (616)957-6036 Fax (616)957-8621
Email: sempres@calvin.edu
Website: www.calvinseminary.edu

Campbell University Divinity School* (Baptist State Convention of North Carolina), Michael G. Cogdill, Dean, 116 T. T. Lanier Street, P.O. Drawer 4050, Buies Creek, NC 27506 Tel. (910)893-1830 Fax (910)893-1835
Website: www.campbell.edu/divinity

Candler School of Theology, Emory University* (The United Methodist Church), Russell E. Richey, Dean, 500 Kilgo Circle NE, Emory Univ., Atlanta, GA 30322 Tel. (404)727-6324 Fax (404)727-3182
Email: candler@emory.edu
Website: www.emory.edu/candler

Capital Bible Seminary* (Nondenominational), Homer Heater Jr., Pres., 6511 Princess Garden Pkwy, Lanham, MD 20706 Tel. (301)552-1400 Fax (301)614-1024
Website: www.bible.edu

Catholic Theological Union at Chicago* (Catholic), Donald Senior, C.P., Pres., 5401 S. Cornell Ave., Chicago, IL 60615-5664 Tel. (773)324-8000 Fax (773)324-8490
Website: www.ctu.edu

Catholic University of America* (Catholic), Rev. Msgr. Stephen Harper, PhD, S.T.D., Dean, 620 Michigan Avenue NE, Washington, D.C. 20064 Tel. (202)319-5683 Fax (202) 319-4967
Email: cua-deansrs@cua.edu
Website: www.religiousstudies.cua.edu

Central Baptist College (Baptist Missionary Association of Arkansas), Charles Attebery, Pres., 1501 College Ave., Conway, AR 72032 Tel. (501)329-6872 Fax (501)329-2941
Email: Cattebery@cbc.edu
Website: www.cbc.edu

Central Baptist Theological Seminary* (Baptist), Thomas E. Clifton, President, 741 N. 31st St., Kansas City, KS 66102-3964 Tel. (913)371-5313 Fax (913)371-8110
Email: central@cbts.edu
Website: www.cbts.edu

Central Baptist Theological Seminary in Indiana (National Baptist Convention USA, Inc.), -vacant-, Pres., 1535 Dr. A. J. Brown Ave. N, Indianapolis, IN 46202- Tel. (317) 636-6622
Email: henriettabrown@webtv.net

Central Bible College (Assemblies of God), M. Wayne Benson, Pres., 3000 N. Grant Ave., Springfield, MO 65803 Tel. (417)833-2551 Fax (417)833-5141
Email: info@cbcag.edu
Website: www.cbcag.edu

Central Christian College of the Bible (Christian Churches and Churches of Christ), Russell N. James III, Pres., 911 E. Urbandale Dr., Moberly, MO 65270-1997 Tel. (660)263-3900 Fax (660)263-3936
Email: develop@cccb.edu
Website: www.cccb.edu

Central Indian Bible College (Assemblies of God), Robert Koscak, Pres., P.O. Box 550, Mobridge, SD 57601 Tel. (605)845-7801 Fax (605)845-7744

Chapman School of Religious Studies of Oakland City University* (General Association of General Baptists), James W. Murray, Chancellor and Pres., 143 Lucretia St., Oakland City, IN 47660 Tel. (812)749-4781 Fax (812)749-1233
Email: @oak.edu

Chicago Theological Seminary* (United Church of Christ), Susan Brooks Thistlethwaite, Pres., 5757 S. University Ave., Chicago, IL 60637-1507 Tel. (773)752-5757 Fax (773)752-5925
Email: sthistle@chgosem.edu
Website: www.chgosem.edu

Christ the King Seminary* (Catholic), Richard W. Siepka, Pres. and Rector, 711 Knox Rd., P.O. Box 607, East Aurora, NY 14052-0607 Tel. (716)652-8900 Fax (716)652-8903
Email: rsiepka@cks.edu
Website: www.cks.edu

Christ the Savior Seminary (The American Carpatho-Russian Orthodox Greek Catholic Church), Nicholas Smisko, Pres., 225 Chandler Ave., Johnstown, PA 15906 Tel. (814)539-8086 Fax (814)536-4699
Email: mrosco2@excite.com

Christian Heritage College† Dr. David Jeremiah, Pres., 2100 Greenfield Dr., El Cajon, CA 92019 Tel. (619)441-2200 Fax (619)440-0209
Email: chcadm@christianheritage.edu
Website: www.christianheritage.edu

Christian Life College† (Nondenominational), Harry Schmidt, Pres., 400 E. Gregory Street, Mount Prospect, IL 60056 Tel. (847)259-1840 Fax (847)259-3888
Email: admissions@christianlifecollege.edu
Website: www.christianlifecollege.edu

Christian Theological Seminary* (Christian Church [Disciples of Christ]), Dr. Edward L.

Wheeler, Pres., 1000 W. 42nd St., Indianapolis, IN 46208-3301 Tel. (317)924-1331 Fax (317)923-1961
Email: wheeler@cts.edu
Website: www.cts.edu

Church Divinity School of the Pacific* (Episcopal Church), Donn F. Morgan, Pres., 2451 Ridge Rd., Berkeley, CA 94709-1217 Tel. (510)204-0700 Fax (510)644-0712
Email: mollyanne@cdsp.edu

Church of God Theological Seminary* (Church of God [Cleveland, Tenn.]), Steven J. Land, Pres., P.O. Box 3330, Cleveland, TN 37320-3330 Tel. (423)478-1131 Fax (423) 478-7711
Email: cogseminary@wingnet.com
Website: www.cogts.edu

Cincinnati Bible College and Seminary* (Christian Churches and Churches of Christ), David M. Faust, Pres., 2700 Glenway Ave., Cincinnati, OH 45204-3200 Tel. (513)244-8120 Fax (513)244-8434
Email: info@cincybible.edu
Website: www.cincybible.edu

Circleville Bible College (Churches of Christ in Christian Union), John Conley, Pres., P.O. Box 458, Circleville, OH 43113 Tel. (614)474-8896 Fax (614)477-7755
Email: cbc@biblecollege.edu
Website: www.biblecollege.edu

Claremont School of Theology* (The United Methodist Church), Philip A. Amerson, Pres., 1325 N. College Ave., Claremont, CA 91711-3199 Tel. (800)626-3521 Fax (909)626-7062
Email: admissions@cst.edu
Website: www.cst.edu

Clear Creek Baptist Bible College (Southern Baptist Convention), President Bill Whittaker, Pres., 300 Clear Creek Rd., Pineville, KY 40977 Tel. (606)337-3196 Fax (606)337-2372
Email: ccbbc@ccbbc.edu
Website: www.ccbbc.edu

Clinton Junior College† Dr. Elaine Johnson Copeland, Pres., 1029 Crawford Road, Rock Hill, SC 29730 Tel. (803)327-7402 Fax (803)327-3261
Email: ecopeland@clintonjrcollege.org
Website: www.clintonjrcollege.org

Colegio Biblico Pentecostal de Puerto Rico (Church of God [Cleveland, Tenn.]), Luz M. Rivera, Pres., P.O. Box 901, Saint Just, PR 00978 Tel. (787)761-0640 Fax (787)748-9228

Colgate Rochester Crozer Divinity School* (American Baptist Churches in the USA), G. Thomas Halbrooks, Pres., 1100 S. Goodman St., Rochester, NY 14620 Tel. (585)271-1320 Fax (585)271-8013
Website: www.crcds.edu

Colorado Christian University (Nondenominational), Larry R. Donnithorne, Pres., 180 S. Garrison St., Lakewood, CO 80226 Tel. (303) 202-0100 Fax (303)274-7560
Website: www.ccu.edu

Columbia Biblical Seminary and School of Missions of Columbia International University* (Inter/Multidenominational), George W. Murray, Pres., P.O. Box 3122, Columbia, SC 29230-3122 Tel. (803)754-4100 Fax (803)786-4209
Website: www.ciu.edu

Columbia International University* (Multidenominational), George W. Murray, Pres., P.O. Box 3122, Columbia, SC 29230-3122 Tel. (803)754-4100 Fax (803)786-4209
Website: www.ciu.edu

Columbia Theological Seminary* (Presbyterian Church [USA]), Laura S. Mendenhall, Pres., 701 Columbia Dr., P.O. Box 520, Decatur, GA 30031 Tel. (404)378-8821 Fax (404)377-9696
Website: www.CTSnet.edu

Concordia Seminary* (The Lutheran Church–Missouri Synod), John Franklin Johnson, Pres., 801 DeMun Ave., St. Louis, MO 63105 Tel. (314)505-7010 Fax (314)505-7002
Email: hollisterr@csl.edu

Concordia Theological Seminary* (The Lutheran Church–Missouri Synod), Dean O. Wenthe, Pres., 6600 N. Clinton St., Ft. Wayne, IN 46825-4996 Tel. (260)452-2100 Fax (260) 452-2121
Email: wenthedo@mail.ctsfw.edu
Website: www.ctsfw.edu

Covenant Theological Seminary* (Prebyterian Church in America), Dr. Bryan Chapell, Pres., 12330 Conway Rd., St. Louis, MO 63141-8697 Tel. (314)434-4044 Fax (314)434-4819
Email: admissions@covenantseminary.edu
Website: www.covenantseminary.edu

Criswell Center for Biblical Studies (Southern Baptist Convention) 4010 Gaston Ave., Dallas, TX 75246 Tel. (214)821-5433 Fax (214)818-1320

Crossroads College (Christian Churches and Churches of Christ; Nondenominational), Dr. Bill J. Luce Jr., Pres., 920 Mayowood Rd. SW, Rochester, MN 55902 Tel. (507)288-4563 Fax (507)288-9046

Email: academic@crossroadscollege.edu
Website: www.crossroadscollege

Crown College (The Christian and Missionary Alliance), Gary M. Benedict, Pres., 6425 County Rd. 30, St. Bonifacius, MN 55375-9001 Tel. (952)446-4100 Fax (952)446-4149
Email: crown@crown.edu
Website: www.crown.edu

Cummins Theological Seminary (Reformed Episcopal Church), James C. West, Pres., 705 S. Main St., Summerville, SC 29483 Tel. (843)873-3451 Fax (843)875-6200
Email: jcw121@aol.com

Dallas Christian College (Christian Churches and Churches of Christ), Dr. John Derry, Pres., 2700 Christian Pkwy, Dallas, TX 75234 Tel. (972)241-3371 Fax (972)241-8021
Email: dcc@dallas.edu
Website: www.dallas.edu

Dallas Theological Seminary* (Inter/Multidenominational), Dr. Mark L. Bailey, Pres., 3909 Swiss Ave., Dallas, TX 75204 Tel. (214)824-3094 Fax (214)841-3625
Website: www.dts.edu

Denver Seminary* (Nondenominational), Craig Williford, Pres., Box 100,000, Denver, CO 80250-0100 Tel. (303)761-2482 Fax (303) 761-8060
Email: info@densem.edu
Website: www.denverseminary.edu

The Disciples Divinity House of the University of Chicago* (Christian Church [Disciples of Christ]), Dr. Kristine A. Culp, Dean, 1156 E. 57th St., Chicago, IL 60637-1536 Tel. (773) 643-4411 Fax (773)643-4413
Email: ddh.uchicago.admin@attglobal.net
Website: ddh.uchicago.edu

Dominican House of Studies* (Catholic), Thomas McCreesh, O.P., Pres., 487 Michigan Ave. NE, Washington, D.C. 20017-1585 Tel. (202)529-5300 Fax (202)636-1700
Email: assistant@dhs.edu
Website: www.dhs.edu

Dominican School of Philosophy and Theology* (Catholic), Gregory Rocca, Pres., 2401 Ridge Rd., Berkeley, CA 94709 Tel. (510)849-2030 Fax (510)849-1372
Website: www.dspt.edu

Dominican Study Center of the Caribbean* (Catholic), P. Felix Struik, O.P., Regent of the Center, Apartado Postal 1968, Bayamon, PR 00960-1968 Tel. (787)787-1826 Fax (787) 798-2712

Drew University (Theological School)* (The United Methodist Church), Maxine C. Beach, Vice Pres. and Dean, 36 Madison Ave., Madison, NJ 07940-4010 Tel. (973)408-3258 Fax (973)408-3534
Email: elopezjr@drew.edu
Website: www.drew.edu/theo

Duke University Divinity School* (The United Methodist Church), L. Gregory Jones, Dean, Box 90968, Durham, NC 27708-0968 Tel. (919)660-3400 Fax (919)660-3474
Email: admissions@div.duke.edu
Website: divinity.duke.edu

Earlham School of Religion* (Interdenominational; Friends), Jay Wade Marshall, Dean, 228 College Ave., Richmond, IN 47374 Tel. (800)432-1377 Fax (765)983-1688
Email: woodna@earlham.edu
Website: www.esr.earlham.edu

Eastern Baptist Theological Seminary* (American Baptist Churches in the USA), Alvin S. Jepson, Pres., 6 Lancaster Ave., Wynnewood, PA 19096 Tel. (610)896-5000 Fax (610)649-3834
Website: www.ebts.edu

Eastern Mennonite Seminary of Eastern Mennonite University* (Mennonite Church), Loren Swartzendruber, Pres., 1200 Park Rd., Harrisonburg, VA 22802 Tel. (540)432-4260 Fax (540)432-4598
Email: info@emu.edu
Website: www.emu.edu/seminary

Eden Theological Seminary* (United Church of Christ), David M. Greenhaw, Pres., 475 E. Lockwood Ave., St. Louis, MO 63119-3192 Tel. (314)961-3627 Fax (314)918-2626
Website: www.eden.edu

Emmanuel School of Religion* (Christian Churches and Churches of Christ), C. Robert Wetzel, Pres., One Walker Dr., Johnson City, TN 37601-9438 Tel. (423)926-1186 Fax (423) 926-6198
Email: wetzelr@esr.edu
Website: www.esr.edu

Emmaus Bible College (Christian Brethren [also known as Plymouth Brethren]), Kenneth Alan Daughters, Pres., 2570 Asbury Rd., Dubuque, IA 52001 Tel. (563)588-8000 Fax (563)588-1216
Email: info@emmaus.edu
Website: www.emmaus.edu

Episcopal Divinity School* (Episcopal Church), The Rt. Rev. Steven Charleston, President and Dean, 99 Brattle St., Cambridge, MA 02138-3494 Tel. (617)868-3450 Fax (617)864-5385

Email: fphillips@episdivschool.org
Website: www.episdivschool.edu

Episcopal Theological Seminary of the Southwest* (Episcopal Church), Titus L. Presler, Dean and Pres., P.O. Box 2247, Austin, TX 78768-2247 Tel. (512)472-4133 Fax (512)472-3098
Email: salexander@etss.edu
Website: www.etss.edu

Erskine Theological Seminary* (Associate Reformed Presbyterian Church [General Synod]), R.J. Gore Jr., Vice Pres. and Dean, P.O. Box 668, Due West, SC 29639 Tel. (864)379-8885 Fax (864)379-2171
Email: gore@erskine.edu
Website: www.erskine.edu/seminary/gore/gore.htm

Eugene Bible College (Open Bible Standard Churches, Inc.), Robert L. Whitlow, Pres., 2155 Bailey Hill Rd., Eugene, OR 97405 Tel. (503)485-1780 Fax (503)343-5801

Evangelical School of Theology* (The Evangelical Congregational Church), Kirby N. Keller, Pres., 121 S. College St., Myerstown, PA 17067 Tel. (717)866-5775 Fax (717)866-4667
Website: www.evangelical.edu

Evangelical Seminary of Puerto Rico* (Inter/Multidenominational), Samuel Pagan, Pres., Ponce de Leon Avenue 776, San Juan, PR 00925 Tel. (787)763-6700 Fax (787)751-0847
Website: http://netministries.org/see/charmin/cm01399

Faith Baptist Bible College and Theological Seminary (General Association of Regular Baptist Churches), Richard W. Houg, Pres., 1900 NW 4th St., Ankeny, IA 50021-2152 Tel. (515)964-0601 Fax (515)964-1638
Website: www.faith.edu

Faith Evangelical Lutheran Seminary† (Conservative Lutheran Association), R. H. Redal, Pres., 3504 N. Pearl St., Tacoma, WA 98407 Tel. (253)752-2020 or (888)777-7675 Fax (253)759-1790
Email: fsinfo@faithseminary.edu
Website: www.faithseminary.edu

Florida Christian College (Christian Churches and Churches of Christ), A. Wayne Lowen, Pres., 1011 Bill Beck Blvd., Kissimmee, FL 34744 Tel. (407)847-8966 Fax (407)847-3925
Email: fcc@fcc.edu
Website: www.fcc.edu

Franciscan School of Theology* (Catholic), William M. Cieslak, Pres., 1712 Euclid Ave., Berkeley, CA 94709 Tel. (510)848-5232 Fax (510)549-9466
Email: wcieslak@fst.edu
Website: www.fst.edu

Free Will Baptist Bible College (National Association of Free Will Baptists), J. Matthew Pinson, Pres., 3606 West End Ave., Nashville, TN 37205 Tel. (615)383-1340 Fax (615)269-6028
Email: president@fwbbc.edu
Website: www.fwbcc.edu

Fuller Theological Seminary* (Interdenominational), Richard J. Mouw, Pres., 135 N. Oakland Ave., Pasadena, CA 91182 Tel. (626) 584-5200 Fax (626)795-8767
Email: lguernse@fuller.edu
Website: www.fuller.edu

Garrett–Evangelical Theological Seminary* (The United Methodist Church), Ted A. Campbell, Pres., 2121 Sheridan Rd., Evanston, IL 60201-3298 Tel. (847)866-3900 Fax (847)866-3957
Email: seminary@garrett.edu
Website: www.garrett.northwestern.edu

The General Theological Seminary* (Episcopal Church), Ward B. Ewing, Pres., 175 Ninth Ave., New York, NY 10011-4977 Tel. (212)243-5150 Fax (212)647-0294
Website: www.gts.edu

George Fox Evangelical Seminary* (Inter/Multidenominational), Ed Stevens, Pres., 12753 SW 68th Ave., Portland, OR 97223 Tel. (503)554-6150 Fax (503)554-6111
Email: seminary@georgefox.edu
Website: www.seminary.georgefox.edu

George Mercer Jr. Memorial School of Theology (Episcopal Church), -vacant-, Pres., 65 Fourth St., Garden City, NY 11530 Tel. (516)248-4800 Fax (516)248-4883

George W. Truett Theological Seminary of Baylor University* (Baptist General Convention of Texas), Paul W. Powell, Dean, P.O. Box 97126, Waco, TX 76798-7126 Tel. (254)710-3755 Fax (254)710-3753
Website: www.baylor.edu/truettseminary.net

God's Bible School and College (Nondenominational), Michael Avery, Pres., 1810 Young St., Cincinnati, OH 45210 Tel. (513)721-7944 Fax (513)721-3971
Email: president@gbs.edu
Website: www.gbs.edu

Golden Gate Baptist Theological Seminary* (Southern Baptist Convention), William O. Crews, Pres., 201 Seminary Dr., Mill Valley,

CA 94941-3197 Tel. (415)380-1300 Fax (415) 380-1302
Email: seminary@ggbts.edu
Website: www.ggbts.edu

Gonzaga University Department of Religious Studies* (Catholic), Fr. Robert Spitzer, S.J., Pres., Spokane, WA 99258-0001 Tel. (509)328-6782 Fax (509)323-5718
Email: www.gonzaga.edu

Gordon–Conwell Theological Seminary* (Inter/Multidenominational), Walter C. Kaiser Jr., Pres., 130 Essex St., South Hamilton, MA 01982 Tel. (978)468-7111 Fax (978)468-6691
Email: info@gcts.edu
Website: www.gordonconwell.edu

Grace Bible College (Grace Gospel Fellowship), Kenneth B. Kemper, Pres., P.O. Box 910, Grand Rapids, MI 49509 Tel. (616)538-2330 Fax (616)538-0599
Email: gbc@gbcol.edu
Website: www.gbcol.edu

Grace Theological Seminary (Fellowship of Grace Brethren Churches), Ronald E. Manahan, Pres., 200 Seminary Dr., Winona Lake, IN 46590-1294 Tel. (574)372-5100 Fax (574)372-5139
Website: www.grace.edu

Grace University (Independent), Dr. James Eckman, Pres., 1311 S. 9th St., Omaha, NE 68108 Tel. (402)449-2809 Fax (402)341-9587
Email: jofast@graceu.edu

Graduate Theological Union* (Interdenominational), James A. Donahue, Pres., 2400 Ridge Rd., Berkeley, CA 94709-1212 Tel. (510)649-2400 Fax (510)649-1417
Email: libref@gtu.edu
Website: www.gtu.edu

Grand Rapids Baptist Seminary* (Baptist, Other), Rex M. Rogers, 1001 E. Beltline NE, Grand Rapids, MI 49525-5897 Tel. (616)222-1422 Fax (616)222-1502

Great Lakes Christian College (Christian Churches and Churches of Christ), Larry Carter, Pres., 6211 W. Willow Hwy, Lansing, MI 48917 Tel. (517)321-0242 Fax (517)321-5902

Greenville College (Free Methodist Church of North America), Robert E. Smith, Pres., 315 E. College Ave., P.O. Box 159, Greenville, IL 62246 Tel. (618)664-2800 Fax (618)664-1748
Email: rsmith@Greenville.edu
Website: www.greenville.edu

Haggard School of Theology at Azusa Pacific University* (Inter/Multidenominational), Kevin W. Mannoia, Dean, 901 E. Alosta Avenue, Azusa, CA 91702-7000 Tel. (626)812-3049 Fax (626)815-3809
Website: www.apu.edu/theology

Harding University Graduate School of Religion* (Churches of Christ), Evertt W. Huffard, Exec. Dir., 1000 Cherry Rd., Memphis, TN 38117-5499 Tel. (901)761-1352 Fax (901)761-1358
Email: dean@hugsr.edu
Website: www.hugsr.edu

Hartford Seminary* (Interdenominational), Heidi Hadsell, Pres., 77 Sherman St., Hartford, CT 06105-2260 Tel. (860)509-9500 Fax (860)509-9509
Email: info@hartsem.edu
Website: www.hartsem.edu

Harvard University Divinity School* (Inter/Multidenominational), Professor William A. Graham, Dean, 45 Francis Ave., Cambridge, MA 02138 Tel. (617)495-5761 Fax (617)495-8026
Website: www.hds.harvard.edu

Hebrew Union College–Jewish Institute of Religion (Jewish), Rabbi David Ellenson, Pres., 3077 University Ave., Los Angeles, CA 90007 Tel. (213)749-3424 Fax (213)747-6128
Website: www.huc.edu

Hebrew Union College–Jewish Institute of Religion, NY (Jewish), Sheldon Zimmerman, Pres., 1 W. 4th St., New York, NY 10012 Tel. (212)674-5300 Fax (212)533-0129

Heritage Bible College† 1747 Bud Hawkins Rd.; P.O. Box 1628, Dunn, NC 28335 Tel. (910)892-3178 Fax (910)892-1809
Email: generalinfo@heritagebiblecollege.org
Website: www.heritagebiblecollege.org

Hillsdale Free Will Baptist College† (National Assoc. of Free Will Baptists), Carl Cheshier, Pres., P.O. Box 7208, Moore, OK 73153-1208 Tel. (405)912-9000 Fax (405)912-9050
Email: hillsdale@hc.edu
Website: www.hc.edu

Hobe Sound Bible College (Nondenominational), P. Daniel Stetler, Pres., P.O. Box 1065, Hobe Sound, FL 33475 Tel. (407)546-5534 Fax (407)545-1421

Holy Cross Greek Orthodox School of Theology* (Greek Orthodox Archdiocese of America), Rev. Nicholas C. Triantafilou, Pres., 50 Goddard Ave., Brookline, MA 02445-7495 Tel. (617)731-3500 Fax (617)850-1460
Email: admissions@hchc.edu
Website: www.hchc.edu

Holy Trinity Orthodox Seminary (The Russian Orthodox Church Outside of Russia), Archbishop Laurus Skurla, Pres., P.O. Box 36, Jordanville, NY 13361 Tel. (315)858-0945 Fax (315)858-0945
Email: seminary@telenet.net

Hood Theological Seminary* (African Methodist Episcopal Zion Church), Albert J.D. Aymer, Pres., 800 W. Thomas St., Salisbury, NC 28144 Tel. (704)636-7611 Fax (704)636-7699
Email: pwells@hoodseminary.edu

Hope International University (Christian Churches and Churches of Christ), E. LeRoy Lawson, Pres., 2500 E. Nutwood Ave., Fullerton, CA 92831 Tel. (714)879-3901 Fax (714)526-0360
Email: slcarter@hiu.edu
Website: www.hiu.edu

Houston Graduate School of Theology* (Friends), Dr. David Robinson, Pres., 1311 Holman, Ste. 200, Houston, TX 77004-3833 Tel. (713)942-9505 Fax (713)942-9506
Email: hgst@hgst.edu
Website: www.hgst.edu

Howard University School of Divinity* (Nondenominational), Evans E. Crawford, Interim Dean, 1400 Shepherd St. NE, Washington, D.C. 20017 Tel. (202)806-0500 Fax (202)806-0711
Website: www.howard.edu/hupage/schools/divinity.html

Huntington College, Graduate School of Christian Ministries (Church of the United Brethren in Christ), G. Blair Dowden, Pres., 2303 College Ave., Huntington, IN 46750 Tel. (219)356-6000 Fax (219)358-3700
Email: gscm@huntington.edu
Website: www.huntington.edu/academics/gscm

Institute for Creation Research Graduate School† 10946 Woodside Avenue North, Santee, CA 92071 Tel. (619)448-0900 Fax (619)448-3469
Email: kcumming@icr.edu
Website: www.icr.org

Iliff School of Theology* (The United Methodist Church), David Maldonado Jr., Pres., 2201 S. University Blvd., Denver, CO 80210-4798 Tel. (303)744-1287 Fax (303) 777-3387
Website: www.iliff.edu

Immaculate Conception Seminary School of Theology* (Catholic), Rev. Msgr. Robert F. Coleman, J. C. D., Rector and Dean, 400 S. Orange Ave., South Orange, NJ 07079 Tel. (973)761-9575 Fax (973)761-9577
Email: theology@shu.edu
Website: www.theology.shu.edu

Indiana Wesleyan University (The Wesleyan Church), James Barnes, Pres., 4201 S. Washington, Marion, IN 46953-4974 Tel. (765) 674-6901 Fax (765)677-2499
Email: james.barnes@indwes.edu
Website: www.indwes.edu

Inter-American Adventist Theological Seminary* (Seventh-day Adventist), Jaime Castrejon, Pres. and Dean, P.O. Box 830518, Miami, FL 33283 Tel. (305)403-4700 Fax (305) 403-4600
Website: www.interamerica.org

Interdenominational Theological Center* (Interdenominational), Dr. Michael A. Battle, Pres., 700 Martin Luther King Jr. Dr. SW, Atlanta, GA 30314-4143 Tel. (404)527-7770 Fax (404)527-0901
Email: info@itc.edu
Website: www.arche.org/institutions/itc.htm

International Baptist College† Dr. Jerry Tetreau, Pres., 2150 E. Southern Avenue, Tempe, AZ 85282-7504 Tel. (480)838-7070 Fax (480)505-3299
Email: ibc4u@juno.com
Website: www.tri-citybaptist.org

International College & Graduate School† 20 Dowsett Ave., Honolulu, HI 96817 Tel. (808) 595-4247 Fax (808)595-4779
Email: icgs@hawaii.rr.com
Website: www.icgshawaii.org

James and Carolyn McAfee School of Theology of Mercer University* (Cooperative Baptist Fellowship), R. Alan Culpepper, Dean of the School of Theology, 3001 Mercer University Dr., Atlanta, GA 30341-4115 Tel. (678)547-6470 Fax (678)547-6478
Website: www.theology.mercer.edu

Jesuit School of Theology at Berkeley* (Catholic), Joseph P. Daoust, Pres., 1735 LeRoy Ave., Berkeley, CA 94709-1193 Tel. (510)549-5000 Fax (510)841-8536
Website: www.jstb.edu

Jewish Theological Seminary of America (Jewish), Ismar Schorsch, Pres., 3080 Broadway, New York, NY 10027-4649 Tel. (212)678-8000 Fax (212)678-8947
Email: webmaster@jtsa.edu
Website: www.jtsa.edu

John Wesley College (Interdenominational), Brian C. Donley, Pres., 2314 N. Centennial St., High Point, NC 27265 Tel. (336)889-2262 Fax (336)889-2261

Email: admissions@johnwesley.edu
Website: www.johnwesley.edu

Johnson Bible College (Christian Churches and Churches of Christ), David L. Eubanks, Pres., 7900 Johnson Dr., Knoxville, TN 37998 Tel. (865)573-4517 Fax (865)251-2336
Email: jbc@jbc.edu
Website: www.jbc.edu

Kansas City College and Bible School (Church of God [Holiness]), Gayle Woods, Pres., 7401 Metcalf Ave., Overland Park, KS 66204 Tel. (913)722-0272 Fax (913)722-2135

Kenrick-Glennon Seminary* (Catholic), Ted L. Wojcicki, Pres.-Rector, 5200 Glennon Dr., St. Louis, MO 63119-4399 Tel. (314)792-6100 Fax (314)792-6500
Website: www.kenrick.edu

Kentucky Christian College (Christian Churches and Churches of Christ), Keith P. Keeran, Pres., 100 Academic Pkwy, Grayson, KY 41143 Tel. (606)474-3000 Fax (606)474-3155
Email: knights@email.kcc.edu
Website: www.kcc.edu

Kentucky Mountain Bible College (Interdenominational), Philip Speas, Pres., Box 10, Vancleve, KY 41385 Tel. (606)666-5000 Fax (606)666-7744

King's College and Seminary† 14800 Sherman Way, Van Nuys, CA 91405 Tel. (818)779-8040 Fax (818)779-8241
Email: registration@kingscollege.edu
Website: www.kingscollege.edu

Knox Theological Seminary* (Presbyterian Church in America), R. Fowler White, Admin. and Dean of the Faculty, 5554 N. Federal Highway, Fort Lauderdale, FL 33308 Tel. (954) 771-0376 Fax (954)351-3343
Email: knox@crpc.org
Website: www.knoxseminary.org

La Sierra University (Seventh-day Adventist Church), Lawrence T. Geraty, Pres., 4700 Pierce St., Riverside, CA 92515-8247 Tel. (909)785-2000 Fax (909)785-2901
Email: pr@lasierra.edu
Website: www.lasierra.edu

Lancaster Bible College (Nondenominational), Peter W. Teague, Pres., P.O. Box 83403, Lancaster, PA 17601 Tel. (717)560-8278 Fax (717)560-8260
Email: president@lbc.edu
Website: www.lbc.edu

Lancaster Theological Seminary* (United Church of Christ), Rev. Dr. Riess W. Potterveld, Pres., 555 W. James St., Lancaster, PA 17603-2897 Tel. (717)393-0654 Fax (717)393-4254
Email: seminary@lancasterseminary.edu
Website: www.lancasterseminary.edu

Lexington Theological Seminary* (Christian Church [Disciples of Christ]), R. Robert Cueni, Pres., 631 S. Limestone St., Lexington, KY 40508 Tel. (859)252-0361 Fax (859)281-6042
Website: www.lextheo.edu

Liberty Baptist Theological Seminary (Independent Baptist), A. Pierre Guillermin, Pres., 1971 University Blvd., Lynchburg, VA 24502-2269 Tel. (804)582-2000 Fax (804) 582-2304

Liberty University† 1971 University Blvd., Lynchburg, VA 24502 Tel. (434)582-2000 Fax (434)582-2304
Email: admissions@liberty.edu
Website: www.liberty.edu

Life Pacific College (International Church of the Foursquare Gospel), Dick Scott, Pres., 1100 Covina Blvd., San Dimas, CA 91773 Tel. (909)599-5433 Fax (909)599-6690
Email: info@lifepacific.edu
Website: www.lifepacific.edu

Lincoln Christian Seminary* (Christian Churches and Churches of Christ), Keith H. Ray, Pres., 100 Campus View Dr., Lincoln, IL 62656 Tel. (217)732-3168 ext.2354 Fax (217)732-1821
Email: ttanner@lccs.edu
Website: www.lccs.edu

Logos Evangelical Seminary* (Evangelical Formosan Church), Felix Liu, Pres., 9358 Telstar Ave., El Monte, CA 91731 Tel. (626) 571-5110 Fax (626)571-5119
Email: logos@les.edu
Website: www.logos-seminary.edu

Louisville Presbyterian Theological Seminary* (Presbyterian Church [USA]), John Kuykendall, Pres., 1044 Alta Vista Rd., Louisville, KY 40205 Tel. (502)895-3411 Fax (502)895-1096
Website: www.lpts.edu

Loyola University Chicago Institute of Pastoral Studies* (Catholic), Mary Elsbernd, OSF, STD, Dir., 6525 N. Sheridan Rd., Chicago, IL 60626 Tel. (773)508-2320 Fax (773)508-2319
Website: www.luc.edu/depts/ips

Luther Rice Bible College & Seminary† Dr. James Flanagan, Pres., 3038 Evans Mill Rd.,

Lithonia, GA 30038 Tel. (770)484-1204 Fax (770)484-1155
Email: lrs@lrs.edu
Website: www.lrs.edu

Luther Seminary* (Evangelical Lutheran Church in America), David L. Tiede, Pres., 2481 Como Ave., St. Paul, MN 55108 Tel. (651)641-3456 Fax (651)641-3425
Email: admissions@luthersem.edu
Website: www.luthersem.edu

Lutheran Bible Institute in California (Intersynodical Lutheran), Samuel Giesy, Acting Pres., 5321 University Dr., Ste. G, Irvine, CA 92612-2942 Tel. (949)262-9222 or (800)261-5242 Fax (949)262-0283 or (877)-381-4245
Email: LBICalifornia@earthlink.net
Website: www.lbic.org

Lutheran Brethren Seminary (Church of the Lutheran Brethren of America), Joel T. Nordtvedt, PhD, Pres., 815 W. Vernon, Fergus Falls, MN 56537 Tel. (218)739-3375 Fax (218) 739-1259
Email: lbs@clba.org
Website: www.lbs.edu

Lutheran School of Theology at Chicago* (Evangelical Lutheran Church in America), James Kenneth Echols, Pres., 1100 E. 55th St., Chicago, IL 60615-5199 Tel. (773)256-0700 Fax (773)256-0782
Email: jboden@lstc.edu
Website: www.lstc.edu

Lutheran Theological Seminary at Gettysburg* (Evangelical Lutheran Church in America), The Rev. Michael L. Cooper-White, Pres., 61 Seminary Ridge, Gettysburg, PA 17325-1795 Tel. (717)334-6286 Fax (717)334-3469
Email: info@ltsg.edu
Website: www.ltsg.edu

Lutheran Theological Seminary at Philadelphia* (Evangelical Lutheran Church in America), Philip D.W. Krey, Pres., 7301 Germantown Ave., Philadelphia, PA 19119 Tel. (215)248-4616 Fax (215)248-4577
Email: mtairy@ltsp.edu
Website: www.ltsp.edu

Lutheran Theological Southern Seminary* (Evangelical Lutheran Church in America), H. Frederick Reisz, Pres., 4201 N. Main St., Columbia, SC 29203 Tel. (803)786-5150 Fax (803)786-6499
Email: Freisz@ltss.edu
Website: www.ltss.edu

M. Christopher White School of Divinity of Gardner-Webb University* (Baptist State Convention of North Carolina), R. Wayne Stacy, Dean, 110 N. Main St., Noel Hall, Boiling Springs, NC 28017 Tel. (704)406-4400 Fax (704)406-3935
Website: www.divinity.gardner-webb.edu

Magnolia Bible College (Churches of Christ), Les Ferguson Sr., Pres., P.O. Box 1109, Kosciusko, MS 39090 Tel. (662)289-2896 Fax (662)289-1850
Email: president@magnolia.edu
Website: www.magnolia.edu

Manhattan Christian College (Christian Churches and Churches of Christ), Kenneth Cable, Pres., 1415 Anderson Ave., Manhattan, KS 66502 Tel. (785)539-3571 Fax (785)539-0832
Website: www.mccks.edu

Maple Springs Baptist Bible College and Seminary† 4130 Belt Rd., Capital Heights, MD 20743 Tel. (301)736-3631 Fax (301)735-6507
Email: larry.jordan@msbbcs.edu
Website: www.msbbcs.edu

Mars Hill Graduate School† (Unaffiliated), Dan B. Allender, PhD, Pres., 2525-220th St., Bothell, WA 98021 Tel. (425)415-0505 Fax (425)806-5599
Email: info@mhgs.edu
Website: www.mhgs.net

McCormick Theological Seminary* (Presbyterian Church [USA]), Cynthia M. Campbell, Pres., 5460 S. University Ave., Chicago, IL 60615-5108 Tel. (773)947-6300 Fax (773) 288-2612
Email: ccampbell@mccormick.edu
Website: www.mccormick.edu

Meadville Lombard Theological School* (Unitarian Universalist Association), Lee Barker, Pres., 5701 S. Woodlawn Ave., Chicago, IL 60637 Tel. (773)256-3000 Fax (773)753-1323
Email: LBarker@meadville.edu
Website: www.meadville.edu

Memphis Theological Seminary* (Cumberland Presbyterian Church), David Hilliard, Interim Pres., 168 E. Parkway S at Union, Memphis, TN 38104-4395 Tel. (901)458-8232 Fax (901) 452-4051
Email: lblakeburn@mtscampus.edu
Website: www.mtscampus.edu

Mennonite Brethren Biblical Seminary* (General Conference of Mennonite Brethren Churches), Henry J. Schmidt, Pres., 4824 E. Butler Ave. (at Chestnut Ave.), Fresno, CA 93727-5097 Tel. (559)251-8628 Fax (559) 251-7212

Email: mbseminary@aol.com
Website: www.mbseminary.com

Messenger College† 300 E. 50th Street, Joplin, MO 64803 Tel. (417)624-7070 Fax (417)624-1689
Email: mc@pcg.org
Website: www.messengercollege.edu

Methodist Theological School in Ohio* (The United Methodist Church), Norman E. Dewire, Pres., 3081 Columbus Pike, P.O. Box 8004, Delaware, OH 43015-8004 Tel. (740)363-1146 Fax (740)362-3135
Email: pres@mtso.edu
Website: www.mtso.edu

Michigan Theological Seminary*† (Non-denominational), Bruce W. Fong, Pres., 41550 E. Ann Arbor Trail, Plymouth, MI 48170 Tel. (734)207-9581 Fax (734)207-9582
Email: mtsregistrar@juno.com
Website: www.mts.edu

Mid-America Christian University (The Church of God), Dr. John D. Fozard, Pres., 3500 SW 119th St., Oklahoma City, OK 73170 Tel. (405)691-3800 Fax (405)692-3165
Email: mbcinfo@mabc.edu
Website: www.mabc.edu

Midwestern Baptist Theological Seminary* (Southern Baptist Convention), Dr. R. Philip Roberts, Pres., 5001 N. Oak Trafficway, Kansas City, MO 64118 Tel. (816)414-3700 Fax (816)414-3799
Website: www.mbts.edu

Moody Bible Institute (Interdenominational), Joseph M. Stowell, Pres., 820 N. La Salle Blvd., Chicago, IL 60610 Tel. (312)329-4000 Fax (312)329-4109
Website: www.moody.edu

Moravian Theological Seminary* (Moravian Church in America [Unitas Fratrum]), Ervin J. Rokke, Pres., 1200 Main St., Bethlehem, PA 18018 Tel. (610)861-1516 Fax (610)861-1569
Email: seminary@moravian.edu
Website: www.moravianseminary.edu

Moreau Seminary **(Congregation of Holy Cross)** (Catholic), Rev. Wilson Miscamble, C.S.C., Pres., Moreau Seminary, Notre Dame, IN 46556 Tel. (574)631-7735 Fax (574)631-9233

Morehouse School of Religion (Interdenominational Baptist), William T. Perkins, Pres., 645 Beckwith St. SW, Atlanta, GA 30314 Tel. (404)527-7777 Fax (404)681-1005

Mount Angel Seminary* (Catholic), Richard Paperini, Pres. Rector, St. Benedict, OR 97373 Tel. (503)845-3951 Fax (503)845-3126
Website: www.mtangel.edu

Mt. St. Mary's Seminary* (Catholic), Very Rev. Kevin C. Rhoades, Rector, 16300 Old Emmitsburg Rd., Emmitsburg, MD 21727-7797 Tel. (301)447-5295 Fax (301)447-5636
Email: rhoades@msmary.edu
Website: www.msmary.edu

Mt. St. Mary's Seminary of the West (Catholic), Gerald R. Haemmerle, Pres., 6616 Beechmont Ave., Cincinnati, OH 45230 Tel. (513)231-2223 Fax (513)231-3254
Email: jhaemmer@mtsm.org
Website: mtsm.org

Multnomah Biblical Seminary* (Multnomah Biblical Seminary), Dr. Daniel R. Lockwood, Pres., 8435 NE Glisan St., Portland, OR 97220 Tel. (503)255-0332 Fax (503)251-6701
Website: www.multnomah.edu

Mundelein Seminary of the Univ. of St. Mary-of-the-Lake (Catholic), John Canary, Rector-Pres., 1000 E. Maple, Mundelein, IL 60060-1174 Tel. (847)566-6401 Fax (847)566-7330
Email: syopusml@usml.edu
Website: www.vocations.org

Nashotah House (Theological Seminary)* (Episcopal Church), Robert S. Munday, Pres. and Dean, 2777 Mission Rd., Nashotah, WI 53058-9793 Tel. (262)646-6500 Fax (262) 646-6504
Email: nashotah@nashotah.edu
Website: www.nashotah.edu

Nazarene Bible College (Church of the Nazarene), Hiram Sanders, Pres., 1111 Academy Park Loop, Colorado Springs, CO 80910-3704 Tel. (719)884-5000 Fax (719) 884-5199
Email: info@nbc.edu
Website: www.nbc.edu

Nazarene Theological Seminary* (Church of the Nazarene), Ron Benefiel, Pres., 1700 E. Meyer Blvd., Kansas City, MO 64131-1246 Tel. (816)333-6254 Fax (816)333-6271
Email: rbenefiel@nts.edu
Website: www.nts.edu

Nebraska Christian College (Christian Churches and Churches of Christ), Richard D. Milliken, Pres., 1800 Syracuse Ave., Norfolk, NE 68701-2458 Tel. (402)379-5000 Fax (402) 391-5100
Email: info@nechristian.edu
Website: www.nechristian.edu

New Brunswick Theological Seminary* (Reformed Church in America), Norman J.

Kansfield, Pres., 17 Seminary Pl., New Brunswick, NJ 08901-1196 Tel. (732)247-5241 Fax (732)249-5412
Email: njk@nbts.edu
Website: www.nbts.edu

New Orleans Baptist Theological Seminary* (Southern Baptist Convention), Charles S. Kelley, Pres., 3939 Gentilly Blvd., New Orleans, LA 70126 Tel. (504)282-4455 Fax (504)816-8023
Email: nobts@nobts.edu
Website: www.nobts.edu

N.Y. City Full Gospel Theological Seminary (Full Gospel Assembly), Frank A. Garofalo, Pres., 6902 11th Ave., Brooklyn, NY 11228 Tel. (908)302-9553 Fax (908)302-9553

New York Theological Seminary* (Inter/Multidenominational), Hillary Gaston Sr., Pres., 475 Riverside Dr., Ste. 500, New York, NY 10115 Tel. (212)870-1211 Fax (212)870-1236
Website: www.nyts.edu

North American Baptist Seminary* (North American Baptist Conference), G. Michael Hagan, Pres., 1525 S. Grange Ave., Sioux Falls, SD 57105-1526 Tel. (605)336-6588 Fax (605)335-9090
Email: train@nabs.edu
Website: www.nabs.edu

North Central Bible College (Assemblies of God), Gordon L. Anderson, Pres., 910 Elliot Ave. S, Minneapolis, MN 55404 Tel. (612) 332-3491 Fax (612)343-4778

North Park Theological Seminary* (The Evangelical Covenant Church), John E. Phelan, Pres. and Dean, 3225 W. Foster Ave., Chicago, IL 60625 Tel. (773)244-6214 Fax (773)244-6244
Email: jphelan@northpark.edu
Website: www.northpark.edu

Northern Baptist Theological Seminary* (American Baptist Churches in the USA), Charles W. Moore, Pres., 660 E. Butterfield Rd., Lombard, IL 60148-5698 Tel. (630)620-2100 Fax (630)620-2194
Email: cwmoore@northern.seminary.edu
Website: www.seminary.edu

Northwest Baptist Seminary† Dr. Mark Wagner, Pres., 4301 N. Stevens, Tacoma, WA 98407 Tel. (253)759-6104 Fax (253)759-3299
Email: nbs@nbs.edu
Website: www.nbs.edu

Northwest College (Assemblies of God), Don H. Argue, EdD, Pres., 5520 108th Ave. NE, P.O. Box 579, Kirkland, WA 98083-0579 Tel. (425)822-8266 Fax (425)827-0148
Email: mail@ncag.edu
Website: www.nwcollege.edu

Northwest Graduate School of the Ministry† Brad Smith, Interim Pres., 1013 Eighth Ave., Seattle, WA 98104 Tel. (206)264-9100 Fax (206)624-8828
Email: nwgs@nwgs.edu
Website: www.nwgs.edu

Notre Dame Seminary* (Catholic), Patrick J. Williams, Pres. and Rector, 2901 S. Carrollton Ave., New Orleans, LA 70118-4391 Tel. (504) 866-7426 Fax (504)866-3119
Website: www.nds.edu

Oak Hills Christian College (Interdenominational), Dr. Daniel Clausen, Pres., 1600 Oak Hills Rd. SW, Bemidji, MN 56601 Tel. (218)751-8670 Fax (218)751-8825
Email: dclausen@aokhills.edu
Website: www.aokhills.edu

Oblate School of Theology* (Catholic), J. William Morell, Pres., 285 Oblate Dr., San Antonio, TX 78216-6693 Tel. (210)341-1366 Fax (210)341-4519
Email: oblate@connecti.com
Website: www.ost.edu

Oral Roberts University School of Theology and Missions* (Inter/Multidenominational), Dr. Thomson K. Mathew, Dean, 7777 S. Lewis Ave., Tulsa, OK 74171 Tel. (918)495-7016 Fax (918)495-6259
Email: jcope@oru.edu
Website: www.oru.edu

St. Vladimir's Orthodox Theological Seminary* (The Orthodox Church in America), John H. Erickson, Dean, 575 Scarsdale Rd., Crestwood, NY 10707-1699 Tel. (914)961-8313 Fax (914)961-4507
Email: info@svots.edu
Website: www.svots.edu

Ozark Christian College (Christian Churches and Churches of Christ), Dr. Kenneth D. Idleman, Pres., 1111 N. Main St., Joplin, MO 64801 Tel. (417)624-2518 Fax (417)624-0090
Email: pres@occ.edu
Website: www.occ.edu

Pacific Lutheran Theological Seminary* (Evangelical Lutheran Church in America), Timothy F. Lull, Pres., 2770 Marin Ave., Berkeley, CA 94708-1597 Tel. (510)524-5264 Fax (510)524-2408
Email: president@plts.edu
Website: www.plts.edu

Pacific School of Religion* (Inter/Multidenominational), William McKinney, Pres., 1798 Scenic Ave., Berkeley, CA 94709 Tel. (510)848-0528 Fax (510)845-8948
Email: comm@psr.edu
Website: www.psr.edu

Payne Theological Seminary* (African Methodist Episcopal Church), Obery M. Hendricks Jr., PhD, Pres., P.O. Box 474, 1230 Wilberforce-Clifton Rd., Wilberforce, OH 45384-0474 Tel. (937)376-2946 Fax (937) 376-3330
Email: dbalsbau@payne.edu
Website: www.payne.edu

Pepperdine University (Churches of Christ), Dr. Randall Chesnutt, Chpsn. of Religion Division, Religion Division, Malibu, CA 90263-4352 Tel. (310)506-4352 Fax (310) 317-7271
Email: randall.chesnutt@pepperdine.edu
Website: http://arachnid.pepperdine.edu/religion div/home.htm

Perkins School of Theology (Southern Methodist University)* (The United Methodist Church), William B. Lawrence, Dean, P.O. Box 750133, Dallas, TX 75275-0133 Tel. (214)768-2293 Fax (214)768-4245
Email: theology@mail.smu.edu
Website: www.smu.edu/theology

Philadelphia Biblical University (Nondenominational), W. Sherrill Babb, Pres., 200 Manor Ave., Langhorne, PA 19047-2990 Tel. (215) 752-5800 Fax (215)702-4341
Email: president@pbu.edu
Website: www.pbu.edu

Phillips Theological Seminary* (Christian Church [Disciples of Christ]), William Tabbernee, Pres., 901 North Mingo Rd., Tulsa, OK 74116 Tel. (918)610-8303 Fax (918)610-8404
Website: www.ptstulsa.edu

Phoenix Seminary* (Nondenominational), Darryl DelHousaye, Pres., 13402 N. Scottsdale Road, Ste. B-185, Scottsdale, AZ 85254 Tel. (480)443-1020 Fax (480)443-1120
Website: www.phoenixseminary.edu

Piedmont Baptist College† (Baptist [Independent]), Charles W. Petitt, Pres., 716 Franklin St., Winston-Salem, NC 27101 Tel. (336)725-8344 Fax (336)725-5522
Email: admissions@pbc.edu
Website: www.pbc.edu

Pittsburgh Theological Seminary* (Presbyterian Church [USA]), Carnegie Samuel Calian, Pres., 616 N. Highland Ave., Pittsburgh, PA 15206 Tel. (412)362-5610 Fax (412)363-3260
Email: calian@pts.edu
Website: www.pts.edu

Point Loma Nazarene College (Church of the Nazarene), Pres., 3900 Lomaland Dr., San Diego, CA 92106 Tel. (619)849-2200 Fax (619) 849-7007
Website: www.ptloma.edu

Pontifical College Josephinum* (Catholic), James F. Garneau, Interim Rector/ Pres. and Academic Dean, 7625 N. High St., Columbus, OH 43235 Tel. (614)885-5585 Fax (614)885-2307
Website: www.pcj.edu

Pope John XXIII National Seminary (Catholic), Francis D. Kelly, Pres., 558 South Ave., Weston, MA 02193 Tel. (617)899-5500 Fax (617)899-9057

Practical Bible College (Independent Baptist), Dale E. Linebaugh, Pres., Box 601, Bible School Park, NY 13737 Tel. (607)729-1581 Fax (607)729-2962
Email: pbc@lakenet.org
Website: www.lakenet.org/~pbc

Princeton Theological Seminary* (Presbyterian Church [USA]), Thomas W. Gillespie, President, P.O. Box 821, Princeton, NJ 08542-0803 Tel. (609)921-8300 Fax (609) 924-2973
Email: comm-pub@ptsem.edu
Website: www.ptsem.edu

Protestant Episcopal Theological Seminary in Virginia* (Episcopal Church), Martha J. Horne, Dean and Pres., 3737 Seminary Rd., Alexandria, VA 22304 Tel. (703)370-6600 Fax (703)370-6234
Email: mhorne@vts.edu
Website: www.vts.edu

Puget Sound Christian College (Christian Churches and Churches of Christ), Randy J. Bridges, PhD, Pres., 7011 226th Pl. SW, Mountlake Terrace, WA 98043-2333 Tel. (425)775-8686 Fax (425)775-8688
Email: president@pscc.edu
Website: www.pscc.edu

Rabbi Isaac Elchanan Theological Seminary (Jewish), Dr. Norman Lamm, Pres., 2540 Amsterdam Ave., New York, NY 10033 Tel. (212)960-5344 Fax (212)960-0061
Website: www.yu.edu/riets/

Reconstructionist Rabbinical College (Jewish), Dan Ehrenkrantz, Pres., Church Rd. and Greenwood Ave., Wyncote, PA 19095 Tel. (215)576-0800 Fax (215)576-6143
Email: rrcinfo@rrc.edu

Reformed Bible College (Interdenominational), Nicholas V. Kroeze, Pres., 3333 E. Beltline NE, Grand Rapids, MI 49525-9749 Tel. (616)222-3000 Fax (616)988-3608
Email: administration@reformed.edu
Website: www.reformed.edu

Reformed Episcopal Seminary (Reformed Episcopal Church), Wayne A. Headman, Pres., 826 Second Ave., Blue Bell, PA 19422-1257 Tel. (610)292-9852 Fax (610)292-9853
Email: info@ptsorec.edu
Website: www.reseminary.edu

Reformed Presbyterian Theological Seminary* (Reformed Presbyterian Church of North America), Jerry F. O'Neill, Pres., 7418 Penn Ave., Pittsburgh, PA 15208-2594 Tel. (412)731-8690 Fax (412)731-4834
Email: rpseminary@aol.com
Website: www.rpts.edu

Reformed Theological Seminary* (Inter/Multidenominational), Dr. Robert C. Cannada Jr., Pres., 5422 Clinton Blvd., Jackson, MS 39209-3099 Tel. (601)923-1600 Fax (601) 923-1654
Email: rts.orlando@rts.edu
Website: www.rts.edu

Regent University School of Divinity* (Interdenominational), Vinson Synan, Dean, 1000 Regent University Dr., Virginia Beach, VA 23464-9870 Tel. (757)226-4537 Fax (757) 226-4597
Email: divschool@regent.edu
Website: www.www.regent.edu/acad/schdiv

Roanoke Bible College (Christian Churches and Churches of Christ), William A. Griffin, Pres., 714 N. Poindexter St., Elizabeth City, NC 27909-4054 Tel. (252)334-2090 or (252)334-2070 Fax (252)334-2071
Email: wag@roanokebible.edu
Website: www.roanokebible.edu

Sacred Heart Major Seminary* (Catholic), The Most Reverend Allen H. Vigneron, Pres., 2701 Chicago Blvd., Detroit, MI 48206 Tel. (313)883-8501 Fax (313)868-6440
Website: www.archdioceseofdetroit.org

Sacred Heart School of Theology* (Catholic), James D. Brackin, S.C.J., Pres./Rector, P.O. Box 429, Hales Corners, WI 53130-0429 Tel. (414)425-8300 Fax (414)529-6999
Email: shst@msn.com
Website: www.shst.edu

St. Bernard's School of Theology and Ministry* (Catholic), Patricia A. Schoelles, Pres., 1100 S. Goodman St., Rochester, NY 14620 Tel. (585)271-3657 Fax (585)271-2045
Email: pschoelles@sbi.edu
Website: www.sbi.edu

St. Charles Borromeo Seminary* (Catholic), Most Rev. Michael F. Burbidge, DD, EdD, Pres. and Rector, 100 E. Wynnewood Rd., Wynnewood, PA 19096-3001 Tel. (610)667-3394 Fax (610)667-0452
Website: www.scs.edu

St. Francis Seminary* (Catholic), Very Rev. Michael G. Witczak, Rector, 3257 S. Lake Dr., St. Francis, WI 53235 Tel. (414)747-6400 Fax (414)747-6442
Email: mwitczak@sfs.edu
Website: www.sfs.edu

St. John's Seminary* (Catholic), Richard G. Lennon, Rector and Pres., 127 Lake St., Brighton, MA 02135 Tel. (617)254-2610 Fax (617)787-2336
Website: www.sjs.edu

St. John's Seminary* (Catholic), Helmut Hefner, Rector and Pres., 5012 Seminary Rd., Camarillo, CA 93012-2598 Tel. (805)482-2755 Fax (805)482-0637
Website: ww.sbi.edu

St. John's University, School of Theology–Seminary* (Catholic), William J. Cahoy, Dean, Box 7288, Collegeville, MN 56321-7288 Tel. (320)363-2100 Fax (320)363-3145
Website: www.csbsju.edu/sot/

St. Joseph's Seminary* (Catholic), Peter G. Finn, Pres., 201 Seminary Ave., (Dunwoodie) Yonkers, NY 10704 Tel. (914)968-6200 Fax (914)968-7912
Website: www.ny-archdiocese.org/pastoral/seminary.cfm

St. Louis Christian College (Christian Churches and Churches of Christ), Kenneth L. Beck, Pres., 1360 Grandview Dr., Florissant, MO 63033 Tel. (314)837-6777 Fax (314)837-8291
Email: questions@slcc4ministry.edu
Website: www.slcc4ministry.edu

St. Mary Seminary and Graduate School of Theology* (Catholic), Thomas W. Tifft, Pres., 28700 Euclid Ave., Wickliffe, OH 44092-2585 Tel. (440)943-7600 Fax (440)943-7577
Website: www.stmarysem.edu

St. Mary's Seminary (Catholic), Rev. Msgr. Chester L. Borski, Rector, 9845 Memorial Dr., Houston, TX 77024-3498 Tel. (713)686-4345 Fax (713)681-7550

St. Mary's Seminary and University* (Catholic), Robert F. Leavitt, Pres. and Rector,

5400 Roland Ave., Baltimore, MD 21210 Tel. (410)864-4000 Fax (410)864-4278
Website: www.stmarys.edu

St. Meinrad School of Theology* (Catholic), Mark O'Keefe, Pres., 200 Hill Drive, St. Meinrad, IN 47577 Tel. (812)357-6611 Fax (812)357-6964
Email: theology@saintmeinrad.edu
Website: www.saintmeinrad.edu

St. Patrick's Seminary* (Catholic), Gerald D. Coleman, Pres. and Rector, 320 Middlefield Rd., Menlo Park, CA 94025 Tel. (650)325-5621 Fax (650)322-0997
Website: www.stpatricksseminary.org

St. Paul School of Theology* (The United Methodist Church), Lovett H. Weems Jr., Pres., 5123 Truman Rd., Kansas City, MO 64127-2499 Tel. (816)483-9600 Fax (816) 483-9605
Email: spst@spst.edu
Website: www.spst.edu

St. Paul Seminary School of Divinity of the University of St. Thomas* (Catholic), Frederick F. Campbell, Vice Pres. and Rector, 2260 Summit Ave., St. Paul, MN 55105 Tel. (651)962-5050 Fax (651)962-5790
Website: www.department.stthomas.edu/sod

St. Tikhon's Orthodox Theological Seminary* (The Orthodox Church in America), Metropolitan Herman (Swaiko), Pres. and Very Rev. Michael G. Dahulich, PhD, Pres. and Dean, Box 130, St. Tikhon's Rd., South Canaan, PA 18459-0121 Tel. (570)937-4411 Fax (570)937-3100
Email: info@stots.edu (General Information)
administration@stots.edu (Administrative Dean)
admissions@stots.edu (Admissions)
academics@stots.edu (Academic Dean)
Website: www.stots.edu

St. Vincent de Paul Regional Seminary* (Catholic), Stephen C. Bosso, Rector and Pres., 10701 S. Military Trail, Boynton Beach, FL 33436-4899 Tel. (561)732-4424 Fax (561)737-2205
Email: p031869b@pb.seflin.org
Website: www.svdp.edu

St. Vincent Seminary* (Catholic), Very Rev. Kurt Belsole, OSB, Rector, 300 Fraser Purchase Rd., Latrobe, PA 15650-2690 Tel. (724)537-4592 Fax (724)532-5052
Email: kurt.belsole@email.stvincent.edu
Website: http://benedictine.stvincent.edu/seminary/

Samuel DeWitt Proctor School of Theology of Virginia Union University* (American Baptist Churches in the USA; National Baptist Convention; Progressive National Baptist Convention), John W. Kinney, Dean, 1500 N. Lombardy Street, Richmond, VA 23330 Tel. (804)257-5715 Fax (804)342-3911
Website: www.vuu.edu

San Francisco Theological Seminary* (Presbyterian Church [USA]), Rev. Dr. Philip W. Butin, Pres., 2 Kensington Rd., San Anselmo, CA 94960 Tel. (415)258-6500 Fax (415)258-6511
Email: sftsinfo@sfts.edu
Website: www.sfts.edu

San Jose Christian College (Christian Churches and Churches of Christ), Bryce L. Jessup, DD, Pres., 790 S. 12th St., P.O. Box 1090, San Jose, CA 95112 Tel. (408)278-4300 Fax (408) 293-7352
Email: BryceJess@aol.com
Website: www.sjchristian.edu

Savonarola Theological Seminary (Polish National Catholic Church of America), Prime Bishop Robert M. Nemkovich, Rector, 1031 Cedar Ave., Scranton, PA 18505 Tel. (570) 343-0100 Fax (570)343-0100
Email: pncccenter@aol.com

Seabury-Western Theological Seminary* (Episcopal Church), James B. Lemler, Dean and Pres., 2122 Sheridan Rd., Evanston, IL 60201-2976 Tel. (847)328-9300 Fax (847) 328-9624
Email: seabury@seabury.edu
Website: www.seabury.edu

Seattle University School of Theology and Ministry* (Catholic Church and 10 Mainline Protestant Denominations and Associations), Rev. Patrick Howell, S.J., Dean, 900 Broadway, Seattle, WA 98122 Tel. (206)296-5330 Fax (206)296-5329
Email: millerdi@seattleu.edu
Website: www.seattleu.edu/theomin

Seminario Evangelico de Puerto Rico (Interdenominational), Samuel Pagán, Pres., 776 Ponce de León Ave., San Juan, PR 00925 Tel. (787)763-6700 Fax (787)751-0847
Email: drspagan@icepr.com or jvaldes@tld.net
Website: netministries.org/see/charmin/CM01399

Seminary of the Immaculate Conception* (Catholic), Msgr. Francis J. Schneider, J.C.D., Pres., 440 West Neck Rd., Huntington, NY 11743 Tel. (631)423-0483 Fax (631)423-2346
Website: www.icseminary.edu

Seventh-day Adventist Theological Seminary of Andrews University* (Seventh-day Adventist Church), John K. McVay, Dean,

Andrews University, Berrien Springs, MI 49104-1500 Tel. (269)471-3537 Fax (269) 471-6202
Email: seminary@andrews.edu
Website: www.andrews.edu/sem

Seventh Day Baptist School of Ministry (Seventh Day Baptist General Conference), Gabriel Bejjani, Dean of School of Ministry, 3120 Kennedy Rd., P.O. Box 1678, Janesville, WI 53547 Tel. (608)752-5055 Fax (608)752-7711
Email: sdbgen@inwave.com

Shasta Bible College and Graduate School† 2951 Goodwater Ave., Redding, CA 96002 Tel. (530) 221-4275 Fax (530) 221-6929
Email: sbcadm@shasta.edu
Website: www.shasta.edu

Shaw University Divinity School* (General Baptist State Convention, N.C.), Talbert O. Shaw, Pres., P.O. Box 2090, Raleigh, NC 27602 Tel. (919)546-8569 Fax (919)546-8571
Website: www.shawuniversity.edu

Simpson College (The Christian and Missionary Alliance), James M. Grant, Pres., 2211 College View Dr., Redding, CA 96003 Tel. (916)224-5600 Fax (916)224-5608

Southeastern Baptist College (Baptist Missionary Association of America), Jentry W. Bond, Pres., 4229 Highway 15N, Laurel, MS 39440 Tel. (601)426-6346 Fax (601)426-6346

Southeastern Baptist Theological Seminary* (Southern Baptist Convention), Leighton Paige Patterson, Pres., P.O. Box 1889, Wake Forest, NC 27588-1889 Tel. (919)556-3101 Fax (919)556-8550
Website: www.sebts.edu

Southeastern Bible College (Interdenominational), John D. Talley, Pres., 3001 Highway 280 E, Birmingham, AL 35243 Tel. (205)969-0880 Fax (205)970-9207
Email: 102064.406@compuserve.com
Website: www.sebc.edu

Southeastern College of the Assemblies of God (Assemblies of God), Mark Rutland, Pres., 1000 Longfellow Blvd., Lakeland, FL 33801 Tel. (863)667-5000 Fax (863)667-5200
Email: info@secollege.edu
Website: www.secollege.edu

Southern Baptist Theological Seminary* (Southern Baptist Convention), R. Albert Mohler Jr., Pres., 2825 Lexington Rd., Louisville, KY 40280 Tel. (502)897-4011 Fax (502)-899-1770
Email: communications@sbts.edu
Website: www.sbts.edu

Southern California Bible College & Seminary† (Nondenominational), Dr. Gary F. Coombs, Pres., 2075 E. Madison Avenue, El Cajon, CA 92019 Tel. (619)442-9841 Fax (619)442-4510
Email: info@scbcs.edu
Website: www.scbcs.edu

Southern Christian University (Churches of Christ), Dr. Rex A. Turner Jr., Pres., 1200 Taylor Rd., Montgomery, AL 36117-3553 Tel. (334)387-3877 Fax (334)387-3878
Email: southernchristian@southernchristian.edu
Website: www.southernchristian.edu

Southern Evangelical Seminary† 3000 Tilley Morris Road, Matthews, NC 28104 Tel. (704) 847-5600 Fax (704) 845-1747
Email: ses@ses.edu
Website: www.ses.edu

Southern Methodist College† 541 Broughton Street P.O. Box 1027, Orangeburg, SC 29116-1027 Tel. (803) 534-7826 Fax (803) 534-7827
Email: smced@smcollege.edu
Website: www.southernmethodistcollege.org

Southern Wesleyan University (The Wesleyan Church), David J. Spittal, Pres., 907 Wesleyan Dr., P.O. Box 1020, Central, SC 29630-1020 Tel. (864)644-5000 Fax (864)644-5900
Email: dspittal@swu.edu
Website: www.swu.edu

Southwestern Assemblies of God University (Assemblies of God), Delmer R. Guynes, Pres., 1200 Sycamore St., Waxahachie, TX 75165 Tel. (972)937-4010 Fax (972)923-0488

Southwestern Baptist Theological Seminary* (Southern Baptist Convention), Kenneth S. Hemphill, Pres., P.O. Box 22000, Fort Worth, TX 76122 Tel. (817)923-1921 Fax (817)923-0610
Website: www.swbts.edu

Southwestern College (Conservative Baptist Association of America), Brent D. Garrison, Pres., 2625 E. Cactus Rd., Phoenix, AZ 85032 Tel. (602)992-6101 Fax (602)404-2159

SS. Cyril and Methodius Seminary* (Catholic), Timothy F. Whalen, Interim Rector, 3535 Indian Trail, Orchard Lake, MI 48324-1623 Tel. (248)683-0310 Fax (248)738-6735
Email: sscms.dean@comcast.net
Website: www.orchardlakeseminary.org

Starr King School for the Ministry* (Unitarian Universalist Association), Rebecca Parker, Pres., 2441 LeConte Ave., Berkeley, CA 94709 Tel. (510)845-6232 Fax (510)845-6273
Website: www.sksm.edu

Swedenborgian House of Studies at the Pacific School of Religion (The Swedenborgian Church), Dr. James F. Lawrence, Dean, 1798 Scenic Ave., Berkeley, CA 94709 Tel. (510)849-8228 Fax (510)849-8296
Email: jlawrence@shs.psr.edu

Talbot School of Theology* (Inter/Multi-denominational), Clyde Cook, Pres., 13800 Biola Ave., La Mirada, CA 90639-0001 Tel. (562)903-4816 Fax (562)903-4759
Email: talbot.receptionist@biola.edu
Website: www.talbot.edu

Temple Baptist Seminary† 1815 Union Ave., Chattanooga, TN 37404 Tel. (423)493-4221 Fax (423)493-4471
Email: tbsinfo@templebaptistseminary.edu
Website: www.templebaptistseminary.edu

Temple Baptist Seminary (Independent Baptist), Barkev Trachian, Pres., 1815 Union Ave., Chattanooga, TN 37404 Tel. (423)493-4221 Fax (423)493-4471

Tennessee Temple University† 1815 Union Ave., Chattanooga, TN 37404 Tel. (423)493-4202 Fax (423)493-4114
Email: ttuinfo@tntemple.edu
Website: www.tntemple.edu

Theological School of the Protestant Reformed Churches (Protestant Reformed Churches in America), Robert D. Decker, Pres., 4949 Ivanrest Ave., Grandville, MI 49418 Tel. (616)531-1490 Fax (616)531-3033
Email: doezema@prca.org
Website: www.prca.org/seminary.html

Toccoa Falls College (The Christian and Missionary Alliance), Donald O. Young, Pres., P.O. Box 800777, Toccoa Falls, GA 30598 Tel. (706)886-6831 Fax (706)282-6005
Email: president@tfc.edu
Website: www.tfc.edu

Trevecca Nazarene University (Church of the Nazarene), Millard Reed, Pres., 333 Murfreesboro Rd., Nashville, TN 37210-2877 Tel. (615)248-1200 Fax (615)248-7728
Website: www.trevecca.edu

Trinity Baptist College† 800 Hammond Blvd., Jacksonville, FL 32221 Tel. (904)596-2400 Fax (904)596-2532
Email: trinity@tbc.edu
Website: www.tbc.edu

Trinity Bible College (Assemblies of God), Dennis D. Niles, Pres., 50 S. 6th Ave., Ellendale, ND 58436 Tel. (701)349-3621 Fax (701)349-5443

Trinity College of Florida (Nondenominational), Bill W. Lanpher, Pres., 2430 Welbilt Blvd., New Port Richey, FL 34655-4401 Tel. (727)376-6911 Fax (727) 376-0781
Email: admissions@trinitycollege.edu
Website: www.trinitycollege.edu

Trinity Episcopal School for Ministry* (Episcopal Church), The Very Rev. Peter C. Moore, Dean and Pres., 311 Eleventh St., Ambridge, PA 15003 Tel. (724)266-3838 Fax (724)266-4617
Email: tesm@tesm.edu
Website: www.tesm.edu

Trinity Evangelical Divinity School of Trinity International University* (Evangelical Free Church of America), Gregory L. Waybright, Pres., 2065 Half Day Rd., Deerfield, IL 60015 Tel. (847)945-8800 Fax (847)317-8141
Website: http://www.tiu.edu/divinity/

Trinity Lutheran College (Interdenominational; Lutheran), John M. Stamm, Pres., 4221 - 228th Ave. SE, Issaquah, WA 98029-9299 Tel. (425)392-0400 Fax (425)392-0404
Email: info@tlc.edu
Website: www.tlc.edu

Trinity Lutheran Seminary* (Evangelical Lutheran Church in America), Mark R. Ramseth, Pres., 2199 E. Main Street, Columbus, OH 43209-2334 Tel. (614)235-4136 Fax (614)238-0263
Website: www.TrinityLutheranSeminary.edu

Union Theological Seminary* (Inter/Multi-denominational), Joseph C. Hough Jr., Pres., 3041 Broadway at 121st St., New York, NY 10027-0003 Tel. (212)280-1403 Fax (212) 280-1440
Website: www.uts.columbia.edu

Union Theological Seminary and Presbyterian School of Christian Education (Union-PSCE)* (Presbyterian Church [USA]), Louis B. Weeks, Pres.
Richmond Campus (main): 3401 Brook Rd., Richmond, VA 23227 Tel. (800)229-2990 Fax (804)355-3919
Charlotte Campus: 1900 Selwyn Ave., Charlotte, NC 28274 Tel. (704)337-2450 Fax (704)337-2451
Email: gbirch@union-psce.edu
Website: www.union-psce.edu

United Theological Seminary* (The United Methodist Church), Rev. Dr. G. Edwin Zeiders, Pres. and Chief Exec. Officer, 1810 Harvard Blvd., Dayton, OH 45406-4599 Tel. (937)278-5817 Fax (937)278-1218
Email: utscom@united.edu
Website: www.united.edu

United Theological Seminary of the Twin Cities* (United Church of Christ), Wilson Yates, Pres., 3000 Fifth St. NW, New Brighton, MN 55112 Tel. (651)633-4311 Fax (651)633-4315
Email: general@unitedseminary-mn.org
Website: www.unitedseminary-mn.org

University of Chicago (Divinity School)* (Interdenominational), Richard Rosengarten, Dean, 1025 E. 58th St., Chicago, IL 60637 Tel. (773)702-8220 Fax (773)702-6048
Website: www.uchicago.edu/divinity

University of Dubuque Theological Seminary* (Presbyterian Church [USA]), Jeffrey Bullock, Pres., 2000 University Ave., Dubuque, IA 52001-5099 Tel. (563)589-3122 Fax (563) 589-3110
Email: udtsadms@dbq.edu
Website: www.UDTSeminary.net

University of Notre Dame, Dept. of Theology* (Catholic), John C. Cavadini, Department Chair, 130 Malloy Hall, Notre Dame, IN 46556-5639 Tel. (574)631-6662 Fax (574) 631-4291
Website: www.nd.edu:80/~theo/

University of St. Thomas School of Theology* (Catholic), Louis T. Brusatti, Pres., 9845 Memorial Dr., Houston, TX 77024 Tel. (713)686-4345 Fax (713)683-8673
Website: www.stthom.edu

University of the South School of Theology* (Episcopal Church), Allan M. Parrent, Interim Dean, 335 Tennessee Ave., Sewanee, TN 37383-0001 Tel. (800)722-1974 Fax (931) 598-1412
Email: aparrent@sewanee.edu
Website: www.sewanee.edu

University of St. Mary of the Lake Mundelein Seminary* (Catholic), John F. Canary, Rector and Pres., 1000 E. Maple Avenue, Mundelein, IL 60060 Tel. (847)566-6401 Fax (847)566-7330
Website: www.vocations.org

Valley Forge Christian College (Assemblies of God), Don Meyer, Pres., 1401 Charlestown Rd., Phoenixville, PA 19460 Tel. (610)935-0450 Fax (610)935-9353
Email: admissions@vfcc.edu
Website: www.vfcc.edu

Vanderbilt University Divinity School* (Inter/Multidenominational), James Hudnut-Beumler, Dean, 411 21st Av. S., Nashville, TN 37240 Tel. (615)322-2776 Fax (615)343-9957
Email: james.hudnut-beumler@vanderbilt.edu
Website: divinity.lib.vanderbilt.edu/vds/vds-home.htm

Vennard College (Interdenominational), W. Edward Rickman, Pres., Box 29, University Park, IA 52595 Tel. (641)673-8391 Fax (641) 673-8365
Email: vennard@vennard.edu
Website: www.vennard.edu

Virginia Union University (School of Theology) (American Baptist Churches in the USA; National Baptist Convention, USA, Inc.; Progressive National Baptist Convention, Inc.) Lott Carey, John W. Kinney, Dean and Pres., 1500 N. Lombardy St., Richmond, VA 23220 Tel. (804)257-5715 Fax (804)342-3911

Walla Walla College (School of Theology) (Seventh-day Adventist Church), Ernest Bursey, Dean and Pres., 204 S. College Ave., College Place, WA 99324-1198 Tel. (509)527-2194 Fax (509)527-2253
Email: burser@wwc.edu
Website: www.wwc.edu

Wartburg Theological Seminary* (Evangelical Lutheran Church in America), Duane H. Larson, Pres., 333 Wartburg Pl., P.O. Box 5004, Dubuque, IA 52004-5004 Tel. (563)589-0200 Fax (563)589-0333
Email: mailbox@wartburgseminary.edu
Website: www.wartburgseminary.edu

Washington Bible College-Capital Bible Seminary (Nondenominational), Homer Heater Jr., Pres., 6511 Princess Garden Pkwy., Lanham, MD 20706 Tel. (301)552-1400 Fax (301)552-2775
Email: bfox@bible.edu
Website: www.bible.edu

Washington Theological Consortium (Nondenominational), Daniel McLellan, O.F.M, Pres., 487 Michigan Ave. NE, Washington, D.C. 20017 Tel. (202)832-2675 Fax (202)526-0818
Email: wtc@washtheocon.org
Website: www.washtheocon.org

Washington Theological Union* (Catholic), Daniel McLellan, O.F.M., Pres., 6896 Laurel St. NW, Washington, D.C. 20012-2016 Tel. (202)726-8800 Fax (202)726-1716
Email: mclellan@wtu.edu
Website: www.wtu.edu

Wesley Biblical Seminary* (Interdenominational), Ronald E. Smith, Pres., P.O. Box 9938, Jackson, MS 39286-0938 Tel. (601)366-8880 Fax (601)366-8832
Website: www.wbs.edu

Wesley Theological Seminary* (The United Methodist Church), David F. McAllister-Wilson, Pres., 4500 Massachusetts Ave. NW, Washington, D.C. 20016-5690 Tel. (800)885-8600 or (800)882-4987 Fax (202)885-8605

Email: caldridge@wesleysem.edu
Website: www.Wesleysem.edu

Western Seminary* (Conservative Baptist Association of America), Bert E. Downs, Pres., 5511 S.E. Hawthorne Blvd., Portland, OR 97215 Tel. (503)517-1800 Fax (503)517-1801
Website: westernseminary.edu

Western Theological Seminary* (Reformed Church in America), Dennis N. Voskuil, Pres., 101 E. 13th St., Holland, MI 49423 Tel. (616)392-8555 Fax (616)392-7717
Website: www.westernsem.org

Westminster Theological Seminary* (Presbyterian Church in America), Samuel T. Logan, Pres., Chestnut Hill, P.O. Box 27009, Philadelphia, PA 19118 Tel. (215)887-5511 Fax (215)887-5404
Email: slogan@wts.edu
Website: www.wts.edu

Westminster Theological Seminary in California* (Nondenominational), W. Robert Godfrey, Pres., 1725 Bear Valley Pkwy, Escondido, CA 92027-4128 Tel. (760)480-8474 Fax (760)480-0252
Email: admissions@wtscal.edu
Website: www.wtscal.edu

Weston Jesuit School of Theology* (Catholic), Robert Manning, Pres., 3 Phillips Pl., Cambridge, MA 02138-3495 Tel. (617)492-1960 Fax (617)492-5833
Email: Admissionsinfo@wjst.edu
Website: www.wjst.edu

William Tyndale College (Interdenominational), Jerry D. Bringard, Acting Pres., 35700 W. Twelve Mile Rd., Farmington Hills, MI 48331 Tel. (248)553-7200 Fax (248)553-5963
Website: www.williamtyndale.edu

Williamson Christian College† 200 Seaboard Lane, Franklin, TN 37067 Tel. (615)771-7821 Fax (615)771-7810
Email: info@williamsoncc.edu
Website: www.williamsoncc.edu

Winebrenner Theological Seminary* (Churches of God, General Conference), David E. Draper, Pres., 701 E. Melrose Ave., P.O. Box 478, Findlay, OH 45839 Tel. (419)422-4824 Fax (419)422-3999
Email: wts@winebrenner.edu
Website: www.winebrenner.edu

Wisconsin Lutheran Seminary (Wisconsin Evangelical Lutheran Synod), David J. Valleskey, Pres., 11831 N. Seminary Dr., 65W, Mequon, WI 53092 Tel. (262)242-8100 Fax (262)242-8110
Website: www.wls.wels.net

Word of Life Bible Institute† P.O. Box 129, 4200 Glendale Road, Pottersville, NY 12860 Tel. (518)494-4723 Fax (518)494-7474
Email: info@wol.org/webmaster@wol.org
Website: www.wol.org

Yale University Divinity School* (Inter/Multidenominational), Harold W. Attridge, Dean, 409 Prospect St., New Haven, CT 06511-2167 Tel. (203)432-5303 Fax (203) 432-5356
Email: divinity.admissions@yale.edu
Website: www.yale.edu/divinity

10. Theological Seminaries and Bible Colleges in Canada

The following list includes theological seminaries and departments in colleges and universities in which ministerial training is provided. Many denominations have additional programs. The list has been developed from direct correspondence with the institutions. Inclusion in or exclusion from this list implies no judgment about the quality or accreditation of any institution. Those schools that are members of the Association of Theological Schools are marked with an asterisk (*). Each of the listings include: the institution name, denominational sponsor when appropriate, location, the president or dean, telephone and fax numbers when known, and email and website addresses when available.

Acadia Divinity College* (Convention of the Atlantic Baptist Church), Lee M. McDonald Wolfville, NS B4P 2R6 Tel. (902)585-2210 Fax (902)585-2233
Email: adcinfo@acadiau.ca
Website: adc.acadiau.ca

Alberta Bible College (Christian Churches and Churches of Christ in Canada), Ronald A. Fraser, 635 Northmount Dr. NW, Calgary, AB T2K 3J6 Tel. (403)282-2994 Fax (403)282-3084
Email: generalinquiries@abc-ca.org
Website: www.abc-ca.org

Arthur Turner Training School (The Anglican Church of Canada), Roy Bowkett, Box 378, Pangnirtung, NT X0A 0R0 Tel. (867)473-8375 Fax (867)473-8064

ACTS Seminaries of Trinity Western University* (Baptist General Conference of Canada; Evangelical Free Church of Canada; The Fellowship of Evangelical Baptist Churches in Canada; Christian and Missionary Alliance; Canadian Conference of Mennonite Brethren Churches), Dr. Phil Zylla, 7600 Glover Rd., Langley, BC V2Y 1Y1 Tel. (604)513-2044 Fax (604)513-2045
Email: acts@twu.ca
Website: www.acts.twu.ca

Atlantic School of Theology* (Interdenominational), Dr. William Close, 660 Francklyn St., Halifax, NS B3H 3B5 Tel. (902)423-6801 Fax (902)492-4048
Website: www.astheology.ns.ca

Baptist Leadership Training School (Canadian Baptist Ministries), Hugh Fraser, 4330 16th St. SW, Calgary, AB T2T 4H9 Tel. (403)243-3770 Fax (403)287-1930
Email: blts@imag.net
Website: www.yet.ca

Bethany Bible College-Canada (The Wesleyan Church), Dr. David S. Medders, 26 Western St., Sussex, NB E4E 1E6 Tel. (506)432-4400 Fax (506)432-4425
Email: meddersd@bethany-ca.edu
Website: www.bethany-ca.edu

Bethany College Bible Institute (Mennonite), Rick Schellenberg, Box 160, Hepburn, SK S0K 1Z0 Tel. (306)947-2175 Fax (306)947-4229
Email: info@bethany.sk.ca
Website: www.bethany.sk.ca

Briercrest Biblical Seminary* (Interdenominational), Paul Magnus, 510 College Dr., Caronport, SK S0H 0S0 Tel. (800)667-5199 Fax (306)756-3366
Email: bbs@compuserve.com
Website: www.briercrest.ca

Briercrest Family of Schools (Bible College & Seminary) (Transdenominational), Dr. Paul Magnus, 510 College Dr., Caronport, SK S0H 0S0 Tel. (800)667-5199 Fax (306)756-3366
Email: enrollment@briercrest.ca
Website: www.briercrest.ca

Canadian Bible College (Christian and Missionary Alliance in Canada), Dr. George Durance, 4400-4th Ave., Regina, SK S4T 0H8 Tel. (306)545-1515 Fax (306)545-0210
Email: gdurance@cbccts.ca
Website: www.cbccts.ca

Canadian Lutheran Bible Institute (Lutheran), Pastor Harold Rust, 4837 52A St., Camrose, AB T4V 1W5 Tel. (780)672-4454 Fax (780) 672-4455
Email: clbi@clbi.edu
Website: www.clbi.edu

Canadian Mennonite University (Mennonite Brethren Churches; Mennonite Church Canada), Gerald Gerbrandt, John Unger, Dean Peachey, 500 Shaftesbury Blvd., Winnipeg, MB R3P 2N2 Tel. (204)487-3300 Fax (204) 487-3858
Email: reception@cmu.ca
Website: www.cmu.ca

Canadian Nazarene University College (Church of the Nazarene Canada), Riley

Coulter, 610, 833 4th Ave. SW, Calgary, AB T2P 3T5 Tel. (403)571-2550 Fax (403)571-2556
Email: cncoff@nuc.edu
Website: www.nuc.edu

Canadian Southern Baptist Seminary* (Canadian Convention of Southern Baptists), G. Richard Blackby, 200 Seminary View, Cochrane, AB T4C 2G1 Tel. (403)932-6622 Fax (403)932-7049
Email: csbs@compuserve.com
Website: www.csbs.edu

Canadian Theological Seminary* (Christian and Missionary Alliance in Canada), Dr. George Durance, 4400-4th Ave., Regina, SK S4T 0H8 Tel. (306)545-1515 Fax (306)545-0210
Email: intouch@cbccts.ca
Website: www.cbccts.ca

Carey Theological Seminary* (Baptist Union of Western Canada), Brian F. Stelck, 5920 Iona Dr., Vancouver, BC V6T 1J6 Tel. (604) 224-4308 Fax (604)2245014
Website: www.interchange.ubc.ca/careytc

Central Pentecostal College, University of Saskatchewan (The Pentecostal Assemblies of Canada), D. Munk, 1303 Jackson Ave., Saskatoon, SK S7H 2M9 Tel. (306)374-6655 Fax (306)373-6968
Email: admissions@cpc-paoc.edu
Website: www.cpc-paoc.edu

Centre for Christian Studies (The Anglican Church of Canada; The United Church of Canada), Caryn Douglas, 60 Maryland, Winnipeg, MB R3G 1K7 Tel. (204)783-4490 Fax (204)786-3012
Email: info@ccsonline.ca
Website: www.ccsonline.ca

College Biblique Québec (The Pentecostal Assemblies of Canada), William Raccah, 740 Lebourgneuf, Ste. 100, Ancienne Lorette, QC G2J 1E2 Tel. (418)622-7552 Fax (418)622-1470

Collège Dominicain de Philosophie et de Théologie (The Roman Catholic Church in Canada), Michel Gourgues, 96 Avenue Empress, Ottawa, ON K1R 7G3 Tel. (613) 233-5696 Fax (613)233-6064

College of Emmanuel and St. Chad (The Anglican Church of Canada), Dr. Walter Deller, 1337 College Dr., Saskatoon, SK S7N 0W6 Tel. (306)975-3753 Fax (306)934-2683
Email: emmanuel.stchad@usask.ca
Website: www.usask.ca/stu/emmanuel

Columbia Bible College (Mennonite), Dr. Paul Wartman, 2940 Clearbrook Rd., Abbotsford, BC V2T 2Z8 Tel. (604)853-3358 Fax (604)853-3063
Email: info@columbiabc.edu
Website: www.columbiabc.edu

Concordia Lutheran Seminary* (Lutheran Church–Canada), Arthur D. Bacon, 7040 Ada Blvd., Edmonton, AB T5B 4E3 Tel. (780)474-1468 Fax (780)479-3067
mail: info@concordiasem.ab.ca
Website: www.connect.ab.ca/~clslib/

Concordia Lutheran Theological Seminary (Lutheran Church–Canada), Jonathan Grothe, 470 Glenridge Ave., St. Catharines, ON L2T 4C3 Tel. (905)688-2362 Fax (905)688-9744
Email: concordia@brocku.ca
Website: www.brocku.ca/concordiaseminary

Covenant Bible College (The Evangelical Covenant Church of Canada), Tel. (Canada) (403)934-6200 Fax (Canada) (403)934-6220 Tel./Fax (Colorado) (970)686-6977
Email: Canada: office@covenantbiblecollege.ab.ca
Colorado: cbc@covbibcolorado.edu
Website: Canada: www.covenantbiblecollege.ab.ca

Emmanuel Bible College (The Evangelical Missionary Church of Canada), Thomas E. Dow, 100 Fergus Ave., Kitchener, ON N2A 2H2 Tel. (519)894-8900 Fax (519)894-5331
Email: dmin@ebcollege.on.ca
Website: www.ebcollege.on.ca

Emmanuel College of Victoria University* (The United Church of Canada), The Rev. Dr. Peter Wyatt, 75 Queens Park Crescent E, Toronto, ON M5S 1K7 Tel. (416)585-4539 Fax (416)585-4516
Email: ec.office@utoronto.ca
Website: vicu.utoronto.ca/emmanuel/index.htm

Faculté De Théologie Évangélique (Union d'Eglises Baptistes Françaises au Canada), Amar Djaballah, 2285 Ave. Papineau, Montréal, QC H2K 4J5 Tel. (514)526-2003 Fax (514)526-6887
Email: reg@fteacadia.com

Faith Alive Bible College (Nondenominational), David Pierce, 637 University Dr., Saskatoon, SK S7N 0H8 Tel. (306)652-2230 Fax (306) 665-1125
Email: faithalive@dlcwest.com

Full Gospel Bible Institute (Apostolic Church of Pentecost of Canada Inc.), Rev. Lauren E. Miller, Box 579, Eston, SK S0L 1A0 Tel. (306)962-3621 Fax (306)962-3810
Email: fgbi.eston@sk.sympatico.ca
Website: fgbi.sk.ca

Gardner College, A Centre for Christian Studies (Church of God [Anderson, Ind.]), John Alan Howard, 4707 56th St., Camrose, AB T4V 2C4 Tel. (780)672-0171 Fax (780) 672-2465
Email: gardnercollege@gardnercollege.org
Website: www.gardnercollege.org

Grand Seminaire de Montréal (The Roman Catholic Church in Canada), Marcel Demers, P.S.S., 2065 Sherbrooke Ouest, Montréal, QC H3H 1G6 Tel. (514)935-1169 Fax (514)935-5497
Email: Information Generale: info@gsdm.qc.ca
Bibliotheque: biblio@gsdm.qc.ca
Website: www.gsdm.qc.ca

Great Lakes Bible College (Churches of Christ in Canada), Mr. Arthur Ford, 62 Hickory St. W, Waterloo, ON N2L 3J4 Tel. (519)884-4310 Fax (519)884-4412
Email: learn@glbc.on.ca
Website: www.glbc.on.ca

Heritage College and Seminary* (The Fellowship of Evangelical Baptist Churches in Canada), Marvin R. Brubacher, 175 Holiday Inn Dr., Cambridge, ON N3C 3T2 Tel. (519)651-2869 or (800)465-1961 Fax (519) 651-2870
Email: recruitment@heritage-theo.edu
Website: www.heritageseminary.net

Huron University College Faculty of Theology* (The Anglican Church of Canada), Dr. Ramona Lumpkin, 1349 Western Rd., London, ON N6G 1H3 Tel. (519)438-7224 Fax (519)438-9981
Email: huron@uwo.ca
Website: www.uwo.ca/huron

Institut Biblique Beree (The Pentecostal Assemblies of Canada), André L. Gagnon, 1711 Henri-Bourassa Est, Montréal, QC H2C 1J5 Tel. (514)385-4238 Fax (514)385-4238

Ecole de Theologie Evangelique de Montreal (Canadian Conference of Mennonite Brethren Churches), Eric Wingender, 1775, boul Édouard-Laurin, Ville Saint-Laurent, QC H4L 2B9 Tel. (514)331-0878 Fax (514)331-0879
Email: iblinstitute@proxyma.net

Institute for Christian Studies (Nondenominational), Harry Fernhout, 229 College St., Suite 200, Toronto, ON M5T 1R4 Tel. (416)979-2331 or (888)326-5347 Fax (416)979-2332
Email: email@icscanada.edu
Website: www.icscanada.edu

International Bible College (Church of God [Cleveland, Tenn.]), Cheryl Busse, 401 Trinity Ln., Moose Jaw, SK S6H 0E3 Tel. (306)692-4041 Fax (306)692-7968
Email: ibc@cofg.net
Website: www.ibc.cofg.net

Joint Board of Theological Colleges* (Inter/Multidenominational), John Vissers, 3473 University St., Montréal, QC H3A 2A8 Tel. (514)849-8511 Fax (514)849-4113
Email: dio@colba.net
Website: www.mcgill.ca/religion/jbtc.htm

Key-Way-Tin Bible Institute (Nondenominational), Dir. Dave Petkau, Box 540, Lac La Biche, AB T0A 2C0 Tel. (780)623-4565 Fax (780)623-1788
Email: kbi@telusplanet.net

Knox College* (The Presbyterian Church in Canada), J. Dorcas Gordon, 59 St. George St., Toronto, ON M5S 2E6 Tel. (416)978-4500 Fax (416)971-2133
Email: knox.college@utoronto.ca
Website: www.utoronto.ca/knox

Living Faith Bible College (Fellowship of Christian Assembies [Canada]), Dan Pope, Box 100, Caroline, AB T0M 0M0 Tel. (403) 722-2225 or (800)838-2975 Fax (403) 722-2459
Email: office@lfbc.net
Website: www.lfbc.net

Lutheran Theological Seminary* (Evangelical Lutheran Church in Canada), Faith E. Rohrbough, 114 Seminary Crescent, Saskatoon, SK S7N 0X3 Tel. (306)966-7850 Fax (306)966-7852
Email: lutheran.seminary@usask.ca
Website: www.usask.ca/stu/luther

Maritime Christian College (Christian Churches and Churches of Christ), Fred C. Osborne, 503 University Ave., Charlottetown, PE C1A 7Z4 Tel. (902)628-8887 Fax (902) 892-3959
Email: registrar@maritimechristiancollege.pe.ca
Website: www.maritimechristiancollege.pe.ca

Master's College and Seminary (The Pentecostal Assemblies of Canada), Dr. Evon G. Horton, 2476 Argentia Rd., Suite 109, Mississauga, ON L5N 6M1 Tel. (705)748-9111 Fax (705)748-3931
Email: info@mcs.edu
Website: www.mcs.edu

McGill University Faculty of Religious Studies* (Interdenominational), B. Barry Levy, 3520 University St., Montréal, QC H3A 2A7 Tel. (514)398-4125 Fax (514)398-6665
Website: www.mcmaster.ca/home.htm

McMaster Divinity College* (Baptist), Stanley E. Porter, 1280 Main St. W, Hamilton, ON L8S 4K1 Tel. (905)525-9140 Fax (905)577-4782
Email: divinity@mcmaster.ca
Website: www.mcmaster.ca/divinity

Millar College of the Bible (Interdenominational), A. Brian Atmore, Box 25, Pambrun, SK S0N 1W0 Tel. (306)582-2033 Fax (306) 582-2027

Montreal Diocesan Theological College (The Anglican Church of Canada), The Most Rev. Andrew Hutchison, 3473 University St., Montreal, QC H3A 2A8 Tel. (514)849-3004 Fax (514)849-4113
Email: diocoll@netrover.com
Website: www.montreal.anglican.org/mdtc

Mount Carmel Bible School (Transdenominational), Gordon King, 4725 106 Ave., Edmonton, AB T6A 1E7 Tel. (780)465-3015 or (800) 561-6443 Fax (780)466-2485
Email: mail@mountcarmel.net
Website: www.mountcarmel.net

National Native Bible College (Elim Fellowship of Evangelical Churches and Ministers), Donovan Jacobs, Box 478, Deseronto, ON K0K 1X0 Tel. (613)396-2311 Fax (613)396-2314

Newman Theological College* (The Catholic Church in Canada), Dr. Christophe Potworowski, 15611 St. Albert Trail, Edmonton, AB T6V 1H3 Tel. (780)447-2993 Fax (780)447-2685
Email: newman@freenet.edmonton.ab.ca
Website: www.newman.edu

Nipawin Bible Institute (Interdenominational), Mark Leppington, Box 1986, Nipawin, SK S0E 1E0 Tel. (306)862-5095 Fax (306)862-3651
Email: info@nipawinbibleinstitute.ca
Website: www.nipawinbibleinstitute.ca

Northwest Baptist Theological College and Seminary (The Fellowship of Evangelical Baptist Churches in Canada), Dr. Larry Perkins, 7600 Glover Rd., Langley, BC V2Y 1Y1 Tel. (604)888-7592 Fax (604)513-8511
Email: nbs@twu.ca
Website: www.nbseminary.com

Northwest Bible College (The Pentecostal Assemblies of Canada), Stephen Hertzog, 11617-106 Ave., Edmonton, AB T5H 0S1 Tel. (780)452-0808 Fax (780)452-5803
Email: info@nwbc.ab.ca
Website: www.nwbc.ab.ca

Ontario Christian Seminary (Christian Churches and Churches of Christ in Canada), James R. Cormode, 260 High Park Ave., Toronto, ON M6P 3J9 Tel. (416)769-7115 Fax (416)769-7047

Pacific Life Bible College (Foursquare), Rob Buzza, 15100 66 A Ave., Surrey, BC V3S 2A6 Tel. (604)597-9082 Fax (604)597-9090
Email: paclife@pacificlife.edu
Website: www.pacificlife.edu

Parole de Vie Bethel/Word of Life Bethel (Nondenominational), Ken Beach, 1175 Chemin Woodward, Lennoxville, QC J1M 2A2 Tel. (819)823-8435 Fax (819)823-2468
Email: quebec@canada.wol.org
Website: www.wol.org

Peace River Bible Institute (Interdenominational), Reuben Kvill, Box 99, Sexsmith, AB T0H 3C0 Tel. (780)568-3962 Fax (780)568-4431
Email: prbi@prbi.edu
Website: www.prbi.edu

Prairie Graduate School* (Interdenominational), Dr. Charlotte Kinvig Bates, 2540 5 Ave. NW, Calgary, AB T2N 0T5 Tel. (403)777-0150 Fax (403)270-2336
Email: prairie@pbi.ab.ca
Website: www.pbi.ab.ca

The Presbyterian College, Montreal (Presbyterian Church in Canada), John Vissers, 3495 University St., Montreal, QC H3A 2A8 Tel. (514)288-5256 Fax (514)288-8072
Email: presbyteriancollege@videotron.ca
Website: www.mcgill.ca/religion/presbcol.htm

Providence College and Theological Seminary* (Inter/Multidenominational), August H. Konkel, General Delivery, Otterburne, MB R0A 1G0 Tel. (204)433-7488 Fax (204)433-7158
Email: info@providence.mb.ca
Website: www.prov.ca

Queens College (The Anglican Church of Canada), Boyd Morgan, 210 Prince Phillip Dr., St. Johns, NF A1B 3R6 Tel. (709)753-0116 Fax (709)753-1214
Email: queens@mun.ca
Website: www.mun.ca/queens

Queen's Theological College (The United Church of Canada), M. Jean Stairs, Room 212 Theological Hall, Kingston, ON K7L 3N6 Tel. (613)533-2110 Fax (613)533-6879
Email: theology@post.queensu.ca
Website: www.queensu.ca/theology

Reformed Episcopal Theological College (Reformed Episcopal Church of Canada), Rt. Rev. Michael Fedechko, 320 Armstrong St., Box 2532, New Liskeard, ON P0J 1P0 Tel. (705)647-4565 Fax (705)647-4565

Email: fed@nt.net
Website: forministry.com/REC-Canada

Reformed Episcopal Theological College (The Reformed Episcopal Church of Canada), Rt. Rev. Michael Fedechko, P.O. Box 2532, Hwy 11 N, New Liskeard, ON P0J 1P0 Tel. (705) 647-4565 Fax (705)647-4565
Email: fed@nt.net
Website: www.retcc.com

Regent College* (Interdenominational), Rod Wilson, PhD, 5800 University Blvd., Vancouver, BC V6T 2E4 Tel. (800)663-8664 or (604)224-3245 Fax (604)224-3097
Email: administration@regent-college.edu
Website: www.regent-college.edu

Regis College* (The Roman Catholic Church in Canada), John Allan Loftus, S.J, 15 St. Mary St., Toronto, ON M4Y 2R5 Tel. (416)922-5474 Fax (416)922-2898
Email: regis.registrar@utoronto.ca
Website: www.utoronto.ca/regis

Rocky Mountain College, Centre for Biblical Studies (The Evangelical Missionary Church of Canada), Gordon Dirks, 4039 Brentwood Rd. NW, Calgary, AB T2L 1L1 Tel. (403)284-5100 Fax (403)220-9567
Email: admissions@rockymountaincollege.ca
Website: www.rockymountaincollege.ca

St. Andrew's College* (The United Church of Canada), Dr. Christopher J. L. Lind, 1121 College Dr., Saskatoon, SK S7N 0W3 Tel. (306)966-8970 Fax (306)966-8981
Website: www.usask.ca/stu

St. Augustine's Seminary of Toronto* (The Roman Catholic Church in Canada), A. Robert Nusca, 2661 Kingston Rd., Toronto, ON M1M 1M3 Tel. (416)261-7207 Fax (416)261-2529
Email: info@staugustines.on.ca
Website: www. staugustines.on.ca

St. John's College, Univ. of Manitoba, Faculty of Theology (The Anglican Church of Canada), Dr. Janet A. Hoskins, 92 Dysart Rd., Winnipeg, MB R3T 2M5 Tel. (204)474-6852 Fax (204)261-1215

Saint Paul University, Faculty of Theology (The Roman Catholic Church), Normand Bonneau, PhD, 223 Main St., Ottawa, ON K1S 1C4 Tel. (613)236-1393 ext. 2246 Fax (613)751-4016
Email: fquesnel@ustpaul.uottawa.ca
Website: www.ustpaul.ca

St. Peter's Seminary* (The Roman Catholic Church in Canada), William T. McGratton, 1040 Waterloo St. North, London, ON N6A 3Y1 Tel. (519)432-1824 Fax (519)432-0964
Website: www.stpetersseminary.ca

St. Stephen's College, Grad. & Continuing Theological Education (The United Church of Canada), Dr. Christopher Lind, 8810 112th St., Edmonton, AB T6G 2J6 Tel. (780)439-7311 Fax (780)433-8875
Email: westema@ualberta.ca
Website: www.ualberta.ca/st.stephens

Salvation Army College for Officer Training (The Salvation Army in Canada), Wayne N. Pritchett, 2130 Bayview Ave., North York, ON M4N 3K6 Tel. (416)481-6131 Fax (416)481-6810 Tel. (Library) (416)481-2895

The Salvation Army William and Catherine Booth College (The Salvation Army in Canada), Dr. Jonathan S. Raymond, 447 Webb Pl., Winnipeg, MB R3B 2P2 Tel. (204)947-6701 Fax (204)942-3856
Email: wcbc@sallynet.org
Website: www.wcbc-sa.edu

Steinbach Bible College (Mennonite), Abe Bergen, Box 1420, Steinbach, MB R0A 2A0 Tel. (204)326-6451 Fax (204)326-6908
Email: info@sbcollege.mb.ca
Website: www.sbcollege.mb.ca

Taylor College of Education (Church Army Canada), Rev. Capt. David Edwards, 230 Hawthorne Ave. Ext, Saint John, NB E2K 3S9 Tel. (506)693-8975 Fax (506)657-8217
Email: edwa@nbnet.ca

Taylor Seminary* (North American Baptist Conference), Dr. Marvin L. Dewey, 11525-23 Ave., Edmonton, AB T6J 4T3 Tel. (780)431-5200 Fax (780)436-9416
Email: marvin.dewey@taylor-edu.ca
Website: www.taylor-edu.ca

Theological College of the Canadian Reformed Churches (Canadian and American Reformed Churches), N. H. Gootjes, 110 W. 27th St., Hamilton, ON L9C 5A1 Tel. (416)575-3688 Fax (416)575-0799

Toronto Baptist Seminary and Bible College (Baptist), Dr. Glendon G. Thompson, 130 Gerrard St. E, Toronto, ON M5A 3T4 Tel. (416)925-3263 Fax (416)925-8305
Email: tbs@tbs.edu
Website: www.tbs.edu

Toronto School of Theology* (Inter/Multi-denominational), Michael G. Steinhauser, 47 Queens Park Crescent E, Toronto, ON M5S 2C3 Tel. (416)978-4039 Fax (416)978-7821
Email: registrar.tst@utoronto.ca
Website: www.tst.edu

Trinity College, Faculty of Divinity* (The Anglican Church of Canada), David Neelands, 6 Hoskin Ave., Toronto, ON M5S 1H8 Tel. (416)978-2146 Fax (416)978-4949
Email: divinity@trinity.utoronto.ca
Website: www.trinity.utoronto.ca/divinity

Tyndale College & Seminary (Trans-denominational), Dr. Brian C. Stiller, 25 Ballyconnor Ct., Toronto, ON M2M 4B3 Tel. (416)226-6380 Fax (416)226-9464
Email: info@tyndale.ca
Website: www.tyndale.ca

United Theological College/Le Séminaire Uni (The United Church of Canada), Rev. Philip Joudrey, 3521 rue Université, Montréal, QC H3A 2A9 Tel. (514)849-2042 Fax (514)849-8634
Email: admin@utc.ca
Website: www.utc.ca

Université Laval, Faculté de Théologie et de Sciences Religieuses (The Roman Catholic Church in Canada), Marc Pelchat, Cité Universitaire, Quebec, QC G1K 7P4 Tel. (418)656-3576 Fax (418)656-3273
Email: ftsr@ftsr.ulaval.ca
Website: www.ftsr.ulaval.ca

Université de Montréal, Faculté de théologie (The Roman Catholic Church in Canada), Jean-Marc Charron, C. P. 6128 Succ. Centre Ville, Montréal, QC H3C 3J7 Tel. (514)343-7160 Fax (514)343-5738
Email: theologie@ere.umontreal.ca
Website: www.theo.umontreal.ca

Université de Sherbrooke, Faculté de theologié, d'éthique et de philosophie (The Roman Catholic Church in Canada), Jean-François Malherbe, 1111, rue Saint-Charles Ouest, Tourquest–Bureau 310, Longueuil, QC J4K 5G4 Tel. (450)670-7157 Fax (450)670-1959
Email: jf.malherbe@sympatico.ca
Website: www.usherb.ca/longueuil

University of St. Michael's College, Faculty of Theology* (Roman Catholic Church), Dr. Anne T. Anderson, CSJ, 81 St. Mary St., Toronto, ON M5S 1J4 Tel. (416)926-7265 Fax (416)926-7294
Website: www.utoronto.ca/stmikes

The University of Winnipeg, Faculty of Theology* (Multidenominational; the United Church of Canada), Gordon E. MacDermid, 515 Portage Ave., Winnipeg, MB R3B 2E9 Tel. (204)786-9390 Fax (204)772-2584
Email: theology@uwinnipeg.ca
Website: www.uwinnipeg.ca/academic/theology

Vancouver School of Theology* (Inter/Multi-denominational), Dr. Kenneth G. MacQueen, 6000 Iona Dr., Vancouver, BC V6T 1L4 Tel. (604)822-9031 Fax (604)822-9212
Email: vstinfo@vst.edu
Website: www.vst.edu

Waterloo Lutheran Seminary* (Evangelical Lutheran Church in Canada), Richard C. Crossman, 75 University Ave. W, Waterloo, ON N2L 3C5 Tel. (519)884-1970 Fax (519)725-2434
Email: seminary@wlu.ca
Website: www.wlu.ca/~wwwsem/index.shtml

Western Christian College (Churches of Christ in Canada), John McMillan, Box 5000, 220 Whitmore Ave. W, Dauphin, MB R7N 2V5 Tel. (204)638-8801 Fax (204)638-7054
Email: president@westernchristian.ca
Website: www.westernchristian.ca

Western Pentecostal Bible College (The Pentecostal Assemblies of Canada), James G. Richards, Box 1700, Abbotsford, BC V2S 7E7 Tel. (604)853-7491 Fax (604)853-8951
Email: wpbcr@uniserve.com
Website: www.wpbc.edu

Wycliffe College* (The Anglican Church of Canada), Rev. Dr. George R. Sumner Jr., 5 Hoskin Ave., Toronto, ON M5S 1H7 Tel. (416)946-3535 Fax (416)946-3545
Email: wycliffe.college@utoronto.ca
Website: www.utoronto.ca/wycliffe

11. Religious Periodicals in the United States

This directory lists publications primarily of the organizations listed in Directory 3, "Religious Bodies in the United States." Some independent publications are also listed. The list does not include all publications prepared by religious bodies, and not all the publications listed here are necessarily the official publication of a particular church. Regional publications and newsletters are not included. A more extensive list of religious periodicals published in the United States can be found in *Gale Directory of Publications and Broadcast Media* (Gale Research, Inc., P.O. Box 33477, Detroit MI 48232-5477).

Each entry in this directory contains the title of the periodical, frequency of publication, religious affiliation, editor's name, address, telephone and fax number, and e-mail and website addresses when available. The frequency of publication, which appears in parenthesis after the name of the publication is represented by a "W." for weekly, "M." for monthly, "Q." for quarterly, "I." for Internet, and "Y." for yearly.

21st Century Christian, (M.) Churches of Christ; M. Norvel Young and Prentice A. Meador Jr., Box 40304, Nashville, TN 37204 Tel. (800)331-5991 Fax (615)385-5915

The A.M.E. Christian Recorder, (bi-W.) African Methodist Episcopal Church; Ricky Spain, 1134-11th St. NW, Suite 202, Washington, D.C. 20001 Tel. (202)216-4294 Fax (202)216-4293
Email: rspain5737@aol.com
Website: www.amecnet.org

Action, (10-Y.) Churches of Christ; Dr. R. H. Tex Williams, P.O. Box 2169, Cedar Park, TX 78630-2169 Tel. (512)345-8191 Fax (512) 345-6634
Email: wbschool@bga.com
Website: www.wbschool.org

Adra Today, (Q.) Seventh-day Adventist Church; Beth Schaefer, 12501 Old Columbia Pike, Silver Spring, MD 20904-6600 Tel. (301)680-6355 Fax (301)680-6370
Email: 74617.2105@compuserve.com
Website: www.adra.org

The Adult Quarterly, (Q.) Associate Reformed Presbyterian Church (General Synod); Mr. W. H. F. Kuykendall PhD, P.O. Box 575, Due West, SC 29639 Tel. (864)379-2284
Email: wkuykend@erskine.edu

Advent Christian News, (M.) Advent Christian Church; Rev. Keith D. Wheaton, P.O. Box 23152, Charlotte, NC 28227 Tel. (704)545-6161 Fax (704)573-0712
Email: Mayerpub@aol.com

The Advent Christian Witness, (M.) Advent Christian Church; Rev. Keith D. Wheaton, P.O. Box 23152, Charlotte, NC 28227 Tel. (704)545-6161 Fax (704)573-0712
Email: Mayerpub@aol.com

The Advent Christian Witness, (6-Y.) Advent Christian Church; Rev. Keith D. Wheaton, P.O. Box 23152, Charlotte, NC 28227 Tel. (704)545-6161 Fax (704)573-0712
Email: Mayerpub@aol.com

Adventist Review, (W.) Seventh-day Adventist Church; W. G. Johnsson, 12501 Old Columbia Pike, Silver Spring, MD 20904-6600 Tel. (301)680-6560 Fax (301)680-6638
Email: 74617,15.compuserve.com
Website: www.adventistreview.com

The Advocate, (10-Y.) Episcopal; Kay Collier McLaughlin, PhD, P.O. Box 610, Lexington, KY 40588-0610 Tel. (606)252-6527 Fax (606) 231-9077
Email: diolex@aol.com
Website: www.diolex.org

Again Magazine, (Q.) The Antiochian Orthodox Christian Archdiocese of North America; R. Thomas Zell, P.O. Box 76, Ben Lomond, CA 95005-0076 Tel. (831)336-5118 Fax (831) 336-8882
Email: marketing@conciliarpress.com
Website: www.conciliarpress.com

Agape Magazine, (6-Y.) Coptic Orthodox Church; Bishop Serapion, P.O.Box 4960, Diamond Bar, CA 91765 Tel. (909)865-8378 Fax (909)865-8348
Email: agape@lacopts.org
Website: lacopts.org

Agenda, (10-Y.) Church of the Brethren; Howard Royer and Walt Wiltschek, 1451 Dundee Ave., Elgin, IL 60120-1694 Tel. (847) 742-5100 Fax (847)742-6103

Email: hroyer_gb@brethren.org or wwiltschek_gb@brethren.org
Website: www.brethren.org

AIM Magazine, (Q.) Free Will Baptists, National Association of; Ida Lewis, Home Missions Office, P.O. Box 5002, Antioch, TN 37011-5002 Tel. (615)731-6812 Fax (615) 731-7655
Email: ida@nafwb.org
Website: www.homemissions.net

Alive Now, (6-Y.) The United Methodist Church; Melissa Tidwell, Editor, P.O. Box 340004, Nashville, TN 37203-0004 Tel. (615)340-7218
Email: alivenow@upperroom.org
Website: www.alivenow.org

The Allegheny Wesleyan Methodist, (M.) The Allegheny Wesleyan Methodist Connection (Original Allegheny Conference); William Cope, P.O. Box 357, Salem, OH 44460 Tel. (330)337-9376 Fax (330)337-9700
Email: awmc@juno.com

Alliance Life, (M.) The Christian and Missionary Alliance; Mark Failing, P.O. Box 35000, Colorado Springs, CO 80935 Tel. (719)599-5999 Fax (719)599-8234
Email: alife@cmalliance.org
Website: www.alliancelife.org

American Baptist In Mission, (4-Y.) American Baptist Churches in the USA; Richard W. Schramm, P.O. Box 851, Valley Forge, PA 19482-0851 Tel. (610)768-2077 Fax (610) 768-2320
Email: richard.schramm@abc-usa.org
Website: www.abc-usa.org

American Baptist Quarterly, (Q.) American Baptist Churches in the USA; Dr. Robert E. Johnson, P.O. Box 851, Valley Forge, PA 19482-0851 Tel. (610)768-2269 Fax (610) 768-2266
Email: dbvanbro@abc-usa.org
Website: www.cbts.edu/rejohnsonweb/AB Quarterly /index.htm

American Bible Society Record, (4-Y.) Nondenominational; Francine Lange, 1865 Broadway, New York, NY 10023-7505 Tel. (212)408-1399 Fax (212)408-1456
Email: absrecord@americanbible.org
Website: www.americanbible.org

El Aposento Alto, (6-Y.) The United Methodist Church; Carmen Gaud, P.O. Box 340004, Nashville, TN 37203-0004 Tel. (615)340-7253 Fax (615)340-7267
Email: ElAposentoAlto@upperroom.org
Website: www.upperroom.org

The Armenian Church, (2-Y.) Diocese of the Armenian Church of America; Arpie McQueen, 630 Second Ave., New York, NY 10016 Tel. (212)686-0710 Fax (212)779-3558

The Associate Reformed Presbyterian, (M.) Associate Reformed Presbyterian Church (General Synod); Mr. Ben Johnston, One Cleveland St., Greenville, SC 29601 Tel. (864)232-8297 Fax (864)271-3729
Email: arpmaged@arpsynod.org
Website: www.arpsynod.org

Attack, A Magazine for Christian Men, (Q.) National Association for Free Will Baptists; James E. Vallance, P.O. Box 5002, Antioch, TN 37011-5002 Tel. (615)731-4950 Fax (615) 731-0771

Awake! (2-M.) Jehovah's Witnesses; Watch Tower Society, 25 Columbia Heights, Brooklyn, NY 11201-2483 Tel. (718)560-5000
Website: watchtower.org

The Banner, (12-Y.) Christian Reformed Church in North America; Editor: -vacant- Interim Editor: Bob De Moor, 2850 Kalamazoo Ave. SE, Grand Rapids, MI 49560 Tel. (616)224-0732 Fax (616)224-0834
Email: editorial@thebanner.org
Website: www.thebanner.org

The Banner of Truth, (M.) Netherlands Reformed Congregations; J. den Hoed, 1113 Bridgeview Dr., Lynden, WA 98264 Tel. (360) 354-4203 Fax (360)354-7565

The Baptist Bible Tribune, (M.) Baptist Bible Fellowship International; Mike Randall, P.O. Box 309, Springfield, MO 65801-0309 Tel. (417)831-3996 Fax (417)831-1470
Email: editors@tribune.org
Website: www.tribune.org

Baptist Bulletin, (M.) General Association of Regular Baptist Churches; David M. Gower, 1300 N. Meacham Rd., Schaumburg, IL 60173-4806 Tel. (847)843-1600 Fax (847) 843-3757
Email: baptistbulletin@garbc.org
Website: www.garbc.org

Baptist History and Heritage, (3-Y.) Baptist History and Heritage Society; Pamela R. Durso, P.O. Box 728, Brentwood, TN 37024-0728 Tel. (615)371-7937 Fax (615)371-7939
Email: pdurso@tubaptist.org
Website: www.baptist history.org

Baptist Peacemaker, (Q.) Baptist; Katie Cook, 4800 Wedgewood Dr., Charlotte, NC 28210 Tel. (704)521-6051 Fax (704)521-6053
Email: bpfna@bpfna.org
Website: www.bpfna.org

Baptist Peacemaker, (Q.) Baptist; Katie Cook, 4800 Wedgewood Drive, Charlotte, NC 28210 Tel. (704)521-6051 Fax (704)521-6053

US PERIODICALS

Email: bpfna@bpfna.org
Website: www.bpfna.org

The Baptist Preacher, (bi-M.) Baptist Bible Fellowship International; Mike Randall, P.O. Box 309 HSJ, Springfield, MO 65801 Tel. (417)831-3996 Fax (417)831-1470
Email: editors@tribune.org
Website: www.tribune.org

The Baptist Preacher's Journal, (Q.) Baptist Bible Fellowship International; Keith Bassham, P.O.Box 309, Springfield, MO 65801 Tel. (417)831-3996 Fax (417)831-1470
Email: editor@tribune.org
Website: tribune.org

Missions Ministry, (Q.) Progresive National Baptist Convention, Inc.; Justus Y. Reeves, 601 50th St. NE, Washington, D.C. 20019 Tel. (202)396-0558 Fax (202)398-4998
Email: justusreeves@aol.com
Website: www.PNBC.org

Baptist Witness, (M.) Primitive Baptists; Lasserre Bradley Jr., Box 17037, Cincinnati, OH 45217 Tel. (513)821-7289 Fax (513)821-7303
Email: bbh45217@aol.com
Website: www.BaptistBibleHour.org

The Bible Advocate, (10-Y.) The Church of God (Seventh Day); Calvin Burrell, P.O. Box 33677, Denver, CO 80233 Tel. (303)452-7973 Fax (303)452-0657
Email: bibleadvocate@cog7.org
Website: www.cog7.org/BA

The Brethren Evangelist, (4-Y.) The Brethren Church (Ashland, Ohio); 524 College Ave., Ashland, OH 44805 Tel. (419)289-1708 Fax (419)281-0450
Email: brethren@brethrenchurch.org
Website: www.brethrenchurch.org

Brethren Journal, (10-Y.) Unity of Brethren; Rev. Milton Maly, 6703 FM 2502, Brenham, TX 77833-9803 Tel. (409)830-8762 Fax
Website: www.unityofthebrethren.org

The Bridegroom's Messenger, (bi-M.) The International Pentecostal Church of Christ; Janice Boyce, 121 W. Hunters Trail, Elizabeth City, NC 27909 Tel. (919)338-3003 Fax (919)338-3003

The Burning Bush, (Q.) The Metropolitan Church Association, Inc. (Wesleyan); Rev. Gary Bowell, The Metropolitan Church Assoc., 415 Broad St. #2, Lake Geneva, WI 53147 Tel. (262)248-6786 Fax

Solia Calendar, (Y.) The Romanian Orthodox Episcopate of America; The Department of Publications of the Romanian Orthodox Episcopate of America, P.O. Box 185, Grass Lake, MI 49240-0185 Tel. (517)522-4800 Fax (517)522-5907
Email: solia@roea.org
Website: roea.org

Call to Unity, (bi-M.) Christian Church (Disciples of Christ); Robert K. Welsh, P.O. Box 1986, Indianapolis, IN 46206-1986 Tel. (317)713-2586 Fax (317)713-2588
Email: rwelsh@ccu.disciples.org
Website: www.disciples.org/ccu

The Calvary Messenger, (M.) Beachy Amish Mennonite Churches; Paul Miller, 7809 Soul Herren Rd., Patridge, KS 67566 Tel. (620)567-2286 Fax (620)567-2286
Email: paulmiller@mindspring.com

Campus Life, (9-Y.) Nondenominational; Christopher Lutes, 465 Gunderson Dr., Carol Stream, IL 60188 Tel. (630)260-6200 Fax (630)260-0114
Email: clmag@campuslife.net
Website: www.campuslife.net

Capsule, (M.) General Association of General Baptists, Jack Eberhardt, 100 Stinson Dr., Poplar Bluff, MO 63901 Tel. (573)785-7746 Fax (573)785-0564

Caring, (4-Y.) Assemblies of God; Owen Wilkie, Gospel Publishing House, 1445 N. Boonville Ave., Springfield, MO 65802 Tel. (417)862-2781 Fax (417)862-4832
Email: benevolences@ag.org
Website: www.benevolences.ag.org

Cathedral Age, (Q.) Interdenominational; Craig W. Stapert, Washington National Cathedral, 3101 Wisconsin Ave. NW, Washington, D.C. 20016-5098 Tel. (202)537-5681 Fax (202) 364-6600
Email: cathedral_age@cathedral.org
Website: www.cathedralage.org

Catholic Chronicle, (bi-W.) The Catholic Church; Christine Alexander, P.O. Box 1866, Toledo, OH 43603-1866 Tel. (419)244-6711 ext. 232 Fax (419)244-0468
Email: calexander@toledodiocese.org
Website: www.catholicchronicle.org

Catholic Digest, (M.) The Catholic Church; Richard Reece, P.O.Box 6001, Mystic, CT 06355 Tel. (860)536-2611 Fax (860)536-5600
Email: rreece@bayardpubs.com
Website: www.CatholicDigest.org

Catholic Herald, (W.) The Catholic Church; Fr. Thomas Brundage, 3501 S. Lake Dr., St. Francis, WI 53235-0913 Tel. (414)769-3500 Fax (414)769-3468

Email: chnonline@archmil.org
Website: www.chnonline@.org

Catholic Light, (bi-W.) The Catholic Church; William R. Genello, 300 Wyoming Ave., Scranton, PA 18503 Tel. (570)207-2229 Fax (570)207-2271
Email: billgenello@worldnet.att.net
Website: www.dioceseofscranton.org

The Catholic New World, (W.) The Catholic Church; Thomas H. Sheridan, 721 N LaSalle Dr. #4, Chicago, IL 60610-3752 Tel. (312)243-1300 Fax (312)243-1526
Email: Neworld201@aol.com
Website: catholicnewworld.com

The Catholic Peace Voice, (bi-M.) The Catholic Church; Dave Robinson, 532 W. 8th Street, Erie, PA 16502 Tel. (814)453-4955 Fax (814)452-4784
Email: mike@paxchristiusa.org
Website: www.paxchristiusa.org

The Catholic Review, (W.) The Catholic Church; Associate Publisher: Daniel L. Medinger, P.O. Box 777, Baltimore, MD 21203 Tel. (443)524-3150 Fax (443)524-3155
Email: mail@catholicreview.org
Website: www.catholicreview.org

Catholic Standard and Times, (W.) The Catholic Church; Rev Paul S. Quinter, 222 N. 17th St., Philadelphia, PA 19103 Tel. (215) 587-3660 Fax (215)587-3979

The Catholic Transcript, (W.) The Catholic Church; Christopher M. Tiano, 467 Bloomfield Ave., Bloomfield, CT 06002 Tel. (203)527-1175 Fax (203)947-6397

Catholic Universe Bulletin, (bi-W.) The Catholic Church; Dennis Sadowski, 1027 Superior Ave. NE, Cleveland, OH 44114-2556 Tel. (216)696-6525 Fax (216)696-6519

Catholic Worker, (7-Y.) The Catholic Church; Managing Eidtors: Joanne Kennedy and Padraic O'Neal, 36 E. First St., New York, NY 10003 Tel. (212)777-9617 Fax (212)677-8627

Cela Biedrs, (10-Y.) The Latvian Evangelical Lutheran Church in America; Rev. Indra Skuja-Grislis, 601-850 Cambridge St., Winnipeg, MB R3M 3W8 Tel. (204)452-3844
Email: celabiedrs@shaw.ca

Celebration: An Ecumenical Worship Resource, (M.) Interdenominational; Patrick Marrin, P.O. Box 419493, Kansas City, MO 64141-6493 Tel. (816)531-0538 Fax (816) 968-2280
Email: patmarrin@aol.com
Website: www.ncrpub.com

The Challenge, (Q.) The Bible Church of Christ, Inc.; A.M. Jones, 1358 Morris Ave., Bronx, NY 10456 Tel. (718)588-2284 Fax (718)992-5597
Website: www.thebiblechurchofchrist.org

Charisma, (M.) Nondenominational; J. Lee Grady, 600 Rinehart Rd., Lake Mary, FL 32746 Tel. (407)333-0600 Fax (407)333-7133
Email: grady@strang.com
Website: www.charismamag.com

The Children's Friend (braille), (Q.) Seventh-day Adventist Church; Gaylena Gibson, P.O. Box 6097, Lincoln, NE 68506 Tel. (402)488-0981 Fax (402)488-7582
Email: editorial@christianrecord.org
Website: www.ChristianRecord.org

Christadelphian Advocate, (M.) Christadelphians; James I. Millay, 27 Delphian Rd., Springfield, VT 05156-9335 Tel. (802)885-2316 Fax (802) 885-2319
Email: jimmillay@sover.net
ebsite: www.advocate@sover.net

Christadelphian Tidings, (M.) Christadelphians; Donald H. Styles, 42076 Hartford Dr., Canton, MI 48187 Tel. (313)844-2426 Fax (313)844-8304

Christadelphian Watchman, (M.) Christadelphians; George Booker, 2500 Berwyn Cir., Austin, TX 78745 Tel. (512)447-8882

The Christian Baptist, (M.) Primitive Baptists; Elder S. T. Tolley, P.O. Box 68, Atwood, TN 38220 Tel. (901)662-7417
Email: cbl@aeneas.net

Christian Bible Teacher, (M.) Churches of Christ; Bob Connel, Box 7385, Ft. Worth, TX 76111 Tel. (817)838-2644 Fax (817)838-2644
Email: bobconnel@aol.com

The Christian Century, (26-Y.) Nondenominational; John Buchanan, 104 S. Michigan Ave., Chicago, IL 60603 Tel. (312) 263-7510 Fax (312)263-7540
Email: main@christiancentury.org
Website: www.christiancentury.org

The Christian Chronicle, (M.) Churches of Christ; Bailey McBride, Box 11000, Oklahoma City, OK 73136-1100 Tel. (405) 425-5070 Fax (405)425-5076

The Christian Community, (8-Y.) International Council of Community Churches; Rev. Michael E. Livingston, 21116 Washington Pkwy., Frankfort, IL 60423 Tel. (815)464-5690 Fax (815)464-5692
Email: ICCC60423@aol.com

Christian Education Counselor, (bi-M.) Assemblies of God; Sylvia Lee, Sunday School Promotion and Training, 1445 Boonville Ave., Springfield, MO 65802-1894 Tel. (417)862-2781 Fax (417)862-0503
Email: salee@publish.ag.org
Website: www.we-build-people.org/cec

The Christian Index, (M.) Christian Methodist Episcopal Church; Dr. Kenneth E. Jones, P.O. Box 431, Fairfield, AL 35064 Tel. (205)929-1640 Fax (205)791-1910
Email: goodoc@aol.com
Website: www.c-m-e.org

Christian Leader, (M.) US Conference of Mennonite Brethren Churches; Carmen Andres, Box 220, Hillsboro, KS 67063 Tel. (316)947-5543 Fax (316)947-3266
Email: chleader@southwind.net

Christian Monthly, (M.) Apostolic Lutheran Church of America; Linda Mattson, P.O. Box 2126, Battle Ground, WA 98604 Tel. (360) 687-6493 Fax (360)687-6493
Email: christianm@apostolic-lutheran.org
Website: www.Apostolic-Lutheran.org

Christian Outlook, (M.) Pentecostal Assemblies of the World, Inc.; Johnna E. Hampton, 3939 Meadows Dr., Indianapolis, IN 46205 Tel. (317)547-9541 Fax (317)543-0512

Christian Reader, (bi-M.) Nondenominational; Managing Editor: Ed Gilbreath, 465 Gundersen Dr., Carol Stream, IL 60188 Tel. (630)260-6200 Fax (630)260-0114
Email: creditor@christianreader.net

Christian Record (braille), (Q.) Seventh-day Adventist Church; Gaylena Gibson, P.O. Box 6097, Lincoln, NE 68506 Tel. (402)488-0981 Fax (402)488-7582
Email: editorial@christianrecord.org
Website: www.ChristianRecord.org

The Christian Science Journal, (M.) Church of Christ, Scientist; Mary M. Trammell, One Norway St., Boston, MA 02115-3195 Tel. (617)450-2000 Fax (617)450-2930
Email: tramellm@csps.com/journal@csps.com
Website: www.csjournal.com

The Christian Science Monitor, (D. & W.) Church of Christ, Scientist; David T. Cook, One Norway St., Boston, MA 02115 Tel. (617)450-2000 Fax (617)450-7575
Website: www.csmonitor.com

Christian Science Quarterly Weekly Bible Lessons, (M. & Q.) Church of Christ, Scientist; Carol Humphry, Circulation Marketing Manager, One Norway St., Boston, MA 02115 Tel. (617)450-2000 Fax (617)450-2930
Email: service@csps.com
Website: www.BibleLesson.com

Christian Science Sentinel, (W.) Church of Christ, Scientist; Mary M. Trammell, One Norway St., Boston, MA 02115-3195 Tel. (617)450-2000 Fax (617)450-2930
Email: sentinel@csps.com/trammellm@csps.com
Website: www.cssentinel.com

Christian Social Action, (bi-M.) The United Methodist Church; Editor: -vacant-, 100 Maryland Ave. NE, Washington, D.C. 20002 Tel. (202)488-5621 Fax (202)488-1617
Website: www.umc-gbcs.org

Christian Standard, (W.) Christian Churches and Churches of Christ; Mark A. Taylor, 8121 Hamilton Ave., Cincinnati, OH 45231 Tel. (513)931-4050 Fax (513)931-0950
Email: christianstd@standardpub.com
Website: www.christianstandard.com

The Christian Union Witness, (M. [except July-Aug.]) Christian Union; Joseph Cunningham, P.O. Box 361, Greenfield, OH 45123 Tel. (937)981-2760
Email: ohiocu@bright.net
Website: christianunionbright.net

Christian Woman, (bi-M.) Churches of Christ; Sandra Humphrey, Box 150, Nashville, TN 37202 Tel. (615)254-8781 Fax (615)254-7411

Christianity & The Arts, (Q.) Nondenominational; Marci Whitney-Schenck, P.O. Box 118088, Chicago, IL 60611 Tel. (312)642-8606 Fax (312)266-7719
Email: chrnarts@aol.com

The Church Advocate, (Q.) Churches of God, General Conference; Rachel L. Foreman, P.O. Box 926, 700 E. Melrose Ave., Findlay, OH 45839 Tel. (419)424-1961 Fax (419)424-3433
Email: communications@cggc.org
Website: www.cggc.org

Church of God Evangel, (M.) Church of God (Cleveland, Tenn.); Bill George, P.O. Box 2250, Cleveland, TN 37320 Tel. (423)478-7592 Fax (423)478-7616
Email: bill_george@pathwaypress.org
Website: www.pathwaypress.org

Church of God Missions, (bi-M.) Church of God (Anderson, Ind.); J. David Reames, Box 2337, Anderson, IN 46018-2337 Tel. (765) 648-2128 Fax (765)642-4279
Email: mbchogvp@aol.com

Church of God Progress Journal, (bi-M.) Church of God General Conference (Oregon,

Ill. & Morrow, Ga.); Steve Taylor, Box 100,000, Morrow, GA 30260 Tel. (404)362-0052 Fax (404)362-9307
Email: info@abc-coggc.org
Website: www.abc-coggc.org

The Church Herald, (11-Y.) Reformed Church in America; Christina Van Eyl, 4500 60th St. SE, Grand Rapids, MI 49512 Tel. (616)698-7071 Fax (616)698-6606
Email: herald@rca.org
Website: www.rca.org/herald/

Church History: Studies in Christianity and Culture, (Q.) Scholarly; Elizabeth A. Clark, Grant Wacker, Hans J. Hillerbrand, and Richard P. Heitzenrater, The Divinity School, Duke University, Box 90975, Durham, NC 27708-0975 Tel. (919)660-3470 Fax (919) 660-3473
Email: church-history@duke.edu
Website: www.churchhistory.org

The Church Messenger, (bi-M.) James S. Dutko, 280 Clinton St., Binghamton, NY 13905

Church School Herald, (Q.) African Methodist Episcopal Zion Church; Ms. Mary A. Love, P.O. Box 26769, Charlotte, NC 28221-6769 Tel. (704)599-4630 ext. 324 Fax (704)688-2548
Email: MaLove@amezhqtr.org

Church & Society Magazine, (bi-M.) Presbyterian Church (USA); Rev. Dr. Bobbi Wells Hargleroad, 100 Witherspoon St., Louisville, KY 40202-1396 Tel. (502)569-5810 Fax (502)569-8116
Email: c-s@ctr.pcusa.org
Website: www.horebpcusa.org/churchsociety

Church Talk, (Q.) General Association of General Baptists; Mike Warren, 100 Stinson Dr., Poplar Bluff, MO 63901 Tel. (573)785-7746 Fax (573)785-0564
Email: cmdir@generalbaptist.com
Website: generalbaptist.com

The Churchman's Human Quest, () Nondenominational; Edna Ruth Johnson, 1074 23rd Ave. N, St. Petersburg, FL 33704 Tel. (813)894-0097

Churchwoman, (Q.) Interdenominational; Annie Llamoso-Songco, 475 Riverside Dr., Suite 500, New York, NY 10115 Tel. (212)870-3339 Fax (212)870-2338
Email: allamoso@churchwomen.org
Website: www.churchwomen.org

Circuit Rider, (6-Y.) The United Methodist Church; Jill S. Reddig, 201 Eighth Ave. S, Nashville, TN 37202 Tel. (615)749-6538 Fax (615)749-6061
Email: jreddig@umpublishing.org
Website: www.cokesbury.com (From "Other Cokesbury Sites" select Circuit Rider)

Clarion Herald, (bi-W.) The Catholic Church; Peter P. Finney Jr., P. O. Box 53247, 1000 Howard Ave. Suite 400, New Orleans, LA 70153 Tel. (504)596-3035 Fax (504)596-3020
Email: clarionherald@clarionherald.org
Website: www.clarionherald.org

Clergy Comminique, (2-Y.) International Council of Community Churches; Michael Livingston, 21116 Washington Pky., Frankfort, IL 60423-3112 Tel. (815)464-5690 Fax (815) 464-5692
Email: iccc60423@aol.com
Website: icccusa.com

The Clergy Journal, (9-Y.) Nondenominational; Managing Editor: Sharilyn A. Figueroa; Executive Editor: Clyde J. Steckel; 6160 Carmen Avenue E, Inver Grove Heights, MN 55076-4422 Tel. (800)328-0200 Fax (651) 457-4617
Email: fig@logostaff.com
Website: www.joinhands.com

Club Connection, (Q.) Assemblies of God; Debby Seler, 1445 Boonville Ave., Springfield, MO 65802-1894 Tel. (417)862-2781 Fax (417)862-0503
Email: clubconnection@ag.org
Website: www.missionettes.ag.org

Coast to Coast on Campus, (Q.) Advent Christian Church; Rev. Keith D. Wheaton, P.O. Box 23152, Charlotte, NC 28227 Tel. (704)545-6161 Fax (704)573-0712
Email: Mayerpub@aol.com

CoLaborer, (bi-M.) National Association of Free Will Baptists; Sarah Fletcher, Women Nationally Active for Christ, P.O. Box 5002, Antioch, TN 37011-5002 Tel. (615)731-6812 Fax (615)731-0771
Email: wnac@nafwb.org

Collegiate Quarterly, (Q.) Seventh-day Adventist Church; Gary B. Swanson, 12501 Old Columbia Pike, Silver Spring, MD 20904 Tel. (301)680-6160 Fax (301)680-6155

Columbia, (M.) The Catholic Church; Tim S. Hickey, One Columbus Plaza, New Haven, CT 06510 Tel. (203)752-4398 Fax (203)752-4109
Email: tim.hickey@kofc-supreme.com
Website: www.kofc.org

The Commission, (7-Y.) International Mission Board, Southern Baptist Convention; Editor-

in-chief: Bill Bangham, Box 6767, Richmond, VA 23230-0767 Tel. (804)219-1253 Fax (804) 219-1410
Email: commission@imb.org
Website: www.tconline.org

Common Lot, (4-Y.) United Church of Christ; Martha J. Hunter, 700 Prospect Ave., Cleveland, OH 44115 Tel. (216)736-2150 Fax (216)736-2156

Commonweal, (bi-W.) The Catholic Church; Paul Baumann, 475 Riverside Dr., Rm 405, New York, NY 10115 Tel. (212)662-4200 Fax (212)662-4183
Email: editors@commonwealmagazine.org
Website: www.commonwealmagazine.org

Communion, (6-Y.) Church of God (Anderson, Indiana); Arthur Kelly, P.O. Box 2420, 1201 E. 5th St., Anderson, IN 46018-2420 Tel. (765) 642-0256 Fax (765)652-5652
Email: akelly@chog.org
Website: chog.org/news/communion.asp

Communique, (M.) National Baptist Convention of America, Inc.; Robert Jeffrey, 1320 Pierre Ave., Shreveport, LA 71103 Tel. (318)221-3701 Fax (318)222-7512

The Congregationalist, (5-Y.) National Association Congregational Christian Churches; Joseph B. Polhemus, 1105 Briarwood Rd., Mansfield, OH 44907 Tel. (419)756-5526 Fax (419)756-5526
Email: jbpedit@aol.com
Website: www.congregationalist.org

Connections, (M.) The Alliance of Baptists in the USA; Rev. Dr. Stan Hastey, 1328 16th St. NW, Washington, D.C. 20036 Tel. (202)745-7609 Fax (202)745-0023
Website: allianceofbaptists.org

Conqueror, (bi-M.) United Pentecostal Church International; John F. Sills, 8855 Dunn Rd., Hazelwood, MO 63042 Tel. (314)837-7300 Fax (314)837-4503
Email: GYouth8855@aol.com

Contact, (M.) National Association of Free Will Baptists; Jack Williams, P.O. Box 5002, Antioch, TN 37011-5002 Tel. (615)731-6812 Fax (615)731-0771
Email: jack@nafwb.org
Website: www.nafwb.org

Context, (22-Y.) Nondenominational; Martin Marty, 205 W. Monroe St., Chicago, IL 60606-5013 Tel. (312)236-7782 Fax (312)236-8207
Email: editors@uscatholic.org
Website: www.contextonline.org

Covenant, (Q.) Presbyterian Church in America; Eileen O'Gorman, 123330 Conway Rd., St. Louis, MO 63141 Tel. (314)434-4044 Fax (314)434-4819
Email: eogorman@covenantseminary.edu
Website: convenantseminary.edu

Cornerstone Connections, (Q.) Seventh-day Adventist Church; Gary B. Swanson, 12501 Old Columbia Pike, Silver Spring, MD 20904 Tel. (301)680-6160 Fax (301)680-6155

Courage in the Struggle for Justice and Peace, (Q.) United Church of Christ; Sandy Sorensen, 110 Maryland Ave., Ste. 207 NE, Washington, D.C. 20002 Tel. (202)543-1517 Fax (202)543-5994

The Covenant Companion, (M.) Evangelical Covenant Church; Managing Eds.: Donald L. Meyer, Jane K. Swanson-Nystrom, 5101 N. Francisco Ave., Chicago, IL 60625 Tel. (773)906-3328 Fax (773)784-4366
Email: communication@covchurch.org
Website: www.covchurch.org/cov/companion

Covenant Home Altar, (Q.) Evangelical Covenant Church; Jane K. Swanson-Nystrom, 5101 N. Francisco Ave., Chicago, IL 60625 Tel. (773)784-3000 Fax (773)784-4366
Email: communication@covchurch.org

Covenant Quarterly, (Q.) Evangelical Covenant Church; Paul E. Koptak, 3225 W. Foster Ave., Chicago, IL 60625-4895 Tel. (773)244-6242
Email: pkoptak@northpark.edu

The Covenanter Witness, (11-Y.) Reformed Presbyterian Church of North America; Drew Gordon and Lynne Gordon, 7408 Penn Ave., Pittsburgh, PA 15208 Tel. (412)241-0436 Fax (412)731-8861
Email: info@psalms4u.com
Website: www.psalms4u.com

Credinta—The Faith, (Q.) The Romanian Orthodox Church in America; V. Rev. Archim. Dr. Vasile Vasilac, 45-03 48th Ave., Woodside, Queens, NY 11377 Tel. (313)893-8390

Credo, (M.) The Antiochian Orthodox Christian Archdiocese of North; Charles Dinkler, P.O. Box 84, Stanton, NJ 08885-0084 Tel. (908) 236-7890

The Criterion, (W.) The Roman Catholic Church; John F. Fink, P. O. Box 1717, 1400 N. Meridian, Indianapolis, IN 46206 Tel. (317) 236-1570

The Cumberland Flag, (M.) Cumberland Presbyterian Church in America; Rev. Robert

Stanley Wood, 226 Church St., Huntsville, AL 35801 Tel. (205)536-7481 Fax (205)536-7482

The Cumberland Presbyterian, (11-Y.) Cumberland Presbyterian Church; Patricia P. Richards, Cumberland Presbyterian Church, 1978 Union Ave., Memphis, TN 38104 Tel. (615)731-5556
Email: cpmag@comcast.net
Website: www.cumberland.org/cpmag/

Currents in Theology and Mission, (6-Y.) Evangelical Lutheran Church in America; Ralph W. Klein, 1100 E. 55th St., Chicago, IL 60615 Tel. (773)256-0751 Fax (773)256-0782
Email: currents@lstc.edu
Website: www.lstc.edu/pub_peo/pub/currents.html

Decision, (M.) Nondenominational; Kersten Beckstrom, Two Parkway Plaza, 4828 Parkway Plaza Blvd, Suite 200, Charlotte, NC 28217 Tel. (612)338-0500 Fax (612)335-1299
Email: decision@bgea.org
Website: www.decisionmag.org

The Disciple, (10-Y.) Christian Church (Disciples of Christ); Patricia R. Case, P.O.Box 179, St. Louis, MO 63166-0179
Email: thedisciple@cbp21.org
Website: www.thedisciple.com

Discipleship Matters, (Q.) International Pentecostal Holiness Church; Harold Dalton, P.O. Box 12609, Oklahoma City, OK 73157-2609 Tel. (405)787-7110 Fax (405)789-3957
Email: dbrewer.iphc.org
Website: iphc.org/cem.html

Discovery, (Q.) (Braille Only, for Youth) Nondenominational; Darcy Quigley, John Milton Society for the Blind, 475 Riverside Dr., Rm 455, New York, NY 10115-0455 Tel. (212)870-3335 Fax (212)870-3226
Email: order@jmsblind.org
Website: www.jmsblind.org

Ecu-Link, (Several times/year) Interdenominational; Sarah Vilankulu, 475 Riverside Dr., 12th Fl., New York, NY 10115-0050 Tel. (212)870-2227 Fax (212)870-2030
Email: sarah@ncccusa.org

Ecumenical Trends, (M.) Nondenominational; Kevin McMorrow, SA, Graymoor Ecumenical & Interreligious Institute, P.O. Box 300, Garrison, NY 10524-0300 Tel. (845)424-3671 ext. 3323 Fax (845)424-2163
Email: kmcmorrow@atonementfriars.org
Website: www.geii.org

Eleventh Hour Messenger, (bi-M.) Wesleyan Holiness Association of Churches; John Brewer, 11411 N US Hwy 27, Fountain City, IN 47341-9757 Tel. (317)584-3199

Elim Herald, (2-Y.) Elim Fellowship; Bernard J. Evans, 1703 Dalton Rd., P.O. Box 57A, Lima, NY 14485 Tel. (585)582-2790 Fax (585)624-1229
Email: executive@elimfellowship.org
Website: www.elimfellowhip.org

Enrichment: A Journal for Pentecostal Ministry, (Q.) Assemblies of God; Managing Eds: Gary Allen, Rick Knoth, 1445 N. Boonville Ave., Springfield, MO 65802 Tel. (417)862-2781 Fax (417)862-0416
Email: gallen@ag.org
Website: www.enrichmentjournal.ag.org

The Ensign, (M.) The Church of Jesus Christ Latter-day Saints; Managing Editor: Brian K. Kelly, 50 E. North Temple Street, 24th Fl, Salt Lake City, UT 84150 Tel. (801)240-2950 Fax (801)240-5732

Epiphany Journal, (Q.) Interdenominational; Nun Macaria, 1516 N. Delaware, Indianapolis, IN 46202 Tel. (317)926-7468

Episcopal Life, (M.) The Episcopal Church; Jerrold Hames, 815 Second Ave., New York, NY 10017-4503 Tel. (800)334-7626 Fax (212)949-8059
Email: jhames@episcopalchurch.org
Website: www.episcopal-life.org

Equip, (6-Y.) Presbyterian Church in America; Rev. Charles Dunahoo, 1700 N. Brown Rd., Ste. 102, Lawerenceville, GA 30043 Tel. (678)825-1100 Fax (678)825-1100
Website: pcanet.org

The Evangel, (6-Y.) American Association of Lutheran Churches; The, Rev. Charles D. Eidum, 801 W. 106th St, Suite 203, Minneapolis, MN 55420-5603 Tel. (952)884-7784 Fax (952)884-7894
Email: aa2aalc@aol.com
ebsite: www.taalc.com

The Evangel, (Q.) The Evangelical Church Alliance; Dr. Henry A. (Hank) Roso, P.O. Box 9, Bradley, IL 60915 Tel. (815)937-0720 Fax (815)937-0001
Email: info@ecainternatinal.org
Website: www.ecainternational.org

The Evangelical Advocate, (M.) Churches of Christ in Christian Union; Ralph Hux, P.O. Box 30, Circleville, OH 43113 Tel. (740)474-8856 Fax (740)477-7766
Email: doc@cccuhg.org
Website: www.cccuhq.org

Evangelical Beacon, (6-Y.) The Evangelical Free Church of America; Ms. Carol Madison, 901 E. 78th St., Minneapolis, MN 55420-1300 Tel. (877)293-5653 Fax (952)853-8488
Email: beacon@efca.org
Website: www.efca.org

Evangelical Challenge, (Q.) The Evangelical Church; John F. Sills, 7733 W. River Rd., Minneapolis, MN 55444 Tel. (763)561-0886 Fax (763)561-0774
Email: jsditzel@juno.com

The Evangelist, (W.) The Roman Catholic Church; James Breig, 40 N. Main Ave., Albany, NY 12203 Tel. (518)453-6688 Fax (518)453-8448
Email: james.breig@rcda.org
Website: www.evangelist.org

Explorations, (4-Y.) Nondenominational; Irvin J. Borowsky, 321 Chestnut St., 4th Floor, Philadelphia, PA 19106-2779 Tel. (215)925-2800 Fax (215)925-3800
Email: aii@interfaith-scholars.org

Extension, (M.) The Roman Catholic Church; Bradley Collins, 150 S. Wacker Drive, 20th Floor, Chicago, IL 60606 Tel. (312)236-7240 Fax (312)236-5276
Email: magazine@catholic-extension.org
Website: www.catholic-extension.org

Face to Face, (4-Yr.) Community of Christ; Richard A. Brown, Herald Publishing House, 1001 W. Walnut, Independence, MO 64050-3562 Tel. (816)833-1000 ext. 2144 Fax (816)521-3043
Email: rbrown@cofchrist.org
Website: www.cofchrist.org

Faith & Fellowship, (M.) Church of the Lutheran Brethren of America; Brent Juliot, P.O. Box 655, Fergus Falls, MN 56538 Tel. (218)736-7357 Fax (218)736-2200
Email: ffpress@clba.org
Website: www.faithandfellowship.org

Faith-Life, (bi-M.) Lutheran; Pastor Marcus Albrecht, 2107 N. Alexander St., Appleton, WI 54911 Tel. (920)733-1839 Fax (920)733-4834
Email: malbrecht@milwpc.com

Faith and Truth, (M.) Pentecostal Fire-Baptized Holiness Church; Edgar Vollratlt, 593 Harris-Lord Rd., Commerce, GA 30529 Tel. (706) 335-5796

Fellowship, (6-Y.) Interfaith; Richard Deats, P.O. Box 271, Nyack, NY 10960-0271 Tel. (845)358-4601 Fax (845)358-4924
Email: fellowship@forusa.org
Website: www.forusa.org/~

Fellowship Focus, (bi-M.) Fellowship of Evangelical Bible Churches; Sharon K. Berg, 3339 N. 109th Plz, Omaha, NE 68164-2908 Tel. (402)965-3860 Fax (402)965-3871
Email: fellowshipfocus@febcministries.org
Website: www.febcministries.org

Fellowship News, (M.) Bible Fellowship Church; Carol Snyder, 3000 Fellowship Dr., Whitehall, PA 18052-3343 Tel. (717)337-3408 Fax (215)536-2120
Email: ccsnyder@supernet.com
Website: www.bfc.org

Fellowship Tidings, (Q.) Full Gospel Fellowship of Churches and Ministers Intern; S. K. Biffle, 1000 N. Beltline Road, Irving, TX 75061 Tel. (214)492-1254 Fax (214)492-1736
Email: FGFCMI@aol.com
Website: www.fgfcmi.org

Firm Foundation, (M.) Churches of Christ; H. A. Dobbs, P.O. Box 690192, Houston, TX 77269-0192 Tel. (713)469-3102 Fax (713) 469-7115
Email: HAD@onramp.net

First Things: A Monthly Journal of Religion & Public Life, (10-Y.) Interdenominational; Richard J. Neuhaus, 156 Fifth Ave., Ste. 400, New York, NY 10010 Tel. (212)627-1985 Fax (212)627-2184
Email: ft@firstthings.com
Website: www.firstthings.com

The Flaming Sword, (M.) Bible Holiness Church; Susan Davolt, 10th St. & College Ave., Independence, KS 67301 Tel. (316)331-2580 Fax (316)331-2580

For the Poor, (bi-M.) Primitive Baptists; W. H. Cayce, P.O. Box 38, Thornton, AR 71766 Tel. (501)352-3694

Foresee, (bi-M.) Conservative Congregational Christian Conference; Carol Wells, 7582 Currell Blvd., #108, St. Paul, MN 55125 Tel. (651)739-1474 Fax (651)739-0750
Email: dmjohnson@ccccusa.org
Website: www.ccccusa.org

Forum Letter, (M.) Independent, Intra-Lutheran (companion publication to the quarterly, Lutheran Forum); Pastor Russell E. Saltzman, Ruskin Heights Lutheran Church, 10801 Ruskin Way, Kansas City, MO 64134 Tel. (816)761-6815 Fax (816)761-6523
Email: Saltzman@integritynetwork.net
Website: www.alpb.org

Forward, (Q.) United Pentecostal Church International; Rev. J. L. Hall, 8855 Dunn Rd., Hazelwood, MO 63042 Tel. (314)837-7300 Fax (314)837-4503

Forward in Christ, (M.) Wisconsin Evangelical Lutheran Synod; Gary Baumler, 2929 N. Mayfair Rd., Milwaukee, WI 53222 Tel. (414) 256-3210 Fax (414)256-3862
Email: fic@sab.wels.net
Website: www.wels.net

Foursquare World Advance, (Q. w/ a bonus issue) International Church of the Foursquare Gospel; Dr. Ron Williams, P.O. Box 26902, 1910 W. Sunset Blvd., Ste 400, Los Angeles, CA 90026-0176 Tel. (213)989-4230 Fax (213) 989-4544
Email: comm@foursquare.org
Website: www.advancemagazine.org

Free Will Baptist Bible College Bulletin, (6-Y.) National Association of Free Will Baptists; Bert Tippett, 3606 West End Ave., Nashville, TN 37205 Tel. (615)383-1340 Fax (615)269-6028
Email: bert@fwbbc.edu
Website: www.fwbbc.edu

Free Will Baptist Gem, (M.) National Association of Free Will Baptists; Nathan Ruble, P.O. Box 991, Lebanon, MO 65536 Tel. (417)532-6537

The Free Will Baptist, (M.) Original Free Will Baptist Church; Tracy A McCoy, P.O. Box 159, 811 N. Lee Street, Ayden, NC 28513 Tel. (919)746-6128 Fax (919)746-9248

Friend Magazine, (M.) The Church of Jesus Christ of Latter-day Saints; Vivian Paulsen, 50 E. South Temple Street, 24th Fl, Salt Lake City, UT 84150 Tel. (801)240-2210 Fax (801)240-2270

Friends Bulletin, (10-Y.) Religious Society of Friends; Anthony Manousos, 5238 Andalucia Ct., Whittier, CA 90601 Tel. (562)699-5670 Fax (562)692-2472
Email: friendsbul@aol.com
Website: www.quaker.org/fb and www.quaker.org/western

Friends Journal, (M.) Religious Society of Friends (Quakers); Publisher & Exec. Editor: Susan Corson-Finnerty, 1216 Arch St., 2A, Philadelphia, PA 19107-2835 Tel. (215)563-8629 Fax (215)568-1377
Email: info@friendsjournal.org
Website: www.friendsjournal.org

The Friends Voice, (3-Y.) Evangelical Friends International–North America Region; Sr. Editor: Becky Towne; Assoc. Editor: Kathy Boblyer; 2748 E. Pikes Peak Ave, Colorado Springs, CO 80909 Tel. (719)632-5721 Fax (719)635-4011
Email: mcrcs@codenet.net
Website: evangelical-friends.org

Front Line, (4-Y.) Conservative Baptist Association of America; Al Russell, P.O. Box 58, Long Prairie, MN 56347 Tel. (320)732-8072 Fax (509)356-7112
Email: chaplruss@earthlink.net
Website: www.cbchaplains.net

Full Gospel Ministries Outreach Report, (Q.) Full Gospel Assemblies International; Simeon Strauser, P.O. Box 1230, Coatsville, PA 19320 Tel. (610)857-2357 Fax (610)857-3109

The Gem, (W.) Churches of God, General Conference; Rachel Foreman, P.O. Box 926, Findlay, OH 45839 Tel. (419)424-1961 Fax (419)424-3433
Email: communications@cggc.org
Website: www.cggc.org

General Baptist Messenger, (M.) General Association of General Baptists; Samuel S. Ramdial, 400 Stinson Dr., Poplar Bluff, MO 63901 Tel. (573)686-9051 Fax (573)686-5198

The Gleaner, (M.) Baptist Missionary Association of America; F. Donald Collins, P.O. Box 193920, Little Rock, AR 72219-3920 Tel. (501)455-4977 Fax (501)455-3636
Email: BMAAM@aol.com

Global Partners, (Q.) Baptist Bible Fellowship International; Loran McAlister, P.O. Box 191, Springfield, MO 65801 Tel. (417)862-5001 Fax (417)865-0794

God's Field, (bi-W.) Polish National Catholic Church of America; Rev. Anthony Mikovsky (English) and Rt. Rev. Casimir Grotnik (Polish), 1006 Pittston Ave., Scranton, PA 18505 Tel. (570)346-9131 Fax (570)346-2188

Good News–Buna Vestire, (Q.) The Romanian Orthodox Episcopate of America; The Romanian Orthodox Deanery of Canada; c/o Psa. Alice Nenson, 2855 Helmsing St., Regina, SK S4V 0W7 Tel. (306)761-2379 Fax (306)525-9650
Email: danenson@accesscomm.ca

Gospel Advocate, (M.) Churches of Christ; Neil W. Anderson, 1006 Elm Hill Pike, Nashville, TN 37202 Tel. (615)254-8781 Fax (615)254-7411
Email: info@gospeladvocate.com
Website: www.gospeladvocate.com

The Gospel Herald, (M.) Church of God, Mountain Assembly, Inc.; Bob Vance, P.O. Box 157, Jellico, TN 37762 Tel. (423)784-8260 Fax (423)784-3258
Email: cgmahdq@jellico.com
Website: www.cgmahdq.org

The Gospel Light, (2-Y.) The Bible Church of Christ, Inc.; Carole Crenshaw, 1358 Morris Ave., Bronx, NY 10456 Tel. (718)588-2284 Fax (718)992-5597
Website: www.thebiblechurchofchrist.org

The Gospel Messenger, (M.) Congregational Holiness Church, Inc.; Cullen L. Hicks, Congregational Holiness Church, 3888 Fayetteville Hwy., Griffin, GA 30223 Tel. (770)228-4833 Fax (770)228-1177
Email: CHChurch@bellsouth.net
Website: www.CHChurch.com

The Gospel News, (M.) The Church of Jesus Christ (Bickertonites); Donald Ross, 201 Royalbrooke Dr., Venetia, PA 15367 Tel. (412)348-6828 Fax (412)348-0919

The Gospel Truth, (bi M.) Church of the Living God, C.W.F.F.; W.E. Crumes, 430 Forest Ave., Cincinnati, OH 45229 Tel. (513)569-5660 Fax (513)569-5661
Email: cwff430@aol.com

Grow Magazine, (4-Y.) Church of the Nazarene; Jim Dorsey, 6401 The Paseo, Kansas City, MO 64131 Tel. (816)333-7000 ext. 2828 Fax (816)361-5202
Email: jdorsey@nazarene.org
Website: www.usamission.org

Guide, (W.) Seventh-day Adventist Church; Randy Fishell, 55 W. Oak Ridge Dr., Hagerstown, MD 21740 Tel. (301)393-4038 Fax (301)393-4055
Email: guide@rhpa.org
Website: www.guidemagazine.org

The Handmaiden, (Q.) The Antiochian Orthodox Christian Archdiocese of North America; Virginia Nieuwsma, P.O. Box 76, Ben Lomond, CA 95005-0076 Tel. (831)336-5118 Fax (831)336-8882
Email: czell@conciliarpress.com
Website: www.conciliarpress.com

The Happy Harvester, (M.) Church of God of Prophecy; Diane Pace, P.O. Box 2910, Cleveland, TN 37320-2910 Tel. (423)559-5435 Fax (423)559-5444
Email: JoDiPace@wingnet.net

Heartbeat, (bi-M.) National Association of Free Will Baptists; Don Robirds, Foreign Missions Office, P.O. Box 5002, Antioch, TN 37011-5002 Tel. (615)731-6812 Fax (615)731-5345
Email: Heartbeat@NAFWB.org

HeartBeat, (M.) The Evangelical Church; John F. Sills, 7733 West River Rd., Minneapolis, MN 55444 Tel. (615)731-6812 Fax (615)760-5345
Email: jsditzel@juno.com
Website: www.nafwb.org/fm

Helping Hand, (bi-M.) International Pentecostal Holiness Church; Mrs. Doris Moore, P.O. Box 12609, Oklahoma City, OK 73157 Tel. (405)787-7110 Fax (405)789-3957

Henceforth, (2-Y.) Advent Christian Church; Rev. Keith D. Wheaton, P.O. Box 23152, Charlotte, NC 28227 Tel. (704)545-6161 Fax (704)573-0712
Email: Mayerpub@aol.com

Herald, (M.) Community of Christ; Linda L. Booth, 1001 W. Walnut, Independence, MO 64050 Tel. (816)833-1000 Fax (816)521-3043
Email: jhannah@cofochrist.org
Website: www.heraldhouse.org/www.cofchrist.org

The Herald of Christian Science, (M. & Q.) Church of Christ, Scientist; Mary M. Trammell, The Christian Science Publishing Society, One Norway St., Boston, MA 02115-3195 Tel. (617)450-2000 Fax (617)450-2930
Email: trammellm@csps.com/herald@csps.com
Website: www.csherald.com

Heritage, (Q.) Assemblies of God; Wayne E. Warner, 1445 Boonville Ave., Springfield, MO 65802 Tel. (417)862-1447 Fax (417)862-6203
Email: wwarner@ag.org
Website: www.agheritage@ag.org

High Adventure, (Q.) Assemblies of God; Jerry Parks, Gospel Publishing House, 1445 N. Boonville Ave., Springfield, MO 65802-1894 Tel. (417)862-2781 Fax (417)831-8230
Email: rangers@ag.org
Website: www.royalrangers.org

Higher Way, (bi-M.) Apostolic Faith Mission of Portland, Oregon; Darrel D. Lee, 6615 S.E. 52nd Ave., Portland, OR 97206 Tel. (503)777-1741 Fax (503)777-1743
Email: kbarrett@apostolicfaith.org
Website: www.apostolicfaith.org

Holiness Digest, (Q.) Nondenominational; Marlin Hotle, 263 Buffalo Rd., Clinton, TN 37716 Tel. (423)457-5978 Fax (423)463-7280

Holiness Today, (M.) Church of the Nazarene; R. Franklin Cook, 6401 The Paseo, Kansas City, MO 64131 Tel. (816)333-7000 Fax (816)333-1748
Email: HolinessToday@nazarene.org
Website: www.holinessTodaymagazine.com

The Holiness Union, (M.) United Holy Church of America, Inc.; Bishop John Lewis, 13102 Morningside Ln., Silver Spring, MD 20904 Tel. (215)724-1346 Fax (215)748-1480

Homiletic and Pastoral Review, (M.) The Roman Catholic Church; Kenneth Baker, 50 S. Franklin Tpk, P.O. Box 297, Ramsey, NJ 07446 Tel. (201)236-9336

Horizons, (7-Y.) Presbyterian Church (USA); Leah Ellison Bradley, Susan Jackson Dowd, Presbyterian Women, 100 Witherspoon St., Louisville, KY 40202-1396 Tel. (502)569-5368 Fax (502)569-8085
Email: lbradley@ctr.pcusa.org
Website: www.pcusa.org/horizons

Horizons, (M.) Christian Churches and Churches of Christ; Reggie Hundley, Box 13111, Knoxville, TN 37920-0111 Tel. (800)655-8524 Fax (865)573-5950
Email: msa@missionservices.org
Website: www.missionservices.org

The Inclusive Pulpit, (1-Y.) International Council of Community Churches; Robert Tuckett, 21116 Washington Pky., Frankfort, IL 60423-3112 Tel. (815)464-5690 Fax (815)464-5692
Email: iccc60423@aol.com
Website: icccusa.com

Insight, (Q.) Advent Christian Church; Dawn Rutan, P.O. Box 23152, Charlotte, NC 28227 Tel. (704)545-6161 Fax (704)573-0712
Email: ACPub@adventchristian.org
Website: www.adventchristian.org

Insight Into, (6-Y.) Netherlands Reformed Congregations; Mr. Schipper, 4732 E. C Avenue, Kalamazoo, MI 49004 Tel. (269)349-9448

InterLit, (4-Y.) Nondenominational magazine on Christian publishing worldwide; Kim A. Pettit, 4050 Lee Vance View Dr., Colorado Springs, CO 80918 Tel. (719)536-0100 Fax (719)536-3266
Email: ccmintl@ccmi.org
Website: www.ccmi.org

International Bulletin of Missionary Research, (Q.) Nondenominational; Jonathan J. Bonk, 490 Prospect St., New Haven, CT 06511-2196 Tel. (203)624-6672 Fax (203) 865-2857
Email: ibmr@OMSC.org
Website: www.omsc.org

Interpretation: A Journal of Bible and Theology, (Q.) Presbyterian Church (USA); William P. Brown, 3401 Brook Rd., Richmond, VA 23227 Tel. (804)278-4296 Fax (804)278-4208
Email: email@interpretation.org
Website: www.interpretation.org

el Intérprete, (6-Y.) The United Methodist Church; Martha E. Rovira Raber, P.O. Box 320, Nashville, TN 37202-0320 Tel. (615)742-5115 Fax (615)742-5460
Email: mraber@umcom.org
Website: www.interpretermagazine.org

Interpreter, (8-Y.) The United Methodist Church; M. Garlinda Burton, P.O. Box 320, Nashville, TN 37202-0320 Tel. (615)742-5102 Fax (615)742-5460
Email: gburton@umcom.org
Website: www.interpretermagazine.org

IssacharFile, (M.) International Pentacostal Holiness Church; Shirley Spencer, P.O. Box 12609, Oklahoma City, OK 73157 Tel. (405)787-7110 Fax (405)789-3957

John Three Sixteen, (Q.) Bible Holiness Church; Mary Cunningham, 10th St. & College Ave., Independence, KS 67301 Tel. (316)331-2580 Fax (316)331-2580

Journal of Adventist Education, (5-Y.) Seventh-day Adventist Church; Beverly J. Robinson-Rumble, 12501 Old Columbia Pike, Silver Spring, MD 20904-6600 Tel. (301)680-5075 Fax (301)622-9627
Email: 74617.1231@compuserve.com or goffc@gc.adventist.org
Website: http://education.gc.adventist.org/jae/

Journal of the American Academy of Religion, (Q.) Nondenominational; Glenn Yocum, Whittier College, P.O. Box 634, Whittier, CA 90608-0634 Tel. (562)907-4200 Fax (562) 907-4910
Email: gyocum@whittier.edu
Website: www.aarweb.org

Journal of Christian Education, (Q.) African Methodist Episcopal Church; Kenneth H. Hill, 500 Eighth Ave. S, Nashville, TN 37203 Tel. (615)242-1420 Fax (615)726-1866
Email: ameced@edge.net
Website: www.ameced.com

Journal of Ecumenical Studies, (Q.) Interdenominational/Interfaith; Leonard Swidler, Temple Univ. (022-38), 1114 West Berks St.-Anderson 511, Philadelphia, PA 19122-6090 Tel. (215)204-7714 Fax (215)204-4569
Email: nkrody@astro.temple.edu

The Journal of Pastoral Care & Counseling, (Q.) Nondenominational; Orlo Strunk Jr., 1068 Harbor Dr. SW, Calabash, NC 28467 Tel. (910)579-5084 Fax (910)579-5084
Email: jpcp@jpcp.org
Website: www.jpcp.org

Journal of Presbyterian History, (Q.) Presbyterian Church (USA); James H. Moorhead; Frederick J. Heuser Jr.; Managing

Editor: Tricia Manning; 425 Lombard St., Philadelphia, PA 19147 Tel. (215)627-1852 Fax (215)627-0509
Email: tmanning@history.pcusa.org
Website: www.history.pcusa.org

Journal From the Radical Reformation, (Q.) Church of God General Conference (Morrow, Ga.); Sr. Editors: Kent Ross and Anthony Buzzard, Box 100,000, Morrow, GA 30260-7000 Tel. (404)362-0052 Fax (404)362-9307
Email: kenthross@cs.com
Website: www.abc-coggc.org

Journal of Theology, (4-Y.) Church of the Lutheran Confession; Prof. Paul Schaller, Immanuel Lutheran College, 501 Grover Rd., Eau Claire, WI 54701-7199 Tel. (715)832-9936 Fax (715)836-6634
Email: schallers@usa.net
Website: www.primenet.com/~clcpub/clc/clc.html

The Joyful Noiseletter, (10-Y.) Interdenominational; Cal Samra, P.O. Box 895, Portage, MI 49081-0895 Tel. (616)324-0990 Fax (616) 324-3984
Email: joyfulnz@aol.com
Website: www._joyful_noiseletter.com

Judaism, (Q.) Jewish; Murray Baumgarten, 15 E. 84th St., New York, NY 10028 Tel. (212)879-4500 Fax (212)249-3672
Email: judaism@cats.ucsc.edu

Keeping in Touch, (2-M.) Universal Fellowship of Metropolitan Community Churches; James N. Birkitt Jr., 8704 Santa Monica Blvd, 2nd Fl., West Hollywood, CA 90069-4548 Tel. (310)360-8640 Fax (310)360-8680
Email: info@mccchurch.org
Website: www.mccchurch.org

Key Lay Notes, (2-Y.) International Council of Community Churches; Stephan Nash, 21116 Washington Pky., Frankfort, IL 60423-3112 Tel. (815)464-5690 Fax (815)464-5692
Email: iccc60423@aol.com
Website: icccusa.com

Kindred Minds, (Q.) Sovereign Grace Baptists; Larry Scouten, P.O. Box 10, Wellsburg, NY 14894 Tel. (607)734-6985

The Lantern, (bi-M.) National Baptist Convention of America, Inc.; Robert Jeffrey, 1320 Pierre Ave., Shreveport, LA 71103 Tel. (318)221-3701 Fax (318)222-7512

Leadership: A Practical Journal for Church Leaders, (Q.) Nondenominational; Marshall Shelley, 465 Gundersen Dr., Carol Stream, IL 60188 Tel. (630)260-6200 Fax (630)260-0114
Email: LJeditor@leadershipjournal.net
Website: www.Leadershipjournal.net

Learning and Living, (4-Y.) Netherlands Reformed Congregations; David Engelsma, 1000 Ball NE, Grandrapids, MI 49505 Tel. (616)458-4367 Fax (616)458-8532
Email: engelsma@plymouthchristian.put.k12.mi.us

Liahona, (varies by language) The Church of Jesus Christ of Latter-day Saints; (49 language editions) Marvin K. Gardner, 50 E. North Temple St., 24th Floor, Salt Lake City, UT 84150-3223 Tel. (801)240-2490 Fax (801)240-4225
Email: CUR-Liahona-IMag@ldschurch.org
Website: www.lds.org

Liberty, (bi-M.) Seventh-day Adventist Church; Clifford R. Goldstein, 12501 Old Columbia Pike, Silver Spring, MD 20904 Tel. (301)680-6691 Fax (301)680-6695

Lifeglow, (Q.) (Large Print) Seventh-day Adventist Church; Gaylena Gibson, P.O. Box 6097, Lincoln, NE 68506 Tel. (402)488-0981 Fax (402)488-7582
Email: editorial@christianrecord.org
Website: www.christianrecord.org

Light and Life Magazine, (bi-M.) Free Methodist Church; Douglas M. Newton, P.O. Box 535002, Indianapolis, IN 46253-5002 Tel. (317)244-3660
Email: llmeditor@fmcna.org
Website: www.freemethodistchurch.org

Liguorian, (10-Y.) The Roman Catholic Church; William J. Parker, C.SS.R., 1 Liguori Dr., Liguori, MO 63057 Tel. (636)464-2500 Fax (636)464-8449
Email: liguorianeditor@liguori.org
Website: www.liguorian.org

Listen, (Sept.-May) Seventh-day Adventist Church; Anita L. Jacobs, 55 W. Oak Ridge Dr., Hagerstown, MD 21740 Tel. (301)393-4010 Fax (301)393-3294
Email: listen@healthconnection.org
Website: www.listenmagazine.org

Living Orthodoxy, (bi-M.) The Russian Orthodox Church Outside of Russia; Fr. Gregory Williams, 1180 Orthodox Way, Liberty, TN 37095 Tel. (615)536-5239 Fax (615)536-5945
Email: info@kronstadt.org
Website: www.kronstadt.org

US PERIODICALS

The Long Island Catholic, (W.) The Roman Catholic Church; Elizabeth O'Connor, P. O. Box 9000, 200 W. Centennial Ave., Suite 201, Roosevelt, NY 11575 Tel. (516)594-1000 Fax (516)594-1092
Website: www.licatholic.org

The Lookout, (W.) Christian Churches and Churches of Christ; Shawn McMullen, 8121 Hamilton Ave., Cincinnati, OH 45231 Tel. (513)931-4050 Fax (513)931-0950
Email: lookout@standardpub.com
Website: www.lookoutmag.com

Lumicon Digital Productions, (I.) Independent, Protestant; Rev. Dr. Tom Boomershine, UMR Communications, P.O. Box 660275, Dallas, TX 75266-0275 Tel. (214) 630-6495 Fax (214)630-0079
Email: tboom@umr.org
Website: www.lumicon.org

The Lutheran, (M.) Evangelical Lutheran Church in America; Rev. David L. Miller, 8765 W. Higgins Rd., Chicago, IL 60631-4183 Tel. (773)380-2540 Fax (773)380-2751
Email: lutheran@elca.org
Website: www.thelutheran.org

The Lutheran Ambassador, (16-Y.) The Association of Free Lutheran Congregations; Craig Johnson, 575 34th Street, Astoria, OR 97103 Tel. (541)687-8643 Fax (541)683-8496
Email: cjohnson@efn.org

The Lutheran Educator, (Q.) Wisconsin Evangelical Lutheran Synod; Prof. John R. Isch, Martin Luther College, 1995 Luther Ct., New Ulm, MN 56073 Tel. (507)354-8221 Fax (507)354-8225
Email: lutheraneducator@mlc-wels.edu

Lutheran Forum, (Q.) Interdenominational Lutheran; Ronald B. Bagnall, 207 Hillcrest Ave., Trenton, NJ 08618 Tel. (856)696-0417

The Lutheran Layman, (6-Y.) The Lutheran Church–Missouri Synod; Gerald Perschbacher, 660 Mason Ridge Center Dr., St. Louis, MO 63141-8557 Tel. (314)317-4100 Fax (314)317-4295

Lutheran Leader, (Q.) Wisconsin Evangelical Lutheran Synod; Pastor Bruce Becker, 2929 N. Mayfair Rd., Milwaukee, WI 53222 Tel. (414)256-3228 Fax (414)256-3899
Email: pegr@sab.wels.net
Website: www.wels.net

Lutheran Parent, (bi-M.) Wisconsin Evangelical Lutheran Synod; Kenneth J. Kremer, 1250 N. 113th St., Milwaukee, WI 53226-3284 Tel. (414)475-6600 Fax (414) 475-7684
Website: www.nph.net

Lutheran Partners, (6-Y.) Evangelical Lutheran Church in America; Editor: -vacant-, 8765 W. Higgins Rd., Chicago, IL 60631-4195 Tel. (773)380-2875 Fax (773)380-2829
Email: lutheran_partners@ecunet.org or lpartmag@elca.org
Website: www.elca.org/lp

Lutheran Sentinel, (M.) Evangelical Lutheran Synod; Theodore Gullixson, 105 Indian Ave., Forest City, IA 50436 Tel. (641)585-1683
Email: elsentinel@wctatel.net

The Lutheran Spokesman, (M.) Church of the Lutheran Confession; Rev. Paul Fleischer, 1741 E. 22nd St., Cheyenne, WY 82001 Tel. (307)638-8006
Email: paulgf@lakes.com
Website: www.lutheranspokeman.org

Lutheran Synod Quarterly, (Q.) Evangelical Lutheran Synod; G.R. Schmeling, Bethany Lutheran Theological Semi, 6 Browns Ct., Mankato, MN 56001 Tel. (507)344-7855 Fax (507)344-7426
Email: elsynod@blc.edu
Website: www.blts.edu

The Lutheran Witness, (M.) The Lutheran Church–Missouri Synod; Rev. David Mahsman, 1333 S. Kirkwood Road, St. Louis, MO 63122-7295 Tel. (314)965-9000 Fax (314)965-1126
Email: lutheran.witness@lcms.org
Website: www.lcms.org/witness

Lutheran Woman Today, (10-Y.) Evangelical Lutheran Church in America; Nancy Goldberger, 8765 W. Higgins Rd., Chicago, IL 60631-4101 Tel. (773)380-2730 Fax (773) 380-2419
Email: lwt@elca.org
Website: www.elca.org/wo/lwthome.html

Lyceum Spotlight, (10-Y.) National Spiritualist Association of Churches; Rev. Cosie Allen, 1418 Hall St., Grand Rapids, MI 49506 Tel. (616)241-2761 Fax (616)241-4703
Email: cosie@grgig.net
Website: www.nsac.org/spotlight

Magyar Egyhaz—Magyar Church, (Q.) Hungarian Reformed Church in America; Stephen Szabo, 464 Forest Ave., Paramus, NJ 7652 Tel. (201)262-2338 Fax (845)359-5771

Mar Thoma Messenger, (Q) Mar Thoma Syrian Church of India; Abraham Mattackal, 2320 S.

Merrick Ave, Merrick, NY 11566 Tel. (516)377-3311 Fax (516)377-3322
Email: marthoma@aol.com

Maranatha, (Q.) Advent Christian Church; Dawn Rutan, P.O. Box 23152, Charlotte, NC 28227 Tel. (704)545-6161 Fax (704)573-0712
Email: acpub@adventchristian.org
Website: www.adventchristian.org

Marriage Partnership, (Q.) Nondenominational; Managing Editor: Ginger Kolbaba, 465 Gundersen Dr., Carol Stream, IL 60188 Tel. (630)260-6200 Fax (630)260-0114
Email: mp@marriagepartnership.com
Website: www.marriagepartnership.com

Maryknoll, (11-Y.) The Roman Catholic Church; Joseph R. Veneroso, Maryknoll Fathers and Brothers, P.O. Box 308, Maryknoll, NY 10545-0308 Tel. (914)941-7590 Fax (914)945-0670
Email: maryknollmag@igc.apc.org

Mature Years, (Q.) The United Methodist Church; Marvin W. Cropsey, 201 Eighth Ave. S, Nashville, TN 37202 Tel. (615)749-6292 Fax (615)749-6512
Email: matureyears@umpublishing.org

Mennonite Historical Bulletin, (Q.) Mennonite Church USA; John E. Sharp, 1700 S. Main St., Goshen, IN 46526 Tel. (574)535-7477 Fax (574)535-7756
Email: archives@goshen.edu
Website: www.mcusa-archives.org

Mennonite Quarterly Review, (Q.) Mennonite Church; John D. Roth, 1700 S. Main St., Goshen, IN 46526 Tel. (574)535-7433 Fax (574)535-7438
Email: MQR@goshen.edu
Website: www.goshen.edu/mgr

The Mennonite, (24-Y.) Mennonite Church USA; Everett Thomas, 1700 S. Main St., Goshen, IN 46526 Tel. (219)535-6051 Fax (219)535-6050
Email: editor@themennonite.org
Website: www.themennonite.org

Message, (bi-M.) Seventh-day Adventist Church; Dr. Ron C. Smith, 55 West Oak Ridge Dr., Hagerstown, MD 21740 Tel. (301)393-4099 Fax (301)393-4103
Email: pharris@rhpa.org
Website: MESSAGEMAGAZINE.org

Message of the Open Bible, (bi-M.) Open Bible Standard Churches, Inc.; Andrea Johnson, 2020 Bell Ave., Des Moines, IA 50315-1096 Tel. (515)288-6761 Fax (515)288-2510
Email: message@openbible.org
Website: www.openbible.org

Messenger, (11-Y.) Church of the Brethren; Fletcher Farrar, 1451 Dundee Ave., Elgin, IL 60120 Tel. (847)742-5100 Fax (847)742-1407
Email: wmcfadden_gb@brethren.org

The Messenger, (M.) Pentecostal Free Will Baptist Church, Inc.; George Thomas, P.O. Box 1568, Dunn, NC 28335 Tel. (910)892-4161 Fax (910)892-6876

The Messenger, (M.) The (Original) Church of God, Inc.; Wayne Jolley and William Dale, P.O. Box 3086, Chattanooga, TN 37404-0086 Tel. (800)827-9234

The Messenger, (M.) The Swedenborgian Church; Patte LeVan, P.O. Box 985, Julian, CA 92036 Tel. (760)765-2915 Fax (760)765-0218
Email: messenger@julianweb.com

Messenger of Truth, (bi-W.) Church of God in Christ (Mennonite); Gladwin Koehn, P.O. Box 230, Moundridge, KS 67107 Tel. (620)345-2532 Fax (620)345-2582
Email: gospub@characterlink.net

Methodist History, (Q.) The United Methodist Church; Charles Yrigoyen Jr., P.O. Box 127, Madison, NJ 07940 Tel. (973)408-3189 Fax (973)408-3909
Email: cyrigoyen@gcah.org
Website: www.gcah.org

Ministry, (M.) Seventh-day Adventist Church; Willmore D. Eva, 12501 Old Columbia Pike, Silver Spring, MD 20904 Tel. (301)680-6510 Fax (301)680-6502
Email: 74532.2425@compuserve.com

Mission, Adult, and Youth Children's Editions, (Q.) Seventh-day Adventist Church; Charlotte Ishkanian, 12501 Old Columbia Pike, Silver Spring, MD 20904 Tel. (301)680-6167 Fax (301)680-6155
Email: 74532.2435@compuserve.com

Mission Connection, (Q.) Wisconsin Evangelical Lutheran Synod; Rev. Gary Baumler, 2929 N. Mayfair Rd., Milwaukee, WI 53222 Tel. (414)256-3210 Fax (414)256-3862
Email: mc@sab.wels.net

Mission Herald, (bi-M.) National Baptist Convention, USA, Inc.; Dr. Bruce N. Alick, 701 S. 19th St., Philadelphia, PA 19146 Tel. (215)735-9853 Fax (215)735-1721

Missionary Church Today, (bi-M.) The Missionary Church; Rev. Thomas Murphy, P.O. Box 9127, Ft. Wayne, IN 46899 Tel. (260)747-2027 Fax (260)747-5331
Email: tom_murphy@mcusa.org
Website: www.mcusa.org

The Missionary Magazine, (9-Y.) Bertha O. Fordham, 800 Risley Ave., Pleasantville, NJ 08232-4250

The Missionary Messenger, (M.) Christian Methodist Episcopal Church; Doris F. Boyd, 213 Viking Dr. W, Cordova, TN 38018 Tel. (901)757-1103 Fax (901)751-2104
Email: doris.boyd@williams.com

The Missionary Messenger, (6-Y.) Cumberland Presbyterian Church; Carol Penn, 1978 Union Ave., Memphis, TN 38104 Tel. (901)276-4572 Fax (901)276-4578
Email: messenger@cumberland.org

Missionary Seer, (bi-M.) African Methodist Episcopal Zion Church; Rev. Kermit J. DeGraffenreidt, 475 Riverside Dr., Rm. 1935, New York, NY 10115 Tel. (212)870-2952 Fax (212)870-2808
Email: domkd5@aol.com

The Missionary Signal, (bi-M.) Churches of God, General Conference; Rachel Foreman, P.O. Box 926, Findlay, OH 45839 Tel. (419)424-1961 Fax (419)424-3433
Email: communications@cggc.org
Website: cggc.org

MissionsUSA, (bi-M.) Southern Baptist Convention; Wayne Grinstead, 4200 North Point Pkwy., Alphretta, GA 30202-4174 Tel. (770)410-6251 Fax (770)410-6006

The Moravian, (10-Y.) Moravian Church in North America (Unitas Fratrum); Dir. Of Communication: Deanna L. Hollenbach, Interprovincial Bd. Of Communication, 1021 Center St., P.O. Box 1245, Bethlehem, PA 18016 Tel. (610)867-0593 Fax (610)866-9223
Email: pubs@mcnp.org
Website: www.moravian.org

The Mother Church, (M.) Western Diocese of the Armenian Church of North America; Rev. Fr. Sipan Mekhsian, 3325 N. Glenoaks Blvd., Burbank, CA 91504 Tel. (818)558-7474 Fax (818)558-6333
Email: armenianchwd@earthlink.net
Website: www.armenianchurchwd.com

Multiply, (Q.) Presbyterian Church in America; Fred Marsh, 1700 N. Brown Road, Mission to North America, Ste. 101, Lawerenceville, GA 30044 Tel. (678)825-1200 Fax (678)825-1201
Email: mna@pcanet.org
Website: pcanet.org/mna

My Soul Sings: A Magazine of Inspirational/ Gospel Music, (Q.) Nondenominational; President and Publisher: Irene C. Franklin, P.O. Box 16181, St. Louis, MO 63105 Tel. (888)862-0179 Fax (888)862-0179
Email: Irene@postnet.com
Website: www.mysoulsings.com

NAE Washington Insight, (M.) Interdenominational; Rev. Richard Cizik, 718 Capitol Square Pl. SW, Washington, D.C. 20024 Tel. (202) 789-1011
Email: rcizik@aol.com
Website: www.nae.net

National Baptist Union Review, (M.) Nondenominational; Willie Paul, 6717 Centennial Blvd., Nashville, TN 37209-1000 Tel. (615)350-8000 Fax (615)350-9018

National Catholic Reporter, (44-Y.) The Catholic Church; Tom Roberts, P.O. Box 419281, Kansas City, MO 64141 Tel. (816)531-0538 Fax (816)968-2280
Email: editor@natcath.org
Website: www.natcath.org

The National Christian Reporter, (W.) Nondenominational; Cynthia B. Astle, UMR Communications, Inc., P.O. Box 660275, Dallas, TX 75266-0275 Tel. (214)630-6495 Fax (214)630-0079
Email: umr4news@umr.org
Website: www.umr.org

The National Spiritualist Summit, (M.) National Spiritualist Association of Churches; Rev. Sandra Pfortmiller, 3521 W. Topeka Dr., Glendale, AZ 85308-2325 Tel. (623)581-6686 Fax (623)581-5544
Email: G2s2pfort@aol.com
Website: www.nsac.org

Network, (4-Yr.) Presbyterian Church in America; Susan Fikse, 1600 N. Brown Rd., Lawrenceville, GA 30047 Tel. (678)823-0004 Fax (678)823-0027
Website: www.pca.org

New Church Life, (M.) General Church of the New Jerusalem; Rev. Donald L. Rose, Box 277, Bryn Athyn, PA 19009 Tel. (215)947-6225 ext. 209 Fax (215)938-1871
Email: DonR@BACS-GC.org
Website: www.newchurch.org

New Horizons in the Orthodox Presbyterian Church, (11-Y.) The Orthodox Presbyterian Church; Larry E. Wilson, 607 N. Easton Rd., Bldg. E, P.O. Box P, Willow Grove, PA 19090-0920 Tel. (215)830-0900 Fax (215)830-0350
Email: wilson.l@opc.org
Website: www.opc.org/

New Oxford Review, (11-Y.) The Catholic Church; Dale Vree, 1069 Kains Ave., Berkeley, CA 94706 Tel. (510)526-5374 Fax (510)526-3492
Website: www.newoxfordreview.org

New World Outlook, (bi-M.) Mission Magazine of The United Methodist Church; Christie R. House, 475 Riverside Dr., Rm. 1476, New York, NY 10115 Tel. (212)870-3765 Fax (212)870-3654
Email: NWO@gbgm-umc.org
Website: gbgm-umc.org/nwo/

The Anchor of Faith, (M.) The Anglican Orthodox Church; The Rt. Rev. Jerry L. Ogles, Anglican Orthodox Church, P.O. Box 128, Statesville, NC 28687-0128 Tel. (704)873-8365 Fax (704)873-5359
Email: aocusa@energyunited.net
Website: www.anglicanorthodoxchurch.org

Newscope, (W.) The United Methodist Church; Andrew J. Schleicher, P.O. Box 801, Nashville, TN 37202 Tel. (615)749-6320 Fax (615)749-6512
Email: aschleicher@umpublishing.org
Website: www.umph.org

NONE, Fellowship of Evangelical Church; 1420 Kerrway Ct., Fort Wayne, IN 46805 Tel. (260)423-3649 Fax (260)420-1905
Email: emchdq@aol.com
Website: www.emctoday.com

North American Baptist Conference, (6-Y) North American Baptist Conference; Marilyn Schaer, 1 S. 210 Summit Ave., Oakbrook Terr., IL 60184 Tel. (630)495-2000 Fax (630)495-3300
Email: serve@nabconference.org
Website: nabconference.org

The North American Catholic, (M.) North American Old Roman Catholic Church; Theodore J. Remalt, 4154 W. Berteau Ave, Chicago, IL 60641 Tel. (312)685-0461 Fax (312)485-0461
Email: chapelhall@aol.com

The North American Challenge, (M.) Home Missions Division of The United Pentecostal Church International; Joseph Fiorino, 8855 Dunn Rd., Hazelwood, MO 63042-2299 Tel. (314)837-7300 Fax (314)837-5632

NRB Magazine, (9-Y.) Nondenominational; Christine Pryor, National Religious Broadcasters, 9510 Technology Dr., Manassas, VA 20110 Tel. (703)330-7000 Fax (703)330-6996
Email: cpryor@nrb.org
Website: www.nrb.org

Nuestra Parroquia, (M.) The Catholic Church; Carmen Aguinaco, 205 W. Monroe St., Chicago, IL 60606-5013 Tel. (312)236-7782 Fax (312)236-8207
Email: USCath@aol.com

On Course, (bi-M.) Assemblies of God; Interim Co-Editors: Kristi Arnold and Amber Weigand-Buckley, 1445 N. Boonville Ave., Springfield, MO 65802-1894 Tel. (417)862-2781 Fax (417)862-1693
Email: oncourse@ag.org
Website: oncourse.ag.org

On the Line, (M.) Mennonite Church; Mary C. Meyer, 616 Walnut Ave., Scottdale, PA 15683 Tel. (724)887-8500 Fax (724)887-3111
Email: otl@mph.org
Website: www.mph.org/otl

Orthodox America, (8-Y.) The Russian Orthodox Church Outside of Russia; Mary Mansur, P.O. Box 383, Richfield Springs, NY 13439-0383 Tel. (315)858-1518
Email: niko@telenet.net
Website: www.roca.org/oa

The Orthodox Church, (M.) The Orthodox Church in America; Managing Editor: Very Rev. John Matusiak, One Wheaton Center #912, Wheaton, IL 60187 Tel. (516)922-0550 Fax (516)922-0954
Email: tocmed@hotmail.com

Orthodox Family, (Q.) The Russian Orthodox Church Outside of Russia; George Johnson and Deborah Johnson, P.O. Box 45, Beltsville, MD 20705 Fax (301)890-3552
Email: 1lew@cais.com
Website: www.roca.org/orthodox

Orthodox Life, (bi-M.) The Russian Orthodox Church Outside of Russia; Fr. Luke, Holy Trinity Monastery, P.O. Box 36, Jordanville, NY 13361-0036 Tel. (315)858-0940 Fax (315)858-0505
Email: 72204.1465@compuserve.com

The Orthodox Observer, (M.) Greek Orthodox Archdiocese of America; Stavros H. Papagermanos, 8 E. 79th St., New York, NY 10021 Tel. (212)570-3555 Fax (212)774-0239
Email: observer@goarch.org
Website: www.observer.goarch.org

Orthodox Russia (English translation of *Pravoslavnaya Rus*), (24-Y.) The Russian Orthodox Church Outside of Russia; Archbishop Laurus, Holy Trinity Monastery, P.O. Box 36, Jordanville, NY 13361-0036 Tel. (315)858-0940 Fax (315)858-0505
Email: orthrus@telenet.net

Orthodox Voices, (4-Y.) The Russian Orthodox Church Outside of Russia; Thomas Webb and Ellen Webb, P.O. Box 23644, Lexington, KY 40523 Tel. (606)271-3877

The Other Side, (bi-M.) Interdenominational; Dee Dee Risher and Douglas Davidson, 300

W. Apsley St., Philadelphia, PA 19144-4221 Tel. (215)849-2178 Fax (215)849-3755
Email: editors@theotherside.org
Website: www.theotherside.org

Our Daily Bread, (M.) The Swedenborgian Church; Lee Woofenden, P.O. Box 396, Bridgewater, MA 02324 Tel. (508)946-1767 Fax (508)946-1757
Email: odb@swedenborg.org
Website: www.swedenborg.org/odb/index.cfm

Our Little Friend, (W.) Seventh-day Adventist Church; Aileen Andres Sox, P.O. Box 5353, Nampa, ID 83653-5353 Tel. (208)465-2500 Fax (208)465-2531
Email: ailsox@pacificpress.com
Website: www.pacificpress.com

US PERIODICALS

Our Sunday Visitor, (W.) The Catholic Church; Gerald Korson, 200 Noll Plaza, Huntington, IN 46750 Tel. (219)356-8400
Email: oursunvis@osv.com
Website: www.osv.com

Outreach, (6-Y.) Armenian Apostolic Church of America; Iris Papazian, 138 E. 39th St., New York, NY 10016 Tel. (212)689-7810 Fax (212) 689-7168
Email: info@armenianprelacy.org
Website: www.armenianprelacy.org

Pastor Talk, (Q.) General Association of General Baptists; Fred Brittian, 100 Stinson Dr., Poplar Bluff, MO 63901 Fax (573)785-0564
Email: pmdir@generalbaptist.com

Pastoral Life, (M.) The Catholic Church; Matthew Roehrig, 9531 Akron-Canfield Rd., Canfield, OH 44406-0595 Tel. (330)533-5503
Email: plmagazine@hotmail.com
Website: www.albahouse.org

The Path of Orthodoxy (Serbian), (M.) Serbian Orthodox Church in the USA and Canada; V. Rev. Nedeljko Lunich, 300 Striker Ave., Joliet, IL 60436 Tel. (815)741-1023 Fax (815)741-1023
Email: nedlunich@.com

Paul, (4-Y.) Netherlands Reformed Congregations; J. Spans, 47 Main St. E, Norwich, ON NOJ 1PO Tel. (519)863-3306 Fax (519)863-2793

Today's Pentecostal Evangel, (W.) Assemblies of God; Hal Donaldson, Gospel Publishing House, 1445 N. Boonville Ave., Springfield, MO 65802-1894 Tel. (417)862-2781 Fax (417)862-0416
Email: pe@ag.org
Website: www.pe.ag.org

Pentecostal Evangel, Missions World Edition, (M.) Assemblies of God; Editor in Chief: Hal Donaldson, Gospel Publishing House, 1445 N. Boonville Ave., Springfield, MO 65802 Tel. (417)862-2781 Fax (417)862-0416
Email: pe@ag.org
Website: www.pe.ag.org

The Pentecostal Herald, (M.) United Pentecostal Church International; Rev. J. L. Hall, 8855 Dunn Rd., Hazelwood, MO 63042 Tel. (314)837-7300 Fax (314)837-4503

Pentecostal Leader, (bi-M.) The International Pentecostal Church of Christ; Clyde M. Hughes, P.O. Box 439, London, OH 43140 Tel. (740)852-4722 Fax (740)852-0348
Email: hqipcc@aol.com
Website: www.IPCC.CC

The Pentecostal Messenger, (M.) Pentecostal Church of God (Joplin, MO); John Mallinak, P.O. Box 850, Joplin, MO 64802 Tel. (417) 624-7050 Fax (417)624-7102
Email: johnm@pcg.org
Website: www.pcg.org

The People's Mouthpiece, (Q.) Apostolic Overcoming Holy Church of God, Inc.; Bishop Franklin McNeil, THB, DD, 1120 North 24th St., Birmingham, AL 35234 Tel. (205)324-2202
Email: bishopmcneil@hotmail.com
Website: www.ricetempleaoh.homestead.com

Perspectives, (10-Y.) Reformed Church in America; Roy M. Anker, David E. Timmer, Leanne Van Dyk (co-editors), P.O. Box 1196, Holland, MI 49422-1196 Tel. (616)957-6528 Fax (616)957-8508
Email: perspectives_@hotmail.com

Perspectives on Science and Christian Faith, (Q.) Nondenominational; Roman J. Miller, 4956 Singers Glen Rd., Harrisonburg, VA 22802 Tel. (540)432-4412 Fax (540)432-4488
Email: millerrj@rica.net
Website: www.asa3.org

The Pillar Monthly, (12-Y.) Donald J. Wolfram and Mark Tomlin, P.O. Box 9045, Zarephath, NJ 08890 Tel. (908)356-0561

The Pilot, (W.) The Catholic Church; Antonio Enrique, 2121 Commonwealth Ave., Brighton, MA 02135 Tel. (617)746-5889 Fax (617)783-2684
Email: editorial@bostonpilot.org
Website: www.rcab.org

Pockets, (11-Y.) The United Methodist Church; Janet R. Knight, P.O. Box 34004, Nashville, TN 37203 Tel. (615)340-7333 Fax (615)340-7267

Email: pockets@upperroom.org
Website: www.upperroom.org/pockets

Polka, (Q.) Polish National Catholic Church of America; Cecelia Lallo, 1127 Frieda St., Dickson City, PA 18519-1304 Tel. (570)489-4364 Fax (570)346-2188

Pravoslavnaya Rus (Russian), (24-Y.) The Russian Orthodox Church Outside of Russia; Archbishop Laurus, Holy Trinity Monastery, P.O. Box 36, Jordanville, NY 13361-0036 Tel. (315)858-0940 Fax (315)858-0505
Email: Orthrus@telenet.net

Pravoslavnaya Zhisn (Monthly Supplement to *Pravoslavnaya Rus*), (M.) The Russian Orthodox Church Outside of Russia; Archbishop Laurus, Holy Trinity Monastery, P.O. Box 36, Jordanville, NY 13361-0036 Tel. (315)858-0940 Fax (315)858-0505
Email: Orthrus@telenet.net

Prayer and Praise, (M.) Advent Christian Church; Rev. Keith D. Wheaton, P.O. Box 23152, Charlotte, NC 28227 Tel. (704)545-6161 Fax (704)573-0712
Email: Mayerpub@aol.com

Preacher's Magazine, (bi-M.) Church of the Nazarene; Randal Denney, 6401 Paseo Blvd., Kansas City, MO 64131-1213

Presbyterian News Service "The News", (26-Y.) Presbyterian Church (USA); Jerry L. VanMarter, 100 Witherspoon St., Rm. 5418, Louisville, KY 40202 Tel. (502)569-5493 Fax (502)569-8073
Email: JVanMart@ctr.pcusa.org
Website: www.pcusa.org/pcnews

Presbyterian Outlook, (43-Y.) Robert H. Bullock Jr., Box 85623, Richmond, VA 23285-5623 Tel. (804)359-8442 Fax (804)353-6369
Email: rbullock@pres-outlook.com
Website: www.pres-outlook.com

Presbyterians Today, (10-Y.) Presbyterian Church (USA); Eva Stimson, 100 Witherspoon St., Louisville, KY 40202-1396 Tel. (502)569-5637 Fax (502)569-8632
Website: www.pcusa.org/today

Primary Treasure, (W.) Seventh-day Adventist Church; Aileen Andres Sox, P.O. Box 5353, Nampa, ID 83653-5353 Tel. (208)465-2500 Fax (208)465-2531
Email: ailsox@pacificpress.com
Website: www.pacificpress.com

The Primitive Baptist, (bi-M.) Primitive Baptists; W. H. Cayce, P.O. Box 38, Thornton, AR 71766 Tel. (501)352-3694

Priority, (M.) The Missionary Church; Dr. Thomas Murphy, P.O. Box 9127, Ft. Wayne, IN 46899 Tel. (260)747-2027 Fax (260)747-5331
Email: mcdenomusa@aol.com
Website: mcusa.org

Providence Visitor, (W.) The Catholic Church; Michael Brown, 184 Broad St., Providence, RI 02903 Tel. (401)272-1010 Fax (401)421-8418
Email: 102344.3235@compuserve.com

Pulse, (M.) The Church of God (Seventh Day); Hope Hais, P.O. Box 33677, 330 W. 152nd Ave., Denver, CO 80233 Tel. (303)452-7973 Fax (303)452-0657
Email: offices@cog7.org
Website: cog7.org

Purpose, (M.) Mennonite Church Canada and USA; James E. Horsch, 616 Walnut Ave., Scottdale, PA 15683 Tel. (724)887-8500 Fax (724)887-3111
Email: horsch@mph.org
Website: www.mph.org

Pursuit, (Q.) The Evangelical Free Church of America; Carol Madison, 901 E. 78th St., Minneapolis, MN 55420-1300 Tel. (612)853-1763 Fax (612)853-8488

Qala min M'Dinkha (Voice from the East), (Q.) Apostolic Catholic Assyrian Church of the East; North A, Shlemon Hesequial, Diocesan Offices, 7201 N. Ashland, Chicago, IL 60626 Tel. (773)465-4777 Fax (773)465-0776

Quaker Life, (10-Y.) Friends United Meeting; Patricia Edwards-Konic, 101 Quaker Hill Dr., Richmond, IN 47374-1980 Tel. (765)962-7573 Fax (765)966-1293
Email: QuakerLife@fum.org
Website: www.fum.org

Quarterly Review, (Q.) The United Methodist Church; Hendrik R. Pieterse, Box 340007, Nashville, TN 37203-0007 Tel. (615)340-7334 Fax (615)340-7048
Email: hpieterse@gbhem.org
Website: www.quarterlyreview.org

Quarterly Review, A.M.E. Zion, (Q.) African Methodist Episcopal Zion Church; Rev. James D. Armstrong, P.O. Box 33247, Charlotte, NC 28233 Tel. (704)599-4630 Fax (704)688-2544
Email: jaarmstrong@amezhqtr.org

Reflections, (bi-M.) United Pentecostal Church International; Melissa Anderson, 8855 Dunn Rd., Hazelwood, MO 63042 Tel. (918)371-2659 Fax (918)371-6320

Email: manderson@tums.org
Website: www.upci.org/ladies

Reformation Today, (bi-M.) Sovereign Grace Baptists; Erroll Hulse, c-o Tom Lutz, 3743 Nichol Ave., Anderson, IN 46011-3008 Tel. (317)644-0994 Fax (317)644-0994

Reformed Herald, (M.) Reformed Church in the United States; David Dawn, 3309 E. 31st ST, Sioux Falls, SC 57103-4407

Reformed Worship, (Q.) Christian Reformed Chuch in North America; Emily R. Brink, 2850 Kalamazoo Ave. SE, Grand Rapids, MI 49560-0001 Tel. (616)224-0785 Fax (616)224-0834
Email: info@reformedworship.org
Website: www.reformedworship.org

Rejoice! (Q.) Mennonite & Mennonite Brethren Church; Philip Wiebe, 1218 Franklin St. NW, Salem, OR 97304 Tel. (503)585-4458 Fax (503)585-4458

Rejoice! (Q.) Mennonite Church; Byron Rempel-Burkholder, 600 Shaftesbury Blvd., Winnipeg, MB R3P 0M4 Tel. (204)888-6781 Fax (204)831-5675
Email: byronrb@mph.org
Website: www.mph.org/rejoice

Report From The Capital, (10-Y.) Baptist Joint Committee; Larry Chesser, 200 Maryland Ave. NE, Washington, D.C. 20002-5797 Tel. (202)544-4226 Fax (202)544-2094
Email: lchesser@bjcpa.org
Website: www.bjcpa.org

Reporter, (M.) The Lutheran Church–Missouri Synod; David Mahsman, 1333 S. Kirkwood Rd., St. Louis, MO 63122-7295 Tel. (314)965-9000 Fax (314)966-1126
Email: REPORTER@lcms.org
Website: http://reporter.lcms.org

Reporter Interactive, (D.) Independent, Protestant; Cynthia B. Astle, UMR Communications, P.O. Box 660275, Dallas, TX 75266-0275 Tel. (214)630-6495 Fax (214) 630-0079
Email: tboom@umr.org
Website: www.lumicon.org

The Rescue Herald, (3-Y.) American Rescue Workers; Rev. Col. Robert N. Coles, National Field Office, 1209 Hamilton Blvd., Hagerstown, MD 21742 Tel. (301)797-0061 Fax (301)797-1480
Email: chiefcoles@aol.com
Website: www.arwus.com

Response, (M.) The United Methodist Church; Dana Jones, 475 Riverside Dr., Room 1356, New York, NY 10115 Tel. (212)870-3755 Fax (212)870-3940

The Restitution Herald, (bi-M.) Church of God General Conference (Oregon, Ill. & Morrow, Ga.); Jeffery Fletcher, Box 100,000, Morrow, GA 30260-7000 Tel. (504)543-0290 Fax (404)362-9307

Restoration Herald, (M.) Christian Churches and Churches of Christ; H. Lee Mason, 7133 Central Parks Blvd., Mason, OH 45040 Tel. (513)229-8003 Fax (513)385-0660
Email: thecra@aol.com
Website: www.thecra.org

Restoration Quarterly, (Q.) Churches of Christ; James W. Thompson, Box 28227, Abilene, TX 79699-8227 Tel. (915)674-3781 Fax (915) 674-3776
Email: rq@bible.acu.edu
Website: www.rq.acu.edu

Review for Religious, (Q.) The Catholic Church; David L. Fleming, S.J., 3601 Lindell Blvd., St. Louis, MO 63108 Tel. (314)977-7363 Fax (314)977-7362
Email: review@slu.edu
Website: www.reviewforreligious.org

Review of Religious Research, (4-Y.) Non-denominational; Patricia Wittberg, Sociology Department, Indiana University Purdue University, Indianapolis, IN 46202 Tel. (317)274-4478 Fax (317)278-3654
Email: pwittber@iupui.edu
Website: http://rra.hartsem.edu

Rocky Mountain Christian, (M.) Churches of Christ; Ron L. Carter, P.O. Box 26620, Colorado Springs, CO 80936 Tel. (719)598-4197 Fax (719)528-1549
Email: 76102.2461@compuserve.com

Sabbath Recorder, (M.) Seventh Day Baptist General Conference, USA and Canada; Rev. Kevin J. Butler, 3120 Kennedy Rd., P.O. Box 1678, Janesville, WI 53547 Tel. (608)752-5055 Fax (608)752-7711
Email: sdbmedia@charter.net
Website: www.seventhdaybaptist.org

Sabbath School Leadership, (M.) Seventh-day Adventist Church; Faith Crumbly, Review and Herald Publishing Assoc., 55 W. Oak Ridge Dr., Hagerstown, MD 21740 Tel. (301)393-4090 Fax (301)393-4055
Email: sabbathschoolleadership@rhpa.org
Website: www.rhpa.org

Saint Anthony Messenger, (M.) The Catholic Church; Jack Wintz, O.F.M., St. Anthony Messenger Editorial, Dept., 28 W. Liberty St.,

Cincinnati, OH 45210 Tel. (513)241-5616 Fax (513)241-0399
Email: StAnthony@AmericanCatholic.org
Website: www.americancatholic.org

Saint Willibrord Journal, (Q.) Christ Catholic Church; The Rev. Monsignor Charles E. Harrison, P.O. Box 271751, Houston, TX 77277-1751 Tel. (713)515-8206 Fax (713) 622-5311
Website: www.christcatholic.org

SBC Life, (10-Y.) Southern Baptist Convention; Bill Merrell, 901 Commerce St., Nashville, TN 37203 Tel. (615)244-2355 Fax (615)782-8684
Email: jrevell@sbc.net
Website: sbc.net

The Schwenkfeldian, (3-Y.) The Schwenkfelder Church; Gerald Heebner, 105 Seminary St., Pennsburg, PA 18073 Tel. (215)679-3103 Fax (215)679-8175
Email: info@schwenfelder.com
Website: www.schwenkfelder.com

Searching Together, (Q.) Sovereign Grace Believers; Jon Zens, Box 548, St. Croix Falls, WI 54024 Tel. (651)465-6516 Fax (651)465-5101
Email: jon@searchingtogether.org
Website: www.searchingtogether.org

The Secret Place, (Q.) American Baptist Churches USA; Senior Editor: Kathleen Hayes, P.O. Box 851, Valley Forge, PA 19482-0851 Tel. (610)768-2240 Fax (610)768-2441
Email: fran.marlin@abc-usa.org

Seeds for the Parish, (bi-M.) Evangelical Lutheran Church in America; Kate Elliott, 8765 W. Higgins Rd., Chicago, IL 60631-4101 Tel. (773)380-2949 Fax (773)380-1465
Email: kelliott@elca.org
Website: www.elca.org/co/seeds/index.html

Shalom! (Q.) Brethren in Christ Church; Harriet Bicksler, 127 Holly Dr., Mechanicsburg, PA 17055-5527 Tel. (717)795-9151
Email: bickhouse@aol.com
Website: bic-church.org/shalom

Shiloh's Messenger of Wisdom, (M.) Israelite House of David; William Robertson, P.O. Box 1067, Benton Harbor, MI 49023

Signs of the Times, (M.) Seventh-day Adventist Church; Marvin Moore, P.O. Box 5353, Nampa, ID 83653-5353 Tel. (208)465-2577 Fax (208)465-2531

The Silver Lining, (M.) Apostolic Christian Churches of America; Bruce Leman, R.R. #2, Box 50, Roanoke, IL 61561-9625 Tel. (309) 923-7777 Fax (309)923-7359

Social Questions Bulletin, (bi-M.) The United Methodist Church; Rev. Kathryn J. Johnson, 212 E. Capitol St. NE, Washington, D.C. 20003 Tel. (202)546-8806 Fax (202)546-6811
Email: mfsa@olg.com
Website: www.olg.com/mfsa

Sojourners, (6-Y.) Ecumenical; Jim Wallis, 2401 15th St. NW, Washington, D.C. 20009 Tel. (202)328-8842 Fax (202)328-8757
Email: sojourners@sojo.net
Website: www.sojo.net

Solia–The Herald, (M.) The Romanian Orthodox Episcopate of America; Rev. Protodeacon David Oancea, P.O. Box 185, Grass Lake, MI 49240-0185 Tel. (517)522-3656 Fax (517) 522-5907
Email: solia@roea.org
Website: www.roea.org

Sound of Grace, (Q.) Soverign Grace Believers; 5317 Wye Creek Dr., Frederick, MD 21703-6938

The Southern Methodist, (bi-M.) Southern Methodist Church; Thomas M. Owens Sr., P.O. Box 39, Orangeburg, SC 29116-0039 Tel. (803)534-9853 Fax (803)535-3881
Email: foundry@bellsouth.net

Spirit, (Q.) Volunteers of America; Arthur Smith and Denis N. Baker, 1809 Carrollton Ave., New Orleans, LA 70118-2829 Tel. (504)897-1731

The Spiritual Sword, (Q.) Churches of Christ; Alan E. Highers, 1511 Getwell Rd., Memphis, TN 38111 Tel. (901)743-0464 Fax (901)743-2197
Email: getwellcc@aol.com
Website: www.getwellchurchofchrist.org

The Standard Bearer, (21-Y.) Protestant Reformed Churches in America; David J. Engelsma, 4949 Ivanrest Ave., Grandville, MI 49418 Tel. (616)531-1490 Fax (616)531-3033
Email: engelsma@prca.org
Website: www.rfpa.org/sb.asp

The Standard, (M.) Baptist General Conference; Bob Putman, 2002 S. Arlington Heights Rd., Arlington Heights, IL 60005 Tel. (847)228-0200 Fax (847)228-5376
Email: gmarsh@baptistgeneral.org
Website: www.bgcworld.org

Star of Zion, (bi-W.) African Methodist Episcopal Zion Church; Mr. Mike Lisby, P.O. Box 26770, Charlotte, NC 28221-6770 Tel. (704)599-4630 ext.318 Fax (704)688-2546

Email: editor@thestarofzion.org
Website: www.thestarofzion.org

Stewardship USA, (Q.) Nondenominational; Raymond Barnett Knudsen II, 4818 Quarton Rd., Bloomfield Hills, MI 48302 Tel. (248) 737-0895 Fax (248)737-0895

Story Friends, (24-Y.) Mennonite Church; Rose Mary Stutzman, 616 Walnut Ave., Scottdale, PA 15683 Tel. (574)887-8500 Fax (574)887-3111
Email: editor@themennonite.org
Website: www.themennonite.org

The Student (Braille & Cassette), (M.) Seventh-day Adventist Church; Jerry Stevens, P.O. Box 6097, Lincoln, NE 68506-0097 Tel. (402)488-0981 Fax (402)488-7582
Email: info@christianrecord.org
Website: www.ChristianRecord.org

Sunday, (Q.) Interdenominational; Timothy A. Norton, 2930 Flowers Rd. S, Atlanta, GA 30341-5532 Tel. (770)936-5376 Fax (770)936-5385
Email: tnorton@ldausa.org
Website: www.sundayonline.org

The Tablet, (W.) The Catholic Church; Ed Wilkinson, 653 Hicks St., Brooklyn, NY 11231 Tel. (718)858-3838 Fax (718)858-2112

Theology Digest, (Q.) The Catholic Church; Co-editors: Bernhard Asen, Rosemary Jermann, 3800 Lindell Blvd., St. Louis, MO 63108 Tel. (314)977-3410 Fax (314)977-3704
Email: thdigest@slu.edu

Theology Today, (Q.) Nondenominational; Patrick D. Miller, Ellen T. Charry, P.O. Box 821, Princeton, NJ 08542-0803 Tel. (609)497-7714 Fax (609)497-1826
Email: theology.today@ptsem.edu
Website: theologytoday.ptsem.edu

These Days, (Q.) Interdenominational; Vince Patton, 100 Witherspoon St., Louisville, KY 40202-1396 Tel. (502)569-5080 Fax (502) 569-5113
Website: www.ppcpub.com

The Three-Fold Vision, (M.) Apostolic Faith Mission Church of God; Alice Walker, 156 Walker Street, Munford, AL 36268 Tel. (256)358-9763 Fax
Email: alicemtwalker156.aol

The Tidings, (W.) The Catholic Church; Tod M. Tamberg, 3424 Wilshire Blvd., Los Angeles, CA 90010 Tel. (213)637-7360 Fax (213)637-6360
Website: www.the-tidings.com

Timbrel: The Publication for Mennonite Women The, (6-Y.) Mennonite Church USA and Mennonite Church Canada; Cathleen Hockman-Wert, 420 SE Richland Ave., Corvallis, OR 97333 Tel. (541)752-0444
Email: timbrel@mennonitewomenUSA.org
Website: www.mennonitewomenusa.org

Today's Christian Woman, (6-Y.) Nondenominational; Jane Johnson Struck, 465 Gundersen Dr., Carol Stream, IL 60188 Tel. (630)260-6200 Fax (630)260-0114
Email: TCWedit@christiantoday.com
Website: www.todayschristianwoman.net

Tomorrow Magazine, (Q.) American Baptist Churches in the USA; Sara E. Hopkins, 475 Riverside Dr., Room 1700, New York, NY 10115-0049 Tel. (800)986-6222 Fax (800) 986-6782

The Tover of St. Cassian, (2-Y.) Apostolic Episcopal Church; Rt. Rev. Francis C. Spataro DD, Order of Corporate Reunion/US Council/Society of St. Cassian, 80-46 234th Street, Jamaica, NY 11427 Tel. (718)740-4134
Email: vil11427@yahoo.com
Website: vgusa.InJesus.com

Truth, (Q.) Grace Gospel Fellowship; Phil Cereghino, 2125 Martindale SW, Grand Rapids, MI 49509 Tel. (616)247-1999 Fax (616)241-2542
Email: ggfinc@aol.com
Website: www.ggfusa.org

Truth Magazine, (bi-W.) Churches of Christ; Mike Willis, Box 9670, Bowling Green, KY 42102 Tel. (800)428-0121
Website: truthmagazine.com

Turnings, (bi-M.) Conservative Baptist Association of America (CBAmerica); Dr. Dennis L. Gorton, 1501 W. Mineral Ave., Suite B, Littleton, CO 80120 Tel. (720)283-3030 ext. 1830 Fax (720)283-3333
Email: CBA@CBAmerica.org
Website: www.CBAmerica.org

Ubique, (Q.) The Liberal Catholic Church–Province of the United States; Rev. James Voirol, 40 Krotona Rd., Ojai, CA 93023
Email: jvoirol@aol.com
Website: www.thelcc.org

Ukrainian Orthodox Herald, Ukrainian Orthodox Church in America (Ecumenical Patria); Rev. Dr. Anthony Ugolnik, P.O. Box 774, Allentown, PA 18105

UMR Communications, Inc., (D., W., bi-W) Independent, Protestant organization which publishes: *The United Methodist Reporter*

(W.), *The United Methodist Reporter* (bi-W.), *The National Christian Reporter* (W.), Lumicon Digital Productions (worship resources), *Reporter Interactive* (daily I.), Cynthia B. Astle, P.O. Box 660275, Dallas, TX 75266-0275 Tel. (214)630-6495 Fax (214)630-0079
Email: umr4news@umr.org
Website: www.umr.org (corporate site)
www.reporterinteractive.org (news site)
www.lumicon.org

United Church News, (10-Y.) United Church of Christ; W. Evan Golder, 700 Prospect Ave., Cleveland, OH 44115 Tel. (216)736-2218 Fax (216)736-2223
Email: goldere@ucc.org
Website: www.ucc.org

The United Methodist Reporter, (W. and bi-W.) Independent, Protestant; Cynthia B. Astle, UMR Communications, P.O. Box 660275, Dallas, TX 75266-0275 Tel. (214)630-6495 Fax (214)630-0079
Email: umr4news@umr.org
Website: www.umr.org

The Upper Room, (6-Y.) The United Methodist Church; Steven D. Bryant, P. O. Box 340004, Nashville, TN 37203-0004 Tel. (877)899-2780 Fax (615)340-7289
Email: sbryant@upperroom.org
Website: www.upperroom.org

U.S. Catholic, (M.) The Catholic Church; Rev. Mark J. Brummel, 205 W. Monroe St., Chicago, IL 60606 Tel. (312)236-7782 Fax (312)236-8207
Email: editors@uscatholic.org
Website: www.uscatholic.org

Vibrant Life, (bi-M.) Seventh-day Adventist Church; Larry Becker, 55 W. Oak Ridge Dr., Hagerstown, MD 21740 Tel. (301)393-4019 Fax (301)393-4055
Email: vibrantlife@rhpa.org
Website: www.vibrantlife.com

Victory (Youth Sunday School/Bible Study Curriculum), (Q.) Church of God of Prophecy; David Bryan, P.O. Box 2910, Cleveland, TN 37320-2910 Tel. (423)559-5321 Fax (423) 559-5461
Email: david@cogop.org
Website: www.cogop.org

The Vindicator, (M.) Old German Baptist Brethren Church; Steven L. Bayer, 6952 N. Montgomery Co. Line Rd., Englewood, OH 45322-9748 Tel. (937)884-7531 Fax (937) 884-7531

Visitor, (6-Y.) Brethren in Christ Church; Ronald C. Ross, P.O. Box A, Grantham, PA 17027 Tel. (717)697-6234 Fax (717)697-7714
Email: rross@messiah.edu
Website: www.bic-church.org

The Visitor, (bi-M.) Brethren in Christ Church; Ron Ross, P.O.Box A, Grantham, PA 17027 Tel. (717)697-2634
Email: rross@messiah.edu
Website: bic-church.org/visitor

Vista, (bi-M.) Christian Church of North America; General Council, Eric Towse, 1294 Rutledge Rd., Transfer, PA 16154 Tel. (412) 962-3501 Fax (412)962-1766
Email: ccna@nauticom.net
Website: www.ccna.org

Voice! (Q.) General Association of General Baptists; Rev. Ron Byrd, 100 Stinson Dr., Poplar Bluff, MO 63901 Tel. (573)785-7746 Fax (573)785-0564
Email: gbnm@pbmo.net
Website: www.generalbaptist.com

Voice of Mission, (Q.) African Methodist Episcopal Church; George Flowers, 1587 Savannah Highway, Ste. A, Charleston, SC 29407 Tel. (843) 852-2645 Fax (843)852-2648
Email: gwmame@bellsouth.net
Website: amegobalmissions.com

The Voice, (Q.) The Bible Church of Christ, Inc.; Montrose Bushrod, 1358 Morris Ave., Bronx, NY 10456 Tel. (718)588-2284 Fax (718)992-5597
Website: www.thebiblechurchofchrist.org

The Voice, (6-Y.) IFCA International, Inc.; Les Lofquist, P.O. Box 810, Grandville, MI 49468-0810 Tel. (616)531-1840 Fax (616) 531-1814
Email: Voice@ifca.org

The War Cry, (bi-W.) The Salvation Army; Marlene Chase, 615 Slaters Ln., Alexandria, VA 22313 Tel. (703)684-5500 Fax (703)684-5539
Email: warcry@usn.salvationarmy.org
Website: publications.salvationarmyusa.org

The Watch Tower Society, (2-M.) Jehovah's Witnesses; Watch Tower Society, 25 Columbia Heights, NY 11201-2483
Website: watchtower.org

Weavings: A Journal of the Christian Spiritual Life, (6-Y.) The United Methodist Church; John S. Mogabgab, 1908 Grand Avenue, Nashville, TN 37212 Tel. (615)340-7254 Fax (615)340-7267
Email: weavings@upperroom.org
Website: www.upperroom.org

The Wesleyan Advocate, (11-Y.) The Wesleyan Church; Norman G. Wilson, P.O. Box 50434,

Indianapolis, IN 46250-0434 Tel. (317)570-5204 Fax (317)570-5260
Email: wilsonn@wesleyan.org
Website: www.wesleyan.org

Wesleyan World, (Q.) The Wesleyan Church; Wayne Derr, P.O. Box 50434, Indianapolis, IN 46250 Tel. (317)570-5172 Fax (317)570-5256
Email: wwm@wesleyan.org
Website: www.wesleyan.org

The White Wing Messenger, (bi-W.) Church of God of Prophecy; Virginia E. Chatham, P.O. Box 3000, Cleveland, TN 37320-3000 Tel. (423)559-5413 Fax (423)559-5444
Email: jenny@wingnet.net
Website: www.cogop.org

Whole Truth, (M.) The Church of God in Christ; Larry Britton, P.O. Box 2017, Memphis, TN 38101 Tel. (901)578-3841 Fax (901)57-6807

Window on the World, (4-Y.) The Evangelical Congregational Church; Patricia Strain, 100 W. Park Ave, Myerstown, PA 17067 Tel. (717)-866-7581 Fax (717)866-7383
Email: ecgmc@eccenter.com
Website: www.eccenter.com

Wineskins, (bi-M.) Churches of Christ; Mike Cope and Rubel Shelly, Box 41028, Nashville, TN 37024-1028 Tel. (615)373-5004 Fax (615) 373-5006
Email: wineskinsmagazine@msn.com
Website: www.wineskins.org

The Winner, (9-Y.) Nondenominational; Anita Jacobs, The Health Connection, P.O. Box 859, Hagerstown, MD 21741 Tel. (301)393-4010 Fax (301)393-3294
Email: winner@healthconnection.org
Website: www.winnermagazine.org

Wisconsin Lutheran Quarterly, (Q.) Wisconsin Evangelical Lutheran Synod; John F. Brug, 11831 N. Seminary Dr., Mequon, WI 53092 Tel. (262)242-8139 Fax (262)242-8110
Email: brugj@wls.wels.net
Website: www.wls.wels.net

With: The Magazine for Radical Christian Youth, (6-Y.) Mennonite Church USA; Carol Duerksen, P.O. Box 347, 722 Main Street, Newton, KS 67114 Tel. (316)283-5100 Fax (316)283-0454
Email: carold@mennoniteusa.org
Website: withonline.org

The Witness, (10-Y.) Nondenominational; Julie A. Wortman, 7000 Michigan Ave., Detroit, MI 48210 Tel. (313)841-1967 Fax (313)841-1956
Email: office@thewitness.org
Website: www.thewitness.org

Woman to Woman, (M.) General Association of General Baptists; Stephana Deckard, 100 Stinson Dr., Poplar Bluff, MO 63901 Tel. (573)785-7746 Fax (573)785-0564
Email: wmdir@generalbaptist.com

The Woman's Pulpit, (Q.) Nondenominational; LaVonne Althouse, 5227 Castor Ave., Philadelphia, PA 19124-1742 Tel. (215)743-4528

Woman's Touch, (bi-M.) Assemblies of God; Arlene Allen, 1445 N. Boonville Ave., Springfield, MO 65802-1894 Tel. (417)862-2781 Fax (417)862-0503
Email: womanstouch@ag.org
Website: www.womanstouch.ag.org

Women's Missionary Magazine, (9-Y.) African Methodist Episcopal Church; Dr. Bettye J. Allen, 17129 Bennett Dr, South Holland, IL 60473 Tel. (708)339-5997 Fax (708)339-5987
Email: bettye1901@aol.com

The Word, (10-Y.) The Antiochian Orthodox Christian Archdiocese of North America; V. Rev. John Abdalah, 1777 Quigg Dr., Pittsburgh, PA 15241-2071 Tel. (412)681-2988 Fax (412)831-5554
Email: frjpa@aol.com
Website: www.antiochian.org

Word and Work, (11-Y.) Churches of Christ; Alex V. Wilson, 2518 Portland Ave., Louisville, KY 40212 Tel. (502)897-2831

The Worker, (Q.) Progressive National Baptist Convention, Inc.; Mattie A Robinson, 601 50th St. NE, Washington, D.C. 20019 Tel. (202) 398-5343 Fax (202)398-4998
Email: info@pnbc.org
Website: www.pnbc.org

World Harvest Today, (Q.) United Pentecostal Church International; J. S. Leaman, 8855 Dunn Rd., Hazelwood, MO 63042 Tel. (314)837-7300 Fax (314)837-2387

World Parish: International Organ of the World Methodist Council, (s-M.) Interdenominational Methodist (Christian World Communion of Methodist and WMC-Related Churches); George Freeman, P.O. Box 518, Lake Junaluska, NC 28745 Tel. (828)456-9432 Fax (828)456-9433
Email: georgefreeman@mindspring.com/george freeman@charter.net
Website: www.worldmethodistcouncil.org

World Vision, (Q.) Nondenominational; Shelly R. Ngo, P.O. Box 9716, Federal Way, WA 98063-9716 Tel. (253)815-1000 Fax (253) 815-3340

Email: wvmagazine@worldvision.org
Website: www.worldvision.org

World Vision Today, (Q.) Nondenominational; Terry Madison, P.O. Box 9716, Federal Way, WA 98063-9716 Tel. (253)815-1000 Fax (253)815-3445
Email: wvtoday@worldvision.org

Worldorama, (M.) Pentecostal Holiness Church, International; Donald Duncan, P.O. Box 12609, Oklahoma City, OK 73157 Tel. (405)787-7110 Fax (405)787-7729
Email: donald@iphc.org

Worship, (6-Y.) The Catholic Church; R. Kevin Seasoltz, St. John's Abbey, Collegeville, MN 56321 Tel. (320)363-3883 Fax (320)363-3145
Email: kseasoltz@csbsju.edu
Website: www.sja.org/worship

Worship Arts, (6-Y.) Nondenominational; David A Wiltse, P.O. Box 6247, Grand Rapids, MI 49516-6247 Tel. (616)459-4503 Fax (616) 459-1051
Email: graphics@iserv.net

Yes! (Q.) Brethren in Christ Church; Ron Ross, P.O.Box A, Grantham, PA 17027 Tel. (717) 697-2634
Email: rross@messiah.edu
Website: bic-church.org/Yes

Young & Alive, (Q.) (Braille and Large Print) Seventh-day Adventist Church; Gaylena Gibson, P.O. Box 6097, Lincoln, NE 68506 Tel. (402)488-0981 Fax (402)488-7582
Email: editorial@christianrecord.org
Website: www.christianrecord.org

Youth Ministry Accent, (Q.) Seventh-day Adventist Church; David S.F. Wong, 12501 Old Columbia Pike, Silver Spring, MD 20904-6600 Tel. (301)680-6180 Fax (301)680-6155
Email: 74532.1426@compuserve.com

YPD Newsletter, (3-M.) African Methodist Episcopal Church; Adrienne A. Morris and Andrea Smith, 327 Washington Ave., Wyoming, OH 45215 Tel. (513)821-1481 Fax (513)821-3073
Email: amconndri@cs.com
Website: ameypd.org

Zion's Advocate, (M.) Church of Christ; Gordon McCann, P.O. Box 472, Independence, MO 64051-0472 Tel. (816)796-6255

12. Religious Periodicals in Canada

The religious periodicals below constitute a basic core of important journals and periodicals circulated in Canada. The list does not include all publications prepared by religious bodies, and not all the publications listed here are necessarily the official publication of a particular church. Each entry gives: the title of the periodical, frequency of publication, religious affiliation, editor's name, address, telephone and fax number, and email and website addresses when available. The frequency of publication, which appears in parenthesis after the name of the publication, is represented by a "W." for weekly, "M." for monthly, "Q." for quarterly, "I." for internet, and "Y." for yearly.

Again, (Q.) The Antiochian Orthodox Christian Archdiocese of North America; R. Thomas Zell, Conciliar Press, P.O. Box 76, Ben Lomond, CA 95005-0076 Tel. (800)967-7377 Fax (831)336-8882
Email: tzell@conciliarpress.com
Website: www.conciliarpress.com

Anglican Journal, (10-Y.) The Anglican Church of Canada; Leanne Larmondin, 600 Jarvis St., Toronto, ON M4Y 2J6 Tel. (416)924-9199 ext. 306 Fax (416)921-4452
Email: editor@national.anglican.ca
Website: www.anglicanjournal.com

The Anglican, (10-Y.) The Anglican Church of Canada; Stuart Mann, 135 Adelaide St. E, Toronto, ON M5C 1L8 Tel. (416)363-6021 Fax (416)363-7678
Email: smann@toronto.anglican.ca
Website: www.toronto.anglican.ca

Armenian Evangelical Church Newsletter, (Q.) Armenian Evangelical Church; Yessayi Sarmazian, 2600 14th Avenue, Markham, ON L3R 3X1 Tel. (905)305-8144 Fax (905)305-8125
Email: aectoronto@yahoo.com

Aujourd'hui Credo, (10-Y.) The United Church of Canada; David Fines, 1332 Victoria, Longueuil, QC J4V 1L8 Tel. (450)446-7733 Fax (450)466-2664
Email: davidfines@egliseunce.org
Website: www.united-church/credo

The Banner, (bi-W.) Christian Reformed Church in North America; John A. Suk, 2850 Kalamazoo Ave. SE, Grand Rapids, MI 49560 Tel. (616)224-0732 Fax (616)224-0834
Email: editorial@thebanner.org
Website: www.thebanner.org

The Baptist Horizon, (M.) Canadian Convention of Southern Baptists; Nancy McGough, P.O. Box 300, Cochrane, AB T0L 0W0 Tel. (403)932-5688 Fax (403)932-4937
Email: office@ccsb.ca

B.C. Fellowship Baptist, (Q.) The Fellowship of Evangelical Baptist Churches in BC and Yukon; Bruce Christensen, #201-26620-56th Ave., Langley, BC V4W 3X5 Tel. (604)607-1192 Fax (604)607-1193
Email: fellowship@shaw.ca

Blackboard Bulletin, (10-Y.) Old Order Amish Church; Old Order Amish Church, Rt. 4, Aylmer, ON N5H 2R3

Die Botschaft, (W.) Old Order Amish Church; James Weaver, Brookshire Publishing, Inc., 200 Hazel St., Lancaster, PA 17603 Tel. (717)392-1321 Fax (717)392-2078

The Budget, (W.) Old Order Amish Church; Fannie Erb-Miller, P.O. Box 249, Sugarcreek, OH 44681 Tel. (330)852-4634 Fax (330)852-4421
Email: budgetnews@aol.com

Cahiers de Spiritualite Ignatienne, (Q.) The Roman Catholic Church in Canada; Rene Champagne, Gaetane Guillemette, 2370 Rue Nicolas-Pinel, Ste-Foy, QC G1V 4L6 Tel. (418)653-6353 Fax (418)653-1208
Email: cahiersi@centremanrese.org
Website: www.centremanrese.org

Canada Lutheran, (8-Y.) Evangelical Lutheran Church in Canada; Editor: -vacant-, 302-393 Portage Avenue, Winnipeg, MB R3B 3H6 Tel. (204)984-9170 Fax (204)984-9185
mail: canaluth@elcic.ca
Website: www.elcic.ca/clweb

Canada Update, (Q.) The Church of God of Prophecy in Canada; Adrian L. Varlack, P. O. Box 457, Brampton, ON L6V 2L4 Tel. (905) 625-1278 Fax (905)843-3990

Canadian Adventist Messenger, (12-Y.) Seventh-day Adventist Church in Canada; Carolyn Willis, 1148 King St. E, Oshawa, ON L1H 1H8 Tel. (905)433-0011 Fax (905)433-0982
Email: cwillis@sdacc.org
Website: www.sdacc.org

The Canadian Baptist, (10-Y.) Baptist Convention of Ontario and Quebec; Larry Matthews, 195 The West Mall, Ste.414,

Etobicoke, ON M9C 5K1 Tel. (416)622-8600 Fax (416)622-0780
Email: thecb@baptist.ca

Canadian Disciple, (4-Y.) Christian Church (Disciples of Christ) in Canada; Stanley Litke, 255 Midvalley Dr. SE, Calgary, AB T2X 1K8 Tel. (403)256-3280 Fax (403)254-6178
Email: litkes@cia.com

The Canadian Friend, (bi-M.) Canadian Yearly Meeting of the Religious Society of Friends; Anne Marie Zilliacus, 218 Third Ave., Ottawa, ON K1S 2K3 Tel. (613)567-8628 Fax (613) 567-1078
Email: zilli@cyberus.ca

The Canadian Lutheran, (9-Y.) Lutheran Church–Canada; Ian Adnams, 3074 Portage Ave., Winnipeg, MB R3K 0Y2 Tel. (204)895-3433 ext.24 Fax (204)897-4319
Email: communications@lutheranchurch.ca
Website: www.lutheranchurch.ca

Canadian Mennonite, (bi-W.) Mennonite Church Canada; Ron Rempel, Suite C5, 490 Dutton Dr., Waterloo, ON N2L 6H7 Tel. (519)884-3810 Fax (519)884-3331
Email: editor@canadianmennonite.org
Website: www.canadianmennonite.org

Canadian Orthodox Messenger, (Q.) Orthodox Church in America (Canada Section); Nun Sophia (Zion), P.O. Box 179, Spencerville, ON K0E 1X0 Tel. (613)925-0645 Fax (613) 925-1521
Email: sophia@ripnet.com

The Catalyst, (6-Y.) Nondenominational; Murray MacAdam, Citizens for Public Justice, 229 College St. #311, Toronto, ON M5T 1R4 Tel. (416)979-2443 Fax (416)979-2458
Email: cpj@cpj.ca
Website: www.cpj.ca

The Catholic Register, (W.) The Roman Catholic Church in Canada; Joseph Sinasac, 1155 Yonge St., Ste. 401, Toronto, ON M4Y 1W2 Tel. (416)934-3410 Fax (416)934-3409
Email: editor@catholicregister.org
Website: www.catholicregister.org

The Catholic Times (Montreal), (10-Y.) The Roman Catholic Church in Canada; Eric Durocher, 2005 St. Marc St., Montreal, QC H3H 2G8 Tel. (514)937-2301 Fax (514)937-3051

Channels, (3-Y) Presbyterian Church in Canada; Calvin Brown, Managing Editor: Dal Shindell, Renewal Fellowship, 3819 Bloor St W, Etobicoke, ON M9B 1K7 Tel. (416)233-6581 Fax (416)233-1743
Email: cbbrown@rogers.com
Website: www.presbycan.ca/rfpc

Chinese Herald, (bi-M.) Canadian Conference of Mennonite Brethren Churches; Joseph Kwan, 8143 Burnlake Dr., Burnaby, BC V5A 3R6 Tel. (604)421-4100 Fax (604)421-4100
Email: chineseherald@mbconf.ca

The Christian Contender, (M.) Mennonite Church (Canada); James Boll, Box 3, Hwy 172, Crockett, KY 41413 Tel. (606)522-4348 Fax (606)522-4896

Christian Courier, (bi-W.) Nondenominational; Harry der Nederlanden, 1 Hiscott, St. Catharines, ON L2R 1C7 Tel. (905)682-8311 Fax (905)682-8313
Email: cceditor@aol.com

Church of God Beacon, (Q.) Church of God (Cleveland, Tenn.); Canute Blake, P.O. Box 2036, Brampton Commercial Service Center, Brampton, ON L6T 3T0 Tel. (905)793-2213 Fax (905)793-2213

Clarion- The Canadian Reformed Magazine, (bi-W.) Canadian and American Reformed Churches; J. Visscher, One Beghin Ave., Winnipeg, MB R2J 3X5 Tel. (204)663-9000 Fax (204)663-9202
Email: clarion@premier.mb.ca
Website: premier.mb.ca/clarion.html

CLBI–Cross Roads, (6 - Y.) Lutheran; Dean J. Rostand, 4837-52A St., Camrose, AB T4V 1W5 Tel. (780)672-4454 Fax (780)672-4455
Email: communications@clbi.edu
Website: www.clbi.edu

College News & Updates, (6-Y.) Church of God (Anderson, Ind.); John Alan Howard, 4707 56th St., Camrose, AB T4V 2C4 Tel. (780) 672-0171 Fax (780)672-2465
Email: garndercollege@gardnercollege.org
Website: www.gardnercollege.org

The Communicator, (3-Y.) The Roman Catholic Church in Canada; P. Giroux, P.O. Box 142, Tantallon, NS B0J 3J0 Tel. (902)826-7236 Fax (902)826-7236

Connexions, (4-Y.) Interdenominational; Ulli Diemer, 489 College St., Suite 305, Toronto, ON M6G 1A5 Tel. (416)964-1511

The Covenant Messenger, (5-Y.) The Evangelical Covenant Church of Canada; Ingrid Wildman, P.O. Box 34025 RPO Fort Richmond, Winnipeg, MB R3T 5T5 Tel. (204) 269-3437 Fax (204)269-3584

Email: messengr@escape.ca
Website: www.canadacovenantchurch.org

Crux, (Q.) Nondenominational; Donald Lewis, Regent College, 5800 University Blvd., Vancouver, BC V6T 2E4 Tel. (604)224-3245 Fax (604)224-3097

Diakonia–A Magazine of Office-Bearers, (4-Y.) Canadian and American Reformed Churches; J. Visscher, Brookside Publishing, 3911 Mt. Lehman Rd., Abbotsford, BC V4X 2M9 Tel. (604)856-4127 Fax (604)856-6724

The Diary, (M.) Old Order Amish Church; Don Carpenter, P.O. Box 98, Gordonville, PA 17529 Tel. (717)529-3938 Fax (717)529-3292

Ecumenism-Oecumenisme, (Q.) Interdenominational; 2065 Sherbrooke St. W, Montreal, QC H3H 1G6 Tel. (514)937-9176 Fax (514)937-4986
Email: ccocce@total.net
Website: www.total.net/~ccocce

The Edge (Christian Youth Magazine), (10-Y.) The Salvation Army in Canada; John McAlister, 2 Overlea Blvd., Toronto, ON M4H 1P4 Tel. (416)422-6116 Fax (416)422-6120
Email: edge@can.salvationarmy.org
Website: www.salvationarmy.ca

Eesti Kirik, (Q.) The Estonian Evangelical Lutheran Church Abroad; Rev. U. Petersoo, 383 Jarvis St., Toronto, ON M5B 2C7 Tel. (416)925-5465 Fax (416)925-5688

EMMC Recorder, (M.) Evangelical Mennonite Mission Conference; Lil Goertzen, Box 52059 Niakwa P.O., Winnipeg, MB R2M 5P9 Tel. (204)253-7929 Fax (204)256-7384
Email: info@emmc.ca

En Avant! (12-Y.) The Salvation Army in Canada; Marie-Michèle Roy, 2050 Rue Stanley, bureau 400, Montreal, QB H3A 3G3 Tel. (514)288-2848 Fax (514)288-4657
Email: enavant@can.salvationarmy.org

The Ensign, (M.) The Church of Jesus Christ of Latter-day Saints; Managing Editor: Brian K. Kelly, 50 E. North Temple St., 24th Floor, Salt Lake City, UT 84150 Tel. (801)240-2950 Fax (801)240-5732
Email: kellybk@ldschurch.org

Esprit, (Q.) Evangelical Lutheran Church in Canada (Evangelical Lutheran Women); Gayle Johannesson, 302-393 Portage Avenue, Winnipeg, MB R3B 3H6 Tel. (204)984-9160 Fax (204)984-9162
Email: esprit@elcic.ca
Website: www.elw.ca

Evangel–The Good News of Jesus Christ, (4-Y.) Canadian and American Reformed Churches; D. Moes, 21804 52nd Ave., Langley, BC V2Y 1L3 Tel. (604)576-2124 Fax (604)576-2101
Email: canrc@uniserve.com or jvisscher@telus.ca

The Evangelical Baptist, (5-Y.) The Fellowship of Evangelical Baptist Churches in Canada; Terry D. Cuthbert, 679 Southgate Dr., Guelph, ON N1G 4S2 Tel. (519)821-4830 Fax (519) 821-9829
Email: president@fellowship.ca
Website: www.fellowship.ca

Faith and Fellowship, (M.) Church of the Lutheran Brethren; Brent Juliot, P.O. Box 655, Fergus Falls, MN 56538 Tel. (218)736-7357 Fax (218)736-2200
Email: ffpress@clba.org
Website: www.faithandfellowship.org

Faith & Friends, (M.) The Salvation Army in Canada; Geoff Moulton, 2 Overlea Blvd., Toronto, ON M4H 1P4 Tel. (416)422-6110 Fax (416)422-6120
Website: faithandfriends.sallynet.org

Faith Today, (bi-M.) Evangelical Fellowship of Canada (a cooperative organization); Gail Reid, M.I.P. Box 3745, Markham, ON L3R 0Y4 Tel. (905)479-5885 Fax (905)479-4742
Email: ft@efc-canada.com
Website: www.faithtoday.ca

Family Life, (11-Y.) Old Order Amish Church; Joseph Stoll and David Luthy, Old Order Amish Church, Rt. 4, Aylmer, ON N5H 2R3

Family Life Network Newsline, (3-Y) Canadian Conference of Mennonite Brethren Churches; Dorothy Siebert, 225 Riverton Ave., Winnipeg, MB R2L 0N1 Tel. (204)667-9576 Fax (204)669-6079
Email: info@fln.ca
Website: www.fln.ca

Fellowship Magazine, (4-Y.) The United Church of Canada; Rev. Diane Walker
Bob McC, Box 237, Barrie, ON L4M 4T2 Tel. (705)737-0114 or (800)678-2607 Fax (705) 737-1086
Email: felmag@csolve.net
Website: www.fellowshipmagazine.org

Foi & Vie, (12-Y.) The Salvation Army in Canada; Marie-Michele Roy, 2050 rue Stanley, Bureau 400, Montreal, QC H3A 3G3 Tel. (514)288-2848 ext. 236 Fax (514)288-4657
Email: foivie@can.salvationarmy.org

The Free Methodist Herald, (bi-M.) Free Methodist Church in Canada; Donna Elford, 3719-44 St. SW, Calgary, AB T3E 3S1 Tel. (403)246-6838 Fax (403)686-3787
Email: fmccan@inforamp.net

Glad Tidings, (6-Y.) Presbyterian Church in Canada; L. June Stevenson, Women's Missionary Society, 50 Wynford Dr., Toronto, ON M3C 1J7 Tel. (800)619-7301 or (416)441-1111 Fax (416)441-2825
Email: jstevenson@presbyterian.ca
Website: www.presbyterian.ca

Global Village Voice, (Q.) The Roman Catholic Church in Canada; Jack J. Panozzo, 420-10 Saint Mary St., Toronto, ON M4Y 1P9 Tel. (416)922-1592 Fax (416)922-0957

Good Tidings, (10-Y.) The Pentecostal Assemblies of Newfoundland and Labrador; H. Paul Foster, 57 Thorburn Rd., P.O. Box 8895, Sta. A, St. John's, NL A1B 3T2 Tel. (709)753-6314 Fax (709)753-4945
Email: paon@paon.nf.ca
Website: www.paon.nf.ca

The Gospel Contact, (4-Y.) Church of God (Anderson, Ind.); Editorial Committee, 4717 56th St., Camrose, AB T4V 2C4 Tel. (780)672-0772 Fax (780)672-6888
Email: wcdncog@cable-lynx.net
Website: www.chog.ca

Gospel Herald, (M.) Churches of Christ in Canada; Wayne Turner and Max E. Craddock, 4904 King St., Beamsville, ON L0R 1B6 Tel. (905)563-7503 Fax (905)563-7503
Email: editorial@gospelherald.org
Website: www.gospelherald.org

The Gospel Standard, (M.) Nondenominational; Perry F. Rockwood, Box 1660, Halifax, NS B3J 3A1 Tel. (902)423-5540

Gospel Tidings, (M.) Independent Holiness Church; R. E. Votary, 1564 John Quinn Rd., Greely, ON K4P 1J9 Tel. (613)821-2237 Fax (613)821-4663
Email: rvotary@hotmail.com
Website: www.holiness.ca

The Grape Vine, (12-Y.) Reformed Episcopal Church in Canada; Richard Montgomery, 626 Blanshard St., Victoria, BC V8W 3G6 Tel. (250)383-8915 Fax (250)383-8916
Email: cool@islandnet.com
Website: www.churchofourlord.org

Hallelujah! (bi-M.) The Bible Holiness Movement; Wesley H. Wakefield, Box 223, Postal Stn. A, Vancouver, BC V6C 2M3 Tel. (250)492-3376

Handmaiden, (Q.) The Antiochian Orthodox Christian Archdiocese of North America; Virginia Nieuwsma and Carla Zell, Conciliar Press, P.O. Box 76, Ben Lomond, CA 95005-0076 Tel. (800)967-7377 Fax (831)336-8882
Email: czell@conciliarpress.com
Website: conciliarpress.com

Herold der Wahrheit, (M.) Old Order Amish Church; Cephas Kauffman, 1827 110th St., Kalona, IA 52247

Horizons, (bi-M.) The Salvation Army in Canada; 2 Overlea Blvd., Toronto, ON M4H 1P4 Tel. (416)425-6118 Fax (416)422-6120

IdeaBank, (Q.) Canadian Conference of Mennonite Brethren Churches; Sharon Johnson, Christian Ed. Office, 3-169 Riverton Ave., Winnipeg, MB R2L 2E5 Tel. (204)669-6575 Fax (204)654-1865
Email: cem@mbconf.ca
Website: www.mbconf.ca

Insight/Insound/In Touch, (6-Y. [Insight], 6-Y. [In Sound], 4-Y. [In Touch]) Interdenominational; Insight (large print newspaper), In Sound (audio magazine), In Touch (braille newspaper), Rebekah Chevalier, Graham Down, John Milton Society for the Blind in Canada, 40 St. Clair Ave. E, Ste. 202, Toronto, ON M4T 1M9 Tel. (416)960-3953 Fax (416)960-3570
Email: admin@jmsblind.ca
Website: www.jmsblind.ca

Intercom, (Q.) The Fellowship of Evangelical Baptist Churches in Canada; Terry D. Cuthbert, 679 Southgate Dr., Guelph, ON N1G 4S2 Tel. (519)821-4830 Fax (519)821-9829
Email: president@fellowship.ca
Website: www.fellowship.ca

ISKRA, (20-Y.) Union of Spiritual Communities of Christ (Orthodox Doukhobors in Canada); Dmitri E. (Jim) Popoff, Box 760, Grand Forks, BC V0H 1H0 Tel. (604)442-8252 Fax (604) 442-3433
Email: iskra@sunshinecable.com

Istocnik, (4-Y.) Serbian Orthodox Church in the USA and Canada; Diocese of Canada, Very Rev. VasilijeTomic, 7470 McNiven Rd., RR 3, Campbellville, ON L0P 1B0 Tel. (905)878-0043 Fax (905)878-1909
Email: vladika@istocnik.com
Website: www.istocnik.com

Le Lien, (11-Y.) Canadian Conference of Mennonite Brethren Churches; Annie Brosseau, 1775 Edouard-Laurin, St. Laurent, QC H4L 2B9 Tel. (514)331-0878 Fax (514) 331-0879

Email: LeLien@total.net
Website: www.mbconf.ca/comm/lelien

Liturgie, Foi et Culture (Bulletin Natl. de Liturgie), (4-Y.) The Roman Catholic Church in Canada; Service des Editions de la CECC, Office national de liturgie, 3530 rue Adam, Montreal, QC H1W 1Y8 Tel. (514)522-4930 Fax (514)522-1557
Email: onl.cecc@ccb.ca
Website: www.cccb.ca

Mandate, (4-Y.) The United Church of Canada; Rebekah Chevalier, 3250 Bloor St. W, Ste. 300, Etobicoke, ON M8X 2Y4 Tel. (416)231-5931 Fax (416)231-3103
Email: rchevali@united-church.ca
Website: www.united-church.ca/mandate

The Mantle, (M.) Independent Assemblies of God International (Canada); Philip Rassmussen, P.O. Box 2130, Laguna Hills, CA 92654-9901 Tel. (514)522-4930 Fax (514) 522-1557

Marketplace, A Magazine for Christians in Business, (bi-M.) Interdenominational Mennonite; Wally Kroeker, 302-280 Smith St., Winnipeg, MB R3C 1K2 Tel. (204)956-6430 Fax (204)942-4001
Website: www.meda.org

Mennonite Brethren Herald, (3-W.) Canadian Conference of Mennonite Brethren Churches; Jim Coggins, 3-169 Riverton Ave., Winnipeg, MB R2L 2E5 Tel. (204)654-5760 Fax (204) 654-1865
Email: mbherald@mbconf.ca
Website: www.mbherald.com

Mennonite Historian, (Q.) Canadian Conference of Mennonite Brethren Churches; Mennonite Church Canada; Abe Dueck and Alf Redekopp, Ctr. for Menn. Brethren Studies, 169 Riverton Ave., Winnipeg, MB R2L 2E5 Tel. (204)669-6575 Fax (204)654-1865
Email: adueck@mbconf.ca
Website: mbconf.ca/mbstudies/

Die Mennonitische Post, (bi-M.) Mennonite Central Committee Canada; Kennert Giesbrecht, Box 1120, 383 Main St., Steinbach, MB R0A 2A0 Tel. (204)326-6790 Fax (204)326-6302
Email: mennpost@mts.net

Mennonitische Rundschau, (M.) Canadian Conference of Mennonite Brethren Churches; Brigitte Penner, Marianne Dulder, 3-169 Riverton Ave., Winnipeg, MB R2L 2E5 Tel. (204)669-6575 Fax (204)654-1865
Email: MR@mbconf.ca
Website: www.mbconf.ca

Messenger (of the Sacred Heart), (M.) The Roman Catholic Church in Canada; F. J. Power, Apostleship of Prayer, 661 Greenwood Ave., Toronto, ON M4J 4B3 Tel. (416)466-1195

Messenger of Truth, (bi-W.) Church of God in Christ (Mennonite); Gladwin Koehn, P.O. Box 230, Moundridge, KS 67107 Tel. (620)345-2532 Fax (620)345-2582
Email: gospub@characterlink.net

The Messenger, (22-Y.) The Evangelical Mennonite Conference; Editor: Terry Smith; Assistant Editor: Becky Buhler; Box 1268, Steinbach, MB R0A 2A0 Tel. (204)326-6401 Fax (204)326-1613
Email: emcmessenger@mts.net
Website: www.emconf.ca/messenger

The Messenger, (Q.) The Reformed Episcopal Church of Canada; Rt. Rev. Michael Fedechko, 320 Armstrong St., New Liskeard, ON P0J 1P0 Tel. (705)647-4565 Fax (705) 647-4565
Email: fed@nt.net
Website: www.forministry.com/REC-Canada

The Messenger, (4-Y.) Church of God in Eastern Canada; Editorial Team c/o Rosemary Krashel, 20625 Winston Churchill Blvd., Alton, ON, L0N 1R0 Tel. (519)938-9994
Email: rosemarykrushel@sympatico.ca

Missions Today, (bi-M.) Roman Catholic; Patricia McKinnon, Society for the Propagation of the Faith, 3329 Danforth Ave., Scarborough, ON M1L 4T3 Tel. (416)699-7077 or (800)897-8865 Fax (416)699-9019
Email: missions@eda.net
Website: www.eda.net/~missions

The Monitor, (M.) The Roman Catholic Church in Canada; Larry Dohey, P.O. Box 986, St. John's, NL A1C 5M3 Tel. (709)739-6553 Fax (709)739-6458
Email: 1dohey@seascape.com
Website: www.delweb.com/rcec/monitor.htm

InfoMission, (Q.) Canadian Baptist Ministries; Jennifer Lau, 7185 Millcreek Dr., Mississauga, ON L5N 5R4 Tel. (905)821-3533 Fax (905) 826-3441
Email: mosaic@cbmin.org
Website: www.cbmin.org

Multiply, (4-Y.) Presbyterian Church in America (Canadian Section); Fred Marsh, 1700 N. Brown, Suite 101, Lawrenceville, GA 30043-8143 Tel. (678)825-1200 Fax (404)982-9108
Email: mna@pcanet.org
Website: www.pcanet.org/mna

NABtoday, (6-Y.) North American Baptist Conference; Marilyn Schaer, 1 S. 210 Summit Ave., Oakbrook Terr., IL 60181 Tel. (630)495-2000 Fax (630)495-3301
Email: NABtoday@nabconf.org
Website: NABConference.org

National Bulletin on Liturgy, (4-Y.) The Roman Catholic Church in Canada; Margaret Bick, 2500 Don Reid Drive, Ottawa, ON K1H 2J2 Tel. (613)241-9461 ext. 221 Fax (613) 241-8117
Email: liturgy@cccb.ca
Website: www.cccb.ca

The New Freeman, (W.) The Roman Catholic Church in Canada; Margie Traftan, One Bayard Dr., Saint John, NB E2L 3L5 Tel. (506)653-6806 Fax (506)653-6818
Email: tnf@nbnet.nb.ca

News of Québec, (3-Y.) Christian Brethren (also known as Plymouth Brethren); Richard E. Strout, P.O. Box 1054, Sherbrooke, QC J1H 5L3 Tel. (819)820-1693 Fax (819)821-9287

Orthodox Way, (M.) Greek Orthodox Metropolis of Toronto (Canada); Orthodox Way Committee, 86 Overlea Blvd., 4th Floor, Toronto, ON M4H 1C6 Tel. (416)429-5757 Fax (416)429-4588
Email: greekomt@on.aibn.com
Website: www.gocanada.org

Passport, (3-Y.) Interdenominational; Lois Penner, Briercrest Family of Schools, 510 College Dr., Caronport, SK S0H 0S0 Tel. (306)756-3200 Fax (306)756-3366
Email: info@briercrest.ca
Website: www.briercrest.ca

Pourastan, (bi-M.) Armenian Holy Apostolic Church–Canadian Diocese; 615 Stuart Ave., Outremont, QC H2V 3H2 Tel. (514)279-3066 Fax (514)276-9960
Email: sourpkrikor@qc.aibn.com
Website: www.sourpkrikor.org

Prairie Messenger, (W.) The Roman Catholic Church in Canada; Andrew M. Britz, O.S.B., Box 190, Muenster, SK S0K 2Y0 Tel. (306)682-1772 Fax (306)682-5285
Email: pm.editor@stpeters.sk.ca
Website: www.stpeters.sk.ca/prairie_messenger

The Presbyterian Message, (10-Y.) Presbyterian Church in Canada; Janice Carter, Kouchibouguac, NB E0A 2A0 Tel. (506)876-4379
Email: mjcarter@nb.sympatico.ca

Presbyterian Record, (11-Y.) The Presbyterian Church in Canada; Rev. David Harris, 50 Wynford Dr., Toronto, ON M3C 1J7 Tel. (416)441-1111 Fax (416)441-2825
Email: pcrecord@presbyterian.ca
Website: www.presbyterian.ca/record

Presence, (8-Y.) The Roman Catholic Church in Canada; Jean-Claude Breton, Presence Magazine, Inc., 2715 chemin de la Cote Ste-Catherine, Montreal, QC H3T 1B6 Tel. (514)739-9797 Fax (514)739-1664
Email: presence@presencemag.qc.ca

The Pulse, (4-Y.) Evangelical Free Church of Canada; Editor-in-Chief: Rev. Terry Kaufman; Managing Editor: Tracy Morris, Box 850, LCDI, Langley, BC V3A 8S6 Tel. (604)888-8668 Fax (604)888-3108
Email: efcc@twu.ca
Website: www.twu.ca/efcc

Quaker Concern, (Q.) Canadian Yearly Meeting of the Religious Society of Friends; Jane Orion Smith, 60 Lowther Ave., Toronto, ON M5R 1C7 Tel. (416)920-5213 Fax (416)920-5214
Email: cfsc-office@quaker.ca
Website: www.cfsc.quaker.ca

Reformed Perspective–A Magazine for the Christian Family, (M.) Canadian and American Reformed Churches; Jon Dykstra, 13820-106 A Avenue, Edmonton, AB T5N 1C9 Tel. (780)452-3978
Email: editor@reformedperspective.ca
Website: www.reformedperspective.ca

Relations, (8-Y.) The Roman Catholic Church in Canada; Jean-Marc Biron, 25 Jarry Ouest, Montreal, QC H2P 1S6 Tel. (514)387-2541 Fax (514)387-0206
Email: relations@cjf.qc.ca
Website: www.cjf.qc.ca

RESCUE, (bi-M.) Association of Gospel Rescue Missions; Philip Rydman, 1045 Swift, N. Kansas City, MO 64116 Tel. (816)471-8020 Fax (816)471-3718
Email: pwydman@agrm.org
Website: www.agrm.org

Revival News, (Q.) Interdenominational; Harold Lutzer, Canadian Revival Fellowship, Box 584, Regina, SK S4P 3A3 Tel. (306)522-3685 Fax (306)522-3686
Email: crfellowship@accesscomm.ca
Website: www.revivalfellowship.com

Rupert's Land News, (10-Y.) The Anglican Church of Canada; Irvin J. Kroeker, Anglican Centre, 935 Nesbitt Bay, Winnipeg, MB R3T 1W6 Tel. (204)992-4205 Fax (204)992-4219
Email: rlnews@rupertsland.ca

Saints Herald, (M.) Community of Christ; Linda Booth, The Herald Publishing House, P.O. Box 1770, Independence, MO 64055-0770 Tel. (816)252-5010 Fax (816)252-3976
Email: comdiv@rlds.org
Website: www.rlds.org

Scarboro Missions, (7-Y.) The Roman Catholic Church in Canada; G. Curry, S.F.M., 2685 Kingston Rd., Scarborough, ON M1M 1M4 Tel. (416)261-7135 or (800)260-4815 (In Canada) Fax (416)261-0820
Email: sfmmag@scarboromissions.ca
Website: www.scarboromissions.ca

Servant Magazine, (4-Y.) Interdenominational; Phil Callaway, Prairie Bible Institute, Box 4000, Three Hills, AB T0M 2N0 Tel. (403)443-5511 Fax (403)443-5540
Website: www.pbi.ab.ca

The Shantyman, (6-Y.) Nondenominational; Editor-in-Chief: Ken Godevenos; Managing Editor: Phil Hood; 1885 Clements Rd., Unite 226, Pickering, ON L1W 3V4 Tel. (905)686-2030 Fax (905)427-0334
Email: shanty@pathcom.com
Website: www.shantymen.org

Sister Triangle, (Q.) Churches of Christ; Marilyn Muller, P.O. 948, Dauphin, MB R7N 3J5 Tel. (204)638-9812 Fax (204)638-6231
Email: dmmuller@mb.sympatico.ca

Solia–The Herald, (M.) The Romanian Orthodox Episcopate of America (Jackson, MI); Rev. Protodeacon David Oancea, P.O. Box 185, Grass Lake, MI 49240-0185 Tel. (517)522-3656 Fax (517)522-5907
Email: solia@roea.org
Website: www.roea.org

SR–Studies in Religion–Sciences religieuses, (Q.) Nondenominational; Dr. Kay Koppedrayer, Dept. of Religion & Culture, Wilfrid Laurier University, Waterloo, ON N2L 3C5 Tel. (780) 492-2879
Email: willi.braun@ualberta.ca

St. Luke Magazine, (M.) Christ Catholic Church International; Donald W. Mullan, 5165 Palmer Ave., Niagara Falls, ON L2E 6S8 Tel. (905)354-2329 Fax (905)354-9934
Email: dmullan1@cogeco.ca

Testimony, (M.) The Pentecostal Assemblies of Canada; Richard P. Hiebert, 2450 Milltower Ct., Mississauga, ON L5N 5Z6 Tel. (905)542-7400 Fax (905)542-7313
Email: testimony@PAOC.org

Topic, (10-Y.) The Anglican Church of Canada; Neale Adams, 580-401 W. Georgia St., Vancouver, BC V6B 5A1 Tel. (604)684-6306 ext. 223 Fax (604)684-7017
Email: nadams@vancouver.anglican.ca
Website: www.vancouver.anglican.ca

United Church Observer, (M.) The United Church of Canada; Muriel Duncan, 478 Huron St., Toronto, ON M5R 2R3 Tel. (416)960-8500 Fax (416)960-8477
Email: general@ucobserver.org
Website: www.ucobserver.org

La Vie Chretienne (French), (M.) Presbyterian Church in Canada; Jean Porret, P.O. Box 272, Suzz. Rosemont, Montreal, QC H1X 3B8 Tel. (514)737-4168

La Vie des Communautes religieuses, (5-Y.) The Roman Catholic Church in Canada; Religious Communities (Consortium), 251 St-Jean-Baptiste, Nicolet, QC J3T 1X9 Tel. (819)293-8736 Fax (819)293-2419
Email: vicar@sogetel.net

Vie Liturgique, (8-Y.) The Roman Catholic Church in Canada; Novalis, 4475, rue Frontenac, Bureau 103, Montreal, QC H2H 2S2 Tel. (800)668-2547 Fax (514)278-3030
Email: info@novalis-inc.com
Website: www.novalis.ca

VIP Communique, Foursquare Gospel Church of Canada; Timothy Peterson, 8459-160th St., Ste. 100, Surrey, BC V3S 3T9 Tel. (604)543-8414 Fax (604)543-8417
Email: foursquare@foursquare.ca
Website: www.foursquare.ca

Visnyk–The Herald, (2-M) Ukrainian Orthodox Church of Canada; Rt. Rev. Fr. William Makarenko, 9 St. John's Ave., Winnipeg, MB R2W 1G8 Tel. (204)586-3093 Fax (204)582-5241
Email: visnky@uocc.ca
Website: www.uocc.ca

Voce Evangelica–Evangel Voice, (Q.) The Italian Pentecostal Church of Canada; Rev. Daniel Costanza, 140 Woodbridge Ave., Suite 400, Woodbridge, ON L4L 4K9 Tel. (905)850-1578 Fax (905)850-1578
Email: bethel@idirect.com
Website: www.the-ipcc.org

The War Cry, (M.) The Salvation Army in Canada and Bermuda; Associate Editor: Major Kenneth Smith, 2 Overlea Blvd., Toronto, ON M4H 1P4 Tel. (416)425-2111 Fax (416)422-6120
Email: warcry@can.salvationarmy.org
Website: salvationarmy.ca

Word Alive, (Q.) Nondenominational; Dwayne Janke/Dave Crough, Wycliffe Bible

Translators of Canada Inc., 4316 10 St. NE, Calgary, AB T2E 6K3 Tel. (403)250-5411 Fax (403)250-2623
Email: editors_wam@wycliffe.ca
Website: www.wycliffe.ca

The Word, (10-Y.) The Antiochian Orthodox Christian Archdiocese of North America; John P. Abdalah, 1777 Quigg Dr., Pittsburgh, PA 15241-2071 Tel. (412)831-7388 Fax (412) 831-5554
Email: wordmag@aol.com
Website: antiochian.org

UU World–The Magazine of the Unitarian Universalist Association, (bi-M.) Unitarian Universalist; Tom Stites, 25 Beacon St., Boston, MA 02108 Tel. (617)742-2100 Fax (617)742-7025
Email: world@uua.org
Website: www.uua.org

Young Companion, (11-Y.) Old Order Amish Church; Joseph Stoll and Christian Stoll, Old Order Amish Church, Rt. 4, Aylmer, ON N5H 2R3

13. Church Archives and Historical Records Collections

American and Canadian history is interwoven with the social and cultural experience of religious life and thought. Most repositories of primary research materials in North America will include some documentation on religion and church communities. This directory is not intended to replace standard bibliographic guides to those resources. The intent is to give a new researcher entry to major archival holdings of religious collections and to programs of national scope. In the interest of space, no attempt has been made to list the specific contents of the archives or to include the numerous specialized research libraries of North America. The repositories listed herein are able to redirect inquirers to significant regional and local church archives, and specialized collections such as those of religious orders, educational and charitable organizations, and personal papers. This directory has been thoroughly re-edited to include updated entries and contact information.

Repositories marked with an asterisk (*) are designated by their denomination as their official archives. The reference departments at these archives will assist researchers in locating primary material of geographic or subject focus of the Episcopal Church, USA

UNITED STATES

Adventist

Adventist Heritage Center, James White Library, Andrews University, Berrien Springs, MI 49104, Curator: Jim Ford Tel. (269)471-3274, Fax (269)471-2646, ahc@andrews.edu, Website: http://www.andrews.edu/library/ahc/index.html

Large collection of Millerite and Seventh-day Adventist materials.

Aurora University, Charles B. Phillips Library, 347 S. Gladstone, Aurora, IL 60506, Volunteer Curator: David T. Arthur Tel. (630)844-5437, Fax (630)844-3848, jhuggins@aurora.edu

Advental archival materials on the Millerite/Early Adventist movement (1830-1860), also denominational archives relating to Advent Christian Church, Life, and Advent Union, and (to a lesser extent) Evangelical Adventists and Age-to-Come Adventists.

Department of Archives and Special Collections/ Ellen G. White Estate Branch Office, Loma Linda University Library, Loma Linda, CA 92350, Chairman/Dir.: Elder Merlin D. Burt Tel. (909)558-4942, Fax (909)558-0381, whiteestate@llu.edu, Website: http://www.llu.edu/llu/library/heritage

Photographs, sound and video recordings, personal papers, and library pertaining to the Seventh-day Adventist Church.

Ellen G. White Estate, Inc., 12501 Old Columbia Pike, Silver Spring, MD 20904, Archivist: Tim Poirier Tel. (301)680-6540, Fax (301)680-6559, Website: http://www.whiteestate.org

Records include letters and manuscripts (1840s to 1915), pamphlets and publications, and the White papers.

*General Conference of Seventh-day Adventists: Archives and Statistics, 12501 Old Columbia Pike, Silver Spring, MD 20904-6600, Dir.: Bert Haloviak Tel. (301)680-5022, Fax (301) 680-5038, HaloviakB@GC.Adventist.org, Website: http://www.adventistarchives.org

Repository of the records created at the world administrative center of the Seventh-day Adventist Church and includes the period from the 1860s to the present.

Assemblies of God

*Flower Pentecostal Heritage Center, 1445 Boonville Ave., Springfield, MO 65802, Dir.: Wayne Warner Tel. (417)862-1447 ext. 4400, Fax (417)862-6203, archives@ag.org, Website: http://www.agheritage.org

Official repository for materials related to the Assemblies of God, as well as materials related to the early Pentecostal movement in general.

Baptist

*American Baptist Archives Center, P.O. Box 851, Valley Forge, PA 19482-0851, Archivist: Betty Layton Tel. (610)768-2374, Fax (610)768-2266, Website: http://www.abc-usa.org/abhs

Repository for the non-current records of the national boards and administrative organizations of American Baptist Churches in the USA. Collections include mission files, publications, correspondence, official minutes, and annual reports.

American Baptist–Samuel Colgate Historical Library, 1106 S. Goodman St., Rochester, NY 14620-2532, Dir.: Stuart W. Campbell Tel. (716)473-1740, Fax (716)473-1740 [Call first], Website: http://www.crds.edu/abhs/default.htm

Manuscript holdings include collections of Baptist ministers, missionaries, and scholars, as well as some records of Baptist churches, associations, and national and international bodies.

Andover Newton Theological School, Franklin Trask Library, 169 Herrick Rd., Newton

CHURCH ARCHIVES

Centre, MA 02459, Associate Dir. for Special Collections: Diana Yount Tel. (617)964-1100 ext. 252, Fax (617)965-9756, dyount@ants.edu, Website: http://www.ants.edu

The collections document Baptist, Congregational, and United Church history, including personal papers relating to national denominational work and foreign missions, with emphasis on New England Church history.

Primitive Baptist Library of Carthage, Illinois, 416 Main St., Carthage, IL 62321, Dir. of Library: Elder Robert Webb Tel. (217)357-3723, Fax (217)357-3723, bwebb9@juno.com, Website: http://www.carthage.lib.il.us/community/churches/primbap/pbl.html

Collects the records of congregations and associations.

*Seventh-day Baptist Historical Society, 3120 Kennedy Rd., P.O. Box 1678, Janesville, WI 53547, Historian: Don A. Sanford Tel. (608)752-5055, Fax (608)752-7711, sdbhist@inwave.com, Website: http://www.seventhday-baptist.org

Serves as a depository for records of Seventh-day Baptists, Sabbath, and Sabbath-keeping Baptists since the mid-seventeenth century.

*Southern Baptists Historical Library & Archives, 901 Commerce St., Suite 400, Nashville, TN 37203-3630, Dir. and Archivist: Bill Sumners Tel. (615)244-0344, Fax (615) 782-4821, bill@sbhla.org, Website: http://www.sbhla.org

Central depository of the Southern Baptist Convention. Materials include official records of denominational agencies, personal papers of denominational leaders and missionaries, records of related Baptist organizations, and annual proceedings of national and regional bodies.

Brethren in Christ

*Brethren in Christ Historical Library and Archives, One College Ave., P.O. Box 3002, Grantham, PA 17027, Dir.: Dori I. Steckbeck Tel. (717)691-6048, Fax (717)691-6042, archives@messiah.edu, Website: http://www.messiah.edu/archives

Records of general church boards and agencies, regional conferences, congregations, organizations, and church institutions, including Messiah College; also includes historical library and special collections (manuscripts, oral history, and photographs).

Church of the Brethren

*Brethren Historical Library and Archives, 1451 Dundee Ave., Elgin IL 60120, Dir.: Kenneth M. Shaffer Jr. Tel. (847)742-5100, Fax (847) 742-6103, kshaffer_gb@brethren.org, Website: http:// www.brethren.org/genbd/bhla

Archival materials dating from 1800-present relating to the cultural, socio-economic, theological, genealogical, and institutional history of the Church of the Brethren.

Churches of Christ

Center for Restoration Studies, Abilene Christian University, 221 Brown Library, P.O. Box 29208, Abilene, TX 79699, Librarian: Craig Churchill Tel. (325)674-2347, Fax (325)674-2202, churchill @ acu.edu, Website: http://www.bible.acu.edu/crs

Materials in various formats including archival materials connected with the Stone-Campbell Restoration Movement. The chief focus is on the Church of Christ in the twentieth century.

Emmanuel School of Religion Library, One Walker Dr., Johnson City, TN 37601-9438, Dir.: Thomas E. Stokes Tel. (423)926-1186, Fax (423)926-6198, library@esr.edu, Website: http://www.esr.edu

Materials related to the Stone-Campbell/Restoration Movement tradition. Collection includes items from the Christian Church and Churches of Christ, the a cappella Churches of Christ, and the Christian Church (Disciples of Christ)

Churches of God, General Conference

*Winebrenner Theological Seminary, 701 E. Melrose Ave., Findlay, OH 45804, Dir. of Library Services: Margaret Hirschy Tel. (419) 422-4824, Fax (419)422-3999, wts@winebrenner.edu, Website: http://www.winebrenner. edu

Archival materials of the Churches of God, General Conference including local conference journals.

Disciples of Christ

Christian Theological Seminary Library, 1000 W. 42nd St., Indianapolis, IN 46208-3301, Serials Librarian and Archivist: Don Haymes Tel. (317)931-2368 (Monday–Thursday), Fax (317)931-2363, don.haymes@cts.edu (Monday–Thursday), Website: http://www.cts.edu

Archival documents, materials, and artifacts of Disciples of Christ, Christian Churches, Churches of Christ, and related movements; documents of Indiana religious history; documents of ecumenical endeavors in Indiana and the American Midwest; documents of local ecumenical organizations and ministries nationwide.

*Disciples of Christ Historical Society, 1101 19th Ave. South, Nashville, TN 37212, Dir. of Library and Archives: Sara Harwell Tel. (615) 327-1444, mail@dishistsoc.org, Website: http://www.dishistsoc.org

Collects documents of the Stone-Campbell Movement.

Episcopal

*Archives of the Episcopal Church, P.O. Box 2247, Austin, TX 78768-2247, Dir.: Mark J.

Duffy Tel. (512)472-6816, Fax (512)480-0437, Research@EpiscopalArchives.org, Website: http://www.EpiscopalArchives.org

Repository for the official records of the national Church, its corporate bodies, and affiliated agencies; personal papers; and some diocesan archives. Contact the Archives for reference to diocesan and parochial church records.

Evangelical Congregation Church

*Archives of the Evangelical Congregational Church, Evangelical School of Theology, Rostad Library, 121 S. College St., Myerstown, PA 17067, Archivist: Terry M. Heisey Tel. (717)866-5775, Fax (717)866-4667, theisey@evangelical.edu, Website: http://www.eccenter.com

Repository of records of the administrative units of the denomination, affiliated organizations, and closed churches. Also collected are records of local congregations and materials related to the United Evangelical Church and the Evangelical Association.

Friends

Friends Historical Library of Swarthmore College, 500 College Ave., Swarthmore, PA 19081-1399, Curator: Christopher Densmore, Tel. (610)328-8496, Fax (610)690-5728, friends@swarthmore.edu, Website: http://www.swarthmore.edu/library/friends

Official depository for records of Philadelphia, Baltimore, New York and Lake Erie Yearly Meetings of the Religious Society of Friends. Also depository for several Quaker organizations, including Friends General Conference and Pendle Hill. Comprehensive collection of printed materials concerning Quakers.

Special Collections/Quaker Collection, Haverford College, 370 Lancaster Ave., Haverford, PA 19041-1392, Quaker Bibliographer: Emma Jones Lapsansky Tel. (610)896-1161, Fax (610)896-1102, elapsans@haverford.edu, Website: http://www.haverford.edu/library/special

Repository for material relating to the Society of Friends (Quakers), especially to the segment known from 1827 to the mid-20th century as "Orthodox," in the Delaware Valley.

Interdenominational

American Bible Society Library and Archives, 1865 Broadway, New York, NY 10023-9980, Dir.: Mary F. Cordat Tel. (212)408-1258, Fax (212)408-1526, mcordato@americanbible.org, Website: http://www.americanbible.org

Billy Graham Center Archives, Wheaton College, 500 College Ave., Wheaton, Il 60187-5593, Dir. of Archives: Paul Ericksen Tel. (630)752-5910, Fax (630)752-5916, bgcarc@wheaton.edu, Website: http://www.wheaton.edu/bgc/archives

Repository of 600+ collections which document the history of evangelism and missions by North American nondenominational Protestants, especially Billy Graham. Extensive resources are available through the Archives Website, including online exhibits. Fee-based services include some short-term borrowing and in-depth research.

David du Plessis Archives, Fuller Theological Seminary, 135 N. Oakland, Pasadena, CA 91182, Archivist: To be appointed, Tel. (626)584-5311, Fax (626)584-5644, archive@fuller.edu, Website: http://www.fuller.edu/archive

Collects material related to the Pentecostal and Charismatic movements, also includes material related to Charles Fuller and the Old Fashioned Revival Hour broadcast, Fuller Theological Seminary, and the Evangelical traditions.

Graduate Theological Union Archives, 2400 Ridge Rd., Berkeley, CA 94709, Archivist: Lucinda Glenn Tel. (510)649-2507, Fax (510) 649-2508, Website: http://library.gtu.edu/archives/index.html

Holy Spirit Research Center, Oral Roberts University (LRC 5E 02), 7777 S. Lewis Ave., Tulsa OK 74171, Dir.: Mark E. Roberts Tel. (918)495-6898, Fax (918)495-6662, hsrc@oru.edu, Website: http://www.oru.edu/university/library/holyspirit

Pentecostal and Charismatic records, with emphasis on divine healing.

National Council of Churches of Christ Archives, Department of History and Records Management Services, Presbyterian Church (USA), 425 Lombard St., Philadelphia, PA 19147-1516, Manager: Margery N. Sly Tel. (215)627-1852, Fax (215)627-0509, preshist@shrsys.hslc.org, Website: http://www.libertynet.org/pacscl/phs/

Schomburg Center for Research in Black Culture, 515 Malcolm X Blvd., New York, NY 10037, Curator: Diana Lachatanere Tel. (212) 491-2224, Fax (212)491-6067, scmarbref@nypl.org, Website: http://www.schomburgcenter.org

Manuscripts, Archives, and Rare Books Division.

Union Theological Seminary, Burke Library, 3041 Broadway, New York, NY 10027, Archivist and Head of Special Collections: Claire McCurdy Tel. (212)280-1502, Fax (212) 280-1456, awt@uts.columbia.edu, Website: http://www.uts.columbia.edu

University of Chicago, Regenstein Library, 1100 E. 57th St., Chicago, IL 60537-1502, Bibliographer for Humanities: Curtis Bochanyin Tel. (773)702-8442, boc7@midway.uchicago.edu, Website: http://www.lib.uchicago.edu/e/su/rel/

Yale Divinity School Library, 409 Prospect St., New Haven, CT 06511, Research Services Librarian: Martha Smalley Tel. (203)432-6374, Fax (203)432-3906, divinity.library@yale.edu, Website: http://www.library.yale.edu/div

Jewish

American Jewish Historical Society, Center for Jewish History, 15 W. 16th St., New York, NY 10011, Dir.: Michael Feldberg Tel. (212)294-6162 (NY), Fax (212)294-6161 (NY), ajhs@ajhs.org, Website: http://www.ajhs.org

Friedman Memorial Library, 2 Thornton Rd., Waltham, MA 02453, Dir.: Michael Feldberg Tel. (781)891-8110, Fax (781)899-9208, mfeldberg@ajhs.cjh.org, Website: http://www.ajhs.org

Archival repositories of the Jewish people in America, including significant religious contributions to American life.

Jacob Rader Marcus Center of the American Jewish Archives, 3101 Clifton Ave., Cincinnati, OH 45220, Associate Archivist: Christine A. Crandall Tel. (513)221-1875 ext. 319, Fax (513)221-7812, ccrandall@huc.edu, Website: http://www.americanjewisharchives.org

Materials documenting the Jewish experience in the Western Hemisphere with emphasis on the Reform movement. Included in the collection are congregational and organizational records, personal papers of rabbis and secular leaders, and genealogical materials.

Latter-day Saints

*Archives, Church of Jesus Christ of the Latter-day Saints, 50 E. North Temple, Salt Lake City, UT 84150-3800, Dir.: Steven R. Sorensen Tel. (801)240-2273, Fax (801)240-6134

Repository of official records of church departments, missions, congregations, and associated organizations. Includes personal papers of church leaders and members.

Family History Library, 35 N. West Temple, Salt Lake City, UT 84150-3400 Tel. (801)240-2331, Fax (801)240-5551, fhl@ldschurch.org, Website: http://www.familysearch.org

International collection of microfilmed records significant to family history. Includes the following subjects: biography, census, civil, court and church records, directories, emigration/ immigration, and genealogy, history (local), Jewish records, land and property, maps, military history, military records, naturalization records, newspapers, obituaries, probate and public records, taxation, and vital records.

Lutheran

*Archives of the Evangelical Lutheran Church in America, 8765 West Higgins Rd., Chicago, IL 60631-4198, Chief Archivist: Elisabeth Wittman Tel. (847)690-9410, Fax (847)690-9502, archives@elca.org, Website: http://www.elca.org/os/archives

Official repository for the churchwide offices of the ELCA and its predecessors. For further information on synod and regional archives, contact the Chicago archives or check the ELCA World Wide Web site. For ELCA college and seminary archives, contact those institutions directly, or consult the ELCA Archives.

*Concordia Historical Institute, Dept. of Archives and History, The Lutheran Church–Missouri Synod, 801 De Mun Ave., St. Louis, MO 63105-3199, Dir.: Martin Noland Tel. (314)505-7900, Fax (314)505-7901, chi@chi.lcms.org, Website: http://chi. lcms.org/

Official repository of The Lutheran Church-Missouri Synod. Collects synodical and congregational records, personal papers, and records of Lutheran agencies.

Mennonite

*Center for Mennonite Brethren Studies, 1717 S. Chestnut, Fresno, CA 93702, Archivist: Kevin Enns-Rempel Tel. (559)453-2225, Fax (559) 453-2124, kennsrem@fresno.edu, Website: http://www.fresno.edu/affiliation/cmbs

Official repository for the General Conference of Mennonite Brethren churches.

*Mennonite Church USA Archives–Goshen, 1700 S. Main, Goshen, IN 46526, Dir.: John E. Sharp Tel. (574)535-7477, Fax (574)535-7756, johnes@goshen.edu, Website: http://www.mcusa-archives.org

One of two repositories of the official organizational records of Mennonite Church USA and personal papers of leaders and members.

*Mennonite Church USA Archives–North Newton, Bethel College, 300 E. 27th St., North Newton, KS 67117-0531, Archivist: John Thiesen Tel. (316)284-5304, Fax (316) 284-5843, mla@bethelks.edu, Website: http://www.bethelks.edu/services/mla

An official repository for the Mennonite Church USA, its predecessor the General Conference Mennonite Church, and several other organizations.

Methodist

B. L. Fisher Library, Asbury Theological Seminary, 204 N. Lexington Ave., Wilmore, KY 40390, Archivist and Special Collections Librarian: Bill Kostlevy Tel. (859)858-2235, Fax (859)858-2350, bill_kostlevy@asbury-seminary.edu

Documents the Holiness Movement and evangelical currents in the United Methodist Church. Holdings include records of related associations, camp meetings, personal papers, and periodicals.

Center for Evangelical United Brethren Heritage, United Theological Seminary, 1810 Harvard Blvd., Dayton, OH 45406-4599, Dir.: Sarah D.

Brooks Blair Tel. (937)278-5817, Fax (937) 275-5701, eubcenter@united.edu, Website: http:// www.united.edu/eubcenter

Documents predecessor and cognate church bodies of the United Methodist Church including the Evangelical Association, United Brethren in Christ, United Evangelical, Evangelical, Evangelical United Brethren, Evangelical Congregational, and Evangelical of North America.

*General Commission on Archives and History, The United Methodist Church, P.O. Box 127, Madison, NJ 07940, Archivist/Records Administrator: L. Dale Patterson Tel. (973) 408-3189, Fax (973)408-3909, gcah@gcah.org, Website: http://www.gcah.org

Collects administrative and episcopal records and personal papers of missionaries and leaders. Holds limited genealogical information on ordained ministers. Will direct researchers to local and regional collections of congregational records and information on United Methodism and its predecessors.

*Heritage Hall at Livingstone College, 701 W. Monroe St., Salisbury, NC 28144, Dir.: Phyllis H. Galloway Tel. (704) 638-5664

Records of the African Methodist Episcopal Zion Church.

*Office of the Historiographer of the African Methodist Episcopal Church, P.O. Box 301, Williamstown, MA 02167, Historiographer: Dennis C. Dickerson Tel. (413)597-2484, Fax (413)597-3673, dennis.c.dickerson@williams.edu

General and annual conference minutes, reports of various departments such as missions and publications, and congregational histories and other local materials. The materials are housed in the office of the historiographer and other designated locations.

Moravian

Moravian Archives, Southern Province, Drawer L, Winston-Salem, NC 27108, Archivist: C. Daniel Crews Tel. (336)722-1742, Fax (336) 725-4514, nblum@mcsp.org, Website: http:// www.moravianarchives.org

Repository of the records of the Moravian Church, Southern Province, its congregations, and its members.

The Moravian Archives, 41 W. Locust St., Bethlehem, PA 18018-2757, Archivist: Vernon H. Nelson Tel. (610)866-3255, Fax (610)866-9210, morarchbeth@enter.net, Website: http:// www.moravianchurcharchives.org

Records of the Northern Province of the Moravian Church in America, including affiliated provinces in the Eastern West Indies, Nicaragua, Honduras, Labrador, and Alaska.

Nazarene

*Nazarene Archives, Church of the Nazarene, 6401 The Paseo, Kansas City, MO 64131, Archives Manager: Stan Ingersol Tel. (816)333-7000 ext. 2437, Fax (816)361-4983, singersol@nazarene.org, Website: http://www.nazarene.org/archives/index.html

While the focus is on collections pertaining to general agencies, leaders, and study commissions, the Archives also has collections on congregations, districts, universities, seminaries, and social ministries in the US and world-wide.

Pentecostal

*Hal Bernard Dixon Jr. Pentecostal Research Center, 260 11th St. NE, Cleveland, TN 37311, Dir.: David G. Roebuck Tel. (423)614-8576, Fax (423)614-8555, dixon_research@leeuniversity.edu, Website: http://www.leeuniversity.edu/library/dixon

Official repository of the Church of God (Cleveland, TN). Also collects other Pentecostal and Charismatic materials.

*International Pentecostal Holiness Church Archives and Research Center, P.O. Box 12609, Oklahoma City, OK 73157, Dir.: Harold D. Hunter Tel. (405)787-7110, Fax (405)789-3957, archives@iphc.org, Website: http://www.pctii.org/arc/archives.html

Official repository for records and publications produced by the international headquarters, conferences, and influential leaders.

United Pentecostal Church International Historical Center, 8855 Dunn Rd., Hazelwood, MO 63042, Chpsn., Historical Committee: J. L. Hall Tel. (314)837-7300, Fax (314)837-4503, main@upci.org, Website: http://www.upci.org

Collects a variety of Pentecostal archives, primarily the United Pentecostal (Oneness) Branch.

Polish National Catholic

*Polish National Catholic Church Commission on History and Archives, 1031 Cedar Ave., Scranton, PA 18505, Chpsn: Joseph Wieczerzak Tel. (570)343-0100, Fax (570) 343-0100 or (570)346-2188, josephwie@aol.com

Documents pertaining to the Church's national office, parishes, Prime Bishop, leaders, and organizations.

Reformed

*Heritage Hall, Calvin College, 1855 Knollcrest Circle SE, Grand Rapids, MI 49546-4402, Curator of Archives: Richard H. Harms Tel. (616)526-6313, Fax (616)526-6470, rharms@calvin.edu, Website: http://www.calvin.edu/hh

Repository of the official records of the Christian Reformed Church in North America, including its classes, congregations, and denominational agencies and committees.

*Historical Foundation of the Cumberland Presbyterian Church and the Cumberland Presbyterian Church in America, 1978 Union

Ave., Memphis, TN 38104, Archivist: Susan Knight Gore Tel. (901)276-8602, Fax (901) 272-3913, skg@cumberland.org, Website: http://www.cumberland.org/hfcpc Official archives of the Cumberland Presbyterian Church and the Cumberland Presbyterian Church in America.

*Reformed Church Archives, 21 Seminary Pl., New Brunswick, NJ 08901-1159, Archivist: Russell Gasero Tel. (732)246-1779, Fax (732) 249-5412, rgasero@rca.org, Website: http://www.rca.org

Official repository for denominational records including congregations, classes, synods, missions, and national offices from 1628 to the present.

*Presbyterian Historical Society, Presbyterian Church (USA) (2 offices): Headquarters, 425 Lombard St., Philadelphia, PA 19147-1516, Deputy Dir.: Margery N. Sly Tel. (215)627-1852, Fax (215)627-0509, refdesk@history.pcusa.org, Website: http://www.history.pcusa.org

Southern Regional Office, P.O. Box 849, Montreat, NC 28757, Deputy Dir.–Southern Regional Office: William Bynum Tel. (828)669-7061, Fax (828)669-5369, refdesk@history.pcusa.org, Website: http://www.history.pcusa.org

Collects the official records of the Church's national offices and agencies, synods, presbyteries, and some congregations. The Society also houses records of the Church's predecessor denominations, personal papers of prominent Presbyterians, and records of ecumenical organizations. The Southern Regional Office in Montreat, NC documents the fourteen southern states.

*Presbyterian Church in America Historical Center, 12330 Conway Rd., St. Louis, MO 63141, Dir.: Wayne Sparkman Tel. (314)469-9077, wsparkman@pcanet.org, Website: http://www.pcanet.org/history

The Historical Center serves as the official archive of the Presbyterian Church in America, and holds records of five other Presbyterian churches: Reformed (Evangelical Synod), Evangelical, Bible, Bible (Columbus Synod), Reformed (General Synod); also includes manuscript collections of some 60 individuals.

Princeton Theological Seminary Libraries, Library Place and Mercer St., P.O. Box 111, Princeton, NJ 08542-0803, Librarian for Archives and Special Collections: William O. Harris Tel. (609)497-7950, Fax (609)497-1826, william.harris@ptsem.edu, Website: http://www.ptsem.edu/grow/library/index.htm

Documents the history of American Presbyterianism, with an extensive collection of alumni biographies, congregational histories, and missionary reports.

Roman Catholic

The Catholic University of America (CUA), The American Catholics History Research Center and University Archives (Life Cycle Institute), 101 LCI, Washington, D.C. 20064, Archivist: Timothy Meagher Tel. (202)319-5065, Fax (202)319-6554, meagher@cua.edu, Website: http://libraries.cua.edu/achrcua/archives.html

Marquette University, Department of Special Collections and Archives, P.O. Box 3141, Milwaukee, WI 93201-3141, Department Head: Charles Elston Tel. (414)288-7256, Fax (414)288-6709, charles.elston@marquette.edu, Website: http://www.marquette.edu/library/collections/archives/index.html

Collection strengths are in the areas of Catholic social action, American missions and missionaries, and other work with Native Americans and African Americans.

US Catholic Documentary Heritage Project. For holdings information on various dioceses and religious orders, see the website. Website: www.uschs.com

University of Notre Dame Archives, 607 Hesburgh Library, Notre Dame, IN 46556, Curator of Manuscripts: William Kevin Cawley Tel. (574)631-6448, Fax (574)631-7980, archives@nd.edu, Website: http://archives.nd.edu

Papers of bishops and prominent Catholics and records of Catholic organizations. Includes parish histories, but few parish records. Covers US only.

Salvation Army

*Salvation Army Archives and Research Center, 615 Slaters Ln., Alexandria, VA 22313, Archivist: Susan Mitchem Tel. (703)684-5500, Fax (703)299-5552, archives@usn.salvationarmy.org, Website: http://www.salvationarmy.org

Holds the documents of Salvation Army history, personalities, and events in the United States from 1880.

Swedenborgian

*Bryn Athyn College of the New Church, Swedenborg Library, 2875 College Dr., P.O. Box 740, Bryn Athyn, PA 19009-0740, Dir.: Carroll C. Odhner Tel. (215)938-2547, Fax (215)938-2637, ccodhner@newchurch.edu, Website: http://www.newchurch.edu/college/facilities/swedlib.html

Unitarian Universalist Association

*Andover–Harvard Theological Library, Harvard Divinity School, 45 Francis Ave., Cambridge, MA 02138, Curator: Frances O'Donnell Tel. (617)496-5153, Fax (617)496-4111, frances_odonnell@harvard.edu, Website: http://www.hds.harvard.edu/library/bms/index. html

Institutional archives of the Unitarian Universalist Association including the Unitarian Universalist Service Committee, also houses records of many congregations, personal papers of ministers and other individuals.

Unitarian and Universalist

Meadville/Lombard Theological School Library, 5701 S. Woodlawn Ave., Chicago, IL 60637, Dir.: Neil W. Gerdes Tel. (773)256-3000 ext. 225, Fax (773)256-3007, ngerdes@meadville.edu, Website: http://www.meadville.edu

Repository for materials relating to Unitarian Universalism in particular and liberal religion in general. Includes personal papers of several noted UU ministers, and church records from many UU churches in the Midwestern USA.

United Church of Christ

Andover Newton Theological School, Franklin Trask Library, 169 Herrick Rd., Newton Centre, MA 02459, Associate Dir. for Special Collections: Diana Yount Tel. (617)964-1100 ext. 252, Fax (617)965-9756, dyount@ants.edu, Website: http://www.ants.edu

Collections document Baptists, Congregational, and UCC history. Some personal papers relating to national denominational work and foreign missionary activity, majority of collections relate to New England history.

Archives of the Evangelical Synod of North America, Eden Theological Seminary, Luhr Library, 475 E. Lockwood Ave., Webster Groves, MO 63119-3192, Assistant Archivist: Val Detjen Tel. (314)918-2515, vdetjen@eden.edu

Archival records include organization records, Evangelical Synod Congregational records, personal papers, and immigration records.

Congregational Library, 14 Beacon St., Boston, MA 02108, Archivist: Jessica Steytler Tel. (617)523-0470, Fax (617)523-0491, jsteytler@14beacon.org, Website: http://www.14beacon.org

Documentation on the Congregational; Congregational Christian; Christian; and United Church of Christ throughout the world; including local church records, associations, charitable organizations, and papers of clergy, missionaries, and others.

Elon University Library, P.O. Box 187, Elon, NC 27244, Archivist/Technical Services Librarian: Connie L. Keller Tel. (336)278-6578, Fax (336) 278-6638, keller@elon.edu

Collection of membership records and other archival material on the predecessor churches of the UCC: Christian Church and the Southern Conference of the Christian Church, also maintains records of churches that no longer exist.

*Evangelical and Reformed Historical Society, Lancaster Theological Seminary, 555 W. James St., Lancaster, PA 17603, Archivist: Richard R. Berg Tel. (717)290-8704, Fax (717)393-4254, erhs@lancasterseminary.edu, Website: http://www.erhs.info

Manuscripts and transcriptions of early German Reformed Church (US) 1725-1863, Reformed Church in the United States 1863-1934, and Evangelical and Reformed Church 1934-1957 records of coetus, synods, classes, pastoral records, and personal papers.

*United Church of Christ Archives, 700 Prospect Ave., Cleveland, OH 44115, Archivist: Bridgette A. Kelly Tel. (216)736-2106, Fax (216)736-2203, kellyb@ucc.org, Website: http://www.ucc.org/aboutus/archives/index.html

Records created in the national setting of the Church since its founding in 1957, including the General Synod, Executive Council, officers, instrumentalities, and bodies created by and/or related to the General Synod.

Standard Guides to Church Archives

Edmund L. Binsfield, "Church Archives in the United States and Canada: A Bibliography," in American Archivist, v. 21, no. 3 (July 1958) pp. 311-332, 219 entries.

Nelson R. Burr, "Sources for the Study of American Church History in the Library of Congress" (1953); 13 pp. Reprinted from Church History, v. XXII, no. 3 (Sept. 1953).

Canadian Archival Resources on the Internet: University of Saskatchewan Archives, Web Site maintained by Cheryl Avery and Steve Billington at http://www.usask.ca/archives/menu.html

Donald L. DeWitt, "Articles Describing Archives and Manuscript Collections in the United States: An Annotated Bibliography," in Bibliographies and Indexes in Library and Information Science, no. 11 (1997).

Andrea Hinding, ed. Women's History Sources: A Guide to Archives and Manuscript Collections in the U.S. (New York, Bowker, 1979) 2 vols.

Kay Kirkham, A Survey of American Church Records, for the Period Before the Civil War, East of the Mississippi River (Salt Lake City, 1959-60) 2 vols. Includes the depositories and bibliographies.

Martha Lund Smalley, "Archives and Manuscript Collections in Theological Libraries," in The American Theological Library Association, ed. by M. Graham (1996) pp. 122-130.

Evangeline Thomas, Women's Religious History Sources: A Guide to Repositories in the United States (New York, Bowker, 1983).

US National Historical Publications and Records Commission, Directory of Archives and Manuscript Repositories in the United States (Washington, D.C., 1988).

US Library of Congress, Washington, D.C., The National Union Catalog of Manuscript Collections, serially published from 1959 to

1993. Contains many entries for collections of church archives. Researchers may consult the cumulative paper indexes or use the NUCMC home page to access the RLIN database of archives and manuscripts collections at http:/lcweb.loc.gov/coll/nucmc/nucmc.html

CANADA

Anglican

*Anglican Church of Canada/General Synod Archives, 600 Jarvis St., Toronto, ON M4Y 2J6—as of 2004 new address: 80 Hayden Street, Toronto, ON M4Y 3G2—Archivist: To be announced, Tel. (416)924-9199 ext. 278, Fax (416)968-7983, archives@national.anglican.ca, Website: http://www.anglican.ca

Collects the permanent records of the General Synod, its committees, and its employees. The Archives has a national scope, and provides referral services on local Church records.

Baptist

*Atlantic Baptist Historical Collection of the Acadia University Archives, Vaughan Memorial Library, Wolfville, NS BOP 1XO, Archivist: Patricia Townsend Tel. (902)585-1412, Fax (902)585-1748, patricia.townsend @acadiau.ca, Website: http://www.acadiau.ca/vaughan/archives

Records of associations and churches of the United Baptist Convention of the Atlantic Provinces, also personal papers of pastors and missionaries.

Canadian Baptist Archives, McMaster Divinity College, Hamilton, ON L8S 4K1, Dir.: Kenneth R. Morgan Tel. (905)525-9140 ext. 23511, Fax (905)577-4782, morgankr@mcmaster.ca, Website: http://www.macdiv.ca

Friends

Canadian Yearly Meeting Archives, Pickering College, 16945 Bayview Ave., New Market, ON L3Y 4X2, Yearly Meeting Archivist: Jane Zavitz-Bond Tel. (905)895-1700, Fax (905) 895-9076

Holds the extant records for Quakers in Canada beginning with Adolphus in 1798 to the present, including the records of the Canadian Friends Service Committee.

Interdenominational

Canadian Council of Churches Archives, on deposit in National Archives of Canada, 395 Wellington, Ottawa, ON K1A 0N3 Tel. Research Services Division: (613)992-3884 or (866)578-7777, Genealogical Assistance: (613)996-7458, Fax (613)995-6274, reference@archives.ca, Website: http://www.archives.ca

National Archives of Canada, 395 Wellington, Ottawa, ON K1A 0N3, Dir.: Ian E. Wilson Tel. Research Services Division: (613)992-388 or (866)578-7777, Genealogical Assistance: (613)996-7458, Fax (613)995-6274, reference @archives.ca, Website: http://www. archives.ca

Records of interdenominational and ecumenical organizations, missionary societies, denominational churches, parish registers, and papers of prominent clergy.

Jewish

Canadian Jewish Congress National Archives, 1590 Ave. Docteur Penfield, Montreal, QC H3G 1C5, Dir. of Archives: Janice Rosen Tel. (514)931-7531 ext. 2, Fax (514)931-0548, archives@cjc.ca, Website: http://www.cjc.ca (see "National Archives" section)

Collects documentation on all aspects of social, political, and cultural history of the Jewish presence in Quebec and Canada.

Lutheran

*Archives of the Evangelical Lutheran Church in Canada, 302-393 Portage Ave., Winnipeg, MB R3B 3H6, Dir. of Administration: Rhonda Lorch Tel. (204)984-9165, Fax (204)984-9185, rlorch@elcic.ca, Website: http://www.elcic.ca

Official repository for the ELCIC and its predecessor bodies, the Evangelical Lutheran Church of Canada and the Evangelical Lutheran Church of America–Canada Section.

Lutheran Historical Institute, 7100 Ada Blvd., Edmonton, Alberta T5B 4E4, Archivist: Karen Baron, kbaron@lccabc.ca, Website: http://www.lccarchives.ca

Mennonite

*Centre for Mennonite Brethren Studies, 1-169 Riverton Ave., Winnipeg, MB R2L 2E5, Dir.: Dr. Heinrich Loewen Tel. (204)669-6575, Fax (204)654-1865, cmbs@mbconf.ca, Website: http://www.mbconf.ca/mbstudies/index.html

Institutional records of the boards and agencies of the Mennonite Brethren Church in Canada with some holdings pertaining to other parts of North America, also personal papers of leaders.

*Mennonite Heritage Centre, 600 Shaftesbury Blvd., Winnipeg, MB R3P 0M4, Dir.: Alf Redekopp Tel. (204)888-6781, Fax (204)831-5675, aredekopp@mennonitechurch.ca, Website: http://www.mennonitechurch.ca/programs/archives/

Institutional records and personal papers of leaders within the Mennonite Community; holdings include the records of the Conference and related agencies.

Pentecostal

*Pentecostal Assemblies of Canada, 2450 Milltower Ct., Mississauga, ON L5N 5Z6,

Dir. of Archives: James D. Craig Tel. (905) 542-7400, Fax (905)542-7313, archives@ paoc.org, Website: http://www. paoc.org

Repository of archival records created by the Pentecostal Assemblies of Canada.

Reformed

*Presbyterian Church in Canada Archives and Records, 50 Wynford Dr., North York, ON M3C 1J7, Archivist/Records Administrator: Kim M. Arnold Tel. (416)441-1111 ext. 310, Fax (416)441-2825, karnold@presbyterian.ca, Website: http://www.presbyterian.ca

Records of the Presbyterian Church in Canada, its officials, ministers, congregations, and organizations.

Roman Catholic

Research Centre for the Religious History of Canada, St. Paul University, 223 Main St., Ottawa, ON K1S 1C4, Dir.: Pierre Hurtubise Tel. (613)236-1393 ext. 2270; Exec. Sec.: Jean-Marie LeBlanc Tel. (613)236-1393 ext. 2225; Fax (613)782-3001, crh-rc-rhc@ustpaul.ca, Website: http://www.ustpaul.ca

Holds 1300 linear feet of documents, mainly records on deposit from other institutions, and also guides to many Canadian Catholic archives.

Salvation Army

The Salvation Army, George Scott Railton Heritage Centre, 2130 Bayview Ave., Toronto, ON M4N 3K6, Dir.: Major Ira Barrow; Archivist: Major Barbara Bawks; Tel. (416) 481-4441, Fax (416)481-6096, heritage_center@ can.salvationarmy.org, Website: http://www. heritage.salvationarmy.ca

Records relative to The Salvation Army include publications; also financial, personnel, social welfare, and immigration records.

United Church of Canada

*United Church of Canada Central Archives, Victoria University, 73 Queen's Park Crescent E, Toronto, ON M5S 1K7, Chief Archivist: Sharon Larade Tel. (416)585-4563, Fax (416) 585-4584, uccvu.archives@utoronto.ca, Website: http://www.united-church.ca/archives/ home.htm

Records of the United Church of Canada and its antecedent denominations (Methodist, Presbyterian, Congregational and Evangelical United Brethren Churches) and local and Conference records of the United Church in Ontario. Call or view the web page for information on the United Church Conference Archives Network.

III

STATISTICAL SECTION

Guide to Statistical Tables

Since questions regarding religious affiliation are no longer a part of the United States Census, the *Yearbook of American & Canadian Churches* is as near an "official" record of denominational statistics as is available.

Because these data represent the most complete annual compilation of church statistics, there is a temptation to expect more than is reasonable. These tables provide the answers to very simple and straightforward questions. Officials in church bodies were asked: "How many members does your organization have?" "How many clergy?" and "How much money does your organization spend?" Each respondent interprets the questions according to the policies of the organization.

Caution should, therefore, be exercised when comparing statistics across denominational lines, comparing statistics from one year to another, and adding together statistics from different denominations.

Some particular methodological issues and therefore cautions in interpretation include the following considerations:

1. Definitions of membership, clergy, and other important characteristics differ from religious body to religious body. In this section, **Full or Confirmed Membership** refers to those with full communicant status. **Inclusive Membership** refers to those who are full communicants or confirmed members plus other members baptized, non-confirmed or non-communicant. Each church determines the age at which a young person is considered a member. Churches also vary in their approaches to statistics. For some, very careful counts are made of members. Other groups only make estimates.

2. Each year the data are collected with the same questions. While most denominations have consistent reporting practices from one year to the next, any change in practices is not noted in the tables. Church mergers and splits can also influence the statistics when they are compared over a number of years. Churches have different reporting schedules and some do not report on a regular basis.

3. The two problems listed above make adding figures from different denominations problematic. However, an additional complication is that individuals who attend two different churches may be included more than once. For example, a person who attends the Church of God in Christ Wednesday evening and an AME service on Sunday morning will likely be included in both counts.

4. Churches were asked to report figures for the full year ending December 31, 2002. Churches actually collect statistics according to their own ecclesial calendars. Data collected consistently from year to year accurately reflect rends over time, irrespective of when customarily collected. Caution should, therefore, be exercised when comparing statistics across denominational line, comparing statistics from one year to another, and adding together statistics from different denominations.

Table 1. Membership Statistics in Canada

Religious Body	Year Reporting	Number of Churches Reporting	Full Communicant or Confirmed Members	Inclusive Membership	Number of Pastors Serving Parishes	Total Number of Clergy	Number of Sunday or Sabbath Schools	Total Enrollment
The Anglican Church of Canada	1999	2,836	686,362	686,362	1,622	3,517	1,794	56,785
The Antiochian Orthodox Christian Archdiocese of North America	2002	15	100,000	100,000	28	29	15	1,290
Apostolic Christian Church (Nazarene)	1985	14		830	49	49		
The Apostolic Church in Canada	2002	20	1,450	1,740	22	28	17	687
Apostolic Church of Pentecost of Canada, Inc.	2002	144	24,000	24,000	317	430		
Armenian Holy Apostolic Church—Canadian Diocese	2000	15	85,000	85,000	10	47	5	424
Associated Gospel Churches	2002	139	10,516	10,516	136	268		
Association of Regular Baptist Churches (Canada)	1994	12			8	11		
Baptist Convention of Ontario and Quebec		373	43,283	57,263	333	625		
Baptist General Conference of Canada	1999	92		7,045	95	143		4,079
Baptist Union of Western Canada	2000	155	20,427	20,427	279	530		
The Bible Holiness Movement	2002	25	751	1,001	14	14	24	
Brethren in Christ Church, Canadian Conference	2001				89	89		

Table 1. Membership Statistics in Canada *(continued)*

Religious Body	Year Reporting	Number of Churches Reporting	Full Communicant or Confirmed Members	Inclusive Membership	Number of Pastors Serving Parishes	Total Number of Clergy	Number of Sunday or Sabbath Schools	Total Enrollment
Canadian and American Reformed Churches	2002	50	8,615	15,620	45	65		
Canadian Baptist Ministries	1996	1,133	129,055	129,055				
Canadian Conference of Mennonite Brethren Churches	2001	232	34,864	34,864	348			21,781
Canadian Convention of Southern Baptists	2002	196	10,622	10,622	150	176	126	5,579
Canadian District of the Moravian Church in America, Northern Province	2000	9	1,138	1,473	8	11	9	396
Canadian Evangelical Christian Churches	2002	27	600	2,000	53	105	40	4,000
Canadian Yearly Meeting of the Religious Society of Friends	2002	24	1,179	17,333	0	0	24	
Christian Brethren (also known as Plymouth Brethren)	2002	585		47,745		250	484	
Christian Church (Disciples of Christ) in Canada	2002	25	1,599	2,631	24	32	23	390
Christian Churches/Churches of Christ	2002	65	5,185	8,825	75	105	60	0
Christian and Missionary Alliance in Canada	2002	419	40,477	117,397	959	1,311	384	38,813
Christian Reformed Church in North America	2002	243	50,557	81,469	187	322		

Table 1. Membership Statistics in Canada *(continued)*

Religious Body	Year Reporting	Number of Churches Reporting	Full Communicant or Confirmed Members	Inclusive Membership	Number of Pastors Serving Parishes	Total Number of Clergy	Number of Sunday or Sabbath Schools	Total Enrollment
Church of God (Anderson, Ind.)	2002	48	3,711	3,711	41	88	37	1,794
Church of God (Cleveland, Tenn.)	2002	135	11,993	11,993	135	175	105	5,599
Church of God in Christ (Mennonite)	2002	49	4,398	4,398	159	168	49	
Church of God of Prophecy in Canada	1995	40	3,107	3,107	98	100	37	
The Church of Jesus Christ of Latter-day Saints in Canada	2002	467	150,371	163,666	1,401	1,578	467	122,076
Church of the Lutheran Brethren	2002	9	376	622	9	10	9	476
Church of the Nazarene in Canada	2002	166	12,660	12,673	152	274	148	16,107
Churches of Christ in Canada		151	6,857	6,587	122	120		
Community of Christ	1995	75	11,264	11,264	1,020	1,020		
Congregational Christian Churches in Canada		95		7,500	174	235		
Convention of Atlantic Baptist Churches	2002	556	63,236	63,236	282	619	314	
The Coptic Orthodox Church in Canada	2002	24	45,000		33	33		
The Estonian Evangelical Lutheran Church Abroad	2002	11	5,536	5,536	8	11	2	77
The Evangelical Covenant Church of Canada	2002	21	1,384	1,384	6	25		1,763

Table 1. Membership Statistics in Canada *(continued)*

Religious Body	Year Reporting	Number of Churches Reporting	Full Communicant or Confirmed Members	Inclusive Membership	Number of Pastors Serving Parishes	Total Number of Clergy	Number of Sunday or Sabbath Schools	Total Enrollment
Evangelical Free Church of Canada	2002	139	7,980	7,980	165	165	132	
Evangelical Lutheran Church in Canada	2002	623	142,865	199,236	485	866	447	17,926
The Evangelical Mennonite Conference	2001	50	7,000	7,000		220	50	
Evangelical Mennonite Mission Conference	1997	44	4,633	4,633	75	201		
The Evangelical Missionary Church of Canada	1993	145	9,923	12,217	172	367	125	7,475
The Fellowship of Evangelical Baptist Churches in Canada	2002	493	71,073					
Foursquare Gospel Church of Canada	1996	54	3,063	3,063	66	103		1,258
Free Methodist Church in Canada	2002	140	7,502	7,502	124	226		4,020
Free Will Baptists	1998	10	347		3	4	8	
Greek Orthodox Metropolis of Toronto (Canada)	1997	76	350,000	350,000	58	71	76	
Independent Assemblies of God International (Canada)	2002	340				705		705
Independent Holiness Church	1994	5		150	4	10	4	118
Jehovah's Witnesses	1998	1,383	113,136	184,787				

Table 1. Membership Statistics in Canada *(continued)*

Religious Body	Year Reporting	Number of Churches Reporting	Full Communicant or Confirmed Members	Inclusive Membership	Number of Pastors Serving Parishes	Total Number of Clergy	Number of Sunday or Sabbath Schools	Total Enrollment
Lutheran Church—Canada	2001	328	58,545	79,178	248	378	2,069	8,911
Mennonite Church—Canada	2002	233	34,478	34,478				14,577
North American Baptist Conference	2002	124	16,873	16,873	133	202	124	
The Old Catholic Church of Canada	2000	4	30	100	4	5	0	0
Old Order Amish Church	1999	24						
Open Bible Faith Fellowship of Canada	2002	87	3,000	10,500	162	236	90	4,600
Orthodox Church in America (Canada Section)	1993	606	1,000,000	1,000,000	740		502	
Patriarchal Parishes of the Russian Orthodox Church in Canada	2000	24	1,200	1,200	5	6	4	116
The Pentecostal Assemblies of Canada	2001	1,108		232,000		1,850	616	30,044
The Pentecostal Assemblies of Newfoundland	2001	126	11,910	25,431	210	312	101	6,067
Presbyterian Church in America (Canadian Section)	2002	17	701	1,067				469
Presbyterian Church in Canada	2001	968	130,287	198,693		1,245	968	
Reformed Church in Canada	2002	42	3,846	5,832	36	78		

Table 1. Membership Statistics in Canada *(continued)*

Religious Body	Year Reporting	Number of Churches Reporting	Full Communicant or Confirmed Members	Inclusive Membership	Number of Pastors Serving Parishes	Total Number of Clergy	Number of Sunday or Sabbath Schools	Total Enrollment
The Reformed Episcopal Church of Canada	2001	11	420	505	10	13	3	25
Reinland Mennonite Church	1995	6	877	1,816	10	13	5	347
The Roman Catholic Church in Canada	2002			12,494,903		8,801		
The Romanian Orthodox Church in America (Canadian Parishes)	2002		3,000	6,500		18	20	270
The Romanian Orthodox Episcopate of America (Jackson, MI)	2000	22	900	1,400	13	16	12	
The Salvation Army in Canada		356	21,645	75,732	567	1,923		
Serbian Orthodox Church in the USA and Canada, Diocese of Canada	1998	23	6,000	230,000	24	27	14	1,876
Seventh-day Adventist Church in Canada	2002	330	51,804	51,804	175	310	391	27,378
Syrian Orthodox Church of Antioch	1995	5	2,500	2,500	3	4		
Ukranian Orthodox Church of Canada	1988	258		120,000	75	91		
Union d'Églises Baptistes Françaises au Canada	2002	32	1,720	1,720	30	39	66	
United Brethren Church in Canada	1992	9	835	835	5	12	9	447

Table 1. Membership Statistics in Canada *(continued)*

Religious Body	Year Reporting	Number of Churches Reporting	Full Communicant or Confirmed Members	Inclusive Membership	Number of Pastors Serving Parishes	Total Number of Clergy	Number of Sunday or Sabbath Schools	Total Enrollment
The United Church of Canada	2002	3,640	625,000	1,518,000	2,003	4,156	2,832	61,380
United Pentecostal Church in Canada	1997	199				340		
Universal Fellowship of Metropolitan Community Churches	1992	12	50	1,500	8	9	1	36
The Wesleyan Church of Canada	2002	89	5,977	6,481	131	201	80	5,306
TOTALS		**20,880**	**16,769,596**	**18,654,511**	**14,203**	**35,836**	**12,922**	**460,890**

Table 2. Membership Statistics in the United States

Religious Body	Year Reporting	Number of Churches Reporting	Full Communicant or Confirmed Members	Inclusive Membership	Number of Pastors Serving Parishes	Total Number of Clergy	Number of Sunday or Sabbath Schools	Total Enrollment
Advent Christian Church	2002		25,277	25,277	285	425	273	12,346
African Methodist Episcopal Church*	1999		1,857,186	2,500,000	7,741	14,428	6,128	303,199
African Methodist Episcopal Zion Church*	2002	3,226	1,209,887	1,430,795	3,235	3,731	2,508	72,969
Albanian Orthodox Diocese of America	2002	2	2,278	2,275	3	3	2	52
The Allegheny Wesleyan Methodist Connection (Original Allegheny Conference)	2002	110	1,663	1,803	81	173	108	5,348
The Alliance of Baptists in the USA*	2002	128	63,870	63,870	286	286		
The American Association of Lutheran Churches	1999	101	14,095	18,252	91	141	83	3,612
The American Baptist Association	1998	1,760		275,000	1,740	1,760		
American Baptist Churches in the USA*	2002	5,836	1,484,291	1,484,291	4,325	8,582		160,954
The American Carpatho-Russian Orthodox Greek Catholic Church	2002	80	13,425	13,425	78	114	76	
American Evangelical Christian Churches	2001	180	15,470	18,412	180	244	180	14,935
American Rescue Workers	2001	15	3,000	3,000	35	35	8	300
The Antiochian Orthodox Christian Archdiocese of North America*	2002	230	380,000	380,000	400	451	230	20,000
Apostolic Catholic Orthodox Church	2002	10	10,000	25,000	13	21	4	

Table 2. Membership Statistics in the United States *(continued)*

Religious Body	Year Reporting	Number of Churches Reporting	Full Communicant or Confirmed Members	Inclusive Membership	Number of Pastors Serving Parishes	Total Number of Clergy	Number of Sunday or Sabbath Schools	Total Enrollment
Apostolic Christian Church (Nazarene)	1993	63	3,723	3,723	217	234	55	
Apostolic Christian Churches of America	2002	86	12,930	12,930	309	404	86	6,650
Apostolic Episcopal Church	2002	250	18,000	18,000	300	320	50	1,150
Apostolic Faith Mission Church of God	2002	23	8,256	10,426	46	94	23	3,911
Apostolic Faith Mission of Portland, Oregon	1994	54	4,500	4,500	60	85	54	
Apostolic Lutheran Church of America	2000	58			61	73		
Apostolic Orthodox Catholic Church of North America	2000	21		2,400	26	32		
Armenian Apostolic Church of America	2002	34	360,000	360,000	32	44	24	1,741
Armenian Apostolic Church, Diocese of America*	1991	72	14,000	414,000	49	70		
Assemblies of God	2002	12,133	1,585,428	2,687,366	19,005	32,556	11,385	1,391,881
Associate Reformed Presbyterian Church (General Synod)	2002	264	35,556	40,905	211	381	202	16,931
The Association of Free Lutheran Congregations	2002	252	27,040	36,431	144	226	236	10,491
Baptist Bible Fellowship International	2002	4,500	1,200,000	1,200,000				
Baptist General Conference	2002	902	145,148	145,148				65,735
Baptist Missionary Association of America	1999	1,334	234,732	234,732	1,525	3,055	1,300	88,921
Beachy Amish Mennonite Churches	2000	153	9,205	9,205	435	453		

Table 2. Membership Statistics in the United States *(continued)*

Religious Body	Year Reporting	Number of Churches Reporting	Full Communicant or Confirmed Members	Inclusive Membership	Number of Pastors Serving Parishes	Total Number of Clergy	Number of Sunday or Sabbath Schools	Total Enrollment
Berean Fundamental Church Fellowship	2000	51	8,000	8,000				
The Bible Church of Christ, Inc.	1993	6	4,150	6,850	11	52	6	
Bible Fellowship Church	2002	57	7,308	7,308	57	115	51	5,351
Brethren in Christ Church	2001	232	20,739	20,739	151	295		12,404
Brethren Church (Ashland, Ohio)	2002	117	10,287	10,287	80	184	108	
The Catholic Church	2002	19,484	66,407,105	66,407,105		44,487		
Christ Catholic Church	2002	6	1,439	1,464	8	8	1	23
Christ Community Church (Evangelical-Protestant)	2000	3	1,027	1,690	5	9	1	369
Christian Brethren (also known as Plymouth Brethren)	2002	1,165		85,050		530	947	
Christian Church (Disciples of Christ) in the United States and Canada*	2002	3,691	504,118	786,334	3,362	7,049	3,321	185,762
Christian Church of North America, General Council	1999	96	7,200	7,200	100	157	96	
Christian Churches and Churches of Christ	1988	5,579		1,071,616	5,525			
The Christian Congregation, Inc.	2000	1,439	119,391	119,391	1,437	1,438	1,295	39,100
Christian Methodist Episcopal Church*	2002	3,300	850,000	850,000	3,001	3,407	2,485	68,155
The Christian and Missionary Alliance	2002	1,963	190,573	389,232				
Christian Reformed Church in North America	2002	762	137,375	197,339	655	1,246		

Table 2. Membership Statistics in the United States *(continued)*

Religious Body	Year Reporting	Number of Churches Reporting	Full Communicant or Confirmed Members	Inclusive Membership	Number of Pastors Serving Parishes	Total Number of Clergy	Number of Sunday or Sabbath Schools	Total Enrollment
Christian Union	2002	111	4,484	6,153	120	220	111	4,811
Church of the Brethren*	2002	1,069	134,844	134,844	925	1,887	825	39,242
The Church of Christ (Holiness) USA	2002	159	10,321	10,321	191	229	145	7,168
Church of Christ, Scientist	2002	2,000						
Church of God (Anderson, Indiana)	2002	2,290	247,007	247,007	3,445	6,114	2,290	137,178
The Church of God in Christ	1991	15,300	5,499,875	5,499,875	28,988	33,593		
Church of God in Christ, Mennonite	2002	115	12,984	12,984	466	493	115	
Church of God (Cleveland, Tennessee)	2002	6,623	944,857	944,857	5,084	15,337	5,199	301,542
Church of God by Faith, Inc.	2002	148	30,000					
Church of God General Conference (Oregon, IL and Morrow, GA)	2002	89	3,860	5,018	66	80	64	2,051
Church of God, Mountain Assembly, Inc.	1994	118	6,140	6,140				
Church of God of Prophecy	2002	1,841	85,000	110,000	3,946		1,715	83,319
The Church of God (Seventh Day), Denver, Colorado	2000	200	9,000	11,000	90	130	200	
The Church of Illumination	1996	4		1,200		16	1	216
The Church of Jesus Christ (Bickertonites)	1989	63		2,707	183	262		
The Church of Jesus Christ of Latter-day Saints	2002	11,879	4,855,255	5,410,544	35,657	40,008	11,879	4,175,801
Church of the Living God (Motto, Christian Workers for Fellowship)	2002	120		20,000	105	214	65	

Table 2. Membership Statistics in the United States *(continued)*

Religious Body	Year Reporting	Number of Churches Reporting	Full Communicant or Confirmed Members	Inclusive Membership	Number of Pastors Serving Parishes	Total Number of Clergy	Number of Sunday or Sabbath Schools	Total Enrollment
Church of the Lutheran Brethren of America	2001	108	8,194	13,702	145	229	101	8,843
Church of the Lutheran Confession	2002	77	6,456	8,492	63	89	67	962
Church of the Nazarene	2002	4,983	639,330	643,649	4,516	9,877	4,765	847,865
Church of Our Lord Jesus Christ of the Apostolic Faith, Inc.	1999	500						
Church of the United Brethren in Christ	2002	217	22,740	22,740	180	323		12,661
Churches of Christ	1999	15,000	1,500,000	1,500,000	14,500	16,350	12,500	1,600,000
Churches of Christ in Christian Union	2002	233	10,473		305	640		9,352
Churches of God, General Conference	2002	337	32,654	32,654	305	460	337	14,521
Community of Christ	2002	951	142,106	142,106		18,337		
Congregational Holiness Church	2002	190	9,565	9,565	190	305	190	
Conservative Baptist Association of America (CBAmerica)	2002	1,200	200,000	200,000	1,800	2,100		
Conservative Congregational Christian Conference	2002	259	40,041	40,041	267	539	229	12,717
Conservative Lutheran Association	2002	3	852	1,267	8	29	3	120
Coptic Orthodox Church*	2000	100	250,000	300,000	140	145	100	5,500
Cumberland Presbyterian Church	2002	780	84,417	84,417	635	884	650	36,559
Cumberland Presbyterian Church in America	1996	152	15,142	15,142	141	156	152	9,465

Table 2. Membership Statistics in the United States *(continued)*

Religious Body	Year Reporting	Number of Churches Reporting	Full Communicant or Confirmed Members	Inclusive Membership	Number of Pastors Serving Parishes	Total Number of Clergy	Number of Sunday or Sabbath Schools	Total Enrollment
Elim Fellowship	2002	100			650	850		
Episcopal Church*	2001	7,344	1,897,004	2,333,628	6,057	16,388	6,294	305,929
The Estonian Evangelical Lutheran Church	1997	21	3,508	3,508	10	12		
The Evangelical Church	2000	133	12,475	12,475	164	255	125	8,000
The Evangelical Congregational Church	2002	150	21,208	21,208	169	247		
The Evangelical Covenant Church	2002	718	103,549	103,549	589	1,096	718	99,687
The Evangelical Free Church of America	1995	1,224	124,499	242,619	1,936	2,436		
Evangelical Friends International—North American Region	2000	278	27,057	27,057				
Evangelical Lutheran Church in America*	2002	10,721	3,757,723	5,038,006	7,354	17,706	8,636	860,349
Evangelical Lutheran Synod	2002	138	16,849	21,442	113	177	125	3,142
Evangelical Methodist Church	1997	123	8,615	8,615	105	215	120	6,547
Evangelical Presbyterian Church	2002	190	64,156	69,351	299	492	165	34,016
Fellowship of Evangelical Bible Churches	2002	17	1,950	1,950	13	40	17	1,595

Table 2. Membership Statistics in the United States *(continued)*

Religious Body	Year Reporting	Number of Churches Reporting	Full Communicant or Confirmed Members	Inclusive Membership	Number of Pastors Serving Parishes	Total Number of Clergy	Number of Sunday or Sabbath Schools	Total Enrollment
Fellowship of Fundamental Bible Churches	1999	22	1,125	1,125	29	46	22	1,036
Fellowship of Grace Brethren Churches	1997	260	30,371	30,371		564		
Fellowship of Evangelical Churches	2002	37	11,604	11,604	87	163	37	4,481
Free Methodist Church of North America	2001	978	61,202	69,342		1,883	866	87,189
Friends General Conference	2002	650	34,000	34,000	0	0	400	
Friends United Meeting*	2002	427	37,595	42,680	306	355	273	
Full Gospel Assemblies International	2002	41	3,075	3,075	224		41	
Full Gospel Fellowship of Churches and Ministers International	2002	902	325,400	326,900	2,210	2,707	899	
Fundamental Methodist Church, Inc.	1993	12	682	787	17	22	12	454
General Association of General Baptists	2001	713	66,636	85,346	1,121	1,305	1,090	23,602
General Association of Regular Baptist Churches	2002	1,415	129,407	129,407				
General Church of the New Jerusalem	2002	35	3,232	6,444	29	65		
General Conference of Mennonite Brethren Churches	1996	368	50,915	82,130	590			34,668
Grace Gospel Fellowship	1992	128		60,000	160	196	128	

Table 2. Membership Statistics in the United States *(continued)*

Religious Body	Year Reporting	Number of Churches Reporting	Full Communicant or Confirmed Members	Inclusive Membership	Number of Pastors Serving Parishes	Total Number of Clergy	Number of Sunday or Sabbath Schools	Total Enrollment
Greek Orthodox Archdiocese of America*		510		1,500,000	599	810	500	
The Holy Eastern Orthodox Catholic and Apostolic Church in North America, Inc.	2002	17	4,138	4,138	9		17	
Hungarian Reformed Church in America*	1998	27		6,000	27	30		
Hutterian Brethren	2000	444	36,800	43,000	600	600		
IFCA International, Inc.	1999	659	61,655	61,655			659	57,768
International Church of the Foursquare Gospel	2001	1,847	235,852	305,852	4,879	8,279	200	51,000
International Council of Community Churches*	2002	192	115,812	115,812	240	340		
The International Pentecostal Church of Christ	2002	67	2,004	4,961	51	157	48	1,918
International Pentecostal Holiness Church	2002	1,905	213,348	213,348	1,956	2,798		122,456
Jehovah's Witnesses	2002	11,876	1,022,397	1,022,397				
Korean Presbyterian Church in America, General Assembly of the*	2002		38,000	55,100	460	572		17,250
The Latvian Evangelical Lutheran Church in America	2002	68	12,124	13,584	43	63		
Liberal Catholic Church (International)	2002	9	1,000	6,000	16	20	3	
The Liberal Catholic Church—Province of the United States of America	2002	24	6,500	6,500	47	47		
The Lutheran Church—Missouri Synod (LCMS)	2002	6,142	1,907,923	2,512,714	5,217	8,505	5,269	469,003

Table 2. Membership Statistics in the United States *(continued)*

Religious Body	Year Reporting	Number of Churches Reporting	Full Communicant or Confirmed Members	Inclusive Membership	Number of Pastors Serving Parishes	Total Number of Clergy	Number of Sunday or Sabbath Schools	Total Enrollment
Mar Thoma Syrian Church of India*	2002	68		32,500	42	47	55	4,000
Mennonite Church USA	2002	964	112,688	112,688	738			
The Missionary Church	2002	386	35,287	35,287	636	951		25,390
Moravian Church in America (Unitas Fratrum)*	2002	93	19,806	25,140	86	164	92	5,918
National Association of Congregational Christian Churches	2002	432	65,392	65,392	507	650		
National Association of Free Will Baptists	2001	2,470	197,919	197,919	2,470	4,104	2,470	132,462
National Baptist Convention of America, Inc.*	2000		3,500,000	3,500,000			9,000	
National Baptist Convention, USA, Inc.*		9,000	5,000,000	5,000,000			9,000	
National Missionary Baptist Convention of America*	1992			2,500,000				
National Organization of the New Apostolic Church of North America	2002	348	37,382		1,647	1,647	287	2,603
National Primitive Baptist Convention, Inc.	2002	1,565	600,000	600,000				
National Spiritualist Association of Churches	2000				156	156	48	
Netherlands Reformed Congregations	2002	27	4,517	9,500	9	10		
North American Baptist Conference	2002	270	47,692	47,692	287	421	270	
North American Old Roman Catholic Church (Archdiocese of New York)	2002	8	590	615	8	9	4	18

Table 2. Membership Statistics in the United States *(continued)*

Religious Body	Year Reporting	Number of Churches Reporting	Full Communicant or Confirmed Members	Inclusive Membership	Number of Pastors Serving Parishes	Total Number of Clergy	Number of Sunday or Sabbath Schools	Total Enrollment
Old German Baptist Brethren Church	2001	55	6,205	6,205	259	259		
Old Order Amish Church	1993	898	80,820	80,820	3,592	3,617	55	
Open Bible Standard Churches	2000	314	38,000	38,000	500	1,028		
The Orthodox Church in America*	2002	725	900,000	900,000	792	873	507	
The Orthodox Presbyterian Church	2002	237	18,746	26,448	14	425		
Patriarchal Parishes of the Russian Orthodox Church in the USA*		31	7,000		45	48		
Pentecostal Assemblies of the World, Inc.	1998	1,750	1,500,000	1,500,000	4,500	4,500		
Pentecostal Church of God	2002	1,197	45,500	104,000		1,762		
Pentecostal Fire-Baptized Holiness Church	1996	27	223	223		28	25	400
Pentecostal Free Will Baptist Church, Inc.	2002	150			259	304		
Philadelphia Yearly Meeting of the Religious Society of Friends*	2000	105	11,871	11,871	0	0		
Polish National Catholic Church of America*	2002	145		60,000	131	147		
Presbyterian Church in America	2002	1,499	254,676	310,750		3,181		115,774
Presbyterian Church (USA)*	2002	11,097	2,451,969	3,407,329	8,725	21,194	8,934	1,127,698

Table 2. Membership Statistics in the United States *(continued)*

Religious Body	Year Reporting	Number of Churches Members	Full Communicant or Confirmed	Inclusive Membership Parishes	Number of Pastors Serving	Total Number of Clergy	Number of Sunday or Sabbath Schools	Total Enrollment
Primitive Advent Christian Church	1993	10	345	345	11	11	10	292
Primitive Methodist Church in the USA	2002	79	4,211	4,399	52	90	65	2,881
Progressive National Baptist Convention, Inc.*	1995	2,000	2,500,000	2,500,000				
Protestant Reformed Churches in America	2002	27	3,976	6,915	24	40	23	
Reformed Catholic Church	1997	100		25,000	80	100		
Reformed Church in America*	2002	901	171,361	281,475	823	1,763		
Reformed Church in the United States	2002	48	3,258	4,369	42	50	48	951
Reformed Episcopal Church	2002	137	8,006	10,665	167	204		
Reformed Mennonite Church	2002	10	295		39			
Reformed Presbyterian Church of North America	1997	86	4,363	6,105	70	137	78	3,373
Religious Society of Friends (Conservative)	1994	1,200		104,000				
The Romanian Orthodox Episcopate of America	2002	22	1,000	1,500	16	19	12	
The Russian Orthodox Church Outside of Russia	1994	177			319	319		
The Salvation Army	2001	1,369	120,209	454,982	2,812	5,481	1,394	104,370

Table 2. Membership Statistics in the United States *(continued)*

Religious Body	Year Reporting	Number of Churches Reporting	Full Communicant or Confirmed Members	Inclusive Membership	Number of Pastors Serving Parishes	Total Number of Clergy	Number of Sunday or Sabbath Schools	Total Enrollment
The Schwenkfelder Church	1995	5	2,524	2,524	8	9	5	701
Separate Baptists in Christ	1992	100	8,000	8,000	95	140	100	
Serbian Orthodox Church in the U.S.A. and Canada*	1986	68		67,000	60	82		
Seventh-day Adventist Church	2002	4,619	918,882	918,882	2,589	4,946	4,921	417,298
Seventh Day Baptist General Conference, USA and Canada	1995	80	4,800		46	74		
Southern Baptist Convention	2002	42,775	16,247,736	16,247,736	94,231	121,417	39,471	8,174,493
Southern Methodist Church	2002	108	6,493	6,493	123	163	108	3,987
Sovereign Grace Believers	2002	350	4,000	4,000	450	450	350	
The Swedenborgian Church*	2002	44	1,532	2,000	34	54		
Syrian (Syriac) Orthodox Church of Antioch*	2002	25	32,500	32,500	21	25	22	1,585
The Syro-Russian Orthodox Catholic Church	2002	125	25,000	26,000	112	127	30	1,150
True Orthodox Church of Greece (Synod of Metropolitan Cyprian), American Exarchate	1993	9	1,095	1,095	18	19		
Ukrainian Orthodox Church of the U.S.A.*	2000	115	8,000	13,000	103	124	65	500

Table 2. Membership Statistics in the United States (*continued*)

Religious Body	Year Reporting	Number of Churches Reporting	Full Communicant or Confirmed Members	Inclusive Membership	Number of Pastors Serving Parishes	Total Number of Clergy	Number of Sunday or Sabbath Schools	Total Enrollment
Unitarian Universalist Association of Congregations	2002	1,010		214,738	1,267	171	1,010	1,819
United Christian Church		10	334	334	8	14	9	448
United Church of Christ*	2002	5,850	1,330,985	1,330,985	4,295	10,364	3,687	310,349
United House of Prayer	2002	135			270	500	135	
The United Methodist Church*	2002	35,102	8,251,042	8,251,042	24,273	44,854	32,245	3,046,198
United Pentecostal Church International	2002	4,100			9,004	9,004		
United Pentecostal Churches of Christ	2000	62	7,059	7,059	466	483	62	2,289
United Zion Church	1998	13	883	883	13	23	11	818
Unity of the Brethren	1998	27	2,548	3,218	25	39	24	1,442
Universal Fellowship of Metropolitan Community Churches	1998	300		44,000	324	372		
Volunteers of America						338		
The Wesleyan Church	2002	1,628	113,570	123,160	1,975	3,198	1,580	532,256
Wisconsin Evangelical Lutheran Synod	2002	1,250	315,312	403,345	1,257	1,806	1,226	40,518
Totals		**325,916**	**147,300,261**	**161,145,004**	**365,021**	**598,420**	**217,131**	**26,054,254**

**National Council of Churches member communion*

Table 3. Membership Statistics for the National Council of the Churches of Christ in the U.S.A.

Religious Body	Year Reporting	Number of Churches Reporting	Inclusive Membership	Number of Pastors Serving Parishes
African Methodist Episcopal Church	1999		2,500,000	7,741
African Methodist Episcopal Zion Church	2002	3,226	1,430,795	3,235
The Alliance of Baptists in the USA	2002	128	63,870	286
American Baptist Churches in the USA	2002	5,836	1,484,291	4,325
The Antiochian Orthodox Christian Archdiocese of North America	2002	230	380,000	400
Armenian Apostolic Church, Diocese of America	1991	72	414,000	49
Christian Church (Disciples of Christ) in the United States and Canada	2002	3,691	786,334	3,362
Christian Methodist Episcopal Church	2002	3,300	850,000	3,001
Church of the Brethren	2002	1,069	134,844	925
Coptic Orthodox Church	2000	100	300,000	140
Episcopal Church	2001	7,344	2,333,628	6,057
Evangelical Lutheran Church in America	2002	10,721	5,038,006	7,354
Friends United Meeting	2002	427	42,680	306
Greek Orthodox Archdiocese of America		510	1,500,000	599
Hungarian Reformed Church in America	1998	27	6,000	27
International Council of Community Churches	2002	192	115,812	240
Korean Presbyterian Church in America, General Assembly of the	2002		55,100	460
Malankara Orthodox Syrian Church, Diocese of America				

Table 3. Membership Statistics for the National Council of the Churches of Christ in the U.S.A. *(continued)*

Religious Body	Year Reporting	Number of Churches Reporting	Inclusive Membership	Number of Pastors Serving Parishes
Mar Thoma Syrian Church of India	2002	68	32,500	42
Moravian Church in America (Unitas Fratrum)	2002	93	25,140	86
National Baptist Convention of America, Inc.	2000		3,500,000	
National Baptist Convention, USA, Inc.		9,000	5,000,000	
National Missionary Baptist Convention of America	1992		2,500,000	
The Orthodox Church in America	2002	725	900,000	792
Patriarchal Parishes of the Russian Orthodox Church in the USA		31		45
Philadelphia Yearly Meeting of the Religious Society of Friends	2000	105	11,871	0
Polish National Catholic Church of America	2002	145	60,000	131
Presbyterian Church (USA)	2001	11,097	3,407,329	8,725
Progressive National Baptist Convention, Inc.	1995	2,000	2,500,000	
Reformed Church in America	2002	901	281,475	823
Serbian Orthodox Church in the USA and Canada	1986	68	67,000	60
The Swedenborgian Church	2002	44	2,000	34
Syrian (Syriac) Orthodox Church of Antioch	2002	25	32,500	21
Ukrainian Orthodox Church of the U.S.A.	2000	115	13,000	103
United Church of Christ	2001	5,888	1,359,105	4,304
The United Methodist Church	2002	35,102	8,251,042	24,273
Totals		**102,280**	**45,378,322**	**77,946**

Table 4. Selected Statistics of Church

				TOTAL CONTRIBUTIONS		
Religious Body	**Year**	**Full or Confirmed Members**	**Inclusive Members**	**Total Contributions**	**Per Capita Full or Confirmed Members**	**Per Capit Inclusive Members**
The Apostolic Church in Canada	2002	1,450	1,740	$1,705,737	$1,176.37	$980.31
Armenian Holy Apostolic Church—Canadian Diocese	2000	85,000	85,000	$855,000	$10.06	$10.06
Baptist Union of Western Canada	1999	20,427	20,427	$5,107,654	$250.04	$250.04
The Bible Holiness Movement	2002	751	1,001	$280,665	$373.72	$280.38
Canadian District of the Moravian Church in America, Northern Province	2002	1,138	1,473	$1,118,024	$982.45	$759.01
Christian Church (Disciples of Christ) in Canada	2002	1,599	2,631	$1,449,009	$906.20	$550.74
Church of the Lutheran Brethren	2002	376	622	$650,359	$1,729.68	$1,045.59
Evangelical Lutheran Church in Canada	2002	142,865	199,236	$61,270,705	$428.87	$307.53
Foursquare Gospel Church of Canada	1996	3,063	3,063	$4,376,923	$1,428.97	$1,428.97
Lutheran Church—Canada	2001	58,545	79,178			
North American Baptist Conference	2002	16,873	16,873	$32,107,050	$1,902.87	$1,902.87
Presbyterian Church in America (Canadian Section)	1997	701	1,067	$1,561,188	$2,227.09	$1,463.16
The Reformed Episcopal Church of Canada	2001	420	505	$221,452	$527.27	$438.52
Seventh-day Adventist Church in Canada	2002	51,804	51,804	$49,582,758	$957.12	$957.12
Union d'Eglises Baptistes Françaises au Canada	2002	1,720	1,720	$584,102	$339.59	$339.59
The United Church of Canada	2002	625,000	1,518,000	$328,501,000	$525.60	$216.40
Totals		1,011,732	1,984,340	$489,371,625	$483.70	$246.62

ᶠinances—Canadian Churches

CONGREGATIONAL FINANCES			BENEVOLENCES			
Total ᶜongregational ᶜontributions	Per Capita Full or Confirmed Members	Per Capita Inclusive Members	Total Benevolences	Per Capita Full or Confirmed Members	Per Capita Inclusive Members	Benevolences as a Percentage of Total Giving
$1,506,104	$1,038.69	$865.58	$199,633	$137.68	$114.73	12%
$430,000	$5.06	$5.06	$425,000	$5.00	$5.00	50%
$562,511	$27.54	$27.54	$4,545,143	$222.51	$222.51	89%
$51,475	$68.54	$51.42	$229,190	$305.18	$228.96	82%
$994,824	$874.19	$675.37	$123,200	$108.26	$83.64	11%
$1,230,384	$769.47	$467.65	$218,625	$136.73	$83.10	15%
$530,911	$1,412.00	$853.55	$119,448	$317.68	$192.04	18%
$52,343,354	$366.38	$262.72	$7,518,028	$52.62	$37.73	12%
$4,248,451	$1,387.02	$1,387.02	$128,472	$41.94	$41.94	3%
$30,813,341	$526.32	$389.17				
$26,408,218	$1,565.12	$1,565.12	$5,698,832	$337.75	$337.75	18%
$1,436,791	$2,049.63	$1,346.57	$124,397	$177.46	$116.59	8%
$96,000	$228.57	$190.10	$125,452	$298.70	$248.42	57%
$14,879,268	$287.22	$287.22	$34,703,490	$669.90	669.90	70%
$237,527	$138.10	$138.10	$346,575	$201.50	$201.50	59%
$284,973,000	$455.96	$187.73	$43,528,000	$69.64	$28.67	13%
$420,742,158	$415.86	$212.03	$98,033,485	$96.90	$49.40	20%

Table 5. Selected Statistics of Church

				TOTAL CONTRIBUTIONS		
Religious Body	**Year**	**Full or Confirmed Members**	**Inclusive Members**	**Total Contributions**	**Per Capita Full or Confirmed Members**	**Per Capit Inclusive Members**
The Allegheny Wesleyan Methodist Connection (Original Allegheny Conference)	2002	1,663	1,803	$5,288,894	$3,180.33	$2,933.39
American Baptist Churches in the USA	2002	1,484,291	1,484,291	$465,276,464	$313.47	$313.47
American Evangelical Christian Churches	2001	15,470	18,412	$2,900,500	$187.49	$157.53
The Antiochian Orthodox Christian Archdiocese of North America	2002	380,000	380,000	$4,285,000	$11.28	$11.28
Apostolic Faith Mission Church of God	2003	8,256	10,426	$1,080,320	$130.85	$103.62
Associate Reformed Presbyterian Church (General Synod)	2002	35,556	40,905	$45,486,055	$1,279.28	$1,111.99
Baptist Missionary Association of America	1998	234,732	234,732	$70,087,434	$298.58	$298.58
Berean Fundamental Church Fellowship	2000	8,000	8,000	$10,309,605	$1,288.70	$1,288.70
Bible Fellowship Church	2002	7,308	7,308	$13,746,622	$1,881.04	$1,881.04
Brethren in Christ Church	2001	20,739	20,739	$36,431,223	$1,756.65	$1,756.65
Christ Community Church (Evangelical-Protestant)	2000	1,027	1,690	$1,107,628	$1,078.51	$655.40
Christian Church (Disciples of Christ) in the United States and Canada	2002	504,118	786,334	$485,087,122	$962.25	$616.90
Christian Union	2002	4,484	6,153	$3,952,933	$881.56	$642.44
Church of the Brethren	2002	134,844	134,844	$93,255,415	$691.58	$691.58
The Church of Christ (Holiness) USA	2002	10,321	10,321	$9,740,580	$943.76	$943.76
Church of the Lutheran Brethren of America	2001	8,194	13,702	$14,103,909	$1,721.25	$1,029.33
Church of the Lutheran Confession	2002	6,456	8,492	$5,685,543	$880.66	$669.52
Church of the Nazarene	2002	639,330	643,649	$719,211,069	$1,124.94	$1,117.40
Churches of Christ	1997	1,500,000	1,500,000	$1,445,000,000	$963.33	$963.33
Churches of God, General Conference	2002	32,654	32,654	$27,158,312	$831.70	$831.70
Community of Christ	2002	142,106	142,106	$42,535,613	$299.32	$299.32
Conservative Congregational Christian Conference	2002	40,041	40,041	44,938,493	$1,122.31	$1,122.31
Cumberland Presbyterian Church	2002	84,417	84,417	$49,446,683	$585.74	$585.74
Cumberland Presbyterian Church in America	1996	15,142	15,142	$40,408,524	$2,668.64	$2,668.64
Episcopal Church	2001	1,897,004	2,333,628	$2,070,493,919	$1,091.45	$887.24
The Evangelical Church	2000	12,475	12,475	$15,632,985	$1,253.15	$1,253.15

Finances—United States Churches

CONGREGATIONAL FINANCES			BENEVOLENCES			
Total Congregation Contributions	Per Capita Full or Confirmed Members	Per Capita Inclusive Members	Total Benevolences	Per Capita Full or Confirmed Members	Per Capita Inclusive Members	Benevolences as a Percentage
$4,117,160	$2,475.74	$2,283.51	$1,171,734	$704.59	$649.88	22%
402,060,918	$270.88	$270.88	$63,215,546	$42.59	$42.59	14%
$2,900,500	$187.49	$157.53	$10,672	$0.69	$0.58	1%
$1,925,000	$5.07	$5.07	$2,360,000	$6.21	$6.21	55%
$308,000	$37.31	$29.54	$722,320	$93.55	$74.08	71%
$37,394,125	$1,051.70	$914.17	$8,091,930	$227.58	$197.82	18%
$57,481,427	$244.88	$244.88	$12,606,007	$53.70	$53.70	18%
$9,277,940	$1,159.74	$1,159.74	$1,031,665	$128.96	$128.96	10%
$10,830,651	$1,482.03	$1,482.03	$2,915,951	$399.01	$399.01	21%
29,566.287	$1,425.64	$1,425.64	$6,864,936	$331.02	$331.02	19%
$904,628	$880.85	$535.28	$203,000	$197.66	$120.12	18%
$438,378,385	$869.59	$557.50	$46,708,737	$92.65	$59.40	10%
$3,197,088	$713.00	$519.60	$755,876	$168.57	$122.85	19%
$70,524,998	$523.01	$523.01	$22,730,417	$168.57	$168.57	24%
$9,178,816	$889.33	$889.33	$561,764	$54.43	$54.43	6%
$11,905,251	$1,452.92	$868.87	$2,198,658	$268.33	$160.46	16%
$4,876,122	$755.29	$574.20	$809,421	$125.38	$95.32	14%
$587,027,991	$918.19	$912.03	$132,183,078	$206.75	$205.37	18%
$1,414,000,000	$942.67	$942.67	$31,000,000	$20.67	$20.67	2%
$22,288,178	$682.56	$682.56	$4,870,134	$149.14	$149.14	18%
$18,217,887	$128.20	$128.20	$24,317,726	$171.12	$171.12	57%
$36,747,983	$917.76	$917.76	$8,190,510	$204.55	$204.55	18%
$42,570,586	$504.29	504.29	$6,876,097	$81.45	$81.45	14%
$34,921,064	$2,306.24	2,306.24	$5,487,460	$362.40	$362.40	14%
$1,787,480,509	$942.27	$765.97	$283,013,410	$149.19	$121.28	14%
12,784,502	$1,024.81	$1,024.81	$2,848,483	$228.34	$228.34	18%

Table 5. Selected Statistics of Church

				TOTAL CONTRIBUTIONS		
Religious Body	**Year**	**Full or Confirmed Members**	**Inclusive Members**	**Total Contributions**	**Per Capita Full or Confirmed Members**	**Per Capita Inclusive Members**
The Evangelical Congregational Church	2002	21,208	21,208	$18,195,387	$857.95	$857.95
The Evangelical Covenant Church	2002	103,549	103,549	$223,340,364	$2,156.86	$2,156.86
Evangelical Lutheran Church in America	2002	3,757,723	5,038,006	$2,472,649,472	$658.02	$490.80
Evangelical Lutheran Synod	2002	16,849	21,442	$12,797,848	$759.56	$596.86
Fellowship of Evangelical Bible Churches	2002	1,950	1,950	$2,128,773	$1,091.68	$1,091.68
Fellowship of Evangelical Churches	2003	11,604	11,604	16,039,843	$1,382.27	$1,382.27
Free Methodist Church of North America	2001	61,202	69,342	$126,011,031	$2,058.94	$1,817.24
General Association of General Baptists	2001	66,636	85,346	$36,335,254	$545.28	$425.74
General Conference of Mennonite Brethren Churches	1996	50,915	82,130	$65,851,481	$1,293.36	$801.80
International Church of the Foursquare Gospel	2002	235,852	305,852	$644,823,024	$2,734.02	$2,108.28
The International Pentecostal Church of Christ	2002	2,004	4,961	$3,551,761	$1,772.34	$715.94
The Latvian Evangelical Lutheran Church in America	2002	12,124	13,584	$3,094,000	$255.20	$227.77
The Lutheran Church Missouri Synod (LCMS)	2002	1,907,923	2,512,714	$1,203,333,537	$630.70	$478.90
Mar Thoma Syrian Church of India	2002		32,500	$2,873,000		$88.40
The Missionary Church	2002	35,287	35,287	$79,747,997	$2,259.98	$2,259.98
Moravian Church in America (Unita Fratrum)	2002	19,806	25,140	$16,257,298	$820.83	$646.67
North American Baptist Conference	2002	47,692	47,692	$65,765,687	$1,378.97	$1,378.97
The Orthodox Presbyterian Church	2002	18,746	26,448	$35,076,000	$1,871.12	$1,326.23
Presbyterian Church in America	2002	254,676	310,750	$505,524,440	$1,984.97	$1,626.79
Presbyterian Church (USA)	2002	2,451,969	3,407,329	$2,902,631,325	$1,183.80	$851.88
Primitive Methodist Church in the USA	2002	4,211	4,399	$4,953,394	$1,176.30	$1,126.03
Reformed Church in America	2002	171,361	281,475	$268,953,148	$1,569.51	$955.51
Reformed Church in the United States	2002	3,258	4,369	$6,241,428	$1,915.72	$1,428.57
Reformed Presbyterian Church of North America	1997	4,363	6,105	$6,446,899	$1,477.63	$1,056.00
Seventh-day Adventist Church	2002	918,882	918,882	$1,072,005,312	$1,166.64	$1,166.64
Southern Baptist Convention	2002	16,247,736	16,247,736	$9,461,603,271	$582.33	$582.33

inances—United States Churches *(continued)*

CONGREGATIONAL FINANCES			BENEVOLENCES			
Total ongregation ontributions	Per Capita Full or Confirmed Members	Per Capita Inclusive Members	Total Benevolences	Per Capita Full or Confirmed Members	Per Capita Inclusive Members	Benevolences as a Percentage
18,195,387	$857.95	$857.95	$2,002,028	$94.40	$94.40	11%
198,202,551	$1,914.09	$1,914.09	$25,137,813	$242.76	$242.76	11%
,238,773,875	$595.78	$444.38	$233,875,597	$62.24	$46.42	9%
11,787,432	$699.59	$549.74	$1,010,416	$59.97	$47.12	8%
$1,689,072	$866.19	$866.19	$439,701	$225.49	$225.49	21%
14,138,539	$1,218.42	$1,218.42	$1,901,304	$163.85	$163.85	12%
111,415,741	$1,820.46	$1,606.76	$14,595,290	$238.48	$210.48	12%
30,152,750	$452.50	$353.30	$3,091,252	$46.39	$36.22	9%
50,832,814	$998.39	$618.93	$15,018,667	$294.98	$182.86	23%
603,266,480	$2,557.82	$1,972.41	$41,556,544	$176.20	$135.87	6%
$2,648,634	$1,321.67	$533.89	$903,127	$450.66	$182.05	25%
$2,598,000	$214.29	$191.25	$496,000	$40.91	$36.51	16%
,086,223,370	$569.32	$432.29	$117,110,167	$61.38	$46.61	10%
$2,403,000		$73.94	$470,000		$14.46	16%
69,735,215	$1,976.23	$1,976.23	$10,012,782	$283.75	$283.75	13%
15,328,513	$773.93	$609.73	$928,785	$46.89	$36.94	6%
56,813,620	$1,191.26	$1,191.26	$8,952,067	$187.71	$187.71	14%
29,251,600	$1,560.42	$1,106,00	$5,216,600	$278.28	$197.24	15%
410,920,946	$1,613.50	$1,322.35	$94,604,494	$371.47	$304.44	19%
,509,677,412	$1,023.54	$736.55	$392,953,913	$160.26	$115.33	14%
$4,264,515	$1,012.71	$969.43	$688,879	$163.59	$156.60	14%
229,560,092	$1,339.63	$815.56	$39,393,056	$229.88	$139.95	15%
$5,309,445	$1,629.66	$1,215.25	$931,983	$286.06	$213.32	15%
$5,792,856	$1,327.72	$948.87	$654,043	$149.91	$107.13	10%
346,825,034	$377.44	$377.44	$725,180,278	$789.20	$789.20	68%
,432,952,589	$519.02	$519.02	$1,028,650,682	$63.31	$63.31	11%

Table 5. Selected Statistics of Churc

				TOTAL CONTRIBUTIONS		
Religious Body	**Year**	**Full or Confirmed Members**	**Inclusive Members**	**Total Contributions**	**Per Capita Full or Confirmed Members**	**Per Capi Inclusive Member**
The Syro-Russian Orthodox Church	2002	25,000	26,000	$89,000	$3.56	$3.42
United Church of Christ	2002	1,330,985	1,330,985	$867,240,642	$651.58	$651.58
The United Methodist Church	2002	8,251,042	8,251,042	$5,043,693,838	$611.28	$611.28
Unity of the Brethren	1998	2,548	3,218	$165,184	$64.83	$51.33
Universal Fellowship of Metropolitan Community Churches	1998		44,000	$1,570,860		$35.70
The Wesleyan Church	2001	113,570	123,160	$235,677,622	$2,223.67	$2,059.74
Wisconsin Evangelical Lutheran Synod	2002	315,312	403,345	$319,771,338	$1,014.14	$792.80

**National Council Churches member communion*

Summary Statitistic

				TOTAL CONTRIBUTIONS		
Nation	**Number Reporting**	**Full or Confirmed Members**	**Inclusive Members**	**Total Contributions**	**Per Capita Full or Confirmed Members**	**Per Capit Inclusive Members**
United States	59	43,694,611	47,773,814	$31,465,090,286	$720.11	$658.63
Canada	16	1,011,732	1,984,340	$486,371,625	$483.70	$246,62

·inances—United States Churches *(continued)*

CONGREGATIONAL FINANCES			BENEVOLENCES			
Total ·ongregation ·ontributions	Per Capita Full or Confirmed Members	Per Capita Inclusive Members	Total Benevolences	Per Capita Full or Confirmed Members	Per Capita Inclusive Members	Benevolences as a Percentage
$35,000	$1.40	$1.35	$54,000	$2.16	$2.08	61%
$789,083,286	$592.86	$592.86	$78,157,356	$58.72	$58.72	9%
·4,067,476,116	$492.97	$492.97	$978,217,722	$118.31	$118.31	19%
$51,465	$20.20	$15.99	$113,719	$44.63	$35.34	69%
$1,415,000		$32.16	$155,860		$3.54	10%
$240,498,251	$2,117.62	$1,952.73	$13,770,178	$121.25	$111.81	5%
$270,619,678	$858.26	$670.94	$49,151,660	$155.88	$121.86	15%

·of Church Finances

CONGREGATIONAL FINANCES			BENEVOLENCES			
Total ·ongregational Contributions	Per Capita Full or Confirmed Members	Per Capita Inclusive Members	Total Belevolences	Per Capita Full or Confirmed Members	Per Capita Inclusive Members	Benevolences as a Percentage of Total Contributions
·26,908,804,274	$615.84	$563.25	$4,555,191,495	$104.25	$95.35	14%
$420,742,158	$415.86	$212.03	$98,033,485	$96.90	$49.40	20%

STATISTICAL SECTION

Trends in Seminary Enrollment

Data Provided by The Association of Theological Schools (ATS) in the United States and Canada

Table 1: ATS total student enrollment figures include the number of individuals enrolled in degree program as well as persons enrolled in non-degree programs of study. Growth in total enrollment is a function of bot increased enrollment in the seminaries and the increased number of member schools in the Association. Th head count enrollment in all member schools increased by 7,635 students, an increase of 11% from fall 199 to fall 2002. Over the same five years, the full-time equivalent (FTE) enrollment increased by almost 8%.

Table 1 Number of Member Schools from 1988 to 2002

Year	Number of Schools	Total Enrollment	Canada Head Count	Canada FTE	United States Head Count	United States FTE	By Membership Accredited	By Membership Non-Accredited
1988	207	55,746	3,995	2,679	51,751	34,827	51,683	4,063
1989	205	56,178	4,142	2,668	52,036	35,013	52,949	3,229
1990	211	59,003	4,053	2,636	54,950	37,590	54,052	4,951
1991	211	59,897	4,648	2,631	55,249	36,456	55,028	4,869
1992	220	63,484	4,897	2,999	58,587	39,554	57,784	5,700
1993	219	63,429	5,040	3,150	58,389	39,506	57,823	5,606
1994	226	65,089	5,241	3,212	59,848	40,293	60,490	4,599
1995	224	64,480	5,203	3,267	59,277	39,834	59,813	4,667
1996	233	65,637	5,568	3,304	60,069	40,111	60,527	5,110
1997	229	65,361	5,544	3,225	59,817	40,022	61,498	3,863
1998	237	68,875	5,847	3,683	63,028	40,994	64,412	4,463
1999	237	70,432	6,010	3,224	64,422	41,528	65,674	4,758
2000	243	72,728	5,868	3,251	68,860	44,627	69,850	2,878
2001	243	73,925	6,254	3,342	67,671	45,094	70,942	2,983
2002	244	76,510	6,643	3,512	69,687	44,557	73,615	2,895

Table 2: ATS computes enrollment both by the total number of individual students (Head Count) and th equivalent of full-time students (FTE). If all students were enrolled full-time, the Head Count number and th full-time equivalency number would be the same. The FTE is calculated by dividing the total number of cred its required for the degree by the number of semesters prescribed for degree duration to determine the averag academic load. The total of credit hours taken by all students in a given degree program in a semester is the divided by the average academic load. During the past five years, full-time equivalent enrollment as a percent age of head count enrollment has generally decreased, indicating an increasing number of part-time students The enrollment figures in the year have reflected this trend.

Table 2 Head Count and FTE for all Member Schools 1988 to 2002

Year	Head Count	% Change	FTE	% Change	FTE % of Head Count
1988	55,746	-0.04	37,506	-2.15	67.3%
1989	56,178	0.77	37,681	0.47	67.1%
1990	59,003	5.03	40,226	6.75	68.2%
1991	59,897	1.52	39,087	-2.83	65.3%
1992	63,484	5.99	42,553	8.87	67.0%
1993	63,429	0.09	42,656	0.24	67.2%
1994	65,089	2.62	43,505	1.99	66.8%
1995	64,480	-0.94	43,101	-0.93	66.8%
1996	65,637	1.79	43,414	0.73	66.1%
1997	65,361	-0.42	43,247	-0.38	66.2%
1998	68,875	5.38	44,678	3.31	64.9%
1999	70,432	2.17	44,845	0.68	63.7%
2000	72,728	3.26	47,876	6.76	65.8%
2001	73,925	1.65	48,435	1.17	65.5%
2002	76,510	3.50	48,069	-0.76	62.8%

Table 3: ATS member schools offer a variety of degree programs, Table 3 displays enrollment by categories f degree programs. The Master of Divinity (MDiv) degree is the normative degree to prepare persons for rdained ministry and for pastoral and religious leadership responsibilities in congregations. Over the past five ears, from fall 1998 to fall 2002, the MDiv experienced the largest increase in the *number* of students enrolled, n increase of 10%. In the same five-year period, the greatest increases by *percentage* in student head count nrollment were in the Master of Arts in a variety of specialized ministry areas (+26%) within the Basic Ministerial Leadership (Non-MDiv) category. This is followed by an increase of 20% in the General heological Studies category.

able 3 Head Count Enrollment by Degree Categories 1988–2002
Categories based on accrediting standards—adopted in 1996)

Year	Basic Ministerial Leadership (M.Div.)	Basic Ministerial Leadership (Non-M.Div.)	General Theological Studies	Advanced Ministerial Leadership	Advanced Theological Research	Others
1988	26,581	5,131	5,423	6,511	4,203	7,897
1989	25,954	5,080	5,485	7,004	4,186	8,469
1990	25,615	5,284	6,144	7,417	5,046	9,497
1991	25,710	5,805	6,105	7,598	5,044	9,635
1992	26,956	5,812	6,872	7,961	5,036	10,847
1993	27,264	6,536	7,131	8,302	5,157	9,039
1994	27,240	6,891	7,229	7,841	5,330	10,558
1995	27,497	6,964	7,211	8,233	5,302	9,273
1996	28,035	7,474	7,157	8,315	5,499	9,157
1997	28,283	7,463	7,048	8,195	5,391	8,981
1998	29,263	8,066	7,601	8,641	5,712	9,591
1999	29,842	8,361	7,862	8,743	5,396	10,228
2000	30,427	9,098	8,436	8,758	5,692	10,317
2001	31,128	8,652	8,503	8,790	5,756	11,096
2002	31,994	9,467	8,610	9,208	5,653	11,578

Table 4: In fall 2002, women constituted 35% of the total enrollment in all ATS schools and 31% of the head ount enrollment in the MDiv degree program. When ATS first began gathering enrollment data by gender in 1972, vomen represented 10.2% of the enrollment and 4.7% of the MDivenrollment. Only once in the past 29 years has he number of women students decreased from one year to the next, that being in 1993, with a 0.65% decrease.

able 4 Women Student Head Count Enrollment 1988-2002

Year	Number of Students	% Annual Increase	% of Total Enrollment
1988	16,326	0.00	29.29%
1989	16,525	1.20	29.42%
1990	17,498	5.56	29.66%
1991	18,188	3.79	30.37%
1992	19,856	8.40	31.28%
1993	19,727	-0.65	31.10%
1994	20,564	4.07	31.59%
1995	20,795	1.12	32.25%
1996	21,523	3.50	32.76%
1997	21,652	0.60	33.10%
1998	23,176	7.04	33.65%
1999	24,057	3.73	34.16%
2000	25,391	5.55	34.91%
2001	25,999	2.39	35.17%
2002	27,315	5.06	35.70%

Tables 5, 6, 7: Enrollment of North American racial/ethnic minority students in ATS schools has grown from 6% of total head count enrollment in 1977 to 21% in 2002. Over the past five years (1998 to 2002), the number of African American students increased by 29%; Hispanic students by 44%; and Pacific/Asian American students by 11%. The number of White students increased 7% over the same period. Tables 5, 6, and 7 show the number of African American, Hispanic, and Pacific/Asian American students enrolled by year.

Table 5 African American Student Head Count Enrollment 1988-2002

Year	Number of Students	% Annual Increase	% of Total Enrollment
1988	3,660	8.72	6.57%
1989	3,925	6.75	6.99%
1990	4,265	7.97	7.23%
1991	4,658	8.44	7.78%
1992	5,558	16.19	8.75%
1993	5,223	-6.41	8.23%
1994	5,526	5.48	8.49%
1995	5,698	3.11	8.84%
1996	5,550	-2.60	8.45%
1997	5,802	4.54	8.87%
1998	6,328	9.07	9.19%
1999	6,854	8.31	9.73%
2000	7,161	4.48	9.85%
2001	7,462	4.20	10.09%
2002	8,192	9.78	10.71%

Table 6 Hispanic Student Head Count Enrollment 1988–2002

Year	Number of Students	% Annual Increase	% of Total Enrollment
1988	1,415	1.13	2.54%
1989	1,485	4.71	2.64%
1990	1,912	22.33	3.24%
1991	1,626	-17.59	2.71%
1992	1,689	3.73	2.66%
1993	1,790	5.64	2.82%
1994	1,799	0.50	2.76%
1995	1,817	1.00	2.82%
1996	1,785	-1.76	2.72%
1997	1,915	7.28	2.93%
1998	2,175	13.58	3.16%
1999	2,256	3.72	3.10%
2000	2,685	19.02	3.69%
2001	2,756	2.64	3.72%
2002	2,449	-11.64	3.20%

Table 7 Pacific/Asian American Student Head Count Enrollment 1988–2002

Year	Number of Students	% Annual Increase	% of Total Enrollment
1988	1,963	13.75	3.52%
1989	2,062	4.80	3.67%
1990	2,437	15.39	4.13%
1991	2,649	8.00	4.42%
1992	3,142	15.69	4.95%
1993	3,631	13.47	5.72%
1994	3,876	6.32	5.95%
1995	4,245	9.52	6.58%
1996	4,492	5.82	6.84%
1997	4,545	1.18	6.95%
1998	4,992	8.95	7.25%
1999	4,932	-1.20	6.78%
2000	5,003	1.44	6.88%
2001	5,021	0.36	6.79%
2002	5,005	-0.32	6.54%

IV

A CALENDAR FOR CHURCH USE

2004–2007

This Calendar presents the major days of religious observances for Christians, Jews, Bahá'ís, and Muslims; and, within the Christian community, major dates observed by Roman Catholic, Eastern and Oriental Orthodox, Episcopal, and Lutheran churches. Within each of these traditions many other observances such as saints' days exist, but only those regarded as the most important are listed. Dates of interest to many Protestant communions are also included.

In the Orthodox dates, immovable observances are listed in accordance with the Gregorian calendar. Movable dates (those depending on the date of Easter) will often differ from Western observance, since the date of Easter (*Pascha*) in the Orthodox communions does not always correlate with the date for Easter of the Western churches. For Orthodox churches that use the old Julian calendar, observances are held thirteen days later than listed here.

Jewish and Muslim holidays begin after sunset the day previous to the date listed in this Calendar. For Jews and Muslims, who follow differing lunar calendars, the dates of major observances are translated into Gregorian dates. Since the actual beginning of a new month in the Islamic calendar is determined by the appearance of the new moon, the corresponding dates given here on the Gregorian calendar may vary by geographic location and practice. Following the lunar calendar, Muslim dates fall roughly eleven days earlier each year on the Gregorian calendar. Practice concerning transliteration of the titles of holidays varies widely as well.

(Note: This listing reflects the first full day of those holidays extending over two or more days. "RC" stands for Roman Catholic, "O" for Orthodox, "E" for Episcopal, "L" for Lutheran, "ECU" for Ecumenical, "M" for Muslim, "J" for Jewish).

Event	**2004**	**2005**	**2006**	**2007**
New Year's Day (RC-Solemnity of Mary; O-Circumcision of Jesus Christ; E-Feast of Holy Name; L-Naming of Jesus) (RC, O, E, L)	Jan 01	Jan 01	Jan 01	Jan. 01
Epiphany Sunday (RC)	Jan 04	Jan 02	Jan 01	Jan. 07
Epiphany (RC,.O, E, L)	Jan 06	Jan 06	Jan 06	Jan 06
Armenian Christmas (O)	Jan 06	Jan 06	Jan 06	Jan 06
First Sunday After Epiphany (Feast of the Baptism of Our Lord) (Christian)	Jan 11	Jan 09	Jan 08	Jan 14
Feast Day of St. John the Baptist (Armenian O)	Jan 13	Jan 13	Jan 13	Jan 13
Week of Prayer for Christian Unity (ECU)	Jan 18	Jan 18	Jan 18	Jan 18
Ecumenical Sunday (ECU)	Jan 18	Jan 16	Jan 15	Jan 21
Week of Prayer for Christian Unity, Canada (ECU)	Jan 19	Jan 17	Jan 16	Jan 22
Theophany (Oriental O)	Jan 19	Jan 19	Jan 19	Jan 19
Waqf al Arafah (Eve of Eid al-Adha) (M)	Jan 31	Jan 19	Jan 08	Dec 29
Presentation of Jesus in the Temple (Candlemas; Purification of the Virgin Mary; O—The Meeting of Our Lord and Savior Jesus Christ) (Christian)	Feb 02	Feb 02	Feb 02	Feb 02
Eid al-Adha (Festival of Sacrifice at time of Pilgrimage to Mecca) (M)	Feb 02	Jan 21	Jan 10	Dec 31
Tu B'Shevat (J)	Feb 07	Jan 25	Feb 13	Feb 03
Brotherhood Week (Interfaith)	Feb 15	Feb 20	Feb 19	Feb 18
Muharram Begins (First Day of the Month of Muharram; Muslim New Year) (M)	Feb 22	Feb 10	Jan 31	Jan 20

Event	2004	2005	2006	2007
Great Lent (First Day of Lent) (O)	Feb 23	Mar 14	Mar 06	Feb 19
Ash Wednesday (Western Churches)	Feb 25	Feb 09	Mar 01	Feb 21
Bahá'í Fasting Season begins (19 days) (Bahá'í)	Mar 02	Mar 02	Mar 02	Mar 02
Ashura' (Martyrdom of Imam Hussein) (M [Shi'a])	Mar 02	Feb 19	Feb 09	Jan 29
World Day of Prayer (ECU)	Mar 05	Mar 04	Mar 3	Mar 02
Purim (J)	Mar 07	Mar 25	Mar 14	Mar 04
Joseph, Husband of Mary (RC, E, L)	Mar 19	Mar 19	Mar 19	Mar 19
Feast of Naw-Ruz (Bahá'í New Year) (Bahá'í)	Mar 21	Mar 21	Mar 21	Mar 21
The Annunciation (Christian)	Mar 25	Mar 25	Mar 25	Mar 25
Holy Week (Western Churches)	Apr 04	Mar 20	Apr 09	Apr 01
Holy Week (O)	Apr 04	Apr 24	Apr 16	Apr 01
Palm Sunday (O)	Apr 04	Apr 24	Apr 16	Apr 01
Passover (Pesach) (8 days) (J)	Apr 06	Apr 24	Apr 13	Apr 03
Holy Thursday (O)	Apr 08	Apr 28	Apr 20	Apr 05
Holy Thursday (Western Churches)	Apr 08	Mar 24	Apr 13	Apr 05
Holy Friday (Good Friday; Burial of Jesus) (O)	Apr 09	Apr 29	Apr 21	Apr 06
Good Friday (Friday of the Passion of Our Lord) (Western Churches)	Apr 09	Mar 25	Apr 14	Apr 06
Pascha (Orthodox Easter) (O)	Apr 11	May 01	Apr 23	Apr 08
Easter (Western Churches)	Apr 11	Mar 27	Apr 16	Apr 08
Yom Hashoah (J)	Apr 18	May 06	Apr 25	Apr 15
Feast of Ridvan (Declaration of Baha'u'llah) (12 days) (Bahá'í)	Apr 21	Apr 21	Apr 21	Apr 21
Yom Haatzmaut (J)	Apr 26	May 12	May 03	Apr 23
Mawlid an-Nabi (Anniversary of the Prophet Muhammed's Birthday) (M)	May 02	Apr 21	Apr 11	Mar 31
National Day of Prayer (ECU)	May 06	May 05	May 04	May 03
May Friendship Day (ECU)	May 07	May 06	May 05	May 04
Lag B'Omer (J)	May 09	May 27	May 16	May 06
Rural Life Sunday (ECU)	May 09	May 08	May 14	May 13
Ascension Thursday (Western Churches)	May 20	May 05	May 25	May 17
Ascension Day (O)	May 20	Jun 02	Jun 11	May 17
Declaration of the Bab (Bahá'í)	May 23	May 23	May 23	May 23
Shavuout (Pentacost) (2 days) (J)	May 26	Jun 13	Jun 02	May 23
Ascension of Baha'u'll ah (Bahá'í)	May 29	May 29	May 29	May 29
Pentecost (Whitsunday) (Western Churches)	May 30	May 15	Jun 04	May 27
Pentecost (O)	May 30	Jun 19	Jun 11	May 27
Visitation of the Blessed Virgin Mary (RC, E, L)	May 31	May 31	May 31	May 31
Holy Trinity (RC, E, L)	Jun 06	May 22	Jun 11	Jun 03
Martyrdom of the Bab (Bahá'í)	Jun 09	Jun 09	Jun 09	Jun 09
Corpus Christi (RC)	Jun 13	May 29	Jun 18	Jun 17
Sacred Heart of Jesus (RC)	Jun 18	Jun 10	Jun 23	Jun 22
Nativity of St. John the Baptist (RC, E, L)	Jun 24	Jun 24	Jun 24	Jun 24
Saint Peter and Saint Paul, Apostles of Christ (O)	Jun 29	Jun 29	Jun 29	Jun 29
Feast Day of the Twelve Apostles of Christ (O)	Jun 30	Jun 30	Jun 30	Jun 30
Tisha B'Av (J)	Jul 27	Aug 14	Aug 03	Jul 24
Transfiguration of the Lord (RC, O, E)	Aug 06	Aug 06	Aug 06	Aug 06
Assumption of the Blessed Virgin Mary (E-Feast of the Blessed Virgin Mary; O-Falling Asleep) (Domition of the Blessed Virgin) (RC, O, E)	Aug 15	Aug 15	Aug 15	Aug 15
The Birth of the Blessed Virgin (RC, O)	Sep 08	Sep 08	Sep 08	Sep 08
Laylat al Miraj (Ascent of the Prophet (M)	Sep 12	Sep 01	Aug 22	Aug 11
Holy Cross Day (RC-Triumph of the Cross); (O-Adoration of the Holy Cross) (Christian)	Sep 14	Sep 14	Sep 14	Sep 14
Rosh Hashanah (New Year) (2 days) (J)	Sep 16	Oct 04	Sep 23	Sep 13
Yom Kippur (Day of Atonement) (J)	Sep 25	Oct 13	Oct 02	Sep 22
Michaelmas (St. Michael and All Angels) (Christian)	Sep 29	Sep 29	Sep 29	Sep 29
Laylat at Bar'a (M)	Sep 30	Sep 19	Sep 09	Aug 29
Sukkot (Tabernacles) (7 days) (J)	Sep 30	Oct 18	Oct 07	Sep 27

Event	2004	2005	2006	2007
World Communion Sunday (ECU)	Oct 03	Oct 02	Oct 01	Oct 07
Sh'mini Atzeret (Solemn Assembly) (J)	Oct 07	Oct 25	Oct 15	Oct 04
Shimchat Torah (Rejoicing of the Law) (J)	Oct 08	Oct 26	Oct 15	Oct 05
Laity Sunday (ECU)	Oct 10	Oct 09	Oct 08	Oct 14
Thanksgiving Day (Canada) (National)	Oct 11	Oct 10	Oct 09	Oct 08
Ramadan Begins (First day of the month of Ramadan) (M)	Oct 15	Oct 04	Sep 24	Sep 13
Birth of the Bab (Bahá'í)	Oct 20	Oct 20	Oct 20	Oct 20
Reformation Sunday (L)	Oct 31	Oct 30	Oct 29	Oct 28
Reformation Day (L)	Oct 31	Oct 31	Oct 31	Oct 31
All Saints Day (RC, E, L)	Nov 01	Nov 01	Nov 01	Nov 01
World Community Day (ECU)	Nov 04	Nov 03	Nov 02	Nov 01
Laylat al Qadr (Night of Destiny, Revelation of the Holy Qur'an) (M)	Nov 10	Oct 30	Oct 20	Oct 09
Birth of Baha'u'llah (Bahá'í)	Nov 12	Nov 12	Nov 12	Nov 12
Eid al- Fitr (Festival of the End of Ramadan; First day of the month of Shawwal) (M)	Nov 14	Nov 03	Oct 24	Oct 13
Bible Sunday (ECU)	Nov 21	Nov 20	Nov 19	Nov 18
National Bible Week (ECU)	Nov 21	Nov 20	Nov 19	Nov 18
Presentation of the Blessed Virgin Mary in the Temple (Presentation of the Theotokos) (O)	Nov 21	Nov 21	Nov 21	Nov 21
Last Sunday After Pentecost (L—Feast of Christ the King) (RC, L)	Nov 21	Nov 20	Nov 26	Nov 25
Thanksgiving Sunday (US) (Christian)	Nov 21	Nov 20	Nov 19	Nov 18
Thanksgiving Day (US) (National)	Nov 25	Nov 24	Nov 23	Nov 22
The Day of the Covenant (Bahá'í)	Nov 26	Nov 26	Nov 26	Nov 26
First Sunday of Advent (Advent Sunday) (Christian)	Nov 28	Nov 27	Dec 03	Dec 02
Ascension of 'Abdu'l-Baha (Bahá'í)	Nov 28	Nov 28	Nov 28	Nov 28
Feast Day of St. Andrew the Apostle (RC, O, E, L)	Nov 30	Nov 30	Nov 30	Nov 30
Immaculate Conception of the Blessed Virgin May (RC)	Dec 08	Dec 08	Dec 08	Dec 08
Hanukkah (Chanukah, Festival of Lights) (8 days) (J)	Dec 08	Dec 26	Dec 16	Dec 05
Fourth Sunday of Advent (Christmas Sunday) (Christian)	Dec 19	Dec 18	Dec 24	Dec 23
Christmas (Christian, Except Armenian)	Dec 25	Dec 25	Dec 25	Dec 25

V

INDEXES
Organizations

AAR (American Academy of Religion) 211
ABCCM (Asheville-Buncombe Community Christian Ministry) 249
Aboriginal Rights Coalition (ARC) 49
ACAT 288
ADRIS-Association for the Development of Religious Information Services 25
Advent Christian Church 58, 365
African Methodist Episcopal Church. . 11, 13, 59, 365, 378
African Methodist Episcopal Zion Church . . . 11, 13, 59, 365, 378
AGAPÉ Deux-Montagnes 287
Akron Area Association of Churches 250
Alaska Christian Conference 226
Alban Institute, Inc., The 21
Albanian Orthodox Archdiocese in America . . 62
Albanian Orthodox Diocese of America. . 62, 365
Allegheny Valley Association of Churches. . . 252
Allegheny Wesleyan Methodist Connection, The (Original Allegheny Conference) . . . 62, 365, 382
Alliance of Baptists in the USA, The 63, 365, 378
Alliance of Churches 250
AMERC (Appalachian Ministries Educational Resource Center) 23
American Academy of Religion (AAR) 211
American Association of Lutheran Churches, The 63, 365
American Baptist Association, The 63, 365
American Baptist Churches in the USA 11, 12, 13, 14, 64, 365, 378, 382
American Bible Society 21
American Buddhist Congress 220
American Carpatho-Russian Orthodox Greek Catholic Church, The 65, 365
American Council of Christian Churches 22
American Evangelical Christian Churches 65, 365, 382
American Friends Service Committee 22
American Hindus Against Defamation 221
American Jewish Committee 223
American Muslim Council, The 222
American Religion Data Archive (ARDA) . . . 212
American Rescue Workers 66, 365
American Theological Library Association, The 23
American Tract Society 23
American Waldensian Society, The 23
Amherst and Area Council of Churches 286
Anglican Church of Canada, The 173, 358
Anti-Defamation League of B'nai B'rith, The 223
Antiochian Orthodox Christian Archdiocese of North America, The 66, 175, 358, 365, 378, 382
Apostolic Catholic Assyrian Church of the East, North American Dioceses 67
Apostolic Catholic Orthodox Church 68, 365
Apostolic Christian Church (Nazarene) . . 68, 175, 358, 366
Apostolic Christian Churches of America 69, 366
Apostolic Church in Canada, The . . 175, 358, 380
Apostolic Church of Pentecost of Canada Inc. 176, 358
Apostolic Episcopal Church 69, 366
Apostolic Faith Mission Church of God 70, 366, 382
Apostolic Faith Mission of Portland, Oregon 70, 366
Apostolic Lutheran Church of America . . 70, 366
Apostolic Orthodox Catholic Church of North America 71, 366
Apostolic Overcoming Holy Church of God, Inc. 72
Appalachian Ministries Educational Resource Center (AMERC) 23
ARC (Aboriginal Rights Coalition) 49
ARDA (American Religion Data Archive) . . . 212
Arizona Ecumenical Council 227
Arkansas Interfaith Conference 227
Armenian Apostolic Church of America . . 72, 366
Armenian Apostolic Church, Diocese of America 72, 366, 378
Armenian Evangelical Church 176
Armenian Holy Apostolic Church—Canadian Diocese 176, 358, 380
Arrowhead Interfaith Council 241
Asheville-Buncombe Community Christian Ministry (ABCCM) 249
Assemblies of God 11, 12, 13, 14, 73, 366
Assemblies of God International Fellowship (Independent/Not affiliated) 74
Associate Reformed Presbyterian Church (General Synod) 74, 366, 382
Associated Church Press, The 24
Associated Churches of Fort Wayne & Allen County, Inc., The 233

INDEX

Associated Gospel Churches, The . . 24, 176, 358
Associated Ministries of Tacoma-Pierce County . . . 259
Associated Ministries of Thurston County . . . 259
Association of Canadian Bible Colleges 49
Association of Catholic Diocesan Archivists . . 24
Association of Christian Churches in Manitoba . . . 286
Association of Christian Churches of South Dakota . . . 256
Association for the Development of Religious Information Services (ADRIS) . . . 25
Association of Free Lutheran Congregations, The . . . 75, 366
Association of Gospel Rescue Missions 25
Association of Regular Baptist Churches (Canada) . . . 177, 358
Association of Religious Communities 229
Association of Statisticians of American Religious Bodies . . . 25
Association of Theological Schools (ATS) . . . 212
Association of Theological Schools in the United States and Canada, The . . . 26
Atlantic Ecumenical Council . . . 287
Atlantic Ecumenical Council of Churches (New Brunswick) . . . 286
Atlantic Ecumenical Council of Churches (Newfoundland) . . . 286
ATS (Association of Theological Schools) . . . 212
Attleboro Area Council of Churches, Inc. . . . 238
Auburn Theological Seminary . . . 213
Austin Area Interreligious Ministries . . . 257
Baha'i National Center of the USA, The 219
Baptist Bible Fellowship International . . . 11, 75, 366
Baptist Convention of Ontario and Quebec . . . 177, 358
Baptist General Conference . . . 76, 366
Baptist General Conference of Canada . . 177, 358
Baptist Missionary Association of America . . . 76, 366, 382
Baptist Union of Western Canada . . 177, 358, 380
BARCA (Border Association for Refugees from Central America, Inc.) . . . 257
Barna Research Group, Ltd. . . . 213
Bay Area Ecumenical Forum . . . 239
Beachy Amish Mennonite Churches 77, 366
Berean Fundamental Church Fellowship . . . 77, 367, 382
Bergen County Council of Churches . . . 244
Berrien County Association of Churches 239
Bible Church of Christ, Inc., The . . . 77, 367
Bible Fellowship Church . . . 78, 367, 382
Bible Holiness Church . . . 78
Bible Holiness Movement, The . . . 177, 358, 380
Bible Way Church of Our Lord Jesus Christ World Wide, Inc. . . . 79
Blanton-Peale Institute . . . 26
Border Association for Refugees from Central America (BARCA), Inc. . . . 257
Bread For The World . . . 26
Brethren in Christ Church . . . 79, 367, 382
Brethren in Christ Church, Canadian Conference . . . 178, 358
Brethren Church (Ashland, Ohio) . . . 79, 367
Bridgewater Inter-Church Council . . . 286
British Methodist Episcopal Church of Canada . . . 178
Brooklyn Council of Churches . . . 245
Broome County Council of Churches, Inc. . . . 245
Buddhist Churches of America . . . 220
Buddhist Council of the Midwest . . . 220
Buddhist Peace Fellowship, The . . . 220
Buddhist Sangha Council of Southern California . . . 220
Burlington Inter-Church Council . . . 287
Calgary Council of Churches . . . 286
Calgary Inter-Faith Community Association . . 286
California Council of Churches-California Church Impact . . . 227
Campus Crusade for Christ International 26
Canadian and American Reformed Churches . . . 178, 359
Canadian Baptist Ministries . . . 179, 359
Canadian Bible Society . . . 49
Canadian Centre for Ecumenism/Centre d'oecuménisme . . . 50, 288
Canadian Conference of Mennonite Brethren Churches . . . 179, 359
Canadian Convention of Southern Baptists . . . 179, 359
Canadian Council of Churches, The . . . 50
Canadian District of the Moravian Church in America, Northern Province 179, 359, 380
Canadian Ecumenical Action . . . 286
Canadian Evangelical Christian Churches . . . 179, 359
Canadian Evangelical Theological Association . . . 50
Canadian Society of Biblical Studies—Société Canadienne des Études Bibliques . . . 51
Canadian Tract Society . . . 51
Canadian Yearly Meeting of the Religious Society of Friends . . . 180, 359
Cape Cod Council of Churches, Inc., The . . . 238
Capital Area Council of Churches, Inc. . . . 245
Capital Region Ecumenical Organization (CREO) . . . 246
Capitol Region Conference of Churches, The . . . 229
CARA–Center for Applied Research in the Apostolate . . . 27
Catholic Church, The 11, 12, 13, 14, 79, 367
CB America (Conservative Baptist Association of America) . . . 101, 369
CEAP (Community Emergency Assistance Program) . . . 241
Center for Applied Research in the Apostolate (CARA) . . . 27
Center City Churches . . . 229
Center for Community Concerns . . . 261
Center on Conscience & War (NISBCO) 27
Center for Parish Development . . . 27
Center for the Prevention of Sexual and Domestic Violence . . . 259
Center for the Study of Religion and American Culture . . . 214

INDEX

Central Maryland Ecumenical Council. 238
Centre Emmaüs 288
Chaplaincy of Full Gospel Churches 27
Chataugua County Rural Ministry 246
Christ Catholic Church 81, 367
Christ Catholic Church International 180
Christ Community Church (Evangelical-Protestant) 81, 367, 382
Christadelphians 82
Christian Associates of Southwest Pennsylvania 252
Christian Brethren (also known as Plymouth Brethren) 82, 181, 359, 367
Christian Church (Disciples of Christ) in Canada. 181, 359, 380
Christian Church (Disciples of Christ) in the United States and Canada . . . 83, 367, 378, 382
Christian Church of North America, General Council 85, 367
Christian Churches/Churches of Christ. . 181, 359
Christian Churches and Churches of Christ. 11, 85, 367
Christian Churches United of the Tri-County Area 252
Christian Community Action 230
Christian Conference of Connecticut 230
Christian Congregation, Inc., The. 86, 367
Christian Council of Delaware and Maryland's Eastern Shore, The. 231
Christian Council of Metropolitan Atlanta . . . 231
Christian Council on Persons with Disabilities . . 28
Christian Endeavor International 28
Christian Leadership Council of Downtown Toronto 287
Christian Management Association 28
Christian Methodist Episcopal Church. 86, 367, 378
Christian Ministries of Delaware County 233
Christian Ministry in the National Parks, A . . . 29
Christian and Missionary Alliance, The . . . 87, 367
Christian and Missionary Alliance in Canada. 182, 359
Christian Reformed Church in North America 88, 182, 359, 367
Christian Service Center for Central Florida, Inc. 231
Christian Union 88, 368, 382
Christian Youth Council. 261
Christians United in Beaver County. 252
Church Army in Canada, The 51
Church of the Brethren. 89, 368, 378, 382
Church of Christ 89
Church of Christ, Scientist. 90, 368
Church of Christ (Holiness) USA, The 90, 368, 382
Church Community Services 233
Church Council of Greater Seattle 259
Church Federation of Greater Indianapolis, Inc., The 233
Church of God (Anderson, Ind.). . 90, 182, 360, 368
Church of God (Cleveland, Tenn.) 11, 13, 92, 183, 360, 368
Church of God, Mountain Assembly, Inc. . . 94, 368
Church of God (Seventh Day), Denver, Colorado, The 95, 368
Church of God in Christ, The 11, 13, 91, 368
Church of God in Christ, International. 92
Church of God in Christ (Mennonite) . . . 92, 183, 360, 368
Church of God by Faith, Inc. 93, 368
Church of God General Conference (Oregon, IL and Morrow, GA) 93, 368
Church of God of Prophecy 94, 368
Church of God of Prophecy in Canada, The 183, 360
Church Growth Center—Home of Church Doctor Ministries. 29
Church of Illumination, The. 95, 368
Church of Jesus Christ (Bickertonites), The 95, 368
Church of Jesus Christ of Latter-day Saints, The. 11, 12, 14, 96, 368
Church of Jesus Christ of Latter-day Saints in Canada, The. 184, 360
Church of the Living God (Motto, Christian Workers for Fellowship) 96, 368
Church of the Lutheran Brethren . . 184, 360, 380
Church of the Lutheran Brethren of America 97, 369, 382
Church of the Lutheran Confession . . . 97, 369, 382
Church of the Nazarene 97, 369, 382
Church of the Nazarene in Canada. 185, 360
Church of Our Lord Jesus Christ of the Apostolic Faith, Inc. 98, 369
Church of the United Brethren in Christ. . 98, 369
Church Women United in the USA 29
Churches of Christ 11, 99, 369, 382
Churches of Christ in Canada. 185, 360
Churches of Christ in Christian Union . . . 99, 369
Churches' Council on Theological Education in Canada, An Ecumenical Foundation, The. . . 51
Churches of God, General Conference 99, 369, 382
Churches United, Inc. 234
Churches United of the Quad City Area. 232
Churches Uniting in Christ 29
Churchpeople for Change and Reconciliation 250
Colorado Council of Churches. 229
Community of Christ . . . 100, 185, 360, 369, 382
Community Emergency Assistance Program (CEAP) 241
Community Ministries of Rockville 238
Community Ministry of Montgomery County. 238
Community Renewal Society. 232
Concerned Ecumenical Ministry to the Upper West Side 246
Congregational Christian Churches in Canada. 186, 360
Congregational Holiness Church 100, 369
Conseil des Églises de Côte-des Neiges (Sept Égliese—une seul Esprit). 288
Conseil interreligieux de Montréal. 288
Conservative Baptist Association of America (CB America). 101, 369

INDEX

Conservative Congregational Christian Conference . . . 101, 369, 382
Conservative Lutheran Association 101, 369
Contact Ministries of Springfield . . . 232
Convention of Atlantic Baptist Churches . . . 186, 360
Cooperative Metropolitan Ministries . . . 238
Coptic Orthodox Church . . . 102, 369, 378
Coptic Orthodox Church in Canada, The . . . 186, 360
Cornwallis District Inter-Church Council . . . 286
Corpus Christi Metro Ministries . . . 257
Cortland County Council of Churches, Inc. . . 246
Council of Christian Communions of Greater Cincinnati . . . 250
Council of Churches of Chemung County, Inc. . . . 246
Council of Churches of the City of New York . . . 246
Council of Churches of Greater Bridgeport, Inc. . . . 230
Council of Churches of Greater Springfield . . 238
Council of Churches of Greater Washington, The . . . 231
Council of Churches of the Ozarks . . . 243
Council of Churches of Santa Clara County, The . . . 227
Council of Churches and Synagogues of Southwestern Connecticut . . . 230
Council of Hindu Temples of North America . . 221
CREO (Capital Region Ecumenical Organization) . . . 246
Cross-Lines Cooperative Council . . . 235
Cumberland Presbyterian Church . . 102, 369, 382
Cumberland Presbyterian Church in America . . . 103, 369, 382
Des Moines Area Religious Council . . . 235
Direction Chrétienne . . . 288
Dutchess Interfaith Council, Inc. . . . 246
East Dallas Cooperative Parish . . . 257
East End Cooperative Ministry . . . 253
Eastern Area Community Ministries . . . 235
Ecclesia . . . 244
Ecumenical Coalition for Economic Justice (ECEJ) . . . 52
Ecumenical Committee (Sault Ste. Marie) . . . 287
Ecumenical Conference of Greater Altoona . . 253
Ecumenical Council of Pasadena Area Churches, The . . . 227
Ecumenical Council of San Diego County . . . 228
Ecumenical Group, The . . . 288
Ecumenical Ministries . . . 243
Ecumenical Ministries of Iowa (EMI) . . . 235
Ecumenical Ministries of Oregon . . . 251
Elim Fellowship . . . 103, 370
Elim Fellowship of Evangelical Churches and Ministers . . . 187
EMI (Ecumenical Ministries of Iowa) . . . 235
empty tomb, inc. . . . 214
Episcopal Church . . . 11, 103, 370, 378, 382
Episcopal Orthodox Church, The . . . 106
Estonian Evangelical Lutheran Church, The . . . 107, 370
Estonian Evangelical Lutheran Church Abroad, The . . . 187, 360
Evangelical Church, The . . . 107, 370, 382
Evangelical Church Alliance, The . . . 107
Evangelical Congregational Church, The . . . 108, 370, 384
Evangelical Council for Financial Accountability . . . 30
Evangelical Covenant Church, The . . . 108, 370, 384
Evangelical Covenant Church of Canada, The . . . 187, 360
Evangelical Fellowship of Canada . . . 52
Evangelical Free Church of America, The . . . 109, 370
Evangelical Free Church of Canada 187, 361
Evangelical Friends International—North American Region . . . 110, 370
Evangelical Lutheran Church in America . . . 11, 12, 14, 110, 370, 378, 384
Evangelical Lutheran Church in Canada . . . 188, 361, 380
Evangelical Lutheran Synod . . . 113, 370, 384
Evangelical Mennonite Conference, The . . . 188, 361
Evangelical Mennonite Mission Conference . . . 189, 361
Evangelical Methodist Church . . . 114, 370
Evangelical Missionary Church of Canada, The . . . 189, 361
Evangelical Presbyterian Church . . . 114, 370
Evangelical Press Association . . . 30
Evanston Ecumenical Action Council . . . 232
Evansville Area Community of Churches, Inc. . . . 234
Faith Community Assistance Center . . . 245
Faith & Values Media . . . 31
Federation of Christian Ministries . . . 31
Federation of Jain Associations in North America . . . 223
Fellowship of Evangelical Baptist Churches in Canada, The . . . 189, 361
Fellowship of Evangelical Bible Churches . . . 114, 370, 384
Fellowship of Evangelical Churches . . . 116, 371. 384
Fellowship of Fundamental Bible Churches . . . 115, 371
Fellowship of Grace Brethren Churches . . 116, 371
Fern Creek-Highview United Ministries . . . 236
First Miramichi Inter-Church Council . . . 286
Florida Council of Churches . . . 231
Foundation for a Conference on Faith and Order in North America . . . 31
Foursquare Gospel Church of Canada . . . 190, 361, 380
Free Christian Zion Church of Christ . . . 117
Free Methodist Church in Canada . . . 190, 361
Free Methodist Church of North America . . . 117, 371, 384
Free Will Baptists . . . 190, 361
Fresno Metro Ministry . . . 227
Friends General Conference . . . 117, 371

INDEX

Friends United Meeting 118, 371, 378
Friends World Committee for Consultation (Section of the Americas) 32
Full Gospel Assemblies International . . . 119, 371
Full Gospel Fellowship of Churches and Ministers International 120, 371
Fund for Theological Education, Inc., The 32
Fundamental Methodist Church, Inc. . . . 120, 371
GEII (Graymoor Ecumenical & Interreligious Institute) 32
General Assembly of the Korean Presbyterian Church in America. 128
General Association of General Baptists 120, 371, 384
General Association of Regular Baptist Churches 121, 371
General Church of the New Jerusalem 121, 190, 371
General Conference of Mennonite Brethren Churches 121, 371, 384
Genesee County Churches United, Inc. 246
Genesee-Orleans Ministry of Concern 247
Georgia Christian Council 232
Glengarry-Prescott-Russell Christian Council 287
Glenmary Research Center 32
GRACE (Grand Rapids Area Center for Ecumenism). 240
Grace Gospel Fellowship 122, 371
Grand Rapids Area Center for Ecumenism (GRACE) 240
Graymoor Ecumenical & Interreligious Institute (GEII) 32
Greater Baton Rouge Federation of Churches and Synagogues. 237
Greater Bethlehem Area Council of Churches 253
Greater Birmingham Ministries 226
Greater Chicago Broadcast Ministries 232
Greater Dallas Community of Churches. 257
Greater Dayton Christian Connections 250
Greater Fairmont Council of Churches. 260
Greater Flint Council of Churches 240
Greater Lawrence Council of Churches 239
Greater Minneapolis Council of Churches . . . 241
Greater New Orleans Federation of Churches . . 237
Greater Rochester Community of Churches . . 247
Greater Toronto Council of Christian Churches, The 287
Greater Victoria Council of Churches 286
Greater Waterbury Interfaith Ministries, Inc.. . . . 230
Greater Wheeling Council of Churches, The. . . 260
Greek Orthodox Archdiocese of America 11, 13, 122, 372, 378
Greek Orthodox Metropolis of Toronto (Canada) 190, 361
Greensboro Urban Ministry 249
Halifax-Dartmouth Council of Churches 286
Hamilton & District Christian Churches Association 287
Hanover Area Council of Churches 253
Hartford Institute for Religion Research of Hartford Seminary, The 215
Hazard-Perry County Community Ministries, Inc. 236
Hemmingford Ecumenical Committee 288
Highlands Community Ministries 236
Holy Eastern Orthodox Catholic and Apostolic Church in North America, Inc., The . . . 124, 372
Holy Ukrainian Autocephalic Orthodox Church in Exile 124
House of God, Which is the Church of the Living God, the Pillar and Ground of the Truth, Inc. 124
Humboldt Clergy Council 288
Hungarian Reformed Church in America 124, 372, 378
Hutterian Brethren 125, 372
Hyde Park & Kenwood Interfaith Council, The 232
ICNA (The Islamic Circle of North America) 222
IFCA International, Inc. 125, 372
IFCO (Interreligious Foundation for Community Organization). 34
Ignace Council of Churches. 287
Illinois Conference of Churches. 232
In One Accord 240
Independent Assemblies of God International (Canada) 191, 361
Independent Holiness Church. 191, 361
Indiana Partners for Christian Unity and Mission 234
Industrial Cape Breton Council of Churches . . . 287
Institute for Ecumenical and Cultural Research 215
Institute for the Study of American Evangelicals (ISAE). 216
Institute for the Study of American Religion . . 216
Inter Church Council of Burlington 287
Interchurch Communications. 53
Inter-Church Council of Greater New Bedford 239
Inter-Church Ministries of Erie County 253
Interchurch Ministries of Nebraska 243
Interfaith Association of Snohomish County, The 260
Interfaith Community Council, Inc. 234
Interfaith Community Services 243
Interfaith Conference of Greater Milwaukee . . . 261
Interfaith Conference of Metropolitan Washington 231
Interfaith Council of Boulder. 229
Interfaith Council of Contra Costa County . . . 227
Interfaith Impact for Justice and Peace. 33
Interfaith Ministries for Greater Houston 257
Inter-Faith Ministries-Wichita 235
Interfaith Mission Service 226
Interfaith Partnership of Metropolitan St. Louis 243
Interfaith Service Bureau 227
International Church of the Foursquare Gospel 125, 372, 384
International Council of Community Churches 126, 372, 378
International Pentecostal Church of Christ, The 127, 372, 384

International Pentecostal Holiness Church . . . 127, 372
International Society for Krishna Consciousness, The . . . 221
InterReligious Council of Central New York. . . 247
Interreligious Foundation for Community Organization (IFCO) . . . 34
Inter-Varsity Christian Fellowship of Canada. . 53
Inter-Varsity Christian Fellowship of the USA . . . 33
Iowa Religious Media Services . . . 235
ISAE (Institute for the Study of American Evangelicals) . . . 216
Islamic Circle of North America (ICNA), The . . . 222
Islamic Society of North America (ISNA), The . . . 222
Italian Pentecostal Church of Canada, The. . . 191
J. M. Dawson Institute of Church-State Studies at Baylor University. . . 217
Jackson County Interfaith Council, The . . . 240
Jehovah's Witnesses . . 11, 13, 128, 191, 361, 372
Jewish-Christian Dialogue of Montreal . . . 288
Jewish Council for Public Affairs. . . 223
Jewish Reconstructionist Federation . . . 224
John Howard Society of Ontario . . . 53
John Milton Society for the Blind in Canada . . 54
Joint Religious Legislative Coalition, The . . . 241
Kairos Institute, Inc., The . . . 34
Kansas Ecumenical Ministries . . . 235
Kentuckiana Interfaith Community . . . 236
Kentucky Council of Churches . . . 236
Kentville Council of Churches. . . 287
Kitchener-Waterloo Council of Churches. . . 287
Korean Presbyterian Church in America, General Assembly of the . . . 128, 372, 378
Lafayette Urban Ministry. . . 234
Lancaster County Council of Churches . . . 253
Latvian Evangelical Lutheran Church in America, The . . . 128, 372, 384
LCMS (The Lutheran Church—Missouri Synod) . . . 11, 12, 14, 129, 372, 384
Lebanon County Christian Ministries. . . 253
Lehigh County Conference of Churches. . . 253
Lewisburg Council of Churches. . . 254
Liberal Catholic Church (International). . . 129, 372
Liberal Catholic Church—Province of the United States of America, The. . . 129, 372
Lincoln Interfaith Council . . . 244
Liturgical Conference, The . . . 34
Lombard Mennonite Peace Center. . . 35
London Inter-City Faith Team . . . 287
Long Island Council of Churches, The. . . 247
Lord's Day Alliance of the United States, The . . . 35
Louisiana Interchurch Conference . . . 237
Louisville Institute, The. . . 217
Lunenburg Queens BA Association . . . 287
Lutheran Church—Canada . . . 191, 362, 380
Lutheran Church—Missouri Synod (LCMS), The. . . 11, 12, 14, 129, 372, 384
Lutheran Council in Canada . . . 54
Lutheran World Relief . . . 35
Madison Area Urban Ministry . . . 261
Mahone Bay Interchurch Council . . . 287
Mahoning Valley Association of Churches. . . 250
Maine Council of Churches . . . 237
Malankara Orthodox Syrian Church, Diocese of America. . . 130, 378
Manchester Area Conference of Churches . . . 230
Mar Thoma Syrian Church of India . . . 131, 373, 379, 384
Marin Interfaith Council . . . 228
Massachusetts Commission on Christian Unity . . . 239
Massachusetts Council of Churches. . . 239
Massey Inter-Church Council . . . 287
MCCC (Mennonite Central Committee Canada) . . . 54
Melville Association of Churches . . . 288
Mennonite Central Committee, The. . . 35
Mennonite Central Committee Canada (MCCC) . . . 54
Mennonite Church Canada. . . 192, 362
Mennonite Church USA. . . 131, 373
Metropolitan Area Church Council . . . 250
Metropolitan Area Religious Coalition of Cincinnati . . . 250
Metropolitan Christian Council: Detroit-Windsor, The. . . 240
Metropolitan Christian Council of Philadelphia. . . 254
Metropolitan Ecumenical Ministry. . . 245
Metropolitan Ecumenical Ministry Community Development Corp. . . 245
Metropolitan Inter Faith Association (MIFA) . . . 256
Metropolitan Interfaith Council on Affordable Housing (MICAH). . . 241
Michigan Ecumenical Forum. . . 240
MIFA (Metropolitan Inter Faith Association). . . 256
Ministries United South Central Louisville (M.U.S.C.L., Inc.) . . . 236
Minnesota Council of Churches. . . 242
Missionary Church, The. . . 132, 373, 384
Mississippi Religious Leadership Conference . . . 242
Moncton Area Council of Churches. . . 286
Montana Association of Churches . . . 243
Montreal Association for the Blind Foundation . . . 288
Montréal Council of Churches. . . 288
Moravian Church in America (Unitas Fratrum) . . . 133, 373, 379, 384
M.U.S.C.L., Inc. (Ministries United South Central Louisville). . . 236
Muskegon County Cooperating Churches . . . 240
Muslim American Society, The . . . 222
Muslim Christian Dialogue . . . 288
NARF (Native American Rights Fund) . . . 225
National Association of Congregational Christian Churches. . . 133, 373
National Association of Ecumenical and Interreligious Staff. . . 36
National Association of Evangelicals, The. . . 36

INDEX

National Association of Free Will Baptists 133, 373
National Baptist Church of America, Inc.. 13
National Baptist Convention of America, Inc. 11, 134, 373, 379
National Baptist Convention, USA., Inc. . . 11, 13, 134, 373, 379
National Bible Association 37
National Conference for Community and Justice, The 37
National Conference on Ministry to the Armed Forces 37
National Congress of American Indians (NCAI) 225
National Council of the Churches of Christ in the USA 38
National Institute of Business and Industrial Chaplains 39
National Interfaith Cable Coalition, Inc. (NICC) 39
National Interfaith Coalition on Aging. 40
National Missionary Baptist Convention of America 11, 13, 135, 373, 379
National Organization of the New Apostolic Church of North America. 135, 373
National Primitive Baptist Convention, Inc. 135, 373
National Religious Broadcasters 40
National Spiritualist Association of Churches 136, 373
National Woman's Christian Temperance Union 40
Native American Rights Fund (NARF) 225
NCAI (National Congress of American Indians) 225
Netherlands Reformed Congregations . . 136, 373
Network of Religious Communities. 247
New Britain Area Conference of Churches (NEWBRACC) 230
New Hampshire Council of Churches 244
New Jersey Council of Churches 245
New Mexico Conference of Churches 245
New York State Community of Churches, Inc. 248
Niagara Council of Churches Inc., The 248
NICA (Northside Inter-Church Agency). 258
NICC (National Interfaith Cable Coalition, Inc.). 39
NISBCO (Center on Conscience & War) 27
North American Baptist Conference 137, 192, 362, 373, 380, 384
North American Baptist Fellowship. 40
North American Old Roman Catholic Church (Archdiocese of New York) 137, 373
North Carolina Council of Churches 249
North Dakota Conference of Churches. 250
North Dallas Shared Ministries 258
North Hills Youth Ministry Counseling Center 254
Northern California Interreligious Conference 228
Northern Kentucky Interfaith Commission, Inc. 236
Northside Common Ministries 254
Northside Inter-Church Agency (NICA). 258
Northwest Harvest–E.M.M. 260
Northwest Interfaith Movement 254
Oak Park-River Forest Community of Congregations 233
Ohio Council of Churches 251
Oikocredit–Ecumenical Development Cooperative Society. 41
Oklahoma Conference of Churches 251
Old Catholic Church of Canada, The . . . 193, 362
Old German Baptist Brethren Church. . . 137, 374
Old Order Amish Church 137, 193, 362, 374
Old Order (Wisler) Mennonite Church. 137
Open Bible Faith Fellowship of Canada 193, 362
Open Bible Standard Churches. 137, 374
(Original) Church of God, Inc., The. 138
Orthodox Church in America, The. . . 11, 13, 138, 374, 379
Orthodox Church in America (Canada Section) 193, 362
Orthodox Presbyterian Church, The 139, 374, 384
Ottawa Christian Council of the Capital Area 287
Pacific and Asian American Center for Theology and Strategies (PACTS). 228
Paducah Cooperative Ministry 237
Parish Resource Center, Inc. 41
Patriarchal Parishes of the Russian Orthodox Church in Canada 193, 362
Patriarchal Parishes of the Russian Orthodox Church in the USA. 139, 374, 379
Pennsylvania Conference on Interchurch Cooperation. 254
Pennsyvania Council of Churches, The 254
Pentecostal Assemblies of Canada, The. . . 173, 362
Pentecostal Assemblies of Newfoundland, The 194, 362
Pentecostal Assemblies of the World, Inc. 11, 13, 139, 374
Pentecostal-Charismatic Churches of North America. 41
Pentecostal Church of God. 139, 374
Pentecostal Fire-Baptized Holiness Church. . 140, 374
Pentecostal Free Will Baptist Church, Inc., The 140, 374
Peoria Friendship House of Christian Service 233
Philadelphia Yearly Meeting of the Religious Society of Friends 140, 374, 379
Pictou Council of Churches 287
Pike County Outreach Council. 251
Pillar of Fire 141
Pluralism Project, The 218
Polish National Catholic Church of America 141, 374, 379
Pomona Inland Valley Council of Churches . . 228
Prairie Centre for Ecumenism 288
Presbyterian Church in America . . . 141, 374, 384
Presbyterian Church in America (Canadian Section) 194, 362, 380

INDEX

Presbyterian Church in Canada 194, 362
Presbyterian Church (USA). 11, 12, 14, 142, 374, 379, 384
Primitive Advent Christian Church. 144, 375
Primitive Baptists 144
Primitive Methodist Church in the USA 144, 375, 384
Progressive National Baptist Convention, Inc. 11, 13, 145, 375, 379
Project of Easton, Inc. 255
Project Equality, Inc. 42
Project Ploughshares 54
Protestant Hour, Inc., The 42
Protestant Reformed Churches in America. 145, 375
Queens County Association of Churches 287
Queens Federation of Churches 248
Radio Ville-Marie 288
Reading Berks Conference of Churches. 255
Reading Urban Ministry 255
Reformed Catholic Church. 145, 375
Reformed Church in America . . 145, 375, 379, 384
Reformed Church in Canada 195, 362
Reformed Church in the United States . . . 146, 375, 384
Reformed Episcopal Church. 147, 375
Reformed Episcopal Church of Canada, The 195, 363, 380
Reformed Mennonite Church. 147, 375
Reformed Methodist Union Episcopal Church. 148
Reformed Presbyterian Church of North America 148, 375, 384
Reformed Zion Union Apostolic Church 148
Regina Council of Churches 288
Regional Council for Christian Ministry, Inc., The 232
Reinland Mennonite Church. 195, 363
Religion In American Life, Inc. 43
Religion Communicators Council, Inc., The . . 43
Religion News Service 44
Religion Newswriters Association 44
Religious Conference Management Association, Inc. 44
Religious Society of Friends (Conservative) 148, 375
Religious Society of Friends (Unaffiliated Meetings) 149
Religious Television Associates 55
Réseau oecuménique justice et paix 288
Rhode Island State Council of Churches, The 256
Roman Catholic Church in Canada, The 196, 363
Romanian Orthodox Church in America, The 149
Romanian Orthodox Church in America (Canadian Parishes) 197, 363
Romanian Orthodox Episcopate of America, The 149, 375
Romanian Orthodox Episcopate of America (Jackson, MI). 197, 363
ROQ 288
Rural Migrant Ministry 248
Russian Orthodox Church Outside of Russia, The 150, 375
Salvation Army, The 150, 375
Salvation Army in Canada, The 198, 363
San Antonio Community of Churches 258
San Antonio Urban Ministries 258
San Fernando Valley Interfaith Council 228
Saskatoon Council of Churches 288
Schenectady Inner City Ministry 248
Schwenkfelder Church, The. 150, 376
Scripture Union 55
SCUPE (The Seminary Consortium for Urban Pastoral Education) 44
SEAM (South East Associated Ministries) . . . 237
SEARCH (Southeast Area Churches). 258
Seminary Consortium for Urban Pastoral Education (SCUPE), The. 44
Separate Baptists in Christ 151, 376
Serbian Orthodox Church in the USA and Canada. 151, 376, 379
Serbian Orthodox Church in the USA and Canada, Diocese of Canada 198, 363
Seventh-day Adventist Church 151, 376, 384
Seventh-day Adventist Church in Canada. 198, 363, 380
Seventh Day Baptist General Conference, USA and Canada 152, 376
Siddhachalam/International Mahavira Jain Mission 223
Sikh Center of Orange County, The 225
South Carolina Christian Action Council, Inc. 256
South Coast Ecumenical Council. 229
South East Associated Ministries (SEAM) . . . 237
South Hills Interfaith Ministries. 255
South Louisville Community Ministries. 237
Southeast Area Churches (SEARCH). 258
Southeast Ecumenical Ministry 249
Southern Baptist Convention. 9, 11, 12, 14, 153, 376, 384
Southern California Ecumenical Council 229
Southern Methodist Church 154, 376
Sovereign Grace Believers 155, 376
Spadina-Bloor Interchurch Council 287
Spokane Council of Ecumenical Ministries . . 260
St. Catharines & Dist. Clergy Fellowship. . . . 287
St. John's Area Council of Churches 286
St. Matthews Area Ministries. 237
St. Paul Area Council of Churches. 242
Staten Island Council of Churches 249
Stratford & District Council of Churches. . . . 287
Student Christian Movement of Canada. 55
Summerside Christian Council. 287
Swedenborgian Church, The. 155, 376, 379
Syriac Orthodox Church of Antioch. 199
Syrian Orthodox Church of Antioch. 363
Syrian (Syriac) Orthodox Church of Antioch 155, 376, 379
Syro-Russian Orthodox Catholic Church, The 156, 376
Syro-Russian Orthodox Church, The 386
Tarrant Area Community of Churches 258

INDEX

Taskforce on the Churches and Corporate Responsibility 55
Ten Days for Global Justice 56
Tennessee Association of Churches 257
Texas Buddhist Council 220
Texas Conference of Churches 258
Thorold Inter-Faith Council 287
Thunder Bay Council of Churches 287
Toledo Ecumenical Area Ministries 251
Tri-Council Coordinating Commission 242
Triumph the Church and Kingdom of God in Christ Inc. (International) 157
Troy Area United Ministries 249
True Orthodox Church of Greece (Synod of Metropolitan Cyprian), American Exarchate 157, 376
Tulsa Metropolitan Ministry 251
Tuscarawas County Council for Church and Community 251
Ukrainian Orthodox Church of Canada . . . 199, 363
Ukrainian Orthodox Church of the USA 158, 376, 379
Union of American Hebrew Congregations . . 224
Union d'Eglises Baptistes Françaises au Canada 199, 363, 380
Union of Orthodox Jewish Congregations of America, The 224
Union of Spiritual Communities of Christ (Orthodox Doukhobors in Canada) 199
Unitarian Universalist Association of Congregations 159, 377
Unitas 288
United Board of Missions 258
United Brethren Church in Canada 200, 363
United Christian Church 159, 377
United Church of Canada, The 200, 364, 380
United Church of Christ . . 11, 160, 377, 379, 386
United Church Maritime Conference—Inter-church Inter-faith Committee 286
United Churches of Lycoming County 255
United Holy Church of America, Inc. 162
United House of Prayer 163, 377
United Methodist Church, The 9, 11, 12, 14, 163, 377, 379, 386
United Ministries 256
United Ministries in Higher Education 45
United Pentecostal Church in Canada . . . 201, 364
United Pentecostal Church International . . . 165, 377
United Pentecostal Churches of Christ, The 166, 377
United Religions Initiative 45
United Religious Community of St. Joseph County 234
United States Conference of Religions for Peace (USCRP), The 46
United Synagogue of Conservative Judaism, The 224
United Zion Church 166, 377
Unity of the Brethren 167, 377, 386
Universal Fellowship of Metropolitan Community Churches . . 167, 201, 364, 377, 386
USCRP (The United States Conference of Religions for Peace) 46
Vancouver Council of Churches 286
Vellore Christian Medical College Board (USA), Inc. 46
Vermont Ecumenical Council and Bible Society 258
Virginia Council of Churches, Inc. 259
Volunteer Ministry Center 257
Volunteers of America 168, 377
Wainwright House 249
Washington Association of Churches 260
Wesleyan Church, The 168, 377, 386
Wesleyan Church of Canada, The 202, 364
Wesleyan Holiness Association of Churches . . . 169
West Central Neighborhood Ministry, Inc. 234
West Side Ecumenical Ministry 251
West Virginia Council of Churches 261
Westside Interfaith Council 229
Wilkinsburg Community Ministry 255
Wisconsin Council of Churches 261
Wisconsin Evangelical Lutheran Church 386
Wisconsin Evangelical Lutheran Synod . 169, 377
Women's Inter-Church Council of Canada 56
Worcester County Ecumenical Council 239
World Council of Churches, United States Office 46
World Day of Prayer 47
World Methodist Council–North American Section 47
World Vision 47
World Vision Canada 56
Wyoming Church Coalition 262
Wyoming Valley Council of Churches 256
YMCA of the USA 48
York County Council of Churches 256
Young Men's Christian Association in Canada 57
Young Women's Christian Association of/du Canada 57
Youth for Christ—Canada 57
Youth for Christ–USA 48
YWCA of the USA 48

Individuals

Abbott, Grant 242
Abbott, Z. Allen 65
Abboud, Jon W.. 147
Abdalah, John P. 338, 347
Aboodi, Timotheos Aphrem 199
Abraham, Raphael. 158
Abuzaakouk, Aly R. 222
Ackerman, Keith L.. 106
Acree, Amos 247
Adams, Don 128
Adams, Dorothy 62
Adams, Gladstone B., III . . 105
Adams, John Hurst 59
Adams, Margaret. 236
Adams, Michael J.. 102
Adams, Neale 346
Adams, Skip 252
Adams, Steven 201
Adams-Smetter, Barbara . . 254
Adcock, Cynthia 260
Addington, James . . . 241, 242
Addington, Timothy 109
Addland, Thomas V. 63
Adira, Titus 118
Adkinson, Oleda 93
Adnams, Ian 192, 341
Adolf, Don 189
Adrian, Marian M.. 247
Aftimios II (Bishop) 71
Agrafiotis, Angelo. 22
Aguinaco, Carmen. 331
Ahonen, E. 173
Aiken, David A., Sr. 61
Aiken, Mike 249
Aja, Antonio (Tony) 236
Aja, Loyda 143
Ajer, Margaret Schmitt . . . 111
Akers, Kenneth 134
Alaexie, Steven M. 133
Alagiah, Sabapath 45
Al-Awady, Nodri 244
Al-Batat, Zainab 244
Albaugh, Freddie. 114
Albers, Frances B.. 231
Alberson, Dobbins. 230
Albert, Leonard. 93
Albrecht, Betty 178
Albrecht, James. 97
Albrecht, Marcus. 323
Albright, Jacob 108, 163
Alchin, Errol 187
Alcosser, Lois 230
Aldred, Ray. 53
Aleksy II. 139
Aleshire, Daniel O. . . . 26, 212
Alexander, Christine 317
Alexander, Darlene 258
Alexander, Jean M. 161
Alexander, John Neil. 105
Alexios (Metropolitan) . . . 123
Alford, Denton 93
Alger, David T. 259
Alguire, Frances M.. 47
Alick, Bruce N. 329
Allard, P. Pierre. 197
Allen, Arlene. 338
Allen, Bettye J. 338
Allen, Cosie 328
Allen, David W.. 201
Allen, David, Jr. 145
Allen, Gary 322
Allen, John 26
Allen, Richard. 59
Allen, Sherman 95, 184
Allen, William B. 85, 261
Allender, Dan B. 299
Allison, Glenn. 228
Allmen, Robert J. 145
Almen, Lowell G. 110
Almquist, Roy G. 113
Alpine, W.H. 134
Alsdurf, Edna 47
Alston, Roosevelt 162
Alston, Wallace M., Jr. 32
Altebarmakian, Varouj. 73
Althouse, LaVonne 338
Alton, Jesse. 78
Alverez, Gracela 47
Alvis, Rick 25
Ambrose, Richard 226
Ambrus, Zoltan 125
Amerson, Philip A. 293
Amik, Isaac. 133
Ammann, Jacob. 116, 193
Ammerman, E.H. Jim 28
Amorim, Nilton D. 198
Amos, Barbara 42
Andenya, Wilson. 118
Anderson, Anne T.. 314
Anderson, Billy. 100
Anderson, Daniel L. 289
Anderson, David (NCN) . . . 98
Anderson, David (RNS) . . . 44
Anderson, David A.. 232
Anderson, Dennis 241
Anderson, Gordon L.. 301
Anderson, James L.. 291
Anderson, Jeffery . . . 109, 187
Anderson, John A.. 63
Anderson, Jon V.. 111
Anderson, Kathy 234
Anderson, Kristi 242
Anderson, Melissa. 333
Anderson, Nancy L. 242
Anderson, Neil W.. . . . 99, 324
Anderson, Paul 103
Anderson, R. Byron. 34
Anderson, Roger G.. 122
Anderson, Scott D. 261
Anderson, Vinton Randolph. . 59
Anderson, Vinton 32
Anderson, Vjuana 248
Anderson, William J.. 174
Anderson-Develrow, Dorothy 258
Andonios (Bishop) 123
Andreas (Bishop) 157
Andres, Carmen 319
Andres, Oseas 66
Andrews, Roger. 116
Andrews, Ruth 52
Andrews, Susan. 143
Andriy (Archimandrite). . . 158
Angeline, Peter 53
Angie, Frank 127
Ankeny, Mark 110
Anker, Roy M. 332
Annie, Frederick P. 261
Annis, Sharon 118
Annunziato, Anne 244
Ansell, Fred A. 64
Anthony (Metropolitan). . . 123
Anthony, Lewis 231
Antony (Archbishop). . 158, 159
Apostola, Nicholas . . 149, 197
Aquila, Dominic 194
Archer, Barbara. 243
Ard, Robert. 228
Argue, David. 73
Argue, Don H.. 301
Armiger, Thomas E. 168
Armstrong, Calvin. 162
Armstrong, George 46
Armstrong, James D. . . 61, 333
Armstrong, Ken. 76
Arnold, Alma 248
Arnold, Don 120
Arnold, Kim M.. 356
Arnold, Kristi 331
Arrington, Juanita R.. 72
Arsenios (Bishop) 69
Arslanian, Hagop. 176
Arthur (Bishop). 124
Arthur, David T. 348
Artis, Lois. 83
Asbury, Francis 59, 163
Asen, Bernhard 336

INDEX

Ashdown, David N. 174
Ashford, Anne. 228
Ashlay, Pamla 136
Astfalk, Carolyn 254
Astin, Claude S., Jr. 66
Astin, Dawn R. 66
Astle, Cynthia B. . . . 330, 334, 337
Atagotaalnuk, Andrew P. . . 174
Atkins, Nancy Lee. 251
Atmore, A. Brian. 312
Atra, Brian 94
Attebery, Charles. 292
Attridge, Harold W. 308
Aubrey, Michael 99
Aucutt, Ronald 109
Augsburger, Bryce. 121
Augsburger, Lynette 116
Augsburger, Rick 39
Augson, Albert 163
Austin, George 139
Austin, Jackie 261
Authier, Kenneth J. 126
Auxentios (Bishop) 158
Avakian, Karl 176
Avery, Michael 295
Avey, Thomas 116
Aymer, Albert J.D. 297
Aymond, Gregory M. 81
Aykazian, Vicken (Bishop) . . 38
Azmy, Isaac Boulos. 102
Baak, David P. 240
Babb, Ruby 248
Babb, W. Sherrill. 302
Babcock, Calvin 153
Bacon, Arthur D. 310
Badi, Izzaldin 244
Bagley, Louis 162
Bagnall, Ronald B. 328
Baha'ullah. 219
Baier, Del 181
Bailey, David. 118
Bailey, Joey. 143
Bailey, Leslee 100
Bailey, Mark L. 294
Bailey, Orrin 101
Bailey, Raymond E. 111
Baillargeon, Gaëtan. 196
Baillie, Kenneth 150
Bainbridge, Harry B. 105
Baird, Bob. 75
Baird, John 114
Baker, Charles. 122
Baker, Denis N. 335
Baker, Kenneth 326
Baker, Kim Nathan 195
Baker, Marsha 24
Baker, Michael L. . . 92, 93, 183
Baldwin, David N. 153
Baldwin, M. Winston, Jr. . . 160
Baldwin, Nancy. 133
Baldwin, Raymond C. 145
Baletka, Jim 167
Ball, David 173
Ball, Frank 250
Ballantyne, V.A. 107
Ballard, M. Russell 96
Ballas, Rhea 251
Ballert, Miriam 46
Balogh, Balint 125
Banaszak, Karen 239
Bancroft, Timothy 39
Bane, David C., Jr. 106
Banek, Walter 147
Bangham, Bill 321
Bankord, Mark A. 28
Banks, Rosa T. 152
Bannister, Kathryn 46
Bansal, Prem 244
Baranowski, Bernice 50
Barber, Jay A., Jr. 91
Barbour, Johnny, Jr. 59
Barcott, Patricia. 260
Barfoot, Gillian 56
Barger, Louise B. 65
Bariteau, Benoît 196
Barkat, Samuel 33
Barker, Lee 299
Barker, Randy 140
Barkman, Len 189
Barna, George 213
Barnabas, Mathews Mar . . 131
Barnes, James 297
Barnes, Ronald B. 254
Barnes, Thane 154
Barnett-Cowan, Alyson. . 32, 174
Barnhouse, James 251
Barnwell, Ray E., Sr. 168
Baron, Karen. 355
Barrentine, Jimmy L. 154
Barrett, Michael 249
Barrow, Ira 356
Barrows, Kenneth 185
Barsamian, Khajag 43, 73
Barsony, Steve. 255
Barth, Karl L. 130
Barthelet, Jacques 196
Bartimaeus (Father). 71
Bartlett, Carol 117
Bartlett, Eileen 237
Bartol, Rachel 235
Barton, Jonathan 259
Bash, Kenneth G. 111
Bass, Richard O., Sr. 87
Bass, Steve 153
Bassett, W. Todd 150
Bassham, Keith 317
Bates, Charlotte Kinvig . . . 312
Bates, Dale 121
Batey, Gary 126
Bathurst, Shirley 248
Batstone, A. Earl 194
Battle, George Edward, Jr. . . 60
Battle, Michael A. 297
Battler, Jack 53
Battram, Janet 234
Batts, Carl. 136
Bauer, Martha 155
Bauer, Scott G. 126
Baughm, Billy. 24
Baughm, Eva. 24
Baum, Mary K. 261
Baumann, Paul 321
Baumgarten, Murray 327
Baumgartner, Dorothy 111
Baumgartner, Will 230
Baumler, Gary . . 169, 324, 329
Bawai (Bishop) 68
Bayer, Steven L. 137, 337
Bayiha, II, Suzie 47
Beach, Ken 312
Beach, Maxine C. 294
Beach, Verda 290
Beacham, A.D., Jr. 128
Beachy, LeRoy 137
Beals, Charlotte. 132
Beard, C. Ronald. 74
Beaupe, Richard 53
Beck, Kenneth L. 303
Beck, Sarai Schnucker. . . . 235
Becker, Bruce 169, 328
Becker, Larry 337
Beckett, Malcolm 186
Beckmann, David 26
Beckstrom, Kersten 322
Beckwith, Peter H. 106
Becton, C.M. 201
Bedford, Kennedy 61
Bedgood, Douglas, Sr. 85
Bediako, Matthew A. 152
Bee, Ernest K., Jr. 153
Behrakis, George. 123
Beinikis, Vilmars. 129
Beirenlaan, Frans 69
Beizer, Lance 68
Bejjani, Gabriel 305
Bekken, Dean 129
Bekker, Gary 88
Belin, Henry Allen, Jr. 59
Bell, Nancy 50, 177
Bellamy, James C. 163
Bellavin, Tikhon 69
Bellefleur, Beverley. 194
Bellinger, Carolyn 190
Bellinger, James 190
Bellous, Ken 177
Belrose, Danny A. 100
Belsky, Martin. 251
Belsole, Kurt. 304
Bender, Robert 227
Benedict, Gary M. 294
Benefiel, Ron 300
Benjamin (Bishop) 157
Benjamin I (Patriarch). 65
Benjamin, Hermenia 78
Benjamin, Waveney. 47
Bennett (Reverend) 24
Bennett, Harold. 21
Bennett, Joe 72

INDEX

Bennett, Robertson H. 43
Bennison, Charles 106
Benoway, Edward R. 113
Benson, M. Wayne 292
Benson, Willie, Jr. 117
Berg, Richard R. 354
Berg, Robert D. 112
Berg, Ron 137
Berg, Sharon K. 323
Berge, Arthur. 185
Bergen, Abe 313
Berger, David G. 243
Bergin, Karen 230
Bergman, John 189
Berkenes, Dave 234
Berlamino, Cheryl 22
Berlin, Sandi 242
Berman, Lowen 252
Bernstine, Gwen Nelson . . 255
Bernthal, Mark 97
Berrieau, Yvon 286
Berstein, Amy 241
Bertalan, Imre 125
Berube, Albert J. 137
Beshara, Sophronios 71
Best, Deb 255
Best, Edna 29
Betancourt, Esdras. 93
Betzer, Dan 73
Betzer, Janet 254
Bevens, Stephen B. 27
Beverley, James. 216
Beverly, Connie Bell 61
Bevilacqua, Anthony Cardinal 81
Beyer, Teresa A. 138
Bhagan, Ken 287
Bianchi, Ed 49
Bibb, Lillie D. 250
Bick, Margaret 345
Bickerton, William 95
Bicksler, Harriet 335
Biebel, William E. 253
Bieniek, Barbara 248
Biffle, Nita 120
Biffle, Steven K. 120, 323
Billard, Ralph 286
Bilyew, Janet. 99
Binda, Andrew 92
Bingham, Maurice D. 90
Birchard, Bruce 117
Birkett, Jim 167
Birkitt, James N., Jr. 327
Birney, Walter 85
Biron, Jean-Marc. 345
Biron, Robert 244
Birse, Douglas. 178
Bishop, Cecil. 47, 60
Bitner, Denver W. 111
Bittle, Michael. 287
Bjork, Bruce 241
Bjornberg, Allan C. 111
Black, Cathy S. 246
Black, Geoffrey A.. . . 161, 248
Black, J.B., Jr. 233
Black, Ron 121
Blackburn, Richard G. 35
Blackby, G. Richard 310
Blackwell, George L. 61
Blades, Wayne. 120
Blair, Sarah D. Brooks. . . . 352
Blaisdell, Charles R. 84
Blake, Bruce P. 165
Blake, Canute 183, 341
Blake, Harry 135
Blake, Ron 98
Blakeman, Jeannine. 236
Blalack, Richard 180
Blanchett, David I. 226
Bland, James C. 142
Blanding, Ann 148
Blanton, Smiley. 26
Blom, Paul J. 112
Bloom, Peter 51
Bloomquist, Nessie S. 248
Blouin, Francis 237
Blount, Bill A. 40
Blount, Robert. 162
Blowers, David 62
Blumhofer, Edith 216
Boardman, Lynda 98
Boatright, Kevin J. 111
Bochanyin, Curtis 350
Boe, Eugene 97
Boehlke, Craig A. 112
Boehm, John Philip 146
Boehm, Martin 98, 200
Boeker, Paul 115
Boerger, Wm. Chris 111
Boersma, Hans 51
Boersma, J. Karel 248
Bogard, Ben M. 63
Boge, Jascha 179
Bohl, Robert 143
Bojey, Fred 200
Boland, J. Kevin 80
Bolduc, Adèle 196
Boles, J.A. 135
Boles, John P. 81
Bolger, Douglas G. 185
Bolger, E. Carl 185
Bolick, Leonard H. 113
Bolinder, Garth T. 109
Boling, Daniel F. 93
Boll, James 341
Bolt, John 88, 182
Boltz, David G. 253
Bombick, Betsy. 133
Bomgardner, LeRoy 160
Bond, Ian 290
Bond, Jane Zavitz 180
Bond, Jentry W. 305
Bond, Jim L. 98
Bond, Linda 150
Bonk, Jonathan J. 326
Bonneau, Normand 313
Bonner, Harrison 30
Bonner, Margie J. 61
Bonner, William L. 98
Book, Robert. 261
Booker, George 318
Boomershine, Tom 328
Boone, Martha Moody 29
Boonstra, John C. 260
Booth, Ballington 168
Booth, Linda L. 325, 346
Booth, Maud 168
Booth, Robert H. 147
Booth, Robert M. 126
Booth, William 66, 150
Borden, M. Daniel. 163
Borden, Paul D. 65
Borgdorff, Peter. 88, 182
Borko, M. Douglas 161
Borowsky, Irvin J. 323
Borski, Chester L. 304
Boschman, Ed 122
Bosh, Larry 150
Bosso, Stephen C. 304
Boto, Augie 153
Bottolfs, Charles 93
Bouchard, Charles E. 289
Bouman, Stephen P. 112
Bouras, Nicholas 123
Bourdeau, Gilles 50, 288
Bourdette, Wesley R. 84
Bourne, Hugh 144
Bowell, Gary. 317
Bowen, Mary Lu 248
Bowie, E.L. 96
Bowkett, Roy 309
Bowman, Christopher D. . . . 89
Bowman, Debra A. 201
Bowman, Locke E., Jr. . . . 104
Boyajcan, Donna 255
Boyce, H. Gene 127
Boyce, Janice. 127, 317
Boyd, Doris F. 330
Boyd, Douglas. 244
Boyd, John E. 286
Boyd, T.B., III 135
Boyer, Wayne W. 100
Boyles, James B. 174
Boyles, Lemuel 37
Boynton, Leonard 246
Bracelin, Frank 81
Brackin, James D. 303
Bradford, Bose 162
Bradley, Curtis 180
Bradley, James G. 230
Bradley, Julie 259
Bradley, Lasserre, Jr. . . 144, 317
Bradsell, Kenneth . . . 146, 195
Brame, Nicholas 126
Brandebura, Michael 173
Branham, Craig 77
Branson, Arlie 120
Bratton, G. Stanford 247
Braun, Alan. 179

INDEX

Braver, Barbara L. 104
Bravo-Guzman, Pedro 69
Brawner, John 110
Braxton, Edward K.. 80
Bray, Donald L.. 168
Brazier, Arthus 139
Breadfires, Edward 141
Bregar, Janet A.. 229
Breig, James 323
Bremer, Calvin L. 88
Brennan, Mary Pat 41
Brennan, Peter P. 69
Brenneman, Howard 132
Brenton, B. Dean. 194
Bresee, Phineas 98
Breton, Jean-Claude 345
Brewer, John 169, 322
Brice, James T. 75
Brickhouse, Smith N. 90
Bridges, Dorothy 241
Bridges, James E. 73, 74
Bridges, Randy J. 302
Briggs, Charles 16
Briggs, Robert L.. 21
Bright, John 93
Brill, Debra 152
Bringard, Jerry D. 308
Brink, Emily R. 334
Brinks, Robert. 143
Brinser, Gerald 160
Brinser, Matthias 166
Briscoe, John A. 38
Britt, Kevin M. 80, 81
Brittain, Fred 121, 332
Britton, Joseph H. 291
Britton, Larry 338
Britz, Andrew M. 345
Broad, Dwayne 190
Broadway, Beth. 247
Brom, Robert H. 81
Brooks, George 139
Brooks, James W. 162
Brooks, John 110
Brooks, Steven 146, 195
Brooks, Susan 292
Brooks, Thomas 70
Brookshire, Mary Sue 63
Broomfield, Oree, Sr. 87
Brosseau, Annie 343
Brown, A.J. 292
Brown, Arthur 117
Brown, Barry R. 54
Brown, Betty. 136
Brown, Carroll E. 230
Brown, Charlotte D. 61
Brown, Cynthia Vasil 62
Brown, Dallas 252
Brown, Don J.. 77
Brown, Donice 70
Brown, E. Lynn. 86
Brown, E. 191
Brown, Elizabeth. 79
Brown, Gary 108
Brown, Gus H. 88
Brown, Harry 234
Brown, J.R. 128
Brown, James R. 66
Brown, Jeffrey P. 87
Brown, John W.. 180
Brown, Joseph C., Jr.. 249
Brown, Mark A. 23
Brown, Michael. 333
Brown, Patricia L. 243
Brown, Richard A.. 323
Brown, Theodore 93
Brown, Tod D. 80
Brown, Vivian W. 61
Brown, W. Wayne 65
Brown, Warner H., Jr. 165
Brown, Warren Matthew . . . 60
Brown, William Adams 16
Brown, William P. 326
Brubacher, Marvin R. 311
Brubaker, John 79
Bruce, George L.R. 175
Bruehl, J. Roger 26
Brug, John F. 338
Brugler, Ronald P. 155
Brummel, Mark J. 337
Brundage, Thomas 318
Bruno, J. Jon 105
Bruno, José 88
Brusatti, Louis T.. 307
Brushaber, George K. . . 76, 291
Brust, Donald M.. 88
Bryan, David. 337
Bryan, Jamie Brooke 167
Bryan, Ron 119
Bryant, David 289
Bryant, John R. 47, 59
Bryant, Juanita 86
Bryant, Roy, Sr. . . . 77, 78, 291
Bryant, S.N. 94
Bryant, Sissieretta 78
Bryant, Steven D. 337
Bucek, Patricia 252
Buchanan, John 106, 318
Buckle, Clarence 194
Buckle, Terry. 175
Buechlein, Daniel M. 81
Bueno, John 73, 74
Buhler, Becky 344
Buick, William W.. 121
Bull, Norman 190
Bulloch, Wendy. 201
Bullock, Jeffrey. 307
Bullock, M. Wyvetta 110
Bullock, Robert H., Jr.. . . . 333
Bullock, Warren 73
Burbidge, Michael F. 303
Burden, Keith 134
Burden, Roy A. 194
Burdick, Brent. 198
Bures, Sally. 41
Burg, Randall S. 87
Burger, Delores 25
Burger, Gail A. 246
Burger, Stephen E. 25
Burgess, David 66
Burgess, Morgan 116
Burgio, Ron. 103
Burgo, Peter 87
Burgonio-Watson, Thelma. . 259
Burke, C. Don 140
Burleigh, Elizabeth F. 68
Burley, Kathy J.. 261
Burney, Artie. 78
Burnham, Gary 94
Burnham, Todd 244
Burns, Donald 287
Burns, Patricia. 51
Burns, Robert J. 51
Burrell, Calvin. 317
Burrell, Willie 139
Burrill, William G. 106
Burris, Glenn C., Jr.. 126
Bursey, Ernest 307
Burt, Merlin D. 348
Burton, Anthony 175
Burton, M. Garlinda 326
Busby, Dan 30
Bush, Richard E. 87
Bushkofsky, Linda Post . . . 111
Bushrod, Montrose 337
Bush-Simmons, La Quetta. . 228
Buslon, Jim 193
Buss, P.M. 121
Busse, Cheryl. . . . 93, 183, 311
Bustle, Louie. 98
Bustram, James 116
Buswell, J. Oliver 125
Butimore, David, Sr. 64
Butin, Philip W.. 304
Butler, Kevin J. 153, 334
Butler, Lisa 136
Butler, Ramsey 139
Butler, Thomas 136
Butts, Calvin O.. 246
Butts, J. Wayman. 250
Buxton, Zane. 143
Buzza, John. 242
Buzza, Rob 312
Buzzard, Anthony 327
Buzzell, Sandra 237
Byers, Verlin 252
Byler, J. Ron 132
Bynum, LaTaunya M. 251
Bynum, William 353
Byrd, Ron 121, 337
Cabana, Denise 230
Cabigting, Ruben. 129
Cable, Kenneth 299
Cabrera, Brigido 146
Cady, Donald D. 168
Cagan, Richard D. 259
Cahoy, William J. 303
Calder, John. 118, 180
Caldwell, Bruce. 106
Calian, Carnegie Samuel . . 302

Caliandro, Arthur 26
Callaway, Phil 346
Callaway, Susan L. 100
Calvin, John. . . . 145, 150, 160
Camp, Peggy 169
Camp, Richard P., Jr. 29
Camp, Steve 161
Campbell, Alexander . . 83, 85, 181
Campbell, Cynthia M. . 26, 299
Campbell, Donald G.. 143
Campbell, Ella. 146
Campbell, Frederick F. . . . 304
Campbell, John D.. 182
Campbell, Joseph 90
Campbell, Roslyn A. 201
Campbell, Scott. 52
Campbell, Stuart W. 348
Campbell, Ted A.. 295
Campbell, Thomas. . 83, 85, 181
Campbell, Virginia 236
Campone, Merv. 53
Campos, Jose Luis. 152
Canary, John F. 300, 307
Canary-Marshall, Deborah 251
Canfield, Paul V. 138
Cannada, Robert C., Jr. . . . 303
Cannaday, Antoinette. 78
Canning, James A.. 29
Cannon, Edward 78
Canon, Rose 124
Caouette, Karen. 237
Caraballo, Ildefonso . . 93, 183
Card, Malcom 186
Carder, Kenneth L. 165
Carey, Lott 307
Carlin, Donald. 254
Carlsen, William A. 64
Carlson, Dennis N. 152
Carlson, Kenneth P. 109
Carlson, Robert W. 40
Carmi, Laila 47
Carmical, Leon J. 76
Carmody, Edmond. 80
Carolson, George G. 112
Caron, Kateri. 260
Carouthers, David 287
Carpenter, Don 342
Carpenter, Paul 115
Carpenter, Ronald, Sr. 128
Carr, Clarence 59, 60
Carriere, Vianney (Sam) . . 174
Carroll, Jeff. 116
Carroll, Leon. 24
Carroo, Winston 38
Carson, John L.. 75
Carson, Kathy 45
Carter, Janice. 345
Carter, Jeff 247
Carter, Larry 296
Carter, Pamela. 141
Carter, Ron L. 334
Cartner, Richard 133
Carver, Hugh. 93
Cary, Lovell R. 93
Cary, Timothy 25
Case, Patricia R. 322
Case, Suzanne 217
Casebolt, James 241, 242
Casey-Lee, Diane 238
Cashwell, G.B. 127
Cassian (Bishop) 124
Casteel, J. Richard. 126
Castle, Gretchen 141
Castrejon, Jaime 297
Cate, William 260
Cauller, William L. 253
Cavadini, John C. 307
Cavalero, Robert 37
Cavanaugh, Donald 22
Cave, Evelyn. 234
Cawley, William Kevin . . . 353
Cayce, W. Hartsel 144
Cayce, W.H. 323, 333
Cazabon, Gilles 197
Cebula, John W. 247
Cecil, James 126
Cell, Howard. 141
Cepure, Uldis 129
Cereghino, Phil 336
Chadden, Shane. 55
Chadwick, Joanne 111
Chafe, Joanne 196
Chamberlain, Larry 116
Chamberlain, Ray W., Jr. . . 165
Chamberlain, Ray 120
Chambers, Clarice L.. 254
Chambers, James R. 166
Chambers, Steven 201
Chamness, Ben R. 164
Champagne, Rene 340
Champion, George L. 59
Champion, Jerrye 29
Champion, Willie C. 86
Chand, Samuel R. . . 45, 127, 291
Chandler, Maurice G. 290
Chane, John B. 106
Chang, Richard 105
Channan, James. 46
Chapell, Bryan. 142, 293
Chapman, Clare. 38
Chapman, John 86
Chapman, Morris H. 153
Chappelle, Richard Allen, Sr. 59
Charland, Dennis. 191
Charles, Mark 85
Charleston, Steven. 294
Charron, Jean-Marc 314
Charry, Ellen T. 336
Chase, Deana 118, 119
Chase, Marlene 337
Chase, Robert 160
Chatham, Virginia E. 338
Chauke, Abner. 117
Chauncey, H. Doyle 154
Cheatham, Shirlie 117
Chell, Ted 286
Chemberlin, Peg 242
Cheney, Charles Edward . . 147
Cherney, Sue 243
Cherry, Conrad 214
Cheshier, Carl 134
Chesnutt, Randall 302
Chesser, Larry 334
Chetti, Samuel S.. 64
Chevalier, Rebekah . . 343, 344
Chidsey, Linda. 118, 119
Childers, John D.. 93
Chiles, Lois. 65
Chisholm, Alvah 244
Chivers, Charlie 28
Chmura, Joyce. 231
Choi, Seung Koo 128
Chol, Keak 244
Choloyan, Oshagan 72
Chondo, Javan. 119
Chow, Rita K. 40
Christensen, Bruce 340
Christensen, Clifford R. . . . 101
Christian, William 96
Christianson, Lawrence . . . 133
Christie, Joyce. 56
Christie, Marge 245
Christie, Paul C. 230
Christopher (Bishop) 124
Christopher (Metropolitan) 151
Christopher, Sharon Brown 163, 164
Chrysostomos (Archbishop) 157, 158
Chu, Thomas. 104
Chuol, Samuel. 244
Church, Ted. 149
Churchill, Craig. 349
Chute, Nilda 287
Chynoweth, George. 245
Ciceva-Aleksic, Marija 47
Cieslak, William M. 295
Cilpam, Ha Giao 88
Cimer, Mary Lee 119
Cinson, Victor 34
Cioffi, Joseph 259
Citronnelli, Eddie 78
Cizik, Richard 36, 330
Clanton, John 121
Clark, Charles 66
Clark, Elizabeth A. 320
Clark, Frank B. 227
Clark, James I., Jr.. 98
Clark, Jeffery A. 154
Clark, Neal 64
Clark, Robert. 34
Clark, Tim. 154
Clarke, John R. 174
Clarke, Levy 94, 184
Clatterbuck, Doug 261

INDEX

Clausen, Daniel 301
Clawson, Douglas B. 139
Clay, Colin 288
Cleave, Dwayne 192
Clement, Marilyn 34
Clements, Kerry 143
Clements, Larry. 64
Clements, Philip J. 37
Clements, Sam. 95, 184
Clifford, Mary Montgomery 136
Clifton, Thomas E. 292
Cline, Douglas M. 93
Cline, Evadna 255
Cline, George 126
Cline, Richard D. 259
Clippard, David. 154
Close, William. 309
Clothier, Patti 252
Cloud, Randy 64, 98
Cloud, Sanford, Jr.. 37
Clouse, Gary A.. 126
Clowes, William 144
Coates, Ken. 228
Coats, John W. 66
Cochran, Sylvenia F. 248
Cochrane, Helen Baily . . . 253
Coffin, Percy D. 175
Coffin, Peter R. 175
Cogdill, Michael G.. 292
Coggins, Jim 344
Cohall, Kirkpatrick 65
Cohen, Albert G. 229
Colas, Ralph 22
Cole, Jack 121
Cole, John K. 139
Cole, John 246
Coleman, Caesar D.. 87
Coleman, Catherine 228
Coleman, Gerald D.. 304
Coleman, James M. 106
Coleman, K. Virginia. 201
Coleman, Robert F. 297
Coles, Robert N. 66, 334
Coll, Roger A.. 201
Collaxo, Manny. 83
Colligan, John 22
Collins, Arnie 48
Collins, Bradley 323
Collins, F. Donald 77, 324
Collins, Jacqueline 178
Collins, Leland C. 232
Collins, Les D. 137
Collins, Michael R. 154
Collins, Sam 91
Collins, Thomas 196
Collins, W. Darwin 85
Collis, John 123
Collymore, Carlisle 163
Colon, John. 104
Combes, Frances 287
Comfort, Marianne 248
Comfort, William 260
Compton, Gordon 29
Conant, Lawrence 155
Conaway, Cosette M.. 126
Condrea, Nicolae 149, 197
Cone, Claude W. 154
Conley, Jean 31
Conley, John 293
Conley, Mike. 31
Conn, C. Paul 93, 183
Connel, Bob 318
Conner, Len 25
Connolly, Alethea 247
Connors, G.C. 173
Constantine (Metropolitan) 158
Contogeorge, Christopher . . 71
Converse, Susan 146, 195
Cook, Charles J. 27
Cook, Clyde 306
Cook, David T. 319
Cook, Frank 256
Cook, Gary 41
Cook, Katie 316, 317
Cook, R. Franklin 325
Cook, William. 22
Cooksey, David 79
Coomas, Doug. 179
Coombs, Gary F. 305
Coop, Linda 110
Cooper, Brian 176
Cooper, Dianne 201
Cooper, Irving S. 129
Cooper-White, Michael L.. 299
Coorilos, Euyakim Mar . . . 131
Cope, Kenneth. 141
Cope, Mike 338
Cope, William 62, 316
Copeland, Elaine Johnson . . 293
Copeland, Shelley 229
Cope-Robinson, Lyn . . 118, 119
Copley, Steve 227
Coplon, David. 249
Corbett, Ardelia M. 162
Corbett, Daniel 95, 184
Corbin, Randall B. 87
Corbitt, James T. 74
Cordat, Mary F. 350
Cordeiro, Wayne 126
Coria, Martin. 39
Corkum, Celest 198
Corkum, Ken. 198
Cormode, James R. 312
Corson-Finnerty, Susan . . . 324
Cortez, Hector. 65
Costanza, Daniel 346
Cotant, William. 245
Côté, P. Richard. 197
Cotton, Edmund G. 115
Cottrell, Ralph. 77
Coulston, James A. 114
Coulter, Riley 310
Court, Anna Lee 238
Cousin, Philip Robert, Sr. . . 59
Couture, Jean-Guy. 196
Cowan, Mattew 151
Cox, Ann. 257
Cox, Jill 261
Cox, William J. 106
Coyner, Michael J.. . . . 164, 250
Crabtree, Charles T. 73, 74
Crabtree, Davida Foy 161
Craddock, Margaret. 256
Craddock, Max E. . . . 185, 343
Craft, Betty Jo. 35
Craft, Roger L. 26
Craig, James D. 356
Cramm, Stassi D. 100
Crandall, Christine A. 351
Crandall, Rick 231
Crane, Charles A. 291
Cranford, Stephen V. 251
Crank, Charles 73
Cranmer, Gilbert 95
Crapson, Winnie 235
Craven, Paul J. 35
Crawford, Bud. 187
Crawford, Evans E. 297
Crawford, Florence L. 70
Crawford, Peggy 36
Crawford, S. Rea. 141
Crawley, David P. 174
Creighton, Michael 105
Creighton, Philip. 54
Crenshaw, Carole 325
Crenshaw, Ray 78
Cress, James A. 152
Cretin, Shan 149
Crews, C. Daniel. 352
Crews, Warren. 243
Crews, William O.. 295
Cribbs, Art C. 228
Crick, Robert D. 93, 183
Crim, Blanche 29
Crisp, John 95
Crist, Jessica 243
Crist, Larry 84
Cristobal (Bishop) 157
Crocker, Richard 77
Crockett, Joseph 22
Croft, Donna 51
Croglio, James. 247
Croneberger, Jack 105
Cronin, Daniel A. 230
Crook, Eleanor Butt 26
Cropsey, Marvin W.. 329
Cross, Roger 48
Crossman, Richard C. . . 52, 314
Crouch, Peter D. 38
Crough, Dave 346
Crouse, David 189
Crout, Valorie 259
Crowder, Sandra B. 61-62
Cruger, Douglas 237
Crum, John 70
Crumbly, Faith 334
Crumes, W.E. 96, 325
Crumpler, A.B. 127
Crutchfield, Carmichael . . . 86

INDEX

Cruver, Rob W. 141
Cruz, John. 21
Cueni, R. Robert 298
Culbertson, Terry. 247
Cullen, Edward P. 81
Cullen, James 174
Culp, Kristine A. 294
Culpepper, R. Alan 297
Cummings, Frank Curtis . . . 59
Cummins, George D.. 147
Cummins, John S. 81
Cunningham, Jack . . . 166, 201
Cunningham, Jeff 259
Cunningham, Jonny. 70
Cunningham, Joseph . . 89, 319
Cunningham, Mary 326
Cunningham, Paul G. 98
Cunningham, Ronald M.
. . . . 30, 87
Cureton, Charles 132
Curry, G.. 346
Curry, Marvin 166
Curry, Michael B. 105
Curtis, Jay 114
Curtis, Larry 257
Cushinberry, Aletha. 139
Cushman, Jim 144
Custer, James. 116
Cuthbert, Richard 66
Cuthbert, Terry D.. . . 189, 342, 343
Cutler, Lelia 136
Cutter, Alan. 241
Cutts, Debbie 261
Cyprian (Metropolitan) . . . 157
Dabrowski, Rajmund. 152
Dadds, David 233
Dadourian, Haig 73
Dahl, Judy. 167
Dahulich, Michael G. 304
Dale, Diana C.. . . . . 39, 68
Dale, William 138, 329
Dalenberg, Jack. 146
Dallenbach, Robert B.. 141
Dalton, Harold. 322
Danhof, Henry. 145
Daniel, Clifton, III. 105
Daniel, W.N. 135
Daniels, Mary Martha 103
Danielson, Duane C. 111
Danna, Rick J.. 126
Danneberger, David D. . . . 256
Daoust, Joseph P.. 297
Darby, John Nelson. 82
Darden, Samuel. 70
Darling, Richard 287
Darr, Steve 259
Dart, Christopher. 242
Dart, Helen 149
Dasa, Anuttama 44, 221
Daugherty, Billy Joe 42
Daughters, Kenneth Alan. . 294
Daum, Roger. 77
Davey, Karen 259
Davidson, Brian 75
Davidson, Douglas 331
Davies, Pat 193
Davies, S.J.P.. 287
Davies, Susan E. 32
Davies-Flindall, Dorothy . . 174
Davis, Ashley 235
Davis, Bessie. 70
Davis, Charles. 139
Davis, Derek 217
Davis, Dollie 140
Davis, Earl 38
Davis, F. Benjamin 135
Davis, G. Lindsey 165
Davis, Gail 227
Davis, George 193
Davis, Jim. 227
Davis, Kathleen. 229
Davis, Randee. 58
Davis, Richard. 166
Davis, Robert 237
Davis, Stephanie 162
Davis, Stephen P.. 154
Davis, Terry 230
Davis, Tyrone T. 86
Davolt, Robert. 79
Davolt, Susan 323
Dawidziuk, Jan 141
Dawidziuk, Robert M.. . . . 141
Dawkins, David. 139
Dawn, David. 334
Day, Jeff 237
de Leon, Linda M.. 44
De Moor, Bob 316
De Paz, Jesus 126
Dearing, Carla. 240
Deats, Richard. 323
Deckard, Stephana. 338
Deckenback, John R.. 161
Decker, Robert D. 306
DeConcini, Barbara 211
Dee, Choe Chong 178
deFreese, David L. 112
DeGraffenreidt, Kermit J.
. . . . 61, 330
DeGroot-Nesdahl, Andrea F.
. . . . 111
DeHaan, M.R.. 125
DeHaas, Ron 114
deJong, H. Wayne 88
Del Turco, John. 85
Del Valle, Harry Fred 143
Delac, Katria. 216
Delaney, Joseph P.. 80
DelHousaye, Darryl. 302
DellaForesta, John. 191
Deller, Walter 310
Delloff, Linda-Marie 17
Delmonte, Elisabeth 47
Delsaut, Phil 189
DeMerchant, Ross A. 168
Demers, Marcel. 311
Demeter, Andor 125
Demetrios (Archbishop)
. . . . 32, 123
Demmitt, Greg 94
Demos, Emanuel G. 123
den Hoed, J. 316
Denis, Mary-Frances 200
Denney, Randal. 333
Dennie, Steve 99
Dennis, Donald R.. 140
Dennison, Don 100
Denny, Jesse W. 91
Densmore, Christopher . . . 350
Denton, A. Louis. 254
Depner, Horst 182
der Nederlanden, Harry . . . 341
Derderian, Hovnan . . . 73, 176
Derr, Wayne 338
Derry, John 294
DeSelm, Joel 132
DeTilla, Paul 133
Detjen, Val 354
Detterick, John J.. 143
DeVeaux, William Phillips . . 59
DeVoe, Jerry M., Jr.. 148
DeVries, Janet 144
Dew, William W.. 165
DeWarf, Martha 29
Dewey, Marvin L. 313
DeWinter, Deborah 47
Dewire, Norman E. 300
Dewling, Gregory R.. 194
Dewling, Robert H.. 194
Diakiw, William. 158, 159
Diaz, Ralph 95
Diaz-Montanez, Cristino . . . 65
Dickerson, Dennis C.. . 59, 352
Dicks, Ronald M. 194
Diefenbach, Joan. 245
Diehl, James H.. 98
Diehl, Paul J., Jr.. 84
Diemer, Ulli 341
Dieterly, John 253
Dietterich, Paul M. 27
Dietz, Harry 255
Diggs, Harold S. 145
Dillaman, Rockwell L. 87
Dilley, Gary 99
Dillon, John 52
Dimick, Gregory 108
Dimitrios (Bishop) 123
Dimitriou, Jerry. 123
Dinatale, Wenda 253
Dinkha IV (Patriarch) 67
Dinkler, Charles 321
Dion, Peter 123
Dirks, Gordon 313
Dirmann, Kimberly 126
DiStaulo, David. 191
Dividson, Janet 195
Dix, Bill 31
Dixon, Brad 99
Dixon, Ian. 177
Dixon, Judy. 251

INDEX

Dixon, Michael A. 98
Djaballah, Amar 310
Dmitri (Archbishop) 138
Dobbs, H.A. 323
Dodds, Edward W. 25
Doderer, John E. 135
Dodson, Christopher 250
Doell, Peter 49
Doezema, Don. 145
Dohey, Larry 344
Dohner, Stephanie 244
Domanik, Janice 117
Donahue, James A. 296
Donald (Bishop) 124
Donaldson, Frederick T. . . 126
Donaldson, Hal 332
Donges, David A. 113
Donley, Brian C. 297
Donnithorne, Larry R. 293
Donohoe, Linda. 50
Donoyan, Avo 72
Dorland, Arthur G. 180
Dorman, Nancy 260
Dorrington, Charles W. 147, 195
Dorsey, Daniel 32
Dorsey, Jim 325
Dortch, Mimi 227
Doster, Dean 154
Dougans, James. 234
Dougherty, Cindy 84
Douglas, Caryn 310
Douglas, Scott. 226
Douglas, William 94
Douglass, Stephen B. 26
Dow, Lorenzo 144
Dow, Thomas E. 310
Dowd, Susan Jackson 326
Dowden, G. Blair 99, 297
Dowhower, Kay S. 254
Dowie, John Alexander 81
Down, Graham 343
Downey, Ray. 182
Downey, William S.H.. . . . 129
Downs, Bert E. 101, 308
Downs, Michael A. 161
Downs, Timothy C. 161
Doyle, Barrie. 182
Draper, David E. 308
Draper, James T., Jr. 153
Dreisback, Frances 141
Dresselhaus, Richard. 73
Drewry, Faye. 259
Driedger, Connie 182
Driggers, B. Carlisle 154
Driscoll, Tom 247
Drummond, C. W. 157
Drur, Stephen 166
Dua, Barbara E.. 245
Duda, Betty 130
Dueck, Abe 344
Duerksen, Carol 338
Duff, Donald J. 139
Duff, Robin M. 185
Duff, Susan 236
Duffy, Mark J. 104, 350
Dufresne, Edward R. 239
Dugas, Jacqueline 52
Duggins, Dominic 32
Duke, Dennis 92
Duke, Thomas. 242
Dulan, C. Garland 152
Dulder, Marianne 344
duMars, Candace. 90
Dunahoo, Charles . . . 142, 322
Dunbar, David G. 291
Duncan, David 50
Duncan, Donald 339
Duncan, Larry 95, 184
Duncan, M. Donald 128
Duncan, Muriel 346
Duncan, Paul. 94
Duncan, Philip M., II. 105
Duncan, Robert W., Jr.. . . . 106
Duncan, Ronald V. 91
Dunkin, Ralph W. 113
Dunn, Craig A. 169
Dunn, Sharon R. 92
Dunnam, Maxie D. . . . 47, 289
Dupcak, Kimberlee 247
Dupras, Diane 197
Durakis, Thomas 22
Durance, George 309, 310
During, Elizabeth C. 38
Durocher, Eric. 341
Durocher, Paul-André 196
Dursi, Elsie L. 250
Durso, Pamela R. 316
Dutko, James S.. 320
Dvorak, Robert C. . . . 109, 230
Dwight, David A. 109
Dyck, Dan. 192
Dyck, Darrell 189
Dyck, Ed. 177
Dykstra, Jon 345
Eads, Ora W.. 86
Early, Margaret 232
Easley, Charles 143
Easley, Homer. 58
Easter, Dennis 126
Eastman, Donald 167
Eatherton, Robert L. 100
Eberhardt, Jack 121, 317
Eberly, Carl. 167
Echohawk, John 225
Echols, James Kenneth . . . 299
Eck, Diana L. 218
Eckhardt, Ellen E. 135
Eckler, Sharon. 235
Eckman, James 296
Eddy, Mary Baker 90
Edgar, Robert W.. 38
Edgar, William J.. 148
Edgren, John Alexis 76
Edlund, Mark 153
Edney, Lowell 162
Edwards, Bruce 243
Edwards, David 239, 313
Edwards, Gregory 39
Edwards, Harold 96
Edwards, James L.. . . . 91, 289
Edwards, Jonathan. 149
Edwards, Larry 143
Edwards, Marion M. 165
Edwards, Neva 47
Edwards, Peg 262
Edwards, Scudder 232
Edwards, William H. 83
Edwards-Konic, Patricia 118, 333
Egby, Robert 136
Egge, Joel 97
Egly, Henry 116
Egnew, Bruce E. 80
Ehninger, Charles 253
Ehrenkrantz, Dan. 302
Ehresman, David. 237
Ehrmantraut, Janet M. 84
Eibl, Shawnda 26
Eidson, E. Larry 35
Eidum, Charles D. 63, 322
Ekemam, Samuel Chuka, Sr. 60
Ekeroth, George E. 74
Ekeroth, M.J.. 74
Elam, Betty 31, 39
Elford, Donna 343
Elford, Keith 47, 190
Elia, Donna 246, 249
Ellenson, David. 296
Elliott, G. Keith. 189
Elliott, Kate. 335
Ellis, Charles, III 139
Ellis, David 120
Ellis, Davis L. 139
Ellis, Howard 187
Ellis, Jerry. 255
Ellis, Jesse Delano, II 166
Ellis, Ken 94
Ellison, Leslie 258
Ellor, James W. 40
Ellyatt, David 191
Elmore, Don 76
Elrod, Rachel 235
Elsbernd, Mary 298
Elsensohn, David. 104
Elston, Charles 353
Ely, Thomas C. 106, 259
El-Yateem, Grace G. 111
Embree, Dorothy 238
Emerson, Daniel E. 48
Emory, M.L. 245
Endecott, Clayton 95, 184
Endel, Leo. 154
Engbrecht, Dave 132
Engebretson, Donn 109
Engel, A. Gayle. 161
Engelhard, David H. . . 88, 182
Engelsma, David J. . . 327, 335

Enger, Cindy 259
Enniss, Jane Hopson 231
Enns-Rempel, Kevin 351
Enrique, Antonio 332
Enslin, Christian 190
Enslin, Jon S. 38
Epp, Gerald 115
Epp, Ruth 115
Eppinger, Paul 227
Epstein, Jerome M. 224
Epting, C. Christopher 104
Erb-Miller, Fannie 340
Erdman, Greg 151
Ericksen, Paul 350
Erickson, C.E. 234
Erickson, Charles R. 257
Erickson, Duane 107
Erickson, Gary 166
Erickson, John H. 301
Erickson, Paul 109
Ericson, Charles 230
Erlandson, Kathy 259
Ervine, Sharon 258
Eschenbrenner, Jim 89
Eslinger, Leslie S. 254
Essey, Basil 67
Estep, Michael 98
Esterle, Stan 236
Estey, David C. 201
Estey, Denise 241
Estocin, Frank 158, 159
Eubanks, David L. 298
Eva, Willmore D. 329
Evangelos (Metropolitan) . . 123
Evans, Alton 138
Evans, Bernard J. . . . 103, 187, 322
Evans, Gene 120
Evans, Irvin 163
Evans, Marie 233
Evans, William 134
Evenson, Carl R. 112
Evison, Ian 21
Evrist, Dale R. 126
Ewell, Thomas C. 237
Ewing, Finis 102
Ewing, Ward B. 295
Eyre, Stephen C. 41
Eyring, Henry B. 96
Fadelle, Norman 82
Failing, Mark 316
Fairchild, Darryl 250
Fairfield, Andrew H. . . 105, 250
Faison, Steve 134
Fallu, Jocelyne 197
Fandrey, James E. 130
Fannin, Robert E. 165
Farabee-Lewis, Iris 238
Farley, Edward 16
Farley, Lawrence 193
Farlow, Gary 119
Farmer, Jeffrey E. 42, 138
Faro, Ira 253
Farrar, Fletcher 329
Fast, Ken 25
Fast, Rick 54
Faurschou, Bruce G. 201
Faust, David M. 293
Faust, James E. 96
Favreau, Claude 187
Fawcett, Bruce 186
Fay, William P. 80
Feamster-Roll, Gerry 236
Fecher, Roger J. 31
Fedak, Wasyly 199
Fedchenkov, Benjamin 71
Fedechko, Michael . . 147, 195, 312, 313, 344
Feldberg, Michael 351
Feldman, James 27
Feliciano, Gloria 47
Feller, Henriette 199
Felter, David 98
Fendt, John W., Jr. 135
Ferber, Otto 180
Ferguson, Christopher 201
Ferguson, Les, Sr. 299
Ferguson, Marylin 260
Ferguson, Tom S. 126
Ferkenstad, Craig 113
Fernhout, Harry 311
Ferree, Cathy 253
Ferree, James W. 249
Ferrell, Douglas G. 261
Ferrell, Ernest 136
Ferrer, Abednego 88
Ferris, Ronald 174
Feshbach, Michael 247
Fetherlin, Robert L. 87
Fewster, Lowell H. 64
Field, Ron 40
Fife, Maureen 259
Figueroa, Sharilyn A. 320
Fikse, Susan 330
Finch, Morris, Jr. 84
Finck, Murray D. 111
Fincke, George B. 147
Fines, David 340
Fink, John F. 321
Finke, Roger 212
Finks, Frederick J. 290
Finlay, Terence E. . . . 174, 175
Finn, Charles W. 129
Finn, Peter G. 303
Finney, Peter P., Jr. 320
Finzel, Hans 101
Fiorino, Joseph 331
Fischer, Harvey 95
Fishell, Randy 325
Fisher, Fred S., Sr. 94, 95 183, 184
Fisher, Gerald 177
Fisher, Violet L. 164
Fisk, J. Victor 119
Fites, Donald V. 47
Fitzgerald, Russell G. 45
Flach, Dennis 114
Flachmeier, Ray 257
Flanagan, James 298
Flanagan, Randall F. 261
Fleischer, Daniel 97
Fleischer, Paul 328
Fleischmann, Konrad 137
Fleming, David L. 334
Flesher, Chuck 24
Fletcher, Alfred 64
Fletcher, James 22
Fletcher, Jeffery 334
Fletcher, Judy R. 144
Fletcher, Ruth A. 84
Fletcher, Sarah 320
Flewelling-Leeds, Ginger . . 257
Flowers, Fort D., Jr. 258
Flowers, George F. . . . 59, 337
Flowers, Marles 91
Flowers, Ronald M. 152
Flu-allen, H. Jay 65
Fluechtling, Rick 261
Fluegel, Elizabeth A. 130
Fluit, Charlie 57
Fluker, Sharon Watson 32
Flynn, Harry J. 81
Folds, Gloria 42
Follett, Don 255
Folts, James E. 106
Fombelle, Douglas W. 291
Fong, Bruce W. 300
Ford, Arthur 311
Ford, Brian 198
Ford, C. Barney 33
Ford, Jim 348
Ford, Lowell 66
Fordham, Bertha O. 330
Foreman, Rachel L. 100, 319, 324, 330
Forlines, James 134
Forlines, Leroy 134
Forro, Alexander 124, 125
Forsberg, Robert 228
Forsee, Tom 226
Fortune, Marie M. 259
Foss, Richard J. 111
Foster, Beryl C. 78
Foster, H. Paul 343
Foster, Julie 233
Foster, Mary Sue 257
Foster, Robert 98
Fouke, Carol J. 38
Foulkes, John R., Sr. 83
Fountain, Peter 181
Fox, Ronald K. 249
Foxman, Abraham H. 223
Fozard, John D. 91, 300
Frade, Leopold 106
Francis, Maureen 37
Franklin, Christian 256
Franklin, Irene C. 330
Franklin, Mark 22, 115
Franklin, Robert M. 32

INDEX

Franks, Lonnie 135
Franzmeier, Briana 241
Frase, Donald M.. 168
Fraser, Hugh 309
Fraser, Margaret 32
Fraser, Ronald A.. 309
Frazier, Susan 127
Frazier-Koontz, Peter 243
Freed, Kathy 235
Freedholm, Herbert M. . . . 109
Freeman, David. 182
Freeman, George. 338
Freeman, Linda Danby 45
Freiheit, Warren D. 112
Freitag, Herbert. 126
Freitag, Merle 130
French, Juletha N. 62
Frenchak, David 44, 45
Frerichs, Jonathan C.. 35
Freund, James P. 126
Freund, Richard C. 135
Frew, Don 46
Frey, Mark 250
Frick, Murray 245
Friend, Kendra 100
Friend, William B.. 80
Friesen, William H. 196
Frisch, Deborah. 148
Fritsche, James 192
Frobisher, Martin. 173
Froehle, Bryan 27
Froehlich, S.H. . . . 68, 69, 175
Frowe, Caroline. 232
Fryling, Robert A. 33
Fuchs, Lorelei F. 33
Fugh, Clement W. 59
Fuller, Roy 236
Fullwood, James 66
Fung, Andrew 260
Funk, Abe 52, 177
Funston, Cammie 235
Futral, James R.. 154
Gabriel (Bishop) 150
Gaddie, Ron 236
Gaddy, Todd 166
Gaewski, David R. 161
Gage, J. Marshall 37
Gagnon, André L. 311
Gagnon, Jean. 196
Galante, Joseph A.. 81
Galegor, Steve. 116
Gallaher, Susan 260
Gallegos, Santiago. 126
Galloway, Phyllis H. . . 61, 352
Galvan, Elias G. 165
Gamble, Rich 260
Gandolfo, Lucian 85
Garbe, Ernest E. 130
Garbidakis, Nicholas 22
Gardiner, Kelvin J. 87
Gardner, Britney 127
Gardner, Harry G. 186
Gardner, Marvin K. 327
Garis, Mark. 79
Garment, Robert 114
Garneau, James F. 302
Garner, Darlene. 167
Garner, Don. 118
Garofalo, Frank A.. 301
Garrett, Phillip. 236
Garrison, Brent D. 305
Garrison, J. Michael 106
Garrison, L. Alton 73
Garrison, Mary Lou. 89
Garriss, Stephen 140
Garton, Jean 130
Gasero, Russell 353
Gast, Mary Susan 161
Gaston, Hillary, Sr. 301
Gaston, Sandra L. 61
Gatrek, Nyalam 244
Gatti, Louis 255
Gaud, Carmen 316
Gaudette, Pierre. 197
Gaumond, André 196
Gautama, Siddhartha 220
Gautier, Haggeo 231
Gautier, Mary 25
Gaw, Catherine H. . . . 201, 288
Gay, Charles 85
Gaydos, John R. 81
Gebet, Russell 231
Geernaert, Donna 32
Geiger, C. Edward. 254
Geldmacher, Joan 246
Genello, Willian R. 318
Gennarelli, Daniel 55, 56
Gensib, Joyce 255
Gensler, Maureen 248
Gentle, Stanley 79
Gentles, Jestina 162
George (Archbishop). 156
George, Barbara 42
George, Bill. 319
George, Ivan 65
George, J. Don 73
George, Richard 85
George, Timothy 290
George, William 86
Georgije (Bishop) . . . 151, 198
Gerasimos (Bishop). 123
Geraty, Lawrence T. 298
Gerbrandt, Gerald 309
Gerdau, Carlson 104
Gerdes, Neil W.. 354
Gerry, Joseph J.. 80
Gethers, Leroy. 148
Getz, Greg. 132
Geulsgeugian, Bernard . . . 176
Geyser, P. 146
Ghabrial, Theresa 230
Ghougassian, Vazken. 72
Giacoletto, Kenneth P.. 65
Gibbens-Rickman, Mark . . 251
Gibbs, Charles P.. 45
Gibbs, Diana 52
Gibbs, Wendell N. 105
Gibson, Frank G., Jr. 23
Gibson, Gaylena 318, 319
327, 339
Gibson, Gordon. 256
Gibson, Marie E. 247
Giesbrecht, Kennert. 344
Giesy, Samuel 299
Gilbert, Jack 32
Gilbert, Wanda 217
Gilbertson, Leon C. 54
Gilbreath, Ed. 319
Giles, Ann. 143
Gill, Deborah 74
Gillan, Stewart 52
Gillespie, Thomas W. . . 32, 302
Gillett, Charisse. 83
Gilley, James W. 152
Gillies, Ann. 43
Gillies, Susan E. 64
Gillming, Keith 76
Gilmore, John 86
Gilmore, Marshall, Sr. 87
Gingerich, Elmer. 77
Gingerich, Melvin 77
Ginter, William 115
Giordano, Sally 248
Giordano, Stephen T. 244
Giroux, P. 341
Girton-Mitchell, Brenda . . . 38
Gist, Lamont 248
Gist, Richard. 41
Gladish, Michael D. 190
Glagau, Ralph R.. 92
Glass, Arless 166
Glenn, Lucinda 350
Glenn, Michael 40
Glickman, Marlene 247
Gliege, Ralph 179
Glodo, Michael 114
Gnassi, Johanne. 196
Gnat, Thomas J. 141
Goatley, David Emmanuel. . 41
Godevenos, Ken 346
Godfrey, W. Robert 308
Goertzen, Lil. 342
Goff, Jim. 151
Goforth, C.W. 140
Goldberger, Nancy 328
Golden, Gary. 22
Golder, Morris. 139
Golder, W. Evan 337
Goldstein, Clifford R. 327
Gomez, Ray 257
Gonyaw, Cheri 259
Gonzales, Gerado 46
Gonzales, Melissa 39
Goodhue, Thomas W. 247
Goodin, David L. 87
Goodpaster, Larry M. 165
Goodyear, Paul 198
Gootjes, N.H.. . . . . . . 179, 313
Gopal, Renee. 250

INDEX

Gorazd (Bishop) 71
Gordon, Drew 321
Gordon, J. Dorcas 311
Gordon, Lynne 321
Gore, Ralph J., Jr. 75, 295
Gore, Susan K. 102, 353
Gorton, Dennis L. . . . 101, 336
Gorzoch, Michael 230
Goslee, Cindi. 118
Gosner, Robert 148
Gossett, George B. 66
Gould, Charles W. 168
Goulet, Mary Jean 196
Gourgues, Michel 310
Gover, Mary Pyke 48
Gower, David M. 121, 316
Grace, C.M.. 163
Grace, Doug 38
Grady, J. Lee. 318
Grady, Joellen W. 250
Grady, Zedekiah LaZett. . . . 59
Graham, Ellen 233
Graham, J.B. 154
Graham, Jack 153
Graham, Jannice 47
Graham, John 150
Graham, Julie 56
Graham, Michael. 239
Graham, Rachel. 249
Graham, Vernon R. 233
Graham, William A. 296
Grainger, David. 232
Granberg-Michaelson, Wesley 146, 195
Granitsas, Nicholas 101
Grant, F.W. 82
Grant, James M. 305
Grant, Sumner M. 65
Graves, Charles 261
Graves, James R.. 63
Graves, Thomas H. 290
Graves, William H., Sr. 86
Gray, Arthur J., II 126
Gray, Davis 102
Gray, Jane 29
Gray, Melva 64
Gray, Stephen C. 161
Graz, John. 152
Greagrey, R. Alan 140
Grecco, Richard 196
Greco, John. 22
Green, Daniel 148
Green, Donald B. 252
Green, Dwight. 91
Green, E. David. 100
Green, Peter 133
Green, S.. 163
Green, Stanley. 132
Greenawald, Patricia 252
Greenhaw, David M. 294
Greening, John 121
Greenleaf, Helen 159
Greenwood, Greg 237
Gregg, William O. 105
Grégoire, Léo 197
Gregory (Reverend). 139
Gregory, Chester, Sr. 162
Gregory, Wilton D. 80, 81
Greiman, Clayton 147
Grein, Richard F.. 32
Grew, J. Clark 106
Grier, David 193
Grieves, Brian 104
Griffin, Arlee. 64
Griffin, Benjamin 289
Griffin, Patricia 248
Griffin, Robert. 167
Griffin, William A. 303
Griffith, Craig 22
Griffiths, Michele 253
Griggs, James 193
Grigsby, Phillip N. . . . 248, 249
Grimard, Roland 199
Grimes, Barry Q.. 194
Grimm, Libby 252
Grimm, Robert. 247
Grinstead, Wayne 330
Griswold, Frank Tracy. . . . 104
Groover, Clarence 98
Groover, Gentle L. 98
Groover, R. Edwin 290
Groseclose, Michael 167
Gross, Glenn M. 148
Gross, Joseph 141
Gross, Philip J. 125
Gross, Trevón 21
Grossman, Leonard 233
Grossman, Randall A. 78
Grossmann, Robert 147
Grossmann, W. 146
Grote, Royal U., Jr. 147
Grothe, Jonathan 310
Grotnik, Casimir 141, 324
Groves, Anthony Norris . . . 82
Grubbs, Bonita 230
Grubbs, J. Perry 91
Grubbs, Lari R. 84
Grudzen, Gerald 31
Guentert, Richard L. 85
Guernsey, Lucy 229
Guffey, Edith A. 160
Guibord, Gwynne 229
Guillebeau, Julie 243
Guillemette, Gaetane 340
Guillermin, A. Pierre 298
Guimond, Arthé. 196
Guinness, Howard. 53
Guirguis, Ammonius 187
Guiterrez, Rosalia 46
Gulick, Edwin F. 105
Gulick, Janet A.. 255
Gullette, Reginald 78
Gullixson, Theodore 328
Gumbs, Carolyn 247
Gunter, Nina 98
Guretzki, David. 51
Gurgel, Karl R. 169
Gurley, Morris. 246
Guskjolen, J.I. 173
Gustafson, James M. 16
Guynes, Delmer R. 305
Gwinn, James A. 29, 40
Habecker, Eugene B. 21
Habegger, Ronald J. 116
Hackett, Charles 73, 74
Hadjinicolaou, John. 193
Hadley, Alvin 250
Hadsell, Heidi 296
Haecker, Elsa 257
Haemmerle, Gerald R. . . . 290, 300
Hagan, G. Michael 301
Hagan, Orville. 92, 183
Hagedorn, Harold J. 169
Haggray, Jeffrey 64, 153
Hahn, Daniel 248
Hai, Iftekhar 46
Haight, David B. 96
Haines, Stephanie Boughton 161
Hais, Hope 333
Halbrooks, G. Thomas. . . . 293
Halde, Fred 240
Hale, Joe 47
Hales, Robert D. 96
Haley, Laura J. 247
Hall, A.Z., Jr.. 91
Hall, Beverly. 95
Hall, David A., Sr.. 92
Hall, Dinah 259
Hall, Gregory V. 91
Hall, J.L. . . 166, 323, 332, 352
Hall, LisaRose. 28
Hall, Marvin 119
Hall, R. Franklin 58
Hall, Will 153
Hallberg, Donald M. 111
Hallman, David. 56
Haloviak, Bert 152, 348
Hamb, Elnora 86
Hamblin, Lloyd D., Jr.. 65
Hambrick, Fred 289
Hamel, William 109
Hamelink, Crystal 248
Hames, Jerrold 322
Hames, Jerry 104
Hamilton, Betty. 78
Hamilton, Karen 50
Hamilton, Thomas. 22
Hamilton, W.W.. 91
Hamlett, James P. 84
Hammer, Bill. 236
Hammock, Cheryl 45
Hammond, F. Melvin 96
Hammons, Roger. 144
Hampton, Charles 129
Hampton, John E. 139
Hampton, Johnna E. 319
Han, Se Won 128

INDEX

Hancock, Carol 47
Hancock, Ginny 235
Handysides, Allan R. 152
Haney, Kenneth F. 166
Hankins, David E. 153
Hanse, Brian W. 35
Hansen, Duane 110
Hansen, Ellen 260
Hansen, Gary L. 112
Hanson, Lloyd. 228
Hanson, Mark S. 110
Hanson, Oscar H. 130
Hanzlik, Darcy 241
Hardenbrook, Jim 89
Hardy, Ralph, Jr. 31, 39
Hargleroad, Bobbi Wells . . 320
Hargrave, Ervin. 127
Harke, Gary L. 254
Harmelink, Herman, III . . . 126
Harms, Forrest. 235
Harms, Richard H.. 352
Harms, Steve. 227
Harper, Bud. 288
Harper, Stephen. 292
Harper, Susan Grine 256
Harper, Terry L.. 154
Harriger, James 25
Harris, Alvin 90
Harris, Annie. 231
Harris, Barbara 105
Harris, David A. 223
Harris, David. 345
Harris, Elsie 162
Harris, Forrest E.. 289
Harris, Jerome V.. 59
Harris, Mark T. 126
Harris, Patricia 261
Harris, Phil 88, 89
Harris, Roger. 177
Harris, Rogers S.. 106
Harris, Virginia S.. 90
Harris, William O.. 353
Harrison, Charles E. 335
Harrison, Matthew. 130
Hart, D.G. 17
Hart, Donald G.. 161
Hart, Jack 50
Hart, Kenneth W.. 126
Hart, Maurice 120
Hart, Stephanie 215
Hartford, Barbara H. 45
Hartke, Gary 98
Hartman, Earl C., Jr. 252
Hartman, Patricia. 108
Hartwig, Raymond L. 130
Harvey, Carole (Kate) H.. . . 65
Harvey, Donald F. 174
Harvey, Jane Hull 33, 34
Harwell, Sara 349
Hasan, John. 227
Haskins, Roger W., Jr. 117
Hassinger, Susan W. 164
Hastey, Stan. 63, 321
Hasty, Robert E. 126
Hatcher, Warren. 148
Haten, C.. 288
Hatfield, Archibald 190
Hatlie, Susan Allers. 241
Hattem, Robb J.. 126
Hauser, Clarence 287
Hawaweeny, Raphael 67
Hawkin, David J.. 51
Hawkins, O.S. 153
Hay, Eleanor 255
Hayes, Kathleen 335
Hayes, Lindsey 127
Hayes, Mona. 29
Hayford, Jack W.. 126
Hayford, James W. 126
Haymes, Don 349
Hayner, Stephen A. 33
Haywood, Marshall 59, 60
Hazuda, Ronald A. 65
Hazzard, David E. 173
Headman, Wayne A. 303
Heagy, David 160
Hearn, Greg. 128
Heaslip, Clifford 201
Heater, Homer, Jr. . . . 292, 307
Heath, Preston. 140
Hebermehl, Rodger W. . . . 130
Heckenmueller, Teri 32
Heckles, Jane E. 161
Heckman, Bud 46
Hedrick, Granville. 89
Heebner, Gerald 335
Heer, Nancy 169
Hefner, Helmut 303
Hein, Marvin. 122
Heinze, Ted. 287
Heisey, Terry M. 350
Heitzenrater, Richard P. . . . 320
Heleine, Berton G. 66
Heller, Ena 22
Helton, Charles L. 87
Helton, James 120
Helton, Mary Beth. 237
Hemachandra, Ramya 56
Heminway, L. Marshall . . . 129
Hemphill, Kenneth S. 305
Henderson, Dorsey F., Jr.. . 106
Henderson, James 143
Henderson, Katharine R. . . 213
Henderson, Veryl F. 153
Hendrick, Sherrill 259
Hendricks, Harry. 96
Hendricks, Obery M., Jr. . . 302
Hendrickson, Mary Lynn. . . 24
Hendrix, Carol S.. 113
Hendrix, Ray. 98
Hendrixson, Joe M. 235
Henkel, Sarah 255
Hennessey, Janet 237
Henning, Cornal Garnett, Sr. . . 59
Henry, Craig 63
Henry, Jennifer 52
Henry, Patrick 215
Henry, Rodney 153
Henze, Charles 245
Heppner, Jack 189
Herbrandson, DeWayne. . . . 28
Heretz, Michael. 159
Herlong, Bertram M. 106
Herman (His Beatitude). . . 138
Herman (Metropolitan) 62
Herman, Alvin. 185
Herman, Harry 139
Hernando, Mirasal. 178
Hernando, Vincente. 178
Herring, Paul L.. 254
Hershkowitz, Thomas 104
Hertzog, Glenn 133
Hertzog, Stephen. 312
Herzog, Daniel W.. 104
Hess, Larry G.. 93
Hessel, Karen M.. 38
Hesselbein, Frances. 168
Hester, Yvonne 239
Heuser, Frederick J., Jr. 143, 327
Hewitt, Bradford L. 130
Heyward, Isaiah 92
Hickcox, Michael A. 43
Hickey, Tim S. 320
Hickman, Holsey. 257
Hicks, Cullen L. 325
Hicks, Daniel 126
Hicks, Maurice M.. 178
Hicks, Roy 190
Hicks, Wayne 100
Hicks, William 95
Hiebert, Richard P. 346
Hiemstra, John E. 246
Higgins, Dave 198
Higgins, Stan. 28
Higham, Susan 147
Highers, Alan E. 335
Hill, Bruce 108
Hill, Darcel 242
Hill, Kenneth H. 59, 326
Hill, R. Eugene 66
Hill, Ronald K. 145
Hill, Ruth Y. 109
Hillerbrand, Hans J.. 320
Hilliard, David 299
Hilliard, William Alexander 60
Hilsden, R.T. 173
Hiltz, Frederick J. 175
Hincke, Karen. 56
Hinckley, Gordon B. 96
Hinkel, George 259
Hinton, Arthur. 103
Hinz, Leo 288
Hinz, Mary Ann 239
Hirschy, Charles A. 100
Hirschy, Margaret 349
Hirschy, Paul. 99
Ho, Esther. 228

Hoak, Don. 258
Hobbs (Reverend) 140
Hobgood, William Chris 83
Hockensmith, David W., Jr. . . 243
Hockman-Wert, Cathleen. . 336
Hodder, Gary. 198
Hodges, Clarence E. 152
Hodges, Douglas 254
Hodges, James. 68, 175
Hodges-Kent, Wendy. 257
Hodgins, Donald E. 202
Hodgson, Robert 22
Hodur, F. 141
Hoefflin, Walter R. 126
Hoeksema, Herman 145
Hoff-Brodowy, Sharon . . . 243
Hoffman, Bud 250
Hoffman, David B. 255
Hoffman, George. 159
Hoffman, James R. 80
Hoffman, Jane Fishler 161
Hoffman, Karl H. 135
Hoffman, Warren L. . . . 79, 178
Hoffs, Vernon 195
Hofstad, Robert D.. 111
Hogan, Ed. 74
Hogston, Delphine. . . 240, 241
Hoke, Kenneth O. 79
Hoke, Terry. 79
Holbrook, Mark G. 28
Holdefer, Helen. 226
Holdeman, John 92
Holden, Ron 186
Holden, Stephen 39
Holdren, David W.. 168
Holland, Grace 79
Holland, Jeffery R. 96
Holland, Melford E., Jr. . . . 104
Hollenbach, Deanna L. 133, 330
Holley, Darrell. 134
Holloway, Callon W., Jr. . . 112
Holloway, Carolyn 246
Hollowell, Barry C.B. 174
Holly, Mary Lynn 163
Holm, Duane 250, 251
Holmberg, Joseph 242
Holme, Mary Swalla 235
Holmes, Carol 246
Holmes, Charles 77, 290
Holmes, Jenny. 252
Holmes, N.J. 127
Holmgren, A.A.. 74
Holmstrom, Virginia 65
Holsinger, James W., Jr.. . . . 47
Holt, Jeanette 63
Holt, John E.. 256
Holt, Michael 46
Holtz, Janet E.. 254
Homoki, Lee 122
Honold, John F. 126
Hood, George 150
Hood, Phil. 346
Hoogendoorn, Case. 45
Hook, Dave. 130
Hoople, William Howard. . . 98
Hoover, Amos B.. 137
Hope, Monica 78
Hopkin, Willis L.. 185
Hopkins, John L. 164, 242
Hopkins, Sara E. 336
Hopyan, Takvor. 73
Horjus, Kenneth 88
Horne, Martha J. 302
Horner, David G.. 109
Horner, R.C. 177
Hornshuh, Fred L. 137
Horsch, James E.. 333
Horton, Charles 231
Horton, Evon G. 311
Horton, Jotham 168
Horvath, Carolyn. 31
Hoskins, Janet A.. 313
Hosler, Mark A.. 100
Hossler, William 132
Hostetter, Steven J. 289
Hotchkiss, Gregory K.. 147
Hotle, Marlin. 325
Houg, Richard W. 295
Hougen, Philip L. 112
Hough, Joseph C., Jr.. 306
Houle, Jacques. 92, 183
House, Alvin 66
House, Christie R. 331
Houseal, Rich 25
Houser, Charles. 22
Houser, Jim 235
Houston, Barbara. 255
Hovsepian, Vatche. 73
How, Gordon. 53, 201
Howard, John Alan . . 311, 341
Howard, Randy 95, 184
Howard, Roscoe J., III. . . . 152
Howe, Bruce H.W. 174
Howe, John H. 105
Howell, Bruce 166
Howell, James R. 148
Howell, Patrick 304
Howell, Stephanie 252
Howerton, Ronnie 120
Howland, William H.. 182
Howlett, Dennis 56
Hoy, G. Philip 234
Hoyle, Gary. 247
Hoyt, Thomas L. 38, 47
Hoyt, Thomas L., Jr. 87
Hubbard, Bede 196
Hubbart, Mike 117
Hucks, John T., Jr. 154
Hudnut-Beumler, James. . . 307
Hudson, Henry 173
Hudson, Jay. 143
Hudson, Steve 109
Huffard, Evertt W. 296
Hugh, Ivor T.. 229
Hughes, Anne 22
Hughes, Clyde M. . . . 127, 332
Hughes, Dustin 127
Hughes, Gethin B. 106
Hughes, H. Merritt 256
Hughes, James L. 142
Hughes, Sarah 236
Hughes, Sherly M.. 162
Huie, Janice Riggle 164
Hull, Rey. 245
Hulse, Erroll 334
Hultquist, Timothy A. 43
Humme, Larryl 146
Hummers, Bill. 256
Humphrey, John 103
Humphry, Carol. 319
Humphry, Sandra. 319
Hundley, Michael 236
Hundley, Reggie 326
Hunerdosse, Marion 89
Hunn, Ken. 79
Hunsberger, David. 255
Hunt, Gerald 54
Hunt, Janet E. 26
Hunt, Raymon. 61
Hunter, A. Scott. 194
Hunter, David 238
Hunter, Harold D. 352
Hunter, Kent R. 29
Hunter, Martha J.. 321
Hunter, Nancy L.. 194
Hunter, Robert. 133
Hunter, Ron. 134
Hunter, Stewart 52
Huntley, Harvey 113
Hurd, Ray 250
Hurley, John 159
Huron, Rod 85
Hurt, Donna 133
Hurtubise, Pierre 356
Hus, Jan 133
Huszagh, Elenie K. 38
Hutchinson, Connie. 28
Hutchinson, Moira. 54
Hutchinson, William W. . . 164
Hutchison, Andrew S. . 174, 312
Hutmire, Louis D. 148
Hutter, Jacob 125
Hux, Ralph 99, 322
Hyvonen, Randall 161
Iakovos (Metropolitan) . . . 123
Ickes, Wayne 110
Idleman, Kenneth D. 301
Ignatieff, Andrew 174
Ignatius Peter III (Patriarch) 156
Ihloff, Bob. 105
Iker, Jack. 105
Ilia (Bishop) 62
Illingworth, Beth 249
Imbens, Annie 46
Imes, William C. 290
Imgram, C.W. 71
Ingersol, Stan 352

INDEX

Ingham, Michael C. 175
Ingham, Susan J. 161
Ingle, Jim 115
Inglis, Charles 173
Ingram, Gregory 30, 59
Ingram, Richard 71
Inskeep, Kenneth W. 111
Inyangu, Frederick. 119
Ionita, Ioan 149, 197
Iorg, Jeff 154
Iosue, Christina J. 256
Ippolito, Luigi 191
Irinev (Reverend) 139
Irish, Carolyn 106
Irish, Esther. 65
Irons, Neil L. 47, 164
Irvio, Wanda 236
Irwin, B.H. 127
Irwin, H.E. 176
Irwin, John W. 55
Isaiah (Metropolitan) 123
Isch, John R. 328
Isenhower, Joe. 130
Ishkanian, Charlotte 329
Isiye, Tom 119
Isom, Beverly 233
Isom, Dotcy I. 87
Iverson, David. 201
Ives, S. Clifton 164
Jaaguste, Evi 187
Jackson, Bernice Powell
. . . . 160, 161
Jackson, Daniel R. 198
Jackson, Hope 287
Jackson, Kitt 245, 246
Jackson, L. Don. 126
Jackson, Mary 78
Jackson, Norman W. 160
Jackson, Phil 133
Jackson, Scott 48
Jackson, Susan 243
Jackson-Skelton, Christina L.
. . . . 110
Jacobs, Anita L. 327, 338
Jacobs, Donovan 312
Jacobs, Sam G. 81
Jacobsen, Michael W. 140
Jacobus, Russell E. 105
Jaggard, Art. 235
Jaharis, Michael 123
Jahr, Armin 97
Jakubik, Arranna 167
James (Archbishop). 124
James II (King) 69
James, Joseph F. 117
James, Russell N., III 292
James, Timothy M. 83
Janes, Burton K. 194
Janke, Dwayne 346
Jansen, Ruth 233
Janssen, Angela 45
Janzen, Gerald. 179
Jarmus, Andrew. 199
Jarrett, Nathaniel, Jr. 60
Jasper, Jeremiah 260
Jeavons, Thomas 118, 141
Jecko, Stephen H. 105
Jeffery, Jim 290
Jeffrey, Robert 321, 327
Jelinek, James L. 105
Jellinek, Nancy 257
Jemerson, Robert. 37
Jenkins, C. Marty 126
Jenkins, Charles E. . . 105, 237
Jenkins, David O. 231
Jenkins, Laurie 249
Jenks, Philip E. 47
Jenness, Jeffery A. 91
Jennings, Charles 66
Jenson, Robert W. 32
Jepson, Alvin S. 294
Jeremiah, David 292
Jerge, Marie C. 112, 248
Jermann, Rosemary 336
Jernigan, C.B. 98
Jesske, T.J. 107
Jessop, William 243
Jessup, Bryce L. 304
Jewel, Bill 237
Jewell, Thomas R. 84
Jewsbury, Will. 234
Jnatiputra, Vardhamana . . . 222
Job (Reverend) 138
Jobson, Harriet Tumlin 43
Johannesson, Gayle 342
John (Archbishop). 156
John (Bishop) 157
John (Chorbishop). 157
John Paul II. 80
John, Esther "Little Dove"
. . . . 260
Johns, Cheryl Bridges 32
Johns-Boehme, Steven . . . 236
Johnson, Alfred 164
Johnson, Andrea 329
Johnson, Arthur F. 74
Johnson, B.M. 74
Johnson, Ben. 71
Johnson, Bill 64
Johnson, Cecil 94
Johnson, Cheryl. 247
Johnson, Craig E. 111
Johnson, Craig. 328
Johnson, David W. 109
Johnson, Deborah 331
Johnson, Del L. 152
Johnson, Diane 101
Johnson, Edna Ruth. 320
Johnson, Eleanor 174
Johnson, Elease W. 61
Johnson, Evelyn M.R. 109
Johnson, Frank 114
Johnson, George 331
Johnson, H.J. 135
Johnson, Harold C. 63
Johnson, Henry L. 139
Johnson, Holly 26
Johnson, Jack 245
Johnson, Jacqueline. 225
Johnson, Jeanette. 261
Johnson, Jeffrey. 117
Johnson, Jeron. 139
Johnson, John Franklin . . . 293
Johnson, Joseph. 60
Johnson, Kathryn J. . . 259, 335
Johnson, Kenneth R. 126
Johnson, M. 131
Johnson, Margaret 64
Johnson, Mel. 167
Johnson, Paul 76
Johnson, Robert E. 316
Johnson, Robert H. 106
Johnson, Robert P. 261
Johnson, Rod. 187
Johnson, Rodney McNeil . . 166
Johnson, Rosie 162
Johnson, Sally A. 109
Johnson, Sharon 343
Johnson, Thomas R. 26
Johnson, Thomas S. 43
Johnson, W. Robert, III . . 59, 60
Johnson, W. Talmadge. 98
Johnson, William E. 148
Johnson, William R. 161
Johnsson, W.G. 315
Johnston, Ben 316
Johnston, E. Benton. 74
Johnston, John. 287
Johnston, Rosemary 228
Joiner, Chris 103
Joiner, Jamie J. 140
Jolley, Wayne 329
Jones, A.M. 78, 318
Jones, Abraham. 78
Jones, Barbara E. 84
Jones, Brooker T. 139
Jones, C. Stephen 245
Jones, Carol. 188
Jones, Cassandra 162
Jones, Clifton 139
Jones, Dale 98
Jones, Dana. 334
Jones, E. Edward. 134
Jones, Elbert 96
Jones, G. Daniel 254
Jones, Gary A. 90
Jones, Greg 186
Jones, Jacqueline. 245
Jones, Jerry 166
Jones, Jesse. 163
Jones, Joyce 198
Jones, Judy 259
Jones, Kenneth E. 86, 319
Jones, L. Bevel, III 43
Jones, L. Gregory 294
Jones, Larry. 187
Jones, Lindsay E. 90
Jones, Noel 139
Jones, Paul Griffin, II 243

Jones, Ralph E. 113
Jones, Stephen M. 100
Jones, Terrence J. 61
Jones, Tim. 93
Jones, Walter D. 90
Jones, Wilbur L. 98
Jones, Wilson 286
Jones-Henry, Barry, Sr. . . . 238
Jordan, Anthony L. 154
Jordan, L.G. 134
Joseph (Archbishop) 156
Joseph (Bishop). 157
Joseph (Hierodeacon) 139
Joseph, Emmanuel. 67
Joseph, John 131
Joshua, Kazi 45
Joudrey, Patricia 287
Joudrey, Philip. 314
Jovan (Bishop) 151
Joy, Norman C. 194
Judd, James. 180
Judd, Peter A. 100
Judge, Beverly. 31, 40
Julien, Tom 116
Juliot, Brent 97, 185, 323, 342
Jump, Rick 260
Jung-Zimmerman, Linda . . 234
Jupin, J. Michael 237
Juras, Julia Sibley 36
Jurgens, Olga. 193
Just, Donald R. 112
Justman, James A. 112
Juuti, Richard C. 71
Kabir. 225
Kaguni, Samuel. 118
Kaiser, John 233
Kaiser, Walter C., Jr. 296
Kalcik, Sharon K. 243
Kalmanek, Edward 31
Kalmanek, Judy. 31
Kamienski, Mikey 255
Kammerer, Charlene P. . . . 165
Kane, Mary 242
Kanouse, Kevin S.. 112
Kansfield, Norman J.. 301
Kapanke, John G. 111
Kapeluck, Michael 159
Kaplan, Clemis Eugene . . . 156
Kapral, Sergei 256
Karim, Cyril Aphrem. 156
Karrott, Sandra 256
Karssen, Paul 146
Karsten, Albert 88
Kaseman, Mansfield M. . . 238
Kashdin, Linda 247
Kashmar, Mary 228
Kashuck, Claire. 238
Kasimer, Sol 57
Katranides, Margaret 118
Katzander, Nina 31
Kauffman, Cephas. 343
Kaufman, Terry 345
Kaur, Amrit 231
Kautz, William 108
Kaye, Edith 238
Kays, Joanne 245
Kays, John 236
Kazanjian, Shant 72
Kearns, Curtis A., Jr. 143
Keating, A.C. 193
Keating, Frank 81
Keaton, Jonathan D. 164
Keefer, Phil 79
Keeler, William Cardinal. 32, 43
Keener, Lamar. 31
Keeney, Mervin B. 89
Keeran, Keith P. 298
Keffer, Anne 288
Keiller, James B. 127
Keith, Judith B. 102
Keith, Raymond J., Jr. 98
Keleher, James P. 81
Keller, Connie L.. 354
Keller, Helen. 54
Keller, Kirby N.. . . . . 108, 295
Keller, Ron L. 240
Kelley, Ann 251
Kelley, Charles S. 301
Kelley, Jack. 128
Kelly, Arlene 118
Kelly, Arthur 321
Kelly, Brian K. 322, 342
Kelly, Bridgette A.. 354
Kelly, Donna 196
Kelly, Doug. 143
Kelly, Francis D. 291, 302
Kelly, John 71
Kelly, Robert L. 16
Kelly, Ronald D. 168
Kelly, Sue 258
Kelly, Thomas 245
Kelly, William. 82
Kelsey, David 17
Kelsey, James 105
Kelshaw, Terence 106
Kemp, John H. 241
Kemper, Bruce 122
Kemper, Kenneth B. 296
Kemper, Nancy Joe 236
Kendall, Michael. 246
Kendall, Ralph 52
Kendall, Stephen 194, 195
Kennaugh, R.S. 193
Kennebrew, Vernon 90
Kennedy, Joanne 318
Kennedy, Johnny. 70
Kennedy, Joy. 56
Kennedy, Leland 290
Kennedy-Wong, Phillip . . . 252
Kent, Allen 66
Kent, Edgar. 127
Kepa, Peter Mar 124
Kersey, Tay 101
Kerslake, Graham . . . 133, 179
Kersten, David 109
Kersten, G.H. 136
Kesohole, Erastus 118
Kessler, Diane C.. 239
Ketcham, Donald. 167
Ketli, Vahe 73
Keurian, Alice 123
Kevern, John R.. 291
Keyes, Randy 166
Keys, Joe. 262
Keyser, Judy E. 89
Khamis, Aprim 67
Khasufa, Sylvester. 119
Khatchadourian, Ashag . . . 229
Khory, George. 46
Khouri, Antoun 67
Khoury, Demetri 67
Khrimian, Mgrditch. 72
Kibble, Alvin M. 152
Kidd, John S.. 230
Kidd, William B. 287
Kidwell, Gary W. 83
Kienitz, Richard 107
Kierman, Jim. 235
Kieschnick, Gerald B. 130
Kiesner, Mary Ellen. 111
Kilgore, Gary 117
Killam, G.. 176
Killam, Gillis 52
Killoren, Eileen. 228
Killpack, Jennifer 100
Kim, Hae-Jong 164
Kim, Nam Soo 74
Kimer, Stan 167
Kind, Kerry D. 168
King, Arthur 103
King, Donald G. 152
King, Eileen 47
King, Eric 91
King, Fred G. 88
King, Gordon 312
King, James R., Jr.. 165
King, Johnny. 201
King, Robert H.. 130
King, Samuel 102
King, Stephen 22
King, William Clinton, Jr. . . 61
Kinkaid, Julie 241
Kinnaman, David 213
Kinney, John W. 304, 307
Kirby, Doryne 52
Kirchhoff, Bernard 38
Kireopoulos, Tony. 38
Kirk, Jennifer 45
Kirkland, Theodore Larry . . 59
Kirkpatrick, Clifton 143
Kirkpatrick, Susan. 119
Kishkovsky, Leonid. . . . 46, 47
Kisia, Joseph 118
Kisner, Elaine 240
Kitui, John. 118
Kivuya, Thomas 119
Klaus, Byron D. 290

INDEX

Klein, Ralph W. 322
Klein, Stephen 241
Kleinfelter, Kenneth 167
Klemm, Ulli 252
Kline, Dale 250
Klinsing, P. David 87
Klombies, Robert G. 185
Klusmeyer, William M. . . . 106
Klutz, C.H. 67
Knapp, Martin Wells 168
Kneece, Brenda 256
Knight, Janet R. 332
Knight, Keith 53, 194
Knipmeyer, Wayne 79
Knoche, H. Gerard 113
Knoedler, Lon 261
Knoppers, Gary 51
Knoth, Rick 322
Knowles, Louis L. 41, 46
Knudsen, Chilton 105
Knudsen, Herbert L. 84
Knudsen, Raymond Barnett II 336
Kobel, Jon 89
Kober, Ted 130
Kochis, Michael 158
Kocian, Dorothy 167
Kocses, Richard 244
Koehn, Dale 92, 183
Koehn, Gladwin 329, 344
Koelpin, Daniel 169
Koh, Linda 152
Kohlbruegge, H. 146
Kokesch, William 53, 196
Koko, Patricia C. 233
Kolb, Leonard R. 135
Kolbaba, Ginger 329
Kolodziej, Jeffrey A. 126
Kolsti, Carol 29
Kondratick, Robert S. 138
Kong, Joe 87
Kong, Joseph S. 88
Konkel, August H. 312
Konsolo, Ephraim 118
Kooistra, Paul D. 142
Koplow, Cordelia 236
Kopp, Herb 122
Koppedrayer, Kay 346
Koptak, Paul E. 321
Korson, Gerald 332
Korz, Geoff 193
Koscak, Robert 292
Kostlevy, Bill 351
Kovalski, Gerald 152
Koziol, Edward 246
Krahn, Robert 177
Krashel, Rosemary 344
Krause, Henry 192
Krawchenko, Oleg 199
Kraybill, J. Nelson 290
Krell, Barbara 232
Kremer, Kenneth J. 328
Krey, Philip D.W. 299
Krick, Brad 31
Krieger, Dorothy 29
Krieger, W.J. 146
Krimm, Joan 250
Kring, S. 177
Kriska, Chloe Ann 250
Kristensen, John 175
Krober, Leslie L. 117
Kroeker, Irvin J. 345
Kroeker, Wally 344
Kroeze, Nicholas V. 303
Krogh, David 93
Krotz, James E. 105
Krueger, Delton 27
Kruschel, Peter 169
Krutz, C. Dana 30, 237
Krywolap, George 159
Kucharek, Wilma S. 113
Kuchta, Thomas 130
Kugars, Girts 129
Kuhlman, Dexter 114
Kuhn, Robert T. 130
Kun, Zolton 125
Kunda, Theresa E. 133
Kunselman, James 62
Kupelian, Gilda 72
Kurima, Andrew H.S. 119
Kurtz, Calvin 255
Kutosi, Peter 119
Kutter, Joseph 65
Kuykendall, John 298
Kuykendall, W.H.F. 315
Kvam, Roger A. 35
Kverno, Trond Hans Farner 180
Kvill, Reuben 312
Kwan, Joseph 341
Kwok, Jack P. 154
Kyrill (Reverend) 138
L'Heureux, N.J., Jr. . . . 246, 248
La Plante, Gerard 180
Labrosse, G. 287
Lacaut, Easton 105
Lacey, Paul 22
Lachatanere, Diana 350
LaCoste, Catherine Louise 25
Lacy, Homer, Jr. 235
Ladehoff, Robert Louis . . . 106
LaFosse, Mona Tokarek . . . 51
Lahey, Raymond 197
Laitner, Christine 155
Lakey, Othal H. 87
Lallo, Cecelia 333
Lamarre-Vincent, David . . 244
Lamb, Jerry A. 105
Lambert, Jerry 98
Lamm, Norman 302
Lance, Paul 229
Lance, Rick 153
Land, Richard D. 153
Land, Steven J. . . 93, 183, 293
Landahl, Paul R. 112
Landers, Bedford F. 154
Landmesser, Leora E. 38
Landon, Dennis L. 83
Lane, Dan G. 237
Lane, Gwendolyn 162
Lane, Hardist 232
Lanes, T.A. 74
Lang, Kristi 95
Lang, Kurt 95
Lange, Francine 316
Langfitt, John N. 144
Langille, Fran 126, 239
Langley, Ken 82
Lanier, Thelma 247
Lanpher, Bill W. 306
Lansing, Steven H. 111
Lapacka, J. Thomas 130
Lapansky, Emma Jones . . . 350
Lapierre, Emmanuel 50
Larade, Sharon 201, 356
Lariviere, Marilyn 29
Larkin, Michael 126
Larmondin, Leanne 340
Larson, April Ulring 112
Larson, Duane H. 307
Larson, Rebecca S. 111
Larson, Ronald 76
Lassen, John 233
Last, Michael A. 112
Lau, David 97
Lau, Jennifer 344
Lauer, Barbara E. 251
Laurence, Steven B. 254
Laursen, Kirsten M. 38, 39
Laurus (Archbishop) 150, 331, 333
Lavallee, Nil 49
Lavigne, David P. 180
Lavine, Bette 237
Law, Bernard Cardinal 81
Law, Sylvia H. 91
Lawrence, Caleb J. 175
Lawrence, James F. 306
Lawrence, William B. 302
Lawson, E. LeRoy 297
Lawson, Phil 228
Lawson, R.C. 98
Layne, Samuel A. 139
Layton, Betty 348
Laza, Kent 167
Lazarus, Frankie 198
Le, Doc 244
Le, Holly Ha 244
Leach, Ed 28
Leach, Norman E. 244
Leag, Riley 243
Leaman, J.S. 338
Leatherman-Young, Sarah 229
Leavitt, Robert F. 304
Leddy, Jennifer 196, 197
Ledeboer (Reverend) 136
Ledesma, Juanita 257

Lee, Arthur 259
Lee, C.R.. 139
Lee, Darrel D. 70, 325
Lee, David H. 154
Lee, Edward L. 106
Lee, Harold L. 152
Lee, Jinwol 46
Lee, Linda. 164
Lee, Luther 168
Lee, Nathan. 97
Lee, Paul H. 87
Lee, Peter J. 106
Lee, Randall R. 111
Lee, Robert L. 75
Lee, Sylvia 319
Leech, David. 257
Leech, Robert E. 143
Legge, W. James 252
Leggett, Harvey E. 135
Leggett, James D. 42, 128
Lehman, Curt 77
Lehman, Edwin. 192
Lehman, Richard. 247
Leibrecht, John J. 27
Leidel, Edward 105
Leiper, Henry Smith 46
Leisey, John 167
Lekic, Mike. 198
Leman, Bruce 335
Lemings, Farrell G. 126
Lemke, Steven. 169
Lemler, James B.. 304
Lemon, Robert E. 152
LeMone, Archie, Jr.. 145
Leney, William T., Jr. 185
Leng, Janet 36
Lennick, Robert B. 43
Lennon, Richard G.. 303
Lenz, Anna Lou. 261
Leonard, Bill J. 24
Leonard, Darnell 253
Leonard, Ellen. 52
Leonhardt, Tom. 31
Leopold, Phyllis J.. 229
Leppington, Mark 312
Lerner, Leigh. 288
Lesher, Thomas 159
Leslie, David A. 252
Lessard, Denis. 193
Lettini, Gabriella 23
Leung, Donna 176
LeValley, Elizabeth A.. . . . 247
LeVan, Patte 329
Levitt, R.A. (Ryan) 185
Levy, B. Barry. 311
Lew, Khristina. 48
Lewis, Beth A.. 111
Lewis, C.A.. 96
Lewis, Donald. 342
Lewis, Ed 116
Lewis, Harry 201
Lewis, Hosea. 157
Lewis, Ida 316
Lewis, James W. 217
Lewis, John. 325
Lewis, Robert L., Jr. . . . 39, 68
Lewis, Vicki L. 62
Lewis, William L. 100
Liebling, Mordechai 224
Liechty, Eric 132
Liegl, Sara. 242
Light, Gordon 174
Lightbody, C. Stuart 182
Liimatta, Michael 25
Likis, Betty 226
Lilande, Joshuah 119
Lillis, John 291
Lima, David 239
Lincoln, John 131
Lind, Christopher J.L. 313
Lindgren, A. Bruce 100
Lindhal, Kay 46
Lindhdm, Charles 246
Lindner, Eileen W.. 38
Lindsay, Emery 90
Lindsay, Joseph 232
Lindsay, R. Rex. 154
Lindsey, W.D. “Doc”. 154
Linebaugh, Dale E. 302
Ling, Mary 95
Lingle, Mark 229
Linsey, Nathaniel 87
Liolin, Arthur E. 62
Lipscomb, John B.. 106
Lipscomb, Oscar H.. 80
Lisby, Micahel 61
Lisby, Mike. 335
Litke, Stanley 341
Little, Darlene 255
Little, Eduard S. 105
Little, Michael D. 40
Little, Vanuel C. 139
Litwin, Paul. 248
Liu, Felix 298
Livingston, John 146, 195
Livingston, Michael E. 126, 319, 320
Llamoso-Songco, Annie . . 320
Llewellyn, Karen MacKay 50
Lloyd, Roy 21
Lobenstine, Clark 231
Locke, Louis J. 126
Lockwood, Daniel R. 300
Loewen, Heinrich 355
Lofquist, Les 125, 337
Lofton-Brook, Oliver. 198
Loftus, John Allan 313
Logan, Samuel T. 308
Logsdon, Gary B. 252
Lohrmann, Marcus C. 112
Lollike, Inge Lise 47
Long, Donald D. 126
Long, Sotello V. 85
Looney, Bill 77
Looper, Kirk 153
Lopez, Hector 161
Lopoukhine, Nikita 193
Lopushinsky, Victor. 194
Lorch, Rhonda. 355
Lord, Frank 230
Lorei, Margaret 253
Lorimer, Paul D. 182
Losten, Basil H. 81
Lotz, Denton 41
Loughran, James 33
Louttit, Henry, Jr. 105
Love, Darrin 255
Love, Mary A.. . . . . . . 61, 320
Love, Ralph E., Sr. 163
Lovett, Sidney 41
Loving, James 139
Lovingood, Vivian. 255
Lowe, Asa 127
Lowe, Grant 143
Lowe, Marvin 78
Lowe, Samuel L. 91
Lowen, A. Wayne 295
Lowery, T.L. 92, 183
Loy, David 234
Lucas, C.B. 145
Lucas, J.P. 92
Lucco, Richard 109
Luce, Bill J., Jr. 293
Luciuk, Rodion 193
Luckett, Catherine 126
Ludwig, John P., Jr. 160
Luedtke, Joel. 242
Luekert, Kathy 143
Luginbuhl, David 52, 198
Luke (Father) 331
Luke, L.M. 134
Lull, Timothy F. 301
Lumpkin, Ramona 311
Lumsden, Jorge 114
Lundgren, Dean A. 109
Lundin, Jack 46
Lundy, Sarah E.. 93
Lung, Wendell. 153
Lunich, Nedeljko 151, 332
Lutes, Carol Christopher . . 317
Luther, Martin. . . 70, 145, 150, 160
Luthy, David 193, 342
Lutterell, Gwen 198
Luttrell, Bill 198
Lutz, Tom 334
Lutzer, Harold. 345
Lyght, Ernest Shaw 164
Lyke, Lonnie. 94
Lykins, Terry. 127
Lyle, Charles. 177
Lynch, Damon, III 250
Lynn, Elizabeth 17
Lynn, Robert W. 16
Lyons, Arthur 45
Lyons, Deborah 141
Lysyj, Anatol. 159
MacAdam, Murray 341

INDEX

Macaria, Nun 322
MacArthur, Earl N. 106
MacArthur, John 125
MacDermid, Gordon E. . . . 314
MacDonald, J. Faber 196
MacDonald, Margaret E. . . 243
MacDonald, Mark 226
Machen, J. Gresham 139
Mack, Alexander 79, 89
Mack, Karen 252
Mack, Paget E.J. 69
MacKenzie, Daryl 186
MacKenzie, Margaret 57
Mackey, Bill F. 154
Mackintosh, C.H. 82
Macklin, Jerry 92
MacLagan, Lynn 238
MacNie, Peggy 256
MacPherson, D. Bruce, Jr. 106
MacPherson, Damian 287
MacQueen, Kenneth G. . . . 314
Madison, Carol 323, 333
Madison, S.C. 163
Madison, Terry 339
Maggs, Robert W., Jr. 143
Magnus, Brian 200
Magnus, Paul 52, 309
Magnus, Richard A., Jr. . . . 111
Magrill, Richard 103
Mahapatra, Amrita 244
Mahavira, Nataputta 222
Mahe, Sally 45
Maher, Philip 57
Mahlman, Margaret 167
Mahon, Chris 141
Mahsman, David . . . 130, 328, 334
Maida, Adam Cardinal 81
Maier, Paul L. 130
Main, A. Donald 113, 254
Mains, Bill 177
Makarenko, William 346
Malayang, José A. . . . 160, 161
Malcolm, Barbara 229
Maldonado, David, Jr. 297
Maldonado, Luis Fernando Hoyos 180
Malenge, Zablon Isaac. . . . 119
Maleske, A. 192
Malherbe, Jean-François . . 314
Malinovic, Mirko 198
Malliet, Jim 33
Mallinak, John 332
Malloy, David, Sr. 80
Maly, Jean 167
Maly, Milton 167, 317
Mammedaty, Kim 161
Manafo, Joseph 191
Manahan, Ronald E. . . 116, 296
Manes, John 95
Mangassarian, Silva 176
Manhard, Mike 241
Mani, Mani M. 46
Manis, H. Lee 22
Mann, Brenda 177
Mann, David 132
Mann, Eric 79
Mann, Gayle 234
Mann, Stuart 340
Manning, Deborah 242
Manning, Robert 308
Manning, Tricia 327
Mannoia, Kevin W. . . . 32, 296
Manon, John C. 114
Manousos, Anthony 324
Manseau, William 31
Mansell, Henry J. 80, 81
Mansholt, Gerald L. 112
Mansur, Mary 331
Mantha, Ray 57
Manthei, Jim 29
Manworren, Donald B. 85
Marani, Samson 119
Marble, Alfred C. 105
Marceil, Christopher 261
Marcum, John P. 25
Mardirossian, Moushegh . . . 72
Mariner, John E. 75
Marini, Chris 85
Mark (Archbishop) 194
Mark (Reverend) 138
Marks, Kirk 108
Markskog, Kyrillos 180
Markus, Carol O. 48
Marquardt, Kami L. 251
Marrin, Patrick 318
Marsh, Fred 330, 344
Marsh, Jack 250
Marsh, Priscilla 246
Marshall, Carolyn M. 163
Marshall, Earl 49
Marshall, Jay Wade 294
Marshall, Jim 52
Marshall, Paul 53, 105
Martens, Ed 189
Martin, Clyde 167
Martin, Gord 181
Martin, J. Bruce 148
Martin, J. Dwayne 258
Martin, John T. 185
Martin, Kenneth 262
Martin, Larry D. 66
Martin, Paul E. 66
Martin, Stephen 51
Martinez, Joel N. 165
Martinez, Margarita 113
Martino, Joseph 254
Martinson, Bradley 97
Martinson, Ronald D. 111
Marty, Martin 321
Marvel, Misha 246
Mary (Queen) 69
Maslo, William 255
Mason, Charles Harrison . . . 91
Mason, Debra 44
Mason, Donald E. 232
Mason, George 257
Mason, H. Lee 334
Mason, Larry D. 64
Mason, Linda J. 91
Massanari, Gregory L. 126
Massey, Anthony 252
Massey, Frank 118
Massey, Stephen K. 66
Mast, Gregg 146
Mathew, Thomson K. 301
Mathies, Ronald J.R. 36
Matigai-Vilitama, Joanna S. . . . 47
Matiz, Jose Ruben Garcia . . 180
Matlack, Lucius C. 168
Matson, Louise 241
Matsuura, Junko 47
Mattackal, Abraham 328
Mattern, Evelyn 249
Mattessich, Tara 242
Matthew, Lamar 118
Matthews, Cecil 114
Matthews, Daniel Paul . . 31, 39
Matthews, F. Clayton 104
Matthews, Larry 340
Matthews, Mary J. 61
Matthews, Victoria 174
Mattoni, Vincent 248
Mattson, Linda 319
Matusiak, John 138, 331
Maudlin, Timothy I. 111
Mauney, James F. 113
Mauney, Patrick 38, 104
Maupin, Tony W. 126
Mawhinney, John A. 23
Maximos (Metropolitan) . . 123
Maxson, Benjamin C. 152
Maxwell, Anita 257
Maxwell, Arthur 49
Maxwell, Laurie 227
Maxwell, Neal A. 96
May, David G. 240
May, Felton Edwin 164
May, Lisa 25
May, Mark A. 16
May, Nareth 87
May, Thomas R. 37
Mayan, Ralph 54, 192
Maybeck, Susan 65
Mayernick, Carol L. 234
Mays, Barbara 118
Mays, Rod 142
Maze, Larry E. 104
Mazur, Francis X. 247
Mbachi, Charles 119
Mbato, Hannington 119
McAdams, Zena S. 84
McAdow, Samuel 102
McAlister, John 342
McAlister, Loran 324
McAlister, Lorne D. 173
McAllister-Wilson, David F. 308
McAnally, Ben 143

INDEX

McAuliffe, Damman 211
McBride, Bailey 318
McBride, Larry 237
McCain, Jacquelyn B. 162
McCain, Paul 130
McCallister, Cline 127
McCann, Gordon. 339
McCann, Jeff. 45
McCardle, Jody 241
McCarrell, Billy 125
McCarrick, Theodore Cardinal 81
McCaskey, Charles 102
McClain, Agnes S. 111
McClain, Gene 66
McCleskey, J. Lawrence . . 165
McClure, George. 118
McClure, Marian. 143
McClurg, Patricia 231
McCoid, Donald J. 32, 111, 113
McColgin, Linda 245
McCollum, Odell. 162
McCombs, Jerry L. 61
McConnell, Alvester 163
McCool, Marilyn. 98
McCowan, JoAnn 247
McCown, Sue 257
McCoy, Bob 259
McCoy, Glenda 258
McCoy, Tracy A. 324
McCreesh, Thomas 294
McCrewy, Leroy 126
McCullough, John L. 38
McCurdy, Claire 350
McCutchen, Retha. 118
McDaniel, Paula 240
McDermott, Pat. 236
McDonald, Lee M. 309
McDonald, Mark. 104
McDonnell, Carol 234
McDonnough, Sheila. 288
McDonough, Linda 121
McDowell, Leon A.. 140
McEntee, Peggy 236
McFadden, Wendy 89
McFerran, L.M. (Mac) . . . 181
McGee, J. Vernon 125
McGibbon, Carol Ann. 45
McGinnis, Robert S., Jr. . . 129
McGough, Nancy 340
McGratton, William T.. . . . 313
McGray, Asa 190
McGuire, Damaris. 248
McHugh, Matthew 26
McIntire, Carl 139
McIntosh, Kenneth W.. . . . 258
McJankin, James E., Jr. 65
McKain, George E., II. 61
McKay, Ginger 167
McKee, David. 247
McKee, Joan 233
McKelvey, Jack. 105
McKenzie, Gilbert E.. 246
McKenzie, Vashti 30, 59
McKinney, Brent 118, 119
McKinney, George D. 42
McKinney, Larry J. 49
McKinney, William 302
McKinnon, Patricia 344
McKnight, James E. 93
McKnight, John. 22
McKnight, William E. 84
McLarty, Alan 161
McLaughlin, John 51
McLaughlin, Kay Collier. . 315
McLaughlin, Scott E.. . 107, 303
McLellan, Daniel. 307
McMillan, John 314
McMillan, Susan 198
McMillen, Bill. 121
McMorrow, Kevin. . . . 33, 322
McMullen, Shawn 328
McMurray, Robert. 139
McMurray, W. Grant . . 100, 185
McNabb, Jerry. 257
McNair, David C. 35
McNally, Beverly 245
McNamara, Dexter 228
McNamara, Mary 26
McNeil, Franklin. 332
McNeil, J.E. 27
McNish, Mary Ellen 22
McPherson, Aimee Semple 125
McQueen, Arpie 316
McRaith, John J. 80
McVay, John K.. 305
Meade, Kenneth 86
Meador, Prentice A., Jr. . . . 315
Meadows-Rogers, Arabella. 250
Meagher, Timothy 353
Mean, John D.. 201
Mecham, Marilyn P. 243
Medders, David S.. 309
Medgyesi, Louis 162
Medinger, Daniel L. 318
Medley, A. Roy 64
Meehan, Bridget Mary 31
Meek, Gary 25
Meekhof, David 260
Mehl, Ronald D. 126
Meier, Gordon F. 87
Mekhsian, Sipan 330
Melanchthon, Phillip 150
Melton, J. Gordon 216
Mendenhall, Laura S. 293
Mendoza, Salvador 42
Menes, Nadia 47
Menitoff, Paul J. 31, 39
Menlove, Coleen K. 96
Menning, Bruce. 146
Meno, John 156
Mercer, David R.. 48
Mercurius (Bishop) 139
Merillat, Pam 132
Merrell, A. William 153
Merrell, Bill 335
Merrill, John 66
Merrill, Nancy. 26, 212
Merritt, Hortense. 248
Merz, Marlene. 253
Meschisen, Eugene 158
Mesiti, Martha. 43
Mesner, Neil 119
Messersmith, Jaclyn 253
Messias, Pedro 127
Messina, Carol 133
Metcalfe, Terri. 85
Methodios (Metropolitan) 123
Metzger, William. 253
Meyer, Don 307
Meyer, Donald L. 321
Meyer, Mary C.. 331
Meyer, William F. 130
Meyerhoffer, Anne Marie 231
Mgonja, Assahe. 47
Micahelius, Domine Jonas 195
Micevych, Paul 159
Michael, Jan 118
Michaelius, Domine Jonas . 146
Micon, Joseph 234
Middendorf, Jesse C.. 98
Middleton, Edward Russell 148
Miericke, Kurt A. 109
Mikovsky, Anthony . . 141, 324
Miley, James E.. 113
Milinowski, Judith W. 249
Millay, James I.. 318
Millen, George 107
Miller, A. Kathleen 287
Miller, Alan C. 161
Miller, Audrey. 38
Miller, Charles S. 110
Miller, Claude E.W.. 174
Miller, David L. 328
Miller, David. 61
Miller, Gene E. 161
Miller, George L.. 108
Miller, Geraldine. 92
Miller, Jean 286
Miller, John Henry, Sr. 60
Miller, John U. 245, 246
Miller, Keith R.. 108
Miller, Lauren E.. 310
Miller, Len 198
Miller, Marcus J.. 112
Miller, Mark H.. 161
Miller, Mary C.. 109
Miller, Mary 27
Miller, Patrick D.. 336
Miller, Paul L.. . . . . 77, 317
Miller, Peter 246
Miller, Rick. 101

INDEX

Miller, Robert J. 120
Miller, Roman J. 332
Miller, Ted. 232
Milliken, Paul 257
Milliken, Richard D. 300
Mills, Wes 176
Miloro, Frank P. 65
Ming, Donald 47
Minnix, Janet. 116
Minor, Ronald R.. 140
Minura, Kyle. 228
Miranda, Jesse. 73
Mirchuk, Nadia 159
Mirek, Art 66
Miscamble, Wilson 300
Missick, Glen 146
Mitchell, James K. 90
Mitchell, Lisa H. 240
Mitchell, Lois P. 186
Mitchem, Susan. 353
Mitrophan (Bishop) 151
Mittman, F. Russell, Jr. . . . 161
Mobley, John P.. 84
Mock, George 239
Moerman, Murray 286
Moes, D.. 342
Moffett, Marilyn 234
Mogabgab, John S. 337
Mogenson, Cris 245
Mohammed, W. Deen 222
Mohler, R. Albert 17
Mohler, R. Albert, Jr.. 305
Mojica, Miguel 95, 184
Moldstad, John A. 113
Moller-Gunderson, Mark R. 110
Moncher, Gary 93
Moncure, Rhymes H., Jr... 165
Monroe, Bill 76
Monson, Thomas S.. 96
Montalvo, Gabriel 80
Montanez, Jose D. 93, 183
Montgomery, Carl Halloway, II 166
Montgomery, Kathleen C. . . 159
Montgomery, Richard. . . . 228, 343
Montgomery, Robert 226
Montmorency-Laval, François de 196
Moody, Carlis L. 91
Moody, Robert M. 106
Moody, William E. 90
Moon, Angelia. 257
Moon, Catherine 253
Mooney, Bernice 25
Moore, Anne 141
Moore, Charles W.. 301
Moore, Clark. 258
Moore, Doris. 325
Moore, Douglas. 173
Moore, Hugh. 233
Moore, Kenneth W. . . . 84, 243
Moore, Larry J. 168
Moore, Marvin 335
Moore, P.J.. . . . . 101, 102
Moore, Peter C. 306
Moore, Ralph E. 126
Moore, Robert A. 93
Moore, Robert L.. 235
Moore, Thomas E.. 66
Moorehead, James H. 327
Moorjani-Vaswani, Shakuntala 46
Morales, Lillian. 253
Mordecai, Patricia C.. 104
Morell, J. William 301
Moretz, Lawrence 150
Morgan, Boyd 312
Morgan, Brent R. 126
Morgan, Dennis. 22
Morgan, Donn F. 293
Morgan, Gerald 240
Morgan, Kenneth R. 355
Morgan, Peter M. 83
Morgan, Peter 193
Morgan, Ronald 76
Morgan-Krick, Valerie. 31
Morgester, Mike 252
Moriah, Lionel 186
Morlino, Robert C. 80, 81
Morris, Adrienne A.. 339
Morris, Calvin S.. 232
Morris, Eli. 114
Morris, Fred 231
Morris, Martha J.. 261
Morris, Tracy 345
Morris, William W. 165
Morrison, Susan M. . . 164, 248
Morrison, William C. 84
Morrissey, James 141
Morrow, William D. 173
Morse, Daniel R.. 147
Mortelliti, Daniel. 191
Morton, Raymond E.. 148
Morushca, Policarp 197
Mosaad, Mohamed 46
Moses, Tom. 94
Mosier, Charles R.. 140
Mosley, Steve 257
Mostert, Thomas J., Jr. . . . 152
Moulton, Geoff 342
Moulton, Lorinda R. 194
Moultrie, Henry A., II 98
Moury, Fred 108
Mouw, Richard J. 32, 295
Mowatt, Ann 57
Moxham, John. 257
Moyer, Bruce 107
Moyer, David 161
Moyer, Dennis. 150
Mstyslav (Archbishop) . . . 158
Mueller, George 82
Mueller, Wayne D. 169
Muganda, Baraka G. 152
Muhammad, Ali 219
Muhlenberg, Henry Melchior 110
Mukulu, Andrew 118
Mukwanja, H.M. 118
Mulama, David A.. 119
Mulama, Joseph Anyonge . . 119
Mulder, Gary. 88
Mullan, Donald W. . . 180, 346
Mullen, David G.. 111
Muller, Marilyn. 346
Mulongo, Andrew Namasaka 119
Mulvaney, Elizabeth 256
Mumford, Ann. 152
Mumford, Stephen. 152
Mummert, Christine S. . . . 111
Munday, Robert S.. 300
Munk, D.. 310
Munro, Victor 287
Munson, Arthur. 65
Muravski, A. 173
Murdoch, John 37
Murdy, Peter 101
Murphy, D.J. 287
Murphy, Sue 232
Murphy, Thomas. . . . 132, 329, 333
Murray, Billy D., Sr. . . . 94, 183
Murray, Edward J. 31, 40
Murray, George V.. 81
Murray, George W. 293
Murray, Hal. 261
Murray, Harold 55
Murray, James W. 292
Murray, Michele 51
Musindi, Meschack 119
Musungu, Philip 118
Mutch, Carol. 195
Mutti, Albert Frederick . . . 164
Muyskens, Samuel. . . . 36, 235
Muzingo, Cathy. 140
Mwanzi, Solomon 119
Myers, Gary 115
Myers, Jerry 66
Myers, Richard 247
Myers-Wirt, Cathy 84
Mylonas, Efstathios 229
N'goma, Joyce 45
Nadauld, Margaret. 96
Nagler, Don. 118
Naik, Deepak 46
Nakasone, Ronald 228
Nakonachny, John . . . 158, 159
Namwembe, Despina 45
Nanak, Guru 225
Nanfelt, Peter N. 87
Nash, Stephen 327
Naten, Loyd L. 140
Nathaniel (Reverend) 138
Navarre, Joy Sorensen. . . . 242

INDEX

Naylor, Susan 185
Neal, Annie Wynn 160
Neal, Joseph C., Jr. 86
Neal, Ricado 238
Neal, Tom 232
Neale, Archie 119
Nederveen, G. 179
Needham, Philip 150
Neelands, David 314
Neely, Constance D. 240
Nees, Tom 98
Neevel, Mary Ann 261
Neff, David 30
Neil, Brad 58
Neils, Michael J. 111
Neilson, Randy 193
Nelson, Arnold C., Jr. 83
Nelson, Beter T. 70
Nelson, Christine L. 253
Nelson, Daniel 149
Nelson, Dean W. 111
Nelson, Elden K. 75
Nelson, Gart 179
Nelson, Gary 41
Nelson, Jodi 242
Nelson, Judy 187
Nelson, Paul D. 30
Nelson, Russell M. 96
Nelson, Steven L. 261
Nelson, Vernon H. 352
Nemkovich, Robert M. 141, 304
Nenson, Alice 324
Nenson, Daniel 197
Nesmith, Virginia 38
Netterfield, Cal 177
Nettleton, Minot B. 230
Neu, Frederick 259
Neufeld, Dietmar 51
Neufeld, John 51
Neuhaus, Richard J. 323
Neuroth, William C. 236
Neville, Robert C. 291
Newhall, Jeffrey 126
Newhouse, Herbert 144
Newman, Greg 193
Newport, Leroy 78
Newsome, Clarence G. 26
Newton, Alan 65
Newton, Alfred, Jr. 94
Newton, Douglas M. 117, 327
Newton, Rita K. 251
Ney, William 192
Ngo, Shelly R. 338
Ngoya, John 119
Nguyen, Tai Anh 88
Nicholas (Metropolitan) . . 123
Nichols, H. Basil 231
Nichols, John D. 93, 183
Nichols, Terence L. 88
Nicholson, Betty 120
Nicholson, William H. 133
Nickerson, Anne 239
Nickson, Sheila 247
Nicodemus, Eugene J. 35
Niebuhr, H. Richard . . . 16, 17
Niederauer, George H. 80
Nielsen, Nancy 45
Nielsen, Niel 142
Nielson, E. Kenneth 33
Nieto, Amelia 229
Nieuwsma, Virginia . . 325, 343
Nighswander, Dan 192
Nikolai (Reverend) 138
Nikon (Reverend) 138
Niles, Dennis D. 306
Nilsson, Harold T. 245
Nippak, Ivar 187
Niswender, Joy 246
Njegovan, James D. 174
Njoroge, James 241
Noffsinger, Stanley J. 89
Nohoolewa, Connie 258
Nolan, Charles 24
Noland, Martin 130, 351
Nolde, Nancy L. 254
Noli, Fan Stylian 62
Noli, Theophan 71
Nolla, Ormara 47
Noonan, Suzanne R. 247
Nordhem, Paula 241
Nordtvedt, Joel T. 299
Norlin, Dennis A. 23
Norman (Bishop) 156
Norman, Clarence 103
Norris, Alfred L. 164
Norris, Dennis E. 64
Norris, Larry R. 100
Norris, Richard Allen 59
Norris, Richard Franklin . . . 59
Northam, Gerald M. 198
Nortness, Michal 260
Norton, Jon 248
Norton, Larry 258
Norton, Timothy A. . . . 35, 336
Norwood, Mathew A. 98
Novak, Mark A. 109
Nunn, Harry, Sr. 74
Nuri, Hussein Ali 219
Nusca, A. Robert 313
Nyenzo, Evans 118
Oakes, Gwyn 166
Oaks, Dallin H. 96
Oancea, David 149, 197, 335, 346
Oates, Lonnie F. 84
Oates, Stephen E. 140
Obengerger, Glenn 113
Obrecht, Margaret M. 41
Obrecht, Patricia 248
O'Brien, Brendan 196
O'Brien, Edwin F. 80
Ochoa-Krueger, Ninfa 257
O'Connor, Elizabeth 328
Odams, John 238
Oden, William B. 164
Odhner, Carroll C. 353
O'Donnell, Frances 353
O'Dowd, Dolores 247
O'Farrell, Mark T. 88
Ofiesh, Aftimios 71, 124
O'Flaherty, Edward 239
Ogle, Jonathan 27
Ogles, Jerry L. 331
O'Gorman, Eileen 321
Oguma, Joseph Lavuna . . . 119
O'Hair, J.C. 122
O'Hara, Robert J., Jr. 254
Ohl, C. Wallis, Jr. 105
O'Keefe, Mark 304
Olfert, Lester 189
Oliver, Vicki 114
Oliver, Willie B. 148
Olsen, Donald P. 133
Olson, Diane 159
Olson, Stanley N. 111
Olubalang, Alan A. 66
O'Malley, Sean P. 80
Omland, Richard R. 111
O'Neal, Grace 126
O'Neal, Padraic 318
O'Neill, Jerry F. 303
Onyewuchi, Rufus 286
Ophoff, George 145
Orens, Elizabeth 231
Orewiler, Teri L. 126
Orser, George 190
Orsi, Robert A. 211
Ortiz, Jose 36
Ort-Marvin, Mary Ellen . . . 231
Osborn, Kenneth W. 152
Osborne, Brenda 66
Osborne, Fred C. 311
Osborne, Linda 261
Osborne, Otis O. 66
Osodo, Lam Kisanya 118
Oswald, Duane 132
Ottenhoff, Don B. 215
Otterbein, Philip William . . 98, 163, 200
Otterson, Michael 96
Otzelberger, E. Ann 136
Ough, Bruce R. 164
Overman, Steve H. 126
Owen, Dean 47
Owen, John 64
Owen, Timothy P. 88
Owens, Chandler D. 91
Owens, Thomas M., Sr. . . . 335
Oyando, Gilbert Akenga . . 118
Oyster, Lisa A. 250
Pace, Connie 235
Pace, Diane 325
Pacheco, Alex J. 126
Packard, George 104
Packer, Boyd K. 96
Padilla, Rafael Malpica . . . 111
Paez, Leticia 48

Pagán, Samuel 295, 304
Pagano, Nicholas 22
Page, Allen 238
Palmberg, Glenn R. 109
Palmer, Floyd 252
Palmer, Gregory V. 164
Palmer, Paul 133
Palmer, Robert M. 68
Palmieri, Paul 95
Palmquist, Gustaf 76
Palumbo, Billie L. 140
Panasuk, Katherine 241
Panozzo, Jack J. 343
Pantupong, Woranut 47
Papagermanos, Stavros H. 331
Papazian, Iris 332
Paperini, Richard 300
Pappajohn, John 123
Pappalas, Thomas 255
Parchia, Earl 139
Pardy, Marion 201
Parish, Donny 77
Park, Michael 152
Parker, Fred 126
Parker, George Lee 85
Parker, Jane 235
Parker, Ken 122
Parker, Rebecca 306
Parker, Ronald L. 84
Parker, William J. 327
Parker, William 148
Parkin, Bonnie D. 96
Parkins, Richard 104
Parks, J.H. 94
Parks, Jerry 325
Parr, Jeb 260
Parrent, Allan M. 307
Parrish, Carol 126
Parrish, Walter L., II 65
Parrott, Rod 229
Parry, Walter P. 227
Parsley, Henry N., Jr. 104
Parsons, Gradye 143
Parsons, Reginald 143
Pastukhiv, Serhij K. 124
Patten, Bebe 183
Patterson, L. Dale 352
Patterson, Leighton Paige . . . 305
Pattillo, Wesley M. 38
Patton, Marcia 64
Patton, Vince 336
Patzer, Jere D. 152
Paul, Willie 330
Paulsen, Jan 152
Paulsen, Vivian 324
Paup, Edward W. 165
Payiavlas, John 123
Payne, Aleta 249
Payne, Claude E. 106
Payne, Margaret G. 112
Payuyo, Patricia 83
Peachey, Dean 309
Peale, Norman Vincent 26
Pearce, Paul 177
Pearson, Jean 242
Pearson, John 28, 29, 238
Peddle, Alvin F. 194
Pedro (Bishop) 157
Peifer, Elvin H. 79
Pelchat, Marc 314
Pell, Archie 51
Pellechia, James N. . . 128, 191
Pelotte, Donald E. 81
Pember, Arlyn 74
Pence, Jerry 168, 169
Pendergast, Arthur J. 287
Pendleton, J.M. 63
Penfield, Jack 230
Penn, Carol 330
Pennel, Joe E., Jr. 165
Penner, A.F. (Bud) 176
Penner, Brigitte 344
Penner, David 189
Penner, Lois 345
Penner, Rick 52
Pennings, Kenneth 261
Pennington, Peter 252
Pennywell, Clarence C. . . . 134
Peper, Mike 76
Peplowski, Thaddeus S. . . . 141
Pepper, Donald R. 35
Perkins, Davis 143
Perkins, Larry 312
Perkins, William T. 300
Perkins-Hughes, Vera 162
Perrin, Clive 230
Perry, L. Tom 96
Perry, Roger 230
Perry, Rufus E. 256
Perry, Troy D. 167, 201
Perschbacher, Gerald 328
Persell, William D. 105
Persson, Bertil 69
Perucca, Kirk P. 42
Perzynska, Kinga 25
Peter (Reverend) 138
Peter, Doug 56
Peter, Raymond 185
Peters, Art 252
Peters, Donald 36, 54
Peters, Judith 251
Peters, Marshall 64
Peterson, Brian 31
Peterson, Curt 109
Peterson, David 37
Peterson, Jay 243
Peterson, Jeanie 259
Peterson, Kathleen 246
Peterson, Robert 109
Peterson, Roland 109
Peterson, Timothy J. . . 190, 346
Peterson, Wendy 53
Petersoo, Udo 187, 342
Petitt, Charles W. 302
Petkau, Dave 311
Petrie, Lou 76
Petrochuk, Sherrie 250
Pettit, Kim A. 326
Pfeifer, Michael 258
Pfortmiller, Gene 136
Pfortmiller, Sandra 330
Phelan, John E., Jr. . . 109, 301
Phillips, A. Blair 255
Phillips, Annie Lee 248
Phillips, Aubrey 187
Phillips, David J. 87
Phillips, Donald D. 175
Phillips, Mary L. 126
Phillips, Stephen 100
Phillips, Sue Watlov 242
Phillips, William Thomas . . 72
Philpott, P.W. 176
Phipps, Ron 132
Piché, Angelika 50
Pickerill, Mark G. 126
Pickle, Claudette 102
Pierce, David 310
Pierce, Ellie J. 218
Pierce, Garland 38
Pierce, R.W. 173
Piescik, Joseph 230
Pieterse, Hendrik R. 333
Pilarezyk, Daniel E. 81
Pile, Gregory R. 113
Pinach, Dennis 193
Pinkston, Ron S. 126
Pinson, J. Matthew . . 134, 295
Piper, O.E. 135
Pishko, Daria 159
Pitt, Benjamin A. 139
Pittman, Wallace B., Jr. . . . 140
Pitts, Clifford R. 162
Pitts, Glen R. 49
Pitts, Tyrone S. 145
Plantinga, Cornelius, Jr. . . . 291
Platt, Allyson D. 239
Plett, Harvey 189
Plouffe, Jean-Louis 197
Plummer, Glenn R. 40
Plummer, Steven 106
Poage, D. 24
Poandl, Robert 32
Poe, James 24
Poesnecker, Gerald E. 95
Pogue, Dirk 108
Pohl, Faye 40
Poirier, Tim 348
Poist, William 62
Poitier, Annette 47
Polasek, Joseph 167
Polding, M. Fred 87
Polhemus, Joseph B. 321
Polite, William 148
Pollema, Vernon 147
Pollington, Cody 65
Polston, Jimmy 151
Polycarpe, Antoine 78
Pomeroy, Betty 245

Pomykal, Janet 167
Ponnaiya, Joyce. 46
Pooler, David 236
Poon, Abraham K.. 88
Pope, Dan 311
Pope, Janet 260
Pope, Kenneth. 66
Poplar, Mildred 49
Popoff, Dmitri E. (Jim) . . . 343
Popovich, Edward 119
Popp, Nathaniel 149, 197
Porch, James M. 154
Porret, Jean 346
Porter, Adlise Ivey. 61
Porter, Jerry D. 98
Porter, John 119
Porter, Nan 255
Porter, Stanley E.. 312
Porter, Waring 114
Posey, Michael E. 126
Posterski, Don. 57
Postuma, Tim 24
Potter, Jim. 186
Potterveld, Riess W. 298
Potworowski, Christophe. . 312
Powell, James L. 83
Powell, Jerry 140
Powell, Joel. 140
Powell, Joseph. 148
Powell, Larry 134
Powell, Paul W.. 295
Powell, Raymond, Sr. 96
Power, F.J.. 344
Powers, Diane 37
Powers, Reggie O.. 140
Prachar, T.. 192
Pratt, John L., Sr.. 245
Premawardhana, Shanta D.
. . . . 38, 63
Prendergast, Terrence 197
Presler, Titus L.. 295
Prestigiacomo, Vincent 85
Prestol, Juan R.. 152
Preus, Christian 130
Preus, Daniel. 130
Price, Donald R. 64
Price, Kenneth. 106
Price, P.. 103
Price, R. 163
Priest, Catherine 288
Primavera, Wendy 245
Prince, T.J. 135
Pritchett, Wayne N. . . 198, 313
Probasco, Ruth 153
Profit, Jim 56
Prosser, Robert 102
Province, Terry 41
Pruter, Karl 81
Pryor, Christine 331
Puckett, John L. 86
Pue, Carson. 52
Pugliese, William 260
Puglisi, Amy 255
Pugsley, John W.. 37
Pulins, Juris. 129
Puryear, Richard 252
Pusateri, John 252
Putman, Bob 335
Putnam, Mai Lan. 247
Pyles, Franklin 182
Quackenbush, David 191
Quattlebaum, Marvin, Jr. . . 256
Quay, Ronald 232
Quessy, Herve L.. 137
Quevedo, Jose Moises
Moncada 181
Quiett, Harry V.. 168
Quigley, Darcy. . 315, 322, 326
Quinn, A. James 80
Quinn, Michaelita 31
Quinn, Thomas 31
Quinter, Paul S.. 318
Quirog, Bonifacio 46
Rabenold, Nelson 253
Raber, Martha E. Rovira . . 326
Rabs, Carol 239
Raccah, William 310
Rader, Sharon Zimmerman
. . . . 163, 164
Radius, Lesley M.. 232
Ragsdale, John 108
Raines, James Ray. 77
Rajan, Frederick E.N. 111
Ralph, Karen 287
Ramdial, Samuel S.. 324
Ramirez, Laura 229
Ramphal, Dwarka 140
Ramseth, Mark R.. 306
Randal, Ed. 114
Randall, Mark 260
Randall, Mike 316, 317
Randels, J. Richard 237
Randolph, Bruce J. 252
Rankin, Jerry A. 153
Ransom, Robert. 132
Rasmussen, Donald R. 65
Rassmussen, Philip 344
Rathbun, Peter. 22
Ravenell, Joseph P. 244
Ray, Keith H. 298
Raymond, Jonathan S.. . . . 313
Read, Glenn 249
Read, James 53
Read, O.J.. 86
Realpe, Marcelo 88
Reames, J. David. 319
Reaney, Dwayne 191
Rebeck, Victoria A.. 24
Reccord, Robert E. 153
Rechter, Elizabeth 231
Redal, R.H. 102, 295
Redd, Eugene 139
Reddick, Lawrence L., III . . 87
Reddig, Jill S. 320
Reddin, George 77
Redding, Phil L. 140
Redding, Sharon K.. 140
Redekopp, Alf 344, 355
Redfield, William C. 247
Redhead, Bob 198
Reece, Richard 317
Reed, J. George 249
Reed, Michael B.. 69
Reed, Millard 306
Reed, Rodger Hall, Sr.. . . . 231
Rees, Seth C.. 168
Reese, Jack R.. 289
Reese, Ron 99
Reese, Rosemary 255
Reeves, Justus Y.. 317
Reeves, Steve 64
Regan, Tom. 286
Regehr, Ernie 54
Regier, Rob. 53
Register, Wayne 29
Regnier, Julie 48
Reichter, Arlo R.. 65
Reid, David. 56
Reid, Gail 342
Reid-MacNevin, Susan 53
Reierson, Gary B. . . . 241, 242
Reilly, Thomas J.. 197
Reimer, Gerald 189
Reimer, Klaas 188
Reimer, Milton 101
Reimer, Ray 115
Reinheimer, Larry 193
Reiser, Virginia Linda 130
Reisz, H. Frederick 299
Reithmaier, Jan 31
Reithmaier, Paul 31
Remalt, Theodore J. 331
Remington, Randy A. 126
Rempel, Ron 132, 341
Rempel, Valerie. 122
Rempel-Burkholder, Byron
. . . . 334
Rendall, Joanne 38
Renshaw, Richard 49
Reshan, Mark 233
Retzman, Alan. 190
Retzr, Gordon L.. 152
Revis, Charles 64
Reyes, Emilio 22
Reyes, José, Sr. 95, 184
Reynolds, Ariene 250
Reynolds, H.F.. . . . . . . 98, 185
Reynolds, Kristine 242
Reynolds, Paul V. 201
Rhéaume, Serge 50
Rhoades, Kevin C.. 300
Rhoads, Armen O.. 169
Rhoden, H. Robert 73
Rhodes, Arthur 93, 183
Rhodes, Schuyler 34
Ricci, Angelo. 71, 72
Rice, Clayton 194
Rice, Gene D. 92, 183

INDEX

Rice, Glenn 58
Richard, Thomas M. 133
Richards, James G. 314
Richards, James W. 154
Richards, Kerry J. 185
Richards, Patricia P.. 322
Richardson, Adam Jefferson
. . . . 59
Richardson, John M. 84
Richardson, Melvin 250
Richardson, Ralph 52
Richert, Jean 230
Riches, Jonathan S. 147
Riches, Leonard W., Sr. 147
Richey, John R. 137
Richey, Mary 262
Richey, Russell E. 292
Richmond, Ben 118
Richmond, Raymond, Jr. 61
Ricker, Robert 41
Rickman, W. Edward 307
Ridgway, Mary 90
Ridings, Dean 31
Rieley-Goddard, Catherine
. . . . 246
Riemenschneider, Dan 132
Rigdon, Sidney 95
Riggs, Ann K. 38
Riggs, Becky 95
Riggs, Don R. 241
Riggs, Tony 95
Riley, Adele M. 61
Riley, E. Roy, Jr. 112
Rimbo, Robert A.. . . . . . 34, 112
Rinard, Gordon 240
Rinden, David 97
Rinderknecht, Daniel 192
Rinehart, Neil 132
Rinnel, Rod 230
Risher, Dee Dee 331
Risser, Paul C. 126
Risser, Terry D. 126
Ritchie, Tracie 252
Rittenhouse, Syl 150
Ritter, Jack 250
Ritts, Kerry R. 144
Rivera, Luz M. 293
Rivera, Regina W. 61
Rivers, Francis 23
Rivers, Willie Mae 92
Robben, Jerome 181
Robbins, Earldean V.S. 143
Robbins, Marj 181
Roberson, Joseph 39
Roberts, B. Ted 126
Roberts, James P., Jr. 129
Roberts, Mark E. 350
Roberts, R. Philip 300
Roberts, Robert H. 64
Roberts, Sharon 22
Roberts, Tom 330
Roberts, Tommy 121
Robertson, Cory 45
Robertson, Creighton 106
Robertson, Kathryn 52
Robertson, William 335
Robinson, Alice Steele 61
Robinson, Anita 78
Robinson, Barbara A. 245
Robinson, Dave 318
Robinson, David 297
Robinson, Densimore 136
Robinson, Ellen 286
Robinson, John 93
Robinson, Judith 174
Robinson, Julian B. 93, 183
Robinson, Kenneth N. 100
Robinson, Kenneth O., Sr.
. . . . 162, 163
Robinson, Leslie 286
Robinson, Mattie A. 338
Robinson, Najla 231
Robinson, Paul 242
Robinson, Thomas 258
Robinson, Tommy 78
Robinson-Rumble, Beverly J.
. . . . 326
Robinson, V. Gene 105
Robirds, Don 325
Roby, Jasper 72
Rocca, Gregory 294
Rochester, Enoch Benjamin . . 60
Rochon, Igumen Irenee 193
Rockwell, David 245
Rockwood, Perry F. 343
Rodgers, George H.. 201
Rodman, Edward 239
Roe, R. Richard 227
Roebuck, David G. 93, 352
Roeder, Renée 247
Roegner, Robert 130
Roehl, Ronald 97
Roehrig, Matthew 332
Rogelstad, David 179
Rogers, Huie 79
Rogers, Joy 240
Rogers, Laura M. 249
Rogers, Rex M. 296
Rogers, Scott 249
Rogers-Witte, Ann C. 161
Rogness, Matthew 97
Rogness, Peter 111
Rohrbough, Faith E. 311
Rokke, Ervin J. 300
Rolf, Kathy 233
Rollins, Richard A. 134
Rollins, Robert L. 162
Roman III-Cruz, Rosilio 87
Romero, Carlos 132
Romero, Daniel F. 161
Ronsvalle, John L.. . . . . 15, 214
Ronsvalle, Sylvia 15, 214
Roop, Eugene F. 291
Roozen, David A. 215
Rorabaugh, Philip A. 155
Rosario, Luis 161
Rose, Donald L.. . . . . . 121, 330
Rose, J. Hugh 166
Rose, Jonathan 46
Rose, Whaid 95
Rosen, Janice 355
Rosengarten, Richard 307
Rosenthal, Hannah 223
Rosier, Bob 261
Rosner, Patrice 38
Roso, Henry A. (Hank) 322
Ross, Brent 58
Ross, David E. 58
Ross, Donald 325
Ross, Eugene 161, 252
Ross, Kent 327
Ross, Mary Jane 215
Ross, Nan 43
Ross, Patricia 226
Ross, Ronald C.. . . . . . 337, 339
Ross, Sean 181
Rost, Nori 167
Rostan, June 23
Rostand, Dean J. 341
Roth, Adam 251
Roth, Jared D. 126
Roth, John D. 329
Rothamel, John, Jr. 136
Rothman, Robert A.. 249
Rothwell, Raymond 120
Rourk, David C. 93
Rousseau, Katherine 229
Roussy, Louis 199
Rowe, Gard 249
Rowell, Leonard 259
Rowley, Robert D. 106
Roy, Marie-Michèle 342
Royer, Howard 316
Royston, James H.. 154
Rozeboom, John A. 88
Rubin, Fred, Sr. 98
Ruble, Nathan 324
Rucker, Jacqueline P. 252
Rucks, Karen L. 238
Rudell, Marilynn 235
Rudy, Frederick J. 28
Ruffier-Farris, Margaret . . . 231
Ruffin, Jeff 96
Rugege, Andrew 22
Rundbraaten, Edwin 185
Rupert, Allan 145
Rupp, Alan 116
Rupp, Gene 116
Rusch, William G. 32
Rusche, Brian A. 241, 242
Rush, Betty 250
Rush, Henry 228
Rush, Robert D.. 102
Russell, Al 324
Russell, Barbara 243
Russell, Charles Taze 128
Russell, Dorothy 40
Russell, Gary E. 88
Russell, Joseph 148

Russell, Keith A. 289
Rust, Harold 185, 309
Rutan, Dawn 326, 329
Ruth, Gary 22
Rutherford, F. Thomas. . 84, 181
Rutland, Mark 305
Ryan, Barb 130
Ryan, James R. 229
Ryan, Skip. 142
Ryan, Sylvester D.. 81
Ryan, Tim 56
Rydman, Philip 25, 345
Ryrie, Charles 125
Ryskamp, Andrew 88
Rystephanuk, David 193
Sadeghian, Janice 231
Saderholm, Mildred J. 249
Sadowski, Dennis 318
Saenz, Agnes. 238
Sage, Russell. 249
Sailors, Ronnette L. 243
Sainten, LaVerne 231
Salge, Carol. 234
Saliba, Philip 67, 175
Salico, Dale V. 65
Sallows, Martha 234
Salmon, Edward L. 106
Salmon, John. 182
Saltzman, Russell E. 323
Salvas, Sylvain 196
Salzman, Ron 137
Samilian, Vida. 227
Sammond, Christopher . . . 118
Samra, Cal 327
Samuel, Athanasius Y. 155
Samuel, Lloyd U. 69
Samuel, S.A. 178
Samuels, T.W. 135
Samuelson, Cecil O., Jr. . . . 96
Sanchagrin, Kenneth M. . . . 32
Sande, Jonathan M. 118
Sanders, Bill 236
Sanders, Hiram 300
Sanders, Kay 236
Sanders, Robert L.. 98
Sandford, Christopher 241
Sandleback, Nancy 24, 25
Sandler, Abraham 88
Sanford, Don A.. . . . . 153, 349
Sanner, Dick 23
Santiago, Felix. 95, 184
Sapp, W. David 35
Sarajian, Richard. 72
Sarly, Robert 239
Sarmazian, Yessayi . . 176, 340
Sartison, Telmore 54
Sarwa, Andrzej J. 181
Satterfield, Ray 62
Sauceda, Sam 261
Sauls, Stacy F. 105
Saunders, Dwight L. 126
Saunders, Willard 139
Savas (Bishop) 123
Sawatzky, Leonard 189
Sawyer, Randy 134
Sawyer, Robert E. 133
Sayre, Larry D. 64
Scali, Jean 244
Scarfe, Alan. 105
Schaal, Wendell J. 35
Schadewald, Tina 253
Schaefer, Beth 315
Schaeffer, John M.. 161
Schaer, Marilyn 137, 192, 331, 345
Schaller, Paul 327
Schearing, Linda 260
Schell, C. Steven. 126
Schellenberg, Rick 309
Schemmel, Wade, Jr. 161
Schiemann, D.. 192
Schierenbeck, John 97
Schilling, Ira 154
Schipper, Mr.. 326
Schlabach, Darrel 132
Schlatter, Michael 146
Schlatter, William R. 69
Schleicher, Andrew J. 331
Schlonecker, William G. . . . 78
Schlosser, Rick 227
Schmeling, G.R. 291, 328
Schmidt, Bill. 232
Schmidt, Harry 120, 292
Schmidt, Henry J. 299
Schmidt, Susannah 55
Schmitt, Bernard W. 261
Schneider, Bette 260
Schneider, Don C. 152
Schneider, Francis J. 305
Schneider, Theodore F. . . . 113
Schoder-Ehri, Bill 118
Schoelles, Patricia A.. 303
Schoeneck, Kathleen 252
Schoenhals, Floyd M. 112
Schofield, John-David 106
Schofield-Bodt, Brian 230
Scholl, Bill 235
Schonenbach, Peter 196
Schoonmaker, Wendy 232
Schori, Katharin Jefferts . . 105
Schorsch, Ismar. 297
Schrader, David. 186
Schrag, James M. 132
Schramm, Richard W. . . 64, 316
Schrock, Simon. 77
Schrock, Wayne 77
Schrodt, Paul. 23
Schroeder, David E.. 289
Schulter, Nancy. 244
Schultz, Harvey. 115
Schultz, Raymond L.. 188
Schultz, Stephen R. 76
Schulz, Wallace R. 130
Schulze, Leonard G. 111
Schuth, Katarina 17
Schutt, David 146
Schwab, David V. 161
Schwarr, Carolyn. 258
Schwich, Kathie Bender . . 111
Scott, Alphonso. 139
Scott, Dick 298
Scott, James C. 126
Scott, John 22
Scott, Molly Davis 29
Scott, Orange 168
Scott, Philip L. 139
Scott, Richard E. 126
Scott, Richard G.. 96
Scott, W. Peter. 201
Scott, Walter 85
Scouten, Larry. 327
Scovil, Larry 101
Scribner, Susan Royce. . . . 238
Scruggs, Endia 103
Scruton, Gordon P. 106
Scudder, Ida S. 46
Seabury, Samuel 103
Seasoltz, R. Kevin. 339
Seater, Robert P. 261
Seeger, Edward B.. 257
Seide, Emmanuel 88
Seifert, Stan. 115
Seler, Debby 320
Sellers, Asbury R. 93
Sellers, Clarence R.. 201
Semel, Rita 46
Senior, Donald 292
Senn, Frank C. 34
Senth, Colin 118
Sentz, Susan 255
Seppala, Ivan M. 70, 71
Seraphim (Bishop). 193
Seraphim (Reverend). 138
Serapion (Bishop) . . . 102, 315
Serber, Jack. 231
Sergeva, Yelena. 252
Serratelli, Arthur J. 81
Sewell, Wayne. 64
Seymour, W.J. 70
Shackelford, Lynne 256
Shada, Doug 77
Shafer, Eric C. 111
Shaffer, Kenneth M., Jr.. . . 349
Shah, Ajay. 221
Shahan, Robert 104
Shaheen, Michael 67
Shahidi, Munirah. 46
Shamana, Beverly J. 165
Shannon, S.E. 96
Shapley, Daniel H.. . . 154, 155
Sharkey, Carole. 33
Sharp, Bill. 114
Sharp, Donald 45
Sharp, John E. 329, 351
Sharp, S. Marion 259
Sharp, Tammy. 25
Sharpe, Michael 102
Shaver, Ruth 238
Shaw, Carla. 42

INDEX

Shaw, Curt. 119
Shaw, M. Thomas 105
Shaw, Milton. 129
Shaw, Richard 238
Shaw, Talbert O. 305
Shaw, William J. 135
Shawl, Sallie 259
Shea, William B. 35
Sheard, J. Drew 92
Sheeks, Bill F. 92, 183
Sheffield, Dan 190
Sheie, Myrna J. 110
Sheldon, William A. 89
Shelley, Marshall. 327
Shelly, Rubel 338
Shelton, Don W. 84
Shelton, Tom 133
Shenouda III 102, 187
Shepard, Raymond 78
Shepherd, D.A. 173
Shepherd, Thomas 238
Sherer, Ann Brookshire . . . 164
Sherer, Knox 114
Sheridan, Thomas H. 318
Sherry, Brian 22
Sherry, Jon 38
Sherry, Paul. 38
Sherwin, Wally 49
Sheveland, Gerald 76
Shimpfky, Richard. 105
Shinachi, Enoch. 119
Shindell, Dal 341
Shipley, Joseph 85
Shipman, Joan G. 254
Shisanya, Jonathan 119
Shivachi, Nilson 119
Shnurr, Dennis M. 81
Shockley, Howard 114
Shockley, Nathan. 169
Short, Betty. 286
Showers, Merle 248
Shreffler, Marilyn 250
Shrenes, Thomas A.. 112
Shuman, Maryellen 255
Shurr, Dan. 189
Shute, Michael 186
Shuttleworth, Frank K. 16
Sibley, Wallace J. 93
Sickbert, Bryan W. 161
Sides, David 74
Sides, Richard 133
Sidner, Art. 242
Sidorak, Stephen J., Jr. . . . 230
Siebert, Dorothy 342
Siepka, Richard W. 292
Sigismund, John 159
Sigman, Michael W. 108
Signer, Ray 45
Sills, John F. . . . 321, 323, 325
Silvey, James L. 77
Simiyu, Benson 119
Simiyu, Maurice 118
Simmons, F. Stan. 126
Simms, John A. 288
Simon, Leon 157
Simon, Mark 126
Simon, Menno. 148
Simon, Paula 261
Simpson, Albert B. . . . 87, 182
Simpson, John 240
Simpson, Susan V.. 121
Sims, John. 93, 183
Sinasac, Joseph 341
Sinclair, Jim 201
Sinclair, L. 71
Sinclair, William 22
Singh, Mohinder 46
Singleton, Richard. 240
Singley, Martin, III 126
Sinkford, William 159
Sisk, Mark. 105
Sitaras, Constantine L.. . . . 123
Skeadas, Georgia. 123
Skelton, William 40
Skidmore, W. Chris Benham 236
Skiles, Neil 89
Skinner, Mrs. Bill 77
Skinner, Douglas. 83
Skinner, Osceola 239
Skitton, William "Bill" . . . 256
Skocypec, Emil 159
Skuja-Grislis, Indra 318
Skurla, Laurus. 297
Skylstad, William S. . . . 80, 81
Slie, Samuel N. 230
Sly, Margery N. 143, 350, 353
Small, Hazel 178
Smalley, Martha 351
Smalley, William E.. 105
Smedberg, Barry 228
Smeeton, Don 93
Smeltzer, James. 252
Smisko, Nicholas. 65, 292
Smith, Alexei 229
Smith, Alycia 233
Smith, Andrea 339
Smith, Andrew D. 105
Smith, Arthur 335
Smith, Autholene. 78
Smith, Bennett W., Sr. 145
Smith, Beth Adams 249
Smith, Brad. 301
Smith, Bruce 184
Smith, Burton E. 126
Smith, Chris 160
Smith, Craig S. 87
Smith, David Charles 253
Smith, Diana E.. 26
Smith, Donald. 229
Smith, Elias Dempsey 157
Smith, Eric 132
Smith, Francis L.. 139
Smith, G. Wayne 105
Smith, Glen. 288
Smith, Glenn. 53
Smith, Guy H., III 74
Smith, Isaac V. 86
Smith, J. Morris. 255
Smith, Jane Orion 345
Smith, Joseph 89, 96, 184
Smith, Leroy, Jr. 96
Smith, Joseph, III 185
Smith, Joseph, Jr.. 185
Smith, Kenneth 346
Smith, Lawrence 129
Smith, Lois L. 252
Smith, Marilyn McCann . . 112
Smith, Marion 185
Smith, R. Bruce. 51
Smith, Rebecca 234
Smith, Robert E. 296
Smith, Robert 181
Smith, Ron C. 329
Smith, Ron 230
Smith, Ronald E. 308
Smith, Ronald 100
Smith, S.S. 149
Smith, Susan J. 226
Smith, Terry M. 189
Smith, Terry 344
Smith, Tom 251
Smith, Velma. 261
Smith, Victor P. 90
Smith, William L. 139
Smith, Zollie 74
Smock, Robert W. 78
Snair, Karen 252
Snead, W.T., Sr.. 135
Snellgrove, P. David 143
Snider, Cindy 132
Snow, Sharon C. 126
Snowman, Sharon L. 136
Snyder, Carol 323
Snyder, Joni 235
Snyder, Richard D. . . . 47, 117
Sobel, Ronald B. 43
Soderquist, Marilyn. 259
Solheim, James 104
Solomon, Frank S.. 98
Sommers, Gordon 43
Soo, Richard 56
Soper, John F. 87
Sophronios (Bishop) 124
Sorensen, Gordon 177
Sorensen, Sandy 321
Sorensen, Steven R.. 351
Sorenson, Eleanor 261
Sotirios (Archbishop) 191
Sovin, Shenork 50
Sowers, Betsy 239
Sox, Aileen Andres . . 332, 333
Spain, Ricky 59, 315
Spans, J. 332
Sparkman, Alan. 140
Sparkman, Wayne 353
Sparks, William. 53
Spataro, Francis C. . . . 69, 336

Speas, Philip 298
Speer, James 77
Spence, Ralph 175
Spencer, Shirley 326
Sperzel, Ceil 234
Spindt, Judith A. 113
Spittal, David J.. 305
Spitzer, Lee 64
Spitzer, Robert 296
Spleth, Richard L. 84
Spousta, Larry R. 126
Sprague, C. Joseph 164
Sprague, Roy. 125
Springgs, J. Wayne 87
Sprinkle, Randy. 154
Spurgeon, Don 99
St. Pierre, Bill 180
Stacy, R. Wayne 299
Stafford, E.E.. 134
Stahl, Robert 108
Stahr, James A. 82, 181
Stair, Randy 142
Stairs, Jean 312
Staller, Thomas 116
Stallings, James O. 64
Stamm, John M. 306
Stamn, John. 159
Stanton, Ivy. 126
Stanton, James M. 105
Stapert, Craig W. 317
Staples, Charles E.. 255
Stark, J. 146
Starnes, Darryl B. 61
Starr, Barbara 136
Statnick, Roger 252
Stauch, Karimah 46
Stavert, Bruce 175
Steadman, J.P. 98
Stearns, Richard 47
Steckbeck, Dori I. 349
Steckel, Clyde 161
Stefanis, Anthony 123
Steib, J. Terry 80
Steinhauser, Michael G.. . . 313
Steinmetz, Larry 26
Steinwand, Randy L. 57
Stelck, Brian F. 177, 310
Stella, Brigitte 245
Stemmle, Carol 236
Stenbakken, Ardis D.. 152
Stenbakken, Richard O.. . . . 152
Stenberg, Luther 185
Stendahl, John K. 111
Stendahl, John. 239
Stenson, Jane. 40
Stephanopoulos, Nikki . . . 123
Stephanopoulos, Robert G.
. . . . 123
Stephen (Archbishop)
. . . . 156, 157
Stephen (Reverend) 156
Stephens, Mary 235
Stephens, P.F. 148
Stephens, Robert 238
Stephenson, Carl H.. 201
Stephenson, Robert E. 100
Stern, George M. 254
Stetler, P. Daniel 296
Stevens, Ed 295
Stevens, Jerry 336
Stevens, Ruth J.. 62
Stevenson, L. June. 343
Stewart, Betty 119
Stewart, Dan R. 126
Stewart, Danny 84
Stewart, Glen J.. 85
Stewart, Jeremy. 253
Stewart, Jewelle 128
Stewart, Jonathan 28
Stewart, Kimberly 167
Stewart, Lois R.. 141
Stewart, Paul A.G., Sr.. 86
Stewart, William E. 185
Stewart-Rhude, Eileen. 53
Steytler, Jessica 354
St-Gelais, Raymond 197
Stiller, Brian C. 52, 314
Stimson, Eva 333
Stinnett, Daniel 178
Stinnett, Daniel, Mrs. 178
Stinnett, J. Dwight. 64
Stinson, Benoni 120
Stites, Tom 347
Stith, Betty V. 61
Stith, Rhandi M. 61
Stoesz, John 257
Stokes, Thomas E.. 349
Stoll, Christian 347
Stoll, Joseph 342, 347
Stolov, Yehuda 46
Stoltzfus, Margaret 119
Stommel, Elizabeth 238
Stone, Barton W. 83, 85
Stone, Jack. . . . 44, 47, 98, 185
Stoners, Edward, Jr.. 43
Stopperich, J.R. 234
Stortz, Dennis 130
Stoudt, John 253
Stowell, Joseph M. 300
Strain, Patricia. 338
Strand, David 130
Strand, Jim 24
Strauser, AnnaMae 119
Strauser, Charles Elwood. . 119
Strauser, Simeon 119, 324
Straut, Charles H., Jr.. 245
Strawser, Craig L. 87
Strayer, Millyellen. 252
Strickland, I. 59, 60
Strickland, Vernon. 106
Strobel, David R.. 112
Strohmaier, Sharon E. 235
Strommen, E. Peter 111
Strope, David 121
Stroup, John 127
Strout, Richard E. 345
Struchen, Shirley W. . . . 38, 43
Struck, Jane Johnson 336
Struik, P. Felix. 294
Strunk, Orlo, Jr.. 326
Strutz, Robert 107
Stuart, Robert F. 231
Stuck, James R. 112
Studivant, G.W.. 148
Stuehrenberg, Paul F.. 23
Stumme-Diers, Paul W. . . . 112
Sturtevant, Elwood 235
Stutzman, Rose Mary 336
Styles, Donald H. 318
Subotic, Zivorad 198
Suhrheinrich, Heidi 237
Suk, John A. 340
Sullivan, Anita. 120
Sullivan, Bernard 61
Sullivan, Jack, Jr. 84
Sullivan, John 153
Sullivan, Linda 239
Sullivan, Rosemari 104
Sumner, George R., Jr.. . . . 314
Sumners, Bill 349
Sunderland, LaRoy 168
Sundquist, Kristin 227
Sure, Heng 46
Sutto, Zoltan S. 240
Sutton, Edgar N. 64
Sutton, Peter A. 196
Sutton, Ray R.. 147
Svennungsen, Ann. 32
Swaiko, Herman 304
Swain, Lawrence O. 65
Swan, Richard. 237
Swan, Sandra 104
Swan, Tina 244
Swank, Sandy 235
Swanson, Douglas 242
Swanson, Gary B. . . . 320, 321
Swanson, Paul R.. 111
Swanson-Nystrom, Jane K.
. . . . 321
Swartling, David D.. 111
Swartz, Fred W.. 89
Swartzendruber, Loren . . . 294
Swatkowski, Ray. 76
Swatsky, Ben. 109
Swedenborg, Emanuel
. . . . 121, 155, 190
Sweeden, Patsie. 84
Sweeting, Don. 114
Swenson, Kristin 45
Swenson, Lester 241
Swenson, Mary Ann 165
Swidler, Leonard 326
Swinburne, R. Douglas, Jr. . 87
Swindle, Zephaniah. 157
Swing, William E. 45, 105
Swor, Ronald E. 126
Sydow, James 97
Syeed, Sayyid M. 222
Sylvest, Tom 237

INDEX

Synan, Vinson 303
Szabo, Stephen 124, 328
Tabbernee, William 302
Taber-Hamilton, Nigel. . . . 260
Tafoya, Arthur N. 80
Taillon, Gerald. 154, 179
Talbert, Melvin G.. 30
Talbot, Frederick Hilborn . . 59
Talbot, Lydia 232
Talcott, Sarah 45
Talley, John D. 305
Talone, Cheryl. 246
Tamberg, Tod M.. 336
Tamer'leng the Mongol 67
Tammen, Mark 143
Tan, David. 244
Tan, Hong Kia. 167
Tandon, Atul 48
Tanis, Justin 167
Tanis, Phil. 146
Tappen, Jerry. 261
Tarr, Rita. 232
Tate, Mary L. 124
Tatum, Craig 240
Tatum, Ed 140
Taylor, Al 93
Taylor, Betty P. 257
Taylor, C. Allen. 185
Taylor, Edwin 286
Taylor, J. Glen. 51
Taylor, J. Graley 260
Taylor, Joyce. 92
Taylor, L. Roy 142
Taylor, Mark A. 99, 319
Taylor, Nancy 161
Taylor, Regina. 258
Taylor, Steve 116, 320
Taylor, Victor 86
Taylor, Wayne 127
Teague, Peter W. 298
Teakle, Debra 177
Tedesco, John 85
Tample, Guy 254
Temple, Jan. 254
Temple, Robert L. (Bobby) 169
Templeton, Beth 256
Templeton, John M., Jr. 37
Teodorovych, Ioan (John) . . 158
Terry, Bob. 24
Tetreau, Jerry. 297
Thell, Barbara 241
Theodosius (Most Blessed) 139
Theriault, Donald J.. 197
Thibodeau, Francois 197
Thiesen, John 351
Thiessen, David. 189
Thiessen, Henry 189
Thirkill, Sharron 250
This, Craig 25
Thoma I (Bishop) 131
Thomann, David A. 78
Thomas, Andrea S. 234
Thomas, Arnold I. 162
Thomas, D. Karl 175
Thomas, Dominic 95
Thomas, Everett 329
Thomas, Floyd 78
Thomas, Freeman M. 139
Thomas, George 329
Thomas, James P. 100
Thomas, John H. 160
Thomas, John 82
Thomas, Millicent D. 62
Thomas, Ralph 33
Thomas, Reginald H.. 144
Thomas, Ronald P. 58
Thomas, T.V.. 182
Thomas, Wendy 49
Thomas-Breitfeld, Leota . . 110
Thomason, Jeanette 31
Thompson, Barbara Ricks . . 38
Thompson, Brice 95, 184
Thompson, Daniel M. 231
Thompson, Doug. 257
Thompson, Else. 111
Thompson, Glendon G. . . . 313
Thompson, Herbert, Jr. . . . 106
Thompson, Houston 234
Thompson, James W.. 334
Thompson, Ken. 115
Thompson, Kenneth 258
Thompson, Leonard, Sr. . . . 64
Thompson, Richard Keith 59, 60
Thomson, H. Rogers 68
Thopil, Markose 139
Thornton, Bobby C.. 77
Thorpe, Debbie 257
Thune, Robert L. 87
Thurman, Barbara 136
Thurton, Winston 52
Tiano, Christopher M. 318
Tidwell, Melissa 316
Tiede, David L. 26, 299
Tiemann, Ray 112
Tifft, Thomas W. 303
Tikhon (Reverend) 138
Timmer, David E. 332
Timmerman, Larry J.. 93
Timmons, Glenn F. 89
Tindal, Douglas. 53
Tinsley, Charles. 227
Tippett, Bert 324
Tipton, Daniel. 99
Tisch, Joseph L. 129
Tisdale, Delores. 252
Tisdale, Janet. 136
Titus, Devorah N. 126
Titus, Richard C. 226
Tizzard, Brian 57
Tkachuk, Rod 193
Tolbert, Rosa. 70
Tolbert, T.C., Jr.. 70
Tolbert, T.C., Sr. 70
Tolle, James A. 126
Tollefson, Rebecca J.. 251
Tolley, S.T. 144, 318
Tolstoy, Leo 200
Tomic, Vasilije 343
Tomlin, Mark 332
Tomlinson, A.J. 94, 183
Tomlinson, M.A. 94, 183
Tomlinson, Susanna M. . . . 253
Tonnos, Anthony F. 196
Toot, Gloria. 155
Tooze, George. 65
Toppins, Helen Garay 119
Torok, Stefan M. 124
Torrance, John. 177
Torrens, Gary 143
Towne, Becky 324
Towns, L. Ferrell. 88
Townsend, Fred. 287
Townsend, Patricia 355
Towse, Eric 337
Toycen, Dave 57
Trachian, Barkev 306
Traftan, Margie 345
Trahan, Randy. 237
Trammell, Mary M. 90, 319, 325
Trapp, Edwin, Jr. 130
Trapp, Hans-Joachim. 90
Trask, Ralph 120
Trask, Thomas E.. . . . . . 42, 73
Traudt, Helen 29
Trautman, Donald W. 80
Treanor, John J.. 25
Trees, Richard J. 126
Treit, Elroy 192
Trejo, José. 242
Tremblay, Anna. 286
Tremblay, Donald 287
Trevino, Max A. 152
Trevino, Yoland. 46
Triantafilou, Nicholas C. 123, 296
Trimmer, Sterling 108
Trine, Melinda. 22
Trinkle, Wanda 236
Tripp, Kevin F. 228
Tripp, Linda 57
Trosen, Robert. 107
Trotta, Michael 85
Trotter, LaTonya 45
Trotti, Melinda 248
Trowbridge, Kathleen 238
Truss, James 70
Trusty, Bill 237
Tsapwe, Simon 119
Tschetter, Charles 115
Tse, James N. 30
Tsimbaki, Matthew 118
Tuan, Jim 117
Tucker, Neville 61
Tucker, Tommy 237
Tuckett, Robert 326

Tuers, Earl. 251
Tune, Leslie C. 38
Tunnicliffe, Geoff 53
Turnage, Juleen 73
Turner, B.G. 127
Turner, Emil 153
Turner, Rex A., Jr. 305
Turner, Wayne 343
Twedt-Ball, Karla 234
Tweet, Margaret 29
Tyler, Robert D. 96
Tyndall, Margaret 48
Tyrrell, Wildfred 35
Tyson, James E.. 139
Udall, William B. 238
Udoh, I.S. 178
Ugoletti, Dennis 252
Ugolnik, Anthony 336
Uiddeke, Paul W.. 130
Ulery, Kent J. 161
Ullestad, Steven L. 112
Ulterino, Gloria 247
Umble, Jeni Hiett 233
Unger, John. 309
Unruh, Ron 188
Up De Graff, Morse 142
Updegrove, John H.. 255
Updegrove, Will 133
Uptain, Misti 260
Upton, John V., Jr. 154
Ursham, N.A. 166
Usgaard, Harold L. 112
Ussery, Daniel K. 126
Ustrzycki, Matthew F. 197
Utterback, J. Michael 93
Valenzuela, Carmen. 242
Vallance, James E.. 316
Vallee, Andre. 50
Valleskey, David J. 308
Van Dyk, Leanne. 332
Van Eyl, Christina 320
van Laar, Erwin. 50
Van Leer, Thomas 241
Van Marter, Jerry. 24
Van Wyngaarden, Bill 45
VanBeusekom, Hein 129
Vanbiber, Craig 114
VanBroekhoven, Deborah B. 65
Vance, Bob 324
Vandee, Daniel 178
Vandee, Daniel, Mrs.. 178
Vanderslice, Kenneth W. 76, 77
Vandervelde, George 32
Vang, Timothy T.. 87
Vanhaverbeke, Sylvia Lisk 47
VanMarter, Jerry L. 333
Vansen, Beatrice 27
Vanyi, Lazlo B. 125
Varecha, Jenny 233
Vargas, David A. 83-84
Varlack, Adrian L. 340
Varsbergs, Anita 129
Vasilac, Vasile 321
Vasquez, Manuel 152
Vasquez, Roberto 29
Vaughan, Anne 247
Veazey, Stephen M. 100
Veenstra, William 88
Veeraswamy, B.. 78
Veillette, Martin 196
Veliko, Lydia. 30
Velozo, Ruth M. 260
Veneroso, Joseph R. 329
Verigin, John J., Sr. 200
Verigin, Peter P.. 200
Verigin, Peter V.. . . . . 199, 200
Verlautz, James 242
Vermillion, William. 107
Vest, R. Lamar. . 21, 42, 92, 183
Vetter, Jay A.. 244
Vettrus, Richard. 97
Vice, Collin 230
Vickery, David 74
Victor (Metropolitan). 124
Vidolo, Japheth 119
Vigneron, Allen H. 303
Vila, Vesna 252
Vilankulu, Sarah 38, 322
Vilathi, Timotheos 156
Villafane, Eldin 32
Vincent, Cheryl L.. 126
Vinton, Samuel 122
Viola, Virginia. 33
Visscher, J. 341, 342
Vissers, John 311, 312
Vitaly (Metropolitan). 150
Vlad, Mike 95
Vladimir (Prince) 71
Vo, Tam. 244
Vogelaar, C.. 136
Vogel-Borne, Jonathan. . . . 119
Voirol, James. 336
Vollratlt, Edgar 323
Volodymyr (Prince) 158
Von Gunten, David 132
von Ossig, Caspar Schwenkfeld 150
Von Rosenberg, Charles. . . 105
Vonicessler, Caroline 256
Voskuil, Dennis N. 308
Votary, R.E. 191, 343
Vree, Dale 330
Vsevolod (Archbishop) . . . 158
Vu, Hung. 243
Wachal, Anne E. 232
Wacker, Grant 320
Wackernagel, Betsy 259
Wade, Charles R.. 154
Wade, Cheryl H. 64
Wade, Melvin V. 135
Wagener, Ginny. 229
Waggoner, James E. 106
Waggoner, Sara Jo 251
Waggoner, Ted 83
Wagner, Jane 167
Wagner, Mark 301
Wagner, Norman L. 139
Wagner, Rebecca. 238
Waites, Bob. 154
Wakefield, M.J. 178
Wakefield, Wesley H. 177, 178, 343
Wakefield, William James Elijah 177
Walden, Mark 44
Waldner, Jacob 125
Walgraeve, Walter M.C. . . . 70
Walhof, Karen 110
Walker, Alice. 336
Walker, Diane 342
Walker, Frank 146, 147
Walker, Gail 34
Walker, George Washington Carver, Sr. 59, 60
Walker, Jewett L.. 61
Walker, LaToya 247
Walker, Orris G. 105
Walker, Paul H. 92, 183
Walker, Paul L. 93, 183
Walker, Reba. 160
Walker, Riley H. 64
Walker-Smith, Angelique. . 233
Walking Elk, Leslie 241
Wall, Jim. 140
Wall, Raymond W.. . . . 92, 183
Wallace, Carl P. 161
Wallace, D. 191
Wallace, Duncan D.. 175
Wallace, E.W. 136
Wallace, Jon R. 290
Wallace, Peter M. 43
Wallace, Robert. 64
Walles, Charles A. 109
Walley, Wendell 291
Wallis, Hope 247
Wallis, Jim 335
Walsh, Gary. 52, 53
Walter, Bob 46
Walter, Don. 98
Walter, Ewa. 47
Walter, Gary B. 109
Walter, Martin 125
Walters, Norman 139
Walther, Bob 137
Waltz, David C.. 154
Walvoord, John 125
Walz, Bob 242
Walz, James 126
Wamala, Francis 119
Wang, Karen 38
Wangberg, Rolf P. 111
Wangensteen, Peg 242
Wantz, Joh. 233
Ward, Marion J.. 259
Ward, Michael, Sr.. 66

INDEX

Ward, Sarah F. 40
Wardlaw, Theodore J. 290
Warfel, Michael W. 80
Warkie, Peter. 139
Warner, Daniel S. 90
Warner, Vincent W. 106
Warner, Wayne E. . . . 325, 348
Warren, Cindy 29
Warren, David 121
Warren, Leodis 139
Warren, Mike. 121, 320
Warren, Patty. 226
Warren, Ronald B. 113
Warren, Thomas S., II 58
Wartman, Paul. 310
Washington, Don A. 238
Wasielewski, Charles. 66
Wasserman, Joseph 229
Watanabe, Hakubun. 220
Waters, Sally 255
Watkins, David J. 78
Watkins, David T. 76
Watkins, Dennis W. 93
Watson, B. Michael 165
Watson, Ralph. 288
Watson, Robert 95
Watt, Laura 234
Watt, Neil 198
Wattson, Paul 33
Wauls, Robert 139
Wawire, Blastus. 119
Waxler, Mel. 257
Waybright, Gregory L. . . . 306
Waynick, Catherine M. . . . 105
Weakland, Rembert G. . . . 261
Weaver, David. 38
Weaver, James. 340
Weaver, Peter D. 164
Weavill, George. 256
Webb, Beth 117
Webb, Ellen. 331
Webb, Robert 349
Webb, Suzanne J. 30, 84
Webb, Thomas 331
Weber, Francis J. 24
Weber, Timothy. 102
Webster, Joe L. 162
Webster, Robert Vaughn . . . 59
Wedgwood, James I. 129
Wedig, Mark E. 290
Weeks, Dewayne. 140
Weeks, Louis B. 306
Weeks, Thomas J. 139
Weeks, Thomas W., Sr. . . . 139
Weems, Lovett H., Jr. 304
Weigand-Buckley, Amber . . 331
Weikel, Calvin. 127
Weiler, Jean-Jacques 48
Weinacht, Alan 119
Weinreb, Tzvi Hersh 224
Weinrich, William C. 130
Weinstein, Judy 254
Weir, Moses 103
Welch, J.M. 173
Welch, Shirley. 61
Wells, Carol. 101, 323
Wells, D.R. 173
Wells, Martin D. 111
Welscott, Richard . . . 146, 195
Welsh, Robert K. 83, 317
Welty, Marcel A. 38
Wenger, Lee 160
Wenski, Thomas G. 80
Wenthe, Dean O. 293
Werner, George L. 104
Werner, Paul 37
Wert, Rita 40
Wesley, John 144, 168
Wesley, Laura 178
Wesley, Richard. 178
West, Barbara J. 147
West, James C. 294
West, James C., Sr. 147
West, Jonathan 23
Westberg, M. Victor 90
Westbrook, Don. 120
Westcott, Barbara Spaulding 240
Wetzel, C. Robert 294
Wetzel, Daniel R. 88
Wexler, Marcie 202
Weyeneth, Benedict. 69
Whalen, Timothy F. 305
Whalon, Pierre W. . . . 104, 106
Whatley, Wesley 28
Wheaton, Keith D. . . . 315, 320, 325, 333
Wheeland, Duane A. 87
Wheeler, Barbara G. . . 17, 213
Wheeler, Edward L. 293
Whitaker, Timothy Wayne. . 165
White, Alma 141
White, Barbara 36
White, Cyrus N. 83
White, David O. 229
White, Ellen G. 95
White, Frank O. 91
White, J. Robert 153
White, J.C. 92
White, Jerry E. 28
White, Jim. 243
White, K. Gordon 239
White, Kent. 141
White, LaDonna 241
White, Marcus. 261
White, Natasha 260
White, Olivia Masih. . . 160, 161
White, Patricia. 103
White, R. Fowler. 298
White, Raymond W. 124
White, Reid R., Jr. 61
White, Richard 91
White, Robert Howell, Jr. . . 143
White, Robert 136, 146
White, Roger J. 105
White, Terry 31
White, Woodie W. 164
WhiteEagle, Sheila 242
Whitfield, D. Max 165
Whitham, Nathan 122
Whiting, Douglas D. 41
Whitlow, Robert L. 295
Whitlow, Roger A. 126
Whitmore, Keith B. 105
Whitney, Dale 229
Whitney-Schenck, Marci . . 319
Whittaker, Bill. 293
Whittaker, Fermin A. 153
Whitted, Annette E. 62
Whittley, LuVoinia 92
Wick, William S. 109
Wickman, David 179
Wickmann, David L. 133
Wideman, James 154
Wiebe, Dave 179
Wiebe, Henry 196
Wiebe, Jim 182
Wiebe, Philip. 334
Wiebe, Virgil. 77
Wieczerzak Joseph 352
Wiederhoeft, Keith 113
Wiemer, Loyal H. 240
Wiens, Dennis 115
Wiens, Hart. 50
Wieser, Walter W. 177
Wigger, Barbara 121
Wiggins, Donald A. 87
Wiggins, James B. 247
Wiggins, Lonnie 64
Wiginton, Melissa 32
Wilbert, Ora 86
Wilcox, Donald M. 246
Wilcox, William 238
Wildman, Ingrid 187, 341
Wiley, Galen 116
Wiley, Jill 239
Wilke, Le Roy. 130
Wilkerson, Jack. 153
Wilkie, Owen 317
Wilkinson, Bruce. 48
Wilkinson, Ed 336
Willard, Pat 256
Willemsma, Tena. 24
William III (King). 69
Williams, Annie M. 61
Williams, Arsenia 136
Williams, Arthur B. 106
Williams, Bertha 162
Williams, Carl E., Sr. 92
Williams, Carolyn 248
Williams, Daniel Day 16
Williams, Dennis L. 84
Williams, Edward 79
Williams, Elijah. 162, 163
Williams, Elvonia 92
Williams, F.W. 70
Williams, Gregory. 327
Williams, Horace K. 92
Williams, Jack. 321

INDEX

Williams, Jesse F. 166
Williams, John L. 143
Williams, John P., Jr. 110
Williams, John 259
Williams, Keith 94
Williams, Larry 244
Williams, Michael A.. 64
Williams, Milton Alexander 60
Williams, Newell. 291
Williams, Oswill . . 42, 95, 184
Williams, Patrick J. 301
Williams, Preston Warren . . 59
Williams, R.H. Tex 315
Williams, Richard D.. 98
Williams, Roger 64, 79
Williams, Ronald D. . . 42, 126, 324
Williams, Roy 132
Williams, Sam. 110
Williams, W. Michelle James 166
Williamson, Edward W. . . . 114
Williamson, Elaine 233
Williamson, Henry M.. 87
Williamson, Jack. 37
Williamson, Portia Turner . . 32
Williamson, Stephen 249
Williford, Craig. 294
Willis, Carolyn 340
Willis, Mike 336
Wills, Susan 257
Wilson, Alex V. 338
Wilson, Dori 229
Wilson, Earle L. 47, 168
Wilson, Glenna 256
Wilson, H.C. 202
Wilson, Helen Tibbs 226
Wilson, Ian E. 355
Wilson, James G.. 104
Wilson, Jeffrey K. 152
Wilson, John 234
Wilson, Larry E. 330
Wilson, Nancy L. 167
Wilson, Norman G. . . 168, 337
Wilson, Robert W.. 169
Wilson, Rod 313
Wilson, Ronald (Bishop) . . 100
Wilson, Ronald 30, 31
Wilson, Stanley M. 126
Wilt, Marge. 31
Wilt, Tom 31
Wiltschek, Walt 89, 316
Wiltse, David A. 339
Winbush, R.L.H. 92
Winbush, Robina. 143
Wind, James P. 21
Windland, Larry D. 185
Wine (Sister) 148
Wine, Dottie 229
Winebrenner, John. 99
Wines, Roger. 144
Wing, David W.. 126
Wingender, Eric. 311
Winger, Brian 200
Winger, Darrell S. 178
Wingren, Gunnar. 74
Winkler, Eugene H. 232
Winn, Douglas K. 289
Winn, Robert. 90
Winnowski, Michael 50
Winsor, Eva M. 194
Winsor, Gary D. 194
Winter, Linda 255
Winter, Roy. 89
Winteregg, Bryce. 116
Winterrowd, William J. . . . 105
Winters, Carolyn M. 226
Winters, Donald 79
Wintz, Jack 334
Wipf, Jacob 125
Wipf, John. 125
Wirt, Douglas 84
Wirthlin, Joseph B. 96
Wise, Phillip 41
Witczak, Michael G. 303
Witman, Mark. 79
Witmer, Joseph W.. 251
Witt, Richard. 248
Wittberg, Patricia. 334
Witte, Frances 150
Wittel, Kim Y. 253
Wittin, Robert 244
Wittman, Elisabeth 351
Wittwer, Joe K. 126
Woelbern, James 26
Woida, Duane 227
Wojcicki, Ted L. 298
Wojtyla, Karol. 80
Wold, David 259
Wold, Mark J. 109
Woldt, Alice. 259, 260
Wolf, Burton 250
Wolf, Geralyn 106
Wolf, Patricia 38
Wolfe, Bennett 90
Wolfe, Robert 202
Wolford, Kathryn F. 35
Wolfram, Donald J. . . 141, 332
Wollersheim, Gary M. 112
Woloschak, Gayle 158
Womack, Anne 23
Wong, David S.F. 339
Wontor, Caryn. 258
Wood, Bertrice Y. 30, 38
Wood, David R.. 185
Wood, David 245
Wood, Edward W. 128
Wood, George O. 73
Wood, Robert Stanley. . . . 103, 322
Woodbury, Clayton R.. 65
Woodrich, Noya 241
Woodring, DeWayne S. 44
Woodruff, James 246
Woods, C. Stacey 33
Woods, Gayle 298
Woodson, Darryl D. 166
Woodward, George 193
Woodward, Jim 237
Woofenden, Lee 332
Woolfolk, Thomas E.. 98
Workman, Marjorie 134
Workowski, Joan. 147
Worley, Lloyd 129
Wormley, Mildred 145
Worthing, Carol M. 258
Worthington, Melvin 44
Wortman, Julie A. 338
Wray, Marina 244
Wright, Abraham. 30
Wright, Benny. 259
Wright, Harold 227
Wright, Hilman 148
Wright, Walter L.. 152
Wright, Wayne P. 105, 231
Wright-Riggins, Aidsand F. . . 65
Wuerch, Harry. 191
Wuerl, Donald W. 81
Wukwanja, Geoffrey M. . . 118
Wulfestieg, Rick 126
Wyatt, Peter. 310
Wylie, Ken 232
Wylie-Kellerman, Bill 45
Wynick, Karmen 22
Yaldezian, John 73
Yanagihara, Akio. 260
Yates, Jonathan 136
Yates, Wilson 307
Yeats, John 153
Yeats, Liz 258
Yeuell, Davis. 143
Yi, Maria Renya 118
Yntema, Philip 192
Yocum, Glenn 326
Yoffie, Eric H.. 224
Yohnka, Betty 232
Yost, Wayne 252
Young, Brigham 184
Young, Donald A. 174
Young, Donald O. 306
Young, M. Norvel 315
Young, Martha 238
Young, McKinley 46, 59
Young, Philip 38
Young, Ronald L. 139
Youngren, Peter. 193
Younis, Omar 244
Yount, Diana 349, 354
Youth, Edwina. 46
Yrigoyen, Charles, Jr. 329
Yuille, William 181
Yury I 69
Zabaidi, Ali 244
Zabel, Nancy. 40
Zacharias, Carl 189
Zachary, Marion 237
Zackrison, James W. 152
Zaffuto, Ferdinand. 191

INDEX

Zain, Thomas 67, 175
Zakian, Chris. 73
Zanders, Lucy 242
Zandier, Don 255
Zapeda, Monica. 260
Zarling, Thomas 169
Zastrow, Dale 63
Zavitz-Bond, Jane 355
Zawierucha, Bazyl. . . 158, 159
Zehlaoui, Joseph 67
Zehr, Marvin 235
Zeiders, G. Edwin 307
Zelenitz, Myrna. 253
Zell, Carla 343
Zell, R. Thomas. 315, 340
Zeller, Stephanie 103
Zellmer, Paul. 154
Zens, Jon 155, 335
Zerbe, Palmer L. 88
Ziadeh, Farhat 260
Zilliacus, Anne Marie 341
Zilmer, Norman D. 82
Zimmerman, Sheldon 296
Zion, Sophia 193, 341
Zipfel, Paul A.. 80
Zobel, Tom 25
Zobler, Donald 256
Zone, Enrique 126
Zottoli, Carmine 85
Zuk (Bishop). 124
Zurek, M. 199
Zwingli, Ulrich 150, 160
Zylla, Phil 309

INDEX